FINANCIAL ACCOUNTING

EIGHTH EDITION

FINANCIAL ACCOUNTING

EIGHTH EDITION

ERNEST I. HANSON
University of Wisconsin, Madison

JAMES C. HAMRE
University of Wisconsin, Madison

The Dryden Press
Harcourt Brace College Publishers

Fort Worth   Philadelphia   San Diego   New York   Orlando   Austin   San Antonio
Toronto   Montreal   London   Sydney   Tokyo

Acquisitions Editor	Mike Reynolds
Developmental Editor	Craig Avery
Project Editor	Kathryn Stewart
Production Manager	Jessica Wyatt
Product Manager	Craig Johnson
Marketing Assistant	Kelly Whidbee
Art Director	Jeanette Barber
Art & Literary Rights Editor	Adele Krause
Copy Editor	JaNoel Lowe
Proofreader	Karen Carriere
Compositor	ETP/Harrison
Text Type	10/12 Times Roman
Cover Image	Dave Cutler © Stock Illustration Source

Address for Orders
The Dryden Press, 6277 Sea Harbor Drive, Orlando, FL 32887-6777
1-800-782-4479, or 1-800-433-0001 (in Florida)

Address for Editorial Correspondence
The Dryden Press, 301 Commerce Street, Suite 3700, Fort Worth, TX 76102

ISBN: 0-03-010309-6

Library of Congress Catalog Card Number: 95-69999

Printed in the United States of America

5 6 7 8 9 0 1 2 3 4   048   9 8 7 6 5 4 3 2 1

The Dryden Press
Harcourt Brace College Publishers

Financial Statements and Related Disclosures from the 1994 Annual Report of General Mills, Inc. reprinted with permission from General Mills, Inc.

THE DRYDEN PRESS SERIES IN ACCOUNTING

Introductory

Bischoff
Introduction to College Accounting
Third Edition

Principles

Hanson, Hamre, and Walgenbach
Principles of Accounting
Sixth Edition

Computerized

Bischoff and Wanlass
The Computer Connection: General Ledger and Practice Sets to accompany Introductory Accounting
Second Edition

Wanlass
Computer Resource Guide: Principles of Accounting
Fourth Edition

Financial

Hanson and Hamre
Financial Accounting
Eighth Edition

Porter and Norton
Financial Accounting: The Impact on Decision Makers

Stickney and Weil
Financial Accounting: An Introduction to Concepts, Methods, and Uses
Seventh Edition

Porter and Norton
Financial Accounting: The Impact on Decision Makers
Alternate Edition

Managerial

Maher, Stickney, and Weil
Managerial Accounting: An Introduction to Concepts, Methods, and Uses
Fifth Edition

Intermediate

Williams, Stanga, and Holder
Intermediate Accounting
Fifth Edition

Advanced

Pahler and Mori
Advanced Accounting: Concepts and Practice
Fifth Edition

Financial Statement Analysis

Stickney
Financial Statement Analysis: A Strategic Perspective
Third Edition

Auditing

Guy, Alderman, and Winters
Auditing
Fourth Edition

Rittenberg and Schwieger
Auditing: Concepts for a Changing Environment

Theory

Belkaoui
Accounting Theory
Third Edition

Bloom and Elgers
Foundations of Accounting Theory and Policy: A Reader

Bloom and Elgers
Issues in Accounting Policy: A Reader

Taxation

Everett, Raabe, and Fortin
1995 Income Tax Fundamentals

Reference

Miller and Bailey
Miller Comprehensive GAAS Guide
College Edition

Williams and Miller
Miller Comprehensive GAAP Guide
College Edition

Miller
Electronic GAAP Guide
College Edition

Governmental and Not-For-Profit

Douglas
Governmental and Nonprofit Accounting: Theory and Practice
Second Edition

Preface

RESPONDING TO THE CALL FOR ACCOUNTING EDUCATION

The Eighth Edition of *Financial Accounting* represents the most extensive revision in the book's history. The changes to the text are based on revisions in the accounting curriculum proposed by the Accounting Education Change Commission and the nation's largest public accounting firms and now being implemented in accounting departments across the country. In an effort to improve the academic preparation of accountants, these groups have suggested a variety of goals for accounting education. These goals, first reflected in the Seventh Edition, have been achieved more fully in the Eighth Edition.

Provide a broad view of the role of accounting in society. Every business function has a relationship to accounting. The pervasive need for accounting information in the business world has been one of the themes of the book in the last two editions. For the Eighth Edition, the importance of the business world is emphasized throughout—its technologies, procedures, applications, and its uses of financial information. Interwoven into the text and end-of-chapter material are well over 150 references and applications of accounting to real-world companies. Students are first introduced to the role of accounting in society in a new section in Chapter 1. **Point of Interest boxes,** integrated within topic areas in each chapter, are based primarily on actual companies.

Provide an overview of the ethical responsibilities of the accountant. Introduced in Chapter 1, a section on ethics and the accounting environment sets the foundation for an **Ethics Case** in each chapter. These cases focus not on general matters of right and wrong but on how the accountant's particular responsibilities may require him or her to confront ethical dilemmas.

Enhance students' analytical skills. A key to success in business is the ability to solve unstructured problems. Multiple opportunities to gain such experience are presented in end-of-chapter **Principles Discussion Questions, Financial Analysis Cases,** and **Business Decision Cases.**

Develop communications skills. For accounting information to be effective, it must be communicated to its users. Writing requirements are integrated throughout the end-of-chapter material.

Gain an understanding of the best practices of other cultures. The effective business-person must see beyond his or her own environment and understand the world beyond. To encourage this, international accounting issues have been integrated into the text as part of the larger integration of real-company processes, technologies, and principles applications. In addition, Appendix A focuses on international accounting issues and practices.

THE THEMES OF THE EIGHTH EDITION

The Eighth Edition builds on these goals for better educated accounting students. We have developed the following themes based on the current state of flux in which accounting educators find themselves. Throughout the revision, we focused on these core themes.

- **Within a traditionally mainstream chapter sequence and rigor, place greater emphasis on concepts, less emphasis on procedures.**   We focused less on procedures without sacrificing the building blocks to understanding accounting activities: journal entries and debits and credits.

- **Greater emphasis on principles as the groundwork for understanding business and accounting.**   We placed coverage of principles and the conceptual framework in Chapter 2 and reinforced their application in **Principle Alert** boxes throughout the text.

- **Greater emphasis on the use of financial information.**   Consistent with the traditional stability that focusing on a single major company provides, we included General Mills' financial statements and disclosures in an end-of-book appendix and emphasized reading and interpretation through **General Mills Annual Report Cases** in every chapter.

- **Coverage of current trends in business.**   We added **Point of Interest** boxes, completely revised the systems Chapter 5, and added new topics such as *limited liability companies, new investment analyses* (current through FAS 115), *impaired assets* (FAS 121), and *just-in-case* and *just-in-time inventories*.

MAJOR CHANGES IN THE EIGHTH EDITION

Within the traditional chapter sequence and teaching approach, the Eighth Edition streamlines the procedural content and strengthens the conceptual underpinnings of the financial accounting course. Although journal entries are retained to provide students with a solid grasp of accounting basics within a business context, changes include the following:

- The accounting cycle occurs in one comprehensive chapter (Chapter 3), with the cycle worksheet placed in chapter-ending Appendix B and reversing entries moved to Appendix C.

- Worksheets are eliminated from the merchandising Chapter 5 and the statement of cash flows Chapter 15.

- Preparation of special journals has been eliminated.

- The Eighth Edition contains a renewed and more focused emphasis on the basic accounting principles. An introduction to principles and the conceptual framework, previously in Chapters 1 and 12, has been consolidated into Chapter 2 and reinforced throughout with Principle Alert boxes and Principles Discussion Questions.

- Instructors teaching the chapter on cash flows (Chapter 15) can now choose between simplified, graphic, free-standing coverage of either the direct or the indirect method of preparing the statement.

- Coverage of investments has been combined into Chapter 14, completely rewritten to incorporate FAS 115, and class-tested by the authors.

- Based on its overwhelming use in business, the perpetual inventory system is emphasized in the merchandising Chapter 4 and the inventories Chapter 7, and the periodic system is relegated to chapter Appendixes D and E.

- Greater emphasis is placed on real-world situations. Throughout the text, boxes, and end-of-chapter material, actual companies are used much more extensively than in the Seventh Edition to illustrate and explore financial accounting issues and practices.

- Problems sets from the Seventh Edition are retained with new numbers and years, but they are augmented by requirements calling for new approaches and formats in student solutions.

- Chapter 5, the accounting systems chapter, has been completely rewritten to emphasize computer-based accounting systems and internal control.

PEDAGOGY

As in the Seventh Edition, the teaching and learning tools have been designed for maximum usefulness by students and instructors alike. For the Eighth Edition, we have included features to support the move to a more conceptual, financial statement user-oriented course within a traditional framework.

Learning Objectives.   As in previous editions, the text and ancillaries are organized around Learning Objectives, which provide the learning and teaching backbone for the course. Learning Objectives are provided at the beginning of every chapter with page references. They are repeated in the margins of the text at the beginning of the section where they are covered. They are the organizing principle behind the Key Points for Chapter Learning Objectives and the end-of-chapter problem material. So that students will be encouraged to take an active learning approach, action words appear in boldface.

Chapter Quotation.   A relevant chapter-opening quotation exposes students to a broader business perspective.

NEW Chapter Focus.   Each chapter begins with a highlighted box that focuses on an introduction to the main topics covered, and uses real companies and situations to initiate the chapter discussion.

NEW Principle Alert.   For this edition, extended boxed extracts have been replaced by shorter boxes that are immediately relevant to the topic at hand. Principle Alert boxes, inserted where appropriate throughout the text, highlight how the topic discussed relates to the relevant accounting principle(s). This emphasis on the core principles, the subject of Chapter 2 and reinforced in these boxes, reflects an increased emphasis on learning and teaching basic concepts.

NEW Point of Interest.   These short boxes, inserted where appropriate in every chapter, highlight the usefulness of accounting information in the real world by depicting actual companies, industries, business processes, technologies, and activities related to the topics just covered.

Financial Analysis.   Coverage of financial statement analysis ratios is extended from Chapter 16 into a section at the end of each of Chapters 4–15. Formerly titled "Analytical Application," this section uses actual financial statement data from major companies to show not only how the ratios are calculated but emphasize what they mean. Wherever possible, the ratios complement the topics in the chapter. The Financial Analysis sections use the same ratios as in Chapter 16, allowing instructors flexibility in how they incorporate ratios into the financial accounting course—in a single chapter, integrated throughout, or a combination of both.

Key Points for Chapter Learning Objectives.   At the end of each chapter, repeated Chapter Learning Objectives and their key points, along with chapter page references, help students organize their review and study time.

Self-Test Questions for Review.   Five multiple-choice self-study questions help students prepare for quizzes and tests. Answers, with page numbers referring to the relevant discussion in the text, appear after the Solution to Demonstration Problem for Review.

Demonstration Problem for Review.   A demonstration problem at the end of each chapter, with complete solution, gives students another opportunity to assess their comprehension of the material.

Glossary of Key Terms Used in This Chapter.   This chapter glossary, with page references to terms' introduction in the chapter, provides a convenient opportunity for vocabulary review. (Terms appearing here are set in color in the text.)

Questions.   Approximately 18 Questions per chapter provide an opportunity for class discussion or single-concept review. Many questions feature a written requirement.

NEW Principles Discussion Question.   These questions (1 per chapter beginning with Chapter 3) help focus discussion and thought on accounting principles.

Exercises.   For use in class or as assignments, Exercises (approximately 8 per chapter) are identified by both topic and Learning Objective.

Problems.   Problems are also identified by topic and Learning Objective. Each chapter contains approximately 8 problems. This edition retains the text's traditional strength of a diversified, clearly-written set of problems.

Alternate Exercises. Alternate Exercises (approximately 8 per chapter) provide an even wider variety of problem material.

Alternate Problems.   Alternate Problems (approximately 8 per chapter) cover the same concepts as the problems with new data to ensure comprehension. In some cases the Alternate Problem tests for an alternative method or concept.

Business Decision Case.   A Business Decision Case, one per chapter, requires the student to analyze a business situation and make a judgment.

Financial Analysis Case.   Formerly titled "Analytical Application Case," one Financial Analysis Case per chapter tests material covered in the Financial Analysis section of Chapters 4–15. Students are asked not only to analyze financial information but to form a conclusion about what their analysis means.

Ethics Case.   One case per chapter challenges students to make an ethical judgment concerning a gray area in an accounting situation related to the material in the chapter.

NEW General Mills Annual Report Case.   This new case, one per chapter, is designed to foster a student's ability to read and interpret financial statements. Students refer to the General Mills annual report found in Appendix K.

Mini Practice Sets I and II.   These extended problems, found after Chapter 3, constitute an extensive accounting cycle assignment. Set I covers the complete accounting cycle; Set II covers the complete accounting cycle with worksheet and reversing entries.

Financial Statements and Related Disclosures from the 1994 Annual Report of General Mills, Inc.   Appendix K reproduces the 1994 financial statements and related disclosures for General Mills. They are used throughout the text in General Mills Annual Report Cases to provide a comprehensive, user-oriented focus for these assignments.

CHAPTER-BY-CHAPTER CHANGES

The chapter-by-chapter changes follow from the increased emphasis on concepts, the streamlining of procedures within the traditional framework, and the greater emphasis on analyzing and understanding real-world companies and their financial statements.

Chapter 1

- "Fields of Accounting Activity" has been deleted and a new section on the role of accounting in society has been added.
- The introduction to basic principles has been moved to Chapter 2.

Chapter 2

- Coverage of errors in transaction analysis has been deleted.
- Chapter 2 now includes the core coverage of accounting principles, moved from Chapter 12. Deleted from Chapter 12 of the Seventh Edition are collection bases of revenue recognition and percentage of completion accounting. Also deleted is the appendix on reporting the impact of changing prices. Financial disclosures has been moved to Appendix J.
- International accounting principles is now covered in Appendix A.

Chapter 3

- Correcting journal errors and erroneous posting has been deleted.
- The appendix on prepayments recorded in revenue and expense accounts has been deleted.
- The accounting cycle is now in a single chapter, with the use of worksheets confined to Appendix B and reversing entries relegated to Appendix C.

Chapter 4

- Coverage of the worksheets for a merchandising firm—periodic, closing entry method, and adjusting entry method—has been deleted.
- The perpetual method of accounting for inventory is emphasized, and the periodic method has been placed in Appendix D.
- Greater emphasis has been placed on the business activities of merchandisers.
- Coverage of the classified balance sheet and the classified income statement has been combined in Chapter 4.

Chapter 5

- The systems chapter has been completely rewritten to focus on computerized systems and control. Internal control, except controls for cash, has been moved up from the Seventh Edition's Chapter 7 on internal control, cash, and short-term investments. Now emphasized are documents used in business transactions, controls in a computerized system, and auditing.
- Preparation of special journals has been deleted.

Chapter 6

- Receivables (previously Chapter 8) have been consolidated into a single chapter with cash and cash controls.
- Petty cash journal entries have been eliminated.
- Internal control for cash received at point of sale has been added.
- The elements of a check, keyed to a check exhibit, has been added as background to bank reconciliations.

Chapter 7

- The perpetual inventory method is used throughout the chapter, and the periodic inventory method is placed in Appendix E.
- Coverage of the retail inventory method and the gross profit method has been deleted.
- Categories of manufacturing inventories are introduced.
- Just-in-case and just-in-time inventories are introduced.

Chapter 8

- Coverage of operating leases and capital leases has been moved to Chapter 10 on long-term liabilities.
- Coverage of the accounting for impaired assets to reflect FAS 121 has been added.

Chapter 9

- Current liabilities has been reorganized and simplified in four classifications: cash obligations of known amount, cash obligations whose amounts are estimated, goods and services obligations of known amount, and goods and services obligations whose amounts are estimated.
- The chapter has been revised to minimize procedural details of payroll. Deleted topics include employee versus independent contractor, remittance and reporting requirements, Fair Labor Standards Act, computation of net pay for an individual employee, payroll records, and payment to employees.
- A new Appendix F is included on the role of taxes on decision making.

Chapter 10

- Accounting for bond sinking funds has been eliminated.
- Straight-line amortization of bond discount and premium on bonds payable has been eliminated.
- Leases have been moved from the plant assets chapter of the Seventh Edition.
- Term loans have been added.
- Capital lease valuation has been added to Appendix G.

Chapter 11

- Limited liability companies have been added due to the increase in popularity of this form of organization.
- Partnerships has been expanded and now forms an entire chapter along with limited liability companies.

Chapter 12

- Stock subscriptions and participating preferred stock have been eliminated.
- Stock issuances by bond conversion has been moved here from the long-term liabilities chapter.

Chapter 13

- Explanations of the retained earnings statement and the statement of stockholders' equity are keyed to the exhibits.

Chapter 14

- All investment coverage now appears in this chapter, along with coverage of consolidated financial statements.
- Coverage of investments has been completely revised to reflect FAS 115, adding trading, available-for-sale, and held-to-maturity securities.
- Consolidation after acquisition date for wholly owned subsidiaries and for majority-held subsidiaries has been eliminated.

Chapter 15

- Worksheets for preparation of the statement of cash flows under both the direct and indirect methods have been eliminated.
- Free-standing modules of both the direct or the indirect method of preparing the statement of cash flows now appear in the chapter.

Chapter 16

- Financial statement disclosures have been moved here from the previous edition's Chapter 12 as Appendix J.
- Operating cash flow to total liabilities ratio has been eliminated.
- Appendixes on the income taxation of corporations and the income taxation of individuals have been eliminated.

SUPPLEMENTS PACKAGE

Solutions Manual. As in past editions, the Solutions Manual has been written, exhaustively revised, proofed, and cross-checked against the textbook by both authors for maximum compatibility and accuracy. The manual includes answers to all end-of-chapter Questions, Principles Discussion Questions, Exercises, Alternate Exercises, Problems, Alternate Problems, and Cases from the textbook.

Computerized Instructor's Manual by Jeffrey D. Ritter (St. Norbert College) and Sandra Halenka-Bitenc (Texas Christian University). For maximum instructional flexibility, the Instructor's Manual will be distributed on a Windows disk. Contains chapter teaching outlines, questions for class discussion, suggested assignment sequences for light, moderate, and heavy amounts of homework, writing assignments, and other aids for instructional support. Also includes 10-Minute Quizzes by Sharyll A. B. Plato (University of Central Oklahoma).

Computerized Test Bank by William Lambert (Houston Community College) and the text authors. Contains true-false, multiple-choice, and problems for every chapter and appendix in the textbook, keyed by chapter objective. Using editing and scrambling, the **EXAMAS-TER+** software allows instructors to customize their tests by selecting items by criteria such as chapter objective and difficulty level. Dryden's RequesTest service allows instructors to call a toll-free number to order custom test masters.

Solutions Transparencies.   Consists of large-type acetate transparencies of numerical Exercises and Alternate Exercises and of all Problems, Alternate Problems, and Cases from the solutions manual.

Study Guide by Imogene A. Posey (University of Tennessee). Contains brief summaries of each chapter with keywords highlighted, chapter review by objective, and a self-test section consisting of true-or-false, multiple-choice, completion, matching items, and exercises in working paper format, all with answers.

Working Papers.   Contains partially filled-out working papers for end-of-chapter Exercises, Alternate Exercises, Problems, Alternate Problems, and Cases.

Checklist of Key Figures.   Key figures for Problems, Alternate Problems, Business Decision Cases, and Financial Analysis Cases give students feedback when solving assignment material.

The Dryden Press will provide complimentary supplements or supplement packages to those adopters qualified under our adoption policy. Please contact your sales representative to learn how you may qualify. If as an adopter or potential user you receive supplements you do not need, please return them to your sales representative or send them to:

Attn: Returns Department
Troy Warehouse
465 South Lincoln Drive
Troy, MO 63379

ACKNOWLEDGMENTS

We are grateful to the following instructors whose comments helped us formulate the themes, pedagogy, and package for the Eighth Edition:

Vern Allen
Central Florida Community College

Tracey Anderson
Indiana University at South Bend

Stanleigh Ayres
Burlington County College

Frank Beigbeder
Rancho Santiago College

Mike Capsuto
Cypress College

Craig Christofferson
Richland College

Paul A. Concilio
McLennon Community College

Walter DeAguero
Saddleback College

Kenneth Duffy
Brookdale Community College

Shirley Glass
Macomb Community College

Gloria Halpern
Montgomery College

John Hartwick
Bucks County College

Tom Hoar
Houston Community College

Don Holloway
Long Beach City College

Thomas Jackson
Cerritos Community College

Ray Krov
Union Community College

William Lambert
Houston Community College

John Martinelli
El Camino College

Janet Matsumaya
Fullerton College

Lyn Mazzola-Paluska
Nassau Community College

William Owens
Golden West College

Imogene Posey
University of Tennessee

David Ravetch
University of California, Los Angeles

Jeffrey Ritter
St. Norbert College

E. Thomas Robinson
University of Alaska—Fairbanks

Steve Rowley
University of Minnesota, Duluth

Jacqueline Sanders
Mercer County Community College

Robbie Sheffy
Tarrant County Junior College, South

Dean Wallace
Collin County Community College

We also wish to thank the team members at The Dryden Press for their tireless efforts on behalf of the book: Mike Reynolds, executive editor; Craig Avery, senior developmental editor; Craig Johnson, product manager; Kathryn Stewart, project editor; Jeanette Barber, designer; Jessica Wyatt, production manager; Adele Krause, art and literary rights editor; Elizabeth Mendoza, editorial assistant; and Kelly Whidbee, marketing assistant.

Contents in Brief

Contents

NOTE: Chapters also contain Key Points for Chapter Learning Objectives, Self-Test Questions for Review, Demonstration Problem for Review (and Solution), Answers to Self-Test Questions, Glossary of Key Terms Used in this Chapter, Questions, Principles Discussion Question, Exercises, Problems, Alternate Exercises, Alternate Problems, Business Decision Case, Financial Analysis Case, Ethics Case, and General Mills Annual Report Case.

CHAPTER 2 THE DOUBLE-ENTRY ACCOUNTING SYSTEM; ACCOUNTING PRINCIPLES 31

CHAPTER 3 THE ACCOUNTING CYCLE 69

CHAPTER 4 MERCHANDISING OPERATIONS AND CLASSIFIED FINANCIAL STATEMENTS 123

CHAPTER 5   ACCOUNTING SYSTEMS AND INTERNAL CONTROL   165

CHAPTER 6   Cash, Cash Controls, and Receivables   193

Chapter 9   Current and Contingent Liabilities   307

CHAPTER 10   LONG-TERM LIABILITIES   342

CHAPTER 11   PARTNERSHIPS AND LIMITED LIABILITY COMPANIES   379

CHAPTER 12   CORPORATIONS: ORGANIZATION AND CAPITAL STOCK   406

Chapter 13   Corporations: Dividends, Retained Earnings, and Earnings Disclosure   435

CHAPTER 14   INVESTMENTS AND CONSOLIDATED FINANCIAL STATEMENTS   467

FINANCIAL ACCOUNTING

EIGHTH EDITION

Accounting: An Information System

CHAPTER LEARNING OBJECTIVES

1 **DESCRIBE** the nature of the accounting process and flows of accounting information (pp. 2–5).

2 **DEFINE** generally accepted accounting principles (p. 5).

3 **DESCRIBE** the role of financial accounting in society (pp. 5–6).

4 **DEFINE** the accounting equation (pp. 6–7).

5 **EXPLAIN** and **ILLUSTRATE** the effects of transactions on the accounting equation (pp. 7–13).

6 **INTRODUCE** the basic financial statements (pp. 13–15).

7 **EXPLAIN** the forms of business organization (pp. 15–16).

8 **IDENTIFY** ethical dimensions related to the accounting environment (pp. 16–17).

CHAPTER FOCUS

The need for financial information leads to a process for creating that information. On a personal level, for example, we need to know how much cash we have available to spend, so we keep a record of our personal checking account. Or we may need to evaluate whether we can afford to attend a particular school, so we prepare a budget showing the expected costs of that school to compare with our expected financial resources. Or we need to determine how much income tax we owe the government, so we prepare an income tax return. In all of these cases, we are engaged in an accounting activity because *the basic purpose of accounting is to provide financial information that is useful in making economic decisions.*

Economic decisions need to be made for organizations as well as individuals. Accounting is the means by which managers and others are informed of the financial status and progress of their organizations. The ability to use the accounting data helps managers and others accomplish their economic objectives. Our study of accounting will emphasize the accounting for organizations, particularly businesses. You will discover the types of economic activities that can be accounted for usefully, the methods used to collect accounting data, and the implications of the resulting information. Furthermore—and often just as important—you will become aware of the limitations of accounting reports. In this chapter, we introduce various aspects of the accounting environment and the analytic process used by accountants.

THE ACCOUNTING PROCESS

OBJECTIVE *1*

DESCRIBE the nature of the accounting process and flows of accounting information.

Accounting may be defined as *the process of measuring the economic activity of an entity in money terms and communicating the results to interested parties.* The accounting process, therefore, consists of two major activities—measurement and communication.

The measurement process requires the accountant to (1) identify the relevant economic activity of the entity, (2) quantify the economic activity, and (3) record the resultant measures in a systematic fashion. Measurement is done in money terms. In the United States, measurements are stated in U.S. dollars. In other countries, measurements are expressed in the local currency. Accounting measurements in Mexico, for example, are stated in pesos.

Because the purpose of accounting is to provide useful financial information, the communication process is extremely important. Engaging in this activity, the accountant (1) prepares financial reports that meet the needs of the user and (2) helps interpret the financial results. To provide reports that serve users well, accountants need to be aware of how users are going to utilize the reports. As we will discuss shortly, there is a variety of user groups; accordingly, there are different types of financial reports prepared by accountants. Accountants employ various techniques to help users interpret the reports. These techniques include the way the report is formatted, the use of charts and graphs to highlight significant trends, and the calculation of ratios to emphasize important financial relationships.

Exhibit 1-1 portrays the accounting process we have just discussed.

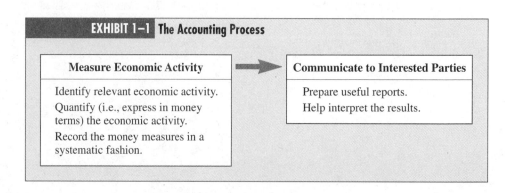

EXHIBIT 1–1 The Accounting Process

Measure Economic Activity	**Communicate to Interested Parties**
Identify relevant economic activity. Quantify (i.e., express in money terms) the economic activity. Record the money measures in a systematic fashion.	Prepare useful reports. Help interpret the results.

INFORMATION FLOWS TO USERS

In today's society, many persons and agencies are involved in the economic life of an organization. The information needs of these parties are fulfilled, in part, by financial information. Information users may be classified by their relationship to the organization—as *internal users* and *external users*. Management at all levels constitute the internal users of financial information. External users include investors, creditors, taxing agencies, regulatory agencies, labor unions, and economic planners. Exhibit 1-2 shows the flow of financial information to these groups.

FLOW A: MANAGERIAL DATA AND REPORTS

A major function of accounting is to provide management with the data needed for decision making and for efficient operation of the firm. While managers do have an interest in the

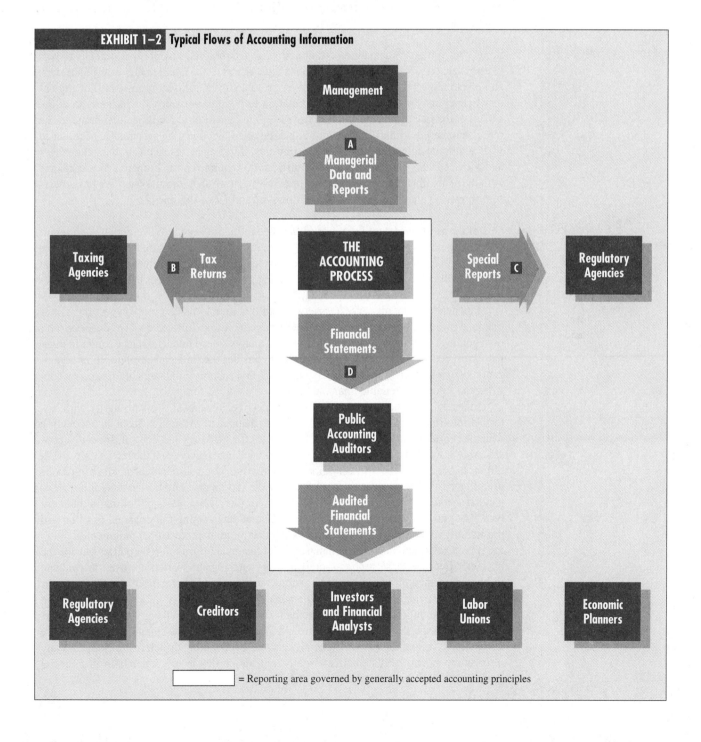

EXHIBIT 1–2 Typical Flows of Accounting Information

= Reporting area governed by generally accepted accounting principles

information reported to external users, managers also require various other information, such as the unit cost of a product, estimates of the profit earned from a specific sales campaign, cost comparisons of alternative courses of action, and long-range budgets. Because of the strategic nature of some of this information, it may be available only to the firm's high-level management. The process of generating and analyzing such data is referred to as **managerial accounting.**

FLOW B: TAX RETURNS

Taxes provide the funds to operate various levels of government. There are many kinds of taxes and, consequently, many kinds of tax returns. Most organizations must file one or more tax returns. A business, for example, may be required to file returns for federal, state, and municipal income taxes, sales and excise taxes, and payroll taxes. The preparation of these returns is governed by the rulings and special reporting requirements of the taxing agencies involved. Proper compliance is generally a matter of law and can be quite complicated.

FLOW C: SPECIAL REPORTS

Some companies, by the nature of their activities, are required to report periodically to regulatory agencies. For example, most banks must report to the Comptroller of the Currency, and most public utility companies must report to a public utility commission. The regulatory agency may use the reported information to monitor solvency (as in the case of the banks) or the rate of income to be earned (as in the case of public utilities). Although these reports are based primarily on accounting data, often they must be prepared in accordance with additional conditions, rules, and definitions. Some agencies, such as stock exchanges and the Securities and Exchange Commission, do require reports prepared in accordance with the generally accepted accounting principles that we shall discuss later. We have therefore shown regulatory agencies in both flows C and D of Exhibit 1-2.

FLOW D: FINANCIAL STATEMENTS

One of the most important functions of the accounting process is to accumulate and report accounting information that shows an organization's financial position, cash flows, and the results of its operations. Publicly owned businesses publish such financial statements at least annually. The subdivision of the accounting process that produces these financial statements is referred to as **financial accounting.**

Financial statements serve a variety of external users. For example, owners must have financial information in order to measure management's performance and to evaluate their own holdings. Potential investors and financial analysts need financial data in order to compare prospective investments. Creditors must consider the financial strength of an organization before lending it funds. Also, labor unions and economic planners often expect a considerable amount of reliable financial data.

Financial accounting is essentially retrospective, because it deals primarily with historical information, or events that have already happened. Although financial accounting data are primarily historical, they are also useful for planning and control. Indeed, a considerable amount of planning must be based on what has happened in the recent past. In addition, historical financial information is inherently a control mechanism, since it can be used to measure the success of past planning. We should also emphasize that, although financial accounting is primarily historical, it is not merely a process of "filling in the numbers." As you study further, you will discover that determining the financial position and profitability of an enterprise is a complex job that requires professional judgment.

Financial statements are the main source of financial information for parties outside the business. Because these reports—prepared by management—often are used to evaluate management, their objectivity could be subject to question. To establish the validity of their financial statements, most firms have them audited by independent public accountants. The independent auditor examines the statements and suggests any changes that may be warranted. He or she then expresses a professional opinion that the financial statements are fairly stated "in conformity with generally accepted accounting principles" or indicates any reservations about the statements. Usually, outside parties have greater faith in financial statements that have been audited.

THE BIG SIX

Independent auditors are licensed by the state in which they do their auditing work and are identified as *certified public accountants* (CPAs). To qualify as a CPA, a person must pass a rigorous examination that is administered nationally and must meet the requirements for education and experience set by the state to ensure high standards of performance. The six largest U.S. public accounting firms, referred to as the *Big Six,* have offices located throughout the world and employ thousands of auditors. These six firms are

Arthur Andersen & Co.
Coopers & Lybrand
Deloitte and Touche
Ernst & Young
KPMG Peat Marwick
Price Waterhouse & Co.

GENERALLY ACCEPTED ACCOUNTING PRINCIPLES

OBJECTIVE 2
DEFINE generally accepted accounting principles.

External users who rely on audited financial statements expect that all companies follow the same standards and procedures in preparing their statements. Accountants have developed an overall set of standards and procedures that apply to the preparation of financial statements. These standards and procedures are called **generally accepted accounting principles (GAAP).** As Exhibit 1-2 indicates, generally accepted accounting principles are primarily relevant to financial accounting.

Because financial accounting is more an art than a science, generally accepted accounting principles are not immutable laws like those in the physical sciences. Instead, they are *guides to action* and may change over time. Sometimes specific principles must be altered or new principles must be formulated to fit changed economic circumstances or changes in business practices.

The most prominent organization concerned with the formulation of generally accepted accounting principles is the Financial Accounting Standards Board (FASB). The FASB is a nongovernmental body whose pronouncements establish GAAP. Consisting of a seven-member board, the FASB follows a process that allows for input from interested parties as it considers a new or changed accounting principle. A new or changed principle requires the support of at least five of the seven board members.

The accounting principles we discuss are generally accepted in the United States. Accounting principles, however, differ in various ways among countries. Energized by the continuing growth of international business, efforts are under way to create more uniformity in worldwide accounting principles.

THE ROLE OF FINANCIAL ACCOUNTING IN SOCIETY

OBJECTIVE 3
DESCRIBE the role of financial accounting in society.

Under any economic system, decisions must be made about how to allocate society's scarce resources for the betterment of its citizens. In the capitalistic, free enterprise system found in the United States, resources are basically allocated by a market system. Individual business entities engage in economic activity to provide various types of goods and services. The owners of these entities are entitled to keep the profits that are generated by their economic activity. Thus, the potential for profits is a motivating force leading to the creation of business entities, and the presence of profits is a critical factor in the continuation of such entities.

Business entities look to investors (i.e., owners) and creditors for financial resources that are needed for the continuation and/or expansion of their economic activity. Investors and creditors, then, need to make decisions about where to direct their financial resources. It doesn't matter whether the investor or creditor is an individual or a large financial institution—the same type of resource allocation decision has to be made. In general, investors and creditors direct their resources to the most profitable, efficient, and productive entities. These are the entities that will provide the highest return for the investor and are the most likely to repay the creditor. Ideally, these allocations result in a healthy economy that meets the needs of its citizens.

To make the appropriate allocation decisions, investors and creditors need to be well informed. Important components of the information they need are the financial statements generated by the financial accounting process. These statements express the economic activity of business entities in money terms and report on the entities' profitability, financial strength, and cash flows. Financial statements that present the results of economic activity fairly and completely should contribute significantly to the best possible allocation decisions by investors and creditors. *Thus, a properly functioning process of financial accounting is crucial to the proper allocation of financial resources in a free enterprise economic system.*

THE ACCOUNTING EQUATION

OBJECTIVE 4
DEFINE the accounting equation.

Accounting analysis takes place within a framework called the *accounting equation.* The **accounting equation** states that the economic resources of a specific entity are equal to the claims on those resources. Another term used to refer to the claims on resources is *equities.* For a business, equities may represent the claims of creditors or of owners. In its basic form, then, the accounting equation appears as follows:

$$\text{Economic Resources} = \text{Claims of Creditors} + \text{Claims of Owners}$$

In stating the accounting equation, accountants use the technical terms *assets, liabilities,* and *owners' equity* to refer, respectively, to a company's economic resources, claims of creditors, and claims of owners. In its technical formulation, then, the accounting equation appears as follows:

$$\text{Assets} = \text{Liabilities} + \text{Owners' Equity}$$

This equation states that an entity's assets equal the sum of its liabilities and owners' equity. *Throughout our accounting analysis, this accounting equation will (and must) remain in balance.*

Accounting Equation for a Business Entity		
Technical Terms:	Assets = Liabilities	+ Owners' Equity
Basic Meanings:	Economic Resources = Claims of Creditors	+ Claims of Owners

We now briefly explain each of the three elements in the accounting equation.

ASSETS Assets are the economic resources of an entity that can be usefully expressed in money terms. Assets may take many forms. Cash is an asset, as are claims to receive cash payments from customers for services or goods provided (accounts receivable). Some assets—such as supplies, land, buildings, and equipment—may have readily identifiable physical characteristics. Others may simply represent prepayments for future services (for example, prepaid advertising) or nonphysical rights (for example, patents and copyrights).

The key characteristic of an asset is that it represents a probable future economic benefit owned or controlled by the entity. Although most items reported as assets are owned by the entity, ownership is not an essential test for an asset. To illustrate, assume that a business with a temporary need for storage space rents warehouse space for one year and prepays the year's rent. Although it does not own the storage space, the firm has paid for the right to use the warehouse for one year. This is a future economic benefit for the firm, which will report the prepaid rent as one of its assets.

LIABILITIES

Liabilities are the obligations, or debts, that an entity must pay in money or services at some time in the future because of past transactions or events. For example, a firm may borrow money and sign a promissory note agreeing to pay it back six months in the future. The firm will report this obligation as a liability called *notes payable.* Similarly, the firm may owe amounts to various suppliers for goods or services already provided (*accounts payable*), or it may owe wages to employees for work already performed (*wages payable*). Notes payable, accounts payable, and wages payable are obligations that will be settled in the relatively near future. Other liabilities may take long periods to settle. For example, a business may borrow funds to finance the construction of a building and agree to pay them back over the next 15 years, with the building serving as collateral for the loan. This transaction results in a liability called *mortgage payable.*

Although most liabilities are payable in cash, some may involve the performance of services. A magazine publisher, for example, may receive advance cash payments for three-year subscriptions. The receipt of these payments creates an obligation for the publisher to provide subscribers with issues of the magazine. The publisher will report a liability (subscriptions received in advance) that will be reduced as the magazines are sent to subscribers.

OWNERS' EQUITY

Owners' equity is the interest of the owners in the assets of an entity. The owners' interest is a *residual claim* on the entity's assets; that is, it is a claim to the assets remaining after the liabilities to creditors have been discharged. For this reason, owners' equity may also be defined as the **net assets** of an entity; net assets is the difference between the assets and the liabilities. Thus,

$$\text{Assets} - \text{Liabilities} = \text{Owners' Equity}$$
$$\text{Net Assets} = \text{Owners' Equity}$$

EFFECT OF TRANSACTIONS ON THE ACCOUNTING EQUATION

OBJECTIVE 5
EXPLAIN and **ILLUSTRATE** the effects of transactions on the accounting equation.

An *accounting transaction* is an economic event that requires accounting recognition. Therefore, an event that affects any of the elements in the accounting equation (assets, liabilities, or owners' equity) must be recorded. Some activities—for example, ordering supplies, bidding for an engagement or contract, and negotiating for the acquisition of assets— may represent economic activities, but an accounting transaction does not occur until such activities result in a change in the firm's assets, liabilities, or owners' equity.

Earlier, we observed that the accounting equation (Assets = Liabilities + Owners' Equity) will always remain in balance. An accounting transaction may affect the components of this equation in various ways, but the equation stays in balance. If assets, liabilities, and owners' equity are computed after each accounting transaction is recorded, the equality of assets and equities will always be confirmed.

TRANSACTIONS NOT AFFECTING OWNERS' EQUITY

Certain transactions may change the character and amounts of assets or liabilities, or both, but have no effect on owners' equity. For example, if a firm purchases equipment for $1,000 cash, the asset Equipment will increase by $1,000, but the asset Cash will decrease by $1,000. This transaction causes only a shift in the composition of individual assets; it does not change total assets. In the same way, collection of accounts receivable causes a shift of assets. Collection of $500 of Accounts Receivable would result in a decrease in this asset and an increase in Cash of $500.

If the $1,000 worth of equipment had been purchased on credit rather than for cash, the result would have been a $1,000 increase in Equipment and an equal increase in the liability Accounts Payable. On the other hand, payment of liabilities reduces both assets and liabilities. If $800 is paid to creditors, both Cash and Accounts Payable would decrease by $800.

TRANSACTIONS AFFECTING OWNERS' EQUITY

The following four types of transactions change the amount of owners' equity:

Transaction	Effect on Owners' Equity
1. Owner contributions	Increase
2. Owner withdrawals	Decrease
3. Revenues	Increase
4. Expenses	Decrease

When an owner contributes cash or other assets to a business firm, the firm's accounting records show an increase in assets and an increase in owners' equity. Conversely, when an owner withdraws assets from the firm, both assets and owners' equity decrease. A major goal of any business, however, is to increase the owners' equity by earning profits, or **net income.** The net income of a firm is determined by subtracting *expenses incurred* from *revenues earned.*

$$\text{Net Income} = \text{Revenues} - \text{Expenses}$$

Owners' equity is increased by revenues and decreased by expenses. Let us examine the nature of revenues and expenses.

REVENUES

Revenues are the increases in owners' equity that a firm earns by providing goods or services for its customers. The revenue earned typically is measured by the assets received in exchange for the goods or services. Sometimes the earning of revenue decreases a liability rather than causing assets to increase. It is important to recognize that *revenue is created at the time that goods or services are provided.* The asset initially received may be cash, but often it is a different asset, such as accounts receivable. For example, if a firm sells goods for $1,500 cash, it has earned $1,500 of revenue and the asset received is $1,500 Cash. If the firm sells other goods for $1,000 on credit (with payment due in 30 days), it has earned another $1,000 of revenue and the asset received is $1,000 Accounts Receivable.

The following example illustrates when the earning of revenue decreases a liability. Suppose a magazine publisher receives $3,600 cash representing 100 one-year subscriptions to its monthly magazine. This event increases Cash by $3,600 and creates a $3,600 Subscriptions Received in Advance liability. When the publisher sends out the magazine each month to the 100 subscribers, it earns $300 of Subscription Revenue ($\frac{1}{12}$ of $3,600) and the Subscriptions Received in Advance liability is decreased by $300.

Receipt of cash by a firm does not necessarily mean that revenue has been earned. As previously noted, the subsequent collection of an account receivable merely results in a shift of assets from Accounts Receivable to Cash—it does not increase revenue. Also as previously noted, payments received in advance for goods or services create a liability because no revenue has yet been earned. Neither is revenue earned when a business borrows money or when the owners contribute cash. Such increases in assets are not earned because the firm has provided no goods or services.

EXPENSES

Expenses are the decreases in owners' equity that a firm incurs in the process of earning revenues. Generally, expenses are measured by the assets that are used up or flow out of a firm as a result of its operating activities. Expenses may also cause an increase in liabilities. For example, if a firm pays $2,000 to an employee as one month's salary, it has incurred $2,000 of Salaries Expense and the asset given up (that is, flowing out of the firm) is $2,000 Cash. If a firm obtains legal services and receives a $500 invoice from the attorney, the firm has incurred $500 of Legal Expense and has increased its liabilities by $500 Accounts Payable. Rent, supplies, advertising, and the costs of heat, light, and telephone are other examples of expenses incurred in producing revenues.

Payments of cash by a firm do not necessarily mean that an expense has been incurred. Cash expenditures made to acquire assets do not represent expenses. Cash expenditures made to pay liabilities, such as the payment of an account payable, also do not represent expenses and do not affect owners' equity. Withdrawals of cash by owners, although they do reduce owners' equity, do not represent expenses. Expenses are directly related to the earning of revenues; owner withdrawals are not part of a firm's efforts to generate revenues.

TRANSACTIONS AND THE ACCOUNTING EQUATION: AN ILLUSTRATION

Now that we have described the effects of transactions on the accounting equation, let us illustrate the effects with an example.

Experienced driver education instructor John King established a private driving school called Westgate Driving School. King intends to buy a lot for vehicle storage and driver instruction but to lease training vehicles. The transactions for June, the first month of operations, are analyzed below. The accounting equation for Westgate Driving School is presented after each transaction so that the effect on the equation may be examined. When a transaction affects owner's equity, the specific type of change will also be shown.

INITIAL INVESTMENT   TRANSACTION 1

On June 1, King invested $40,000 of his personal funds in the school. This first business transaction increased the asset Cash and increased King's equity (J. King, Capital).

	Assets	=	Liabilities	+	Owner's Equity	
	Cash	=			J. King, Capital	Type of Change
1	+ $40,000	=			+ $40,000	Investment

PURCHASE OF LAND   TRANSACTION 2

On June 2, Westgate Driving School paid $26,000 cash for a lot to be used for storing vehicles and for some driving instruction. This transaction reduced the asset Cash and created another asset, Land, for an equivalent amount. This transaction was merely the conversion of one asset to another.

	Assets			=	Liabilities	+	Owner's Equity	
	Cash	+	Land	=			J. King, Capital	Type of Change
Balance	$40,000			=			$40,000	
2	– 26,000		+ $26,000					
Balance	$14,000	+	$26,000	=			$40,000	

PAYMENT OF RENT   TRANSACTION 3

On June 3, the school paid $800 to rent a furnished office (including utilities) near the parking lot for June. This expenditure is a June expense, representing the cost of using office space for the month. The transaction reduced assets (Cash) and owner's equity (J. King, Capital) by $800.

	Assets			=	Liabilities	+	Owner's Equity	
	Cash	+	Land	=			J. King, Capital	Type of Change
Balance	$14,000	+	$26,000	=			$40,000	
3	– 800						– 800	Expense: Rent
Balance	$13,200	+	$26,000	=			$39,200	

PAYMENT OF LEASE TRANSACTION 4

On June 3, the school paid $3,500 to lease cars for the month of June. This payment permits the driving school to use the automobiles during June and is an expense for June. The transaction reduced assets (Cash) and owner's equity (J. King, Capital) by $3,500.

	Assets			=	Liabilities	+	Owner's Equity	
	Cash	+	Land	=			J. King, Capital	Type of Change
Balance	$13,200	+	$26,000	=			$39,200	
4	−3,500						−3,500	Expense: Car Lease
Balance	$ 9,700	+	$26,000	=			$35,700	

PURCHASE OF ADVERTISING ON ACCOUNT TRANSACTION 5

On June 10, the school received a $300 invoice from the local newspaper for a driving school advertisement that will run in the newspaper four times during June. The invoice will be paid on June 30. The cost of advertising services is an expense incurred to generate revenues, and this $300 is an expense for June. As a result of this transaction, liabilities (Accounts Payable) are increased and owner's equity (J. King, Capital) is decreased by $300.

	Assets			=	Liabilities	+	Owner's Equity	
	Cash	+	Land	=	Accounts Payable	+	J. King, Capital	Type of Change
Balance	$9,700	+	$26,000	=			$35,700	
5					+$300		−300	Expense: Advertising
Balance	$9,700	+	$26,000	=	$300	+	$35,400	

BILLING FOR FEE REVENUE TRANSACTION 6

On June 26, students were billed $16,000 for June instructional fees. Providing instruction during the month generated an asset, Accounts Receivable, and revenue, which increased owner's equity (J. King, Capital), even though payment will not be received until later.

	Assets					=	Liabilities	+	Owner's Equity	
	Cash	+	Accounts Receivable	+	Land	=	Accounts Payable	+	J. King, Capital	Type of Change
Balance	$9,700			+	$26,000	=	$300	+	$35,400	
6			+$16,000						+16,000	Revenue: Instructional Fees Earned
Balance	$9,700	+	$16,000	+	$26,000	=	$300	+	$51,400	

PAYMENT OF SALARIES TRANSACTION 7

On June 30, the school paid instructors' salaries of $9,000 for June. This amount was a June expense, because it represented the cost of employees' services used during June. Therefore, Cash and J. King, Capital were both reduced by $9,000.

	Assets			=	Liabilities	+	Owner's Equity	
	Cash	+ Accounts Receivable	+ Land	=	Accounts Payable	+	J. King, Capital	Type of Change
Balance	$9,700	+ $16,000	+ $26,000	=	$300	+	$51,400	
7	−9,000						−9,000	Expense: Salaries
Balance	$ 700	+ $16,000	+ $26,000	=	$300	+	$42,400	

COLLECTION OF ACCOUNTS RECEIVABLE

TRANSACTION **8**

On June 30, the school collected $10,000 on account from students billed in transaction **6**. This transaction increased Cash and decreased Accounts Receivable—merely a shift in assets. Note that the revenue, which increased owner's equity, had already been reflected when the month's billings were made on June 26.

	Assets			=	Liabilities	+	Owner's Equity	
	Cash	+ Accounts Receivable	+ Land	=	Accounts Payable	+	J. King, Capital	Type of Change
Balance	$ 700	+ $16,000	+ $26,000	=	$300	+	$42,400	
8	+ 10,000	− 10,000						
Balance	$10,700	+ $ 6,000	+ $26,000	=	$300	+	$42,400	

RECEIPT OF INVOICE FOR GAS AND OIL

TRANSACTION **9**

On June 30, the school received a $400 invoice from the local service station for gas and oil charged to the school's account during June. The invoice will be paid in July. Gas and oil used during the month represent a June expense. Consequently, liabilities (Accounts Payable) are increased and owner's equity (J. King, Capital) is decreased by $400.

	Assets			=	Liabilities	+	Owner's Equity	
	Cash	+ Accounts Receivable	+ Land	=	Accounts Payable	+	J. King, Capital	Type of Change
Balance	$10,700	+ $6,000	+ $26,000	=	$300	+	$42,400	
9					+400		−400	Expense: Gas and Oil
Balance	$10,700	+ $6,000	+ $26,000	=	$700	+	$42,000	

PAYMENT OF ACCOUNTS PAYABLE

TRANSACTION **10**

On June 30, the school paid the $300 invoice for advertising that was received on June 10. This transaction reduced assets (Cash) and liabilities (Accounts Payable) by $300.

	Assets			=	Liabilities	+	Owner's Equity	
	Cash	+ Accounts Receivable	+ Land	=	Accounts Payable	+	J. King, Capital	Type of Change
Balance	$10,700	+ $6,000	+ $26,000	=	$700	+	$42,000	
10	−300			=	−300			
Balance	$10,400	+ $6,000	+ $26,000	=	$400	+	$42,000	

BORROWING OF CASH TRANSACTION **11**

On June 30, the school borrowed $3,000 from a bank and King, as owner of Westgate Driving School, signed a promissory note agreeing to pay it back in six months. (The school will use the money to buy a video projection unit so that instructional videotapes may be shown to students.) This borrowing transaction increased both assets (Cash) and liabilities (Notes Payable) by $3,000.

	Assets				=	Liabilities			+	Owner's Equity	
	Cash	+	Accounts Receivable	+	Land	=	Notes Payable	+	Accounts Payable	+	J. King, Capital	Type of Change
Balance	$10,400	+	$6,000	+	$26,000	=			$400	+	$42,000	
11	+3,000						+$3,000					
Balance	$13,400	+	$6,000	+	$26,000	=	$3,000	+	$400	+	$42,000	

WITHDRAWAL BY OWNER TRANSACTION **12**

On June 30, King withdrew $1,400 from the firm for personal use. This withdrawal reduced Cash and J. King, Capital by $1,400. Note that the effect of this transaction was the reverse of transaction **1**, in which King invested personal funds in the school.

	Assets				=	Liabilities			+	Owner's Equity	
	Cash	+	Accounts Receivable	+	Land	=	Notes Payable	+	Accounts Payable	+	J. King, Capital	Type of Change
Balance	$13,400	+	$6,000	+	$26,000	=	$3,000	+	$400	+	$42,000	
12	−1,400										−1,400	Withdrawal
Balance	$12,000	+	$6,000	+	$26,000	=	$3,000	+	$400	+	$40,600	

SUMMARY OF JUNE ACTIVITIES

Exhibit 1-3 summarizes the June activities of the Westgate Driving School. At the end of June, total assets of $44,000 are equaled by a $44,000 total for liabilities plus owner's

---

EXHIBIT 1–3 Summary of June Activities and Their Effect on the Accounting Equation

	Assets				=	Liabilities			+	Owner's Equity	
Transaction	Cash	+ Receivable	+ Land		=	Notes Payable	+	Accounts Payable	+	J. King, Capital	Type of Change
1	+$40,000									+$40,000	Investment
2	−26,000		+$26,000								
3	−800									−800	Rent Expense
4	−3,500									−3,500	Car Lease Expense
5								+$300		−300	Advertising Expense
6		+$16,000								+16,000	Instructional Fees Earned
7	−9,000									−9,000	Salaries Expense
8	+10,000	−10,000									
9								+400		−400	Gas and Oil Expense
10	−300							−300			
11	+3,000						+$3,000				
12	−1,400									−1,400	Withdrawal
	$12,000	+ $ 6,000	+ $26,000		=	$3,000	+	$400	+	$40,600	
		$44,000			=		$44,000				

equity. As a result of the driving school's June activities, John King's capital increased from his original investment of $40,000 to $40,600, an increase of $600. Had King not withdrawn $1,400 for personal use, the increase would have been $2,000, which represents the net income, or net earnings, for June.

BASIC FINANCIAL STATEMENTS

OBJECTIVE 6
INTRODUCE the basic financial statements.

The basic set of statements that are communicated to interested parties comprise four financial statements. They are the income statement, the statement of owners' equity, the balance sheet, and the statement of cash flows. Exhibit 1-4 shows these financial statements for Westgate Driving School.

Note that each financial statement begins with a heading. The heading gives the name of the company and the name of the financial statement. In addition, the balance sheet heading identifies the specific date of the balance sheet, while the headings for the other three financial statements identify the time period that they cover. Note also that the totals in the various financial statements have been double ruled. Accountants do this principally to signify that all necessary calculations have been performed and to emphasize final amounts for the benefit of readers.

Although financial statements are the end result of the financial accounting process, we introduce them in simplified form here, early in our study. Having some knowledge of the ultimate objective of financial accounting will help you understand the various steps in the accounting process.

INCOME STATEMENT

The **income statement** reports the results of operations for a period. The income statement lists the revenues and expenses of the firm. When total revenues exceed total expenses, the resulting amount is net income; when expenses exceed revenues, the resulting amount is a net loss. Westgate Driving School reports a net income of $2,000 for June because its revenues exceed its expenses by that amount.

STATEMENT OF OWNERS' EQUITY

The **statement of owners' equity** presents information on the events causing a change in owners' equity during a period. The statement starts with owners' equity at the beginning of the period, then reports the events causing increases and decreases in the owners' equity, and ends with owners' equity at the end of the period. Owners' equity is increased when owners make investments in the firm and when operations achieve a net income. Owners' equity is decreased when owners make withdrawals from the firm and when operations result in a net loss. During June, the owner's equity of Westgate Driving School increased by $40,000 from owner investments and $2,000 from net income. Withdrawals of $1,400 decreased owner's equity. At the end of June, owner's equity was $40,600.

BALANCE SHEET

The **balance sheet**, sometimes called the **statement of financial position,** is a listing of a firm's assets, liabilities, and owners' equity on a given date. Each of these categories represents a section in a balance sheet. The balance sheet for Westgate Driving School illustrates the typical format for a balance sheet—total assets ($44,000) are shown to be equal to the sum of liabilities and owner's equity ($44,000). This equality, of course, is the equality presented by the accounting equation. For this reason, the accounting equation is sometimes called the *balance sheet equation.*

STATEMENT OF CASH FLOWS

The **statement of cash flows** reports information about cash inflows and outflows during a period of time. The cash flows are grouped into three categories of activities: operating, investing, and financing. The cash flows from operating activities show the cash effects of a firm's efforts to generate revenues. The cash flows from investing activities include the cash payments and receipts that occur when a firm buys and sells assets that it uses in its operations, such as land, buildings, and equipment. The cash flows from financing activities identify owner investments and withdrawals of cash, as well as cash borrowed and repaid.

EXHIBIT 1–4 Financial Statements for Westgate Driving School

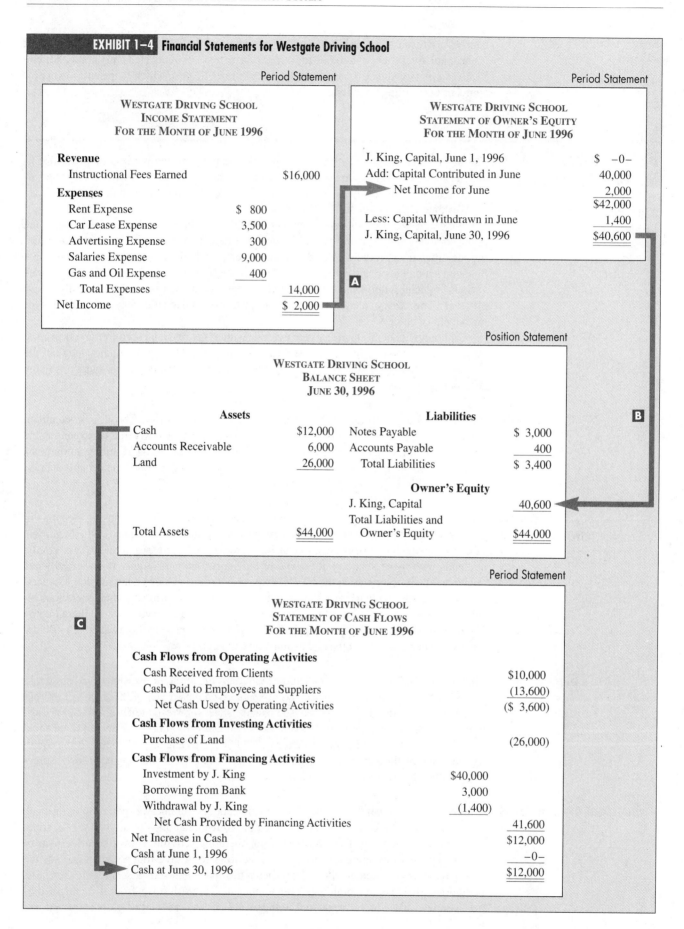

Period Statement

WESTGATE DRIVING SCHOOL
INCOME STATEMENT
FOR THE MONTH OF JUNE 1996

Revenue

Instructional Fees Earned	$16,000

Expenses

Rent Expense	$ 800	
Car Lease Expense	3,500	
Advertising Expense	300	
Salaries Expense	9,000	
Gas and Oil Expense	400	
Total Expenses		14,000
Net Income		$ 2,000

Period Statement

WESTGATE DRIVING SCHOOL
STATEMENT OF OWNER'S EQUITY
FOR THE MONTH OF JUNE 1996

J. King, Capital, June 1, 1996	$ –0–
Add: Capital Contributed in June	40,000
Net Income for June	2,000
	$42,000
Less: Capital Withdrawn in June	1,400
J. King, Capital, June 30, 1996	$40,600

A

Position Statement

WESTGATE DRIVING SCHOOL
BALANCE SHEET
JUNE 30, 1996

Assets		Liabilities	
Cash	$12,000	Notes Payable	$ 3,000
Accounts Receivable	6,000	Accounts Payable	400
Land	26,000	Total Liabilities	$ 3,400
		Owner's Equity	
		J. King, Capital	40,600
		Total Liabilities and	
Total Assets	$44,000	Owner's Equity	$44,000

B

Period Statement

WESTGATE DRIVING SCHOOL
STATEMENT OF CASH FLOWS
FOR THE MONTH OF JUNE 1996

Cash Flows from Operating Activities

Cash Received from Clients	$10,000
Cash Paid to Employees and Suppliers	(13,600)
Net Cash Used by Operating Activities	($ 3,600)

Cash Flows from Investing Activities

Purchase of Land	(26,000)

Cash Flows from Financing Activities

Investment by J. King	$40,000	
Borrowing from Bank	3,000	
Withdrawal by J. King	(1,400)	
Net Cash Provided by Financing Activities		41,600
Net Increase in Cash		$12,000
Cash at June 1, 1996		–0–
Cash at June 30, 1996		$12,000

C

RELATIONSHIPS AMONG THE FINANCIAL STATEMENTS

The income statement, the statement of owners' equity, the balance sheet, and the statement of cash flows complement one another. To illustrate, refer again to the financial statements of Westgate Driving School in Exhibit 1-4. Observe that **A** the net income (or net loss) for a period is an input into the statement of owner's equity, and **B** the ending owner's equity is an input into the balance sheet. Further, the statement of cash flows explains the reasons for a change in cash for a period, and **C** its ending cash amount agrees with the cash amount in the balance sheet. When financial statements are prepared, the sequence suggested by these relationships is customarily followed; that is, *the income statement is prepared first, then the statement of owners' equity, then the balance sheet, and then the statement of cash flows.*

Three of the basic financial statements present information covering a specific period of time. They are the income statement, the statement of owners' equity, and the statement of cash flows. For this reason, these financial statements are referred to as **period statements.** In contrast, the balance sheet shows information as of a specific date. The balance sheet, therefore, is referred to as a **position statement.**

FORMS OF BUSINESS ORGANIZATION

OBJECTIVE *7*
EXPLAIN the forms of business organization.

The principal forms of business organization are the sole proprietorship, the partnership, and the corporation.[1] Although each of these organizational units is treated as an accounting entity, only the corporation is viewed under the law as a legal entity separate from its owners. A **sole proprietorship** is a business owned by one person; it is the most numerous of the three forms of business organization. A **partnership** is a voluntary association of two or more persons for the purpose of conducting a business. A **corporation** is a separate legal entity created under the laws of a state or the federal government. Owners of a corporation receive shares of stock as evidence of their ownership and, consequently, the owners are referred to as *stockholders* or *shareholders.* The corporation is the most dominant organizational form in terms of the volume of business activity conducted.

The principal differences in the financial statements for the three types of business organizations just described appear in the owners' equity section of the balance sheet. State corporation laws require that corporations segregate, in their balance sheets, the owners' investment (the amount paid for their stock) and any accumulated earnings. Because there are no comparable legal restrictions on sole proprietorships and partnerships, these types of businesses do not have to distinguish between amounts invested by owners and undistributed earnings.

The following illustrations demonstrate the variations in the balance sheet presentation of owners' equity for the three forms of business organization.

CASE I: SOLE PROPRIETORSHIP

George Taylor originally invested $50,000 in a graphics business. Subsequent earnings left in the business amounted to $30,000. The owner's equity section of the firm's balance sheet would appear as follows:

Owner's Equity

G. Taylor, Capital $80,000

CASE II: PARTNERSHIP

George Taylor, Eva Williams, and John Young invested $25,000, $15,000, and $10,000, respectively, in a graphics business. Each partner's share of the subsequent earnings of $30,000 not withdrawn from the business was $10,000. The owners' equity section of this firm's balance sheet would appear as follows:

---

[1]Variations on these basic organizational forms are driven by liability and/or tax considerations. We discuss the limited liability company (LLC) and limited liability partnership (LLP) in Chapter 11.

OPEN AND CLOSED CORPORATIONS

Corporations may be classified as an open corporation or a closed corporation. An **open corporation** sells its stock to the general public. The stock of a **closed corporation** is not available to the general public. Also known as a **closely held corporation,** the closed corporation either has relatively few shareholders (such as family members) or shareholders who are members of a select group (such as company executives). Most well-known corporations, such as General Motors, IBM, and Wal-Mart Stores, are open corporations. However, the ranks of closed corporations include such companies as United Parcel Service, Montgomery Ward & Co., Levi Strauss & Co., Hallmark Cards, Penske Corp., Russell Stover Candies, Rayovac, Bose, Packard Bell Electronics, and Jockey International.

Owners' Equity

G. Taylor, Capital	$35,000
E. Williams, Capital	25,000
J. Young, Capital	20,000
Total Owners' Equity	$80,000

CASE III: CORPORATION

George Taylor, Eva Williams, and John Young began a corporation investing $25,000, $15,000, and $10,000, respectively, and receiving shares of stock for those amounts, totaling $50,000. This amount, called Capital Stock, is not available for distribution to the owners (stockholders). Unlike sole proprietorships and partnerships, in which owners are personally liable for the firm's debts, corporate stockholders' liability is usually limited to their investment. Therefore, the capital stock amount is kept intact to protect the firm's creditors. Because there may be many shareholders and because the shares of stock are freely transferable, the identity of the stockholders is not shown in the balance sheet. Corporate earnings, amounting to $30,000, that have not been distributed are identified as *retained earnings* in the corporate balance sheet. Ordinarily, this is the maximum amount that can be distributed to the shareholders. The stockholders' equity section of the firm's balance sheet would appear as follows:

Stockholders' Equity

Capital Stock	$50,000
Retained Earnings	30,000
Total Stockholders' Equity	$80,000

In sole proprietorships and partnerships, the owners may make withdrawals at their own discretion. A withdrawal results in a decrease in cash and a decrease in the owner's capital. In a corporation, a formal procedure is needed. The board of directors, elected by the stockholders, must meet and "declare a dividend" before the distribution can be made to the stockholders. If the firm in our illustration declared and paid a dividend of $5,000, both cash and retained earnings would be reduced by that amount, and the retained earnings balance would be $25,000.

ETHICS AND THE ACCOUNTING ENVIRONMENT

Ethics deals with the values, rules, and justifications that govern one's way of life. Although fundamental ethical concepts such as right and wrong, good and evil, justice, and morality tend to be abstract, many of the issues we face in our daily lives have ethical dimensions. The way we respond to these issues defines our ethical profile. In both our personal and professional lives, our goal should be to act ethically and responsibly.

Ethical behavior has not always been the case in the business world. Business history reveals such unethical activities as price-gouging customers, using inside information for

OBJECTIVE 8

IDENTIFY ethical dimensions related to the accounting environment.

personal gain, paying bribes to government officials, ignoring safety regulations, selling arms to aggressor governments, polluting the environment, and issuing misleading financial information.

Increasingly, however, business managements recognize the importance of ethical behavior from their employees. It is now common for businesses to develop written codes of ethics to guide their employees. About 75% of the top 1,200 U.S. companies have written ethical codes. Similarly, professional organizations of accountants have written ethical codes. The American Institute of Certified Public Accountants (AICPA) has a professional code of ethics to guide the conduct of member CPAs. The Institute of Management Accountants (IMA) has formulated written standards of ethical conduct for accountants employed in private accounting.

Accountants face several unique ethical dimensions as a result of their work. These dimensions include the following:

1. The output produced by accountants may have significant financial implications for one or more persons. These situations may generate pressures on the accountant to "improve" the outcome. The amount of income taxes to be paid by an individual or organization, the amount of a bonus to be received by an employee, the price to be paid by a customer, and the amount of money to be distributed to owners are examples of situations in which the financial implications may lead to efforts to influence the outcome. *Ethical behavior mandates that accountants should ignore these pressures.*

2. Accountants have access to confidential and sensitive information. Tax returns, salary data, details of financial arrangements, planned acquisitions, and proposed price changes illustrate these types of information. *Ethically, accountants must respect the confidentiality of the data used in their work.*

3. An emphasis on short-term profits may contribute to ethical breakdowns within businesses. One of the criticisms of U.S. business practices is that they are too "bottom-line" (that is, short-term profit) oriented. This orientation may lead to unethical actions by management to increase reported short-term profits. Because accountants compute and report firms' profits, they should be particularly concerned about these ethical breakdowns. *Both accountants and managements must recognize the importance of a long-run perspective.* Indeed, studies indicate that, over the long term, successful companies and ethical practices go hand in hand.

KEY POINTS FOR CHAPTER LEARNING OBJECTIVES

1 **DESCRIBE** the nature of the accounting process and flows of accounting information (pp. 2–5).
- Accounting is the process of measuring the economic activity of an entity in money terms and communicating the results to interested parties.
- The basic purpose of accounting is to provide financial information that is useful in making economic decisions.
- Reporting to management, taxing agencies, and regulatory agencies is in accordance with their directives or regulations; reporting to most other users is in accordance with generally accepted accounting principles.

2 **DEFINE** generally accepted accounting principles (p. 5).
- Generally accepted accounting principles (GAAP) are the standards and procedures that guide the preparation of financial statements.
- The Financial Accounting Standards Board (FASB) is an organization in the private sector that has responsibility for formulating generally accepted accounting principles.

3 **DESCRIBE** the role of financial accounting in society (pp. 5–6).
- In a capitalistic, free enterprise economy, investors and creditors decide how they will allocate their financial resources to business entities.
- The financial statements resulting from the financial accounting process contribute significantly to the allocation decisions made by investors and creditors.

4 **DEFINE** the accounting equation (pp. 6–7).
- The accounting equation, Assets = Liabilities + Owners' Equity, is the basic framework within which accounting analysis takes place.

- Assets are the economic resources of an entity that can be usefully expressed in money terms.
- Liabilities are the obligations that an entity must pay in money or services in the future because of past transactions or events.
- Owners' equity is the interest of owners in the assets of an entity.

5 **EXPLAIN** and **ILLUSTRATE** the effects of transactions on the accounting equation (pp. 7–13).
- Certain transactions may change the character and amount of assets and liabilities but have no effect on owners' equity.
- Owners' equity is increased by contributions from owners and by revenues. It is decreased by owner withdrawals and expenses.
- Net income (or loss) is the difference between revenues and expenses. The computation of net income using accrual accounting matches expenses incurred with revenues earned.

6 **INTRODUCE** the basic financial statements (pp. 13–15).
- *Income statement:* Presents revenues and expenses for a period of time.
- *Statement of owners' equity:* Reports events causing a change in owners' equity during a period of time.
- *Balance sheet:* Presents the assets, liabilities, and owners' equity on a given date.
- *Statement of cash flows:* Reports information about cash inflows and outflows during a period of time.

7 **EXPLAIN** the forms of business organization (pp. 15–16).
- Sole proprietorships, partnerships, and corporations are the major forms of business organization.
- In sole proprietorships and partnerships, the balance sheet reports a single amount of equity for each owner.
- For a corporation, state laws require the owners' investment to be shown separately, as capital stock, and the undistributed net income shown separately as retained earnings.

8 **IDENTIFY** ethical dimensions related to the accounting environment (pp. 16–17).
- Certain accounting data may have significant financial implications for individuals.
- Accountants have access to confidential and sensitive information.
- An emphasis on short-term profits may contribute to ethical breakdowns within business firms.

SELF-TEST QUESTIONS FOR REVIEW

(Answers follow the Solution to Demonstration Problem.)

1. To which area of accounting are generally accepted accounting principles primarily relevant?
   a. Managerial accounting
   b. Financial accounting
   c. Tax accounting
   d. Financial reporting to all regulatory agencies

2. To what are net assets equal?
   a. Assets minus liabilities
   b. Assets plus liabilities
   c. Assets minus owners' equity
   d. Assets plus owners' equity

3. What are increases in owners' equity that a firm earns by providing goods or services for its customers called?
   a. Assets
   b. Revenues
   c. Expenses
   d. Liabilities

4. Which of the following transactions does not affect the balance sheet totals?
   a. Purchasing $500 supplies on account
   b. Paying a $3,000 note payable
   c. Collecting $4,000 from customers on account
   d. Withdrawal of $800 by the firm's owner

5. The beginning and ending balances of owner's equity for the year were $30,000 and $35,000, respectively. If owner's withdrawals exceeded contributions during the year by $3,000, what was the net income or net loss for the year?
   a. $8,000 net loss
   b. $14,000 net income
   c. $2,000 net income
   d. $8,000 net income

DEMONSTRATION PROBLEM FOR REVIEW

Ford Aerobics Studio, Inc., operates as a corporation. The firm rents studio space (including a sound system) and specializes in offering aerobics classes to various groups. On January 1, 1996, the assets, liabilities, and stockholders' equity of the business were as follows: Cash, $5,000; Accounts Receivable, $5,200; Notes Payable, $2,500; Accounts Payable, $1,000; Capital Stock, $5,500; and Retained Earnings, $1,200. The January business activities were as follows:

(1) Paid $600 on accounts payable.
(2) Paid January rent, $3,600.
(3) Billed clients for January classes, $11,500.
(4) Received $500 invoice from supplier for T-shirts given to January class members as an advertising promotion.
(5) Collected $10,000 on account from clients.
(6) Paid employees' wages $2,400.
(7) Received $680 invoice for January utilities.
(8) Paid $20 to bank as January interest on note payable.
(9) Declared and paid $900 cash dividend to stockholders.
(10) Paid $4,000 on January 31 to purchase sound system equipment that will replace the rental system.

REQUIRED

a. Set up an accounting equation in columnar form with the following individual assets, liabilities, and stockholders' equity: Cash, Accounts Receivable, Equipment, Notes Payable, Accounts Payable, Capital Stock, and Retained Earnings. Enter January 1 amounts below each item. (*Note:* Equipment amount is $0.)
b. Show the impact (increase or decrease) of transactions (1)–(10) on the beginning amounts, and total the columns to prove that total assets equal liabilities plus stockholders' equity at January 31.
c. Prepare an income statement for January.
d. Prepare a balance sheet at January 31, 1996.

SOLUTION TO DEMONSTRATION PROBLEM

		Cash	+	Accounts Receivable	+	Equipment	=	Notes Payable	+	Accounts Payable	+	Capital Stock	+	Retained Earnings
a.		$ 5,000	+	$ 5,200	+	$ –0–	=	$2,500	+	$1,000	+	$5,500	+	$ 1,200
b.	(1)	–600								–600				
	(2)	–3,600												–3,600
	(3)			+11,500										+11,500
	(4)									+500				–500
	(5)	+10,000		–10,000										
	(6)	–2,400												–2,400
	(7)									+680				–680
	(8)	–20												–20
	(9)	–900												–900
	(10)	–4,000				+4,000								
		$ 3,480	+	$ 6,700	+	$4,000	=	$2,500	+	$1,580	+	$5,500	+	$ 4,600

$14,180   = $14,180

c.

FORD AEROBICS STUDIO, INC.
INCOME STATEMENT
FOR THE MONTH OF JANUARY 1996

Revenue		
Aerobics Fees Earned		$11,500
Expenses		
Rent Expense	$3,600	
Advertising Expense	500	
Wages Expense	2,400	
Utilities Expense	680	
Interest Expense	20	
Total Expenses		7,200
Net Income		$ 4,300

d.

FORD AEROBICS STUDIO, INC.
BALANCE SHEET
JANUARY 31, 1996

Assets		**Liabilities**		
Cash	$ 3,480	Notes Payable		$ 2,500
Accounts Receivable	6,700	Accounts Payable		1,580
Equipment	4,000	Total Liabilities		$ 4,080
		Stockholders' Equity		
		Capital Stock	$5,500	
		Retained Earnings	4,600	10,100
Total Assets	$14,180	Total Liabilities and Stockholders' Equity		$14,180

ANSWERS TO SELF-TEST QUESTIONS

1. b, p. 5   **2.** a, p. 7   **3.** b, p. 8   **4.** c, p. 7   **5.** d, p. 13

GLOSSARY OF KEY TERMS USED IN THIS CHAPTER

accounting   The process of measuring the economic activity of an entity in money terms and communicating the results to interested parties. The purpose is to provide financial information that is useful in making economic decisions (p. 2).

accounting equation   An expression of the equivalency of the economic resources and the claims upon those resources of a specific entity; often stated as Assets = Liabilities + Owners' Equity (p. 6).

assets   The economic resources of an entity that can be usefully expressed in money terms (p. 6).

balance sheet   A financial statement showing an entity's assets, liabilities, and owners' equity at a specific date; sometimes called a *statement of financial position* (p. 13).

closed corporation   A corporation whose stock is not available for sale to the general public; also called a *closely held corporation* (p. 16).

closely held corporation   See *closed corporation.*

corporation   A legal entity created under the laws of a state or the federal government. Owners of a corporation receive shares of stock as evidence of their ownership (p. 15).

ethics   An area of inquiry dealing with the values, rules, and justifications that govern one's way of life (p. 16).

expenses   Decreases in owners' equity incurred by a firm in the process of earning revenues (p. 8).

financial accounting   The area of accounting activities dealing with the preparation of financial statements showing an entity's results of operations, financial position, and cash flows (p. 4).

generally accepted accounting principles (GAAP)   A set of standards and procedures that guide the preparation of financial statements (p. 5).

income statement   A financial statement reporting an entity's revenues and expenses for a period of time (p. 13).

liabilities   The obligations, or debts, that an entity must pay in money or services at some time in the future because of past transactions or events (p. 7).

managerial accounting   The accounting activities carried out by a firm's accounting staff primarily to furnish management with accounting data for decisions related to the firm's operations (p. 4).

net assets   The difference between an entity's assets and liabilities. Net assets are equal to owners' equity (p. 7).

net income   The excess of a firm's revenues over its expenses (p. 8).

open corporation   A corporation whose stock is available for sale to the general public (p. 16).

owners' equity   The interest of owners in the assets of an entity; equal to the difference between the entity's assets and liabilities (p. 7).

partnership   A voluntary association of two or more persons for the purpose of conducting a business (p. 15).

period statement   A financial statement accumulating information for a specific period of time; examples are the income statement, the statement of owners' equity, and the statement of cash flows (p. 15).

position statement   A financial statement presenting information as of a particular date; the balance sheet is a position statement (p. 15).

revenues   Increases in owners' equity a firm earns by providing goods or services for its customers (p. 8).

sole proprietorship   A form of business organization in which one person owns the business (p. 15).

statement of cash flows   A financial statement showing a firm's cash inflows and outflows for a specific period, classified into operating, investing, and financing categories (p. 13).

statement of financial position   A financial statement showing a firm's assets, liabilities, and owners' equity at a specific date; also called a *balance sheet* (p. 13).

statement of owners' equity   A financial statement presenting information on the events causing a change in owners' equity during a period. The statement presents the beginning balance, additions to, deductions from, and the ending balance of owners' equity for the period (p. 13).

QUESTIONS

1-1 Define *accounting*. What is the basic purpose of accounting?

1-2 What is the distinction between *financial* and *managerial* accounting?

1-3 Who are some outside groups that may be interested in a company's financial data and what are their particular interests?

1-4 What are *generally accepted accounting principles* and what organization has primary responsibility for their formulation?

1-5 Why do business firms frequently keep more than one set of records on certain aspects of their financial activities?

1-6 What role does financial accounting play in the allocation of society's financial resources?

1-7 What is the accounting equation? Define *assets, liabilities,* and *owners' equity.*

1-8 What is an *accounting transaction*?

1-9 What is a transaction that would
   a. Increase one asset but not change the amount of total assets?
   b. Decrease an asset and a liability?
   c. Decrease an asset and owners' equity?
   d. Increase an asset and a liability?

1-10 Would each of the following increase, decrease, or have no effect on owners' equity?
   a. Purchased supplies for cash.
   b. Withdrew supplies for personal use.
   c. Paid salaries.
   d. Purchased equipment for cash.
   e. Invested cash in business.
   f. Rendered service to customers, on account.
   g. Rendered service to customers, for cash.

1-11 What are *revenues* and *expenses*?

1-12 What is the purpose of an income statement? a statement of owners' equity? a balance sheet? a statement of cash flows?

1-13 The owner's capital on a particular balance sheet is $80,000. Without seeing the rest of this financial statement, can you say that the owner should be able to withdraw $80,000 cash from the business? Justify your answer.

1-14 What is a *period statement*? Give three examples.

1-15 What is a *position statement*? Give one example.

1-16 How does the presentation of owners' equity in the balance sheet of a corporation differ from that of a sole proprietorship?

1-17 On December 31, 1996, Miller Company had $700,000 in total assets and owed $220,000 to creditors. If this corporation's capital stock amounted to $300,000, what amount of retained earnings should appear on a December 31, 1996, balance sheet?

1-18 What are three aspects of the accounting environment that may create ethical pressure on accountants?

EXERCISES

ACCOUNTING EQUATION
— OBJ. 4 —

1-19 Determine the missing amount in each of the following cases.

	Assets	Liabilities	Owners' Equity
a.	$200,000	$85,000	?
b.	?	$32,000	$28,000
c.	$93,000	?	$52,000

TRANSACTION ANALYSIS
— OBJ. 5 —

1-20 Following the example shown in (a) below, indicate the effects of the listed transactions on the assets, liabilities, and owners' equity of Joyce Martin, certified public accountant, a sole proprietorship.
   (a) Purchased, for cash, a typewriter for use in office.
      ANSWER: Increase assets (Office Equipment)
                     Decrease assets (Cash)

(b) Rendered accounting services and billed client.
(c) Paid rent for month.
(d) Rendered tax services to client for cash.
(e) Received amount due from client in (b).
(f) Purchased an office desk on account.
(g) Paid employees' salaries for month.
(h) Paid for desk purchased in (f).
(i) Withdrew cash for personal use.

TRANSACTION ANALYSIS
— OBJ. 5 —

1-21 The accounting equation of Liang Chen, attorney, at the beginning of an accounting period is given below, followed by seven transactions whose effects on the equation are shown. Describe each transaction that occurred. Of the transactions affecting L. Chen, Capital, transaction (e) had no effect on net income for the period.

	Cash	+	Accounts Receivable	+	Supplies	=	Notes Payable	+	Accounts Payable	+	L. Chen, Capital
Balance	$4,100	+	$9,000	+	$700	=	$2,500	+	$800	+	$10,500
(a)	+6,500		−6,500								
(b)					+400				+400		
(c)			+7,000								+7,000
(d)	−800								−800		
(e)	−4,900										−4,900
(f)	−300				+300						
(g)	+1,200								+1,200		

BALANCE SHEET AND NET
INCOME DETERMINATION
— OBJ. 5, 6 —

1-22 At the beginning of 1996, Flynn's Parking Lots had the following balance sheet:

Assets		Liabilities	
Cash	$ 4,800	Accounts Payable	$12,000
Accounts Receivable	14,700		
Land	60,000	**Owner's Equity**	
		A. Flynn, Capital	67,500
Total Assets	$79,500	Total Liabilities and Owner's Equity	$79,500

a. At the end of 1996, Flynn had the following assets and liabilities: Cash, $8,800; Accounts Receivable, $17,400; Land, $60,000; and Accounts Payable, $7,500. Prepare a year-end balance sheet for Flynn's Parking Lots.
b. Assuming that Flynn did not invest any money in the business during the year but withdrew $12,000 for personal use, what was the net income or net loss for 1996?
c. Assuming that Flynn invested an additional $13,500 early in the year but withdrew $21,000 before the end of the year, what was the net income or net loss for 1996?

DETERMINATION OF RETAINED
EARNINGS AND NET INCOME
— OBJ. 5, 7 —

1-23 The following information appears in the records of Bock Corporation at the end of 1996:

Accounts Receivable	$ 23,000	Retained Earnings	$?
Accounts Payable	11,000	Supplies	9,000
Cash	8,000	Equipment	138,000
Capital Stock	110,000		

a. Calculate the amount of retained earnings at the end of 1996.
b. If the amount of the retained earnings at the beginning of 1996 was $30,000, and $12,000 in dividends were declared and paid during 1996, what was the net income for 1996?

FINANCIAL STATEMENTS
— OBJ. 6 —

1-24 Heather Meier operates The Print Shop as a sole proprietorship. For each of the following financial items related to her business, indicate the financial statement (or statements) in which the item would be reported.
a. Cash (at year-end)
b. Advertising expense
c. H. Meier, capital (at year-end)
d. Printing fees, earned
e. Cash withdrawn by H. Meier for personal use

      f. Accounts payable
      g. Cash paid to purchase equipment
      h. Equipment

ETHICS
— OBJ. 8 —

1-25 In each of the following cases, (a) identify the aspect of the accounting environment primarily responsible for the ethical pressure on the accountant and (b) indicate the appropriate response for the accountant.

    1. James Jehring, tax accountant, is preparing an income tax return for a client. The client wants Jehring to take a sizable deduction on the return for business-related travel, even though the client states that he has no documentation to support the deduction. "I don't think the IRS will audit my return," declares the client.

    2. Willa English, accountant for Dome Construction Company, has just finished putting the numbers together for a construction project on which the firm is going to submit a bid next month. At a social gathering that evening, a friend casually asks English what Dome's bid is going to be. English knows the friend's brother works for a competitor.

    3. The manager of Cross Department Store is ending his first year with the firm. December's business was slower than expected, and the firm's annual results are trailing last year's results. The manager instructs Kyle Tarpley, store accountant, to include revenues from the first week of January in the December data. "This way, we'll show an increase over last year," declares the manager.

PROBLEMS

TRANSACTION ANALYSIS
— OBJ. 5 —

1-26 An analysis of the transactions of Hewit Detective Agency for the month of May appears below. Line 1 summarizes Hewit's accounting equation data on May 1; lines 2–10 represent the transactions for May.

	Cash	+	Accounts Receivable	+	Supplies	+	Equipment	=	Notes Payable	+	Accounts Payable	+	P. Hewit, Capital
(1)	$2,400	+	$7,600	+	$500	+	$8,000	=	$5,000	+	$300	+	$13,200
(2)	+2,000								+2,000				
(3)	+6,100		−6,100										
(4)					+980						+980		
(5)			+6,800										+6,800
(6)	−300										−300		
(7)	+1,500												+1,500
(8)	−800												−800
(9)	−750						+750						
(10)	−2,500								−2,500				

REQUIRED

    a. Prove that assets equal liabilities plus owner's equity at May 1.

    b. Describe the apparent transaction indicated by each line. (For example, line 2: Borrowed $2,000, giving a note payable.) If any line could reasonably represent more than one type of transaction, describe each type.

    c. Prove that assets equal liabilities plus owner's equity at May 31.

TRANSACTION ANALYSIS,
INCOME STATEMENT, OWNER'S
EQUITY STATEMENT, AND
BALANCE SHEET
— OBJ. 5, 6 —

1-27 Grant Appraisal Service is a sole proprietorship providing commercial and industrial appraisals and feasibility studies. On January 1, 1996, assets and liabilities of the business were the following: Cash, $6,700; Accounts Receivable, $14,800; Notes Payable, $2,500; and Accounts Payable, $600. The following transactions occurred during January:

    (1) Paid rent for January, $950.
    (2) Received $8,800 on customers' accounts.
    (3) Paid $500 on accounts payable.
    (4) Received $1,600 for services performed for cash customers.
    (5) Borrowed $5,000 from bank and signed note payable for that amount.
    (6) Billed the city for a feasibility study performed, $6,200, and various other credit customers, $1,900.
    (7) Paid salary of assistant, $4,000.
    (8) Received invoice for January utilities, $410.
    (9) Lindsey Grant withdrew $6,000 cash for personal use.
    (10) Purchased van (on January 31) for business use, $9,800.
    (11) Paid $50 to bank as January interest on notes payable.

REQUIRED

a. Set up an accounting equation in columnar form with the following individual assets, liabilities, and owner's equity: Cash, Accounts Receivable, Van, Notes Payable, Accounts Payable, and L. Grant, Capital. Enter January 1 amounts below each item. (*Note:* Van amount is $0.)

b. Show the impact (increase or decrease) of transactions 1–11 on the beginning amounts, and total the columns to prove that assets equal liabilities plus owner's equity at January 31, 1996.

c. Prepare an income statement for the month of January 1996.

d. Prepare a statement of owner's equity for the month of January 1996.

e. Prepare a balance sheet at January 31, 1996.

TRANSACTION ANALYSIS AND INCOME STATEMENT FOR A CORPORATION
— OBJ. 5, 6, 7 —

1-28 On June 1, 1996, a group of bush pilots in Thunder Bay, Ontario, formed the Outpost Fly-In Service, Inc., by selling $50,000 capital stock for cash. The group then leased several amphibious aircraft and docking facilities, equipping them to transport campers and hunters to outpost camps owned by various resorts. The following transactions occurred during June 1996:

(1) Sold capital stock for cash, $50,000.

(2) Paid June rent for aircraft, dockage, and dockside office, $4,800.

(3) Received invoice for the cost of a dinner and reception the firm gave to entertain resort owners, $1,600.

(4) Paid for June advertising in various sport magazines, $900.

(5) Paid insurance premium for January, $1,800.

(6) Rendered fly-in services for various groups for cash, $22,700.

(7) Billed the Ministry of Natural Resources for transporting mapping personnel, $2,900, and billed various firms for fly-in services, $13,000.

(8) Paid $1,500 on accounts payable.

(9) Received $13,200 on account from clients.

(10) Paid June wages, $16,000.

(11) Received invoice for the cost of fuel used during June, $3,500.

(12) Declared and paid a cash dividend, $3,000.

REQUIRED

a. Set up an accounting equation in columnar form with the following column headings: Cash, Accounts Receivable, Accounts Payable, Capital Stock, and Retained Earnings.

b. Show how the June transactions affect the items in the accounting equation, and total all columns to prove that assets equal liabilities plus stockholders' equity at June 30. (*Note:* Revenues, expenses, and dividends affect Retained Earnings.)

c. Prepare an income statement for June.

INCOME STATEMENT, OWNER'S EQUITY STATEMENT, AND BALANCE SHEET
— OBJ. 6 —

1-29 On March 1, 1996, Amy Dart began Dart Delivery Service, which provides delivery of bulk mailings to the post office, neighborhood delivery of weekly papers, data delivery to computer service centers, and various other delivery services via leased vans. On February 28, Dart invested $19,000 of her own funds in the firm and borrowed $6,000 from her father on a six-month, noninterest-bearing note payable. The following information is available at March 31 (*Note:* Owner's capital reflects March 1, 1996, amount):

Accounts Receivable	$9,700	Delivery Fees Earned	$19,300
Rent Expense	1,500	Cash	12,900
Advertising Expense	900	Supplies	6,500
Supplies Expense	2,700	Notes Payable	6,000
Accounts Payable	1,200	Insurance Expense	800
Salaries Expense	6,300	A. Dart, Capital (March 1)	19,000
Miscellaneous Expense	200		

Dart made a $1,000 additional investment during March but withdrew $5,000 during the month.

REQUIRED

a. Prepare an income statement for the month of March 1996.

b. Prepare a statement of owner's equity for the month of March 1996.

c. Prepare a balance sheet at March 31, 1996.

BALANCE SHEETS AND INCOME DETERMINATION
— OBJ. 5, 6 —

1-30 Balance sheet information for Jordan Packaging Service at the end of 1995 and 1996 is as follows:

	December 31, 1996	December 31, 1995
Accounts Receivable	$22,800	$17,500
Accounts Payable	1,800	1,600
Cash	10,000	8,000
Equipment	32,000	27,000
Supplies	4,700	4,200
Notes Payable	25,000	25,000
N. Jordan, Capital	?	?

REQUIRED

a. Prepare balance sheets for December 31 of each year.

b. Noel Jordan contributed $5,000 to the business early in 1996 but withdrew $17,000 in December 1996. Calculate the net income for 1996.

BALANCE SHEETS FOR A CORPORATION
— OBJ. 5, 6, 7 —

1-31 The following balance sheet data are given for Normandy Catering Service, a corporation, at May 31, 1996:

Accounts Receivable	$18,300	Accounts Payable	5,200
Notes Payable	20,000	Cash	12,200
Equipment	55,000	Capital Stock	42,500
Supplies	16,400	Retained Earnings	?

Assume that on June 1, 1996, only the following transactions occurred:

June 1   Purchased additional equipment costing $15,000, giving $2,000 cash and a $13,000 note payable.

   1   Declared and paid a cash dividend of $7,000.

REQUIRED

a. Prepare a balance sheet at May 31, 1996.

b. Prepare a balance sheet at June 1, 1996.

ALTERNATE EXERCISES

ACCOUNTING EQUATION
— OBJ. 4, 7 —

1-19A Determine the following:

a. The owner's equity of a sole proprietorship that has assets of $450,000 and liabilities of $326,000.

b. The equity of partner Fisk in the Fisk & Blake partnership that has assets of $618,000, liabilities of $225,000, and Y. Blake, Capital of $165,000.

c. The assets of a corporation that has liabilities of $400,000, capital stock of $200,000, and retained earnings of $185,000.

TRANSACTION ANALYSIS
— OBJ. 5 —

1-20A Following the example shown in (a) below, indicate the effects of the listed transactions on the assets, liabilities, and owner's equity of Martin Andrews, attorney, a sole proprietorship.

(a) Rendered legal services to clients for cash.
   ANSWER: Increase assets (Cash)
         Increase owner's equity (M. Andrews, Capital)

(b) Purchased office supplies on account.

(c) Andrews invested cash into the firm.

(d) Paid amount due on account for office supplies purchased in (b).

(e) Borrowed cash (and signed a six-month note) from bank.

(f) Rendered legal services and billed clients.

(g) Purchased, for cash, a desk lamp for the office.

(h) Paid interest on note payable to bank.

(i) Received invoice for month's utilities.

TRANSACTION ANALYSIS
— OBJ. 5 —

1-21A On October 1, Alice Bloom started a consulting firm. The asset, liability, and owner's equity amounts after each of her first six transactions are shown below. Describe each of these six transactions.

Amounts after Transaction	Cash	+	Accounts Receivable	+	Supplies	+	Equipment	=	Notes Payable	+	A. Bloom, Capital
(a)	$6,000	+	$ –0–	+	$ –0–	+	$ –0–	=	$ –0–	+	$6,000
(b)	4,000	+	–0–	+	2,000	+	–0–	=	–0–	+	6,000
(c)	7,500	+	–0–	+	2,000	+	–0–	=	3,500	+	6,000
(d)	2,500	+	–0–	+	2,000	+	5,000	=	3,500	+	6,000
(e)	2,500	+	1,000	+	2,000	+	5,000	=	3,500	+	7,000
(f)	3,000	+	500	+	2,000	+	5,000	=	3,500	+	7,000

DETERMINATION OF NET INCOME AND ENDING CAPITAL
— OBJ. 5, 6 —

1-22A The following income statement and balance sheet information is available for Lloyd Appraisers at the end of the current month:

Supplies	$ 4,900	Accounts Payable	$ 4,000
Accounts Receivable	18,000	Salaries Expense	15,000
Utilities Expense	700	Appraisal Fees Earned	31,000
Supplies Expense	1,300	C. Lloyd, Capital (at	
Rent Expense	2,500	beginning of month)	18,000
Cash	3,600		

a. Calculate the net income or net loss for the month.
b. If C. Lloyd made no additional investment during the month but withdrew $7,000, what is the amount of his capital at the end of the month?

DETERMINATION OF OMITTED FINANCIAL STATEMENT DATA
— OBJ. 5, 6 —

1-23A For the four unrelated situations A–D below, compute the unknown amounts indicated by the letters appearing in each column.

	A	B	C	D
Beginning				
Assets	$28,000	$12,000	$28,000	$ (d)
Liabilities	18,600	5,000	19,000	9,000
Ending				
Assets	30,000	26,000	34,000	40,000
Liabilities	17,300	(b)	15,000	19,000
During Year				
Capital Contributed	2,000	4,500	(c)	3,500
Revenues	(a)	28,000	18,000	24,000
Capital Withdrawn	5,000	1,500	1,000	6,500
Expenses	8,500	21,000	11,000	17,000

FINANCIAL STATEMENTS
— OBJ. 6 —

1-24A Karl Flury operates a golf driving range as a sole proprietorship. For each of the following financial items related to his business, indicate the financial statement (or statements) in which the item would be reported.
a. Accounts receivable.
b. Cash received from sale of land.
c. Net income
d. Cash invested in business by Flury.
e. Notes payable.
f. Supplies expense.
g. Land.
h. Supplies.

ETHICS
— OBJ. 8 —

1-25A In each of the following cases, (a) identify the aspect of the accounting environment primarily responsible for the ethical pressure on the accountant and (b) indicate the appropriate response for the accountant.
1. Patricia Kelly, accountant for Wooden Company, is reviewing the costs charged to a government contract that Wooden worked on this year. Wooden is manufacturing special parts for the government and is allowed to charge the government for the actual manufacturing costs plus a fixed fee. Kelly notes that $75,000 worth of art objects purchased for the president's office is buried among the miscellaneous costs charged to the contract. Upon inquiry, the firm's vice president replies, "This sort of thing is done all the time."
2. Barry Marklin, accountant for Smith & Wesson partnership, is working on the 1996 year-end financial data. The partnership agreement calls for Smith and Wesson to share the firm's 1996 net income equally. In 1997, the partners will share the net income 60% to

Smith and 40% to Wesson (Wesson plans to cut back his involvement in the firm). Smith wants Marklin to delay recording revenue from work done at the end of 1996 until January 1997. "We haven't received the cash yet from these services," declares Smith.

3. The St. Louis Wheelers, a new professional football franchise, has just signed its first-round draft pick to a multiyear contract that is reported in the newspapers as a four-year, $20 million contract. Johanna Factor, Wheelers' accountant, receives a call from the agent of another team's first-round pick. "Just calling to confirm the terms reported in the papers," states the agent. "My client should receive a similar contract, and I'm sure you don't want him to get shortchanged."

ALTERNATE PROBLEMS

TRANSACTION ANALYSIS
— OBJ. 5 —

1-26A Appearing below is an analysis of the June transactions for Gary Rhode, consulting engineer. Line 1 summarizes Rhode's accounting equation data on June 1; lines 2–10 are the transactions for June.

	Cash	+	Accounts Receivable	+	Supplies	+	Equipment	=	Notes Payable	+	Accounts Payable	+	G. Rhode, Capital
(1)	$3,500	+	$5,200	+	$820	+	$9,000	=	$3,000	+	$600	+	$14,920
(2)					+670						+670		
(3)							+5,000		+5,000				
(4)	+4,200		−4,200										
(5)			+7,800										+7,800
(6)	−600										−600		
(7)	−200				+200								
(8)	−4,600												−4,600
(9)	+2,000								+2,000				
(10)							+750						+750

REQUIRED

a. Prove that assets equal liabilities plus owner's equity at June 1.
b. Describe the apparent transaction indicated by each line. For example, line 2: Purchased supplies on account, $670. If any line could reasonably represent more than one type of transaction, describe each type.
c. Prove that assets equal liabilities plus owner's equity on June 30.

TRANSACTION ANALYSIS, INCOME STATEMENT, OWNER'S EQUITY STATEMENT, AND BALANCE SHEET
— OBJ. 5, 6 —

1-27A Grace Main began the Main Answering Service, a sole proprietorship, during December 1995. The firm provides services for professional people and is currently operating with leased equipment. On January 1, 1996, the assets and liabilities of the business were Cash, $4,400; Accounts Receivable, $6,900; Notes Payable, $1,500; and Accounts Payable, $600. The following transactions occurred during January.

(1) Paid rent on office and equipment for January, $800.
(2) Collected $4,500 on account from clients.
(3) Borrowed $2,000 from bank and signed note payable for that amount.
(4) Billed clients for work performed on account, $9,500.
(5) Paid $400 on accounts payable.
(6) Received invoice for January advertising, $550.
(7) Paid January salaries, $3,800.
(8) Paid January utilities, $430.
(9) Main withdrew $2,600 cash for personal use.
(10) Purchased fax machine (on January 31) for business use, $1,400.
(11) Paid $30 to bank as January interest on notes payable.

REQUIRED

a. Set up an accounting equation in columnar form with the following individual assets, liabilities, and owner's equity: Cash, Accounts Receivable, Equipment, Notes Payable, Accounts Payable, and G. Main, Capital. Enter January 1 amounts below each item. (*Note:* Equipment amount is $0.)
b. Show the impact (increase or decrease) of the January transactions on the beginning amounts, and total all columns to prove that assets equal liabilities plus owner's equity at January 31.

c. Prepare an income statement for the month of January 1996.
d. Prepare a statement of owner's equity for the month of January 1996.
e. Prepare a balance sheet at January 31, 1996.

TRANSACTION ANALYSIS AND INCOME STATEMENT — OBJ. 5, 6 —

1-28A On December 1, 1996, Peter Allen started Career Services, a sole proprietorship furnishing career and vocational counseling services. The following transactions took place during December:

(1) Allen invested $7,000 in the business.
(2) Paid rent for December on furnished office space, $750.
(3) Received invoice for December advertising, $500.
(4) Borrowed $15,000 from bank and signed note payable for that amount.
(5) Received $1,200 for counseling services rendered for cash.
(6) Billed certain governmental agencies and other clients for counseling services, $6,800.
(7) Paid secretary's salary, $2,200.
(8) Paid December utilities, $370.
(9) Allen withdrew $900 cash for personal use.
(10) Purchased land for cash to use as a site for own facility, $13,000.
(11) Paid $100 to bank as December interest on note payable.

REQUIRED

a. Set up an accounting equation in columnar form with the following column headings: Cash, Accounts Receivable, Land, Notes Payable, Accounts Payable, and P. Allen, Capital.
b. Show how the December transactions affect the items in the accounting equation, and total all columns to prove that assets equal liabilities plus owner's equity at December 31.
c. Prepare an income statement for the month of December 1996.

INCOME STATEMENT, OWNER'S EQUITY STATEMENT, AND BALANCE SHEET — OBJ. 6 —

1-29A After all transactions have been reflected for 1996, the records of R. Levy, interior decorator, show the following information (*Note:* Owner's capital reflects January 1, 1996, amount):

Notes Payable	$ 4,000	Supplies	$ 6,100
Decorating Fees Earned	67,600	Cash	4,200
Supplies Expense	9,700	Accounts Receivable	10,600
Insurance Expense	1,500	Advertising Expense	1,700
Miscellaneous Expense	200	Salaries Expense	30,000
R. Levy, Capital		Rent Expense	7,500
(January 1)	10,200	Accounts Payable	1,800

Levy made an additional investment of $1,400 in the business during the year and withdrew $13,500 near the end of the year.

REQUIRED

a. Prepare an income statement for 1996.
b. Prepare a statement of owner's equity for 1996.
c. Prepare a balance sheet at December 31, 1996.

BALANCE SHEETS AND INCOME DETERMINATION FOR A CORPORATION — OBJ. 5, 6, 7 —

1-30A Following is balance sheet information for Lynch Janitorial Service, Inc., at the end of 1995 and 1996:

	December 31, 1996	December 31, 1995
Accounts Payable	$ 6,000	$ 9,000
Cash	23,000	20,000
Accounts Receivable	42,000	33,000
Land	40,000	40,000
Building	250,000	260,000
Equipment	43,000	45,000
Mortgage Payable	90,000	100,000
Supplies	20,000	18,000
Capital Stock	220,000	220,000
Retained Earnings	?	?

REQUIRED

a. Prepare balance sheets at December 31 of each year.
b. The firm declared and paid a dividend of $10,000 in December 1996. Calculate the net income for 1996. (*Hint:* The net increase in retained earnings is equal to the net income less the dividend.)

**BALANCE SHEETS FOR A
CORPORATION
— OBJ. 5, 6, 7 —**

1-31A The following balance sheet data are given for Bettis Plumbing Contractors, Inc., at June 30, 1996.

Accounts Payable	$ 8,900	Capital Stock	$100,000
Cash	14,700	Retained Earnings	?
Supplies	30,500	Notes Payable	30,000
Equipment	98,000	Accounts Receivable	9,200
Land	25,000		

Assume that, during the next two days, only the following transactions occurred:

July 1 Paid noninterest-bearing note due today, $5,000
   2 Purchased equipment for $10,000, paying $2,000 cash and giving a note payable for the balance.
   2 Declared and paid a cash dividend, $5,500.

REQUIRED
a. Prepare a balance sheet at June 30, 1996.
b. Prepare a balance sheet at July 2, 1996.

CASES

**BUSINESS
DECISION CASE**

Paul Seale, a friend of yours, is negotiating the purchase of an extermination firm called Total Pest Control. Seale has been employed by a national pest control service and knows the technical side of the business. However, he knows little about accounting, so he asks for your assistance. The sole owner of the firm, Greg Krey, has provided Seale with income statements for the past three years, which show an average net income of $72,000 per year. The latest balance sheet shows total assets of $285,000 and liabilities of $45,000. Seale brings the following matters to your attention:

1. Krey is asking $300,000 for the firm. He has told Seale that, because the firm has been earning 30% on the owner's investment, the price should be higher than the net assets on the balance sheet.
2. Seale has noticed no salary for Krey on the income statements, even though he worked half-time in the business. Krey explained that because he had other income, he withdrew only $18,000 each year from the firm for personal use. If he purchases the firm, Seale will hire a full-time manager for the firm at an annual salary of $36,000.
3. Krey's tax returns for the past three years report a lower net income for the firm than the amounts shown in the financial statements. Seale is skeptical about the accounting principles used in preparing the financial statements.

REQUIRED
a. How did Krey arrive at the 30% return figure given in point 1? If Seale accepts Krey's average annual income figure of $72,000, what would Seale's percentage return be, assuming that the net income remained at the same level and that the firm was purchased for $300,000?
b. Should Krey's withdrawals affect the net income reported in the financial statements? What will Seale's percentage return be if he takes into consideration the $36,000 salary he plans to pay a full-time manager?
c. Could there be legitimate reasons for the difference between net income shown in the financial statements and net income reported on the tax returns, as mentioned in point 3? How might Seale obtain additional assurance about the propriety of the financial statements?

ETHICS CASE

Jack Hardy, CPA, has a brother, Ted, in the retail clothing business. Ted ran the business as a sole proprietor for 10 years. During this 10-year period, Jack helped Ted with various accounting matters. For example, Jack designed the accounting system for the company, prepared Ted's personal income tax returns (which included financial data about the clothing business), and recommended various cost control procedures. Ted paid Jack for all these services. A year ago, Ted expanded the business and incorporated. Ted is president of the corporation and also chairs the corporation's board of directors. The board of directors has overall responsibility for corporate affairs. When the corporation was formed, Ted asked Jack to serve on its board of directors. Jack accepted. In addition, Jack now prepares the corporation's income tax returns and continues to advise his brother on accounting matters.

Recently, the corporation applied for a large bank loan. The bank wants audited financial statements for the corporation before it will decide on the loan request. Ted asked Jack to perform the audit. Jack replied that he cannot do the audit because the code of ethics for CPAs requires that he be independent when providing audit services.

REQUIRED

Why is it important that a CPA be independent when providing audit services? Which of Jack's activities or relationships impair his independence?

GENERAL MILLS ANNUAL REPORT CASE

Refer to the annual report of General Mills, Inc., presented in Appendix K.

REQUIRED

a. Refer to the consolidated balance sheets.
   1. What form of business organization does General Mills use? What evidence supports your answer?
   2. What is the date of the most recent balance sheet presented?
   3. For the most recent balance sheet, what is the largest asset reported? the largest liability?

b. Refer to the consolidated statements of earnings (an alternate name for income statements).
   1. What time period is covered by the most recent statement of earnings presented?
   2. What total amount of revenues from sales did General Mills generate in the most recent period presented? What is the change in sales revenues from the year ended May 30, 1993, to the year ended May 29, 1994?
   3. What is the net income (i.e., net earnings) for the most recent period presented? What is the change in net earnings from the year ended May 30, 1993, to the year ended May 29, 1994?

c. Refer to the consolidated statements of cash flows.
   1. For the most recent period presented, what are the amount and direction of the cash flow from operating activities?
   2. For the most recent period presented, what are the amount and direction of the cash flow from investing (i.e., investment) activities?
   3. For the most recent period presented, what are the amount and direction of the cash flow from financing activities?

d. Refer to the independent auditors' report.
   1. Who are the independent auditors for General Mills?
   2. To whom is the independent auditors' report addressed?

2

The Double-Entry Accounting System; Accounting Principles

CHAPTER LEARNING OBJECTIVES

1 **EXPLAIN** the nature and format of an account (pp. 32–35).

2 **DEFINE** permanent and temporary accounts (p. 35).

3 **DESCRIBE** the system of debits and credits (pp. 35–37).

4 **ILLUSTRATE** debit and credit analysis of transactions (pp. 37–41).

5 **EXPLAIN** the nature and format of a general ledger and trial balance (pp. 41–42).

6 **DISCUSS** the historical development of accounting principles and the nature of the conceptual framework (pp. 42–44).

7 **IDENTIFY** and **DISCUSS** the basic principles of accounting (pp. 45–50).

CHAPTER FOCUS

Analyzing and recording transactions in columnar fashion within the accounting equation framework is a useful way to convey a basic understanding of how transactions affect a firm's financial data. It is not a feasible approach, however, once the total number of individual assets, liabilities, and owners' equity becomes large. Imagine the size of the accounting equation listing individual assets, liabilities, and owners' equity for Honeywell, Inc., a global enterprise operating in 95 countries on six continents! Therefore, an efficient, formal system of classification and recording is required so that financial data may be gathered for day-to-day management needs and timely accounting reports for interested parties. In this chapter, we examine the classification and recording system called *double-entry* accounting.

Also in this chapter, we introduce the fundamental and pervasive principles of financial accounting. An understanding of these principles is indispensable to anyone who uses financial accounting data. Throughout the remaining chapters of the textbook we use *Principle Alerts* to demonstrate the impact of these principles on financial accounting practices.

THE DOUBLE-ENTRY ACCOUNTING SYSTEM

THE ACCOUNT

OBJECTIVE 1
EXPLAIN the nature and format of an account.

The basic component of the formal accounting system is the **account,** which is an individual record of increases and decreases in specific assets, liabilities, and owners' equity. An account is created for each individual asset, liability, and owners' equity.

Most transactions of business firms involve the earning of revenues or the incurring of expenses. The income statement reports information about revenues and expenses for a specific time period. Because of the importance of revenues and expenses, individual accounts are created for each type of revenue and expense. As discussed earlier, revenues increase owners' equity and expenses decrease owners' equity. Revenue and expense accounts, therefore, are considered temporary subdivisions within the owners' equity category.

In sole proprietorships and partnerships, each owner's equity is reflected in an owner's capital account. Investments by an owner increase the owner's capital and will be immediately shown in the owner's capital account. Withdrawals by an owner decrease the owner's equity. Generally, owner withdrawals occur often enough that a separate account, called a **drawing account,** is created for each owner to accumulate information about withdrawals for a period of time. Drawing accounts are considered temporary subdivisions within owners' equity. Information about withdrawals appears in the statement of owners' equity.

The stockholders' equity of a corporation is represented by its capital stock and retained earnings. A corporation opens an account for each type of capital stock and for retained earnings. Corporation revenue and expense accounts are considered temporary subdivisions of the corporation's retained earnings. Cash dividends declared and paid to stockholders decrease retained earnings and cash. When dividends are declared and paid several times a year (each quarter, for example), a *Cash Dividends* account is used to accumulate information about dividends for the year. The Cash Dividends account is a temporary subdivision of retained earnings. The Cash Dividends account serves the same role in corporation accounting as that provided by drawing accounts in sole proprietorships and partnerships.

Exhibit 2-1 shows the form of a *two-column* account, a form often used in a manual record-keeping system. The form is called a two-column account because it has two money columns. Another popular form, called a *running balance* (or *three-column*) account, is illustrated later in this chapter.

EXHIBIT 2–1 Form for Two-Column Account

(ACCOUNT TITLE)   ACCOUNT NO. _____

Date	Description	Post. Ref.	Amount	Date	Description	Post. Ref.	Amount

Most account forms facilitate recording the following information:

1. The account title and number
2. Amounts reflecting increases and decreases
3. Cross-references to other accounting records
4. Dates and descriptive notations

Each account has a short account title that describes the item whose data are being recorded in that account. Some common account titles are Cash, Accounts Receivable, Notes Payable, Professional Fees Earned, and Rent Expense. Increases and decreases are recorded in the appropriate money columns. These amounts are referred to as *entries*. In other words, making an entry in an account consists of recording an amount in a particular place to represent either an increase or a decrease in the account. Accounts also contain space for presentation of other types of information—for example, the date of any entry, a description section to record any memoranda explaining a particular entry, and a posting reference column (indicated by Post. Ref.). The posting reference column is used for noting the records from which entries into this account have been taken. This practice will be explained more fully in the next chapter.

A two-column Cash account for Westgate Driving School is presented in Exhibit 2-2. In our example, there is no beginning amount (balance) because June was the first month of business. Increases in cash from the June transactions have been placed on the left side

EXHIBIT 2–2 Two-Column Cash Account for Westgate Driving School

CASH   ACCOUNT NO. 11

Date	Description	Post. Ref.	Amount	Date	Description	Post. Ref.	Amount
1996				1996			
June 1			40,000	June 2			26,000
30			10,000	3			800
30			3,000	3			3,500
				30			9,000
				30			300
				30			1,400
	Total		53,000		Total		41,000
30	Balance		12,000				

of the Cash account and the decreases on the right side. Periodically, the balance of the account is determined and shown in the account.

An account balance is determined by totaling the left side and right side money columns and entering the difference on the side with the largest total. At June 30, 1996, Westgate Driving School's Cash account shows a $12,000 balance on the left side of the account. This amount is the difference between the $53,000 left-side column total and the $41,000 right-side column total.

The account is an extremely simple record that can be summarized in terms of four money elements:

1. Beginning balance

2. Additions

3. Deductions

4. Ending balance

If any three elements are known, the fourth can easily be computed. Normally, after transactions have been recorded, only the ending balance needs to be computed. Accountants, however, are sometimes confronted with situations in which available data are incomplete and reconstruction of accounts is necessary. Let us demonstrate such an analysis with the following example:

	A	B	C	D
Beginning balance	$10	$70	$ 40	$?
Additions	40	30	?	100
Deductions	20	?	160	120
Ending balance	?	10	0	40

In column A, the ending balance must be $20 greater than the beginning balance, because the additions exceed the deductions by $20. The ending balance is therefore $30. In B, the account balance decreased by $60, so the deductions must exceed the additions by $60. Therefore, total deductions are $90. Show that the unkonwn variable in column C is $120 and in column D is $60.

A simplified form often used to represent the account in accounting textbooks and in the classroom is referred to as the **T account** (because it resembles the letter T). This is merely a skeleton version of the account illustrated for actual record keeping. A T-account form with the June changes in Cash entered for Westgate Driving School follows:

CASH

(1)	40,000	(2)	26,000
(8)	10,000	(3)	800
(11)	3,000	(4)	3,500
		(7)	9,000
		(10)	300
		(12)	1,400
Total	53,000	Total	41,000
Bal.	12,000		

Because dates and other related data are usually omitted in T accounts, it is customary to "key" the entries with a number or a letter to identify the transactions or entry. This permits a systematic review of the entries in the event that an error has been made. It also enables anyone to review a set of such accounts and match related entries. The numerical keys in this T account are the ones used to identify the June transactions for the Westgate Driving School example in the previous chapter.

The printed account form in Exhibit 2-1 is appropriate for classifying accounting data in manual record-keeping systems. In accounting systems using computers, the account form may not be obvious because the actual data might be stored on media such as magnetic tapes or disks. Every accounting system, however, whether manual or automated, must provide for the retrieval and printing out of the types of information shown in the manual form.

NUMBER OF ACCOUNTS

The number of accounts used by a business entity depends on the complexity of its operations and the degree of detail needed by the information users. For complex organizations, the degree of detail needed for managerial purposes exceeds what is needed by external users, such as owners. For example, Morgan Stanley Group, Inc., an international securities firm, reports six major revenue categories in the annual financial statements submitted to its shareholders: investment banking, principal transactions—trading, principal transactions—investments, commissions, interest and dividends, and asset management and administration. Supporting these six revenue categories are at least 32 different revenue accounts used to gather the detail about revenues that is useful to management.

PERMANENT AND TEMPORARY ACCOUNTS

OBJECTIVE 2
DEFINE permanent and temporary accounts.

All accounts may be classified as either permanent accounts or temporary accounts. The **permanent accounts** are the accounts presented in the balance sheet. They consist of the accounts for assets, liabilities, owners' capital (for sole proprietorships and partnerships), and capital stock and retained earnings (for corporations). The distinguishing feature of a permanent account is that any balance in the account at the end of an accounting period is carried forward to the next accounting period.

As discussed earlier, accounts for revenues, expenses, owners' drawings (for sole proprietorships and partnerships), and cash dividends (for corporations) are temporary subdivisions of owners' equity. These accounts compose a firm's temporary accounts. **Temporary accounts** are used to gather information for a particular accounting period; at the end of the accounting period, temporary account balances are transferred to a permanent owners' equity account. The specific procedures used to transfer temporary account balances to a permanent owners' equity account are explained in a later chapter.

The following schedule summarizes the classification of permanent and temporary accounts.

Permanent Accounts	Temporary Accounts
Assets	Revenues
Liabilities	Expenses
Owners' Capital*	Owners' Drawings*
Capital Stock†	Cash Dividends†
Retained Earnings†	

*Accounts unique to sole proprietorships and partnerships.
†Accounts unique to corporations.

THE SYSTEM OF DEBITS AND CREDITS

OBJECTIVE 3
DESCRIBE the system of debits and credits.

One basic characteristic of all account forms is that entries recording increases and decreases are separated. In some accounts, such as the Cash account illustrated in Exhibit 2-2, increases are recorded on the left side of the account and decreases on the right side; in other accounts the reverse is true. The method used in different types of accounts is a matter of convention; that is, a simple set of rules is followed. We will now discuss and illustrate these rules.

The terms **debit** and **credit** are used to refer to the left side and the right side of an account, as shown below.

(ANY TYPE OF ACCOUNT)

Debit	Credit
Always the left side	Always the right side

Regardless of what is recorded in an account, an entry made on the left side is a debit to the account; an entry recorded on the right side is a credit to the account. The words *debit* and *credit* are abbreviated *dr.* (from the Latin *debere*) and *cr.* (from the Latin *credere*), respectively.

The rules of debit and credit identify which accounts are increased by debits and reduced by credits, and which accounts are increased by credits and reduced by debits. Exhibit 2-3 summarizes these rules for each of six categories of accounts: assets, liabilities, permanent owners' equity, owner withdrawals, revenues, and expenses.

Observe the following relationships in Exhibit 2-3:

1 *Debit* always refers to the left side of any account; *credit* refers to the right side.

2 Increases in asset, owner withdrawal, and expense accounts are debit entries, while increases in liability, permanent owners' equity, and revenue accounts are credit entries.

3 Decreases are logically recorded on the side opposite increases.

4 The normal balance of any account is on the side on which increases are recorded; asset, owner withdrawal, and expense accounts normally have debit balances; the other three groups normally have credit balances. This result occurs because increases in an account are usually greater than or equal to decreases.

EXHIBIT 2–3 | **Pattern of Increases and Decreases, Debits and Credits, and Normal Balances**

Categories of Accounts

	ASSETS		LIABILITIES		PERMANENT OWNERS' EQUITY★		OWNER WITHDRAWALS†		REVENUES		EXPENSES	
	Debit	Credit	Debit	Credit	Debit	Credit	Debit	Credit	Debit	Credit	Debit	Credit
1 Always true												
2 Increases	+			+		+	+			+	+	
3 Decreases		–	–		–			–	–			–
4 Normal balance	*			*		*	*			*	*	

★Owners' Capital accounts for sole proprietorships and partnerships; Capital Stock and Retained Earnings accounts for corporations.
†Owners' Drawing accounts for sole proprietorships and partnerships; Cash Dividends account for corporations.

Note that the pattern for assets is opposite that for liabilities and permanent owners' equity. Also observe that the pattern for revenues is the same as for permanent owners' equity. This is to be expected, because revenues are a temporary subdivision of owners' equity and increase owners' equity. Following the same logic, the pattern for owner withdrawals and expenses is opposite that of permanent owners' equity, because owner withdrawals and expenses are temporary subdivisions of owners' equity and reduce owners' equity.

POINT OF INTEREST

FRA LUCA PACIOLI

The first treatise on the art of systematic bookkeeping appeared in 1494, in Venice. "Everything about Arithmetic, Geometry, Proportions and Proportionality" (*Summa de Arithmetica, Geometria, Proportioni et Proportionalita*) was written by the Franciscan monk, Fra Luca Pacioli, one of the most celebrated mathematicians of his day. The work was intended to summarize the existing knowledge of mathematics. Included in the arithmetical part of the work was a section that explained in detail the double-entry system of accounting. Although Pacioli made no claim to developing the art of bookkeeping, he is considered the father of double-entry accounting. All of today's accounting textbooks have their foundation in this system described over 500 years ago by Pacioli.

The system of debits and credits illustrated here is known as the **double-entry system,** so called because at least two entries, a debit and a credit, are made for each transaction. For the accounting equation to remain in balance (and it must), the dollar amount of debits must equal the dollar amount of credits for each transaction.

THE RUNNING BALANCE ACCOUNT

A different account form, the **running balance,** or three-column, account is often used rather than the symmetrical two-column form illustrated in Exhibit 2-1. The Cash account for Westgate Driving School in running balance form is shown in Exhibit 2-4. Notice that the account contains all the information shown in the two-column account but also provides a balance after each transaction.

EXHIBIT 2–4	Running Balance Cash Account for Westgate Driving School

CASH   ACCOUNT No. 11

Date		Description	Post. Ref.	Debit*	Credit	Balance
1996 June	1			40,000		40,000
	2				26,000	14,000
	3				800	13,200
	3				3,500	9,700
	30				9,000	700
	30			10,000		10,700
	30				300	10,400
	30			3,000		13,400
	30				1,400	12,000

*Designates normal balance.

The major advantage of this type of account over the two-column account is that the account balance is apparent for any date during the period. A slight disadvantage is that one must be careful to note whether the account has a normal balance or not. An abnormal account balance should be placed in parentheses. For example, if we overdrew our bank balance, the Cash account balance would be abnormal (a credit balance).

We will use the running balance account in our formal illustrations throughout the succeeding chapters. *To assist you in the earlier chapters, we have placed an asterisk (*) in the column of the account that designates its normal balance.* In illustrations in which detail is not needed and concepts are emphasized, we will use T accounts.

ILLUSTRATION OF DEBIT AND CREDIT ANALYSIS

OBJECTIVE 4
ILLUSTRATE debit and credit analysis of transactions.

The following illustration of debit and credit analysis uses the transactions given in the previous chapter for the first month's operations of Westgate Driving School. Each transaction is stated, analyzed, and followed by an illustration of the appropriate debit and credit entries in the various accounts, using T accounts for simplicity. We have numbered each transaction for reference. In the transaction analysis and the resulting debits and credits, each entry resulting from a particular transaction is parenthetically keyed to the transaction number. Refer to Exhibit 2-3 for an explanation of the use of debits and credits in the analysis.

Transaction 1

On June 1, John King deposited $40,000 of his personal funds in a special checking account for the Westgate Driving School.

ANALYSIS   In the first transaction of Westgate Driving School, King's contribution of capital increases both the assets and the equities of the firm. Specifically, Cash increases by

$40,000, and the permanent owner's equity account, J. King, Capital, increases by the same amount. The entries are

Debit Cash $40,000   **Credit** J. King, Capital $40,000

The related accounts appear as follows:

CASH		J. KING, CAPITAL	
(1) 40,000			(1) 40,000

Transaction 2

On June 2, Westgate Driving School paid $26,000 for a lot to be used for storing vehicles and for some driving instruction.

ANALYSIS   This transaction represents the conversion of one asset to another, causing an increase in the asset Land and a decrease in the asset Cash. The entries are

Debit Land $26,000   **Credit** Cash $26,000

The related accounts appear as follows:

LAND		CASH	
(2) 26,000		(1) 40,000	(2) 26,000

Transaction 3

On June 3, the school paid $800 to rent a furnished office near the parking lot for June.

ANALYSIS   The cost of using the office is a June operating expense. When financial statements are prepared at the end of June, the month's rent appears on the income statement as an expense. The transaction increases Rent Expense and reduces Cash. The entries are

Debit Rent Expense $800   **Credit** Cash $800

The related accounts appear as follows:

RENT EXPENSE		CASH	
(3) 800		(1) 40,000	(2) 26,000
			(3) 800

Transaction 4

On June 3, the school paid $3,500 to lease cars for the month of June.

ANALYSIS   This payment permits the driving school to use the automobiles during June and, therefore, is a June operating expense. The transaction increases Car Lease Expense and reduces Cash. The entries are

Debit Car Lease Expense $3,500   **Credit** Cash $3,500

The related accounts appear as follows:

CAR LEASE EXPENSE		CASH	
(4) 3,500		(1) 40,000	(2) 26,000
			(3) 800
			(4) 3,500

Transaction 5

On June 10, the school received a $300 invoice from the local newspaper for a driving school advertisement that will run in the newspaper four times during June. The invoice will be paid on June 30.

ANALYSIS   Advertising for the month of June is a June operating expense. Receipt of the invoice indicates that an amount is owed to the newspaper for this advertising. Therefore, this transaction increases an expense, Advertising Expense, and increases a liability, Accounts Payable. The entries are

Debit Advertising Expense $300   **Credit** Accounts Payable $300

The related accounts appear as follows:

ADVERTISING EXPENSE		ACCOUNTS PAYABLE	
(5)	300	(5)	300

Transaction 6

On June 26, the school's students were billed $16,000 for June instructional fees.

ANALYSIS   Providing instruction during the month generates an asset, Accounts Receivable, and revenue, Instructional Fees Earned. Note that the revenue is reflected in the month that instruction is given, even though the students may not pay the fees until a later period. The entries are

Debit Accounts Receivable $16,000   **Credit** Instructional Fees Earned $16,000

The related accounts appear as follows:

ACCOUNTS RECEIVABLE		INSTRUCTIONAL FEES EARNED	
(6)	16,000	(6)	16,000

Transaction 7

On June 30, the school paid instructors' salaries for June of $9,000.

ANALYSIS   The services received from driving instructors during the month represent an expense that will be shown on the June income statement. Therefore, this transaction increases an expense, Salaries Expense, and decreases an asset, Cash. The entries are

Debit Salaries Expense $9,000   **Credit** Cash $9,000

The related accounts appear as follows:

SALARIES EXPENSE		CASH			
(7)	9,000	(1)	40,000	(2)	26,000
				(3)	800
				(4)	3,500
				(7)	**9,000**

Transaction 8

On June 30, the school collected $10,000 on account from students billed in transaction 6.

ANALYSIS   Receipt of this amount represents the collection of students' accounts, not new revenue. Recall that the related revenue was recorded in transaction 6, when the claims against students were recognized as the asset Accounts Receivable. This transaction converts one asset (accounts receivable) into another asset (cash). Cash increases by $10,000 and Accounts Receivable decreases by the same amount. The entries are

Debit Cash $10,000   **Credit** Accounts Receivable $10,000

The related accounts appear as follows:

CASH				ACCOUNTS RECEIVABLE			
(1)	40,000	(2)	26,000	(6)	16,000	(8)	**10,000**
(8)	**10,000**	(3)	800				
		(4)	3,500				
		(7)	9,000				

Transaction 9

On June 30, the school received a $400 invoice from the local service station for gas and oil charged to the school's account during June. The invoice will be paid in July.

ANALYSIS   Under generally accepted accounting principles, expenses are recorded in the period they help to generate revenues, regardless of when payment is made. The gas and oil were used in the school's activities during June, and their cost is a June expense. This transaction increases Gas and Oil Expense and increases the liability Accounts Payable. The entries are

Debit Gas and Oil Expense $400   Credit Accounts Payable $400

The related accounts appear as follows:

GAS AND OIL EXPENSE			ACCOUNTS PAYABLE		
(9)	400			(5)	300
				(9)	**400**

Transaction 10

On June 30, the school paid the $300 invoice for advertising that was received on June 10.

ANALYSIS   This payment settles a previously recorded obligation. Therefore, this transaction reduces both a liability, Accounts Payable, and an asset, Cash, by $300. The entries are

Debit Accounts Payable $300   Credit Cash $300

The related accounts appear as follows:

ACCOUNTS PAYABLE				CASH			
(10)	300	(5)	300	(1)	40,000	(2)	26,000
		(9)	400	(8)	10,000	(3)	800
						(4)	3,500
						(7)	9,000
						(10)	**300**

Transaction 11

On June 30, the school borrowed $3,000 from a bank and King, as owner of Westgate Driving School, signed a promissory note agreeing to pay it back in six months.

ANALYSIS   Borrowing $3,000 in exchange for a promissory note increases both the asset Cash and the liability Notes Payable by $3,000. The entries are

Debit Cash $3,000   Credit Notes Payable $3,000

The related accounts appear as follows:

CASH				NOTES PAYABLE	
(1)	40,000	(2)	26,000	(11)	**3,000**
(8)	10,000	(3)	800		
(11)	**3,000**	(4)	3,500		
		(7)	9,000		
		(10)	300		

Transaction 12

On June 30, King withdrew $1,400 from the firm for personal use.

ANALYSIS

The withdrawal of cash by King reduces King's equity in Westgate Driving School. King will use a drawing account to accumulate information about his withdrawals from the firm. Recall that a drawing account is a temporary subdivision of owner's equity. Because the drawing account accumulates information about a type of event (owner asset withdrawals) that reduces owner's equity, the account is increased by debit entries. King's withdrawal of $1,400 cash, therefore, increases the drawing account, J. King, Drawing, and reduces Cash by $1,400. The entries are

Debit J. King, Drawing $1,400   Credit Cash $1,400

The related accounts appear as follows:

J. KING, DRAWING				CASH			
(12)	**1,400**			(1)	40,000	(2)	26,000
				(8)	10,000	(3)	800
				(11)	3,000	(4)	3,500
						(7)	9,000
						(10)	300
						(12)	**1,400**

The entries for each of the foregoing transactions have total debits equal to total credits. This equality of debits and credits is the distinguishing characteristic of the double-entry system of accounting.

THE GENERAL LEDGER AND THE TRIAL BALANCE

OBJECTIVE 5

EXPLAIN the nature and format of a general ledger and trial balance.

A grouping of a firm's accounts is referred to as a *ledger.* Although firms may use various ledgers to accumulate certain detailed information, all firms have a general ledger. A **general ledger** is the grouping of all of the accounts that are used to prepare the basic financial statements. In a manual system, the general ledger consists of a loose-leaf binder or a tray of cards, with each page or card representing an account. The general ledger in a computerized accounting system is maintained on magnetic tapes or disks.

The left portion of Exhibit 2-5 shows the general ledger of Westgate Driving School. The accounts in the general ledger usually are grouped by category in the following

---

EXHIBIT 2–5 General Ledger and Trial Balance for Westgate Driving School

GENERAL LEDGER

CASH			
(1)	40,000	(2)	26,000
(8)	10,000	(3)	800
(11)	3,000	(4)	3,500
		(7)	9,000
		(10)	300
		(12)	1,400
Tot.	53,000	Tot.	41,000
Bal.	12,000		

ACCOUNTS RECEIVABLE			
(6)	16,000	(8)	10,000
Bal.	6,000		

LAND			
(2)	26,000		

NOTES PAYABLE			
		(11)	3,000

ACCOUNTS PAYABLE			
(10)	300	(5)	300
		(9)	400
Tot.	300	Tot.	700
		Bal.	400

J. KING, CAPITAL			
		(1)	40,000

J. KING, DRAWING			
(12)	1,400		

INSTRUCTIONAL FEES EARNED			
		(6)	16,000

RENT EXPENSE			
(3)	800		

CAR LEASE EXPENSE			
(4)	3,500		

ADVERTISING EXPENSE			
(5)	300		

SALARIES EXPENSE			
(7)	9,000		

GAS AND OIL EXPENSE			
(9)	400		

WESTGATE DRIVING SCHOOL
TRIAL BALANCE
JUNE 30, 1996

	Debit	Credit
Cash	$12,000	
Accounts Receivable	6,000	
Land	26,000	
Notes Payable		$ 3,000
Accounts Payable		400
J. King, Capital		40,000
J. King, Drawing	1,400	
Instructional Fees Earned		16,000
Rent Expense	800	
Car Lease Expense	3,500	
Advertising Expense	300	
Salaries Expense	9,000	
Gas and Oil Expense	400	
	$59,400	$59,400

order: (1) assets, (2) liabilities, (3) permanent owners' equity, (4) owner withdrawals, (5) revenues, and (6) expenses.

The **trial balance** is a list of the account titles in the general ledger with their respective debit or credit balances. It is prepared at the close of an accounting period after transactions have been recorded. The right side of Exhibit 2-5 illustrates a trial balance for Westgate Driving School at the end of June 1996. Note that the sequence of accounts and the dollar amounts are taken directly from the general ledger. The debit and credit columns balance; that is, each column totals to the same amount ($59,400).

The two main reasons for preparing a trial balance are

1. To serve as an interim mechanical check to determine if the debits and credits in the general ledger are equal.

2. To show all general ledger account balances on one concise record. This is often convenient when preparing financial statements. The trial balance itself, though, is not a financial statement.

Note that a trial balance should be dated; the trial balance of Westgate Driving School was taken at June 30, 1996.

ACCOUNTING PRINCIPLES

HISTORICAL DEVELOPMENT

OBJECTIVE 6

DISCUSS the historical development of accounting principles and the nature of the conceptual framework.

In contrast to the physical sciences, accounting has no immutable or natural laws, such as the law of gravity. The closest approximation to a law in accounting is probably the use of arithmetic functions and logic. Because no basic natural accounting law exists, accounting principles have developed on the basis of their *usefulness*. Consequently, the growth of accounting is more closely related to experience and practice than to the foundation provided by ultimate law. As such, accounting principles tend to evolve rather than be discovered, to be flexible rather than precise, and to be subject to relative evaluation rather than be ultimate or final.

Conventional accounting comprises a relatively recent body of knowledge. Although the origin of double-entry bookkeeping has been traced back to the fourteenth century, most important accounting developments have occurred in the last century.

The recent rapid development of accounting as an information system is largely explained by the economic history of the last 8 to 10 decades. This period included (1) the development of giant industrial firms, (2) the existence of large stockholders' groups, (3) the pronounced separation of ownership and management of large corporate firms, (4) the rapid growth of industrial and economic activity, and (5) the expansion of government regulation of industry. These factors helped create the large groups of interested parties who require a constant stream of reliable financial information concerning the economic entities they own, finance, manage, or regulate. This information is meaningful only when prepared according to some agreed-on standards and procedures.

Accounting principles—like common law—originate from problem situations such as changes in the law, tax regulations, new business organizational arrangements, or new financing or ownership techniques. In response to the effect such problems have on financial reports, certain accounting techniques or procedures are tried. Through comparative use and analysis, one or more of these techniques are judged most suitable, obtain substantial authoritative support, and are then considered a generally accepted accounting principle. Organizations such as the Financial Accounting Standards Board (FASB), the American Institute of Certified Public Accountants (AICPA), and the Securities and Exchange Commission (SEC) have been instrumental in the development of most accounting principles.

An accounting principle must have substantial authoritative support to qualify as generally accepted. References to a particular accounting principle in authoritative accounting literature constitute substantive evidence of its general acceptance.

Pronouncements by the FASB are the most direct evidence of whether or not a specific accounting principle is generally accepted. Organized in 1973, the FASB has issued more than 120 *Statements of Financial Accounting Standards* dealing with generally accepted accounting principles.[1] Before the creation of the FASB, pronouncements by the AICPA—many of which are still in effect—represented the most authoritative indicators of general acceptance.[2]

During the two decades ending in 1959, the Committee on Accounting Procedures of the AICPA issued 51 *Accounting Research Bulletins.* These bulletins dealt with a variety of problems and, although they lacked formal legal status, considerably influenced generally accepted practice. In 1959, the AICPA established the Accounting Principles Board (APB) to issue authoritative opinions on problems related to generally accepted accounting principles. During its existence, the APB issued 31 *Opinions of the Accounting Principles Board.* These opinions increased in importance in 1964 when the AICPA required that any departure from an APB opinion be disclosed in a footnote to the financial statements or in the accompanying auditor's report. When the FASB succeeded the APB in 1973, this requirement was extended to cover FASB pronouncements.

As a federal agency, the SEC's primary focus is to regulate the interstate sale of stocks and bonds. The SEC requires companies under its jursdiction to submit annual audited financial statements. The SEC has the power to set the accounting principles used by these companies, but, for the most part, the SEC has relied upon the FASB (and earlier, the AICPA) to formulate accounting principles. Because of its interest in full and fair financial reporting, the SEC interacts regularly with the FASB about various accounting problems.

CONCEPTUAL FRAMEWORK

The FASB has developed an overall conceptual framework to guide the formulation of specific accounting principles. The **conceptual framework** is a cohesive set of interrelated objectives and fundamentals for external financial reporting. For business enterprises, the framework consists of (1) financial reporting objectives, (2) financial statement elements, (3) recognition criteria for financial statement items, and (4) qualitative characteristics of accounting information. A recurrent theme throughout the conceptual framework is the importance of providing information that is useful to financial statement readers.

The **financial reporting objectives** focus primarily on information useful to investors and creditors. Financial statements should provide information that is (1) useful in making investment, credit, and similar decisions and (2) helpful in assessing the ability of enterprises to generate future cash flows. Finally, financial statements should (3) contain information about a firm's economic resources, the claims to these resources, and the effects of events that change these resources and claims. This latter information enhances the efforts of investors and creditors to identify financial strengths and weaknesses, predict future performance, or evaluate earlier expectations.

Financial statement elements are the significant components used to put financial statements together. These elements include assets, liabilities, owners' equity, investments by owners, distributions to owners, revenues, expenses, gains, losses, and comprehensive income.[3] The conceptual framework identifies and defines these elements, noting that they reflect the economic resources, claims to resources, and events that are relevant to decisions made by investors and creditors.

---

[1]Paralleling the FASB structure, the Governmental Accounting Standards Board (GASB) was organized in 1984 to formulate accounting principles for state and local government financial reporting.

[2]For a hierarchy of sources of generally accepted accounting principles, see *Statement on Auditing Standards No. 69,* "The Meaning of 'Present Fairly in Conformity with Generally Accepted Accounting Principles' in the Independent Auditor's Report," in *Journal of Accountancy,* March 1992, pp. 108–111.

[3]We discuss gains and losses in later chapters. Comprehensive income is a concept not yet achieved in practice.

The **recognition criteria** specify in broad terms the criteria that must be satisfied before a particular asset, liability, revenue, expense, or the like may be recorded in the accounts. Essentially, the item under consideration must meet the definition of an element and be measurable, and information about the item must achieve the primary qualitative characteristics of accounting information.

The **qualitative characteristics of accounting information** are qualities that contribute to decision usefulness. The two primary qualities are **relevance** and **reliability.** To be relevant, information must contribute to the predictive and evaluative decisions made by investors and creditors. Reliable information contains no bias or material error and faithfully portrays what it intends to represent.

Exhibit 2-6 summarizes the conceptual framework. Various pieces of this conceptual framework were already part of the accounting discipline before their consideration by the FASB. Integrating the pieces into a cohesive framework is important, however. The FASB's intent is to solve individual accounting issues and formulate specific accounting principles within the context of the conceptual framework. Consequently, accounting principles based on this framework should form a consistent and coherent set of guidelines for financial reporting.

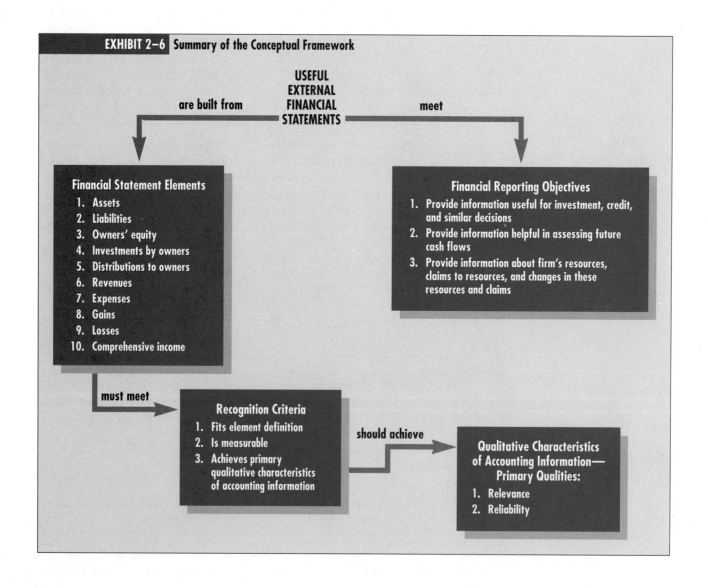

EXHIBIT 2–6 Summary of the Conceptual Framework

USEFUL EXTERNAL FINANCIAL STATEMENTS

are built from

meet

Financial Statement Elements
1. Assets
2. Liabilities
3. Owners' equity
4. Investments by owners
5. Distributions to owners
6. Revenues
7. Expenses
8. Gains
9. Losses
10. Comprehensive income

Financial Reporting Objectives
1. Provide information useful for investment, credit, and similar decisions
2. Provide information helpful in assessing future cash flows
3. Provide information about firm's resources, claims to resources, and changes in these resources and claims

must meet

Recognition Criteria
1. Fits element definition
2. Is measurable
3. Achieves primary qualitative characteristics of accounting information

should achieve

Qualitative Characteristics of Accounting Information— Primary Qualities:
1. Relevance
2. Reliability

JOHNSON & JOHNSON ACCOUNTING ENTITY

Johnson & Johnson, a manufacturer of health care products, produces such consumer items as Tylenol and Band-Aids. In a recent annual report to stockholders, the company profile showed that the firm had 81,600 employees in 168 operating companies in more than 50 countries. For purposes of reporting to its owners, Johnson & Johnson viewed this cluster of companies as one accounting entity, which means that the financial data of the 168 companies were consolidated into one set of financial statements.

BASIC PRINCIPLES

OBJECTIVE 7

IDENTIFY and **DISCUSS** the basic principles of accounting.

In this section, we consider several fundamental principles that underlie the preparation of accounting data. Accountants vary somewhat in the way they refer to these basic guides; terms such as *principle, concept, standard, assumption,* and *convention* have been used to refer to one or more of them. Regardless of the term selected, however, each of these items influences the practice of accounting.

ACCOUNTING ENTITY CONCEPT

Accounting reports are compiled for clearly defined economic units.

The most fundamental concept in accounting is the entity. An **accounting entity** is an economic unit with identifiable boundaries for which accountants accumulate and report financial information. Before accountants can analyze and report activities, they must identify the particular entity (and its boundaries) for which they are accounting. Every financial report specifies the entity in its heading.

Each proprietorship, partnership, and corporation is a separate entity, and separate accounting records should be kept for each unit. In accumulating financial information, we must separate the activities of an accounting entity from the other economic and personal activities of its owners. For example, Matt and Lisa Cook own Good Cook Inn restaurant as partners. The Good Cook Inn partnership is an accounting entity. Matt Cook is also an attorney whose activities constitute a proprietorship. Therefore, he keeps a set of accounting records for his legal activities separate from Good Cook Inn's records of its business activities. Lisa Cook's activities as a realtor also constitute a proprietorship. She keeps a set of accounting records for her realty activities separate from both the records of Good Cook Inn and of Matt Cook, attorney.

An accounting entity may be a unit other than a proprietorship, partnership, or corporation. Data for two or more corporations may be combined to provide financial reports for a larger economic entity. For example, a parent corporation and its wholly owned subsidiaries (corporations in their own right) may consolidate their individual financial reports into a set of consolidated statements covering the group of corporations. In contrast, internal reports to corporate management may contain financial data concerning the activities of units as small as a division, a department, a profit center, or a plant. In this type of financial reporting, the entity is the division, the department, the profit center, or the plant.

ACCOUNTING PERIOD CONCEPT

The economic life of an accounting entity can be divided into specific periods—typically, one year for financial reporting purposes.

The operations of most businesses are virtually continuous except for some changes associated with cyclical time periods, seasons, or dates. Thus, any division of the total life of a business into segments based on annual periods is somewhat artificial. However, the concept of **accounting periods** is useful. Many taxes are assessed on an annual basis, and comprehensive reports to corporation stockholders are made annually. In addition, many other noneconomic factors tend to consider the year a natural division of time.

Accounting reports may cover other periods. For instance, investors and creditors may receive quarterly *interim* financial reports and management may receive monthly financial reports.

The combined effect of the entity and period concepts is illustrated in Exhibit 2-7, which uses Good Cook Inn and its two owners as an example. The shaded box isolates Good Cook Inn's activities for 1997. Proper accounting requires that both the entity and the period be identified in financial reports.

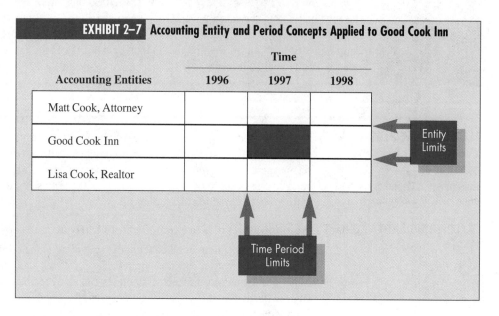

EXHIBIT 2–7　Accounting Entity and Period Concepts Applied to Good Cook Inn

Accounting Entities	Time		
	1996	1997	1998
Matt Cook, Attorney			
Good Cook Inn			
Lisa Cook, Realtor			

MEASURING UNIT CONCEPT

The unit of measure in accounting is the basic unit of money.

The economic activity that accountants record must be expressed in a common unit of measure so that the data may be easily classified, summarized, and reported. The **measuring unit concept** specifies that a monetary unit (the dollar in the United States) is to be used to measure and record an entity's economic activity. When all assets, liabilities, and owners' equity are stated in monetary terms, they may be easily added or subtracted, as necessary, to prepare financial statements. Also, various relationships among financial statement components may be easily calculated and presented to help interpret the statements.

Recording and reporting in monetary terms imposes two limitations on the financial accounting process. First, only items that may be expressed in monetary terms are brought into the information system. Some economic resources and obligations may be excluded from the accounting information system because there is no agreement as to how to express them monetarily. For example, the human resource (that is, a firm's employees) is not recorded and reported as an asset in conventional financial statements. Accountants recognize that a firm's workforce is an economic resource, but accountants have not yet determined an appropriate way to measure this resource in monetary terms. Unitl this measurement issue is resolved, the human resource will not be reported among a firm's assets.

The second limitation is that the U.S. dollar (as well as the currencies of other countries) is not a stable unit of measure. Inflation causes a currency's purchasing power to decline through time. Failure to adjust for this may cause some distortion in a firm's financial statements because the amounts appearing in the statements are expressed in dollars of different vintages. For example, in computing total assets at December 31, 1996, supplies purchased in 1996 may be added to land purchased in 1970; both supplies and land are measured in U.S. dollars, but they are dollars from two quite different points in time (1996 and 1970) and, thus, represent quite different units of purchasing power. Some persons believe that using dollars with different purchasing powers limits the usefulness of financial data. However, no adjustments are made to U.S. basic financial statements to reflect the impact of purchasing power changes in the unit of measure. The measuring unit concept specifies that the U.S. dollar's purchasing power, while not completely stable, is stable enough so that no adjustments are necessary.

OBJECTIVITY PRINCIPLE

Whenever possible, accounting entries must be based on objectively determined evidence.

The usefulness of accounting reports is enhanced when the underlying data are objective and verifiable. The **objectivity principle** dictates that the recording of transactions should be based on reliable and verifiable evidence. Amounts recorded should be supported by actual invoices, physical counts, and other relatively bias-free evidence whenever possible. Undocumented opinions of management or others do not provide a good basis for accounting determinations. As we shall see throughout our discussion of accounting, however, it is often necessary to incorporate estimates into our analyses. Even when a certain amount of subjectivity cannot be avoided, it is important that such estimates be supported by some type of objective analysis if possible.

COST PRINCIPLE

Asset measures are based on the prices paid to acquire the assets.

The **cost principle** states that assets are initially recorded at the amounts paid to acquire the assets. Land, for example, may be purchased for $75,000 cash. The land is recorded at its $75,000 cost. Cost is considered the proper initial measure because, at the time an asset is acquired, cost represents the fair value of the asset as agreed to by both the buyer and seller.

In general, cost also is the basis used to report an asset at subsequent times while it is still held by a firm. A year later, for example, the land purchased above may be appraised at $90,000. The firm continues to report the land at $75,000, because that amount was verified by engaging in an exchange transaction with another entity; the $90,000 amount has not been verified by an exchange transaction. In this context, the cost measure is often referred to as *historical cost* (a cost measure that continues to be utilized through time). Accountants have long recognized that historical cost is probably the most objective and verifiable basis for reporting assets. As you will learn, historical costs are often *reduced* over time to reflect asset expirations. You will also learn of a few cases in which current market values (rather than historical costs) are used to measure assets at dates after their acquisition date.

GOING CONCERN CONCEPT

In the absence of evidence to the contrary, a business is assumed to have an indefinite life.

The **going concern concept** assumes that an entity will continue to operate indefinitely and will not be sold or liquidated. This assumption supports the use of historical cost to measure assets, such as supplies and equipment, that will be used in operating the business. The going concern concept implies that the firm will operate long enough to use up the supplies and equipment. As they are used up, their costs will be reflected as costs of operations. Information about the current market values or liquidation values of assets that are going to be used in operations rather than sold is not considered to be particularly relevant information.

Sometimes accountants have strong evidence that the entity is not going to operate indefinitely into the future. If this is the case, the going concern assumption is not used, and amounts other than historical cost may become useful data. For example, a firm that is bankrupt and in the process of liquidating will find estimated liquidation values for its assets to be more useful information than historical costs. Throughout this book, however, we will use the going concern concept.

CONSISTENCY PRINCIPLE

Unless otherwise disclosed, accounting reports are prepared on a basis consistent with the preceding period.

In many instances, more than one method of applying a generally accepted accounting principle is possible. In other words, two firms that have identical operating situations might each choose a different—but equally acceptable—accounting method and report different amounts for the same types of transactions.

Changes in accounting procedures that lead to different reported values may affect the amount of reported income. Under certain circumstances, a firm could, by design, increase or decrease its reported earnings simply by changing from one generally accepted accounting principle to another that yields different values. This situation justifies the consistency principle. **Consistency** means that the same accounting methods are used from one accounting period to the next. Consistency enhances the utility of financial statements when comparative data for a firm are analyzed.

Sometimes it is appropriate for a firm to change an accounting method. Indeed, progress in improving accounting data almost dictates that some changes will occur. In these cases, financial statement users should know when and to what extent reported earnings result from changes in accounting techniques.

REVENUE RECOGNITION PRINCIPLE

In general, revenue is recognized when services are performed or goods are sold.

Business entities exist to provide services and/or sell goods to their customers. The **revenue recognition principle** states that revenue should be recorded when the services are performed or the goods are sold.

The revenue recognition principle requires two conditions to exist before revenue may be recorded: the revenue must be *earned* and *realized.* Normally, both conditions are not met until services are performed or goods are sold. An entity *earns* revenue by putting forth the economic effort to provide services or to sell goods. A department store, for example, earns revenue by doing such things as buying merchandise, displaying it in convenient locations, and providing sales clerks to answer questions.

An entity *realizes* revenue either by receiving payment for the services and goods or by establishing a claim to receive payment. The involvement of a customer creates realization; that is, services are provided *for* a customer and goods are sold *to* a customer. The customer is a party outside the entity whose involvement confirms the amount of revenue. A department store realizes revenue, for example, when it sells goods to a specific customer. Realization occurs at this point because the customer either pays immediately or the store has a claim to receive payment (an account receivable).

MATCHING CONCEPT

To the extent feasible, all expenses related to given revenue are matched with and deducted from that revenue in the determination of net income.

The **matching concept** states that net income is determined by linking, or matching, expenses incurred with the related revenues recognized. Expenses are recorded in the period they help to generate the recorded revenues. There is a linkage, therefore, between expenses and revenues: expenses are incurred to generate revenues.

Together, the revenue recognition principle and the matching concept define accrual accounting. In **accrual accounting,** revenues are recognized when they are both earned and realized (revenue recognition principle) and expenses are recorded in the period they help to generate the recorded revenues (matching concept). The recording of accrual revenues and expenses does not rely on the receipt or payment of cash. For example, a driving school records revenue when driving instruction is provided to a client, regardless of when it receives cash payment for the instruction. Similarly, store rent for March helps a hardware store generate revenues during March; the rent is an expense for March regardless of when it is actually paid in cash.

Cash-basis accounting contrasts with accrual accounting. Under **cash-basis accounting,** revenues are recorded when cash is received from operating activities and expenses are recorded when cash payments related to operating activities are made. Net income, therefore, becomes the difference between operating cash receipts and cash payments. Cash-basis accounting is a relatively simple system for determining net income. There is no attempt, however, to match expenses with revenues; thus, cash-basis accounting is not consistent with generally accepted accounting principles.

Exhibit 2-8 compares the net income of Westgate Driving School for June 1996 using accrual accounting and cash-basis accounting. Accrual accounting shows a $2,000 net in-

| EXHIBIT 2–8 | Accrual and Cash-Basis Income Statements Compared |

WESTGATE DRIVING SCHOOL
ACCRUAL INCOME STATEMENT
FOR THE MONTH OF JUNE 1996

Revenue		
Instructional Fees Earned		$16,000
Expenses		
Rent Expense	$ 800	
Car Lease Expense	3,500	
Advertising Expense	300	
Salaries Expense	9,000	
Gas and Oil Expense	400	
Total Expenses		14,000
Net Income		$ 2,000

WESTGATE DRIVING SCHOOL
CASH-BASIS INCOME STATEMENT
FOR THE MONTH OF JUNE 1996

Revenue		
Instructional Fees Received		$10,000
Expenses		
Rent Expense	$ 800	
Car Lease Expense	3,500	
Advertising Expense	300	
Salaries Expense	9,000	
Total Expenses		13,600
Net Loss		($ 3,600)

come while the cash-basis approach shows a net loss of $3,600. The $5,600 difference between the two approaches exists because the accrual approach (1) recognizes revenue of $6,000 from services provided for which no cash has yet been received and (2) records an expense of $400 (gas and oil expense) that has been incurred but not yet paid in cash.

Although cash-basis accounting is unacceptable for net income computations, information about cash flows is useful because cash is a particularly important asset. As noted in Chapter 1, a basic set of financial statements includes both an income statement and a statement of cash flows.

CONSERVATISM CONCEPT **Accounting measurements take place in a context of significant uncertainties, and possible errors in measurement of net assets and income should tend toward understatement rather than overstatement.**

Accounting determinations are often based on estimates of future events and are therefore subject to a range of optimistic or pessimistic interpretations. In the early 1900s, many abuses were perpetrated on financial statement users who were given overly optimistic measurements of assets and estimates of income. Consequently, the investor was reassured when a company used the "most conservative" accounting procedures. In some instances, banks would report handsome multistory office buildings on the balance sheet at a nominal value of $1. The intention was to emphasize the understatement of assets as evidence of conservative accounting and financial strength.

More recently, accountants have recognized that intentional understatement of net assets and income can be as misleading as overly optimistic accounting treatments. Today, **conservatism** is the accountant's reaction to situations in which significant uncertainties exist about the outcomes of transactions still in progress. In contrast to the intentional understatements of net assets and income, accountants follow conservative accounting procedures when they are unsure of the proper measure to use. For example, if two estimates of future amounts to be received are about equally likely, conservatism requires the less optimistic estimate be used. Thus, possible errors in measuring net assets and income should tend toward understatement rather than overstatement.

MATERIALITY CONCEPT **Accounting transactions so insignificant that they would not affect the actions of financial statement users are recorded as is most expedient.**

Applying sound accounting procedures requires effort and costs money. When the amounts involved are too small to affect the overall picture significantly, the application of theoretically correct accounting procedures is hardly worth its cost. For example, assets represent items with future economic benefit to an entity. Yet the costs of some assets are so small that it makes little sense to track them in the accounts for their entire future economic lives. Thus, the concept of **materiality** permits a firm to expense the costs of such items as small tools, pencil sharpeners, and waste paper baskets when acquired because they are "immaterial" in amount. Many firms set dollar limits—such as $25 or $100—below which the costs of all items are expensed.

The concept of materiality is relative—an immaterial amount for General Motors Corporation may be material for smaller companies. Note also that although a given series of transactions might *each* be considered immaterial in amount, their aggregate effect could be material in certain circumstances.

FULL DISCLOSURE PRINCIPLE

All information necessary for the users' understanding of the financial statements must be disclosed.

Accounting's purpose is to provide useful information to various parties interested in a firm's financial performance and position. Often facts or conditions exist that, although not specifically part of the data in the accounts, have considerable influence on the understanding and interpretation of the financial statements. For example, assume that a corporation is a defendant in a $100 million product liability lawsuit. Or suppose a company has signed noncancelable lease contracts that will cost $75 million per year for five years. To inform users properly, the **full disclosure principle** requires that firms disclose all significant financial facts and circumstances, including lawsuits and lease commitments.

KEY POINTS FOR CHAPTER LEARNING OBJECTIVES

1 **EXPLAIN** the nature and format of an account (pp. 32–35).
- An account is an individual record of increases and decreases in specific assets, liabilities, permanent owners' equity, owner withdrawals, revenues, and expenses.
- Information provided by the account includes title, amounts reflecting increases and decreases, cross-references to other accounting records, and dates and descriptive notations.

2 **DEFINE** permanent and temporary accounts (p. 35).
- Permanent accounts are the balance sheet accounts—assets, liabilities, and permanent owners' equity; any balance in a permanent account at the end of an accounting period is carried forward to the next period.
- Temporary accounts consist of revenue, expense, and owner withdrawal accounts; they gather information for an accounting period and at the end of the period, their balances are transferred to a permanent owners' equity account.

3 **DESCRIBE** the system of debits and credits (pp. 35–37).
- The left side of an account is always the debit side; the right side is always the credit side.
- Increases in assets, owner withdrawals, and expenses are debit entries; increases in liabilities, permanent owners' equity, and revenues are credit entries. Decreases are the opposite.
- The normal balance of any account appears on the side for recording increases.

4 **ILLUSTRATE** debit and credit analysis of transactions (pp. 37–41).
- Each accounting transaction should be analyzed into equal debits and credits.
- All accounting transactions are analyzed using one or more of the basic account categories: (1) assets, (2) liabilities, (3) permanent owners' equity, (4) owner withdrawals, (5) revenues, and (6) expenses.

5 **EXPLAIN** the nature and format of a general ledger and trial balance (pp. 41–42).
- A general ledger is the grouping of all of the accounts that are used to prepare the basic financial statements.
- A trial balance is a list of the accounts in the general ledger with their respective debit or credit balances; it is prepared after transactions have been recorded for an accounting period.
- A trial balance serves as a check to determine the equality of debits and credits.
- Showing all the account balances on one concise record (that is, a trial balance) facilitates preparation of the financial statements.

6 **DISCUSS** the historical development of accounting principles and the nature of the conceptual framework (pp. 42–44).
- The FASB, the AICPA, and the SEC have been instrumental in the development of generally accepted accounting principles.
- The conceptual framework is a cohesive set of interrelated objectives and fundamentals for external financial reporting.

7 **IDENTIFY** and **DISCUSS** the basic principles of accounting (pp. 45–50).
  ■ Each of the following is an important basic accounting principle:

accounting entity	consistency
accounting period	revenue recognition
measuring unit	matching
objectivity	conservatism
cost	materiality
going concern	full disclosure

  ■ Revenue is usually recognized when services are performed or goods are sold because it is then both earned and realized.

SELF-TEST QUESTIONS FOR REVIEW

(Answers follow the Solution to Demonstration Problem.)

1. The ending balance of the Accounts Receivable account was $12,000. Services billed to customers for the period were $21,500, and collections on account from customers were $23,600. What was the beginning balance of Accounts Receivable?
   a. $33,500   **b.** $14,100   **c.** $9,900   **d.** $33,100

2. Which of the following accounts is a temporary account?
   a. Accounts Receivable
   b. Notes Payable
   c. P. Reilly, Capital
   d. Advertising Expense

3. In applying the rules of debit and credit, which of the following statements is correct?
   a. The word *debit* means to increase and the word *credit* means to decrease.
   b. Asset, expense, and owner drawing accounts are debited for increases.
   c. Liability, revenue, and owner drawing accounts are debited for increases.
   d. Asset, expense, and owner capital accounts are debited for increases.

4. Which of the following is not included in the overall conceptual framework for business enterprises?
   a. Financial reporting objectives
   b. Financial statement elements
   c. Ethical characteristics of the reporting process
   d. Qualitative characteristics of accounting information

5. Land is reported in the balance sheet at its purchase price of $20,000 rather than its estimated current market value of $35,000. Which basic principle of accounting does this procedure reflect?
   a. Full disclosure
   b. Matching
   c. Consistency
   d. Cost

DEMONSTRATION PROBLEM FOR REVIEW

For each of the transactions listed below for Thomas Company, a sole proprietorship, fill in the blank spaces to answer the following questions:

1. Which specific accounts are affected by the transaction?
2. What type of account is each account affected (that is, is it an asset, liability, owner capital, owner drawing, revenue, or expense account)?
3. Should the account be increased or decreased?
4. Should the account be debited or credited?

Transactions:

(A) The company received $1,300 cash from clients for services rendered.
(B) The company paid $2,400 of salaries to employees.
(C) The company collected $600 from clients on account.
(D) The owner, F. Thomas, withdrew $400 cash for personal use.
(E) The company purchased $700 of supplies on account.

(F) The company billed clients $900 for services rendered.

(G) The company paid $500 to suppliers on account.

Transaction	Accounts Affected	Type of Account	Increase or Decrease	Debit or Credit
(A)	1. _____	1. _____	1. ____	1. ____
	2. _____	2. _____	2. ____	2. ____
(B)	1. _____	1. _____	1. ____	1. ____
	2. _____	2. _____	2. ____	2. ____
(C)	1. _____	1. _____	1. ____	1. ____
	2. _____	2. _____	2. ____	2. ____
(D)	1. _____	1. _____	1. ____	1. ____
	2. _____	2. _____	2. ____	2. ____
(E)	1. _____	1. _____	1. ____	1. ____
	2. _____	2. _____	2. ____	2. ____
(F)	1. _____	1. _____	1. ____	1. ____
	2. _____	2. _____	2. ____	2. ____
(G)	1. _____	1. _____	1. ____	1. ____
	2. _____	2. _____	2. ____	2. ____

SOLUTION TO DEMONSTRATION PROBLEM

Transaction	Accounts Affected	Type of Account	Increase or Decrease	Debit or Credit
(A)	1. Cash	1. Asset	1. Increase	1. Debit
	2. Service Fees Earned	2. Revenue	2. Increase	2. Credit
(B)	1. Salaries Expense	1. Expense	1. Increase	1. Debit
	2. Cash	2. Asset	2. Decrease	2. Credit
(C)	1. Cash	1. Asset	1. Increase	1. Debit
	2. Accounts Receivable	2. Asset	2. Decrease	2. Credit
(D)	1. F. Thomas, Drawing	1. Owner Drawing	1. Increase	1. Debit
	2. Cash	2. Asset	2. Decrease	2. Credit
(E)	1. Supplies	1. Asset	1. Increase	1. Debit
	2. Accounts Payable	2. Liability	2. Increase	2. Credit
(F)	1. Accounts Receivable	1. Asset	1. Increase	1. Debit
	2. Service Fees Earned	2. Revenue	2. Increase	2. Credit
(G)	1. Accounts Payable	1. Liability	1. Decrease	1. Debit
	2. Cash	2. Asset	2. Decrease	2. Credit

ANSWERS TO SELF-TEST QUESTIONS   **1.** b, p. 34   **2.** d, p. 35   **3.** b, p. 36   **4.** c, p. 44   **5.** d, p. 47

International Accounting Principles

A topic of importance to an increasing number of accountants is the development and implementation of a set of international accounting principles. The term **international accounting principles** refers to a set of accounting guidelines that are acceptable for financial statements that will be presented and utilized in different countries.

NEED FOR INTERNATIONAL ACCOUNTING PRINCIPLES

Two major reasons for interest in a set of international accounting principles are (1) to improve the operation of international capital markets and (2) to reduce the information-generating costs of multinational companies.

IMPROVE THE OPERATION OF INTERNATIONAL CAPITAL MARKETS

Accompanying the movement to a global economy has been the development of an international capital market. A U.S. company in need of funds, for example, may seek financing in one or more foreign countries, or a foreign company may seek financing in the United States. Similarly, a U.S. investor may invest in foreign securities, or a foreign investor may invest in U.S. securities. The movement of capital across borders is sizable, amounting to hundreds of billions of dollars each year.

At present, there are differences in accounting principles among countries. These differences create barriers to, and cause inefficiencies in, the operation of the international capital market. For example, some foreign companies are unwilling to offer their securities in the United States because they do not want to incur the costs of restating their financial data to comply with U.S. accounting principles. Also, in trying to compare corporate performances across borders, U.S. investors and lenders incur extra costs as they adjust their analyses to compensate for the lack of comparability in underlying accounting principles. Lenders may even increase the rate of interest charged to compensate for the uncertainty created by the use of different (and not completely understood) accounting principles. A set of international accounting principles, understood and interpreted consistently throughout the world, would eliminate these types of problems and encourage the flow of capital across borders.

Even the existence of the large amounts of capital currently flowing in the international market does not reduce the need for increased harmonization of accounting principles among countries. Accounting's role in the allocation of resources in capital markets is to provide investors and creditors with relevant and reliable financial information so that informed decisions may be made as to where resources should be allocated. If the underlying accounting data are not comparable across countries (as is currently the case), then it is likely that investors and creditors at present are not making the optimal allocation decisions.

REDUCE THE INFORMATION-GENERATING COSTS OF MULTINATIONAL COMPANIES

A multinational corporation has subsidiary units located outside the firm's home country. To the extent that each country in which a subsidiary is located has different accounting principles, the multinational firm's costs of generating accounting information are increased. For example, a different accounting system must be established for each country in which the firm operates so that local reporting requirements may be met, various personnel must be trained in the similarities and differences in accounting principles used by subsidiary units, and subsidiary financial data must be converted to the home country accounting principles whenever the data from all units are to be merged into one overall set of financial statements. Costs associated with these activities would be eliminated with the implementation of a set of international accounting principles.

OBSTACLES TO INTERNATIONAL ACCOUNTING PRINCIPLES

Getting a set of international accounting principles identified and accepted by different countries is a difficult task. Among the obstacles are (1) cultural differences among countries, (2) differences among countries as to who establishes accounting principles, and (3) nationalistic tendencies of principle-setting bodies.

CULTURAL DIFFERENCES

Countries differ in economic environment, political structure, and language. These differences contribute to the diversity in accounting principles among countries, and this diversity makes it harder to agree on a common set of principles.

An economic environment with a high rate of inflation, for example, may generate an accounting principle that requires inflation adjustments to the financial statements, but a country with a low inflation rate may not require such adjustments. As an illustration, Mexican accounting principles require inflation adjustments to financial statements, but U.S. principles do not. Similarly, an economy dominated by publicly held corporations may require accounting principles that are not needed in an economy influenced by small, family-owned businesses.

Some political systems place more emphasis on private ownership of property than do other systems, and this may lead to differences in accounting principles. The relationship between tax law and accounting principles also differs among countries. In some countries, financial statements must conform to tax returns, but in other countries, such as the United States, tax returns and financial statements may differ significantly.

Language differences create problems in establishing a uniformly understood set of international accounting principles. Accounting contains many technical terms and not all languages can easily assimilate the fine points of technical definitions. Also, the interpretation of certain concepts, such as the *timeliness* of reporting or the *reliability* of data, may differ among countries.[1]

DIFFERENCES IN NATIONAL PRINCIPLE-SETTING BODIES

The nature of the group with primary responsibility for formulating accounting principles varies from one country to the next. The group may be a committee in the private sector (such as the Financial Accounting Standards Board in the United States and the Accounting Standards Committee in Canada), or it may be a governmental body (in Germany, for example, Parliament sets accounting standards through the Ministry of Finance), or it may be a combined effort of a private-sector committee and a governmental body.[2] The group's membership may consist of accountants only, or it may be a mix of accountants and nonaccountants. A governmental body containing nonaccountants is likely to have a different perspective about appropriate accounting principles than is a private-sector committee composed of accountants only. The variety among countries in the nature and composition of principle-setting bodies, then, contributes to the problem of achieving agreement on international accounting principles.

NATIONALISTIC TENDENCIES OF PRINCIPLE-SETTING BODIES

To achieve a set of international accounting principles that is acceptable to all countries, each country's principle-setting body will probably have to compromise its views somewhat. These compromises may be difficult to achieve. For example, although the FASB supports the development of international accounting principles, situations may arise in which it believes its current accounting principles are best and should not be "watered down" to

---

[1]John M. Turner, "International Harmonization: A Professional Goal," *The Journal of Accountancy,* January 1983, pp. 59–60.

[2]S. E. C. Purvis, Helen Gernon, and Michael A. Diamond, "The IASC and Its Comparability Project: Prerequisites for Success," *Accounting Horizons,* June 1991, p. 25.

meet a proposed international standard. Further, the appropriate role for a nation's principle-setting body once international principles are in place is still open to question. A strong national principle-setting group, for example, may not want its role to be only that of advocate for its country's interests at the international level. Concerns about compromise and future roles create a tendency in principle-setting bodies to resist, or slow down, the movement toward international harmonization of accounting principles. For substantial progress toward international harmonization to occur, however, nationalistic attitudes would have to be modified.

INTERNATIONAL ACCOUNTING STANDARDS COMMITTEE

Although several organizations are working to increase international harmonization in accounting, the organization that has taken the lead in formulating international accounting principles is the *International Accounting Standards Committee (IASC)*. Organized in 1973 and headquartered in London, the IASC's membership covers more than 100 professional accounting organizations from 80 countries. The IASC has no authoritative status in any country, nor does it have any enforcement powers. Instead, the IASC depends on its members to persuade the principle setters in their home countries that financial statements should comply with the international accounting standards it formulates.

The IASC is governed by a 14-member board, and standards must be approved by at least 75% of the board members. Through the late 1980s, most of the standards identified a range of acceptable practice—usually two acceptable alternatives were established—rather than specifying a single accounting principle for each situation considered. For the most part, the practices allowed by these standards were compatible with generally accepted accounting principles (GAAP) in the United States.

Beginning in 1988 and continuing to the present, the IASC has worked to eliminate a large number of the alternatives allowed in its existing standards. Some of the revised standards may well conflict with current GAAP. These conflicts will likely bring pressure on the FASB to conform U.S. standards to the international standards.

The *International Organization of Securities Commissions (IOSCO)* supports the IASC's efforts to eliminate alternatives in its standards. IOSCO comprises securities regulators from all over the world (the U.S. member is the Securities and Exchange Commission). Should the IASC develop a set of principles acceptable to securities regulators, then an intermediate approach to accounting internationalism may be possible. Under this approach, the securities regulators would adopt the principles as a set of international standards. Foreign companies wishing to issue securities in a particular country would then be required to reconcile their financial statements to the international standards (not the local country's standards).[3] As a result, the international flow of capital would be improved without requiring national principle setters to compromise their standards for domestic companies. The late 1990s should reveal whether this intermediate approach will be successful.

GLOSSARY OF KEY TERMS USED IN THIS CHAPTER AND APPENDIX

account   A record of the additions, deductions, and balances of individual assets, liabilities, permanent owners' equity, owner drawings, revenues, and expenses (p. 32).

accounting entity   An economic unit that has identifiable boundaries and that is the focus for the accumulation and reporting of financial information (p. 45).

accounting period   The time period, typically one year, to which periodic accounting reports are related (p. 45).

accrual accounting   Accounting procedures whereby revenues are recorded when they are earned and realized and expenses are recorded in the period in which they help to generate revenues (p. 48).

cash-basis accounting   Accounting procedures whereby revenues are recorded when cash is received from operating activities and expenses are recorded when cash payments related to operating activities are made (p. 48).

---

[3]Philip R. Lochner, Jr., "The Role of U.S. Standard Setters in International Harmonization of Accounting Standards," *The Journal of Accountancy,* September 1991, p. 108.

conceptual framework   A cohesive set of interrelated objectives and fundamentals for external financial reporting developed by the FASB (p. 43).

conservatism   An accounting principle stating that judgmental determinations should tend toward understatement rather than overstatement of net assets and income (p. 49).

consistency   An accounting principle stating that, unless otherwise disclosed, accounting reports should be prepared on a basis consistent with the preceding period (p. 48).

cost principle   An accounting principle stating that asset measures are based on the prices paid to acquire the assets (p. 47).

credit (entry)   An entry on the right side (or in the credit column) of any account (p. 35).

debit (entry)   An entry on the left side (or in the debit column) of any account (p. 35).

double-entry system   A method of accounting that recognizes the duality of a transaction such that the analysis results in a recording of equal amounts of debits and credits (p. 37).

drawing account   A temporary owners' equity account used to accumulate owner withdrawals from the business (p. 32).

financial reporting objectives   A component of the conceptual framework that specifies that financial statements should provide information (1) useful for investment and credit decisions, (2) helpful in assessing an entity's ability to generate future cash flows, and (3) about an entity's resources, claims to those resources, and the effects of events causing changes in these items (p. 43).

financial statement elements   A part of the conceptual framework that identifies the significant components—such as assets, liabilities, owners' equity, revenues, and expenses—used to put financial statements together (p. 43).

full disclosure principle   An accounting principle stipulating the disclosure of all facts necessary to make financial statements useful to readers (p. 50).

general ledger   A grouping of all of an entity's accounts that are used to prepare the basic financial statements (p. 41).

going concern concept   An accounting principle that assumes that, in the absence of evidence to the contrary, a business entity will have an indefinite life (p. 47).

international accounting principles   A set of accounting guidelines that is acceptable for financial statements that will be presented and used in different countries (p. 53).

matching concept   An accounting guideline that states that income is determined by relating expenses, to the extent feasible, with revenues that have been recorded (p. 48).

materiality   An accounting guideline that states that transactions so insignificant that they would not affect a user's actions may be recorded in the most expedient manner (p. 50).

measuring unit concept   An accounting guideline noting that the accounting unit of measure is the basic unit of money (p. 46).

objectivity principle   An accounting principle requiring that, whenever possible, accounting entries be based on objectively determined evidence (p. 47).

permanent account   An account used to prepare the balance sheet; that is, asset, liability, and owner capital (or, for a corporation, capital stock and retained earnings) accounts. Any balance in a permanent account at the end of an accounting period is carried forward to the next period (p. 35).

qualitative characteristics of accounting information   The characteristics of accounting information that contribute to decision usefulness. The primary qualities are *relevance* and *reliability* (p. 44).

recognition criteria   The criteria that must be met before a financial statement element may be recorded in the accounts. Essentially, the item must meet the definition of an element and must be measurable, and the resultant information about the item must be relevant and reliable (p. 48).

relevance   A qualitative characteristic of accounting information; relevant information contributes to the predictive and evaluative decisions made by financial statement users (p. 44).

reliability   A qualitative characteristic of accounting information; reliable information contains no bias or error and faithfully portrays what it intends to represent (p. 44).

revenue recognition principle   An accounting principle requiring that, with few exceptions, revenue be recognized when services are performed or goods are sold (p. 44).

running balance account   An account form having money columns for debit entries, credit entries, and the account balance. Sometimes called the *three-column account* (p. 37).

T account   An abbreviated form of the formal account in the shape of a *T;* use is usually limited to illustrations of accounting techniques and analysis (p. 34).

temporary account   An account used to gather information for an accounting period; at the end of the period, the balance is transferred to a permanent owners' equity account. Revenue, expense, and owners' drawing accounts are temporary accounts (p. 35).

trial balance   A list of the account titles in the general ledger, their respective debit or credit balances, and the totals of the debit and credit amounts (p. 42).

QUESTIONS

2-1 What is an *account?*

2-2 What information is recorded in an account?

2-3 What is the justification for using a separate owner's drawing account?

2-4 Define *permanent account.* What is an example?

2-5 What is the type of permanent owners' equity account used in sole proprietorships and partnerships? Identify the types used in corporations.

2-6 Define *temporary account.* What is an example?

2-7 What does the term *debit* mean? What does the term *credit* mean?

2-8 What type of account—asset, liability, permanent owner's equity, owner withdrawal, revenue, or expense—is each of the following accounts? Indicate whether a debit entry or a credit entry increases the balance of the account.

Professional Fees Earned	S. Adams, Capital
Accounts Receivable	Advertising Expense
Accounts Payable	Supplies
Cash	S. Adams, Drawing

2-9 How is the normal side of an account determined?

2-10 What is the normal balance (debit or credit) of each account in Question 2-8?

2-11 What are one advantage and one disadvantage of the running balance, or three-column, account form compared with the two-column form?

2-12 Explain the terms *general ledger* and *trial balance.* What are the reasons for preparing a trial balance?

2-13 How would you determine whether a particular accounting procedure is a generally accepted accounting principle?

2-14 Why has the FASB developed a conceptual framework?

2-15 What are two primary qualities of accounting information that contribute to decision usefulness?

2-16 How would you describe, in one sentence, each of the following accounting principles?

accounting entity	consistency
accounting period	revenue recognition
measuring unit	matching
objectivity	conservatism
cost	materiality
going concern	full disclosure

2-17 Why is the accounting entity the most fundamental accounting concept?

2-18 Why do accounting principles emphasize historical cost as a basis for measuring assets?

2-19 How do accountants justify recognizing revenue when services are performed or goods are sold?

2-20 How do accrual accounting and the cash basis of accounting differ? To which of these accounting approaches does the matching concept relate?

EXERCISES

**ANALYSIS OF ACCOUNTS
— OBJ. 1 —**

2-21 Compute the unknown amount required in each of the following five independent situations. The answer to situation (a) is given as an example.

Account	Beginning Balance	Ending Balance	Other Information
(a) Cash	$ 6,100	$ 5,250	Total cash disbursed, $5,400.
(b) Accounts Receivable	8,500	9,300	Services on account, $16,500.
(c) Notes Payable	15,000	20,000	Funds borrowed by notes, $30,000.
(d) Accounts Payable	3,280	1,720	Payments on account, $2,900.
(e) M. Ventura, Capital	32,000	46,000	Capital contributions, $5,000.

Unknown Amounts Required

a. Total cash received	$4,550
b. Total cash collected from credit customers	
c. Notes payable repaid during the period	
d. Goods and services received from suppliers on account	
e. Net income, if no withdrawals were made	

NATURE OF ACCOUNTS,
DEBIT AND CREDIT RULES
— OBJ. 2, 3 —

2-22 For each of the accounts listed below, indicate whether the account (1) is increased by a debit or a credit and (2) is a permanent or a temporary account.

Accounts Payable	G. Frankel, Capital
Advertising Expense	G. Frankel, Drawing
Cash	Land
Equipment	Service Fees Earned

TRANSACTION ANALYSIS
— OBJ. 4 —

2-23 Match each of the following transactions of L. Boyd, a printer, with the appropriate letters, indicating the debits and credits to be made. The key for letters follows the transaction list. The correct answer for transaction 1 is given.

		Answer
(1)	The owner contributed cash to the business.	a, f
(2)	Purchased equipment on account.	_____
(3)	Received and immediately paid advertising bill.	_____
(4)	Purchased supplies for cash.	_____
(5)	Borrowed money from bank, giving a note payable.	_____
(6)	Billed customers for services rendered.	_____
(7)	Made partial payment on account for equipment.	_____
(8)	Paid employee's salary.	_____
(9)	Collected amounts due from customers billed in transaction 6.	_____

Effect of Transaction

a.	Debit an asset	f.	Credit owner's capital
b.	Credit an asset	g.	Debit a revenue
c.	Debit a liability	h.	Credit a revenue
d.	Credit a liability	i.	Debit an expense
e.	Debit owner's capital	j.	Credit an expense

TRANSACTION ANALYSIS
— OBJ. 4 —

2-24 The accounts below are from the general ledger of Tiffany Bast, an architect. For each letter given in the T accounts, describe the type of business transaction(s) or event(s) that would most probably be reflected by entries on that side of the account. For example, the answer to (a) is Amounts of services performed for clients on account.

ACCOUNTS RECEIVABLE		NOTES PAYABLE	
(a)	(b)		(c)

OFFICE EQUIPMENT		ACCOUNTS PAYABLE	
(d)		(e)	(f)

PROFESSIONAL FEES EARNED		T. BAST, DRAWING	
	(g)	(h)	

T. BAST, CAPITAL		SALARIES EXPENSE	
	(i)	(j)	

TRANSACTION ANALYSIS
AND TRIAL BALANCE
— OBJ. 4, 5 —

2-25 Make T accounts for the following accounts that appear in the general ledger of Pet Hospital, owned by R. Mead, a veterinarian: Cash; Accounts Receivable; Supplies; Office Equipment; Accounts Payable; R. Mead, Capital; R. Mead, Drawing; Professional Fees Earned; Salaries Expense; and Rent Expense. Record the following December 1996 transactions in the T accounts and key all entries with the number identifying the transaction. Finally, determine the balance in each account and prepare a trial balance at December 31, 1996.
   (1) Mead opened a checking account on December 1 at United Bank in the name of Pet Hospital and deposited $20,000 cash.
   (2) Paid rent for December, $1,100.
   (3) Purchased office equipment on account, $2,900.
   (4) Purchased supplies for cash, $1,700.
   (5) Billed clients for services rendered, $7,300.
   (6) Paid secretary's salary, $1,950.
   (7) Paid $1,500 on account for the equipment purchased in transaction 3.
   (8) Collected $5,800 from clients previously billed for services.
   (9) Mead withdrew $2,200 cash for personal use.

CONCEPTUAL FRAMEWORK
— OBJ. 6 —

2-26 The Financial Accounting Standards Board worked several years to develop a conceptual framework.
    a. What is the basic purpose of a conceptual framework?
    b. Identify the financial reporting objectives that are specified in the conceptual framework.

BASIC PRINCIPLES
— OBJ. 7 —

2-27 Indicate the basic principle or principles of accounting that underlie each of the following independent situations:
    a. Dr. Kline is a practicing pediatrician. Over the years, she has accumulated a personal investment portfolio of securities, virtually all of which have been purchased from her earnings as a pediatrician. The investment portfolio is not reflected in the accounting records of her medical practice.
    b. A company purchases a desk tape dispenser for use by the office secretary. The tape dispenser cost $10 and has an estimated useful life of 25 years. The purchase is debited to the Office Supplies Expense account.
    c. A company sells a product that has a two-year warranty covering parts and labor. In the same period that revenues from product sales are recorded, an estimate of future warranty costs is debited to the Product Warranty Expense account.
    d. A company is sued for $1 million by a customer claiming that a defective product caused an accident. The company believes that the lawsuit is without merit. Although the case will not be tried for a year, the company adds a note describing the lawsuit to its current financial statements.

REVENUE RECOGNITION
— OBJ. 7 —

2-28 For each of the following situations, determine whether the criteria for revenue recognition have been met by December 31, 1996.
    a. A manufacturing company received $50,000 cash on December 31, 1996, as an advance payment on a special order piece of equipment. The equipment will be manufactured by March 31, 1997.
    b. A television dealer acquired six new high-definition television sets for $8,400 cash on December 31, 1996, and advertised their availability, at $2,000 each, in that evening's newspaper.
    c. A snow removal service signed a contract on November 15, 1996, with a shopping mall to clear its parking lot of all snowfalls over 1 inch during the months of December 1996 through March 1997. The cost is $600 per month and payment is due in two $1,200 installments: January 2, 1997, and February 1, 1997. By December 31, 1996, no snowfall over 1 inch had occurred.

INTERNATIONAL
ACCOUNTING PRINCIPLES
— APPENDIX A —

2-29 The acceptance by nations of a set of international accounting principles will provide certain benefits.
    a. What group has taken the lead in developing a set of international accounting principles?
    b. Identify and briefly discuss two major benefits that would result from the adoption by nations of a set of international accounting principles.

PROBLEMS

TRANSACTION ANALYSIS
AND TRIAL BALANCE
— OBJ. 4, 5 —

2-30 James Behm, electrical contractor, began business on May 1, 1996. The following transactions occurred during May:
    (1) Behm invested $18,000 of his personal funds in the business.
    (2) Purchased equipment on account, $4,200.
    (3) Returned $200 of equipment that was not satisfactory. The return reduced the amount owed to the supplier.
    (4) Purchased supplies on account, $860.
    (5) Purchased a truck for $10,500. Behm paid $5,500 cash and gave a note payable for the balance.
    (6) Paid rent for May, $875.
    (7) Paid fuel cost for truck, $60.
    (8) Billed customers for services rendered, $13,700.
    (9) Paid $3,000 on account for equipment purchased in transaction 2.
    (10) Paid cost of utilities for May, $210.
    (11) Received invoice for May advertising, to be paid in June, $280.
    (12) Paid employees' wages, $3,350.
    (13) Collected $8,600 on accounts receivable.
    (14) Behm withdrew $1,500 cash for personal expenses.
    (15) Paid interest for May on note payable, $40.
    REQUIRED
    a. Record the above transactions in T accounts, and key entries with the numbers of the transactions. The following accounts will be needed to record the transactions for May: Cash; Accounts Receivable; Supplies; Equipment; Truck; Notes Payable; Accounts Payable; J. Behm, Capital; J. Behm, Drawing; Service Revenue; Rent Expense; Wages Expense; Utilities Expense; Truck Expense; Advertising Expense; and Interest Expense.
    b. Prepare a trial balance of the general ledger as of May 31, 1996.

TRIAL BALANCE AND
FINANCIAL STATEMENTS
— OBJ. 5 —

2-31 The following account balances, in alphabetical order, are from the general ledger of Morgan's Waterproofing Service at January 31, 1997. The firm's accounting year began on January 1. All accounts have normal balances.

Accounts Payable	$ 2,600	Notes Payable	$ 6,000
Accounts Receivable	21,000	Rent Expense	1,700
Advertising Expense	420	Salaries Expense	8,000
Cash	10,400	Service Fees Earned	25,760
Interest Expense	50	Supplies	8,960
K. Morgan, Capital (January 1)	29,740	Supplies Expense	10,250
K. Morgan, Drawing	3,000	Utilities Expense	320

REQUIRED

a. Prepare a trial balance in good form from the given data.
b. Prepare an income statement for the month of January 1997.
c. Prepare a statement of owner's equity for the month of January 1997.
d. Prepare a balance sheet at January 31, 1997.

TRANSACTION ANALYSIS
AND THE EFFECT OF
ERRORS ON TRIAL BALANCE
— OBJ. 4, 5 —

2-32 The following T accounts contain numbered entires for the May transactions of Carol Marsh, a market analyst, who opened her offices on May 1, 1996:

CASH					C. MARSH, CAPITAL		
(1)	13,000	(2)	4,800			(1)	13,000
(9)	3,700	(4)	810				
		(6)	1,950				
		(8)	600				

ACCOUNTS RECEIVABLE					C. MARSH, DRAWING		
(5)	6,400	(9)	3,700	(8)	600		

OFFICE SUPPLIES				PROFESSIONAL FEES EARNED		
(3)	2,800				(5)	6,400

OFFICE EQUIPMENT				RENT EXPENSE		
(2)	4,800		(4)	810		

ACCOUNTS PAYABLE					UTILITIES EXPENSE		
(6)	1,950	(3)	2,800	(7)	270		
		(7)	270				

REQUIRED

a. Give a reasonable description of each of the nine numbered transactions entered in the above accounts. Example: (1) Carol Marsh invested $13,000 of her personal funds in her business.
b. The following trial balance, taken for Marsh's firm on May 31, contains several errors. Itemize the errors and indicate the correct totals for the trial balance.

CAROL MARSH, MARKET ANALYST
TRIAL BALANCE
MAY 31, 1996

	Debit	Credit
Cash	$ 8,450	
Accounts Receivable	3,700	
Office Supplies	2,800	
Office Equipment	4,800	
Accounts Payable		$ 1,120
C. Marsh, Capital		13,000
C. Marsh, Drawing		600
Professional Fees Earned		6,400
Rent Expense	810	
	$20,560	$21,120

TRANSACTION ANALYSIS,
TRIAL BALANCE, AND
FINANCIAL STATEMENTS
— OBJ. 4, 5 —

2-33 Pam Brown owns Art Graphics, a firm providing designs for advertisers, market analysts, and others. On July 1, 1996, her general ledger showed the following normal account balances:

Cash	$ 8,500	Notes Payable	$ 5,000
Accounts Receivable	9,800	Accounts Payable	2,100
		P. Brown, Capital	11,200
	$18,300		$18,300

The following transactions occurred in July:

July 2   Paid July rent, $670

2   Collected $7,100 on account from customers.

5   Paid $2,500 installment due on the $5,000 noninterest-bearing note payable to a relative.

9   Billed customers for design services rendered on account, $16,550.

12   Rendered design services and collected from cash customers, $1,200.

15   Paid $1,400 to creditors on account.

18   Collected $12,750 on account from customers.

21   Paid a delivery service for delivery of graphics to commercial firms, $400.

30   Paid July salaries, $4,600.

30   Received invoice for July advertising expense, to be paid in August, $600.

31   Paid cost of utilities for July, $350.

31   Brown withdrew $2,000 cash for personal use.

31   Received invoice for supplies used in July, to be paid in August, $2,260.

31   Purchased computer for $4,300 cash to be used in the business starting next month.

REQUIRED

a. Set up running balance accounts for the general ledger accounts with July 1 balances and enter the beginning balances. Also provide the following running balance accounts: Equipment; P. Brown, Drawing; Service Fees Earned; Rent Expense; Salaries Expense; Delivery Expense; Advertising Expense; Utilities Expense; and Supplies Expense. Record the listed transactions in the accounts.

b. Prepare a trial balance at July 31, 1996.

c. Prepare an income statement for the month of July 1996.

d. Prepare a statement of owner's equity for the month of July 1996.

e. Prepare a balance sheet at July 31, 1996.

TRANSACTION ANALYSIS,
TRIAL BALANCE, AND
FINANCIAL STATEMENTS
— OBJ. 4, 5 —

2-34 Outpost Fly-In Service, Inc., operates leased amphibious aircraft and docking facilities, equipping the firm to transport campers and hunters from Thunder Bay, Ontario, to outpost camps owned by various resorts in Ontario. On August 1, 1996, the firm's trial balance was as follows:

OUTPOST FLY-IN SERVICE, INC.
TRIAL BALANCE
AUGUST 1, 1996

	Debit	Credit
Cash	$52,600	
Accounts Receivable	23,200	
Notes Payable		$ 3,000
Accounts Payable		1,700
Capital Stock		50,000
Retained Earnings		21,100
	$75,800	$75,800

During August the following transactions occurred:

Aug. 1   Paid August rental cost for aircraft, dockage, and dockside office, $5,000.

3   Paid insurance premium for August, $1,800.

5   Paid for August advertising in various sports magazines, $1,000.

6   Rendered fly-in services for various groups for cash, $13,750.

8   Billed the Ministry of Natural Resources for services in transporting mapping personnel, $3,200.

13   Received $17,400 on account from clients.

16   Paid $1,500 on accounts payable.

24 Billed various clients for services, $16,400.
31 Paid interest on note payable for August, $25.
31 Paid August wages, $12,800.
31 Received invoice for the cost of fuel used during August, $3,200.
31 Declared and paid a cash dividend, $4,500 (debit Retained Earnings).

REQUIRED

a. Set up running balance accounts for each item in the August 1 trial balance and enter the beginning balances. Also provide similar accounts for the following items: Service Fees Earned, Wages Expense, Advertising Expense, Rent Expense, Fuel Expense, Insurance Expense, and Interest Expense. Record the transactions for August in the accounts, using the dates given.
b. Prepare a trial balance at August 31, 1996.
c. Prepare an income statement for the month of August 1996.
d. Prepare a balance sheet at August 31, 1996. (*Note:* The month's net income increases Retained Earnings.)

BASIC PRINCIPLES — OBJ. 7 —

2-35 The following are certain unrelated accounting situations and the accounting treatment that has been followed in each firm's records.

1. Martin Company mounts a $600,000 year-long advertising campaign on a new national cable television network. The firm's annual accounting period is the calendar year. The television network required full payment in December at the beginning of the campaign. Accounting treatment is

   Increase Advertising Expense, $600,000
   Decrease Cash, $600,000

2. Because of a local bankruptcy, machinery worth $200,000 was acquired at a "bargain" purchase price of $180,000. Accounting treatment is

   Increase Machinery, $180,000
   Decrease Cash, $180,000

3. Tim Vagly, a consultant operating a sole proprietorship, withdrew $20,000 from the business and purchased stocks as an investment gift to his wife. Accounting treatment is

   Increase Investments, $20,000
   Decrease Cash, $20,000

4. The Solid State Bank, by action of the board of directors, wrote down the recorded amount of its home office building from its cost of $2,500,000 to the nominal amount of $100. The objective was to bolster its customers' confidence in the bank's financial strength by obviously understating bank assets. Accounting treatment is

   Increase Building Write-Down Expense, $2,499,900
   Decrease Buildings, $2,499,900

5. Sioux Company received a firm offer of $96,000 for a parcel of land it owns that cost $68,000 two years ago. The offer was refused, but the indicated gain was recorded in the accounts. Accounting treatment is

   Increase Land, $28,000
   Increase Revenue from Change in Land Value, $28,000

REQUIRED

a. In each of the given situations, indicate which basic generally accepted accounting principles apply and whether they have been used appropriately.
b. If you decide the accounting treatment is not generally accepted, discuss the effect of the departure on the balance sheet and the income statement.

ALTERNATE EXERCISES

NATURE OF ACCOUNTS, DEBIT AND CREDIT RULES — OBJ. 2, 3 —

2-21A Refer to the schedule of account categories on page 63. In the first blank column, enter *permanent* or *temporary* to describe the nature of an account in the category shown to the left. In the last three blank columns, enter *debit* or *credit* to describe the entry necessary to increase and decrease an account in the category shown to the left, and which side of the account represents the normal balance.

	Permanent or Temporary	Increase	Decrease	Normal Balance
Asset	_____	_____	_____	_____
Liability	_____	_____	_____	_____
Owner, Capital	_____	_____	_____	_____
Owner, Drawing	_____	_____	_____	_____
Revenue	_____	_____	_____	_____
Expense	_____	_____	_____	_____

NATURE OF ACCOUNTS, DEBIT AND CREDIT RULES — OBJ. 2, 3 —

2-22A For each of the accounts listed below, indicate whether the account (1) is increased by a debit or a credit and (2) is a permanent or temporary account.

Accounts Receivable	Notes Payable
Advertising Revenue	Retained Earnings
Building	Supplies
Capital Stock	Utilities Expense

TRANSACTION ANALYSIS — OBJ. 4 —

2-23A Match each of the following transactions of S. Lesch, a landscape architect, with the appropriate letters, indicating the debits and credits to be made. The key for the letters follows the transaction list. The correct answer for transaction 1 is given.

	Answer
(1) Purchased supplies on account.	a, d
(2) Paid interest on note payable.	_____
(3) The owner withdrew cash from the business for personal use.	_____
(4) Returned some defective supplies and received a reduction in the amount owed.	_____
(5) Made payment to settle note payable.	_____
(6) Received an invoice for monthly utilities used.	_____
(7) Received payment in advance from client for work to be done next month.	_____
(8) The owner contributed a number of landscape design books to the business.	_____

Effect of Transaction

a. Debit an asset	g. Debit owner's drawing
b. Credit an asset	h. Credit owner's drawing
c. Debit a liability	i. Debit a revenue
d. Credit a liability	j. Credit a revenue
e. Debit owner's capital	k. Debit an expense
f. Credit owner's capital	l. Credit an expense

TRANSACTION ANALYSIS — OBJ. 4 —

2-24A Make T accounts for the following accounts that appear in the general ledger of Daniel Kelly, an attorney: Cash; Accounts Receivable; Office Equipment; Legal Database Subscription; Accounts Payable; D. Kelly, Capital; D. Kelly, Drawing; Legal Fees Earned; Salaries Expense; Rent Expense; and Utilities Expense. Record the following October transactions in the T accounts and key all entries with the number identifying the transaction. Determine the balance in each account.

(1) Kelly started his law practice by contributing $19,500 cash to the business on October 1, 1996.
(2) Purchased office equipment on account, $10,400.
(3) Paid office rent for October, $700.
(4) Paid $9,600 to access on-line legal database for two years.
(5) Billed clients for services rendered, $11,300.
(6) Made $6,000 payment on account for the equipment purchased in transaction 2.
(7) Paid legal assistant's salary, $2,800.
(8) Collected $9,400 from clients previously billed for services.
(9) Received invoice for October utilities, $180; it will be paid in November.
(10) Kelly withdrew $1,500 cash for personal use.

TRIAL BALANCE — OBJ. 5 —

2-25A After recording the transactions in the previous exercise, prepare a trial balance for Daniel Kelly, attorney, at October 31, 1996.

CONCEPTUAL FRAMEWORK
— OBJ. 6 —

2-26A The Financial Accounting Standards Board worked several years to develop a conceptual framework.

a. Identify the financial statement elements that are specified in the conceptual framework.

b. Before a financial statement element may be recorded in the accounts, certain recognition criteria must be met. What are these recognition criteria?

BASIC PRINCIPLES
— OBJ. 7 —

2-27A Indicate the basic principle or principles of accounting that underlie each of the following independent situations:

a. Ford Motor Company reports in its annual report to stockholders that revenues from automotive sales "are recorded by the company when products are shipped to dealers."

b. The annual financial report of Chrysler Corporation and subsidiaries includes the financial data of its significant subsidiaries, including Chrysler Financial Corporation (which provides financing for dealers and customers), Chrysler Technologies Corporation (which manufactures high-technology electronic products), and Pentastar Transportation Group, Inc. (which includes Thrifty Rent-A-Car System, Inc., and Dollar Rent A Car Systems, Inc.). All significant intercompany transactions are eliminated when the data are combined.

c. A company purchased a parcel of land several years ago for $65,000. The land's estimated current market value is $80,000. The Land account balance is not increased but remains at $65,000.

d. A company has a calendar-year accounting period. On January 8, 1997, a tornado destroyed its largest warehouse, causing a $1,800,000 loss. This information is reported in a footnote to the 1996 financial statements.

ACCRUAL VERSUS CASH-BASIS
ACCOUNTING
— OBJ. 7 —

2-28A On December 31, Jayne Leigh completed her first year as a financial planner. The following data are available from the accounting records:

Fees billed to clients for services rendered	$97,000
Cash received from clients	85,000
Supplies purchased for cash	4,500
Supplies used during the year	3,300
Cash paid for rent (rent is paid through February of next year)	12,600
Rent expense for year just ended	10,800
Utility expense incurred	2,500
Utility bills paid	2,200
Salary earned by assistant	30,000
Salary paid to assistant	27,500

a. Compute Leigh's net income for the year just ended using accrual accounting.

b. Compute Leigh's net income for the year just ended using cash-basis accounting.

c. Which net income amount is computed in accordance with generally accepted accounting principles?

INTERNATIONAL ACCOUNTING
PRINCIPLES
— APPENDIX A —

2-29A Although there are benefits to the acceptance by nations of a set of international accounting principles, several obstacles would have to be overcome before such acceptance could occur.

a. Identify and briefly discuss three obstacles to the acceptance by nations of a set of international accounting principles.

b. What role might the International Organization of Securities Commissions play in implementing a set of international accounting principles?

ALTERNATE PROBLEMS

TRANSACTION ANALYSIS AND
TRIAL BALANCE
— OBJ. 4, 5 —

2-30A Mary Aker opened a tax practice on June 1, 1996. The following accounts will be needed to record her transactions for June: Cash; Accounts Receivable; Office Supplies; Tax Library; Office Furniture and Fixtures; Notes Payable; Accounts Payable; M. Aker, Capital; M. Aker, Drawing; Professional Fees Earned; Rent Expense; Salaries Expense; Advertising Expense; Utilities Expense; and Interest Expense. The following transactions occurred in June:

(1) Aker opened a special checking account at the bank for the business, investing $16,000 in her practice.

(2) Purchased office furniture and fixtures for $9,800, paid $2,800 cash, and gave a note payable for the balance.

(3) Purchased books and software for tax library on account, $3,700.

(4) Purchased office supplies for cash, $560.

(5) Paid rent for June, $750.

(6) Returned $300 of books with defective bindings. The return reduced the amount owed to the supplier.

(7) Billed clients for professional services rendered, $7,600.

(8) Paid $1,700 on account for the library items purchased in transaction 3.

(9) Collected $5,900 on account from clients billed in transaction 7.

(10) Paid June salaries, $2,900.

(11) Received invoice for June advertising, to be paid in July, $300.

(12) Aker withdrew $800 cash for personal use.

(13) Paid utilities for June, $160.

(14) Paid interest for June on note payable, $60.

REQUIRED

a. Record the above transactions in T accounts, and key entries with the numbers of the transactions.

b. Prepare a trial balance of the general ledger as of June 30, 1996.

TRIAL BALANCE AND FINANCIAL STATEMENTS — OBJ. 5 —

2-31A The following account balances were taken (out of order) from the general ledger of R. Ladd, dog trainer, at January 31, 1997. Ladd trains dogs for competitive championship field trials. The firm's accounting year began on January 1. All accounts have normal balances.

Land	$21,000	Office Rent Expense	$ 800
Maintenance Expense	460	Supplies Expense	760
Supplies	1,640	Utilities Expense	200
Advertising Expense	350	Fees Earned	16,470
R. Ladd, Capital (January 1)	29,000	Accounts Receivable	8,200
Cash	7,300	Salaries Expense	4,480
Accounts Payable	820	R. Ladd, Drawing	1,100

REQUIRED

a. Prepare a trial balance in good form from the given data.

b. Prepare an income statement for the month of January 1997.

c. Prepare a statement of owner's equity for the month of January 1997.

d. Prepare a balance sheet at January 31, 1997.

TRANSACTION ANALYSIS AND THE EFFECT OF ERRORS ON TRIAL BALANCE — OBJ. 4, 5 —

2-32A The following T accounts contain numbered entries for the May transactions of Flores Corporation, an architectural firm, which opened its offices on May 1, 1997:

CASH					ACCOUNTS PAYABLE			
(1)	20,000	(4)	1,400		(5)	310	(3)	1,530
(10)	5,200	(7)	5,950		(8)	1,000	(9)	290
		(8)	1,000					

CAPITAL STOCK		
	(1)	20,000

ACCOUNTS RECEIVABLE			
(6)	8,750	(10)	5,200

PROFESSIONAL FEES EARNED		
	(6)	8,750

SUPPLIES			
(3)	1,530	(5)	310

RENT EXPENSE	
(4)	1,400

OFFICE EQUIPMENT	
(2)	5,000

UTILITIES EXPENSE	
(9)	290

NOTES PAYABLE		
	(2)	5,000

SALARIES EXPENSE	
(7)	5,950

REQUIRED

a. Give a reasonable description of each of the 10 numbered transactions entered in the above accounts. Example: (1) Flores Corporation issued capital stock for cash, $20,000.

b. The following trial balance, taken for Flores Corporation on May 31, contains several errors. Itemize the errors, and indicate the correct totals for the trial balance.

FLORES CORPORATION
TRIAL BALANCE
MAY 31, 1997

	Debit	Credit
Cash	$61,850	
Accounts Receivable	3,550	
Supplies	1,220	
Office Equipment		$ 5,000
Notes Payable		50,000
Accounts Payable		510
Capital Stock		2,000
Professional Fees Earned		8,570
Rent Expense	1,400	
Utilities Expense	290	
Salaries Expense	5,950	
	$74,260	$66,080

TRANSACTION ANALYSIS, TRIAL BALANCE, AND FINANCIAL STATEMENTS — OBJ. 4, 5 —

2-33A Angela Mehl operates the Mehl Dance Studio. On June 1, 1997, her general ledger contained the following information:

Cash	$ 5,930	Notes Payable	$ 3,000
Accounts Receivable	7,420	Accounts Payable	480
		A. Mehl, Capital	9,870
	$13,350		$13,350

The following transactions occurred in June:

June 2   Paid June rent for practice and performance studio, $975.
      3   Paid June piano rental, $90 (Rent Expense).
      6   Collected $5,320 from students on account.
      10 Borrowed $1,500 and signed a promissory note payable due in six months.
      15 Billed students for June instructional fees, $5,600.
      18 Paid interest for June on notes payable, $30.
      20 Paid $350 for advertising ballet performances.
      21 Paid costume rental, $400 (Rent Expense).
      25 Collected $2,100 admission fees from ballet performances given today.
      27 Paid $480 owed on account.
      30 Received invoice for June utilities, to be paid in July, $280.
      30 Mehl withdrew $750 cash for personal expenses.
      30 Purchased piano for $5,000 cash, to be used in business starting in July.

REQUIRED

a. Set up running balance accounts for the general ledger accounts with June 1 balances and enter the beginning balances. Also provide the following accounts: Piano; A. Mehl, Drawing; Instructional Fees Earned; Performance Revenue; Rent Expense; Utilities Expense; Advertising Expense; and Interest Expense. Record the listed transactions in the accounts.
b. Prepare a trial balance at June 30, 1997.
c. Prepare an income statement for the month of June 1997.
d. Prepare a statement of owner's equity for the month of June 1997.
e. Prepare a balance sheet as of June 30, 1997.

TRANSACTION ANALYSIS, TRIAL BALANCE, AND FINANCIAL STATEMENTS — OBJ. 4, 5 —

2-34A On December 1, 1996, a group of individuals formed a corporation to establish the *Beeper,* a neighborhood weekly newspaper featuring want ads of individuals and advertising of local firms. The free paper will be mailed to about 8,000 local residents; revenue will be generated from advertising and want ads. The December transactions are summarized below:

Dec. 1   Sold capital stock of Beeper, Inc., for cash, $25,000.
      2   Paid December rent on furnished office, $1,000.
      3   Purchased for $750, on account, T-shirts displaying company logo. The T-shirts were distributed at a grand opening held today.

Dec. 5   Paid to creditor on account, $750
   8   Collected want ad revenue in cash, $2,800
  12   Paid post office for cost of bulk mailing, $910.
  14   Billed various firms for advertising in first two issues of the newspaper, $5,300.
  15   Paid Acme Courier Service for transporting newspapers to post office, $50.
  16   Paid for printing newspaper, $2,900.
  18   Collected want ad revenue in cash, $2,570.
  31   Received invoice for December utilities, to be paid in January, $310.
  31   Paid for printing newspaper, $2,900.
  31   Paid December salaries, $4,100.
  31   Billed various firms for advertising in two issues of the newspaper, $6,850.
  31   Paid post office for cost of bulk mailing, $930.
  31   Paid Acme Courier Service for transporting newspapers to post office, $50.
  31   Collected $5,100 on accounts receivable.
  31   Purchased fax machine for office in exchange for a six-month note payable, $1,100.

REQUIRED

a. Set up running balance accounts for the following: Cash, Accounts Receivable, Office Equipment, Notes Payable, Accounts Payable, Capital Stock, Advertising Revenue, Want Ad Revenue, Printing Expense, Advertising Expense, Utilities Expense, Salaries Expense, Rent Expense, and Delivery Expense. Record the foregoing transactions in the accounts.
b. Take a trial balance at December 31, 1996.
c. Prepare an income statement for the month of December 1996.
d. Prepare a balance sheet as of December 31, 1996. (*Note:* In this problem, the net income for December becomes the amount of retained earnings at December 31, 1996.)

**BASIC PRINCIPLES
— OBJ. 7 —**

2-35A The following are several unrelated accounting practices:

1. A recession has caused slow business and low profits for Balke Company. Consequently, the firm delays making its payments for December's rent and utilities until January and does not record either of these expenses in December.
2. Gail Derry, a consultant operating a sole proprietorship, used her business car for a personal, month-long vacation. A full year's gas and oil expenditures on the car are charged to the firm's gas and oil expense account.
3. Vine Company purchased a new $18 snow shovel that is expected to last six years. The shovel is used to clear the firm's front steps during the winter months. The shovel's cost is debited to the Snow Shovel asset account.
4. Filene Corporation has been named as the defendant in a $40,000,000 pollution lawsuit. Because the lawsuit will take several years to resolve and the outcome is uncertain, Filene's management decides not to mention the lawsuit in the current year financial statements.
5. The management of Newell Corporation, a U.S. company, prepares and issues its financial statements in constant units of purchasing power rather than the U.S. dollar unadjusted for the effect of inflation.

REQUIRED

a. For each of the given practices, indicate which basic generally accepted accounting principles apply and whether they have been used appropriately.
b. For each inappropriate accounting practice, indicate the proper accounting procedure.

CASES

**BUSINESS
DECISION CASE**

Sarah Penney operates the Wildlife Picture Gallery, selling original art and signed prints received on consignment (rather than purchased) from recognized wildlife artists throughout the country. The firm receives a 30% commission on all art sold and remits 70% of the sales price to the artists. All art is sold on a strictly cash basis.

Sarah began the business on March 1, 1996. She received a $10,000 loan from a relative to help her get started in business. Sarah signed a note agreeing to pay the loan back in one year. No interest is being charged on the loan, but the relative does want to receive a set of financial statements each month. On April 1, 1996, Sarah asks for your help in preparing the statements for the first month.

Sarah has carefully kept the firm's checking account up to date and provides you with the following complete listing of the cash receipts and disbursements for March 1996:

Cash Receipts

Original investment by Sarah Penney	$ 6,500	
Loan from relative	10,000	
Sales of art	95,000	
Total cash receipts		$111,500

Cash Disbursements

Payments to artists for sales made	$54,000	
Payment of March rent for gallery space	900	
Payment of March wages to staff	4,900	
Payment of airfare for personal vacation of Sarah Penney (vacation will be taken in April)	500	
Total cash disbursements		60,300
Cash balance, March 31, 1996		$ 51,200

Sarah also gives you the following documents she has received:

1. A $350 invoice for March utilities; payment is due by April 15, 1996.
2. A $1,700 invoice from Careful Express for the shipping of the artwork sold during March; payment is due by April 10, 1996.
3. The one-year lease she signed for the gallery space; as an incentive to sign the lease, the landlord reduced the first month's rent by 25%; the monthly rent starting in April is $1,200.

In your discussions with Sarah, she tells you that she has been so busy that she is behind in sending artists their share of the sales proceeds. She plans to catch up within the next week.

REQUIRED

From the above information, prepare the following financial statements for Wildlife Picture Gallery: (a) income statement for the month of March 1996; (b) statement of owner's equity for the month of March 1996; and (c) balance sheet as of March 31, 1996. To obtain the data needed, you may wish to use T accounts to construct the company's accounts.

ETHICS CASE   Andy Frame and his supervisor are sent on an out-of-town assignment by their employer. At the supervisor's suggestion, they stay at the Spartan Inn (across the street from the Luxury Inn). After three days of work, they settle their lodging bills and leave. On the return trip, the supervisor gives Andy what appears to be a copy of a receipt from the Luxury Inn for three nights of lodging. Actually, the supervisor indicates that he prepared the Luxury Inn receipt on his office computer and plans to complete his expense reimbursement request using the higher lodging costs from the Luxury Inn.

REQUIRED

What are the ethical considerations that Andy faces when he prepares his expense reimbursement request?

GENERAL MILLS ANNUAL REPORT CASE   Refer to the annual report of General Mills, Inc., presented in Appendix K.

REQUIRED

a. Refer to the consolidated statements of earnings and consolidated balance sheets.
   1. Identify four accounts from these financial statements that are temporary accounts.
   2. Identify four accounts from these financial statements that are permanent accounts.
   3. What accounting principle supports General Mills' presentation of land, buildings, and equipment in the balance sheets?

b. Income tax expense is one of the accounts shown in the statement of earnings.
   1. What is the increase side for this account?
   2. What is the decrease side for this account?
   3. What is the normal balance side for this account?

c. Accounts payable is one of the accounts shown in the balance sheets.
   1. What is the increase side for this account?
   2. What is the decrease side for this account?
   3. What is the normal balance side for this account?

d. Refer to Note 1 to the financial statements dealing with a Summary of Significant Accounting Policies.
   1. How does General Mills determine the ending date for its fiscal year?
   2. What is the length of General Mills' accounting period for fiscal year 1994? fiscal year 1993? fiscal year 1992?

3

The Accounting Cycle

CHAPTER LEARNING OBJECTIVES

1 **IDENTIFY** the five major steps in the accounting cycle (pp. 70–71).

2 **EXPLAIN** the role of source documents in transaction analysis (pp. 71–72).

3 **DESCRIBE** the process of journalizing and posting transactions (pp. 72–78).

4 **DESCRIBE** the adjusting process and **ILLUSTRATE** typical adjusting entries (pp. 78–83).

5 **ILLUSTRATE** the financial statements prepared from adjusted data (pp. 83–87).

6 **DESCRIBE** the process of closing the temporary accounts (pp. 87–90).

7 **SUMMARIZE** a manual accounting cycle and **DESCRIBE** a computerized accounting cycle (pp. 91–92).

CHAPTER FOCUS

The double-entry accounting system provides a basic framework for the analysis of business activities. Now we wish to go into greater detail about the procedures used to account for the operations of a business entity during a specific period of time. Regardless of its size or complexity, the entity engages in certain basic steps, called the *accounting cycle,* in order to accumulate and report its financial information. All business entities, whether it be a specialty coffee company like Starbucks Corporation, a manufacturer of microcomputer components like Intel Corporation, or a retailer like Sears, Roebuck and Co., go through the basic steps of the accounting cycle. We examine the accounting cycle in this chapter.

THE MAJOR STEPS IN THE ACCOUNTING CYCLE

OBJECTIVE *1*

IDENTIFY the five major steps in the accounting cycle.

Business entities engage in economic activity. The accountant analyzes this activity for its impact on the basic accounting equation and enters the results of the analysis into the company's information system. When management needs financial statements, the accountant reviews the financial data and makes any adjustments necessary for a proper presentation. The financial statements are then prepared. At the end of the annual accounting period, the accountant "closes the books," a process that prepares the records for the next accounting period.

The accounting activities described in the preceding paragraph constitute the major steps in the **accounting cycle**—a sequence of activities by accountants to accumulate and report financial information. Stated succinctly, these steps are analyze, record, adjust, report, and close. Exhibit 3-1 shows the sequence of these major steps in the accounting cycle.

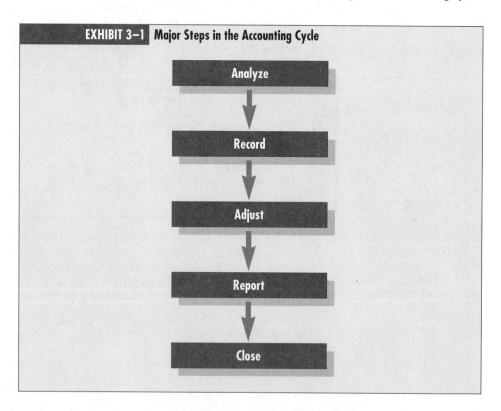

EXHIBIT 3–1 Major Steps in the Accounting Cycle

Analyze → Record → Adjust → Report → Close

These major steps in the accounting cycle do not occur with equal frequency. Accountants analyze and record daily throughout the accounting period. They adjust and report whenever management needs financial statements, usually at monthly or quarterly intervals, but at least annually. Closing occurs once, at the end of each accounting period.

ZZZZ BEST COMPANY

The significance of source documents has not been overlooked by various embezzlers and swindlers who try to cover up their schemes with false accounting entries and documents. A prominent example is the fraud perpetrated upon investors and creditors by Barry Minkow during the mid-1980s. Minkow was the founder of ZZZZ Best Company. Starting with a legitimate carpet cleaning business, Minkow later created a fictitious building restoration business. According to the accounting records and source documents, ZZZZ Best did millions of dollars' worth of restoration work, yet no restoration work was actually ever done. An elaborate facade of false documents concealed the fraud. Using a copy machine, Minkow and his accomplices created invoices, contracts, letterheads, remittance advices, and the like to support the recording of the restoration work. When the fraud was finally uncovered, investors and lenders in ZZZZ Best lost over $100,000,000. For a complete story, see Joe Domanick, *Faking It in America: Barry Minkow and the Great ZZZZ Best Scam* (Chicago: Contemporary Books, 1989) or Daniel Ankst, *Wonder Boy: Barry Minkow, The Kid Who Swindled Wall Street* (New York: Scribner's, 1990).

The annual accounting period adopted by a business firm is known as its **fiscal year.** Business firms whose fiscal year ends on December 31 are said to be on a **calendar-year** basis. About 60% of business firms are on a calendar-year basis. Many firms prefer to have their accounting year coincide with their "natural" year; that is, the fiscal year ends when business is slow and, for merchandisers, inventory quantities are low and easy to count. Year-end accounting procedures are most efficiently accomplished at this time. The "natural" year does not necessarily coincide with the calendar year. For example, Lands' End, a catalog retailer of casual clothing, ends its fiscal year on the Friday nearest January 31; its busiest period occurs during November, December, and January. The Boston Celtics, a professional basketball team, ends its fiscal year on June 30.

The major steps in the accounting cycle are accomplished whether the business entity uses a manual accounting system or a computer-based system. We will illustrate the accounting cycle using a manual system. Our example will be the December 1996 transactions of Landen TV Service, a repair business begun by Mark Landen on December 1, 1996. Landen TV Service's fiscal year-end will be December 31, so the first accounting period will be only one month long.

ANALYZE TRANSACTIONS FROM SOURCE DOCUMENTS

OBJECTIVE 2

EXPLAIN the role of source documents in transaction analysis.

Source documents are printed forms or computer records that are generated when the firm engages in business transactions. Even a brief source document usually specifies the dollar amounts involved, the date of the transaction, and possibly the party dealing with the firm. Some examples of source documents are (1) a supplier's invoice showing evidence of a purchase of supplies on account, (2) a bank check indicating payment of an obligation, (3) a deposit slip showing the amount of funds turned over to a bank, and (4) a cash receipt form indicating the amount of cash received from a customer for services rendered.

Accounting systems for many companies utilize computers to maintain a number of source documents electronically. For example, a company may pay an invoice by electronically transferring funds to a supplier; thus, no paper check is prepared. Regardless of whether a source document is a paper form or an electronic record, the source document serves as the basis for the accountant's analysis of the underlying event.

Exhibit 3-2 lists the December transactions of Landen TV Service, together with their related source documents. Ordinarily, source documents such as those listed in Exhibit 3-2 alert the accountant to the need for an entry in the records. The accountant analyzes the transaction by examining the documents to determine the appropriate accounts to be increased or decreased. For example, in transaction 2, the seller's invoice would probably indicate both the cost of the supplies and parts and the down payment. The check copy (most businesses keep a copy of checks issued) would further confirm the amount paid. The

| EXHIBIT 3–2 | Transactions of Landen TV Service for December 1996 |

Transaction	Date	Brief Description	Related Source Documents
(1)	Dec. 1	Mark Landen deposited $10,000 in the firm's bank account to start the business.	Bank deposit slip
(2)	1	Purchased supplies and parts for $950; paid $250 down; remainder to be paid in 60 days.	Seller's invoice, bank check
(3)	1	Paid rent for six months, December–May, $3,600.	Bank check, lease contract
(4)	1	Purchased truck for $10,800 and signed two-year note payable for $10,800. Annual interest at 10% is due each November 30.	Seller's invoice, promissory note
(5)	2	Signed contract to perform service work for a local TV dealer for four months, December–March, at $250 per month. Received $1,000 in advance.	Contract, dealer's check
(6)	2	Signed one-year contract with cable TV company to provide Landen TV's customers with cable TV promotional literature. For distributing the literature, Landen TV will receive a $50 monthly commission, payable at the end of every three months. The first $150 commission will be paid February 28, 1997.	Contract
(7)	10	Performed TV service for various customers and received $650 cash.	Duplicates of cash receipt forms
(8)	13	Billed various customers for TV service rendered on account, $1,580.	Invoices to customers
(9)	13	Paid employee's wages for first two weeks of December, $540.	Bank check
(10)	19	Received $800 on account from customers.	Customers' checks
(11)	21	Performed TV service for various customers and received $520 cash.	Duplicates of cash receipt forms
(12)	27	Paid employee's wages for second two weeks of December, $540.	Bank check
(13)	29	Withdrew $800 cash for personal use.	Bank check
(14)	30	Paid December truck expenses (gas and oil), $160.	Seller's invoice, bank check
(15)	31	Billed various customers for TV service rendered on account, $2,700.	Invoices to customers

analysis by the accountant, then, debits Supplies and Parts for $950, credits Cash for $250, and credits Accounts Payable for $700.

Many transactions affect several accounting periods, and the accounting for these transactions after their initial occurrence may require the accountant to refer back to previously received documents and the accounting records themselves. Examples from Exhibit 3-2 include transaction 3, where the rent payment covers six months; transaction 4, where the truck will be useful for several years and the note payable extends two years; transaction 5, where the contract runs for four months; and transaction 6, where the contract runs for one year. To ensure the proper analysis in accounting for these transactions later on, the accountant may refer back to the original source documents or review the entry made at the time of the initial transaction. We illustrate the subsequent accounting for the above transactions later in this chapter.

RECORD RESULTS OF TRANSACTION ANALYSIS

RECORD TRANSACTIONS IN A JOURNAL

For simplicity, the entries used to this point have been made directly in the general ledger accounts. This method would not prove feasible, however, for even a modest-sized business. For instance, suppose an owner wished to investigate a $1,000 credit in the Cash account. If entries were actually recorded directly in the general ledger, the purpose of the $1,000 expenditure could be difficult to determine. The owner might be forced to search through the entire general ledger to discover the offsetting debit of $1,000. Consequently, accounting records include a journal, which shows the total effect of a business transaction in one location.

OBJECTIVE *3*

DESCRIBE the process of journalizing and posting transactions.

A **journal**, or *book of original entry*, is a tabular record in which business activities are analyzed in terms of debits and credits and recorded in chronological order before they are entered in the general ledger. A journal, therefore, organizes information by date rather than by account. The complete analysis for one transaction is shown in a journal before the next transaction analysis is recorded. The word *journalize* means to record a transaction in a journal.

CHART OF ACCOUNTS

A chart of accounts is prepared to facilitate the analysis of activities and the formulation of journal entries. The **chart of accounts** is a list of the titles and numbers of all accounts found in the general ledger. The account titles should be grouped by, and in order of, the five major sections of the general ledger (assets, liabilities, owners' equity, revenues, and expenses). Exhibit 3-3 shows a chart of accounts for Landen TV Service, indicating the account numbers that will now be used.

| **EXHIBIT 3–3** | **Chart of Accounts for Landen TV Service** |

Assets	**Owner's Equity**
11 Cash	31 M. Landen, Capital
12 Accounts Receivable	32 M. Landen, Drawing
13 Commissions Receivable	33 Income Summary
14 Supplies and Parts	
15 Prepaid Rent	**Revenues**
18 Truck	41 Service Fees Earned
19 Accumulated Depreciation—Truck	42 Commissions Earned
Liabilities	**Expenses**
21 Accounts Payable	51 Rent Expense
22 Interest Payable	52 Wages Expense
23 Wages Payable	53 Supplies and Parts Expense
24 Unearned Service Fees	54 Truck Expense
25 Long-Term Notes Payable	55 Depreciation Expense—Truck
	56 Interest Expense

Each company has its own system for numbering accounts. In Exhibit 3-3, accounts in each major category start with the same digit: all asset accounts begin with 1, liabilities with 2, and so on. A numbering system permits easy reference to accounts even if the account title contains several words. For example, the account Supplies and Parts Expense might be referred to simply as account No. 53.

GENERAL JOURNAL

The **general journal** is a journal with enough flexibility so that any type of business transaction may be recorded in it. (We discuss other journals later in the text.) Exhibit 3-4 shows the first transaction from Exhibit 3-2 as it would be recorded in Landen TV Service's general journal.

The procedure for recording entries in the general journal is as follows:

1 Indicate the year, month, and date of the entry. Usually the year and month are rewritten only at the top of each page of the journal or at the point where they change.

2 Enter titles of the accounts affected in the Description column. Accounts to receive debits are entered close to the left margin and are recorded first. Accounts to receive credits are then recorded and indented slightly.

3 Place the appropriate money amounts in the left (Debit) and right (Credit) money columns.

EXHIBIT 3–4	General Journal Form with First Entry of Landen TV Service

GENERAL JOURNAL   PAGE 1

Date		Description	Post. Ref.	Debit	Credit
1996 Dec. **1**	1	Cash **2** M. Landen, Capital Owner invested cash to start business. **4**		10,000	**3** 10,000

4 Write an explanation of the transaction below the account titles. The explanation should be as brief as possible, disclosing all the information necessary to understand the event being recorded.

Each transaction entered in the journal should be stated in terms of equal dollar amounts of debits and credits. The account titles cited in the Description column should correspond to those used for the related general ledger accounts. To separate clearly the various entries, we leave a line blank between entries.

POST JOURNAL ENTRIES TO GENERAL LEDGER ACCOUNTS

After transactions have been journalized, the debits and credits in each journal entry are transferred to the appropriate general ledger accounts. This transcribing process is called **posting** to the general ledger. When records are kept by hand, posting from the general journal may be done daily, every few days, or at the end of each month. Journalizing and posting occur simultaneously when the record-keeping process is automated.

It is important to be able to trace any entry appearing in a ledger account to the journal location from which it was posted. Consequently, both the general journal and ledger accounts have **posting reference** columns. Entries in the Posting Reference column of the general journal indicate the account to which the related debit or credit has been posted. Posting references appearing in ledger accounts identify the journal location from which the related entry was posted. The posting references in the general journal and ledger accounts are entered when the journal entries are posted to the ledger accounts.

To keep accounting records uncluttered, we make posting references simple. For example, the posting reference of the general journal might be simply J. Thus, a posting reference of J9 appearing on the line with a $1,000 debit entry in the Cash account means that the ninth page of the general journal contains the entire entry in which the $1,000 debit to Cash appears. Every entry appearing in a ledger account should have a related posting reference. Posting references appearing in the journal are usually the numbers that have been assigned to the general ledger accounts.

ILLUSTRATION OF POSTING

Exhibit 3-5 diagrams the posting of Landen TV Service's first transaction from the general journal to the ledger accounts. Each debit entry and each credit entry are posted as follows:

1 The date (year, month, and day) is entered in the appropriate account. Note that this is the date of the journal entry, not necessarily the date of the actual posting. As with journals, the year and month are restated only at the top of a new account page or at the point where they change.

2 The amount is entered in the account as a debit or a credit, as indicated in the journal's money columns.

3 The new account balance is calculated.

4 The posting reference from the journal (both symbol and page number) is placed in the Posting Reference column of the ledger account.

5 The account number is placed in the Posting Reference column of the journal.

EXHIBIT 3–5 | Illustration of Posting to Ledger Accounts

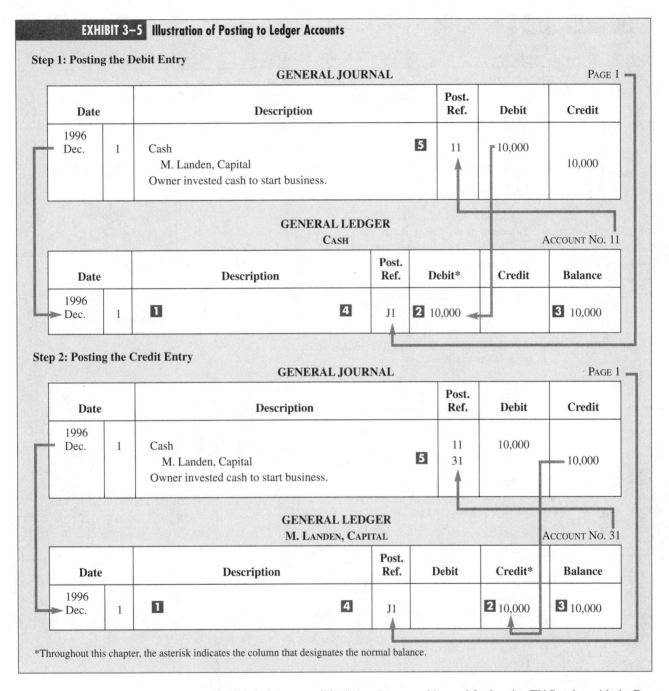

Step 1: Posting the Debit Entry

GENERAL JOURNAL   PAGE 1

Date		Description	Post. Ref.	Debit	Credit
1996 Dec.	1	Cash	**5** 11	10,000	
		M. Landen, Capital			10,000
		Owner invested cash to start business.			

GENERAL LEDGER
CASH   ACCOUNT NO. 11

Date		Description	Post. Ref.	Debit*	Credit	Balance
1996 Dec.	1	**1** **4**	J1	**2** 10,000		**3** 10,000

Step 2: Posting the Credit Entry

GENERAL JOURNAL   PAGE 1

Date		Description	Post. Ref.	Debit	Credit
1996 Dec.	1	Cash	11	10,000	
		M. Landen, Capital	**5** 31		10,000
		Owner invested cash to start business.			

GENERAL LEDGER
M. LANDEN, CAPITAL   ACCOUNT NO. 31

Date		Description	Post. Ref.	Debit	Credit*	Balance
1996 Dec.	1	**1** **4**	J1		**2** 10,000	**3** 10,000

*Throughout this chapter, the asterisk indicates the column that designates the normal balance.

Exhibit 3-6 (on page 76) shows the general journal for Landen TV Service with the December transactions from Exhibit 3-2 properly journalized and posted. Note that the account numbers in the Posting Reference column are not entered when the journal entry is recorded; they are inserted when the entry is posted. You should review each transaction in the illustration for (1) the nature of the transaction and (2) the related journal entry. We comment on transactions 2, 3, 5, and 6 from Exhibit 3-2 below.

A journal entry that involves more than just two accounts is called a **compound journal entry.** The journal entry for transaction 2 in Exhibit 3-6 is an example of a compound journal entry involving three accounts. The debit of $950 to Supplies and Parts is offset by credits of $250 to Cash and $700 to Accounts Payable. Any number of accounts may appear in a compound entry; but, regardless of how many accounts are used, the total of the debit amounts must always equal the total of the credit amounts.

Transaction 3 is the payment of rent for six months; the journal entry debits Prepaid Rent for $3,600 and credits Cash for $3,600. Prepaid Rent is an asset account; it is debited

EXHIBIT 3–6	Journalizing Landen TV Service Transactions

GENERAL JOURNAL

PAGE 1

Date		Description	Post. Ref.	Debit	Credit
1996 Dec.	1	Cash	11	10,000	
		M. Landen, Capital	31		10,000
See text explanation:		Owner invested cash to start business.			
	1	Supplies and Parts	14	950	
Transaction (2)		Cash	11		250
		Accounts Payable	21		700
		Purchased supplies and parts for $950.			
		Terms: $250 down, remainder due in 60 days.			
Transaction (3)	1	Prepaid Rent	15	3,600	
		Cash	11		3,600
		Paid rent for December–May.			
	1	Truck	18	10,800	
		Long-Term Notes Payable	25		10,800
		Purchased truck for two-year note payable; annual interest rate is 10%.			
Transaction (5)	2	Cash	11	1,000	
		Unearned Service Fees	24		1,000
		Received advance on four-month contract at $250 per month.			
	10	Cash	11	650	
		Service Fees Earned	41		650
		Services rendered for cash.			
	13	Accounts Receivable	12	1,580	
		Service Fees Earned	41		1,580
		Services rendered on account.			
	13	Wages Expense	52	540	
		Cash	11		540
		Paid wages for first two weeks of December.			
	19	Cash	11	800	
		Accounts Receivable	12		800
		Received $800 on account from credit customers.			
	21	Cash	11	520	
		Service Fees Earned	41		520
		Services rendered for cash.			
	27	Wages Expense	52	540	
		Cash	11		540
		Paid wages for second two weeks of December.			
	29	M. Landen, Drawing	32	800	
		Cash	11		800
		Withdrew $800 for personal use.			
	30	Truck Expense	54	160	
		Cash	11		160
		Gas and oil for December.			
	31	Accounts Receivable	12	2,700	
		Service Fees Earned	41		2,700
		Services rendered on account.			

because the time period covered by the rental payment extends beyond the current accounting period (which is the month of December). Asset accounts should be debited when payments are made in advance for services to be received over more than just the current accounting period. Other examples include the payment in advance of insurance premiums for coverage that extends beyond the current accounting period (debit Prepaid Insurance) and the payment in advance for advertising services that extend beyond the current period (debit Prepaid Advertising).

Transactions 5 and 6 relate to contracts entered into by Landen TV Service. The mere signing of a contract does not normally require a journal entry, because a contract is just an agreement by each party to do something, and neither party has performed yet. This is the case in transaction 6; no entry is made in the general journal because the cable TV company has not paid anything yet, and Landen TV Service has not yet distributed any promotional literature. In transaction 5, however, Landen TV Service receives payment in advance for four months of services. The receipt of this payment requires a journal entry debiting Cash for $1,000 and crediting Unearned Service Fees for $1,000. Unearned Service Fees is a liability account and represents the obligation of Landen TV Service to provide four months of service for which payment has already been received.

Exhibit 3-7 presents the general ledger accounts of Landen TV Service that have received the postings from the journal entries in Exhibit 3-6. You should trace several of the

---

EXHIBIT 3–7 **General Ledger and Unadjusted Trial Balance for Landen TV Service**

GENERAL LEDGER BEFORE ADJUSTMENTS

CASH ACCOUNT No. 11

Date	Description	Post. Ref.	Debit*	Credit	Balance
1996					
Dec. 1		J1	10,000		10,000
1		J1		250	9,750
1		J1		3,600	6,150
2		J1	1,000		7,150
10		J1	650		7,800
13		J1		540	7,260
19		J1	800		8,060
21		J1	520		8,580
27		J1		540	8,040
29		J1		800	7,240
30		J1		160	7,080

ACCOUNTS RECEIVABLE ACCOUNT No. 12

Date	Description	Post. Ref.	Debit*	Credit	Balance
1996					
Dec. 13		J1	1,580		1,580
19		J1		800	780
31		J1	2,700		3,480

SUPPLIES AND PARTS ACCOUNT No. 14

Date	Description	Post. Ref.	Debit*	Credit	Balance
1996					
Dec. 1		J1	950		950

PREPAID RENT ACCOUNT No. 15

Date	Description	Post. Ref.	Debit*	Credit	Balance
1996					
Dec. 1		J1	3,600		3,600

TRUCK ACCOUNT No. 18

Date	Description	Post. Ref.	Debit*	Credit	Balance
1996					
Dec. 1		J1	10,800		10,800

ACCOUNTS PAYABLE ACCOUNT No. 21

Date	Description	Post. Ref.	Debit	Credit*	Balance
1996					
Dec. 1		J1		700	700

UNEARNED SERVICE FEES ACCOUNT No. 24

Date	Description	Post. Ref.	Debit	Credit*	Balance
1996					
Dec. 2		J1		1,000	1,000

LONG-TERM NOTES PAYABLE ACCOUNT No. 25

Date	Description	Post. Ref.	Debit	Credit*	Balance
1996					
Dec. 1		J1		10,800	10,800

M. LANDEN, CAPITAL ACCOUNT No. 31

Date	Description	Post. Ref.	Debit	Credit*	Balance
1996					
Dec. 1		J1		10,000	10,000

M. LANDEN, DRAWING ACCOUNT No. 32

Date	Description	Post. Ref.	Debit*	Credit	Balance
1996					
Dec. 29		J1	800		800

SERVICE FEES EARNED ACCOUNT No. 41

Date	Description	Post. Ref.	Debit	Credit*	Balance
1996					
Dec. 10		J1		650	650
13		J1		1,580	2,230
21		J1		520	2,750
31		J1		2,700	5,450

WAGES EXPENSE ACCOUNT No. 52

Date	Description	Post. Ref.	Debit*	Credit	Balance
1996					
Dec. 13		J1	540		540
27		J1	540		1,080

TRUCK EXPENSE ACCOUNT No. 54

Date	Description	Post. Ref.	Debit*	Credit	Balance
1996					
Dec. 30		J1		160	160

UNADJUSTED TRIAL BALANCE

LANDEN TV SERVICE
UNADJUSTED TRIAL BALANCE
DECEMBER 31, 19 96

	Debit	Credit
Cash	$ 7,080	
Accounts Receivable	3,480	
Supplies and Parts	950	
Prepaid Rent	3,600	
Truck	10,800	
Accounts Payable		$ 700
Unearned Service Fees		1,000
Long-Term Notes Payable		10,800
M. Landen, Capital		10,000
M. Landen, Drawing	800	
Service Fees Earned		5,450
Wages Expense	1,080	
Truck Expense	160	
	$27,950	$27,950

postings from the general journal to these ledger accounts. Note the reference J1 in the posting reference columns of the ledger accounts. This refers to the page number used in the general journal illustrated in Exhibit 3-6.

ADJUST THE GENERAL LEDGER ACCOUNTS

OBJECTIVE *4*
DESCRIBE the adjusting process and **ILLUSTRATE** typical adjusting entries.

It is important that accounts appearing in financial statements be properly stated. For many accounts, the balances showing in the general ledger after all transactions have been posted are not the proper balances for financial statements. Thus, when it is time to prepare financial statements, the accountant will review account balances and make appropriate adjustments to these balances. The specific adjustments that are made flow from the accountant's understanding of accrual accounting and generally accepted accounting principles.

PREPARE UNADJUSTED TRIAL BALANCE

The adjustment process begins with a trial balance of all general ledger accounts that show a balance. Because this trial balance shows account balances before any adjustments have been made, it is called an **unadjusted trial balance.** We want to be sure the general ledger is in balance before we start to adjust the accounts. Also, showing all the general ledger account balances in one place makes it easier to review the accounts and determine which account balances need to be adjusted. The unadjusted trial balance of Landen TV Service at December 31 is shown in Exhibit 3-7.

TYPES OF ADJUSTMENTS

Four general types of adjustments are made at the end of an accounting period:

1. Allocating assets to expense to reflect expenses incurred during the period.
2. Allocating revenues received in advance to revenue to reflect revenues earned during the period.
3. Accruing expenses to reflect expenses incurred during the period that are not yet paid or recorded.
4. Accruing revenues to reflect revenues earned during the period that are not yet received or recorded.

The journal entries made to give effect to these various adjustments are known as **adjusting entries.** Each adjusting entry usually affects a balance sheet account (an asset or liability account) and an income statement account (an expense or revenue account). Adjustments in the first two categories—allocating various assets to expense and allocating revenues received in advance to revenue—are often referred to as **deferrals.** The distinguishing characteristic of a deferral is that the adjustment deals with an amount that has previously been recorded in a balance sheet account; the adjusting entry, in effect, decreases the balance sheet account and increases an income statement account. Adjustments in the last two categories—accruing expenses and accruing revenues—are often referred to as **accruals.** The unique characteristic of an accrual is that the adjustment deals with an amount that has not previously been recorded in any account; the adjusting entry, therefore, increases both a balance sheet account and an income statement account.

ALLOCATING ASSETS TO EXPENSE

Many business outlays may benefit a number of accounting periods. Some common examples are purchases of buildings, equipment, and supplies; prepayments of rent and advertising; and payments of insurance premiums covering a period of years. Ordinarily, these outlays are debited to an asset account at the time of expenditure. Then, at the end of each accounting period, the estimated portion of the outlay that has expired during the period or that has benefited the period is transferred to an expense account.

Under most circumstances, we can discover when adjustments of this type are needed by inspecting the unadjusted trial balance for costs that benefit several periods. By looking at the December 31 trial balance of Landen TV Service (Exhibit 3-7), for example, we would find that adjustments are required to apportion the costs of the supplies and parts, the prepaid rent, and the truck between December and subsequent periods.

SUPPLIES AND PARTS During December, Landen TV Service purchased supplies and parts and recorded the outlay in an asset account, Supplies and Parts, as follows:

PRINCIPLE ALERT

REVENUE RECOGNITION PRINCIPLE AND MATCHING CONCEPT

As introduced in Chapter 2, the revenue recognition principle and the matching concept are the key accounting principles that define the nature of net income under accrual accounting. In general, accrual accounting recognizes revenues when services are performed or goods are sold (*revenue recognition principle*) and recognizes expenses in the period that they help to generate the recorded revenues (*matching concept*). Under these principles, many of the transactions reflected in the general ledger accounts affect the net income of more than one period. Other events, not yet recorded in the accounts, affect the current period's net income. It is the adjusting process that identifies these situations and causes the proper revenue and expense amounts to be recorded in the current period.

Dec. 1	Supplies and Parts	950	
	Cash		250
	Accounts Payable		700
	Purchased supplies and parts for $950.		
	Terms: $250 down, remainder due in 60 days.		

During December, supplies and parts were used up as repair services were provided. The cost of supplies and parts used is an expense for December that reduces the amount of supplies and parts on hand. It is not necessary, however, to record the expense as each individual supply item or part is used. Instead, at the end of December, the firm counts the items still on hand. Suppose that the count shows $510 worth of supplies and parts on hand at the end of the month, indicating that $440 ($950 – $510) worth of supplies and parts have been used in service work during the month. Therefore, at the end of the period, an adjusting entry transfers this amount to an expense account, Supplies and Parts Expense, as follows:

Dec. 31	Supplies and Parts Expense	440	
	Supplies and Parts		440
	To record expense of supplies and parts used in December.		

When this adjusting entry is posted, it properly reflects the $440 December expense for supplies and parts and reduces the asset account Supplies and Parts to $510, the actual amount of the asset remaining at December 31.

PREPAID RENT   On December 1, Landen TV Service paid six months' rent in advance and debited the $3,600 payment to Prepaid Rent, an asset account. As each day passes and the rented space is occupied, rent expense is being incurred, and the prepaid rent is decreasing. It is not necessary to record rent expense on a daily basis because financial statements are not prepared daily. At the end of an accounting period, however, an adjustment must be made to recognize the proper amount of rent expense for the period just ended and to decrease the prepaid rent.

On December 31, one month's rent has been used up, so Landen TV Service transfers $600 ($3,600/6) from Prepaid Rent to Rent Expense, as follows:

Dec. 31	Rent Expense	600	
	Prepaid Rent		600
	To record rent expense for December.		

The posting of this adjusting entry creates the proper rent expense ($600) for December in the Rent Expense ledger account and reduces the Prepaid Rent balance to the amount that is prepaid as of December 31 ($3,000).

Examples of other prepaid expenses for which similar adjustments are made include prepaid insurance and prepaid advertising. When insurance premiums are paid, the amount is debited to Prepaid Insurance. At the end of an accounting period, the adjusting entry to record the portion of the insurance coverage that expired during the period debits Insurance Expense and credits Prepaid Insurance. Similarly, when advertising services are purchased in advance, the payment is debited to Prepaid Advertising. At the end of an accounting period, an adjustment is needed to recognize the cost of any of the prepaid advertising that was used during the period. The adjusting entry debits Advertising Expense and credits Prepaid Advertising.

DEPRECIATION   The process of allocating the costs of a firm's equipment, vehicles, and buildings to the periods benefiting from their use is called **depreciation accounting.** Because these long-lived assets help generate revenue in a company's operations, each accounting period in which the assets are used should reflect a portion of their cost as expense. This periodic expense is known as *depreciation expense.*

Periodic depreciation expense must be estimated by accountants. The procedure we use here estimates the annual amount of depreciation expense by dividing the cost of the asset by its estimated useful life in years. This method is called **straight-line depreciation.** (We will explore other methods in a later chapter.)

When recording depreciation expense, the asset amount is not reduced directly. Instead, the reduction is recorded in a contra account called *Accumulated Depreciation.* **Contra accounts** are so named because they are used to record reductions in or offsets against a related account. The Accumulated Depreciation account normally has a credit balance and appears in the balance sheet as a deduction from the related asset amount. Use of the contra account Accumulated Depreciation allows the original cost of the related asset to be shown in the balance sheet, followed by the accumulated amount of depreciation.

Let us assume that the truck purchased by Landen TV Service for $10,800 is expected to last six years. Straight-line depreciation recorded on the truck is therefore $1,800 ($10,800/6) per year, or $150 ($1,800/12) per month. At the end of December, we make the following adjusting entry:

Dec. 31	Depreciation Expense—Truck	150
	Accumulated Depreciation—Truck	150
	To record December depreciation on truck.	

When the preceding entry is posted, it properly reflects the cost of using this asset during December, and the correct expense ($150) appears in the December income statement.

On the balance sheet, the accumulated depreciation amount is subtracted from the related asset amount. The resulting balance (cost less accumulated depreciation), which is the asset's **book value,** represents the unexpired asset cost to be applied as an expense against future operating periods. For example, the December 31, 1996, balance sheet would show the truck with a book value of $10,650, presented as follows:

Truck	$10,800	
Less: Accumulated Depreciation	150	$10,650

ALLOCATING REVENUES RECEIVED IN ADVANCE TO REVENUE

Sometimes a business receives fees for services before service is rendered. Such transactions are ordinarily recorded by debiting Cash and crediting a liability account for the **unearned revenue.** The liability account in this situation may also be referred to as **deferred revenue** and shows the obligation for performing future service. As the service is performed, the revenue is earned by the firm. When it is time to make adjustments, an entry is made to record the revenue that was earned in the current accounting period and to reduce the liability account.

DEFERRED SERVICE REVENUE   During December, Landen TV Service entered one transaction that generated an advance receipt of revenues. On December 2, the firm signed a four-month contract to perform service for a local TV dealer at $250 per month, with the entire contract price of $1,000 received in advance. The entry made on December 2 was as follows:

Dec. 2	Cash	1,000
	Unearned Service Fees	1,000
	Received advance on four-month contract at $250 per month.	

On December 31, the following adjusting entry is made to transfer $250, the revenue earned in December, to Service Fees Earned and reduce the liability Unearned Service Fees by the same amount:

Dec. 31	Unearned Service Fees	250	
	Service Fees Earned		250
	To record portion of advance earned in December.		

After the entry is posted, the liability account shows a balance of $750, the amount of future services still owing, and the Service Fees Earned account reflects the $250 earned in December.

Other examples of revenues received in advance include rental payments received in advance by real estate management companies, insurance premiums received in advance by insurance companies, subscription revenues received in advance by magazine and newspaper publishers, and membership fees received in advance by health clubs. In each case, a liability account should be established when the advance payment is received. Later, an adjusting entry will be made to reflect the revenues earned from the services provided or products delivered during the period.

Accruing Expenses

A firm often incurs expenses before paying for them. Wages, salaries, interest, utilities, and taxes are examples of expenses that are incurred before payment is made. Usually the cash payments are made at regular intervals of time, such as weekly, monthly, quarterly, or annually. If the accounting period ends on a date that does not coincide with a scheduled cash payment date, an adjusting entry is needed to reflect the expense incurred since the last cash payment. Such an expense is often referred to as an **accrued expense.** Landen TV Service has two such adjustments to make at December 31—wages and interest.

Accrued Wages   A Landen TV Service employee is paid every two weeks at the rate of $270 for each six-day work week. The employee was paid $540 on December 13 and December 27. Let us assume that both these dates fell on Saturday and that Sunday is the employee's day off. At the close of business on Wednesday, December 31, the employee will have worked three days (Monday, Tuesday, and Wednesday) during December for which wages will not be paid until January. Because the employee's wages are $45 per day ($270/6 days), additional wages expense of $135 should be reflected in the income statement for December. The adjusting entry at the end of December would be as follows:

Dec. 31	Wages Expense	135	
	Wages Payable		135
	To record accrued wages for December 29, 30, and 31.		

This adjustment enables the firm to reflect as December expense the cost of all wages *incurred* during the month rather than just the wages *paid.* In addition, the balance sheet shows the liability for unpaid wages at the end of the period.

When the employee is paid on the next regular payday in January, the accountant must make sure that the three days' pay accrued at the end of December is not again charged to expense. If we assume that the employee is paid $540 on Saturday, January 10, the following entry can be made:

Jan. 10	Wages Payable	135	
	Wages Expense	405	
	Cash		540
	To record wages paid.		

This entry eliminates the liability recorded in Wages Payable at the end of December and debits January Wages Expense for only those wages earned by the employee in January. Another method of avoiding dual charges, that of reversing entries, is explained in Appendix C.

Accrued Interest   On December 1, 1996, Landen TV Service signed a two-year note payable for $10,800 to finance the purchase of its truck. The annual interest rate on the note is 10%, with interest payable each November 30. The first year's interest of $1,080 ($10,800 × 10%) is due on November 30, 1997. Because interest accumulates as time passes, an adjusting entry is needed at December 31, 1996, to reflect the interest expense for December. December's interest is $90 ($1,080/12), and the adjusting entry at December 31 is as follows:

Dec. 31	Interest Expense	90	
	Interest Payable		90
	To record interest expense for December.		

When this entry is posted to the general ledger, the accounts show the correct interest expense for December as well as a liability for the one month's interest that has accrued by December 31.

When the first year's interest of $1,080 is paid on November 30, 1997, the accountant must not forget that $90 of that amount relates to 1996. Assume, for example, that Landen TV Service is going to prepare only annual financial statements in 1997 and makes no 1997 adjustments for interest through the end of November. On November 30, 1997, the following entry to record the interest payment on that date can be made:

Nov. 30	Interest Payable	90	
	Interest Expense	990	
	Cash		1,080
	To record payment of annual interest.		

This entry eliminates the interest payable that was accrued on December 31, 1996, and debits Interest Expense for $990, the correct interest expense for the first 11 months of 1997. Another way to handle the accounting for interest in 1997, using reversing entries, is discussed in Appendix C.

ACCRUING REVENUES

Revenues from services should be recognized in the period the services are performed. Yet a company may provide services during a period that are neither paid for by clients or customers nor billed at the end of the period. The value of these services represents revenue that should be included in the firm's current period accrual income statement. To accomplish this, end-of-period adjusting entries are made to reflect any revenues for the period that have been earned and realized, but are not yet paid for or billed. Such accumulated revenue is often called **accrued revenue.**

ACCRUED COMMISSIONS   Landen TV Service entered into a contract with a cable TV company on December 2 that requires a December 31 adjusting entry to accrue revenue. Under the one-year contract, Landen TV Service agreed to distribute cable TV promotional literature to customers in exchange for a monthly commission of $50, payable at the end of every three months. (A commission represents a payment to an employee or agent for specific services rendered and usually is a percentage of the amounts involved in the related transaction, such as a commission to a real estate broker for selling a home; a commission may be a fixed amount, as is true for Landen TV Service's contract with the cable TV company.) By December 31, Landen TV Service has earned one month's commission, and the following adjusting entry is made:

Dec. 31	Commissions Receivable	50	
	Commissions Earned		50
	To record commissions earned for December.		

After this entry is posted, a $50 normal balance is created in a new asset account, Commissions Receivable, to reflect Landen TV Service's claim to receive revenues already earned. A new revenue account, Commissions Earned, also has a $50 normal balance created. A different revenue account is used because a different activity generates the revenue—distributing promotional literature as contrasted with repairing television sets.

When Landen TV Service receives the first $150 commission payment on February 28, 1997, the accountant must be alert to the fact that $50 was earned and recorded in 1996. Assuming that Landen TV Service accrues no more commissions before February 28, 1997, the following entry can be made to record the commissions received on that date.

Feb. 28	Cash	150	
	Commissions Receivable		50
	Commissions Earned		100
	To record receipt of quarterly commission.		

This entry eliminates the Commissions Receivable that was established on December 31, 1996, and records $100 of commissions earned, the proper amount of revenue from commissions for the first two months of 1997. Another way to account for the commissions earned in 1997, using reversing entries, is discussed in Appendix C.

Another example of an adjusting entry to accrue revenue involves a firm that has loaned money on which interest has been earned that is not collected by the end of the period. The amount of the interest should be reflected in the net income of the period in which it is earned. In this situation, an adjusting entry is made debiting Interest Receivable and crediting Interest Income for the amount of interest earned.

Exhibit 3-8 shows Landen TV Service's adjusting journal entries recorded on page 2 of its general journal. As shown by the account numbers in the posting reference column, these adjustments have also been posted to the general ledger.

EXHIBIT 3–8 **Adjusting Entries for Landen TV Service**

GENERAL JOURNAL PAGE 2

Date		Description	Post. Ref.	Debit	Credit
1996 Dec.	31	Supplies and Parts Expense	53	440	
		Supplies and Parts	14		440
		To record expense of supplies and parts used in December.			
	31	Rent Expense	51	600	
		Prepaid Rent	15		600
		To record rent expense for December.			
	31	Depreciation Expense—Truck	55	150	
		Accumulated Depreciation—Truck	19		150
		To record December depreciation on truck.			
	31	Unearned Service Fees	24	250	
		Service Fees Earned	41		250
		To record portion of advance earned in December.			
	31	Wages Expense	52	135	
		Wages Payable	23		135
		To record accrued wages for December 29, 30, and 31.			
	31	Interest Expense	56	90	
		Interest Payable	22		90
		To record interest expense for December.			
	31	Commissions Receivable	13	50	
		Commissions Earned	42		50
		To record commissions earned for December.			

REPORT ADJUSTED DATA IN FINANCIAL STATEMENTS

PREPARE ADJUSTED TRIAL BALANCE

After the adjustments are posted, the accountant prepares an adjusted trial balance. The **adjusted trial balance** lists all the general ledger account balances after adjustments. Much of the content for a firm's financial statements is taken from the adjusted trial balance. Exhibit 3-9 shows the general ledger accounts after adjustments and the adjusted trial balance at December 31 for Landen TV Service.

EXHIBIT 3–9	General Ledger and Adjusted Trial Balance for Landen TV Service

GENERAL LEDGER AFTER ADJUSTMENTS

CASH   ACCOUNT NO. 11

Date		Description	Post. Ref.	Debit*	Credit	Balance
1996 Dec.	1		J1	10,000		10,000
	1		J1		250	9,750
	1		J1		3,600	6,150
	2		J1	1,000		7,150
	10		J1	650		7,800
	13		J1		540	7,260
	19		J1	800		8,060
	21		J1	520		8,580
	27		J1		540	8,040
	29		J1		800	7,240
	30		J1		160	7,080

ACCOUNTS RECEIVABLE   ACCOUNT NO. 12

Date		Description	Post. Ref.	Debit*	Credit	Balance
1996 Dec.	13		J1	1,580		1,580
	19		J1		800	780
	31		J1	2,700		3,480

COMMISSIONS RECEIVABLE   ACCOUNT NO. 13

Date		Description	Post. Ref.	Debit*	Credit	Balance
1996 Dec.	31	(adjusting)	J2	50		50

SUPPLIES AND PARTS   ACCOUNT NO. 14

Date		Description	Post. Ref.	Debit*	Credit	Balance
1996 Dec.	1		J1	950		950
	31	(adjusting)	J2		440	510

PREPAID RENT   ACCOUNT NO. 15

Date		Description	Post. Ref.	Debit*	Credit	Balance
1996 Dec.	1		J1	3,600		3,600
	31	(adjusting)	J2		600	3,000

TRUCK   ACCOUNT NO. 18

Date		Description	Post. Ref.	Debit*	Credit	Balance
1996 Dec.	1		J1	10,800		10,800

ACCUMULATED DEPRECIATION— TRUCK   ACCOUNT NO. 19

Date		Description	Post. Ref.	Debit	Credit*	Balance
1996 Dec.	31	(adjusting)	J2		150	150

ACCOUNTS PAYABLE   ACCOUNT NO. 21

Date		Description	Post. Ref.	Debit	Credit*	Balance
1996 Dec.	1		J1		700	700

INTEREST PAYABLE   ACCOUNT NO. 22

Date		Description	Post. Ref.	Debit	Credit*	Balance
1996 Dec.	31	(adjusting)	J2		90	90

WAGES PAYABLE   ACCOUNT NO. 23

Date		Description	Post. Ref.	Debit	Credit*	Balance
1996 Dec.	31	(adjusting)	J2		135	135

UNEARNED SERVICE FEES   ACCOUNT NO. 24

Date		Description	Post. Ref.	Debit	Credit*	Balance
1996 Dec.	2		J1		1,000	1,000
	31	(adjusting)	J2	250		750

LONG-TERM NOTES PAYABLE   ACCOUNT NO. 25

Date		Description	Post. Ref.	Debit	Credit*	Balance
1996 Dec.	1		J1		10,800	10,800

M. LANDEN, CAPITAL   ACCOUNT NO. 31

Date		Description	Post. Ref.	Debit	Credit*	Balance
1996 Dec.	1		J1		10,000	10,000

M. LANDEN, DRAWING   ACCOUNT NO. 32

Date		Description	Post. Ref.	Debit*	Credit	Balance
1996 Dec.	29		J1	800		800

SERVICE FEES EARNED   ACCOUNT NO. 41

Date		Description	Post. Ref.	Debit	Credit*	Balance
1996 Dec.	10		J1		650	650
	13		J1		1,580	2,230
	21		J1		520	2,750
	31		J1		2,700	5,450
	31	(adjusting)	J2		250	5,700

COMMISSIONS EARNED   ACCOUNT NO. 42

Date		Description	Post. Ref.	Debit	Credit*	Balance
1996 Dec.	31	(adjusting)	J2		50	50

RENT EXPENSE   ACCOUNT NO. 51

Date		Description	Post. Ref.	Debit*	Credit	Balance
1996 Dec.	31	(adjusting)	J2	600		600

WAGES EXPENSE   ACCOUNT NO. 52

Date		Description	Post. Ref.	Debit*	Credit	Balance
1996 Dec.	13		J1	540		540
	27		J1	540		1,080
	31	(adjusting)	J2	135		1,215

SUPPLIES AND PARTS EXPENSE   ACCOUNT NO. 53

Date		Description	Post. Ref.	Debit*	Credit	Balance
1996 Dec.	31	(adjusting)	J2	440		440

TRUCK EXPENSE   ACCOUNT NO. 54

Date		Description	Post. Ref.	Debit*	Credit	Balance
1996 Dec.	30		J1	160		160

DEPRECIATION EXPENSE—TRUCK   ACCOUNT NO. 55

Date		Description	Post. Ref.	Debit*	Credit	Balance
1996 Dec.	31	(adjusting)	J2	150		150

INTEREST EXPENSE   ACCOUNT NO. 56

Date		Description	Post. Ref.	Debit*	Credit	Balance
1996 Dec.	31	(adjusting)	J2	90		90

ADJUSTED TRIAL BALANCE

LANDEN TV SERVICE
ADJUSTED TRIAL BALANCE
DECEMBER 31, 1996

	Debit	Credit
Cash	$ 7,080	
Accounts Receivable	3,480	
Commissions Receivable	50	
Supplies and Parts	510	
Prepaid Rent	3,000	
Truck	10,800	
Accumulated Depreciation—Truck		$ 150
Accounts Payable		700
Interest Payable		90
Wages Payable		135
Unearned Service Fees		750
Long-Term Notes Payable		10,800
M. Landen, Capital		10,000
M. Landen, Drawing	800	
Service Fees Earned		5,700
Commissions Earned		50
Rent Expense	600	
Wages Expense	1,215	
Supplies and Parts Expense	440	
Truck Expense	160	
Depreciation Expense—Truck	150	
Interest Expense	90	
	$28,375	$28,375

OBJECTIVE 5

ILLUSTRATE the financial statements prepared from adjusted data.

PREPARE FINANCIAL STATEMENTS

The financial statements prepared from the adjusted trial balance and other data are the income statement, statement of owners' equity, balance sheet, and statement of cash flows. We will illustrate these financial statements for Landen TV Service.

INCOME STATEMENT   The income statement presents a firm's revenues and expenses. Landen TV Service's adjusted trial balance contains two revenue accounts and six expense accounts. These revenues and expenses are reported in Landen TV Service's income statement for December shown in Exhibit 3-10. As shown in this income statement, the firm's net income for December is $3,095.

EXHIBIT 3–10

LANDEN TV SERVICE
INCOME STATEMENT
FOR THE MONTH OF DECEMBER 1996

Revenues		
Service Fees Earned	$5,700	
Commissions Earned	50	
Total Revenues		$5,750
Expenses		
Wages Expense	$1,215	
Truck Expense	160	
Supplies and Parts Expense	440	
Rent Expense	600	
Depreciation Expense—Truck	150	
Interest Expense	90	
Total Expenses		2,655
Net Income		$3,095

STATEMENT OF OWNER'S EQUITY   The statement of owner's equity reports the events causing the owner's capital to change during the accounting period. Exhibit 3-11 presents Landen TV Service's statement of owner's equity for December. A review of the owner's capital account in the general ledger provides some of the information for this statement; namely, the capital balance at the beginning of the period and capital contributions during the period. (Because December is the first month of Landen TV Service's existence, the beginning capital balance is zero.) The net income (or net loss) amount comes from the income statement. Capital withdrawn during the period is summarized in the drawing account balance shown in the adjusted trial balance.

EXHIBIT 3–11

LANDEN TV SERVICE
STATEMENT OF OWNER'S EQUITY
FOR THE MONTH OF DECEMBER 1996

M. Landen, Capital, December 1, 1996		$ –0–
Add: Capital Contributed in December	$10,000	
Net Income for December	3,095	13,095
		$13,095
Less: Capital Withdrawn in December		800
M. Landen, Capital, December 31, 1996		$12,295

BALANCE SHEET   The balance sheet reports an entity's assets, liabilities, and owners' equity. The assets and liabilities for Landen TV Service's balance sheet at December 31, 1996, shown in Exhibit 3-12, come from the adjusted trial balance (Exhibit 3-9). The amount reported as M. Landen, Capital ($12,295) in the balance sheet is taken from the statement of owner's equity for December (Exhibit 3-11).

EXHIBIT 3–12

LANDEN TV SERVICE
BALANCE SHEET
DECEMBER 31, 1996

Assets				**Liabilities**	
Cash		$ 7,080		Accounts Payable	$ 700
Accounts Receivable		3,480		Interest Payable	90
Commissions Receivable		50		Wages Payable	135
Supplies and Parts		510		Unearned Service Fees	750
Prepaid Rent		3,000		Long-Term Notes Payable	10,800
Truck	$10,800			Total Liabilities	$12,475
Less: Accumulated Depreciation	150	10,650			
				Owner's Equity	
				M. Landen, Capital	12,295
Total Assets		$24,770		Total Liabilities and Owner's Equity	$24,770

STATEMENT OF CASH FLOWS The statement of cash flows reports information about cash inflows and outflows for a period of time. The cash flows are classified into operating, investing, and financing categories. The procedures for preparing a statement of cash flows are discussed in a later chapter. For completeness, we present Landen TV Service's statement of cash flows for December in Exhibit 3-13 (there were no investing cash flows in December).

EXHIBIT 3–13

LANDEN TV SERVICE
STATEMENT OF CASH FLOWS
FOR THE MONTH OF DECEMBER 1996

Cash Flows from Operating Activities		
Cash Received from Customers		$2,970
Cash Paid to Employees and Suppliers		(5,090)
Net Cash Used by Operating Activities		($2,120)
Cash Flows from Financing Activities		
Investment by M. Landen	$10,000	
Withdrawal by M. Landen	(800)	
Net Cash Provided by Financing Activities		9,200
Net Increase in Cash		$7,080
Cash at December 1, 1996		–0–
Cash at December 31, 1996		$7,080

ACCOUNTING PERIOD CONCEPT

The income statement, statement of owners' equity, and statement of cash flows are financial statements covering specific periods of time. These statements illustrate the *accounting period concept;* that is, the concept that useful financial statements can be prepared for arbitrary time periods within an entity's total life span. The entity does not complete all of its transactions at the end of each accounting period. Accounting principles, therefore, must provide a procedure to cut through the entity's continuing transactions at the end of a period so that useful periodic statements may be prepared. The procedure provided by accrual accounting is the adjustment process. A major purpose of adjusting entries is to ensure that proper amounts of revenue and expense are assigned to the accounting period ending on the date of the adjustments.

CLOSE THE TEMPORARY ACCOUNTS

OBJECTIVE 6

DESCRIBE the process of closing the temporary accounts.

Temporary accounts consist of revenue, expense, and owner withdrawal accounts. These accounts accumulate data that relate to a specific accounting period; as such, their balances are reported in period financial statements—the income statement and the statement of owners' equity. At the end of each accounting year, the balances of these temporary accounts are transferred to a permanent owners' equity account—the owner's capital account for a sole proprietorship and the Retained Earnings account for a corporation. This part of the accounting cycle is referred to as the **closing procedures.**

A temporary account is *closed* when an entry is made that changes its balance to zero— that is, the entry is equal in amount to the account's balance but is opposite to the balance as a debit or credit. An account that is closed is said to be closed *to* the account that receives the offsetting debit or credit. Thus, a closing entry simply transfers the balance of one account to another account. Because closing entries bring temporary account balances to zero, the temporary accounts are then ready to start accumulating data for the next accounting period.

JOURNALIZE AND POST CLOSING ENTRIES

A summary account is traditionally used to close the temporary revenue and expense accounts. For our illustration, we will use an account titled Income Summary, although a variety of titles is found in practice (Revenue and Expense Summary, Income and Expense Summary, or Profit and Loss Summary, for example). The entries for opening and closing Income Summary are quite simple and occur only during the closing procedures. The entries that close the temporary accounts are as follows:

1 **Close the revenue accounts.** Debit each revenue account for an amount equal to its balance, and credit Income Summary for the total amount of revenues.

2 **Close the expense accounts.** Credit each expense account for an amount equal to its balance, and debit Income Summary for the total amount of expenses.

After these temporary accounts have been closed, the balance of the Income Summary account is equal to the period's net income (if a credit balance) or net loss (if a debit balance). The remaining closing steps depend on the form of business organization and are as follows:

3 **Close the Income Summary account.**
    a. *For sole proprietorships:* In the case of a net income, debit Income Summary and credit the owner's capital account for the net income amount. In the case of a net loss, debit the owner's capital account and credit Income Summary for the net loss amount.
    b. *For corporations:* In the case of a net income, debit Income Summary and credit Retained Earnings for the net income amount. In the case of a net loss, debit Retained Earnings and credit Income Summary for the net loss amount.

4 **Close the owner drawing account (sole proprietorships) or close the dividends account (corporations).**

a. *For sole proprietorships:* Debit the owner's capital account and credit the owner's drawing account for an amount equal to the debit balance in the owner's drawing account.

b. *For corporations:* Debit Retained Earnings and credit Cash Dividends for the debit balance in the Cash Dividends account.

SOLE PROPRIETORSHIP CLOSING

In Exhibit 3-14, we illustrate the entries for closing the revenue and expense accounts to the Income Summary account of Landen TV Service as they would be recorded in the general journal. The effect of these two entries is shown using T accounts.

At this point, the balance of the Income Summary is a credit equal to the net income of $3,095. The closing procedure is completed by closing the Income Summary and

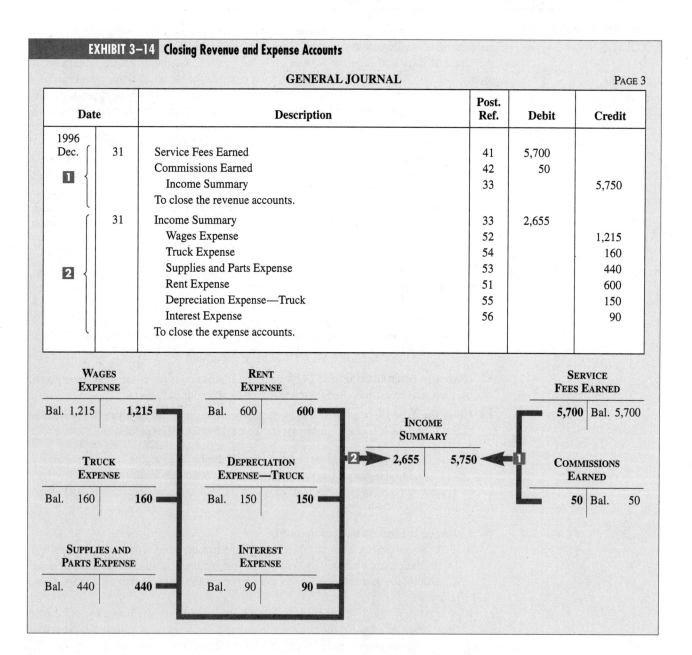

EXHIBIT 3–14 **Closing Revenue and Expense Accounts**

GENERAL JOURNAL PAGE 3

Date		Description	Post. Ref.	Debit	Credit
1996 Dec.	31	Service Fees Earned	41	5,700	
1		Commissions Earned	42	50	
		Income Summary	33		5,750
		To close the revenue accounts.			
	31	Income Summary	33	2,655	
		Wages Expense	52		1,215
		Truck Expense	54		160
2		Supplies and Parts Expense	53		440
		Rent Expense	51		600
		Depreciation Expense—Truck	55		150
		Interest Expense	56		90
		To close the expense accounts.			

WAGES EXPENSE
Bal. 1,215 | **1,215**

TRUCK EXPENSE
Bal. 160 | **160**

SUPPLIES AND PARTS EXPENSE
Bal. 440 | **440**

RENT EXPENSE
Bal. 600 | **600**

DEPRECIATION EXPENSE—TRUCK
Bal. 150 | **150**

INTEREST EXPENSE
Bal. 90 | **90**

INCOME SUMMARY
2 → **2,655** | **5,750** ← **1**

SERVICE FEES EARNED
5,700 | Bal. 5,700

COMMISSIONS EARNED
50 | Bal. 50

M. Landen, Drawing accounts to the M. Landen, Capital account. These two entries are recorded in the general journal as shown in Exhibit 3-15. The effect of these entries on the general ledger is also diagrammed.

EXHIBIT 3–15   **Closing the Income Summary and Drawing Accounts**

GENERAL JOURNAL   PAGE 3

Date		Description	Post. Ref.	Debit	Credit
1996 Dec. **3**	31	Income Summary	33	3,095	
		M. Landen, Capital	31		3,095
		To close the Income Summary account.			
4	31	M. Landen, Capital	31	800	
		M. Landen, Drawing	32		800
		To close the drawing account.			

M. LANDEN, DRAWING		M. LANDEN, CAPITAL		INCOME SUMMARY	
Bal. 800	**800** ➡**4**➡ **800**	Bal. 10,000	2,655	5,750
		3,095 ⬅**3**⬅3,095		

CORPORATION CLOSING

To illustrate the unique aspects of a corporation closing, assume that a corporation has exactly the same revenues and expenses as Landen TV Service. (Because a corporation is subject to an income tax, it has an additional expense account called *Income Tax Expense;* we will disregard income taxes for this illustration.) During the period, cash dividends of $800 were declared and paid (creating a Cash Dividends account with an $800 debit balance). After closing the revenue and expense accounts (exactly as shown in Exhibit 3-14), the final two closing entries are as follows:

Income Summary	3,095	
Retained Earnings		3,095
To close the Income Summary account.		
Retained Earnings	800	
Cash Dividends		800
To close the Cash Dividends account.		

PREPARE POST-CLOSING TRIAL BALANCE

After the closing entries for Landen TV Service have been recorded and posted to the firm's general ledger, all temporary accounts have zero balances. At this point a **post-closing trial balance** is taken. The balancing of this trial balance is evidence that an equality of debits and credits has been maintained in the general ledger throughout the adjusting and closing process and that the general ledger is in balance to start the next accounting period. Because the temporary accounts have been closed, only balance sheet accounts appear in a post-closing trial balance. Exhibit 3-16 presents the general ledger accounts after closing and the post-closing trial balance for Landen TV Service. Closing entries are identified by the parenthetical notation (closing).

EXHIBIT 3–16 General Ledger and Post-Closing Trial Balance for Landen TV Service

GENERAL LEDGER AFTER CLOSING

CASH   ACCOUNT NO. 11

Date		Description	Post. Ref.	Debit*	Credit	Balance
1996						
Dec.	1		J1	10,000		10,000
	1		J1		250	9,750
	1		J1		3,600	6,150
	2		J1	1,000		7,150
	10		J1	650		7,800
	13		J1	.	540	7,260
	19		J1	800		8,060
	21		J1	520		8,580
	27		J1		540	8,040
	29		J1		800	7,240
	30		J1		160	7,080

ACCOUNTS RECEIVABLE   ACCOUNT NO. 12

Date		Description	Post. Ref.	Debit*	Credit	Balance
1996						
Dec.	13		J1	1,580		1,580
	19		J1		800	780
	31		J1	2,700		3,480

COMMISSIONS RECEIVABLE   ACCOUNT NO. 13

Date		Description	Post. Ref.	Debit*	Credit	Balance
1996						
Dec.	31	(adjusting)	J2	50		50

SUPPLIES AND PARTS   ACCOUNT NO. 14

Date		Description	Post. Ref.	Debit*	Credit	Balance
1996						
Dec.	1		J1	950		950
	31	(adjusting)	J2		440	510

PREPAID RENT   ACCOUNT NO. 15

Date		Description	Post. Ref.	Debit*	Credit	Balance
1996						
Dec.	1		J1	3,600		3,600
	31	(adjusting)	J2		600	3,000

TRUCK   ACCOUNT NO. 18

Date		Description	Post. Ref.	Debit*	Credit	Balance
1996						
Dec.	1		J1	10,800		10,800

ACCUMULATED DEPRECIATION—TRUCK   ACCOUNT NO. 19

Date		Description	Post. Ref.	Debit	Credit*	Balance
1996						
Dec.	31	(adjusting)	J2		150	150

ACCOUNTS PAYABLE   ACCOUNT NO. 21

Date		Description	Post. Ref.	Debit	Credit*	Balance
1996						
Dec.	1		J1		700	700

INTEREST PAYABLE   ACCOUNT NO. 22

Date		Description	Post. Ref.	Debit	Credit*	Balance
1996						
Dec.	31	(adjusting)	J2		90	90

WAGES PAYABLE   ACCOUNT NO. 23

Date		Description	Post. Ref.	Debit	Credit*	Balance
1996						
Dec.	31	(adjusting)	J2		135	135

UNEARNED SERVICE FEES   ACCOUNT NO. 24

Date		Description	Post. Ref.	Debit	Credit*	Balance
1996						
Dec.	2		J1		1,000	1,000
	31	(adjusting)	J2	250		750

LONG-TERM NOTES PAYABLE   ACCOUNT NO. 25

Date		Description	Post. Ref.	Debit	Credit*	Balance
1996						
Dec.	1		J1		10,800	10,800

M. LANDEN, CAPITAL   ACCOUNT NO. 31

Date		Description	Post. Ref.	Debit	Credit*	Balance
1996						
Dec.	1		J1		10,000	10,000
	31	(closing)	J3		3,095	13,095
	31	(closing)	J3	800		12,295

M. LANDEN, DRAWING   ACCOUNT NO. 32

Date		Description	Post. Ref.	Debit*	Credit	Balance
1996						
Dec.	29		J1	800		800
	31	(closing)	J3		800	–0–

INCOME SUMMARY   ACCOUNT NO. 33

Date		Description	Post. Ref.	Debit	Credit*	Balance
1996						
Dec.	31	(closing)	J3		5,750	5,750
	31	(closing)	J3	2,655		3,095
	31	(closing)	J3	3,095		–0–

SERVICE FEES EARNED   ACCOUNT NO. 41

Date		Description	Post. Ref.	Debit	Credit*	Balance
1996						
Dec.	10		J1		650	650
	13		J1		1,580	2,230
	21		J1		520	2,750
	31		J1		2,700	5,450
	31	(adjusting)	J2		250	5,700
	31	(closing)	J3	5,700		–0–

COMMISSIONS EARNED   ACCOUNT NO. 42

Date		Description	Post. Ref.	Debit	Credit*	Balance
1996						
Dec.	31	(adjusting)	J2		50	50
	31	(closing)	J3	50		–0–

RENT EXPENSE   ACCOUNT NO. 51

Date		Description	Post. Ref.	Debit*	Credit	Balance
1996						
Dec.	31	(adjusting)	J2	600		600
	31	(closing)	J3		600	–0–

WAGES EXPENSE   ACCOUNT NO. 52

Date		Description	Post. Ref.	Debit*	Credit	Balance
1996						
Dec.	13		J1	540		540
	27		J1	540		1,080
	31	(adjusting)	J2	135		1,215
	31	(closing)	J3		1,215	–0–

SUPPLIES AND PARTS EXPENSE   ACCOUNT NO. 53

Date		Description	Post. Ref.	Debit*	Credit	Balance
1996						
Dec.	31	(adjusting)	J2	440		440
	31	(closing)	J3		440	–0–

TRUCK EXPENSE   ACCOUNT NO. 54

Date		Description	Post. Ref.	Debit*	Credit	Balance
1996						
Dec.	30		J1	160		160
	31	(closing)	J3		160	–0–

DEPRECIATION EXPENSE—TRUCK   ACCOUNT NO. 55

Date		Description	Post. Ref.	Debit*	Credit	Balance
1996						
Dec.	31	(adjusting)	J2	150		150
	31	(closing)	J3		150	–0–

INTEREST EXPENSE   ACCOUNT NO. 56

Date		Description	Post. Ref.	Debit*	Credit	Balance
1996						
Dec.	31	(adjusting)	J2	90		90
	31	(closing)	J3		90	–0–

POST-CLOSING TRIAL BALANCE

LANDEN TV SERVICE
POST-CLOSING TRIAL BALANCE
DECEMBER 31, 1996

	Debit	Credit
Cash	$ 7,080	
Accounts Receivable	3,480	
Commissions Receivable	50	
Supplies and Parts	510	
Prepaid Rent	3,000	
Truck	10,800	
Accumulated Depreciation—Truck		$ 150
Accounts Payable		700
Interest Payable		90
Wages Payable		135
Unearned Service Fees		750
Long-Term Notes Payable		10,800
M. Landen, Capital		12,295
	$24,920	$24,920

SUMMARY OF THE ACCOUNTING CYCLE

OBJECTIVE 7

SUMMARIZE a manual accounting cycle and **DESCRIBE** a computerized accounting cycle.

MANUAL SYSTEM

The sequence of accounting procedures known as the *accounting cycle* occurs each fiscal year and represents a systematic process for accumulating and reporting the financial data of a business entity. Exhibit 3-17 summarizes the five major steps in the accounting cycle as well as the specific steps in the manual accounting cycle discussed in the chapter.

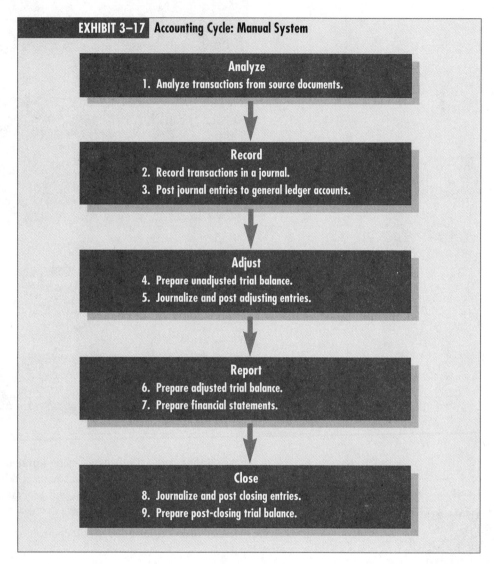

EXHIBIT 3–17   Accounting Cycle: Manual System

Analyze
1. Analyze transactions from source documents.

Record
2. Record transactions in a journal.
3. Post journal entries to general ledger accounts.

Adjust
4. Prepare unadjusted trial balance.
5. Journalize and post adjusting entries.

Report
6. Prepare adjusted trial balance.
7. Prepare financial statements.

Close
8. Journalize and post closing entries.
9. Prepare post-closing trial balance.

COMPUTERIZED SYSTEMS

Many businesses today use computers to process accounting data. Computers permit data to be processed quickly and accurately. Although the major steps of the accounting cycle are embedded within a computerized system, the specific procedures vary from those of a manual system.

Exhibit 3-18 outlines the procedures used to process accounting data in a computerized system. Similar to that of the manual system, the first step involves analyzing data to be processed through the system. Internally generated data, such as payroll information, are identified, but the related source documents are usually not manually prepared. Instead, they are prepared as part of the computer processing. Both the internally generated data and the data from external source documents are entered in the computer.

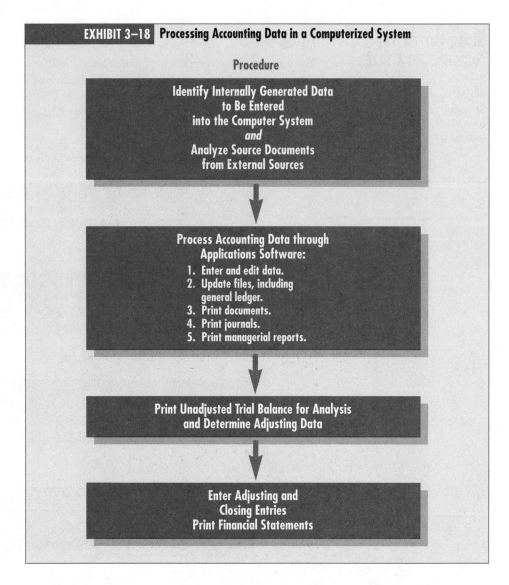

EXHIBIT 3–18 Processing Accounting Data in a Computerized System

Procedure

Identify Internally Generated Data
to Be Entered
into the Computer System
and
Analyze Source Documents
from External Sources

Process Accounting Data through
Applications Software:
1. Enter and edit data.
2. Update files, including
   general ledger.
3. Print documents.
4. Print journals.
5. Print managerial reports.

Print Unadjusted Trial Balance for Analysis
and Determine Adjusting Data

Enter Adjusting and
Closing Entries
Print Financial Statements

Next, the accounting data are processed using **applications programs**. Usually there are separate programs for sales invoicing, accounts receivable, cash receipts, accounts payable, check preparation, payroll, inventory, and general ledger.

Each applications program incorporates five primary functions:

1. Data are entered and processed through edit controls to ensure that the data are valid and reasonable.

2. Files maintained by the computer system on either magnetic disk or magnetic tape, including the general ledger, are updated.

3. Documents such as sales invoices, payment checks to vendors, and employee payroll checks are printed.

4. Chronological records, such as the general journal, are printed.

5. Various managerial reports are printed.

After the data have been processed, an unadjusted trial balance is printed so that a staff member can analyze the trial balance and prepare the necessary adjusting entries. The adjusting and closing entries are then entered in the computer system. The computer updates its files and makes them ready for future processing; this is often done only at the end of the accounting year. The computer also prints the financial statements using formats stored in the applications programs.

KEY POINTS FOR CHAPTER LEARNING OBJECTIVES

1 **IDENTIFY** the five major steps in the accounting cycle (pp. 70–71).
- The five major steps in the accounting cycle are
  a. Analyze.   **b.** Record.   **c.** Adjust.   **d.** Report.   **e.** Close.

2 **EXPLAIN** the role of source documents in transaction analysis (pp. 71–72).
- Source documents usually provide the basis for analyzing business transactions.
- Source documents are printed forms or computer records that are generated when a transaction occurs.

3 **DESCRIBE** the process of journalizing and posting transactions (pp. 72–78).
- Accounting entries are initially recorded in a journal; the entries are in chronological order, and the journal shows the total effect of each transaction or adjustment.
- Posting is the transfer of information from a journal to the general ledger accounts.
- Posting references are used to cross-reference the information in journals and the general ledger accounts.

4 **DESCRIBE** the adjusting process and **ILLUSTRATE** typical adjusting entries (pp. 78–83).
- Adjusting entries made to achieve the appropriate recognition of revenues and matching of expenses and revenues are summarized as follows:

Adjustment Category	Nature of Adjusting Entry	Examples from Chapter		
		Entry		
Allocating assets to expense	Increase expense Decrease asset	Supplies and Parts Expense Supplies and Parts	440	440
		Rent Expense Prepaid Rent	600	600
	Increase expense Increase contra asset (which decreases asset's book value)	Depreciation Expense—Truck Accumulated Depreciation—Truck	150	150
Allocating revenues received in advance to revenue	Decrease liability Increase revenue	Unearned Service Fees Service Fees Earned	250	250
Accruing expenses	Increase expense Increase liability	Wages Expense Wages Payable	135	135
		Interest Expense Interest Payable	90	90
Accruing revenues	Increase asset Increase revenue	Commissions Receivable Commissions Earned	50	50

5 **ILLUSTRATE** the financial statements prepared from adjusted data (pp. 83–87).
- An income statement, statement of owners' equity, balance sheet, and statement of cash flows may be prepared from an adjusted trial balance and other information.
- The owner's capital account may need to be reviewed to obtain information on the beginning capital balance and owner capital contributions during the period for the statement of owner's equity.

6 **DESCRIBE** the process of closing the temporary accounts (pp. 87–90).
- *Closing the books* means closing the revenue, expense, and other temporary accounts. Revenue and expense account balances are transferred to the Income Summary account. The balances of the Income Summary account and the owner's drawing accounts are closed to the owner's capital account. For corporations, the Income Summary account and Cash Dividends account are closed to Retained Earnings.

7 **SUMMARIZE** a manual accounting cycle and **DESCRIBE** a computerized accounting cycle (pp. 91–92).
- Manual and computerized accounting cycles contain quite different specific procedures. However, both systems accomplish the five major steps of an accounting cycle.

SELF-TEST QUESTIONS FOR REVIEW

(Answers follow the Solution to Demonstration Problem.)

1. A journal entry that contains more than just two accounts is called
   a. A posted journal entry.
   b. An adjusting journal entry.
   c. An erroneous journal entry.
   d. A compound journal entry.

2. *Posting* refers to the process of transferring information from
   a. A journal to general ledger accounts.
   b. General ledger accounts to a journal.
   c. Source documents to a journal.
   d. A journal to source documents.

3. Which of the following is an example of an adjusting entry?
   a. Recording the purchase of supplies on account
   b. Recording depreciation expense on a truck
   c. Recording the billing of customers for services rendered
   d. Recording the payment of wages to employees

4. An adjusting entry to record utilities used during a month for which no bill has yet been received is an example of
   a. Allocating assets to expense to reflect expenses incurred during the accounting period.
   b. Allocating revenues received in advance to revenue to reflect revenues earned during the accounting period.
   c. Accruing expenses to reflect expenses incurred during the accounting period that are not yet paid or recorded.
   d. Accruing revenues to reflect revenues earned during the accounting period that are not yet received or recorded.

5. Which of the following closing procedures is unique to a corporation?
   a. Close each revenue account to the Income Summary account.
   b. Close each expense account to the Income Summary account.
   c. Close the Income Summary account to the Retained Earnings account.
   d. Close the owner's drawing account to the owner's capital account.

DEMONSTRATION PROBLEM FOR REVIEW

Balke Laboratory began operations on July 1, 1994, and provides various diagnostic services for physicians and clinics. Its fiscal year ends on June 30 and the accounts are adjusted annually on this date. Its unadjusted trial balance at June 30, 1997, is as follows:

BALKE LABORATORY
UNADJUSTED TRIAL BALANCE
JUNE 30, 1997

	Debit	Credit
Cash	$ 1,000	
Accounts Receivable	9,200	
Prepaid Insurance	6,000	
Supplies	31,300	
Laboratory Equipment	270,000	
Accumulated Depreciation—Laboratory Equipment		$ 60,000
Accounts Payable		3,100
Diagnostic Fees Received in Advance		4,000
P. Balke, Capital		110,000
Diagnostic Fees Revenue		220,400
Wages Expense	58,000	
Rent Expense	22,000	
	$397,500	$397,500

The following information is also available:

1. The Prepaid Insurance account balance represents a premium paid on January 1, 1997, for two years of fire and casualty insurance coverage. Before 1997, Balke Laboratory had no insurance protection.

2. The supplies on hand were counted at June 30, 1997. The total count was $6,300.

3. All laboratory equipment was purchased on July 1, 1994. It is expected to last nine years.

4. Balke Laboratory received a $4,000 cash payment on April 1, 1997, from Boll Clinic for diagnostic services to be provided uniformly over the four months beginning April 1, 1997. Balke credited the payment to Diagnostic Fees Received in Advance. The services for April, May, and June have been provided to Boll Clinic.

5. Unpaid wages at June 30 were $600.

6. Balke Laboratory rents facilities for $2,000 per month. Because of cash flow problems, Balke was unable to pay the rent for June 1997. The landlord gave Balke permission to delay the payment until July.

REQUIRED

Make the adjusting entries, in general journal form, needed at June 30, 1997.

SOLUTION TO DEMONSTRATION PROBLEM

June 30	Insurance Expense		1,500	
	Prepaid Insurance			1,500
	To record 6 months' insurance expense ($6,000/4 = $1,500).			
30	Supplies Expense		25,000	
	Supplies			25,000
	To record supplies expense for the year ($31,300 − $6,300 = $25,000).			
30	Depreciation Expense—Laboratory Equipment		30,000	
	Accumulated Depreciation—Laboratory Equipment			30,000
	To record depreciation for the year ($270,000/9 years = $30,000).			
30	Diagnostic Fees Received in Advance		3,000	
	Diagnostic Fees Revenue			3,000
	To record portion of advance payment that has been earned ($4,000 × $\frac{3}{4}$ = $3,000).			
30	Wages Expense		600	
	Wages Payable			600
	To record unpaid wages at June 30.			
30	Rent Expense		2,000	
	Rent Payable			2,000
	To record rent expense for June.			

ANSWERS TO SELF-TEST QUESTIONS   **1.** d, p. 75   **2.** a, p. 74   **3.** b, p. 80   **4.** c, p. 81   **5.** c, p. 87

B

Use of a Worksheet

Accountants often use a worksheet. A **worksheet** is an informal document that helps in compiling the information needed for financial reports. A worksheet is a tool of the accountant; it is not part of a company's formal accounting records. In this appendix, we will explain how a worksheet may be used to help compile information for a set of financial statements.

PREPARING A WORKSHEET

The accountant prepares a worksheet at that stage in the accounting cycle when it is time to adjust the accounts and prepare financial statements. The basic structure of the worksheet is presented in Exhibit B-1, which includes an explanation of the format used. The worksheet is prepared in the order indicated by the boxed numbers in the exhibit. A completed worksheet for Landen TV Service (the company illustrated in the chapter) appears in Exhibit B-2. Refer to both of these exhibits when reading through the following procedures for preparing a worksheet.

EXHIBIT B-1 **Basic Structure of a Worksheet**

1
(HEADING FOR WORKSHEET)

Description	Unadjusted Trial Balance		Adjustments		Adjusted Trial Balance		Income Statement		Balance Sheet	
	Debit	Credit	Debit	Credit	Debit	Credit	Debit	Credit	Debit	Credit
2 The unadjusted trial balance			**3** Amounts of adjustments		**4** Amounts of all account balances		**5** Extension of adjusted trial balance			
							Income statement accounts		Balance sheet accounts	
Titles of accounts not in unadjusted trial balance, added as needed							**6** Balancing of columns for each statement			

1 HEADING

The worksheet *heading* should include (1) the name of the accounting entity involved, (2) the term *Worksheet* to indicate the type of analysis performed, and (3) a date describing the period covered. The worksheet includes both income statement data (for the period described) and balance sheet data (for the end of the period described). Exhibit B-2 illustrates the heading for Landen TV Service's worksheet.

EXHIBIT B–2 **Example of Completed Worksheet**

LANDEN TV SERVICE
WORKSHEET
FOR THE MONTH ENDED DECEMBER 31, 1996

Description	Unadjusted Trial Balance Debit	Credit	Adjustments Debit	Credit	Adjusted Trial Balance Debit	Credit	Income Statement Debit	Credit	Balance Sheet Debit	Credit
Cash	7,080				7,080				7,080	
Accounts Receivable	3,480				3,480				3,480	
Supplies and Parts	950			(1) 440	510				510	
Prepaid Rent	3,600			(2) 600	3,000				3,000	
Truck	10,800				10,800				10,800	
Accounts Payable		700				700				700
Unearned Service Fees		1,000	(4) 250			750				750
Long-Term Notes Payable		10,800				10,800				10,800
M. Landen, Capital		10,000				10,000				10,000
M. Landen, Drawing	800				800				800	
Service Fees Earned		5,450		(4) 250		5,700		5,700		
Wages Expense	1,080		(5) 135		1,215		1,215			
Truck Expense	160				160		160			
	27,950	27,950								
Supplies & Parts Expense			(1) 440		440		440			
Rent Expense			(2) 600		600		600			
Depreciation Expense —Truck			(3) 150		150		150			
Accumulated Depreciation—Truck				(3) 150		150				150
Wages Payable				(5) 135		135				135
Interest Expense			(6) 90		90		90			
Interest Payable				(6) 90		90				90
Commissions Receivable			(7) 50		50				50	
Commissions Earned				(7) 50		50		50		
			1,715	1,715	28,375	28,375	2,655	5,750	25,720	22,625
Net Income							3,095			3,095
							5,750	5,750	25,720	25,720

The worksheet form we have illustrated has a description column and 10 amount (money) columns. A set of Debit and Credit columns is provided for each of the five headings, Unadjusted Trial Balance, Adjustments, Adjusted Trial Balance, Income Statement, and Balance Sheet.

2 Unadjusted Trial Balance

The unadjusted trial balance becomes the starting point for the accounting analysis on the worksheet. It is entered in the worksheet's Description column and the first pair of money columns. Once this trial balance is placed on the worksheet and double ruled, it reflects the state of the general ledger at the time the worksheet is prepared. Exhibit B-2 shows the worksheet placement of Landen TV Service's unadjusted trial balance at December 31, 1996.

3 Adjustments

When a worksheet is used, all adjustments are first entered on the worksheet. This procedure permits the adjustment to be reviewed for completeness and accuracy. To adjust accounts already appearing in the unadjusted trial balance, we simply enter the amounts in the appropriate side (debit or credit) of the Adjustments columns on the lines containing the accounts. When accounts not appearing in the unadjusted trial balance require adjustment, their titles are listed as needed in the Description column below the accounts already listed. Note that adjustments entered on the worksheet are not yet journalized; journalizing the adjustments occurs later.

The adjustments recorded on Landen TV Service's worksheet in Exhibit B-2 are identical to those illustrated in the chapter. (See Exhibit 3-8). It is common practice to "key" the amounts of each adjusting entry with the same letter or number. Note that the numbers (1) through (7) are used in Exhibit B-2. This procedure makes it easy to check the equality of debits and credits in each entry and to identify all the amounts related to a particular adjustment.

We repeat the adjusting entries made at the end of December for Landen TV Service and explain their placement on the worksheet (Exhibit B-2). Remember that because we are preparing a worksheet, these adjustments are entered on the worksheet first; they are not yet recorded in the general journal.

(1)	Supplies and Parts Expense	440	
	Supplies and Parts		440

Because $510 worth of supplies were on hand at December 31, we reduce the asset Supplies and Parts from $950 to $510 and record the $440 difference as expense. Note that the expense account, Supplies and Parts Expense, does not appear in the unadjusted trial balance and must be added below the accounts already listed on the worksheet.

(2)	Rent Expense	600	
	Prepaid Rent		600

This adjustment records the rent expense for December ($600) and reduces the prepaid rent to an amount representing five months' prepayment ($3,000). The Rent Expense account is not in the unadjusted trial balance and, therefore, must be added below the Supplies and Parts Expense account on the worksheet.

(3)	Depreciation Expense—Truck	150	
	Accumulated Depreciation—Truck		150

The truck depreciation for December is reflected by this adjustment. The two accounts used in the adjustment, Depreciation Expense—Truck and Accumulated Depreciation—Truck, do not appear in the unadjusted trial balance. Therefore, these two accounts must be listed in the worksheet's Description column below the Rent Expense account.

(4)	Unearned Service Fees	250	
	Service Fees Earned		250

This adjustment is made to reflect the portion of a $1,000 advance earned in December. The liability account Unearned Service Fees, originally credited for the $1,000 advance, is reduced by a $250 debit, and a corresponding credit is made to the revenue account Service Fees Earned. Since both accounts appear in the unadjusted trial balance, we record this adjustment on the lines already provided for these accounts.

(5)	Wages Expense	135	
	Wages Payable		135
(6)	Interest Expense	90	
	Interest Payable		90

These adjustments reflect expenses incurred in December 1996 that will not be paid until 1997. Wages are accrued for the last three days in December, and interest is accrued for the month of December. The accounts Wages Payable, Interest Expense, and Interest Payable do not appear in the unadjusted trial balance; they are added beneath the Accumulated Depreciation—Truck account on the worksheet.

| (7) | Commissions Receivable | 50 | |
| | Commissions Earned | | 50 |

This adjustment reflects the commission earned during December 1996 that will not be received until 1997. Neither of the accounts in this adjustment appears in the unadjusted trial balance, so both the Commissions Receivable and Commissions Earned accounts are added to the worksheet below the Interest Payable account.

After recording all the adjusting entries on the worksheet, we total the adjustments columns to prove that debits equal credits.

4 ADJUSTED TRIAL BALANCE

Once the adjustments have been entered on the worksheet, there is sufficient information available to compile an adjusted trial balance. The adjusted figures are determined by combining horizontally, line by line, the amounts in the first four money columns—that is, the unadjusted trial balance and the adjustments.

We review the calculations for three lines of Exhibit B-2 to illustrate this process. The first line shows Cash with a debit amount of $7,080 in the unadjusted trial balance. Because Cash is not affected by any adjustments, the $7,080 appears in the Debit column of the adjusted trial balance. On the third line, Supplies and Parts begins with a debit of $950 in the unadjusted trial balance and then shows a credit of $440 in the Adjustments columns. The $440 credit is subtracted from the $950 debit, and the remaining $510 is shown as a debit in the adjusted trial balance. Service Fees Earned, on the eleventh line, shows a $5,450 credit balance in the unadjusted trial balance and a $250 credit in the Adjustments columns. These two credit amounts are added, and the $5,700 sum is shown in the Credit column of the adjusted trial balance.

After computing the adjusted trial balance amounts for all the accounts on the worksheet, we total the two columns of the adjusted trial balance to confirm that they are equal and that, therefore, our worksheet still balances.

5 EXTENSION OF ADJUSTED TRIAL BALANCE

The amounts in the Adjusted Trial Balance columns are extended into the two remaining pairs of columns as follows:

Expenses	$\longrightarrow$	Debit column of income statement
Revenues	$\longrightarrow$	Credit column of income statement
Assets, owner's drawing, and cash dividends	$\longrightarrow$	Debit column of balance sheet
Liabilities, owner's capital, capital stock, retained earnings, and contra assets, such as accumulated depreciation	$\longrightarrow$	Credit column of balance sheet

Expense and revenue account balances are extended to the Income Statement columns because these accounts will be used to prepare the income statement. Similarly, asset, contra asset, liability, and owner's capital accounts are balance sheet accounts, so their balances are extended to the Balance Sheet columns. Although not a balance sheet account, an owner's drawing account debit balance is also extended to the appropriate Balance Sheet column (the Debit column). We will use the owner's drawing account balance in deriving the proper end-of-period owner's capital amount.

If the worksheet is for a corporation, a cash dividends debit balance is extended to the Balance Sheet Debit column. Credit balances in the capital stock and retained earnings accounts are extended to the Balance Sheet Credit column.

Exhibit B-2 shows the extension of Landen TV Service's adjusted trial balance to the worksheet's Income Statement and Balance Sheet columns. Once the proper extensions are made, the worksheet is complete except for balancing the two pairs of statement columns containing the adjusted balances.

6   BALANCING THE WORKSHEET

The first step in balancing is to add each of the Income Statement and Balance Sheet columns and record their respective totals on the same line as the totals of the Adjusted Trial Balance columns. The difference between the total debits and total credits in the Income Statement columns is the difference between total revenues and total expenses—that is, the net income or net loss for the period. The net income or net loss should also be the amount by which the Debit and Credit columns for the balance sheet differ. This is true because the owner's capital account balance, as extended, does not yet reflect the net income or net loss for the current period.

When revenues exceed expenses, we balance the two pairs of statement columns by adding the net income figure to both the Debit column of the income statement and the Credit column of the balance sheet. Exhibit B-2 illustrates this balancing situation with Landen TV Service's net income for December of $3,095. If expenses exceed revenues, we add the amount of net loss to the Credit column of the income statement and to the Debit column of the balance sheet. After we have added the net income (or loss) to the proper columns, we total and double rule the four columns. The worksheet is now complete.

A completed worksheet aids in the last three major steps of the accounting cycle—adjust, report, and close.

Adjust: The adjusting entries to be journalized and posted may be taken from the information in the Adjustments columns. Because the adjustments have first been entered on the worksheet, they can be reviewed for their financial effects before being journalized. Thus, the likelihood of incorrect adjustments appearing in the formal accounting records is reduced.

Report: The income statement may be prepared from the data in the Income Statement columns. Two pieces of information for the statement of owner's equity are available in the worksheet—the net income (or net loss) and the owner's drawings. The assets and liabilities needed for the balance sheet are available in the Balance Sheet columns (the ending owner's capital amount for the balance sheet will be obtained from the statement of owner's equity).

Close: The closing entries to be journalized and posted may be prepared from data in the worksheet because it displays all the temporary account balances. The revenue and expense account balances are shown in the Income Statement columns and the owner's drawing (or cash dividends) account balance is shown in the Balance Sheet Debit column.

Reversing Entries

In our discussion of adjusting entries for accrued items in the chapter, we pointed out that certain precautions are necessary to avoid reflecting the same expense or revenue in two successive periods. We now review two alternative procedures for recording the settlement of accrued items in the period after their accrual. We illustrate these procedures using wages expense for Landen TV Service.

WAGES EXPENSE IN DECEMBER

Recall that the Landen TV Service employee received wages of $270 for each six-day work week ($45 per day) and that the employee was paid every other Saturday. We assumed that the two paydays in December 1996 fell on December 13 and 27. Wages expense of $135 was accrued for December 29, 30, and 31. We made the following adjusting entry to reflect the proper expense for December:

1996

Dec. 31	Wages Expense	135	
	Wages Payable		135
	To record accrued wages for December 29, 30, and 31.		

After this adjusting entry was posted, the Wages Expense account had a debit balance of $1,215. This consisted of two debits of $540 made on December 13 and 27 and the $135 accrual on December 31. Along with other expenses, the Wages Expense account was closed to Income Summary on December 31. After the closing procedures, the Wages Expense and Wages Payable accounts appeared in the ledger as follows:

WAGES EXPENSE   ACCOUNT NO. 52

Date		Description	Post. Ref.	Debit*	Credit	Balance
1996 Dec.	13		J1	540		540
	27		J1	540		1,080
	31	(adjusting)	J2	135		1,215
	31	(closing)	J3		1,215	–0–

WAGES PAYABLE   ACCOUNT NO. 23

Date		Description	Post. Ref.	Debit	Credit*	Balance
1996 Dec.	31	(adjusting)	J2		135	135

JANUARY ACCOUNTING WITHOUT USING REVERSALS

On January 10, 1997, the employee will receive another $540 wage payment. Of this amount, only $405 should be reflected as January expense since only nine days were worked in January (the other three days were worked in December and accrued as December wages expense). We may record the wage payment and the correct January wages expense by making the following entry:

1997

Jan. 10	Wages Payable	135	
	Wages Expense	405	
	Cash		540
	To record wages paid.		

This procedure, however, requires extreme vigilance in recording routine transactions on the part of the accountant, who must keep in mind previously made accruals in order to record subsequent payments correctly. Many accountants find this a nuisance and avoid the problem by reversing adjustments made for accruals.

JANUARY ACCOUNTING USING REVERSALS

As an alternative to the preceding procedure, then, an accountant may use **reversing entries.** Reversing entries are made after all closing procedures have been completed and the post-closing trial balance has been prepared. Reversing entries are dated the first day of the following period and, therefore, are the first journal entries in that period. A reversing entry is so named because the entry exactly reverses the debits and credits of an adjusting entry. For example, the reversing entry for the accrual of wages would be

1997

Jan. 1	Wages Payable	135	
	Wages Expense		135
	To reverse accrual made December 31.		

This entry reduces the liability Wages Payable to zero and results in a $135 abnormal credit balance in the Wages Expense account at the start of the new accounting period. On the next payday, however, the wage payment of $540 is recorded as all wage payments are recorded, as follows:

Jan. 10	Wages Expense	540	
	Cash		540
	Paid wages for two weeks ended January 10.		

When this entry is posted to the Wages Expense account, the $540 debit is combined with the $135 credit balance created by the reversing entry. As a result, the account balance is the proper wages expense for January 1–10 ($405). After the January 1 reversing entry and the January 10 payment have been posted, the Wages Expense and Wages Payable accounts appear as follows. Note that the $135 abnormal balance is placed in parentheses.

WAGES EXPENSE   ACCOUNT No. 52

Date		Description	Post. Ref.	Debit*	Credit	Balance
1996 Dec.	13		J1	540		540
	27		J1	540		1,080
	31	(adjusting)	J2	135		1,215
	31	(closing)	J3		1,215	–0–
1997 Jan.	1	(reversing)	J4		135	(135)
	10		J5	540		405

WAGES PAYABLE   ACCOUNT No. 23

Date		Description	Post. Ref.	Debit	Credit*	Balance
1996 Dec.	31	(adjusting)	J2		135	135
1997 Jan.	1	(reversing)	J4	135		–0–

Both of the alternative procedures for handling the December accrued wages in January give the same result—the elimination of the $135 wages payable and the portrayal of $405 of wages expense for the first 10 days in January. By using reversals, however, the accountant can record the first January payroll without having to consider the amount of wages accrued at December 31.

OTHER REVERSALS

A reversing entry simplifies the recording of a transaction that relates to an earlier adjusting entry. The appropriate adjustments to reverse are *accruals* of revenues and expenses. Of the adjustments made by Landen TV Service (in addition to the accrual of wages), reversing entries are employed for the two other accruals—the $90 interest expense and the $50 commissions earned. The accountant therefore makes two additional entries after the books are closed.

1997

Jan. 1 Interest Payable   90
    Interest Expense   90
    To reverse accrual made December 31.

Jan. 1 Commissions Earned   50
    Commissions Receivable   50
    To reverse accrual made December 31.

These entries eliminate the accrued amounts from the liability and asset accounts and create an abnormal credit balance of $90 in Interest Expense and an abnormal debit balance of $50 in Commissions Earned.

The credit balance in Interest Expense will be eliminated when the annual interest of $1,080 on the note payable is paid on November 30, 1997. The entry to record this interest payment is as follows:

Nov. 30 Interest Expense   1,080
    Cash   1,080
    To record payment of annual interest.

After the entry for payment is posted, Interest Expense has a $990 debit balance, the proper amount of interest expense on the note payable for the first 11 months of 1997.

The debit balance in Commissions Earned is eliminated when Landen TV Service receives its three-month commission payment of $150 on February 28, 1997. This receipt is recorded as follows:

Feb. 28 Cash   150
    Commissions Earned   150
    To record receipt of quarterly commission.

This entry leaves a credit balance of $100 in the Commissions Earned revenue account, reflecting the proper amount of revenue for commission work performed in January and February 1997.

Although the use of reversing entries is optional, it does permit us to analyze certain transactions the same way all the time. For example, if reversals are used, an accountant may be instructed (or a computer programmed) to debit Wages Expense and credit Cash every time wages are paid. Similarly, every interest payment may be analyzed as a debit to Interest Expense and a credit to Cash, and every receipt of commissions may be recorded as a debit to Cash and a credit to Commissions Earned. Reversals eliminate the need to remember the effects of previous accruals and, therefore, contribute to the more efficient processing of data.

GLOSSARY OF KEY TERMS USED IN THIS CHAPTER AND APPENDIXES

accounting cycle   A series of basic steps followed to process accounting information during a fiscal year (p. 70).

accruals   Adjustments that reflect revenues earned but not received or recorded and expenses incurred but not paid or recorded (p. 78).

accrued expense   An expense incurred but not yet paid; recognized with an adjusting entry (p. 81).

accrued revenue   Revenue earned but not yet billed or received; recognized with an adjusting entry (p. 82).

adjusted trial balance   A list of general ledger accounts and their balances taken after adjustments have been made (p. 83).

adjusting entries   Entries made at the end of an accounting period under accrual accounting to ensure the proper matching of expenses incurred with revenues earned for the period (p. 78).

applications programs   Computer programs that direct the processing of data, including accounting data, through a computer system (p. 92).

book value   The dollar amount carried in the accounts for a particular item. The book value of a depreciable asset is derived by deducting the contra account Accumulated Depreciation from the balance in the depreciable asset account (p. 80).

calendar year   A fiscal year that ends on December 31 (p. 71).

chart of accounts   A list of all the general ledger account titles and their numerical code (p. 73).

closing procedures   A step in the accounting cycle in which the balances of all temporary accounts are transferred to the owner's capital account or the Retained Earnings account, leaving the temporary accounts with zero balances (p. 87).

compound journal entry   A journal entry containing more than just one debit and one credit (p. 75).

contra account   An account related to, and deducted from, another account when financial statements are prepared or when book values are computed (p. 80).

deferrals   Adjustments that allocate various assets and revenues received in advance to the proper accounting periods as expenses and revenues (p. 78).

deferred revenue   A liability representing revenues received in advance. Also called *unearned revenue* (p. 80).

depreciation accounting   The process of allocating the cost of equipment, vehicles, and buildings to expense over the time period benefiting from their use (p. 80).

fiscal year   The annual accounting period used by a business firm (p. 71).

general journal   A journal with enough flexibility so that any type of business transaction may be recorded in it (p. 73).

journal   A tabular record in which business transactions are analyzed in debit and credit terms and recorded in chronological order (p. 73).

post-closing trial balance   A list of general ledger accounts and their balances after closing entries have been recorded and posted (p. 89).

posting   The transfer of information from the journal to the ledger accounts (p. 74).

posting references   A series of abbreviations used in posting to indicate to where or from where a journal entry is posted (p. 74).

reversing entries   Journal entries made the first day of an accounting period that reverse the debits and credits of accrual adjusting entries made at the end of the preceding period (p. 102).

source document   Any written document or computer record evidencing an accounting transaction, such as a bank check or deposit slip, sales invoice, or cash register tape (p. 71).

straight-line depreciation   A depreciation procedure that allocates uniform amounts of depreciation expense to each full period of a depreciable asset's useful life (p. 80).

unadjusted trial balance   A list of general ledger accounts and their balances taken before adjustments have been made (p. 78).

unearned revenue   A liability representing revenues received in advance. Also called *deferred revenue* (p. 80).

worksheet   An informal accounting document used to facilitate the preparation of financial statements (p. 96).

QUESTIONS

3-1 What are the five major steps in the accounting cycle? List them in their proper order.

3-2 What does the term *fiscal year* mean?

3-3 What are three examples of source documents that underlie business transactions?

3-4 What are the nature and purpose of a general journal?

3-5 Explain the technique of posting references. What is the justification for their use?

3-6 What is a compound journal entry?

3-7 What is a chart of accounts? Give an example of a coding system for identifying different types of accounts.

3-8 Why is the adjusting step of the accounting cycle necessary?

3-9 What four different types of adjustments are frequently necessary at the close of an accounting period? Give examples of each type.

3-10 On January 1, Prepaid Insurance was debited with the cost of a two-year premium, $1,872. What adjusting entry should be made on January 31 before financial statements are prepared for the month?

3-11 What is a contra account? What contra account is used in reporting the book value of a depreciable asset?

3-12 At the beginning of January, the first month of the accounting year, the Supplies account had a debit balance of $825. During January, purchases of $260 worth of supplies were debited to the account. Although only $630 worth of supplies were on hand at the end of January, the necessary adjusting entry was omitted. How will the omission affect (a) the income statement for January and (b) the balance sheet prepared at January 31?

3-13 The publisher of *International View,* a monthly magazine, received two-year subscriptions totaling $9,720 on January 1. (a) What entry should be made to record the receipt of the $9,720? (b) What entry should be made at the end of January before financial statements are prepared for the month?

3-14 Globe Travel Agency pays an employee $475 in wages each Friday for the five-day work week ending on that day. The last Friday of January falls on January 27. What adjusting entry should be made on January 31, the fiscal year-end?

3-15 The Bayou Company earns interest amounting to $360 per month on its investments. The company receives the interest every six months, on December 31 and June 30. Monthly financial statements are prepared. What adjusting entry should be made on January 31?

3-16 Which period financial statements include information as of the beginning of the period?

3-17 Which groups of accounts are closed at the end of the accounting year?

3-18 How do closing entries for a corporation differ from closing entries for a proprietorship?

3-19 What is the purpose of a post-closing trial balance? Which of the following accounts should *not* appear in the post-closing trial balance: Cash; Unearned Revenue; R. Davis, Drawing; Depreciation Expense; Utilities Payable; Supplies Expense; and Retained Earnings?

3-20 What primary functions are incorporated into most computer application programs?

PRINCIPLES DISCUSSION QUESTION

3-21 W.H. Brady Co., headquartered in Milwaukee, Wisconsin, is an international manufacturer of coated films and industrial identification products. Included among its prepaid expenses is an account titled Prepaid Catalog Costs; in recent years, this account's size has ranged between $2,500,000 and $4,000,000. The company states that catalog costs are initially capitalized and then written off over the estimated useful lives of the publications (generally eight months). Identify and briefly discuss the accounting principles that support W.H. Brady's handling of its catalog costs.

EXERCISES

TRANSACTION ENTRIES — OBJ. 3 —

3-22 Creative Designs, a firm providing art services for advertisers, began business on June 1, 1996. The following accounts in its general ledger are needed to record the transactions for June: Cash; Accounts Receivable; Supplies; Office Equipment; Accounts Payable; L. Ryan, Capital; L. Ryan, Drawing; Service Fees Earned; Rent Expense; Utilities Expense; and Salaries Expense. Record the following transactions for June in a general journal:

June 1   Lisa Ryan invested $12,000 cash to begin the business.

2   Paid rent for June, $950.

3   Purchased office equipment on account, $6,400.

June 6   Purchased art materials and other supplies costing $3,800; paid $1,800 down with the remainder due within 30 days.

11   Billed clients for services, $4,700.

17   Collected $3,250 from clients on account.

19   Paid $3,000 on account to office equipment firm (see June 3).

25   Lisa Ryan withdrew $2,000 cash for personal use.

30   Paid utilities bill for June, $350.

30   Paid salaries for June, $2,500.

**SOURCE DOCUMENTS
— OBJ. 2 —**

3-23   For each transaction in Exercise 3-22, indicate the related source document or documents that evidence the transaction.

**TRANSACTION ENTRY AND
ADJUSTING ENTRIES
— OBJ. 3, 4 —**

3-24   Deluxe Building Services offers janitorial services on both a contract basis and an hourly basis. On January 1, 1996, Deluxe collected $20,100 in advance on six-month contracts for work to be performed evenly during the next six months.

a. Give the general journal entry on January 1 to record the receipt of $20,100 for contract work.

b. Give the adjusting entry to be made on January 31, 1996, for the contract work done during January.

c. At January 31, a total of 30 hours of hourly rate janitor work was unbilled. The billing rate is $19 per hour. Give the adjusting entry needed on January 31, 1996. (*Note:* The firm uses the account Fees Receivable to reflect amounts due but not yet billed.)

**ADJUSTING ENTRIES
— OBJ. 4 —**

3-25   Selected accounts of Ideal Properties, a real estate management firm, are shown below as of January 31, 1996, before any adjusting entries have been made.

	Debit	Credit
Prepaid Insurance	$6,660	
Supplies	1,930	
Office Equipment	5,952	
Unearned Rent Revenue		$ 5,250
Salaries Expense	3,100	
Rent Revenue		15,000

Monthly financial statements are prepared. Using the following information, record in a general journal the adjusting entries necessary on January 31:

a. Prepaid Insurance represents a three-year premium paid on January 1, 1996.

b. Supplies of $850 were on hand January 31.

c. Office equipment is expected to last eight years.

d. On January 1, 1996, the firm collected six months' rent in advance from a tenant renting space for $875 per month.

e. Accrued salaries not recorded as of January 31 are $490.

**ADJUSTING ENTRIES
— OBJ. 4 —**

3-26   For each of the following unrelated situations, prepare the necessary adjusting entry in general journal form.

a. Unrecorded depreciation on equipment is $610.

b. The Supplies account has a balance of $2,990. Supplies on hand at the end of the period total $1,100.

c. On the date for preparing financial statements, an estimated utilities expense of $390 has been incurred, but no utility bill has yet been received.

d. On the first day of the current month, rent for four months was paid and recorded as a $2,800 debit to Prepaid Rent and a $2,800 credit to Cash. Monthly statements are now being prepared.

e. Nine months ago, Solid Insurance Company sold a one-year policy to a customer and recorded the receipt of the premium by debiting Cash for $624 and crediting Unearned Premium Revenue for $624. No adjusting entries have been prepared during the nine-month period. Annual financial statements are now being prepared.

f. At the end of the accounting period, employee wages of $965 have been incurred but not paid.

g. At the end of the accounting period, $300 of interest has been earned but not yet received on notes receivable that are held.

**STATEMENT OF OWNER'S
EQUITY
— OBJ. 5 —**

3-27   On January 1, 1996, the credit balance of the M. Strife, Capital account was $48,000, and on December 31, 1996, the credit balance before closing was $54,000. The M. Strife, Drawing account had a debit balance of $9,700 on December 31, 1996. After revenue and expense accounts were closed, the Income Summary account had a credit balance of $29,900. Prepare a 1996 statement of owner's equity for Mark Strife, architect.

**CLOSING ENTRIES FOR
SOLE PROPRIETORSHIP
— OBJ. 6 —**

3-28 The adjusted trial balance prepared December 31, 1996, for Phyllis Howell, consultant, contains the following revenue and expense accounts:

	Debit	Credit
Service Fees Earned		$80,300
Rent Expense	$20,800	
Salaries Expense	45,700	
Supplies Expense	5,600	
Depreciation Expense	10,200	
P. Howell, Capital		67,000
P. Howell, Drawing	9,000	

Prepare journal entries to close the accounts. After these entries are posted, what is the balance of the P. Howell, Capital account?

**CLOSING ENTRIES FOR
CORPORATION
— OBJ. 6 —**

3-29 In the midst of closing procedures, Echo Corporation's accountant became ill and was hospitalized. You have volunteered to complete the closing of the books, and you find that all revenue and expense accounts have zero balances and that the Income Summary account has a single debit entry for $308,800 and a single credit entry for $347,400. The Cash Dividends account has a debit balance of $18,000, and the Retained Earnings account has a credit balance of $117,000. Prepare journal entries to complete the closing procedures at December 31, 1996.

**WORKSHEET
— APPENDIX B —**

3-30 Identify each of the 10 amount columns of the worksheet and indicate to which column the adjusted balance of the following accounts would be extended:
   a. Accounts Receivable   **f.** Rent Receivable
   b. Accumulated Depreciation   **g.** Prepaid Insurance
   c. W. Biggs, Drawing   **h.** Service Fees Earned
   d. Wages Payable   **i.** Capital Stock
   e. Depreciation Expense   **j.** Retained Earnings

**REVERSING ENTRIES
— APPENDIX C —**

3-31 Fibre Company closes its accounts on December 31 each year. The company works a five-day work week and pays its employees every two weeks. On December 31, 1996, Fibre accrued $4,700 of salaries payable. On January 9, 1997, the company paid salaries of $12,000 to employees. Prepare journal entries to (a) accrue the salaries payable on December 31; (b) close the Salaries Expense account on December 31 (the account has a year-end balance of $250,000 after adjustments); (c) reverse the December 31 salary accrual on January 1; and (d) record the salary payment on January 9.

PROBLEMS

**SOURCE DOCUMENTS,
TRANSACTION ENTRIES,
POSTING, TRIAL BALANCE,
AND ADJUSTING ENTRIES
— OBJ. 2, 3, 4 —**

3-32 Mark Ladd opened Ladd Roofing Service on April 1, 1996. Transactions for April are as follows:

Apr. 1 Ladd contributed $11,500 of his personal funds to begin the business.
      2 Purchased a used truck for $6,100 cash.
      2 Purchased ladders and other equipment for a total of $3,100, paid $1,000 cash, with the balance due in 30 days.
      3 Paid two-year premium on liability insurance, $2,880.
      5 Purchased supplies on account, $1,200.
      5 Received an advance payment of $1,800 from a customer for roof repair work to be done during April and May.
     12 Billed customers for roofing services, $5,500.
     18 Collected $4,900 on account from customers.
     29 Paid bill for truck fuel used in April, $75.
     30 Paid April newspaper advertising, $100.
     30 Paid assistants' wages, $2,500.
     30 Billed customers for roofing services, $4,000.

REQUIRED
a. For each transaction, indicate the related source document or documents that evidence the transaction.
b. Set up a general ledger with the following accounts, using the account numbers shown: Cash (11); Accounts Receivable (12); Supplies (13); Prepaid Insurance (14); Trucks (15); Accumulated Depreciation—Trucks (16); Equipment (17); Accumulated Depreciation—Equipment (18); Accounts Payable (21); Unearned Roofing Fees (22); M. Ladd, Capital

(31); Roofing Fees Earned (41); Fuel Expense (51); Advertising Expense (52); Wages Expense (53); Insurance Expense (54); Supplies Expense (55); Depreciation Expense—Trucks (56); and Depreciation Expense—Equipment (57).

c. Record these transactions in general journal form and post to the ledger accounts.

d. Take an unadjusted trial balance at April 30, 1996.

e. Make the journal entries to adjust the books for insurance expense, supplies expense, depreciation expense on the truck, depreciation expense on the equipment, and roofing fees earned. Supplies on hand on April 30 amounted to $400. Depreciation for April was $125 on the truck and $35 on the equipment. One-fourth of the roofing fee received in advance was earned by April 30. Post the adjusting entries.

TRANSACTION ENTRIES, POSTING, TRIAL BALANCE, AND ADJUSTING ENTRIES — OBJ. 3, 4 —

3-33 The Wellness Catering Service had the following transactions in July 1996, its first month of operations:

July   1   Kelly Foster contributed $15,000 of personal funds to the business.

1   Purchased the following items for cash from a catering firm that was going out of business (make a compound entry): delivery van, $3,780; equipment, $3,240; and supplies, $1,600.

2   Paid premium on a one-year liability insurance policy, $1,080.

2   Entered into a contract with a local service club to cater weekly luncheon meetings for one year at a fee of $750 per month. Received six months' fees in advance.

3   Paid rent for July, August, and September, $2,340.

12   Paid employee's two weeks' wages (five-day week), $1,700.

15   Billed customers for services rendered, $4,500.

18   Purchased supplies on account, $3,400.

26   Paid employee's two weeks' wages, $1,700.

30   Paid July bill for gas, oil, and repairs on delivery van, $690.

30   Collected $3,700 from customers on account.

31   Billed customers for services rendered, $4,800.

31   Foster withdrew $1,900 cash for personal use.

REQUIRED

a. Set up a general ledger that includes the following accounts, using the account numbers shown: Cash (11); Accounts Receivable (12); Supplies (13); Prepaid Rent (14); Prepaid Insurance (15); Delivery Van (16); Accumulated Depreciation—Delivery Van (17); Equipment (18); Accumulated Depreciation—Equipment (19); Accounts Payable (21); Wages Payable (22); Unearned Catering Fees (23); K. Foster, Capital (31); K. Foster, Drawing (32); Catering Fees Revenue (41); Wages Expense (51); Rent Expense (52); Supplies Expense (53); Insurance Expense (54); Delivery Van Expense (55); Depreciation Expense—Delivery Van (56); and Depreciation Expense—Equipment (57).

b. Record July transactions in general journal form and post to the ledger accounts.

c. Take an unadjusted trial balance at July 31, 1996.

d. Record adjusting journal entries in the general journal and post to the ledger accounts. The following information is available on July 31, 1996:

> Supplies on hand, $1,500
>
> Accrued wages, $510
>
> Estimated life of delivery van, three years
>
> Estimated life of equipment, six years

Also, make any necessary adjusting entries for insurance, rent, and catering fees indicated by the July transactions.

TRIAL BALANCE AND ADJUSTING ENTRIES — OBJ. 4 —

3-34 Photomake, Inc., a commercial photography studio, has just completed its first full year of operations on December 31, 1996. The general ledger account balances before year-end adjustments follow. No adjusting entries have been made to the accounts at any time during the year. Assume that all balances are normal.

Cash	$ 2,150	Accounts Payable	$ 1,910
Accounts Receivable	3,800	Unearned Photography Fees	2,600
Prepaid Rent	12,600	Capital Stock	24,000
Prepaid Insurance	2,970	Photography Fees Earned	34,480
Supplies	4,250	Wages Expense	11,000
Equipment	22,800	Utilities Expense	3,420

An analysis of the firm's records discloses the following items:

1. Photography services of $925 have been rendered, but customers have not yet been billed. The firm uses the account Fees Receivable to reflect amounts due but not yet billed.
2. The equipment, purchased January 1, 1996, has an estimated life of 10 years.
3. Utilities expense for December is estimated to be $400, but the bill will not arrive until January of next year.
4. The balance in Prepaid Rent represents the amount paid on January 1, 1996, for a two-year lease on the studio.
5. In November, customers paid $2,600 in advance for pictures to be taken for the holiday season. When received, these fees were credited to Unearned Photography Fees. By December 31, all these fees are earned.
6. A three-year insurance premium paid on January 1, 1996, was debited to Prepaid Insurance.
7. Supplies on hand at December 31 are $1,520.
8. At December 31, wages expense of $375 has been incurred but not paid.

REQUIRED

a. Prove that debits equal credits for Photomake's unadjusted account balances by preparing an unadjusted trial balance at December 31, 1996.
b. Record adjusting entries in general journal form.

ADJUSTING ENTRIES — OBJ. 4 —

3-35 Dole Carpet Cleaners ended its first month of operations on June 30, 1996. Monthly financial statements will be prepared. The unadjusted account balances are as follows:

DOLE CARPET CLEANERS
UNADJUSTED TRIAL BALANCE
JUNE 30, 1996

	Debit	Credit
Cash	$ 1,180	
Accounts Receivable	450	
Prepaid Rent	3,100	
Supplies	2,520	
Equipment	4,440	
Accounts Payable		$ 760
T. Dole, Capital		7,500
T. Dole, Drawing	200	
Service Fees Earned		4,650
Wages Expense	1,020	
	$12,910	$12,910

The following information is also available:

1. The balance in Prepaid Rent was the amount paid on June 1 for the first four months' rent.
2. Supplies on hand at June 30 were $820.
3. The equipment, purchased June 1, has an estimated life of five years.
4. Unpaid wages at June 30 were $210.
5. Utility services used during June were estimated at $300. A bill is expected early in July.
6. Fees earned for services performed but not yet billed on June 30 were $380. The firm uses the account Fees Receivable to reflect amounts due but not yet billed.

REQUIRED

In general journal form, make the adjusting entries needed at June 30, 1996.

ADJUSTING ENTRIES — OBJ. 4 —

3-36 The following information relates to December 31 adjustments for Finest Print, a printing company. The firm's fiscal year ends on December 31.

1. Weekly salaries for a five-day week total $1,800, payable on Fridays. December 31 of the current year is a Tuesday.
2. Finest Print has $20,000 of notes payable outstanding at December 31. Interest of $200 has accrued on these notes by December 31, but will not be paid until the notes mature next year.
3. During December, Finest Print provided $900 of printing services to clients who will be billed on January 2. The firm uses the account Fees Receivable to reflect amounts due but not yet billed.
4. Starting December 1, all maintenance work on Finest Print's equipment is handled by Prompt Repair Company under an agreement whereby Finest Print pays a fixed monthly charge of $90. Finest Print paid six months' service charge in advance on December 1, debiting Prepaid Maintenance for $540.

5. The firm paid $900 on December 15 for a series of radio commercials to run during December and January. One-third of the commercials have aired by December 31. The $900 payment was debited to Prepaid Advertising.

6. Starting December 16, Finest Print rented 400 square feet of storage space from a neighboring business. The monthly rent of $0.80 per square foot is due in advance on the first of each month. Nothing was paid in December, however, because the neighbor agreed to add the rent for one-half of December to the January 1 payment.

7. Finest Print invested $5,000 in securities on December 1 and earned interest of $38 on these securities by December 31. No interest will be received until January.

8. The annual depreciation on the firm's equipment is $2,175. No depreciation has been recorded during the year.

REQUIRED

Prepare the required December 31 adjusting entries in general journal form.

FINANCIAL STATEMENTS AND
CLOSING ENTRIES
— OBJ. 5, 6 —

3-37 The adjusted trial balance shown below is for Fine Consulting Service at December 31, 1996. Byran Fine made no capital contributions during 1996.

Adjusted Trial Balance

	Debit	Credit
Cash	$ 2,700	
Accounts Receivable	3,270	
Supplies	3,060	
Prepaid Insurance	1,500	
Equipment	6,400	
Accumulated Depreciation—Equipment		$ 1,080
Accounts Payable		845
Long-Term Notes Payable		7,000
B. Fine, Capital		7,205
B. Fine, Drawing	2,900	
Service Fees Earned		58,400
Rent Expense	12,000	
Salaries Expense	33,400	
Supplies Expense	4,700	
Insurance Expense	3,250	
Depreciation Expense—Equipment	720	
Interest Expense	630	
	$74,530	$74,530

REQUIRED

a. Prepare an income statement and a statement of owner's equity for 1996 and a balance sheet at December 31, 1996.

b. Prepare closing entries in general journal form.

CLOSING ENTRIES AND
CORPORATION ACCOUNTS
— OBJ. 6 —

3-38 The adjusted trial balance shown below is for Bayou, Inc., at December 31, 1996.

Adjusted Trial Balance

	Debit	Credit
Cash	$ 3,500	
Accounts Receivable	8,000	
Prepaid Insurance	3,600	
Equipment	72,000	
Accumulated Depreciation		$12,000
Accounts Payable		600
Capital Stock		30,000
Retained Earnings		14,100
Cash Dividends	5,000	
Service Fees Earned		97,200
Miscellaneous Income		4,200

	Debit	Credit
Salaries Expense	$ 42,800	
Rent Expense	13,400	
Insurance Expense	1,800	
Depreciation Expense	8,000	
Income Tax Expense	8,800	
Income Tax Payable		$ 8,800
	$166,900	$166,900

REQUIRED

a. Prepare closing entries in general journal form.

b. After the closing entries are posted, what is the balance in the Retained Earnings account?

c. Which accounts in the adjusted trial balance would not appear if the company were organized as a sole proprietorship rather than as a corporation?

WORKSHEET
— APPENDIX B —

3-39 The following unadjusted trial balance was taken at March 31, 1997:

FOCUS TRAVEL AGENCY
UNADJUSTED TRIAL BALANCE
MARCH 31, 1997

	Debit	Credit
Cash	$ 2,400	
Commissions Receivable	5,000	
Supplies	1,750	
Prepaid Insurance	1,800	
Equipment	13,000	
Accumulated Depreciation		$ 2,600
Accounts Payable		550
Unearned Commissions		600
G. Owen, Capital		10,000
G. Owen, Drawing	900	
Commissions Earned		18,990
Salaries Expense	4,500	
Rent Expense	1,770	
Advertising Expense	1,000	
Utilities Expense	620	
	$32,740	$32,740

Focus Travel Agency's fiscal year ends on March 31. The following additional information is available:

1. Depreciation for the year is $1,300.

2. Supplies on hand at March 31 amount to $820.

3. By March 31, $400 of the unearned commissions were earned. The remainder will be earned in the next year.

4. Insurance expense for the year is $1,200

5. Accrued salaries payable total $600 at March 31.

REQUIRED

Enter the trial balance on a worksheet and complete the worksheet using the adjustment data given above.

ADJUSTING AND REVERSING
ENTRIES
— APPENDIX C —

3-40 The following selected accounts appear in Shaw Company's unadjusted trial balance at December 31, 1996, the end of the fiscal year (all accounts have normal balances):

Prepaid Advertising	$ 1,200	Unearned Service Fees	$ 5,400
Wages Expense	43,800	Service Fees Earned	87,000
Prepaid Insurance	3,420	Rental Income	4,900

REQUIRED

a. Make the necessary adjusting entries in general journal form at December 31, 1996, assuming the following:

1. Prepaid advertising at December 31 is $800.

2. Unpaid wages earned by employees in December are $1,300.

3. Prepaid insurance at December 31 is $2,280.

4. Unearned service fees at December 31 are $3,000.

5. Rent revenue of $1,000 owed by a tenant is not recorded at December 31.

b. Assume that the company makes reversing entries. Which of the adjustments in part (a) should be reversed? Make the proper reversing entries on January 1, 1997.

c. Assume that reversing entries have been made. Prepare the journal entries on January 4, 1997, to record (1) the payment of $2,400 in wages and (2) the receipt from the tenant of the $1,000 rent revenue

d. Assume that reversing entries have not been made. Prepare the journal entries on January 4, 1997, to record (1) the payment of $2,400 in wages and (2) the receipt from the tenant of the $1,000 rent revenue.

ALTERNATE EXERCISES

**TRANSACTION ENTRIES
— OBJ. 3 —**

3-22A Thoro Clean, a firm providing house cleaning services, began business on April 1, 1996. The following accounts in its general ledger are needed to record the transactions for April: Cash; Accounts Receivable; Supplies; Prepaid Van Lease; Equipment; Notes Payable; Accounts Payable; R. Storm, Capital; R. Storm, Drawing; Cleaning Fees Earned; Wages Expense; Advertising Expense; and Van Fuel Expense. Record the following transactions for April in a general journal:

April 1 Randy Storm invested $9,000 cash to begin the business.

2 Paid six months' lease on van, $2,850.

3 Borrowed $10,000 from bank and signed note payable agreeing to repay the $10,000 in one year plus 10% interest.

3 Purchased $5,500 of cleaning equipment; paid $2,500 down with the remainder due within 30 days.

4 Purchased cleaning supplies for $4,300 cash.

7 Paid $350 for advertisements to run in newspaper during April.

21 Billed customers for services, $3,500.

23 Paid $3,000 on account to cleaning equipment firm (see April 3).

28 Collected $2,300 from customers on account.

29 Randy Storm withdrew $1,000 cash from the firm.

30 Paid wages for April, $1,750.

30 Paid service station for gasoline used during April, $95.

**SOURCE DOCUMENTS
— OBJ. 2 —**

3-23A For each transaction in Exercise 3-22A, indicate the related source document or documents that evidence the transaction.

**ANALYSIS OF ADJUSTED DATA
— OBJ. 4 —**

3-24A Selected T-account balances for Coyle Company are shown below as of January 31, 1997; adjusting entries have already been posted. The firm uses a calendar-year accounting period and makes monthly adjustments.

SUPPLIES		SUPPLIES EXPENSE	
Jan. 31 Bal. 800		Jan. 31 Bal. 960	

PREPAID INSURANCE		INSURANCE EXPENSE	
Jan. 31 Bal. 574		Jan. 31 Bal. 82	

WAGES PAYABLE		WAGES EXPENSE	
	Jan. 31 Bal. 500	Jan. 31 Bal. 3,200	

TRUCK		ACCUMULATED DEPRECIATION—TRUCK	
Jan. 31 Bal. 8,700			Jan. 31 Bal. 2,610

a. If the amount in Supplies Expense represents the January 31 adjustment for the supplies used in January, and $620 worth of supplies were purchased during January, what was the January 1 balance of Supplies?

b. The amount in the Insurance Expense account represents the adjustment made at January 31 for January insurance expense. If the original insurance premium was for one year, what was the amount of the premium and on what date did the insurance policy start?

c. If we assume that no balance existed in Wages Payable or Wages Expense on January 1, how much cash was paid as wages during January?

d. If the truck has a useful life of five years, what is the monthly amount of depreciation expense and how many months has Coyle owned the truck?

ADJUSTING ENTRIES
— OBJ. 4 —

3-25A Judy Brock began Brock Refinishing Service on July 1, 1996. Selected accounts are shown below as of July 31, before any adjusting entries have been made.

	Debit	Credit
Prepaid Rent	$5,700	
Prepaid Advertising	630	
Supplies	3,000	
Unearned Refinishing Fees		$ 600
Refinishing Fees Revenue		2,500

Using the following information, record in a general journal the adjusting entries necessary on July 31:

a. On July 1, the firm paid one year's rent of $5,700.

b. On July 1, $630 was paid to the local newspaper for an advertisement to run daily for the months of July, August, and September.

c. Supplies on hand at July 31 total $1,100.

d. At July 31, refinishing services of $800 have been performed but not yet billed to customers. The firm uses the account Fees Receivable to reflect amounts due but not yet billed.

e. One customer paid $600 in advance for a refinishing project. At July 31, the project is one-half complete.

ANALYSIS OF THE IMPACT
OF ADJUSTMENTS ON
FINANCIAL STATEMENTS
— OBJ. 4, 5 —

3-26A At the end of the first month of operations, Bradley Company's accountant prepared financial statements that showed the following amounts:

Assets	$60,000
Liabilities	20,000
Owners' Equity	40,000
Net Income	9,000

In preparing the statements, the accountant overlooked the following items:

a. Depreciation for the month, $1,000.

b. Service revenue earned but unbilled at month-end, $1,500.

c. Employee wages earned but unpaid at month-end, $250.

Determine the correct amounts of assets, liabilities, and owners' equity at month-end and net income for the month.

STEPS IN MANUAL
ACCOUNTING CYCLE
— OBJ. 7 —

3-27A Listed below, out of order, are the steps in a manual accounting cycle.

1. Prepare unadjusted trial balance.
2. Post journal entries to general ledger accounts.
3. Analyze transactions from source documents.
4. Journalize and post adjusting entries.
5. Prepare financial statements.
6. Record transactions in a journal.
7. Prepare post-closing trial balance.
8. Prepare adjusted trial balance.
9. Journalize and post closing entries.

(a) Place the numbers from the above list in the order in which the steps in the manual accounting cycle are performed, and (b) identify the steps in the accounting cycle that occur daily.

CLOSING ENTRIES FOR
SOLE PROPRIETORSHIP
— OBJ. 6 —

3-28A The adjusted trial balance prepared December 31, 1996, for Cheryl Fontaine, agent, contains the following accounts:

	Debit	Credit
Commissions Earned		$84,900
Wages Expense	$36,000	
Insurance Expense	1,900	
Utilities Expense	8,200	
Depreciation Expense	9,800	
C. Fontaine, Drawing	12,000	
C. Fontaine, Capital		72,100

Prepare journal entries to close the accounts. After these entries are posted, what is the balance of the C. Fontaine, Capital account?

CLOSING ENTRIES FOR CORPORATION — OBJ. 6 —

3-29A The adjusted trial balance of Rose Corporation, prepared December 31, 1996, contains the following accounts:

	Debit	Credit
Service Fees Earned		$92,500
Interest Income		2,200
Salaries Expense	$41,800	
Advertising Expense	4,300	
Depreciation Expense	8,700	
Income Tax Expense	9,900	
Capital Stock		75,000
Retained Earnings		57,700
Cash Dividends	15,000	

Prepare journal entries to close the accounts. After these entries are posted, what is the balance of the Retained Earnings account?

WORKSHEET, CORPORATION — APPENDIX B —

3-30A The adjusted trial balance columns of a worksheet for Bonn Corporation are shown below. The worksheet is prepared for the year ended December 31, 1996.

	Adjusted Trial Balance	
	Debit	Credit
Cash	4,000	
Accounts Receivable	6,500	
Equipment	78,000	
Accumulated Depreciation		14,000
Notes Payable		10,000
Capital Stock		43,000
Retained Earnings		20,600
Cash Dividends	8,000	
Service Fees Earned		71,000
Rent Expense	18,000	
Salaries Expense	37,100	
Depreciation Expense	7,000	
	158,600	158,600

Complete the worksheet by (a) entering the adjusted trial balance on paper, (b) putting in the worksheet income statement and balance sheet columns, (c) extending the adjusted trial balance to the income statement and balance sheet columns, and (d) balancing the worksheet.

REVERSING ENTRIES — APPENDIX C —

3-31A Lewis Company closes its accounts on December 31 each year. On December 31, 1996, Lewis accrued $600 of interest income that was earned on an investment but not yet received or recorded (the investment will pay interest of $900 on January 31, 1997). On January 31, 1997, the company received the $900 cash as interest on the investment. Prepare journal entries to (a) accrue the interest earned on December 31; (b) close the Interest Income account on December 31 (the account has a year-end balance of $2,400 after adjustments); (c) reverse the December 31 interest accrual on January 1; and (d) record the cash receipt of interest on January 31.

ALTERNATE PROBLEMS

SOURCE DOCUMENTS, TRANSACTION ENTRIES, POSTING, TRIAL BALANCE, AND ADJUSTING ENTRIES — OBJ. 2, 3, 4 —

3-32A Huang Karate School began business on June 1, 1997. Transactions for June were as follows:

June 1 Po Huang contributed $7,500 of his personal funds to begin the business.

2 Purchased equipment for $2,750, paying $750 cash, with the balance due in 30 days.

2 Paid six months' rent, $3,450.

3 Paid one-year premium on liability insurance, $876.

8 Paid June newspaper advertising, $225.

June 15   Billed participants for karate lessons to date, $2,200.

20   Received $555 from a local company to conduct a special three-session class on self-defense for its employees. The three sessions will be held on June 29, July 6, and July 13, at $185 per session.

21   Collected $1,800 on account from participants.

25   Paid $275 to repair damage to wall caused by an errant kick.

30   Billed participants for karate lessons to date, $2,000.

30   Paid assistant's wages, $650.

REQUIRED

a. For each transaction, indicate the related source document or documents that evidence the transaction.

b. Set up a general ledger with the following accounts, using the account numbers shown: Cash (11); Accounts Receivable (12); Prepaid Rent (13); Prepaid Insurance (14); Equipment (15); Accumulated Depreciation—Equipment (16); Accounts Payable (21); Utilities Payable (22); Unearned Karate Fees (23); P. Huang, Capital (31); Karate Fees Earned (41); Advertising Expense (51); Repairs Expense (52); Wages Expense (53); Rent Expense (54); Insurance Expense (55); Depreciation Expense—Equipment (56); and Utilities Expense (57).

c. Record these transactions in general journal form and post to the ledger accounts.

d. Take an unadjusted trial balance at June 30, 1997.

e. Make the adjusting entries for rent expense, insurance expense, depreciation expense, utilities expense, and karate fees earned. Depreciation expense for June is $50, and estimated utilities expense for June is $120. Post the adjusting entries.

TRANSACTION ENTRIES,
POSTING, TRIAL BALANCE,
AND ADJUSTING ENTRIES
— OBJ. 3, 4 —

3-33A   Market-Probe, a market research firm, had the following transactions in June 1997, its first month of operations.

June 1   J. Witson invested $24,000 of personal funds in the firm.

1   The firm purchased the following from an office supply company: office equipment, $11,040; office supplies, $2,840. Terms called for a cash payment of $4,000, with the remainder due in 60 days. (Make a compound entry.)

2   Paid June rent, $875.

2   Contracted for three months' advertising in a local newspaper at $310 per month and paid for the advertising in advance.

2   Signed a six-month contract with an electronics firm to provide research consulting services at a rate of $3,200 per month. Received two months' fees in advance. Work on the contract started immediately.

10   Billed various customers for services rendered, $5,800.

12   Paid two weeks' salaries (five-day week) to employees, $3,600.

15   Paid J. Witson's travel expenses to business conference, $1,240.

18   Paid post office for bulk mailing of survey research questionnaire, $520 (postage expense).

26   Paid two weeks' salaries to employees, $3,600.

28   Billed various customers for services rendered, $5,200.

30   Collected $7,800 from customers on account.

30   J. Witson withdrew $1,500 cash for personal use.

REQUIRED

a. Set up a general ledger that includes the following accounts, using the account numbers shown: Cash (11); Accounts Receivable (12); Office Supplies (14); Prepaid Advertising (15); Office Equipment (16); Accumulated Depreciation—Office Equipment (17); Accounts Payable (21); Salaries Payable (22); Unearned Service Fees (23); J. Witson, Capital (31); J. Witson, Drawing (32); Service Fees Earned (41); Salaries Expense (51); Advertising Expense (52); Supplies Expense (53); Rent Expense (54); Travel Expense (55); Depreciation Expense—Office Equipment (56); and Postage Expense (57).

b. Record June transactions in general journal form and post to the ledger accounts.

c. Take an unadjusted trial balance at June 30, 1997.

d. Record adjusting journal entries in general journal form, and post to the ledger accounts. The following information is available on June 30, 1997:

Office supplies on hand, $1,530.

Accrued salaries, $725.

Estimated life of office equipment, eight years.

Also, make any necessary adjusting entries for advertising and for service fees indicated by the June transactions.

TRIAL BALANCE AND ADJUSTING ENTRIES — OBJ. 4 —

3-34A   Deliverall, a mailing service, has just completed its first full year of operations on December 31, 1996. The firm's general ledger account balances before year-end adjustments are given below. No adjusting entries have been made to the accounts at any time during the year. Assume that all balances are normal.

Cash	$ 2,300	Accounts Payable	$ 2,700
Accounts Receivable	5,120	V. Pryor, Capital	9,530
Prepaid Advertising	1,680	Mailing Fees Earned	86,000
Supplies	6,270	Wages Expense	38,800
Equipment	42,240	Rent Expense	6,300
Notes Payable	7,500	Utilities Expense	3,020

An analysis of the firm's records reveals the following:
1. The balance in Prepaid Advertising represents the amount paid for newspaper advertising for one year. The agreement, which calls for the same amount of space each month, covers the period from February 1, 1996, to January 31, 1997. Deliverall did not advertise during its first month of operations.
2. The equipment, purchased January 1, has an estimated life of eight years.
3. Utilities expense does not include expense for December, estimated at $325. The bill will not arrive until January 1997.
4. At year-end, employees have earned $1,200 in wages that will not be paid until January.
5. Supplies on hand at year-end amounted to $1,520.
6. At year-end, unpaid interest of $450 has accrued on the notes payable.
7. The firm's lease calls for rent of $525 per month payable on the first of each month, plus an amount equal to $\frac{1}{2}\%$ of annual mailing fees earned. The rental percentage is payable within 15 days after the end of the year.

REQUIRED
a. Prove that debits equal credits for the unadjusted account balances shown above by preparing an unadjusted trial balance at December 31, 1996.
b. Record adjusting entries in general journal form.

ADJUSTING ENTRIES — OBJ. 4 —

3-35A   The Wheel Place, Inc., began operations on March 1, 1996, to provide automotive wheel alignment and balancing services. On March 31, 1996, the unadjusted balances of the firm's accounts are as follows:

THE WHEEL PLACE, INC.
UNADJUSTED TRIAL BALANCE
MARCH 31, 1996

	Debit	Credit
Cash	$ 1,900	
Accounts Receivable	3,820	
Prepaid Rent	4,770	
Supplies	3,700	
Equipment	36,180	
Accounts Payable		$ 2,510
Unearned Service Revenue		1,000
Capital Stock		38,400
Service Revenue		12,360
Wages Expense	3,900	
	$54,270	$54,270

The following information is also available:
1. The balance in Prepaid Rent was the amount paid on March 1 to cover the first six months' rent.
2. Supplies on hand on March 31 amounted to $1,720.
3. The equipment has an estimated life of nine years.
4. Unpaid wages at March 31 were $560.
5. Utility services used during March were estimated at $390. A bill is expected early in April.
6. The balance in Unearned Service Revenue was the amount received on March 1 from a new car dealer to cover alignment and balancing services on all new cars sold by the dealer in March and April. The Wheel Place agreed to provide the services at a fixed fee of $500 each month.

REQUIRED

In general journal form, make the adjusting entries needed at March 31, 1996.

**ADJUSTING ENTRIES
— OBJ. 4 —**

3-36A The following information relates to the December 31, 1996, adjustments for Water Barrier, a firm providing waterproofing services for commercial and residential customers. The firm's fiscal year ends December 31; no adjusting entries have been made during 1996.

1. The firm paid a $2,340 premium for a three-year insurance policy, coverage to begin October 1, 1996. The premium payment was debited to Prepaid Insurance.
2. Weekly wages for a five-day work week total $1,225, payable on Fridays. December 31, 1996, is a Thursday.
3. Water Barrier received $3,600 in November 1996 for services to be performed during December 1996 through February 1997. When received, this amount was credited to Unearned Service Fees. By December 31, one-third of this amount was earned.
4. Water Barrier receives a 5% commission from the manufacturer on sales of a waterproofing agent to Water Barrier's customers. By December 31, 1996, Water Barrier had sales of $9,000 (during November and December) for which no commissions had yet been received or recorded.
5. During December, fuel oil costs of $495 were incurred to heat the firm's buildings. Because the monthly bill from the oil company has not yet arrived, no entry has been made for this amount (fuel oil costs are charged to Utilities Expense).
6. The Supplies account has a balance of $16,900 on December 31. A count of supplies on December 31 indicates that $3,500 worth of supplies are still on hand.
7. On December 1, 1996, Water Barrier borrowed $9,000 from the bank, giving a note payable. Interest is not payable until the note is due near the end of January 1997. However, the interest for December is $75.
8. Water Barrier rents parking spaces in its lot to firms in the office building next door. On December 1, 1996, Water Barrier received $10,000 as advance payments to cover parking privileges in the lot for December 1996 through March 1997. When received, the $10,000 was credited to Unearned Parking Fees.

REQUIRED

Prepare the necessary December 31, 1996, adjusting entries in general journal form.

**FINANCIAL STATEMENTS AND
CLOSING ENTRIES FOR
CORPORATION
— OBJ. 5, 6 —**

3-37A Trails, Inc., publishes magazines for skiers and hikers. The firm has the following adjusted trial balance at December 31, 1996.

TRAILS, INC.
ADJUSTED TRIAL BALANCE
DECEMBER 31, 1996

	Debit	Credit
Cash	$ 3,400	
Accounts Receivable	8,600	
Supplies	4,200	
Prepaid Insurance	930	
Office Equipment	66,000	
Accumulated Depreciation		$ 11,000
Accounts Payable		2,100
Unearned Subscription Revenue		10,000
Salaries Payable		3,500
Capital Stock		25,000
Retained Earnings		23,220
Subscription Revenue		168,300
Advertising Revenue		49,700
Salaries Expense	100,230	
Printing and Mailing Expense	85,600	
Rent Expense	8,800	
Supplies Expense	6,100	
Insurance Expense	1,860	
Depreciation Expense	5,500	
Income Tax Expense	1,600	
	$292,820	$292,820

REQUIRED

a. Prepare an income statement for 1996 and a balance sheet at December 31, 1996.

b. Prepare closing entries in general journal form.

CLOSING ENTRIES FOR SOLE PROPRIETORSHIP
— OBJ. 6 —

3-38A The adjusted trial balance for Okay Moving Service at December 31, 1996, is shown below.

	Adjusted Trial Balance	
	Debit	**Credit**
Cash	$ 3,800	
Accounts Receivable	5,250	
Supplies	2,300	
Prepaid Advertising	3,000	
Trucks	28,300	
Accumulated Depreciation—Trucks		$ 10,000
Equipment	7,600	
Accumulated Depreciation—Equipment		2,100
Accounts Payable		1,200
Unearned Service Fees		2,700
S. Warner, Capital		26,050
S. Warner, Drawing	5,500	
Service Fees Earned		72,500
Wages Expense	29,800	
Rent Expense	10,200	
Insurance Expense	2,900	
Supplies Expense	5,100	
Advertising Expense	6,000	
Depreciation Expense—Trucks	4,000	
Depreciation Expense—Equipment	800	
	$114,550	$114,550

REQUIRED

a. Prepare the closing entries at December 31 in general journal form.

b. After the closing entries are posted, what is the balance in the S. Warner, Capital account?

c. Prepare a post-closing trial balance.

WORKSHEET
— APPENDIX B —

3-39A The July 31, 1997, unadjusted trial balance of Sharp Outfitters, a firm renting various types of equipment to canoeists and campers, follows.

SHARP OUTFITTERS
UNADJUSTED TRIAL BALANCE
JULY 31, 1997

	Debit	**Credit**
Cash	$ 3,750	
Supplies	8,600	
Prepaid Insurance	3,200	
Equipment	95,000	
Accumulated Depreciation		$ 16,500
Accounts Payable		3,500
Unearned Rental Fees		8,850
C. Sharp, Capital		39,000
C. Sharp, Drawing	1,200	
Rental Fees Earned		78,150

	Debit	Credit
Wages Expense	$ 27,800	
Rent Expense	3,300	
Advertising Expense	2,300	
Travel Expense	850	
	$146,000	$146,000

Sharp Outfitters' fiscal year ends on July 31. The following additional information is available:
1. Supplies on hand at July 31 amount to $3,300.
2. Insurance expense for the year is $1,600.
3. Depreciation for the year is $8,250.
4. The unearned rental fees consist of deposits received from customers in advance when reservations are made. During the year, $4,850 of the unearned rental fees were earned. The remaining deposits apply to rentals for August and September 1997.
5. At July 31, revenue from rental services earned during July but not yet billed or received amounts to $2,500. (*Note:* Debit Fees Receivable.)
6. Accrued wages payable for equipment handlers and guides amounts to $900 at July 31.

REQUIRED

Enter the trial balance in a worksheet and complete the worksheet using the adjustment data given above.

ADJUSTING AND REVERSING ENTRIES
— APPENDIX C —

3-40A The following selected accounts appear in Birch Company's unadjusted trial balance at December 31, 1996, the end of the fiscal year (all accounts have normal balances):

Prepaid Maintenance	$2,700	Commission Fees Earned	$84,000
Supplies	8,400	Rent Expense	10,800
Unearned Commission Fees	8,500		

REQUIRED

a. Make the necessary adjusting entries in general journal form at December 31, assuming the following:
1. On September 1, 1996, the company entered into a prepaid equipment maintenance contract. Birch Company paid $2,700 to cover maintenance service for six months, beginning September 1, 1996. The $2,700 payment was debited to Prepaid Maintenance.
2. Supplies on hand at December 31 are $3,200.
3. Unearned commission fees at December 31 are $4,000.
4. Commission fees earned but not yet billed at December 31 are $2,800. (*Note:* Debit Fees Receivable.)
5. Birch Company's lease calls for rent of $900 per month payable on the first of each month, plus an annual amount equal to 1% of annual commissions earned. This additional rent is payable on January 10 of the following year. (*Note:* Be sure to use the adjusted amount of commissions earned in computing the additional rent.)
b. Assume that the company makes reversing entries. Which of the adjustments in (a) should be reversed? Make the proper reversing entries on January 1, 1997.
c. Assume that reversing entries have been made. Prepare the journal entries on January 10, 1997, to record (1) the billing of $4,600 of commissions earned (an amount that includes the $2,800 of commissions earned but not billed at December 31) and (2) the payment of the additional rent owed for 1996.
d. Assume that reversing entries have not been made. Prepare the journal entries on January 10, 1997, to record (1) the billing of $4,600 of commissions earned (an amount that includes the $2,800 of commissions earned but not billed at December 31) and (2) the payment of the additional rent owed for 1996.

CASES

BUSINESS DECISION CASE

Wyland Consulting Services, a firm started three years ago by Bruce Wyland, offers consulting services for material handling and plant layout. The balance sheet prepared by the firm's accountant at the close of 1996 is shown on the following page.

WYLAND CONSULTING SERVICES
BALANCE SHEET
DECEMBER 31, 1996

Assets			Liabilities	
Cash		$ 3,400	Notes Payable	$30,000
Accounts Receivable		22,875	Accounts Payable	4,200
Supplies		13,200	Unearned Consulting Fees	11,300
Prepaid Insurance		4,500	Wages Payable	400
Equipment	$68,500		Total Liabilities	$45,900
Less: Accumulated			**Owner's Equity**	
Depreciation	23,975	44,525	B. Wyland, Capital	42,600
			Total Liabilities and	
Total Assets		$88,500	Owner's Equity	$88,500

Earlier in the year, Wyland obtained a bank loan of $30,000 for the firm. One of the provisions of the loan is that the year-end debt-to-equity ratio (ratio of total liabilities to total owner's equity) shall not exceed 1.0. Based on the above balance sheet, the ratio at the end of 1996 is 1.08.

Wyland is concerned about being in violation of the loan agreement and asks your assistance in reviewing the situation. Wyland believes that his rather inexperienced accountant may have overlooked some items at year-end.

In discussions with Wyland and the accountant, you learn the following:

1. On January 1, 1996, the firm paid a $4,500 insurance premium for two years of coverage. The amount in Prepaid Insurance has not been adjusted.
2. Depreciation on the equipment should be 10% of cost per year. The accountant inadvertently recorded 15% for 1996.
3. Interest on the bank loan has been paid through the end of 1996.
4. The firm concluded a major consulting engagement in December, doing a plant layout analysis for a new factory. The $6,000 fee has not been billed or recorded in the accounts.
5. On December 1, 1996, the firm received an $11,300 advance payment from Croy Corporation for consulting services to be rendered over a two-month period. This payment was credited to the Unearned Consulting Fees account. One-half of this fee was earned by December 31, 1996.
6. Supplies costing $4,800 were on hand on December 31. The accountant filed the record of the count but made no entry in the accounts.

REQUIRED
What is the correct debt-to-equity ratio at December 31, 1996? Is the firm in violation of the loan agreement? Prepare a schedule to support your computation of the correct total liabilities and total owner's equity at December 31, 1996.

ETHICS CASE I   It is the end of an accounting year for Juliet Kravetz, controller of a medium-sized, publicly held corporation specializing in toxic waste cleanup. Within the corporation, only Kravetz and the president know that the firm has been negotiating for several months to land a very large contract for waste cleanup in Western Europe. The president has hired another firm with excellent contacts in Western Europe to help with the negotiations. The outside firm will charge an hourly fee plus expenses, but has agreed not to submit a bill until the negotiations are in their final stages (expected to occur in another three to four months). Even if the contract falls through, the outside firm is entitled to receive payment for its services. Based upon her discussion with a member of the outside firm, Kravetz knows that its charge for services provided to date will be $150,000. This is a material amount for the company.

Kravetz knows that the president wants the negotiations to remain as secret as possible so that competitors will not learn of the contract the company is pursuing in Europe. Indeed, the president recently stated to her, "This is not the time to reveal our actions in Western Europe to other staff members, our auditors, or readers of our financial statements; securing this contract is crucial to our future growth." No entry has been made in the accounting records for the cost of the contract negotiations. Kravetz now faces an uncomfortable situation. The company's outside auditor has just asked her if she knows of any year-end adjustments that have not yet been recorded.

REQUIRED
What are the ethical considerations that Kravetz faces in answering the auditor's question? How should she respond to the question?

ETHICS CASE II

Ed Finlay is controller for ServiceView, Inc., a corporation that provides cable television service throughout the Midwest. His son-in-law, Bryan Foote, owns and manages a printing company, Total Print. Foote has plans to develop a specialty for Total Print in printing corporate annual reports for stockholders. Foote has asked Finlay many questions about this possible specialty, including questions about ServiceView's cost of using an outside company to do the printing of its annual reports. Finlay has been quite candid and helpful in answering Foote's questions and providing prices of the current supplier and has encouraged his son-in-law to pursue this line of business.

This morning, Finlay received a call from ServiceView's president. "I need your help, Ed," stated the president. "I am reviewing a recommendation from the purchasing department for the printing of this year's annual report. The purchasing department recommends that we continue to use Excelprint, which has been printing our annual report for the last decade and with which we have a very good relationship. However, Excelprint is not the low bidder this year; an outfit called Total Print has bid $15,000 less to do the job. Total Print's sample of its work looks very good, and I am inclined to go with the lowest bid. What do you recommend, Ed?"

REQUIRED

What are the ethical considerations that Finlay faces in answering the president's question?

GENERAL MILLS ANNUAL REPORT CASE

Refer to the annual report of General Mills, Inc., presented in Appendix K. Review the consolidated balance sheets and Note 6 dealing with balance sheet information.

REQUIRED

a. Identify two assets listed in the consolidated balance sheets that indicate that General Mills makes deferral-type adjustments. Which accounts of General Mills are affected by these adjustments?

b. Identify two liabilities listed in the consolidated balance sheets that indicate that General Mills makes accrual-type adjustments. Which accounts of General Mills are affected by these adjustments?

MINI PRACTICE SET I

COMPLETE ACCOUNTING CYCLE

Keith Howe, tax consultant, began business on December 1, 1996. December transactions were as follows.

Dec. 1 Howe invested $20,000 in the business.

2 Paid rent for December to Star Realty, $1,200.

2 Purchased various supplies on account, $1,080.

3 Purchased $9,500 of office equipment, paying $4,700 down with the balance due in 30 days.

8 Paid $1,080 on account for supplies purchased December 2.

14 Paid assistant's wages for two weeks, $900.

20 Performed consulting services for cash, $3,000.

28 Paid assistant's wages for two weeks, $900.

30 Billed clients for December consulting services, $7,200.

31 Howe withdrew $1,800 cash from the business.

REQUIRED

a. Open the following general ledger accounts, using the account numbers shown: Cash (11); Accounts Receivable (12); Fees Receivable (13); Supplies (14); Office Equipment (15); Accumulated Depreciation (16); Accounts Payable (21); Wages Payable (22); K. Howe, Capital (31); K. Howe, Drawing (32); Income Summary (33); Consulting Revenue (41); Supplies Expense (51); Wages Expense (52); Rent Expense (53); and Depreciation Expense (54).

b. Journalize the December transactions, and post to the ledger.

c. Prepare an unadjusted trial balance at December 31, 1996.

d. Journalize and post the adjusting entries at December 31, using the following information:

1. Supplies on hand at December 31 are $710.

2. Accrued wages payable at December 31 are $270.

3. Depreciation for December is $120.

4. Howe has spent 30 hours on an involved tax fraud case during December. When completed in January, his work will be billed at $75 per hour. (*Note:* The firm uses the account Fees Receivable to reflect amounts earned but not yet billed.)

e. Prepare an adjusted trial balance at December 31, 1996.

f. Prepare a December 1996 income statement and statement of owner's equity and a December 31, 1996, balance sheet.

g. Journalize and post the closing entries.

h. Prepare a post-closing trial balance at December 31, 1996.

MINI PRACTICE SET II

COMPLETE ACCOUNTING CYCLE WITH WORKSHEET AND REVERSING ENTRIES

Keith Howe, tax consultant, began business on December 1, 1996. December transactions were as follows.

Dec. 1   Howe invested $20,000 in the business.

2   Paid rent for December to Star Realty, $1,200.

2   Purchased various supplies on account, $1,080.

3   Purchased $9,500 of office equipment, paying $4,700 down with the balance due in 30 days.

8   Paid $1,080 on account for supplies purchased December 2.

14   Paid assistant's wages for two weeks, $900.

20   Performed consulting services for cash, $3,000.

28   Paid assistant's wages for two weeks, $900.

30   Billed clients for December consulting services, $7,200.

31   Howe withdrew $1,800 cash from the business.

REQUIRED

a. Open the following general ledger accounts, using the account numbers shown: Cash (11); Accounts Receivable (12); Fees Receivable (13); Supplies (14); Office Equipment (15); Accumulated Depreciation (16); Accounts Payable (21); Wages Payable (22); K. Howe, Capital (31); K. Howe, Drawing (32); Income Summary (33); Consulting Revenue (41); Supplies Expense (51); Wages Expense (52); Rent Expense (53); and Depreciation Expense (54).

b. Journalize the December transactions, and post to the ledger.

c. Prepare an unadjusted trial balance directly on a worksheet, and complete the worksheet using the following information:

1. Supplies on hand at December 31 are $710.

2. Accrued wages payable at December 31 are $270.

3. Depreciation for December is $120.

4. Howe has spent 30 hours on an involved tax fraud case during December. When completed in January, his work will be billed at $75 per hour. (*Note:* The firm uses the account Fees Receivable to reflect amounts earned but not yet billed.)

d. Prepare a December 1996 income statement and statement of owner's equity and a December 31, 1996, classified balance sheet.

e. Journalize and post adjusting and closing entries.

f. Prepare a post-closing trial balance at December 31, 1996.

g. Journalize and post the appropriate reversing entries.

4

Merchandising Operations and Classified Financial Statements

CHAPTER LEARNING OBJECTIVES

1 DESCRIBE the nature of merchandising operations and DISCUSS the operating cycle of a merchandising firm (pp. 124–126).

2 DEFINE and ILLUSTRATE trade discounts and cash discounts (pp. 126–127).

3 INTRODUCE the perpetual inventory system and ILLUSTRATE the accounting entries for merchandising transactions using the perpetual inventory system (pp. 127–132).

4 OUTLINE the procedure for taking a year-end physical inventory (p. 133).

5 DISCUSS the net price method of accounting for merchandising transactions and ILLUSTRATE its use with the perpetual inventory system (pp. 133–135).

6 DESCRIBE and ILLUSTRATE classified financial statements (pp. 135–140).

7 Financial Analysis DEFINE *gross profit percentage* and EXPLAIN its use (pp. 140–141).

CHAPTER FOCUS

In previous chapters, we described accounting for service firms. In this chapter, we introduce and discuss accounting for merchandising firms. Merchandising firms use the same accounting concepts as service firms with some additional concepts related to merchandise inventory. **Merchandise inventory** is a stock of products that a company buys from another company and makes available for sale to its customers. Merchandise inventory can include groceries for companies such as Safeway and A&P, clothing for Marshall Field's and Macy's, and household products for Wal-Mart and Walgreen's.

THE NATURE OF MERCHANDISING OPERATIONS

OBJECTIVE *1*

DESCRIBE the nature of merchandising operations and **DISCUSS** the operating cycle of a merchandising firm.

Manufacturers, wholesale distributors, and retailers are companies that deal with products rather than services. Exhibit 4-1 illustrates a typical relationship among these types of companies and the ultimate buyer, the individual consumer. The manufacturer of a product sells the product to a wholesale distributor, the wholesale distributor sells the product to a retailer, and the retailer sells the product to individual consumers.

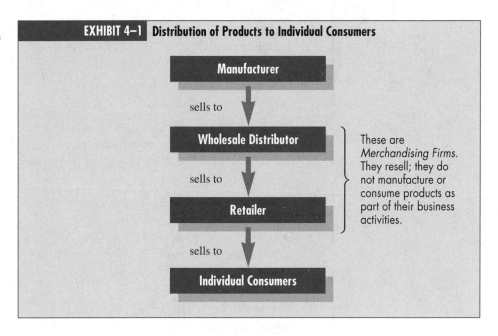

EXHIBIT 4-1 Distribution of Products to Individual Consumers

Manufacturer

sells to

Wholesale Distributor

sells to

Retailer

sells to

Individual Consumers

These are *Merchandising Firms.* They resell; they do not manufacture or consume products as part of their business activities.

CLASSIFICATION OF FIRMS

Manufacturers convert raw materials and components into finished products through the application of skilled labor and machine operations. For example, General Motors converts raw materials such as sheets of steel and components such as tires into automobiles; Del Monte converts raw materials such as fresh peaches and components such as metal cans into canned peaches. Manufacturers typically sell their products to wholesale distributors.

Wholesale distributors buy finished products from manufacturing firms in large quantities. After storing the product for a period of time, the wholesale distributor sells the product to various retailers in small quantities. Some wholesale distributors handle the products of only one manufacturer; others handle the products of multiple manufacturers. Examples of large wholesale distributors are W. W. Grainger, Inc., and Sysco Foods.

Retailers typically buy products from wholesale distributors and sell the products to individual consumers, the general public. The retailer usually has one or more store locations where it displays the products and customers view and buy the products. Radio, television, and newspaper advertisements inform potential customers of product availability and price. Retailers range in size from small, with one store location, to large, with thousands of store locations. In the U.S. economy, there are many more retailers than either manufacturers or wholesale distributors.

Some retailers, such as authorized dealerships and national retailers, buy product directly from manufacturers. **Authorized dealerships** are independent retailers that have been designated by the manufacturer to sell the manufacturer's product in a specific geographic area. Ford-authorized dealerships buy automobiles directly from Ford Motor Company and John Deere-authorized dealerships buy tractors directly from John Deere & Company.

National retailers are large retailers with hundreds of stores located throughout the United States. National retailers such as Kmart and Wal-Mart buy such huge quantities of product that they are able to require manufacturers to sell products directly to them. These products either have the **manufacturer's brand name** (such as Kleenex) on them or the retailer's **private label brand name** (such as Kmart) on them. In some cases, the manufacturer ships products to the retailer's central warehouse and the retailer distributes the product to its individual retail stores. In other cases, the manufacturer ships products directly to the individual retail stores; this approach is known as **drop-shipping.**

Wholesale distributors and retailers are both merchandising firms. **Merchandising firms** buy finished products, store the products for varying periods of time, and then resell the products. Merchandising firms do not manufacture products, nor do they consume the products that they purchase. Merchandising firms may provide services to their customers as well, but their primary business is the resale of products.

THE OPERATING CYCLE OF MERCHANDISING FIRMS

Exhibit 4-2 presents an overview of the operating cycle of a merchandising firm. There are three primary transactions in the merchandising firm's operating cycle referenced in Exhibit 4-2. These transactions are to **1** purchase merchandise for resale and place it in inventory, **2** remove merchandise from inventory and ship it to the customer, and **3** receive cash from the customer to pay accounts receivable. These transactions are related to three asset accounts: cash, inventory, and accounts receivable. Cash is used to pay for the merchandise purchased; the merchandise becomes part of the inventory; an account receivable is created when the product is shipped to the customer; and cash is received when the customer pays for the merchandise.

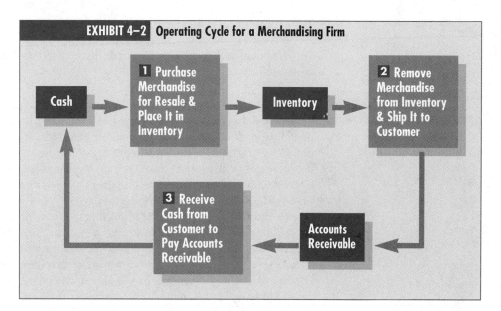

EXHIBIT 4–2 **Operating Cycle for a Merchandising Firm**

The three sequential transactions repeat frequently, creating the cycle depicted in Exhibit 4-2. The timing of the cash collection depends on the type of company making the sale and the terms of the sale. When wholesale distributors sell to retailers, they usually make the sale on a credit basis. That is, the retailer has some period of time after the sale, frequently 30 days, to pay cash to the wholesale distributor. Some retailers call a credit sale a **sale on account.** "On account" means on a credit basis.

When retailers such as Macy's or Neiman Marcus sell to individual consumers, the consumer may (1) pay cash at the time of the sale, (2) use a credit card issued by a financial institution, or (3) use an open account with the retailer. The retailer may have its own credit card to implement the open account sale. If the customer pays cash, the retailer receives cash immediately. If the customer uses a financial institution credit card, the retailer turns the credit card slips over to a financial institution and collects cash from the financial institution either the same day or within a few days of the sale. If the customer uses an open account, the retailer may not collect cash from the customer for 30 to 45 days.

TRADE DISCOUNTS ON PURCHASES AND SALES OF MERCHANDISE

OBJECTIVE 2

DEFINE and **ILLUSTRATE** trade discounts and cash discounts.

Many companies publish a catalog or price list that presents each item of merchandise that is offered for sale and its list price. **List price** is the suggested price or reference price in a catalog or price list, not necessarily the price that a purchaser will have to pay. Most sellers allow purchasers, under certain conditions, to subtract a trade discount from the list price.

A **trade discount** is an amount, usually based on quantity of merchandise purchased, that the seller subtracts from the list price to determine the invoice price. The **invoice price** is the price that the seller charges the purchaser. Often, a company states its trade discounts as a percentage of the list price. For example, Asian Electronics Manufacturing Company quotes the list price of a particular computer disk drive at $300 each. Asian Electronics also offers the following trade discount schedule for the disk drive:

1 to 29 units	10%
30 to 59 units	20%
60 or more units	30%

If Barton Wholesale Electronics Company orders 100 of these disk drives, Asian Electronics determines the invoice price in the following way:

List price ($300 × 100 units)	$30,000
Less 30% trade discount	9,000
Invoice price	$21,000

The trade discount is 30% because the order is for 60 or more units.

A system of list prices and trade discounts allows a merchandising firm to revise its invoice prices merely by changing its trade discounts. It does not have to issue a new catalog or new price list.

CASH DISCOUNTS ON PURCHASES AND SALES OF MERCHANDISE

When merchandise is sold on credit, the **credit period** is the maximum amount of time, usually stated in days, that the purchaser has to pay the seller. The length of the credit period varies from one industry to another and from one firm to another. A typical credit period for wholesale distributors is 30 days. The credit period is frequently described as the net credit period, or net terms. A merchandising firm uses the notation "n/" followed by the number of days in the credit period to designate the credit period. For example, n/30 indicates that the credit period is 30 days.

To encourage early payment of bills, many firms offer a cash discount if payment is made within a designated discount period. A **cash discount** is the amount that the seller deducts from the invoice price if the payment is made within the discount period. Sellers usually state cash discounts as a percentage of invoice price. The **discount period** is the maximum amount of time, usually stated in days, that the purchaser has to pay the seller if the purchaser wants to claim the cash discount. The discount period is always shorter than the credit period. A merchandising firm uses the format "cash discount percent/discount period" to designate the cash discount and the discount period. For example, 2/10 indicates a cash discount of 2% of invoice price and a discount period of 10 days after the date of the sale.

Merchandising companies usually combine the notation for the cash discount and the discount period with the notation for the credit period. For example, 2/10, n/30 represents a cash discount of 2% if paid within 10 days of the sale with a total credit period of 30 days after the date of the sale. Extending the example presented above, assume that Asian Electronics Manufacturing Company and Barton Wholesale Electronics Company agree on terms of 2/10, n/30 and that the sale took place on November 10. Barton may deduct 2% of the $21,000 invoice price ($420) if it pays Asian by November 20. In that case, Barton would pay $20,580. If Barton pays Asian anytime after November 20 but no later than December 10, the amount to pay is $21,000. After December 10, the $21,000 amount would be overdue. The following discussion of the perpetual inventory system contains additional examples of cash discounts.

THE PERPETUAL INVENTORY SYSTEM

OBJECTIVE *3*

INTRODUCE the perpetual inventory system and **ILLUSTRATE** the accounting entries for merchandising transactions using the perpetual inventory system.

There are two basic systems for accounting for merchandise transactions: the perpetual inventory system and the periodic inventory system. The perpetual inventory system is presented and discussed in this chapter. The periodic inventory system is presented and discussed in Appendix D. Today, more merchandising firms use the perpetual inventory system than the periodic inventory system. Companies usually implement the perpetual inventory system in a computerized environment.

The **perpetual inventory system** records the cost of merchandise inventory in the Inventory account at the time of the purchase. This system also updates the Inventory account for subsequent transactions related to merchandise as they occur. The following examples present the different types of transactions that affect the Inventory account. All of the illustrations in this chapter assume that purchasers and sellers of merchandise execute merchandise inventory transactions on a credit basis (on account) rather than a cash basis.

PURCHASES OF MERCHANDISE

When a company using the perpetual inventory system purchases merchandise, it debits the cost of the merchandise purchased to the Inventory account to reflect an increase in the inventory and credits the cost to Accounts Payable to reflect an increase in the amount owed others. Extending the preceding example, Barton Wholesale Electronics Company records its purchase of merchandise from Asian Electronics Manufacturing Company on November 10 by making the following entry:

Nov. 10	Inventory	21,000	
	Accounts Payable		21,000
	To record the purchase of 100 disk drives from Asian		
	Electronics Manufacturing Company with 2/10, n/30 terms.		

Barton Wholesale uses the gross price method of recording purchases. The **gross price method of recording purchases** records purchases of merchandise at invoice price. (In the preceding example, list price is $30,000, invoice price is $21,000, and the amount paid if the cash discount is taken is $20,580.) The gross price method of recording purchases results in the Inventory account containing a dollar amount that is net of the trade discount (the trade discount is subtracted from the list price) and gross of the cash discount (the cash discount is *not* subtracted).

TRANSPORTATION COSTS FOR MERCHANDISE

Transportation costs incurred by a merchandising company to acquire goods should be included as part of the cost of inventory. Assume Barton Wholesale Electronics Company pays $126 to a freight company on November 12 for transportation cost on the purchase of 100 disk drives. Barton makes the following entry to record the payment of $126:

Nov. 12	Inventory	126	
	Cash		126
	To record the payment of $126 of transportation costs on the		
	purchase of 100 disk drives.		

COST PRINCIPLE

The inclusion of transportation cost in the cost of inventory is consistent with the *cost principle.* The cost principle states that assets are initially recorded at the amounts paid to acquire the assets. There may be more than one expenditure associated with an asset acquisition. All such expenditures that are reasonable and necessary to acquire the asset are added into the asset's initial dollar measure.

PURCHASES RETURNS AND ALLOWANCES

Occasionally, a purchaser is dissatisfied with some or all of the merchandise that the seller has shipped. The purchaser may be dissatisfied because the merchandise was defectively manufactured, the wrong merchandise was shipped, or the merchandise was damaged during shipping. The purchaser and the seller can agree either on a merchandise return or a merchandise allowance to remedy the situation.

With a **merchandise return,** the purchaser ships the unsatisfactory merchandise back to the seller and receives a credit against the amount due for the invoice price of the merchandise returned. With a **merchandise allowance,** the purchaser keeps the merchandise, and the seller reduces the amount that the purchaser owes the seller for the shipment, in effect reducing the price.

A retailer may also return merchandise even though there is nothing wrong with it. For example, a college bookstore returns unsold textbooks to the publisher. The bookstore is unable to sell all of the textbooks it purchased and, with the consent of the publisher, returns the unsold items.

Merchandise returns and merchandise allowances are accounted for the same way: the purchaser reduces its Inventory account balance by the invoice price of the merchandise returned or the price reduction granted. Extending the previous example, assume that on November 15, Barton Wholesale returns 10 of the 100 disk drives that were purchased on November 10 because Barton Wholesale believes it can only sell 90 disk drives to its customers. There is nothing wrong the with the disk drives that Barton Wholesale returns to Asian Electronics. Assuming that Barton Wholesale has not yet paid Asian Electronics, Barton Wholesale makes the following entry on November 15 to record the merchandise return:

Nov. 15	Accounts Payable	2,100	
	Inventory		2,100
	To record the return of 10 disk drives at an invoice price of		
	$210 each.		

This entry reduces the balance in the Inventory account for the units returned and reduces the amount owed to Asian Electronics. When the purchaser and seller reach agreement on how to handle a merchandise return, they also have to agree about which party should pay the freight on the merchandise being returned. Usually, the seller pays the freight when the goods are returned because of the purchaser's dissatisfaction.

POINT OF INTEREST

BAR CODES ON INVENTORY

Merchandising firms with many items in their inventories are using bar codes with computerized inventory systems. The merchandising firm prints bar codes on the outside of cartons containing merchandise. Humans with bar code scanners or robots with built-in scanners read these bar codes to identify the contents of the cartons as they are moved into and out of the warehouse.

PAYMENTS FOR MERCHANDISE PURCHASED

The purchaser makes a timely cash payment to the seller either between the date of sale and the end of the discount period or between the date after the end of the discount period and the end of the credit period. However, the cash discount is taken only if the cash payment is made between the date of sale and the end of the discount period.

Extending the previous example, Barton Wholesale Electronics Company owes $18,900 to Asian Electronics Manufacturing Company ($21,000 purchase – $2,100 return = $18,900). Assume that Barton Wholesale makes the cash payment on November 20, the last day of the discount period. (November 11, the first day after the date of the sale, is the first day of the discount period, and November 20 is the tenth or last day of the discount period.) Barton Wholesale records the cash payment with the following entry:

Nov. 20	Accounts Payable	18,900	
	Inventory		378
	Cash		18,522
	To record the payment to Asian Electronics within the discount period.		

This entry reduces to zero the amount that Barton Wholesale owes Asian Electronics. It also records the cash discount of 2% ($18,900 × 2% = $378) as a reduction of the cost in the Inventory account. Finally, the entry reveals that $18,522 of cash was paid by Barton Wholesale to Asian Electronics ($18,900 – $378 = $18,522). It is important to note two aspects of this transaction. First, the cash discount applies only to the cost of the merchandise, not to the transportation cost. Second, the invoice price of the merchandise returned is subtracted from the total invoice price before the cash discount is calculated.

If Barton Wholesale makes the payment within the discount period, the net total cost in Barton Wholesale's Inventory account related to the disk drives is:

November 10 purchase (+100 units)	+ $21,000
November 12 transportation	+ 126
November 15 purchase return (–10 units)	– 2,100
November 20 cash discount	– 378
	$18,648

The previous transactions assigned a total cost of $18,648 to the 90 disk drives in the inventory (100 purchased – 10 purchase return). This results in an average cost per disk drive of $207.20 ($18,648/90 disk drive). Note that the preceding schedule includes only the inventory costs related to the disk drives. The Inventory account also includes costs related to other items of merchandise.

If Barton Wholesale had made the cash payment sometime between November 21 and December 10 (after the discount period), the cash discount would not apply. Barton Wholesale would have recorded a cash payment on November 25 with the following entry:

Nov. 25	Accounts Payable	18,900	
	Cash		18,900
	To record the payment to Asian Electronics outside the discount period.		

In this situation, when Barton Wholesale makes the payment outside the discount period, the net total cost in Barton Wholesale's Inventory account related to the disk drives would be as follows:

November 10 purchase (+100 units)	+ $21,000
November 12 transportation	+ 126
November 15 purchase return (–10 units)	– 2,100
	$19,026

A total cost of $19,026 would be assigned to the 90 disk drives in the inventory. This would result in an average cost per disk drive of $211.40 ($19,026/90 disk drives). The cost per disk drive would be higher in this situation because Barton Wholesale did not take the cash discount.

POINT OF INTEREST

CASH DISCOUNTS VERSUS INTEREST ON BORROWINGS

Companies try to maintain a good cash position so they can take advantage of cash discounts. If a purchaser makes a purchase with 2/10, n/30 terms, the purchaser has 10 days to make the payment within the discount period or 30 days to make the payment outside the discount period. Passing up the discount is the same as paying 2% interest to use the amount owed for 20 days, which is equivalent to paying 36.5% for 365 days (365/20 × 2% = 36.5%). This annual interest rate is significantly higher than the 12% to 15% annual rate a company would pay a bank for a loan.

SALES OF MERCHANDISE

Manufacturing firms and merchandising firms use the Sales account to record the revenue from sale of product. These firms credit Sales when they sell merchandise, either on a credit basis or a cash basis. The Sales account has a normal credit balance. Manufacturing firms and merchandising firms record only sales of merchandise in the Sales account.

Extending the previous example, assume that Barton Wholesale Electronics Company sells 15 of the computer disk drives purchased from Asian Electronics Manufacturing Company (cost per unit = $207.20) to Computer Outlet Company at a sales price per unit of $280 each. Barton Wholesale makes the credit sale on December 12 with 1/10, n/15 terms. Computer Outlet Company pays for the shipping cost. Barton Wholesale makes the following two entries to record the sale:

Dec. 12	Accounts Receivable	4,200	
	Sales		4,200
	To record the sale of 15 disk drives at a sales price of $280 each to Computer Outlet Company with credit terms of 1/10, n/15.		
12	Cost of Goods Sold	3,108	
	Inventory		3,108
	To record the sale of 15 disk drives with a unit cost of $207.20 to Computer Outlet Company.		

The first entry records $4,200 revenue ($280 × 15 disk drives) from the sale. The debit to Accounts Receivable increases the amount due from customers, and the credit to Sales increases the total revenue from sales of merchandise during the accounting period. The Sales account shows the total invoice price charged to customers for all goods sold during the current accounting period.

Selling merchandise creates a new expense: cost of goods sold. **Cost of goods sold** is the total cost of the merchandise sold to customers during the accounting period. The second entry transfers the $3,108 cost of the merchandise sold ($207.20 × 15 disk drives) from Inventory to Cost of Goods Sold. The debit to Cost of Goods Sold increases the total cost of all the merchandise sold during the accounting period and the credit to Inventory removes the cost of the merchandise sold from the Inventory account.

PRINCIPLE ALERT

REVENUE RECOGNITION PRINCIPLE AND MATCHING CONCEPT

The entry to record sales revenue when 15 disk drives are sold to Computer Outlet Company illustrates the *revenue recognition principle*. For a merchandising firm, the revenue recognition principle states that revenue should be recorded when goods are sold. Normally, this is the earliest point in time that the revenue is both earned (entity has made the economic effort to sell goods) and realized (entity has received payment or has a claim to receive payment for the goods).

The entry to record the cost of goods sold illustrates the *matching concept*. The matching concept states that expenses should be recorded in the same accounting period as the revenues they help generate. As an expense, cost of goods sold may be related (or matched) with specific sales revenue. The matching concept requires that cost of goods sold be recorded in the same accounting period as the related sales revenue.

After recording the sale of merchandise, the net total cost in Barton Wholesale's Inventory account related to the disk drives is $15,540 ($21,000 November 10 purchase + $126 transportation cost − $2,100 purchase return − $378 cash discount on purchase − $3,108 cost of units sold on December 12). The $15,540 cost relates to the 75 disk drives (100 purchased − 10 returned − 15 sold) remaining in the inventory. The average cost per disk drive is still $207.20 ($15,540/75 disk drives).

DELIVERY EXPENSE

A merchandising firm may bear the cost of shipping goods to a buyer. When this occurs, the seller charges the payment to *Delivery Expense*. Sometimes a seller will pay the shipping costs even though it is a cost that is to be borne by the buyer. This frequently happens, for example, when goods are sold through the mail. In these cases, the seller debits the shipping payment to Accounts Receivable.

SALES RETURNS AND ALLOWANCES

Occasionally, a customer is dissatisfied with some or all of the merchandise purchased. As previously noted, the customer may be dissatisfied because wrong or defective merchandise was shipped, the merchandise was damaged during shipping, or the customer may have ordered too much merchandise. The customer and the seller can agree either on a merchandise return or a merchandise allowance to remedy the situation. With a merchandise return, the customer ships the merchandise back to the seller and the customer receives a reduction in the amount due to the seller. With a merchandise allowance, the customer keeps the merchandise, and the seller reduces the amount the customer owes it, in effect reducing the price.

Accounting for sales returns and allowances requires two entries. The first entry offsets the revenue generated from the sale and reduces the amount owed by the customer. The second entry transfers the cost of the merchandise from cost of goods sold back to the inventory. Extending the previous example, assume that on December 15, Computer Outlet Company returned five of the disk drives that it had bought on December 12. Computer Outlet returns the units because it ordered five too many; there is nothing wrong with the disk drives. Barton Wholesale records the sales return by making the following two entries:

Dec. 15	Sales Returns and Allowances	1,400	
	Accounts Receivable		1,400
	To record the return of 5 disk drives by Computer Outlet Company; sales price was $280 each.		
15	Inventory	1,036	
	Cost of Goods Sold		1,036
	To record the return of 5 disk drives with a unit cost of $207.20 from Computer Outlet Company.		

The first December 15 entry, based on sales price, offsets the revenue generated from the sale by debiting Sales Returns and Allowances and reduces the amount the customer owes by crediting Accounts Receivable. Sales Returns and Allowances is a contra revenue account.

POINT OF INTEREST

MONITORING SALES RETURNS AND ALLOWANCES

Companies accumulate sales in one account and sales returns and allowances in another account so they can compare the two amounts. A high ratio of sales returns and allowances to sales is undesirable, often indicating a problem in the quality of the merchandise or its packaging. A company compares the ratio for the current year to prior year ratios and the target ratio set for the current year to determine how well the company is doing.

The second December 15 entry, based on cost, transfers the cost of the merchandise from cost of goods sold back to the inventory by debiting Inventory (increasing it) and by crediting Cost of Goods Sold (decreasing it). After recording the transfer from cost of goods sold to the inventory, the net total cost in Barton Wholesale's Inventory account related to the disk drives is

November 10 purchase (+100 units)	+	$21,000
November 12 transportation	+	126
November 15 purchase return (−10 units)	−	2,100
November 20 cash discount	−	378
December 12 sale (−15 units)	−	3,108
December 15 sales return (+5 units)	+	1,036
		$16,576

The $16,576 total cost relates to 80 units (100 purchased − 10 purchase return − 15 sold + 5 sales return). The average cost of the disk drives is still $207.20 ($16,576/80 disk drives).

PAYMENTS RECEIVED FROM CUSTOMERS

When making a cash payment, the customer takes a cash discount only if the payment is made between the date of sale and the end of the discount period. If a cash discount is taken, the seller records it in a separate account, Sales Discounts.

Continuing the previous example, assume Computer Outlet Company pays the amount due Barton Wholesale Electronics Company after deducting a 1% cash discount on December 22, the last day of the cash discount period (December 13 is the first day of the discount period and December 22 is the tenth or last day of the discount period.) Barton Wholesale makes the following entry to record the cash received from Computer Outlet:

Dec. 22	Cash	2,772	
	Sales Discounts	28	
	Accounts Receivable		2,800
	To record the cash payment from Computer Outlet Company within the discount period.		

This entry reduces the amount the customer, Computer Outlet, owes the seller, Barton Wholesale, to zero. The total amount due from Computer Outlet Company is $2,800 ($4,200 sale − $1,400 sales return). The terms of the sale are 1/10, n/15. The cash discount, or sales discount, is $28 ($2,800 × 1%). The amount of cash collected, $2,772, is the amount due less the sales discount ($2,800 − $28).

Just as companies accumulate sales returns and allowances in a separate account, they also accumulate sales discounts in still another account. This allows management to monitor the dollar amount of sales discounts being taken by customers. Sales Discounts is a contra revenue account, like Sales Returns and Allowances. Both accounts are contra to (or offset against) the Sales account. Note two important aspects of the sales discount computation. First, the cash discount applies only to the sales price of the merchandise, not to any transportation cost. Second, the sales price of any merchandise returned must be subtracted from the total amount before calculating the cash discount.

Net sales is the total revenue generated through merchandise sales less the revenue given up through sales returns and allowances and through sales (cash) discounts. A company calculates net sales for an accounting period by subtracting the balances of the Sales Returns and Allowances account (normal debit balance) and the Sales Discounts account (normal debit balance) from the balance of the Sales account (normal credit balance).

If Computer Outlet Company makes the cash payment anytime after December 22 (after the discount period), the cash discount does not apply. For example, Barton Wholesale records cash received as full payment from Computer Outlet on December 27 with the following entry:

Dec. 27	Cash	2,800	
	Accounts Receivable		2,800
	To record the cash payment from Computer Outlet Company outside the discount period.		

PHYSICAL INVENTORY

OBJECTIVE 4
OUTLINE the procedure for taking a year-end physical inventory.

As the preceding entries illustrate, the perpetual inventory system updates the balance of the Inventory account as each transaction related to the merchandise inventory occurs. When a company reaches the end of the accounting period, however, it usually wants to verify that the ending balance in the Inventory account is correct. It is possible that changes in the quantity of particular items could have taken place without a transaction being recognized. For example, quantities of various items may have been stolen. Also, the seller might have shipped an incorrect quantity to a customer even though the seller reflected the correct quantity in the journal entry.

A company takes a physical inventory to verify the inventory balance. The **physical inventory,** often taken at year-end, consists of the following steps:

1. Count the number of each individual item of merchandise in stock at the end of the year.
2. Determine the unit cost of each individual item and multiply its quantity times its unit cost to obtain the total cost for each individual item.
3. Add together the total costs of all the individual items to obtain the total cost of the complete inventory.

If the physical inventory results in a total that does not agree with the balance in the Inventory account, the company makes a year-end adjusting entry. If the physical inventory total is less than the Inventory account balance, the company makes an entry debiting Cost of Goods Sold and crediting Inventory for the difference between the physical inventory total and the balance in the Inventory account. This entry decreases the balance in the Inventory account and adds the cost of the inventory shortage to Cost of Goods Sold. The cost associated with the inventory shortage is known as **inventory shrinkage.**

If the physical inventory total is greater than the Inventory account balance, the company makes an entry debiting Inventory and crediting Cost of Goods Sold for the difference between the physical inventory and the Inventory account balance. This entry increases the balance in the Inventory account and subtracts the cost of the inventory overage from Cost of Goods Sold.

Assume that the December 31 balance of Barton Wholesale Electronic Company's Inventory account (including all items) is $120,600. Also assume that the physical inventory total cost at December 31 is $120,000. Barton Wholesale makes the following adjusting entry at December 31 to adjust the balance in the Inventory account from $120,600 to $120,000:

Dec. 31	Cost of Goods Sold	600	
	Inventory		600
	To adjust the perpetual inventory balance in the Inventory account to the total cost determined by the physical inventory.		

Barton Wholesale makes this adjusting entry at the same time it makes other year-end adjusting entries.

THE NET PRICE METHOD OF RECORDING PURCHASES

OBJECTIVE 5
DISCUSS the net price method of accounting for merchandising transactions and **ILLUSTRATE** its use with the perpetual inventory system.

The prior examples in this chapter use the gross price method of recording merchandise purchases. Some merchandising firms use the net price method of recording purchases instead. A firm using the **net price method of recording purchases** anticipates taking cash discounts on merchandise purchases and initially records such purchases at net price (net of the cash discount). Exhibit 4-3 shows the relationship among list price, gross price, and net price. List price minus trade discount equals gross price, also known as *invoice price*. Gross price minus cash discount available equals net price.

The net price method is used with both the perpetual inventory system and the periodic inventory system. A company uses the net price method if it expects to take cash discounts on merchandise purchased. The principal advantage of the net price method is that it focuses

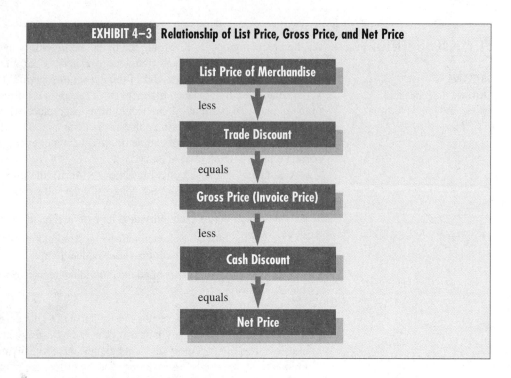

EXHIBIT 4–3 Relationship of List Price, Gross Price, and Net Price

attention on cash discounts not taken. The following discussion points out the three entries in the prior examples that are different if Barton Wholesale Electronics Company uses the net price method.

PURCHASE OF MERCHANDISE

If Barton Wholesale uses the net price method, it records the November 10 purchase net of the cash discount:

Nov. 10	Inventory	20,580	
	Accounts Payable		20,580
	To record the purchase of 100 disk drives from Asian		
	Electronics Manufacturing Company with 2/10, n/30 terms.		

This entry records both the increase in the Inventory account and the increase in the amount owed. The dollar amounts are net of the trade discount *and* net of the cash discount.

PURCHASES RETURNS AND ALLOWANCES

If Barton Wholesale uses the net price method, it also records the merchandise return net of the cash discount:

Nov. 15	Accounts Payable	2,058	
	Inventory		2,058
	To record the return of 10 disk drives at an invoice price of		
	$210 each less a 2% cash discount.		

PAYMENT FOR MERCHANDISE PURCHASED

If Barton Wholesale uses the net price method, it also records the payment on November 20 net of the cash discount:

Nov. 20	Accounts Payable	18,522	
	Cash		18,522
	To record the payment to Asian Electronics within the discount		
	period.		

If, instead, the payment is made on November 25, outside the discount period, Barton Wholesale makes the following entry:

Nov. 25	Accounts Payable	18,522	
	Inventory	378	
	Cash		18,900
	To record the payment to Asian Electronics outside the		
	discount period.		

In this situation, Barton Wholesale did not take the cash discount even though it had been anticipated. The entry adds the amount of the cash discount lost to the previously recorded cost of the inventory ($20,580 purchase − $2,058 return + $378 discount lost = $18,900). This total cost agrees with the cost of the inventory acquired ($30,000 list price − $9,000 trade discount − $2,100 returned at invoice price − $0 cash discount).

CLASSIFIED FINANCIAL STATEMENTS

OBJECTIVE *6*
DESCRIBE and **ILLUSTRATE**
classified financial statements.

In previous chapters, we have presented simple financial statements. On the income statement, we grouped items as revenues and expenses. On the balance sheet, we grouped items as assets, liabilities, and owners' equity. To make financial statements more useful to management, creditors, owners, and potential investors, the items on these financial statements should be classified into defined subgroups. Financial statements constructed in this manner are called classified financial statements. In this chapter, we describe and illustrate the classified income statement and classified balance sheet.

CLASSIFIED INCOME STATEMENT

A **classified income statement** presents revenues and expenses in distinct categories to facilitate financial analysis and management decision making. Exhibit 4-4 presents the

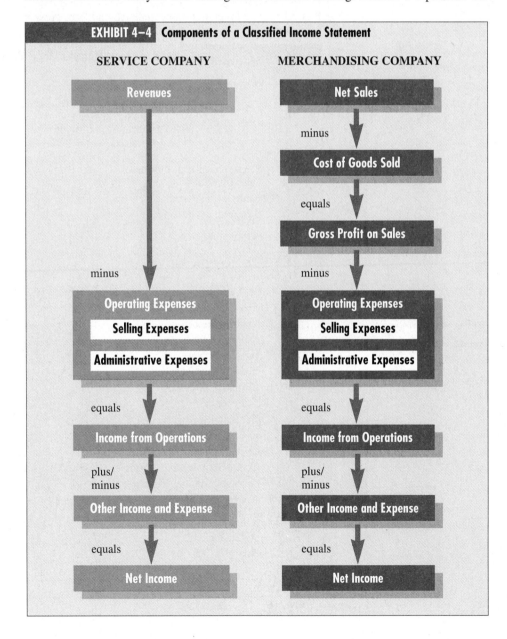

EXHIBIT 4–4 **Components of a Classified Income Statement**

components of a classified income statement for a service company and the components of a classified income statement for a merchandising company. For a service company, total operating expenses are subtracted from total revenues to determine income from operations. Operating expenses are those expenses that relate to the primary functions of the business. Operating expenses are classified as either selling expenses or administrative expenses. Revenue and expense items that do not relate to the primary operating activities of the company appear in a separate grouping called *other income and expense*. The net amount of other income and expense is either added to or subtracted from income from operations to determine net income.

For a merchandising company, cost of goods sold is subtracted from net sales to determine gross profit on sales. **Gross profit on sales** is defined as the difference between net sales and cost of goods sold. **Gross margin** is an alternative title for gross profit on sales. The remainder of the structure of a merchandising company's classified income statement is basically the same as the structure of the service company's classified income statement.

Exhibit 4-5 presents a classified income statement for Barton Wholesale Electronics Company, a merchandising company, for the year ended December 31, 1996. The revenue or net sales section includes total sales reduced by sales returns and allowances and sales discounts. Cost of goods sold is typically the largest expense for a merchandising company. It is subtracted directly from net sales to highlight gross profit on sales.

EXHIBIT 4–5 **Classified Income Statement for a Merchandising Company**

BARTON WHOLESALE ELECTRONICS COMPANY
INCOME STATEMENT
FOR THE YEAR ENDED DECEMBER 31, 1996

Sales			$433,000
Less: Sales Returns and Allowances		$2,500	
Sales Discounts		5,500	8,000
Net Sales			$425,000
Cost of Goods Sold			255,000
Gross Profit on Sales			$170,000
Operating Expenses			
Selling Expenses			
Sales Salaries Expense	$64,500		
Delivery Expense	19,250		
Advertising Expense	6,170		
Depreciation Expense	6,000		
Insurance Expense	280		
Total Selling Expenses		$96,200	
Administrative Expenses			
Rent Expense	$16,500		
Office Salaries Expense	26,800		
Insurance Expense	1,700		
Supplies Expense	1,200		
Total Administrative Expenses		46,200	
Total Operating Expenses			142,400
Income from Operations			$ 27,600
Other Income and Expense			
Interest Expense			2,100
Net Income			$ 25,500

The operating expenses section includes those expenses that relate to the primary operating functions of the business. All operating expenses are classified as either selling expenses or administrative expenses. In Exhibit 4-5, sales salaries expense, delivery expense, advertising expense, depreciation expense, and insurance expense are selling expenses. Rent expense, office salaries expense, insurance expense, and supplies expense are administrative expenses.

Certain types of operating expenses appear under both the selling and administrative categories. In Exhibit 4-5, notice that insurance expense appears under selling expenses ($280) and under administrative expenses ($1,700). Part of insurance expense applies to the selling function (for example, insurance on salespersons' cars) and part of it applies to the administrative function (for example, insurance on administrative computers). An allocation assigns insurance expense on the basis of benefit received by the selling function and the administrative function. Classified income statements for other companies might show items such as depreciation expense, supplies expense, and rent expense allocated between the selling and administrative categories.

Examples of revenues and expenses that do not relate to the primary operating activities of a merchandising firm include interest income, interest expense, dividend income, and foreign currency gains and losses. These items are reported in the other income and expense section that follows the information on the primary operating activities.

CLASSIFIED BALANCE SHEET

A **classified balance sheet** presents assets and liabilities in defined subgroups to facilitate financial analysis and management decision making. Exhibit 4-6 presents the available components for a classified balance sheet; each company uses the components it needs to report its financial position. Assets are classified into five subgroups: current assets, plant assets, investments, natural resources, and intangible assets. Liabilities are classified into two subgroups: current liabilities and long-term liabilities.

CURRENT ASSETS

Current assets are cash and other assets that will be converted to cash or used up during the normal operating cycle of the business or one year, whichever is longer. The **normal operating cycle** of a business is the average period of time between the use of cash in its typical operating activity and the subsequent collection of cash from customers. In a service business, the operating cycle includes two steps: (1) the firm uses cash to provide services which create accounts receivable, and (2) the firm generates cash when receivables are collected. As discussed earlier, the operating cycle for a merchandising business includes three steps: (1) the firm uses cash to buy merchandise, (2) the firm sells merchandise to its customers which create accounts receivable, and (3) the firm generates cash when receivables are collected. For most service and merchandising businesses, the normal operating cycle is less than one year.

Current assets are listed on a classified balance sheet in the order of their liquidity. Liquidity is determined by the ability to be converted into cash. Exhibit 4-6 lists five examples of current assets in the order of their liquidity: cash, accounts receivable, inventory, supplies, and prepaid expenses. Accounts receivable and inventory are converted to cash during normal operations. Supplies and prepaid expenses are normally consumed during the operating cycle rather than converted into cash.

POINT OF INTEREST

DIFFERENT LEVELS OF CURRENT ASSETS

The level of various current assets differs dramatically between companies. In recent annual reports, OshKosh B'Gosh, Inc., reported $99,999,000 of inventory (which represented 65.9% of its current assets) and Clark Equipment Company reported $123,728,000 of inventory (which represented only 25.0% of its current assets).

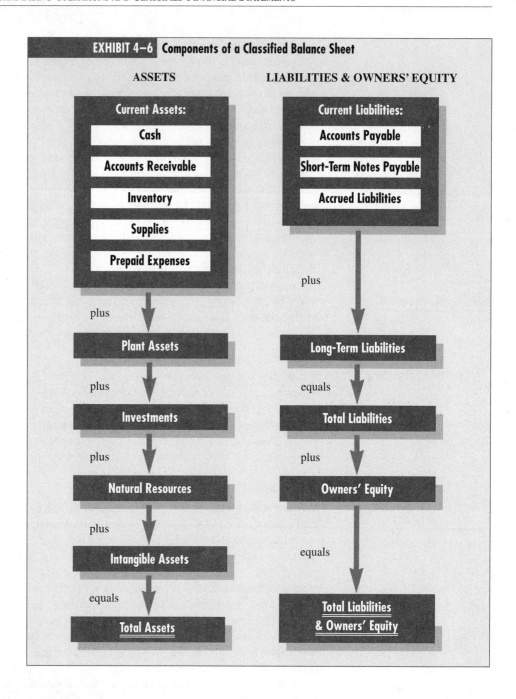

EXHIBIT 4–6 Components of a Classified Balance Sheet

ASSETS

LIABILITIES & OWNERS' EQUITY

Current Assets:
- Cash
- Accounts Receivable
- Inventory
- Supplies
- Prepaid Expenses

plus

Plant Assets

plus

Investments

plus

Natural Resources

plus

Intangible Assets

equals

Total Assets

Current Liabilities:
- Accounts Payable
- Short-Term Notes Payable
- Accrued Liabilities

plus

Long-Term Liabilities

equals

Total Liabilities

plus

Owners' Equity

equals

Total Liabilities & Owners' Equity

PLANT ASSETS

Plant assets are the land, buildings, equipment, vehicles, furniture, and fixtures that a firm uses in its operations. This section of a classified balance sheet may also be labeled *property and equipment* or *property, plant, and equipment.*

OTHER ASSET CATEGORIES

Other categories of assets include investments, natural resources, and intangible assets. We discuss and illustrate these types of assets in later chapters.

CURRENT LIABILITIES

Current liabilities are liabilities that must be settled within the normal operating cycle or one year, whichever is longer. Exhibit 4-6 lists three types of current liabilities: accounts payable, short-term notes payable, and accrued liabilities. Accrued liabilities may include wages, utilities, interest, income tax, and property tax. Current liabilities may also include advance payments received from customers that will be earned as revenue within the normal operating cycle or one year, whichever is longer.

LONG-TERM LIABILITIES

Long-term liabilities are debt obligations not due to be settled within the normal operating cycle or one year, whichever is longer. Long-term notes payable and bonds payable are two examples of long-term liabilities. Any portion of a long-term liability that is due within the next year is classified as a current liability.

OWNERS' EQUITY

The owners' interest in the assets of a firm appears in the owners' equity section of a classified balance sheet. For sole proprietorships and partnerships, the interest is reflected in a capital account for each owner. A corporation labels its owners' equity as *stockholders' equity* or *shareholders' equity.* This equity is divided into two main categories: amounts invested by owners (capital stock) and cumulative net incomes not yet distributed to owners as dividends (retained earnings). These two categories are examined in greater detail in later chapters.

BALANCE SHEET FORMAT

The two acceptable formats for presenting classified balance sheets are the account form and the report form. Exhibit 4-7 presents the account form of a classified balance sheet for Barton Wholesale Electronics Company as of December 31, 1996. In the *account form,* assets are displayed on the left side and liabilities and owners' equity are displayed on the

---

EXHIBIT 4–7 **Account Form of a Classified Balance Sheet**

BARTON WHOLESALE ELECTRONICS COMPANY
BALANCE SHEET
DECEMBER 31, 1996

Assets			Liabilities		
Current Assets			**Current Liabilities**		
Cash	$ 23,210		Accounts Payable	$ 17,500	
Accounts Receivable	32,000		Salaries Payable	500	
Inventory	120,000		Total Current Liabilities		$ 18,000
Supplies	1,600		**Long-Term Liabilities**		
Prepaid Insurance	990		Long-Term Notes Payable		20,000
Total Current Assets		$177,800	Total Liabilities		$ 38,000
Plant Assets					
Delivery Equipment	$ 30,000		**Owner's Equity**		
Less: Accumulated			J. Barton, Capital		159,500
Depreciation	10,300	19,700	Total Liabilities and		
Total Assets		$197,500	Owner's Equity		$197,500

---

right side. Exhibit 4-8 presents the *report form* of a classified balance sheet for Barton Wholesale Electronics Company as of December 31, 1996. In the report form, assets are displayed first. Liabilities are then displayed below assets, and owners' equity is displayed below liabilities. Both formats are widely used.

EXHIBIT 4–8	Report Form of a Classified Balance Sheet

BARTON WHOLESALE ELECTRONICS COMPANY
BALANCE SHEET
DECEMBER 31, 1996

Assets

Current Assets

Cash	$ 23,210	
Accounts Receivable	32,000	
Inventory	120,000	
Supplies	1,600	
Prepaid Insurance	990	
Total Current Assets		$177,800

Plant Assets

Delivery Equipment	$ 30,000	
Less: Accumulated Depreciation	10,300	19,700
Total Assets		$197,500

Liabilities

Current Liabilities

Accounts Payable	$ 17,500	
Salaries Payable	500	
Total Current Liabilities		$ 18,000

Long-Term Liabilities

Long-Term Notes Payable		20,000
Total Liabilities		$ 38,000

Owner's Equity

J. Barton, Capital		159,500
Total Liabilities and Owner's Equity		$197,500

FINANCIAL ANALYSIS

GROSS PROFIT PERCENTAGE

Managers, investors, and outsiders monitor gross profit on sales very closely. They know that if gross profit on sales decreases from one year to the next, net income for the second year probably will be lower than for the first year. People who monitor gross profit on sales are usually also very interested in the **gross profit percentage,** the rate at which a company earns gross profit on sales. A merchandising company calculates its gross profit percentage as follows:

$$\text{Gross Profit Percentage} = \frac{\text{Gross Profit on Sales}}{\text{Net Sales}}$$

The income statement for Barton Wholesale Electronics Company for the year ended December 31, 1996 (Exhibit 4-5), includes the following amounts:

Net Sales	$425,000
Cost of Goods Sold	255,000
Gross Profit on Sales	$170,000

The gross profit percentage for Barton Wholesale Electronics Company for 1996 is $170,000/$425,000 = 0.40, or 40%. We could also calculate the **cost of goods sold percentage** for Barton Company by dividing cost of goods sold by net sales ($255,000/ $425,000 = 0.60, or 60%).

The following display summarizes these percentages for Barton Wholesale:

Net Sales	$425,000	100%
Cost of Goods Sold	255,000	60%
Gross Profit on Sales	$170,000	40%

This display highlights the relationship among net sales, cost of goods sold, and gross profit on sales. Note that a gross profit percentage of 40% means that 60% of Barton Wholesale's sales dollars were needed to cover the cost of the merchandise sold and only 40% were available to cover other expenses and to generate net income.

Financial analysis of the gross profit percentage for a particular company frequently involves a comparative analysis among multiple years or among multiple companies in the same industry. Abbott Laboratories, a diversified health care company well known for its pharmaceutical products, had the following operating results over three recent, consecutive years (in millions of dollars—Year 3 is the most recent year):

	Year 3	Year 2	Year 1
Net Sales	$8,408	$7,852	$6,877
Cost of Goods Sold	3,685	3,505	3,140
Gross Profit on Sales	4,723	4,347	3,737

We calculate the gross profit percentage for each of the three years as follows:

$$\text{Year 3: } \$4,723/\$8,408 = 56.2\%$$
$$\text{Year 2: } \$4,347/\$7,852 = 55.4\%$$
$$\text{Year 1: } \$3,737/\$6,877 = 54.3\%$$

Over the three-year period, the gross profit percentage increased from 54.3% to 55.4% to 56.2%. This trend is clearly favorable. It indicates that revenues from sales increased faster than the cost of the merchandise sold.

KEY POINTS FOR CHAPTER LEARNING OBJECTIVES

1 **DESCRIBE** the nature of merchandising operations and **DISCUSS** the operating cycle of a merchandising firm (pp. 124–126).
- Merchandise inventory is a stock of products that a company buys from another company and makes available for sale to its customers.
- Merchandising firms sell merchandise. There are two types of merchandising firms: wholesale distributors and retailers.
- Manufacturers convert raw materials and components into finished products through the application of skilled labor and machine operations; wholesale distributors buy finished product from manufacturing firms in large quantities and sell smaller quantities to retailers; retailers sell the products to individual consumers.
- The operating cycle of a merchandising firm consists of three types of transactions: purchase merchandise for resale and place in inventory, remove from inventory and ship to customer, and receive cash from customer.

2 **DEFINE** and **ILLUSTRATE** trade discounts and cash discounts (pp. 126–127).
- A trade discount is an amount, usually based on quantity of merchandise purchased, that the seller subtracts from the list price to determine the invoice price.
- A cash discount is the amount that the seller deducts from the invoice price if the payment is made within the discount period.
- Cash discount terms are usually presented in the form 2/10, n/30, which means that a 2% discount can be taken if the amount due is paid within 10 days; no cash discount can be taken if the amount is paid between 11 and 30 days from the date of sale.

3 **INTRODUCE** the perpetual inventory system and **ILLUSTRATE** the accounting entries for merchandising transactions using the perpetual inventory system (pp. 127–132).
- The perpetual inventory system records the cost of merchandise in the Inventory account at the time of purchase and updates the Inventory account for subsequent transactions as they occur.
- When the perpetual inventory system is used with the gross price method, the Inventory account is affected by merchandise transactions as follows:
  - Debited for the invoice price of purchases.
  - Debited for transportation costs.
  - Credited for the cost of purchases returns and allowances.

- Credited for cash discounts taken.
- Credited for the cost of the merchandise sold.
- Debited for the cost of any sales returns.

4 **OUTLINE** the procedure for taking a year-end physical inventory (p. 133).
- The year-end physical inventory is taken to verify the inventory balance. It consists of three steps:
    - Count the number of each individual item of merchandise in stock at the end of the year.
    - Determine the unit cost of each individual item and multiply its quantity times its unit cost to obtain the total cost for each individual item of merchandise.
    - Add together the total costs of all the individual items to obtain the total cost of the complete inventory.
- If the result of the physical inventory does not agree with the perpetual inventory balance, an adjusting journal entry is required to adjust the balance in the Inventory account to the amount of the physical inventory.

5 **DISCUSS** the net price method of accounting for merchandising transactions and **ILLUSTRATE** its use with the perpetual inventory system (pp. 133–135).
- The net price method of recording purchases anticipates taking cash discounts on merchandise purchases and initially records such purchases at net price (net of the cash discount).
- If the cash discount is subsequently lost, it is added back to the Inventory account.

6 **DESCRIBE** and **ILLUSTRATE** classified financial statements (pp. 135–140).
- A classified income statement for a merchandising firm often includes one section for revenues; two sections for expenses: cost of goods sold and operating expenses; and an other income and expense section.
- A classified balance sheet contains five subgroups of assets (current assets, plant assets, investments, natural resources, and intangible assets), two subgroups of liabilities (current liabilities and long-term liabilities), and one group of owners' equity accounts.
- A classified balance sheet can be presented in the account form or the report form.

7 **Financial Analysis** **DEFINE** *gross profit percentage* and **EXPLAIN** its use (pp. 140–141).
- The gross profit percentage is the rate at which a company earns gross profit on sales.
- The gross profit percentage is calculated by dividing Gross Profit on Sales by Net Sales.

SELF-TEST QUESTIONS FOR REVIEW

1. Bennett's Fashion Store purchased 100 pairs of pants with a list price of $30 each from Steinberg Wholesale. Steinberg offers a 10% trade discount for quantities of 50 to 90 and 20% for quantities greater than 90. Steinberg also offers 2/10, n/30 credit terms. What is the total invoice price for the pants?
   a. $3,000
   b. $2,400
   c. $2,352
   d. $2,340

2. On March 1, 1996, Troy Company purchased merchandise with an invoice price of $2,700 and 2/10, n/30 terms. On March 3, Troy pays $100 transportation cost. On March 10, Troy pays for the merchandise. What is Troy's total cost of the merchandise?
   a. $2,700
   b. $2,744
   c. $2,746
   d. $2,800

3. Newman Company started business on January 1, 1996. During 1996, it purchased merchandise with an invoice price of $500,000. Newman also paid $20,000 freight on the merchandise. During the year, Newman returned $80,000 of the merchandise to its suppliers. All purchases were paid for during 1996, and a $10,000 cash discount was taken. $418,000 of the merchandise was sold for $627,000. What is the December 31, 1996, balance in the Inventory account?
   a. $82,000
   b. $32,000
   c. $12,000
   d. $2,000

4. Saber Company uses the perpetual inventory system with the net price method of recording purchases. Saber purchased merchandise with an invoice price of $800, terms 2/10, n/30. If Saber returns merchandise with an invoice price of $200 to the supplier, what should the entry to record the return include?

    a. Debit to Inventory of $200
    b. Debit to Inventory of $196
    c. Credit to Inventory of $200
    d. Credit to Inventory of $196
5. On a classified balance sheet, Equipment appears in which subgroup?
    a. Current assets
    b. Plant assets
    c. Investments
    d. Intangible assets

DEMONSTRATION PROBLEM FOR REVIEW

Williams Distributing Company is a merchandising company. Williams uses the perpetual inventory system. Record each of the following transactions related to purchasing and selling merchandise two ways: (1) assume that the gross price method of recording purchases is used and (2) assume that the net price method of recording purchases is used:

March	1	Purchased on account merchandise for resale for $6,000; terms were 2/10, n/30.
	3	Paid $200 cash for freight on the March 1 purchase.
	6	Returned merchandise costing $300 (part of the $6,000 purchase).
	10	Paid for merchandise purchased on March 1.
	12	Sold merchandise on account costing $8,000 for $10,000; terms were 2/10, n/30.
	15	Accepted returned merchandise from customer costing $400 that had been sold on account for $500 (part of the $10,000 sale).
	20	Received payment from customer for merchandise sold on March 12.

SOLUTION TO DEMONSTRATION PROBLEM

		Gross Price Method				**Net Price Method**		
March 1	Inventory	6,000			Inventory	5,880	
	Accounts Payable		6,000		Accounts Payable		5,880
	Purchased merchandise with 2/10, n/30 terms.				Purchased merchandise with 2/10, n/30 terms.		
3	Inventory	200			Inventory	200	
	Cash		200		Cash		200
	Paid freight on March 1 purchase.				Paid freight on March 1 purchase.		
6	Accounts Payable	300			Accounts Payable	294	
	Inventory		300		Inventory		294
	Returned merchandise from March 1 purchase.				Returned merchandise from March 1 purchase.		
10	Accounts Payable	5,700			Accounts Payable	5,586	
	Inventory		114		Cash		5,586
	Cash		5,586		Paid for merchandise purchased on March 1 within the discount period.		
	Paid for merchandise purchased on March 1 within the discount period [($6,000 − $300) × 2% = $114].						
12	Accounts Receivable	10,000			Accounts Receivable	10,000	
	Sales		10,000		Sales		10,000
	To record revenue from sale of merchandise.				To record revenue from sale of merchandise.		
12	Cost of Goods Sold	8,000			Cost of Goods Sold	8,000	
	Inventory		8,000		Inventory		8,000
	To record cost of merchandise sold and to reduce inventory.				To record cost of merchandise sold and to reduce inventory.		
15	Sales Returns and Allowances	500			Sales Returns and Allowances	500	
	Accounts Receivable		500		Accounts Receivable		500
	To record revenue lost from return by customer.				To record revenue lost from return by customer.		

Gross Price Method			**Net Price Method**		
15 Inventory	400		Inventory	400	
Cost of Goods Sold		400	Cost of Goods Sold		400
To record cost of goods returned by customer.			To record cost of goods returned by customer.		
20 Cash	9,310		Cash	9,310	
Sales Discounts	190		Sales Discounts	190	
Accounts Receivable		9,500	Accounts Receivable		9,500
To record receipt of cash from customer within the discount period.			To record receipt of cash from customer within the discount period.		

ANSWERS TO SELF-TEST QUESTIONS

1. b, pp. 126–127   **2.** c, pp. 126–127   **3.** c, pp. 127–131   **4.** d, pp. 133–135
5. b, pp. 136–137

D

The Periodic Inventory System

A less-used alternative to the perpetual inventory system is the periodic inventory system. The **periodic inventory system** does not update the Inventory account or the Cost of Goods Sold account as transactions related to merchandise occur during the year. Instead, the Inventory account and the Cost of Goods Sold account are updated only at the end of the accounting year. Other accounts are used to record purchases, transportation costs, purchases returns and allowances, and purchases discounts.

THE PERIODIC INVENTORY SYSTEM

For many companies, the periodic inventory system is an unacceptable system because up-to-date inventory amounts are not available during the year for managerial analysis and decision making. However, the periodic inventory system is less costly to operate than a perpetual inventory system and may be an acceptable system for some companies. The following sections illustrate the journal entries that Barton Wholesale Electronics Company would make if it used the periodic inventory system. We use the same data that we used to illustrate the perpetual inventory system to allow easy comparison of the two systems.

PURCHASES OF MERCHANDISE

When a company using the periodic inventory system purchases merchandise, it records the purchase by debiting the cost of the merchandise to the Purchases account (rather than the Inventory account) and crediting the cost to Accounts Payable. On November 10, Barton Wholesale records the purchase of 100 disk drives with a list price of $300 each, a 30% trade discount, and terms of 2/10, n/30 by making the following entry:

Nov. 10	Purchases	21,000	
	Accounts Payable		21,000
	To record the purchase of 100 disk drives from Asian		
	Electronics Manufacturing Company with 2/10, n/30 terms.		

The Purchases account has a normal debit balance.

Barton Wholesale uses the gross price method to record purchases. That is, Barton Wholesale subtracts the trade discount from the list price but does not subtract the cash discount. Barton Wholesale used the same approach with the perpetual inventory system. Note that only merchandise acquisitions are recorded in the Purchases account. Companies record acquisitions of other types of assets in the appropriate asset accounts.

TRANSPORTATION COSTS FOR MERCHANDISE

When a purchaser using the periodic inventory system bears the cost of transporting the merchandise from the seller, the purchaser records the transportation cost in the Transportation In account (rather than the Inventory account). Barton Wholesale makes the following entry on November 12 to record payment of $126 of transportation cost on the purchase of 100 disk drives:

Nov. 12	Transportation In	126	
	Cash		126
	To record the payment of $126 of transportation costs on the		
	purchase of 100 disk drives.		

The Transportation In account has a normal debit balance.

PURCHASES RETURNS AND ALLOWANCES

If the purchaser is dissatisfied with merchandise that was purchased and a purchase return or allowance is granted, the purchaser records the return or allowance using the Purchases Returns and Allowances account (rather than the Inventory account). On November 15, Barton Wholesale records the return of 10 disk drives to Asian Electronics by making the following entry:

Nov. 15	Accounts Payable	2,100	
	Purchases Returns and Allowances		2,100
	To record the return of 10 disk drives at a list price of $300 less a 30% trade discount.		

Purchases Returns and Allowances is a contra purchases account with a normal credit balance. This account permits the purchaser to accumulate data on returns and allowances in a separate account.

PAYMENTS FOR MERCHANDISE PURCHASED

If a purchaser makes a cash payment to the seller by the end of the discount period, the purchaser deducts a cash discount. Otherwise, the purchaser pays the full invoice price. When a purchaser takes a cash discount, the purchaser credits the Purchases Discounts account (rather than the Inventory account). Barton Wholesale makes the following entry on November 20 to record the cash payment to Asian Electronics after deducting the cash discount:

Nov. 20	Accounts Payable	18,900	
	Purchases Discounts		378
	Cash		18,522
	To record the payment to Asian Electronics within the discount period.		

Purchases Discounts is a contra purchases account with a normal credit balance. Under the periodic inventory system, the purchaser typically isolates cash discounts on purchases in this contra account.

If Barton Wholesale makes the payment sometime between November 21 and December 10 (after the discount period), the cash discount does not apply. Barton Wholesale records a cash payment on November 25 with the following entry:

Nov. 25	Accounts Payable	18,900	
	Cash		18,900
	To record the payment to Asian Electronics outside the discount period.		

SALES OF MERCHANDISE

Under the periodic inventory system, the seller makes only one entry to record a sale of merchandise. The entry records the receivable from the customer and the revenue from the sale by debiting Accounts Receivable and crediting Sales. Barton Wholesale records the December 12 sale of 15 disk drives to Computer Outlet Company at a sales price of $280 each with terms of 1/10, n/15 by making the following entry:

Dec. 12	Accounts Receivable	4,200	
	Sales		4,200
	To record the sale of 15 disk drives at a sales price of $280 each to Computer Outlet Company with credit terms of 1/10, n/15.		

The same entry is made under the perpetual inventory system. Under the periodic inventory system, however, there is no concurrent entry to transfer the cost of merchandise sold from the Inventory account to the Cost of Goods Sold account.

SALES RETURNS AND ALLOWANCES

Under the periodic inventory system, only one entry is used to record a sales return or allowance. The entry records the reduction of the revenue from the sale and the reduction of the receivable from the customer by debiting Sales Returns and Allowances and crediting

Accounts Receivable. Barton Wholesale records the December 15 return by Computer Outlet Company of five disk drives by making the following entry:

Dec. 15	Sales Returns and Allowances	1,400	
	Accounts Receivable		1,400
	To record the return of 5 disk drives by Computer Outlet		
	Company; sales price was $280 each.		

This entry is the same as the first entry under the perpetual inventory system. However, Barton Wholesale does not make the second entry made under the perpetual inventory system. Under the periodic inventory system, there is no immediate reinstatement of the returned merchandise to the Inventory account and corresponding reduction in the Cost of Goods Sold account.

PAYMENTS RECEIVED FROM CUSTOMERS

The entry to record the receipt of a cash payment from a customer is exactly the same under either the perpetual inventory system or the periodic inventory system. If the payment is made within the discount period, the entry includes a debit to Sales Discounts, a contra sales account. Barton Wholesale records the cash received from Computer Outlet Company on December 22 (within the discount period) as follows:

Dec. 22	Cash	2,772	
	Sales Discounts	28	
	Accounts Receivable		2,800
	To record the cash payment from Computer Outlet Company		
	within the discount period.		

If Computer Outlet Company makes the cash payment any time between December 23 and December 27 (after the discount period), the cash discount does not apply. Barton Wholesale records the cash received from Computer Outlet on December 27 with the following entry:

Dec. 27	Cash	2,800	
	Accounts Receivable		2,800
	To record the cash payment from Computer Outlet Company		
	outside the discount period.		

YEAR-END ADJUSTING ENTRY

As the preceding entries illustrate, the periodic inventory system does not update the balance of the Inventory account as each transaction related to merchandise occurs during the year. As a result, the unadjusted balance of the Inventory account at the end of each year is the same as the balance at the beginning of the year. Further, the periodic inventory system makes no entries to the Cost of Goods Sold account during the year. As a result, its balance at the end of the year before adjustment is zero.

Barton Wholesale must make an adjusting entry at the end of the year to create proper balances in the Inventory account and the Cost of Goods Sold account. Assume the following data for Barton Wholesale Electronics Company for the year ended December 31, 1996:

Physical inventory at December 31, 1995 (1996 beginning inventory)	$115,000
Physical inventory at December 31, 1996 (1996 ending inventory)	$120,000
Account balances at December 31, 1996, before adjusting entries:	
Inventory	$115,000 debit
Cost of Goods Sold	–0–
Purchases	259,500 debit
Purchases Returns and Allowances	4,800 credit
Purchases Discounts	4,400 credit
Transportation In	9,700 debit

Under the periodic inventory system, the year-end balance in the Inventory account, prior to any adjusting entries, is $115,000, the beginning balance for 1996. The December 31, 1996, account balances for Purchases, Purchases Returns and Allowances, Purchases Discounts, and Transportation In all represent the cumulative transactions in those accounts during 1996. The balance in Cost of Goods Sold is zero because the periodic inventory system transferred no cost to it as Barton Wholesale sold merchandise.

Barton Wholesale makes the following adjusting entry at December 31, 1996, to adjust the balances of the Inventory account and the Cost of Goods Sold account:

1996

Dec. 31	Cost of Goods Sold	255,000	
	Purchases Returns and Allowances	4,800	
	Purchases Discounts	4,400	
	Inventory	120,000	
	Purchases		259,500
	Transportation In		9,700
	Inventory		115,000
	To remove the beginning inventory balance ($115,000), to record the ending inventory balance ($120,000), and to determine and record cost of goods sold.		

After posting this adjusting entry, Barton Wholesale will show the following account balances at December 31, 1996:

Inventory	$120,000 debit
Cost of Goods Sold	255,000 debit
Purchases	–0–
Purchases Returns and Allowances	–0–
Purchases Discounts	–0–
Transportation In	–0–

The Inventory account now agrees with the total cost from the December 31, 1996, physical inventory, and all costs of merchandise sold during 1996 have been transferred to the Cost of Goods Sold account.

Exhibit D-1 presents the components that were used to develop the 1996 balance in the Cost of Goods Sold account. The net cost of purchases during 1996 is added to the cost of the inventory at January 1, 1996 (the same as the December 31, 1995, physical inventory), to determine cost of goods available for sale for 1996. Net cost of purchases is determined by subtracting purchases returns and allowances and purchases discounts from purchases and then adding any transportation-in costs. Then the cost of the inventory at December 31, 1996 (the physical inventory at December 31, 1996), is subtracted to determine cost of goods sold for 1996. Exhibit D-2 shows the computation of cost of goods sold for Barton Wholesale for 1996.

CLASSIFIED FINANCIAL STATEMENTS

The classified income statement and the classified balance sheet for a merchandising firm are the same whether the firm uses the perpetual inventory system or the periodic inventory system. Therefore, Exhibit 4-5 in the chapter illustrates the classified income statement and Exhibit 4-7 illustrates the classified balance sheet for Barton Wholesale Electronics Company at December 31, 1996, if Barton used the periodic inventory system.

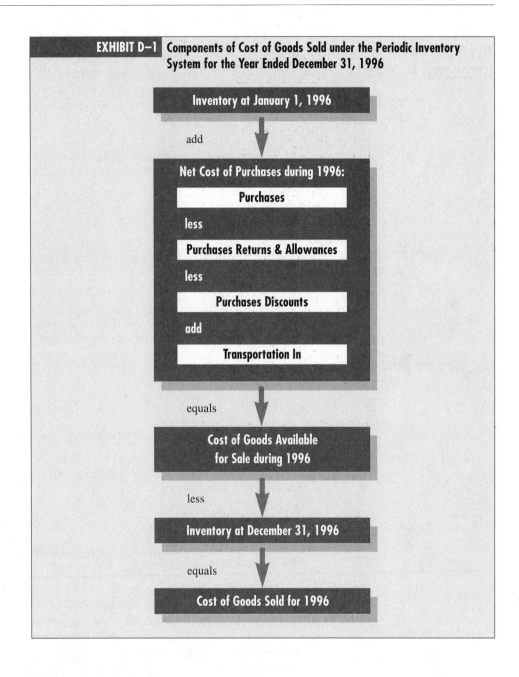

EXHIBIT D–1 Components of Cost of Goods Sold under the Periodic Inventory System for the Year Ended December 31, 1996

Inventory at January 1, 1996

add

Net Cost of Purchases during 1996:

Purchases

less

Purchases Returns & Allowances

less

Purchases Discounts

add

Transportation In

equals

Cost of Goods Available for Sale during 1996

less

Inventory at December 31, 1996

equals

Cost of Goods Sold for 1996

EXHIBIT D–2 Determination of Cost of Goods Sold for Barton Wholesale Electronics Company

Inventory at January 1, 1996			$115,000
Add: Net cost of purchases made during 1996			
Purchases		$259,500	
Less: Purchases returns and allowances	$4,800		
Purchases discounts	4,400	9,200	
		$250,300	
Add: Transportation In		9,700	260,000
Cost of goods available for sale during 1996			$375,000
Less: Inventory at December 31, 1996			120,000
Cost of goods sold for 1996			$255,000

NET PRICE METHOD OF RECORDING PURCHASES

Barton Wholesale records three of the preceding transactions differently if it uses the net price method with the periodic inventory system.

PURCHASES OF MERCHANDISE

Barton Wholesale records the November 10 purchase net of the cash discount:

Nov. 10	Purchases	20,580	
	Accounts Payable		20,580
	To record the purchase of 100 disk drives from Asian Electronics Manufacturing Company with 2/10, n/30 terms.		

The increase in the Purchases account and the increase in the amount owed are both recorded net of the trade discount *and* net of the cash discount (the cash discount is subtracted from the invoice price).

PURCHASES RETURNS AND ALLOWANCES

Barton Wholesale also records the merchandise return on November 15 net of the cash discount:

Nov. 15	Accounts Payable	2,058	
	Purchases Returns and Allowances		2,058
	To record the return of 10 disk drives at a list price of $300 less a 30% trade discount and a 2% cash discount.		

PAYMENTS FOR MERCHANDISE PURCHASED

Barton Wholesale also records the payment for the merchandise on November 20 net of the cash discount:

Nov. 20	Accounts Payable	18,522	
	Cash		18,522
	To record the payment to Asian Electronics within the discount period.		

If the payment is made on November 25, outside the discount period, Barton Wholesale makes the following entry:

Nov. 25	Accounts Payable	18,522	
	Discounts Lost	378	
	Cash		18,900
	To record the payment to Asian Electronics outside the discount period.		

Note that Barton Wholesale uses a separate account, Discounts Lost, to accumulate the total cash discounts not taken on purchases of merchandise. This account has a normal debit balance. Most companies treat the balance of this account as a cost element in the determination of cost of goods sold. The adjusting entry that creates the balance in the Cost of Goods Sold account will include the Discount Lost account.

GLOSSARY OF KEY TERMS USED IN THIS CHAPTER AND THE APPENDIX

authorized dealerships   Independent retailers that have been designated by a manufacturer to sell the manufacturer's product in a specific geographic area (p. 125).

cash discount   An amount that a purchaser of merchandise may deduct from the purchase price for paying within the discount period (p. 126).

classified balance sheet   A balance sheet in which items are classified into subgroups to facilitate financial analysis and management decision making (p. 136).

classified income statement   An income statement in which items are classified into subgroups to facilitate financial analysis and management decision making (p. 135).

cost of goods sold   The total cost of merchandise sold to customers during the accounting period (p. 130).

cost of goods sold percentage   The ratio of goods sold divided by net sales (p. 140).

credit period   The maximum amount of time, usually stated in days, that the purchaser of merchandise has to pay the seller (p. 126).

current assets   Cash and other assets that will be converted to cash or used up during the normal operating cycle of the business or one year, whichever is longer (p. 136).

current liabilities   Liabilities that must be settled within the normal operating cycle or one year, whichever is longer (p. 139).

discount period   The maximum amount of time, usually stated in days, that the purchaser of merchandise has to pay the seller if the purchaser wants to claim the cash discount (p. 126).

drop-shipping   Shipment of product from a manufacturer directly to individual retail stores rather than to wholesale distributors (p. 125).

gross margin   The difference between net sales and cost of goods sold; also called *gross profit* (p. 136).

gross price method of recording purchases   An accounting procedure by which merchandise purchases are recorded at invoice price (p. 127).

gross profit on sales   The difference between net sales and cost of goods sold; also called *gross margin* (p. 136).

gross profit percentage   The ratio of gross profit on sales divided by net sales (p. 140).

inventory shrinkage   The cost associated with an inventory shortage; the amount by which the perpetual inventory exceeds the physical inventory (p. 133).

invoice price   The price that a seller charges the purchaser for merchandise (p. 126).

list price   The suggested price or reference price of merchandise in a catalog or price list (p. 126).

long-term liabilities   Debt obligations not due to be settled within the normal operating cycle or one year, whichever is longer (p. 139).

manufacturers   Companies that convert raw materials and components into finished products through the application of skilled labor and machine operations (p. 124).

manufacturer's brand name   A brand name owned by a manufacturer that is placed on products that it manufactures (p. 125).

merchandise allowance   A reduction in the selling price of merchandise granted by the seller due to dissatisfaction of the purchaser (p. 128).

merchandise inventory   A stock of products that a company buys from another company and makes available for sale to its customers (p. 124).

merchandise return   Shipping unsatisfactory merchandise from the purchaser back to the seller (p. 128).

merchandising firm   A company that buys finished products, stores the products for varying periods of time, and then resells the products (p. 125).

national retailers   Large retailing companies with thousands of stores located throughout the United States (p. 125).

net price method of recording purchases   An accounting procedure by which merchandise purchases are recorded at amounts equal to invoice price less the anticipated cash discount (p. 133).

net sales   The total revenue generated by a company through merchandise sales less the revenue given up through sales returns and allowances and less the revenue given up through sales discounts (p. 132).

normal operating cycle   For a particular business, the average period of time between the use of cash in its typical operating activity and the subsequent collection of cash from customers (p. 136).

periodic inventory system   A system that records merchandise transactions in a variety of accounts; the Inventory account and Cost of Goods Sold account are not updated until the end of the year (p. 145).

perpetual inventory system   A system that records the cost of merchandise inventory in the Inventory account at the time of purchase and updates the Inventory account for subsequent transactions related to merchandise as they occur (p. 127).

physical inventory   A year-end procedure that involves counting the quantity of each inventory item, determining the unit cost of each item, multiplying the unit cost times quantity, and summing the costs of all the items to determine the total inventory at cost (p. 133).

plant assets   Land, buildings, equipment, vehicles, furniture, and fixtures that a firm uses in its operations (p. 138).

private label brand name   A brand name owned by a manufacturer's customer that is placed on products manufactured by the manufacturer (p. 125).

retailers   Companies that buy products from wholesale distributors and sell the products to individual customers, the general public (p. 124).

sale on account   A sale of merchandise made on a credit basis (p. 126).

trade discount   An amount, usually based on quantity of merchandise purchased, that the seller subtracts from the list price of merchandise to determine the invoice price (p. 126).

wholesale distributors   Companies that buy finished products from manufacturing firms in large quantities and resell the products to retailers (p. 124).

QUESTIONS

4-1 What are the differences among (a) manufacturer, (b) wholesale distributor, and (c) retailer?

4-2 What are the three primary transactions in the operating cycle of a merchandising firm?

4-3 What is the difference between a credit period and a discount period? What is the difference between a cash discount and a trade discount?

4-4 Sprague Company bought merchandise with a list price of $2,000 from Thompson Company. Thompson offers a 15% trade discount and a 2% cash discount. What is the invoice price of the merchandise?

4-5 Krane Company purchased $4,000 of merchandise and paid $250 of transportation costs to a trucking company to deliver the merchandise. Krane then returned $1,000 of the merchandise before paying the supplier within the discount period. Krane was entitled to a 2% cash discount. How much did Krane pay the supplier?

4-6 What is the primary difference between a merchandise return and a merchandise allowance?

4-7 What are the three steps that make up the year-end physical inventory?

4-8 The net price method of recording purchases anticipates taking cash discounts on merchandise purchases. Describe the three types of transactions that are recorded differently if a company uses the net price method rather than the gross price method.

4-9 What are the components of a classified income statement for a merchandising firm?

4-10 Define *gross profit on sales*. What is an alternate name for it?

4-11 For each item listed below, indicate whether it is an element of (a) cost of goods sold, (b) selling expense, (c) administrative expense, (d) both selling and administrative expense—allocated between them—or (e) other income and expense: insurance expense, transportation cost on merchandise purchases, interest expense, office salaries expense, depreciation expense, and advertising expense.

4-12 What are the five asset subgroups that may be found in the asset section of the classified balance sheet?

4-13 Define *current asset* and *normal operating cycle*.

4-14 Which of the following assets are current assets: land, cash, prepaid expense, building, accounts receivable, inventory, and equipment?

4-15 Define *gross profit percentage*. How is it used?

PRINCIPLES DISCUSSION QUESTION

4-16 When merchandisers and manufacturers prepare income statements for their annual reports to stockholders, they usually begin the statements with net sales. For internal reporting purposes, however, the income statements will show gross sales and the related contra revenue accounts (sales returns and allowances and sales discounts). What might explain this difference in the financial information disclosed to external parties and management? Do you consider the more limited disclosure in the annual reports to be inconsistent with the full disclosure principle? Briefly explain.

EXERCISES

TRADE AND CASH DISCOUNT CALCULATIONS — OBJ. 2 —

4-17 On June 1, 1996, Forest Company sold merchandise with a list price of $24,000. For each of the sales terms below, determine (a) the amount recorded as a sale and (b) the proper amount of cash received. Forest Company uses the gross price method.

	Applicable Trade Discount (%)	Credit Terms	Date Paid
1.	30	2/10, n/30	June 8
2.	40	1/10, n/30	June 15
3.	—	2/10, n/30	June 11
4.	20	1/15, n/30	June 14
5.	40	n/30	June 28

ENTRIES FOR SALE, RETURN, AND REMITTANCE — OBJ. 2, 3 —

4-18 On September 13, 1996, Brady Company sold merchandise with an invoice price of $900 ($600 cost), terms 2/10, n/30, to Dalton Company. On September 17, $150 of the merchandise ($100 cost) was returned because it was the wrong model. On September 23, Brady Company received a check for the amount due from Dalton Company.

Record the journal entries made by Brady Company for these transactions. Brady uses the perpetual inventory system and the gross price method.

ENTRIES FOR PURCHASE, RETURN, AND REMITTANCE — OBJ. 3 —

4-19 On April 13, 1996, Kesselman Company purchased $22,000 of merchandise from Krausman Company, terms 1/10, n/30. On April 15, Kesselman paid $300 to Ace Trucking Company for freight on the shipment. On April 18, Kesselman Company returned $1,000 of merchandise for credit. Final payment was made to Krausman on April 22. Kesselman Company records purchases using the gross price method and the perpetual inventory system.

Prepare the journal entries that Kesselman Company should make on April 13, 15, 18, and 22.

ENTRIES FOR MERCHANDISE
TRANSACTIONS ON SELLER'S
AND BUYER'S RECORDS
— OBJ. 2, 3 —

4-20 The following are selected transactions of Lamont, Inc., during 1996:

June 21   Sold and shipped on account to Lowery Company, $2,880 ($2,000 cost) of merchandise, terms 2/10, n/30.

28   Lowery Company returned defective merchandise billed at $280 on June 21 ($210 cost).

30   Received from Lowery Company a check for full settlement of the June 21 transaction.

Record, in general journal form, these transactions as they would appear on the books of (a) Lamont, Inc., and (b) Lowery Company. Both companies use the perpetual inventory system and Lowery records purchases using the gross price method.

NET PRICE METHOD OF
RECORDING PURCHASES
— OBJ. 5 —

4-21 Alvarez, Inc., uses the net price method of recording purchases. On July 1, 1996, the firm purchased merchandise for $1,800, terms 2/10, n/30. On July 5, the firm returned $600 of the merchandise to the seller. Payment of the account occurred on July 8. Alvarez uses the perpetual inventory system.
a. Give the general journal entries for July 1, July 5, and July 8.
b. Assuming that the account was paid on July 14, give the entry for payment on that date.

YEAR-END
PHYSICAL INVENTORY
— OBJ. 4 —

4-22 The December 31, 1996, inventory for Hayes Company included five products. The year-end count revealed the following:

Product	Quantity on Hand
A	26
B	50
C	34
D	75
E	40

The related unit costs follow: A, $10; B, $6; C, $5; D, $8; and E, $7. Calculate the total cost of the December 31, 1996, physical inventory.

CLASSIFIED
INCOME STATEMENT
— OBJ. 6 —

4-23 From the following accounts, listed in alphabetic order, prepare a classified income statement for Karlman Distributors for the year ended December 31, 1996. All accounts have normal balances.

Advertising Expense	$ 18,000	Salaries Expense (office)	$ 35,000
Cost of Goods Sold	330,000	Salaries Expense (sales)	83,000
Delivery Expense	25,000	Sales	560,000
Interest Expense	3,000	Sales Discounts	10,000
Rent Expense (office)	21,000	Supplies Expense (office)	4,000

CLASSIFIED BALANCE SHEET
— OBJ. 6 —

4-24 From the following accounts, listed in alphabetical order, prepare a classified balance sheet for Berkly Wholesalers at December 31, 1996. All accounts have normal balances.

Accounts Payable	$43,000	Inventory	$117,000
Accounts Receivable	40,000	Land	45,000
Accumulated Depreciation—		Mortgage Payable	
Building	23,000	(long term)	78,000
Accumulated Depreciation—		Office Equipment	21,000
Office Equipment	5,000	Office Supplies	2,000
Building	90,000	Salaries Payable	7,000
Cash	26,000	T. Berkly, Capital	185,000

ENTRIES FOR SALE,
RETURN, AND
REMITTANCE—PERIODIC
— APPENDIX D —

4-25 On June 8, 1996, Stevens Company sold merchandise listing for $1,600 to Dalton Company, terms 2/10, n/30. On June 12, $400 worth of the merchandise was returned because it was the wrong color. On June 18, Stevens Company received a check for the amount due.

Record the general journal entries made by Stevens Company for these transactions. Stevens uses the periodic inventory system.

ENTRIES FOR PURCHASE, RETURN, AND REMITTANCE—PERIODIC — APPENDIX D —

4-26 On March 10, 1996, Horton Company purchased $18,000 worth of merchandise from James Company, terms 1/10, n/30. On March 12, Horton paid $160 freight on the shipment. On March 15, Horton returned $200 of merchandise for credit. Final payment was made to James on March 19. Horton Company uses the gross price method of recording purchases and the periodic inventory system.

Prepare the general journal entries that Horton should make on March 10, March 12, March 15, and March 19.

ENTRIES FOR MERCHANDISE TRANSACTIONS ON SELLER'S AND BUYER'S RECORDS— PERIODIC — APPENDIX D —

4-27 The following are selected transactions of Franklin, Inc., during 1996:

April 20   Sold and shipped on account to Lind Stores merchandise listing for $2,400, terms 2/10, n/30.

27   Lind Stores returned defective merchandise billed at $200 on April 20.

29   Received from Lind Stores a check for full settlement of the April 20 transaction.

Record, in general journal form, these transactions as they would appear on the books of (a) Franklin, Inc., and (b) Lind Stores. Lind Stores records purchases using the gross price method. Both companies use the periodic inventory system.

PROBLEMS

ENTRIES FOR MERCHANDISE TRANSACTIONS ON SELLER'S AND BUYER'S RECORDS — OBJ. 2, 3 —

4-28 The following transactions occurred between Decker Company and Mann Stores, Inc., during March 1996.

Mar. 8   Decker sold $13,200 worth of merchandise ($8,800 cost) to Mann Stores, terms 2/10, n/30.

10   Mann Stores paid freight charges on the shipment from Decker Company, $200.

12   Mann Stores returned $1,200 of the merchandise ($800 cost) shipped on March 8.

17   Decker received full payment for the net amount due from the March 8 sale.

20   Mann Stores returned goods that had been billed originally at $600 ($400 cost). Decker issued a check for $588.

REQUIRED

Record these transactions in general journal form as they would appear on (a) the books of Decker Company and (b) the books of Mann Stores, Inc. Assume that both companies use the perpetual inventory system and the gross price method.

ENTRIES FOR MERCHANDISE TRANSACTIONS — OBJ. 2, 3 —

4-29 Rockford Corporation, which began business on August 1, 1996, sells on terms of 2/10, n/30. Credit terms for its purchases vary with the supplier. Selected transactions for August are given below. Unless noted, all transactions are on account and involve merchandise held for resale. All purchases are recorded using the gross price method, and the perpetual inventory system is used.

Aug. 1   Purchased merchandise from Norris, Inc., $3,400, terms 2/10, n/30.

5   Paid freight on shipment from Norris, Inc., $160.

7   Sold merchandise to Denton Corporation, $4,800 ($3,400 cost).

7   Paid $240 freight on August 7 shipment and billed Denton for the charges.

9   Returned $600 worth of the merchandise purchased August 1 from Norris, Inc., because it was defective. Norris approved the return.

9   Received $800 of returned merchandise ($600 cost) from Denton Corporation. Rockford approved the return.

10   Paid Norris, Inc., the amount due.

14   Purchased from Chambers, Inc., goods with a list price of $8,000. Rockford Corporation was entitled to a 25% trade discount; terms 1/10, n/30.

15   Paid freight on shipment from Chambers, Inc., $280.

17   Received the amount due from Denton Corporation.

18   Sold merchandise to Weber, Inc., $9,600 ($6,600 cost).

20   Paid $320 freight on August 18 shipment and billed Weber for the charges.

24   Paid Chambers, Inc., the amount due.

28   Received the amount due from Weber, Inc.

REQUIRED

Record these transactions for Rockford Corporation in general journal form.

EFFECT OF TRANSACTIONS ON INVENTORY ACCOUNT — OBJ. 2, 3 —

4-30 Watt Wholesale Company purchases merchandise from a variety of manufacturers and sells the merchandise to a variety of retailers. All sales are subject to a trade discount (10% for sales up to $1,000, 15% for sales from $1,000 to $5,000, and 20% for sales greater than $5,000) and a cash discount (2/10, n/30). Watt has a perpetual inventory system that incorporates the gross price method of recording merchandise purchases. The May 1, 1996, balance in Watt's Inventory account was a $60,000 debit. The following transactions occurred during May 1996:

May	2	Purchased $4,500 of merchandise from Ajax Manufacturing; terms are 1/10, n/30.
	4	Paid $160 freight on the May 2 purchase.
	12	Paid Ajax for the May 2 purchase.
	14	Purchased $3,000 of merchandise from Baker Manufacturing; terms are 2/10, n/45.
	16	Received a $200 allowance on the May 14 purchase since some of the merchandise was the wrong color. All of the merchandise is salable at regular prices.
	18	Purchased $2,500 of merchandise from Charles Industries; terms are 2/10, n/30.
	19	Sold merchandise with a list price of $2,000 ($1,200 cost) to Daytime Industries.
	22	Daytime Industries returned 30% of the merchandise from the May 19 sale.
	26	Paid Baker Manufacturing for the May 14 purchase.
	29	Paid Charles Industries for the May 18 purchase.

REQUIRED

Prepare a schedule that shows the impact of these transactions on Watt's Inventory account. Use the following headings:

Date	Transaction	Debit Amount	Credit Amount	Account Balance

GROSS PRICE METHOD AND NET PRICE METHOD — OBJ. 3, 5 —

4-31 Cushing Distributing Company uses the perpetual inventory system. Cushing had the following transactions related to merchandise during the month of June 1996:

June	1	Purchased on account merchandise for resale for $8,000; terms were 2/10, n/30.
	3	Paid $350 cash for freight on the June 1 purchase.
	7	Returned merchandise costing $500 (part of the $8,000 purchase).
	10	Paid for merchandise purchased on June 1.
	13	Sold merchandise on account costing $7,000 for $10,000; terms were 2/10, n/30.
	16	Customer returned merchandise costing $650 that had been sold on account for $900 (part of the $10,000 sale).
	22	Received payment from customer for merchandise sold on June 13.

REQUIRED

Record each of the following transactions related to purchasing and selling merchandise two ways: (1) assume that the gross price method of recording purchases is used and (2) assume that the net price method of recording purchases is used.

PHYSICAL INVENTORY CALCULATIONS AND ADJUSTING ENTRY — OBJ. 4 —

4-32 Apache Stores conducted a physical inventory at December 31, 1996. The items counted during the physical inventory are listed below. Apache's accountant provided the unit costs.

Item Description	December 31, 1996 Count	Unit Cost
Colorado wool sweaters	48	$32
Magnum wool sweaters	27	34
Johnson jackets	50	28
Magnum caps	45	12
Evans caps	26	10
Colorado shirts	72	18
Johnson shirts	68	15
Magnum boots	40	60

REQUIRED

a. Prepare a schedule to determine the total cost of each item in the inventory and the total cost of the complete inventory at December 31, 1996.

b. Assume that the perpetual inventory records show a $9,520 debit balance in the Inventory account at December 31, 1996. Prepare the general journal entry to adjust the perpetual inventory to the total cost determined by the physical inventory.

CLASSIFIED FINANCIAL STATEMENTS — OBJ. 6 —

4-33 The adjusted trial balance of Crane Distributors on December 31, 1996, is shown below; the perpetual inventory system has been used. Crane contributed no capital during 1996.

CRANE DISTRIBUTORS
ADJUSTED TRIAL BALANCE
DECEMBER 31, 1996

	Debit	Credit
Cash	$ 15,200	
Accounts Receivable	110,200	
Inventory	114,000	
Prepaid Insurance	2,400	
Supplies	6,400	
Delivery Equipment	80,000	
Accumulated Depreciation		$ 35,000
Accounts Payable		70,000
H. Crane, Capital		168,000
H. Crane, Drawing	26,000	
Sales		812,000
Sales Returns and Allowances	11,600	
Sales Discounts	14,600	
Cost of Goods Sold	513,400	
Salaries Expense (60% selling)	118,000	
Rent Expense (30% selling)	40,000	
Supplies Expense (100% administrative)	8,400	
Utilities Expense (40% selling)	4,000	
Depreciation Expense (100% selling)	16,000	
Insurance Expense (50% selling)	4,800	
	$1,085,000	$1,085,000

REQUIRED

a. Prepare a classified income statement for the year ended December 31, 1996.
b. Prepare a statement of owner's equity for the year ended December 31, 1996.
c. Prepare a classifed balance sheet as of December 31, 1996, for Crane Distributors.

CLASSIFIED FINANCIAL STATEMENTS AND ADJUSTING ENTRIES
— OBJ. 6 —

4-34 Boston Trading Company, whose accounting year ends on December 31, had the following normal balances in its general ledger at December 31, 1996:

Cash	$ 13,000	Sales	$640,000
Accounts Receivable	65,600	Sales Returns and	
Inventory	73,000	Allowances	4,400
Prepaid Insurance	6,000	Sales Discounts	5,600
Office Supplies	4,200	Cost of Goods Sold	404,000
Furniture and Fixtures	21,000	Utilities Expense	4,800
Accumulated Depreciation—		Sales Salaries Expense	82,000
Furniture and Fixtures	5,000	Delivery Expense	10,800
Delivery Equipment	84,000	Advertising Expense	5,600
Accumulated Depreciation—		Rent Expense	14,400
Delivery Equipment	12,000	Office Salaries Expense	56,000
Accounts Payable	41,000		
Long-Term Notes Payable	30,000		
M. Boston, Capital	136,000		
M. Boston, Drawing	9,600		

Rent expense and utilities expense are 60% administrative and 40% selling. During the year, the accounting department prepared monthly statements but no adjusting entries were made in the journals and ledgers. Data for the year-end procedures are as follows:

1. Prepaid insurance, December 31, 1996 (75% of insurance expense is classified as selling expense, and 25% is classified as administrative expense) $ 1,200

2. Depreciation expense on furniture and fixtures for 1996 (an administrative expense)   1,800
3. Depreciation expense on delivery equipment for 1996   13,000
4. Salaries payable, December 31, 1996 ($1,800 sales and $1,200 office)   3,000
5. Office supplies on hand, December 31, 1996   1,000

REQUIRED

a. Record the necessary adjusting entries in general journal form at December 31, 1996.
b. Prepare a classified income statement for 1996.
c. Prepare a classified balance sheet at December 31, 1996.

ENTRIES FOR MERCHANDISE TRANSACTIONS ON SELLER'S AND BUYER'S RECORDS—PERIODIC
— APPENDIX D —

4-35 The following transactions occurred between Southwick Company and Mann Stores, Inc., during March 1996.

Mar. 8   Southwick sold $6,600 worth of merchandise to Mann Stores, terms 2/10, n/30.
10   Mann Stores paid freight charges on the shipment from Southwick Company, $100.
12   Mann Stores returned $600 of the merchandise shipped on March 8.
17   Southwick received full payment for the net amount due from the March 8 sale.
20   Mann Stores returned goods that had been billed originally at $200. Southwick issued a check for $196.

REQUIRED

Record these transactions in general journal form as they would appear on (a) the books of Southwick Company and (b) the books of Mann Stores, Inc. Mann Stores, Inc., records purchases using the gross price method. Assume that both companies use the periodic inventory system.

ENTRIES FOR MERCHANDISE TRANSACTIONS—PERIODIC
— APPENDIX D —

4-36 Malvado Corporation, which began business on August 1, 1996, sells on terms of 2/10, n/30. Credit terms for its purchases vary with the supplier. Selected transactions for August are given below. Unless noted, all transactions are on account and involve merchandise held for resale. All purchases are recorded using the gross price method; the periodic inventory system is used.

Aug. 1   Purchased merchandise from Norris, Inc., $1,700, terms 2/10, n/30.
5   Paid freight on shipment from Norris, Inc., $80.
7   Sold merchandise to Denton Corporation, $2,400.
7   Paid freight on shipment to Denton Corporation, $120, and billed Denton for the charges.
9   Returned $300 worth of the merchandise purchased August 1 from Norris, Inc., because it was defective. Norris approved the return.
9   Received $400 of returned merchandise from Denton Corporation.
10   Paid Norris, Inc., the amount due.
14   Purchased from Chambers, Inc., goods with a list price of $4,000. Malvado Corporation was entitled to a 25% trade discount; terms 1/10, n/30.
15   Paid freight on shipment from Chambers, Inc., $140.
17   Received the amount due from Denton Corporation.
18   Sold merchandise to Weber, Inc., $4,800.
20   Paid freight on August 18 shipment to Weber, Inc., $160.
24   Paid Chambers, Inc., the amount due.
28   Received the amount due from Weber, Inc.

REQUIRED

Record these transactions for Malvado Corporation in general journal form.

ALTERNATE EXERCISES

4-17A On April 1, 1996, Fitzgerald Company sold merchandise with a list price of $40,000. For each of the sales terms below, determine (a) the amount recorded as a sale and (b) the proper amount of cash received.

TRADE AND CASH DISCOUNT CALCULATIONS — OBJ. 2 —

		Applicable Trade Discount (%)	Credit Terms	Date Paid
	1.	20	1/15, n/30	April 14
	2.	40	n/30	April 28
	3.	—	2/10, n/30	April 11
	4.	30	2/10, n/30	April 8
	5.	40	1/10, n/30	April 15

ENTRIES FOR SALE, RETURN, AND REMITTANCE — OBJ. 2, 3 —

4-18A On October 14, 1996, Patrick Company sold merchandise with an invoice price of $1,000 ($750 cost), terms 2/10, n/30, to Baxter Company. On October 18, $200 of merchandise ($150 cost) was returned because it was the wrong size. On October 24, Patrick Company received a check for the amount due from Baxter Company.

Record the journal entries made by Patrick Company for these transactions. Patrick uses the perpetual inventory system and the gross price method.

ENTRIES FOR PURCHASE, RETURN, AND REMITTANCE — OBJ. 3 —

4-19A On May 15, 1996, Monique Company purchased $25,000 of merchandise from Terrell Company, terms 1/10, n/30. On May 17, Monique paid $260 to Swift Trucking Company for freight on the shipment. On May 20, Monique Company returned $500 of merchandise for credit. Final payment was made to Terrell on May 24. Monique Company records purchases using the gross price method and the perpetual inventory system.

Prepare the journal entries that Monique Company should make on May 15, 17, 20, and 24.

ENTRIES FOR MERCHANDISE TRANSACTIONS ON SELLER'S AND BUYER'S RECORDS — OBJ. 2, 3 —

4-20A The following are selected transactions of Candello, Inc., during 1996.

June 18 Sold and shipped on account to Dante Company $4,000 ($3,000 cost) of merchandise, terms 2/10, n/30.

25 Dante Company returned defective merchandise billed at $400 on June 18 ($300 cost).

27 Received from Dante Company a check for full settlement of the June 18 transaction.

Record, in general journal form, these transactions as they would appear on the books of (a) Candello, Inc., and (b) Dante Company. Both companies use the perpetual inventory system and Dante records purchases using the gross price method.

NET PRICE METHOD OF RECORDING PURCHASES — OBJ. 5 —

4-21A Evans, Inc., uses the net price method of recording purchases. On September 12, 1996, the firm purchased merchandise for $3,000, terms 2/10, n/30. On September 16, the firm returned $900 of the merchandise to the seller. Payment of the account occurred on September 19. Evans uses the perpetual inventory system.

a. Give the general journal entries for September 12, September 16, and September 19.

b. Assuming that the account was paid on September 25, give the entry for payment on that date.

YEAR-END PHYSICAL INVENTORY — OBJ. 4 —

4-22A The December 31, 1996, inventory for Simmons Company included five products. The year-end count revealed the following:

Product	Quantity on Hand
K	40
L	36
M	60
N	52
P	55

The related unit costs are K, $7; L, $10; M, $8; N, $5; and P, $4. Calculate the total cost of the December 31, 1996, physical inventory.

CLASSIFIED INCOME STATEMENT — OBJ. 6 —

4-23A From the following accounts, listed in alphabetical order, prepare a classified income statement for Kokomo Wholesale for the year ended December 31, 1996. All accounts have normal balances.

Advertising Expense	$ 22,000	Salaries Expense (office)	$ 45,000
Cost of Goods Sold	400,000	Salaries Expense (sales)	95,000
Delivery Expense	30,000	Sales	670,000
Interest Expense	4,000	Sales Discounts	12,000
Rent Expense (office)	26,000	Supplies Expense (office)	5,000

CLASSIFIED BALANCE SHEET
— OBJ. 6 —

4-24A From the following accounts, listed in alphabetical order, prepare a classified balance sheet for Balford Wholesalers at December 31, 1996. All accounts have normal balances.

Accounts Payable	$ 52,000	Inventory	$142,000
Accounts Receivable	54,000	Land	58,000
Accumulated Depreciation—		Mortgage Payable	
Building	28,000	(long-term)	100,000
Accumulated Depreciation—		Office Equipment	26,000
Office Equipment	7,000	Office Supplies	2,000
Building	100,000	Salaries Payable	8,000
Cash	40,000	V. Balford, Capital	227,000

ENTRIES FOR SALE,
RETURN, AND
REMITTANCE—PERIODIC
— APPENDIX D —

4-25A On March 10, 1996, Sharon Company sold merchandise listing for $2,000 to Dillard Company, terms 2/10, n/30. On March 14, $500 of merchandise was returned because it was the wrong size. On March 20, Sharon Company received a check for the amount due.

Record the general journal entries made by Sharon Company for these transactions. Sharon uses the periodic inventory system.

ENTRIES FOR PURCHASE,
RETURN, AND
REMITTANCE—PERIODIC
— APPENDIX D —

4-26A On August 15, 1996, Harris Company purchased $20,000 of merchandise from Jason Company, terms 2/10, n/30. On August 17, Harris paid $200 freight on the shipment. On August 20, Harris returned $300 worth of the merchandise for credit. Final payment was made to Jason on August 24. Harris Company records purchases using the gross price method and the periodic inventory system.

Give the general journal entries that Harris should make on August 15, August 17, August 20, and August 24.

ENTRIES FOR MERCHANDISE
TRANSACTIONS ON SELLER'S
AND BUYER'S RECORDS—
PERIODIC
— APPENDIX D —

4-27A The following are selected transactions of Fenton, Inc., during 1996:

Jan. 18   Sold and shipped on account to Lawrence Stores merchandise listing for $1,500, terms 2/10, n/30.

25   Lawrence Stores was granted a $200 allowance on goods shipped January 18.

27   Received from Lawrence Stores a check for full settlement of the January 18 transaction.

Record, in general journal form, these transactions as they would appear on the books of (a) Fenton, Inc., and (b) Lawrence Stores. Lawrence Stores records purchases using the gross price method. Both companies use the periodic inventory system.

ALTERNATE PROBLEMS

ENTRIES FOR MERCHANDISE
TRANSACTIONS ON SELLER'S
AND BUYER'S RECORDS
— OBJ. 2, 3 —

4-28A Riggs Distributing Company had the following transactions with Arlington, Inc., during 1996:

Nov. 10   Riggs sold and shipped $6,000 worth of merchandise ($4,200 cost) to Arlington, terms 2/10, n/30.

12   Arlington, Inc., paid freight charges on the shipment from Riggs Company, $320.

14   Riggs received $600 of merchandise returned by Arlington ($420 cost) from the November 10 sale.

19   Riggs received payment in full for the net amount due on the November 10 sale.

24   Arlington returned goods that had originally been billed at $300 ($210 cost). Riggs issued a check for $294.

REQUIRED
Record these transactions in general journal form as they would appear (a) on the books of Riggs Distributing Company and (b) on the books of Arlington, Inc. Assume that both companies use the perpetual inventory system and the gross price method.

ENTRIES FOR MERCHANDISE
TRANSACTIONS
— OBJ. 2, 3 —

4-29A Webster Company was established on July 1, 1996. Its sales terms are 2/10, n/30. Credit terms for its purchases vary with the supplier. Selected transactions for the first month of operations are given below. Unless noted, all transactions are on account and involve merchandise held for resale. All purchases are recorded using the gross price method and the perpetual inventory system.

July   1   Purchased goods from Dawson, Inc., $1,900; terms 1/10, n/30.

2   Purchased goods from Penn Company, $4,200, terms 2/10, n/30.

3   Paid freight on shipment from Dawson, $100.

5   Sold merchandise to Ward, Inc., $1,300 ($975 cost).

5   Paid freight on shipment to Ward, Inc., $60.

8   Returned $300 worth of the goods purchased July 1 from Dawson, Inc., because some goods were damaged. Dawson approved the return.

9   Received returned goods from Ward, Inc., worth $200 ($150 cost).

10   Paid Dawson, Inc., the amount due.

10   Purchased goods from Dorn Company with a list price of $2,400. Webster was entitled to a $33\frac{1}{3}\%$ trade discount; terms 2/10, n/30.

11   Paid freight on shipment from Dorn Company, $130.

15   Received the amount due from Ward, Inc.

15   Sold merchandise to Colby Corporation, $3,200 ($2,400 cost).

16   Mailed a check to Penn Company for the amount due on its July 2 invoice.

18   Received an allowance of $100 from Dorn Company for defective merchandise purchased on July 10.

19   Paid Dorn Company the amount due.

25   Received the amount due from Colby Corporation.

REQUIRED

Record these transactions for Webster Company in general journal form.

EFFECT OF TRANSACTIONS ON INVENTORY ACCOUNT — OBJ. 2, 3 —

4-30A Rand Wholesale Company purchases merchandise from a variety of manufacturers and sells the merchandise to a variety of retailers. All sales are subject to a trade discount (10% for sales up to $1,000; 15% for sales from $1,000 to $5,000; and 20% for sales of more than $5,000) and a cash discount (2/10, n/30). Rand has a perpetual inventory system that incorporates the gross price method of recording merchandise purchases. The February 1, 1996, balance in Rand's Inventory account was a $50,000 debit. The following transactions occurred during February 1996:

Feb.   2   Purchased $7,600 of merchandise from Sweet Manufacturing; terms are 1/10, n/30.

5   Paid $270 freight on the February 2 purchase.

11   Paid Sweet for the February 2 purchase.

13   Purchased $5,000 of merchandise from Tayler Manufacturing; terms are 2/10, n/45.

16   Received a $300 allowance on the February 13 purchase since some of the merchandise was the wrong size. All of the merchandise is salable at regular prices.

17   Purchased $4,200 of merchandise from Zorn Industries; terms are 2/10, n/30.

20   Sold merchandise with a list price of $4,000 ($2,200 cost) to Valley Mart.

22   Valley Mart returned 20% of the merchandise from the February 20 sale.

23   Paid Tayler Manufacturing for the February 13 purchase.

28   Paid Zorn Industries for the February 17 purchase.

REQUIRED

Prepare a schedule that shows the impact of these transactions on Rand's Inventory account. Use the following headings:

Date	Transaction	Debit Amount	Credit Amount	Account Balance

GROSS PRICE METHOD AND NET PRICE METHOD — OBJ. 3, 5 —

4-31A Janetto Distributing Company uses the perpetual inventory system. Janetto had the following transactions related to merchandise during the month of August 1996:

Aug. 10   Purchased on account merchandise for resale for $3,000; terms were 2/10, n/30.

12   Paid $120 cash for freight on the August 10 purchase.

16   Returned merchandise costing $200 (part of the $3,000 purchase).

19   Paid for merchandise purchased on August 10.

22   Sold merchandise on account costing $1,000 for $1,600; terms were 2/10, n/30.

25   Customer returned merchandise costing $65 that had been sold on account for $100 (part of the $1,600 sale).

31   Received payment from customer for merchandise sold on August 22.

REQUIRED

Record each of the following transactions related to purchasing and selling merchandise two ways: (1) assume that the gross price method of recording purchases is used and (2) assume that the net price method of recording purchases is used.

PHYSICAL INVENTORY CALCULATIONS AND ADJUSTING ENTRY — OBJ. 4 —

4-32A Furniture City conducted a physical inventory at December 31, 1996. The items counted during the physical inventory are listed below. Furniture City's accountant provided the unit costs.

Item Description	December 31, 1996 Count	Unit Cost
Taylor sofas	10	$250
Georgia sofas	8	300
Taylor chairs	22	175
Taylor recliners	12	200
Georgia recliners	4	210
Carolina lamps	16	30
Chicago lamps	18	28
Georgia tables	8	150

REQUIRED

a. Prepare a schedule to determine the total cost of each item in the inventory and the total cost of the complete inventory at December 31, 1996.

b. Assume that the perpetual inventory records show a $14,360 debit balance in the Inventory account at December 31, 1996. Prepare the general journal entry to adjust the perpetual inventory to the total cost determined by the physical inventory.

CLASSIFIED FINANCIAL STATEMENTS — OBJ. 6 —

4-33A The adjusted trial balance of Marshall Corporation on December 31, 1996, is shown below; the perpetual inventory system has been used. Marshall had no stock transactions during 1996.

MARSHALL CORPORATION
ADJUSTED TRIAL BALANCE
DECEMBER 31, 1996

	Debit	Credit
Cash	$ 46,400	
Accounts Receivable	95,200	
Inventory	90,000	
Prepaid Insurance	300	
Furniture and Fixtures	32,000	
Accumulated Depreciation—Furniture and Fixtures		$ 6,800
Delivery Equipment	65,000	
Accumulated Depreciation—Delivery Equipment		32,000
Accounts Payable		17,400
Capital Stock		200,000
Retained Earnings		59,600
Sales		374,000
Sales Returns and Allowances	4,800	
Sales Discounts	4,000	
Cost of Goods Sold	214,800	
Salaries Expense (70% selling)	92,000	
Rent Expense (40% selling)	20,800	
Utilities Expense (30% selling)	6,800	
Insurance Expense (60% administrative)	1,500	
Depreciation Expense—Furniture and Fixtures (100% administrative)	3,200	
Depreciation Expense—Delivery Equipment (100% selling)	13,000	
	$689,800	$689,800

REQUIRED

a. Prepare a classified income statement for the year ended December 31, 1996.

b. Prepare a classified balance sheet as of December 31, 1996.

CLASSIFIED FINANCIAL STATEMENTS AND ADJUSTING ENTRIES — OBJ. 6 —

4-34A Oregon Distributors, whose accounting year ends on December 31, had the following normal balances in its ledger accounts at December 31, 1996:

Cash	$ 32,800		W. Oregon, Drawing	$ 8,000
Accounts Receivable	103,000		Sales	1,180,000
Inventory	82,000		Sales Returns and	
Prepaid Insurance	7,200		Allowances	9,600
Office Supplies	4,800		Sales Discounts	16,400
Furniture and Fixtures	28,000		Cost of Goods Sold	821,200
Accumulated Depreciation—			Utilities Expense	8,600
Furniture and Fixtures	10,800		Sales Salaries Expense	108,000
Delivery Equipment	70,000		Delivery Expense	36,800
Accumulated Depreciation—			Advertising Expense	26,200
Delivery Equipment	24,400		Rent Expense	30,000
Accounts Payable	69,400		Office Salaries Expense	72,000
Long-Term Notes Payable	30,000			
W. Oregon, Capital	150,000			

Rent expense and utilities expense are 70% administrative and 30% selling. During the year, the accounting department prepared monthly statements, but no adjusting entries were made in the journals and ledgers. Data for the year-end procedures are as follows:

1. Prepaid insurance, December 31, 1996 (insurance expense is classified as a selling expense) $ 2,400
2. Depreciation expense on furniture and fixtures for the year (an administrative expense) 2,000
3. Depreciation expense on delivery equipment for 1996 10,000
4. Salaries payable, December 31, 1996 ($1,000 sales and $600 office) 1,600
5. Office supplies on hand, December 31, 1996 1,800

REQUIRED

a. Record the necessary adjusting entries in general journal form at December 31, 1996.
b. Prepare a classified income statement for 1996.
c. Prepare a classified balance sheet at December 31, 1996.

ENTRIES FOR MERCHANDISE TRANSACTIONS ON SELLER'S AND BUYER'S RECORDS— PERIODIC — APPENDIX D —

4-35A Fortune Distributing Company had the following transactions with Arlington, Inc., during 1996:

Nov. 10 Fortune sold and shipped $6,000 worth of merchandise to Arlington, terms 2/10, n/30.

12 Arlington, Inc., paid freight charges on the shipment from Fortune Company, $360.

14 Fortune received $600 of merchandise returned by Arlington from the November 10 sale.

19 Fortune received payment in full for the net amount due on the November 10 sale.

24 Arlington returned goods that had originally been billed at $500. Fortune issued a check for $490.

REQUIRED

Record these transactions in general journal form as they would appear (a) on the books of Fortune Distributing Company and (b) on the books of Arlington, Inc. Arlington, Inc., records purchases using the gross price method. Assume that both companies use the periodic inventory system.

ENTRIES FOR MERCHANDISE TRANSACTIONS—PERIODIC — APPENDIX D —

4-36A Polidor Company was established on July 1, 1996. Its sales terms are 2/10, n/30. Credit terms for its purchases vary with the supplier. Selected transctions for the first month of operations are given below. Unless noted, all transactions are on account and involve merchandise held for resale. All purchases are recorded using the gross price method and the periodic inventory system.

July 1 Purchased goods from Dawson, Inc., $1,900; terms 1/10, n/30.

2 Purchased goods from Penn Company, $4,200, terms 2/10, n/30.

3 Paid freight on shipment from Dawson, $80.

5 Sold merchandise to Ward, Inc., $1,300.

5 Paid freight on shipment to Ward, Inc., $60.

July 8   Returned $300 worth of the goods purchased July 1 from Dawson, Inc., because some goods were damaged. Dawson approved the return.

9   Received returned merchandise from Ward, Inc., $200.

10   Paid Dawson, Inc., the amount due.

10   Purchased goods from Dorn Company with a list price of $2,400. Polidor was entitled to a $33\frac{1}{3}\%$ trade discount; terms 2/10, n/30.

11   Paid freight on shipment from Dorn Company, $130.

15   Received the amount due from Ward, Inc.

15   Sold merchandise to Colby Corporation, $3,200.

16   Mailed a check to Penn Company for the amount due on its July 2 invoice.

18   Received an allowance of $100 from Dorn Company for defective merchandise purchased on July 10.

19   Paid Dorn Company the amount due.

25   Received the amount due from Colby Corporation.

REQUIRED

Record these transactions for Polidor Company in general journal form.

CASES

BUSINESS DECISION CASE

Northwestern Corporation started a retail clothing business on July 1, 1996. During 1996, Northwestern Corporation had the following summary transactions related to merchandise inventory:

	Purchases	Sales
July	$240,000	$ 360,000
August	384,000	696,000
September	312,000	576,000
October	360,000	660,000
November	900,000	1,020,000
December	264,000	1,344,000

On average, Northwestern's cost of goods sold is 50% of sales. Assume that there were no sales returns and allowances or purchases returns and allowances during this six-month time period.

REQUIRED

a. Calculate the ending merchandise inventory for each of the six months.
b. Northwestern's purchases peaked during November; its sales peaked during December. Did Northwestern plan its purchases wisely? Should Northwestern expect a similar pattern in future years?

FINANCIAL ANALYSIS CASE

Johnson & Johnson is a worldwide manufacturer of health care products, including BAND-AID bandages and MYLANTA antacid. It reported the following results (in millions of dollars) for three recent years (Year 3 is the most recent):

	Year 3	Year 2	Year 1
Net Sales	$14,138	$13,753	$12,447
Cost of Goods Sold	4,791	4,678	4,204

Assume that similar-sized companies in the same basic industries have experienced an average gross profit percentage of 66% each year.

REQUIRED

a. Calculate the gross profit percentage for Johnson & Johnson for the three years.
b. Compare the three-year trend in gross profit percentage for Johnson & Johnson to the assumed industry average. Analyze the trend and evaluate the performance of Johnson & Johnson compared to the assumed industry average.

ETHICS CASE

During the last week of 1996, George Connors, controller of the We 'R' Appliances, received a memorandum from the firm's president, Jane Anderson. The memorandum stated that Anderson had negotiated a very large sale with a new customer and directed Connors to see that the order was processed and the goods shipped before the end of the year. Anderson noted that she had to depart from the usual credit terms of n/30 and allow terms of n/60 to clinch the sale. Although the credit terms were unusual for the company, Connors was particularly pleased with the news because business had been somewhat slow. The goods were shipped on December 29 and the sale was incorporated into the 1996 financial data.

It is now mid-February 1997, and two events have occurred recently that, together, cause concern for Connors. First, he was inadvertently copied on a letter from the firm's bank to Anderson. The letter stated that the bank had reconsidered its decision to deny a loan to the company and is now granting the loan based on the new, and favorable, sales data supplied by the president. The bank was "particularly impressed with the sales improvement shown in December." Although Connors had been involved in the initial loan application that was denied, he had been unaware that the president had reapplied for the loan.

The second event was that all of the goods shipped on December 29, 1996, to the new customer had just been returned.

REQUIRED

What are the ethical considerations George Connors faces as a result of the recent events?

GENERAL MILLS ANNUAL REPORT CASE

Refer to the annual report of General Mills, Inc., presented in Appendix K.

REQUIRED

a. At May 29, 1994, what was the total cost of inventory on hand?

b. What percent of total current assets was inventory at May 29, 1994?

c. The consolidated balance sheets are classified balance sheets.
    (1) What were the three major subgroups of assets at May 29, 1994?
    (2) What were the five types of current assets at May 29, 1994?

d. According to note 6, what were the descriptions and dollar amounts of the components that made up the Land, Buildings and Equipment total at May 29, 1994?

Accounting Systems and Internal Control

CHAPTER LEARNING OBJECTIVES

1 **DESCRIBE** the features of an accounting system (p. 166).

2 **EXPLAIN** the use of subsidiary ledgers (pp. 166–168).

3 **INTRODUCE** the special journal system, **DISCUSS** its advantages, and **CONTRAST** manual and computerized special journal systems (pp. 168–170).

4 **IDENTIFY** documents used in business transactions and **DESCRIBE** their flow through accounting transactions (pp. 170–174).

5 **DESCRIBE** electronic data interchange and electronic funds transfer and **DISCUSS** their use in computerized accounting systems (pp. 174–175).

6 **DEFINE** internal control, **DISCUSS** concepts used in designing internal controls, **PRESENT** examples of their application, and **DESCRIBE** control failures (pp. 175–178).

7 **PRESENT** controls in a computerized accounting system, including terminal access controls and application controls (pp. 179–180).

8 **DESCRIBE** financial statement audits and operational audits (pp. 180–181).

9 **Financial Analysis** **DEFINE** *return on sales* and **EXPLAIN** its use (pp. 181–182).

CHAPTER FOCUS

In 1981, IBM Corporation introduced its first personal computer. Prior to that time, only large organizations operated their own computerized accounting systems. During the 1980s and 1990s, many small companies acquired computerized accounting systems that used personal computers manufactured by Apple, IBM, Compaq, Gateway, Dell, Digital Equipment, and Hewlett-Packard. This chapter describes important features of computerized accounting systems, including subsidiary ledgers, special journals, business documents, electronic data interchange, electronic funds transfer, internal controls, and audits.

FEATURES OF ACCOUNTING SYSTEMS

OBJECTIVE 1

DESCRIBE the features of an accounting system.

The **accounting system** is a structured collection of people, policies, procedures, equipment, files, and records that a company uses to collect, record, classify, process, store, report, and interpret financial data. Some companies call their accounting system a *transaction processing system* because transactions generate data for the accounting system.

People are the most important element of an accounting system or transaction processing system. Accountants decide when and how to recognize and record transactions. They also establish accounting policies and procedures. Managers select computers and instruct programmers to program them to run the accounting system. Managers also identify and design the reports that they want the accounting system to produce. Analysts decide how to interpret financial data.

Policies and procedures are the rules that allow an accounting system to operate efficiently and correctly. The sequential steps in the accounting cycle are an example of an accounting procedure. Most accounting systems use equipment of some type. Manual accounting systems incorporate adding machines, calculators, and typewriters. Today, most accounting systems utilize computers. As a result, many accounting systems store files and records on magnetic tapes and magnetic disks rather than in the paper journals and ledgers described in the prior chapters.

The next section describes various types of manual accounting systems. Many computerized accounting systems used today are patterned after these manual systems. We need to understand the basics of manual accounting systems to fully understand the functioning of today's computerized accounting systems.

MANUAL ACCOUNTING SYSTEMS

The basic manual accounting system uses a general journal and a general ledger for recording and posting transactions and adjustments. This type of accounting system is satisfactory for presenting basic accounting concepts in an introductory accounting class. However, this system has two shortcomings for a business with even a moderate volume of accounting transactions.

First, the general ledger does not contain enough detail for required management analyses and decisions. For example, the accounts receivable account in the general ledger reveals the total amount that all customers owe the entity for credit sales. However, it does not reveal which customers owe the entity or how much each customer owes. The subsidiary ledgers described in this chapter provide this type of detail.

Second, recording all transactions in the general journal seriously limits the number of transactions that a company can record each day. Only one person at a time can make entries in this single journal. The multiple journal system we describe in this chapter overcomes this shortcoming.

SUBSIDIARY LEDGERS

A **subsidiary ledger** is a set of accounts or records that contains detailed information about the items included in the balance of one general ledger account. For example, each customer

OBJECTIVE *2*

EXPLAIN the use of subsidiary ledgers.

has one account or record in the accounts receivable subsidiary ledger. The balance of an account in the accounts receivable subsidiary ledger is the amount that one particular customer owes. Each accounts receivable subsidiary ledger account also contains other information about the customer, such as name, address, date and amount of each credit sale, and date and amount of each payment received.

A **control account** is a general ledger account that summarizes the accounts in a subsidiary ledger. The balance of a control account in the general ledger should equal the sum of the balances of all the accounts in the related subsidiary ledger. The general ledger account provides the control total for the subsidiary ledger accounts.

Most accounting systems maintain several subsidiary ledgers, each one providing details about a different general ledger account. Exhibit 5-1 provides a list of general ledger accounts (control accounts) that usually have subsidiary ledgers. Exhibit 5-1 also indicates the organization of each subsidiary ledger. For example, the inventory subsidiary ledger has one account for each item of merchandise and the accounts payable subsidiary ledger has one account for each supplier.

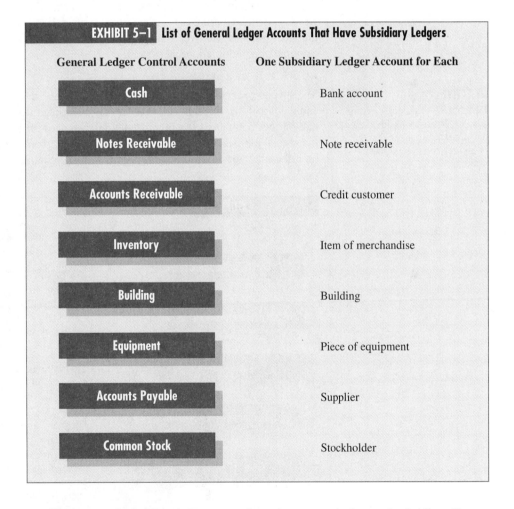

EXHIBIT 5–1 **List of General Ledger Accounts That Have Subsidiary Ledgers**

General Ledger Control Accounts	One Subsidiary Ledger Account for Each
Cash	Bank account
Notes Receivable	Note receivable
Accounts Receivable	Credit customer
Inventory	Item of merchandise
Building	Building
Equipment	Piece of equipment
Accounts Payable	Supplier
Common Stock	Stockholder

The names of subsidiary ledgers sometimes do not contain the word subsidiary. For example, the accounts receivable subsidiary ledger may be called the *accounts receivable ledger* or the *customer ledger.*

CODING SUBSIDIARY LEDGER DATA IN JOURNAL ENTRIES

When a company records a journal entry that affects one or more subsidiary ledgers, the company must provide detailed information in the journal entry to enable posting to the subsidiary accounts. The company can attach the detailed data to the general ledger account names in the journal entry:

Inventory—Product 2	1,000	
Inventory—Product 4	600	
Accounts Payable—Supplier 1		1,600
To record the purchase of merchandise on account.		

or place the detailed data in the explanation:

Inventory	1,600	
Accounts Payable		1,600
To record the purchase of merchandise on account. Inventory ledger postings: product 2 = $1,000 debit and product 4 = $600 debit; accounts payable ledger posting: supplier 1 = $1,600 credit.		

Either approach is acceptable.

MULTIPLE JOURNAL SYSTEMS

When a company records all its transactions in the general journal, the company can record only a limited number of transactions each day. With the single journal, only one person at a time can make journal entries. Companies have designed many different types of multiple journal systems to overcome this problem. We discuss the special journal system as an example of a multiple journal system.

THE SPECIAL JOURNAL SYSTEM

OBJECTIVE 3

INTRODUCE the special journal system, **DISCUSS** its advantages, and **CONTRAST** manual and computerized special journal systems.

The **special journal system** consists of five journals: the credit sales journal, the cash receipts journal, the payables journal, the cash disbursements journal, and the general journal. Various companies use other (but similar) names for these journals. A company using the special journal system records each transaction in only one of the journals. Exhibit 5-2 describes the types of transactions recorded in each journal.

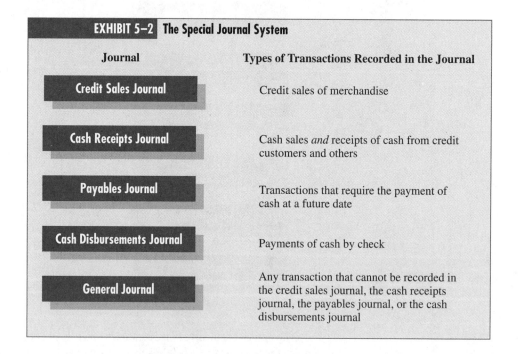

EXHIBIT 5–2   The Special Journal System

Journal	Types of Transactions Recorded in the Journal
Credit Sales Journal	Credit sales of merchandise
Cash Receipts Journal	Cash sales *and* receipts of cash from credit customers and others
Payables Journal	Transactions that require the payment of cash at a future date
Cash Disbursements Journal	Payments of cash by check
General Journal	Any transaction that cannot be recorded in the credit sales journal, the cash receipts journal, the payables journal, or the cash disbursements journal

All special journals have four distinguishing features. First, a company records transactions in a special journal in date sequence as they occur. Second, each transaction is recorded on one or more lines of the journal. Third, a company does not enter account titles in a special journal for most transactions. Instead, the company records dollar amounts in columns with account titles. Fourth, each special journal provides a structured format for recording subsidiary ledger data.

ADVANTAGES OF THE SPECIAL JOURNAL SYSTEM

Using special journals enables a division of labor in recording transactions. A company using the special journal system can divide the recording function among several people, each of whom records one particular type of transaction. Using special journals also reduces recording time. There is no need to enter account titles or explanations for the entries due to the columnar structure.

Posting is more streamlined and usually more efficient when a company uses special journals. First, the special journal organizes the data for easy posting daily to the subsidiary ledgers. Second, a company typically waits until the end of the month and then posts only the column totals to the appropriate general ledger accounts.

COMPUTERIZED SPECIAL JOURNAL SYSTEMS

An integrated computerized special journal system is made up of multiple software modules. A *software module* is a separate computer program that processes one particular group of transactions. Many computerized special journal systems have separate software modules for accounts receivable, accounts payable, cash receipts, cash disbursements, general ledger, payroll, and plant assets. Each software module maintains one or more master files. A *master file* is a computer file of detailed data, such as a subsidiary ledger or the general ledger. An *integrated computer system* provides programmed links between the various software modules. These programmed links allow automatic updating of multiple master files with only one entry of data.

To illustrate, Exhibit 5-3 displays the major steps a company follows in processing credit sales through an integrated computerized special journal system. The company enters

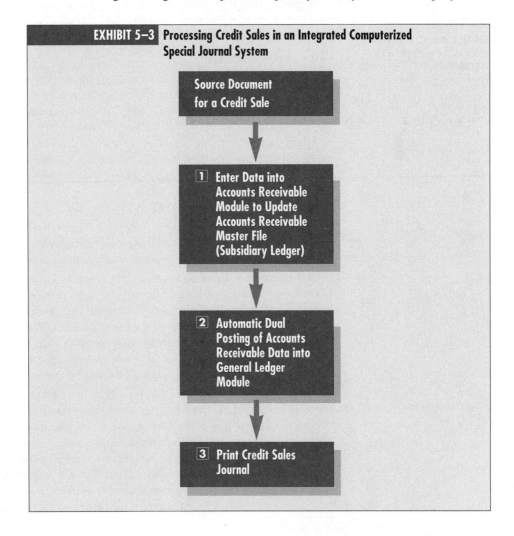

EXHIBIT 5–3 **Processing Credit Sales in an Integrated Computerized Special Journal System**

Source Document for a Credit Sale

1 Enter Data into Accounts Receivable Module to Update Accounts Receivable Master File (Subsidiary Ledger)

2 Automatic Dual Posting of Accounts Receivable Data into General Ledger Module

3 Print Credit Sales Journal

data related to the credit sale into the accounts receivable software module **1**. This module uses the data to update the accounts receivable master file (accounts receivable subsidiary ledger). The accounts receivable module then automatically transfers a copy of the data to the general ledger module, which uses the data to post the transaction to the general ledger master file **2**.

The last major step is printing the credit sales journal **3**. The computer system usually prints the credit sales journal daily, including only the transactions for that day.

DOCUMENTS USED IN BUSINESS TRANSACTIONS

OBJECTIVE 4

IDENTIFY documents used in business transactions and **DESCRIBE** their flow through accounting transactions.

Most companies use a variety of **business documents** to capture data related to business transactions. People in all business disciplines prepare and use these paper forms. Each company defines the format of each document that it uses. However, the various forms used by different companies have basically the same data documented on them. Some of these documents trigger the recording of transactions in the accounting system.

FLOW OF BUSINESS DOCUMENTS

A merchandising firm may encounter eight business documents when it purchases merchandise and returns some of the merchandise: purchase requisition, purchase order, packing list, receiving report, invoice, payment approval form, credit memo, and check. Exhibit 5-4 portrays the flow of these business documents between a retailer (purchaser) and a wholesaler (seller). This flow has 14 steps. In the following paragraphs, we discuss each step and present samples of some of the documents. We key our discussion to Exhibit 5-4 by referring to step numbers such as **1**. We assume that the retailer and wholesaler are both using the perpetual inventory system.

PURCHASE REQUISITION In step **1**, the retailer recognizes a need to order additional merchandise and prepares a purchase requisition. A **purchase requisition** is an internal document that requests that the purchasing department order particular items of merchandise. After management approves the form, it is sent to the retailer's purchasing department.

PURCHASE ORDER A **purchase order** is a document that formally requests a supplier to sell and deliver specific quantities of particular items of merchandise at specified prices. The purchasing department prepares this document after consulting price lists, catalogs, or quotations to determine which wholesaler to use **2**. The purchasing department sends the original copy of the purchase order to the wholesaler. The retailer's purchasing department sends duplicate copies to the retailer's receiving department and accounting department, where the copies are filed for later use. Exhibit 5-5 presents a sample purchase order.

PACKING LIST The wholesaler receives the purchase order, reviews it, and approves extending credit to the retailer **3**. The wholesaler then removes the merchandise from its inventory, packages it in cartons for shipping, and prepares a packing list **4**. The **packing list** is a document that lists the items of merchandise contained in the cartons and the quantity of each item. The wholesaler includes the retailer's purchase order number on the packing list for the convenience of the retailer. Typically, the wholesaler attaches the packing list to the outside of one of the cartons so the retailer can retrieve it without opening any of the cartons. The wholesaler then ships the cartons to the retailer.

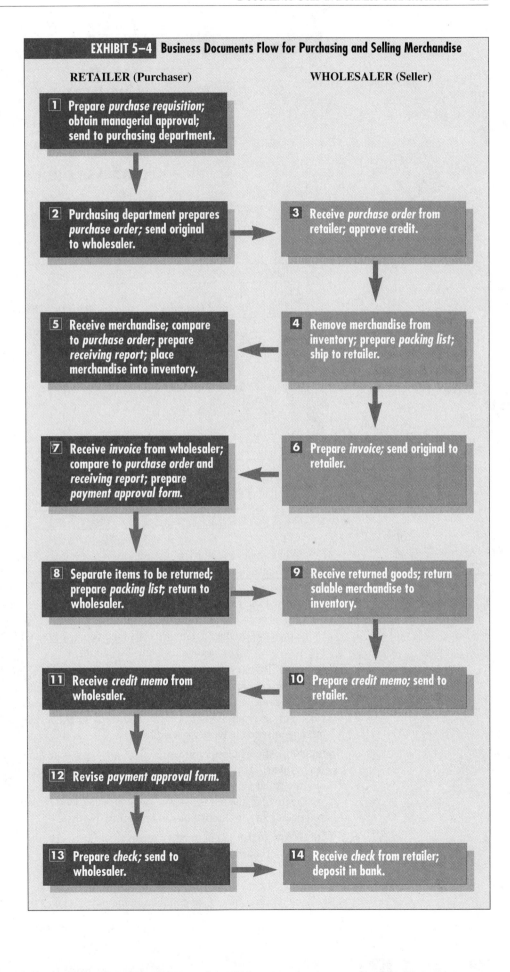

EXHIBIT 5–4 Business Documents Flow for Purchasing and Selling Merchandise

RETAILER (Purchaser)   WHOLESALER (Seller)

1 Prepare *purchase requisition*; obtain managerial approval; send to purchasing department.

2 Purchasing department prepares *purchase order*; send original to wholesaler.

3 Receive *purchase order* from retailer; approve credit.

5 Receive merchandise; compare to *purchase order*; prepare *receiving report*; place merchandise into inventory.

4 Remove merchandise from inventory; prepare *packing list*; ship to retailer.

7 Receive *invoice* from wholesaler; compare to *purchase order* and *receiving report*; prepare *payment approval form*.

6 Prepare *invoice*; send original to retailer.

8 Separate items to be returned; prepare *packing list*; return to wholesaler.

9 Receive returned goods; return salable merchandise to inventory.

11 Receive *credit memo* from wholesaler.

10 Prepare *credit memo*; send to retailer.

12 Revise *payment approval form*.

13 Prepare *check*; send to wholesaler.

14 Receive *check* from retailer; deposit in bank.

EXHIBIT 5–5 Sample Purchase Order

Hudson Stores

1300 Forest Acres Drive
Foothills, California 97608-4124

Number **3758**

Telephone 928-555-8600

PURCHASE ORDER

TO: Arden Supply Company
3508 Dobson Road
San Diego, California 95286-2770

Order Date: 6/10/96   Buyer: Brenda Gomez   Payment Terms: 2/10, n/30

Line	Item Number	Quantity	Item Description	Unit Price
1	268	10	Men's shirt, style JQ, size L	18.00
2	290	25	Men's shirt, style RG, size L	20.00
3	355	20	Men's shirt, style RG, size XL	20.00

Buyer's Signature: _____*Brenda Gomez*_____

When the cartons arrive, the retailer's receiving department removes the packing list from the cartons and compares it to the duplicate copy of the purchase order on file to determine whether the retailer had ordered the merchandise that was shipped **5**. After determining that the retailer had ordered the merchandise, the receiving department opens the cartons, inspects the merchandise, counts the quantity of each item, and compares the count to the quantity on the packing list. If all the counts agree with the quantities on the packing list, the receiving department accepts the shipment.

RECEIVING REPORT The receiving department then prepares the receiving report. The **receiving report** lists the details of the shipment, including date received, shipper name, supplier name, retailer's purchase order number, and, for each item received, the item number, item description, and quantity received. The receiving department then transfers the merchandise to the warehouse and sends the receiving report to the accounting department.

INVOICE The wholesaler prepares an invoice and sends the original copy to the retailer **6**. An **invoice** is a document that the seller sends to the purchaser to request payment for items that the seller shipped to the purchaser. Exhibit 5-6 presents a sample invoice. After issuing the invoice, the wholesaler records the sale (debit Accounts Receivable and credit Sales *and* debit Cost of Goods Sold and credit Inventory).

THREE-WAY MATCH The retailer receives the invoice in the mail from the wholesaler **7**. The retailer's accounting department then undertakes a process known as the *three-way match*. The three-way match is a process in which a person in the accounting department compares the invoice to the duplicate copy of the related purchase order and the related receiving report. The person conducting the match makes two important comparisons.

First, he or she compares item description and quantity on the invoice to item description and quantity on the receiving report to ensure that the items and quantities billed are the same as those actually received. Second, he or she compares item description, price, and credit terms on the invoice to item description, price, and credit terms on the purchase order to ensure that the prices billed agree with those specified on the purchase order and that the credit terms are those originally agreed upon. During the three-way match, all calculations on the invoice are recomputed to ensure mathematical accuracy.

PAYMENT APPROVAL FORM   If the comparisons reveal no discrepancies, accounting personnel prepare the payment approval form. The accounting department must reconcile any discrepancies before authorizing payment. The **payment approval form** is a document that authorizes the payment of an invoice. Some companies call this form a **voucher.** Data recorded on this form include (1) name of vendor to be paid, (2) scheduled date to pay, (3) amount to be paid, (4) invoice number, and (5) account distribution.

Account distribution is the list of the general ledger accounts and related dollar amounts to be debited and credited to record the approved payment. For example, the account distribution for a merchandise purchase is

Debit Inventory $500
Credit Accounts Payable $500

The person preparing the payment approval form attaches the duplicate copy of the purchase order, the receiving report, and the invoice to the payment approval form and then signs or initials the form. The retailer then records the purchase of merchandise. The retailer has made no accounting entry for the purchase of merchandise prior to this point.

EXHIBIT 5–6 Sample Invoice

Arden Supply Company
3508 Dobson Road
San Diego, California 95286-2770

Telephone 802-555-7825

Number **4692**

INVOICE

SOLD TO: Hudson Stores
1300 Forest Acres Drive
Foothills, California 97608-4124

Invoice Date: 6/18/96		P.O. Number 3758		Payment Terms: 2/10, n/30	
Line	**Item Number**	**Quantity**	**Item Description**	**Unit Price**	**Extended Price**
1	268	10	Men's shirt, style JQ, size L	$18.00	$180.00
2	290	25	Men's shirt, style RG, size L	20.00	500.00
3	355	20	Men's shirt, style RG, size XL	20.00	400.00
			Invoice Total		$1,080.00

POINT OF INTEREST

CREDIT SALES WITHOUT INVOICES

Some companies have eliminated some of the traditional business documents from their operations. Cummins Engine Co., Inc., ships truck engines to Freightliner Corp. each week. Cummins does not send invoices to Freightliner for any of the shipments. Instead, Cummins and Freightliner have agreed to use a technique known as *evaluated receipts settlement* (ERS). With ERS, Freightliner authorizes payment to Cummins based only on its receiving report. The recurring nature of the shipments makes ERS a feasible approach.

CREDIT MEMO   Steps **8** through **12** exist only if the retailer returns merchandise to the wholesaler. In step **8**, the retailer places the merchandise being returned in cartons, attaches a packing list, and ships it back to the wholesaler. The wholesaler receives the returned merchandise, returns it to inventory if it is salable or throws it away if it is damaged **9**, prepares a credit memo, and sends the credit memo to the retailer **10**. A **credit memo** is a document prepared by a seller to inform the purchaser that the seller has reduced the amount owed by the purchaser to the seller. The seller issues a credit memo to reflect a merchandise return or a merchandise allowance.

The credit memo is so named because the wholesaler credits (reduces) the retailer's account in the wholesaler's accounts receivable subsidiary ledger. The wholesaler also records the return in its general ledger accounts (debit Sales Returns and Allowances and credit Accounts Receivable *and* debit Inventory and credit Cost of Goods Sold). When the retailer (purchaser) receives the credit memo **11**, the retailer revises its payment approval form to reduce the amount to be paid **12**. The retailer also makes a journal entry (debit Accounts Payable and credit Inventory).

CHECK   Subsequently, the retailer prepares and sends a check to the wholesaler **13**. This step causes the retailer to make another journal entry (debit Accounts Payable and credit Cash). The wholesaler then receives the check and deposits it in the bank **14**. The wholesaler records the cash receipt as a debit to Cash and a credit to Accounts Receivable.

PRINCIPLE ALERT

OBJECTIVITY PRINCIPLE

The *objectivity principle* states that the recording of transactions should be based on reliable and verifiable evidence. The business documents and the processing of these documents described in this chapter illustrate the implementation of this basic principle for transactions involving the purchase and sale of merchandise. The documents provide the objective support for the accounts that are used and the dollar amounts that are entered into the accounting records.

USING ELECTRONIC DATA INTERCHANGE

OBJECTIVE 5

DESCRIBE electronic data interchange and electronic funds transfer and **DISCUSS** their use in computerized accounting systems.

Today, many companies use electronic data interchange instead of paper documents. **Electronic data interchange** is the computer-to-computer transmission of computer records that represent business documents other than checks. Electronic data interchange, commonly known as *EDI*, replaces a paper document with an electronic computer record that contains the data that traditionally have been recorded on a paper document. For example, instead of sending a paper purchase order to a wholesaler via mail, a retailer using EDI has its computer format a computer record containing the purchase order data. The retailer's computer then sends the computer record to the wholesaler's computer via telephone line or satellite transmission.

Companies often use EDI for purchase orders, invoices, and credit memos. Some major retailers have notified their suppliers that, in the future, the retailer will purchase merchandise only from suppliers willing and able to use EDI for ordering and invoicing. Most large companies are either using or investigating EDI because it has many advantages. EDI eliminates the costs of printing documents, of preparing and mailing documents, and of handling and filing documents. These three costs savings are usually very significant. Some companies using EDI have reduced their ordering and processing costs per transaction by over 50%.

EDI transfers information between companies much faster than paper documents flow. A company can send a computer record by telephone or satellite in less than a minute; sending a paper document by mail may take several days. A company can also obtain this time advantage by using a fax machine with a paper document. However, the cost advantages listed above are not available when using paper documents and a fax machine.

POINT OF INTEREST

STANDARDIZED "ELECTRONIC DOCUMENTS"

The American National Standards Institute, known as ANSI, has developed a set of standard document formats for EDI called *ANSI X.12 Standards*. These standards specify the structure of the electronic records for different types of documents. A company using EDI translates business document data from its own computer format into the ANSI X.12 computer format before sending the data to another company via telephone or satellite. The company receiving the business document data translates it from the ANSI X.12 computer format to its own computer format before placing the data in its computer files.

USING ELECTRONIC FUNDS TRANSFER

Many companies use electronic funds transfer to pay suppliers rather than writing and mailing checks. **Electronic funds transfer,** commonly known as EFT, involves sending an electronic message from one computer to another to cause a transfer of money from one financial institution to another. Actually, two electronic messages are sent. Assume a company wants to use EFT to transfer money to a second company to pay an invoice. The paying company has its computer send a message to its bank's computer to request the funds transfer. This is known as *retail EFT.* Then, the paying company's bank uses EFT to transfer funds to the receiving company's bank. This is known as *wholesale EFT* or *bank-to-bank EFT.* Wholesale EFT usually involves a central bank (such as a federal reserve bank) that acts as an automated clearing house by increasing the balance of one bank and decreasing the balance of the other bank.

INTERNAL CONTROLS

OBJECTIVE 6
DEFINE internal control, **DISCUSS** concepts used in designing internal controls, **PRESENT** examples of their application, and **DESCRIBE** control failures.

Internal controls are the measures undertaken by a company to ensure the reliability of its accounting data, protect its assets from theft or unauthorized use, make sure that employees are following the company's policies and procedures, and evaluate the performance of employees, departments, divisions, and the company as a whole. A company installs internal controls to improve the chances that the employees will function according to the plans developed by the management team.

Management is responsible for designing, installing, and monitoring internal controls throughout the company. In designing the controls, management tries to attain "reasonable assurance" rather than "absolute assurance" that the controls will meet their objectives. Management does this by balancing the benefit derived from installing a control against the cost of installing and maintaining the control. The benefit should exceed the cost.

Internal controls exist in many forms, including policies, procedures, records, equipment, supervision, and insurance. An internal control can be either a prevention control or a detection control. A company establishes a **prevention control** to deter problems before they arise. A company establishes a **detection control** to discover problems soon after they arise. Prevention controls are generally more desirable than detection controls.

A company should incorporate the following concepts when it designs its prevention and detection controls:

1. Establish clear lines of authority and responsibility.
2. Separate incompatible work functions.
3. Hire competent personnel.
4. Use control numbers on all business documents.
5. Develop plans and budgets.
6. Maintain adequate accounting records.
7. Provide physical and electronic controls.
8. Conduct internal audits.

We discuss each of these concepts in the following paragraphs and provide examples of their use.

ESTABLISH CLEAR LINES OF AUTHORITY AND RESPONSIBILITY

The organization structure of a company defines the lines of authority and responsibility within the company. When a company assigns authority to an employee to perform certain functions, it also makes that employee responsible for accomplishing certain objectives. This structure provides the overall framework for planning, directing, and controlling the company's operations. It informs the employees about who is in charge of what functions and to whom each person reports.

Supervision is a very important internal control. The existence of an identified supervisor is a preventive control: employees know that the supervisor is evaluating their performance so they are more likely to perform according to the rules. Supervision is also a detection control: the supervisor is likely to discover errors or irregularities when he or she reviews the work performance of employees.

Management must make sure that all of the company's employees understand management's philosophy and operating style as well as the authority and responsibility relationships. To guide employees in performing their duties, top management develops written policy statements, procedure manuals, and job descriptions. These control items are very important guidelines to employees so they properly record accounting transactions and perform related duties.

SEPARATE INCOMPATIBLE WORK FUNCTIONS

When allocating various duties within the transaction processing system, management should make sure that too much responsibility is not assigned to any one employee. No individual employee should be able to perpetrate and conceal irregularities in the transaction processing system. To accomplish this, management must separate three functions: the authorization function, the recording function, and the custody function. Ideally, for any particular transaction, an individual employee should have authority to perform only one of these three functions.

For example, if an employee "authorizes" a sales transaction by approving the customer's credit, that employee should not "record" the transaction in the accounting records or have physical "custody" of the merchandise sold or the cash received from the customer. This separation is an important preventive control. For another example, the employee preparing a purchase order for merchandise "authorizes" the transaction. The employee preparing the receiving report gains "custody" of the merchandise. Neither of these employees should be allowed to "record" this transaction in the accounting records.

HIRE COMPETENT PERSONNEL

Because people are the most important element of an accounting system, it is vital that a company hire competent personnel. Management must screen each applicant for a job to determine that he or she has sufficient education, training, and experience to qualify for the job. After hiring the employee, the company should provide specific formal training so the employee is able to do all the tasks the job requires. The training should refer to the written policy statements, procedure manuals, and job descriptions so the employee becomes familiar with them.

Some companies routinely rotate personnel among various jobs. For example, a company might switch jobs between an employee working exclusively with the accounts receivable subsidiary ledger and an employee working exclusively on the accounts payable subsidiary ledger. This rotation may disclose errors or irregularities resulting from over-familiarity with the job or carelessness. Requiring employees to take vacations of at least one week in duration may also disclose errors or irregularities when another employee performs the vacationing employee's duties. These two controls—job rotation and mandatory vacations—also develop backup personnel for important processing jobs within the accounting system.

USE CONTROL NUMBERS ON ALL BUSINESS DOCUMENTS

All business documents such as purchase orders, invoices, credit memos, and checks should have control numbers preprinted on them. Each control number should be unique for that type of document. The bank checks that you use to pay your personal bills have control numbers on them, usually in the upper right-hand corner. You refer to them as *check numbers.*

To provide proper control to the accounting process, a company should use the following three rules related to control numbers on business documents. First, have a commercial printer place the control numbers on the documents when they are printed. Second, use the documents in strict numerical sequence. That is, use number 101 first, then 102, then 103, and so on. Third, for each type of business document, periodically account for all the numbers in the sequence to make sure that all of them were processed. Use of control numbers with this type of reconciliation helps to ensure that a company records all transactions and it does not record a transaction multiple times. This important preventive control contributes to the accuracy of the data in the accounting system.

POINT OF INTEREST

COMPUTERIZED RESTAURANT SYSTEMS

Restaurant chains such as The Olive Garden, Applebee's, and T.G.I.Fridays are using computer systems rather than prenumbered customer order slips. After taking a customer's order, the server enters it into a computer terminal. The computer assigns a sequential control number to the order. The drink order then appears on a video screen in the bar and the food order appears on a video screen in the kitchen. When the customer is ready to pay, the server instructs the terminal to print the final bill, which has the sequential control number printed on it. This system speeds up the operation of the restaurant and provides good control over the ordering process and cash collection process.

DEVELOP PLANS AND BUDGETS

Top management should initiate the planning and budget process to establish forward thinking about the business and to provide a basis for evaluating performance. Every company should prepare an annual operating plan and budget. These items provide guidance for all levels of managers on how to respond to various situations. The budget also provides a basis for comparing actual operating results when management evaluates performance. Examples of evaluating performance are comparing actual sales to budgeted sales and comparing actual advertising expense to budgeted advertising expense.

MAINTAIN ADEQUATE RECORDS

We have already discussed many controls that help ensure that a company has adequate accounting records. These controls include using the double-entry approach to recording transactions (debits = credits), preparing trial balances (total debits = total credits), maintaining a control account in the general ledger for each separate subsidiary ledger (control account balance = sum of the subsidiary ledger account balances), and taking physical inventory counts (physical inventory total = perpetual inventory total).

Many internal controls related to maintaining adequate records involve comparisons. A company periodically makes a physical inspection to compare the data in the plant assets subsidiary ledger to plant assets actually in use. This inspection identifies missing assets and assets not recorded in the subsidiary ledger. Both require adjustment of the subsidiary ledger and related general ledger accounts. Similarly, a company periodically confirms the amounts owed to suppliers (accounts payable subsidiary ledger) and amounts due from customers (accounts receivable subsidiary ledger) by contacting the suppliers and customers.

Occasionally, someone else makes the comparisons for the company. For example, each time the company issues a payroll check to an employee, the company also issues a statement to the employee detailing gross pay, deductions, and net pay. The employee then compares these data to the results that he or she expected. This approach identifies errors quickly.

PROVIDE PHYSICAL AND ELECTRONIC CONTROLS

Physical and electronic controls take many forms. Locked doors are a very important physical control. Locked doors help prevent the theft of assets and protect the integrity of the accounting system. Many companies install safes and vaults to store cash prior to depositing it in the bank and to hold important business documents such as mortgages and securities. Safes and vaults should be installed so they can withstand significant fires and natural disasters such as tornados. Fencing all company property and assigning security guards at the gates are other commonly used physical controls.

Electronic controls are widely used today. Merchandising firms use electronic cash registers to ensure that each salesperson records each transaction as it occurs and that the salesperson stores cash in a locked drawer. Retailers, convenience stores, and banks use observation cameras to monitor their operations. Retailers also attach to merchandise special plastic tags that activate electronic sensors and ring alarms if a person attempts to leave the store without having the plastic tag removed by a salesperson.

A wide variety of companies issues employee name badges with magnetic stripes on the back. Employees use these badges to gain entry into various parts of the company by placing the card in a reader with electronic sensors. These readers can also record the time that each employee arrives and departs. Many electronic controls are built into computer-based systems. We discuss these controls in later sections of this chapter.

CONDUCT INTERNAL AUDITS

In a small company, internal auditing is a function that a company assigns to an employee who has other duties as well. In a large company, internal auditing is assigned to an independent department that reports to top management or the board of directors of a corporation. **Internal auditing** is a company function that provides independent appraisals of the company's financial statements, its internal controls, and its operations.

The appraisal of its internal controls involves two phases. First, the internal auditor determines whether sufficient internal controls are in place. Second, the internal auditor determines whether the internal controls in place are actually functioning as planned. After completing the appraisal, the internal auditor makes recommendations to management on additional controls that are needed and improvements that are required in existing controls.

CONTROL FAILURES

Occasionally, internal controls fail. For example, an employee forgets to lock a door and a thief steals merchandise. Or an employee with custody responsibilities steals cash received from customers. A company cannot absolutely prevent these types of incidents. Instead, the company acquires insurance to compensate it if these types of incidents occur. Casualty insurance provides financial compensation for losses from fire, natural disasters, and theft. A **fidelity bond** is an insurance policy that provides financial compensation for theft by employees specifically covered by the insurance.

Another reason that internal controls fail is employee collusion. When two or more employees work together to get around or avoid prescribed internal controls, this act is known as *employee collusion*. For example, an employee with custody of an asset can work with an employee with recording responsibilities to steal the asset and cover up the theft in the accounting records. Employee collusion is difficult to prevent or detect. Hiring high-quality employees and paying them at least market salaries and wages is the best approach to avoid collusion. Close supervision is also important.

CONTROLS IN A COMPUTERIZED ACCOUNTING SYSTEM

OBJECTIVE 7

PRESENT controls in a computerized accounting system, including terminal access controls and application controls.

Many companies have computerized their accounting systems. A computerized accounting system processes accounting transactions one of two ways: batch processing or on-line real-time processing. In a **batch processing system,** a company accumulates a group of transactions, usually recorded on business documents, for a period of time, usually one day. The company enters all of the transactions into the computer at one time and then processes the entire group of transactions. Frequently, the data entry and processing occur at night. As a result, accounting files are up-to-date only after the night processing.

In an **on-line real-time system,** a company enters each transaction into the computer as it occurs. The computer then processes the transaction immediately. Most newly designed accounting systems available today incorporate on-line real-time processing. This approach maintains accounting files that are always up-to-date. Batch processing systems and on-line real-time systems both require special internal controls related only to computer systems.

TERMINAL ACCESS CONTROLS

Most companies use computer terminals to enter accounting data into a computer system. A computer terminal is a piece of equipment consisting of a keyboard, a video screen, and internal electronic devices that translate keyboard input into digital signals that the terminal sends to a computer via a cable or telephone line connection. A microcomputer can function as a computer terminal if it is equipped with special electronic devices. A company must devise **terminal access controls** to provide internal control over entering accounting data via a terminal.

User identification codes, passwords, and access control matrix are three examples of terminal access controls. The first data item that a user enters into a computer terminal is his or her *user identification code.* This code identifies to the computer who is doing the data entry. For example, William J. Chang's user identification code might be WJC465 (Chang's initials plus his employee number). Employees usually know the user identification codes of other employees.

The second data item that a user enters into a computer terminal is his or her **password.** A password is a string of characters that the user enters to prove to the computer that the user is truly the person associated with the user identification code. Passwords are confidential; each employee should know only his or her password. Chang's password might be 2XM3Q, a meaningless combination of numbers and letters. If he is unable to enter his user identification number and password, the computer will not allow him to enter accounting data.

POINT OF INTEREST

CUSTOMER ACCESS TO BANK COMPUTER TERMINALS

Many banks such as Chase Manhattan and Bank One have installed automated teller machines (sometimes called *cash machines*) to allow their customers to make deposits and withdraw cash from checking or savings accounts without having to visit a bank location. A bank provides each customer with a plastic card with a magnetic stripe on its back. When the customer inserts the card into the machine (actually a computer terminal), it reads the customer number (user identification code) from the magnetic stripe. The machine then asks the customer to enter his or her personal identification number (PIN), which is really a password. The PIN, known only to the customer, prevents another person from using the card unless the customer reveals the PIN.

After entering his user identification code and password, Chang then informs the computer what tasks he wants to perform on the computer system. The computer then checks the access control matrix to determine whether Chang will be allowed to do what he requested. An **access control matrix** is a computerized file that lists the type of access that each user is entitled to have to each file and program in the computer system. Chang may have "inquire-only access" (can look at data but cannot post transactions or change existing data) to payroll files, "update access" (can look at data and post transactions but cannot change existing data) to general ledger files, and "maintenance access" (can look at data, post transactions, and change existing data) to accounts payable files. The access control matrix allows Chang to perform only those computer tasks that management has authorized.

APPLICATION CONTROLS

In a computerized accounting system, many internal controls are built into the computer programs. These controls reject data items that do not meet predefined conditions before the data enter the accounting system. An **edit check** examines each piece of data to determine whether it has the correct sign (positive or negative), the correct type of characters (alphabetic or numeric), and the correct number of characters (for example, exactly six characters). A **sequence check** examines each piece of data to determine if the data are being entered in the correct sequence (for example, item 101 before item 102).

A **validity check** determines whether an entered value for a code (such as customer number) is among the possible values. The computer makes this check by referring to a table of possible values stored in the computer. A **limit check** determines whether an entered value is greater than an established maximum value. For example, the number of hours worked by one employee in one week cannot be greater than 60 (the limit set by management). These controls, and other similar controls, help ensure that users are entering correct data into the accounting system.

AUDITING

OBJECTIVE 8

DESCRIBE financial statement audits and operational audits.

One of the internal control concepts we mentioned previously was conducting internal audits. Internal audits provide appraisals of the company's financial statements, its internal controls, and its operations. Company employees conduct internal audits under the direction of top management or the board of directors. Parties outside the company, such as bankers and stockholders, want independent appraisals of the company's performance. These parties are usually unwilling to accept an audit report prepared by company-employed internal auditors.

Outsiders frequently require that an independent, professional auditing firm conduct a financial statement audit, usually at the end of each year. Federal laws require all corporations whose common stock is publicly traded on an interstate basis to have an independent firm of certified public accountants (CPAs) audit their annual financial statements. The company being audited pays the CPA firm for conducting the audit.

FINANCIAL STATEMENT AUDITS

A **financial statement audit** is an examination of a company's financial statements (usually annual financial statements) by a firm of independent certified public accountants. The CPA firm conducts this examination so it can prepare a report that expresses an opinion on whether the financial statements fairly present the operating results, cash flows, and financial position of the company. The CPAs must be "independent"; that is, they cannot be owners, investors, or employees of the company they are auditing.

AUDIT PROCEDURES

The CPA firm conducts the audit according to standards established by the American Institute of Certified Public Accountants. The audit includes many different stages of work. During an early stage of the audit, the auditors review and evaluate the internal controls in the company's accounting system and other systems. The review and evaluation help the auditors determine what additional steps should be included in the audit. Then the auditors collect and analyze data that substantiates the amounts in the financial statements. The auditors obtain most of these data from accounting records (such as journals and ledgers), business documents (such as purchase orders, invoices, and payment approval forms), and outside sources (such as banks, insurance companies, and suppliers).

THE AUDIT REPORT

The **audit report** that the auditors issue specifies the financial statements that were audited, summarizes the audit process, and states the auditors' opinion on the financial statements.

The opinion usually states that the financial statements "fairly present" the operating results, cash flows, and financial position of the company. The auditors do not conduct the audit to determine whether the financial statements are absolutely correct. Instead, they conduct the audit to determine whether the financial statements are fair presentations of operating results, cash flows, and financial position.

PRINCIPLE ALERT

GOING CONCERN CONCEPT

The *going concern concept* assumes that the business entity will continue to operate indefinitely. As part of their annual audit, auditors must assess the likelihood that the firm they are auditing will continue as a going concern for a reasonable period. Events such as recurring losses, pending litigation, and the loss of a major customer or supplier may raise concern about the firm's ability to maintain its going concern status. In such cases, auditors should assess management's response to the problem and the type of financial statement disclosure being made about the problem. When substantial doubt exists about the going concern status, auditors may include a paragraph in the audit report expressing their concern.

The primary purpose of a financial statement audit is *not* the discovery of fraudulent acts by management or employees of the company. Many audit procedures use statistical samples of transactions and data rather than examining the complete population. The auditors use samples to minimize the time required to conduct the audit and its cost. As a result, there is the possibility that errors or irregularities exist in the transactions and data that the auditors did not review or evaluate. However, auditors carefully design their procedures to detect errors and irregularities that are material in relation to the financial statements. Therefore, it is unlikely that the auditors will not detect a material error or irregularity.

OPERATIONAL AUDITS

Both internal audit departments and independent CPA firms perform operational audits. An **operational audit** is an evaluation of activities, systems, and internal controls within a company to determine their efficiency, effectiveness, and economy. Operational auditing goes beyond accounting records and financial statements to obtain a full understanding of the operations of the company. Companies dedicated to continuous quality improvement often use operational audits to identify specific areas where they need to improve the quality of operations or products.

Auditors design operational audits to assess the quality and efficiency of operational performance, identify opportunities for improvement, and develop specific recommendations for improvement. Each operational audit is unique. The scope of an operational audit can be very narrow (review and evaluate the procedures for processing cash receipts) or quite broad (review and evaluate all the internal controls in a computerized accounting system).

An operational audit report is usually treated as a confidential document that a company restricts to internal use. The operational audit report can take a variety of forms. The report should include the purpose of the operational audit, the areas reviewed, the procedures followed, the results obtained from the procedures, the conclusions, and any recommendations for improvements. The report should indicate that the auditors discussed the conclusions and recommendations with personnel from the departments subject to the operational audit. The report should also state how the personnel in the audited departments reacted to the conclusions and recommendations. The report should note any significant disagreements.

FINANCIAL ANALYSIS

RETURN ON SALES

Many people view the income statement as the most important financial statement. The income statement determines and presents net income, referred to as *the bottom line*. Most

OBJECTIVE 9

· **DEFINE** *return on sales* and **EXPLAIN** its use.

companies share the goal of generating a profit, that is, a positive net income. In addition to looking at the net income amount, managers, analysts, and investors also look at **return on sales,** or percent profit. Return on sales is calculated as follows:

$$\text{Return on Sales} = \frac{\text{Net Income}}{\text{Net Sales}}$$

The consolidated financial statements of Abbott Laboratories for three recent years (Year 3 is the most recent) reveal the following information (in millions of dollars):

	Year 3	Year 2	Year 1
Net Sales	$8,407.8	$7,851.9	$6,876.6
Net Income	$1,399.1	$1,239.1	$1,088.7

The return on sales for Year 3 is calculated as follows:

Return on Sales = $1,399.1/$8,407.8 = 0.166, or 16.6%

This percentage means that 16.6% of each dollar of net sales remains after deducting cost of goods sold, operating expenses, and income taxes. The return on sales for each of the three years is

	Year 3	Year 2	Year 1
Return on Sales	16.6%	15.8%	15.8%

During the three-year period, Abbott Laboratories has increased its net sales and its net income. In addition, Abbott Laboratories has increased its return on sales from 15.8% to 16.6%. This increase of 0.8% is very significant. The net income for Year 3 is $67,262,400 higher because the return on sales percentage increased from 15.8% to 16.6% ($8,407,800,000 × 0.8% = $67,262,400). Pharmaceutical and nutritional products represent more than 50% of Abbott Laboratories' sales. Compared with most other industries, companies in the pharmaceutical industry tend to have high returns on sales.

KEY POINTS FOR CHAPTER LEARNING OBJECTIVES

1 **DESCRIBE** the features of an accounting system (p. 166).
- An accounting system is a structured collection of people, policies, procedures, equipment, files, and records that a company uses to collect, record, classify, process, store, report, and interpret financial data.

2 **EXPLAIN** the use of subsidiary ledgers (pp. 167–168).
- A subsidiary ledger is a set of accounts that contains detailed information about the items included in the balance of one general ledger account, known as a *control account.*

3 **INTRODUCE** the special journal system, **DISCUSS** its advantages, and **CONTRAST** manual and computerized special journal systems (pp. 168–170).
- The special journal system consists of five journals: the credit sales journal, the cash receipts journal, the payables journal, the cash disbursements journal, and the general journal.
- The special journal system enables a division of labor, reduces recording time, and streamlines posting.
- A computerized special journal system uses software modules to update detailed data on master files. The processing sequence involves updating (posting) the master files before preparing a printed journal.

4 **IDENTIFY** documents used in business transactions and **DESCRIBE** their flow through accounting transactions (pp. 170–174).
- Business documents capture data related to business transactions.
- A merchandising firm may encounter eight business documents (listed below in usual order of occurrence).
  - Purchase requisition—an internal document that requests that the purchasing department order specific items.
  - Purchase order—a document that requests a supplier to sell and deliver specific quantities of particular items at specified prices.
  - Packing list—a document prepared by the seller that lists the contents of the carton to which it is attached.

- Receiving report—a document prepared by the buyer that lists the details of a shipment received from a supplier.
- Invoice—a document that the seller sends to the buyer to request payment for items sold.
- Payment approval form—a document that authorizes payment of an invoice. This form is completed after determining that the invoice, receiving report, and invoice agree (three-way match).
- Credit memo—a document prepared by the seller to inform the buyer of a reduction in the amount owed due to a return or an allowance.
- Check—a written order to transfer cash.

5 **Describe** electronic data interchange and electronic funds transfer and **Discuss** their use in computerized accounting systems (pp. 174–175).
- Electronic data interchange (EDI) is the computer-to-computer transmission of computer records that represent business documents other than checks.
- Electronic funds transfer (EFT) is the sending of an electronic message from one computer to another to cause a transfer of cash.

6 **Define** *internal control,* **Discuss** concepts used in designing internal controls, **Present** examples of their application, and **Describe** control failures (pp. 175–178).
- Internal controls are the measures undertaken by a company to ensure the reliability of its accounting data, protect its assets from theft or unauthorized use, make sure that employees are following the company's policies and procedures, and evaluate the performance of employees, departments, divisions, and the company as a whole.
- A prevention control is designed to deter problems before they arise. A detection control is designed to discover problems soon after they arise. Prevention controls are generally more desirable than detection controls.
- A company should incorporate the following concepts when it designs its controls:
  - Establish clear lines of authority and responsibility.
  - Separate incompatible work functions.
  - Hire competent personnel.
  - Use control numbers on all business documents.
  - Develop plans and budgets.
  - Maintain adequate accounting records.
  - Conduct internal audits.

7 **Present** controls in a computerized accounting system, including terminal access controls and application controls (pp. 179–180).
- Terminal access controls provide internal control over entering accounting data via a computer terminal. Computer systems incorporate three types of terminal access controls: user identification code, password, and access control matrix.
- Application controls are internal controls built into computer programs. Edit checks, sequence checks, validity checks, and limit checks are examples.

8 **Describe** financial statement audits and operational audits (pp. 180–181).
- A financial statement audit is an examination of a company's financial statements by a firm of independent certified public accountants. The firm issues an audit report upon completion of the audit.
- An operational audit is an evaluation of activities, systems, and internal controls within a company to determine their efficiency, effectiveness, and economy.

9 **Financial Analysis** **Define** *return on sales* and **Explain** its use (pp. 181–182).
- Return on sales is calculated as follows:

$$\text{Return on Sales} = \frac{\text{Net Income}}{\text{Net Sales}}$$

SELF-TEST QUESTIONS FOR REVIEW

1. Which business document would Jacobs Stores use to document the receipt of merchandise from a supplier?
   a. Purchase order
   b. Packing list
   c. Receiving report
   d. Invoice

2. Which of the following documents would Ramirez Company not use in the three-way match process to authorize payment of an invoice?
   a. Purchase order
   b. Packing list
   c. Receiving report
   d. Invoice

3. Burton Company should utilize all except one of the following concepts related to placing control numbers on business documents. Which concept should Burton *not* use?
   a. Write the control number on the document when it is used.
   b. Place control numbers on all business documents.
   c. Use the documents in strict numerical sequence.
   d. Periodically account for all numbers used.

4. Helen Wong enters accounting transaction data into an on-line real-time computer system for Arlington Stores. What is the confidential data item that she enters to prove her identity to the computer system called?
   a. Limit check
   b. Sequence check
   c. User identification code
   d. Password

5. Bill Williams enters cash receipts via a computer terminal. What is the application control that determines whether each customer number that Bill enters is a real customer number?
   a. Limit check
   b. User identification code
   c. Validity check
   d. Terminal access control

DEMONSTRATION PROBLEM FOR REVIEW

The accounting systems terms listed below are used in this chapter. Select the statement that best defines the term and place the letter associated with the statement in the space to the left of the term.

__ 1. Control account	__ 7. Fidelity bond
__ 2. Subsidiary ledger	__ 8. Employee collusion
__ 3. Purchase requisition	__ 9. Access control matrix
__ 4. Packing list	__ 10. Limit check
__ 5. Invoice	__ 11. Validity check
__ 6. Electronic data interchange	__ 12. Operational audit

a. An application control in a computer program that determines whether an entered value is greater than an established maximum value.
b. An internal document that requests that the purchasing department order particular items of merchandise.
c. An insurance policy that provides compensation for theft by an employee.
d. The computer-to-computer transmission of computer records that represent business documents other than checks.
e. A general ledger account that summarizes the accounts in the related subsidiary ledger.
f. An evaluation of activities, systems, and internal controls within a company to determine efficiency, effectiveness, and economy.
g. Two or more employees working together to get around or avoid prescribed internal controls.
h. A set of accounts or records that contains detailed information about the items included in the balance of one general ledger account.
i. An application control in a computer program that determines whether an entered value for a code is among the possible values.
j. A document that the seller sends to the purchaser to request payment for items that the seller shipped to the purchaser.
k. A computerized file that lists the type of access that each computer user is entitled to have to each file and program in the computer system.
l. A document that lists the items of merchandise contained in a carton and the quantity of each item.

SOLUTION TO DEMONSTRATION PROBLEM

1. e   2. h   3. b   4. l   5. j   6. d   7. c   8. g   9. k   10. a   11. i   12. f

ANSWERS TO SELF-TEST QUESTIONS

1. c, p. 172   2. b, pp. 172–173   3. a, p. 177   4. d, p. 179   5. c, p. 180

GLOSSARY OF KEY TERMS USED IN THIS CHAPTER

access control matrix   A computerized file that lists the type of access that each computer user is entitled to have to each file and program in the computer system (p. 179).

accounting system   The structured collection of people, policies, procedures, equipment, files, and records that a company uses to collect, record, classify, process, store, report, and interpret financial data (p. 166).

audit report   A report issued by independent auditors that includes the final version of the financial statements, accompanying notes, and the auditor's opinion on the financial statements (p. 180).

batch processing system   A computer system that processes a group of transactions periodically rather than each transaction as it occurs (p. 179).

business documents   Printed forms used by a company to capture data related to business transactions (p. 170).

control account   A general ledger account that summarizes the accounts in the related subsidiary ledger (p. 167).

credit memo   A document prepared by a seller to inform the purchaser that the seller has reduced the amount owed by the purchaser due to a return or an allowance (p. 174).

detection control   An internal control designed to discover problems soon after they arise (p. 175).

edit check   An application control in a computer program that examines each piece of input data to determine whether it has the correct sign, the correct type of characters, and the correct number of characters (p. 180).

electronic data interchange   The computer-to-computer transmission of computer records that represent business documents other than checks (p. 174).

electronic funds transfer   Sending an electronic message from one computer to another to cause a transfer of money from one financial institution to another (p. 175).

fidelity bond   An insurance policy that provides financial compensation for theft by employees specifically covered by the insurance (p. 178).

financial statement audit   An examination of a company's financial statements by a firm of independent certified public accountants (p. 180).

internal auditing   A company function that provides independent appraisals of the company's financial statements, its internal controls, and its operations (p. 178).

internal controls   The measures undertaken by a company to ensure the reliability of its accounting data, protect its assets from theft or unauthorized use, make sure that employees are following the company's policies and procedures, and evaluate the performance of employees, departments, divisions, and the company as a whole (p. 175).

invoice   A document that the seller sends to the purchaser to request payment for items that the seller shipped to the purchaser (p. 172).

limit check   An application control in a computer program that determines whether an entered value is greater than an established maximum value (p. 180).

on-line real-time system   A computer system that processes each transaction as it occurs; accounting files are always up-to-date (p. 179).

operational audit   An evaluation of activities, systems, and internal controls within a company to determine their efficiency, effectiveness, and economy (p. 181).

packing list   A document that lists the items of merchandise contained in a carton and the quantity of each item; the packing list is usually attached to the outside of the carton (p. 170).

password   A string of characters that a computer user enters into a computer terminal to prove to the computer that the person using the computer is truly the person named in the user identification code (p. 179).

payment approval form   A document that authorizes the payment of an invoice (p. 173).

prevention control   An internal control designed to discover problems before they arise (p. 175).

purchase order   A document that formally requests a supplier to sell and deliver specific quantities of particular items of merchandise at specified prices (p. 170).

purchase requisition   An internal document that requests that the purchasing department order particular items of merchandise (p. 170).

receiving report   A document that lists the details of a shipment received from a supplier, including date received, shipper name, supplier name, purchase order number, and, for each item received, the item number, item description, and quantity received (p. 172).

return on sales   The ratio obtained by dividing Net Income by Net Sales (p. 182).

sequence check   An application control in a computer program to determine whether the data in a file is in the correct sequence (p. 182).

special journal system   A manual accounting system that includes five journals (books of original entry): the credit sales journal, the cash receipts journal, the payables journal, the cash disbursements journal, and the general journal (p. 168).

subsidiary ledger   A set of accounts or records that contains detailed information about the items included in the balance of one general ledger account (p. 166).

terminal access controls   Internal controls built into computer programs to provide control over entering accounting data via a computer terminal (p. 179).

validity check   An application control in a computer program that determines whether an entered value for a code is among the possible values (p. 180).

voucher   Another name for the payment approval form (p. 173).

QUESTIONS

5-1 Define *accounting system.* What is the most important element of an accounting system?

5-2 What is a subsidiary ledger? What is a control account?

5-3 What three subsidiary ledgers does a merchandising firm that uses the perpetual inventory system need to post the details of merchandise transactions?

5-4 Name the five journals in the special journal system. What type of transactions can be recorded in each journal?

5-5 What are the benefits of using the special journal system rather than only the general journal?

5-6 Nordquist Company is considering installing an integrated computerized special journal system. What are the major steps that this type of system would follow in processing credit sales data?

5-7 How are a purchase requisition and a purchase order similar and different?

5-8 How are a packing list and a receiving report similar and different?

5-9 What three business documents are used when the three-way match is performed? What two important comparisons should be made?

5-10 Hartman Company is considering adding electronic data interchange (EDI) to its accounting system. How does EDI work? Do any EDI standards exist?

5-11 What is electronic funds transfer (EFT)? What are retail EFT and wholesale EFT?

5-12 Define and contrast *prevention controls* and *detection controls*. Which are more desirable?

5-13 Yates Company is reviewing its internal procedures to try to improve internal control. It specifically wants to separate incompatible work functions. What three types of work functions must be separated to improve internal control?

5-14 Kwong Industries is redesigning its business documents. What three rules should Kwong follow relative to the use of control numbers on business documents?

5-15 Portland Company has an on-line real-time computer system. Employees use terminals to enter data into Portland's accounting system. What are three terminal access controls that Portland should incorporate into its computer system? Describe them.

5-16 How are a financial statement audit and an operational audit similar and different?

5-17 What does the term *return on sales* mean? Explain its use.

PRINCIPLES DISCUSSION QUESTION

5-18 Carter Manufacturing Company makes a variety of consumer products. For the year just ended (and the two prior years), sales of private label product to Mega-Mart (1,200 stores nationwide) have made up 60% to 65% of total sales. On December 31 of the year just ended, Mega-Mart informed Carter that it would be buying all private label products from another manufacturer under a five-year contract. Losing this business will result in a 50% to 55% reduction in total gross profit.
   a. What is the going concern concept and how does it apply to this situation?
   b. How should the full disclosure principle be applied when preparing the annual report for the year just ended?
   c. What is the independent auditor's responsibility in this situation?

EXERCISES

SUBSIDIARY LEDGERS
— OBJ. 2 —

5-19 Finestein Company uses the perpetual inventory system, makes all purchases and sales of merchandise on a credit basis, and maintains the following subsidiary ledgers:
   a. Notes Receivable
   b. Accounts Receivable
   c. Inventory
   d. Building
   e. Autos and Trucks
   f. Accounts Payable
   For each of the following transactions, place the letter of each subsidiary ledger updated by the transaction in the space to the left of the number of the transaction. Each letter may be used more than once; there may be more than one letter for each transaction.
   __ **1.** Paid cash to a supplier.
   __ **2.** Sold merchandise to a customer.
   __ **3.** Purchased a new truck for cash.
   __ **4.** Customer returned merchandise for credit.
   __ **5.** Sold a building for cash.

SPECIAL JOURNALS
— OBJ. 3 —

5-20 Alpine Company makes all purchases of merchandise on a credit basis. Alpine uses the special journal system. Each of Alpine's transactions is recorded in one of the following journals: (a) credit sales journal, (b) cash receipts journal, (c) payables journal, (d) cash disbursements journal, and (e) general journal. For each of the following transactions, place the letter of the best answer in the space to the left of the transaction's number.

__ **1.** Which journal would be used to record the purchase of merchandise from a supplier?

__ **2.** Which journal would be used to record the sale of a piece of used equipment for cash?

__ **3.** Which journal would be used to record the sale of merchandise on account?

__ **4.** Which journal would be used to record the payment of an amount due to a supplier?

BUSINESS DOCUMENTS
— OBJ. 4 —

5-21 Ferring Company, a merchandising firm, has used the following business documents in its business:

> Payment approval form to pay supplier
> Packing list for return to supplier
> Packing list for shipment from supplier
> Purchase requisition
> Invoice from supplier
> Purchase order to supplier
> Check to pay supplier
> Receiving report for shipment from supplier
> Credit memo from supplier

Place these documents in the normal order of occurrence. Assume that the return occurred before the approval of the payment to the supplier.

TERMINAL ACCESS CONTROLS
— OBJ. 7 —

5-22 Zander Company uses an on-line real-time computer system to maintain its accounting records. All accounting transaction data are entered into the computer system via terminals. Zander's president wants to make sure that only authorized employees in the accounting department are able to access the accounting files. Prepare a brief memo that answers the following questions:

a. What are the first two data elements a user enters when using a computer terminal?

b. Which of these is commonly known and which is confidential?

c. What is an access control matrix?

d. What are three possible different types of access that an employee may be granted to the accounting files?

INTERNAL CONTROL
— OBJ. 6 —

5-23 Each of the following unrelated procedures has been designed to strengthen internal control. Explain how each of these procedures strengthens internal control.

a. After preparing a check for a cash disbursement, the accountant for Travis Lumber Company cancels the supporting business documents (purchase order, receiving report, and invoice) by stamping them PAID.

b. The salespeople for Davis Department Store give each customer a cash register receipt along with the proper change. A sign on each cash register states that no refunds or exchanges are allowed without the related cash register receipt.

c. The ticket-taker at the Esquire Theater tears each admission ticket in half and gives one half back to the ticket purchaser. The seat number is printed on each half of the ticket.

d. John Renaldo's restaurant provides servers with prenumbered customers' checks. The servers are to void checks with mistakes on them and issue new ones rather than make corrections on them. Voided checks must be given to the manager every day.

PROBLEMS

SUBSIDIARY LEDGERS
— OBJ. 2 —

5-24 Wild Rose Distributing, which uses the perpetual inventory system, makes all sales and purchases of merchandise on account. Wild Rose maintains five subsidiary ledgers: accounts receivable, inventory, building, equipment, and accounts payable. Wild Rose had the following transactions during March:

Mar. 15 Paid $4,000 cash to Hosta Company, a supplier.

17 Purchased a $22,000 forklift to move merchandise around the warehouse. This purchase was paid for with cash received from a bank loan.

20 Sold six-foot-long fence boards with a cost of $1,700 to Home Supply (an existing customer) for $3,000.

21 Received $2,500 cash from The Greenery, a frequent customer.

25 Purchased $3,500 of six-foot-long fence boards from James Company, a long-time supplier.

REQUIRED

For each of the transactions described above, indicate which subsidiary ledger(s) would be affected and what the effect(s) would be.

BUSINESS DOCUMENTS
— OBJ. 4 —

5-25 Marston Company distributes a variety of products to retailers. All purchases and sales of merchandise are made on a credit basis. Marston uses the perpetual inventory system. The following events took place during August 1996:

Aug. 11   Received merchandise from Hall Manufacturing, reviewed the shipment, and placed the merchandise into inventory.

15   Regas Manufacturing packed merchandise for Marston and shipped the cartons via Ajax Trucking Company.

17   Marston packed and returned some of the merchandise received from Hall Manufacturing on August 11. Hall had authorized the return.

19   After receiving the returned goods, Hall notified Marston that its account with Hall had been reduced by the selling price of the returned goods.

22   Marston's accountant reviewed the necessary documentation for a bill received from London Company and authorized its payment on August 30.

24   Marston's office manager made a request that a new printer be purchased for the company computer.

25   Marston billed Jupiter Stores for merchandise that Marston shipped to Jupiter.

27   Marston received some of the merchandise back from Jupiter Stores. Jupiter's account with Marston was reduced by the sales price of the merchandise returned.

29   Karlson Company paid Marston the balance of its account.

REQUIRED

For each event, name the business document that records the event and which company prepared the document. Use the following three-column format:

Date of Event   Business Document   Preparer

INTERNAL CONTROL
— OBJ. 4, 6 —

5-26 Regent Company encountered the following situations:

a. The person who opens the mail for Regent, Bill Stevens, stole a check from a customer and cashed it. To cover up the theft, he debited Sales Returns and Allowances and credited Accounts Receivable in the general ledger. He also posted the amount to the customer's account in the accounts receivable subsidiary ledger.

b. The purchasing agent, Susan Martin, used a company purchase order to order building materials from Builders Mart. Later, she telephoned Builders Mart and changed the delivery address to her home address. She told Builders Mart to charge the material to the company. At month-end, she approved the invoice from Builders Mart for payment.

c. Nashville Supply Company sent two invoices for the same order: the first on June 10 and the second on July 20. The accountant authorized payment of both invoices and both were paid.

d. On January 1, Jack Monty, a junior accountant for Regent, was given the responsibility of recording all general journal entries. At the end of the year, the auditors discovered that Monty had made 150 serious errors in recording transactions. The chief accountant was unaware that Monty had been making mistakes.

REQUIRED

For each situation, describe any violations of good internal control procedures and identify the steps that you would take to prevent each situation.

INTERNAL CONTROL
— OBJ. 6 —

5-27 Each of the following lettered paragraphs briefly describes an independent situation involving some aspect of internal control.

REQUIRED

Answer the questions at the end of each paragraph or numbered section.

a. Robert Flynn is the office manager of Oswald Company, a small wholesaling company. Flynn opens all incoming mail, makes bank deposits, and maintains both the general ledger and the accounts receivable subsidiary ledger. An assistant records transactions in the credit sales journal and the cash receipts journal. The assistant also prepares a monthly statement for each customer and mails the statements to the customers. These statements list the beginning balance, credit sales, cash receipts, adjustments, and ending balance for the month.

1. If Flynn stole Customer A's $200 check (payment in full) and made no effort to conceal his embezzlement in the ledgers, how would the misappropriation probably be discovered?

2. What routine accounting procedure would disclose Flynn's $200 embezzlement in part (1), even if Flynn destroyed Customer A's subsidiary ledger account?

3. What circumstances might disclose Flynn's theft if he posted a payment to Customer A's account in the accounts receivable subsidiary ledger and set up a $200 account for a fictitious customer?

4. In part (3), why might Flynn be anxious to open the mail himself each morning?

5. In part (3), why might Flynn want to have the authority to write off accounts considered uncollectible?

b. A doughnut shop uses a cash register that produces a printed receipt for each sale. The register also prints each transaction on a paper tape that is locked inside the cash register. Only the supervisor has access to the locked-in tape. A prominently displayed sign promises a free doughnut to any customer who is not given the cash register receipt with his or her purchase. How is this procedure an internal control device for the doughnut shop?

c. Jason Miller, a swindler, sent several businesses invoices requesting payment for office supplies that had never been ordered or delivered to the businesses. A 5% discount was offered for prompt payment. What internal control procedures should prevent this swindle from being successful?

d. The cashier for Uptown Cafeteria is located at the end of the food line. After customers have selected their food items, the cashier rings up the prices of the food and the customer pays the bill. The customer line frequently stalls while the person paying searches for the correct amount of cash. To speed things up, the cashier often collects money from the next customer or two who have the correct change without ringing up their food on the register. After the first customer finally pays, the cashier rings up the amounts for the customers who have already paid.

1. What is the internal control weakness in this procedure?
2. How might the internal control over the collection of cash from the cafeteria customers be strengthened?

ALTERNATE EXERCISES

SUBSIDIARY LEDGERS — OBJ. 2 —

5-19A Pratt Company uses the perpetual inventory system, makes all purchases and sales of merchandise on a credit basis, and maintains subsidiary ledgers for (a) accounts receivable, (b) inventory, (c) building, (d) equipment, and (e) accounts payable. Place the letters of the answers in the space to the left of each question.

__ **1.** Which subsidiary ledger(s) would be affected by the purchase of a new building for cash?

__ **2.** Which subsidiary ledger(s) would be affected by the purchase on account of merchandise from a supplier?

__ **3.** Which subsidiary ledger(s) would be affected by the sale of a piece of equipment for cash?

__ **4.** Which subsidiary ledger(s) would be affected by the receipt of cash from a customer?

__ **5.** Which subsidiary ledger(s) would be affected by the return of merchandise by a customer for credit?

SPECIAL JOURNALS — OBJ. 3 —

5-20A Cherokee Company makes all purchases of merchandise on a credit basis. Cherokee uses the special journal system. Each of Cherokee's transactions is recorded in one of the following journals:

a. Credit sales journal
b. Cash receipts journal
c. Payables journal
d. Cash disbursements journal
e. General journal

For each of the following transactions, place the letter of the journal that would be used to record the transaction in the space to the left of the transaction number.

__ **1.** Purchased merchandise from a supplier.

__ **2.** Received cash from a customer on account.

__ **3.** Received merchandise returned by a customer for credit.

__ **4.** Sold merchandise to a customer for cash.

BUSINESS DOCUMENTS — OBJ. 4 —

5-21A Hoskins Company, a merchandising firm, has used the following business documents in its business:

> Invoice to customer
> Purchase order from customer
> Packing list for return from customer
> Packing list for shipment to customer
> Check from customer
> Credit memo to customer
> Receiving report for goods returned by customer

Place these documents in the normal order of occurrence. Assume that the return occurred before the customer paid Hoskins.

COMPUTER APPLICATION CONTROLS — OBJ. 7 —

5-22A Vardanski Company uses an on-line real-time computer system to maintain its accounting records. Employees in operational departments use terminals to enter accounting data directly into the computer as the transactions occur. Vardanski uses user identification codes, passwords, and an access control matrix to control access to the terminals. Vardanski's controller wants to build internal controls into the accounts receivable programs that will reject data items that do not meet predefined conditions. Prepare a memo that defines each of the following application controls and give an example of how each would be used to control the entry of cash receipts from credit customers.

> Edit check
> Validity check
> Limit check

INTERNAL CONTROL — OBJ. 6 —

5-23A Each of the following unrelated procedures has been designed to strengthen internal control. Explain how each of these procedures strengthens internal control.

a. Western Corporation's photocopy machines are activated by keying a code number. Each employee is assigned a different, confidential code number. Each copy machine keeps track of the number of copies run under each employee number.

b. Picket Company's bank requires a signature card on file for each Picket Company employee who is authorized to sign checks.

c. Fast Stop Convenience Stores have programmed their cash registers to imprint a blue star on every 300th receipt printed. A sign by each cash register states that the customer will receive $2 if his or her receipt has a blue star on it.

d. Wilson Corporation has a policy that every employee must take two weeks of vacation each year.

ALTERNATE PROBLEMS

SUBSIDIARY LEDGERS — OBJ. 2 —

5-24A Colorific Paint Distributing maintains four subsidiary ledgers: accounts receivable, inventory, plant assets, and accounts payable. Colorific makes all purchases and sales of merchandise on account. It also uses the perpetual inventory system. Colorific had the following transactions during June:

June 10 Received $600 cash from Paint World, a frequent customer.

12 Purchased $1,100 of exterior white paint from Thomas Moore Paint Company, a long-time supplier. Colorific continually stocks this item.

16 Paid $850 cash to Franklin Industries, a supplier.

22 Sold interior blue paint with a cost of $500 to Sanchez Lumber for $800. Sanchez is a frequent customer.

26 Purchased a delivery truck for $25,000. The truck dealer provided 100% financing with a 36-month term.

REQUIRED

For each of the transactions described above, indicate which subsidiary ledger(s) would be affected and what the effect(s) would be.

BUSINESS DOCUMENTS — OBJ. 4 —

5-25A Horton Company distributes a variety of products to retailers. All purchases and sales of merchandise are made on a credit basis. Horton uses the perpetual inventory system. The following events took place during October 1996:

Oct. 12 Horton's accountant reviewed the documents related to a bill received from Brennen Company and authorized its payment on October 20.

14 Horton billed Walton Stores for merchandise that Horton had shipped to Walton.

18 Horton received some of the merchandise back from Walton Stores. Walton's account with Horton was reduced by the sales price of the merchandise returned.

20 Received merchandise from Davidson Manufacturing, inspected the merchandise, and placed it into inventory.

21 Stock Manufacturing packed merchandise for Horton and shipped the cartons via XRX Trucking Company.

23 Carolina Company paid Horton the balance of its account.

26 Horton packed and returned some of the merchandise received from Davidson Manufacturing on October 20. Davidson had authorized the return.

29 After receiving the returned goods, Davidson notified Horton that its account with Davidson had been reduced by the selling price of the returned goods.

30 Horton's warehouse manager made a request that a new desk be purchased for the warehouse.

REQUIRED

For each event, name the business document that records the event and which company prepared the business document. Use the following three-column format:

Date of Event	Business Document	Preparer

INTERNAL CONTROL
— OBJ. 4, 6 —

5-26A Wheeler Company encountered the following situations:

a. Jenny Farrell, head of the receiving department, created a fictitious company named Quick Forms and used it to send invoices to Wheeler Company for business documents that Wheeler never ordered or received. Farrell prepared receiving reports that stated that the business documents had been received. Wheeler's controller compared the receiving reports to the invoices and paid each one.

b. Wheeler Company lost one day's cash receipts. An employee took the receipts to the bank after the bank's closing hours to deposit them in the night depository slot. A creative thief had placed a sign on the slot saying it was out of order and all deposits should be placed in a metal canister placed next to the building. Wheeler's employee placed the deposit in the canister and left. Employees from two other companies did the same thing. Later that night, the thief returned and stole the deposits from the canister. (This is an actual case.)

c. Wheeler Company does not prenumber the sales invoices used for over-the-counter sales. A cashier pocketed cash receipts and destroyed all copies of the related sales invoices.

REQUIRED

For each situation, describe any violations of good internal control procedures and identify the steps that you would take to prevent each situation.

INTERNAL CONTROL
— OBJ. 6 —

5-27A The Mountain Twister amusement ride has the following system of internal control over cash receipts. All persons pay the same price for a ride. A person taking the ride pays cash to the cashier and receives a prenumbered ticket. The tickets are issued in strict number sequence. The individual then walks to the ride site, hands the ticket to a ticket-taker (who controls the number of people getting on each ride), and passes through a turnstile. At the end of each day, the beginning ticket number is subtracted from the ending ticket number to determine the number of tickets sold. The cash is counted and compared with the number of tickets sold. The turnstile records how many people pass through it. At the end of each day, the beginning turnstile count is subtracted from the ending count to determine the number of riders that day. The number of riders is compared with the number of tickets sold.

REQUIRED

Which internal control feature would reveal each of the following irregularities?

a. The ticket-taker lets her friends on the ride without tickets.

b. The cashier gives his friends tickets without receiving cash from them.

c. The cashier gives too much change.

d. The ticket-taker returns the tickets she has collected to the cashier. The cashier then resells these tickets and splits the proceeds with the ticket-taker.

e. A person sneaks into the ride line without paying the cashier.

CASES

BUSINESS
DECISION CASE

Qualitec Electronics Company is a distributor of microcomputers and related electronic equipment. The company has grown very rapidly. It is located in a large building near Chicago, Illinois. Jack Flanigan, the president of Qualitec, has hired you to perform an internal control review of the company. You conduct interviews of key employees, tour the operations, and observe various company functions. You discover the following:

1. Qualitec has not changed its ordering procedures since it was formed eight years ago. Anyone in the company can prepare a purchase order and send it to the vendor without getting any managerial approval. When the invoice arrives from the vendor, it is compared only to the purchase order before authorizing payment.

2. Qualitec does not have an organization chart. In fact, employees are encouraged to work on their own, without supervision. Flanigan believes that this approach increases creativity.

3. Business documents have been carefully designed by the controller. When the printer prints the documents, no control numbers are printed on them. Instead, employees using a form write the next sequential number on the form. The controller believes that this approach ensures that a proper sequencing of numbers will be maintained.

4. No budgets are prepared for the company.

5. All doors to the building remain unlocked from 7:00 a.m. to 11:00 p.m. Employees normally work from 7:30 a.m. to 5:00 p.m. A private security firm drives to the building to unlock it each morning and lock it each night. The security firm's employee leaves immediately after unlocking or locking. The company does not use time clocks or employee badges.

6. Flanigan believes that audits (either external or internal) are a waste of time. He has resisted the bank president's urging to hire a CPA firm to conduct an audit.
7. Qualitec has installed an on-line real-time microcomputer network. All employees have access to all computer application programs. Flanigan has told each employee which programs to use and which programs not to use. The first thing that appears on the terminal screen is a menu asking the employee which program he or she wants to use.
8. The employees who enter accounting data are expected to manually review the data for three types of errors: (1) alphabetic characters in the customer number or vendor number, (2) quantities that exceed allowed maximums, and (3) invalid product numbers, customer numbers, and vendor numbers.

REQUIRED

Analyze the findings listed above. Then list all the internal control weaknesses that you can identify. For each weakness, describe one or more internal controls that Qualitec should install to overcome the weakness.

FINANCIAL ANALYSIS CASE

Johnson & Johnson is a worldwide manufacturer of health care products, including BAND-AID bandages and MYLANTA antacid. It has 81,600 employees and 168 operating companies in 50 countries. The consolidated statement of earnings for Johnson & Johnson for three recent years (Year 3 is the most recent) reveals the following information (in millions of dollars):

	Year 3	Year 2	Year 1
Net Sales	$14,138	$13,753	$12,447
Cost of Goods Sold	4,791	4,678	4,204
Income Taxes	545	582	577
Net Income	1,787	1,030	1,461

REQUIRED

a. Calculate the return on sales for each of the three years.
b. What trend, if any, is evident in the three years?

ETHICS CASE

Donald Keane is an employee in the central purchasing department of Home Centers, a large retail hardware chain. His job includes recommending suppliers to the purchasing supervisor. This recommendation is only one of the many factors the supervisor considers when making the final decision for a supplier.

Keane is offered an all-expenses-paid weekend at a resort by Tools-N-Stuff, a new supplier that wants to increase the amount of business it does with Home Centers. Tools-N-Stuff owns a condominium at this resort and frequently offers similar weekend trips to customers. Keane does not know what Home Center's policy, if any, is on the acceptance of such gifts.

REQUIRED

What are the ethical considerations facing Donald Keane? What are his alternatives?

GENERAL MILLS ANNUAL REPORT CASE

Refer to The Report of Management Responsibilities and the Independent Auditors' Report in the annual report of General Mills, Inc., presented in Appendix K.

REQUIRED

a. What party is responsible for the fairness and accuracy of the company's financial statements?
b. Why has management established a system of internal controls?
c. What firm was retained to audit the financial statements?
d. What opinion did the auditors express about the financial statements of General Mills, Inc.?
e. How much time elapsed between the end of the accounting year and the date the auditors issued their report?

Cash, Cash Controls, and Receivables

CHAPTER LEARNING OBJECTIVES

1 **DEFINE** cash and **DISCUSS** accounting for cash (p. 194).

2 **DESCRIBE** internal controls for cash received on account and cash received from retail cash sales (pp. 195–199).

3 **DISCUSS** checking accounts, bank statements, bank reconciliations, and petty cash (pp. 199–205).

4 **PRESENT** an overview of accounts receivable, **DEFINE** losses from uncollectible accounts, and **DISCUSS** the allowance method of accounting for credit losses (pp. 205–208).

5 **DESCRIBE** and **ILLUSTRATE** two methods for estimating credit losses—the percentage of net sales method and the accounts receivable aging method (pp. 208–210).

6 **INTRODUCE** the direct write-off method and **CONTRAST** it to the allowance method (pp. 210–211).

7 **DISCUSS** the accounting treatment of credit card sales (pp. 211–212).

8 **ILLUSTRATE** a promissory note, **DISCUSS** the calculation of interest on promissory notes receivable, and **PRESENT** journal entries to record notes receivable and interest (pp. 212–215).

9 **Financial Analysis** **DEFINE** *accounts receivable turnover* and *average collection period* and **EXPLAIN** their use (pp. 215–216).

CHAPTER FOCUS

Cash and accounts receivable are two assets that play a major role in most businesses. Recently, for example, cash and accounts receivable represented over 50% of the assets of Kelly Services, Inc. (staffing services), and Sybase, Inc. (client/server software and services). In this chapter, we define cash and examine internal controls related to cash, including cash handling controls and procedural controls such as bank reconciliations and petty cash funds. Then we discuss accounts receivable and accounting for uncollectible accounts expense. Accounting for credit card sales and promissory notes receivable are also covered.

ACCOUNTING FOR CASH

OBJECTIVE *1*
DEFINE cash and **DISCUSS** accounting for cash.

Cash includes coins, currency (paper money), checks, money orders, traveler's checks, and funds on deposit at a financial institution in checking accounts and savings accounts. An item is considered to be an element of cash if (1) it is acceptable to a bank for deposit and (2) it is free from restrictions that would prevent its use for paying debts.

Many near-cash items such as certificates of deposit, postdated checks, not-sufficient-funds checks, and IOUs are not considered to be cash. **Certificates of deposit** (CDs) are securities issued by a bank when cash is invested for a short period of time, typically six months or one year. CDs pay a fixed interest rate. A **postdated check** is a check from another person or company with a date that is later than the current date. A postdated check does not become cash until the date of the check. A **not-sufficient-funds check** (NSF check) is a check from an individual or company that had an insufficient cash balance in the bank when the holder of the check presented it to the bank for payment. **IOU** is a slang term for a note receivable, a written document that states that one party promises to pay the other party a certain amount of cash at a certain date. CDs are investments and postdated checks, NSF checks, and IOUs are receivables rather than cash.

CASH IN THE BALANCE SHEET

A company may have only one Cash account in the general ledger or it may have multiple cash accounts, such as Cash in Bank, Cash on Hand, and Petty Cash. Cash in Bank includes checking accounts and savings accounts. Cash on Hand includes cash items not yet deposited in the bank. Petty Cash is used for small disbursements.

When a company has several bank accounts, it may maintain a separate general ledger account for each account rather than one overall Cash in Bank account. Although a company may prepare for internal use only a balance sheet that shows each individual bank account separately, the balance sheet that the company prepares for external users typically shows the combined balances of all bank accounts and other cash accounts under the single heading Cash. Management wants the detail so it can monitor and control the various accounts and on-hand amounts. Most external users are interested only in the total amount of cash and its relationship to other items on the financial statements.

Cash is a current asset and is shown first in the balance sheet listing of assets. Sometimes a company's total cash includes one or more compensating balances. A **compensating balance** is a minimum amount that a bank requires a firm to maintain in a bank account as part of a borrowing arrangement. Compensating balances related to short-term borrowings are current assets, which, if significant, are reported separately from the cash amount among the current assets. Compensating balances related to long-term borrowings are reported as long-term assets.

CASH AND CASH EQUIVALENTS

A company may combine certain short-term, highly liquid investments with cash and present a single amount called **cash and cash equivalents** in the balance sheet. Treasury bills and money market funds are examples of investments that may be considered as cash equivalents. A company presents this combined amount on the balance sheet so it ties to the statement of cash flows. The statement of cash flows explains the changes during an accounting period in a firm's total cash and cash equivalents.

INTERNAL CONTROL OF CASH RECEIPTS TRANSACTIONS

OBJECTIVE *2*

DESCRIBE internal controls for cash received on account and cash received from retail cash sales.

Most companies develop elaborate internal controls to protect cash because it is their most liquid asset. Cash is highly desirable, easily taken and concealed, and quickly converted into other assets. In addition, a high percentage of a company's transactions involve cash. Cash is received from customers and cash is paid to suppliers and employees. A company receives cash from customers, for example, as payments on account and as payments for cash sales. The following sections describe cash-handling procedures and related internal controls for these two types of cash receipts.

CASH RECEIVED ON ACCOUNT

A company receives cash through the mail from customers who are making payments on their accounts receivable balances. Four departments play major roles in processing cash receipts that arrive via the mail: the mailroom, the treasurer's department, the controller's department, and the internal audit department. Exhibit 6-1 and the following paragraphs describe the role that each department plays in processing mail cash receipts.

MAILROOM

A company often sets up a separate post office box and asks all its customers to mail cash payments on account to that post office box. All other mail and company correspondence

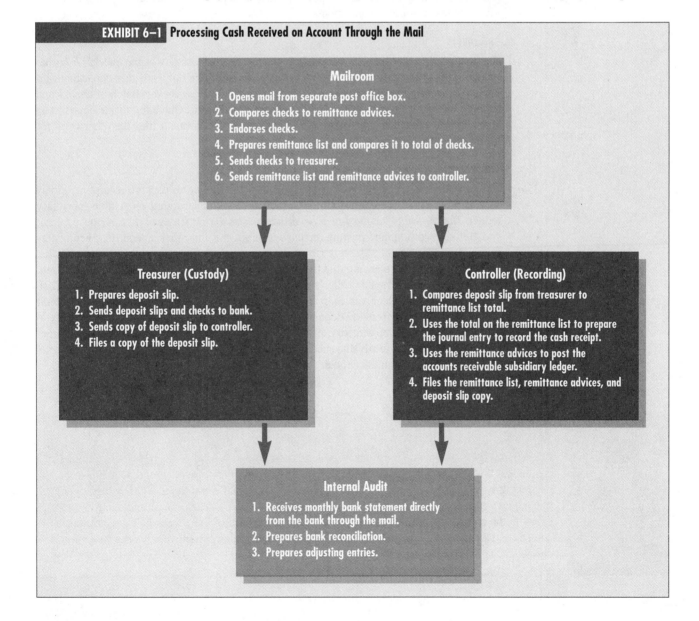

EXHIBIT 6-1   **Processing Cash Received on Account Through the Mail**

Mailroom
1. Opens mail from separate post office box.
2. Compares checks to remittance advices.
3. Endorses checks.
4. Prepares remittance list and compares it to total of checks.
5. Sends checks to treasurer.
6. Sends remittance list and remittance advices to controller.

Treasurer (Custody)
1. Prepares deposit slip.
2. Sends deposit slips and checks to bank.
3. Sends copy of deposit slip to controller.
4. Files a copy of the deposit slip.

Controller (Recording)
1. Compares deposit slip from treasurer to remittance list total.
2. Uses the total on the remittance list to prepare the journal entry to record the cash receipt.
3. Uses the remittance advices to post the accounts receivable subsidiary ledger.
4. Files the remittance list, remittance advices, and deposit slip copy.

Internal Audit
1. Receives monthly bank statement directly from the bank through the mail.
2. Prepares bank reconciliation.
3. Prepares adjusting entries.

are directed to the company address or a different post office box. This approach automatically sorts the mail into two groups: (1) cash receipts from customers and (2) all other mail.

Mailroom employees open the envelopes containing cash receipts from customers. Each envelope should contain two items: a check and a remittance advice. A **remittance advice** is a form that accompanies a check to inform the person receiving the check the purpose of the check. The remittance advice includes the customer's name, the amount paid, and reference numbers such as invoice number and customer account number.

Mailroom employees make sure the dollar amounts on each check and its related remittance advice are the same and then place the two documents in separate piles. They endorse each check "For Deposit Only" so that no one else can cash the check. The mailroom employees also prepare a remittance list. A **remittance list** is a list of the checks received. For each check, the list includes customer name and/or number, check number, and amount received. A mailroom employee computes the total of the dollar amounts and records the total on the remittance list.

A mailroom employee compares this total to an adding machine total of the checks and another adding machine total of the remittance advices to make sure that the check amounts are listed correctly and that they agree with the remittance advices. The mailroom then sends the checks to the treasurer's department and the remittance list and the remittance advices to the controller's department.

TREASURER

The treasurer's department is a *custody* department. It has custody of the checks. *It has no responsibilities for any recording or posting activities.* The duties of this department include preparing a bank deposit slip (original plus two copies) for this batch of checks and sending the original deposit slip and the checks to the bank. One copy of the deposit slip is sent to the controller's department. The treasurer's department files the other copy for future reference.

CONTROLLER

The controller's department is a *recording* department. It records the cash receipts in a journal and posts the cash receipts to the general ledger and the accounts receivable subsidiary ledger. *The controller's department never has access to or custody of the checks.*

Before recording and posting the cash receipts, the controller's department compares the total on the deposit slip copy (from the treasurer's department) to the remittance list (from the mailroom) to ensure that the treasurer's department deposited all the checks sent from the mailroom. The controller's department then prepares a journal entry (debit Cash and credit Accounts Receivable) to record the cash receipt. The dollar amount of the debit and credit is the total from the deposit slip.

The controller's department uses the individual remittance advices to post the cash payments to the accounts receivable subsidiary ledger. After processing, the remittance list, the remittance advices, and the deposit slip copy are filed for future reference.

CASH COLLECTIONS PROCESSED DIRECTLY BY THE BANK

Large banks such as Citicorp and Bank of America offer lockbox cash collection services to their customers. With this approach, a company instructs its customers to send payments to a post office box that only the bank can open. The bank retrieves the mail from the post office box, opens it, compares each check to the remittance advice, makes a record of each check, and deposits each check in the company's account. The bank then sends a record of the checks and the remittance advices to the company. This approach eliminates having company employees handle customers' checks and speeds up the depositing of checks.

INTERNAL AUDIT

Internal audit is an independent department; it has no recurring custody, recording, or authorization duties related to accounting transactions. Once each month, it performs independent review and reconciliation duties related to cash received. The internal auditor receives the monthly bank statement directly from the bank through the mail. This ensures that no one alters any of the information returned with the bank statement. The internal audit department uses the bank statement to prepare the monthly bank reconciliation and create any needed journal entries. Later sections in this chapter describe the preparation of the bank reconciliation and related journal entries.

CASH RECEIVED FROM RETAIL CASH SALES

A retailer receives cash from customers when the retailer sells merchandise. The retailer must design internal controls to protect the cash. Five groups play major roles in collecting, protecting, processing, and recording cash received from retail customers: the retail sales area, retail sales supervisors, the treasurer's department, the controller's department, and the internal audit department. Exhibit 6-2 and the following paragraphs describe the role that each group plays.

RETAIL SALES AREA

Sales associates use cash registers to record cash sales and to control and protect the cash collected from customers. A retailer places multiple cash registers on its sales floor to allow customers to pay for their purchases. Some retailers such as Safeway Food Stores place all the cash registers near the store exit. Other retailers such as Macy's Department Stores place the cash registers throughout the store in the various departments such as men's suits, cosmetics, and women's coats.

Each sales associate uses a unique password or key to identify himself or herself to the cash register. Each person should have a separate cash drawer for collecting cash from customers and making change. Each sales associate begins each day with a fixed amount of change in his or her cash drawer. The sales associates enter details of each sale into the cash register and place cash received from customers into the assigned cash drawer. The cash register prints a paper tape listing the description and price of the items sold and the total amount due. The cash register also records this information either in the memory of the cash register or in computer memory that the cash register accesses.

POINT OF INTEREST

RETAIL GROCERY CHAIN POINT-OF-SALE SYSTEM

Large grocery chains such as A&P use cash registers attached to a plate scanner, an on-line scale, and a central computer. The **plate scanner** is built into the checkout counter and uses a laser to read the **universal product code (UPC) bar code** on products such as canned corn and shampoo. The central computer looks up the product number represented in the bar code and sends the item description and price to the cash register.

The **on-line scale** records the weight of items such as bananas after the salesperson enters a **price-look-up (PLU) code** (usually a three-digit number) into the cash register. Both the weight and the PLU code are sent to the computer, which looks up the item description and price per pound, calculates the amount of the purchase, and sends the item description and purchase amount to the cash register.

Using UPC bar codes and PLU codes speeds the checkout process and increases the accuracy of entering price data.

RETAIL SALES SUPERVISOR

The retail sales supervisor observes the sales operation during the day. Throughout the day, the supervisor approves any unusual transactions such as merchandise returns and complaints. At the end of the day, the supervisor counts the contents of each cash drawer. He or she compares the amount of cash in the drawer in excess of the beginning amount of change

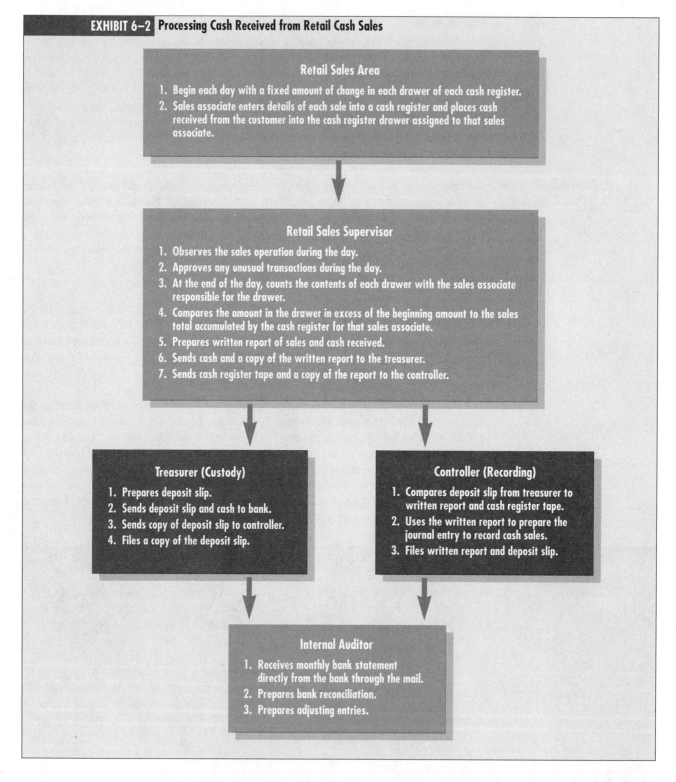

EXHIBIT 6–2 Processing Cash Received from Retail Cash Sales

Retail Sales Area

1. Begin each day with a fixed amount of change in each drawer of each cash register.
2. Sales associate enters details of each sale into a cash register and places cash received from the customer into the cash register drawer assigned to that sales associate.

Retail Sales Supervisor

1. Observes the sales operation during the day.
2. Approves any unusual transactions during the day.
3. At the end of the day, counts the contents of each drawer with the sales associate responsible for the drawer.
4. Compares the amount in the drawer in excess of the beginning amount to the sales total accumulated by the cash register for that sales associate.
5. Prepares written report of sales and cash received.
6. Sends cash and a copy of the written report to the treasurer.
7. Sends cash register tape and a copy of the report to the controller.

Treasurer (Custody)

1. Prepares deposit slip.
2. Sends deposit slip and cash to bank.
3. Sends copy of deposit slip to controller.
4. Files a copy of the deposit slip.

Controller (Recording)

1. Compares deposit slip from treasurer to written report and cash register tape.
2. Uses the written report to prepare the journal entry to record cash sales.
3. Files written report and deposit slip.

Internal Auditor

1. Receives monthly bank statement directly from the bank through the mail.
2. Prepares bank reconciliation.
3. Prepares adjusting entries.

to the sales total accumulated by the cash register for that particular sales associate. The supervisor then prepares a written report (three copies) to document total sales and total cash received.

The supervisor delivers the cash in excess of the initial change amount and a copy of the written report to the treasurer's department. The cash register tape and another copy of the written report are taken to the controller's department. The supervisor files the other copy of the written report.

TREASURER

The treasurer's department takes custody of the cash from the supervisor after signing a receipt that the supervisor keeps. Employees of the treasurer's department count the cash and prepare a deposit slip (original plus two copies). They send the original deposit slip and the cash to the bank. One copy of the deposit slip is sent to the controller's department. The treasurer's department files the other copy for future reference.

CONTROLLER

The controller's department is responsible for recording cash sales. The controller's department never has access to or custody of the checks. Before recording and posting the cash receipts, the controller's department compares the total on the deposit slip copy (from the treasurer's department) to the written report (from the retail sales supervisor) to ensure that the treasurer's department deposited all the cash. The controller's department then prepares a journal entry to record the cash sales. This entry reflects any shortage or overage of cash.

INTERNAL AUDIT

We described the duties of the internal audit department in our discussion of cash received on account. Note again that the bank sends the monthly bank statement to the internal auditor. If a company does not have an internal auditor, the bank sends the monthly bank statement to an appropriate person designated by the company, usually someone who does not have custody or recording responsibilities for cash.

POINT OF INTEREST

FAST-FOOD RESTAURANT COMPUTERIZED CASH REGISTER SYSTEM

Fast-food restaurants such as McDonald's use cash registers with preset keys. A **preset key** on a cash register identifies a specific product, such as a hamburger or a milk shake. The sales associate presses the hamburger key to record the sale of a hamburger. The internal mechanisms in the cash register look up the item description and price in memory, display them for the customer to see, and add them to the cumulative sales totals in the cash register.

Use of preset keys speeds data entry and increases the accuracy of recording prices. Preset keys are also used by convenience stores and other retailers that have a small number of items that make up most of their sales.

RECONCILING THE BANK ACCOUNT

OBJECTIVE 3

DISCUSS checking accounts, bank statements, bank reconciliations, and petty cash.

When a company opens a checking account at a bank, the bank requires each company employee who will sign checks to sign a signature card. The bank files the signature cards. Occasionally, a bank employee compares the signatures on checks to the authorized signatures on the signature cards.

CHECKS

A **check** is a written order signed by a checking account owner (also known as the *maker*) directing the bank (also known as the *payer*) to pay a specified amount of money to the person or company named on the check (also known as the *payee*). A check is a negotiable instrument; it can be transferred to another person or company by writing "pay to the order of" and the name of the other person or company on the back of the check and then signing the back of the check.

Exhibit 6-3 is a sample check. As noted in the previous chapter, proper internal control requires that business documents such as checks be prenumbered in numerical sequence. The printed check number appears in two locations in Exhibit 6-3: in standard type in the upper right corner **1** and in MICR (magnetic ink character recognition) form on the bottom of the check **2**. Also printed twice on the check are alternative formats of the routing number for the check, a fraction format **3** and an MICR format **4**. (See the following

Point of Interest.) The check printer also places the customer's account number on the check in MICR form **5**. When the check is processed by the banking system, the MICR check amount **6** is added at the bottom right of the check. Banks use special equipment that reads MICR codes directly into computer files.

EXHIBIT 6–3 **Sample Check**

WILSON CORPORATION	**1** 157

WILSON CORPORATION
1847 Elmwood Avenue
Madison, Wisconsin 53712

3 79-123/759

November 5, 19 96

PAY
TO THE
ORDER OF   Sterling Manufacturing Corporation $ 233.26

Two Hundred Thirty Three and 26/100 ----------------------------------- DOLLARS

Anchor National Bank
Madison, Wisconsin 53701

Memo Invoice 5247   *Leslie Marten*

4 ⑆075901238⑆   **5** ⑈27⑈31020558⑈   **2** 0157   **6** ⑆00000023326⑆

POINT OF INTEREST

MAGNETIC CHARACTERS ON BANK CHECKS

The routing number on a check tells the various banks handling the check how to route it through the federal reserve system to properly transfer cash between bank accounts. The routing number has two formats: the fraction format (item **3** in Exhibit 6-3) and the MICR format (item **4** in Exhibit 6-3). Both formats are printed on each check. In the fraction format in Exhibit 6-3, 79 represents the state in which the bank is located, 123 represents the number of the bank where the checking account is located, and 759 represents the federal reserve district and bank through which the check must clear. In the MICR format, 0759 identifies the federal reserve district and bank, 0123 identifies the specific bank, and 8 is the check digit. The MICR format must be exactly nine digits long.

THE BANK STATEMENT

At the end of each month, the bank prepares a bank statement for each checking account and sends it to the person or company that owns the checking account. Exhibit 6-4 is the bank statement from Anchor National Bank for Wilson Corporation's checking account as of November 30, 1996. The bank prints Wilson Corporation's name, address, account number, and statement date at the top of the statement.

In the body of the statement, the bank lists Wilson's deposits and other credits on the left, Wilson's checks (in numerical order) and other debits in the center, and Wilson's daily account balance on the right. Daily balance is the balance in the account as of the end of each day listed. The bank presents a summary calculation of Wilson's ending account balance near the bottom of the statement.

The bank defines a series of code letters at the bottom of the statement. These code letters identify debits and credits not related to paying checks or making deposits. These code

| EXHIBIT 6–4 | Bank Statement of Wilson Corporation |

ANCHOR NATIONAL BANK
123 Center Street
Madison, Wisconsin 53701

Wilson Corporation
1847 Elmwood Avenue
Madison, Wisconsin 53712

Account Number 27-31020558
Statement Date November 30, 1996

Deposits and Credits		Checks and Debits			Daily Balance	
Date	**Amount**	**Number**	**Date**	**Amount**	**Date**	**Amount**
Nov 01	420.00	149	Nov 02	125.00	Nov 01	6,060.30
Nov 02	630.00	154	Nov 03	56.25	Nov 02	6,565.30
Nov 07	560.80	155	Nov 10	135.00	Nov 03	6,509.05
Nov 10	480.25	156	Nov 08	315.10	Nov 07	6,801.19
Nov 14	525.00	157	Nov 07	233.26	Nov 08	6,486.09
Nov 17	270.25	158	Nov 11	27.14	Nov 10	6,831.34
Nov 21	640.20	159	Nov 18	275.00	Nov 11	6,804.20
Nov 26	300.00CM	160	Nov 15	315.37	Nov 14	7,329.20
Nov 26	475.00	161	Nov 17	76.40	Nov 15	7,013.83
Nov 30	471.40	162	Nov 21	325.60	Nov 17	7,207.68
		163	Nov 21	450.00	Nov 18	6,932.68
		164	Nov 23	239.00	Nov 21	6,731.58
		165	Nov 21	65.70	Nov 23	6,492.58
		166	Nov 28	482.43	Nov 26	7,262.58
		169	Nov 28	260.00	Nov 28	6,520.15
		170	Nov 30	122.50	Nov 30	6,488.95
		171	Nov 30	370.10		
			Nov 07	35.40RT		
			Nov 26	5.00DM		
			Nov 30	10.00SC		

Beginning Balance	+	Deposits and Credits	–	Checks and Debits	=	Ending Balance
$5,640.30	+	$4,772.90	–	$3,924.25	=	$6,488.95

Item Codes:	EC: Error Correction	DM: Debit Memo	CM: Credit Memo
	SC: Service Charge	OD: Overdraft	RT: Returned Item
	IN: Interest Earned		

POINT OF INTEREST

DEBITS OR CREDITS?

Debit and credit terminology may seem backward on a bank statement. Debits decrease the account balance and credits increase the account balance. When a company deposits cash in its checking account, the bank debits Cash and credits a liability account. The subsidiary ledger for this liability contains the customers' account balances. The statement sent to each company is a statement of its account in the bank's liability subsidiary ledger. As with any liability, debits decrease its balance and credits increase its balance.

letters are not standard from bank to bank. In Exhibit 6-4, EC identifies corrections of errors made by the bank; DM (debit memo) identifies automatic loan payments and bank charges for items such as collecting notes; CM (credit memo) identifies amounts collected by the bank for the depositor; SC (service charge) identifies fees charged by the bank for the checking account; OD (overdraft) indicates a negative balance in the account; RT (returned item) identifies items such as posted checks and NSF checks for which the bank could not collect cash; and IN (interest earned) identifies interest added to the account. The bank statement for Wilson Corporation does not show any interest because federal regulations do not allow corporate checking accounts to earn interest.

THE BANK RECONCILIATION

The internal auditor or other designated employee prepares a bank reconciliation as of the end of each month. A **bank reconciliation** is a schedule that (1) accounts for all differences between the ending balance on the bank statement and the ending balance of the Cash account in the general ledger and (2) determines the reconciled cash balance as of the end of the month. The person preparing the bank reconciliation needs access to the bank statement, the general ledger, cash receipts records (such as the cash receipts journal), and cash disbursements records (such as the cash disbursements journal) to prepare the reconciliation.

BANK RECONCILIATION STRUCTURE   Exhibit 6-5 outlines the structure of a company's bank reconciliation. The bank reconciliation is really two schedules prepared side-by-side. The

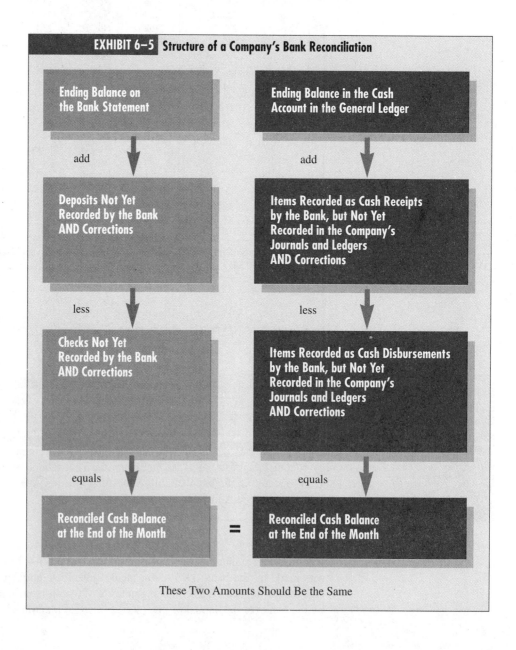

EXHIBIT 6–5 | **Structure of a Company's Bank Reconciliation**

These Two Amounts Should Be the Same

schedule on the left includes bank items, and the schedule on the right includes items related to the company's general ledger.

The schedule on the left begins with the ending balance of the bank statement (the month-end balance according to the bank's records). The person preparing the reconciliation adds (1) deposits not yet recorded by the bank, called **deposits in transit,** and (2) any corrections not yet made by the bank that will increase the bank balance. The preparer subtracts (1) checks not yet recorded by the bank, called **outstanding checks,** and (2) any corrections not yet made by the bank that will decrease the bank balance. The resulting total is the *reconciled cash balance at the end of the month.*

The schedule on the right begins with the ending balance in the Cash account in the company's general ledger. The preparer adds (1) items recorded as cash receipts by the bank but not yet recorded in the company's journals and ledgers and (2) any corrections not yet made by the company that will increase the general ledger cash balance. The preparer subtracts (1) items recorded as cash disbursements by the bank but not yet recorded in the company's journals and ledgers and (2) any corrections not yet made by the company that will decrease the general ledger cash balance. The resulting total is the *reconciled cash balance at the end of the month.* The totals of the two schedules should be the same.

BANK RECONCILIATION PROCEDURE Assume that the internal auditor of Wilson Corporation is preparing the November 30, 1996, bank reconciliation. He or she uses the following procedures to reconcile the November 30, 1996, bank statement balance of $6,488.95 to the November 30, 1996, general ledger balance of $5,322.69:

1. **Trace outstanding items on the bank reconciliation for the previous month to the current bank statement.** Any item on the previous reconciliation that still has not been processed by the bank must appear on the current reconciliation. The October 31, 1996, reconciliation included the following:

Deposit in transit		$420.00
Outstanding checks:	Number 149	$125.00
	Number 154	56.25
	Number 155	135.00

   The November 30, 1996, bank statement includes the $420 deposit and all three checks listed above. Therefore, none of these items will appear on the November 30 reconciliation.

2. **Compare the deposits made during the month to the deposits on the bank statement.** Wilson Corporation made the following deposits during November:

November 2	$630.00		November 21	$640.20
November 7	560.80		November 26	475.00
November 10	480.25		November 29	471.40
November 14	525.00		November 30	225.00
November 17	270.25			

   All of these deposits appear on the bank statement except for the November 30 deposit of $225. The $225 deposit will appear on the left side of the November 30 reconciliation as a deposit in transit.

3. **Compare the checks issued during the month to the checks on the bank statement.** Wilson Corporation issued the following checks during November:

Number 156	$315.10		Number 161	$ 76.40
Number 157	233.26		Number 162	325.60
Number 158	27.14		Number 163	450.00
Number 159	275.00		Number 164	239.00
Number 160	315.37		Number 165	65.70

Number 166	$482.43		Number 170	$122.50
Number 167	301.66		Number 171	370.10
Number 168	149.50		Number 172	450.00
Number 169	260.00		Number 173	240.50

Four of the checks—numbers 167, 168, 172, and 173—do not appear on the bank statement. These four checks will appear on the left side of the November 30 reconciliation as outstanding checks.

4. **Scan the bank statement for charges and credits not yet reflected in the general ledger.** Wilson Corporation's bank statement contains a charge of $35.40 for a returned item, a debit memo of $5.00, and a service charge of $10.00 in the checks and other debits column. The deposits and other credits column contains a credit memo for $300.00. Supplemental information sent by the bank with the bank statement reveals that the bank charged a $35.40 NSF check against Wilson's account, that the bank collected a $300.00 note for Wilson, and charged a $5.00 collection fee, and that the service charge for the month of November was $10.00. These four items have not yet been recorded by Wilson Corporation. Therefore, they must be listed on the right side of the reconciliation.

After the four preceding procedures have been completed, the November 30, 1996, bank reconciliation for Wilson Corporation appears as shown in Exhibit 6-6. Note that both the left side and the right side of the reconciliation end with a reconciled cash balance and that the two amounts are the same. This reconciled cash balance is the amount that will appear in the November 30, 1996, balance sheet.

EXHIBIT 6–6 November 30, 1996, Bank Reconciliation for Wilson Corporation

WILSON CORPORATION
BANK RECONCILIATION
NOVEMBER 30, 1996

Ending balance from bank statement		$6,488.95	Balance from general ledger		$5,322.69
Add: Deposits in transit		225.00	Add: Collection of note	$300.00	
			Less: Collection fee	5.00	295.00
		$6,713.95			$5,617.69
Less: Outstanding checks:			Less: NSF check	$35.40	
No. 167	$301.66		Service charge	10.00	45.40
No. 168	149.50				
No. 172	450.00				
No. 173	240.50	1,141.66			
Reconciled cash balance		$5,572.29	Reconciled cash balance		$5,572.29

Before Wilson Corporation prepares its financial statements for November, Wilson must make journal entries to bring the balance in the cash account into agreement with the reconciled cash balance on the bank reconciliation. These entries incorporate the items on the company's side of the reconciliation. Wilson makes the following entries:

Nov. 30	Cash	295.00	
	Miscellaneous Expense	5.00	
	Notes Receivable		300.00
	To record a note collected by the bank, less a collection fee.		

Nov. 30	Accounts Receivable	35.40	
	Cash		35.40
	To reclassify an NSF check as an account receivable.		
30	Miscellaneous Expense	10.00	
	Cash		10.00
	To record bank service charge for November.		

THE PETTY CASH FUND

Most businesses find it inconvenient and expensive to write checks for small expenditures. Instead, these businesses establish a petty cash fund. A **petty cash fund** is a small amount of cash, such as $300, that is placed in a box to be used to pay for small expenditures such as postage, delivery service charges, and minor purchases of supplies. The size of the petty cash fund depends on how often it is used and the amount of the disbursements. Firms often select an amount that will last for three or four weeks. All payments from the fund are made in currency and coin.

Although the use of a petty cash fund violates the rule that all cash payments should be made by check, control can be maintained by handling the fund on an imprest basis with documented procedures. An *imprest* fund contains a fixed amount of cash. A business establishes a petty cash fund by writing a check against the firm's checking account and cashing the check at the bank. All replenishments of the petty cash fund are also made by check. As a result, all expenditures are ultimately controlled by check.

ACCOUNTS RECEIVABLE

OBJECTIVE *4*

PRESENT an overview of accounts receivable, **DEFINE** losses from uncollectible accounts, and **DISCUSS** the allowance method of accounting for credit losses.

Many businesses sell products and services to their customers on a credit basis, allowing the customer a specific number of days to make a cash payment. **Accounts receivable** is the current asset that is created by a sale or service on a credit basis. Another name for an account receivable is *trade receivable*.

A company debits Accounts Receivable and credits Sales when it records a credit sale. This transaction is posted to the general ledger, increasing both Accounts Receivable and Sales balances. It is also posted as a debit in the customer's account in the accounts receivable subsidiary ledger.

Accounts receivable includes only amounts due that relate to the sale of products or services. Other amounts, such as loans or advances to employees or affiliated companies, should be included with Other Receivables. These other receivables may be current or noncurrent.

Sometimes an individual customer account in the accounts receivable subsidiary ledger may have a credit balance. This can happen when the customer overpays its account or is granted a credit for returned merchandise after the customer has paid the amount due prior to the return. If the customer's credit balance is significant, the selling company should reclassify it as a current liability when the company prepares its balance sheet.

LOSSES FROM UNCOLLECTIBLE ACCOUNTS

Businesses that make credit sales anticipate reasonable credit losses. The size of such losses is usually related to the firm's credit policy. A company may deliberately liberalize its credit policy to obtain increased sales, fully anticipating an increase in credit losses.

Most large companies have credit departments to administer management's credit policies. Credit personnel conduct investigations, establish credit limits, and follow up on unpaid accounts. They also decide, following written collection procedures, when a debt is uncollectible.

Credit losses, considered operating expenses of the business, are debited to an appropriately titled account such as **Uncollectible Accounts Expense.** Other account titles frequently used are *Loss from Uncollectible Accounts, Loss from Doubtful Accounts,* or *Bad Debts Expense.* Normally, the expense is classified as a selling expense on the income statement, although some companies include it with administrative expenses.

CREDIT SCORING SYSTEMS

Many companies use a computerized credit scoring system to decide whether to extend credit to a potential customer. The computerized system is a set of formulas with multiple variables. The person working with the system enters data from the potential customer's credit application and from credit reporting services. The system then calculates the credit score, compares the score to predetermined limits, and recommends whether credit should be extended.

If credit is to be extended, the scoring system often recommends the amount of credit to be extended. Scoring systems focus on the potential customer's ability to generate net income and cash flow, its current level of debt and required repayment schedule, and its current assets. Many of the financial statement ratios discussed throughout this text are incorporated into the scoring systems.

THE ALLOWANCE METHOD

Credit losses are incurred in the process of generating sales revenues. At the time a specific credit sale is made, the seller does not know whether the account receivable will be collected in full, in part, or not at all. Any loss from an uncollectible account may not be known for several months, or even a year or more. To get the credit loss in the appropriate accounting period, accountants must estimate the amount of uncollectible accounts expense to report in the income statement. The estimate is reported in an end-of-period adjusting entry. The overall process of estimating uncollectible accounts expense is called the **allowance method.**

MATCHING CONCEPT

The *matching concept* states that expenses should be linked with the revenues they help to generate. A company sells on credit because it attracts more customers and, therefore, more sales revenues than if sales were for cash only. One of the costs of extending credit is the uncollectible accounts expense. The matching concept requires that this expense should be reported in the same accounting period as the related sales revenues. To accomplish the matching, accountants estimate this expense because all of the specific accounts that will be uncollectible may not be known until a later period.

The allowance method receives its name because the adjusting entry credits a contra asset account called *Allowance for Uncollectible Accounts.* The allowance method not only matches credit losses with the related sales but also reports accounts receivable at their estimated realizable value in the end-of-period balance sheet. To illustrate, assume that a firm estimates its uncollectible accounts expense for 1995 to be $4,000 and makes the following adjusting entry:

1995

Dec. 31	Uncollectible Accounts Expense	4,000	
	Allowance for Uncollectible Accounts		4,000
	To record uncollectible accounts expense for the year.		

The credit is made to the **Allowance for Uncollectible Accounts** account rather than to Accounts Receivable for two reasons. First, when the firm makes the adjusting entry, it does not know which accounts in the accounts receivable subsidiary ledger will be uncollectible. If the Accounts Receivable control account is credited and no entries are made in the subsidiary ledger, then the two records no longer agree in total. Second, because the amount involved is only an estimate, it is preferable not to reduce Accounts Receivable directly.

Allowance for Uncollectible Accounts is a contra asset account with a normal credit balance. To present the expected collectible amount of accounts receivable, we deduct Allowance for Uncollectible Accounts from Accounts Receivable in the balance sheet.

Assuming that the firm had $100,000 of accounts receivable (and a zero balance in Allowance for Uncollectible Accounts before the December 31, 1995, adjusting entry), the year-end balance sheet presentation is as follows:

Current Assets		
Cash		$ 52,000
Accounts Receivable	$100,000	
Less: Allowance for Uncollectible Accounts	4,000	96,000
Inventory		125,000
Other Current Assets		31,000
Total Current Assets		$304,000

PRINCIPLE ALERT

GOING CONCERN CONCEPT

Accounts receivable are presented in the balance sheet at the number of dollars the company expects to collect in the future from its credit customers. This presentation assumes the company will be in existence long enough to collect its accounts receivable and, therefore, relies on the *going concern concept*. As a basic principle of accounting, the going concern concept assumes the business entity will continue to operate indefinitely.

WRITING OFF SPECIFIC ACCOUNTS UNDER THE ALLOWANCE METHOD

The credit manager usually authorizes writing off a specific account. Assume, for example, that the credit manager authorizes a $300 write-off of Monroe Company's receivable. When the accounting department is notified it makes the following entry:

1996

Jan. 5	Allowance for Uncollectible Accounts	300	
	Accounts Receivable—Monroe Company		300
	To write off Monroe Company's account.		

The credit in this entry is made to Monroe Company's account in the accounts receivable subsidiary ledger as well as to the Accounts Receivable control account.

The entry to write off an account does not affect net income or total assets. By means of the year-end adjusting entry, the expense is reflected in the period when the related revenue is recorded. Because Allowance for Uncollectible Accounts is deducted from Accounts Receivable in the balance sheet, the *net* realizable value of accounts receivable is not changed by the write-off. After Monroe Company's account has been written off, the Accounts Receivable and Allowance for Uncollectible Accounts general ledger accounts appear as follows:

ACCOUNTS RECEIVABLE   ACCOUNT NO. 12

Date		Description	Post. Ref.	Debit	Credit	Balance
1996 Jan.	1	Balance				100,000
	5	Write-off, Monroe Company			300	99,700

ALLOWANCE FOR UNCOLLECTIBLE ACCOUNTS   ACCOUNT NO. 13

Date		Description	Post. Ref.	Debit	Credit	Balance
1996 Jan.	1	Balance				4,000
	5	Write-off, Monroe Company		300		3,700

In these accounts, the net realizable value of accounts receivable on January 1, 1996, is $96,000 ($100,000 – $4,000 allowance). After the January 5, 1996, writeoff, the net realizable value of accounts receivable is still $96,000 ($99,700 – $3,700 allowance).

ESTIMATING CREDIT LOSSES

When the allowance method is used, estimates of credit losses are generally based on past experience, with additional consideration given to forecasts of sales activity, economic conditions, and planned changes in credit policy. The most commonly used calculations are related either to credit sales for the period or to the amount of accounts receivable at the end of the period.

PERCENTAGE OF NET SALES METHOD

OBJECTIVE 5

DESCRIBE and **ILLUSTRATE** two methods for estimating credit losses—the percentage of net sales method and the accounts receivable aging method.

Through experience, many companies can determine the approximate percentage of credit sales that will be uncollectible. At the end of an accounting period, the amount of the adjusting entry is determined by multiplying the total credit sales by this percentage. Suppose that credit sales for 1996 are $500,000 and that past experience indicates a 2% loss. The adjusting entry for expected losses for 1996 (2% × $500,000) appears as follows:

1996		
Dec. 31	Uncollectible Accounts Expense	10,000
	Allowance for Uncollectible Accounts		10,000
	To record uncollectible accounts expense.	

Because the periodic estimates for uncollectible accounts under this procedure are related to sales, a firm should review its allowance account regularly to ensure a reasonable balance. If the allowance account balance is too large or too small, the percentage used for the periodic estimates should be revised accordingly.

A company that uses the **percentage of net sales method** usually applies the uncollectible percentage only to credit sales, excluding cash sales, since only credit sales will be subject to credit losses. Further, sales discounts and sales returns and allowances should be deducted from the credit sales before applying the percentage.

ACCOUNTS RECEIVABLE AGING METHOD

A firm may estimate uncollectible accounts expense indirectly by determining the appropriate balance in the Allowance for Uncollectible Accounts account at the end of the year. The year-end balance in Allowance for Uncollectible Accounts represents the firm's estimate of the year-end accounts receivable that will prove uncollectible. The **accounts receivable aging method** uses this approach. When using the accounts receivable aging method, a company would determine the amount needed in the allowance account by analyzing the age structure of the account balances. An aging schedule similar to the one in Exhibit 6-7 would be used. An **aging schedule** is simply an analysis that shows how long customers' balances have remained unpaid. Assume that the firm whose aging schedule appears

EXHIBIT 6–7	Aging Schedule of Customer Balances, December 31, 1996						
				Past Due			
Customer	Account Balance	Current	0–30 Days	31–60 Days	61–120 Days	121 Days –6 Mos.	Over 6 Mos.
Alton, J.	$ 320	$ 320					
Bailey, C.	400		$ 400				
⋯	⋯	⋯	⋯	⋯	⋯	⋯	⋯
Wall, M.	150				50	100	
Zorn, W.	210			210			
	$50,000	$42,000	$4,000	$2,000	$1,000	$800	$200

in Exhibit 6-7 sells on net terms of 30 days. Alton's account is current, which means that the $320 billing was made within the last 30 days. Bailey's account is 0–30 days *past due,* which means that the account is from 31 to 60 days old. Wall's balance consists of a $50 billing made from 91 to 150 days ago and a $100 billing made from 151 days to seven months ago, and so on.

Companies that analyze their uncollectible accounts experience with the aged balances may develop percentages of each age group that are likely to prove uncollectible. At the end of each period, these percentages are applied to the totals of each age group to determine the allowance account balance. For our example, these percentages are shown in the table below. Applying the percentages to the totals in our aging schedule, we calculate an allowance requirement of $1,560.

	Amount	Percent Doubtful	Allowance Required
Current	$42,000	2	$ 840
0–30 days past due	4,000	3	120
31–60 days past due	2,000	5	100
61–120 days past due	1,000	20	200
121 days–6 months past due	800	25	200
Over 6 months past due	200	50	100
Total allowance required			$1,560

Suppose that the allowance account has a $400 credit balance before adjustment. The adjusting entry is

1996
Dec. 31	Uncollectible Accounts Expense	1,160	
	Allowance for Uncollectible Accounts		1,160
	To record uncollectible accounts expense.		

This entry brings the credit balance in the allowance account to the required amount—$1,560, as shown below:

ALLOWANCE FOR UNCOLLECTIBLE ACCOUNTS   ACCOUNT No. 13

Date		Description	Post. Ref.	Debit	Credit	Balance
1996 Dec.	31	Balance before adjusting entry				400
	31	Adjusting entry			1,160	1,560

It is possible to have a debit balance in the allowance account before adjustment. This would occur whenever the write-off of specific accounts during the year exceeded the credit balance in the account at the beginning of the year. Assume, for example, that the allowance account had a $350 debit balance before the December 31, 1996, adjusting entry and that the aging schedule showed that the allowance account should have a $1,560 credit balance. The adjusting entry would then be as follows:

1996
Dec. 31	Uncollectible Accounts Expense	1,910	
	Allowance for Uncollectible Accounts		1,910
	To record uncollectible accounts expense.		

The following Allowance for Uncollectible Accounts ledger account shows that this entry creates the desired year-end credit balance of $1,560.

ALLOWANCE FOR UNCOLLECTIBLE ACCOUNTS   ACCOUNT NO. 13

Date		Description	Post. Ref.	Debit	Credit	Balance
1996 Dec.	31	Balance before adjusting entry				(350)
	31	Adjusting entry			1,910	1,560

RECOVERIES OF ACCOUNTS WRITTEN OFF UNDER THE ALLOWANCE METHOD

Occasionally, accounts written off against the Allowance for Uncollectible Accounts later prove to be wholly or partially collectible. In such situations, a firm should reinstate the customer's account for the amount recovered before recording the collection. Then the payment can be recorded in the customer's account. The entry made for the write-off is reversed to the extent of the recovery and the receipt is recorded in the usual manner. For example, assume that a company using the allowance method wrote off Monroe Company's $300 account on January 5, 1996, but received a $200 payment on April 20, 1996. The following entries (including write-off) illustrate the recovery procedure.

To write off the account

1996

Jan. 5	Allowance for Uncollectible Accounts	300	
	Accounts Receivable—Monroe Company		300
	To write off Monroe Company's account.		

To reinstate the account

Apr. 20	Accounts Receivable—Monroe Company	200	
	Allowance for Uncollectible Accounts		200
	To reinstate Monroe Company's account to the extent of the recovery.		

To record receipt of cash

Apr. 20	Cash	200	
	Accounts Receivable—Monroe Company		200
	To record collection of cash on account.		

These last two entries are prepared the same way even if the recovery occurs in a year after the year in which the account was written off.

POINT OF INTEREST

LEVELS OF ALLOWANCES

Different companies have very different levels of allowances for doubtful accounts. At the end of a recent year, OshKosh B'Gosh, Inc., reported accounts receivable of $22,787,000 with an allowance for doubtful accounts of $3,310,000 (14.5% of accounts receivable). At the end of the same year, Clark Equipment reported accounts receivable of $115,545,000 with an allowance for doubtful accounts of $6,000,000 (5.2% of accounts receivable).

DIRECT WRITE-OFF METHOD

OBJECTIVE 6

INTRODUCE the direct write-off method and **CONTRAST** it to the allowance method.

The direct write-off method of accounting for credit losses is an alternative to the allowance method. Under the **direct write-off method,** uncollectible accounts are charged to expense in the period in which they are determined to be uncollectible. There is no estimate of uncollectible accounts expense, no allowance account, and no year-end adjusting entry. For most companies, the direct write-off method is not an acceptable method of accounting for credit losses, because it does not properly match credit losses with sales. However, the direct write-off method is used by virtually all companies for income tax purposes.

The entries made when the direct write-off method is used are illustrated below, using the data from the previous example:

To write off the account

1996

Jan. 5   Uncollectible Accounts Expense   300
           Accounts Receivable—Monroe Company   300
           To write off Monroe Company's account.

To reinstate the account

Apr. 20   Accounts Receivable—Monroe Company   200
           Uncollectible Accounts Expense   200
           To reinstate Monroe Company's account to the extent of the
           recovery.

To record remittance

Apr. 20   Cash   200
           Accounts Receivable—Monroe Company   200
           To record collection of cash on account.

If an account written off in a prior year is reinstated during the current year, and the Uncollectible Accounts Expense account has no balance from other write-offs (and no more write-offs are expected), then the account credited in the reinstatement entry would be Uncollectible Accounts Recovery, a revenue account.

The major shortcoming of the direct write-off method is that credit losses are not matched with related sales. The use of the direct write-off method also causes consistent overstatement of accounts receivable on the balance sheet. Because generally accepted accounting principles prescribe that accounts receivable be shown at the amount that the firm expects to collect, the direct write-off method is usually inappropriate except for income tax calculations.

CREDIT CARD SALES

OBJECTIVE 7

DISCUSS the accounting treatment of credit card sales.

Many businesses, especially retailers, allow their customers to use credit cards. Popular credit cards include VISA, MasterCard, Discover, American Express, Carte Blanche, and Diners Club. When a purchaser uses a credit card to make a purchase, the seller collects cash from the credit card company, and the purchaser pays cash to the credit card company. To facilitate this process, the seller prepares a sales slip using the credit card. The seller either imprints the card number on a slip using the card or uses an electronic device such as a cash register with a card reader to read the card number from the magnetic strip on the back of the card and print a sales slip with the card number on it. The second approach also allows for electronic accumulation and transmission of credit card sales data. In either case, the purchaser is usually asked to sign the sales slip.

The issuer of a credit card, frequently a financial institution or one of its subsidiaries, charges the seller a fee each time a card is used. This **credit card fee** usually ranges from 1% to 5% of credit card sales. Sellers are willing to incur this fee because credit cards provide benefits to the seller: the seller does not have to evaluate creditworthiness of customers using credit cards; the seller avoids risks of noncollection of the account; and the seller typically receives the cash from the credit card issuer faster than if the customer were granted credit by the seller.

Depending on the type of credit card, there are two ways that the seller may collect from the credit card issuer: immediately upon deposit of the credit card sales slips or delayed until paid subsequently by the credit card company. For cards issued by a financial institution, cash is received immediately upon deposit of the sales slips at the financial institution. The entry to record a $1,000 credit card sale of this type on March 15, with a 3% credit card fee, follows:

Mar. 15   Cash   970
           Credit Card Fee Expense   30
             Sales   1,000
           To record credit card sales and collection, less a 3% fee.

If, instead, sales slips are sent to a credit card company for subsequent cash settlement, the entries to record the $1,000 credit card sale with subsequent collection on March 23 is as follows:

Mar. 15	Accounts Receivable—Credit Card Company		970	
	Credit Card Fee Expense		30	
	Sales			1,000
	To record credit card sales.			
23	Cash		970	
	Accounts Receivable—Credit Card Company			970
	To record collection from credit card company.			

NOTES RECEIVABLE

OBJECTIVE *8*

ILLUSTRATE a promissory note, **DISCUSS** the calculation of interest on promissory notes receivable, and **PRESENT** journal entries to record notes receivable and interest.

Promissory notes are often used in transactions when the credit period is longer than the 30 or 60 days typical for accounts receivable. Although promissory notes are used frequently in sales of equipment and real property, a note is sometimes exchanged for merchandise. Occasionally, a note is substituted for an account receivable when an extension of the usual credit period is granted. Also, promissory notes are normally prepared when financial institutions make loans.

A **promissory note** is a written promise to pay a certain sum of money on demand or at a fixed and determinable future date. The note is signed by the **maker** and made payable to the order of either a specific **payee** or the **bearer.** The interest rate specified on the note is typically an annual rate. A promissory note is illustrated in Exhibit 6-8.

EXHIBIT 6–8	A Promissory Note

$2,000.00   Chicago, Illinois   May 3, 1996

Sixty days   after date   I   promise to pay to

the order of   Susan Robinson

Two Thousand and no/100-- dollars

for value received with interest at   9%

payable at   First Bank of Chicago, Illinois

James Stone

A note from a debtor is called a **note receivable** by the holder. A note is usually regarded as a stronger claim against a debtor than an account receivable because the terms of payment are specified in writing.

FACTORING AND DISCOUNTING

A company can accelerate the collection of cash on an account receivable or a note receivable by selling the receivable to another company. Selling an account receivable to another company is called **factoring** and selling a note receivable is called **discounting.** Receivables are typically sold to finance companies or financial institutions.

The finance company or financial institution pays the selling company the amount of the account receivable or note receivable less a fee, often ranging from 2% to 5%. The finance company or financial institution then collects the payments directly from the customers who originally owed the company that sold the receivable. This approach speeds the collection of cash to the selling company and releases it from the work of billing and collecting the account.

INTEREST ON NOTES RECEIVABLE

Interest is a charge for the use of money. Interest incurred on a promissory note is interest income to the holder or payee of the note. Since business firms want to distinguish between operating and nonoperating items in their income statements, they place interest income under the Other Income and Expense heading in the income statement.

Interest on a short-term promissory note is paid at the maturity date of the note. The formula for determining the amount of interest follows:

$$\text{Interest} = \text{Principal} \times \frac{\text{Interest}}{\text{Rate}} \times \frac{\text{Interest}}{\text{Time}}$$

The principal is the face amount of a note. The interest rate is the annual rate of interest. Interest time is the fraction of a year that the note is outstanding.

When a note is written for a certain number of months, time is expressed in twelfths of a year. For example, interest on a six-month note for $2,000 with a 9% annual interest rate is

$$\text{Interest} = \$2,000 \times 0.09 \times \frac{6}{12} = \$90$$

When a note's duration is given in days, time is expressed as a fraction of a year; the numerator is the number of days the note will be outstanding and the denominator is 360 days. (Some lenders use 360 days; others use 365 days; we will use 360 days in our examples, exercises, and problems). For example, interest on a 60-day note for $2,000 with a 9% annual interest rate is

$$\text{Interest} = \$2,000 \times 0.09 \times \frac{60}{360} = \$30$$

DETERMINING MATURITY DATE

When a note's duration is expressed in days, we count the exact days in each calendar month to determine the **maturity date.** For example, a 90-day note dated July 21 has an October 19 maturity date, which we determine as follows:

10 days in July (remainder of month—31 days minus 21 days)
31 days in August
30 days in September
<u>19</u> days in October (number of days required to total 90)
<u><u>90</u></u>

If the duration of a note is expressed in months, we find the maturity date simply by counting the months from the date of issue. For example, a two-month note dated January 31 would mature on March 31, a three-month note of the same date would mature on April 30 (the last day of the month), and a four-month note would mature on May 31.

RECORDING NOTES RECEIVABLE AND INTEREST

When a note is exchanged to settle an account receivable, an entry is made to reflect the note receivable and to reduce the balance of the related account receivable. For example, suppose that Jordon Company sold $12,000 of merchandise on account to Bowman Company. On October 1, after the regular credit period had elapsed, Bowman Company gave Jordon Company a 60-day, 9% note for $12,000. Jordon Company makes the following entry to record receiving the note:

Oct. 1	Notes Receivable—Bowman Company	12,000	
	Accounts Receivable—Bowman Company		12,000
	Received 60-day, 9% note in payment of account.		

If Bowman Company pays the note on the November 30 maturity date, Jordon Company makes the following entry:

Nov. 30   Cash   12,180
     Interest Income   180
     Notes Receivable—Bowman Company   12,000
    Collected Bowman Company note
    ($12,000 × 0.09 × $\frac{60}{360}$ = $180).

RECORDING DISHONORED NOTES

The interest for 60 days at 9% is recorded on the maturity date of the note, even if the maker defaults on (dishonors) the note. When a note is dishonored at maturity, the amount of the combined principal plus interest is converted to an account receivable. This procedure leaves only the current, unmatured notes in the holder's Notes Receivable control account. If Bowman Company did not pay the note on November 30, Jordon Company makes the following entry:

Nov. 30   Accounts Receivable—Bowman Company   12,180
     Interest Income   180
     Notes Receivable—Bowman Company   12,000
    To record the dishonoring of a note by Bowman Company.

ADJUSTING ENTRY FOR INTEREST

When the term of a promissory note extends beyond the end of an accounting period, an adjusting entry is necessary to reflect interest in the proper accounting period. Year-end adjusting entries are made to record interest income on notes receivable.

Assume that Jordon Company has one note receivable outstanding at December 31, 1996. The note receivable from Garcia Company is dated December 21, 1996, has a principal amount of $6,000, an interest rate of 12%, and a maturity date of February 19, 1997. The adjusting entry that Jordon Company makes at December 31, 1996, follows:

Dec. 31   Interest Receivable   20
     Interest Income   20
    To accrue interest income on the note from Garcia
    Company ($6,000 × 0.12 × $\frac{10}{360}$ = $20).

PRINCIPLE ALERT

REVENUE RECOGNITION PRINCIPLE

The adjustment to accrue interest income at year-end illustrates the *revenue recognition principle.* This principle states that, in general, revenue is recognized when services are performed or goods are sold. The holder of a promissory note provides the maker of the note with a service: the use of money for a specified time period. This service is provided each day the note is outstanding; interest is the payment for this service. Interest income is not recorded each day. Normally, interest income for the note's full term is recorded when it is collected at the note's maturity. If the accounting period ends before the maturity date, though, the adjusting entry records the revenue for the services provided in the current period.

When the note is subsequently paid on February 19, 1997, Jordon Company makes the following entry (assuming that no reversing entries were made on January 1, 1997):

Feb. 19   Cash   6,120
     Interest Income   100
     Interest Receivable   20
     Notes Receivable—Garcia Company   6,000
    Received payment of principal and interest from
    Garcia Company ($6,000 × 0.12 × $\frac{50}{360}$ = $100).

NOTES RECEIVABLE IN FINANCIAL STATEMENTS

A business shows short-term notes receivable as current assets in the balance sheet; because they can normally be converted to cash fairly easily, these notes usually are placed above accounts receivable. As with accounts receivable, notes receivable are separated from notes from officers and employees and notes representing advances to affiliated companies. If such notes are not truly short term, they should not be classified as current assets. Interest Receivable is also a current asset.

Sometimes companies with a large volume of notes receivable must provide for possible losses on notes. Frequently, the provision for credit losses also covers losses on notes as well. In such cases, the Allowance for Uncollectible Accounts account is deducted from the sum of Accounts Receivable and Notes Receivable in the balance sheet.

FINANCIAL ANALYSIS

OBJECTIVE 9

DEFINE *accounts receivable turnover* and *average collection period* and **EXPLAIN** their use.

ACCOUNTS RECEIVABLE TURNOVER AND AVERAGE COLLECTION PERIOD

Most companies make the majority of their sales on credit. Doing so creates accounts receivable. Management and financial analysts monitor trade accounts receivable using a variety of measures, including accounts receivable turnover and the average collection period. **Accounts receivable turnover** indicates how many times a year a firm collects its average accounts receivable and, thus, measures how fast accounts receivable are converted into cash. Accounts receivable turnover is computed as follows:

$$\text{Accounts Receivable Turnover} = \frac{\text{Net Sales}}{\text{Average Accounts Receivable}}$$

The numerator in this ratio is net sales. Ideally, the numerator should be net credit sales, but financial information available to analysts and other external users does not usually divide net sales into credit sales and cash sales. Average accounts receivable (net of the allowance for uncollectible accounts) is calculated by summing the beginning and ending accounts receivable (net) and dividing the sum by 2.

Chrysler Corporation reported the following results for two recent years (Year 2 is the more recent; amounts in millions):

	Year 2	Year 1
Net Sales	$40,831	$33,548
Beginning accounts receivable (net)	1,848	1,948
Ending accounts receivable (net)	1,799	1,848

Chrysler's accounts receivable turnover for Year 2 is $40,831/[$1,848 + $1,799)/2] = 22.39. Chrysler's accounts receivable turnover for Year 1 is $33,548/[($1,948 + $1,848)/2] = 17.68. The higher the turnover ratio is, the faster accounts receivable are being converted into cash. The increase from Year 1 to Year 2 is a positive sign.

A variation (or extension) of accounts receivable turnover is the **average collection period,** computed as follows:

$$\text{Average Collection Period} = \frac{365}{\text{Accounts Receivable Turnover}}$$

This ratio indicates how many days it takes on average to collect an account receivable. During Year 2, Chrysler's average collection period was 365/22.39 = 16.3 days. During Year 1, Chrysler's average collection period was 365/17.68 = 20.6 days.

The average collection period may be used to evaluate the effectiveness of a firm's credit policies. One rule of thumb states that the average collection should not exceed the credit period by more than 15 days. Therefore, if a firm grants net 30 credit terms, its average collection period should not exceed 45 days.

KEY POINTS FOR CHAPTER LEARNING OBJECTIVES

1 **DEFINE** *cash* and **DISCUSS** accounting for cash (p. 194).
- Cash includes coins, currency (paper money), checks, money orders, traveler's checks, and funds on deposit at a financial institution in checking accounts and savings accounts.
- A company can have one or more cash accounts in its general ledger. Cash is a current asset.
- A company may combine certain short-term, highly liquid investments with cash and present a single amount called *cash and cash equivalents.*

2 **DESCRIBE** internal controls for cash received on account and cash received from retail cash sales (pp. 195–199).
- Companies develop elaborate internal controls to protect cash, their most liquid asset.
- Four departments play major roles in processing cash received on account: the mailroom (open mail, endorse checks, list checks), the treasurer's department (deposit checks), the controller's department (update general ledger and subsidiary ledger), and the internal audit department (reconcile bank statement).
- Five departments play major roles in processing cash received from retail sales: the retail sales area (enter sales in cash register and place cash in drawer), the retail sales supervisor (count cash and prepare reports), the treasurer's department (deposit cash), the controller's department (update general ledger), and the internal audit department (reconcile bank statement).

3 **DISCUSS** checking accounts, bank statements, bank reconciliations, and petty cash (pp. 199–205).
- A check is a written order signed by the checking account owner directing the bank to pay a specified amount of money to the person or company named on the check. Some of the data on the check are printed with magnetic ink so they can be read by equipment that transfers the data directly to a computer.
- Each month, the bank sends a statement that lists deposits received and checks paid along with various bank charges and credits.
- A bank reconciliation is a schedule that (1) accounts for all differences between the ending balance of the bank statement and the ending balance of the Cash account in the general ledger and (2) determines the reconciled cash balance as of the end of the month.
- The procedure used to prepare the bank reconciliation involves four steps.
  - Trace outstanding items on the bank reconciliation for the previous month to the current bank statement.
  - Compare the deposits made during the month to the deposits on the bank statement.
  - Compare the checks issued during the month to the checks on the bank statement.
  - Scan the bank statement for charges and credits not yet reflected in the general ledger.
- A petty cash fund is a small amount of cash placed in a box to be used to pay for small expenditures such as postage and delivery service.
- The fund should be replenished at least once each month so that the accumulated expenses can be recorded in the journal.

4 **PRESENT** an overview of accounts receivable, **DEFINE** losses from uncollectible accounts, and **DISCUSS** the allowance method of accounting for credit losses (pp. 205–208).
- Accounts receivable is the current asset created by a sale or service on a credit basis. It is also called *trade receivable.*
- Accounts receivable does not include items such as loans or advances to employees.
- The credit department of a company is responsible for conducting credit investigations, establishing credit limits, and following up on overdue accounts.
- The allowance method is designed to record uncollectible accounts expense in the same accounting period as the related credit sales are made.
- When the allowance method is used, specific accounts are written off by debiting Allowance for Uncollectible Accounts and crediting Accounts Receivable.

5 **DESCRIBE** and **ILLUSTRATE** two methods for estimating credit losses—the percentage of net sales method and the accounts receivable aging method (pp. 208–210).
- The percentage of net sales method is used to determine estimated credit losses directly. Estimated credit losses are determined by multiplying credit sales (net of discounts and returns and allowances) times the estimated percentage of uncollectible credit sales.
- The accounts receivable aging method determines the estimated credit loss indirectly. The balance in Accounts Receivable is segmented into age categories. Then the balance of each category is multiplied times the estimated uncollectible percentage for that age category. The results are added to obtain the desired balance in Allowance for Uncollectible Accounts. The desired balance is then compared to the existing balance in Allowance for Uncollectible Accounts to determine the estimated credit losses.
- Occasionally, accounts written off against Allowance for Uncollectible Accounts later prove to be wholly or partially collectible. When this happens, the account is reinstated to the extent of the recovery (debit Accounts Receivable and credit Allowance for Uncollectible Accounts), and the collection is recorded (debit Cash and credit Accounts Receivable).

6 **INTRODUCE** the direct write-off method and **CONTRAST** it with the allowance method (pp. 210–211).
- Under the direct write-off method, uncollectible accounts are charged to expense in the period in which they are determined to be uncollectible.
- For most companies, the direct write-off method is not an acceptable method of accounting for credit losses; however, most companies use the direct write-off method for income tax purposes.

7 **DISCUSS** the accounting treatment of credit card sales (pp. 211–212).
- The issuer of the credit card can reimburse the merchant accepting the credit card immediately upon deposit or subsequently after processing the sales slip.
- In both situations, the credit card fee expense is recognized when the credit card sales slips are remitted to the credit card issuer.

8 **ILLUSTRATE** a promissory note, **DISCUSS** the calculation of interest on promissory notes receivable, and **PRESENT** journal entries to record notes receivable and interest (pp. 212–215).
- Interest on a short-term promissory note is determined using the following formula:

$$\text{Interest} = \text{Principal} \times \frac{\text{Interest}}{\text{Rate}} \times \frac{\text{Interest}}{\text{Time}}$$

- When a note is received in payment of an account, Notes Receivable is debited and Accounts Receivable is credited.
- The holder of the note recognizes interest income at the maturity date or in an end-of-period adjusting entry.

9 **Financial Analysis** **DEFINE** *accounts receivable turnover* and *average collection period* and **EXPLAIN** their use (pp. 215–216).
- $\text{Accounts Receivable Turnover} = \dfrac{\text{Net Sales}}{\text{Average Accounts Receivable}}$
- $\text{Average Collection Period} = \dfrac{365}{\text{Accounts Receivable Turnover}}$
- *Accounts receivable turnover* indicates how many times a year a firm collects its average accounts receivable. *Average collection period* indicates how many days it takes to collect an account receivable.

SELF-TEST QUESTIONS FOR REVIEW

(Answers follow the Solution to Demonstration Problem 2.)

1. What is a bank reconciliation?
   a. A formal financial statement that lists all of a firm's bank account balances
   b. A merger of two banks that previously were competitors
   c. A statement sent monthly by a bank to a depositor that lists all deposits, checks paid, and other credits and charges to the depositor's account for the month
   d. A schedule that accounts for differences between a firm's cash balance as shown on its bank statement and the balance shown in its general ledger Cash account

2. Which of the following statements about a petty cash fund is *not* true?
   a. The fund is managed on an imprest basis.
   b. The fund is used to pay for minor items such as postage and delivery charges.
   c. The fund should have a balance large enough to support one replenishment per year.
   d. All replenishments are made by check.

3. A firm using the allowance method of recording credit losses wrote off a customer's account of $500. Later, the customer paid the account. The firm reinstated the account by means of a journal entry and then recorded the collection. What is the result of these procedures?
   a. Increases total assets by $500
   b. Decreases total assets by $500
   c. Decreases total assets by $1,000
   d. Has no effect on total assets

4. A firm has accounts receivable of $90,000 and a debit balance of $900 in Allowance for Uncollectible Accounts. Two-thirds of the accounts receivable are current and one-third is past due. The firm estimates that 2% of the current accounts and 5% of the past due accounts will prove to be uncollectible. The adjusting entry to provide for uncollectible accounts expense under the aging method should be for what amount?
   a. $2,700
   b. $3,600
   c. $1,800
   d. $4,500

5. A firm receives a six-month note from a customer. The note has a face amount of $4,000 and an interest rate of 9%. What is the total amount of interest to be received?
   a. $1,080
   b. $30
   c. $360
   d. $180

DEMONSTRATION PROBLEM 1 FOR REVIEW

At December 31, 1996, the Cash account in Tyler Company's general ledger had a debit balance of $18,434.27. The December 31, 1996, bank statement showed a balance of $19,726.40. In reconciling the two amounts, you discover the following:

1. Bank deposits made by Tyler on December 31, 1996, amounting to $2,145.40 do not appear on the bank statement.
2. A noninterest-bearing note receivable from Smith Company for $2,000, left with the bank for collection, was collected by the bank near the end of December. The bank credited the proceeds, less a $5 collection charge, on the bank statement. Tyler Company has not recorded the collection.
3. Accompanying the bank statement is a debit memorandum indicating that John Miller's check for $450 was charged against Tyler's bank account on December 30 because of insufficient funds.
4. Check No. 586, written for advertising expense of $869.10, was recorded as $896.10 by Tyler Company.
5. A comparison of the paid checks returned by the bank with the recorded disbursements revealed the following checks still outstanding at December 31, 1996:

No. 561	$306.63	No. 591	$190.00
No. 585	440.00	No. 592	282.50
No. 588	476.40	No. 593	243.00

6. The bank mistakenly charged Tyler Company's account for check-printing costs of $30.50, which should have been charged to Taylor Company.
7. The bank charged Tyler Company's account $42.50 for rental of a safe deposit box. No entry has been made in Tyler's records for this expense.

REQUIRED

a. Prepare a bank reconciliation at December 31, 1996.
b. Prepare any necessary journal entries at December 31, 1996.

SOLUTION TO DEMONSTRATION PROBLEM 1

a.

TYLER COMPANY
BANK RECONCILIATION
DECEMBER 31, 1996

Ending balance from bank statement		$19,726.40	Balance from general ledger		$18,434.27
Add: Deposits not credited by bank		2,145.40	Add: Collection of note	$2,000.00	
Error by bank (Check printing			Less: Collection charge	5.00	1,995.00
charge of Taylor Co.)		30.50	Error in recording check No. 586		27.00
		$21,902.30			$20,456.27
Less: Outstanding checks:			Less:		
No. 561	$306.63		NSF check	$450.00	
No. 585	440.00		Charge for safe deposit box	42.50	492.50
No. 588	476.40				
No. 591	190.00				
No. 592	282.50				
No. 593	243.00	1,938.53			
Reconciled cash balance		$19,963.77	Reconciled cash balance		$19,963.77

b.

Dec. 31	Cash		1,995.00	
	Miscellaneous Expense		5.00	
	Notes Receivable—Smith Company			2,000.00
	To record collection of Smith Company's note by bank, less collection charge.			
31	Cash		27.00	
	Advertising Expense			27.00
	To correct error in recording advertising expense.			
31	Accounts Receivable—John Miller		450.00	
	Cash			450.00
	To reclassify NSF check as an account receivable.			
31	Miscellaneous Expense		42.50	
	Cash			42.50
	To record rental expense of safe deposit box.			

DEMONSTRATION PROBLEM 2 FOR REVIEW

At December 31, 1995, the following selected accounts appeared in Delta Company's unadjusted trial balance:

Accounts Receivable	$81,000
Allowance for Uncollectible Accounts	1,200 (credit)
Notes Receivable (Jason, Inc.)	12,000

Net credit sales for 1995 were $250,000. The $12,000 note receivable was a 90-day, 8% note dated December 13, 1995. The following adjusting entries and transactions occurred at the end of 1995 and during the following year, 1996:

1995

Dec. 31 Recorded the adjusting entry for uncollectible accounts expense, at $1\frac{1}{2}$% of net credit sales.

31 Recorded the adjusting entry for interest on the $12,000 note receivable.

1996

Mar. 12 Received payment on the $12,000 note receivable from Jason, Inc., plus interest.

Apr. 5 Wrote off the account of Abilene Company, $2,850.

July 9 Wrote off the account of Acme Suppliers, $1,450.

Sept. 5 Received payment from Acme Suppliers, which is in bankruptcy proceedings, for $450 in final settlement of the account written off on July 9.

Dec. 6 Wrote off the account of Walton, Inc., $1,300.

31 Changed from the percent-of-net-sales method of providing for uncollectible accounts to an estimate based on aged accounts receivable. The firm's analysis indicated a desired credit balance of $4,500 in Allowance for Uncollectible Accounts.

REQUIRED

Prepare the journal entries for these adjustments and transactions.

SOLUTION TO DEMONSTRATION PROBLEM 2

1995

Dec. 31 Uncollectible Accounts Expense   3,750
      Allowance for Uncollectible Accounts   3,750
    To provide for uncollectible accounts expense at $1\frac{1}{2}$% of net credit sales, $250,000.

31 Interest Receivable   48
      Interest Income   48
    To accrue interest on Jason, Inc., note receivable ($12,000 \times 0.08 \times \frac{18}{360} = \$48$).

1996

Mar. 12 Cash   12,240
      Interest Income   192
      Interest Receivable   48
      Notes Receivable—Jason, Inc.   12,000
    To record receipt of payment of Jason, Inc., note receivable ($12,000 \times 0.08 \times \frac{72}{360} = \$192$).

Apr. 5 Allowance for Uncollectible Accounts   2,850
      Accounts Receivable—Abilene Company   2,850
    To write off the account of Abilene Company as uncollectible.

July 9 Allowance for Uncollectible Accounts   1,450
      Accounts Receivable—Acme Suppliers   1,450
    To write off the account of Acme Suppliers as uncollectible.

Sept. 5 Accounts Receivable—Acme Suppliers   450
      Allowance for Uncollectible Accounts   450
    To reinstate $450 of the account of Acme Suppliers that proved collectible.

5 Cash   450
      Accounts Receivable—Acme Suppliers   450
    To record payment of Acme Suppliers' account.

Dec. 6 Allowance for Uncollectible Accounts   1,300
      Accounts Receivable—Walton, Inc.   1,300
    To write off the account of Walton, Inc., as uncollectible.

Dec. 31	Uncollectible Accounts Expense	4,700	
	Allowance for Uncollectible Accounts		4,700
	To provide for uncollectible accounts expense ($4,500 desired balance + $200 existing debit balance = $4,700).		

ANSWERS TO SELF-TEST QUESTIONS

1. d, pp. 202–204   **2.** c, p. 205   **3.** d, p. 210   **4.** b, pp. 208–209   **5.** d, p. 213

GLOSSARY OF KEY TERMS USED IN THIS CHAPTER

accounts receivable A current asset that is created by a sale on a credit basis. It represents the amount owed the company by the customer (p. 205).

accounts receivable aging method A procedure that uses an aging schedule to determine the year-end balance needed in the Allowance for Uncollectible Accounts account (p. 208).

accounts receivable turnover Annual net sales divided by average accounts receivable (p. 215).

aging schedule An analysis that shows how long customers' accounts receivable balances have remained unpaid (p. 208).

Allowance for Uncollectible Accounts A contra asset account with a normal credit balance shown on the balance sheet as a deduction from accounts receivable to reflect the expected realizable amount of accounts receivable (p. 206).

allowance method An accounting procedure whereby the amount of uncollectible accounts expense is estimated and recorded in the period in which the related credit sales occur (p. 206).

average collection period Determined by dividing 365 days by accounts receivable turnover (p. 215).

bank reconciliation A procedure or analysis explaining the various items—such as deposits in transit, checks outstanding, bank charges, and errors—that lead to differences between the balance shown on a bank statement and the related Cash account in the general ledger (p. 202).

bearer One of the terms that may be used to designate the payee on a promissory note; means the note is payable to whoever holds the note (p. 212).

cash An asset category representing the amount of a firm's paper money, coins, checks, money orders, traveler's checks, and funds on deposit at a bank in checking accounts and savings accounts (p. 194).

cash and cash equivalents The sum of cash plus short-term, highly liquid investments such as treasury bills and money market funds (p. 194).

certificate of deposit (CD) An investment security available at financial institutions generally offering a fixed rate of return for a specified period of time (p. 194).

check A written order signed by a checking account owner directing the bank to pay a specified amount of money to the person or company named on the check (p. 199).

compensating balance A minimum amount that a financial institution requires a firm to maintain in its account as part of a borrowing arrangement (p. 194).

credit card fee A fee charged retailers for credit card services provided by financial institutions. The fee is usually stated as a percentage of credit card sales (p. 211).

deposits in transit Cash deposits made to a bank account near the end of a month that do not appear on that month's bank statement (p. 202).

direct write-off method An accounting procedure whereby the amount of uncollectible accounts expense is not recorded until specific uncollectible accounts are identified (p. 210).

discounting The exchanging of notes receivable for cash at a financial institution (p. 212).

factoring Selling an account receivable to another company, typically a finance company or a financial institution (p. 212).

IOU A slang term for a note receivable (p. 194).

maker The signer of a promissory note (p. 212).

maturity date The date on which a note or bond matures (p. 213).

note receivable A promissory note held by the note's payee (p. 212).

not-sufficient-funds check A check from an individual or company that had an insufficient cash balance in the bank when the holder of the check presented it to the bank for payment (p. 194).

on-line scale A device attached to a point-of-sale system that registers the weight of items such as produce and transmits the weight to a computer to determine the amount to charge the customer (p. 197).

outstanding checks Checks issued by a firm that have not yet been presented to its bank for payment (p. 202).

payee The company or individual to whom a promissory note is made payable (p. 212).

petty cash fund A special, relatively small cash fund established for making minor cash disbursements in the operation of a business (p. 205).

percentage of net sales method A procedure that determines the uncollectible accounts expense for the year by multiplying net credit sales by the estimated uncollectible percentage (p. 208).

plate scanner   A device built into a checkout counter in a retail store that uses a laser to read bar codes on products (p. 197).

postdated check   A check from another person or company with a date that is later than the current date. A postdated check does not become cash until the date of the check (p. 194).

preset keys   Keys on a cash register that represent a particular product. Pressing the key causes the computer to look up the item description and price in the computer's files (p. 199).

price-look-up code   A numeric code entered by a salesperson into a point-of-sale system to instruct the computer to look up the price of a particular product (p. 197).

promissory note   A written promise to pay a certain sum of money on demand or at a determinable future time (p. 212).

remittance advice   A form that accompanies a check to inform the person receiving the check the purpose of the check (p. 196).

remittance list   A list of the checks received from customers to pay their accounts receivable (p. 196).

Uncollectible Accounts Expense   The expense stemming from the inability of a business to collect an amount previously recorded as a receivable. Sometimes called *bad debts expense*. Normally classified as a selling or administrative expense (p. 205).

universal product code (UPC) bar code   The bar code placed on consumer products by manufacturers to facilitate point-of-sale systems in retail stores (p. 197).

QUESTIONS

6-1 What types of items are included in cash? What are the two important characteristics of an item of cash?

6-2 Which of the following are considered to be cash: paper money, certificates of deposit, postdated checks, traveler's checks, funds in a checking account, and money orders?

6-3 What is a remittance advice? What types of data are included on a remittance advice?

6-4 How does a company use a lockbox collection service?

6-5 What is the purpose of a bank reconciliation?

6-6 In preparing a bank reconciliation, how should you determine (a) deposits not recorded in the bank statement and (b) outstanding checks?

6-7 Indicate whether the following bank reconciliation items should be (1) added to the bank statement balance, (2) deducted from the bank statement balance, (3) added to the ledger account balance, or (4) deducted from the ledger account balance:
  a. Bank service charge.
  b. NSF check.
  c. Deposit in transit.
  d. Outstanding check.
  e. Bank error charging company's account with another company's check.
  f. Difference of $270 in amount of check written for $410 but recorded by the company as $140.

6-8 Which of the items listed in Question 6-7 require a journal entry on the company's books?

6-9 What is an imprest petty cash fund? How is such a fund established and replenished?

6-10 In dealing with receivables, what do the terms *factoring* and *discounting* mean?

6-11 How does a credit scoring system work?

6-12 How do the allowance method and the direct write-off method of handling credit losses differ with respect to the timing of expense recognition?

6-13 When a firm provides for credit losses under the allowance method, why is Allowance for Uncollectible Accounts credited rather than Accounts Receivable?

6-14 What are the two most commonly used methods of estimating uncollectible accounts expense when the allowance method is employed? Describe them.

6-15 Murphy Company estimates its uncollectibles by aging its accounts and applying percentages to various age groups of the accounts. Murphy calculated a total of $2,100 in possible losses as of December 31, 1996. Accounts Receivable has a balance of $98,000, and Allowance for Uncollectible Accounts has a credit balance of $500 before adjustment at December 31, 1996. What is the December 31, 1996, adjusting entry to provide for credit losses? Determine the net amount of Accounts Receivable included in current assets.

6-16 On June 15, 1995, Rollins, Inc., sold $750 worth of merchandise to Dell Company. On November 20, 1995, Rollins, Inc., wrote off Dell's account. On March 10, 1996, Dell Company paid the account in full. What are the entries Rollins, Inc., makes for the write-off and the recovery, assuming that Rollins, Inc., uses (a) the allowance method of handling credit losses and (b) the direct write-off method?

6-17   Wood Company sold a $675 refrigerator to a customer who charged the sale with a VISA bank credit card. Wood Company deposits credit card sales slips daily; cash is deposited in Wood Company's checking account at the same time. Wood Company's bank charges a credit card fee of 4% of sales. What entry should Wood Company make to record the sale?

6-18   Volter, Inc., received a 60-day, 9% note for $15,000 on March 5, 1996, from a customer. What is the maturity date of the note?

6-19   Stanley Company received a 150-day, 8% note for $15,000 on December 1, 1996. What adjusting entry is needed to accrue interest on December 31, 1996?

6-20   Define *accounts receivable turnover* and explain its use. How is the *average collection period* determined?

PRINCIPLES DISCUSSION QUESTION

6-21   At a recent board of directors meeting of Ascot, Inc., one of the directors expressed concern over the Allowance for Uncollectible Accounts appearing in the company's balance sheet. "I don't understand this account," he said. "Why don't we just show accounts receivable at the amount we would receive if we sold them to a financial institution and get rid of that allowance account?"

Prepare a written response to the director. Include in your response (1) an explanation of why the company has an allowance account, (2) what the balance sheet presentation of accounts receivable is supposed to show, and (3) how the basic principles of accounting relate to the analysis and presentation of accounts receivable.

EXERCISES

INTERNAL CONTROLS FOR CASH RECEIVED ON ACCOUNT
— OBJ. 2 —

6-22   Hudson Company sells supplies to restaurants. Most sales are made on open account (credit sales). Hudson has requested your help in designing procedures for processing checks received from its customers. Briefly describe the procedures that should be used in the following departments:
a. Mailroom
b. Treasurer's department
c. Controller's department

BANK RECONCILIATION
— OBJ. 3 —

6-23   Use the following information to prepare a bank reconciliation for Young Company at June 30, 1996.
1. Balance per Cash account, June 30, $7,055.80.
2. Balance per bank statement, June 30, $7,300.25.
3. Deposits not reflected on bank statement, $725.
4. Outstanding checks, June 30, $1,260.45.
5. Service charge on bank statement not recorded in books, $11.
6. Error by bank—Yertel Company check charged on Young Company's bank statement, $550.
7. Check for advertising expense, $250, incorrectly recorded in books as $520.

BANK RECONCILIATION COMPONENTS
— OBJ. 3 —

6-24   Identify the amount asked for in each of the following situations.
a. Munsing Company's May 31 bank reconciliation shows deposits in transit of $1,400. The general ledger Cash in Bank account shows total cash receipts during June of $57,300. The June bank statement shows total cash deposits of $55,900 (and no credit memos). What amount of deposits in transit should appear in the June 30 bank reconciliation?
b. Sandusky Company's August 31 bank reconciliation shows outstanding checks of $2,100. The general ledger Cash in Bank account shows total cash disbursements (all by check) during September of $50,300. The September bank statement shows $49,200 of checks clearing the bank. What amount of outstanding checks should appear in the September 30 bank reconciliation?
c. Fremont Corporation's March 31 bank reconciliation shows deposits in transit of $800. The general ledger Cash in Bank account shows total cash receipts during April of $38,000. The April bank statement shows total cash deposits of $37,100 (including $1,300 from the collection of a note; the note collection has not yet been recorded by Fremont). What amount of deposits in transit should appear in the April 30 bank reconciliation?

CREDIT LOSSES BASED ON SALES
— OBJ. 4, 5 —

6-25   Lewis Company uses the allowance method of handling credit losses. It estimates losses at 1% of credit sales, which were $900,000 during 1996. On December 31, 1996, the Accounts Receivable balance was $150,000, and Allowance for Uncollectible Accounts had a credit balance of $1,200 before adjustment.
a. Prepare the adjusting entry to record credit losses for 1996.
b. Show how Accounts Receivable and Allowance for Uncollectible Accounts would appear in the December 31, 1996, balance sheet.

CREDIT LOSSES BASED ON ACCOUNTS RECEIVABLE
— OBJ. 5 —

6-26 Hunter, Inc., analyzed its Accounts Receivable balances at December 31, 1996, and arrived at the aged balances listed below, along with the percentage that is estimated to be uncollectible.

Age Group	Balance	Estimated Loss %
0–30 days past due	$ 90,000	1
31–60 days past due	20,000	2
61–120 days past due	11,000	5
121 days–six months past due	6,000	10
Over six months past due	4,000	25
	$131,000	

The company handles credit losses with the allowance method. The credit balance of Allowance for Uncollectible Accounts is $520 on December 31, 1996, before any adjustments.
a. Prepare the adjusting entry for estimated credit losses on December 31, 1996.
b. Prepare the entry to write off Rose Company's account on April 10, 1997, $425.

ALLOWANCE VS. DIRECT WRITE-OFF METHODS
— OBJ. 5, 6 —

6-27 On March 10, 1996, Gardner, Inc., declared a $900 account receivable from Gates Company uncollectible and wrote off the account. On November 18, 1996, Gardner received a $400 payment on the account from Gates.
a. Assume that Gardner uses the allowance method of handling credit losses. Prepare the entries to record the write-off and the subsequent recovery of Gates' account.
b. Assume that Gardner uses the direct write-off method of handling credit losses. Prepare the entries to record the write-off and the subsequent recovery of Gates' account.
c. Assume that the payment from Gates arrives on February 5, 1997, rather than on November 18, 1996. (1) Prepare the entries to record the write-off and subsequent recovery of Gates' account under the allowance method. (2) Prepare the entries to record the write-off and subsequent recovery of Gates' account under the direct write-off method. Assume that Gardner expects to write off several accounts in 1997.

CREDIT CARD SALES
— OBJ. 7 —

6-28 Ruth Anne's Fabrics accepts cash, personal checks, and two credit cards when customers buy merchandise. With the Great American Bank Card, Ruth Anne's Fabrics receives an immediate deposit in its checking account when credit card sales slips are deposited at the bank. The bank charges a 4% fee. With the United Merchants card, Ruth Anne's Fabrics mails the credit card sales slips to United Merchants' regional processing center each day. United Merchants accumulates these slips for three days and then mails a check to Ruth Anne's Fabrics, after deducting a 3% fee. Prepare journal entries to record the following:
a. Sales for March 15, 1996, were as follows:

Cash and checks	$ 850
Great American Bank Card (Deposited at the end of the day)	1,100
United Merchants Card (Mailed at the end of the day)	700
	$2,650

b. Received a check for $3,978 from United Merchants on March 20, 1996.

MATURITY DATES OF NOTES RECEIVABLE
— OBJ. 8 —

6-29 Determine the maturity date and compute the interest for each of the following notes:

	Date of Note	Principal	Interest Rate (%)	Term
a.	August 5	$ 6,000	8	120 days
b.	May 10	16,800	7	90 days
c.	October 20	24,000	9	45 days
d.	July 6	4,500	10	60 days
e.	September 15	9,000	8	75 days

COMPUTING ACCRUED INTEREST
— OBJ. 8 —

6-30 Compute the interest accrued on each of the following notes receivable held by Northland, Inc., on December 31, 1996:

Maker	Date of Note	Principal	Interest Rate (%)	Term
Maple	11/21/96	$18,000	10	120 days
Wyman	12/13/96	14,000	9	90 days
Nahn	12/19/96	21,000	8	60 days

PROBLEMS

**INTERNAL CONTROLS FOR
CASH RECEIVED ON ACCOUNT
— OBJ. 2 —**

6-31 Schoff Company sells plumbing supplies to plumbing contractors on account. The procedures that Schoff uses to handle checks received from customers via the mail are described below.

a. Schoff instructs its customers to send payment checks to its street address, 619 Main Street, Scottsdale, Arizona.

b. Schoff does not provide a remittance advice to its customers for return with payment checks.

c. Checks are endorsed by the treasurer's office just prior to sending the checks to the bank for deposit.

d. The mailroom prepares a remittance list of all the checks received and files the only copy of the remittance list in a mailroom file cabinet.

e. The checks are sent to the controller's office. The controller's office uses the checks to post the accounts receivable subsidiary ledger and prepare the journal entry to record cash receipts. The checks are then sent to the treasurer's office.

f. The treasurer's office prepares the deposit slip (two copies) and sends one copy and the checks to the bank. The other copy of the deposit slip is filed in the treasurer's file cabinet.

g. The bank statement is sent to the controller, who prepares the bank reconciliation.

REQUIRED

For each of these procedures, indicate how Schoff could improve it. (Refer to Exhibit 6-1 in the chapter to help you generate ideas).

**BANK RECONCILIATION
— OBJ. 3 —**

6-32 On July 31, 1996, Sullivan Company's Cash in Bank account had a balance of $7,216.60. On that date, the bank statement indicated a balance of $9,098.55. Comparison of returned checks and bank advices revealed the following:

1. Deposits in transit July 31 amounted to $3,576.95.

2. Outstanding checks July 31 totaled $1,467.90.

3. The bank erroneously charged a $325 check of Solomon Company against the Sullivan bank account.

4. A $25 bank service charge has not yet been recorded by Sullivan Company.

5. Sullivan neglected to record $4,000 borrowed from the bank on a 10% six-month note. The bank statement shows the $4,000 as a deposit.

6. Included with the returned checks is a memo indicating that J. Martin's check for $640 had been returned NSF. Martin, a customer, had sent the check to pay an account of $660 less a $20 discount.

7. Sullivan Company recorded a $109 payment for repairs as $1,090.

REQUIRED

a. Prepare a bank reconciliation for Sullivan Company at July 31, 1996.

b. Prepare the general journal entry or entries necessary to bring the Cash in Bank account into agreement with the reconciled cash balance on the bank reconciliation.

**BANK RECONCILIATION
— OBJ. 3 —**

6-33 The bank reconciliation made by Winton, Inc., on August 31, 1996, showed a deposit in transit of $1,280 and two outstanding checks, No. 597 for $830 and No. 603 for $640. The reconciled cash balance on August 31 was $14,110.

The following bank statement is available for September:

BANK STATEMENT							
TO Winton, Inc. St. Louis, MO						September 30, 1996 STATE BANK	
Date	**Deposits**	**No.**	**Date**	**Charges**		**Date**	**Balance**
						Aug. 31	$14,300
Sept. 1	$1,280	597	Sept. 1	$ 830		Sept. 1	14,750
2	1,120	607	5	1,850		2	15,870
5	850	608	5	1,100		5	13,770
9	744	609	9	552		8	13,130
15	1,360	610	8	640		9	13,322
17	1,540	611	17	488		15	14,008
25	1,028	612	15	674		17	15,060
30	680	614	25	920		25	15,168
		NSF	29	1,028		29	14,140
		SC	30	36		30	14,784

A list of deposits made and checks written during September is shown below:

Deposits Made		Checks Written	
Sept. 1	$1,120	No. 607	$1,850
4	850	608	1,100
8	744	609	552
12	1,360	610	640
16	1,540	611	488
24	1,028	612	746
29	680	613	310
30	1,266	614	920
	$8,588	615	386
		616	420
			$7,412

The Cash in Bank account balance on September 30 was $15,286. In reviewing checks returned by the bank, the accountant discovered that check No. 612, written for $674 for advertising expense, was recorded in the cash disbursements journal as $746. The NSF check for $1,028, which Winton deposited on September 24, was a payment on account from customer D. Walker.

REQUIRED

a. Prepare a bank reconciliation for Winton, Inc., at September 30, 1996.

b. Prepare the necessary journal entries to bring the Cash in Bank account into agreement with the reconciled cash balance on the bank reconciliation.

ALLOWANCE VS. DIRECT WRITE-OFF METHODS — OBJ. 5, 6 —

6-34 Fullerton Company, which has been in business for three years, makes all of its sales on account and does not offer cash discounts. The firm's credit sales, collections from customers, and write-offs of uncollectible accounts for the three-year period are summarized below:

Year	Sales	Collections	Accounts Written Off
1	$300,000	$287,000	$2,100
2	385,000	380,000	3,350
3	420,000	407,000	3,650

REQUIRED

a. If Fullerton Company had used the direct write-off method of recognizing credit losses during the three years, what amount of Accounts Receivable would appear on the firm's balance sheet at the end of the third year? What total amount of uncollectible accounts expense would have appeared on the firm's income statement during the three-year period?

b. If Fullerton Company had used an allowance method of recognizing credit losses and had provided for such losses at the rate of 1.2% of sales, what amounts in Accounts Receivable and Allowance for Uncollectible Accounts would appear on the firm's balance sheet at the end of the third year? What total amount of uncollectible accounts expense would have appeared on the firm's income statement during the three-year period?

c. Comment on the use of the 1.2% rate to provide for losses in part (b).

ENTRIES FOR CREDIT LOSSES — OBJ. 4, 5 —

6-35 At the beginning of 1996, Whitney Company had the following accounts on its books:

Accounts Receivable	$122,000 (debit)
Allowance for Uncollectible Accounts	7,900 (credit)

During 1996, credit sales were $1,173,000 and collections on account were $1,150,000. The following transactions, among others, occurred during the year:

Feb. 17 Wrote off R. Lowell's account, $3,600.

May 28 Wrote off G. Boyd's account, $2,400.

Oct. 13 Received $600 from G. Boyd, who is in bankruptcy proceedings, in final settlement of the account written off on May 28. This amount is not included in the $1,150,000 collections.

Dec. 15 Wrote off K. Marshall's account, $1,500.

31 In an adjusting entry, recorded the provision for uncollectible accounts at 0.8% of credit sales for the year.

REQUIRED

a. Prepare general journal entries to record the credit sales, the collections on account, and the preceding transactions and adjustment.

b. Show how Accounts Receivable and Allowance for Uncollectible Accounts would appear in the December 31, 1996, balance sheet.

CREDIT LOSSES BASED ON ACCOUNTS RECEIVABLE — OBJ. 4, 5 —

6-36 At December 31, 1996, Schuler Company had a balance of $370,000 in its Accounts Receivable account and a credit balance of $4,200 in the Allowance for Uncollectible Accounts account. The accounts receivable subsidiary ledger consisted of $375,000 in debit balances and $5,000 in credit balances. The company has aged its accounts as follows:

Current	$304,000
0–60 days past due	44,000
61–180 days past due	18,000
Over six months past due	9,000
	$375,000

In the past, the company has experienced losses as follows: 1% of current balances, 5% of balances 0–60 days past due, 15% of balances 61–180 days past due, and 40% of balances over six months past due. The company bases its provision for credit losses on the aging analysis.

REQUIRED
a. Prepare the adjusting journal entry to record the provision for credit losses for 1996.
b. Show how Accounts Receivable (including the credit balances) and Allowance for Uncollectible Accounts would appear in the December 31, 1996, balance sheet.

CREDIT CARD SALES — OBJ. 7 —

6-37 Valderi's Gallery sells quality art work, with prices for individual pieces ranging from $500 to $25,000. Sales are infrequent, typically three to five pieces per week. The following transactions occurred during the first week of June 1996. Perpetual inventory is used.

On June 1, sold an $800 framed print ($500 cost) to Kerwin Antiques on open account, with 2/10, n/30 terms.

On June 2, sold three framed etchings totaling $2,400 ($1,500 cost) to Maria Alvado, who used the United Merchants Card to charge the etchings. Valderi mailed the credit card sales slip to United Merchants the same day. United Merchants will send a check within seven days after deducting a 1% fee.

On June 4, sold an $1,800 oil painting ($1,000 cost) to Shaun Chandler, who paid with a personal check.

On June 5, sold a $2,000 watercolor ($1,300 cost) to Julie and John Malbie, who used their Great American Bank Card to charge the purchase. Valderi deposited the credit card sales slip the same day and received immediate credit in the company's checking account. The bank charged a 2% fee.

On June 6, received payment from Kerwin Antiques for its June 1 purchase.

On June 7, received a check from United Merchants for the June 2 sale.

REQUIRED
Prepare journal entries to record these transactions.

VARIOUS ENTRIES FOR ACCOUNTS AND NOTES RECEIVABLE — OBJ. 4, 5, 8 —

6-38 Lancaster Inc., began business on January 1, 1996. Certain transactions for 1996 follow:

June 8 Received a $15,000, 60-day, 8% note on account from R. Elliot.

Aug. 7 Received payment from R. Elliot on her note (principal plus interest).

Sept. 1 Received an $18,000, 120-day, 9% note from B. Shore Company on account.

Dec. 16 Received a $14,400, 45-day, 10% note from C. Judd on account.

30 B. Shore failed to pay its note.

31 Wrote off B. Shore's account as uncollectible. Lancaster, Inc., uses the allowance method of providing for credit losses.

31 Recorded expected credit losses for the year by an adjusting entry. Write-offs of accounts during this first year have created a debit balance in Allowance for Uncollectible Accounts of $22,600. Analysis of aged receivables indicates that the desired balance of the allowance account is $19,500.

31 Made the appropriate adjusting entries for interest.

REQUIRED
Record the foregoing transactions and adjustments in general journal form.

ALTERNATE EXERCISES

INTERNAL CONTROLS FOR CASH RECEIVED FROM RETAIL SALES — OBJ. 2 —

6-22A Edwards Company operates a retail department store. Most customers pay cash for their purchases. Edwards has asked you to help it design procedures for processing cash received from customers for cash sales. Briefly describe the procedures that should be used in the following departments:
a. Retail sales departments
b. Retail sales supervisor

c. Treasurer's department

d. Controller's department

BANK RECONCILIATION
— OBJ. 3 —

6-23A Use the following information to prepare a bank reconciliation for Dillon Company at April 30, 1996.

1. Balance per Cash account, April 30, $6,042.10.
2. Balance per bank statement, April 30, $6,300.28.
3. Deposits not reflected on bank statement, $650.
4. Outstanding checks, April 30, $1,140.18.
5. Service charge on bank statement not recorded in books, $12.
6. Error by bank—Dillard Company check charged on Dillon Company's bank statement, $400.
7. Check for advertising expense, $130, incorrectly recorded in books at $310.

BANK RECONCILIATION
COMPONENTS
— OBJ. 3 —

6-24A Identify the amount asked for in each of the following situations:

a. Howell Company's August 31 bank reconciliation shows deposits in transit of $2,400. The general ledger Cash in Bank account shows total cash receipts during September of $91,200. The September bank statement shows total cash deposits of $88,000 (and no credit memos). What amount of deposits in transit should appear in the September 30 bank reconciliation?

b. Wright Corporation's March 31 bank reconciliation shows deposits in transit of $1,600. The general ledger Cash in Bank account shows total cash receipts during April of $63,100. The April bank statement shows total cash deposits of $66,200 (including $2,000 from the collection of a note; the note collection has not yet been recorded by Wright). What amount of deposits in transit should appear in the April 30 bank reconciliation?

c. Braddock Company's October 31 bank reconciliation shows outstanding checks of $2,600. The general ledger Cash in Bank account shows total cash disbursements (all by check) during November of $68,700. The November bank statement shows $67,200 of checks clearing the bank. What amount of outstanding checks should appear in the November 30 bank reconciliation?

CREDIT LOSSES BASED ON
SALES
— OBJ. 4, 5 —

6-25A Highland Company uses the allowance method of handling credit losses. It estimates losses at 1% of credit sales, which were $1,200,000 during 1996. On December 31, 1996, the Accounts Receivable balance was $280,000, and Allowance for Uncollectible Accounts had a credit balance of $1,700 before adjustment.

a. Prepare the adjusting entry to record credit losses for 1996.

b. Show how Accounts Receivable and Allowance for Uncollectible Accounts would appear in the December 31, 1996, balance sheet.

CREDIT LOSSES BASED ON
ACCOUNTS RECEIVABLE
— OBJ. 5 —

6-26A Maxwell, Inc., analyzed its Accounts Receivable balances at December 31, 1996, and arrived at the aged balances listed below, along with the percentage that is estimated to be uncollectible.

Age Group	Balance	Estimated Loss %
0–30 days past due	$100,000	1
31–60 days past due	18,000	3
61–120 days past due	20,000	6
121 days–six months past due	7,000	10
Over six months past due	2,000	20
	$147,000	

The company handles credit losses with the allowance method. The credit balance of Allowance for Uncollectible Accounts is $840 on December 31, 1996, before any adjustments.

a. Prepare the adjusting entry for estimated credit losses on December 31, 1996.

b. Prepare the entry to write off Porter Company's account on May 12, 1997, $480.

ALLOWANCE VS. DIRECT
WRITE-OFF METHODS
— OBJ. 5, 6 —

6-27A On April 12, 1996, Maddox Company declared a $1,000 account receivable from Ward Company uncollectible and wrote off the account. On December 5, 1996, Maddox received a $700 payment on the account from Ward.

a. Assume that Maddox uses the allowance method of handling credit losses. Prepare the entries to record the write-off and the subsequent recovery of Ward's account.

b. Assume that Maddox uses the direct write-off method of handling credit losses. Prepare the entries to record the write-off and the subsequent recovery of Ward's account.

c. Assume that the payment from Ward arrives on January 18, 1997, rather than on December 5, 1996. (1) Prepare the entries to record the write-off and subsequent recovery of Ward's account under the allowance method. (2) Prepare the entries to record the write-off and subsequent recovery of Ward's account under the direct write-off method. Assume that Maddox expects to write off several accounts in 1997.

CREDIT CARD SALES
— OBJ. 7 —

6-28A Historically, 60% of customer bills at Andrews Supper Club have been paid with cash or check, and 40% have been charged using either the Great American Bank Card or the United Merchants Card. Andrews pays a 4% fee with both cards. Great American Bank deposits cash in Andrews' checking account when the credit card sales slips are deposited. United Merchants makes an electronic funds transfer three days after the sales slips are mailed. Prepare journal entries to record the following:

a. Sales for September 10, 1996, were as follows:

Cash and checks	$1,340
Great American Bank Card (Deposited at the end of the day)	500
United Merchants Card (Mailed at the end of the day)	300
	$2,140

b. On September 13, 1996, received an electronic funds transfer from United Merchants for the September 10, 1996, sales.

MATURITY DATES OF
NOTES RECEIVABLE
— OBJ. 8 —

6-29A Determine the maturity date and compute the interest for each of the following notes:

	Date of Note	Principal	Interest Rate (%)	Term
a.	July 10	$ 7,200	9	90 days
b.	April 14	12,000	8	120 days
c.	May 19	11,200	$7\frac{1}{2}$	120 days
d.	June 10	5,400	8	45 days
e.	October 29	30,000	8	75 days

COMPUTING ACCRUED
INTEREST
— OBJ. 8 —

6-30A Compute the interest accrued on each of the following notes receivable held by Galloway, Inc., on December 31, 1996:

Maker	Date of Note	Principal	Interest Rate (%)	Term
Barton	12/4/96	$10,000	8	120 days
Lawson	12/13/96	24,000	9	90 days
Riley	12/19/96	9,000	10	60 days

ALTERNATE PROBLEMS

INTERNAL CONTROLS FOR CASH
RECEIVED FROM RETAIL SALES
— OBJ. 2 —

6-31A Midland Stores is a retailer of men's clothing. Most customers pay cash for their purchases. The procedures that Midland uses for handling cash are described below.

a. Each department begins the day with whatever amount of cash remains in the cash register from the prior day. This is not a predetermined amount.

b. All sales associates share one cash drawer.

c. Each sales associate can handle all transactions, including returns and unusual transactions, without approval from a supervisor.

d. At the end of each day, one of the sales associates takes the cash drawer and the cash register totals to a private area where no one can observe what is being done, counts the cash in the drawer, and prepares a written report of sales and cash received. The cash, the register tape, and a copy of the report are sent to the controller's department.

e. The controller prepares the deposit slip and sends the deposit to the bank. The controller then prepares the journal entry to record the cash sales.

f. The controller does not keep any copies of the written report or the deposit slip.

g. The bank statement is sent to the controller, who prepares the bank reconciliation.

REQUIRED

For each of these procedures, indicate how Midland could improve it. (Refer to Exhibit 6-2 in the chapter to help you generate ideas).

BANK RECONCILIATION
— OBJ. 3 —

6-32A On May 31, 1996, the Cash in Bank account of Wallace Company, a sole proprietorship, had a balance of $6,122.50. On that date, the bank statement indicated a balance of $7,933.50. Comparison of returned checks and bank advices revealed the following:

1. Deposits in transit May 31 totaled $2,709.05.

2. Outstanding checks May 31 totaled $3,088.25.

3. The bank added to the account $27.80 of interest income earned by Wallace during May.
4. The bank collected a $2,400 note receivable for Wallace and charged a $20 collection fee. Both items appear on the bank statement.
5. Bank service charges in addition to the collection fee, not yet recorded, were $20.
6. Included with the returned checks is a memo indicating that L. Ryder's check for $686 had been returned NSF. Ryder, a customer, had sent the check to pay an account of $700 less a 2% discount.
7. Wallace Company recorded the payment of an account payable as $690; the check was for $960.

REQUIRED

a. Prepare a bank reconciliation for Wallace Company at May 31, 1996.
b. Prepare the general journal entry or entries necessary to bring the Cash in Bank account into agreement with the reconciled cash balance on the bank reconciliation.

BANK RECONCILIATION — OBJ. 3 —

6-33A The bank reconciliation made by Sandler Company, a sole proprietorship, on March 31, 1996, showed a deposit in transit of $1,100 and two outstanding checks, No. 797 for $450 and No. 804 for $890. The reconciled cash balance on March 31, 1996, was $11,720.

The following bank statement is available for April 1996:

BANK STATEMENT							
TO Sandler Company Fairbanks, AK					**April 30, 1996** FAIRBANKS NATIONAL BANK		
Date	**Deposits**	**No.**	**Date**	**Charges**		**Date**	**Balance**
						Mar. 31	$11,960
Apr. 1	$1,100	804	Apr. 2	$ 890		Apr. 1	13,060
3	1,680	807	3	730		2	12,170
7	1,250	808	7	1,140		3	13,120
13	1,020	809	7	838		7	12,392
18	840	810	16	1,040		13	13,086
23	790	811	13	326		16	12,046
27	1,340	813	27	540		18	12,386
30	1,160	814	23	600		23	12,576
30	60IN	NSF	18	500		27	13,376
		SC	30	40		30	14,556

A list of deposits made and checks written during April is shown below:

Deposits Made		Checks Written	
Apr. 2	$1,680	No. 807	$ 730
6	1,250	808	1,140
10	1,020	809	838
17	840	810	1,040
22	790	811	272
24	1,340	812	948
29	1,160	813	540
30	1,425	814	600
	$9,505	815	372
		816	875
			$7,355

The Cash in Bank account balance on April 30 was $13,870. In reviewing checks returned by the bank, the accountant discovered that check No. 811, written for $326 for delivery expense, was recorded in the cash disbursements journal as $272. The NSF check for $500 was that of customer R. Koppa, deposited in April. Interest for April added to the account by the bank was $60.

REQUIRED

a. Prepare a bank reconciliation for Sandler Company at April 30, 1996.
b. Prepare the necessary journal entries to bring the Cash in Bank account into agreement with the reconciled cash balance on the bank reconciliation.

ALLOWANCE VS. DIRECT WRITE-OFF METHODS — OBJ. 5, 6 —

6-34A Steinbrook Company, which has been in business for three years, makes all of its sales on account and does not offer cash discounts. The firm's credit sales, collections from customers, and write-offs of uncollectible accounts for the three-year period are summarized below:

Year	Sales	Collections	Accounts Written Off
1	$751,000	$733,000	$5,300
2	876,000	864,000	5,800
3	972,000	938,000	6,500

REQUIRED

a. If Steinbrook Company used the direct write-off method of recognizing credit losses during the three years, what amount of Accounts Receivable appears on the firm's balance sheet at the end of the third year? What total amount of uncollectible accounts expense appeared on the firm's income statements during the three-year period?
b. If Steinbrook Company used an allowance method of recognizing credit losses and provided for such losses at the rate of 1% of sales, what amounts of Accounts Receivable and Allowance for Uncollectible Accounts appear on the firm's balance sheet at the end of the third year? What total amount of uncollectible accounts expense appeared on the firm's income statement during the three-year period?
c. Comment on the use of the 1% rate to provide for losses in part (b).

ENTRIES FOR CREDIT LOSSES — OBJ. 4, 5 —

6-35A At January 1, 1996, Griffin Company had the following accounts on its books:

Accounts Receivable	$126,000 (debit)
Allowance for Uncollectible Accounts	6,800 (credit)

During 1996, credit sales were $811,000 and collections on account were $794,000. The following transactions, among others, occurred during the year:

Jan. 11   Wrote off J. Wolf's account, $2,800.
Apr. 29   Wrote off B. Avery's account, $1,000.
Nov. 15   Received $1,000 from B. Avery to pay a debt that had been written off April 29. This amount is not included in the $794,000 collections.
Dec. 5   Wrote off D. Wright's account, $2,150.
      31   In an adjusting entry, recorded the provision for uncollectible accounts at 1% of credit sales for the year.

REQUIRED

a. Prepare general journal entries to record the credit sales, the collections on account, the transactions, and the adjustment.
b. Show how Accounts Receivable and Allowance for Uncollectible Accounts appear in the December 31, 1996, balance sheet.

CREDIT LOSSES BASED ON ACCOUNTS RECEIVABLE — OBJ. 4, 5 —

6-36A At December 31, 1996, Rinehart Company had a balance of $304,000 in its Accounts Receivable account and a credit balance of $2,800 in the Allowance for Uncollectible Accounts account. The accounts receivable subsidiary ledger consisted of $309,600 in debit balances and $5,600 in credit balances. The company has aged its accounts as follows:

Current	$262,000
0–60 days past due	28,000
61–180 days past due	11,200
Over six months past due	8,400
	$309,600

In the past, the company has experienced losses as follows: 2% of current balances, 6% of balances 0–60 days past due, 15% of balances 61–180 days past due, and 30% of balances more than six months past due. The company bases its provision for credit losses on the aging analysis.

REQUIRED

a. Prepare the adjusting journal entry to record the provision for credit losses for 1996.
b. Show how Accounts Receivable (including the credit balances) and Allowance for Uncollectible Accounts appear in the December 31, 1996, balance sheet.

**CREDIT CARD SALES
— OBJ. 7 —**

6-37A Captain Paul's Marina sells boats and other water recreational vehicles (approximately three vehicles are sold each week). The following transactions occurred during the third week of May 1996:

On May 15, sold a $600 boat trailer ($400 cost) to Sam and Myrna Marston, who paid using a personal check.

On May 16, sold a $10,000 boat ($6,500 cost) to the Calumet Lake Patrol on open account, with 2/10, n/30 terms.

On May 18, sold a $1,200 water scooter ($700 cost) to Kyle Bronson, who used the United Merchants Card to charge the water scooter. Captain Paul's mailed the credit card sales slip to United Merchants the same day. United Merchants will send a check within seven days, net of a 2% fee.

On May 19, sold a $5,000 fishing boat ($3,000 cost) to Michael Ferguson, who used the Great American Bank Card to pay for the boat. Captain Paul's deposited the credit card sales slip the same day and received an immediate credit in the company's checking account, net of a 2% fee.

On May 20, received payment from Calumet Lake Patrol for the boat purchased on May 16.

On May 21, received payment from United Merchants for the May 18 transaction.

REQUIRED

Prepare journal entries to record these transactions. Captain Paul's Marina uses the perpetual inventory system.

**VARIOUS ENTRIES FOR
ACCOUNTS AND
NOTES RECEIVABLE
— OBJ. 4, 5, 8 —**

6-38A Armstrong, Inc., began business on January 1, 1996. Several transactions for 1996 follow:

May 2 Received a $14,400, 60-day, 10% note on account from Holt Company.

July 1 Received payment from Holt for its note plus interest.

1 Received a $27,000, 120-day, 10% note from B. Rich Company on account.

Oct. 30 B. Rich failed to pay its note.

Dec. 9 Wrote off B. Rich's account as uncollectible. Armstrong, Inc., uses the allowance method of providing for credit losses.

11 Received a $21,000, 90-day, 9% note from W. Maling on account.

31 Recorded expected credit losses for the year by an adjusting entry. Allowance for Uncollectible Accounts has a debit balance of $28,300 as a result of write-offs of accounts during this first year. Analysis of aged receivables indicates that the desired balance of the allowance account is $5,800.

31 Made the appropriate adjusting entries for interest.

REQUIRED

Record the foregoing transactions and adjustments in general journal form.

CASES

**BUSINESS
DECISION CASE**

On December 15, 1996, Sharon Taylor, who owns Taylor Company, asks you to investigate the cash-handling activities in her firm. She believes that an employee might be stealing funds. "I have no proof," she says, "but I'm fairly certain that the November 30, 1996, undeposited receipts amounted to more than $12,000, although the November 30 bank reconciliation prepared by the cashier (who works in the treasurer's department) shows only $7,238.40. Also, the November bank reconciliation doesn't show several checks that have been outstanding for a long time. The cashier told me that these checks needn't appear on the reconciliation because he had notified the bank to stop payment on them and he had made the necessary adjustment on the books. Does that sound reasonable to you?"

At your request, Taylor shows you the following November 30, 1996, bank reconciliation prepared by the cashier:

**TAYLOR COMPANY
BANK RECONCILIATION
NOVEMBER 30, 1996**

Ending balance from bank statement		$ 4,843.69	Balance from general ledger		$10,893.89
Add: Deposits in transit		7,238.40			
		$12,082.09			
Less:			Less:		
Outstanding checks:			Bank service charge	$ 60.00	
No. 2351	$1,100.20		Unrecorded credit	1,200.00	1,260.00
No. 2353	578.32				
No. 2354	969.68	2,448.20			
Reconciled cash balance		$ 9,633.89	Reconciled cash balance		$ 9,633.89

You discover that the $1,200 unrecorded bank credit represents a note collected by the bank on Taylor's behalf; it appears in the deposits column of the November bank statement. Your investigation also reveals that the October 31, 1996, bank reconciliation showed three checks that had been outstanding longer than 10 months: No. 1432 for $600, No. 1458 for $466.90, and No. 1512 for $253.10. You also discover that these items were never added back into the Cash account in the books. In confirming that the checks shown on the cashier's November 30 bank reconciliation were outstanding on that date, you discover that check No. 2353 was actually a payment of $1,658.32 and had been recorded on the books for that amount.

To confirm the amount of undeposited receipts at November 30, you request a bank statement for December 1–12 (called a *cut-off bank statement*). This indeed shows a December 1 deposit of $7,238.40.

REQUIRED

a. Calculate the amount of funds stolen by the cashier.

b. Describe how the cashier concealed the theft.

c. What sort of entry or entries should be made when a firm decides that checks outstanding for a long time should no longer be carried in the bank reconciliation?

d. What suggestions would you make to Sharon Taylor about cash control procedures?

FINANCIAL ANALYSIS CASE

Abbott Laboratories is a diversified health care company devoted to the discovery, development, manufacture, and marketing of innovative products that improve diagnostic, therapeutic, and nutritional practices. Abbott markets products in more than 130 countries and employs 50,000 people. Pfizer Inc is a research-based, global health care company. Its mission is to discover and develop innovative, value-added products that improve the quality of life of people around the world. Pfizer manufactures products in 31 countries and markets these products worldwide. These two companies reported the following information in their financial reports for two recent years (Year 2 is the more recent year; amounts in millions of dollars):

	Year 2	Year 1
Abbott Laboratories		
Net Sales	$8,407.8	$7,851.9
Beginning Accounts Receivable (net)	1,244.4	1,150.9
Ending Accounts Receivable (net)	1,336.2	1,244.4
Pfizer Inc		
Net Sales	$7,477.7	$7,230.2
Beginning Accounts Receivable (net)	1,400.3	1,403.9
Ending Accounts Receivable (net)	1,468.7	1,400.3

REQUIRED

a. Calculate the accounts receivable turnover and the average collection period for Abbott Laboratories and Pfizer Inc for Year 1 and Year 2.

b. Compare the average collection periods for the two companies and comment on possible reasons for the difference in average collection periods for the two companies.

ETHICS CASE I

Gina Pullen is the petty cash cashier of a large family-owned restaurant. She has been presented on numerous occasions with properly approved receipts for reimbursement from petty cash that she believes are personal expenses of one of the five owners. She reports to the controller of the company. The controller is also a family member and is the person who approves the receipts for payment out of petty cash.

REQUIRED

What are the accounting implications if Pullen is correct? What alternatives should she consider?

ETHICS CASE II

Tractor Motors' best salesperson is Marie Glazer. Glazer's largest sales have been to Farmers Cooperative, a customer she brought to the company. Another salesperson, Bryan Blanchard, has been told in confidence by his cousin (an employee of Farmers Cooperative) that Farmers Cooperative is experiencing financial difficulties and may not be able to pay Tractor Motors what is owed to it.

Both Glazer and Blanchard are being considered for promotion to a new sales manager position.

REQUIRED

What are the ethical considerations that face Bryan Blanchard? What alternatives does he have?

GENERAL MILLS ANNUAL REPORT CASE

Refer to the consolidated balance sheets in the annual report of General Mills, Inc., presented in Appendix K.

REQUIRED

a. What was the amount of cash and cash equivalents at the beginning of the most recent year?

b. What was the amount of cash and cash equivalents at the end of the most recent year?

c. By what amount did cash and cash equivalents increase or decrease during the most recent year?

d. What statement elsewhere in the annual report contains an explanation of the increase or decrease in the cash and cash equivalents amount? In that statement, what amount of net cash was provided or used by (1) operating activities, (2) investment activities, and (3) financing activities?

e. What was the amount of total receivables and the amount of allowance for doubtful accounts at the end of each of the two years?

f. What percent of receivables was the allowance for doubtful accounts at the end of each of the two years?

Inventories

CHAPTER LEARNING OBJECTIVES

1 **REVIEW** concepts related to inventories for merchandising firms and **INTRODUCE** concepts related to inventories for manufacturing firms (pp. 235–236).

2 **DISCUSS** the need for inventories and **INTRODUCE** the quick response and just-in-time approaches to inventory management (p. 236).

3 **DESCRIBE** inventory costing under a perpetual inventory system using the specific identification method, moving average method, FIFO method, and LIFO method (pp. 237–241).

4 **ANALYZE** the effects the different inventory costing methods have on gross profit, matching of expenses with revenues, and income taxes (pp. 241–244).

5 **DESCRIBE** alternative treatments of freight costs (pp. 244–245).

6 **EXPLAIN** when inventories are measured at less than cost (pp. 245–246).

7 **DISCUSS** accounting for merchandise imports and exports (pp. 247–250).

8 **Financial Analysis** **DEFINE** *inventory turnover* and *day's sales in inventory* and **EXPLAIN** their use (p. 250).

Chapter Focus

In the notes to its financial statements, Intel Corporation reveals that it uses the first-in, first-out inventory costing method; DuPont reveals that it uses the last-in, first-out inventory costing method. Why did these companies choose these methods and how are they calculated? In this chapter, we expand on our previous discussions of merchandise inventories, introduce manufacturing inventories, and describe specific approaches to determining inventory cost. We also introduce basic concepts for dealing with imports and exports, a major issue for most companies, including Intel and DuPont.

INVENTORY CONCEPTS

OBJECTIVE *1*

Review concepts related to inventories for merchandising firms and **Introduce** concepts related to inventories for manufacturing firms.

In a previous chapter, we defined *merchandise inventory* as a stock of products that a merchandising company buys from another company and makes available for sale to its customers. All costs necessary to acquire the merchandise and bring it to the site of the sale are part of inventory costs. Inventory costs include the purchase price, plus any transportation or freight in costs, less purchases returns and allowances and purchases discounts.

MERCHANDISING FIRMS

Wholesale distributors and retailing firms are the two major types of merchandising firms. These types of firms have three primary transactions in their operating cycle. First, the company purchases merchandise and places it in inventory. Second, the firm removes the merchandise from inventory and ships it to a customer. Third, the customer pays the merchandising firm for the merchandise. These three transactions repeat frequently during the year.

A merchandising firm using the perpetual inventory system records the cost of the merchandise in the Inventory account. When the merchandise is sold to a customer, the cost of the items sold is transferred from the Inventory account to the Cost of Goods Sold account. At the same time, the selling price of the items sold is recorded in the Accounts Receivable account and the Sales account. When the customer pays, the amount received is recorded in the Cash account and the balance of the Accounts Receivable account is reduced by the amount of the payment and the sales discount, if any, which is recorded in the Sales Discounts account.

MANUFACTURING FIRMS

Manufacturing firms do not purchase merchandise that is ready for sale. Instead, they purchase various materials and components and convert them into merchandise in their factories. At any point in time, manufacturing operations have units of product at various stages of completion.

A manufacturing firm usually maintains three separate inventories: materials inventory, work in process inventory, and finished goods inventory. Each is accounted for using the perpetual inventory system.

The **materials inventory** includes materials and components that have been purchased for use in the factory but have not yet been placed into production. Sheets of steel and coils of wire are examples of materials, and computer chips and electric motors are examples of components. A **component** is an item in the materials inventory that was a finished product for the manufacturer that produced it. For example, Intel manufactures computer chips that other manufacturers incorporate into their products. All items in the materials inventory are recorded at their net delivered cost and stored in an area often called the *storeroom*.

The **work in process inventory** consists of units of product that have been started in production in the factory but have not yet been completed. All of the costs related to materials and components, human labor in the factory, factory utilities, use of factory assets, and other factory-related resources are included in the work in process inventory. Items in this inventory are not yet salable because they are not finished products.

The **finished goods inventory** includes all product that has been completed and is ready to be sold to customers. The cost of each item in the finished goods inventory was accumulated in the work in process inventory and transferred to the finished goods inventory.

A manufacturing firm using the perpetual inventory system records the cost of materials and components in the Materials Inventory account. When material and components are transferred from the storeroom to the factory, their cost is transferred from the Materials Inventory account to the Work in Process Inventory account. When a product is completed, its cost is transferred from the Work in Process Inventory to the Finished Goods Inventory account. When finished goods are sold to a customer, the cost of the items sold is transferred from the Finished Goods Inventory account to the Cost of Goods Sold account. At the same time, the selling price of the items sold is recorded in the Accounts Receivable account and the Sales account.

THE NEED FOR INVENTORIES

OBJECTIVE 2

DISCUSS the need for inventories and **INTRODUCE** the quick response and just-in-time approaches to inventory management.

Merchandising companies find it necessary and desirable to maintain a large and varied inventory of merchandise. For example, consumers want a wide assortment of colors, sizes, styles, and qualities available to them when they shop in a retail store. Consumer preferences tend to force the retailer to keep inventories at fairly high levels.

JUST-IN-CASE INVENTORIES

Manufacturing companies have traditionally maintained inventories (materials, work in process, and finished goods) as buffers against unforeseen delays and unplanned needs. For example, a manufacturer would keep an extra supply of various materials on hand to protect against a supplier being late in the delivery of materials needed to produce a particular product or to provide materials if the manufacturer decides to make product that it had not previously planned to make. This extra quantity is known as **just-in-case inventory** (just in case the supplier does not deliver when scheduled or just in case the manufacturer decides to make a previously unplanned product).

Just-in-case inventories create inventory carrying costs for the manufacturer. **Inventory carrying costs** include casualty insurance, building usage costs, and the cost of the capital invested in the inventory. Higher levels of just-in-case inventories cause higher levels of inventory carrying costs. On an annual basis, these costs often are 20% to 25% of the cost of the inventory itself.

JUST-IN-TIME INVENTORY PHILOSOPHY

The just-in-time inventory philosophy seeks to eliminate or minimize the just-in-case inventory quantities. A manufacturing company strictly following the **just-in-time inventory philosophy** would have no inventories at the end of each day. That is, the balances of the Materials Inventory, the Work in Process Inventory, and the Finished Goods Inventory accounts would all be zero at the end of each day.

Materials and components would be ordered so that only the materials and components needed for production each day would be received each morning. Production would be scheduled so that all products started during the day would be completed by the end of the day (resulting in no work in process inventory). All completed products would be shipped to customers the same day they were completed (resulting in no finished goods inventory).

The keys to just-in-time (JIT) inventories are careful planning and sophisticated management of the manufacturing process. Managerial accounting and cost accounting texts cover the details of this planning and management. Many manufacturing companies have been unable to reach the absolute zero inventories of the JIT philosophy. However, they have been able to significantly reduce the just-in-case quantities.

QUICK RESPONSE SYSTEMS

Many retailers have installed point-of-sale checkout systems that incorporate a computer. These systems either read Universal Product Code bar codes or specially formed characters using either a plate scanner built into the counter or a hand-held scanner to identify the product to the computer system.

Many of these retailers use a quick response system to optimize their inventory. A **quick response system** is designed to make sure that the retailer quickly orders more of the items that are selling and quickly gets rid of the items that are not selling. Special software on the computer identifies and lists fast-selling and slow-selling items. The retailer then reviews the list from the computer and orders more of the highly desirable items that are selling quickly. The retailer then uses one or both of the following approaches to get rid of the slow-moving items: (1) return the item to the supplier (if possible) and (2) reduce the price. The quick response system will tend to reduce the size of the total inventory and increase the dollar amount of sales, both desirable results.

INVENTORY COSTING METHODS WITH THE PERPETUAL INVENTORY SYSTEM

OBJECTIVE 3

DESCRIBE inventory costing under a perpetual inventory system using the specific identification method, moving average method, FIFO method, and LIFO method.

In general, inventories are entered into and maintained in the accounting records at historical cost. Inventory costing is simple when acquisition cost remains constant. For example, assume that Fletcher Company purchased electric motors four times during the year:

February 10 purchase	100 motors at $180 each
April 25 purchase	150 motors at $180 each
July 16 purchase	150 motors at $180 each
October 8 purchase	200 motors at $180 each

The December 31 inventory for Fletcher Company includes 40 electric motors, some from the July 16 purchase and some from the October 8 purchase. It is easy to determine the cost assigned to these 40 motors ($40 \times \$180 = \$7,200$) because all of the purchases were made at the same price: $180.

In a real business situation, however, the purchase prices of items change during the year. The trend is usually toward increasing prices, but some purchase price changes may be decreases. When purchase prices change during the year, a company must either keep track of the cost of each specific unit or make assumptions about which units have been sold and which units are still on hand in the inventory. Most companies make assumptions about which units have been sold and which are still on hand.

Two terms are useful in considering the problem of assigning cost to inventories when purchase prices are changing. *Goods flow* describes the actual physical movement of product in the firm's operation. Goods flow is the result of various physical events. *Cost flow* is the actual or assumed assignment of costs to goods sold and in inventory. The cost flow does not always reflect the actual goods flow. Generally accepted accounting principles permit the use of a cost flow that does not reflect the actual goods flow.

In this section, we introduce and illustrate four generally accepted methods of costing inventories under the perpetual inventory system: (1) specific identification, (2) moving average, (3) first-in, first out (FIFO), and (4) last-in, first-out (LIFO). Each of these four methods uses historical costs. After we present the four methods, we present a comparative evaluation.

To compare the four methods easily, we illustrate all four with the same data. Assume that a company had the following experience during the year for a particular inventory item:

Jan.	1	Beginning inventory	60	units @ $10 = $ 600
Mar.	27	Purchase	90	units @ $11 = $ 990
May	2	Sell	(130)	units

Aug. 15	Purchase	100	units @ $13 = $1,300
Nov. 6	Purchase	50	units @ $16 = $ 800
Dec. 10	Sell	(90)	units
	Ending inventory	80	units

Under all four perpetual inventory costing methods, the Inventory account is increased each time a purchase occurs (by the cost of the purchase) and decreased each time a sale occurs (by the cost of goods sold). The methods differ in the way the cost of goods sold amounts are computed. Each method will result in a year-end Inventory account balance that represents the cost of the 80 units on hand.

SPECIFIC IDENTIFICATION METHOD

When the **specific identification method** is used, the actual costs of the specific units sold are identified and used to compute the cost of goods sold. To illustrate, assume that (1) 50 of the units sold on May 2 came from the beginning inventory and 80 units came from the purchase on March 27 and (2) 10 of the units sold on December 10 came from the purchase on March 27 and 80 units came from the purchase on August 15. With these data, the specific identification method gives the results shown in Exhibit 7-1. Cost of goods sold for this inventory item when the specific identification method is used is $2,530 for the year (the sum of the Sold Total column). The year-end inventory cost is $1,160 (the last amount in the Inventory Balance Total column).

EXHIBIT 7–1 Specific Identification Method (Perpetual Inventory System)

Date	Purchased			Sold			Inventory Balance		
	Units	Unit Cost	Total	Units	Unit Cost	Total	Units	Unit Cost	Total
Jan. 1							60	$10	$ 600
Mar. 27	90	$11	$ 990				60 90	10 11	1,590
May 2				50 80	$10 11	$ 500 880	10 10	10 11	210
Aug. 15	100	13	1,300				10 10 100	10 11 13	1,510
Nov. 6	50	16	800				10 10 100 50	10 11 13 16	2,310
Dec. 10				10 80	11 13	110 1,040	10 20 50	10 13 16	1,160
TOTAL						$2,530			

MOVING AVERAGE METHOD

When the **moving average method** is used, each time goods are purchased, a new average unit cost is computed for the goods on hand (total cost divided by total units on hand). Cost of goods sold for each sale is computed by multiplying the average unit cost at the time of sale by the number of units sold. Exhibit 7-2 shows how the moving average method works.

Average unit cost is recomputed each time a purchase occurs. This happens three times in the example in Exhibit 7-2. On March 27, 90 units were purchased at a unit cost of $11. The new average unit cost on March 27 is calculated as follows:

$$\frac{\$600 \; + \; \$990}{60 \text{ Units} \; + \; 90 \text{ Units}} = \$10.60$$

On August 15, 100 units were purchased at a unit cost of $13. The new average unit cost on August 15 is calculated as follows:

$$\frac{\$212 \; + \; \$1,300}{20 \text{ Units} \; + \; 100 \text{ Units}} = \$12.60$$

On November 6, 50 units were purchased at a unit cost of $16. The new average unit cost on November 6 is calculated as follows:

$$\frac{\$1,512 \; + \; \$800}{120 \text{ Units} \; + \; 50 \text{ Units}} = \$13.60$$

Cost of goods sold for this inventory item using the moving average method is $2,602 (the sum of the Sold Total column). The year-end inventory is $1,088 (the last amount in the Inventory Balance Total column).

EXHIBIT 7–2 **Moving Average Method (Perpetual Inventory System)**

Date	Purchased Units	Unit Cost	Total	Sold Units	Unit Cost	Total	Inventory Balance Units	Unit Cost	Total
Jan. 1							60	$10.00	$ 600
Mar. 27	90	$11	$ 990				150	10.60	1,590
May 2				130	$10.60	$1,378	20	10.60	212
Aug. 15	100	13	1,300				120	12.60	1,512
Nov. 6	50	16	800				170	13.60	2,312
Dec. 10				90	13.60	1,224	80	13.60	1,088
TOTAL						$2,602			

FIRST-IN, FIRST-OUT (FIFO) METHOD

Under the **first-in, first-out (FIFO) method,** each time a sale is made the costs of the oldest goods on hand are charged to cost of goods sold. Using the data from our illustration, FIFO gives the results shown in Exhibit 7-3.

The FIFO method handles the May 2 sale of 130 units as follows. The oldest units on hand are the units in the January 1 inventory. These are the first 60 units assumed to be sold. The next oldest units are the units purchased on March 27. Seventy units are needed from this purchase (130 Total Sale – 60 from January 1) to provide all of the units needed for the May 2 sale. After the May 2 sale, only 20 units remain, all from the March 27 purchase.

The December 10 sale of 90 units is handled in a similar manner. The oldest units at December 10 are the 20 units remaining from the March 27 purchase. These are the first units assumed to be sold. The next oldest units are the 100 units purchased on August 15. Seventy additional units are needed for the sale (90 total sale – 20 from the March 27 purchase). Therefore, 70 of the 100 units from the August 15 purchase are assumed to be included in the units sold on December 10. After the sale, 30 units remain from the August 15 purchase, and 50 units remain from the November 6 purchase.

Cost of goods sold using the first-in, first-out method (FIFO method) is $2,500 (the sum of the Sold Total column). The year-end inventory is $1,190 (the last amount in the Inventory Balance Total column).

EXHIBIT 7–3	First-In, First-Out Method (Perpetual Inventory System)

	Purchased			Sold			Inventory Balance		
Date	Units	Unit Cost	Total	Units	Unit Cost	Total	Units	Unit Cost	Total
Jan. 1							60	$10	$ 600
Mar. 27	90	$11	$ 990				60 / 90	10 } / 11 }	1,590
May 2				60 / 70	$10 / 11	$ 600 / 770	20	11	220
Aug. 15	100	13	1,300				20 / 100	11 } / 13 }	1,520
Nov. 6	50	16	800				20 / 100 / 50	11 } / 13 } / 16 }	2,320
Dec. 10				20 / 70	11 / 13	220 / 910	30 / 50	13 } / 16 }	1,190
TOTAL						$2,500			

LAST-IN, FIRST-OUT (LIFO) METHOD

When the **last-in, first-out (LIFO) method** is used, each time a sale is made, the costs of the most recent purchases are charged to cost of goods sold. Exhibit 7-4 shows the results obtained using the LIFO method.

The LIFO method handles the May 2 sale of 130 units as follows. The most recently purchased units (newest units) on hand are the units from the March 27 purchase. These are the first 90 units assumed to be sold. The next newest units are the units in the January 1 inventory. Forty of the January 1 units are needed (130 total sale – 90 from the March 27 purchase) to provide all of the units needed for the May 2 sale. After the May 2 sale, only 20 units remain, all from the January 1 inventory.

The December 10 sale of 90 units is handled in a similar manner. The newest units at December 10 are the 50 units purchased on November 6. These are the first units assumed

POINT OF INTEREST

VARIETY OF INVENTORY METHODS

A company may have many different inventories and, as a result, may use more than one inventory costing method. Sears, Roebuck and Co., for example, uses LIFO for domestic inventories and FIFO for inventories of international operations, Western Auto, and Puerto Rico. Birmingham Steel Corporation measures steel inventories using FIFO whereas bolt inventory costs are determined using LIFO. And for a recent year, The Quaker Oats Company used LIFO for 53% of its inventory, average cost for 35%, and FIFO for 12%. Although more than one method may be used, the same method is to be used for each inventory category from one year to the next.

to be sold. The next newest units are the 100 units purchased on August 15. Forty additional units are needed for the sale (90 Total Sale – 50 from November 6 Purchase). Therefore, 40 of the 100 units from the August 15 purchase are assumed to be included in the units sold on December 10. After the sale, 20 units remain from the January 1 inventory and 60 units remain from the August 15 purchase.

Cost of goods sold using the last-in, first-out (LIFO) method is $2,710 (the sum of the Sold Total column). The year-end inventory is $980 (the last amount in the Inventory Balance Total column).

| **EXHIBIT 7–4** | **Last-In, First-Out Method (Perpetual Inventory System)** | | | | | | | | | |

	Purchased			**Sold**			**Inventory Balance**		
Date	**Units**	**Unit Cost**	**Total**	**Units**	**Unit Cost**	**Total**	**Units**	**Unit Cost**	**Total**
Jan. 1							60	$10	$ 600
Mar. 27	90	$11	$ 990				60 90	10 11 }	1,590
May 2				90 40	$11 10	$ 990 400	20	10	200
Aug. 15	100	13	1,300				20 100	10 13 }	1,500
Nov. 6	50	16	800				20 100 50	10 13 16 }	2,300
Dec. 10				50 40	16 13	800 520	20 60	10 13 }	980
TOTAL						$2,710			

COMPARATIVE ANALYSIS OF INVENTORY COSTING METHODS

OBJECTIVE 4

ANALYZE the effects the different inventory costing methods have on gross profit, matching of expenses with revenues, and income taxes.

The data used in our prior examples had an important characteristic: the purchase cost per unit increased each time a purchase was made. This is the situation typically encountered in the real world where price inflation is common and price deflation is uncommon. Exhibit 7-5 summarizes the results of applying the four inventory costing methods to the example data. The FIFO method produces the lowest cost of goods sold, and the LIFO method produces the highest cost of goods sold.

| **EXHIBIT 7–5** | **Summary of Results of Different Inventory Costing Methods** | |

Costing Method	**Year-End Inventory Cost**	**Cost of Goods Sold**
Specific identification	$1,160	$2,530
Moving average	1,088	2,602
FIFO	1,190	2,500
LIFO	980	2,710

COST FLOWS

Each company is able to select one or more of these methods for assigning cost to its inventory and cost of goods sold. Which method a particular company selects depends on a number of factors.

SPECIFIC IDENTIFICATION METHOD

The specific identification method is typically used by companies that have products with relatively high unit values. Automobiles, jewelry, and construction equipment are examples of products that would justify the cost of tracking the specific unit cost of each inventory item. Specific identification is usually not feasible with products that have low unit costs or involve high volumes. A company using the specific identification method can maximize reported income by choosing to sell the specific units with the lowest unit cost. This provides a low cost of goods sold and a high year-end inventory. Alternatively, the company can minimize reported income by choosing to sell the specific units with the highest unit cost. This provides a high cost of goods sold and a low year-end inventory.

MOVING AVERAGE METHOD

The moving average method is best suited for operations that store a large volume of undifferentiated goods in a common area. Liquid fuels, grains, and other commodities are examples. The moving average method typically generates a cost of goods sold amount that is neither high nor low compared to the results of the other methods.

FIFO METHOD

Many companies, especially those with perishable or style-affected merchandise, attempt to sell their oldest merchandise first. This is especially true for companies that sell food products, chemicals, and drugs. For these types of companies, the assumed cost flow of the FIFO method most closely matches the actual flow of goods. Even though the FIFO actual flow of goods is the most common, FIFO is not the most common method chosen.

LIFO METHOD

The LIFO method is the most popular of the four methods discussed here. However, it is difficult to find examples of actual LIFO flows of goods. Purchases of coal or a similar commodity may all be dumped onto one pile from an overhead trestle, and sales may be taken from the top of the pile by a crane. If beginning inventories have been maintained or increased, we conclude that the firm's oldest purchases are still in inventory. In this case, LIFO represents the actual goods flow. Although LIFO is not the actual goods flow for most businesses, an estimated 50% or more of major businesses use LIFO to cost some of their inventories. We explore the reasons for this choice later in this chapter.

SUMMARY

To summarize:

1. In a physical sense, the specific identification method best presents actual cost of goods sold and ending inventory.
2. The moving average method can best be associated with business operations in which like goods are commingled.
3. FIFO approximates the actual goods flow for most firms.
4. Although LIFO represents the least likely goods flow, many firms use it.

VARIATIONS IN GROSS PROFIT

For comparative purposes, let us assume that the 220 units sold in our previous illustrations were sold for $20 each. Exhibit 7-6 shows the differences among gross profit figures resulting from each of the inventory costing methods. Remember that these differences in reported gross profit result from assumptions made about cost flows, not from any difference in actual goods flows. Each of the inventory costing methods is in accord with generally accepted accounting principles, yet one method's impact on income determination may be quite different from the impact of another method.

| | | EXHIBIT 7–6 | Gross Profit on Sales Based on Various Inventory Pricing Methods |

	Specific Identification	Moving Average	FIFO	LIFO
Sales (220 units @ $20)	$4,400	$4,400	$4,400	$4,400
Cost of goods sold	2,530	2,602	2,500	2,710
Gross profit on sales	$1,870	$1,798	$1,900	$1,690
Increased gross profit compared with LIFO	$ 180	$ 108	$ 210	

MATCHING EXPENSES WITH REVENUES

As Exhibit 7-6 shows, LIFO results in the smallest gross profit among the alternative inventory costing methods. This is because our illustration assumed that the purchase cost of merchandise was increasing throughout the year. Most accountants agree that when costs are rising, FIFO tends to overstate gross profit (and income) because older, lower unit costs are included in the cost of goods sold and matched with current sales prices. In other words, in our example, all of the units sold are charged to costs of goods sold under FIFO at unit costs of $10, $11, and $13. If our latest purchases reflect current acquisition costs, the units sold must be replaced by units costing $16 (or more if costs continue to rise). Thus, we can argue that LIFO better matches current costs with current revenues, because the cost of the most recent purchases constitutes cost of goods sold.

However, while LIFO associates the current, most significant, unit costs with cost of goods sold, it assigns costs to the ending inventory using the older, less realistic unit costs. Because of this, the LIFO inventory figure on the balance sheet is often meaningless in terms of current costs. As we noted earlier, when inventory quantities are maintained or increased, the LIFO method prevents the older costs from appearing in the cost of goods sold. No doubt, some firms still carry LIFO inventories at unit costs that existed more than 25 years ago. Under FIFO, in contrast, the ending inventory is measured at relatively recent costs.

PRINCIPLE ALERT

CONSISTENCY PRINCIPLE AND FULL DISCLOSURE PRINCIPLE

Inventory costing requires the application of two basic principles of accounting: *consistency* and *full disclosure*. Because of the possible variation in income and asset amounts from the use of different inventory costing methods, it is important that a firm use the same inventory costing method from one accounting period to the next. This application of the consistency principle enhances the comparability of a firm's cost of goods sold, gross profit, net income, inventory, current assets, and total assets over time.

In addition, a firm should disclose which inventory costing method it is using, either in its financial statements or in the additional information included with the financial statements. This information, required by the full disclosure principle, is important to users who are trying to compare financial data for two or more firms.

INCOME TAX ADVANTAGE OF LIFO

As noted, during periods of rising costs, LIFO generally results in a lower gross profit than the alternative pricing methods. Lower gross profits (and incomes) mean lower amounts of income taxes to pay to the government. The desire to reduce current income tax payments is a major reason for the widespread usage of LIFO. (Corporations pay income taxes on their pretax incomes; although sole proprietorships and partnerships do not pay income taxes, the owners pay income taxes on their share of the entity's net income.)

A highly simplified example compares FIFO with LIFO to illustrate the advantage of using LIFO during times of rising costs. Assume that a corporation has an opening inventory of 10 units costing $500 each. Only two transactions take place. First, the corporation purchases 10 more units costing $630 each. Second, the corporation sells 10 units for $700 each. All transactions are for cash and, for simplicity, we also assume that operating expenses are zero and the applicable income tax rate is 35%. Exhibit 7-7 shows the income statements and cash flows under both FIFO and LIFO.

EXHIBIT 7–7	FIFO-LIFO Comparison: Phantom Profit Effect and Tax Benefit			

	FIFO		LIFO	
	Income Statement	Cash In (Out)	Income Statement	Cash In (Out)
Sales (10 @ $700)	$ 7,000	$7,000	$ 7,000	$7,000
Cost of goods sold:				
Beginning inventory (10 @ $500)	$ 5,000		$ 5,000	
Purchases (10 @ $630)	6,300	(6,300)	6,300	(6,300)
Goods available (20 units)	$11,300		$11,300	
Ending inventory				
10 @ FIFO	6,300			
10 @ LIFO			5,000	
Cost of goods sold	$ 5,000		$ 6,300	
Pretax income	$ 2,000		$ 700	
Income tax at 35%	700	(700)	245	(245)
Net income	$ 1,300		$ 455	
Net cash proceeds		$ 0		$ 455

Note that under FIFO, $1,300 of net income is reported, but the amount of cash from sales is only enough to replace the inventory sold and pay the income tax on the $2,000 pretax income. Thus, the net income of $1,300 is not realized in cash that can be declared as dividends or reinvested in the business; it is considered *phantom* (or *inventory*) *profit.* We can easily imagine how the phantom profit element causes problems in planning corporate dividend policy and using net income as a funding source for capital investments.

As Exhibit 7-7 shows, LIFO results in a smaller ending inventory and larger cost of goods sold than FIFO. This translates directly into a smaller amount of income subject to tax and smaller cash outflows for income taxes under LIFO. The attractiveness of LIFO during periods of rising cost of purchases is evidenced by its more favorable cash flows compared with FIFO. Use of LIFO during times of falling cost of purchases, however, has the opposite tax consequence.

FREIGHT COSTS

OBJECTIVE 5

DESCRIBE alternative treatments of freight costs.

When merchandise is shipped by a common carrier—a railroad, a trucking company, or an airline—the carrier prepares a *freight bill* in accordance with the instructions of the party making the transportation arrangements. The freight bill designates which party bears the shipping costs and whether the shipment is *freight prepaid* (freight paid for before the shipment) or *freight collect* (freight paid for after the shipment).

Freight bills usually show shipping terms of F.O.B. shipping point or F.O.B. destination. *F.O.B.* is an abbreviation for "free on board." When the freight terms are F.O.B. shipping point, the purchaser bears the shipping costs; when the terms are F.O.B. destination, the seller bears the shipping costs. Often, the party bearing the freight cost pays the carrier. Thus, goods are typically shipped *freight collect* when the terms are F.O.B. shipping point and *freight prepaid* when the terms are F.O.B. destination. Sometimes, as a matter of convenience, the firm not bearing the freight cost pays the carrier. When this situation occurs, the seller and buyer simply adjust the amount of the payment for the merchandise. Exhibit 7-8 shows which party—the buyer or the seller—pays the shipper and bears the freight cost for various freight terms.

EXHIBIT 7–8	Treatment of Freight Costs	
Freight Terms	**Pays Shipper**	**Bears Freight Cost**
F.O.B. Shipping Point, Freight Collect	Buyer	Buyer
F.O.B. Destination, Freight Prepaid	Seller	Seller
F.O.B. Shipping Point, Freight Prepaid	Seller	Buyer
F.O.B. Destination, Freight Collect	Buyer	Seller

DEPARTURES FROM COST

OBJECTIVE 6

EXPLAIN when inventories are measured at less than cost.

The four methods discussed earlier in this chapter—specific identification, moving average, FIFO, and LIFO—are used to assign cost to inventories. Inventories are generally measured at cost. The measurement may be reduced below cost, however, if there is evidence that the inventory's utility has fallen below cost. Such *inventory write-downs* may occur when (1) merchandise must be sold at reduced prices because it is damaged or otherwise not in normal salable condition or (2) the cost of replacing items in the ending inventory has declined below their recorded cost.

NET REALIZABLE VALUE

Damaged, physically deteriorated, or obsolete merchandise should be measured and reported at net realizable value when this value is less than cost. **Net realizable value** is the estimated selling price less the expected cost of disposal. For example, assume that an inventory item cost $300 but can be sold for only $200 because it is damaged. Related selling costs are an estimated $20. We should write down the item to $180 ($200 estimated selling price less $20 estimated disposal cost) and reflect a $120 loss for this period.

LOWER OF COST OR MARKET

The **lower of cost or market (LCM)** rule provides for the recognition of a loss when costs decline on new inventory items. Under this rule, the loss is reported in the period when the costs decline, rather than during a subsequent period of sale. *Market* is defined as the current replacement cost of the merchandise. This procedure assumes that decreases in replacement costs will be accompanied by proportionate decreases in selling prices. If applicable, the LCM rule simply measures inventory at the lower (replacement) market figure. Consequently, reported income decreases by the amount that the ending inventory has been written down. When the ending inventory becomes part of the cost of goods sold in a future period of lower selling prices, its reduced carrying value helps maintain normal profit margins in the period of sale.

To illustrate, let us assume an inventory item that cost $80 has been selling for $100 during the year, yielding a gross profit of 20% on sales. At year-end, the item's replacement cost has dropped to $60—a 25% decline—and a proportionate reduction in the selling price to $75 is expected. In this case, the inventory would be written down to the $60 replacement cost, reducing the current period's net income by the $20 loss. When the item is sold in a subsequent period for $75, a normal gross profit of 20% on sales will be reported ($75 – $60 = $15 gross profit).[1]

We may apply the LCM rule to (1) each inventory item, (2) the totals of major inventory classes or categories, or (3) the total inventory. Exhibit 7-9 shows the application of these alternatives and indicates that the inventory amount obtained depends on how the rule is applied.

EXHIBIT 7–9 Application of the Lower of Cost or Market Rule

Inventory Item	Quantity	Per Unit Cost	Per Unit Market	Total Cost	Total Market	Lower of Cost or Market by Individual Items	Lower of Cost or Market by Major Categories	Lower of Cost or Market by Total Inventory
Cameras								
Model V70	40	$80	$75	$3,200	$3,000	$3,000		
Model V85	30	60	64	1,800	1,920	1,800		
Subtotal				$5,000	$4,920		$4,920	
Calculators								
Model C20	90	13	15	$1,170	$1,350	1,170		
Model C40	50	20	17	1,000	850	850		
Subtotal				$2,170	$2,200		2,170	
Total				$7,170	$7,120	$6,820	$7,090	$7,120

In Exhibit 7-9, if we apply LCM to the total inventory, our result is $7,120. Applied by item, however, the LCM amount is $6,820, and applied by major category, the LCM amount is $7,090. Although the item-by-item procedure is used most often, any of the three ways is acceptable. In any case, one method should be used consistently. Inventory market values appear in such sources as current catalogs, purchase contracts with suppliers, and other forms of price quotations.

PRINCIPLE ALERT

CONSERVATISM CONCEPT

The lower of cost or market rule for inventory applies the *conservatism concept*. When the current replacement cost for an inventory item falls below its historical cost, there is increased uncertainty about the future profitability of this item. Conservatism is the accountant's reaction to significant uncertainties in the measurement of net assets and net income. In choosing between alternative financial measures, conservatism causes the less optimistic measure to be selected. When market (current replacement cost of inventory) falls below historical cost, the less optimistic measure is the lower market amount.

---

[1]Because of the scale and complexity of modern markets, not all decreases in replacement prices are followed by proportionate reductions in selling prices. In these cases, the application of the LCM rule is modified. These modifications are covered in more advanced accounting courses.

ACCOUNTING FOR IMPORTS AND EXPORTS

OBJECTIVE 7
DISCUSS accounting for merchandise imports and exports.

The market today for consumer and capital goods is truly a world market. An individual in the United States, for example, may drink Brazilian coffee, jog in German running shoes, drive a Japanese automobile, snack on a Swiss chocolate bar, and enjoy music played on a stereo system with Danish components.

U.S. export and import levels indicate the extensive involvement of U.S. firms in international trade. Annual merchandise exports and imports each amount to several hundred billion dollars. The existence of world markets affects accounting because currencies other than the U.S. dollar may be involved in the transactions. Financial data stated in a foreign currency must be converted to U.S. dollars. Before examining these transactions, however, we consider foreign currency exchange rates.

FOREIGN CURRENCY EXCHANGE RATES

Exchange rates are used to convert one currency into a different currency. An **exchange rate** states the price, in terms of one currency, at which one unit of another currency may be bought or sold. Because our focus is on accounting in U.S. dollars, we express foreign currency exchange rates in terms of the U.S. dollar.

Exhibit 7-10 presents exchange rates for several foreign currencies. The exhibit shows, for example, that one Canadian dollar converts to $0.7270; that is, it takes $0.7270 to purchase one Canadian dollar. Currencies are bought and sold like other goods. Thus, a currency's price (its exchange rate) is determined by the supply and demand for that currency. Exchange rates change frequently, so the rates in Exhibit 7-10 (which are for a particular date) are illustrative only. Current exchange rates, no doubt, are different.

EXHIBIT 7–10	**Exchange Rates with the U.S. Dollar**

Country	Currency Unit	Price of One Unit in U.S. Dollars
Brazil	Real	$1.0881
Canada	Dollar	0.7270
Denmark	Kroner	0.1856
France	Franc	0.2065
Germany	Mark	0.7247
Hong Kong	Dollar	0.1292
Italy	Lira	0.0006133
Japan	Yen	0.01184
Netherlands	Guilder	0.6472
Switzerland	Franc	0.8726

SOURCE: *The Wall Street Journal*, June 30, 1995.

IMPORTS AND EXPORTS DENOMINATED IN A FOREIGN CURRENCY

Transactions a U.S. business may have with a foreign entity include the purchase (import) or sale (export) of goods. A transaction is a **foreign currency transaction** if it is *denominated* in a foreign currency; that is, if its terms are fixed in the amount of foreign currency to be paid or received. An import of television sets from a Japanese firm requiring payment of a fixed number of yen is a foreign currency transaction. Similarly, an export of computers to an English enterprise that requires settlement in a fixed number of British pounds is a foreign currency transaction.

ACCOUNTING AT TRANSACTION DATE

A U.S. firm keeps its financial records in U.S. dollars. All foreign currency transactions, therefore, must be translated into U.S. dollars so they may be properly recorded. When journalized, each transaction component is translated into U.S. dollars using the exchange rate at the transaction date.

IMPORTS   To illustrate, assume that a U.S. firm using the perpetual inventory system purchases merchandise on account from a Canadian firm on June 1, 1996. The cost is 10,000 Canadian dollars (C$). Payment is due in 30 days. Assume the exchange rate for Canadian dollars on June 1 is $0.73 per Canadian dollar. Using the June 1 exchange rate, the U.S. firm translates the C$10,000 to $7,300 (C$10,000 × $0.73) and makes the following entry:

June 1	Inventory	7,300	
	Accounts Payable		7,300
	To record purchase of merchandise on account		
	(C$10,000 × $0.73 = $7,300).		

EXPORTS   Assume that on June 1, 1996, our U.S. firm also sells merchandise costing $7,500 to a French firm on account, billing the firm 60,000 French francs (FF) due in 30 days. Assume that the exchange rate for French francs on June 1 is $0.21 per franc. Using this exchange rate, the U.S. firm makes the following entry on June 1:

June 1	Accounts Receivable	12,600	
	Sales		12,600
	To record sale of merchandise on account		
	(FF60,000 × $0.21 = $12,600).		
1	Cost of Goods Sold	7,500	
	Inventory		7,500
	To record the cost of the goods sold.		

ACCOUNTING AT SETTLEMENT DATE

Exchange rates may change before the settlement date for a foreign currency payable or receivable. Should this occur, a **foreign exchange gain or loss** is recorded at the settlement date. The foreign exchange gain or loss measures the change in the U.S. dollar equivalent required to settle the transaction. Foreign exchange gains and losses are reported in the income statement. A company experiencing both foreign exchange gains and foreign exchange losses during the same period may combine them and report a net foreign exchange gain or loss in its income statement.

SETTLEMENT OF ACCOUNTS PAYABLE   Continuing our previous example, assume that on July 1, the U.S. company settles its account payable with the Canadian firm, and the exchange rate on that date is $0.71 per Canadian dollar. On July 1, it costs the U.S. firm $7,100 to purchase the 10,000 Canadian dollars needed to settle the account. The exchange rate decline creates a $200 foreign exchange gain ($7,300 − $7,100) for the U.S. firm. The July 1 settlement is recorded as follows:

July 1	Accounts Payable	7,300	
	Cash		7,100
	Foreign Exchange Gain		200
	To record payment of account payable		
	(C$10,000 × $0.71 = $7,100) and foreign exchange gain.		

SETTLEMENT OF ACCOUNTS RECEIVABLE   Assume that on July 1, the U.S. company also receives 60,000 French francs from the French firm as payment of its account receivable. Assume further the exchange rate with the French franc on July 1 has fallen to $0.20 per franc. This exchange rate decline creates a $600 foreign exchange loss for the U.S. firm. The July 1 receipt is recorded as follows:

July 1	Cash	12,000	
	Foreign Exchange Loss	600	
	Accounts Receivable		12,600
	To record collection of account receivable		
	(FF60,000 × $0.20 = $12,000) and foreign exchange loss.		

UNSETTLED FOREIGN CURRENCY TRANSACTIONS

Foreign currency receivables and payables that are not settled at a balance sheet date are adjusted to reflect the exchange rate at that date. Such adjustments place foreign exchange gains and losses in the period when exchange rates change. Any foreign exchange gain or loss at the settlement date, then, relates only to exchange rate changes since the latest balance sheet date.

To illustrate, assume that on December 15, 1996, our U.S. firm purchases more merchandise on a 30-day account from the Canadian firm. The merchandise costs 15,000 Canadian dollars. The U.S. firm's accounting period ends on December 31, 1996. The account payable is settled on January 14, 1997. Exchange rates for the Canadian dollar are assumed to be as follows:

December 15	$0.82 per Canadian dollar
December 31	0.84
January 14	0.81

The U.S. firm accounts for this foreign currency transaction as follows:

1996

Dec. 15	Inventory	12,300	
	Accounts Payable		12,300
	To record purchase of merchandise on account (C$15,000 × $0.82 = $12,300).		
31	Foreign Exchange Loss	300	
	Accounts Payable		300
	To adjust accounts payable to current exchange rate (C$15,000 × $0.84 = $12,600; $12,600 – $12,300 = $300) and record foreign exchange loss.		

1997

Jan. 14	Accounts Payable	12,600	
	Cash		12,150
	Foreign Exchange Gain		450
	To record payment of account payable (C$15,000 × $0.81 = $12,150) and foreign exchange gain.		

On December 31, 1996, a $300 foreign exchange loss is recorded to reflect the impact of the strengthening of the Canadian dollar between December 15 and December 31. Because the account payable is not settled on this date, the loss is unrealized. It is included, however, in the 1996 income statement. The account payable is settled on January 14, 1997. The Canadian dollar has weakened since December 31, 1996, so a $450 foreign exchange gain is recorded and included in the 1997 income statement.

POINT OF INTEREST

FINANCING INTERNATIONAL TRADE

When a company in the United States sells merchandise to another U.S. company, it typically does so on a credit basis. However, when a U.S. company sells merchandise to a company in a foreign country, it is reluctant to do so on a credit basis for a number of reasons, such as increased lag times for international shipments, currency risks, and different laws covering the transaction. Many exporting companies rely on an international letter of credit to finance the transaction. A **letter of credit** is a document issued by a bank guaranteeing the payment of a specific amount of money on completion of certain conditions.

A typical international letter of credit arrangement includes the following steps: (1) the importer requests its bank to issue a letter of credit, (2) the importer's bank issues the letter of credit to the exporter's bank, (3) the exporter ships the goods after being notified that the letter of credit has been received and deemed to be valid by its bank, (4) the exporter and shippers prepare documents that prove that the shipment was made according to the agreement detailed in the letter of credit, (5) the exporter's bank pays the exporter, and (6) the exporter's bank collects from the importer's bank. The letter of credit in effect substitutes the credit of the importer's bank for the credit of the importer.

TRANSACTIONS DENOMINATED IN U.S. CURRENCY

A U.S. firm's transactions with foreign entities that are denominated in U.S. dollars are *not* foreign currency transactions. No translation is required (the transaction is initially stated in U.S. dollars), and no foreign exchange gains or losses develop. For example, assume that a U.S. firm sells merchandise to a Swiss firm on account. The sales price is $6,000 U.S. dollars, due in 30 days. Because the transaction is denominated in U.S. dollars, the U.S. firm accounts for the transaction no differently than if the customer were in the United States. The Swiss firm, in contrast, must translate its foreign currency transaction into Swiss francs and faces gains and losses from exchange rate changes.

FINANCIAL ANALYSIS

OBJECTIVE 8

DEFINE inventory turnover *and* days' sales in inventory *and* **EXPLAIN** their use.

INVENTORY TURNOVER AND DAYS' SALES IN INVENTORY

The inventory turnover ratio indicates how many times a year a firm sells its average inventory. **Inventory turnover** is computed as follows:

$$\text{Inventory Turnover} = \frac{\text{Cost of Goods Sold}}{\text{Average Inventory}}$$

This ratio relates data from two financial statements: the income statement and the balance sheet. Cost of goods sold is taken from the income statement. Average inventory is calculated from balance sheet data; the beginning and ending inventories are summed and the total is divided by 2.

In general, the faster a company can turn over its inventory, the better. The higher the inventory turnover ratio, the less time a firm has funds tied up in its inventory and the less risk the firm faces of trying to sell out-of-date merchandise. What is considered to be a satisfactory inventory turnover varies by industry; a grocery store, for example, should have a much higher inventory turnover than a jewelry shop.

Wal-Mart Stores, Inc., one of the nation's largest retail chains, reported the following financial data for three recent years (Year 3 is the most recent year; amounts in thousands):

	Year 3	Year 2	Year 1
Cost of goods sold	$53,443,743	$44,174,685	$34,786,119
Beginning inventory	9,268,309	7,384,299	5,808,416
Ending inventory	11,013,706	9,268,309	7,384,299

Wal-Mart's Year 3 inventory turnover is $53,443,743/[($9,268,309 + $11,013,706)/2] = 5.27. Similar computations reveal the inventory turnover is 5.31 for Year 2 and 5.27 for Year 1. During this three-year period, Wal-Mart's inventory turnover was very stable.

Inventory turnover is a ratio that is affected by a firm's inventory costing method. Inventory amounts computed using LIFO will typically be smaller than the same inventory computed using FIFO. A person who is going to compare inventory turnover ratios among firms in the same industry needs to be alert to the inventory costing method used by each firm.

A variation (or extension) of inventory turnover is **days' sales in inventory,** computed as follows:

$$\text{Days' Sales in Inventory} = \frac{365}{\text{Inventory Turnover}}$$

This ratio indicates how many days it takes a firm to sell its average inventory. During Year 3 for Wal-Mart Stores, Inc., for example, the days' sales in inventory were 365/5.27 = 69.3.

KEY POINTS FOR CHAPTER LEARNING OBJECTIVES

1 **REVIEW** concepts related to inventories for merchandising firms and **INTRODUCE** concepts related to inventories for manufacturing firms (pp. 235–236).
- Merchandise inventory is a stock of products that a merchandising company buys from another company and makes available for sale to its customers.
- A manufacturing firm maintains three different inventories: materials inventory, work in process inventory, and finished goods inventory.

2 **DISCUSS** the need for inventories and **INTRODUCE** the quick response and just-in-time approaches to inventory management (p. 236).
- Merchandising firms find it necessary and desirable to maintain a large and varied inventory of merchandise to satisfy customer demand.
- Many retailers use a quick response system with their point-of-sale checkout systems to facilitate quickly ordering more of items that are selling and getting rid of items that are not selling.
- Traditionally, manufacturers have maintained just-in-case inventories of material and finished goods to provide for unplanned production. This results in high levels of inventory carrying costs.
- Today, many manufacturers have adopted the just-in-time (JIT) inventory philosophy, which is designed to eliminate or minimize materials, work in process, and finished goods inventories. The key to JIT inventories is careful planning and sophisticated management.

3 **DESCRIBE** inventory costing under a perpetual inventory system using the (a) specific identification method, (b) moving average method, (c) FIFO method, and (d) LIFO method (pp. 237–241).
- To assign cost to units sold (cost of goods sold) and units on hand (inventory), a company must either keep track of the cost of each specific unit (specific identification method) or make assumptions about which units have been sold (moving average, FIFO, and LIFO methods).
- The moving average method assumes that a mix of the goods on hand is sold; the FIFO method assumes that the oldest goods on hand are sold; and the LIFO method assumes that the newest goods on hand are sold.

4 **ANALYZE** the effects the different inventory costing methods have on gross profit, matching of expenses with revenues, and income taxes (pp. 241–244).
- Each of the different inventory costing methods produces a different cost of goods sold and gross profit.
- When costs are rising, the LIFO method does the best job of matching current costs with revenues; LIFO also produces a lower gross profit and lower income taxes than moving average or FIFO.

5 **DESCRIBE** alternative treatments of freight costs (pp. 244–245).
- Freight terms of *F.O.B. shipping point* indicate that the purchaser bears the shipping cost; freight terms of *F.O.B. destination* indicate that the seller bears the shipping cost.
- *Freight prepaid* means that the seller pays the freight bill before shipping the goods; either the seller or the buyer may ultimately bear these costs. *Freight collect* means that the buyer pays the freight bill when the goods are delivered; either the seller or the buyer may ultimately bear these costs.

6 **EXPLAIN** when inventories are measured at less than cost (pp. 245–246).
- Damaged, physically deteriorated, or obsolete merchandise should be measured and reported at net realizable value (estimated selling price less expected cost of disposal).
- The lower of cost or market rule provides for losses to be recorded in the period that replacement costs of inventory items decline.
- The lower of cost or market rule may be applied to (a) each inventory item, (b) major inventory categories, or (c) the total inventory.

7 **DISCUSS** accounting for merchandise imports and exports (pp. 247–250).
- Imports and exports denominated in a foreign currency result in foreign exchange gains and losses if the exchange rate changes between the transaction date and the settlement date.
- International letters of credit are often used to finance international sales.

8 **Financial Analysis** **DEFINE** inventory turnover and days' sales in inventory and **EXPLAIN** their use (p. 250).
- Inventory turnover and days' sales in inventory indicate, respectively, how many times during the year a firm sells its average inventory and how many days it takes to sell the firm's average inventory.
- Inventory turnover and days' sales in inventory help in the evaluation of a firm's ability to sell its inventory.

SELF-TEST QUESTIONS FOR REVIEW

(Answers follow the Solution to Demonstration Problem.)

1. Which of the following concepts relates to the elimination or minimization of inventories by a manufacturing firm?
   a. Quick response
   b. Just in time
   c. Just in case
   d. Specific identification

2. Which inventory costing method assumes that the most recently purchased merchandise is sold first?
   a. Specific identification
   b. Moving average
   c. FIFO
   d. LIFO

3. Which inventory costing method results in the largest ending inventory cost during a period of rising unit costs?
   a. Specific identification
   b. Moving average
   c. FIFO
   d. LIFO

4. Under which of the following freight terms would the seller both pay and bear the freight costs?
   a. F.O.B. shipping point, freight collect
   b. F.O.B. shipping point, freight prepaid
   c. F.O.B. destination, freight collect
   d. F.O.B. destination, freight prepaid

5. On April 1, 1996, Drew Company purchased goods from a French supplier for 100,000 French francs, payable in 60 days. On May 29, 1996, Drew's bank sent the supplier a bank draft for 100,000 francs and charged Drew's account for the cost of the francs. Assume that the exchange rate for the franc was $0.176 on April 1, 1996, and $0.169 on May 29, 1996. The purchase and settlement of this import results in Drew Company showing a
   a. $16,900 foreign exchange loss.
   b. $700 foreign exchange gain.
   c. $17,600 foreign exchange gain.
   d. $700 foreign exchange loss.

DEMONSTRATION PROBLEM FOR REVIEW

Montclair Corporation had the following transactions for its only product during 1996:

Purchases	
February 15	2,000 units @ $27.00 each
April 20	3,000 units @ $28.40 each
October 25	1,200 units @ $31.25 each
Sales	
March 1	1,200 units @ $50.00 each
June 12	2,000 units @ $52.00 each
August 10	1,000 units @ $53.00 each
December 14	1,600 units @ $55.00 each

Montclair Corporation had 1,000 units in its January 1, 1996, inventory with a unit cost of $24 each. Montclair uses the perpetual inventory system.

REQUIRED

a. Determine the cost assigned to Montclair's December 31, 1996, inventory and Montclair's cost of goods sold for 1996 under each of the following costing methods:
   1. Moving average
   2. FIFO
   3. LIFO

b. Determine Montclair's gross profit for 1996 under each of the following costing methods:
   1. Moving average
   2. FIFO
   3. LIFO

SOLUTION TO DEMONSTRATION PROBLEM

a. 1. Moving average method

Date	Purchased Units	Purchased Unit Cost	Purchased Total	Sold Units	Sold Unit Cost	Sold Total	Inventory Balance Units	Inventory Balance Unit Cost	Inventory Balance Total
Jan. 1							1,000	$24.00	$ 24,000
Feb. 15	2,000	$27.00	$54,000				3,000	26.00	78,000
Mar. 1				1,200	$26.00	$ 31,200	1,800	26.00	46,800
Apr. 20	3,000	28.40	85,200				4,800	27.50	132,000
Jun. 12				2,000	27.50	55,000	2,800	27.50	77,000
Aug. 10				1,000	27.50	27,500	1,800	27.50	49,500
Oct. 25	1,200	31.25	37,500				3,000	29.00	87,000
Dec. 14				1,600	29.00	46,400	1,400	29.00	40,600
TOTAL						$160,100			

2. FIFO method

Date	Purchased Units	Purchased Unit Cost	Purchased Total	Sold Units	Sold Unit Cost	Sold Total	Inventory Balance Units	Inventory Balance Unit Cost	Inventory Balance Total
Jan. 1							1,000	$24.00	$ 24,000
Feb. 15	2,000	$27.00	$54,000				1,000 2,000	24.00 27.00 }	78,000
Mar. 1				1,000 200	$24.00 27.00	$ 24,000 5,400	1,800	27.00	48,600
Apr. 20	3,000	28.40	85,200				1,800 3,000	27.00 28.40 }	133,800
Jun. 12				1,800 200	27.00 28.40	48,600 5,680	2,800	28.40	79,520
Aug. 10				1,000	28.40	28,400	1,800	28.40	51,120
Oct. 25	1,200	31.25	37,500				1,800 1,200	28.40 31.25 }	88,620
Dec. 14				1,600	28.40	45,440	200 1,200	28.40 31.25 }	43,180
TOTAL						$157,520			

3. LIFO method

Date	Purchased Units	Purchased Unit Cost	Purchased Total	Sold Units	Sold Unit Cost	Sold Total	Inventory Balance Units	Inventory Balance Unit Cost	Inventory Balance Total
Jan. 1							1,000	$24.00	$24,000
Feb. 15	2,000	$27.00	$54,000				1,000 2,000	24.00 27.00	} 78,000
Mar. 1				1,200	$27.00	$ 32,400	1,000 800	24.00 27.00	} 45,600
Apr. 20	3,000	28.40	85,200				1,000 800 3,000	24.00 27.00 28.40	} 130,800
Jun. 12				2,000	28.40	56,800	1,000 800 1,000	24.00 27.00 28.40	} 74,000
Aug. 10				1,000	28.40	28,400	1,000 800	24.00 27.00	} 45,600
Oct. 25	1,200	31.25	37,500				1,000 800 1,200	24.00 27.00 31.25	} 83,100
Dec. 14				1,200 400	31.25 27.00	37,500 10,800	1,000 400	24.00 27.00	} 34,800
TOTAL						$165,900			

b.

Sales for 1996

March 1	1,200 units × $50 =	$ 60,000
June 12	2,000 units × $52 =	104,000
August 10	1,000 units × $53 =	53,000
December 14	1,600 units × $55 =	88,000
Total sales		$305,000

	Moving Average	FIFO	LIFO
Sales	$305,000	$305,000	$305,000
Cost of goods sold	160,100	157,520	165,900
Gross profit	$144,900	$147,480	$139,100

ANSWERS TO SELF-TEST QUESTIONS   **1.** b, p. 236   **2.** d, pp. 240–241   **3.** c, p. 242   **4.** d, p. 245   **5.** b, p. 248

Costing Methods with the Periodic Inventory System

INVENTORY COSTING METHODS WITH THE PERIODIC INVENTORY SYSTEM

In this appendix, we introduce four generally accepted methods of costing inventories under a periodic inventory system: (1) specific identification; (2) weighted average; (3) first-in, first-out; and (4) last-in, first-out. Each of the four methods illustrated uses historical costs. Initially, we will concentrate primarily on the computational technique of each method. A comparative evaluation is presented in a later section.

To compare more easily the four inventory methods, we illustrate all four with the same data used with the perpetual methods:

Jan. 1	Beginning inventory	60 units @ $10 =	$ 600
Mar. 27	Purchase	90 units @ 11 =	990
Aug. 15	Purchase	100 units @ 13 =	1,300
Nov. 6	Purchase	50 units @ 16 =	800
	Goods available for sale	300 units	$3,690
	Sales	220 units	
Dec. 31	Ending inventory	80 units	

Therefore, in each illustration,

1. Beginning inventory is costed at $600.

2. Three purchases are made during the period, as listed above.

3. Goods available for sale during the period amount to 300 units at a total cost of $3,690.

4. During the period, 220 units are sold, leaving an ending inventory of 80 units.

The four inventory costing methods differ in the way they assign costs to the units in the ending inventory. Under the periodic inventory system, the Inventory account and the Cost of Goods Sold account are updated only at the end of the accounting year. Once the total cost of the ending inventory is determined, the ending inventory amount is subtracted from the cost of goods available for sale to derive the period's total cost of goods sold.

SPECIFIC IDENTIFICATION METHOD

The periodic **specific identification method** involves (1) keeping track of the purchase cost of each specific unit available for sale and (2) costing the ending inventory at the actual costs of the specific units not sold. Assume that the 80 unsold units consist of 10 units from beginning inventory, 20 units from the August 15 purchase, and all 50 of the units purchased on November 6. The costs assigned to the ending inventory and cost of goods sold are shown in Exhibit E-1. Note that the full $3,690 cost of the goods available for sale has been assigned as either ending inventory or as cost of goods sold.

EXHIBIT E–1	Specific Identification Method (Periodic Inventory System)										
		Goods Available					**Ending Inventory**				
		Units		Cost		Total		Units		Cost		Total
Jan. 1 Beginning inventory	60 @	$10 =	$ 600	10 @	$10 =	$ 100
Mar. 27 Purchase	90 @	11 =	990			
Aug. 15 Purchase	100 @	13 =	1,300	20 @	13 =	260
Nov. 6 Purchase	50 @	16 =	800	50 @	16 =	800
	300		$3,690	80		$1,160
Cost of goods available for sale			$3,690			
Less: Ending inventory			1,160			
Cost of goods sold			$2,530			

WEIGHTED AVERAGE METHOD

The **weighted average method** spreads the total dollar cost of the goods available for sale equally among all units. In our illustration, this figure is $3,690/300, or $12.30 per unit. Exhibit E-2 diagrams the assignment of costs under this method. Note again that the entire cost of goods available for sale has been divided between ending inventory and cost of goods sold.

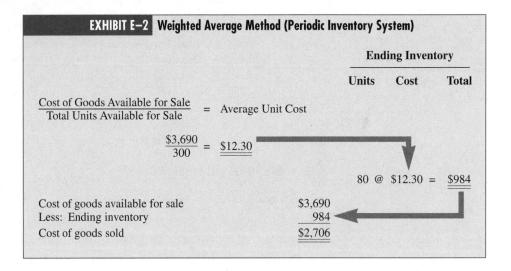

EXHIBIT E–2	Weighted Average Method (Periodic Inventory System)

$$\frac{\text{Cost of Goods Available for Sale}}{\text{Total Units Available for Sale}} = \text{Average Unit Cost}$$

$$\frac{\$3,690}{300} = \$12.30$$

80 @ $12.30 = $984

Cost of goods available for sale $3,690
Less: Ending inventory   984
Cost of goods sold $2,706

It would be incorrect to use a *simple* average of the costs. The simple average unit cost is ($10 + $11 + $13 + $16)/4 = $12.50; this figure fails to take into account the different numbers of units available at the various prices. This average yields the same figure as the weighted average only when the same number of units are purchased at each price.

FIRST-IN, FIRST-OUT (FIFO) METHOD

The **first-in, first-out (FIFO)** method assumes that the oldest goods on hand (or earliest purchased) are sold first. Thus, ending inventories are always made up of the most recent purchases. The periodic FIFO method would result in the cost allocations as shown in Exhibit E-3. This method assumes the first 220 units acquired are sold and the last 80 units purchased are still on hand.

| EXHIBIT E-3 | First-In, First-Out Method (Periodic Inventory System) |

	Goods Available			Ending Inventory		
	Units	**Cost**	**Total**	**Units**	**Cost**	**Total**
Jan. 1 Beginning inventory	60 @	$10 =	$ 600			
Mar. 27 Purchase	90 @	11 =	990			
Aug. 15 Purchase	100 @	13 =	1,300	30 @	$13 =	$ 390
Nov. 6 Purchase	50 @	16 =	800	50 @	16 =	800
	300		$3,690	80		$1,190
Cost of goods available for sale			$3,690			
Less: Ending inventory			1,190			
Cost of goods sold			$2,500			

LAST-IN, FIRST-OUT (LIFO) METHOD

The **last-in, first-out (LIFO)** method assumes that the most recent purchases are sold first. Exhibit E-4 shows how periodic LIFO works. This method assumes the 220 units most recently purchased are sold, and the 80 oldest units available for sale remain on hand at the end of the period.

| EXHIBIT E-4 | Last-In, First-Out Method (Periodic Inventory System) |

	Goods Available			Ending Inventory		
	Units	**Cost**	**Total**	**Units**	**Cost**	**Total**
Jan. 1 Beginning inventory	60 @	$10 =	$ 600	60 @	$10 =	$600
Mar. 27 Purchase	90 @	11 =	990	20 @	11 =	220
Aug. 15 Purchase	100 @	13 =	1,300			
Nov. 6 Purchase	50 @	16 =	800			
	300		$3,690	80		$820
Cost of goods available for sale			$3,690			
Less: Ending inventory			820			
Cost of goods sold			$2,870			

COMPARISON OF METHODS

Exhibit E-5 summarizes the results of applying the periodic and perpetual costing methods to the same example data. Note that specific identification and FIFO yield the same results with periodic and perpetual.

| EXHIBIT E-5 | Summary of Results of Different Inventory Costing Methods |

Costing Method	Year-End Inventory Cost	Cost of Goods Sold
Specific identification:		
Periodic	$1,160	$2,530
Perpetual	1,160	2,530
Average:		
Periodic	984	2,706
Perpetual	1,088	2,602
FIFO:		
Periodic	1,190	2,500
Perpetual	1,190	2,500
LIFO:		
Periodic	820	2,870
Perpetual	980	2,710

GLOSSARY OF KEY TERMS USED IN THIS CHAPTER AND APPENDIX

component An item in the materials inventory of a manufacturing firm that was a finished product to the firm that manufactured it (p. 235).

days' sales in inventory A ratio computed by dividing 365 by Inventory Turnover; this ratio indicates the number of days it takes to sell a firm's average inventory (p. 250).

exchange rate The price, in terms of one currency, at which one unit of another currency may be bought or sold (p. 247).

finished goods inventory A manufacturer's inventory that includes all products that have been completed and are ready for sale to customers (p. 236).

first-in, first-out (FIFO) method An inventory costing method that assumes that the oldest (earliest purchased) goods on hand are sold first (pp. 239, 256).

foreign currency transaction A transaction whose terms are fixed in the amount of a foreign currency to be paid or received (p. 247).

foreign exchange gain or loss A gain or loss arising from a change in exchange rates before a foreign currency transaction is settled (p. 248).

inventory carrying costs Costs created by just-in-case inventories, including casualty insurance, building usage costs, and the cost of capital invested in the inventory (p. 236).

inventory turnover A ratio computed by dividing cost of goods sold by average inventory (p. 250).

just-in-case inventory An extra quantity of inventory that a firm carries just in case suppliers do not deliver when scheduled or just in case the company decides to make previously unplanned product (p. 236).

just-in-time inventory philosophy A philosophy that a manufacturer would follow, seeking to minimize or eliminate just-in-case inventory quantities, through careful planning (p. 236).

last-in, first-out (LIFO) method An inventory costing method that assumes that the newest (most recently purchased) goods are sold first (pp. 240, 257).

letter of credit A document issued by a bank guaranteeing the payment of a specific amount of money upon completion of certain conditions (p. 249).

lower of cost or market (LCM) A measurement guideline that, when applied to inventory, provides for inventory to be presented in the balance sheet at the lower of its acquisition cost or current replacement cost (p. 245).

materials inventory A manufacturer's inventory that includes materials and components that have been purchased for use in the factory but have not yet been placed into production (p. 235).

moving average method An inventory costing method that recomputes average unit cost each time a purchase occurs and uses that average unit cost to determine the cost of goods sold for subsequent sales (p. 238).

net realizable value An asset measure computed by subtracting expected disposal cost from the asset's expected selling price (p. 245).

quick response system A system used with a point-of-sale system that is designed to make sure that a retailer quickly orders more of the items that are selling and quickly gets rid of the items that are not selling (p. 237).

specific identification method An inventory costing method involving the physical identification of goods sold and goods remaining on hand and costing these amounts at their actual costs (pp. 238, 255).

weighted average method An inventory costing method that computes an average unit purchase cost and uses that average unit cost to determine cost of goods sold for all sales (p. 256).

work in process inventory A manufacturer's inventory that consists of units of product that have been started into production in the factory but have not yet been completed (p. 235).

QUESTIONS

7-1 What are the three inventory accounts maintained by a manufacturing firm? Define each.

7-2 ShopMart Stores uses point-of-sale equipment at its checkouts to read universal bar codes. It also uses a quick response system. What is a quick response system? Describe it.

7-3 What are *just-in-case inventory* and *inventory carrying cost?* Define them.

7-4 What is the *just-in-time inventory philosophy?* Describe it.

7-5 What is meant by *goods flow* and *cost flow?*

7-6 How is each of the following inventory costing methods used with the perpetual inventory system: (a) specific identification; (b) moving average; (c) first-in, first-out; and (d) last-in, first-out?

7-7 What is an appropriate operating situation (that is, goods flow corresponds with cost flow) for each of the following approaches to inventory costing: specific identification, moving average, FIFO, and LIFO?

7-8 Why do relatively stable purchase prices reduce the significance of the choice of an inventory pricing method?

7-9 What is the nature of *phantom profits* during periods of rising merchandise purchase costs?

7-10 If costs have been rising, which inventory costing method—moving average; first-in, first-out; or last-in, first-out—yields (a) the lowest inventory amount? (b) the lowest net income? (c) the largest inventory amount? (d) the largest net income?

7-11 Even though it does not represent their goods flow, why might firms adopt last-in, first-out inventory pricing during periods when costs are consistently rising?

7-12 What are two situations in which merchandise may be inventoried at an amount less than cost?

7-13 At year-end, The Appliance Shop has a refrigerator on hand that has been used as a demonstration model. The refrigerator cost $350 and sells for $500 when new. In its present condition, the refrigerator will be sold for $325. Related selling costs are an estimated $15. At what amount should the refrigerator be carried in inventory?

7-14 What is the effect on reported income of applying the lower of cost or market rule to inventory?

7-15 How do the accounting principles of consistency and full disclosure apply to inventory costing?

7-16 Which party, the seller or the buyer, bears the freight cost when the terms are F.O.B. shipping point? When the terms are F.O.B. destination?

7-17 What event causes a foreign exchange loss to occur when accounting for an import, purchased on account, that is denominated in a foreign currency?

7-18 Moyer Company has a 1996 inventory turnover of 4.51. What is Moyer's 1996 days' sales in inventory?

PRINCIPLES DISCUSSION QUESTION

7-19 In a recent annual report, Craftmade International, Inc., describes its inventory accounting policies as follows:

> Inventories are stated at the lower of cost or market, with inventory cost determined using the first-in, first-out (FIFO) method. The cost of inventory includes freight-in and duties on imported goods.

Also in a recent annual report, Kaiser Aluminum Corporation made the following statement in discussing its inventories:

> The Company recorded pretax charges of approximately $19.4 million because of a reduction in the carrying values of its inventories caused principally by prevailing lower prices for alumina, primary aluminum, and fabricated products.

What basic accounting principle causes Craftmade International to include the costs of freight-in and duties on imported goods in its inventory account? Briefly describe how a firm determines which costs to include in its inventory account. What basic accounting principle caused Kaiser Aluminum to record the $19.4 million pretax charge? Briefly describe the rationale for this principle.

EXERCISES

JUST-IN-TIME INVENTORIES
— OBJ. 2 —

7-20 Raymond Manufacturing Company, which uses the perpetual inventory system, plans to use materials costing $600,000 in making its products during 1996. Raymond will operate its factory 300 days during 1996. Currently, Raymond follows the just-in-case philosophy with its materials inventory, keeping materials costing $15,000 in its materials inventory. Raymond plans to switch to the just-in-time philosophy by keeping only the materials needed for the next two days of production. Calculate the new materials inventory level after Raymond implements the just-in-time philosophy.

INVENTORY COSTING
METHODS
— OBJ. 3 —

7-21 Lippert Company uses the perpetual inventory system. The following July data are for an item in Lippert's inventory:

July 1   Beginning inventory, 30 units @ $8 per unit.
    10   Purchased 50 units @ $9 per unit.
    15   Sold 60 units.
    26   Purchased 25 units @ $10 per unit.

Compute the cost of goods sold for the July 15 sale using (a) first-in, first-out, (b) last-in, first-out, and (c) moving average.

INVENTORY COSTING
METHODS
— OBJ. 3 —

7-22   Archer Company is a retailer that uses the perpetual inventory system. Archer has 300 items in its inventory. On August 1, it had 80 units of product A on hand at a total cost of $1,600. On August 5, Archer purchased 100 units of A for $2,116. On August 8, it purchased 200 units of A for $4,416. On August 11, it sold 150 units of A for $4,800. Compute the inventory cost of item A on August 11 (after the sale) using (a) first-in, first-out, (b) last-in, first-out, and (c) moving average.

FREIGHT TERMS
— OBJ. 5 —

7-23   For each of the following Columbus Company purchases of merchandise, assume that the credit terms are 2/10, n/30 and that the cash discount applies only to the merchandise, not the freight.

Date	Purchase Amount	Shipping Terms	Freight Prepaid by Seller
Jan. 3	$1,200	F.O.B. shipping point	$100
5	2,400	F.O.B. destination	240
12	2,800	F.O.B. shipping point	—
16	4,000	F.O.B. shipping point	300

In each case, determine (a) the cash discount available and (b) the cash paid if the payment is made within the cash discount period.

DEPARTURES FROM COST
— OBJ. 6 —

7-24   Determine the proper total inventory amount for each of the following items in Viking Company's year-end inventory.
a. Viking has 600 video games in stock. The games cost $36 each, but their year-end replacement cost is $30. Viking has been selling these games for $60, but competitors are now selling them for $50. Viking plans to drop its price to $50. Viking's normal gross profit rate on video games is 40%.
b. Viking has 300 rolls of camera film that are past the expiration date marked on each film's box. The films cost $1.65 each and are normally sold for $3.30. New replacement films still cost $1.65. To clear out these old films, Viking will drop their selling price to $1.40. There are no related selling costs.
c. Viking has five cameras in stock that have been used as demonstration models. The cameras cost $180 and normally sell for $280. Because these cameras are in used condition, Viking has set the selling price at $160 each. Expected selling costs are $10 per camera. New models of the camera (on order) will cost Viking $200 and will be priced to sell at $320.

IMPORTS AND EXPORTS
— OBJ. 7 —

7-25   **a.** National Company, a U.S. firm, purchased merchandise on account from Soytan Company, a Japanese supplier, for 800,000 yen. On the purchase date, the exchange rate was $0.00765 per yen. On the payment date, the exchange rate was $0.00788 per yen. What are (1) the cost of the merchandise purchased and (2) the foreign exchange gain or loss from the settlement?
b. Starr Company, a U.S. firm, sold merchandise on account to Brinker Company, a Danish firm, for 50,000 kroner. On the sale date, the exchange rate was $0.1522 per kroner. On the settlement date, the exchange rate was $0.1548 per kroner. What are (1) the sales revenue and (2) the foreign exchange gain or loss from the settlement?

INVENTORY COSTING
METHODS—PERIODIC
— APPENDIX E —

7-26   The following information is for Bloom Company for 1996. Bloom sells just one product.

	Units	Unit Cost
Beginning inventory	200	$10
Purchases: Feb. 11	500	14
May 18	400	16
Oct. 23	100	20

At December 31, 1996, there was an ending inventory of 360 units. Assume periodic inventory procedures and compute the ending inventory and the cost of goods sold for the year using (a) first-in, first-out, (b) last-in, first-out, and (c) weighted average.

PROBLEMS

JUST-IN-TIME INVENTORY
— OBJ. 2 —

7-27   Dixon Manufacturing Company uses the perpetual inventory system with its material inventory. During 1996, Dixon plans to include material costing $1,960,000 in the products that it produces. John Dixon, president of the company, wants to adopt the just-in-time inventory philosophy for the materials inventory during 1996. He wants to have only the material needed for the next day's production on hand at the end of each day. The factory operates 280 days each year. Historically, the materials inventory balance at the end of the day has averaged $50,000 cost. Dixon has an annual inventory carrying cost equal to 20% of inventory cost.

REQUIRED

a. What is the anticipated inventory carrying cost (in dollars) if Dixon does not adopt the just-in-time inventory philosophy?

b. Compute the average level (in dollars) for the materials inventory if Dixon adopts the just-in-time philosophy.

c. Compute the reductions in the materials inventory level and the materials inventory annual carrying cost if Dixon adopts the just-in-time philosophy.

d. What other factors or situations should John Dixon consider before deciding to have only one day's supply of material on hand? (*Hint:* Consider factors and situations related to environment, supplier problems, labor problems, and so on.)

INVENTORY COSTING METHODS — OBJ. 3 —

7-28 Fortune Stores uses the perpetual inventory system for its merchandise inventory. The April 1 inventory for one of the items in the merchandise inventory consisted of 120 units with a unit cost of $325. Transactions for this item during April were as follows:

April   9   Purchased 40 units @ $345 per unit.

  14   Sold 80 units @ $550 per unit.

  23   Purchased 20 units @ $350 per unit.

  29   Sold 40 units @ $550 per unit.

REQUIRED

a. Prepare a schedule similar to the one in Exhibit 7-2 to compute cost of goods sold and inventory cost for the month of April using the moving average method.

b. Prepare a schedule similar to the one in Exhibit 7-3 to compute cost of goods sold and inventory cost for the month of April using the first-in, first-out method.

c. Prepare a schedule similar to the one in Exhibit 7-4 to compute cost of goods sold and inventory cost for the month of April using the last-in, first-out method.

INVENTORY COSTING METHODS — OBJ. 3 —

7-29 Chen Sales Corporation uses the perpetual inventory system. On January 1, 1996, Chen had 1,000 units of product A on hand with a unit cost of $20. A summary of purchases and sales during 1996 follows:

	Unit Cost	Units Purchased	Units Sold
Feb. 2			400
Apr. 6	$22	1,800	
July 10			1,600
Aug. 9	26	800	
Oct. 23			800
Dec. 30	29	1,200	

REQUIRED

a. Assume that Chen uses the first-in, first-out method. Compute the cost of goods sold for 1996 and the inventory balance at December 31, 1996, for product A.

b. Assume that Chen uses the last-in, first-out method. Compute the cost of goods sold for 1996 and the inventory balance at December 31, 1996, for product A.

c. Assume that Chen uses the moving average method. Compute the cost of goods sold for 1996 and the inventory balance at December 31, 1996, for product A.

d. Which of these three inventory costing methods would you choose

   1. To reflect what is probably the physical flow of goods?

   2. To minimize income tax for the period?

   3. To report the largest amount of income for the period?

   Justify your answers.

FREIGHT COSTS — OBJ. 5 —

7-30 Cardinal Wholesale Company sells merchandise to a variety of retailers. Cardinal uses different freight terms with its various customers and suppliers. All sales are made on account with 2/10, n/30 terms.

REQUIRED

For each of the following transactions, indicate which company pays the freight company and which ultimately bears the freight cost.

a. Cardinal sold merchandise to X-Mart Stores, with shipping terms of F.O.B. shipping point, freight collect.

b. Cardinal purchased merchandise from Zendo Manufacturing Company, with shipping terms of F.O.B. destination, freight prepaid.

c. Cardinal sold merchandise to Mary's Boutique, with shipping terms of F.O.B. destination, freight collect.

d. Sunshine Manufacturing Company sold merchandise to Cardinal, with shipping terms of F.O.B. shipping point, freight prepaid.

e. Cardinal purchased merchandise from Warfield Manufacturing Company, with freight terms of F.O.B. shipping point, freight collect.

f. Stevenson Stores purchased merchandise from Cardinal, with shipping terms of F.O.B. shipping point, freight prepaid.

LOWER OF COST OR MARKET RULE — OBJ. 6 —

7-31 Venner Company had the following inventory at December 31, 1996.

	Quantity	Unit Price Cost	Unit Price Market
Fans			
Model X1	300	$18	$19
Model X2	250	22	24
Model X3	400	29	26
Heaters			
Model B7	500	24	28
Model B8	290	35	32
Model B9	100	41	38

REQUIRED

a. Determine the ending inventory amount by applying the lower of cost or market rule to
  1. Each item of inventory.
  2. Each major category of inventory.
  3. The total inventory.

b. Which of the LCM procedures from requirement (a) results in the lowest net income for 1996? Explain.

IMPORT ACCOUNTING — OBJ. 7 —

7-32 On June 18, 1996, Talon, Inc., a U.S. company using the perpetual inventory system, purchased merchandise on account from Bourne Company, a French firm. The merchandise cost was 80,000 French francs. Talon paid the amount due (in francs) on July 10, 1996. Talon's fiscal year ends on June 30. Assume that the exchange rates for the French franc were the following:

June 18, 1996 $0.176
June 30, 1996   0.165
July 10, 1996   0.157

REQUIRED

a. Prepare the journal entries to account for the Bourne Company transaction on Talon's records for June 18, 1996, June 30, 1996, and July 10, 1996.

b. Assume that Talon's accounting year ends December 31 rather than June 30. Prepare the necessary journal entries on Talon's records in 1996 to account for the foreign currency transaction with Bourne Company.

c. Assume that Talon's accounting year ends June 30 and the exchange rates for the French franc were as follows:

June 18, 1996 $0.154
June 30, 1996   0.172
July 10, 1996   0.149

Prepare the journal entries to account for the Bourne Company transaction on Talon's records for June 18, 1996, June 30, 1996, and July 10, 1996.

INVENTORY COSTING METHODS—PERIODIC — APPENDIX E —

7-33 Using the data in Problem 7-29, assume that Chen Sales Corporation uses the periodic inventory system.

REQUIRED

a. Assume that Chen uses the first-in, first-out method. Compute the cost of goods sold for 1996 and the inventory balance at December 31, 1996, for product A.

b. Assume that Chen uses the last-in, first-out method. Compute the cost of goods sold for 1996 and the inventory balance at December 31, 1996, for product A.

c. Assume that Chen uses the weighted average method. Compute the cost of goods sold for 1996 and the inventory balance at December 31, 1996, for product A.

d. Which of these three inventory costing methods would you choose
  1. To reflect what is probably the physical flow of goods?
  2. To minimize income tax for the period?
  3. To report the largest amount of income for the period?
  Justify your answers.

ALTERNATE EXERCISES

JUST-IN-TIME INVENTORIES
— OBJ. 2 —

7-20A Carson Manufacturing Company, which uses the perpetual inventory system, plans to use material costing $1,650,000 in making its products during 1996. Carson will operate its factory 275 days during 1996. Currently, Carson follows the just-in-case philosophy with its materials inventory, keeping materials costing $35,000 in its materials inventory. Carson plans to switch to the just-in-time philosophy by keeping only the materials needed for the next two days of production. Calculate the new materials inventory level after Carson implements the just-in-time philosophy.

INVENTORY COSTING
METHODS
— OBJ. 3 —

7-21A Merritt Company uses the perpetual inventory system. The following May data are for an item in Merritt's inventory:

May 1   Beginning inventory, 150 units @ $30 per unit.
     12   Purchased 100 units @ $35 per unit.
     16   Sold 180 units.
     24   Purchased 160 units @ $36 per unit.

Compute the cost of goods sold for the May 16 sale using (a) first-in, first-out, (b) last-in, first-out, and (c) moving average.

INVENTORY COSTING
METHODS
— OBJ. 3 —

7-22A Spangler Company is a retailer that uses the perpetual inventory system. Spangler has 250 items in its inventory. On March 1, it had 100 units of product M on hand at a total cost of $1,590. On March 6, Spangler purchased 200 units of M for $3,600. On March 10, it purchased 150 units of M for $3,000. On March 15, it sold 180 units of M for $5,400. Compute the inventory cost of item M on March 15 (after the sale) using (a) first-in, first-out, (b) last-in, first-out, and (c) moving average.

FREIGHT TERMS
— OBJ. 5 —

7-23A For each of the following Clarenden Company purchases of merchandise, assume that the credit terms are 2/10, n/30 and that the cash discount applies only to the merchandise, not the freight.

Date	Purchase Amount	Shipping Terms	Freight Prepaid by Seller
Apr. 3	$3,000	F.O.B. shipping point	—
6	4,500	F.O.B. shipping point	$400
13	2,500	F.O.B. destination	300
17	1,500	F.O.B. shipping point	100

In each case, determine (a) the cash discount available and (b) the cash paid if the payment is made within the cash discount period.

LOWER OF COST
OR MARKET
— OBJ. 6 —

7-24A The following data refer to Froning Company's ending inventory:

Item Code	Quantity	Unit Cost	Unit Market
LXC	60	$45	$48
KWT	210	38	34
MOR	300	22	20
NES	100	27	32

Determine the ending inventory amount by applying the lower of cost or market rule to (a) each item of inventory and (b) the total inventory.

IMPORTS AND EXPORTS
— OBJ. 7 —

7-25A a. Storm Company, a U.S. firm, purchased merchandise on account from Downe Company, an Australian supplier, for 80,000 Australian dollars. On the purchase date, the exchange rate was $0.798 per Australian dollar. On the payment date, the exchange rate was $0.823 per Australian dollar. What are (1) the cost of the merchandise purchased and (2) the foreign exchange gain or loss from the settlement?

b. Banner Company, a U.S. firm, sold merchandise on account to Zurich Industries, a Swiss customer, for 100,000 Swiss francs. On the sale date, the exchange rate was $0.698 per Swiss franc. On the settlement date, the exchange rate was $0.672 per Swiss franc. What are (1) the sales revenue and (2) the foreign exchange gain or loss from the settlement?

INVENTORY COSTING
METHODS—PERIODIC
— APPENDIX E —

7-26A Toon Company, which uses the periodic inventory system, has the following records for 1996:

	Units	Unit Cost
Beginning inventory	100	$46
Purchases: Jan. 6	650	42
July 15	550	38
Dec. 28	200	36

Ending inventory at December 31, 1996, was 350 units. Compute the ending inventory and the cost of goods sold for the year using (a) first-in, first out, (b) weighted average, and (c) last-in, first-out.

ALTERNATE PROBLEMS

JUST-IN-TIME INVENTORY
— OBJ. 2 —

7-27A Field Manufacturing Company uses the perpetual inventory system with its material inventory. During 1996, Field plans to include material costing $2,400,000 in the products that it produces. Henry Field, president of the company, wants to adopt the just-in-time inventory philosophy for the materials inventory during 1996. He wants to have only the material needed for the next day's production on hand at the end of each day. The factory operates 300 days each year. Historically, the materials inventory balance at the end of the day has averaged $60,000 cost. Field has an annual inventory carrying cost equal to 22% of inventory cost.

REQUIRED

a. What is the anticipated annual inventory carrying cost (in dollars) if Field does not adopt the just-in-time inventory philosophy?

b. Compute the average level (in dollars) for the materials inventory if Field adopts the just-in-time philosophy.

c. Compute the reductions in the materials inventory level and the materials inventory annual carrying cost if Field adopts the just-in-time philosophy.

d. What other factors or situations should Henry Field consider before deciding to have only one day's supply of material on hand? (*Hint:* Consider factors and situations related to environment, supplier problems, labor problems, and so on.)

INVENTORY COSTING
METHODS
— OBJ. 3 —

7-28A Shiloh Company uses the perpetual inventory system for its merchandise inventory. The June 1 inventory for one of the items in the merchandise inventory consisted of 60 units with a unit cost of $40. Transactions for this item during June were as follows:

June 5   Purchased 40 units @ $50 per unit.
  13   Sold 50 units @ $90 per unit.
  25   Purchased 30 units @ $52 per unit.
  29   Sold 20 units @ $100 per unit.

REQUIRED

a. Prepare a schedule similar to the one in Exhibit 7-2 to compute cost of goods sold and inventory cost for the month of June using the moving average method.

b. Prepare a schedule similar to the one in Exhibit 7-3 to compute cost of goods sold and inventory cost for the month of June using the first-in, first-out method.

c. Prepare a schedule similar to the one in Exhibit 7-4 to compute cost of goods sold and inventory cost for the month of June using the last-in, first-out method.

INVENTORY COSTING
METHODS
— OBJ. 3 —

7-29A Gleem Sales Corporation uses the perpetual inventory system. On January 1, 1996, Gleem had 2,600 units of product B on hand with a unit cost of $40. A summary of purchases and sales during 1996 follows:

	Unit Cost	Units Purchased	Units Sold
Jan. 3			1,600
Mar. 8	$44	3,000	
June 13			2,000
Sept. 19	50	800	
Nov. 23	55	1,200	
Dec. 28			1,800

REQUIRED

a. Assume that Gleem uses the first-in, first-out method. Compute the cost of goods sold for 1996 and the inventory balance at December 31, 1996, for product B.

b. Assume that Gleem uses the last-in, first-out method. Compute the cost of goods sold for 1996 and the inventory balance at December 31, 1996, for product B.

c. Assume that Gleem uses the moving average method. Compute the cost of goods sold for 1996 and the inventory balance at December 31, 1996, for product B.

d. Which of these three inventory costing methods would you choose
   1. To reflect what is probably the physical flow of goods?
   2. To minimize income tax for the period?
   3. To report the largest amount of income for the period?
   Justify your answers.

FREIGHT COSTS
— OBJ. 5 —

7-30A Marshall Distributors sells merchandise to a variety of retailers. Marshall uses different freight terms with its various customers and suppliers. All sales are made on account with 2/10, n/30 terms.

REQUIRED

For each of the following transactions, indicate which company pays the freight company and which company ultimately bears the freight cost.

a. Marshall sold merchandise to Clay Boutique, with shipping terms of F.O.B. destination, freight collect.

b. Marshall purchased merchandise from Campbell Manufacturing Company, with freight terms of F.O.B. shipping point, freight collect.

c. Marshall sold merchandise to Save-A-Lot Stores, with shipping terms of F.O.B. shipping point, freight prepaid.

d. Marshall purchased merchandise from Central Manufacturing Company, with shipping terms of F.O.B. destination, freight prepaid.

e. Levinson Stores purchased merchandise from Marshall, with shipping terms of F.O.B. shipping point, freight prepaid.

f. Connor Manufacturing Company sold merchandise to Marshall, with shipping terms of F.O.B. shipping point, freight collect.

LOWER OF COST OR
MARKET RULE
— OBJ. 6 —

7-31A Crane Company had the following inventory at December 31, 1996:

		Unit Price	
	Quantity	Cost	Market
Desks			
Model 9001	70	$190	$210
Model 9002	45	280	268
Model 9003	20	350	360
Cabinets			
Model 7001	120	60	64
Model 7002	80	95	88
Model 7003	50	130	126

REQUIRED

a. Determine the ending inventory amount by applying the lower of cost or market rule to
  1. Each item of inventory.
  2. Each major category of inventory.
  3. The total inventory.

b. Which of the LCM procedures from requirement (a) results in the lowest net income for 1996? Explain.

EXPORT ACCOUNTING
— OBJ. 7 —

7-32A On December 20, 1996, Bluemound, Inc., a U.S. firm using the perpetual inventory system, sold merchandise costing $46,000 on account to Mitsison Company, a Japanese company. The sale price was 8,000,000 yen. Bluemound received the amount due (in yen) on January 18, 1997. Bluemound ends its accounting year on December 31. Assume that the exchange rates for the Japanese yen were the following:

December 20, 1996	$0.00725 per yen
December 31, 1996	0.00759
January 18, 1997	0.00792

REQUIRED

a. Prepare the journal entries to account for the Mitsison Company transaction on Bluemound's records for December 20, 1996, December 31, 1996, and January 18, 1997.

b. Assume that Bluemound's accounting year ends October 31 rather than December 31. Prepare the necessary journal entries on Bluemound's records in 1996 and 1997 to account for the foreign currency transaction with Mitsison Company.

c. Assume that Bluemound's accounting year ends December 31 and the exchange rates for the Japanese yen were as follows:

December 20, 1996	$0.00788 per yen
December 31, 1996	0.00756
January 18, 1997	0.00713

Prepare the journal entries to account for the Mitsison Company transaction on Bluemound's records for December 20, 1996, December 31, 1996, and January 18, 1997.

**INVENTORY COSTING
METHODS—PERIODIC
— APPENDIX E —**

7-33A   Using the data in Problem 7-29A, assume that Gleem Sales Corporation uses the periodic inventory system.

REQUIRED

a. Assume that Gleem uses the first-in, first-out method. Compute the cost of goods sold for 1996 and the inventory balance at December 31, 1996, for product B.

b. Assume that Gleem uses the last-in, first-out method. Compute the cost of goods sold for 1996 and the inventory balance at December 31, 1996, for product B.

c. Assume that Gleem uses the weighted average method. Compute the cost of goods sold for 1996 and the inventory balance at December 31, 1996, for product B.

d. Which of these three inventory costing methods would you choose

  1. To reflect what is probably the physical flow of goods?

  2. To minimize income tax for the period?

  3. To report the largest amount of income for the period?

  Justify your answers.

CASES

**BUSINESS
DECISION CASE**

Mackenzie Company is a wholesaler that uses the perpetual inventory system. On January 1, 1996, Mackenzie had 3,000 units of its only product on hand at a cost of $5 per unit. Transactions related to inventory during 1996 were as follows:

Purchases			**Sales**		
Feb. 5	9,000 units @ $6		Mar. 8	8,000 units @ $ 9	
May 19	20,000 units @ 7		June 21	19,000 units @ 10	
Dec. 15	3,000 units @ 9		Dec. 28	4,000 units @ 12	

Mackenzie is trying to decide whether to use first-in, first-out (FIFO) costing or last-in, first-out (LIFO) costing.

REQUIRED

a. Assume that Mackenzie decides to use the FIFO costing method.

  1. What would gross profit be for 1996?

  2. How would Mackenzie's gross profit and ending inventory for 1996 change if the December 15, 1996, purchase had been made on January 3, 1997?

  3. How would Mackenzie's gross profit and ending inventory for 1996 change if the December 15, 1996, purchase had been made for 6,000 units instead of 3,000 units?

b. Assume that Mackenzie decides to use the LIFO costing method.

  1. What would gross profit be for 1996?

  2. How would Mackenzie's gross profit and ending inventory for 1996 change if the December 15, 1996, purchase had been made on January 3, 1997?

  3. How would Mackenzie's gross profit and ending inventory for 1996 change if the December 15, 1996, purchase had been made for 6,000 units instead of 3,000 units?

c. Which method should Mackenzie choose and why?

FINANCIAL ANALYSIS CASE

Pfizer Inc is a research-based, global health care company. The company has four business segments: health care, consumer health care, food science, and animal health. Abbott Laboratories is a diversified health care company well known for its pharmaceutical products. The two companies are in similar industries. Recent financial data for these two companies follow (Year 2 is the more recent; amounts are in millions of dollars):

	Year 2		**Year 1**	
	Pfizer	**Abbott**	**Pfizer**	**Abbott**
Cost of goods sold	$1,772.0	$3,684.7	$2,024.3	$3,505.3
Beginning inventory	1,067.8	863.8	1,171.5	815.4
Ending inventory	1,093.5	940.5	1,067.8	863.8

REQUIRED

a. Compute the inventory turnover and days' sales in inventory for Pfizer Inc and Abbott Laboratories for Years 1 and 2.

b. What conclusions can be drawn about the two companies from inventory turnover and days' sales in inventory?

c. In evaluating the Year 2 inventory turnover and days' sales in inventory for Pfizer Inc, is it appropriate to compare these ratios to (1) the Year 1 ratios for Pfizer Inc and (2) the Year 2 ratios for Abbott Laboratories? Why or why not?

ETHICS CASE   Reed Kohler is in his last year, before retiring, as controller for Quality Sales Corporation. As a member of top management, Kohler participates in an attractive company bonus plan. The overall size of the bonus is a function of the firm's income before bonus and income taxes (the larger the income, the larger the bonus).

Due to a slowdown in the economy, Quality Sales Corporation has encountered difficulties in managing its cash flows. To improve cash flows (by reducing cash payments for income taxes), the firm's auditors have recommended that the firm change its inventory pricing method from FIFO to LIFO. This change would cause a significant increase in the cost of goods sold for the year. Kohler believes the firm should not switch to LIFO this year because its inventory quantities are too large. He believes the firm should work to reduce its inventory quantities and then switch to LIFO (the switch could be made in a year or two). After expressing this opinion to the firm's treasurer, Kohler is stunned when the treasurer replies: "Reed, I can't believe that after all these years with the firm, you put your personal interests ahead of the firm's interests."

REQUIRED

Explain why Kohler may be viewed as holding a position that favors his personal interests. What can Kohler do to increase his credibility when the possible change to LIFO is discussed at a meeting of the firm's top management next week?

GENERAL MILLS ANNUAL   Refer to the annual report of General Mills, Inc., presented in Appendix K.
REPORT CASE   **REQUIRED**

a. Refer to Note 1, parts C and G.
   (1) Which inventory costing method does General Mills use?
   (2) Where are gains and losses from foreign currency transactions reported?
b. Refer to Note 5.
   (1) What was the total cost of raw materials, work in process, and supplies at May 29, 1994?
   (2) What was the total cost of finished goods at May 29, 1994?
   (3) At May 29, 1994, how much inventory was valued at LIFO?

8

Plant Assets, Natural Resources, and Intangible Assets

CHAPTER LEARNING OBJECTIVES

1 **DISCUSS** the nature of plant asset accounting and **IDENTIFY** the guidelines relating to the initial measurement of plant assets (pp. 269–273).

2 **DISCUSS** the nature of the depreciation process, **ILLUSTRATE** four depreciation methods, and **EXPLAIN** impairment losses (pp. 273–281).

3 **DISCUSS** the distinction between revenue and capital expenditures (pp. 281–283).

4 **EXPLAIN** and **ILLUSTRATE** the accounting for disposals of plant assets (pp. 283–285).

5 **DISCUSS** the nature of and the accounting for natural resources (pp. 285–286).

6 **DISCUSS** the nature of and the accounting for intangible assets (pp. 286–289).

7 **ILLUSTRATE** the balance sheet presentation of plant assets, natural resources, and intangible assets (p. 289).

8 Financial Analysis **DEFINE** *return on assets* and *asset turnover* and **EXPLAIN** their use (p. 290).

CHAPTER FOCUS

Consider, for a moment, the asset structure of Georgia-Pacific Corporation. More than 80% of the assets used to fulfill its mission of manufacturing and distributing building products, pulp, and paper are in three long-term categories: *plant assets, natural resources,* and *intangible assets.* **Plant assets,** or **fixed assets,** refer to a firm's *property, plant, and equipment.* Utilizing more than 400 facilities, Georgia-Pacific's plant assets exceed $5.4 billion. The firm's wood fiber requirements are supplied from its 5.7 million acres of timberland—a natural resource measured at more than $1.3 billion. And when Georgia-Pacific acquired control of Great Northern Nekoosa Corporation in 1990, it recorded about $2 billion of an intangible asset called goodwill. Most of this goodwill is still on Georgia-Pacific's balance sheet. The benefits to a firm from its plant assets, natural resources, and intangible assets extend over many accounting periods. In this chapter, we discuss the accounting guidelines for these asset categories.

The carrying values of these long-term assets are normally based on historical costs. The costs related to the use of these long-term assets must be properly calculated and matched with the revenues they help generate so that periodic net income is determined correctly. Each period's expired portion of the asset's cost is called *depreciation, depletion,* or *amortization,* depending on the type of asset involved. All of these terms have the same meaning in accounting: that is, periodic charging to expense.

Exhibit 8-1 gives several specific examples within each asset category. The exhibit also associates the term for the periodic write-off to expense with the proper asset category. Note that site land—that is, a place on which to operate—usually has an indefinite useful life and therefore does not require any periodic write-off to expense.

EXHIBIT 8–1	Long-Term Assets Requiring Periodic Write-Off	
Asset Category	**Examples**	**Term for Periodic Write-Off to Expense**
Plant Assets	Buildings, equipment, tools, furniture, fixtures, and vehicles	Depreciation
	Exception: Land for site use considered to have an indefinite life and is not depreciated	
Natural Resources	Oil, timber, coal, and other mineral deposits	Depletion
Intangible Assets	Patents, copyrights, leaseholds, franchises, trademarks, and goodwill	Amortization

OVERVIEW OF PLANT ASSET PROBLEMS

OBJECTIVE *1*

DISCUSS the nature of plant asset accounting and **IDENTIFY** the guidelines relating to the measurement of plant assets.

We consider the problems associated with plant assets in the order shown in Exhibit 8-2. This exhibit is a graphic presentation of the typical accounting problems created by plant assets in relation to an asset's life cycle.

Measurement problems associated with plant assets include **1** identifying the types and amounts of expenditures that make up the original recorded cost of the particular asset. **2** During the use period of a limited-life asset, it is important to charge the appropriate amounts against yearly revenue to reflect the asset's consumption. This involves estimating

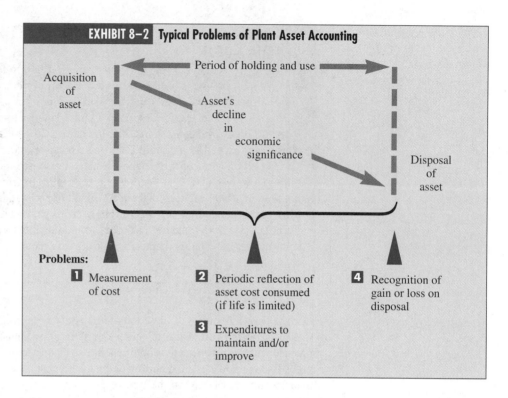

EXHIBIT 8–2 Typical Problems of Plant Asset Accounting

the asset's useful life and its probable salvage value at disposal. **3** Also during the use period, expenditures for simple maintenance (expense) must be properly differentiated from expenditures that increase the capacity or extend the life of the asset (added to asset costs). **4** On disposal, the adjusted accounting cost of the asset must be compared with the net proceeds from disposal to determine any related gain or loss.

ORIGINAL MEASUREMENT OF PLANT ASSETS

Plant assets are originally recorded at their cost. These measures are also called *historical costs* because they provide the basis for accounting for the assets in subsequent periods. Usually we do not attempt to reflect subsequent changes in market values for plant assets. In general, the initial cost of a plant asset equals the cash and/or the cash equivalent of that which is given up to acquire the asset *and* to prepare it for use. In other words, initial cost includes the asset's (1) implied cash price and (2) cost of preparation for use.

The expenditures to acquire and prepare the asset for use must be reasonable and necessary to be considered part of the asset's cost. Accountants do not capitalize (charge to an asset account) wasteful or inefficient expenditures. Costs of waste and inefficiency are expensed when incurred. For example, suppose equipment is damaged while it is being installed or a firm's receiving dock is damaged while equipment is being unloaded. Expenditures made to repair these damages are not part of the cost of the equipment; they are instead charged to expense.

PRINCIPLE ALERT

COST PRINCIPLE

Note the application of the *cost principle* to the initial measurement of plant assets. To measure plant assets at cost, accountants not only must identify the asset's cash purchase price but also must consider several other factors. Were there additional costs incurred to get the plant asset in condition and location for use? If so, were these costs reasonable and necessary? If the answer to these two questions is yes, the additional costs are added to the plant asset's account and are considered part of the asset's cost.

CASH PURCHASES Often an asset's historical cost is simply the amount of cash paid when the asset is acquired and readied for use. Consider, for example, the following expenditures for a certain piece of equipment:

Purchase price factors		
Gross invoice price	$10,000	
Less: Cash discount (1/10, n/30)	(100)	
Sales tax	500	$10,400
Related expenditures		
Freight charges	$ 200	
Installation costs	500	
Testing of installed machine	300	1,000
Cost of equipment		$11,400

The total initial equipment cost is $11,400, consisting of a cash purchase price of $10,400 and preparation costs of $1,000. The sales tax is a necessary component of the purchase price and should not be charged to a tax expense account. Similarly, the costs of freight, installation, and testing are expenditures necessary to get the asset to the location and in condition for use.

DEFERRED PAYMENT PURCHASES If an asset's purchase price is not immediately paid in cash, we determine the cash equivalent purchase price at the acquisition date and record that amount in the asset account. Suppose that we purchased this equipment on a financing plan requiring a $400 cash down payment and a 9%, $10,000 note payable due in one year. The implied cash price remains $10,400, even though more than $10,400 is eventually disbursed under the financing plan ($400 down payment + $10,000 principal payment on note + $900 interest payment = $11,300). Because the equipment is ready for immediate use, the extra $900 paid as interest will be charged to interest expense. The entry to record the purchase of the asset under the financing plan is as follows:

Equipment	10,400	
Cash		400
Notes Payable		10,000
To record purchase of equipment.		

Of course, the expenditures for freight, installation, and testing are still debited to the Equipment account when they are incurred.

PACKAGE PURCHASES Sometimes several types of assets are purchased concurrently as a package. For example, assume that a company purchased a small freight terminal including land, a building, and some loading equipment for a total price of $190,000. For accounting purposes, the total purchase price should be divided among the three asset forms because (1) they are reported in different accounts, (2) only the building and equipment are subject to depreciation, and (3) the equipment will have an estimated useful life different from that of the building.

The price of package purchases is commonly allocated on the basis of relative market or appraisal values. We assume estimated market values to illustrate this approach.

Asset	Estimated Market Value	Percent of Total	Allocation of Purchase Price	Estimated Useful Life
Land	$ 60,000	30	$ 57,000	Indefinite
Building	120,000	60	114,000	30 years
Equipment	20,000	10	19,000	8 years
Totals	$200,000	100	$190,000	

Actually, the firm may obtain realistic market values from a professional appraiser or from assessed values on related property tax bills.

CAPITALIZATION OF INTEREST

Interest cost is part of an asset's initial cost if a period of time is required to get the asset ready for use. The process that adds interest cost to an asset's initial cost is called the **capitalization of interest.** For example, the construction of a factory building takes time to complete. Accordingly, an appropriate portion of the actual interest cost incurred during the construction period is added to the factory building's cost. We compute the amount of interest capitalized by multiplying the periodic interest rate times the period's average accumulated construction expenditures. The average accumulated construction expenditures for a period are usually determined by summing the accumulated expenditures at the beginning of the period and the end of the period and dividing the sum by 2.

To illustrate, let us assume that Miller Company borrowed $500,000 at 12% to finance the construction of a factory building. Interest of $5,000 is paid monthly. During the first month, construction expenditures total $300,000. The interest cost capitalized this first month is $1,500, computed as follows:

Average accumulated construction expenditures

Accumulated construction expenditures, beginning of month	$ –0–
Accumulated construction expenditures, end of month	300,000
Average accumulated construction expenditures for the month	$300,000 ÷ 2 = $150,000
Monthly interest rate (1%)	0.01
Interest capitalized for the month	$ 1,500

Interest is capitalized until the factory building is completed. Of course, in subsequent months, the average accumulated construction expenditures increase, so larger amounts of interest cost are capitalized.

RELATED EXPENDITURES

A purchase of land often raises some interesting questions about related expenditures. Suppose that a firm retains a local real estate broker at a fee of $2,000 to locate an appropriate site for its new office building. The property eventually chosen has an old residence on it, which will be razed. The terms of the sale include a payment of $40,000 to the seller, with the buyer paying off an existing mortgage of $10,000 and $300 of accrued interest. In addition, the buyer agrees to pay accrued real estate taxes of $800. Other related expenditures include legal fees of $400 and a title insurance premium of $500. A local salvage company will raze the old residence, level the lot, keep all the materials, and pay the firm $200. If we apply the general plant asset measurement rule, we compute the initial cost of the land as follows:

Payment to the seller	$40,000
Commission for finding property	2,000
Payment of mortgage and interest due at time of sale	10,300
Payment of property taxes owed by seller	800
Legal fees	400
Title insurance premium	500
	$54,000
Less: Net recovery from razing	(200)
Cost of land	$53,800

Again, expenditures for the taxes, insurance, legal fees, and interest should be capitalized as part of the land, because they were necessary for its acquisition and preparation for use. Removing the old residence prepares the land for its intended use. The $200 net recovery from razing, therefore, *reduces* the land's cost. A net payment to remove the old building would have *increased* the land's cost.

When a land site is acquired in an undeveloped area, the firm may pay special assessments to the local government for such property improvements as streets, sidewalks, and sewers. These improvements are normally maintained by the local government and, accordingly, are considered relatively permanent improvements by the firm. In these circumstances, the company capitalizes the special assessments as part of the cost of the land.

The firm may make property improvements that have limited lives. Classified as **land improvements,** they include such improvements as paved parking lots, driveways, private sidewalks, and fences. Expenditures for these items are charged to separate land improvement accounts, which are depreciated over the estimated lives of the improvements.

LEASEHOLD IMPROVEMENTS

Expenditures made by a business entity to alter or improve leased property are called **leasehold improvements.** For example, a merchandising firm may make improvements, with the permission of the owner, to a leased building. Toys "R" Us, a children's specialty retail chain, leases a portion of its more than 1,000 stores and reports over $600 million of leasehold imrovements in its balance sheet. The improvements or alterations become part of the leased property and revert to the owner of the property at the end of the lease. The cost of leasehold improvements is capitalized to the *Leasehold Improvements* account. Leasehold improvements are depreciated over the life of the lease or the life of the improvements, whichever is shorter.

THE NATURE OF DEPRECIATION

OBJECTIVE *2*

DISCUSS the nature of the depreciation process, **ILLUSTRATE** four depreciation methods, and **EXPLAIN** impairment losses.

With the exception of site land, the use of plant assets to generate revenue consumes their economic potential. At some point of reduced potential—usually before they are totally worthless—these assets are disposed of and possibly replaced. We can diagram the typical pattern of plant asset utilization as follows:

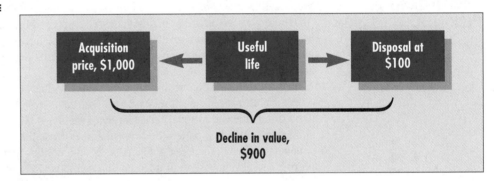

The asset is acquired for $1,000, used for several accounting periods, and then sold for $100. The $900 decline in value is called **depreciation** and, in every sense of the word, is an expense of generating the revenues recognized during the periods that the asset was used. Therefore, if the periodic income figures are to be meaningful, $900 of expense must be allocated to these periods and matched with the revenues. Failure to do so would overstate income for these periods.

Note that in this process we estimate an asset's useful life and salvage value as well as properly determine its acquisition cost. **Useful life** is the expected period of economic usefulness to the current entity—the period from date of acquisition to expected date of disposal. **Salvage value** (or *residual value*) is the expected net recovery (sales proceeds – disposal costs) when the asset is sold or removed from service. When the salvage value is insignificant, it may be ignored in the depreciation process.

ALLOCATION VERSUS VALUATION

Although the idea is theoretically appealing, accountants do not specifically base depreciation on the changes in market value or on the measured wear of assets—primarily because a reliable, objective, and practical source for such data rarely exists. Rather, **depreciation accounting** attempts to allocate in a *systematic* and *rational* manner the difference between acquisition cost and estimated salvage value over the *estimated* useful life of the asset. Depreciation accounting techniques are convenient expedients for measuring asset expirations and are therefore not precise. Though imprecise, depreciation estimates clearly

PRINCIPLE ALERT

MATCHING CONCEPT

Depreciation accounting represents an application of the *matching concept.* Depreciable plant assets are used in an entity's operating activities to help generate revenues. These assets help generate revenues for their entire useful lives. Each period that benefits from a plant asset's use is assigned part of the asset's cost as depreciation expense. Thus, depreciation expense is being matched with the revenues that it helps to generate. The matching that occurs through depreciation accounting extends throughout a plant asset's useful life.

provide better income determination than would result from completely expensing the asset at either the date of acquisition or the date of disposal.

Several factors are naturally related to the periodic allocation of depreciation. Depreciation can be caused by wear from use, from natural deterioration through interaction of the elements, and from technical obsolescence. Each factor reduces the value of the asset. To some extent, maintenance (lubrication, adjustments, parts replacements, and cleaning) may partially arrest or offset wear and deterioration. Quite logically, then, when useful life and salvage values are estimated, a given level of maintenance is assumed.

COMPUTATIONS OF PERIODIC DEPRECIATION

We now illustrate four widely used methods of computing periodic depreciation. For each illustration, we assume that the asset costs $1,000 and has an estimated useful life of five years. The estimated salvage value at the end of the five-year period is $100. Our computations illustrate different ways to *allocate* the amount depreciated among each of the five accounting periods in the asset's life.

How to allocate depreciation expense to individual accounting periods is just one facet of the overall task of matching expenses with revenues. As noted earlier, the allocation is to be systematic and rational. The four methods that we illustrate are systematic. A rational allocation results in a pattern of depreciation expense that is congruent with the pattern of benefits from using the asset. Plant assets benefit entities in different patterns; thus, it is appropriate to have a variety of depreciation methods.

STRAIGHT LINE

The **straight-line method** is probably the simplest depreciation method to use. An equal amount of depreciation expense is allocated to each full period of the asset's useful life. Using straight-line depreciation,

$$\text{Annual Depreciation} = \frac{\text{Original Cost} - \text{Salvage Value}}{\text{Periods of Useful Life}}$$

which in our example is

$$\frac{\$1,000 - \$100}{5 \text{ years}} = \$180 \text{ per year}$$

The basic entry to record each period's depreciation expense is

Depreciation Expense—Equipment	180	
Accumulated Depreciation—Equipment		180
To record depreciation expense for the year.		

Like other expense accounts, Depreciation Expense is deducted from revenues in determining net income and is closed at year-end to the Income Summary account. The offsetting credit is posted to the contra account, Accumulated Depreciation, which is deducted from the related asset account on the balance sheet to compute the asset's book value, or carrying value. In this manner, the original cost of an asset is maintained in the asset account, and the cumulative balance of depreciation taken is carried in the contra account as long as the asset is in service. When an asset is disposed of, the related cost and accumulated depreciation are removed from the accounts.

For our simple illustration, the following table shows account balances and the progression of certain amounts during the asset's five-year life.

			End-of-Period Balance	
Year of Useful Life	Balance of Asset Account	Annual Depreciation Expense	Accumulated Depreciation Account	Asset's Book Value
1	$1,000	$180	$180	$820
2	1,000	180	360	640
3	1,000	180	540	460
4	1,000	180	720	280
5	1,000	180	900	100
		Total $900		

Observe that (1) the asset account always shows the original cost of the asset, (2) each period reflects $180 of depreciation expense, (3) the Accumulated Depreciation account balance is cumulative and shows the portion of the original cost taken as depreciation to date, (4) the asset's book value is the original cost less total accumulated depreciation to date, and (5) the asset's book value at the end of five years equals the estimated salvage value. Thus, the book value decreases to the estimated salvage value as the asset is depreciated during its useful life.

For periods of less than one year, straight-line depreciation amounts are simply proportions of the annual amount. For example, if the asset had been acquired on April 1, depreciation for the period ended December 31 would be $\frac{9}{12} \times \$180 = \$135$. Assets acquired or disposed of during the first half of any month are usually treated as if the acquisition or disposal occurred on the first of the month. When either event occurs during the last half of any month, we assume that it occurred on the first of the following month.

Straight-line depreciation is best suited to an asset with a relatively uniform periodic usage and a low obsolescence factor. Examples include pipelines, storage tanks, fencing, and surface paving. These types of assets can provide approximately equal utility during all periods of their useful lives.

PRINCIPLE ALERT

GOING CONCERN CONCEPT

Note the role of the *going concern concept* in the process of depreciation accounting. Absent evidence to the contrary, the going concern concept assumes that the business entity has an indefinite life. Depreciation accounting allocates a plant asset's depreciable cost to expense over the asset's useful life *to the entity*. A depreciation schedule that allocates cost over many years—whether it be 5 years or 25 years (or more)—relies on an assumption that the entity will be in existence for at least that number of years.

UNITS OF PRODUCTION   The **units-of-production method** allocates depreciation in proportion to the asset's use in operations. First, the depreciation per unit of production is computed by dividing the total expected depreciation (in our example, $900) by the asset's projected units-of-production capacity. Therefore,

$$\text{Depreciation per Unit} = \frac{\text{Original Cost} - \text{Salvage Value}}{\text{Estimated Total Units of Production}}$$

Units-of-production capacity may represent miles driven, tons hauled, hours used, or number of cuttings, drillings, or stampings of parts. Assume that our example is a drilling tool that will drill an estimated 45,000 parts during its useful life. The depreciation per unit of production is

$$\frac{\$1,000 - \$100}{45,000 \text{ parts}} = \$0.02 \text{ per part}$$

To find periodic depreciation expense, we multiply the depreciation per unit of production by the number of units produced during the period. Therefore,

Annual Depreciation = Depreciation per Unit × Units of Production for the Year

Assuming that the parts drilled over the five years were 8,000, 14,000, 10,000, 4,000, and 9,000, respectively, we calculate each year's depreciation expense as follows:

Year of Useful Life	Depreciation per Unit		Annual Units of Production		Annual Depreciation Expense
1	$0.02	×	8,000	=	$160
2	0.02	×	14,000	=	280
3	0.02	×	10,000	=	200
4	0.02	×	4,000	=	80
5	0.02	×	9,000	=	180
				Total	$900

The units-of-production method is particularly appropriate when wear is the major cause of depreciation and the amount of use varies from period to period. Of course, if use is uniformly spread over the asset's life, the same allocation of depreciation would result from either the straight-line or units-of-production method. The units-of-production method may necessitate some extra record keeping to express the periodic use in terms of production capacity. However, these data may already be tabulated as part of a periodic production report.

SUM OF THE YEARS' DIGITS

The **sum-of-the-years'-digits (SYD) method** accelerates depreciation expense so that the amounts recognized in the early periods of an asset's useful life are greater than those recognized in the later periods. This type of depreciation pattern (larger amounts in early periods) identifies an **accelerated depreciation method.** The SYD is found by estimating an asset's useful life in years, assigning consecutive numbers to each year, and totaling these numbers. For n years,

$$SYD = 1 + 2 + 3 + \ldots + n$$

In our example, the SYD for a five-year asset life is $1 + 2 + 3 + 4 + 5 = 15$.

Determining the SYD factor by simple addition can be somewhat laborious for long-lived assets. For these assets, the formula $n(n + 1)/2$, where n equals the number of periods in the asset's useful life, can be applied to derive the SYD. In our example,

$$\frac{5(5 + 1)}{2} = \frac{30}{2} = 15$$

The yearly depreciation is then calculated by multiplying the total depreciable amount for the asset's useful life by a fraction whose numerator is the remaining useful life and whose denominator is the SYD. Thus, the formula for yearly depreciation is

$$\text{Annual Depreciation} = (\text{Original Cost} - \text{Salvage Value}) \times \frac{\text{Remaining Useful Life}}{\text{SYD}}$$

NOT BAD FOR A TEN-YEAR-OLD

Born in Brunswick, Germany, in 1777, Carl Friedrich Gauss ranks among the greatest mathematicians of all time. An episode that occurred when Gauss was 10 years old relates to our study of depreciation accounting. One day during arithmetic class, the teacher assigned the students the task of finding the sum of all the numbers 1 through 100. The students did their assignments on slate tablets. As they finished an assignment, they would each place their tablet on a large table. The teacher had barely finished giving this assignment when Gauss placed his tablet on the table, exclaiming "Ligget se!" [There it is]. While the other students were still busy writing and computing, the teacher finally took a look at Gauss's slate. There was only one number written on it—5,050, the correct answer!

Gauss got his answer so quickly because he noted a particular numerical relationship: if he paired the first number and the last number (1, 100), the second number and the next to last number (2, 99), the third number and the third from the last number (3, 98), and so on, the sum of each pair was the same, 101. Out of the 100 numbers, there were 50 such pairs. Thus, the sum of all the numbers is 50×101, or 5,050.

This brilliantly simple solution to the problem of adding up a set of whole numbers explains the formula used in summing up an asset's years in sum-of-the-years'-digits depreciation. If we let n equal the number of years of useful life, the number of "Gaussian" pairs is $n/2$ and the sum of each pair is $n + 1$. The sum of the numbers, therefore, is $(n/2)(n + 1)$, or, alternatively, $n(n + 1)/2$.

SOURCE: This episode and other details of Gauss's life may be found in G. Waldo Dunnington, *Carl Friedrich Gauss: Titan of Science* (New York: Exposition Press, 1955).

The calculations for our example follow:

Year of Useful Life	Fraction of Total Depreciation Taken Each Year		Original Cost Less Salvage Value		Annual Depreciation Expense
1	$\frac{5}{15}$	×	$900	=	$300
2	$\frac{4}{15}$	×	900	=	240
3	$\frac{3}{15}$	×	900	=	180
4	$\frac{2}{15}$	×	900	=	120
5	$\frac{1}{15}$	×	900	=	60
SYD 15					Total $900

When the acquisition of an asset does not coincide with the beginning of the fiscal period, the annual depreciation amounts are allocated proportionately to the appropriate fiscal periods. For example, assume that we purchased the asset on April 1. Depreciation for the period ended December 31 would be $\frac{9}{12} \times \$300 = \$225$. For the next fiscal year, a full year's depreciation would be calculated as $(\frac{3}{12} \times \$300) + (\frac{9}{12} \times \$240) = \$255$.

As an accelerated depreciation method, the SYD approach is most appropriate when the asset renders greater utility during its early life and less in its later life. Accelerated depreciation is suitable for assets with either a high technological obsolescence factor in the early life phase or a high maintenance factor in the late life phase.

DECLINING BALANCE   Another accelerated depreciation method is the **declining-balance method.** It computes depreciation expense as a constant percentage of the asset's book value at the beginning of each year. An asset's book value (initial cost – accumulated depreciation) decreases, or declines, each year (hence, the reason for the method's name). Salvage value is not considered in the calculations, except that depreciation stops when the asset's book value equals its estimated salvage value.

The declining-balance method is an accelerated method because the constant percentage it uses is a multiple of the straight-line rate (the straight-line rate = 100%/Years of useful life). There are different versions of the declining-balance method because different multiples of the straight-line rate may be used. *Double declining-balance depreciation* uses a rate that is twice the straight-line rate; *150% declining-balance depreciation* uses a rate that is one and one-half times the straight-line rate.

For example, the straight-line rate for our asset with a five-year useful life is 100%/5 = 20%. Thus, to depreciate such an asset, the double declining-balance method uses a 40% rate (2 × 20%); the 150% declining-balance method uses a 30% rate (1.5 × 20%).

We will illustrate the declining-balance method using the double declining-balance version. Under this approach, then,

$$\text{Annual Depreciation} = \text{Book Value at Beginning of Year} \times \text{Double Declining-Balance Rate}$$

Computing annual depreciation this way in our example results in the accelerated depreciation pattern shown in the following table (amounts to the nearest dollar):

Year of Useful Life	Original Cost	Beginning Accumulated Depreciation	Beginning Book Value		Twice Straight-Line Percentage		Annual Depreciation Expense
1	$1,000	$–0–	$1,000	×	40%	=	$400
2	1,000	400	600	×	40%	=	240
3	1,000	640	360	×	40%	=	144
4	1,000	784	216	×	40%	=	86
5	1,000	870	130				30
							Total $900

Observe that in the fifth year, depreciation expense is only $30, the amount needed to reduce the asset's book value to the estimated salvage value of $100. Assets are not depreciated below their salvage values. If no salvage value has been estimated, the double declining-balance technique automatically provides one. When a fraction (40%, or $\frac{4}{10}$, for example) is applied to an asset's book value, the entire original cost can never be depreciated; some balance, though small, will always remain.

If an asset is purchased during the fiscal period, a pro rata allocation of the first year's depreciation is necessary. If we acquired our asset on April 1, depreciation for the period ended December 31 would be $\frac{9}{12} \times (40\% \times \$1,000) = \$300$. In subsequent periods, the usual procedure is followed; that is, the asset's book value at the beginning of the period is multiplied by the constant rate. The next year, for example, depreciation would be $40\% \times (\$1,000 - \$300) = \$280$.

Because double declining-balance depreciation is also an accelerated depreciation method, it is appropriate in the same situations as the SYD method.

COMPARISON OF DEPRECIATION METHODS

The following chart compares the periodic depreciation expense from our example for the straight-line method, the sum-of-the-years'-digits method, and the double declining-balance method. The chart visually displays the accelerated nature of the latter two methods. The units-of-production method is not shown in the chart because there is no general pattern for the annual depreciation. The annual depreciation using the units-of-production method depends on the yearly productive activity of the asset, and this activity will vary from asset to asset.

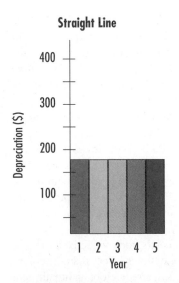

Straight Line

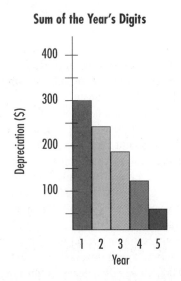

Sum of the Year's Digits

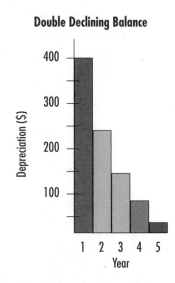

Double Declining Balance

POPULARITY OF STRAIGHT-LINE DEPRECIATION

The straight-line method is by far the most widely used depreciation method for financial reporting purposes. This method represents about 75% of the depreciation methods in use at 600 companies surveyed each year by the American Institute of Certified Public Accountants. A fairly recent convert to the straight-line method is Ford Motor Company. Beginning in 1993, plant assets placed in service at Ford are depreciated using straight line. Older plant assets are depreciated using an accelerated method. Ford changed to straight line because improvements in the design and flexibility of its machinery and equipment resulted in more uniform productive capacities over their useful lives.

REVISION OF DEPRECIATION

We have stressed that depreciation allocations are based on estimates of both useful lives and salvage values. Circumstances change, however, and original estimates may be too high or too low. Once it is determined that original estimates are wrong, the computation of periodic depreciation expense for the asset's remaining useful life must be revised. We revise a depreciation estimate by allocating the revised undepreciated balance of the asset over the revised remaining useful life. To illustrate this revision procedure, we use the data from our previous examples in which an asset costing $1,000 has a five-year life and an estimated salvage value of $100.

If, based on the original estimates, straight-line depreciation of $180 has been recorded for each of the first three years, the accumulated depreciation would be 3 × $180 = $540. Now suppose that just before recording the fourth year's depreciation, circumstances indicate that the asset's life will be six years instead of five and that its salvage value at the end of the sixth year will be $40. The revised depreciation expense to be taken during the revised remaining useful life is computed as follows:

Original asset cost	$1,000
Depreciation already recorded (3 years @ $180)	540
Book value at start of fourth year	$ 460
Revised salvage value	40
Revised remaining depreciation	$ 420
Revised remaining useful life	3 years
Revised periodic depreciation expense for fourth, fifth, and sixth years	$420/3 = $140 per year

IMPAIRMENT LOSSES

Sometimes the change in circumstances relating to a depreciable asset is so severe that future cash flows from its use and disposal are estimated to be *less* than its book value. If the book value will not be recovered through future cash flows, the asset is considered *impaired* and an impairment loss is recorded. The **impairment loss** is the difference between the asset's book value and its current fair value.[1]

To illustrate, assume that two years ago the Good Health Clinic purchased diagnostic equipment for $500,000 with an estimated useful life of six years and salvage value of $20,000. The equipment's book value today is $340,000 ($500,000 cost less $160,000 accumulated depreciation). Unanticipated technological advances in equipment acquired by competitors, however, now severely limit the diagnostic uses of Good Health's equipment. The clinic now expects the net cash flows from the use and disposal of its equipment over the next four years to be $300,000. The limited diagnostic uses of the equipment cause its current fair value to be $200,000.

Good Health's diagnostic equipment is impaired because its book value is not recoverable through future cash flows—the $300,000 of future cash flows is less than the equipment's $340,000 book value. An asset must be identified as impaired before an impairment loss may be recorded. The impairment loss is then computed by comparing the equipment's book value with its current fair value, as follows:

Equipment book value	$340,000
Equipment current fair value	200,000
Impairment loss	$140,000

The journal entry to record the loss follows:

Impairment Loss on Equipment	140,000	
Accumulated Depreciation—Equipment		140,000
To record impairment loss on equipment.		

PRINCIPLE ALERT

CONSERVATISM CONCEPT

The accounting analysis relating to impaired plant assets illustrates the *conservatism concept.* In selecting between alternative accounting measures, this basic principle of accounting states that the less optimistic measure should be used. When a plant asset is impaired, it ends up being reported on the balance sheet at its current fair value, an amount lower than its book value before the impairment loss is recorded. Unimpaired plant assets remain at book value even though current fair values are higher.

DEPRECIATION FOR TAX PURPOSES

Depreciation expense is deducted by a business on its federal income tax return. The amount on the tax return, however, may differ substantially from the amount reported in the firm's income statement because the calculation of tax depreciation follows income tax regulations. The specific procedures for tax purposes depend on the year the asset was acquired. Assets acquired before 1981 are depreciated over their useful lives, and the acceptable methods include straight line, units of production, sum of the years' digits, and double declining balance. For property acquired from 1981 through 1986, tax depreciation is calculated under a special accelerated method called the **accelerated cost recovery system (ACRS).** The ACRS procedures are modified, and referred to as the **modified accelerated**

---

[1]*Statement of Financial Accounting Standards No. 121,* "Accounting for the Impairment of Long-Lived Assets and for Long-Lived Assets to Be Disposed Of," (Norwalk, CT: Financial Accounting Standards Board, 1995).

cost recovery system (MACRS), for assets acquired after 1986. Both ACRS and MACRS permit firms the option of using a straight-line method. However, salvage value is ignored under ACRS, MACRS, and the straight-line options to these procedures.

ACRS and MACRS establish classes of property with prescribed write-off periods. For assets acquired after 1986, MACRS establishes eight property classes with prescribed write-off periods ranging from 3 years to 31.5 years. Most machinery and equipment, for example, are in a seven-year class. When acquired, property is placed in the appropriate class (per tax guidelines) and depreciated over the prescribed period following the method specified for that class.[2]

ACRS was introduced into the tax law to encourage companies to invest in plant assets. Because the write-off period under ACRS and MACRS is usually shorter than an asset's useful life, these methods provide larger depreciation deductions during an asset's early years than was previously possible. In a sense, these accelerated deductions provide an interest-free loan to the firm because they allow the firm to pay less tax in the early phase of an asset's life and more in the later phase. During the intervening time, the firm can use the amount of funds equal to the postponed income tax payments.

Change and modification characterize the history of U.S. tax law. Tax depreciation guidelines will likely be modified again in the future. Keep in mind, however, that depreciation changes in the tax law do not affect the depreciation methods a firm may use in preparing its financial statements.

REVENUE EXPENDITURES

OBJECTIVE 3
DISCUSS the distinction between revenue and capital expenditures.

Revenue expenditures are expenditures relating to plant assets that are expensed when incurred. The following list identifies three common types of revenue expenditures:

1. Expenditures for ordinary maintenance and repairs of existing plant assets.
2. Expenditures to acquire low-cost items that benefit the firm for several periods.
3. Expenditures considered unnecessary or unreasonable in the circumstances.

MAINTENANCE AND REPAIRS

Some level of maintenance and repairs must be assumed when estimating useful lives and salvage values of property, plant, and equipment. For example, a plant asset that is not maintained or repaired will have a shorter useful life than a similar asset that is properly maintained. Periodic upkeep—such as lubrication, cleaning, and replacement of minor parts—is necessary to maintain an asset's expected level and length of usefulness. These periodic upkeep costs are charged to expense as they are incurred.

LOW-COST ITEMS

Most businesses purchase items that provide years of service at a relatively small cost, such as paperweights, ashtrays, and wastebaskets. Because of the small dollar amounts involved, establishing these items as assets and depreciating them over their expected useful lives really serve no useful purpose. The effect on the financial statements is not significant. Consequently, expensing these expenditures at the time of purchase is more efficient. The accounting for such low-cost items is thus completed in the period they are purchased.

UNNECESSARY OR UNREASONABLE COSTS

As noted earlier, costs of waste and inefficiency related to the acquisition of plant assets are expensed when incurred. Because an asset's initial cost includes only necessary and reasonable expenditures, any unnecessary or unreasonable outlays are expensed. An accountant may need to exercise considerable judgment, however, in determining whether a particular expenditure is necessary and reasonable. Identical expenditures may be treated

---

[2]Depreciation in most classes must follow a half-year convention whereby one-half of the first year's depreciation is taken in the first year (regardless of when the asset was acquired) and one-half of the last year's depreciation is taken in the year of disposal. The half-year convention means that assets in the 3-year property class are depreciated in four different accounting periods, assets in the 5-year property class are depreciated in six different accounting periods, and so on.

PRINCIPLE ALERT

MATERIALITY CONCEPT

The practice of accounting for small dollar transactions in the most expedient fashion follows the *materiality concept.* Under this concept, generally accepted accounting principles apply only to items of significance to the users of financial statements. Because the judgment of users will not be affected by the accounting for immaterial dollar amounts, their immediate expensing does not lessen the usefulness of financial statements.

differently, depending on the circumstances. For example, assume that a company pays an overtime premium to have a piece of equipment delivered on a holiday. If it is essential that the equipment be available for use on the next workday, the overtime premium should be added to the equipment's cost as a necessary and reasonable expenditure. In contrast, if the equipment could just as well be delivered on the next workday, the overtime premium is an unnecessary and wasteful expenditure that should be expensed.

CAPITAL EXPENDITURES

Capital expenditures increase the book value of long-term assets. To *capitalize* an amount, then, means to increase an asset's book value by that amount. Following are typical capital expenditures related to property, plant, and equipment:

1. Initial acquisitions and additions.
2. Betterments.
3. Extraordinary repairs.

INITIAL ACQUISITIONS AND ADDITIONS

Earlier in this chapter, we discussed the guidelines governing the initial measurement of plant assets. Expenditures equal to the asset's implied cash price plus the costs necessary to prepare the asset for use were debited to the asset account. These amounts were capital expenditures.

The same guidelines apply in accounting for additions to existing plant assets. Adding a new wing to a building or expanding the size of an asphalt parking lot are examples of additions. These capital expenditures should also be debited to an asset account. A separate account (and depreciation schedule) should be used for an addition when its estimated useful life differs from the remaining useful life of the existing plant asset.

BETTERMENTS

Betterments improve the quality of services rendered by a plant asset but do not necessarily extend its useful life. Examples include adding a power winch to a highway service truck or air conditioning to an automobile. In each instance, the vehicle's services are enhanced, but its useful life is not changed. Expenditures for betterments are debited to the appropriate asset account, and the subsequent periodic depreciation expense is increased to allocate the additional cost over the asset's remaining useful life.

Betterments may involve replacing a significant asset component with an improved component. Again, the cost of the new asset component should be added to the asset account and depreciated over the asset's remaining useful life. Further, the cost and accumulated depreciation of the replaced asset component should be removed from the accounts. For example, if a building's gas furnace is replaced by a more efficient model, the cost of the new furnace is added to the Building account, and the cost and applicable depreciation on the old furnace are removed from the accounts. The book value of the old asset component may be difficult to determine if it is not accounted for separately, but a reasonable estimate frequently can be made.

EXTRAORDINARY REPAIRS

Extraordinary repairs are expenditures that extend an asset's expected useful life beyond the original estimate. These capital expenditures are debited to the asset's Accumulated

Depreciation account (which increases the asset's book value). We charge Accumulated Depreciation because some of the previous years' depreciation presumably is recovered by the expenditures that extend the asset's useful life. Depreciation entries after an extraordinary repair should lead to the salvage value at the end of the revised (extended) useful life.

In practice, the distinctions among additions, betterments, and extraordinary repairs to plant assets often become blurred. Some expenditures, for example, may improve an asset's quality of services *and* extend its useful life. Accountants must use reasonable judgment to identify (and account for) the primary effect of the transaction.

DISPOSALS OF PLANT ASSETS

OBJECTIVE 4
EXPLAIN and **ILLUSTRATE** the accounting for disposals of plant assets.

A firm may dispose of a plant asset in a variety of ways. The asset may be sold, retired, or exchanged as partial payment for a new asset. The asset's usefulness to the firm may be ended by an unfavorable and unanticipated event—the asset may be stolen or destroyed by a natural disaster.

Depreciation must extend through an asset's total useful life to a firm. Therefore, depreciation must be recorded up to the disposal date, regardless of the manner of the asset's disposal. Should the disposal date not coincide with the end of an accounting period, a journal entry must record depreciation for a partial period (the period from the date depreciation was last recorded to the disposal date). We illustrate this partial period depreciation in our first example.

We use the following basic data to illustrate disposals of plant assets:

Equipment's original cost	$1,000
Estimated salvage value after five years	100
Annual straight-line depreciation	180
(Unless stated otherwise, assume that depreciation to the date of disposal has been recorded.)	

SALE OF PLANT ASSETS

Most sales of plant assets involve the following related factors:

1. The sale transaction exchanges a used plant asset for cash. Because the plant asset sold is no longer on hand, the journal entry must remove from both the asset and the accumulated depreciation accounts all amounts related to that asset. These amounts reflect the asset's book value.

2. Because plant assets are most often sold for amounts either higher or lower than their book values, gains or losses are produced. Sales proceeds in excess of book values create gains from the sales. Book values in excess of sales proceeds cause losses from the sales.

SOLD FOR MORE THAN BOOK VALUE

Assume that the equipment is sold for $230 midway through its fifth year. Depreciation was last recorded at the end of the fourth year. The related entries are

Depreciation Expense—Equipment	90	
Accumulated Depreciation—Equipment		90
To record depreciation expense for six months.		
Cash	230	
Accumulated Depreciation—Equipment	810	
Equipment		1,000
Gain on Sale of Plant Assets		40
To record sale of equipment for $230.		

Note that recording depreciation to the date of sale adds $90 to the Accumulated Depreciation account, which totals $(4 \times \$180) + \$90 = \$810$. To reflect the sale properly, we must remove this entire amount of accumulated depreciation from the books. The gain is the proceeds of $230 minus the asset's book value of $190.

SOLD FOR LESS THAN BOOK VALUE

Assume the equipment is sold for $30 at the end of the fifth year. The correct entry to record this sale is

Cash	30	
Loss on Sale of Plant Assets	70	
Accumulated Depreciation—Equipment	900	
Equipment		1,000
To record sale of equipment for $30.		

The loss equals the book value of $100 minus the sales proceeds of $30. The cash receipt is recorded, and balances from both accounts related to the asset—the asset account and its contra account—are removed from the books.

If the equipment is sold for an amount exactly equal to its book value, no gain or loss is involved. Should the equipment be abandoned, stolen, or destroyed (with no insurance coverage) before the end of its expected useful life, a loss equal to its book value will be recorded. Similarly, if the equipment is retired at the end of its useful life and has no sales value, we record a loss equal to its book value. Ideally, any asset that is scrapped at retirement has had a zero estimated salvage value and, thus, has a zero book value at retirement.

EXCHANGE OF PLANT ASSETS

A plant asset may be traded in for another plant asset. The seller of the new asset establishes a trade-in allowance for the used asset with the balance of the selling price due in cash. Normally, the cash payment represents a significant portion of the new asset's selling price. In these cases, the new plant asset is recorded at its fair value (its cash equivalent price).[3] The book value of the asset traded in is removed from the accounts. We determine any gain or loss on the exchange transaction by comparing the old asset's book value with its trade-in allowance. There is a gain if the trade-in allowance exceeds the old asset's book value; a loss exists if the book value exceeds the trade-in allowance. No gain or loss is recorded if the two amounts being compared are equal.

GAIN ON EXCHANGE

To illustrate an exchange of plant assets resulting in a recorded gain, assume that our equipment ($1,000 cost and $100 salvage value) is traded in after two years (accumulated depreciation, $360) on new equipment that has a $1,200 cash price. The old equipment receives a $700 trade-in allowance, so a $500 cash payment is required. The following entry records the exchange:

Equipment (New)	1,200	
Accumulated Depreciation—Equipment	360	
Equipment (Old)		1,000
Cash		500
Gain on Exchange of Plant Assets		60
To record trade of equipment.		

The $60 gain on the transaction is the excess of the old equipment's trade-in allowance ($700) over its book value ($640).

LOSS ON EXCHANGE

Now assume that the old equipment exchanged in the preceding example receives a $400 trade-in allowance. With this allowance, an $800 cash payment is required. The journal entry for this exchange of plant assets shows a loss on the exchange, as follows:

---

[3]When the cash payment is less than 25% of the total fair value exchanged, accounting guidelines require, in certain instances, that any gain inherent in the transaction not be recognized and that the new asset be recorded at the sum of the book value of the asset traded in plus any cash paid. See *EITF Abstracts, A Summary of Proceedings of the FASB Emerging Issues Task Force,* Issue No. 86-29 (Norwalk, CT: Financial Accounting Standards Board, 1994). The guidelines for these nonroutine exchanges are best covered in more advanced accounting courses.

Equipment (New)	1,200	
Accumulated Depreciation—Equipment	360	
Loss on Exchange of Plant Assets	240	
Equipment (Old)		1,000
Cash		800
To record trade of equipment.		

The $240 loss on the transaction is the excess of the old equipment's book value ($640) over its trade-in allowance ($400).

TRADE-IN AND TAX REGULATIONS

The Internal Revenue Code specifies that any gains or losses on trade-in transactions involving similar assets not be reported in the year of exchange. Under income tax guidelines, the new asset acquired when similar plant assets are exchanged is recorded at the book value of the asset given up plus any cash paid. This treatment differs from the accounting guidelines just discussed. Accounting guidelines recognize all losses and most gains on trade-in transactions involving similar plant assets. Some firms, however, may follow the income tax method when losses and gains are immaterial to avoid keeping a separate record for income tax purposes.

NATURAL RESOURCES

OBJECTIVE 5

DISCUSS the nature of and the accounting for natural resources.

Natural resources are assets occurring in a natural state, such as timber, petroleum, natural gas, coal, and other mineral deposits mined by the extractive industries. These resources are also known as **wasting assets**. As with plant assets, natural resources are initially accounted for at their cost. When known deposits are purchased, the initial measurement is quite simple. When the natural resource is discovered after extensive exploration, however, determining its initial cost is more difficult. Because not all exploration activities are successful, we must determine which activities were necessary to discover the resource. Expenditures for these activities are capitalized as the cost of the resource, and the remaining amounts are expensed. The cost of developing the site so the natural resource may be extracted is another component of initial cost. Expenditures to remove layers of soil and clay, build access roads, and construct mine entrances illustrate these development costs.

DEPLETION

The term **depletion** refers to the allocation of the cost of natural resources to the units extracted from the ground or, in the case of timberland, the board feet of timber cut. Accounting for the depletion of natural resources is comparable to units-of-production depreciation of plant assets. The average depletion cost per unit of natural resource is computed as follows:

$$\text{Depletion per Unit} = \frac{\text{Cost of Natural Resource} - \text{Residual Value}}{\text{Estimated Total Units of Resource}}$$

The unit measure used depends on the natural resource; the unit may be barrels, tons, board feet, cubic feet, or some other unit appropriate for the resource. Residual value is the expected net recovery (sales proceeds – restoration costs) when the property is eventually sold. Once depletion per unit is computed, periodic depletion is determined as follows:

$$\text{Periodic Depletion} = \text{Depletion per Unit} \times \text{Units Extracted in Current Period}$$

For example, assume that a company acquires for $520,000 a parcel of land whose major commercial value is a soft coal mine that contains an estimated 800,000 tons of extractable coal. Development costs of $100,000 are incurred to prepare the site for mining coal. The property's estimated residual value is $20,000 ($115,000 expected sales value – $95,000 estimated costs to recondition the land). The coal deposit's initial cost is $620,000 ($520,000 acquisition cost + $100,000 development costs). We calculate the depletion per ton of mined coal as follows:

$$\frac{\$620,000 - \$20,000}{800,000 \text{ tons}} = \$0.75 \text{ per ton}$$

If, during the first period, 60,000 tons are extracted, that period's depletion charge would be $60,000 \times \$0.75 = \$45,000$. We would make the following entry:

Depletion of Coal Deposit	45,000	
Accumulated Depletion—Coal Deposit		45,000
To record depletion of coal deposit.		

In the balance sheet, Accumulated Depletion is a contra account deducted from the cost of the natural resource. The disposition of the periodic depletion charge depends on whether the extracted units are sold or on hand at the end of the period. The depletion amount of units sold is deducted in the income statement as part of the cost of the resource sold. Units on hand at year-end, however, constitute inventory items, so their depletion charge appears in the balance sheet as part of the inventory cost. In addition to the depletion charge, the costs of extracting and processing the natural resource are part of the inventory cost.

Assume, for example, that $81,000 of extracting and processing costs are incurred the first period to mine the 60,000 tons of coal. The total cost of the 60,000 mined tons is $126,000 ($45,000 depletion + $81,000 extracting and processing costs); the average cost per ton is $2.10 ($126,000/60,000 tons). If 40,000 tons are sold during the first period, $84,000 (40,000 tons × $2.10 per ton) is expensed in the income statement as the cost of coal sold. The year-end balance sheet will show a mined coal inventory of $42,000 (20,000 tons × $2.10 per ton).

DEPRECIATION OF ON-SITE EQUIPMENT

The extraction of many natural resources requires the construction of *on-site* equipment, such as drilling and pumping devices, crushing equipment, and conveyor systems. Often in remote places, this equipment may be abandoned when the natural resource is exhausted. If the useful life of these assets expires before the resources are exhausted, ordinary depreciation techniques are appropriate. When the reverse is true—natural resources are exhausted, and the asset is abandoned before the end of its physical life—depreciation should be based on the length of the extraction period. Alternatively, we could use the units-of-production approach based on the estimated total resource to be extracted.

For example, assume coal mining equipment was acquired at a cost of $210,000 in our preceding example. The equipment has an estimated $10,000 salvage value after the coal is mined. If the units-of-production method were used, depreciation per ton for the first year would be

$$\frac{\$210,000 - \$10,000}{800,000 \text{ tons}} = \$0.25 \text{ per ton}$$

The first year's depreciation, when 60,000 tons are mined, is $60,000 \times \$0.25 = \$15,000$.

INTANGIBLE ASSETS

OBJECTIVE 6
DISCUSS the nature of and the accounting for intangible assets.

In accounting, **intangible assets** include certain resources that benefit an enterprise's operations but lack physical substance. Several intangible assets are exclusive rights or privileges obtained from a governmental unit or by legal contract—such as patents, copyrights, franchises, trademarks, and leaseholds. Other intangible assets (1) arise from the creation of a business enterprise—namely, organization costs—or (2) reflect a firm's ability to generate above-normal earnings—that is, goodwill.

The term *intangible asset* is not used with precision in accounting literature. By convention, only certain assets are included in the intangible category. Some resources that lack physical substance—such as prepaid insurance, receivables, and investments—are not classified as intangible assets. Because intangible assets lack physical characteristics, the related accounting procedures may be more subjective and arbitrary than for tangible assets.

MEASUREMENT OF INTANGIBLE ASSETS

A firm should record intangible assets acquired from outside entities initially at their cost. Similarly, some intangible assets created internally by a firm are measured at their cost. For example, the costs of forming a business are charged to an Organization Costs account, and the costs to secure a trademark—such as attorney's fees, registration fees, and design costs—are charged to a Trademarks account.

The accounting for other expenditures related to intangible assets varies, depending on the type of expenditure and the nature of the intangible asset. *Research and development costs* are not capitalized as part of any intangible assets, because accounting guidelines require that these expenditures be expensed when incurred.[4] Thus, many significant costs incurred by a firm in developing a patentable product or process are not capitalized. Legal costs associated with patent work may be capitalized, however. The costs of developing, maintaining, or restoring an intangible asset are also expensed when incurred, provided the asset is not specifically identifiable, has an indeterminate life, or is inherent in the business as a whole—such as goodwill. As a result of these procedures, some companies may have important intangible assets that are carried at a nominal amount or may even fail to appear on the firm's financial statements.

AMORTIZATION OF INTANGIBLES

The **amortization** of an intangible asset is the periodic write-off to expense of the asset's cost over the term of its expected useful life. Because salvage values are ordinarily not involved, amortization typically entails (1) determining the asset's cost, (2) estimating the period over which it benefits the firm, and (3) allocating the cost in equal amounts to each accounting period involved. *Accounting principles modify this general approach by specifying that the period of amortization for intangibles should not exceed 40 years.*[5] As a result, intangibles are treated as if they have a limited life—even though some, such as trademarks, may legally have indefinite lives. Straight-line amortization must be used for intangible assets unless another method is shown to be more appropriate.

The amortization entry debits the appropriate amortization expense account. The entry's credit normally goes directly to the intangible asset account. An accumulated amortization account could be used for the credit, but generally there is no particular benefit to financial statement users from accumulating amortization in a separate contra asset account. In our examples, we will credit the asset account directly for its periodic amortization.

EXAMPLES OF INTANGIBLE ASSETS

A **patent** is an exclusive privilege granted to an inventor by the federal government for a period of 20 years from the date the patent application was filed. The patent gives the patent holder the right to exclude others from making, using, or selling the invention. Patent laws were originated to encourage inventors by protecting them from imitators who might usurp the invention for commercial gain. Just what a patentable idea is has become quite complex in the modern realm of technical knowledge. Consequently, long periods of patent "searching" and, frequently, successful defense of infringement suits may precede the validation of a patent. Even though patents have a legal life of 20 years from application date, changes

POINT OF INTEREST

GATT CHANGES PATENT LIFE

As a result of the implementation of the General Agreement on Tariffs and Trade (GATT), the term of U.S. patents changed beginning June 8, 1995. Effective that date, U.S. patents that are granted run for 20 years starting from the date the patent application was filed. Patents granted before June 8, 1995, run for 17 years from the date the patent was issued. Many patent applications, especially those in biotechnology and other high-tech areas, take more than three years to process and issue. Thus, the GATT agreement has shortened the economic useful life for many U.S. patents.

---

[4]*Statement of Financial Accounting Standards No. 2,* "Accounting for Research and Development Costs" (Stamford, CT: Financial Accounting Standards Board, 1974).

[5]*Opinions of the Accounting Principles Board, No. 17,* "Accounting for Intangible Assets" (New York: American Institute of Certified Public Accountants, 1970).

in technology or consumer tastes may shorten their economic life. Because of their uncertain value, patents should probably be accounted for conservatively. When patents are purchased some time after having been granted, the buyer enjoys the privilege at most for only the remaining legal life.

To illustrate the accounting for patents, assume that, early in January, a company pays $30,000 legal costs incurred to obtain a patent on a new product. The journal entry is

Patents	30,000	
Cash		30,000
To record legal costs of acquiring patent.		

The company expects the patent to provide benefits for 15 years. The following entry records the first year's straight-line amortization:

Amortization Expense—Patents	2,000	
Patents		2,000
To record patent amortization ($30,000/15 = $2,000).		

Because an accumulated amortization account is not used, the asset account balance reflects the asset's book value. The balance sheet presentation at year-end would be

Patents (cost less amortization to date) $28,000

A **copyright** protects its owner against the unauthorized reproduction of a specific written work or artwork. A copyright lasts for the life of the author plus 50 years. The purchase price of valuable copyrights can be substantial, and proper measurement and amortization are necessary for valid income determination. But even with the related legal fees, the cost of most copyrights is seldom sufficiently material to present accounting problems.

Franchises most often involve exclusive rights to operate or sell a specific brand of products in a given geographic area. Franchises may be for definite or indefinite periods. Although many franchises are agreements between two private firms, various governmental units award franchises for public utility operations within their legal jurisdictions. The right to operate a Kentucky Fried Chicken restaurant or to sell Midas Mufflers in a specific area illustrates franchise agreements in the private sector.

Some franchise agreements require a substantial initial payment by the party acquiring the franchise. This amount should be debited to the intangible asset account Franchise and amortized on a straight-line basis over the franchise period or 40 years, whichever is shorter.

Trademarks and **trade names** represent the exclusive and continuing right to use certain terms, names, or symbols, usually to identify a brand or family of products. An original trademark or trade name can be registered with the federal government at nominal cost. A company may spend considerable time and money to determine an appropriate name or symbol for a product. Also, the purchase of well-known, and thus valuable, trademarks or trade names may involve substantial amounts of funds. When the cost of a trademark or trade name is material, the amount is debited to an appropriate intangible asset account—Trademarks, for example—and amortized over the period of expected benefit (not exceeding 40 years).

Expenditures incurred in launching a business (usually a corporation) are called **organization costs.** These expenditures, which may include attorney's fees, fees paid to the state, and other costs related to preparation for operations, are debited to the intangible asset account Organization Costs. Theoretically, these expenditures benefit the firm throughout its operating life, but all intangibles must be amortized over 40 years or less. Most firms amortize organization costs over a 5- to 10-year period. Income tax guidelines reinforce this practice by permitting the amortization of organization costs for tax purposes over a period of at least five years.

Goodwill is the value derived from a firm's ability to earn more than a normal rate of return on the fair market value of its specific, identifiable net assets. The measurement of

GOODWILL CAN BE A SIGNIFICANT ASSET

Even though accountants only record goodwill when an entire business entity is purchased (to the extent that the purchase price exceeds the fair value of the identifiable net assets acquired), the balance sheets of many major corporations contain significant amounts of goodwill. Recent balance sheets, for example, show the following amounts of goodwill: Ford Motor Company, $2.6 billion; The Black & Decker Corporation, $2.3 billion; Union Pacific Corporation, $1.32 billion; Hershey Foods Corporation, $473.4 million; Pitney Bowes Inc, $231.3 million, and Pfizer Inc, $231.1 million. These amounts are evidence of the active acquisition efforts of major corporations.

goodwill is complex, because it can stem from any factor that can make income rates high relative to investment. Examples of such factors include exceptional customer relations, advantageous location, operating efficiency, superior personnel relations, favorable financial sources, and even monopolistic position. Furthermore, goodwill cannot be severed from a firm and sold separately. Because measuring goodwill is difficult, a firm records it in the accounts only when another firm is purchased and the amount paid exceeds the recognized fair market value of the identifiable net assets acquired. Determining the amount of goodwill often requires complex negotiations, but the agreed-on amount is almost always based on the anticipated above-normal earnings.

BALANCE SHEET PRESENTATION

OBJECTIVE 7

ILLUSTRATE the balance sheet presentation of plant assets, natural resources, and intangible assets.

Plant assets, natural resources, and intangible assets usually are presented in the balance sheet below the sections for current assets and investments. Exhibit 8-3 shows how these assets may appear on a balance sheet.

EXHIBIT 8-3	Balance Sheet Presentation of Plant Assets, Natural Resources, and Intangible Assets (in Thousands of Dollars)

Plant Assets		
Land		$ 800
Buildings	$4,600	
Less: Accumulated Depreciation	1,200	3,400
Fixtures	$ 90	
Less: Accumulated Depreciation	20	70
Equipment	$1,400	
Less: Accumulated Depreciation	300	1,100
Leasehold Improvements	$ 226	
Less: Accumulated Depreciation	81	145
Total Plant Assets		$5,515
Natural Resources		
Timberland	$ 500	
Less: Accumulated Depletion	200	$ 300
Coal Deposit	$ 900	
Less: Accumulated Depletion	150	750
Total Natural Resources		$1,050
Intangible Assets (Cost less amortization to date)		
Patents		$ 200
Goodwill		500
Organization Costs		100
Total Intangible Assets		$ 800

FINANCIAL ANALYSIS

OBJECTIVE 8

DEFINE return on assets *and* asset turnover *and* **EXPLAIN** *their use.*

RETURN ON ASSETS AND ASSET TURNOVER

The ability of a firm to use its assets effectively and efficiently in its operations is a sign of a healthy, well-managed company. The rate of return on assets, generally referred to as *return on assets,* is a widely used ratio that focuses on this dimension of a firm's financial profile. In practice, there is some variation in the computation of this ratio. One typical computation of **return on assets** is as follows:

$$\text{Return on Assets} = \frac{\text{Net Income}}{\text{Average Total Assets}}$$

This ratio relates data from two financial statements—the income statement and the balance sheet. The numerator consists of the net income for the year.[6] The denominator in the ratio is the average amount of assets used during the year (sum total assets at the beginning of the year and total assets at the end of the year and divide the sum by 2).

To illustrate the computation of return on assets, we use data from a recent year for The Coca-Cola Company. The company reported, in millions, a net income of $2,176, total assets at the beginning of the year of $11,052, and year-end total assets of $12,021. Coca-Cola's return on assets for the year is 18.9%, computed as $2,176/[($11,052 + $12,021)/2].

To evaluate a firm's return on assets, we should consider the trend in the ratio, the return for other firms in the industry, the industry average, and the economic environment. For example, in the year that The Coca-Cola Company generated an 18.9% return on assets, competitor PepsiCo, Inc., had a 7.1% return on assets. For that year, The Coca-Cola Company utilized its assets more profitably than did PepsiCo, Inc.

The **asset turnover** ratio is another ratio that deals with the use of assets. This ratio measures how effectively a firm generates sales revenue from its investment in assets. The asset turnover ratio is computed as follows:

$$\text{Asset Turnover} = \frac{\text{Net Sales}}{\text{Average Total Assets}}$$

Continuing our use of data from a recent year for The Coca-Cola Company, the firm reported net operating revenues (which is equivalent to net sales), in millions, of $13,957. Coca-Cola's asset turnover for the year is 1.21, computed as $13,957/[($11,052 + $12,021)/2]. The higher the asset turnover is, the more effective the company is in using its assets to generate sales revenue. For the preceding year, Coca-Cola's asset turnover was 1.23. The decrease in Coca-Cola's ratio from 1.23 to 1.21, therefore, indicates that the firm declined slightly in the second year in the revenue-generating effectiveness of its assets.

KEY POINTS FOR CHAPTER LEARNING OBJECTIVES

1 **DISCUSS** the nature of plant asset accounting and **IDENTIFY** the guidelines relating to the initial measurement of plant assets (pp. 269–273).
  - Plant asset accounting involves the proper handling of a plant asset's initial measurement, depreciation, subsequent capital expenditures, and disposal.
  - The initial cost of a plant asset is its implied cash price plus the expenditures necessary to prepare it for use.
  - A portion of actual interest cost is included in a plant asset's initial cost if a period of time is required to get the asset ready for use.

2 **DISCUSS** the nature of the depreciation process, **ILLUSTRATE** four depreciation methods, and **EXPLAIN** impairment losses (pp. 273–281).
  - Depreciation is a cost allocation process; it allocates a plant asset's depreciable cost (acquisition cost less salvage value) in a systematic and rational manner over the asset's estimated useful life.
  - The most commonly used depreciation methods are straight line, units of production, sum of the years' digits, and declining balance.

---

[6]An alternate computation adds interest expense to net income in the ratio's numerator. This variation keeps the method of financing the assets from influencing the ratio.

- Revisions of depreciation are accomplished by recalculating depreciation charges for current and subsequent periods.
- When a plant asset is impaired, a loss is recognized equal to the difference between the asset's book value and current fair value.

3 **DISCUSS** the distinction between revenue and capital expenditures (pp. 281–283).
- Revenue expenditures, expensed as incurred, include the performance of ordinary repairs and maintenance, the purchase of low-cost items, and the incurrence of unnecessary or unreasonable outlays.
- Capital expenditures, which increase a plant asset's book value, include initial acquisitions, additions, betterments, and extraordinary repairs.

4 **EXPLAIN** and **ILLUSTRATE** the accounting for disposals of plant assets (pp. 283–285).
- When a firm disposes of a plant asset, depreciation must be recorded on the asset up to the disposal date.
- Gains and losses on plant asset dispositions are determined by comparing the assets' book values to the proceeds received.

5 **DISCUSS** the nature of and the accounting for natural resources (pp. 285–286).
- Natural resources are initially measured at their cost.
- Depletion is the allocation of a natural resource's cost to the resource units as they are mined, cut, or otherwise extracted from their source.
- The units-of-production depreciation method may be appropriate for equipment used exclusively in the mining and extracting of natural resources.

6 **DISCUSS** the nature of and the accounting for intangible assets (pp. 286–289).
- Intangible assets acquired from outside entities are initially measured at their cost. Some internally created intangible assets are also measured at their cost (such as organization costs and trademarks), but most expenditures related to internally created intangible assets are expensed rather than capitalized.
- Research and development costs related to a firm's products and its production processes are expensed as incurred.
- Amortization is the periodic write-off to expense of an intangible asset's cost over the asset's useful life or 40 years, whichever is shorter.
- Goodwill reflects a firm's ability to generate above-normal earnings. Goodwill may be shown in the accounts only when it has been purchased.

7 **ILLUSTRATE** the balance sheet presentation of plant assets, natural resources, and intangible assets (p. 289).
- Plant assets, natural resources, and intangible assets usually appear in the balance sheet after current assets and investments.

8 **Financial Analysis** **DEFINE** *return on assets* and *asset turnover* and **EXPLAIN** their use (p. 290).
- Return on assets is computed by dividing net income by average total assets.
- Asset turnover is computed by dividing net sales by average total assets. It measures the effectiveness of assets in generating sales revenues.

SELF-TEST QUESTIONS FOR REVIEW

(Answers follow the Solution to Demonstration Problem.)

1. The initial cost of a plant asset is equal to the asset's implied cash price and
   a. The interest paid on any debt incurred to finance the asset's purchase.
   b. The market value of any noncash assets given up to acquire the plant asset.
   c. The reasonable and necessary costs incurred to prepare the asset for use.
   d. The asset's estimated salvage value.

2. On January 1, 1996, Rio Company purchased a delivery truck for $10,000. The company estimates the truck will be driven 80,000 miles over its eight-year useful life. The estimated salvage value is $2,000. The truck was driven 12,000 miles in 1996. Which method results in the largest 1996 depreciation expense?
   a. Sum of the years' digits   c. Straight line
   b. Units of production   d. Double declining balance

3. On the first day of the current year, Blakely Company sold equipment for less than its book value. Which of the following is part of the journal entry to record the sale?
   a. A debit to Equipment
   b. A credit to Accumulated Depreciation—Equipment
   c. A credit to Gain on Sale of Plant Assets
   d. A debit to Loss on Sale of Plant Assets

4. Accounting for the periodic depletion of natural resources is similar to which depreciation method?
   - **a.** Straight line
   - **b.** Units of production
   - **c.** Sum of the years' digits
   - **d.** Double declining balance

5. The value derived from a firm's ability to earn more than a normal rate of return on its specific, identifiable net assets is called
   - **a.** A franchise.
   - **b.** Goodwill.
   - **c.** A patent.
   - **d.** Organization costs.

DEMONSTRATION PROBLEM FOR REVIEW

Segman Company purchased a machine in 1996 for $24,300. The machine has an expected useful life of three years and a salvage value of $900. The company expects to use the machine for 1,400 hours the first year, 2,000 hours the second year, and 1,600 hours the third year.

REQUIRED

a. Assume that the machine was purchased on January 2, 1996. Compute each year's depreciation expense for 1996–1998 using each of the following depreciation methods: (1) straight line, (2) units of production (actual usage equals expected usage), (3) sum of the years' digits, and (4) double declining balance.

b. Assume that the machine was purchased June 1, 1996. Compute each year's depreciation expense for 1996–1999 using each of the following depreciation methods: (1) straight line, (2) sum of the years' digits, and (3) double declining balance.

SOLUTION TO DEMONSTRATION PROBLEM

a. 1. Straight line:
   1996: ($24,300 − $900)/3 = $7,800
   1997: ($24,300 − $900)/3 = $7,800
   1998: ($24,300 − $900)/3 = $7,800

2. Units of production:
   Depreciation per hour = ($24,300 − $900)/5,000 hours = $4.68 per hour
   1996: 1,400 hours × $4.68 = $6,552
   1997: 2,000 hours × $4.68 = $9,360
   1998: 1,600 hours × $4.68 = $7,488

3. Sum of the years' digits:
   SYD = 3 + 2 + 1 = 6
   1996: ($24,300 − $900) × 3/6 = $11,700
   1997: ($24,300 − $900) × 2/6 = $7,800
   1998: ($24,300 − $900) × 1/6 = $3,900

4. Double declining balance:
   Twice straight-line rate = (100%/3) × 2 = $66\frac{2}{3}\%$
   1996: $24,300 × $66\frac{2}{3}\%$ = $16,200
   1997: ($24,300 − $16,200) × $66\frac{2}{3}\%$ = $5,400
   1998: ($24,300 − $21,600) × $66\frac{2}{3}\%$ = $1,800

b. 1. Straight line REFER TO CALCULATIONS IN (a)1.
   1996: $7,800 × $\frac{7}{12}$ = $4,550
   1997: $7,800 (full year's depreciation)
   1998: $7,800 (full year's depreciation)
   1999: $7,800 × $\frac{5}{12}$ = $3,250

2. Sum of the years' digits REFER TO CALCULATIONS IN (a)3.
   1996: $11,700 × $\frac{7}{12}$ = $6,825
   1997: ($11,700 × $\frac{5}{12}$) + ($7,800 × $\frac{7}{12}$) = $9,425
   1998: ($7,800 × $\frac{5}{12}$) + ($3,900 × $\frac{7}{12}$) = $5,525
   1999: $3,900 × $\frac{5}{12}$ = $1,625

3. Double declining balance REFER TO CALCULATIONS IN (a)4.
   1996: $16,200 × $\frac{7}{12}$ = $9,450
   1997: ($24,300 − $9,450) × $66\frac{2}{3}\%$ = $9,900
   1998: ($24,300 − $19,350) × $66\frac{2}{3}\%$ = $3,300
   1999: $750 [This amount reduces the machine's book value to its salvage value of $900 and is the maximum depreciation expense for 1999. ($24,300 − $22,650) × $66\frac{2}{3}\%$ = $1,100 gives an amount in excess of the maximum $750 depreciation.]

ANSWERS TO SELF-TEST QUESTIONS   **1.** c, p. 270   **2.** d, p. 278   **3.** d, p. 284   **4.** b, p. 285   **5.** b, p. 288

GLOSSARY OF KEY TERMS USED IN THIS CHAPTER

accelerated cost recovery system (ACRS, MACRS)   A system of accelerated depreciation for tax purposes introduced in 1981 (ACRS) and modified starting in 1987 (MACRS); it prescribes depreciation rates by asset classification for assets acquired after 1980 (p. 280).

accelerated depreciation method   Any depreciation method under which the amounts of depreciation expense taken in the early years of an asset's life are larger than the amounts expensed in the later years (p. 276).

amortization   The periodic writing off of an account balance to expense; usually refers to the writing off of an intangible asset (p. 287).

asset turnover   Net sales divided by average total assets (p. 290).

betterments   Capital expenditures that improve the quality of services rendered by a plant asset but do not necessarily extend its useful life (p. 282).

capital expenditures   Expenditures that increase the book value of long-term assets (p. 282).

capitalization of interest   A process that adds interest to an asset's initial cost if a period of time is required to prepare the asset for use (p. 272).

copyright   An exclusive right that protects an owner against the unauthorized reproduction of a specific written work or artwork (p. 288).

declining-balance method   An accelerated depreciation method that allocates depreciation expense to each year by applying a constant percentage to the declining book value of the asset (p. 277).

depletion   The allocation of the cost of natural resources to the units extracted from the ground or, in the case of timberland, the board feet of timber cut (p. 285).

depreciation   The decline in economic potential of plant assets originating from wear, deterioration, and obsolescence (p. 273).

depreciation accounting   The process of allocating the cost of plant assets (less salvage value) to expense in a systematic and rational manner over the time period benefitting from their use (p. 273).

extraordinary repairs   Expenditures that extend a plant asset's useful life beyond the original estimate (p. 282).

fixed assets   An alternate label for plant assets; may also be called *property, plant, and equipment* (p. 269).

franchise   Generally, an exclusive right to operate or sell a specific brand of products in a given geographic area (p. 288).

goodwill   The value that derives from a firm's ability to earn more than a normal rate of return on the fair market value of its specific, identifiable net assets (p. 288).

impairment loss   A loss recognized on an impaired asset equal to the difference between its book value and current fair value (p. 280).

intangible assets   A term applied to a group of long-term assets, including patents, copyrights, franchises, trademarks, and goodwill, that benefit an entity but do not have physical substance (p. 286).

land improvements   Improvements with limited lives made to land sites, such as paved parking lots and driveways (p. 273).

leasehold improvements   Expenditures made by a lessee to alter or improve leased property (p. 273).

modified accelerated cost recovery system   See *accelerated cost recovery system* (p. 280).

natural resources   Assets occurring in a natural state, such as timber, petroleum, natural gas, coal, and other mineral deposits (p. 285).

organization costs   Expenditures incurred in launching a business (usually a corporation), including attorney's fees and various fees paid to the state (p. 288).

patent   An exclusive privilege granted for 20 years to an inventor that gives the patent holder the right to exclude others from making, using, or selling the invention (p. 287).

plant assets   A firm's property, plant, and equipment (p. 269).

return on assets   A financial ratio computed as net income divided by average total assets (p. 290).

revenue expenditures   Expenditures related to plant assets that are expensed when incurred (p. 281).

salvage value   The expected net recovery when a plant asset is sold or removed from service. Also called *residual value* (p. 273).

straight-line method   A depreciation method that allocates equal amounts of depreciation expense to each full period of an asset's useful life (p. 274).

sum-of-the-years'-digits method   An accelerated depreciation method that allocates depreciation expense to each year in a fractional proportion, the denominator of which is the sum of the years' digits in the useful life of the asset and the numerator of which is the remaining useful life of the asset at the beginning of the current depreciation period (p. 276).

trademark   An exclusive and continuing right to use a certain symbol to identify a brand or family of products (p. 288).

trade name   An exclusive and continuing right to use a certain term or name to identify a brand or family of products (p. 288).

units-of-production method   A depreciation method that allocates depreciation expense to each operating period in proportion to the amount of the asset's expected total production capacity used each period (p. 275).

useful life   The period of time an asset is used by an entity in its operating activities, running from date of acquisition to date of disposal (or removal from service) (p. 273).

wasting assets   Another name for natural resources. See *natural resources* (p. 285).

QUESTIONS

8-1 What are the three major types of long-term assets that require a periodic write-off? Present examples of each, and indicate for each type the term that denotes the periodic write-off to expense.

8-2 In what way is land different from other plant assets?

8-3 In general, what amounts constitute the initial cost of plant assets?

8-4 Wyler Company borrowed $3,500,000 to finance the purchase of a new office building, which was ready for immediate use. May Wyler add a portion of the interest cost on the $3,500,000 to the building's cost? Explain.

8-5 Foss Company bought land with a vacant building for $400,000. Foss will use the building in its operations. Must Foss allocate the purchase price between the land and building? Why or why not? Would your answer be different if Foss intends to raze the building and build a new one? Why or why not?

8-6 Why is the recognition of depreciation expense necessary to match revenue and expense properly?

8-7 What is the pattern of plant asset utility (or benefit) that is appropriate for each of the following depreciation methods: (a) straight line, (b) units of production, (c) sum of the years' digits, and (d) double declining balance?

8-8 How should we handle a revision of depreciation charges due to a change in an asset's estimated useful life or salvage value? Which periods—past, present, or future—are affected by the revision?

8-9 When is a plant asset considered to be impaired? How is an impairment loss calculated?

8-10 What is the benefit of accelerating depreciation for income tax purposes when the total depreciation taken is no more than if straight-line depreciation were used?

8-11 Identify three types of revenue expenditures. What is the proper accounting for revenue expenditures?

8-12 Identify three types of capital expenditures. What is the proper accounting for capital expenditures?

8-13 What is the difference between an ordinary repair and an extraordinary repair? What is the rationale for charging extraordinary repairs to accumulated depreciation?

8-14 What factors determine the gain or loss on the sale of a plant asset?

8-15 What is the definition of *depletion?* The total depletion charge for a period may not all be expensed in the same period. Explain.

8-16 Folger Company installed a conveyor system that cost $192,000. The system can be used only in the excavation of gravel at a particular site. Folger expects to excavate gravel at the site for 10 years. Over how many years should the conveyor be depreciated if its physical life is estimated at (a) 8 years and (b) 12 years?

8-17 What are six different types of intangible assets? Briefly explain the nature of each type.

8-18 How should a firm account for research and development costs?

8-19 What is the maximum amortization period for an intangible asset?

8-20 Under what circumstances is goodwill recorded?

8-21 How is *return on assets* computed? What does this ratio show?

8-22 How is the *asset turnover ratio* computed? What does this ratio show?

PRINCIPLES DISCUSSION QUESTION

8-23 Prairie Laboratories provides laboratory services for a number of medical clinics. It has just purchased new equipment for $250,000 that will be used in a test designed to detect the presence of certain human genes. Prairie has just started to provide this particular testing service. Demand for this type of test is modest right now, but Prairie expects a significant expansion of demand over the next several years. Prairie also expects the new equipment will be technically obsolete in four years. The controller suggests to you that the new equipment's depreciable cost be assigned to depreciation expense over the four years as follows: 10% the first year, 20% the second year, 30% the third year, and 40% the fourth year. Calling this method "reverse sum of the years' digits," the controller asks for your comments on his suggestion.

Prepare a reply to the controller indicating whether his proposed depreciation method is appropriate. In your response, consider the purpose of depreciation accounting and the criteria used to evaluate the propriety of a depreciation method.

EXERCISES

INITIAL COST OF PLANT ASSET
— OBJ. 1 —

8-24 The following data relate to a firm's purchase of a machine used in the manufacture of its product:

Invoice price	$20,000
Applicable sales tax	1,200
Cash discount taken for prompt payment	400
Freight paid	260
Cost of insurance coverage on machine while in transit	125
Installation costs	1,000
Testing and adjusting costs	475
Repair of damages to machine caused by the firm's employees	550
Prepaid maintenance contract for first year of machine's use	300

Compute the initial amount at which the machine should be carried in the firm's accounts.

ALLOCATION OF PACKAGE PURCHASE PRICE
— OBJ. 1 —

8-25 Tamock Company purchased a small established plant from one of its suppliers. The $975,000 purchase price included the land, a building, and factory machinery. Tamock also paid $5,000 in legal fees to negotiate the purchase of the plant. Various property tax bills for the plant showed the following assessed values for the items purchased:

Property	Assessed Value
Land	$126,000
Building	486,000
Machinery	288,000
Total	$900,000

Using the assessed valuations on the property tax bill as a guide, allocate the total purchase price of the plant to the land, building, and machinery accounts in Tamock Company's records.

CAPITALIZATION OF INTEREST
— OBJ. 1 —

8-26 On April 1, 1996, Florida Company borrowed $600,000 at 9% to finance the construction of a new wing on its headquarters office building. The construction will take several months. Interest of $4,500 is paid monthly. Construction begins April 1, 1996, and accumulated construction expenditures are $160,000 at April 30, 1996. Determine how much interest cost should be capitalized for April.

DEPRECIATION METHODS
— OBJ. 2 —

8-27 A delivery truck costing $18,000 is expected to have a $1,500 salvage value at the end of its useful life of four years or 125,000 miles. Assume that the truck was purchased on January 2, 1996. Compute the depreciation expense for 1997 using each of the following depreciation methods: (a) straight line, (b) sum of the years' digits, (c) double declining balance, and (d) units of production (assume that the truck was driven 28,000 miles in 1997).

REVISION OF DEPRECIATION
— OBJ. 2 —

8-28 On January 2, 1993, Mosler, Inc., purchased new equipment for $66,000. The equipment was expected to have a $6,000 salvage value at the end of its estimated six-year useful life. Straight-line depreciation has been recorded. Before adjusting the accounts for 1997, Mosler decided that the useful life of the equipment should be extended by two years and the salvage value decreased to $4,000.
a. Prepare a general journal entry to record depreciation expense on the equipment for 1997.
b. What is the book value of the equipment at the end of 1997 (that is, after recording the depreciation expense for 1997)?

IMPAIRMENT LOSS
— OBJ. 2 —

8-29 On July 1, 1993, Okin Company purchased equipment for $225,000; the estimated useful life was 10 years and the expected salvage value was $25,000. Straight-line depreciation is used. On July 1, 1997, economic factors cause the market value of the equipment to decrease to $90,000. On this date, Okin checks to see if the equipment is impaired and estimates future cash flows relating to the use and disposal of the equipment to be $125,000.

a. Is the equipment impaired at July 1, 1997? Explain.
b. If the equipment is impaired at July 1, 1997, compute the impairment loss.
c. If the equipment is impaired at July 1, 1997, prepare the journal entry to record the impairment loss.

REVENUE AND CAPITAL EXPENDITURES
— OBJ. 3 —

8-30 Shively Company built an addition to its chemical plant. Indicate whether each of the following expenditures related to the addition is a revenue expenditure or a capital expenditure.
   a. Shively's initial application for a building permit was denied by the city as not conforming to environmental standards. Shively disagreed with the decision and spent $6,000 in attorney's fees to convince the city to reverse its position and issue the permit.
   b. Due to unanticipated sandy soil conditions, and on the advice of construction engineers, Shively spent $58,000 to extend the footings for the addition to a greater depth than originally planned.
   c. Shively spent $3,000 to send each of the addition's subcontractors a side of beef as a thank-you gift for completing the project on schedule.
   d. Shively invited the mayor to a ribbon-cutting ceremony to open the plant addition. It spent $25 to purchase the ribbon and scissors.
   e. Shively spent $4,100 to have the company logo sandblasted into the concrete above the entrance to the addition.

SALE OF PLANT ASSET
— OBJ. 4 —

8-31 Raine Company has a machine that originally cost $68,000. Depreciation has been recorded for five years using the straight-line method, with a $5,000 estimated salvage value at the end of an expected nine-year life. After recording depreciation at the end of the fifth year, Raine sells the machine. Prepare the journal entry to record the machine's sale for
   a. $37,000 cash.
   b. $33,000 cash.
   c. $28,000 cash.

EXCHANGE OF PLANT ASSET
— OBJ. 4 —

8-32 Assume that Hawkeye Company trades a used machine for a new machine with a cash price of $28,000. The old machine originally cost $24,000 and has $19,000 of accumulated depreciation. The seller allows a trade-in for the old machine and Hawkeye pays the balance in cash. Prepare the journal entry to record Hawkeye's trade-in transaction assuming the following:
   a. The trade-in allowance is $4,000.
   b. The trade-in allowance is $7,500.

COMPUTING AND RECORDING AMORTIZATION EXPENSE
— OBJ. 6 —

8-33 For each of the following unrelated situations, calculate the annual amortization expense and present a general journal entry to record the expense. Assume that contra accounts are not used for accumulated amortization.
   a. A patent with a 15-year remaining legal life was purchased for $270,000. The patent will probably be commercially exploitable for another nine years.
   b. A trademark is carried at a cost of $260,000, which represents the out-of-court settlement paid to another firm that has agreed to refrain from using or claiming the trademark or one similar to it. The company expects to actively use the trademark as long as the company exists.
   c. A patent was acquired on a device designed by a production worker. Although the cost of the patent to date consisted of $42,300 in legal fees for handling the patent application, the patent should be commercially valuable during its entire remaining legal life of 18 years and is currently worth $378,000.
   d. A franchise granting exclusive distribution rights for a new solar water heater within a three-state area for four years was obtained at a cost of $63,000. Satisfactory sales performance over the four years permits renewal of the franchise for another four years (at an additional cost determined at renewal).

PROBLEMS

INITIAL COST OF PLANT ASSETS
— OBJ. 1 —

8-34 The following items represent expenditures (or receipts) related to the construction of a new home office for Lowrey Company.

Cost of land site, which included an old apartment building appraised at $75,000	$165,000
Legal fees, including fee for title search	2,100
Payment of apartment building mortgage and related interest due at time of sale	9,300
Payment for delinquent property taxes assumed by the purchaser	4,000
Cost of razing the apartment building	17,000
Proceeds from sale of salvaged materials	(3,800)

Grading to establish proper drainage flow on land site	$ 1,900
Architect's fees on new building	300,000
Proceeds from sale of excess dirt (from basement excavation) to owner of adjoining property (dirt was used to fill in a low area on property)	(2,000)
Payment to building contractor	5,000,000
Interest cost incurred during construction (based on average accumulated construction expenditures)	230,000
Payment of medical bills of employee accidentally injured while inspecting building construction	1,400
Special assessment for paving city sidewalks (paid to city)	18,000
Cost of paving driveway and parking lot	25,000
Cost of installing lights in parking lot	9,200
Premium for insurance on building during construction	7,500
Cost of open house party to celebrate opening of new building	8,000

REQUIRED

From the given data, compute the proper balances for the Land, Building, and Land Improvements accounts of Lowrey Company. Land Improvements is a control account for all the separate land improvement accounts.

ALLOCATION OF PACKAGE PURCHASE PRICE AND DEPRECIATION METHODS — OBJ. 1, 2 —

8-35 To expand its business, Small Company paid $754,000 for most of the property, plant, and equipment of a small trucking company that was going out of business. Before agreeing to the price, Small hired a consultant for $6,000 to appraise the assets. The appraised values were as follows:

Land	$120,000
Building	440,000
Trucks	144,000
Equipment	96,000
Total	$800,000

Small issued two checks totaling $760,000 to acquire the assets and pay the consultant on July 1, 1996. Small depreciated the assets using the straight-line method on the building, the double declining-balance method on the trucks, and the sum-of-the-years'-digits method on the equipment. Estimated useful lives and salvage values were as follows:

	Useful Life	Salvage Value
Building	20 years	$42,000
Trucks	4 years	15,000
Equipment	7 years	10,000

REQUIRED

a. Compute the amounts allocated to the various types of plant assets acquired on July 1, 1996.
b. Prepare the July 1, 1996, general journal entries to record the purchase of the assets and the payment to the consultant.
c. Prepare the December 31, 1996, general journal entries to record 1996 depreciation expense on the building, trucks, and equipment.

DEPRECIATION METHODS — OBJ. 2 —

8-36 On January 2, Roth, Inc., purchased a laser cutting machine to be used in the fabrication of a part for one of its key products. The machine cost $80,000, and its estimated useful life was four years or 1,000,000 cuttings, after which it could be sold for $5,000.

REQUIRED

Compute the depreciation expense for each year of the machine's useful life under each of the following depreciation methods:

a. Straight line.
b. Sum of the years' digits.
c. Double declining balance.
d. Units of production. (Assume annual production in cuttings of 200,000; 350,000; 260,000; and 190,000.)

COMPREHENSIVE PROBLEM — OBJ. 1, 2, 3 —

8-37 During the first few days of 1996, Coast Company entered into the following transactions:
1. Purchased a parcel of land with a building on it for $900,000 cash. The building, which will be used in operations, has an estimated useful life of 25 years and a salvage value of $60,000.

The assessed valuations for property tax purposes show the land at $80,000 and the building at $720,000.

2. Paid $30,000 for the construction of an asphalt parking lot for customers. The parking lot is expected to last 12 years and have no salvage value.
3. Paid $25,000 for the construction of a new entrance to the building.
4. Purchased store equipment, paying the invoice price (including 7% sales tax) of $74,900 in cash. The estimated useful life of the equipment is eight years, and the salvage value is $6,000.
5. Paid $220 freight on the new store equipment.
6. Paid $1,500 to repair damages to floor caused when the store equipment was accidentally dropped as it was moved into place.
7. Paid $40 for an umbrella holder to place inside front door (customers may place wet umbrellas in the holder). The holder is expected to last 20 years.

REQUIRED
a. Prepare general journal entries to record these transactions.
b. Prepare the December 31, 1996, general journal entries to record the proper amounts of depreciation expense for the year. Sum-of-the-years'-digits depreciation is used for the equipment, and straight-line depreciation is used for the building and parking lot.

COMPREHENSIVE PROBLEM
— OBJ. 1, 2, 3 —

8-38 Basin Corporation had the following transactions related to its delivery truck:

1996
Jan. 5   Purchased for $14,300 cash a new truck with an estimated useful life of four years and a salvage value of $2,300.
Feb. 20 Installed a new set of side-view mirrors at a cost of $68 cash.
June 9   Paid $285 for an engine tune-up, wheel balancing, and a periodic lubrication.
Aug. 2   Paid a $250 repair bill for the uninsured portion of damages to the truck caused by Basin's own driver.
Dec. 31 Recorded 1996 depreciation on the truck.

1997
May 1   Installed a set of parts bins in the truck at a cost of $800 cash. This expenditure was not expected to increase the salvage value of the truck.
Dec. 31 Recorded 1997 depreciation on the truck.

1998
July 1   Paid $1,830 for a major engine overhaul on the truck. The overhaul should extend the useful life of the truck an additional two years (to December 31, 2001) with a salvage value now estimated at $1,100.
Dec. 31 Recorded 1998 depreciation on the truck.

Basin's depreciation policies include (1) using straight-line depreciation, (2) recording depreciation to the nearest whole month, and (3) expensing all truck expenditures of $75 or less.

REQUIRED
Prepare general journal entries to record these transactions and adjustments.

DISPOSALS OF PLANT ASSET
— OBJ. 4 —

8-39 Citano Company has a used executive charter plane that originally cost $800,000. Straight-line depreciation on the plane has been recorded for six years, with an $80,000 expected salvage value at the end of its estimated eight-year useful life. The last depreciation entry was made at the end of the sixth year. Eight months into the seventh year, Citano disposes of the plane.

REQUIRED
Prepare journal entries to record
a. Depreciation expense to the date of disposal.
b. Sale of the plane for cash at its book value.
c. Sale of the plane for $215,000 cash.
d. Sale of the plane for $195,000 cash.
e. Exchange of the plane for a new aircraft costing $900,000. The trade-in allowance received is $230,000, and the balance is paid in cash.
f. Destruction of the plane in a fire. Citano expects a $190,000 insurance settlement.
g. Exchange of the plane for a new yacht costing $860,000. The trade-in allowance received is $188,000, and the balance is paid in cash.

DEPLETION ACCOUNTING
— OBJ. 5 —

8-40 Pitt Gravel, Inc., has just purchased a site containing an estimated 2,000,000 tons of high-grade aggregate rock. Pitt makes the following expenditures before starting production:

Purchase price of property	$2,876,000
Legal fees to acquire title and secure proper zoning for operations	10,300
Removal of topsoil and grading for drainage	73,700
Construction of on-site crushing, washing, and loading facilities	700,000

Once the rock deposits are no longer commercially valuable, Pitt estimates the company will spend $70,000 to recondition the land. The land will then sell for an estimated $190,000. Certain parts of the on-site crushing, washing, and loading facilities have an estimated salvage value of $100,000 when operations are terminated.

REQUIRED

a. Prepare the journal entry to record the total depletion charge for the first year, during which 200,000 tons of rock are extracted from the quarry.

b. Prepare the journal entry to record the depreciation of the crushing, washing, and loading facilities for the first year, in which 200,000 tons of rock are extracted. Use the units-of-production depreciation method.

c. Compute the cost of a 40,000-ton inventory of rock at the end of the first year for which all extraction and processing costs except depletion and depreciation of crushing, washing, and loading facilities average $0.90 per ton.

d. At the beginning of the second year, Pitt estimates that only 1,200,000 tons of rock remain in the quarry. Compute the revised (1) depletion per ton of rock and (2) depreciation per ton of rock. (*Hint:* The procedures for revising depletion per ton and depreciation per ton are similar.)

ACCOUNTING FOR INTANGIBLE ASSETS AND LEASEHOLD IMPROVEMENTS
— OBJ. 1, 2, 6 —

8-41 Berdahl Company owns several retail outlets. In 1996, it expanded operations and entered into the following transactions:

Jan. 2   Signed an eight-year lease for additional retail space for an annual rent of $23,400. Paid the first year's rent on this date. (*Hint:* Debit the first year's rent to Prepaid Rent.)

     3   Paid $22,800 to a contractor for installation of a new oak floor in the leased facility. The oak floor's life is an estimated 50 years with no salvage value.

Mar. 1   Paid $45,000 to obtain an exclusive area franchise for five years to distribute a new line of perfume.

July 1   Paid $38,000 to LogoLab, Inc., for designing a trademark for a new line of gourmet chocolates that Berdahl will distribute nationally. Berdahl will use the trademark for as long as the firm (and the chocolates) remain in business. Berdahl expects to be in business for at least another 50 years.

     1   Paid $25,000 for advertisement in a national magazine (June issue) introducing the new line of chocolates and the trademark.

REQUIRED

a. Prepare general journal entries to record these transactions.

b. Prepare the necessary adjusting entries on December 31, 1996, for these transactions. Berdahl makes adjusting entries once a year. Berdahl uses straight-line depreciation and amortization but does not use contra accounts when amortizing intangible assets.

PREPARATION OF BALANCE SHEET
— OBJ. 7 —

8-42 Dooley Company's December 31, 1996, post-closing trial balance contains the following normal balances:

Cash	$9,000
Accounts Payable	18,000
Stone Quarry	405,000
Building	439,500
Long-Term Notes Payable	785,000
H. Dooley, Capital	970,000
Accumulated Depreciation—Equipment	180,000
Accumulated Depletion—Stone Quarry	144,000
Land	81,000
Accounts Receivable	22,500
Timberland	690,000
Accumulated Depreciation—Building	135,000
Wages Payable	6,000
Patent (net of amortization)	120,000

Accumulated Depletion—Timberland	$202,500
Notes Payable (short term)	131,000
Inventory	206,000
Equipment	600,000
Allowance for Uncollectible Accounts	1,500

REQUIRED

Prepare a December 31, 1996, classified balance sheet for Dooley Company.

ALTERNATE EXERCISES

INITIAL COST OF PLANT ASSET
— OBJ. 1 —

8-24A Fischer Construction purchased a used front-end loader for $28,000, terms 1/10, n/30, F.O.B. shipping point, freight collect. Fischer paid the freight charges of $270 and sent the seller a check for $27,720 one week after the machine was delivered. The loader required a new battery, which cost Fischer $150. Fischer also spent $240 to have the company name printed on the loader and $375 for one year's insurance coverage on it. Fischer hired a new employee to operate it at a wage of $19 per hour; the employee spent one morning (four hours) practicing with the machine and went to work at a construction site that afternoon. Compute the initial amount at which the front-end loader should be carried in the firm's accounts.

ALLOCATION OF PACKAGE PURCHASE PRICE
— OBJ. 1 —

8-25A Andrew Lupino went into business by purchasing a car lubrication station, consisting of land, a building, and equipment. The seller's original asking price was $210,000. Lupino hired an appraiser for $2,000 to appraise the assets. The appraised valuations were land, $38,000; building, $95,000, and equipment, $57,000. After receiving the appraisal, Lupino offered $175,000 for the business. The seller refused this offer. Lupino then offered $185,000 for the business, which the seller accepted. Using the appraisal values as a guide, allocate the total purchase price of the car lubrication station to the land, building, and equipment accounts.

CAPITALIZATION OF INTEREST
— OBJ. 1 —

8-26A On May 1, 1996, Iowa Company borrowed $850,000 at 12% to finance the construction of a new warehouse. Interest of $8,500 is paid monthly. The construction that began during the first week of May will take several months. At May 31, the accumulated construction expenditures were $275,000. At June 30, the accumulated construction expenditures were $425,000. Determine how much interest cost should be capitalized for June.

DEPRECIATION METHODS
— OBJ. 2 —

8-27A A machine costing $145,800 was purchased May 1, 1996. The machine should be obsolete after three years and, therefore, no longer useful to the company. The estimated salvage value is $5,400. Compute each year's depreciation expense for 1996–1999 using each of the following depreciation methods: (a) straight line, (b) sum of the years' digits, and (c) double declining balance.

REVISION OF DEPRECIATION
— OBJ. 2 —

8-28A Associated Clinic purchased a special machine for use in its laboratory on January 2, 1996. The machine cost $84,000 and was expected to last 10 years. Its salvage value was estimated to be $6,000. By early 1998, it was evident that the machine will be useful for a total of only seven years. The salvage value after seven years was estimated to be $7,500. Associated Clinic uses straight-line depreciation. Compute the proper depreciation expense on the machine for 1998.

IMPAIRMENT LOSS
— OBJ. 2 —

8-29A On May 1, 1994, Silky, Inc., purchased machinery for $315,000; the estimated useful life was eight years and the expected salvage value was $15,000. Straight-line depreciation is used. On May 1, 1996, economic factors cause the market value of the machinery to decrease to $190,000. On this date, Silky checks to see if the machinery is impaired.
  a. Assume that on May 1, 1996, Silky estimates future cash flows relating to the use and disposal of the machinery to be $260,000. Is the machinery impaired at May 1, 1996? Explain. If it is impaired, what is the amount of the impairment loss?
  b. Assume that on May 1, 1996, Silky estimates future cash flows relating to the use and disposal of the machinery to be $230,000. Is the machinery impaired at May 1, 1996? Explain. If it is impaired, what is the amount of the impairment loss?

REVENUE AND CAPITAL EXPENDITURES
— OBJ. 3 —

8-30A Indicate whether each of the following expenditures is a revenue expenditure or a capital expenditure for Blare Company.
  a. Paid $280 to replace a truck windshield that was cracked by a stone thrown up by another vehicle while the truck was being used to make a delivery.
  b. Paid $10 for a no-smoking sign for the conference room.
  c. Paid $900 to add a hard disk to an employee's computer.
  d. Paid $15 for a dust cover for a computer printer.
  e. Paid $280 to replace a cracked windshield on a used truck that was just purchased for company use. The company bought the truck knowing the windshield was cracked.

f. Paid $100 for a building permit from the city for a storage shed the company is going to have built.

SALE OF PLANT ASSET
— OBJ. 4 —

8-31A Noble Company has equipment that originally cost $63,000. Depreciation has been recorded for six years using the straight-line method, with a $7,000 estimated salvage value at the end of an expected eight-year life. After recording depreciation at the end of the sixth year, Noble sells the equipment. Prepare the journal entry to record the equipment's sale for
a. $27,000 cash.
b. $21,000 cash.
c. $18,000 cash.

EXCHANGE OF PLANT ASSET
— OBJ. 4 —

8-32A Holden Company exchanges used equipment costing $75,000 (on which $60,000 of depreciation has accumulated) for similar new equipment. The new equipment's cash price, with no trade-in, is $84,000. Prepare the journal entry to record Holden's trade-in transaction when
a. The equipment's trade-in allowance is $14,000, and the balance is paid in cash.
b. The equipment's trade-in allowance is $25,000, and the balance is paid in cash.

COMPUTING DEPLETION
AND DEPRECIATION
— OBJ. 2, 5 —

8-33A Savage Mining Company purchased Hidden Valley Mine for $12,000,000. The mine contains an estimated 3,000,000 tons of ore. Savage also purchased mining equipment for $660,000 that will be useful only at Hidden Valley Mine. The equipment will be worthless when the ore is depleted. Upon completion of the mining operations, Savage estimates the land can be sold for $350,000 after spending $50,000 to restore the land site.
a. Compute the proper depletion charge for a period during which 280,000 tons of ore are extracted and sold.
b. Compute the proper depreciation charge on the mining equipment, using the units-of-production method, for a period during which 280,000 tons of ore are extracted and sold.

ALTERNATE PROBLEMS

8-34A The following items represent expenditures (or receipts) related to the construction of a new home office for Secrest Investment Company.

INITIAL COST OF PLANT
ASSETS
— OBJ. 1 —

Cost of land site, which included an abandoned railroad spur	$ 175,000
Legal fees, including title search, relating to land purchase	4,300
Cost of surveying land to confirm boundaries	1,100
Cost of removing railroad tracks	6,500
Payment of delinquent property taxes assumed by the purchaser	6,000
Proceeds from sale of timber from walnut trees cut down to prepare site for construction	(18,000)
Proceeds from sale of salvaged railroad track	(3,500)
Grading to prepare land site for construction	4,000
Cost of basement excavation (contracted separately)	3,700
Architect's fees on new building	128,000
Payment to building contractor—original contract price	3,200,000
Cost of changes during construction to make building more energy efficient	91,000
Interest cost incurred during construction (based on average accumulated construction expenditures)	115,000
Cost of replacing windows broken by vandals	2,400
Cost of paving driveway and parking lot	17,000
Out-of-court settlement for mud slide onto adjacent property	10,000
Special assessment for paving city sidewalks (paid to city)	22,000
Cost of brick and wrought iron fence installed across front of property	16,500

REQUIRED

From the given data, compute the proper balances for the Land, Building, and Land Improvements accounts of Secrest Investment Company. Land Improvements is a control account for all the separate land improvement accounts.

ALLOCATION OF PACKAGE PURCHASE PRICE AND DEPRECIATION METHODS — OBJ. 1, 2 —

8-35A In an expansion move, Beam Company paid $2,180,000 for most of the property, plant, and equipment of a small manufacturing firm that was going out of business. Before agreeing to the price, Beam hired a consultant for $20,000 to appraise the assets. The appraised values were as follows:

Land	$ 384,000
Building	912,000
Equipment	960,000
Trucks	144,000
Total	$2,400,000

Beam issued two checks totaling $2,200,000 to acquire the assets and pay the consultant on April 1, 1996. Beam depreciated the assets using the straight-line method on the building, the sum-of-the-years'-digits method on the equipment, and the double declining-balance method on the trucks. Estimated useful lives and salvage values were as follows:

	Useful Life	Salvage Value
Building	15 years	$86,000
Equipment	9 years	70,000
Trucks	5 years	13,000

REQUIRED

a. Compute the amounts allocated to the various types of plant assets acquired on April 1, 1996.

b. Prepare the April 1, 1996, general journal entries to record the purchase of the assets and the payment of the consultant.

c. Prepare the December 31, 1996, general journal entries to record the 1996 depreciation expense on the building, equipment, and trucks.

DEPRECIATION METHODS — OBJ. 2 —

8-36A On January 2, 1996, Alvarez Company purchased an electroplating machine to help manufacture a part for one of its key products. The machine cost $218,700 and was estimated to have a useful life of six years or 700,000 platings, after which it could be sold for $23,400.

REQUIRED

a. Compute each year's depreciation expense for 1996–2001 under each of the following depreciation methods:
  1. Straight line.
  2. Sum of the years' digits.
  3. Double declining balance.
  4. Units of production. (Assume annual production in platings of 140,000, 180,000, 100,000, 110,000, 80,000, and 90,000).

b. Assume that the machine was purchased on September 1, 1996. Compute each year's depreciation expense for 1996–2002 under each of the following depreciation methods:
  1. Straight line.
  2. Sum of the years' digits.
  3. Double declining balance.

COMPREHENSIVE PROBLEM — OBJ. 1, 2, 3 —

8-37A Stellar Delivery Service had the following transactions related to its delivery truck:

1995

Mar. 1 Purchased for $28,500 cash a new delivery truck with an estimated useful life of five years and a $2,800 salvage value.

      2 Paid $580 for painting the company name and logo on the truck.

Dec. 31 Recorded 1995 depreciation on the truck.

1996

July 1 Installed air conditioning in the truck at a cost of $1,808 cash. Although the truck's estimated useful life was not affected, its estimated salvage value was increased by $400.

Sept. 7 Paid $430 for truck tune-up and safety inspection.

Dec. 31 Recorded 1996 depreciation on the truck.

1997

May 2 Paid $2,220 for a major overhaul of the truck. The overhaul should extend the truck's useful life one year (to February 28, 2001), when the revised salvage value should be $3,000.

Sept. 3 Installed a set of front and rear bumper guards at a cost of $130 cash.

Dec. 31 Recorded 1997 depreciation on the truck.

1998

Dec. 31 Recorded 1998 depreciation on the truck.

Stellar's depreciation policies include (1) using straight-line depreciation, (2) recording depreciation to the nearest whole month, and (3) expensing all truck expenditures of $150 or less.

REQUIRED

Prepare general journal entries to record these transactions and adjustments.

REVISION OF DEPRECIATION AND CAPITAL EXPENDITURE — OBJ. 2, 3 —

8-38A Richter Company uses straight-line depreciation in accounting for its machines. On January 2, 1991, Richter purchased a new machine for $122,000 cash. The machine's estimated useful life was seven years with a $10,000 salvage value. In 1996, the company decided its original useful life estimate should be increased by three years. Beginning in 1996, depreciation was based on a 10-year total useful life, and no change was made in the salvage value estimate. On January 3, 1997, Richter added an automatic cut-off switch and a self-sharpening blade mechanism to the machine at a cost of $8,800 cash. These improvements did not change the machine's useful life but did increase the estimated salvage value to $11,200.

REQUIRED

a. Prepare general journal entries to record (1) the purchase of the machine, (2) 1991 depreciation expense, (3) 1996 depreciation expense, (4) the 1997 improvements, and (5) 1997 depreciation expense.

b. Compute the book value of the machine at the end of 1997 (that is, after recording the depreciation expense for 1997).

DISPOSALS OF PLANT ASSET — OBJ. 4 —

8-39A Canyon Company has a used delivery truck that originally cost $27,200. Straight-line depreciation on the truck has been recorded for three years, with a $2,000 expected salvage value at the end of its estimated six-year useful life. The last depreciation entry was made at the end of the third year. Four months into the fourth year, Canyon disposes of the truck.

REQUIRED

Prepare journal entries to record

a. Depreciation expense to the date of disposal.

b. Sale of the truck for cash at its book value.

c. Sale of the truck for $15,000 cash.

d. Sale of the truck for $12,000 cash.

e. Exchange of the truck for a new truck costing $24,400. The trade-in allowance received is $11,400, and the balance is paid in cash.

f. Theft of the truck. Canyon carries no insurance for theft.

g. Exchange of the truck for golf carts costing $32,500 for the company golf course. The trade-in allowance received is $14,400, and the balance is paid in cash.

DEPLETION ACCOUNTING — OBJ. 5 —

8-40A Longview Mining Company has just purchased a site containing an estimated 3,000,000 tons of coal. Longview makes the following expenditures before starting operations:

Cost of land survey	$ 26,000
Purchase price of property	4,160,000
Legal fees to acquire title and secure proper zoning for operations	14,000
Construction of on-site conveyance and loading facilities	650,000

After all the coal has been extracted, Longview expects to spend $150,000 to restore the land site and then sell it for $450,000. Longview also expects to sell certain parts of the conveyance and loading facilities for $50,000.

REQUIRED

a. Prepare the journal entry to record the total depletion charge for the first year, during which 400,000 tons of coal are extracted from the mine.

b. Prepare the journal entry to record the depreciation of the conveyance and loading facilities for the first year, in which 400,000 tons of coal are extracted. Use the units-of-production depreciation method.

c. Compute the cost of a 60,000-ton inventory of coal at the end of the first year for which all extraction and processing costs except depletion and depreciation of conveyance and loading facilities average $1.75 per ton.

d. At the beginning of the second year, Longview estimates that only 2,000,000 tons of coal remain underground. Compute the revised (1) depletion per ton of coal and (2) depreciation per ton of coal. (*Hint:* The procedures for revising depletion per ton and depreciation per ton are similar.)

**ACCOUNTING FOR PLANT
AND INTANGIBLE ASSETS
— OBJ. 1, 2, 4, 6 —**

8-41A Selected 1997 transactions of Continental Publishers, Inc., are given below:

Jan. 2 Paid $90,000 to purchase copyrights to a series of romantic novels. The copyrights expire in 40 years, although sales of the novels are expected to stop after 10 years.

Mar. 1 Discovered a satellite dish antenna has been destroyed by lightning. The loss is covered by insurance and a claim is filed today. The antenna cost $9,180 when installed on July 1, 1995, and was being depreciated over 12 years with a $900 salvage value. Straight-line depreciation was last recorded on December 31, 1996. Continental expects to receive an insurance settlement of $8,100.

Apr. 1 Paid $120,000 to remodel space to create an employee exercise area on the lower level in a leased building. The building's remaining useful life is 40 years; the lease on the building expires in 12 years (March 31, 2009).

July 1 Paid $270,000 to acquire a patent on a new publishing process. The patent has a remaining legal life of 15 years. Continental estimates the new process will be utilized for 6 years before it becomes obsolete.

Oct. 1 Exchanged old printing equipment for new printing equipment. The old equipment cost $102,000 and had accumulated depreciation of $76,800 (through September 30, 1997). The new equipment's cash price was $144,000. Continental's trade-in allowance was $24,000, and the company paid $120,000 cash. Continental estimates an eight-year useful life and a $12,000 salvage value for the new equipment.

Nov. 1 Paid $63,000 to obtain a four-year franchise to sell a new series of computerized do-it-yourself manuals.

REQUIRED

a. Prepare general journal entries to record these transactions.

b. Prepare the December 31, 1997, general journal entries to record the proper amounts of depreciation and amortization expense for assets acquired during the year. Continental uses straight-line depreciation and amortization but does not use contra accounts when amortizing intangible assets.

**PREPARATION OF
BALANCE SHEET
— OBJ. 7 —**

8-42A Conlon Corporation's December 31, 1996, post-closing trial balance contains the following normal account balances:

Interest Payable	$ 24,000
Allowance for Uncollectible Accounts	1,000
Accumulated Depreciation—Equipment	130,000
Inventory	137,000
Organization Costs (net of amortization)	19,000
Copper Deposit	800,000
Notes Payable (short term)	80,000
Cash	2,000
Accumulated Depletion—Coal Deposit	126,000
Building	280,000
Accounts Receivable	21,000
Patent (net of amortization)	50,000
Equipment	266,000
Capital Stock	400,000
Retained Earnings	353,000
Accumulated Depreciation—Building	70,000
Accounts Payable	13,000
Leasehold Improvements	140,000
Accumulated Depletion—Copper Deposit	320,000
Land	174,000
Long-Term Notes Payable	950,000
Coal Deposit	600,000
Accumulated Depreciation—Leasehold Improvements	22,000

REQUIRED
Prepare a December 31, 1996, classified balance sheet for Conlon Corporation.

CASES

BUSINESS DECISION CASE

Lyle Fleming, president of Fleming, Inc., wants you to resolve his dispute with Mia Gooden over the amount of a finder's fee due Gooden. Fleming hired Gooden to locate a new plant site to expand the business. By agreement, Gooden's fee was to be 15% of the "cost of the property (excluding the finder's fee) measured according to generally accepted accounting principles."

Gooden located Site 1 and Site 2 for Fleming to consider. Each site had a selling price of $150,000, and the geographic locations of both sites were equally acceptable to Fleming. Fleming employed an engineering firm to conduct the geological tests necessary to determine the relative quality of the two sites for construction. The tests, which cost $10,000 for each site, showed that Site 1 was superior to Site 2.

The owner of Site 1 initially gave Fleming 30 days—a reasonable period—to decide whether or not to buy the property. However, Fleming procrastinated in contracting the geological tests, and the results were not available by the end of the 30-day period. Fleming requested a two-week extension. The Site 1 owner granted Fleming the additional two weeks but charged him $6,000 for the extension (which Fleming paid). Fleming eventually bought Site 1.

Fleming sent Gooden a fee of $24,000, which was 15% of a cost computed as follows:

Sales price, Site 1	$150,000
Geological tests, Site 1	10,000
Total	$160,000

Gooden believes that she is entitled to $26,400, based on a cost computed as follows:

Sales price, Site 1	$150,000
Geological tests, Site 1	10,000
Geological tests, Site 2	10,000
Fee for time extension	6,000
Total	$176,000

REQUIRED

What fee is Gooden entitled to under the agreement? Explain.

FINANCIAL ANALYSIS CASE

Best Buy Co., Inc., is headquartered in Minneapolis, Minnesota. The company sells brand name consumer electronics, personal computers, home office products, major appliances, entertainment software, and photographic equipment. Selected financial data for Best Buy Co. for three recent years follow (amounts in thousands; Year 3 is the most recent year).

	Year 3	Year 2	Year 1
Total assets, beginning of year	$ 439,142	$ 337,218	$185,528
Total assets, end of year	952,494	439,142	337,218
Revenues for the year	3,006,534	1,619,978	929,692
Net income for the year	41,285	19,855	9,601

REQUIRED

a. Compute the return on assets for Years 1, 2, and 3.
b. In Years 1, 2, and 3, Best Buy's total assets grew by 82%, 30%, and 117%, respectively. With such a rapid growth in assets, was Best Buy able to maintain its rate of profitability in the utilization of assets throughout the three years? Explain.

ETHICS CASE

Linda Tristan, assistant controller for Ag-Growth, Inc., a biotechnology firm, has concerns about the accounting analysis for the firm's purchase of a land site and building from Hylite Corporation. The price for this package purchase was $1,800,000 cash. A memorandum from the controller, Greg Fister, stated that the journal entry for this purchase should debit Land for $1,350,000, debit Building for $450,000, and credit Cash for $1,800,000. The building, a used laboratory facility, is to be depreciated over 10 years with a zero salvage value.

The source documents supporting the transaction include two appraisals of the property, one done for Ag-Growth and one done for Hylite Corporation. The appraisal for Ag-Growth valued the land at $1,000,000 and the building at $500,000. The appraisal for Hylite Corporation (done by a different appraiser) valued the land at $1,500,000 and the building at $750,000. Negotiations between the two firms finally settled on an overall price of $1,800,000 for the land and the building.

Tristan asked Fister how he arrived at the amounts to be recorded for the land and building since each appraisal valued the land at only twice the building's value. "Well," replied Fister, 'I used the $1,500,000 land value from Hylite's appraiser and the $500,000 building value from our appraiser. That relationship shows the land to be worth three times the building's value. Using that relationship,

I assigned 75% of our actual purchase price of $1,800,000 to the land and 25% of the purchase price to the building."

"But why do it that way?" asked Tristan.

"Because it will improve our profits, before income taxes, by $150,000 over the next decade," replied Fister.

"But it just doesn't seem right," commented Tristan.

REQUIRED

a. How does the accounting analysis by Fister improve profits, before income taxes, by $150,000 over the next decade?

b. Is the goal of improving profits a sufficient rationale to defend the accounting analysis by Fister?

c. Do you agree with Fister's analysis? Briefly explain.

d. What actions are available to Tristan to resolve her concerns with Fister's analysis?

GENERAL MILLS ANNUAL REPORT CASE

Refer to the annual report of General Mills, Inc., presented in Appendix K. Review the consolidated statements of earnings, the consolidated balance sheets, and Notes 1 and 6.

REQUIRED

a. What is General Mills' gross cost of land, buildings, and equipment at May 29, 1994?

b. What depreciation method is used in the financial statements?

c. How much depreciation and amortization were expensed in fiscal 1994?

d. How much depreciation has accumulated by May 29, 1994?

e. How much research and development cost was expensed in fiscal 1994?

f. What is General Mills' return on assets for fiscal 1994?

Current and Contingent Liabilities

CHAPTER LEARNING OBJECTIVES

1 **DESCRIBE** the nature of liabilities and **DEFINE** current liabilities (pp. 308–309).

2 **DISCUSS** and **ILLUSTRATE** cash obligations of known amount (pp. 309–315).

3 **DISCUSS** and **ILLUSTRATE** cash obligations whose amounts are estimated (pp. 315–317).

4 **DISCUSS** and **ILLUSTRATE** goods and services obligations of known amount (pp. 317–318).

5 **DISCUSS** and **ILLUSTRATE** goods and services obligations whose amounts are estimated (pp. 318–319).

6 **DEFINE** contingent liabilities, **OUTLINE** criteria for their treatment on financial statements, and **PRESENT** illustrations (pp. 319–322).

7 **Financial Analysis** **DEFINE** *current ratio* and *quick ratio* and **EXPLAIN** their use (pp. 322–323).

CHAPTER FOCUS

Companies create obligations to nonowners in the normal course of business. General Motors owes money to its suppliers for materials built into cars, the New York Yankees owe games to season ticket holders, and Time-Life owes magazines to subscribers. In this chapter, we discuss two categories of obligations: current liabilities and contingent liabilities.

THE NATURE OF LIABILITIES

OBJECTIVE *1*

DESCRIBE the nature of liabilities and **DEFINE** current liabilities.

Liabilities are obligations resulting from past transactions or events that require the firm to pay money, provide goods, or perform services in the future. The existence of a past transaction or event is an important element in the definition of liabilities.

Consider two examples. In the first example, a buyer agrees to purchase inventory from a seller. This purchase commitment is actually an agreement between a buyer and a seller to enter into a *future* transaction. The performance of the seller that will create the obligation on the part of the buyer is, at this point, a future transaction. Therefore, a purchase commitment is not a liability. Another example is a company's long-term salary contract with an executive. When the agreement is signed, each party is committed to perform in the future—the executive to render services and the company to pay for those services. The company does not record a liability when the contract is signed because the executive has not yet rendered any services.

These examples are not reported as liabilities because they are related to future transactions. However, items such as significant purchase commitments and executive compensation commitments should be disclosed in notes to the balance sheet.

Items shown as liabilities are often not legally due and payable on the balance sheet date. For example, the accrual of wages expense incurred but not paid during the period results in a credit balance account titled Wages Payable. Accrued wages are not typically due until several days after the balance sheet date. In the case of other accrued expenses—such as property taxes and executive bonuses—payment may not be due until months after the balance sheet date. Bonds payable, although shown as liabilities, actually may not be payable for several decades. These items are all reported as liabilities, however, because they are obligations resulting from past transactions that will be settled as the business continues to operate.

The determination of liabilities is basic to accounting properly for a firm's operations. For example, if a liability is omitted, either an asset or an expense has been omitted also. If expense is involved, net income and owners' equity are misstated as well. Thus, the balance sheet or the income statement, or both, may be affected if liabilities are not reported correctly.

Most liabilities are satisfied by the eventual payment of cash. Some may require a firm to furnish goods—for instance, a publisher obligated to provide issues of a magazine to customers who have subscribed in advance. Other liabilities may be obligations to provide services, for example, product warranties and maintenance contracts that accompany a new appliance or automobile.

CURRENT LIABILITIES

Current liabilities are all obligations that will require within the coming year or the normal operating cycle, whichever is longer, (1) the use of existing current assets or (2) the creation of other current liabilities. Most current liabilities will be settled by using current assets, but sometimes a current liability is settled by the issuance of another current liability. A past-due account payable, for example, may be settled by issuing a short-term note payable. Liabilities are classified as current using the same time frame as is used to classify current assets—the longer of one year or the firm's normal operating cycle.

For purposes of discussion, current liabilities may be divided into four categories: cash obligations of known amount, cash obligations whose amounts are estimated, goods and services obligations of known amount, and goods and services obligations whose amounts are estimated. In the following sections, we review common types of current liabilities in each of these categories.

CASH OBLIGATIONS OF KNOWN AMOUNT

Short-term cash obligations of known amount include accounts payable, notes payable, interest payable, dividends payable, current portions of long-term debt, sales and excise taxes payable, and payroll-related liabilities. All of these liabilities represent obligations that will be settled by cash payments in the future. Further, the dollar amount of each obligation may be accurately determined by an accountant.

ACCOUNTS PAYABLE

OBJECTIVE 2

DISCUSS and **ILLUSTRATE** cash obligations of known amount.

In a balance sheet listing of current liabilities, amounts due to short-term creditors on notes payable and accounts payable are commonly shown first. Most of the accounting procedures for accounts payable are fairly routine and have been discussed in previous chapters.

Short-term creditors send invoices specifying the amounts owed for the goods or services they have provided. As a result, the amount of the accounts payable liability is easily determined because it is based on the invoices received from creditors. If a creditor allows a cash discount for prompt payment (with terms such as 2/10, n/30, for example), the accounts payable may be recorded net of the available cash discount.

At the end of an accounting period, accountants need to know whether any significant amounts of goods are in transit to the company and what the shipping terms are for such goods. If the goods are shipped F.O.B. shipping point, ownership of the goods has transferred to the buyer and an account payable needs to be recorded at year-end (as well as an increase in inventory) even though the goods and an invoice have not yet arrived.

NOTES PAYABLE AND INTEREST PAYABLE

Promissory notes are often used in transactions when the credit period is longer than the 30 or 60 days typical for accounts payable. Although promissory notes are used frequently in sales of equipment and real property, a note is sometimes exchanged for merchandise. Occasionally, a note is substituted for an account payable when an extension of the usual credit period is granted. Promissory notes are normally prepared when loans are obtained from financial institutions.

Interest is a charge for the use of money. Interest incurred on a promissory note is interest expense to the maker of the note. Since business firms want to distinguish between operating and nonoperating items in their income statements, they place interest expense under the other income and expense heading in the income statement.

Interest on promissory notes is structured one of two ways: it is an amount paid that is in addition to the face amount of the note (the add-on interest method) or it is an amount that is included in the face amount of the note (the discount method). We illustrate both methods in the following sections.

ADD-ON INTEREST METHOD

Interest on a short-term note payable using the *add-on interest method* is paid at the maturity date of the note.

INTEREST FORMULA   The formula for determining the amount of interest follows:

$$\text{Interest} = \text{Principal} \times \frac{\text{Interest}}{\text{Rate}} \times \frac{\text{Interest}}{\text{Time}}$$

The principal or face amount of a note with add-on interest is the amount borrowed. The interest rate is the annual rate of interest. Interest time is the fraction of a year that the note is outstanding.

When a note is written for a certain number of months, time is expressed in twelfths of a year. For example, interest on a three-month note for $4,000 with a 9% annual interest rate is

$$\text{Interest} = \$4,000 \times 0.09 \times \frac{3}{12} = \$90$$

When a note's duration is given in days, time is expressed as a fraction of a year; the numerator is the number of days the note will be outstanding and the denominator is 360 days. (Some lenders use 360 days; others use 365 days; we will use 360 days in our examples, exercises, and problems.) For example, interest on a 60-day note for $3,000 with a 9% annual interest rate is

$$\text{Interest} = \$3,000 \times 0.09 \times \frac{60}{360} = \$45$$

DETERMINING MATURITY DATE   When a note payable's duration is expressed in days, we count the exact days in each calendar month to determine the **maturity date.** For example, a 90-day note dated July 21 has an October 19 maturity date, which we determine as follows:

> 10 days in July (remainder of month—31 days minus 21 days)
> 31 days in August
> 30 days in September
> <u>19</u> days in October (number of days required to total 90)
> <u>90</u>

If the duration of a note is expressed in months, we find the maturity date simply by counting the months from the date of issue. For example, a two-month note dated January 31 matures on March 31, a three-month note of the same date matures on April 30 (the last day of the month), and a four-month note matures on May 31.

RECORDING NOTE PAYABLE AND INTEREST   When a note payable is exchanged to settle an account payable, an entry is made to reflect the note payable and to reduce the balance of the related account payable. For example, suppose Jordon Company sold $12,000 of merchandise on account to Bowman Company. On October 1, after the regular credit period had elapsed, Bowman Company gave Jordon Company a 60-day, 9% note for $12,000. Bowman Company makes the following entry on October 1:

Oct. 1	Accounts Payable—Jordon Company	12,000	
	Notes Payable—Jordon Company		12,000
	Gave 60-day, 9% note in payment of account.		

If Bowman Company pays the note on the November 30 maturity date, Bowman Company makes the following entry:

Nov. 30	Notes Payable—Jordon Company	12,000	
	Interest Expense	180	
	Cash		12,180
	Paid note to Jordon Company		
	($12,000 × 0.09 × $\frac{60}{360}$ = $180).		

RECORDING DISHONORED NOTE PAYABLE   The interest for 60 days at 9% is recorded by the respective parties on the maturity date of the note, even if the maker defaults on (dishonors) the note. When a note is dishonored at maturity, the amount of the combined principal plus interest is converted to an open account. This procedure leaves only the current, unmatured notes in the holder's Notes Receivable account and the maker's Notes Payable account. If Bowman Company did not pay the note on November 30, it makes the following entry:

Nov. 30	Notes Payable—Jordon Company	12,000	
	Interest Expense	180	
	Accounts Payable—Jordon Company		12,180
	To record the nonpayment of a note due to Jordon Company.		

DISCOUNT METHOD

Interest is included in the face amount of a note payable under the *discount method.* Thus, when a company **borrows at a discount,** the face amount of the note payable is equal to its maturity value and the amount borrowed is less than the note's face amount.

CASH PROCEEDS FORMULA   The cash proceeds of the borrowing is determined using the following formula:

$$\text{Proceeds} = \frac{\text{Maturity}}{\text{Value}} - \text{Discount}$$

The formula for determining the amount of discount follows:

$$\text{Discount} = \frac{\text{Maturity}}{\text{Value}} \times \frac{\text{Discount}}{\text{Rate}} \times \frac{\text{Discount}}{\text{Time}}$$

RECORDING NOTE PAYABLE AND DISCOUNT   Suppose that Bowman Company agrees to borrow at a discount and signs a 12%, $8,000, 60-day note payable at Great American Bank. The note is dated December 16. The calculation of discount and proceeds are as follows:

$$\text{Discount} = \$8,000 \times 0.12 \times \frac{60}{360} = \$160$$

$$\text{Proceeds} = \$8,000 - \$160 = \$7,840$$

Bowman Company makes the following entry to record the signing of the note and the receipt of the $7,840 cash proceeds:

Dec. 16	Cash	7,840	
	Discount on Notes Payable	160	
	Notes Payable—Great American Bank		8,000
	To record the note signed at Great American Bank and the receipt of the proceeds.		

Note that the $160 is debited to **Discount on Notes Payable** rather than Interest Expense. Discount on Notes Payable is a contra account that is subtracted from the Notes Payable amount on the balance sheet. As the life of the note elapses, the discount is reduced and charged to Interest Expense. We illustrate this adjustment procedure later in the chapter.

EFFECTIVE INTEREST RATE   Because the cash proceeds of this type of note payable are less than the maturity value, the **effective interest rate** for the loan is greater than the stated discount rate. The effective interest rate may be calculated by the following formula:

$$\text{Effective Interest Rate} = \frac{\text{Maturity Value of Note} \times \text{Stated Discount Rate}}{\text{Cash Proceeds from Note}}$$

Therefore, the effective interest rate on the Bowman Company note is computed as follows:

$$\frac{\$8,000 \times 12\%}{\$7,840} = 12.24\%$$

INTEREST PAYABLE

At the end of the fiscal year, adjusting entries are made to reflect accrued interest expense. Adjusting entries are made for notes payable with add-on interest and for notes payable which resulted from borrowing at a discount.

ADJUSTING ENTRY FOR ADD-ON INTEREST METHOD   Assume that Bowman Company has one note payable with add-on interest outstanding at December 31, 1996. This note payable to Garcia Company is dated December 21, 1996, has a principal amount of $6,000, an interest rate of 12%, and a maturity date of February 19, 1997. The adjusting entry that Bowman Company makes at December 31, 1996, follows:

1996

Dec. 31	Interest Expense	20	
	Interest Payable		20
	To accrue interest expense on the note to		
	Garcia Company ($6,000 × 0.12 × $\frac{10}{360}$ = $20).		

When the note payable to Garcia Company is subsequently paid on February 19, 1997, Bowman Company makes the following entry (assuming that a reversing entry was not made on January 1, 1997):

1997

Feb. 19	Notes Payable—Garcia Company	6,000	
	Interest Payable	20	
	Interest Expense	100	
	Cash		6,120
	Paid principal and interest to Garcia Company		
	($6,000 × 0.12 × $\frac{50}{360}$ = $100).		

ADJUSTING ENTRY FOR DISCOUNT METHOD   Earlier in this chapter, we illustrated borrowing at a discount by having Bowman Company sign an $8,000 note in exchange for $7,840 cash. The entry that Bowman Company made to record the note (assume that the date of the note was December 16, 1996) follows:

1996

Dec. 16	Cash	7,840	
	Discount on Notes Payable	160	
	Notes Payable—Great American Bank		8,000
	To record the note signed at Great American Bank		
	and the receipt of the proceeds.		

The following is the adjusting entry that Bowman Company makes at December 31, 1996:

1996

Dec. 31	Interest Expense	40	
	Discount on Notes Payable		40
	To record interest expense on the note to		
	Great American Bank ($160 × $\frac{15 \text{ days}}{60 \text{ days}}$ = $40).		

In its December 31, 1996, balance sheet, Bowman Company shows the $120 remaining Discount on Notes Payable as a contra liability account, subtracted from the Notes Payable amount.

When the note is paid off on February 14, 1997, Bowman Company makes the following entry (assuming that a reversing entry was not made on January 1, 1997):

1997

Feb. 14	Notes Payable—Great American Bank	8,000	
	Interest Expense	120	
	Discount on Notes Payable		120
	Cash		8,000
	Payment of note to Great American Bank at maturity.		

DIVIDENDS PAYABLE   Ordinary dividends are distributions of corporate earnings to stockholders. Because the corporate board of directors determines the timing and amounts of dividends, they do not accrue as does interest expense. Instead, dividends are shown as liabilities only after a formal declaration. Once declared, however, dividends are binding obligations of the corporation. Dividends are current liabilities because they are usually paid within several weeks of the time they are declared.

PORTIONS OF LONG-TERM DEBT   The repayment of many long-term obligations involves a series of installments over several years. To report liabilities involving installments properly, we should show the principal amount of the installments due within one year (or the operating cycle, if longer) as a current liability.

SALES AND EXCISE TAXES PAYABLE

Many products and services are subject to sales and excise taxes. The laws governing these taxes usually require the selling firm to collect the tax at the time of sale and to send the collections periodically to the appropriate taxing agency. Assume that a particular product selling for $1,000 is subject to a 6% state sales tax and a 10% federal excise tax. Each tax should be figured on the basic sales price only. We record this sale as follows:

Accounts Receivable (*or* Cash)	1,160	
Sales		1,000
Sales Tax Payable		60
Excise Tax Payable		100
To record sales and related taxes.		

Recording this transaction as a $1,160 sale is incorrect, because this overstates revenue and may lead to the omission of the liabilities for the taxes collected. The selling firm periodically completes a tax reporting form and sends the period's tax collections with it. The tax liability accounts are then debited and Cash is credited.

Some firms record sales at the gross amount, including taxes collected. Then, to convert the total amount to actual sales, they divide the transaction total by 1.00 plus the tax percentages. In our example, the transaction total of $1,160 divided by 1.16 (1.00 + 0.06 + 0.10) yields $1,000 as the correct sales revenue. The remaining $160 ($1,160 − $1,000) is the total taxes payable.

PAYROLL-RELATED LIABILITIES

Salaries and wages represent a major element in the cost structure of many businesses. For service firms, the largest expense category is usually the compensation paid to employees and the related payroll taxes and fringe benefits paid by the employer. Three types of current liabilities arise from payroll: (1) accrued salaries and wages payable (discussed in previous chapters), (2) amounts withheld from employees' paychecks by the employer, and (3) payroll taxes and fringe benefits paid by the employer.

AMOUNTS WITHHELD FROM EMPLOYEE PAYCHECKS

When a business firm hires an employee, the firm establishes the employee's rate of pay either as a salary (a fixed amount per time period, regardless of hours worked, such as $2,000 per month) or as a wage (a fixed amount per hour worked, such as $12 per hour). Each pay period, the employer uses the salary or wage to determine each employee's **gross pay,** the amount earned before any withholdings. The employer then subtracts withheld amounts to determine **net pay,** the amount of the paycheck. Exhibit 9-1 demonstrates this relationship.

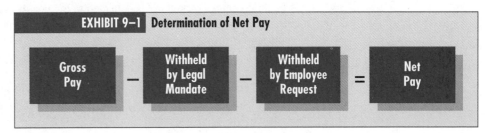

EXHIBIT 9–1 Determination of Net Pay

$$\text{Gross Pay} - \text{Withheld by Legal Mandate} - \text{Withheld by Employee Request} = \text{Net Pay}$$

AMOUNTS WITHHELD BY LEGAL MANDATE Some amounts withheld by the employer are mandated by law. These amounts include federal income tax, state income tax, social security, and medicare.

The amount of federal income tax withheld from a particular employee's paycheck is determined by referencing a table or a formula that uses the amount of the employee's gross pay, the employee's marital status, and the number of withholding allowances to which the employee is entitled to calculate the amount to be withheld. Most states require employers to use similar information in calculating state income tax withholding.

The **Federal Insurance Contributions Act (FICA)** dictates the percentages to be used in calculating the withholding amounts for social security and medicare. The rates for employee withholding for 1995 were 6.2% of the first $61,200 of gross pay for social security and 1.45% of all gross pay for medicare.

AMOUNTS WITHHELD BY EMPLOYEE REQUEST   Other amounts are withheld by employee request. These amounts include premiums for life or health insurance, contributions to charitable organizations, union dues, payments into a retirement plan, or payments on a loan from a financial institution. The employer will withhold these amounts only if the employee has authorized the employer to do so.

RECORDING GROSS PAY AND NET PAY

Assume that the payroll for the week ended August 15 for Centerline Company totaled $6,000. Amounts withheld were $1,200 for federal income tax, $405 for state income tax, $372 for social security, and $87 for medicare. In addition, Centerline withheld $100 for United Way and $320 for health insurance premiums. Centerline would make the following entry to record the payroll:

Aug. 15	Salaries and Wages Expense	6,000	
	Federal Income Tax Withholding Payable		1,200
	State Income Tax Withholding Payable		405
	FICA Taxes Payable		459
	United Way Contributions Payable		100
	Health Insurance Premiums Payable		320
	Payroll Payable		3,516
	To record the payroll for the week ended August 15.		

At the appropriate times, the employer company remits the amounts withheld from employees to the proper recipients. Typically, income and FICA taxes withheld are sent to a designated financial institution, insurance premiums withheld are sent to the insurance company, and United Way contributions withheld are sent to United Way. To the extent that any of the payable amounts are not paid at the end of an accounting period, they are current liabilities.

PAYROLL TAXES PAID BY THE EMPLOYER

The employer pays three types of taxes on the gross payroll amount: FICA taxes, federal unemployment tax, and state unemployment tax.

Each employer is required to pay an amount equal to the FICA taxes withheld from the employees' gross pay (1995 rates were 6.2% of the first $61,200 of gross pay for social security and 1.45% of all gross pay for medicare). As a result, the total social security collected in 1995 for each employee was 12.4% of the first $61,200 of gross pay, and the total medicare collected was 2.9% of all gross pay.

Federal unemployment tax is collected to finance the administration of the unemployment programs of the individual states. State unemployment tax is collected to fund the benefits paid by the state unemployment programs. Federal and state unemployment taxes are levied only on the employers as a percentage of the gross payrolls, subject to various limits.

The current federal unemployment tax rate is 6.2% of the first $7,000 of an employee's gross pay. However, the employer is entitled to a credit against this tax for unemployment taxes paid to the state. The maximum credit allowed is 5.4% of the first $7,000 of gross pay. Many states set their basic unemployment tax rate at this maximum credit. In these states, the effective federal unemployment tax rate is 0.8% (6.2% − 5.4%), and the effective state unemployment tax rate is 5.4%.

RECORDING PAYROLL TAXES PAID BY THE EMPLOYER   Assume that the payroll for the week ended August 15 for Centerline Company totaled $6,000. Amounts withheld included $372 for social security and $87 for medicare. Federal unemployment tax payable for this week was $48 (0.8%) and state unemployment tax payable was $324 (5.4%). Centerline makes the following entry to record the payroll taxes:

Aug. 15	Payroll Tax Expense	777	
	FICA Taxes Payable		405
	Federal Unemployment Tax Payable		48
	State Unemployment Tax Payable		324
	To record the payroll taxes for the week ended August 15.		

If payroll taxes have not been remitted to the proper government agency by the end of the accounting period, they are classified as current liabilities in the balance sheet.

FRINGE BENEFITS PAID BY THE EMPLOYER

Some companies pay for some or all of the fringe benefits enjoyed by the employees. These fringe benefits might include health insurance, life insurance, and pension plans. Any amount the employer pays is an expense of the company. The costs of providing many of these fringe benefits are readily determinable because they are either established by entities that provide the benefits (insurance companies establish the health and life insurance premiums) or the amount is specified by contractual agreement (one popular type of pension plan defines how much the employer corporation will contribute each year to the employees' retirement accounts).

RECORDING FRINGE BENEFITS PAID BY THE EMPLOYER   Assume that the payroll for the week ended August 15 for Centerline Company totaled $6,000. Centerline is responsible for paying the life insurance premium for its employees. The premium for this week is $680. Centerline makes the following entry to record this expense:

Aug. 15	Life Insurance Expense	680	
	Life Insurance Payable		680
	To record the life insurance expense for the week ended August 15.		

Fringe benefit obligations recorded by an employer that have not been remitted to insurance or pension companies by the end of an accounting period are classified as current liabilities.

TOTAL COMPENSATION COST

A company's **total compensation cost** is the sum of gross pay and payroll taxes and fringe benefits paid by the employer. Exhibit 9-2 summarizes this relationship.

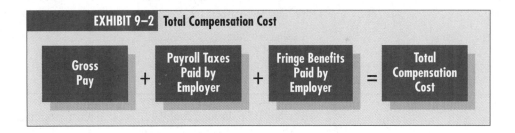

EXHIBIT 9–2 Total Compensation Cost

Gross Pay + Payroll Taxes Paid by Employer + Fringe Benefits Paid by Employer = Total Compensation Cost

---

CASH OBLIGATIONS WHOSE AMOUNTS ARE ESTIMATED

Short-term cash obligations whose amounts are estimated include property taxes payable, income taxes payable, and liability for vacation benefits. These obligations require settlement in cash but the amounts must be estimated when they are recorded.

PROPERTY TAXES PAYABLE

OBJECTIVE 3
DISCUSS and **ILLUSTRATE** cash obligations whose amounts are estimated.

Property taxes are a primary source of revenue for city and county governments. The property taxes paid by business firms represent the cost of the many governmental services from which the firms benefit. As a result, property taxes are considered an operating expense.

Often, firms do not know in advance the amount of tax to be paid. These firms must accrue an estimated amount of property tax expense (and the related liability) each month until they know their actual tax liability.

To illustrate, assume that Morton Company, which ends its accounting year on December 31, is located in the City of Liberty, whose fiscal year runs from July 1 to June 30. City taxes are assessed on October 1 (for the fiscal year started the preceding July 1) and are paid by November 15. The relationship of Morton Company's and Liberty's accounting years is diagrammed as follows:

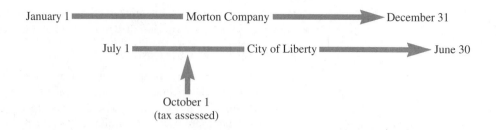

January 1 ━━━━━━━━━ Morton Company ━━━━━━▶ December 31

July 1 ━━━━━━━ City of Liberty ━━━━━▶ June 30

October 1
(tax assessed)

For example, on October 1, 1996, Morton Company knows the amount of its property taxes for the last six months of 1996 and the first six months of 1997. Consequently, property tax expense must be estimated for July, August, and September 1996. Morton Company estimates in July 1996 that its property taxes for the next 12 months will be $18,000. At the end of July, August, and September 1996, the following entry would be made to reflect the estimated monthly property taxes ($18,000/12 = $1,500):

Property Tax Expense	1,500	
Estimated Property Tax Payable		1,500
To record estimated property tax expense for the month.		

On October 1, 1996, Morton Company receives a $19,008 property tax bill from the City of Liberty. Morton's estimate for July–September is too low by $252 ($19,008/12 = $1,584; $1,584 – $1,500 = $84; $84 × 3 months = $252). The $252 difference may be handled as an increase in the property taxes for October. The entry to record the October taxes would be the following:

Property Tax Expense ($1,584 + $252)	1,836	
Estimated Property Tax Payable		1,836
To record property tax expense for October.		

The Estimated Property Tax Payable account has a balance of $6,336 after the October entry. The following is the entry on November 15 to record the property tax payment in full:

Estimated Property Tax Payable	6,336	
Prepaid Property Tax	12,672	
Cash		19,008
To record payment of property taxes.		

The balance in the Prepaid Property Tax account is amortized to Property Tax Expense from November 1996 through June 1997 at $1,584 per month ($12,672/8 = $1,584).

INCOME TAXES PAYABLE The federal government, most states, and some municipalities levy income taxes against corporations, individuals, estates, and trusts. Sole proprietorships and partnerships are not taxable entities—their owners include the businesses' income on their personal tax returns. In the United States, income is generally reported annually on one or more income tax forms, and taxpayers compute the amount of tax due.

The tax due is determined in accordance with various tax laws, rulings of the taxing agencies, and many applicable court decisions. Because administration of tax laws is quite complex and many honest differences exist in their interpretation, the tax obligation reported on a tax return is only an estimate until the government reviews and accepts the firm's calculations. On occasion, the government disagrees with some aspect of a tax return and assesses additional taxes. If the firm challenges the government's position, the issue is litigated and the final tax liability may not be settled until several years after a given tax year.

Because corporations are separate taxable entities, they ordinarily incur a legal obligation for income taxes whenever corporate income is earned. Therefore, corporate financial statements routinely include income tax liabilities. Income taxes of $8,000 are recorded as follows:

Income Tax Expense	8,000	
Income Tax Payable		8,000
To record estimated income tax.		

Corporations usually pay estimates of their income taxes quarterly, with an annual tax return and final payment due within a few months after the end of the year. Thus, any liability for income taxes in the financial statements is classified properly as a current liability.

LIABILITY FOR VACATION BENEFITS

Most employees enjoy vacation privileges—typically, at least two weeks per year with regular pay. Depending on the particular agreement, an employee may earn some fraction of his or her annual vacation each payroll period. Other contracts may require a full year's employment before any vacation is given. In the latter case, the proportion of employees who earn annual vacations depends on the employee turnover rate.

Generally, an employer accrues **vacation benefits expense** if the employees' vacation benefits relate to service already rendered and they accrue over time, as long as payment is probable and can be estimated.[1]

Assume that a firm provides an annual two-week vacation for employees who have worked 50 weeks. Because of employee turnover, only 80% of the staff will receive vacation benefits. These employees earn the two weeks' vacation pay during the 50 weeks worked each year, or at the rate of 4% (2 weeks vacation/50 weeks worked). The proper accrual of vacation benefits expense for a $10,000 payroll is

$$\$10,000 \times 0.04 \times 0.8 = \$320$$

The employing firm makes the following entry at the same time the payroll is recorded:

Vacation Benefits Expense	320	
Estimated Liability for Vacation Benefits		320
To record estimated vacation benefits earned by employees during the current payroll period.		

When the vacation benefits are paid, the amount is recorded as follows (assume that vacation benefit of $150 is paid):

Estimated Liability for Vacation Benefits	150	
Cash		150
To record payment of vacation benefits.		

This treatment assigns the annual vacation expense to the appropriate accounting periods and recognizes throughout the year the accrued liability for vacation benefits.

GOODS AND SERVICES OBLIGATIONS OF KNOWN AMOUNT

OBJECTIVE 4
DISCUSS and **ILLUSTRATE** goods and services obligations of known amount.

Some obligations of known dollar amount require a company to ship goods or provide services rather than pay cash. These obligations result from advance payments received from customers. Another name for this type of obligation is *unearned revenue.*

When a company receives advance payments, it debits Cash and credits a liability that identifies the source of the unearned revenue. Later, when the revenue is earned, the company debits the liability (unearned revenue) and credits an earned revenue account. If the goods or services will be provided within the next year (or operating cycle, if longer), the liability is classified as a current liability.

ADVANCE PAYMENTS FOR GOODS

Magazine and newspaper subscriptions are examples of advance payments for goods. The customer pays cash in advance and the company agrees to ship product (magazines or newspapers) in the future. As an example, assume that *Newsweek* magazine receives $5,200 of one-year subscriptions on June 15. *Newsweek* makes the following entry to record the unearned revenue:

June 15	Cash	5,200	
	Unearned Subscription Revenue		5,200
	To record subscriptions received.		

---

[1]*Statement of Financial Accounting Standards No. 43,* "Accounting for Compensated Absences" (Stamford, CT: Financial Accounting Standards Board, 1980).

As the magazines are sent to these subscribers each week, *Newsweek* makes the following entry:

Aug. 1	Unearned Subscription Revenue	100	
	Subscription Revenue		100
	To record subscription revenue.		

SUBSCRIPTIONS TO THE NEW YORK TIMES

In a recent set of financial statements, The New York Times Company reported total current liabilities of $553,730,000. This total included $130,627,000 of unexpired subscriptions.

ADVANCE PAYMENTS FOR SERVICES

Airline tickets, cruise line tickets, season football tickets, and telephone charges in advance are examples of advance payments for services. The customer pays cash in advance and the company agrees to provide services (travel, football games, or basic telephone services) in the future. As an example, assume that Northwest Airlines sells a ticket for $400 on March 20 for travel on May 25. Northwest Airlines makes the following entry when the ticket is sold:

Mar. 20	Cash	400	
	Unearned Ticket Revenue		400
	To record the sale of an airline ticket.		

When the passenger takes the scheduled flight, Northwest Airlines makes this entry:

May 25	Unearned Ticket Revenue	400	
	Ticket Revenue		400
	To record ticket revenue earned.		

ROYAL CARIBBEAN DEPOSITS FROM CUSTOMERS

In a recent set of financial statements, Royal Caribbean Cruises Ltd. reported total current liabilities of $351,788,000. This total included $163,276,000 of customer deposits.

GOODS AND SERVICES OBLIGATIONS WHOSE AMOUNTS ARE ESTIMATED

Some of the most interesting current liabilities are the goods and services obligations whose amounts are estimated. Liabilities for product warranties and frequent use awards are two examples of this type of current liability.

LIABILITIES FOR PRODUCT WARRANTIES

OBJECTIVE 5

DISCUSS and **ILLUSTRATE** goods and services obligations whose amounts are estimated.

Many firms guarantee their products for a period of time after the sale. Proper matching of expenses with revenue requires that the estimated costs of providing these **product warranties** be recognized as an expense in the period of sale rather than in a later period when the warranty costs may actually be paid.

Suppose that a firm sells a product for $300 per unit, which includes a 30-day warranty against defects. Past experience indicates that 3% of the units will prove defective and that the average repair cost is $40 per defective unit. Furthermore, during a particular month, product sales were $240,000, and 13 of the units sold in this month were defective and were repaired during the month. Using this information, we calculate the accrued liability for product warranties at the end of the month as follows:

Number of units sold ($240,000/$300)	800
Rate of defective units	× 0.03
Total units expected to fail	24
Less: Units failed in month of sale	13
Units expected to fail in the remainder of the warranty period	11
Average repair cost per unit	×$ 40
Estimated liability for product warranty at end of month	$440

This accrued liability is recorded at the end of the month of sale as follows:

Product Warranty Expense	440	
Estimated Liability for Product Warranty		440
To record estimated warranty expense.		

When a unit fails in a future period, the repair costs will be recorded by debiting Estimated Liability for Product Warranty and crediting Cash, Supplies, and so forth.

PRINCIPLE ALERT

MATCHING CONCEPT

As noted in the preceding discussion, the accounting for product warranties is influenced by the *matching concept*. This basic principle of accounting states that expenses must be recorded in the same accounting period as the revenues they help generate. Product warranties make products more attractive to buyers than products without warranties. The warranties, therefore, help generate sales revenues. One of the expenses that needs to be matched with the sales revenues is the cost of servicing the product warranties. Because most of these costs will be incurred in periods after the period of sale, it is necessary to estimate these costs and record them as illustrated in our discussion.

LIABILITIES FOR FREQUENT USE AWARDS

To attract additional business, many companies offer incentives to customers in the form of frequent use awards. Airlines offer frequent flyer awards, hotel and motel chains offer frequent traveler awards, and some restaurants even offer frequent dining awards. When certain levels of use are achieved by a customer (such as miles flown, nights stayed, or meals eaten), the customer is entitled to additional services or goods at no additional cost to the customer.

When customers achieve a level of use that entitles them to receive frequent use awards, the company should estimate the cost of providing the awards and record an expense and estimated current liability for that amount. For example, assume that the Good Nite Motel chain offers customers a free night of lodging for every 10 nights of paid lodging. During the month of December 1996, 120 customers complete 10 nights of paid lodging with Good Nite. Good Nite estimates that the incremental cost of providing these customers with a free night of lodging is $2,160. At December 31, 1996, Good Nite makes the following entry:

Dec. 31	Frequent Traveler Awards Expense	2,160	
	Estimated Liability for Frequent Traveler Awards		2,160
	To record estimated cost of frequent traveler awards earned in December.		

The Estimated Liability for Frequent Traveler Awards is reduced as customers use their free nights of lodging.

Sometimes a product warranty extends for several years or customers have several years to utilize their frequent use awards. When financial statements are prepared in these cases, the estimated liabilities for product warranties and frequent use awards should be divided between the current and long-term liability sections in the balance sheet.

DELTA'S FREQUENT FLYER LIABILITY

A footnote to a recent set of financial statements from Delta Air Lines, Inc., describes the accounting for its Frequent Flyer program as follows:

> The Company sponsors a travel incentive program whereby frequent travelers accumulate mileage credits that entitle them to certain awards, including free travel. The Company accrues the estimated incremental cost of providing free travel awards under its Frequent Flyer program when free travel award levels are achieved. The accrued incremental cost is included in accounts payable and miscellaneous accrued liabilities as a current liability.

CONTINGENT LIABILITIES

OBJECTIVE *6*

DEFINE contingent liabilities, **OUTLINE** criteria for their treatment on financial statements, and **PRESENT** illustrations.

Previously, we defined *liabilities* as obligations resulting from past transactions or events that require the firm to pay money, provide goods, or perform services in the future. Even though a past transaction or event has taken place, the existence of some liabilities still depends on the occurrence of a future event. These types of liability are called **contingent liabilities.** Whether or not a contingent liability is currently recorded in the accounts depends on the likelihood of the future event occurring and the measurability of the obligation.

If the future event will *probably occur* and the amount of the liability can be *reasonably estimated,* an estimated liability should be recorded in the accounts.[2] The estimated liability for product warranty discussed earlier in the chapter is an example of this situation. Our analysis assumed that customers were likely to make claims under warranties for goods they had purchased and that a reasonable estimate of the amount of warranty obligation could be made.

ESTIMATED LIABILITIES RESULTING FROM LAWSUITS

Kaiser Aluminum & Chemical Corporation (KACC) presented the following note to its 1993 financial statements under the heading Asbestos Contingencies:

> KACC is a defendant in a number of lawsuits in which the plaintiffs allege that certain of their injuries were caused by exposure to asbestos during, and as a result of, their employment with KACC or to products containing asbestos produced or sold by KACC. The lawsuits generally relate to products KACC has not manufactured for at least 15 years.
>
> At year-end 1993, the number of such lawsuits pending was approximately 23,400 (approximately 11,400 of which were received in 1993). The number of such lawsuits instituted against KACC increased substantially in 1993, and management believes the number of such lawsuits will continue at approximately the same rate for the next few years.
>
> In connection with such litigation, during 1993, 1992, and 1991, KACC made cash payments for settlement and other related costs of $7.0, $7.1, and $6.1 million, respectively. Based upon prior experience, KACC estimates annual future cash payments in connection with such litigation of approximately $8.0 to $13.0 million for the years 1994 through 1998, and an aggregate of approximately $88.4 million thereafter through 2006. Based upon past experience and reasonably anticipated future activity, KACC has established an accrual for estimated asbestos-related costs for claims filed and estimated to be filed and settled through 2006.

---

[2]*Statement of Financial Accounting Standards No. 5,* "Accounting for Contingencies" (Stamford, CT: Financial Accounting Standards Board, 1975).

Some contingent liabilities are not recorded in the accounts but must be disclosed in a note to the financial statements. Contingent liabilities disclosed in this manner are (1) those for which the likelihood of the future event occurring is probable but no reasonable estimate of the future obligation is determinable or (2) those for which the likelihood of the future event occurring is *reasonably possible* (but not probable), regardless of the ability to measure the future amount. When the future amount is not determinable, the note should state that the amount cannot be estimated.

If the likelihood of the future event occurring is *remote,* the contingent liability is not recorded in the accounts or disclosed in a note to the financial statements, regardless of the ability to measure the future amount. One exception to this guideline, however, is when a company guarantees the credit of others (discussed in the following section). Even remote contingent liabilities associated with credit guarantees must be disclosed in a note to the financial statements.

PRINCIPLE ALERT

MEASURING UNIT CONCEPT AND FULL DISCLOSURE PRINCIPLE

The accounting guidelines for contingent liabilities illustrate the application of two basic principles of accounting: the *measuring unit concept* and the *full disclosure principle.* The measuring unit concept requires that information reported in the body of financial statements be expressed in money terms. If a reasonable estimate of a contingent liability's dollar amount cannot be made, the measuring unit concept prevents the item from appearing in the balance sheet, even if its future occurrence is probable. However, the full disclosure principle requires that firms disclose all significant financial facts and circumstances to financial statement users. This principle leads to the reporting of likely, but unmeasurable contingent liabilities in the notes to the financial statements.

EXAMPLES OF CONTINGENT LIABILITIES

Situations that may create contingent liabilities are discussed in the following sections. In each of these situations, accountants must assess the likelihood of the future event occurring and the measurability of the future amount because these factors determine the proper accounting treatment.

LAWSUITS

In the course of its operations, a firm may prosecute a claim in a court of law by filing a **lawsuit.** At any point, a firm may also be the defendant in one or more lawsuits involving potentially sizable settlements. Examples of litigation issues include product liability, patent infringement, unfair labor practices, breach of contract, environmental matters, and tax issues. The resolution of a lawsuit may take several years. During the time a lawsuit is pending, the defendant has a contingent liability for any future settlement or damages.

ENVIRONMENTAL CLEANUP COSTS

Past actions by many companies in disposing of various types of industrial waste, such as acids, solvents, and isotopes, have caused subsequent environmental damage. The magnitude of the problem led to the passage of federal laws and the creation of a federal agency, the Environmental Protection Agency, to ensure that damaged sites are cleaned up. Some estimates of the total cleanup cost run as high as $100 billion. Firms owning sites that require cleanup or that may require cleanup face a contingent liability for the cleanup costs. Cleanup costs for a particular site may be very difficult to estimate. The party responsible for bearing the cost—the company or its insurance company—may also be at issue.

ADDITIONAL INCOME TAX ASSESSMENTS

Earlier in this chapter, we explained that many aspects of income tax laws and rulings are subject to a significant degree of interpretation. Consequently, many firms do not know their final income tax liability for a given tax period until the related return has been audited or until the applicable statute of limitations becomes effective. The federal statute of limitations for income taxes is three years. No statute of limitations exists in cases of fraud or

POINT OF INTEREST

HOW MUCH WILL IT COST?

In its *1993 Report to Shareholders*, Chrysler Corporation includes in its Commitments and Contingent Liabilities note to its financial statements a paragraph on environmental matters. It states that "the United States Environmental Protection Agency and various state agencies have notified Chrysler that it may be a potentially responsible party ("PRP") for the cost of cleaning up hazardous waste storage or disposal facilities pursuant to the Comprehensive Environmental Response, Compensation and Liability Act ("CERCLA") and other federal and state environmental laws. . . . Chrysler may ultimately incur significant expenditures over an extended period of time . . . and therefore has established reserves for the estimated costs. . . . Future developments could cause Chrysler to change its estimate of the total costs associated with these matters, and such changes could be material to Chrysler's consolidated results of operations for the period in which such developments occur."

failure to file returns. After a firm's income tax return has been audited, the government may determine an **additional income tax assessment.** Proposed assessments for additional taxes often are contested in court for extended periods. During this time, the taxpaying firm is contingently liable for the proposed additional tax.

CREDIT GUARANTEES

To accommodate important but less financially secure suppliers or customers, a firm may create a **credit guarantee** by cosigning a note payable. Until the original debtor satisfies the obligation, the cosigning firm is contingently liable for the debt. Even when the likelihood of default by the debtor is considered remote, the contingent liability associated with credit guarantees must still be disclosed in a note to the financial statements.

CRITERIA FOR FINANCIAL STATEMENT TREATMENT

Exhibit 9-3 summarizes the criteria for identifying various types of liabilities and the related financial statement treatment. Observe that all liabilities—noncontingent and contingent—arise from a past transaction or event involving the firm. The unique feature of a contingent liability is that it depends on the occurrence of a future event. When it is probable that the future event will occur and that the future obligation is reasonably estimable, the contingent liability is recorded in the accounts and appears in the firm's balance sheet.

FINANCIAL ANALYSIS

CURRENT RATIO AND QUICK RATIO

OBJECTIVE 7
DEFINE current ratio and quick ratio and **EXPLAIN** their use.

The **working capital** of a firm is the difference between its current assets and current liabilities. In analyzing the adequacy of a firm's working capital, the current ratio is a widely used financial statistic. The **current ratio** is computed as follows:

$$\text{Current Ratio} = \frac{\text{Current Assets}}{\text{Current Liabilities}}$$

Historically, a current ratio of 2.00 has often been considered an acceptable current ratio. This is a general guide only. Successful operation with a current ratio below 2.00 is possible for many companies, particularly service firms, because they do not have large amounts of inventory among their current assets.

In evaluating a specific firm's current ratio, one should consider such things as the nature of the business, the industry average, the composition of the current assets, and the recent trend in the current ratio. Indeed, one might even conclude that a firm's current ratio is too high; that is, the firm may have far more current assets than are needed to provide adequate coverage of current liabilities. The excess resources might better be directed to more profitable uses.

| EXHIBIT 9–3 | Liabilities: Criteria and Financial Statement Treatment |

Criterion	Liability Recorded in Accounts and Reported in Balance Sheet		Contingent Liability: Disclosed in Footnote to Financial Statements		Contingent Liability: No Disclosure Required
	Noncontingent	Contingent			
Arises out of past transaction or event	Yes	Yes	Yes	Yes	Yes	Yes
Dependent on occurrence of future event	No	No	Yes	Yes	Yes	Yes
Likelihood of future event occurring	Not applicable	Not applicable	Probable	Probable	Reasonably possible	Remote
Amount of future obligation	Known	Reasonably estimable	Reasonably estimable	Not reasonably estimable	Known, reasonably estimable, or not reasonably estimable	Known, reasonably estimable, or not reasonably estimable
Examples	Notes payable, accounts payable, dividends payable	Income tax payable, estimated liability for frequent use awards	Estimated liability for product warranty	Lawsuits, environmental cleanup costs, additional income tax assessments, and guarantees of others' credit. Exact classification depends on likelihood of future event occurring and measurability of future amount. Guarantees of others' credit must be disclosed even if likelihood of future event occurring is remote.		

The **quick ratio** is another ratio used to analyze a company's working capital position. The quick ratio (sometimes called the *acid test ratio*) is calculated using the following formula:

$$\text{Quick Ratio} = \frac{\text{Cash and Cash Equivalents} + \text{Short-Term Investments} + \text{Current Receivables}}{\text{Current Liabilities}}$$

Cash and cash equivalents, short-term investments, and current receivables (notes, accounts, and others) are known as *quick assets*. Quick assets are converted to cash more quickly than inventory and prepaid assets.

Comparing the quick ratio to the current ratio, the main items omitted from the numerator when calculating the quick ratio are inventory and prepaid assets. The quick ratio is used because it may give a better picture than the current ratio of a company's ability to pay current liabilities and take advantage of cash discounts. When the quick ratio is 1.00 (or 1:1), the quick assets available are equal to the current liabilities.

Following are examples of recent ratios for companies in different industries:

	Current Ratio	Quick Ratio
GTE Corporation (telecommunications)	0.75	0.53
Johnson & Johnson (health care products)	1.62	0.80
Minnesota Power (multistate utility)	1.87	1.57
W.H. Brady Co. (coated films manufacturer)	3.81	2.63

KEY POINTS FOR CHAPTER LEARNING OBJECTIVES

1 **DESCRIBE** the nature of liabilities and **DEFINE** *current liabilities* (pp. 308–309).
- Liabilities are obligations resulting from past transactions or events that require the firm to pay money, provide goods, or perform services in the future.
- Items shown on the balance sheet as liabilities are often not legally due and payable on the balance sheet date.
- Current liabilities are obligations that will require within the coming year or the normal operating cycle, whichever is longer, (1) the use of existing current assets or (2) the creation of other current liabilities.

2 **DISCUSS** and **ILLUSTRATE** cash obligations of known amount (pp. 309–315).
- Accounts payable are amounts due to short-term creditors on open account.
- Notes payable are used in transactions when the credit period is longer than the typical 30 or 60 days for accounts payable.
  - We use the following formula to calculate the amount of interest on a note payable with add-on interest:

$$\text{Interest} = \text{Principal} \times \text{Interest Rate} \times \text{Interest Time}$$

- A company records payment of a note payable with add-on interest by debiting Notes Payable for the principal amount, debiting Interest Expense for interest not yet accrued, debiting Interest Payable for interest previously accrued, and crediting Cash for the total amount paid.
- If a company defaults on a note payable with add-on interest, the company records the default by debiting Notes Payable for the principal amount, debiting Interest Expense for accrued interest, and crediting Accounts Payable for the sum of the principal and the accrued interest.
- When a company borrows at a discount from a financial institution, it uses the following formula to calculate the amount of the discount:

$$\text{Discount} = \text{Maturity Value} \times \text{Discount Rate} \times \text{Discount Time}$$

- A company records a note payable resulting from borrowing at a discount by debiting Cash for the cash proceeds received, debiting Discount on Notes Payable (a contra account to Notes Payable) for the amount of the discount, and crediting Notes Payable for the maturity value (face amount) of the note. A company records interest expense when borrowing at a discount by debiting Interest Expense and crediting Discount on Notes Payable.
- Dividends Payable is a current liability that is recorded when the board of directors of a corporation declares the dividend. Dividends are usually paid within several weeks of the time they are declared.
- The principal amount of long-term debt to be paid within one year (or the operating cycle, if longer) is treated as a current liability.
- Sales taxes payable and excise taxes payable are also current liabilities. They are usually paid within several weeks of being recorded.
- Three types of current liabilities arise from payroll: (1) accrued salaries and wages payable, (2) amounts withheld from employees' paychecks, and (3) payroll taxes and fringe benefits paid by the employer.
  - Amounts withheld by legal mandate include federal income tax, state income tax, social security, and medicare. Amounts withheld by employee request include premiums for health or life insurance, contributions to charitable organizations, union dues, payments into a retirement plan, or payments on a loan from a financial institution.
  - Payroll taxes paid by the employer include social security, medicare, federal unemployment tax, and state unemployment tax. Fringe benefits paid by the employer may include life insurance, health insurance, and pension plan contributions.

3 **DISCUSS** and **ILLUSTRATE** cash obligations whose amounts are estimated (pp. 315–317).
- Estimated liabilities for property tax, income tax, and vacation benefits need to be recorded to properly match expenses with revenues.

4 **DISCUSS** and **ILLUSTRATE** goods and services obligations of known amount (pp. 317–318).
- Advance payments for goods include magazine and newspaper subscriptions.
- Advance payments for services include airline tickets, cruise line tickets, season football tickets, and telephone charges in advance.
- This type of liability is also known as unearned revenue.

5 **DISCUSS** and **ILLUSTRATE** goods and services obligations whose amounts are estimated (pp. 318–319).
- To facilitate proper matching of expenses with revenues, a firm selling products with warranties must recognize the estimated cost of future warranty repairs in the period the product is sold. This recognition creates an estimated liability.
- The estimated cost of frequent use awards earned is recorded so it can be matched against revenue generated from the promotion.

6 **DEFINE** *contingent liabilities,* **OUTLINE** criteria for their treatment on financial statements, and **PRESENT** illustrations (pp. 319–322).

- Even though a past transaction or event has taken place, the existence of some liabilities, called *contingent liabilities,* depends on the occurrence of a future event. Whether or not a contingent liability is currently recorded in the accounts depends on the likelihood of the future event occurring and the measurability of the obligation.
  1. If the future event will probably occur and the amount of the liability can be reasonably estimated, the contingent liability should be recorded in the accounts.
  2. If the likelihood of the future event occurring is probable, but no reasonable estimate of the future obligation is determinable or the likelihood of the future event occurring is reasonably possible (but not probable), regardless of the ability to measure the future amount, the contingent liability should be disclosed in a note to the financial statements, not recorded in the accounts.
  3. If the likelihood of the future event occurring is remote, the contingent liability is not recorded in the accounts or disclosed in a note to the financial statements. The only exception is a credit guarantee, which must be disclosed in a note to the financial statements.

7 **Financial Analysis** **DEFINE** *current ratio* and *quick ratio* and **EXPLAIN** their use (pp. 322–323).

- The current ratio is computed as follows:

$$\text{Current Ratio} = \frac{\text{Current Assets}}{\text{Current Liabilities}}$$

- The quick ratio (sometimes called the *acid test ratio*) is calculated using the following formula:

$$\text{Quick Ratio} = \frac{\text{Cash and Cash Equivalents} + \text{Short-Term Investments} + \text{Current Receivables}}{\text{Current Liabilities}}$$

- Both of these ratios measure a firm's ability to pay its current liabilities.

SELF-TEST QUESTIONS FOR REVIEW

(Answers follow the Solution to Demonstration Problem.)

1. Goldsteen Corporation obtained a $5,000 loan from a bank by borrowing at a discount. The discount rate was 9% and the term of the loan was six months. How much cash did Goldsteen receive from the bank?
   a. $4,525
   b. $5,000
   c. $5,225
   d. $4,775

2. Wong, Inc., sold merchandise on account for $1,840, which included a 10% excise tax and a 5% sales tax. What would the entry to record this sale include?
   a. A debit of $1,600 to Accounts Receivable
   b. A debit of $2,116 to Accounts Receivable
   c. A credit of $1,600 to Sales
   d. A credit of $1,840 to Sales

3. Jansen Company sells a product for $400 per unit, which includes a 30-day warranty against defects. Experience indicates that 4% of the units will prove defective, requiring an average repair cost of $50 per unit. During the first month of business, product sales were $320,000, and 20 of the units sold were defective and repaired during the month. What is the accrued liability for product warranties at month-end?
   a. $1,000
   b. $600
   c. $1,600
   d. $2,000

4. Which of the following payroll-related taxes are not withheld from the employees' earnings?
   a. Medicare taxes
   b. Income taxes
   c. Federal unemployment taxes
   d. Social Security taxes

5. Which of the following is *not* considered to be a contingent liability?
   a. Environmental cleanup costs
   b. Notes payable
   c. Credit guarantees
   d. Lawsuit

DEMONSTRATION PROBLEM FOR REVIEW

Archer Corporation had the following payroll data for April 1996:

Office salaries	$ 40,000
Sales salaries	86,000
Federal income taxes withheld	25,600
Health insurance premiums withheld	1,850
United Way contributions withheld	950
Salaries (included above)	
Subject to both FICA taxes	126,000
Subject to federal unemployment taxes	76,000
Subject to state unemployment taxes	88,000

The combined FICA tax rate is 7.65% (6.2% plus 1.45%), the federal unemployment compensation tax rate is 0.8%, and the state unemployment compensation tax rate is 5.4%. The amounts subject to these taxes are given above.

REQUIRED

Present general journal entries to record the following on April 30:

a. Accrual of the payroll.
b. Payment of the net payroll.
c. Accrual of employer's payroll taxes.
d. Payment of all liabilities related to the payroll. (Assume that all are settled at the same time.)

SOLUTION TO DEMONSTRATION PROBLEM

a. Apr. 30

Office Salaries Expense	40,000	
Sales Salaries Expense	86,000	
Federal Income Tax Withholding Payable		25,600
FICA Tax Payable		9,639
Health Insurance Premiums Payable		1,850
United Way Contributions Payable		950
Payroll Payable		87,961

To accrue payroll for April (FICA taxes = 0.0765 × $126,000 = $9,639).

b. 30

Payroll Payable	87,961	
Cash		87,961

To pay April payroll.

c. 30

Payroll Tax Expense	14,999	
FICA Tax Payable		9,639
Federal Unemployment Tax Payable		608
State Unemployment Tax Payable		4,752

To record employer's payroll taxes (FICA Tax = 0.0765 × $126,000 = $9,639; Federal Unemployment Tax = 0.008 × $76,000 = $608; State Unemployment Tax = 0.054 × $88,000 = $4,752).

d. 30

Federal Income Tax Withholding Payable	25,600	
FICA Tax Payable	19,278	
Health Insurance Premiums Payable	1,850	
United Way Contributions Payable	950	
Federal Unemployment Tax Payable	608	
State Unemployment Tax Payable	4,752	
Cash		53,038

To record payment of payroll-related liabilities.

ANSWERS TO SELF-TEST QUESTIONS

1. d, p. 311   **2.** c, p. 313   **3.** b, p. 318   **4.** c, p. 314   **5.** b, pp. 321–322

APPENDIX

F

The Role of Taxes in Decision Making

Federal, state, and local government are much like businesses in the sense that they need revenue to operate. While the primary purpose of taxation is to raise revenue, taxes also serve many other purposes such as economic control, special interest promotion, and wealth and income redistribution. Various types of taxes lend themselves to each of these purposes.

TYPES OF TAXES THAT AFFECT BUSINESS DECISIONS

Federal, state, and local governing units collect many different types of taxes from businesses. The federal government collects income taxes, payroll taxes, excise taxes, and tariffs. State governments collect income taxes, payroll taxes, excise and sales taxes, and property taxes. Local governments collect income taxes, sales taxes, and property taxes.

INCOME TAXES

Income taxes are levied on the taxable income of the taxpayer. Income taxes are usually considered progressive taxes because the tax rate typically increases as the income subject to taxation increases. This is based on the theory that as income rises, the taxpayer has a greater ability to pay. Taxable income differs from pretax financial income due to provisions in the tax laws that provide for different methods of computing items such as depreciation and amortization.

Income taxes apply directly to the earnings of corporations but not sole proprietorships, partnerships, and limited liability companies. The income of sole proprietorships, partnerships, and limited liability companies is added to the taxable income of the owners and taxed at the income tax rate applicable to the owners. A corporation uses the following tax rate schedule to determine its tax amount:

1994 FEDERAL TAX RATE SCHEDULE FOR CORPORATIONS			
Taxable Income		**Tax Amount**	
Over	But Not Over		
$ 0	$ 50,000	$ 0 + 15% of amount over	$ 0
50,000	75,000	7,500 + 25% of amount over	50,000
75,000	100,000	13,750 + 34% of amount over	75,000
100,000	335,000	22,250 + 39% of amount over	100,000
335,000	10,000,000	113,900 + 34% of amount over	335,000
10,000,000	15,000,000	3,400,000 + 35% of amount over	10,000,000
15,000,000	18,333,333	5,150,000 + 38% of amount over	15,000,000
18,333,333		0 + 35% of amount over	0

MARGINAL AND AVERAGE INCOME TAX RATES

The *average income tax rate* is found by dividing the total tax liability by the taxable income of the taxpayer and represents an arithmetic mean tax rate. The *marginal income tax rate* is the tax rate that will be charged on the next dollar of taxable income. The marginal income tax rate is usually higher than the average income tax rate and should be used when evaluating the tax consequences of decisions.

Assume that a corporation has $60,000 of taxable income. The federal income tax liability, the average income tax rate, and the marginal income tax rate are determined as follows, using rates from the 1994 tax rate schedule:

	Taxable Income		Tax Rate		Tax Liability
First	$50,000	×	15%	=	$ 7,500
Next	10,000	×	25%	=	2,500
	$60,000				$10,000

Average income tax rate: $10,000/$60,000 = 0.1667 or 16.67%
Marginal income tax rate: 25%

Additional income will not be taxed at the average income tax rate but at the marginal income tax rate.

PAYROLL TAXES

Payroll taxes are collected for retirement (social security), health care (Medicare), and unemployment benefits. The employee pays half of the social security and Medicare taxes and the employer pays the other half. Unemployment taxes (both federal and state) are usually paid only by the employer. The federal unemployment tax is levied on the first $7,000 of each employee's wages. The rates and salary bases used by states vary widely.

EXCISE AND SALES TAXES

Excise taxes are similar to sales taxes in that both are levied on transfer transactions. While sales taxes are usually state and local taxes levied against all sales, excise taxes are levied on specific transactions. Examples of federal excise taxes are taxes on gasoline and aviation fuel, trucks and trailers, highway use tires, telephone calls, alcohol, tobacco, firearms, air travel, certain motor vehicles, chemicals, ozone-depleting chemicals, and wagering. State and local governments levy excise taxes on items such as tobacco, firearms, alcohol, gasoline and aviation fuel, trucks and trailers, and telephone calls.

Because excise taxes are levied against the sale and use of specific items, the rates are raised and lowered with the political and economic desirability of the items' use. Many excise taxes are levied at the wholesale level so end-consumers are often unaware of these taxes because they are included in the retail price of goods. They are, therefore, referred to as hidden taxes.

TARIFFS

Tariffs are charges made on import and export transactions. Tariffs have become an economic and political weapon, and form entry and exit barriers for foreign trade. They have become significant costs and often affect the competitiveness of prices.

PROPERTY TAXES

Property taxes are usually assessed at the local level annually based upon the ownership of tangible and real property. They are a major source of revenue for local governments. Because they are not derived from income or transfer transactions, these taxes require other income sources for the owner of the property.

AFTER-TAX CONSIDERATIONS IN DECISION MAKING

Whenever decision alternatives are considered by a decision-making body, the after-tax effect should be considered the basis for the decision. This consideration should not be limited to the income tax effects but should include all of the taxes previously discussed.

PURCHASE OF ASSET

For example, Roberts Trucking Corporation is considering the purchase of a truck that will require a full-time driver. Assume that the 65,000 pound truck will cost $85,000 plus a 12% federal excise tax and a 3% state sales tax. Annual highway motor vehicle tax is $100 per year plus $22 for every one thousand pounds over 55,000 pounds. The vehicle license tag (a personal property tax) will cost $750 per year. The driver will be paid an annual salary of $46,000 per year with a benefits package that is equivalent to 13 percent of salary. The company pays social security tax of 6.2% of the first \$61,200 of salary per employee; Medicare tax of 1.45% of the salary per employee; federal unemployment tax of 0.8% of the first \$7,000 of salary per employee; and state unemployment tax of 1.2% of the first \$9,000 of salary per employee. The corporation has a marginal federal income tax rate of 34% and a marginal state income tax rate of 5%. Tax-basis depreciation will be 20% of the truck's cost for the first year. The president of the corporation wants to know the after-tax cost of the decision for the next tax year assuming the purchase and hiring occur on January 2. The costs can be summarized as follows:

Purchase cost of the truck:

Cost of the truck	\$85,000
12% Federal excise tax	10,200
3% State sales tax	2,550
Total purchase cost of the truck	\$97,750

Annual income tax deduction for the truck:

Depreciation (20% × \$97,750)	\$19,550
Road taxes (\$100 + [\$22 × 10])	320
License tag	750
Annual deduction for the truck	\$20,620

Annual cost of the driver:

Salary	\$46,000
Social security (6.2% × \$46,000)	2,852
Medicare (1.45% × \$46,000)	667
Federal unemployment (0.8% × \$7,000)	56
State unemployment (1.2% × \$9,000)	108
Benefits package (13% × \$46,000)	5,980
Annual cost of the driver	\$55,663

Total net annual cost:

Annual deduction for the truck	\$20,620
Annual cost of the driver	55,663
Annual cost before income tax	\$76,283
Less: Tax savings (0.34 + 0.05) × \$76,283	29,750 (rounded)
Net annual after-tax cost	\$46,533

To generalize, the after-tax cost of a business expenditure is the total annual tax-basis cost (before income tax) multiplied by one minus the marginal tax rate.

$$AT = \text{After-tax effect}$$
$$AC = \text{Annual cost before income tax}$$
$$MR = \text{Marginal income tax rate (federal and state)}$$
$$AT = AC \times (1 - MR)$$
$$\$46,533 = \$76,283 \times (1 - 0.39)$$

BUYING VERSUS LEASING When comparing the costs of alternative courses of action, it is important to compare the costs on an after-tax basis. The difference in after-tax costs will often be smaller than the difference in costs before taxes. Identifying the proper cost differential between alternative actions is important because the decision to select an alternative will consider qualitative factors as well as costs. When assessing whether qualitative factors will outweigh cost differentials, it is important to have identified the proper cost amounts.

For example, assume that the president of Roberts Trucking Corporation wants to compare leasing with buying the \$85,000 truck described previously. The total purchase cost of the truck was \$97,750. Assume the entire \$97,750 is borrowed from a bank at 10% interest. Tax-basis depreciation for the first year of \$19,550 plus \$320 for road taxes and \$750 for license tag fees resulted in an annual income tax deduction for the truck of \$20,620.

Assume the truck will be used for five years and will have no salvage value at the end of five years.

If the truck is leased for five years, the annual lease cost will be $32,000. The leasing company will pay road taxes and license tag fees. An analysis of the annual after-tax costs of buying versus leasing follows:

	Buy	Lease
Annual deduction for the truck	$20,620	
Interest deduction ($97,750 × 10%)	9,775	
Annual lease cost		$32,000
Annual cost of the driver	55,663	55,663
Annual cost before income tax	$86,058	$87,663
Less: Tax savings (0.34 + 0.05)	33,563	34,189 (rounded)
Net annual after-tax cost	$52,495	$53,474

Before allowing for income taxes, the annual cost of leasing exceeds the buying alternative by $1,605 ($87,663 – $86,058). Comparing the after-tax costs, the annual leasing cost exceeds the buying alternative by $979 ($53,474 – $52,495). Cost will be one of many factors that the president considers in selecting whether to lease or buy. The proper cost differential for the president to consider in arriving at a decision is the $979.

HIRING VERSUS LEASING

A similar decision situation relates to one of the newer practices: leasing employees from organizations that (1) pay the employee; (2) pay the related payroll taxes and fringe benefits; and (3) prepare the appropriate tax reports to the federal, state, and local governments. This practice has become popular because of the considerable costs beyond salaries and wages of hiring employees, including payroll taxes, benefit packages, and administrative costs of the personnel department.

Assume, for example, that the president of Roberts Trucking Corporation has determined that he can lease a driver for $4,600 per month from a firm that provides many other corporations with drivers. In addition, the corporation is only obligated on a monthly basis, with no severance pay required. The firm has experienced average turnover of similar personnel every 24 months with a severance cost of 10% of annual wages and annual administrative costs of 2% of salaries. An analysis of costs appears on the following page:

	Hire	Lease
Annual salary	$46,000	
Annual lease cost ($4,600 × 12)		$55,200
Social security (6.2% × $46,000)	2,852	
Medicare (1.45% × $46,000)	667	
Federal unemployment (0.8% × $7,000)	56	
State unemployment (1.2% × $9,000)	108	
Benefits package (13% × $46,000)	5,980	
Administrative cost (2% × $46,000)	920	
Severance cost (5% × $46,000)	2,300	
Total annual costs	$58,883	$55,200
Less: Tax savings at 39% (0.34 + 0.05)	22,964	21,528 (rounded)
Net annual after-tax cost	$35,919	$33,672

Before allowing for income taxes, the hiring alternative cost exceeds the leasing alternative cost by $3,683 ($58,883 – $55,200). Comparing the after-tax costs, the hiring alternative exceeds the leasing alternative by $2,247 ($35,919 – $33,672). Cost will be one of many factors the president considers in selecting whether to lease or hire. The proper cost differential for the president to consider in arriving at a decision is the $2,247. Also note that the corporation could pay up to $58,883 to lease an employee before the costs would equal hiring the employee.

GLOSSARY OF KEY TERMS USED IN THIS CHAPTER

additional income tax assessment   An assessment by taxing authorities for an increased income tax payment; if contested by the taxpayer, it is disclosed as a contingent liability by the company that is assessed the additional tax (p. 322).

borrows at a discount   When the face amount of the note is reduced by a calculated cash discount to determine the cash proceeds (p. 311).

contingent liabilities   A potential obligation, the eventual occurrence of which usually depends on some future event beyond the control of the firm. Contingent liabilities may originate with such things as lawsuits, credit guarantees, and contested income tax assessments (p. 320).

credit guarantee   A guarantee of another company's debt by cosigning a note payable; a guarantor's contingent liability that is usually disclosed in a balance sheet footnote (p. 322).

current liabilities   Obligations that will require within the coming year or operating cycle, whichever is longer, (1) the use of existing current assets or (2) the creation of other current liabilities (p. 308).

current ratio   Current assets divided by current liabilities (p. 322).

Discount on Notes Payable   A contra account that is subtracted from the Notes Payable amount on the balance sheet. As the life of the note elapses, the discount is reduced and charged to Interest Expense (p. 311).

effective interest rate   The rate determined by dividing the total discount amount by the cash proceeds on a note payable when the borrower borrowed at a discount (p. 311).

Federal Insurance Contributions Act (FICA)   Under this act, the income of an individual is taxed to support the national social security program providing retirement income, medical care, and death benefits. Employers pay a matching amount of tax on their eligible employees (p. 313).

gross pay   The amount an employee earns before any withholdings or deductions (p. 313).

lawsuit   A prosecution of a claim in a court of law; may lead to a financial statement footnote disclosure by the defendant as a contingent liability (p. 321).

liabilities   Present obligations resulting from past transactions that require the firm to pay money, provide goods, or perform services in the future (p. 308).

maturity date   The date on which a note payable is due to be paid (p. 310).

net pay   The amount of an employee's paycheck, after subtracting withheld amounts (p. 313).

product warranties   Guarantees against product defects for a designated period of time after sale (p. 318).

quick ratio   The sum of (1) cash and cash equivalents, (2) short-term investments, and (3) current receivables divided by current liabilities (p. 323).

total compensation cost   The sum of gross pay, payroll taxes, and fringe benefits paid by the employer (p. 315).

vacation benefits expense   An expense reflecting the cost of employee vacation privileges; this expense is generally accrued over the period in which employees earn vacation (p. 317).

working capital   The difference between current assets and current liabilities (p. 322).

QUESTIONS

9-1 For accounting purposes, how are liabilities defined?

9-2 At what amount are current liabilities presented on the balance sheet?

9-3 What does the term *current liabilities* mean?

9-4 What formula should Hardy Company use to calculate the total amount of interest on a note payable that uses add-on interest?

9-5 Gordon Company signed a note payable with add-on interest on November 20, 1996. Gordon has a December 31 year-end. It paid the note, including interest, on the maturity date, February 20, 1997. What accounts did Gordon debit and what account did it credit on February 20, 1997?

9-6 On September 17, 1997, Davis Company defaulted on a note payable with add-on interest signed on March 17, 1997. Davis has a December 31 year-end. What accounts should it debit and credit to record the default?

9-7 What formula should MacDonald Company's bank use to calculate the total discount amount on a note payable when MacDonald borrows at a discount?

9-8 What type of account is Discount on Notes Payable? Where will it appear in the financial statements?

9-9 One of Jordow Company's notes payable to First United Bank has a discount rate of 10%. The maturity value of the note is $5,000, and the cash proceeds were $4,800. What is the effective interest rate on this note payable?

9-10 On July 18, 1996, James Brown borrowed at a discount at the bank, signing a 90-day note for $8,000 at 9%.
   a. What is the maturity date of the note?
   b. What is the maturity value of the note?
   c. What are the cash proceeds of the note?

9-11 On December 10, 1996, Mary Reed signed a 90-day note for $12,000 at the bank at 8% and charged the discount to Discount on Notes Payable. What adjusting entry is necessary on December 31, 1996?

9-12 Jack Swanson gave a creditor a 90-day, 8% note payable for $7,200 on December 16, 1996. What adjusting entry should Swanson make on December 31, 1996?

9-13 What are five examples of voluntary deductions from an employee's gross pay?

9-14 On whom is the FICA tax levied? What does the FICA tax finance?

9-15 On whom are the federal and state unemployment insurance taxes levied? What do these taxes finance?

9-16 If earned but unpaid wages are accrued at year-end, should employer payroll taxes on these wages be accrued at the same time? Explain.

9-17 What is the difference between accounting for product warranties on (a) failed units repaired in the month of sale and (b) failed units repaired in a subsequent month but that are still covered by the warranty?

9-18 What are *contingent liabilities?* List three examples of contingent liabilities. When should contingent liabilities be recorded in the accounts?

9-19 What do the terms *current ratio* and *quick ratio* mean? How is each used?

PRINCIPLES DISCUSSION QUESTION

9-20 American Paging, Inc., is the seventh largest paging company in the United States. In a recent balance sheet, it reported a current liability of $8,452,379 that was labeled Unearned Revenues and Deposits. A note to the financial statements explained:

> Unearned revenues and deposits primarily represent monthly charges to customers for radio paging rental and dispatch billed in advance. Such revenues and deposits are recognized in the following month when service is provided or are applied against the customer's final bill or last month's rent.

What basic principle of accounting guides American Paging's handling of its unearned revenues and deposits? Briefly explain.

EXERCISES

LIABILITIES IN THE BALANCE SHEET
— OBJ. 1, 3 —

9-21 For each of the following situations, indicate the amount shown as a liability on the balance sheet of Kane, Inc., at December 31, 1996.
   a. Kane has accounts payable of $110,000 for merchandise included in the 1996 ending inventory.
   b. Kane agreed to purchase a $28,000 drill press in January 1997.
   c. During November and December of 1996, Kane sold products to a firm and guaranteed them against product failure for 90 days. Estimated costs of honoring this provision during 1997 are $2,200.
   d. On December 15, 1996, Kane declared a $70,000 cash dividend payable on January 15, 1997, to stockholders of record on December 31, 1996.
   e. Kane provides a profit-sharing bonus for its executives equal to 5% of the reported before-tax income for the current year. The estimated before-tax income for 1996 is $600,000.

MATURITY DATES OF NOTES PAYABLE
— OBJ. 2 —

9-22 Determine the maturity date and compute the interest for each of the following notes payable with add-on interest:

	Date of Note	Principal	Interest Rate (%)	Term
a.	August 5	$15,000	8	120 days
b.	May 10	8,400	7	90 days
c.	October 20	12,000	9	45 days
d.	July 6	4,500	10	60 days
e.	September 15	13,500	8	75 days

**NOTE PAYABLE—DISCOUNT
METHOD
— OBJ. 2 —**

9-23 On November 21, 1996, Tilden Company signed an 8%, $14,400, 60-day note payable at the bank; Tilden borrowed at a discount.
  a. What is the maturity date of the note?
  b. What are the proceeds of the note?
  c. What is the effective interest rate on the note?

**COMPUTING ACCRUED
INTEREST PAYABLE
— OBJ. 2 —**

9-24 Compute the interest accrued on each of the following notes payable owed by Northland, Inc., on December 31, 1996:

Lender	Date of Note	Principal	Interest Rate (%)	Term
Maple	11/21/96	$18,000	10	120 days
Wyman	12/13/96	14,000	9	90 days
Nahn	12/19/96	16,000	12	60 days

**ADJUSTING ENTRIES
FOR INTEREST
— OBJ. 2 —**

9-25 The following note transactions occurred during 1996 for Towell Company:

Nov. 25 Towell issued a 90-day, 9% note payable for $8,000 to Hyatt Company for merchandise.

Dec. 7 Towell signed a 120-day, $12,000 note at the bank at 10%, charging the discount to Discount on Notes Payable.

   22 Towell gave Barr, Inc., a $12,000, 10%, 60-day note in payment of account.

Prepare the general journal entries necessary to adjust the interest accounts at December 31, 1996.

**EXCISE AND SALES TAX
CALCULATIONS
— OBJ. 2 —**

9-26 Barnes Company has just billed a customer for $1,044, an amount that includes a 10% excise tax and a 6% state sales tax.
  a. What amount of revenue is recorded?
  b. Prepare a general journal entry to record the transaction on the books of Barnes Company on June 15, 1996.

**ADVANCE PAYMENTS FOR GOODS
— OBJ. 4 —**

9-27 The Chicago Daily Times Corporation (CDT) publishes a daily newspaper. A 52-week subscription sells for $208. Assume that CDT sells 100 subscriptions on January 1. None of the subscriptions are cancelled as of March 31.
  a. Prepare a journal entry to record the receipt of the subscriptions on January 1.
  b. Prepare a journal entry to record one week of earned revenue on March 25.

**PROVIDING FOR
WARRANTY COSTS
— OBJ. 5 —**

9-28 Milford Company sells a motor that carries a 60-day unconditional warranty against product failure. Based on a reliable statistical analysis, Milford knows that between the sale and lapse of the product warranty, 2% of the units sold will require repair at an average cost of $50 per unit. The following 1996 data reflect Milford's recent experience:

	October	November	December	Dec. 31 Total
Units sold	23,000	22,000	25,000	70,000
Known product failures from sales of				
October	120	180	160	460
November		130	220	350
December			210	210

Calculate and prepare a general journal entry to record properly the estimated liability for product warranties at December 31, 1996. Assume that warranty costs of known failures have already been reflected in the records.

**PROVIDING FOR VACATION
BENEFITS
— OBJ. 3 —**

9-29 Franklin, Inc.'s current vacation policy for its production workers provides four weeks paid vacation for employees who have worked 48 weeks. An analysis of the company's employee turnover rates indicates that approximately 10% of the employees will forfeit their vacation benefits.
  a. Compute the proper provision for estimated vacation benefits for a four-week period in which the total pay earned by the employee group was $110,000.
  b. Present a general journal entry to recognize the above provision on March 20, 1996.

PROBLEMS

BORROWING AT A DISCOUNT
— OBJ. 2 —

9-30 Gordon Products, Inc., had the following transactions and adjustment for 1996 and 1997:

1996

May 18   Borrowed at a discount from Bank Wisconsin, signing a $36,000, 90-day note at 8%.

Aug. 16   Paid Bank Wisconsin the amount due on the May 18 note payable.

Oct.   2   Borrowed at a discount from Bank Wisconsin, signing a $33,600, 120-day note at 9%.

Dec. 31   Made the appropriate adjusting entry for interest expense on the note payable to Bank Wisconsin.

1997

Jan. 30   Paid Bank Wisconsin the amount due on the October 2, 1996, note payable.

REQUIRED

a. Record these transactions and the adjustment in general journal form.

b. Calculate the effective interest rate for the May 18, 1996, note and the October 2, 1996, note.

VARIOUS ENTRIES FOR
ACCOUNTS AND NOTES PAYABLE
— OBJ. 2 —

9-31 Logan Company had the following transactions during 1996:

Apr.   8   Issued a $4,800, 75-day, 8% note payable in payment of an account with Bennett Company.

May 15   Borrowed at a discount from Lincoln Bank, signing a $36,000, 60-day note at 9%.

June 22   Paid Bennett Company the principal and interest due on the April 8 note payable.

July   6   Purchased $12,000 of merchandise from Bolton Company; signed a 90-day note with 10% add-on interest.

     14   Paid the May 15 note due Lincoln Bank.

Oct.   2   Borrowed at a discount from Lincoln Bank, signing a $24,000, 120-day note at 12%.

     4   Defaulted on the note payable to Bolton Company.

REQUIRED

a. Record these transactions in general journal form.

b. Record any adjusting entries for interest in general journal form. Logan Company has a December 31 year-end.

ADJUSTING ENTRIES FOR
INTEREST
— OBJ. 2 —

9-32 At December 31, 1995, Hoffman Corporation had two notes payable outstanding (notes 1 and 2). At December 31, 1996, Hoffman also had two notes payable outstanding (notes 3 and 4). These notes are described below.

	Date of Note	Principal Amount	Interest Rate %	Number of Days
December 31, 1995				
Note 1 (borrowed at a discount)	11/16/95	$12,000	8%	120
Note 2 (add-on interest)	12/4/95	16,000	9	60
December 31, 1996				
Note 3 (borrowed at a discount)	12/7/96	9,000	9	60
Note 4 (add-on interest)	12/21/96	18,000	10	30

REQUIRED

a. Prepare the adjusting entries for interest at December 31, 1995.

b. Assume that the adjusting entries were made at December 31, 1995, and that no reversing or adjusting entries were made during 1996. Prepare the 1996 journal entries to record payment of the notes that were outstanding at December 31, 1995.

c. Prepare the adjusting entries for interest at December 31, 1996.

RECORDING PAYROLL AND
PAYROLL TAXES
— OBJ. 2 —

9-33 Beamon Corporation had the following payroll for April 1996:

Officers' salaries	$32,000
Sales salaries	67,000
Federal income taxes withheld	19,000
FICA taxes withheld	7,500
Health insurance premiums withheld	1,600
United Way contributions withheld	1,200
Salaries (included above) subject to federal unemployment taxes	55,000
Salaries (included above) subject to state unemployment taxes	60,000

REQUIRED

Prepare general journal entries on April 30, 1996, to record

a. Accrual of the monthly payroll.

b. Payment of the net payroll.

c. Accrual of employer's payroll taxes. (Assume that the FICA tax matches the amount withheld, the federal unemployment tax is 0.8%, and the state unemployment tax is 5.4%.)

d. Payment of all liabilities related to this payroll. (Assume that all are settled at the same time.)

RECORDING PAYROLL AND PAYROLL TAXES
— OBJ. 2 —

9-34 The following data are taken from Fremont Wholesale Company's May 1996 payroll:

Administrative salaries	$34,000
Sales salaries	47,000
Custodial salaries	7,000
Total payroll	$88,000
Salaries subject to 1.45% medicare tax	$88,000
Salaries subject to 6.2% social security tax	74,000
Salaries subject to federal unemployment taxes	14,000
Salaries subject to state unemployment taxes	20,000
Federal income taxes withheld from all salaries	17,800

Assume that the company is subject to a 2% state unemployment tax (due to a favorable experience rating) and a 0.8% federal unemployment tax.

REQUIRED

Record the following in general journal form on May 31, 1996:

a. Accrual of the monthly payroll.

b. Payment of the net payroll.

c. Accrual of the employer's payroll taxes.

d. Payment of these payroll-related liabilities. (Assume that all are settled at the same time.)

PROPERTY TAX CALCULATIONS
— OBJ. 3 —

9-35 Estrella Company prepares monthly financial statements and ends its accounting year on December 31. Its headquarters is located in the city of Bayfield. City taxes are assessed on September 1 each year, are paid by October 15, and relate to the city's fiscal year that ends the next June 30 (10 months after assessment). For the city tax year July 1, 1995–June 30, 1996, Estrella paid $20,000 in property taxes on its headquarters building.

REQUIRED

a. What amount of property tax expense should be accrued on the financial statements for July 1996, if property taxes for July 1, 1996–June 30, 1997, are an estimated 5% higher than the preceding year?

b. Assume that the 1996–1997 tax bill received on September 1, 1996, was for $22,800 and that the estimate in part (a) was used through August. What is the proper monthly property tax expense for September 1996 if the deficiencies in the monthly property tax estimates through August are handled as an increase in the property tax expense for September 1996?

c. How does the payment of the tax bill on October 15, 1996, affect the amount of property tax expense recognized for October?

EXCISE AND SALES TAX CALCULATIONS
— OBJ. 2 —

9-36 Fulton Corporation initially records its sales at amounts that exclude any related excise and sales taxes. During June 1996, Fulton recorded total sales of $400,000. An analysis of June sales indicated the following:

1. Thirty percent of sales were subject to both a 10% excise tax and a 6% sales tax.

2. Fifty percent of sales were subject only to the sales tax.

3. The balance of sales was for labor charges not subject to either excise or sales tax.

REQUIRED

a. Calculate the related liabilities for excise and sales taxes for June 1996.

b. Prepare the necessary journal entry at June 30 to record the monthly payment of excise tax and sales tax to the government.

NONCONTINGENT AND CONTINGENT LIABILITIES
— OBJ. 3, 6 —

9-37 The following independent situations represent various types of liabilities:

1. One of the employees of Martin Company was severely injured when hit by one of Martin's trucks in the parking lot. The 35-year-old employee will never be able to work again. Insurance coverage is minimal. The employee has sued Martin Company and a jury trial is scheduled.

2. A stockholder has filed a lawsuit against Sweitzer Corporation. Sweitzer's attorneys have reviewed the facts of the case. Their review revealed that similar lawsuits have never resulted in a cash award and it is highly unlikely that this lawsuit will either.

3. Armstrong Company signed a 60-day, 10% note when it purchased merchandise from Fischer Company.

4. Richmond Company has been notified by the Department of Environment Protection (DEP) that a state where it has a plant is filing a lawsuit for groundwater pollution against Richmond and another company that has a plant adjacent to Richmond's plant. Test results have not identified the exact source of the pollution. Richmond's manufacturing process can produce by-products that pollute ground water.

5. Fredonia Company has cosigned a note payable to a bank for one of its customers. The customer received all of the proceeds of the note. Fredonia will have to repay the loan if the customer fails to do so. Fredonia Company believes that it is unlikely that it will have to pay the note.

6. Holt Company manufactured and sold products to Z-Mart, a retailer that sold the products to consumers. The manufacturer's warranty offers replacement of the product if it is found to be defective within 90 days of the sale to the consumer. Historically, 1.2% of the products are returned for replacement.

REQUIRED

Prepare a multicolumn analysis that presents the following information for each of these situations:

a. Number of the situation.

b. Type of liability: (1) noncontingent or (2) contingent.

c. Accounting treatment: (1) record in accounts, (2) disclose in a footnote to financial statements, or (3) neither record nor disclose.

TAX CONSIDERATIONS IN DECISION MAKING — APPENDIX F —

9-38 The vice-president of production for Jonstone Framing Corporation has proposed that the company invest in a new machine that will increase the output of metal frames. The new machine will cost $120,000 plus 5% state sales tax. The old machine it will replace has a tax-basis book value of $25,000 and can be sold for $14,000. The new machine requires only one worker; the old machine required two workers. These workers earn $25,000 per year and have a benefits package that costs the company 11.5% of their salary. The company's total payroll tax burden is 8% of the gross salary for these employees and the combined marginal federal and state income tax rate is 39%. Assume that the first year's tax-basis depreciation will be 20% of cost.

REQUIRED

Assume that the new machine would be purchased at the start of 1996. Compute the effect on 1996 income tax.

TAX CONSIDERATIONS IN DECISION MAKING — APPENDIX F —

9-39 Ann Williams Corporation is considering the lease or purchase of automobiles for its sales representatives. The cars can be purchased for $9,000 each plus state sales tax of 5% (which is added to the cost) and an annual license tag fee of $400 (which is a deductible expense). The automobiles will be used for three years and can be sold for $2,000 on the last day of the third year. With a special financing plan, the cars can be purchased with no money down. Interest expense in years 1 through 3 will be $800, $500, and $300, respectively. The same cars can be leased for 3 years at $4,000 per year. The leasing company will pay the sales tax and the license tag fees. Assume that the tax-basis depreciation will be $3,100 per car per year. The corporation's marginal income tax rate is 38%.

REQUIRED

a. Compute the net after-tax cost of each car for each of the 3 years if the cars are purchased.

b. Compute the net after-tax cost of each car for each of the 3 years if the cars are leased.

ALTERNATE EXERCISES

LIABILITIES IN THE BALANCE SHEET — OBJ. 1, 3 —

9-21A For each of the following situations, indicate the amount shown as a liability on the balance sheet of Anchor, Inc., at December 31, 1996.

a. Anchor's general ledger shows a credit balance of $125,000 in Long-Term Notes Payable; of this amount, a $25,000 installment becomes due on June 30, 1997.

b. Anchor estimates its unpaid income tax liability for 1996 is $34,000; it plans to pay this amount in March 1997.

c. On December 31, 1996, Anchor received a $15,000 invoice for merchandise shipped on December 28. The merchandise has not yet been received. The merchandise was shipped F.O.B. shipping point.

d. During 1996, Anchor collected $10,500 of state sales tax. At year-end, it has not yet remitted $1,400 of these taxes to the state department of revenue.

e. On December 31, 1996, Anchor's bank approved a $5,000, 90-day loan. Anchor plans to sign the note and receive the money on January 2, 1997.

MATURITY DATES OF NOTES PAYABLE — OBJ. 2 —

9-22A Determine the maturity date and compute the interest for each of the following notes payable with add-on interest:

	Date of Note	Principal	Interest Rate (%)	Term
a.	July 10	$7,200	9	90 days
b.	April 14	6,000	8	120 days
c.	May 19	5,600	$7\frac{1}{2}$	120 days
d.	June 10	5,400	8	45 days
e.	October 29	7,500	8	75 days

NOTE PAYABLE—DISCOUNT METHOD — OBJ. 2 —

9-23A On April 21, 1996, Prospect Company borrowed at a discount, signing a $9,000, 60-day note at the bank at 9%.
a. What is the maturity date of the note?
b. What are the proceeds of the note?
c. What is the effective interest rate on the note?

COMPUTING ACCRUED INTEREST PAYABLE — OBJ. 2 —

9-24A Compute the interest accrued on each of the following notes payable owed by Galloway, Inc., on December 31, 1996:

Lender	Date of Note	Principal	Interest Rate (%)	Term
Barton	12/4/96	$10,000	12	120 days
Lawson	12/13/96	12,000	9	90 days
Riley	12/19/96	15,000	10	60 days

ADJUSTING ENTRIES FOR INTEREST — OBJ. 2 —

9-25A The following note transactions occurred during 1996 for Zuber Company:

Nov. 25 Zuber issued a 90-day, 12% note payable for $6,000 to Porter Company for merchandise.
Dec. 10 Zuber signed a 120-day, $7,200 note at the bank at 10%, charging the discount to Discount on Notes Payable.
      23 Zuber gave Dale, Inc., a $9,000, 10%, 60-day note in payment of account.

Prepare the general journal entries necessary to adjust the interest accounts at December 31, 1996.

EXCISE AND SALES TAX CALCULATIONS — OBJ. 2 —

9-26A Allied Company has just billed a customer for $1,102, an amount that includes a 10% excise tax and a 6% state sales tax.
a. What amount of revenue is recorded?
b. Prepare a general journal entry to record the transaction on the books of Allied Company on November 6, 1996.

ADVANCE PAYMENT FOR SERVICES — OBJ. 4 —

9-27A The Columbus Bluebirds football team sells a 12-game season ticket for $180. Assume that the team sells 1,000 season tickets on August 10. The tickets are all used for admission.
a. Prepare a journal entry to record the sale of the season tickets on August 10.
b. Prepare a journal entry to record one game of earned revenue on September 12.

PROVIDING FOR WARRANTY COSTS — OBJ. 5 —

9-28A Brigham Company sells an electric timer that carries a 60-day unconditional warranty against product failure. Based on a reliable statistical analysis, Brigham knows that between the sale and lapse of the product warranty, 3% of the units sold will require repair at an average cost of $35 per unit. The following 1996 data reflect Brigham's recent experience:

	October	November	December	Dec. 31 Total
Units sold	36,000	34,000	45,000	115,000
Known product failures from sales of				
October	320	550	210	1,080
November		230	360	590
December			410	410

Calculate and prepare a general journal entry to record properly the estimated liability for product warranties at December 31, 1996. Assume that warranty costs of known failures have already been reflected in the records.

PROVIDING FOR VACATION BENEFITS
— OBJ. 3 —

9-29A Dalton, Inc.'s current vacation policy for its production workers provides two weeks paid vacation for employees who have worked 50 weeks. An analysis of the company's employee turnover rates indicates that approximately 15% of the employees will forfeit their vacation benefits.

 a. Compute the proper provision for estimated vacation benefits for a four-week period in which the total pay earned by the employee group was $170,000.

 b. Present a general journal entry to recognize the above provision on April 15, 1996.

ALTERNATE PROBLEMS

BORROWING AT A DISCOUNT
— OBJ. 2 —

9-30A Peabody Products, Inc., had the following transactions and adjustment for 1996 and 1997:

1996

Mar. 6   Borrowed at a discount from United Bank, signing a $40,000, 60-day note at 9%.

May 5   Paid United Bank the amount due on the March 6 note payable.

Nov. 16   Borrowed at a discount from United Bank, signing a $50,000, 90-day note at 8%.

Dec. 31   Made the appropriate adjusting entry for interest expense on the note payable to United Bank.

1997

Feb. 14   Paid United Bank the amount due on the November 16, 1996, note payable.

REQUIRED

 a. Record these transactions and the adjustment in general journal form.

 b. Calculate the effective interest rate for the March 6, 1996, note and the November 16, 1996, note.

VARIOUS ENTRIES FOR ACCOUNTS AND NOTES PAYABLE
— OBJ. 2 —

9-31A Simon Company had the following transactions during 1996:

Apr. 15   Issued a $6,000, 75-day, 8% note payable in payment of an account with Marion Company.

May 22   Borrowed at a discount from Sinclair Bank, signing a $30,000, 60-day note at 9%.

June 29   Paid Marion Company the principal and interest due on the April 15 note payable.

July 13   Purchased $12,000 of merchandise from Sharp Company; signed a 90-day note with 10% add-on interest.

     21   Paid the May 22 note due Sinclair Bank.

Oct.   2   Borrowed at a discount from Sinclair Bank, signing a $36,000, 120-day note at 12%.

     11   Defaulted on the note payable to Sharp Company.

REQUIRED

 a. Record these transactions in general journal form.

 b. Record any adjusting entries for interest in general journal form. Simon Company has a December 31 year-end.

ADJUSTING ENTRIES FOR INTEREST
— OBJ. 2 —

9-32A At December 31, 1995, Portland Corporation had two notes payable outstanding (notes 1 and 2). At December 31, 1996, Portland also had two notes payable outstanding (notes 3 and 4). These notes are described below.

	Date of Note	Principal Amount	Interest Rate %	Number of Days
December 31, 1995				
Note 1 (borrowed at a discount)	11/25/95	$27,000	8%	90
Note 2 (add-on interest)	12/16/95	16,800	9	60
December 31, 1996				
Note 3 (borrowed at a discount)	12/11/96	15,400	9	120
Note 4 (add-on interest)	12/7/96	18,000	10	90

REQUIRED

 a. Prepare the adjusting entries for interest at December 31, 1995.

 b. Assume that the adjusting entries were made at December 31, 1995, and that no reversing or adjusting entries were made during 1996. Prepare the 1996 journal entries to record payment of the notes that were outstanding at December 31, 1995.

 c. Prepare the adjusting entries for interest at December 31, 1996.

RECORDING PAYROLL AND PAYROLL TAXES
— OBJ. 2 —

9-33A Manchester, Inc., had the following payroll for March 1996:

Officers' salaries	$39,000
Sales salaries	65,000
Federal income taxes withheld	21,000
FICA taxes withheld	7,900
Health insurance premiums withheld	2,200
Salaries (included above) subject to federal unemployment taxes	65,000
Salaries (included above) subject to state unemployment taxes	70,000

REQUIRED
Prepare general journal entries on March 31, 1996, to record:
a. Accrual of the monthly payroll.
b. Payment of the net payroll.
c. Accrual of employer's payroll taxes. (Assume that the FICA tax matches the amount withheld, the federal unemployment tax is 0.8%, and the state unemployment tax is 5.4%.)
d. Payment of all liabilities related to this payroll. (Assume that all are settled at the same time.)

RECORDING PAYROLL AND PAYROLL TAXES
— OBJ. 2 —

9-34A The following data are taken from Jefferson Distribution Company's March 1996 payroll:

Administrative salaries	$29,000
Sales salaries	55,000
Custodial salaries	8,000
Total payroll	$92,000
Salaries subject to FICA tax (6.2% + 1.45%)	$92,000
Salaries subject to federal unemployment taxes	68,000
Salaries subject to state unemployment taxes	76,000
Federal income taxes withheld from all salaries	18,600

Assume that the company is subject to a 5.4% state unemployment tax and an 0.8% federal unemployment tax.

REQUIRED
Record the following in general journal form on March 31, 1996:
a. Accrual of the monthly payroll.
b. Payment of the net payroll.
c. Accrual of the employer's payroll taxes.
d. Payment of these payroll-related liabilities. (Assume that all are settled at the same time.)

PROPERTY TAX CALCULATIONS
— OBJ. 3 —

9-35A Bryant Company prepares monthly financial statements and ends its accounting year on December 31. The company owns a factory in the city of Ashton, where city taxes are assessed on March 1 each year, are paid by May 1, and relate to the city's fiscal year that ends the next June 30 (four months after assessment). For the city tax year July 1, 1995–June 30, 1996, Bryant paid $24,000 in property taxes on its factory.

REQUIRED
a. What amount of property tax expense should be accrued on the financial statements for July 1996, if property taxes for July 1, 1996–June 30, 1997, are an estimated 6% higher than they were the preceding year?
b. Assume that the 1996–1997 tax bill received on March 1, 1997, was for $26,400 and that the estimate in part (a) was used through February. What is the proper monthly property tax expense for March 1997 if the deficiencies in the monthly property tax estimates through February are handled as an increase in the property tax expense for March 1997?
c. How does the payment of the tax bill on May 1, 1997, affect the amount of property tax expense recognized for May?

EXCISE AND SALES TAX CALCULATIONS
— OBJ. 2 —

9-36A Madison Corporation initially records its sales at amounts that exclude any related excise and sales taxes. During May 1996, Madison recorded total sales of $600,000. An analysis of May sales indicated the following:
1. Twenty percent of sales were subject to both a 10% excise tax and a 5% sales tax.
2. Sixty percent of sales were subject only to the sales tax.
3. The balance of sales was for labor charges not subject to either excise or sales tax.

REQUIRED

a. Calculate the related liabilities for excise and sales taxes for May 1996.

b. Prepare the necessary journal entry at May 31, 1996, to record the monthly payment of excise tax and sales tax to the government.

NONCONTINGENT AND
CONTINGENT LIABILITIES
— OBJ. 3, 6 —

9-37A The following independent situations represent various types of liabilities:

1. Marshall Company has a manufacturing plant located in a small rural community. The only other major employer in the area is Baker Company, which is experiencing financial problems. Marshall agrees to guarantee a loan for Baker so Baker will remain in the community. Baker will receive all the proceeds of the loan. However, Marshall will have to repay the loan if Baker fails to do so. Marshall believes that Baker will repay the loan.

2. The village of High Creek and the town of Middlebury have been jointly using a rural dump site for 25 years. The state department of natural resources has notified the two municipalities that wells on the nearby farms are polluted and that the dump site will be closed while further testing is done. Cleanup could cost as much as $25 million.

3. Two people walking on the sidewalk in front of the building owned by First United Bank were injured when part of the building collapsed on them. They are 25 years old and both are totally disabled. The building had been in poor condition for a long time. Insurance coverage is minimal. Both are suing First United Bank, and a jury trial is scheduled.

4. Winters Company sells garden tractors through 120 dealers located throughout the United States. Winters provides a two-year warranty for all parts and labor on these tractors. Each year, the average warranty cost per tractor sold is approximately $40.

5. Cronnin Company signed a 90-day note when it bought a new delivery truck for $25,000.

6. The CPA firm of Boyd and Lampe is being sued by one of the owners of an audit client that went bankrupt three years after Boyd and Lampe conducted an audit. The CPA firm has no insurance for this type of lawsuit. The attorneys for the CPA firm have stated that similar cases have never been successful, and they expect the same result here.

REQUIRED

Prepare a multicolumn analysis that presents the following information for each of these situations:

a. Number of the situation.

b. Type of liability: (1) noncontingent or (2) contingent.

c. Accounting treatment: (1) record in accounts, (2) disclose in a footnote to financial statements, or (3) neither record nor disclose.

TAX CONSIDERATIONS IN
DECISION MAKING
— APPENDIX F —

9-38A Louis Corporation is currently planning to hire three new employees. Louis Corporation has a benefit package that costs 12.5% of salaries with a maximum cost of $7,500 per employee. Assume that social security is 6.2% of the first $53,400 per employee; Medicare is 1.45%; federal unemployment is 0.8% of the first $7,000 per employee; and state unemployment is 2.1% of the first $8,500 per employee. The marginal income tax rate for Louis Corporation is 34% federal and 7% state. Louis Corporation enjoys an average income tax rate of 30% federal and 6% state.

REQUIRED

Compute the annual after-tax cost of each of three employees whose respective salaries are listed below. Round all calculations to the nearest dollar.

a. $25,000.

b. $52,000.

c. $85,000.

TAX CONSIDERATIONS IN
DECISION MAKING
— APPENDIX F —

9-39A For each salary level in problem 9-38A, determine at what amount the corporation could lease an employee and incur the same after-tax cost. Round your answers to the nearest dollar.

CASES

BUSINESS
DECISION CASE

Statz Enterprises manages office buildings in several Midwestern cities. The firm maintains its own janitorial staff for all buildings managed. The firm manages 10 buildings in Center City, where it maintains a staff of 40 janitorial people, with a total annual payroll of $710,000. All members of the staff earn more than $16,000 per year each. FICA tax rates are 6.2% of the first $61,200 of earnings plus 1.45% of total earnings per employee. Only one employee's earnings exceeds the $61,200 maximum amount by the amount of $2,000. Statz is subject to a 5.4% state unemployment tax on the first $10,000 wages earned by each employee. Its federal unemployment compensation tax rate is 0.8% of the first $7,000 earned by each employee. The firm's contribution to health insurance cost averages $200 per employee. Annual nonpayroll costs of the Center City operation follow:

Supplies	$25,000
Depreciation on equipment	46,000
Insurance	22,000
Miscellaneous	5,000
	$98,000

The firm has a high employee turnover rate and has not always kept tenants happy with the janitorial service. President Robert Statz has been approached by Maintenance, Inc., a commercial janitorial service chain, which has submitted a bid of $875,000 annually to provide janitorial service for the 10 buildings in Center City. This firm is noted for efficiency and satisfactory service. Statz estimates that hiring an outside firm would save $10,000 annually in accounting costs and costs of contracting with other commercial firms for substitutes for regular help. These costs are not included in the preceding list of nonpayroll costs.

REQUIRED

Prepare a cost analysis for Statz to help him decide whether to accept the bid of Maintenance, Inc.

FINANCIAL ANALYSIS CASE Abbott Laboratories is a diversified health care company devoted to the discovery, development, manufacture, and marketing of innovative products that improve diagnostic, therapeutic, and nutritional practices. The company's balance sheet for three recent years contains the following data (Year 3 is the most recent; dollar amounts in thousands):

	Year 3	Year 2	Year 1
Cash and Cash Equivalents	$ 300,676	$ 116,576	$ 60,395
Investment Securities	78,149	141,601	85,838
Trade Receivables (net of allowance)	1,336,222	1,244,396	1,150,894
Inventories	940,533	863,808	815,385
Prepaids	929,955	865,357	778,556
Total Current Assets	$3,585,535	$3,231,738	$2,891,068
Total Current Liabilities	$3,094,933	$2,782,508	$2,229,337

REQUIRED

a. Compute the current ratio for years 1, 2, and 3.
b. Compute the quick ratio for years 1, 2, and 3.
c. Comment on the three-year trend in these two ratios.

ETHICS CASE Sunrise Pools, Inc., is being sued by the Crescent Club for negligence when installing a new pool on Crescent Club's property. Crescent Club alleges that the employees of Sunrise Pools damaged the foundation of the clubhouse and part of the golf course while operating heavy machinery to install the pool.

The lawsuit is for $1.5 million. At the time of the alleged incident, Sunrise Pools carried only $600,000 of liability insurance.

While reviewing the draft of Sunrise Pools' annual report, its president deletes all references to this lawsuit. She is concerned that disclosure of this lawsuit in the annual report will be viewed by Crescent Club as admission of Sunrise's wrongdoing, even though she privately admits that Sunrise employees were careless and believes that Sunrise Pools will be found liable for an amount in excess of $1 million. The president sends the amended draft of the annual report to the vice-president of finance with a note stating that the lawsuit will not be disclosed in the annual report and that the lawsuit will not be disclosed to the board of directors.

REQUIRED

Is the president's concern valid? What ethical problems will the vice-president of finance face if he follows the president's instructions?

GENERAL MILLS ANNUAL REPORT CASE Refer to the annual report of General Mills, Inc., presented in Appendix K.

REQUIRED

a. What was the total dollar amount of current liabilities at May 29, 1994?
b. What percent of long-term debt was considered current at May 29, 1994?
c. What were the current ratio and quick ratio at May 29, 1994?

10

Long-Term Liabilities

CHAPTER LEARNING OBJECTIVES

1 **IDENTIFY** the reasons for issuing bonds and **DESCRIBE** various types of bonds (pp. 343–345).

2 **DISCUSS** the relationship of bond prices to interest rates (pp. 345–346).

3 **ILLUSTRATE** accounting for bond issuance, interest, and effective interest amortization (pp. 347–353).

4 **ILLUSTRATE** the classification of bonds on the balance sheet and the early retirement of bonds (p. 353).

5 **DESCRIBE** and **ILLUSTRATE** accounting for term loans (p. 354).

6 **DEFINE** *capital* and *operating leases* and **DISTINGUISH** between them (pp. 354–356).

7 **DESCRIBE** the basic ideas of accounting for post-retirement benefits (pp. 356–357).

8 **DESCRIBE** and **ILLUSTRATE** deferred income taxes (pp. 357–359).

9 Financial Analysis **DEFINE** *times interest earned ratio* and **EXPLAIN** its use (pp. 359–360).

CHAPTER FOCUS

Have you borrowed money to finance your college education? Do you have a car loan? A home mortgage? If so, you have a long-term liability, a debt obligation that will be settled more than one year in the future. Although some busines entities, like some individuals, are able to avoid long-term liabilities (at this writing, for example, neither Microsoft Corporation nor Kelly Services, Inc., report any long-term liabilities), most business entities have significant amounts of long-term obligations. In this chapter, we examine several of these long-term liabilities: bonds payable, term loans, capital lease liabilities, postretirement liabilities, and deferred tax liabilities.

BONDS PAYABLE

OBJECTIVE 1

IDENTIFY the reasons for issuing bonds and **DESCRIBE** various types of bonds.

At various times in the course of business operations, particularly during phases of expansion, firms must secure additional long-term funds. When they choose long-term borrowing, it is often accomplished by issuing bonds. A **bond** is a long-term debt instrument that promises to pay interest periodically as well as a principal amount at maturity. The interest is usually paid semiannually. The principal amount is referred to as the bond's *face value* (because it is printed on the face of the bond certificate) or *par value*.

Bonds are used most often when a borrower receives funds from a large number of lenders contributing various amounts. Consequently, bonds are usually drawn up to be negotiable. Because many parties are involved, the borrower should select a *trustee*—often a large bank—to represent the group of bondholders. As a third party to the transaction, the trustee may take security title to any pledged property and is likely to initiate any action necessitated by failure to meet the terms of the bond agreement. The trustee may also maintain a record of current bond owners and may act as a disbursing agent for the interest and principal payments.

ADVANTAGES AND DISADVANTAGES OF ISSUING BONDS

A corporation is the type of business entity that issues bonds. Issuing bonds or issuing capital stock are alternative ways for corporations to obtain long-term funds. The advantages and disadvantages of issuing bonds, then, result from a comparison of these two ways of obtaining funds. When a corporation issues only one type of capital stock, that stock is called *common stock*. The following discussion compares the issuance of bonds with the issuance of common stock.

The advantages of obtaining long-term funds by issuing bonds rather than common stock include the following:

1. **No dilution of ownership interest.** Bondholders are creditors, not owners, of a corporation. Issuing bonds rather than common stock, therefore, maintains outstanding shares of stock at their current level.

2. **Tax deductibility of bond interest expense.** Interest expense is currently deductible as an expense on a corporation's income tax return. Dividend payments to stockholders are not tax deductible. With combined federal and state income tax rates approaching 40% for many corporations, the tax deductibility of bond interest expense is an attractive aspect of financing through bonds.

3. **Income to common stockholders may increase.** The term **trading on the equity** or **leveraging** identifies the use of borrowed funds, particularly long-term debt, in the capital structure of a firm. Trading *profitably* on the equity means that the borrowed funds generate a higher rate of return than the interest rate paid for the use of the funds. The excess accrues to the benefit of the common shareholders because it increases their earnings without any increase in the number of issued shares of common stock.

343

For example, assume a firm can earn 15% on $5,000,000 obtained by issuing bonds that have a 10% interest rate. If this firm pays income taxes at a 40% rate, then net income will increase $150,000 each year, as follows:

Earnings on funds borrowed: 15% × $5,000,000	$750,000
Interest cost on funds borrowed: 10% × $5,000,000	500,000
Increase in income before income tax expense	$250,000
Income tax expense on increase: 40% × $250,000	100,000
Increase in net income	$150,000

Because no stock was issued to obtain the $5,000,000, the $150,000 increase in net income benefits the current stockholders.

Not all aspects of issuing bonds are necessarily desirable for the borrowing company. Among the disadvantages of issuing bonds are the following:

1. **Bond interest expense is a contractual obligation.** In contrast with dividends on common stock, bond interest represents a fixed periodic expenditure that the firm is contractually obligated to make. Fixed interest charges can be a financial burden when operations do not develop as favorably as expected.

2. **Funds borrowed have a specific repayment date.** Because bonds normally have a definite maturity date, the borrower has a specific obligation to repay the face value of the bonds at maturity. This obligation, too, can be a significant burden when a company's financial performance does not reach expected levels. Funds received from issuing common stock, on the other hand, have no specific repayment date; instead, they usually represent a permanent increase in a firm's owners' equity.

3. **Borrowing agreement may restrict company actions.** The legal document setting forth the terms of a bond issue is called a *bond indenture.* Among the provisions in the bond indenture may be restrictions on dividend payments, restrictions on additional financing, specification of a minimum cash balance, and specification of minimum financial ratios that must be maintained. These provisions are intended to provide protection for the bondholders, but they do limit management's flexibility to act.

TYPES OF BONDS

Bond agreements may be formulated to capitalize on certain lending situations, appeal to special investor groups, or provide special repayment patterns. We now list several types of bonds and discuss their characteristics.

Secured bonds pledge some specific property as security for meeting the terms of the bond agreement. The specific title of the bonds may indicate the type of property pledged— for example, real estate mortgage bonds (land or buildings), chattel mortgage bonds (machinery or equipment), and collateral trust bonds (negotiable securities). If property is subject to two or more mortgages, the relative priority of each mortgage is denoted by its identification as a "first," "second," or even "third" mortgage.

Bonds that have no specific property pledged as security for their repayment are **debenture bonds.** Holders of such bonds rely on the borrower's general credit reputation. Because the lender's risk is usually greater than with secured bonds, the sale of unsecured bonds may require offering a higher interest rate.

The maturity dates of **serial bonds** are staggered over a series of years. For example, a serial bond issue of $15 million may provide for $1 million of the bonds to mature each year for 15 years. An advantage of serial bonds is that lenders can choose bonds with maturity dates that correspond with their desired length of investment.

The issuing corporation (or its trustee) maintains a record of the owners of **registered bonds.** At appropriate times, interest payments are mailed to the registered owners. Interest on **coupon bonds** is paid in a different manner. A coupon for interest payable to the bearer is attached to the bond for each interest period. When interest is due, the bondholder detaches a coupon and deposits it with his or her bank for collection.

Convertible bonds grant the holder the right to convert them to capital stock at some specific exchange ratio. This provision gives an investor the security of being a creditor during a certain stage of a firm's life, with the option of becoming a stockholder if the firm becomes sufficiently profitable. Because the conversion feature is attractive to potential investors, a company may issue convertible bonds at a lower interest rate than it would pay without the conversion feature.

Zero coupon bonds are bonds that offer no periodic interest payments but are issued at a substantial discount from their face value. The face value is paid to the lender at maturity. The total interest in the bond contract is the difference between the issue price and the face value. For example, a five-year, $1,000 zero coupon bond issued for $713 will pay the lender $1,000 at the end of five years. The total interest associated with this bond is $287 ($1,000 − $713). Zero coupon bonds are particularly helpful to a borrower when the project being financed with the bond proceeds provides no cash inflows until the bond maturity date (constructing and finding tenants for a shopping mall, for example).

POINT OF INTEREST

BOND RATINGS AND JUNK BONDS

The quality of bonds varies a great deal. Lenders who want to know the relative quality of a particular bond issue can consult a bond rating service. Two major firms that rate bonds are Standard & Poor's Corporation (S&P) and Moody's Investors Service (Moody's). The rating categories used by these firms are similar. The schedule below shows the relationship between the ratings and the degree of risk, using Standard & Poor's rating system.

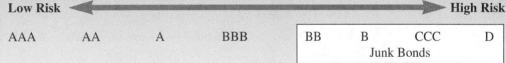

Low Risk				High Risk
AAA AA A BBB			BB B CCC D	
			Junk Bonds	

Junk bonds are low-quality, high-yield bonds. In the S&P rating system, junk bonds are any bonds rated BB and lower. Generally, bonds with poor ratings must offer higher interest rates than highly rated bonds. Junk bonds, then, offer relatively high interest rates. Junk bonds were quite prominent in the 1980s when they were used to finance many corporate takeovers and buyouts.

BOND FEATURES   Bonds with a **call provision** allow the borrower to call in the bonds for redemption. Usually, an extra amount or premium must be paid to the holders of the called bonds. A call provision offers borrowers an additional flexibility that may be significant if funds become available at interest rates substantially lower than those being paid on the bonds. To some degree, borrowers can in effect "call" any of their bonds by buying them in the open market.

A **sinking fund provision** requires the borrower to retire a portion of the outstanding bonds each year or, in some bond issues, to make payments each year to a trustee who is responsible for managing the resources needed to retire the bonds at maturity. The orderly retirement of bonds or accumulation of funds needed at maturity required by a sinking fund provision is generally viewed as making the bonds safer for the bondholders.

BOND PRICES   Most bonds are sold in units of $1,000 face (maturity) value, and the market price is expressed as a percentage of face value. For example, a $1,000 face value bond quoted at 98 sells for $980, and a bond quoted at 103 sells for $1,030. Generally, bond prices fluctuate in response to changes in market interest rates, which are determined by government monetary policies (managing the demand and supply of money) and economic expectations. They are also affected by the outlook for the issuing firm. Market prices are quoted in the financial news at the nearest $\frac{1}{8}$% of the true market price.

OBJECTIVE 2

DISCUSS the relationship of bond prices to interest rates.

A bond specifies a pattern of future cash flows: a series of interest payments and a single payment at maturity equal to the face value. The amount of the periodic interest payment is determined by the **nominal** or **contract rate** stated on the bond certificate. Interest rates are stated as annual rates, so the nominal rate needs to be converted to fit the interest period when interest is paid more than once a year. For example, bond interest is usually paid semiannually, with the payments six months apart. Thus, the amount of interest paid semiannually is calculated by multiplying one-half the nominal rate of interest times the bond's face value.

A bond's market price is determined by discounting the bond's future cash flows to the present using the current **market rate** of interest for the bond as the discount rate, a process known as *computing the bond's present value.* The market rate is the rate of return investors expect on their investment. Present value factors are available in tables to help simplify the calculations (also, certain calculators are programmed to compute present values). When issued, a bond's price may be equal to, less than, or more than its face value. Bonds sell at *face value* when the market rate of interest equals the nominal rate. Bonds sell at a *discount* (less than face value) when the market interest rate exceeds the nominal rate, and bonds sell at a *premium* (more than face value) when the market interest rate is less than the nominal rate.

Since bonds are usually printed and sold at different times, the two interest rates often differ. Also, a firm may desire a nominal rate expressed in even percentages or in easily recognized fractions of a percent (that is, 10% or $9\frac{1}{2}\%$), whereas the market rate for a particular bond issue may be expressed in a more complex fraction or decimal amount.

Exhibit 10-1 shows the calculation of a bond's price using different market rates of interest. (See the appendix to this chapter for a discussion of the calculation of a bond's present value.) The bond is a $1,000, 8%, four-year bond with interest payable semiannually; the periodic interest payment is $40 ($1,000 × 0.08 × $\frac{1}{2}$). As shown in the exhibit, the bond will

1. Sell at a *discount* ($936 bond price) when the market rate (10%) exceeds the nominal rate (8%).

2. Sell at *face value* ($1,000 bond price) when the market rate (8%) equals the nominal rate (8%).

3. Sell at a *premium* ($1,070 bond price) when the market rate (6%) is less than the nominal rate (8%).

EXHIBIT 10–1   Calculation of Bond Price at Different Interest Rates

The bond being priced is a $1,000, 8%, four-year bond with interest payable semiannually. There are eight semiannual interest payments of $40 ($1,000 × 8% × $\frac{1}{2}$).

	Priced to Yield Investor an Interest Rate, Compounded Semiannually, of		
	10%	8%	6%
Present value of $1,000 due at maturity:			
$1,000 × 0.677 present value factor* =	$677		
$1,000 × 0.731 present value factor =		$ 731	
$1,000 × 0.789 present value factor =			$ 789
Present value of eight $40 interest payments (rounded to nearest dollar):			
$40 × 6.463 present value factor* =	259		
$40 × 6.733 present value factor =		269	
$40 × 7.020 present value factor =			281
Bond price	$936	$1,000	$1,070
Bond priced at	Discount	Face value	Premium

*See the appendix to this chapter for a discussion of present value factors and present value tables.

Recording Bond Issues

OBJECTIVE 3

ILLUSTRATE accounting for bond issuance, interest, and effective interest amortization.

Firms often authorize more bonds than they actually anticipate issuing at one time. Authorization of bonds usually includes (1) formal action by the board of directors, (2) application to and approval of some government agency, (3) retention of a trustee, and (4) all the attendant negotiations and legalities. For secured bonds, the total value of the bonds authorized is typically some fraction of the value of the property pledged. The difference between the dollar amount of the bonds issued and the value of the pledged property represents a margin of safety to bondholders.

Because individual bond issues may have widely varying characteristics, separate accounts with reasonably descriptive titles should be used for each bond issue. When the bonds are authorized, an account is opened in the general ledger, and a notation may be made in the account stating the total amount of bonds authorized.

Bonds Issued at Face Value

To provide a simple illustration, we will use a short bond life. Assume that on December 31, 1996, Reid, Inc., issues at face value $100,000 of 8% bonds that mature in four years with interest paid on June 30 and December 31. The following entry records the bond issue:

1996
Dec. 31	Cash	100,000	
	Bonds Payable		100,000
	To record issuance of bonds.		

Interest of $4,000 ($100,000 \times 0.08 \times \frac{6}{12}$) will be paid on each of the eight payment dates (four years, semiannual payments). For example, the entry on June 30, 1997, the first interest payment date, is

1997
June 30	Bond Interest Expense	4,000	
	Cash		4,000
	To record payment of semiannual interest on bonds payable.		

When the bonds mature, Reid, Inc., records their retirement in the following manner:

2000
Dec. 31	Bonds Payable	100,000	
	Cash		100,000
	To record retirement of bonds.		

Issuance between Interest Dates

Not all bonds are sold on the exact day on which their interest begins to accumulate (the date on the bond certificates). For example, issuance may be delayed in anticipation of a more favorable bond market. Investors who buy bonds after the interest begins to accrue are expected to "buy" the accrued interest. Such bonds are said to be sold at some price "plus accrued interest." The accrued interest is returned to the investor on the next interest payment date. This procedure simplifies the bond issuer's administrative work. Regardless of when bonds are issued, a full six months' interest is paid to all bondholders on each interest payment date.

To illustrate, let us assume that Reid, Inc., sold its $100,000, 8%, four-year bonds at 100 plus accrued interest on February 28, 1997, instead of on December 31, 1996, the date on the bond certificates. The following entry is made:

1997
Feb. 28	Cash	101,333	
	Bonds Payable		100,000
	Bond Interest Payable		1,333
	To record bond issuance at 100 plus two months' accrued interest.		

The interest accrued on the bonds on February 28 is $1,333 ($100,000 \times 0.08 \times \frac{2}{12}$, rounded). On the first interest payment date, June 30, 1997, Reid, Inc., makes the following entry:

1997
June 30   Bond Interest Payable   1,333
          Bond Interest Expense   2,667
              Cash   4,000
          To record payment of semiannual interest on bonds payable.

Note that the bond interest expense recorded by Reid, Inc., relates to the four months since the bonds were issued.

BONDS ISSUED AT A DISCOUNT

If the nominal rate of interest on the bonds issued is less than the current market rate of interest for the type and quality of the bonds, they can be sold only at a price less than their face value. In such cases, investors "discount" the bonds to earn the amount of interest reflected in the current money market. For example, assume that Reid, Inc.'s $100,000 issue of 8%, four-year bonds is sold on December 31, 1996, for $93,552. This price permits investors to earn an interest rate of 10% (for computations, see the appendix to this chapter). The following entry records the issuance:

1996
Dec. 31   Cash   93,552
          Discount on Bonds Payable   6,448
              Bonds Payable   100,000
          To record issuance of bonds.

The $6,448 discount is not an immediate loss or expense to Reid, Inc. Rather, it represents an adjustment of interest expense over the life of the bonds. We illustrate this by comparing the funds that Reid, Inc., receives with the funds it must pay to the bondholders. Regardless of their selling price, the bonds are an agreement to pay $132,000 to the bondholders ($100,000 principal plus eight semiannual interest payments of $4,000 each).

Total funds paid to bondholders	$132,000
Total funds received from bond sale	93,552
Difference equals total interest expense	$ 38,448
Total semiannual interest payments	32,000
Increase in interest expense beyond semiannual interest payments	$ 6,448

The total interest expense for this four-year bond issue is $38,448, the difference between the total cash paid to the bondholders and the proceeds from the sale of the bonds. The semiannual interest payments to bondholders total $32,000, so an additional $6,448 needs to be recognized as interest expense over the life of the bonds. The $6,448 is the amount of the bond discount. To reflect the larger periodic interest expense, the bond discount is *amortized*. Amortization of bond discount means that periodically an amount is transferred from Discount on Bonds Payable to Bond Interest Expense.

There are two methods of amortization: the straight-line method and the effective interest method. Under the *straight-line method,* equal amounts are transferred from bond discount to interest expense for equal periods of time. The *effective interest method* reflects a constant rate of interest over the life of the bonds. We will use the effective interest method in this chapter.[1]

EFFECTIVE INTEREST METHOD OF DISCOUNT AMORTIZATION   The **effective interest method** of amortization recognizes a constant percentage of the book value of bonds as interest expense for each interest period. For bonds issued at a discount, their book value is the balance in the Bonds Payable account less the balance in the Discount on Bonds Payable account. To obtain a period's interest expense under the effective interest method, we mul-

---

[1]The bond investor acquired the bonds at a discount and faces a similar amortization need when computing periodic interest income. We illustrate the straight-line method of amortization in Chapter 14 when we discuss the accounting for bond investments.

MATERIALITY CONCEPT

Accounting standards state that the effective interest method of amortization should be used. It is the appropriate method because it uses the periodic rate of interest that was used to price the bonds when they were issued. The effective interest method is somewhat more complex than the straight-line method. Accounting standards permit the straight-line method of amortization to be used when the results are not materially different from those achieved under the effective interest method. This represents an application of the *materiality concept.* As previously discussed, this concept permits insignificant accounting transactions to be recorded most expediently. Here, the materiality concept permits a simpler (and, thus, more expedient) straight-line method to be used when it results in insignificant differences from the theoretically superior effective interest method.

tiply the bonds' book value at the beginning of each period by the effective interest rate. The **effective rate** is the market rate of interest used to price the bonds when they were issued. The difference between this amount and the amount of interest paid (Nominal Interest Rate × Face Value of Bonds) is the amount of discount amortized. When using the effective interest method of amortization, accountants often prepare an amortization schedule similar to the one in Exhibit 10-2. This schedule covers the four-year life of the Reid, Inc., bonds issued at a discount.

EXHIBIT 10–2	Bonds Sold at a Discount: Periodic Interest Expense, Effective Interest Amortization, and Book Value of Bonds

$100,000 of 8%, four-year bonds with interest payable semiannually issued on December 31, 1996, at $93,552 to yield 10%.

Year	Interest Period	A Interest Paid (4% of face value)	B Interest Expense (5% of bond book value)	C Periodic Amortization (B − A)	D Balance of Unamortized Discount (D − C)	E Book Value of Bonds, End of Period ($100,000 − D)
(at issue)					$6,448	$ 93,552
1997	1	$4,000	$4,678	$678	5,770	94,230
	2	4,000	4,712	712	5,058	94,942
1998	3	4,000	4,747	747	4,311	95,689
	4	4,000	4,784	784	3,527	96,473
1999	5	4,000	4,824	824	2,703	97,297
	6	4,000	4,865	865	1,838	98,162
2000	7	4,000	4,908	908	930	99,070
	8	4,000	4,930*	930	–0–	100,000

*Adjusted for cumulative rounding error of $24.

The schedule shows six-month interest periods; therefore, the interest rates shown in columns A and B are one-half the annual rates. Column A lists the constant amounts of interest paid each six months, that is, the nominal interest rate times face value (4% × $100,000). The amounts in column B are obtained by multiplying the book value at the beginning of each period (column E) by the 5% effective interest rate. For example, the $4,678 interest expense for the first period is 5% of $93,552; for the second period, it is 5% of $94,230, or $4,712, and so on. Note that the amount changes each period. For discounted bonds, the amount increases each period because the book value increases over the life of the bonds until it reaches face value at the maturity date. The amount of discount amortization for each period, given in column C, is the difference between the corresponding amounts in columns A and B. Column D lists the amount of unamortized discount at the end of each period.

The amounts recorded for each interest payment can be read directly from the amortization schedule. The following entries record the interest expense and discount amortization at the time of the first two interest payments:

1997

June 30	Bond Interest Expense	4,678	
	Discount on Bonds Payable		678
	Cash		4,000
	To record semiannual interest payment and amortization of bond discount.		
Dec. 31	Bond Interest Expense	4,712	
	Discount on Bonds Payable		712
	Cash		4,000
	To record semiannual interest payment and amortization of bond discount.		

Amortizing the bond discount over the four-year life of the bonds leaves a zero balance in the Discount on Bonds Payable account at the maturity date of the bonds. The retirement of the bonds is then recorded by debiting Bonds Payable and crediting Cash for $100,000, the amount of their face value.

BONDS ISSUED AT A PREMIUM

If the market rate of interest had been below the 8% offered by Reid, Inc.'s bonds, investors would have been willing to pay a premium for them. Suppose that the effective interest rate was 6%. Reid, Inc.'s $100,000 of 8%, four-year bonds would then sell for $106,980 (for computations, see the appendix to this chapter). The issuance of the bonds on December 31, 1996, is recorded as follows:

1996

Dec. 31	Cash	106,980	
	Bonds Payable		100,000
	Premium on Bonds Payable		6,980
	To record issuance of bonds.		

When bonds are issued at a premium, the book value of the bond liability is determined by adding the Premium on Bonds Payable account balance to the Bonds Payable account balance. The initial book value of the bond issuance that is recorded in the preceding entry, then, is $106,980.

Like a bond discount, a bond premium is considered an adjustment of interest expense over the life of the bonds. We just saw that a bond discount represents the excess of total interest expense over the total semiannual interest payments; a similar analysis shows that a bond premium represents the amount by which the total semiannual interest payments exceed the total interest expense. The analysis begins by comparing the total funds that will be paid to the bondholders over the four years (again, it is $132,000) with the proceeds received when the bonds are issued.

Total funds paid to bondholders	$132,000
Total funds received from bond sale	106,980
Difference equal total interest expense	$ 25,020
Total semiannual interest payments	32,000
Decrease in interest expense below semiannual interest payments	$ 6,980

The total interest expense for this four-year bond issue is $25,020, an amount that is $6,980 less than the total semiannual interest payments made to bondholders. The $6,980 is the amount of the bond premium. The bond premium is amortized, then, to cause the periodic interest expense to be *less* than the semiannual interest payment.

EFFECTIVE INTEREST METHOD OF PREMIUM AMORTIZATION   The effective interest method of amortizing a bond premium is handled the same way as a bond discount amortization. Each interest period, a constant percentage of the bonds payable book value at the beginning of the period is recognized as interest expense; the difference between the interest expense amount and the semiannual interest payment is the amount of the premium amortization.

Exhibit 10-3 shows the amortization schedule for the four-year life of the Reid, Inc., bonds that were issued at a premium. The nominal interest rate of 4% in column A and the effective interest rate of 3% in column B are one-half the annual rates because the calculations are for six-month periods.

EXHIBIT 10–3	Bonds Sold at a Premium: Periodic Interest Expense, Effective Interest Amortization, and Book Value of Bonds

$100,000 of 8%, four-year bonds with interest payable semiannually issued on December 31, 1996, at $106,980 to yield 6%.

Year	Interest Period	A Interest Paid (4% of face value)	B Interest Expense (3% of bond book value)	C Periodic Amortization (A – B)	D Balance of Unamortized Discount (D – C)	E Book Value of Bonds, End of Period ($100,000 + D)
(at issue)					$6,980	$106,980
1997	1	$4,000	$3,209	$791	6,189	106,189
	2	4,000	3,186	814	5,375	105,375
1998	3	4,000	3,161	839	4,536	104,536
	4	4,000	3,136	864	3,672	103,672
1999	5	4,000	3,110	890	2,782	102,782
	6	4,000	3,083	917	1,865	101,865
2000	7	4,000	3,056	944	921	100,921
	8	4,000	3,079*	921	–0–	100,000

*Adjusted for cumulative rounding error of $51.

The journal entries for each interest payment may be taken directly from the amortization schedule. The entries for the first two interest payments (June 30 and December 31, 1997) follow. Note that the periodic interest expense is less than the semiannual interest payment.

1997

June 30	Bond Interest Expense	3,209	
	Premium on Bonds Payable	791	
	Cash		4,000
	To record semiannual interest payment and amortization of bond premium.		

Dec. 31	Bond Interest Expense	3,186	
	Premium on Bonds Payable	814	
	Cash		4,000
	To record semiannual interest payment and amortization of bond premium.		

After amortizing the bond premium over the four-year life of the bonds, the balance in the Premium on Bonds Payable account is zero. When the bonds are retired at the end of four years, then, the entry debits Bonds Payable and credits Cash for the $100,000 face value of the bonds.

YEAR-END ADJUSTMENTS

When a periodic interest payment does not correspond with the fiscal year-end, adjustment of the general ledger accounts should include an entry reflecting the amount of interest expense incurred but not yet recorded. The adjusting entry includes a pro rata amortization of bond discount or bond premium for the portion of the year involved.

PRINCIPLE ALERT

MATCHING CONCEPT

The adjustment to reflect interest expense incurred but not yet recorded is an application of the *matching concept.* This basic principle of accounting states that an expense should be recorded in the period that benefits from its incurrence, regardless of when the expense is paid in cash. Interest is the charge for the use of money, and this charge is incurred every day that the borrower has use of, and benefits from, the funds.

Our previous bond discount and bond premium examples have assumed that Reid, Inc., was on a calendar-year basis. To illustrate adjusting entries, let us assume that Reid, Inc.'s accounting year ends on September 30. Recall that the four-year bonds were issued on December 31, 1996, with semiannual interest payments on June 30 and December 31. On September 30, 1997, for example, Reid, Inc., is three months into the second six-month interest period. An adjusting entry to recognize three months of interest expense is made on September 30, 1997.

ADJUSTMENT FOR BONDS ISSUED AT A DISCOUNT   For periods of less than six months, the adjustment amounts are proportionate allocations of the six-month amounts. The adjustment at September 30, 1997, covering three months will be one-half of the amounts for the six-month period ending December 31, 1997. The amounts can be computed from those shown for the second interest period in the amortization schedules. For our first example (bonds issued at a discount), one-half of the amount shown for the second interest period in Exhibit 10-2, column A, [($4,000/2) = $2,000] is the interest payable. In the same fashion, from column B, [($4,712/2) = $2,356] is the interest expense, and from column C, [($712/2) = $356] is the discount amortization. The year-end adjusting entry follows:

1997

Sept. 30	Bond Interest Expense	2,356	
	Discount on Bonds Payable		356
	Bond Interest Payable		2,000
	To accrue interest for three months and amortize one-half of the discount for the interest period.		

When interest is paid at the next interest payment date, the remaining amounts of bond interest expense and discount amortization for the six-month period are recognized. Assuming that Reid, Inc., does not use reversing entries, the entry to record the interest payment on December 31, 1997, is as follows:

1997

Dec. 31	Bond Interest Payable	2,000	
	Bond Interest Expense	2,356	
	Discount on Bonds Payable		356
	Cash		4,000
	To record semiannual interest payment and discount amortization for three months.		

ADJUSTMENT FOR BONDS ISSUED AT A PREMIUM   For our second example (bonds issued at a premium), we follow the same procedure, using the second interest period in Exhibit 10-3. Again, we use one-half of the amounts shown to derive the amounts for our year-end adjusting entry:

1997

Sept. 30	Bond Interest Expense	1,593	
	Premium on Bonds Payable	407	
	Bond Interest Payable		2,000
	To accrue interest for three months and amortize one-half of the premium for the interest period.		

Here, too, the remaining amounts of bond interest expense and premium amortization for the six-month period are recognized at the next interest payment date. Assuming that Reid, Inc., does not use reversing entries, the entry on December 31, 1997, to record the interest payment is the following:

1997

Dec. 31	Bond Interest Payable	2,000	
	Bond Interest Expense	1,593	
	Premium on Bonds Payable	407	
	Cash		4,000
	To record semiannual interest payment and premium amortization for three months.		

BONDS PAYABLE ON THE BALANCE SHEET

OBJECTIVE 4

ILLUSTRATE the classification of bonds on the balance sheet and the early retirement of bonds.

Bonds payable that mature more than one year in the future are classified as long-term liabilities on the balance sheet. Bonds payable maturing within the next year should be classified within the current liabilities section. The Discount on Bonds Payable and Premium on Bonds Payable accounts are classified properly as a deduction from and as an addition to, respectively, the face value of the bonds in the balance sheet.

At December 31, 1997, the Reid, Inc., bonds issued at a discount (see Exhibit 10-2) appear on the firm's balance sheet as follows:

Bonds Payable	$100,000	
Less: Discount on Bonds Payable	5,058	$94,942

On the same date, the bonds issued at a premium (see Exhibit 10-3) appear as follows:

Bonds Payable	$100,000	
Add: Premium on Bonds Payable	5,375	$105,375

RETIREMENT OF BONDS BEFORE MATURITY

Bonds are usually retired at their maturity dates with an entry debiting Bonds Payable and crediting Cash for the amount of the face value of the bonds. However, bonds may be retired before maturity—for example, to take advantage of more attractive financing terms.

In accounting for the retirement of bonds before maturity, the following analysis should be used:

1. Remove the book value of the bonds being retired from the accounts (that is, remove the Bonds Payable amount and any related bond premium or discount).

2. Record the cash paid to retire the bonds.

3. Recognize any difference between the bonds' book value and the cash paid as a gain or loss on bond retirement.

To illustrate, assume that the bonds issued for $106,980 in our previous example were called for retirement at 105 at the end of 1999, just after paying the semiannual interest on December 31, 1999. According to Exhibit 10-3, the bonds' book value at the end of 1999 is $101,865. The following entry properly reflects the bond retirement:

1999

Dec. 31	Bonds Payable	100,000	
	Premium on Bonds Payable	1,865	
	Loss on Bond Retirement	3,135	
	Cash		105,000
	To retire bonds at 105 and record loss on retirement.		

Accounting guidelines require that a gain or loss on bond retirement, if material, be classified as an extraordinary item on the income statement.[2]

---

[2]Extraordinary items are discussed in Chapter 13.

TERM LOANS

OBJECTIVE 5
DESCRIBE and **ILLUSTRATE**
accounting for term loans.

When long-term borrowing is arranged with a single lender, the borrower signs a note payable and the debt is referred to as a **term loan.** Because the borrower works directly with the lender (such as a bank or insurance company), arranging a term loan is a faster process than getting bonds ready for public issuance.

Term loans are often repaid in equal periodic installments. Mortgage loans, for example, are repaid in equal installments. The agreement may require installment payments to be made monthly, quarterly, or semiannually. Each payment contains an interest amount and a repayment of principal. Because the installment payments are equal, each installment payment contains different amounts of interest and principal repayment. These component amounts change with each installment because the interest is computed on the unpaid principal, and the unpaid principal is reduced with each payment.

To illustrate, assume that on December 31, 1996, Reid, Inc., borrows $100,000 from a bank on a 12%, 10-year mortgage note payable. The note is to be repaid with equal quarterly installments of $4,326 (for computation, see the appendix to this chapter). Thus, there will be 40 quarterly payments; the quarterly interest rate is 3%. Exhibit 10-4 shows the first eight quarterly payments and their division between interest expense and principal repayment. The journal entry to record the first quarterly payment follows:

1997
Mar. 31	Interest Expense	3,000	
	Mortgage Note Payable	1,326	
	Cash		4,326
	To record quarterly mortgage loan payment.		

EXHIBIT 10–4 **Partial Mortgage Note Payment Schedule**

$100,000 mortgage note payable with quarterly payments of $4,326 and quarterly interest rate of 3%.

Payment Date	A Cash Payment	B Interest Expense (3% × D)*	C Principal Repaid (A – B)	D Book Value of Note (Unpaid Principal)
1996				
December 31 (issue date)				$100,000
1997				
March 31	$4,326	$3,000	$1,326	98,674
June 30	4,326	2,960	1,366	97,308
September 30	4,326	2,919	1,407	95,901
December 31	4,326	2,877	1,449	94,452
1998				
March 31	4,326	2,834	1,492	92,960
June 30	4,326	2,789	1,537	91,423
September 30	4,326	2,743	1,583	89,840
December 31	4,326	2,695	1,631	88,209

*3% × unpaid principal after previous payment, rounded to the nearest dollar.

LEASES

OBJECTIVE 6
DEFINE capital and operating leases and **DISTINGUISH** between them.

A firm may rent property for a specified period under a contract called a **lease.** The company acquiring the right to use the property is the **lessee;** the owner of the property is the **lessor.** The rights transferred to the lessee are called a **leasehold.** Examples of leased assets are land, buildings, trucks, factory machinery, office equipment, planes, and automobiles. A lessee's accounting treatment depends on whether a lease is a capital lease or an operating lease.

POINT OF INTEREST

CAPITAL LEASES IN THE AIRLINE INDUSTRY

Companies in the airline industry use capital leases to finance some of their flight equipment as well as other plant assets. Following are the dollar amounts of liabilities from capital leases reported by several airlines in their balance sheets at the end of a recent year:

American	$2,233,000,000
Northwest	890,300,000
United	883,000,000
Continental	445,943,000
TWA	414,223,000
Southwest	204,904,000
USAir	105,389,000
Delta	97,000,000

CAPITAL LEASE   A **capital lease** transfers to the lessee substantially all of the benefits and risks related to the ownership of the property. A lease meeting at least one of the following criteria is a capital lease.[3]

1. The lease transfers ownership of the property to the lessee by the end of the lease term.

2. The lease contains a bargain purchase option.

3. The lease term is at least 75% of the estimated economic life of the leased property.

4. The present value of the lease payments[4] is at least 90% of the fair value of the leased property.

The economic effect of a capital lease is similar to that of an installment purchase. The lessee accounts for a capital lease by recording the leased property as an asset and establishing a liability for the lease obligation. The present value of the future lease payments determines the dollar amount of the entry. For example, assume that Reid, Inc., leases equipment under a capital lease for 10 years at $40,000 per year, and that the proper initial valuation of this lease for accounting purposes is $226,000 (for computation, see the appendix to this chapter). Reid, Inc., records the capital lease as follows:

Leased Equipment	226,000	
Lease Obligation		226,000
To record 10-year capital lease.		

The leased equipment is depreciated over the period it benefits the lessee and appears among the firm's plant assets in the balance sheet. The lease obligation is divided between the current and long-term liabilities in the balance sheet based on the settlement dates for the obligation. The accounting for each lease payment is similar to the accounting for an installment note payment illustrated in the previous section. Part of each lease payment made by the lessee is charged to interest expense, and the remainder reduces the lease obligation.

OPERATING LEASE   The typical rental agreement illustrates an **operating lease:** the lessee pays for the use of an asset for a limited period, and the lessor retains the usual risks and rewards of owning the property. The lessee usually charges each lease payment to rent expense. No leased asset or lease obligation is recorded.

Lessees usually prefer to have their leases classified as operating leases rather than capital leases because this classification avoids showing a lease obligation among the balance

---

[3]*Statement of Financial Accounting Standards No. 13,* "Accounting for Leases" (Stamford, CT: Financial Accounting Standards Board, 1976).

[4]Present values are discussed in the appendix to this chapter.

sheet liabilities. Having fewer balance sheet liabilities may make it easier to borrow money from lenders. Structuring a lease so that no liability is recorded (that is, having it qualify as an operating lease) is an example of a practice known as **off-balance-sheet financing.**

We have identified the basic differences between capital and operating leases. Accounting for capital leases may be quite complex. The lease complexities are covered in intermediate accounting texts.

PENSION PLANS AND OTHER POSTRETIREMENT BENEFITS

PENSION PLANS

OBJECTIVE *7*

DESCRIBE the basic ideas of accounting for postretirement benefits.

Many companies have established plans to pay benefits to their employees after they retire. The cost of these **pension plans** may be paid entirely by the employer. Sometimes, the employees pay part of the cost through deductions from their salaries and wages. The employer and employee contributions are usually paid into a pension fund that is managed by another company. Retirement benefits are paid from the assets in the pension fund.

The employer's pension plan cost must be expensed during the years the employees work for the company. For some plans, this accounting analysis is fairly simple; for other plans, it is not. In a *defined contribution plan,* for example, the employer's responsibility is to contribute a certain defined amount to the pension fund each year (a percentage of employee salaries, perhaps). The assets available in the pension fund, then, determine the size of each employee's retirement benefits. The employer's pension accounting analysis is straightforward—when the required contribution is made, Pension Expense is debited and Cash is credited. The employer corporation has no pension liability in its balance sheet as long as it makes the proper defined contribution each year. The Proctor & Gamble Company and Dell Computer Corporation are among the companies that offer defined contribution plans.

The analysis becomes more complex in *defined benefit plans.* These plans specify the retirement benefits to be received in the future; typically, the retirement benefits are a function of the number of years an employee works for the company and the salary or wage level at or near retirement. One complexity under such plans is the determination of the periodic pension expense and contribution amounts. These amounts are influenced by such factors as employee turnover, employee life expectancies, future salary and wage levels, and pension fund investment performance. Actuaries make the required pension estimates.

When a defined benefit plan is first adopted, the company usually gives employees credit for their years of employment prior to the plan's adoption. The cost of providing the retirement benefits earned by this earlier service is called *prior service cost.* Prior service cost may be quite sizable, and the company may take many years to fund it. A similar situation may develop when a company amends a plan to increase benefit levels. Another complexity in a defined benefit plan, then, is that the accumulated pension retirement benefits may exceed the assets in the pension fund. In such cases, accounting standards require companies to record a liability equal to the excess amount. Recently, for example, Norfolk Southern Corporation reported a pension liability related to its defined benefit plans of $105,700,000.

OTHER POSTRETIREMENT BENEFITS

In addition to pensions, employers may provide retired employees with other benefits, such as health care and life insurance. Accounting guidelines require companies to expense the cost of providing these benefits during the years the employees work for the company. The benefits are not paid until after the employees retire, so a long-term liability for these benefits accrues during the employees' working years. As with pension plans, this liability for other postretirement benefits must appear in the balance sheet to the extent that it is not funded by the company.

The accounting standard requiring these postretirement benefits other than pensions to be accrued as a liability prior to payment did not take effect until the early 1990s. Many companies have funded only a small portion (or no portion at all) of the accumulated liability. Given that these postretirement benefits often include some future health care benefits, the unfunded liability can be quite sizable. Recently, for example, General Motors Corporation and AT&T reported postretirement benefit liabilities (other than pensions) of $37,920,000,000 and $8,161,000,000, respectively!

MATCHING CONCEPT

Current accounting standards for defined benefit pension plans and other postretirement benefits require companies to record the costs of providing these benefits during the years the covered employees work for the company. These guidelines went into effect in the late 1980s for defined benefit pension plans and the early 1990s for other postretirement benefit plans. Both guidelines represent applications of the *matching concept,* a basic principle that states that expenses should be recorded in the periods that benefit from their incurrence. Before the current guidelines became effective, companies accounted for the cost of these postretirement plans by expensing the benefit payments as they were made, a system known as "pay-as-you-go" accounting. This was not proper matching because a company benefits from these plans while the covered employees work for the company, not when the employees are retired. Among the benefits to a company are an improved morale among employees and a system that permits older employees to retire.

DEFERRED INCOME TAXES

Corporations pay income taxes based on the amount of taxable income they report on their income tax returns. Most of the revenues and expenses used to compute taxable income are exactly the same as the firm reports in its income statement. There are several areas, however, in which the tax law either requires or permits a firm to report revenues and expenses in a different pattern on the tax return than on the income statement.

DEFERRED TAX LIABILITIES

OBJECTIVE 8
DESCRIBE and **ILLUSTRATE**
deferred income taxes.

Following are two examples of differences between when a transaction affects taxable income and when it affects the income statement:

1. A company purchases a plant asset in the current year that it is allowed to expense immediately on its income tax return. In its current year financial statements, the company establishes an asset that will be depreciated over its useful life. On the current year tax return, the company immediately expenses the entire payment.

2. A company purchases a plant asset in the current year and depreciates it in its financial statements using the straight-line method with no expected salvage value. On the tax return, the company depreciates the asset using the *modified accelerated cost recovery system (MACRS).* The first year's MACRS depreciation exceeds the straight-line amount.

Both transactions create a situation in which, at the end of the current year, the book value of the related plant asset exceeds the asset's tax basis (that is, the remaining amount that can be expensed on future tax returns). The difference is only temporary, however, because eventually both the asset's book value and its tax basis will be zero (as the expensing of the asset is completed in the financial statements and on the tax return). Further, in the future year(s) when the temporary difference (excess of book value over tax basis) is expensed in the financial statements, the company will owe income taxes on that amount (because there will not be any corresponding expense in that year's tax return). These future income taxes payable represent a deferred tax consequence, therefore, from a situation in which an asset's book value temporarily exceeds its tax basis.

Accounting standards require that a **deferred tax liability** be recorded for the deferred tax consequences of temporary differences. In other words, an accounting liability must be recognized when a temporary difference between an asset's book value and its tax basis will result in future taxable amounts. The deferred tax liability is an appropriate liability to report in the balance sheet: it repesents an estimate of future income taxes payable resulting from an already existing temporary difference. The deferred tax liability is computed by applying the proper income tax rate to the future taxable amount.

To illustrate, assume that on January 2, 1996, Lenscape, Inc., purchases equipment for $10,000 and debits the expenditure to the Equipment account. The equipment is expected to last two years with no salvage value and will be depreciated in 1996 and 1997 using the straight-line method. Lenscape deducts the full $10,000 as an expense on its 1996 income tax return. Lenscape owns no other plant assets. This is the only difference between Lenscape's financial statements and tax returns. The income tax rate is 40% for 1996 and 1997.

Assume that Lenscape's income before depreciation expense and income taxes is $50,000 in 1996 and $70,000 in 1997. Lenscape's pretax financial income and taxable income for 1996 and 1997 will then be as follows:

	1996		1997	
	Financial Income	Taxable Income	Financial Income	Taxable Income
Income before depreciation expense and income taxes	$50,000	$50,000	$70,000	$70,000
Depreciation expense	5,000	10,000	5,000	–0–
Pretax financial income	$45,000		$65,000	
Taxable income		$40,000		$70,000

The book value and tax basis of the equipment at December 31, 1996, and December 31, 1997, are as follows:

	December 31, 1996		December 31, 1997	
	Book Value	Tax Basis	Book Value	Tax Basis
Equipment	$5,000	–0–	–0–	–0–

The following observations may be drawn from Lenscape's handling of the equipment expenditure:

1. Deducting the equipment on 1996's tax return causes a $5,000 difference between the book value and tax basis of the equipment at December 31, 1996.

2. The $5,000 difference at December 31, 1996, between the equipment's book value and its tax basis is temporary. It is eliminated in 1997.

3. The elimination of the $5,000 temporary difference in 1997 causes taxable income that year to be $5,000 higher than pretax financial income. Lenscape, therefore, will pay an income tax on the $5,000 in 1997 of $2,000 (0.40 × $5,000). This is the liability that must recognized at December 31, 1996, as a deferred tax liability.

The journal entry to record income taxes at December 31, 1996, is

1996

Dec. 31	Income Tax Expense	18,000	
	Income Tax Payable		16,000
	Deferred Tax Liability		2,000
	To record 1996 income taxes.		

The entry to Deferred Tax Liability is the amount necessary to establish the proper year-end account balance. At December 31, 1996, there should be a deferred tax liability of $2,000 (0.40 × $5,000). Lenscape has no previous balance in the Deferred Tax Liability account, so the credit entry is for the full $2,000. The entry to Income Tax Payable reflects the income taxes currently due to the government; it is computed by multiplying the 1996 taxable income by the 1996 tax rate ($40,000 × 0.40 = $16,000). The debit to Income Tax Expense is the balancing amount in the journal entry; in this case, it is determined by combining the income tax payable and deferred tax liability amounts.

The journal entry to record income taxes at December 31, 1997, is

1997

Dec. 31	Income Tax Expense	26,000	
	Deferred Tax Liability	2,000	
	Income Tax Payable		28,000
	To record 1997 income taxes.		

The $2,000 debit to Deferred Tax Liability brings this account balance to zero. This is the correct balance at December 31, 1997, because the temporary difference is eliminated in 1997. The $28,000 credit to Income Tax Payable correctly records the 1997 income tax owed to the government ($70,000 × 0.40 = $28,000). The balancing debit to Income Tax Expense is determined by netting the income tax payable and deferred tax liability amounts.

INCOME TAX RATE

The proper income tax rate to use in determining a deferred tax liability is the tax rate scheduled to be in effect when the future taxable amount occurs. If a new tax rate has been enacted into law for the future year, then that tax rate is used. To illustrate using the Lenscape, Inc., example, assume that the tax rates enacted into law are 40% for 1996 and 35% for 1997. The journal entries to record income taxes for 1996 and 1997 are then as follows:

1996

Dec. 31	Income Tax Expense	17,750	
	Income Tax Payable		16,000
	Deferred Tax Liability		1,750
	To record 1996 income taxes		

[Deferred Tax liability: $5,000 × 0.35 = $1,750; Income tax payable: $40,000 × 0.40 = $16,000; Income tax expense: $1,750 + $16,000 = $17,750].

1997

Dec. 31	Income Tax Expense	22,750	
	Deferred Tax Liability	1,750	
	Income Tax Payable		24,500
	To record 1997 income taxes		

[Deferred tax liability: to eliminate account balance; Income tax payable: $70,000 × 0.35 = $24,500; Income tax expense: $24,500 − $1,750 = $22,750].

If tax rates change after a deferred tax liability has been recorded, a journal entry is necessary to revise the account balance to its proper amount (with an offsetting debit or credit to Income Tax Expense).

BALANCE SHEET PRESENTATION

Deferred income tax accounts are classified on a firm's balance sheet as current or noncurrent based on the classification of the related asset or liability. For example, Lenscape's deferred tax liability at December 31, 1996, would be classified as a noncurrent liability because the related asset, Equipment, is classified as a noncurrent asset.

The amounts reported as deferred tax liabilities may be quite large, often millions of dollars (or more) for major corporations. As one example, Phillip Morris Companies, Inc., reported deferred tax liabilities of $3,067,000,000 in a recent balance sheet.

OTHER TEMPORARY DIFFERENCES

Some temporary differences cause an asset's book value to be *less* than its tax basis. For example, a firm may use the allowance method in its financial statements to account for uncollectible accounts expense and use the direct write-off method for tax purposes. Also, some temporary differences may create a liability with a book value larger than its tax basis. For example, a company may receive an advance payment for future services to be performed (crediting a liability account for the advance payment) but include the payment in taxable income in the year it is received. These temporary differences create deferred tax assets (future reductions or refunds of income taxes). The guidelines for measuring deferred tax assets, however, are more complex than those that apply to deferred tax liabilities and are beyond the scope of this textbook.

FINANCIAL ANALYSIS

TIMES INTEREST EARNED RATIO

A financial ratio of particular interest to present and potential long-term creditors is the times interest earned ratio (also known as the *interest coverage ratio*). The **times interest earned ratio** is computed as follows:

OBJECTIVE 9

DEFINE times interest earned ratio and **EXPLAIN** its use.

$$\text{Times Interest Earned Ratio} = \frac{\text{Income before Interest Expense and Income Taxes}}{\text{Interest Expense}}$$

The principal on long-term debt such as bonds payable is not due until maturity, which may be many years into the future. Interest payments, however, are due each year. Thus, creditors look at the times interest earned ratio to help assess the ability of a firm to meet its annual interest commitments. The ratio shows the number of times the fixed interest charges were earned during the year. Many financial analysts consider that the times interest earned ratio should be at least in the range of 3.0–4.0 for the extension of long-term credit to be considered a safe investment. The trend of the ratio in recent years and the nature of the industry (volatile or stable, for example) may also influence the interpretation of this ratio.

Both the numerator and denominator in the times interest earned ratio come from the income statement. The numerator uses income before interest expense and income taxes, because that is the amount available to cover the interest charges. The denominator is the firm's total interest expense for the period. To illustrate, Reid, Inc., in this chapter's first example, issued $100,000 of 8% bonds at face value. The annual interest expense was $8,000. If this were Reid's only interest expense and Reid's income before interest expense and income taxes the first year were $28,000, Reid's times interest earned ratio that year would be $28,000/$8,000 = 3.5.

The times interest earned ratio may differ considerably among firms. Following are examples of recent times interest earned ratios for several companies in different industries.

The Quaker Oats Company (grocery products)	8.1
The Mead Corporation (paper and paper products)	2.3
Southwestern Bell Corporation (communications)	5.2
Lands' End, Inc. (direct mail merchandising)	195.6
Motorola, Inc. (semiconductors and electronics)	9.4

KEY POINTS FOR CHAPTER LEARNING OBJECTIVES

1 **IDENTIFY** the reasons for issuing bonds and **DESCRIBE** various types of bonds (pp. 343–345).
  ■ The advantages of issuing bonds rather than common stock include (1) no dilution of ownership interest, (2) tax deductibility of interest expense, and (3) possible increase in return on stockholders' equity.
  ■ *Trading on the equity* means that borrowed funds are used in the expectation that they will generate a rate of return higher than the interest rate.
  ■ The disadvantages of issuing bonds include the following: (1) interest is a contractual obligation, (2) the funds borrowed have a specific repayment date, and (3) the borrowing agreement may restrict company actions.
  ■ Bonds permit borrowing from a large number of investors, who are usually represented by a trustee. Bonds may be secured or unsecured (debenture bonds). Bonds may all come due at the same time or may have staggered maturities (serial bonds). For registered bonds, the issuer keeps records of owners and mails them interest payments. Owners of coupon bonds detach the interest coupons when due and deposit them in a bank. Some bonds are convertible into the firm's stock at a specified exchange ratio, and zero coupon bonds are issued at a substantial discount from their face value.

2 **DISCUSS** the relationship of bond prices to interest rates (pp. 345–346).
  ■ Bond prices are expressed as a percentage of face value.
  ■ The nominal rate of interest, stated on the bond certificate, dictates the amount of interest paid each period. The effective, or market, rate of interest is the rate investors expect to receive on their investment.
  ■ When the market interest rate exceeds the nominal rate on bonds, they are sold at a discount; when the nominal rate exceeds the market rate, the bonds are sold at a premium.

3 **ILLUSTRATE** accounting for bond issuance, interest, and effective interest amortization (pp. 347–353).
  ■ Discounts and premiums are recorded when the bonds are issued.
  ■ Discounts and premiums are amortized each interest date under the effective interest method.
  ■ The effective interest method results in a constant rate of interest on the bond book value throughout the life of the bonds.

4 **ILLUSTRATE** the classification of bonds on the balance sheet and the early retirement of bonds (p. 353).
- Bonds payable are shown in the long-term liabilities section of the balance sheet, with unamortized premium added or unamortized discount deducted.
- The entry for retirement of bonds removes both the bonds payable and any related bond premium or bond discount from the accounts at the date of retirement and recognizes any gain or loss on retirement.

5 **DESCRIBE** and **ILLUSTRATE** accounting for term loans (p. 354).
- A term loan is long-term borrowing obtained from a single source, with the borrower signing a note payable.
- Term loans are often repaid in equal periodic installments, with each payment containing different amounts of interest and principal.

6 **DEFINE** *capital* and *operating leases* and **DISTINGUISH** between them (pp. 354–356).
- A capital lease transfers most of the usual risks and rewards of property ownership to the lessee. At the inception of the lease, the lessee records an asset (a leased asset) and a liability (a lease obligation). The asset is depreciated over its useful life to the lessee, and the liability is reduced as the periodic lease payments are made.
- Under an operating lease, the lessor retains the usual risks and rewards of owning the property. The lessee records no liability at the start of the lease. Each lease payment made by the lessee is charged to rent expense.

7 **DESCRIBE** the basic ideas of accounting for postretirement benefits (pp. 356–357).
- In a defined contribution pension plan, the employer contributes a defined amount to the pension fund each year, debiting Pension Expense and crediting Cash. The fund assets determine the size of benefits.
- Defined benefit pension plans specify retirement benefits to be received in the future. They are often a function of years worked and the salary or wage level at retirement. Pension expense and contributions are influenced by such variables as employee turnover, life expectancies, and future salary and wage levels, and actuaries are needed to make estimates.
- Other postretirement benefits, such as health care and life insurance, must be accounted for by expensing the cost of providing these benefits during the years of employee service.

8 **DESCRIBE** and **ILLUSTRATE** deferred income taxes (pp. 357–359).
- When a difference in tax accounting and financial reporting results in the related asset having a book value in excess of its tax basis, a deferred tax liability results.
- The deferred tax liability is phased out as the difference in book value and tax basis disappears.

9 **Financial Analysis** **DEFINE** *times interest earned ratio* and **EXPLAIN** its use (pp. 359–360).
- The times interest earned ratio is computed as income before interest expense and income taxes divided by interest expense. It measures the ability of a firm to meet its annual interest commitments.

SELF-TEST QUESTIONS FOR REVIEW

(Answers follow the Solution to Demonstration Problem.)

1. On May 1, 1996, a firm issued $400,000 of 12-year, 9% bonds payable at $96\frac{1}{2}$ plus accrued interest. The bonds are dated January 1, 1996, and interest is payable on January 1 and July 1 of each year. The amount the firm receives on May 1 is
   a. $386,000.   **b.** $422,000.   **c.** $392,000.   **d.** $398,000.

2. A firm issued $250,000 of 10-year, 12% bonds payable on January 1, 1996, for $281,180, yielding an effective rate of 10%. Interest is payable on January 1 and July 1 each year. The firm records amortization on each interest date. Bond interest expense for the first six months of 1996, using effective interest amortization, is
   a. $15,000.   **b.** $16,870.80.   **c.** $14,059.   **d.** $14,331.

3. In financial statement presentations, the Discount on Bonds Payable account is
   a. Added to Bond Interest Expense.
   b. Deducted from Bonds Payable.
   c. Added to Bonds Payable.
   d. Deducted from Bond Interest Expense.

4. An example of off-balance-sheet financing is a(n)
   a. Term loan.
   b. Operating lease.
   c. Zero coupon bond.
   d. Capital lease.

5. A firm started operations in 1996. In 1996, it expensed $6,000 on its income tax return that it will not deduct in its financial statements until 1997. The firm's pretax financial income in 1996 was $100,000. The income tax rate for 1996 is 35%; the enacted tax rate for 1997 is 40%. In its December 31, 1996, balance sheet, the company should show a deferred tax liability of
    a. $35,000.   **b.** $2,100.   **c.** $40,000.   **d.** $2,400.

DEMONSTRATION PROBLEM FOR REVIEW

The following are selected transactions of Tyler, Inc., for 1996 and 1997. The firm closes its books on December 31.

1996

Dec. 31   Issued $500,000 of 12%, 10-year bonds for $562,360, yielding an effective rate of 10%. Interest is payable June 30 and December 31.

1997

June 30   Paid semiannual interest and recorded semiannual premium amortization on bonds.

Dec. 31   Paid semiannual interest and recorded semiannual premium amortization on bonds.

    31   Called one-half of the bonds in for retirement at 104.

REQUIRED

Record these transactions in general journal form. Use effective interest amortization. Round amounts to nearest dollar.

SOLUTION TO DEMONSTRATION PROBLEM

a.   **1996**

Dec. 31	Cash	562,360	
	Bonds Payable		500,000
	Premium on Bonds Payable		62,360
	Issued $500,000 of 12%, 10-year bonds for $562,360.		

b.   **1997**

June 30	Bond Interest Expense	28,118	
	Premium on Bonds Payable	1,882	
	Cash		30,000
	To record semiannual interest payment and premium amortization [$562,360 × 0.05 = $28,118].		
Dec. 31	Bond Interest Expense	28,024	
	Premium on Bonds Payable	1,976	
	Cash		30,000
	To record semiannual interest payment and premium amortization [($562,360 − $1,882) × 0.05 = $28,024, rounded].		
31	Bonds Payable	250,000	
	Premium on Bonds Payable	29,251	
	Cash		260,000
	Gain on Bond Retirement		19,251
	To record retirement of $250,000 of bonds; book value of bonds retired:		

Face amount	$250,000
Add: Premium (50% × $58,502)	29,251
Book value	$279,251

Retirement payment: $250,000 × 1.04 = $260,000.

ANSWERS TO SELF-TEST QUESTIONS

1. d, p. 347   **2.** c, p. 351   **3.** b, p. 353   **4.** b, p. 356   **5.** d, p. 359

G

Present Values and Future Values

In this appendix, we explain the concept of present value and the techniques of bond valuation, installment payment computation, and capital lease valuation. We also introduce the concept of future value.

PRESENT VALUES

CONCEPT OF PRESENT VALUE

Would you rather receive a dollar now or a dollar one year from now? Most persons would answer, "a dollar now." Intuition tells us that a dollar received now is more valuable than the same amount received sometime in the future. Sound reasons exist for choosing the earlier dollar, the most obvious of which concerns risk. Because the future is always uncertain, some event may prevent us from receiving the dollar at the later date. To avoid this risk, we choose the earlier date.

A second reason for choosing the earlier date is that the dollar received now could be invested; one year from now, we could have not only the dollar but also the interest income for the period. Using these risk and interest factors, we can generalize that (1) the right to receive an amount of money now—its **present value**—is normally worth more than the right to receive the same amount later—its future value; (2) the longer we must wait to receive an amount, the less attractive the receipt is; and (3) the difference between the present value of an amount and its future value is a function of interest (Principal × Interest Rate × Interest Time). The more risk associated with any situation, the higher the appropriate interest rate.

We support these generalizations with an illustration. What amount could we accept now that would be as valuable as receiving $100 one year from now if the appropriate interest rate is 10%? We recognize intuitively that with a 10% interest rate, we should accept less than $100, or approximately $91. We base this estimate on the realization that the $100 received in the future must equal the present value (100%) plus 10% interest on the present value. Thus, in our example, the $100 future receipt must be 1.10 times the present value. Dividing ($100/1.10), we obtain a present value of $90.90. In other words, under the given conditions, we would do as well to accept $90.90 now as to wait one year and receive $100. To confirm the equality of a $90.90 receipt now to a $100 receipt one year later, we calculate the future value of $90.90 at 10% for one year as follows:

$$\$90.90 \times 1.10 \times 1 \text{ year} = \$100 \text{ (rounded)}$$

Thus, we compute the present value of a future receipt by discounting (deducting an interest factor) the future receipt back to the present at an appropriate interest rate. We present this schematically below:

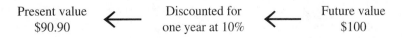

Present value		Discounted for		Future value
$90.90	←	one year at 10%	←	$100

If either the time period or the interest rate were increased, the resulting present value would decrease. If more than one time period is involved, compound interest computations are appropriate.

USE OF PRESENT VALUE TABLES

Because present value tables, such as Table I (on page 368) are widely available, we need not present here the various formulas for interest computations. Table I can be used to compute the present value amounts in the illustrations and problem materials that follow. Simply stated, present value tables provide a multiplier for many combinations of time periods and interest rates that, when applied to the dollar amount of a future cash flow, determines its present value.

Present value tables are used as follows. First, determine the number of interest compounding periods involved (three years compounded annually are 3 periods, three years compounded semiannually are 6 periods, three years compounded quarterly are 12 periods, and so on). The extreme left-hand column indicates the number of periods covered in the table.

Next, determine the interest rate per compounding period. Note that interest rates are usually quoted on a *per year* basis. Therefore, only in the case of annual compoundings is the quoted interest rate the interest rate per compounding period. In other cases, the rate per compounding period is the annual rate divided by the number of compounding periods in a year. For example, an interest rate of 10% per year would be 10% for one compounding period if compounded annually, 5% for two compounding periods if compounded semiannually, and $2\frac{1}{2}\%$ for four compounding periods if compounded quarterly.

Locate the factor that is to the right of the appropriate number of compounding periods and beneath the appropriate interest rate per compounding period. Multiply this factor by the number of dollars involved.

Note the logical progressions among multipliers in Table I. All values are less than 1.0 because the present value is always smaller than the $1 future amount if the interest rate is greater than zero. Also, as the interest rate increases (moving from left to right in the table) or the number of periods increases (moving from top to bottom), the multipliers become smaller.

EXAMPLE 1

Compute the present value of $100 one year hence, at 10% interest compounded annually:

Number of periods (one year, annually) = 1

Rate per period (10%/1) = 10%

Multiplier = 0.909

Present value = $100.00 × 0.909 = $90.90

(Note that this agrees with our earlier illustration.)

EXAMPLE 2

Compute the present value of $116.99 two years hence, at 8% compounded semiannually:

Number of periods (two years, semiannually) = 4

Rate per period (8%/2) = 4%

Multiplier = 0.855

Present value = $116.99 × 0.855 = $100 (rounded)

ANNUITY FORM OF CASH FLOW

Using present value tables like Table I, we can compute the present value of any single future cash flow or series of future cash flows. One frequent pattern of cash flows, however, is subject to a more convenient treatment. This pattern, known as an **annuity,** can be described as *equal amounts equally spaced over a period.*

For example, $100 is to be received at the end of each of the next three years as an annuity. When annuity cash flows occur at the end of each period, the annuity is called an *ordinary annuity.* As shown below, the present value of this ordinary annuity can be computed from Table I by computing the present value of each of the three individual receipts and summing them (assuming 5% annual interest).

Future Receipts (ordinary annuity)				PV Multiplier (Table I)		Present Value
Year 1	Year 2	Year 3				
$100			×	0.952	=	$ 95.20
	$100		×	0.907	=	90.70
		$100	×	0.864	=	86.40
				Total present value		$272.30

Table II (on page 368) provides a single multiplier for computing the present value of a series of future cash flows in the ordinary annuity form. Referring to Table II in the three periods hence row and the 5% column, we see that the multiplier is 2.723. When applied to the $100 annuity amount, the multiplier gives a present value of $272.30. As shown above, the same present value is derived from the several multipliers of Table I. For annuities of 5, 10, or 20 years, considerable computations are avoided by using annuity tables.

BOND VALUATIONS

We have explained previously that (1) a bond agreement specifies a pattern of future cash flows—usually a series of interest payments and a single payment at maturity equal to the face value—and (2) bonds are sold at premiums or discounts to adjust their effective interest rates to the prevailing market rate when they are issued.

Because of the role played by interest, the selling price (or valuation) of a bond that is necessary to yield a specific rate can be determined as follows:

1. Use Table I to compute the present value of the future principal repayment at the desired (or effective) rate of interest.

2. Use Table II to compute the present value of the future series of interest payments at the desired (or effective) rate of interest.

3. Add the present values obtained in steps 1 and 2.

We illustrate in Exhibit G-1 the pricing of a $100,000 issue of 8%, four-year bonds paying interest semiannually and sold on the date of issue to yield (1) 8%, (2) 10%, and (3) 6%. Note that the price of 8% bonds sold to yield 8% is the face (or par) value of the bonds. The bonds will issue for $93,552 to yield 10%. An issue price of $106,980 will cause the bonds to yield 6%.

INSTALLMENT PAYMENT COMPUTATION

When a creditor lends money that is repaid in equal periodic installments, such as a mortgage note payable, the creditor needs to determine the amount of the installment payment. This is done by dividing the amount loaned (a present value amount) by the present value factor for an annuity at the desired rate of interest.

For example, a creditor lends $100,000 on a 10-year mortgage note to be repaid in equal quarterly payments. The creditor wants to earn a return of 12% annually. Because there are four payments each year, the present value factor selected is for 40 periods at 3%. From Table II, this factor is 23.115. The quarterly payment, then, is determined as follows:

Present Value	÷	Factor	=	Periodic Payment
$100,000	÷	23.115	=	$4,326 (rounded)

CAPITAL LEASE VALUATION

At the time a lessee enters into a capital lease, a leased asset and a lease liability are recorded on the lessee's books. The amount is determined by calculating the present value of the future lease payments. Most lease payment schedules take the form of an annuity. The

EXHIBIT G–1	Calculation of Bond Price Using Present Value Tables

(1) $100,000 of 8%, four-year bonds with interest payable semiannually priced to yield 8%.

Future Cash Flows	Multiplier (Table I)	Multiplier (Table II)	Present Values at 4% Semiannually
Principal repayment, $100,000 (a single amount received eight semiannual periods hence)	0.731		$ 73,100
Interest payments, $4,000 at end of each of eight semiannual interest periods		6.733	26,900 (rounded)
Total present value (or issue price) of bonds			$100,000

(2) $100,000 of 8%, four-year bonds with interest payable semiannually priced to yield 10%.

Future Cash Flows	Multiplier (Table I)	Multiplier (Table II)	Present Values at 5% Semiannually
Principal repayment, $100,000 (a single amount received eight semiannual periods hence)	0.677		$67,700
Interest payments, $4,000 at end of each of eight semiannual interest periods		6.463	25,852
Total present value (or issue price) of bonds			$93,552

(3) $100,000 of 8%, four-year bonds with interest payable semiannually priced to yield 6%.

Future Cash Flows	Multiplier (Table I)	Multiplier (Table II)	Present Values at 3% Semiannually
Principal repayment, $100,000 (a single amount received eight semiannual periods hence)	0.789		$ 78,900
Interest payments, $4,000 at end of each of eight semiannual interest periods		7.020	28,080
Total present value (or issue price) of bonds			$106,980

interest rate used in the calculation is usually the lessee's current interest rate on borrowed funds.

Assume, for example, that a firm leases equipment for 10 years under a capital lease. Annual lease payments of $40,000 will be made at the end of each year, and the lessee's current interest rate to borrow money is 12%. The present value factor to be used in the calculation is for an annuity of $1 for 10 periods at 12%. From Table II, this factor is 5.650. The initial valuation of the capital lease, then, is calculated as follows:

Annual Lease Payments	×	Present Value Factor	=	Lease Valuation
$40,000	×	5.650	=	$226,000

FUTURE VALUES

FUTURE VALUE OF A SINGLE AMOUNT

The **future value** of a single sum is the amount a specified investment will be worth at a future date if invested at a given rate of compound interest. Suppose that we decide to invest $6,000 in a savings account that pays 6% annual interest and that we intend to leave the principal and interest in the account for five years. We assume that interest is credited to the account at the end of each year. The balance in the account at the end of five years is determined using Table III (on page 369), which furnishes the future value of a dollar after a given number of time periods, as follows:

Principal	×	Factor	=	Future Value
$6,000	×	1.338	=	$8,028

The factor 1.338 is in the row for five periods and the column for 6%.

Suppose that the interest is credited to the account semiannually rather than annually. In this situation, there are 10 compounding periods, and we use a 3% rate (one-half the annual rate). The future value calculation is as follows:

Principal	×	Factor	=	Future Value
$6,000	×	1.344	=	$8,064

FUTURE VALUE OF AN ANNUITY

If, instead of investing a single amount at the beginning of a series of periods, we invest a specified amount each period, we are investing in the annuity form. Suppose that we decide to invest $2,000 at the end of each year for five years at an 8% annual rate of return. To determine the accumulated amount of principal and interest, we refer to Table IV (on page 369), which furnishes the future value of a dollar invested at the end of each period. The factor 5.867 is in the row for five periods and the column for 8%, and the calculation is as follows:

Periodic Payment	×	Factor	=	Future Value
$2,000	×	5.867	=	$11,734

If we decide to invest $1,000 at the end of each six months for five years at an 8% annual rate of return, we would use the factor for 10 periods at 4%, as follows:

Periodic Payment	×	Factor	=	Future Value
$1,000	×	12.01	=	$12,010

INSTALLMENT PAYMENT COMPUTATION

When the future value is some desired amount and the periodic payment is to be calculated, you need only to *divide* the future value by the factor to determine the periodic payment.

For example, a corporation issued $100,000 of 10-year bonds payable and agreed to contribute the necessary amounts to a sinking fund at the end of each year to retire the bonds in 10 years. It is expected that the sinking fund will earn a 12% annual rate of return over the period. The factor for 10 periods at 12%, taken from Table IV, is 17.55. The annual contribution to the sinking fund is as follows:

Future Value	÷	Factor	=	Periodic Payment
$100,000	÷	17.55	=	$5,698 (rounded)

PRESENT VALUE TABLES

TABLE I | Present Value of $1

Periods Hence	Rate per Compounding Period									
	2%	3%	4%	5%	6%	8%	10%	12%	15%	20%
1	0.980	0.971	0.962	0.952	0.943	0.926	0.909	0.893	0.870	0.833
2	0.961	0.943	0.925	0.907	0.890	0.857	0.826	0.797	0.756	0.694
3	0.942	0.915	0.889	0.864	0.840	0.794	0.751	0.712	0.658	0.579
4	0.924	0.889	0.855	0.823	0.792	0.735	0.683	0.636	0.572	0.482
5	0.906	0.863	0.822	0.784	0.747	0.681	0.621	0.567	0.497	0.402
6	0.888	0.838	0.790	0.746	0.705	0.630	0.564	0.507	0.432	0.335
7	0.871	0.813	0.760	0.711	0.665	0.583	0.513	0.452	0.376	0.279
8	0.854	0.789	0.731	0.677	0.627	0.540	0.467	0.404	0.327	0.233
9	0.837	0.766	0.703	0.645	0.592	0.500	0.424	0.361	0.284	0.194
10	0.821	0.744	0.676	0.614	0.558	0.463	0.386	0.322	0.247	0.162
11	0.804	0.722	0.650	0.585	0.527	0.429	0.350	0.287	0.215	0.135
12	0.789	0.701	0.625	0.557	0.497	0.397	0.319	0.257	0.187	0.112
13	0.773	0.681	0.601	0.530	0.469	0.368	0.290	0.229	0.163	0.093
14	0.758	0.661	0.577	0.505	0.442	0.340	0.263	0.205	0.141	0.078
15	0.743	0.642	0.555	0.481	0.417	0.315	0.239	0.183	0.123	0.065
16	0.728	0.623	0.534	0.458	0.394	0.292	0.218	0.163	0.107	0.054
17	0.714	0.605	0.513	0.436	0.371	0.270	0.198	0.146	0.093	0.045
18	0.700	0.587	0.494	0.416	0.350	0.250	0.180	0.130	0.081	0.038
19	0.686	0.570	0.475	0.396	0.331	0.232	0.164	0.116	0.070	0.031
20	0.673	0.554	0.456	0.377	0.312	0.215	0.149	0.104	0.061	0.026
30	0.552	0.412	0.308	0.231	0.174	0.099	0.057	0.033	0.015	0.004
40	0.453	0.307	0.208	0.142	0.097	0.046	0.022	0.011	0.004	0.001
50	0.372	0.228	0.141	0.087	0.054	0.021	0.009	0.003	0.001	—

TABLE II | Present Value of an Ordinary Annuity of $1 per Period

Periods Hence	Rate per Compounding Period									
	2%	3%	4%	5%	6%	8%	10%	12%	15%	20%
1	0.980	0.971	0.962	0.952	0.943	0.926	0.909	0.893	0.870	0.833
2	1.942	1.914	1.886	1.859	1.833	1.783	1.736	1.690	1.626	1.528
3	2.884	2.829	2.775	2.723	2.673	2.577	2.487	2.402	2.283	2.106
4	3.808	3.717	3.630	3.546	3.465	3.312	3.170	3.037	2.855	2.589
5	4.714	4.580	4.452	4.330	4.212	3.993	3.791	3.605	3.352	2.991
6	5.601	5.417	5.242	5.076	4.917	4.623	4.355	4.111	3.784	3.326
7	6.472	6.230	6.002	5.786	5.582	5.206	4.868	4.564	4.160	3.605
8	7.326	7.020	6.733	6.463	6.210	5.747	5.335	4.968	4.487	3.837
9	8.162	7.786	7.435	7.108	6.802	6.247	5.760	5.328	4.772	4.031
10	8.983	8.530	8.111	7.722	7.360	6.710	6.145	5.650	5.019	4.192
11	9.787	9.253	8.761	8.306	7.887	7.139	6.495	5.988	5.234	4.327
12	10.575	9.954	9.385	8.863	8.384	7.536	6.814	6.194	5.421	4.439
13	11.348	10.635	9.986	9.394	8.853	7.904	7.103	6.424	5.583	4.533
14	12.106	11.296	10.563	9.899	9.295	8.244	7.367	6.628	5.724	4.611
15	12.849	11.938	11.118	10.380	9.712	8.560	7.606	6.811	5.847	4.675
16	13.578	12.561	11.652	10.838	10.106	8.851	7.824	6.974	5.954	4.730
17	14.292	13.166	12.166	11.274	10.477	9.122	8.022	7.120	6.047	4.775
18	14.992	13.754	12.659	11.690	10.828	9.372	8.201	7.250	6.128	4.812
19	15.679	14.324	13.134	12.085	11.158	9.604	8.365	7.366	6.198	4.844
20	16.351	14.878	13.590	12.462	11.470	9.818	8.514	7.469	6.259	4.870
30	22.397	19.600	17.292	15.373	13.765	11.258	9.427	8.055	6.566	4.979
40	27.356	23.115	19.793	17.159	15.046	11.925	9.779	8.244	6.642	4.997
50	31.424	25.730	21.482	18.256	15.762	12.234	9.915	8.304	6.661	4.999

FUTURE VALUE TABLES

TABLE III Future Value of $1

Periods Hence	Rate per Compounding Period									
	2%	3%	4%	5%	6%	8%	10%	12%	15%	20%
1	1.020	1.030	1.040	1.050	1.060	1.080	1.100	1.120	1.150	1.200
2	1.040	1.061	1.082	1.103	1.124	1.166	1.210	1.254	1.323	1.440
3	1.061	1.093	1.125	1.158	1.191	1.260	1.331	1.405	1.521	1.728
4	1.082	1.126	1.170	1.216	1.262	1.360	1.464	1.574	1.749	2.074
5	1.104	1.159	1.217	1.276	1.338	1.469	1.611	1.762	2.011	2.488
6	1.126	1.194	1.265	1.340	1.419	1.587	1.772	1.974	2.313	2.986
7	1.149	1.230	1.316	1.407	1.504	1.714	1.949	2.211	2.660	3.583
8	1.172	1.267	1.369	1.477	1.594	1.851	2.144	2.476	3.059	4.300
9	1.195	1.305	1.423	1.551	1.689	1.999	2.358	2.773	3.518	5.160
10	1.219	1.344	1.480	1.629	1.791	2.159	2.594	3.106	4.046	6.192
11	1.243	1.384	1.539	1.710	1.898	2.332	2.853	3.479	4.652	7.430
12	1.268	1.426	1.601	1.796	2.012	2.518	3.138	3.896	5.350	8.916
13	1.294	1.469	1.665	1.886	2.133	2.720	3.452	4.363	6.153	10.699
14	1.319	1.513	1.732	1.980	2.261	2.937	3.798	4.887	7.076	12.839
15	1.346	1.558	1.801	2.079	2.397	3.172	4.177	5.474	8.137	15.407
16	1.373	1.605	1.873	2.183	2.540	3.426	4.595	6.130	9.358	18.488
17	1.400	1.653	1.948	2.292	2.693	3.700	5.054	6.866	10.761	22.186
18	1.428	1.702	2.026	2.407	2.854	3.996	5.560	7.690	12.375	26.623
19	1.457	1.754	2.107	2.527	3.026	4.316	6.116	8.613	14.232	31.948
20	1.486	1.806	2.191	2.653	3.207	4.661	6.728	9.646	16.367	38.338
30	1.811	2.427	3.243	4.322	5.743	10.06	17.45	29.96	66.212	237.376
40	2.208	3.262	4.801	7.040	10.29	21.72	45.26	93.05	267.864	1,469.772
50	2.692	4.384	7.107	11.47	18.42	46.90	117.4	289.0	1,083.657	9,100.438

TABLE IV Future Value of an Ordinary Annuity of $1 per Period

Periods Hence	Rate per Compounding Period									
	2%	3%	4%	5%	6%	8%	10%	12%	15%	20%
1	1.000	1.000	1.000	1.000	1.000	1.000	1.000	1.000	1.000	1.000
2	2.020	2.030	2.040	2.050	2.060	2.080	2.100	2.120	2.150	2.200
3	3.060	3.091	3.122	3.153	3.184	3.246	3.310	3.374	3.473	3.640
4	4.122	4.184	4.246	4.310	4.375	4.506	4.641	4.779	4.993	5.368
5	5.204	5.309	5.416	5.526	5.637	5.867	6.105	6.353	6.742	7.442
6	6.308	6.468	6.633	6.802	6.975	7.336	7.716	8.115	8.754	9.930
7	7.434	7.662	7.898	8.142	8.394	8.923	9.487	10.09	11.07	12.92
8	8.583	8.892	9.214	9.549	9.897	10.64	11.44	12.30	13.73	16.50
9	9.755	10.16	10.58	11.03	11.49	12.49	13.58	14.78	16.79	20.80
10	10.95	11.46	12.01	12.58	13.18	14.49	15.94	17.55	20.30	25.96
11	12.17	12.81	13.49	14.21	14.97	16.65	18.53	20.65	24.35	32.15
12	13.41	14.19	15.03	15.92	16.87	18.98	21.38	24.13	29.00	39.58
13	14.68	15.62	16.63	17.71	18.88	21.50	24.52	28.03	34.35	48.50
14	15.97	17.09	18.29	19.60	21.02	24.21	27.98	32.39	40.50	59.20
15	17.29	18.60	20.02	21.58	23.28	27.15	31.77	37.28	47.58	72.04
16	18.64	20.16	21.82	23.66	25.67	30.32	35.95	42.75	55.72	87.44
17	20.01	21.76	23.70	25.84	28.21	33.75	40.54	48.88	65.08	105.9
18	21.41	23.41	25.65	28.13	30.91	37.45	45.60	55.75	75.84	128.1
19	22.84	25.12	27.67	30.54	33.76	41.45	51.16	63.44	88.21	154.7
20	24.30	26.87	29.78	33.07	36.79	45.76	57.28	72.05	102.4	186.7
30	40.57	47.58	56.08	66.44	79.06	113.3	164.5	241.3	434.7	1,181.2
40	60.40	75.40	95.03	120.8	154.8	259.1	442.6	767.1	1,779	7,343
50	84.58	112.8	152.7	209.3	290.3	573.8	1,164	2,400	7,218	45,497

GLOSSARY OF KEY TERMS USED IN THIS CHAPTER AND THE APPENDIX

annuity　A pattern of cash flows in which equal amounts are spaced equally over a number of periods (p. 364).

bond　A long-term debt instrument that promises to pay interest periodically and a principal amount at maturity, usually issued by the borrower to a group of lenders. Bonds may incorporate a wide variety of provisions relating to security for the debt involved, methods of paying the periodic interest, and retirement provisions (p. 343).

call provision　A bond feature that allows the borrower to retire (call in) the bonds after a stated date (p. 345).

capital lease　A lease that transfers to the lessee substantially all of the benefits and risks related to ownership of the property. The lessee records the leased property as an asset and establishes a liability for the lease obligation (p. 355).

contract rate　The rate of interest stated on a bond certificate (p. 346).

convertible bond　A bond incorporating the holder's right to convert the bond to capital stock under prescribed terms (p. 345).

coupon bond　A bond with coupons for interest payable to bearer attached to the bond for each interest period. Whenever interest is due, the bondholder detaches a coupon and deposits it with his or her bank for collection (p. 344).

debenture bond　A bond that has no specific property pledged as security for the repayment of funds borrowed (p. 344).

deferred tax liability　A liability representing the estimated future income taxes payable resulting from an existing temporary difference between an asset's book value and its tax basis (p. 357).

effective interest method　A method of amortizing bond premium or discount that results in a constant rate of interest each period and varying amounts of premium or discount amortized each period (p. 348).

effective rate　The current rate of interest in the market for a bond or other debt instrument. When issued, a bond is priced to yield the market rate of interest at the date of issuance (p. 349).

future value　The amount a specified investment (or series of investments) will be worth at a future date if invested at a given rate of compound interest (p. 366).

lease　A contract between a lessor (owner) and lessee (tenant) for the rental of property (p. 354).

leasehold　The rights transferred from the lessor to the lessee by a lease (p. 354).

lessee　The party acquiring the right to the use of property by a lease (p. 354).

lessor　The owner of property who transfers the right to use the property to another party by a lease (p. 354).

leveraging　The use of borrowed funds in the capital structure of a firm. The expectation is that the funds will earn a return higher than the rate of interest on the borrowed funds (p. 343).

market rate　The current rate of interest in the market for a bond or other debt instrument (p. 346).

nominal rate　The rate of interest stated on a bond certificate or other debt instrument (p. 346).

off-balance-sheet financing　The structuring of a financing arrangement so that no liability shows on the borrower's balance sheet (p. 356).

operating lease　A lease by which the lessor retains the usual risks and rewards of owning the property (p. 355).

pension plan　A plan to pay benefits to employees after they retire from the company. The plan may be a defined contribution plan or a defined benefit plan (p. 356).

present value　The current worth of amounts to be paid (or received) in the future; computed by discounting the future payments (or receipts) at a specified interest rate (p. 363).

registered bond　A bond for which the issuer (or the trustee) maintains a record of owners and, at the appropriate times, mails out interest payments (p. 344).

secured bond　A bond that pledges specific property as security for meeting the terms of the bond agreement (p. 344).

serial bond　A bond issue that staggers the bond maturity dates over a series of years (p. 344).

sinking fund provision　A bond feature that requires the borrower to retire a portion of the bonds each year or, in some cases, to make payments each year to a trustee who is responsible for managing the resources needed to retire the bonds at maturity (p. 345).

term loan　A long-term borrowing, evidenced by a note payable, that is arranged with a single lender (p. 354).

times interest earned ratio　Income before interest expense and income taxes divided by interest expense. Sometimes called *interest coverage ratio* (p. 359).

trading on the equity　The use of borrowed funds in the capital structure of a firm. The expectation is that the funds will earn a return higher than the rate of interest on the borrowed funds (p. 343).

zero coupon bond　A bond that offers no periodic interest payments but that is issued at a substantial discount from its face value (p. 345).

QUESTIONS

10-1 What do the following terms mean? (a) term loan, (b) bonds payable, (c) trustee, (d) secured bonds, (e) serial bonds, (f) call provision, (g) convertible bonds, (h) face value, (i) nominal rate, (j) bond discount, (k) bond premium, and (l) amortization of bond premium or discount.

10-2 What are the advantages and disadvantages of issuing bonds rather than common stock?

10-3 A $3,000,000 issue of 10-year, 9% bonds was sold at 98 plus accrued interest three months after the bonds were dated. What net amount of cash is received?

10-4 How does issuing bonds at a premium or discount "adjust the nominal rate to the applicable market rate of interest"?

10-5 Regardless of whether premium or discount is involved, what generalization can be made about the change in the book value of bonds payable during the period in which they are outstanding?

10-6 If the effective interest amortization method is used for bonds payable, how does the periodic interest expense change over the life of the bonds when they are issued (a) at a discount and (b) at a premium?

10-7 How should premium and discount on bonds payable be presented in the balance sheet?

10-8 On April 30, 1996, one year before maturity, Eastern Company retired $200,000 of 9% bonds payable at 101. The book value of the bonds on April 30 was $197,600. Bond interest was last paid on April 30, 1996. What is the gain or loss on the retirement of the bonds?

10-9 Sax Company borrowed money by issuing a 20-year mortgage note payable. The note will be repaid in equal monthly installments. The interest expense component of each payment decreases with each payment. Why?

10-10 What is the difference between an operating lease and a capital lease?

10-11 How is the initial valuation determined for the asset and liability in a capital lease?

10-12 Over what time period should the cost of providing retirement benefits to employees be expensed?

10-13 What accounting analysis is required when the accumulated retirement benefits under a firm's pension plan exceed the assets in the pension fund?

10-14 What are two examples of temporary differences that will result in the recognition of deferred tax liabilities?

10-15 During 1997, its first year of operations, Hunter, Inc., recorded $20,000 of sales revenue in its financial statements that will not be reported as revenue on its income tax return until 1998. The tax rate is 40% for 1997 and 1998. What amount of deferred tax liability related to this temporary difference should appear in Hunter's December 31, 1997, balance sheet?

10-16 A firm records an outlay as an asset in 1996 but deducts the outlay as an expense on its 1996 income tax return. In 1997 the entire amount will be expensed for financial reporting. In 1996, tax rates enacted into law were 35% for 1996 and 40% for 1997. Which rate is used in determining the deferred tax liability at December 31, 1996? Explain.

10-17 When are deferred tax liabilities classified as current liabilities? as long-term liabilities?

10-18 What does the times interest earned ratio show and how is it used?

PRINCIPLES DISCUSSION QUESTION

10-19 A recent annual report from Briggs & Stratton Corporation discloses the following guidelines regarding accrued employee benefits:

> The Company's life insurance program includes payment of a death benefit to beneficiaries of retired employees. The Company accrues for the estimated cost of these benefits over the estimated working life of the employee. Past service costs for all retired employees have been fully provided for and the Company also accrues for the estimated cost of supplemental retirement and death benefit agreements with executive officers.

What is the basic accounting principle that causes Briggs & Stratton to accrue the estimated cost of providing death benefit payments over the estimated working lives of the covered employees? Briefly explain how this principle leads to the accounting treatment Briggs & Stratton uses. The past service costs referred to by Briggs & Stratton relate to the firm's defined benefit pension plan. What are past service costs? Over what time period is Briggs & Stratton recognizing the expense of providing supplemental retirement and death benefit agreements with executive officers?

EXERCISES

10-20 On December 31, 1996, Daggett Company issued $800,000 of 10-year, 9% bonds payable for $750,232, yielding an effective interest rate of 10%. Interest is payable semiannually on June 30 and December 31. Prepare journal entries to reflect (a) the issuance of the bonds, (b) the semiannual interest payment and discount amortization (effective interest method) on June 30, 1997, and (c) the semiannual interest payment and discount amortization on December 31, 1997. Round amounts to the nearest dollar.

10-21 On December 31, 1996, Coffey Company issued $300,000 of 15-year, 10% bonds payable for $351,780, yielding an effective interest rate of 8%. Interest is payable semiannually on June 30 and December 31. Prepare journal entries to reflect (a) the issuance of the bonds, (b) the semiannual interest payment and premium amortization (effective interest method) on June 30, 1997, and (c) the semiannual interest payment and premium amortization on December 31, 1997. Round amounts to the nearest dollar.

10-22 Indicate the proper financial statement classification for each of the following accounts:

> Gain on Bond Retirement (material amount)
> Discount on Bonds Payable
> Mortgage Notes Payable
> Bonds Payable
> Bond Interest Expense
> Bond Interest Payable
> Premium on Bonds Payable

10-23 Elston Corporation issued $400,000 of 11%, 20-year bonds at 108 on January 1, 1996. Interest is payable semiannually on July 1 and January 1. Through January 1, 2001, Elston amortized $5,000 of the bond premium. On January 1, 2001, Elston retired the bonds at 103 (after making the interest payment on that date). Prepare the journal entry to record the bond retirement on January 1, 2001.

10-24 On December 31, 1996, Thomas, Inc., borrowed $700,000 on a 12%, 15-year mortgage note payable. The note is to be repaid in equal semiannual installments of $50,854 (payable on June 30 and December 31). Prepare journal entries to reflect (a) the issuance of the mortgage note payable, (b) the payment of the first installment on June 30, 1997, and (c) the payment of the second installment on December 31, 1997. Round amounts to the nearest dollar.

10-25 On January 1, 1996, Spider, Inc., entered into two lease contracts. The first lease contract was a six-year lease for a computer with $15,000 annual lease payments due at the end of each year. Spider took possession of the computer on January 1, 1996. The second lease contract was a six-month lease, beginning January 1, 1996, for some warehouse storage space with $1,000 monthly lease payments due the first of each month. Spider made the first month's payment on January 1, 1996. The present value of the lease payments under the first contract is $74,520. The present value of the lease payments under the second contract is $5,853.
a. The first lease contract is a capital lease. Prepare the appropriate journal entry for this lease on January 1, 1996.
b. The second lease contract is an operating lease. Prepare the proper journal entry for this lease on January 1, 1996.

10-26 Fisk, Inc., purchased $600,000 of construction equipment on January 1, 1996. The equipment is being depreciated on a straight-line basis over six years with no expected salvage value. MACRS depreciation is being used on the firm's tax returns. At December 31, 1998, the equipment's book value is $300,000 and its tax basis is $173,000 (this is Fisk's only temporary difference). Over the next three years, straight-line depreciation will exceed MACRS depreciation by $31,000 in 1999, $31,000 in 2000, and $65,000 in 2001. The income tax rate in effect for all years is 40%.
a. What amount of deferred tax liability should appear in Fisk's December 31, 1998, balance sheet?
b. What amount of deferred tax liability should appear in Fisk's December 31, 1999, balance sheet?
c. What amount of deferred tax liability should appear in Fisk's December 31, 2000, balance sheet?
d. Where should the deferred tax liability accounts be classified in Fisk's 1998, 1999, and 2000 year-end balance sheets?

10-27 Lunar, Inc., plans to issue $900,000 of 10% bonds that will pay interest semiannually and mature in five years. Assume that the effective interest rate is 12% per year compounded semiannually. Compute the selling price of the bonds. Use Tables I and II (on page 368).

PROBLEMS

BONDS PAYABLE ENTRIES; ISSUED AT PAR PLUS ACCRUED INTEREST
— OBJ. 3, 4 —

10-28 Askew, Inc., which closes its books on December 31, is authorized to issue $500,000 of 9%, 15-year bonds dated May 1, 1996, with interest payments on November 1 and May 1.

REQUIRED

Prepare general journal entries to record the following events, assuming that the bonds were sold at 100 plus accrued interest on October 1, 1996.

a. The bond issuance.
b. Payment of the first semiannual period's interest on November 1, 1996.
c. Accrual of bond interest expense at December 31, 1996.
d. Payment of the semiannual interest on May 1, 1997. (The firm does not make reversing entries.)
e. Retirement of $300,000 of the bonds at 101 on May 1, 2001 (immediately after the interest payment on that date).

EFFECTIVE INTEREST AMORTIZATION
— OBJ. 3 —

10-29 On December 31, 1996, Caper, Inc., issued $250,000 of 8%, 9-year bonds for $220,900, yielding an effective interest rate of 10%. Semiannual interest is payable on June 30 and December 31 each year. The firm uses the effective interest method to amortize the discount.

REQUIRED

a. Prepare an amortization schedule showing the necessary information for the first two interest periods. Round amounts to the nearest dollar.
b. Prepare the journal entry for the bond issuance on December 31, 1996.
c. Prepare the entry to record the bond interest payment and discount amortization at June 30, 1997.
d. Prepare the entry to record the bond interest payment and discount amortization at December 31, 1997.

EFFECTIVE INTEREST AMORTIZATION
— OBJ. 3 —

10-30 On March 31, 1996, Eagle, Inc., issued $800,000 of 9%, 20-year bonds for $878,948, yielding an effective interest rate of 8%. Semiannual interest is payable on September 30 and March 31 each year. The firm uses the effective interest method to amortize the premium.

REQUIRED

a. Prepare an amortization schedule showing the necessary information for the first two interest periods. Round amounts to the nearest dollar.
b. Prepare the journal entry for the bond issuance on March 31, 1996.
c. Prepare the entry to record the bond interest payment and premium amortization at September 30, 1996.
d. Prepare the adjusting entry to record interest expense and premium amortization at December 31,1996, the close of the firm's accounting year.
e. Prepare the entry to record the bond interest payment and premium amortization at March 31, 1997. (The firm does not make reversing entries.)

INSTALLMENT TERM LOAN
— OBJ. 5, APPENDIX G —

10-31 On December 31, 1997, Finley Corporation borrowed $500,000 on a 10%, 10-year mortgage note payable. The note is to be repaid with equal semiannual installments, beginning June 30, 1998.

REQUIRED

a. Compute the amount of the semiannual installment payment. Use Table II (on page 368) and round amount to the nearest dollar.
b. Prepare the journal entry to record Finley's borrowing of funds on December 31, 1997.
c. Prepare the journal entry to record Finley's installment payment on June 30, 1998.
d. Prepare the journal entry to record Finley's installment payment on December 31, 1998. (Round amounts to the nearest dollar.)

DEFERRED INCOME TAXES
— OBJ. 8 —

10-32 Early in January 1997, Wade, Inc., purchased equipment costing $16,000 and debited the amount to the Equipment account. The equipment had a two-year useful life and was depreciated $8,000 in each of the years 1997 and 1998. Wade deducted the entire $16,000 as an expense on its 1997 income tax return. Wade had no other plant assets and the accounting for this equipment represented the only difference between Wade's financial statements and income tax returns. Wade's income before depreciation expense and income taxes was $236,000 in 1997 and $245,000 in 1998. Tax rates enacted into law at December 31, 1997, were 40% for both 1997 and 1998.

REQUIRED

a. What amount of deferred tax liability should be reported in Wade's year-end balance sheets for 1997 and 1998?
b. Prepare journal entries to record income taxes at December 31, 1997, and December 31, 1998.
c. Assume that the tax rates enacted into law at December 31, 1997, are 35% for 1997 and 40% for 1998. Prepare journal entries to record income taxes at December 31, 1997, and December 31, 1998.

COMPUTING VARIOUS
PRESENT VALUES
— APPENDIX G —

10-33 Refer to Tables I and II on page 368.

REQUIRED

Compute the present value of each of the following items.

a. $90,000 10 years hence if the annual interest rate is
   1. 8% compounded annually.
   2. 8% compounded semiannually.
   3. 8% compounded quarterly.

b. $1,000 received at the end of each year for the next eight years if money is worth 10% per year compounded annually.

c. $600 received at the end of each six months for the next 15 years if the interest rate is 8% per year compounded semiannually.

d. $500,000 inheritance 10 years hence if money is worth 10% per year compounded annually.

e. $2,500 received each half-year for the next 10 years plus a single sum of $85,000 at the end of 10 years if the interest rate is 12% per year compounded semiannually.

ALTERNATE EXERCISES

BONDS PAYABLE ENTRIES;
EFFECTIVE INTEREST
AMORTIZATION
— OBJ. 3 —

10-20A On December 31, 1996, Blair Company issued $600,000 of 20-year, 11% bonds payable for $554,718, yielding an effective interest rate of 12%. Interest is payable semiannually on June 30 and December 31. Prepare journal entries to reflect (a) the issuance of the bonds, (b) the semiannual interest payment and discount amortization (effective interest method) on June 30, 1997, and (c) the semiannual interest payment and discount amortization on December 31, 1997. Round amounts to the nearest dollar.

BONDS PAYABLE ENTRIES;
EFFECTIVE INTEREST
AMORTIZATION
— OBJ. 3 —

10-21A On December 31, 1996, Kay Company issued $400,000 of five-year, 13% bonds payable for $446,372, yielding an effective interest rate of 10%. Interest is payable semiannually on June 30 and December 31. Prepare journal entries to reflect (a) the issuance of the bonds, (b) the semiannual interest payment and premium amortization (effective interest method) on June 30, 1997, and (c) the semiannual interest payment and premium amortization on December 31, 1997. Round amounts to the nearest dollar.

BONDS PAYABLE ON
BALANCE SHEET
— OBJ. 4 —

10-22A The adjusted trial balance for the Lancer Corporation at the end of 1996 contains the following accounts:

Bond Interest Payable	$ 25,000
9% Bonds Payable due 1999	600,000
10% Bonds Payable due 2005	500,000
Discount on 9% Bonds Payable	19,000
Premium on 10% Bonds Payable	15,000
Zero Coupon Bonds Payable due 2001	170,500
8% Bonds Payable due 1997	100,000

Prepare the long-term liabilities section of the balance sheet. Indicate the proper balance sheet classification for accounts listed above that do not belong in the long-term liabilities section.

EARLY RETIREMENT OF BONDS
— OBJ. 4 —

10-23A Norwich, Inc., issued $250,000 of 8%, 15-year bonds at 96 on June 30, 1996. Interest is payable semiannually on December 31 and June 30. Through June 30, 2002, Norwich amortized $3,000 of the bond discount. On June 30, 2002, Norwich retired the bonds at 101 (after making the interest payment on that date). Prepare the journal entry to record the bond retirement on June 30, 2002.

INSTALLMENT TERM LOAN
— OBJ. 5 —

10-24A On December 31, 1996, Beam, Inc., borrowed $500,000 on an 8%, 10-year mortgage note payable. The note is to be repaid in equal quarterly installments of $18,278 (beginning March 31, 1997). Prepare journal entries to reflect (a) the issuance of the mortgage note payable, (b) the payment of the first installment on March 31, 1997, and (c) the payment of the second installment on June 30, 1997. Round amounts to the nearest dollar.

POSTRETIREMENT BENEFITS
— OBJ. 7 —

10-25A Hall Corporation has a defined contribution pension plan for its employees. Each year, Hall contributes to the plan an amount equal to 4% of the employee payroll for the year. Hall's 1997 payroll was $400,000. Hall also provides a life insurance benefit that pays a $50,000 death benefit to the beneficiaries of retired employees. At the end of 1997, Hall estimates that its liability under the life insurance program is $625,000. Hall has assets with a fair value of $175,000 in a trust fund that are available to meet the death benefit payments.

a. Prepare the journal entry at December 31, 1997, to record Hall's 1997 defined contribution to a pension trustee who will manage the pension funds for the firm's employees.

b. What amount of liability for death benefit payments must Hall report in its December 31, 1997, balance sheet?

DEFERRED INCOME TAXES
— OBJ. 8 —

10-26A Miner Corporation paid $12,000 on December 31, 1996, for equipment with a three-year useful life (1997–1999) and debited the payment to Equipment. The equipment will be depreciated $4,000 per year in 1997, 1998, and 1999. Miner took the $12,000 payment as an expense on its 1996 income tax return. This amount is Miner's only temporary difference between its books and its tax return. Miner's income tax rate is 40%.
  a. What amount of deferred tax liability should appear in Miner's December 31, 1996, balance sheet?
  b. Where should the deferred tax liability be classified in the balance sheet at December 31, 1996?
  c. What amount of deferred tax liability should appear in Miner's December 31, 1997, balance sheet?

DETERMINING BOND PRICE
— APPENDIX G —

10-27A Tide, Inc., plans to issue $500,000 of 9% bonds that will pay interest semiannually and mature in 10 years. Assume that the effective interest is 8% per year compounded semiannually. Compute the selling price of the bonds. Use Tables I and II (on page 368).

ALTERNATE PROBLEMS

BONDS PAYABLE ENTRIES;
ISSUED AT PAR PLUS ACCRUED
INTEREST
— OBJ. 3, 4 —

10-28A Cheney, Inc., which closes its books on December 31, is authorized to issue $800,000 of 9%, 20-year bonds dated March 1, 1996, with interest payments on September 1 and March 1.
REQUIRED
Prepare general journal entries to record the following events, assuming that the bonds were sold at 100 plus accrued interest on July 1, 1996.
  a. The bond issuance.
  b. Payment of the semiannual interest on September 1, 1996.
  c. Accrual of bond interest expense at December 31, 1996.
  d. Payment of the semiannual interest on March 1, 1997. (The firm does not make reversing entries.)
  e. Retirement of $200,000 of the bonds at 101 on March 1, 2006 (immediately after the interest payment on that date).

EFFECTIVE INTEREST
AMORTIZATION
— OBJ. 3 —

10-29A On December 31, 1996, Echo, Inc., issued $720,000 of 11%, 10-year bonds for $678,852, yielding an effective interest rate of 12%. Semiannual interest is payable on June 30 and December 31 each year. The firm uses the effective interest method to amortize the discount.
REQUIRED
  a. Prepare an amortization schedule showing the necessary information for the first two interest periods. Round amounts to the nearest dollar.
  b. Prepare the journal entry for the bond issuance on December 31, 1996.
  c. Prepare the entry to record bond interest expense and discount amortization at June 30, 1997.
  d. Prepare the entry to record bond interest expense and discount amortization at December 31, 1997.

EFFECTIVE INTEREST
AMORTIZATION
— OBJ. 3 —

10-30A On April 30, 1996, Raines, Inc., issued $250,000 of 6%, 15-year bonds for $206,690, yielding an effective interest rate of 8%. Semiannual interest is payable on October 31 and April 30 each year. The firm uses the effective interest method to amortize the discount.
REQUIRED
  a. Prepare an amortization schedule showing the necessary information for the first two interest periods. Round amounts to the nearest dollar.
  b. Prepare the journal entry for the bond issuance on April 30, 1996.
  c. Prepare the entry to record the bond interest payment and discount amortization at October 31, 1996.
  d. Prepare the adjusting entry to record bond interest expense and discount amortization at December 31, 1996, the close of the firm's accounting year.
  e. Prepare the entry to record the bond interest payment and discount amortization at April 30, 1997. (The firm does not make reversing entries.)

INSTALLMENT TERM LOAN
— OBJ. 5, APPENDIX G —

10-31A On December 31, 1997, Comray Corporation borrowed $950,000 on an 8%, five-year mortgage note payable. The note is to be repaid with equal quarterly installments, beginning March 31, 1998.
REQUIRED
  a. Compute the amount of the quarterly installment payment. Use Table II (on page 368) and round amount to the nearest dollar.

b. Prepare the journal entry to record the borrowing of funds by Comray Corporation on December 31, 1997.

c. Prepare the journal entry to record the installment payment by Comray Corporation on March 31, 1998.

d. Prepare the journal entry to record the installment payment by Comray Corporation on June 30, 1998.

DEFERRED INCOME TAXES
— OBJ. 8 —

10-32A Viking Corporation paid $12,000 on December 31, 1996, for special equipment with a two-year useful life and debited the payment to Equipment. The equipment was depreciated $6,000 per year in 1997 and 1998. Viking owned no other plant assets. Viking deducted the entire $12,000 as an expense on its 1996 income tax return. This represented the only difference between Viking's financial statements and income tax returns. Viking's income before depreciation expense and income taxes was $320,000 in 1996, $400,000 in 1997, and $420,000 in 1998. Tax rates enacted into law at December 31, 1996, were 35% for 1996, 35% for 1997, and 40% for 1998.

REQUIRED

a. What is the book value of equipment at December 31, 1996; December 31, 1997; and December 31, 1998?

b. What is the tax basis of equipment at December 31, 1996; December 31, 1997; and December 31, 1998?

c. What amount of deferred tax liability should be reported in the year-end balance sheets for 1996, 1997, and 1998?

d. Prepare journal entries to record income taxes at December 31, 1996; December 31, 1997; and December 31, 1998.

DETERMINING BOND SINKING-
FUND CONTRIBUTION AND
VARIOUS FUTURE VALUES
— APPENDIX G —

10-33A Refer to Tables III and IV on page 369.

REQUIRED

Compute the amounts specified below.

a. A firm issued $800,000 of 10-year bonds payable. The bond agreement requires annual year-end contributions to a sinking fund in order to accumulate $800,000 to retire the bonds at maturity. Calculate the amount of the annual contribution if an 8% rate of return is expected.

b. Calculate the future value of a single amount of $7,000 invested for 15 years at 10% compounded annually.

c. Calculate the future value of a single amount of $7,000 invested for 15 years at 10% compounded semiannually.

d. Calculate the future value of an annuity of $20,000 invested at the end of each year for eight years at an annual rate of 8%.

e. Calculate the future value of an annuity of $10,000 invested at the end of each six months for eight years at an annual rate of 8%.

CASES

BUSINESS
DECISION CASE

Kingston Corporation has total assets of $5,200,000 and has been earning an average of $800,000 before income taxes the past several years. The firm is planning to expand plant facilities to manufacture a new product and needs an additional $2,000,000 in funds, on which it expects to earn 18% before income tax. The income tax rate is expected to be 40% for the next several years. The firm has no long-term debt outstanding and presently has 75,000 shares of common stock outstanding. The firm is considering three alternatives:

1. Obtain the $2,000,000 by issuing 25,000 shares of common stock at $80 per share.

2. Obtain the $2,000,000 by issuing $1,000,000 of 10%, 20-year bonds at face value and 12,500 shares of common stock at $80 per share.

3. Obtain the $2,000,000 by issuing $2,000,000 of 10%, 20-year bonds at face value.

REQUIRED

As a stockholder of Kingston Corporation, which alternative would you prefer if your main concern is enhancing the firm's earnings per share? (*Hint:* Divide net income by the number of outstanding common shares to determine earnings per share.)

FINANCIAL ANALYSIS CASE

Merck & Co., headquartered in Whitehouse Station, New Jersey, is a pharmaceutical products and services company. Royal Caribbean Cruises Ltd., headquartered in Miami, Florida, provides more than 50 different cruise itineraries on its fleet of passenger ships. Selected financial information for three years for these two companies are presented below (Year 3 is the most recent year; amounts in millions).

	Year 3	Year 2	Year 1
Merck & Co.			
Interest expense	$ 124.4	$ 84.7	$ 72.7
Income before income taxes	4,415.2	3,102.7	3,563.6
Royal Caribbean Cruises			
Interest expense	43.3	54.4	82.2
Income before income taxes	142.2	106.7	60.6

REQUIRED

a. Compute the times interest earned ratio for Merck & Co. for Years 1 through 3 and comment on the trend.

b. Compute the times interest earned ratio for Royal Caribbean Cruises for Years 1 through 3 and comment on the trend.

c. Assume that you were going to acquire $200,000 of 10-year bonds issued by one of these two companies. Based on the ratios computed in requirements (a) and (b), to which company would you prefer to lend your money?

ETHICS CASE

Sexton Corporation is in the third quarter of the current year, and projections are that net income will be down about $600,000 from the previous year. Sexton's return on assets is also projected to decline from its usual 15% to approximately 13%. If earnings do decline, this year will be the second consecutive year of decline. Sexton's president is quite concerned about these projections (and his job) and has called a meeting of the firm's officers for next week to consider ways to "turn things around and fast."

Shane Smith, treasurer of Sexton Corporation, has received a memorandum from his assistant, Ann Hathaway. Smith had asked Hathaway if she had any suggestions as to how Sexton might improve its earnings performance for the current year. Hathaway's memo reads as follows:

> As you know, we have $3,000,000 of 8%, 20-year bonds payable outstanding. We issued these bonds 10 years ago at face value. When they mature, we would probably replace them with other bonds. The economy right now is in a phase of high inflation, and interest rates for bonds have soared to about 16%. My proposal is to replace these bonds right now. More specifically, I propose:
>
> **1.** Immediately issue $3,000,000 of 20-year, 16% bonds payable. These bonds will be issued at face value.
>
> **2.** Use the proceeds from the new bonds to buy back and retire our outstanding 8% bonds. Because of the current high rates of interest, these bonds are trading in the market at $1,900,000.
>
> **3.** The benefits to Sexton are that (a) the retirement of the old bonds will generate a $1,100,000 gain for the income statement and (b) there will be an extra $1,100,000 of cash available for other uses.

Smith is intrigued by the possibility of generating a $1,100,000 gain for the income statement. However, he is not sure this proposal is in the best long-run interests of the firm and its stockholders.

REQUIRED

a. How is the $1,100,000 gain calculated from the retirement of the old bonds? Where would this gain be reported in Sexton's income statement?

b. Why might this proposal not be in the best long-run interests of the firm and its stockholders?

c. What possible ethical conflict is present in this proposal?

GENERAL MILLS ANNUAL REPORT CASE

Refer to the annual report of General Mills, Inc., presented in Appendix K. Refer to the consolidated statement of earnings, the consolidated balance sheets, and Notes 8, 11, 12, 13, 15, and 16.

REQUIRED

a. What is the total amount of long-term liabilities reported by General Mills at May 29, 1994?

b. How much of General Mills' long-term debt is maturing within one year of May 29, 1994? Where is this amount classified in the financial statements?

c. What amount of zero coupon notes does General Mills have outstanding at May 29, 1994? When do these notes mature?

d. In 1992, General Mills called in sinking fund debentures that matured in 2009. Did this early retirement of debt result in a gain or a loss?

e. *Accrued pension cost* is the term used by General Mills to identify the pension liability related to defined benefit pension plans. Some of General Mills' defined benefit plans are underfunded. What is the amount of accrued pension cost for the underfunded plans at May 29, 1994?

f. What amount of pension expense in the year ended May 29, 1994, was the result of General Mills making contributions to defined contribution plans? How does General Mills determine the amount of its defined contributions?

g. General Mills provides health care benefits to the majority of its retirees. Some of these plans are underfunded. What is the amount of accrued postretirement benefits liability for the underfunded health benefit plans at May 29, 1994?

h. What total amount of deferred tax liabilities does General Mills report in its May 29, 1994, balance sheet? What amount of deferred tax assets is reported?

i. Are General Mills' leases capital leases or operating leases? Explain.

j. What is General Mills' times interest earned ratio for the year ended May 29, 1994?

Partnerships and Limited Liability Companies

CHAPTER LEARNING OBJECTIVES

1 **DEFINE** the different types of partnerships, **LIST** the characteristics of a partnership, and **DEFINE** a limited liability company (pp. 380–382).

2 **DESCRIBE** the advantages and disadvantages of a partnership and **INTRODUCE** accounting for a partnership (p. 382).

3 **PRESENT** an overview of the formation of a partnership (pp. 382–383).

4 **ILLUSTRATE** various methods for dividing profits and losses among partners (pp. 383–386).

5 **PRESENT** the methods for admitting a new partner (pp. 386–388).

6 **DESCRIBE** the alternatives when a partner retires (pp. 388–389).

7 **EXPLAIN** how partnerships are liquidated (pp. 390–392).

8 Financial Analysis **DEFINE** *debt-to-equity ratio* and **EXPLAIN** its use (pp. 392–393).

CHAPTER FOCUS

Many businesses are formed as partnerships. Professional people, such as physicians, attorneys, architects, public accountants, and engineers, often operate as partnerships. In addition, many shopping centers, office buildings, and apartment complexes are owned by partnerships. Partnerships also own some professional sports teams. In this chapter, we discuss partnerships and related entities, how they are formed, how new partners are admitted, how the partnership handles the retirement of a partner, and how partnerships are liquidated.

CHARACTERISTICS OF A PARTNERSHIP

OBJECTIVE *1*

DEFINE the different types of partnerships, **LIST** the characteristics of a partnership, and **DEFINE** a limited liability company.

A **partnership** is a voluntary association of two or more persons for the purpose of conducting a business for profit. The Uniform Partnership Act governs the formation and operation of partnerships in many states. A partnership is easily formed; the parties need only agree to it. The ease of formation makes the partnership an attractive form of organization for a business that requires more capital than a single proprietor can provide or for persons who want to combine specialized talents. Each partnership is an accounting entity.

Partnership agreements may be oral, but sound business practice demands a written agreement to avoid misunderstandings. A written partnership agreement constitutes the **articles of copartnership.** The articles of copartnership should detail the important provisions of the partnership arrangement, including the name and location of the partnership; the nature and duration of the business; the duties of partners; the capital contribution of each partner; the understanding for sharing profits and losses and permitted withdrawal of assets; the method of accounting; the procedure for withdrawals of partners; and the procedure for dissolving the business.

PRINCIPLE ALERT

OBJECTIVITY PRINCIPLE

A written partnership agreement is supported by the *objectivity principle.* This basic accounting principle requires that accounting entries be based on objectively determined evidence whenever possible. Many partnership accounting entries are influenced by the content of the partnership agreement, such as the division of profits and losses among the partners. A written partnership agreement provides more objective evidence on these matters than does an oral agreement.

MUTUAL AGENCY

An important characteristic of a partnership is mutual agency. Mutual agency means that every partner is an agent for the firm with the authority to bind the partnership to contracts. This authority applies to all acts of a partner engaging in the usual activities of the firm. Although the partners may limit the authority of one or more partners to act on customary matters, a partner acting contrary to a restriction may still contractually bind the partnership if the other party to the contract is unaware of the limitation. The partnership would not be bound, however, if the other party knew of the restriction.

LIABILITY

There are three primary types of partnerships: general partnership, limited partnership, and limited liability partnership. In a **general partnership,** each partner is individually liable for all of the firm's debt, regardless of the amount of the partner's investment in the firm. This characteristic is known as **unlimited liability.** Creditors of a general partnership unable to pay its debts may obtain payments from the personal assets of the individual partners. Each partner is a general partner, and each general partner is an agent of the firm, able to bind the firm to contracts.

A **limited partnership** has two classes of partners: general partners and limited partners. There must be at least one **general partner** to assume unlimited liability for the firm's debts. Normally, the **limited partners** are investors who participate in the profits and losses of the firm. Their liability for firm debt is limited to the amount of their investment. Limited partners usually do not participate actively in the management of the firm. Today, few firms use the limited partnership form. Instead, they organize as limited liability partnerships or limited liability companies. We discuss limited liability partnerships next and limited liability companies in a later section of this chapter.

In a **limited liability partnership,** there are no general partners. The firm remains liable for all debts, including any malpractice judgments against the firm. In addition, each partner remains personally liable (unlimited liability) for any judgments against the firm for his or her own professional malpractice. However, each partner's liability for the other partners' professional malpractice or the debts of the firm is limited to the partner's investment in the firm.

The limited liability partnership is a relatively new type of partnership. During the past five years, many states have passed laws to allow this type of entity. The other states are considering passing laws to allow this form of entity. Professional firms, such as CPA firms, are adopting this type of partnership.

POINT OF INTEREST

Large CPA Firms Are LLPs

During 1994, many of the largest CPA firms in the United States changed their form of organization from a general partnership to a limited liability partnership. Changes in state laws and the rules of the American Institute of Certified Public Accountants allowed these changes. All of the Big 6 CPA firms are now limited liability partnerships. These firms have added LLP to the end of their firm name (for example, Ernst & Young LLP) to designate this new form of organization.

LIMITED LIFE Because a partnership is a voluntary association of persons, many events may cause its dissolution. These events include the expiration of the agreed-on partnership term; the accomplishment of the business objective; the admission of a new partner; the withdrawal, death, or bankruptcy of an existing partner; and the issuance of a court decree because of a partner's incapacity or misconduct. Even though a change in membership dissolves a partnership, business continuity is often unaffected. A new partnership often continues the operations of the former partnership without interruption.

CO-OWNERSHIP OF PROPERTY Assets contributed by partners become partnership property jointly owned by all partners. Individual partners no longer separately own the specific resources invested in the firm. Unless an agreement to the contrary exists, each partner has an equal right to the firm's property for partnership purposes.

NONTAXABLE ENTITY Although a partnership must file an information return for federal income tax purposes, the partnership itself is not a taxable entity. The information return shows the distributive shares of the partnership's net income that the partners should include on their individual tax returns. The individual partners pay income taxes on their respective shares of partnership earnings whether or not these amounts have been withdrawn from the firm.

LIMITED LIABILITY COMPANY

Most states have recently allowed another type of entity called a **limited liability company.** A limited liability company, often called an *LLC,* is an entity in which each owner's liability for all debts of the firm is limited to that owner's investment in the firm. The LLC form of organization (where allowed by state law) is used for all types of business: manufacturer, wholesaler, retailer, service firm, and real estate investment.

A limited liability company is a hybrid form of organization that has some of the characteristics of a partnership and some of the characteristics of a corporation. The LLC is nontaxable like a partnership; however, the liability of the individual owners is limited the same way it is with a corporation. Further, the accounting for a limited liability company is basically the same as the accounting for a partnership.

ADVANTAGES AND DISADVANTAGES OF A PARTNERSHIP

OBJECTIVE 2

DESCRIBE the advantages and disadvantages of a partnership, and **INTRODUCE** accounting for a partnership.

In contrast with a corporation, a partnership is easier and less expensive to organize and is subject to less government regulation and fewer reporting requirements. Certain actions by a corporation require the approval of stockholders or directors; partners have fewer constraints on their actions. Businesses of modest size or of planned short duration may find these features advantageous. The same may be true for new businesses hesitant to incur the cost of incorporation until their ventures prove successful.

Disadvantages of the partnership form of organization are mutual agency, unlimited liability, and limited life. The first two in particular underscore the importance of selecting partners with great care and are no doubt partially responsible for the rule that no person may be admitted to a partnership without the consent of all existing partners. A corporation, which offers limited liability to all investors, is better able than a general partnership to raise large amounts of capital.

The impact of taxes varies from one circumstance to the next. A partnership is a nontaxable entity; a corporation is a taxable entity. Partners' earnings are taxable whether distributed to the partners or not. A corporation pays income tax on the corporation's net income when it is earned. The stockholders pay income tax on any dividends paid by the corporation. This results in double taxation of earnings distributed to stockholders. Determination of the most advantageous form of organization for tax purposes requires careful analysis of existing tax laws and the tax status of the persons going into business.

CAPITAL, DRAWING, AND LOAN ACCOUNTS

Accounting for partnerships is similar in most respects to accounting for sole proprietorships. Each partner has a capital account and a drawing account that serve the same functions as the related accounts for a sole proprietor. A partner's capital account is credited for his or her investments, and each individual drawing account is debited to reflect assets withdrawn from the partnership. At the end of each accounting period, the balances in the drawing accounts are closed to the related capital accounts.

Occasionally, a partner may lend cash or other assets to the partnership beyond the intended permanent investment. These loans should be credited to the partner's loan account and classified among the liabilities, separate from liabilities to outsiders. Similarly, if a partner withdraws money with the intention of repaying it, the debit should be made to the partner's advance (or loan receivable) account and be classified separately among the partnership's receivables.

The formation of partnerships, the division of profits and losses, the admission and retirement of partners, and the liquidation of partnerships represent areas of particular interest in accounting for these entities. We focus on these issues in the remainder of this chapter.

FORMATION OF A PARTNERSHIP

OBJECTIVE 3

PRESENT an overview of the formation of a partnership.

A partnership's books are opened with an entry reflecting the net contribution of each partner to the firm. Asset accounts are debited for assets invested in the partnership, liability accounts are credited for any liabilities assumed by the partnership, and separate capital accounts are credited for the amount of each partner's net investment.

Assume that Earl Ames, a sole proprietor, and John Baker form a partnership. Ames invests $8,000 cash, office equipment with a current fair value of $25,000, and office supplies worth $2,000. The partnership agrees to assume the $5,000 balance on a note payable signed by Ames when he acquired the equipment. Baker invests $10,000 cash. The following entries on the books of the partnership record the investments of Ames and Baker:

Cash	8,000	
Office Equipment	25,000	
Office Supplies	2,000	
Notes Payable		5,000
E. Ames, Capital		30,000

To record Ames' investment in the partnership of Ames and Baker.

Cash	10,000	
J. Baker, Capital		10,000

To record Baker's investment in the partnership of Ames and Baker.

Assets invested in the partnership should be recorded at their current fair values. These assets (less any liabilities assumed by the partnership) determine the opening capital balances for each partner. If the assets are not recorded initially at their fair values, inequities develop among the partners in terms of their respective capital balances.

For example, assume that the office equipment invested by Ames was recorded incorrectly at $22,000 (its book value from his proprietorship records). If the partnership immediately sold the equipment for its current fair value of $25,000, the resulting $3,000 gain, on closing, would increase the capital balances of both Ames and Baker. This is not equitable. The $3,000 "gain" was not added to the asset by the operations of the partnership. Baker should not be credited with any part of this amount. A similar inequity develops if the equipment is used in operations rather than sold. Owing to a lower total depreciation over the life of the equipment, income would be $3,000 higher over the same period. To avoid such inequities, the partnership records the office equipment initially at $25,000. The values assigned to assets invested in a partnership should be agreeable to all partners.

DIVISION OF PARTNERSHIP PROFITS AND LOSSES

OBJECTIVE 4
ILLUSTRATE the various methods for dividing profits and losses among partners.

If the partners do not agree on a profit and loss sharing formula, partnership profits and losses are divided equally. Partners who do not wish to share profits and losses equally must specify, preferably in a formal written agreement, the manner in which profit and loss distributions are made. Such arrangements may specify a fixed ratio (such as $\frac{2}{3}$ to $\frac{1}{3}$, 60% to 40%, or 5:3) or a sharing formula of some kind based on the relative financial participation of the partners, the services performed by the partners, or both. Any arrangement can be made. Losses may be shared differently from profits. If an agreement specifies the manner of sharing profits but is silent on the sharing of losses, losses will be divided in the same manner as profits. In the following sections, we discuss several common arrangements.

CAPITAL RATIOS

When the services performed or skills provided by the various partners are considered equal, profits and losses may be divided according to the partners' relative investments in the firm. Assume that the Ames and Baker partnership had a profit of $18,000 for 1996 and that the partners' capital accounts, before any profit distribution at year-end, show the following amounts:

E. AMES, CAPITAL		J. BAKER, CAPITAL	
1996		1996	
Jan. 1	30,000	Jan. 1	10,000
		July 1	10,000

The $18,000 profit might be divided according to the beginning capital investment ratio or the average capital investment ratio for the year.

BEGINNING CAPITAL RATIO

At the beginning of 1996, the total capital investment in the firm was $40,000: $30,000 for Ames and $10,000 for Baker. If they shared according to the ratio of *beginning* capital balances, the profit distribution would be 3:1, or $13,500 for Ames and $4,500 for Baker, computed as follows:

	Beginning Capital	Percent of Total	Division of Profit
Ames	$30,000	75	$13,500
Baker	10,000	25	4,500
	$40,000	100	$18,000

The following entry is made to distribute the credit balance in the Income Summary account (which represents the partnership's net income):

Income Summary	18,000	
E. Ames, Capital		13,500
J. Baker, Capital		4,500
To close the Income Summary account.		

AVERAGE CAPITAL RATIO

Because partners' investments may change during the year, the partners may decide that using *average* capital balances rather than beginning capital balances provides a more equitable division of profits. Under this scheme, investment balances are *weighted* by multiplying the amount of the investment by the portion of the year that these funds were invested. Because Baker invested an additional $10,000 on July 1, 1996, his average capital would be based on a $10,000 investment for the first six months and a $20,000 investment for the last six months. The computation is as follows:

Dollars × Months		Average Investment		
Ames				
$30,000 × 12 months =		$360,000 ÷ 12 =	$30,000	
Baker				
$10,000 × 6 months =	$ 60,000			
$20,000 × 6 months =	120,000	$180,000 ÷ 12 =	15,000	
			$45,000	

Profit Distribution

Ames: $\dfrac{\$30,000}{\$45,000} \times \$18,000 = \$12,000$

Baker: $\dfrac{\$15,000}{\$45,000} \times \$18,000 = \dfrac{6,000}{\$18,000}$

The entry to close the Income Summary account would credit E. Ames, Capital with $12,000 and J. Baker, Capital with $6,000.

SALARY AND INTEREST ALLOWANCES

A sharing agreement may provide for variations in the personal services contributed by partners and in their relative investments. **Salary allowances** provide for differences in personal services; **interest allowances** on capital balances provide for differences in the financial participation of partners.

The terms *salary allowances* and *interest allowances* describe only the process of dividing net income among partners. These terms should not be confused with any salary expense and interest expense appearing in the firm's records or with any cash withdrawals the partners make. For example, the partnership agreement may provide that partners may make withdrawals equal to their salary allowances. These withdrawals would be debited to each partner's drawing account, which is eventually closed to his or her capital account. The cash withdrawals in no way affect net income or the division of net income among partners; the division of net income is governed by the sharing agreement.

SALARY ALLOWANCE

Suppose Ames and Baker provide different levels of personal services and therefore specify a salary allowance in their sharing agreement, $6,000 for Ames and $4,000 for Baker. The remainder of net income is divided equally. The division of the $18,000 net income is as follows:

	Ames	Baker	Total
Earnings to be divided			$18,000
Salary allowances			
Ames	$ 6,000		
Baker		$4,000	10,000
Remainder			$ 8,000
Remainder ($8,000) divided equally	4,000	4,000	
Partners' shares	$10,000	$8,000	

The $18,000 balance in the Income Summary account would be distributed by crediting E. Ames, Capital for $10,000 and J. Baker, Capital for $8,000.

SALARY AND INTEREST ALLOWANCES

Assume, instead, that Ames and Baker wish to acknowledge the differences in their financial involvement as well as in their personal services. They have the following sharing agreement: salaries of $6,000 to Ames and $4,000 to Baker; 8% interest on *average* capital balances; and the remainder divided equally. We computed average investments for Ames and Baker earlier at $30,000 and $15,000, respectively. The $18,000 net income would therefore be divided as follows:

	Ames	Baker	Total
Earnings to be divided			$18,000
Salary allowances			
Ames	$ 6,000		
Baker		$4,000	10,000
			$ 8,000
Allowance for interest on average capital			
Ames ($30,000 × 0.08)	2,400		
Baker ($15,000 × 0.08)		1,200	3,600
Remainder			$ 4,400
Remainder ($4,400) divided equally	2,200	2,200	
Partners' shares	$10,600	$7,400	

The entry distributing the $18,000 net income in the Income Summary account would credit E. Ames, Capital for $10,600 and J. Baker, Capital for $7,400.

If Ames and Baker had withdrawn cash equal to their salary allowances, their drawing accounts at the end of the year would contain debit balances of $6,000 and $4,000, respectively. The entry to close the drawing accounts would be

E. Ames, Capital	6,000	
J. Baker, Capital	4,000	
E. Ames, Drawing		6,000
J. Baker, Drawing		4,000
To close the partners' drawing accounts.		

ALLOWANCES EXCEED EARNINGS

Unless a special provision is included in the sharing agreement, the same allocation procedures apply in the event of a loss or of earnings insufficient to cover allowances for salary and interest. For example, assume that net income for the year was only $8,000. After salary and interest allowances are allocated, a *sharing agreement loss* of $5,600 would be divided equally between the partners to fulfill their agreement. The following are the computations:

	Ames	Baker	Total
Earnings to be divided			$ 8,000
Salary allowances	$6,000	$4,000	
Interest allowances	2,400	1,200	
Total salary and interest	$8,400	$5,200	13,600
Remainder (sharing agreement loss)			($ 5,600)
Remainder divided equally	(2,800)	(2,800)	
Partners' shares	$5,600	$2,400	

The entry distributing the $8,000 net income in the Income Summary account would credit E. Ames, Capital with $5,600 and J. Baker, Capital with $2,400.

PARTNERSHIP FINANCIAL STATEMENTS

A few unique features of partnership financial statements arise because a partnership consists of co-owners. The partnership income statement may show, at the bottom, how the net income is divided among the partners. A capital account for each partner appears in the owners' equity section of the balance sheet. The statement of partners' capital portrays the changes in the capital balances of each partner, as shown in Exhibit 11-1.

EXHIBIT 11–1 **The Statement of Partners' Capital**

AMES AND BAKER
STATEMENT OF PARTNERS' CAPITAL
FOR THE YEAR ENDED DECEMBER 31, 1996

	Ames	Baker	Total
Capital Balances, January 1, 1996	$30,000	$10,000	$40,000
Add: Additional Contributions during 1996		10,000	10,000
Net Income for 1996	10,600	7,400	18,000
Totals	$40,600	$27,400	$68,000
Less: Withdrawals during 1996	6,000	4,000	10,000
Capital Balances, December 31, 1996	$34,600	$23,400	$58,000

ADMISSION OF A PARTNER

OBJECTIVE 5
PRESENT the methods for admitting a new partner.

New partners may be admitted to a partnership either by purchasing an interest from current partners or by investing in the firm. When a person buys an interest from one or more of the current partners, the assets of the firm are not affected. Payment is made personally to the member or members from whom the interest is obtained, resulting in merely a transfer among capital accounts. When an investment is made in the firm, however, total assets increase by the amount contributed.

Economic circumstances usually dictate a new partner's mode of entry. A firm with sufficient capital may seek the skills and services of a particular new partner. Or current partners may wish to liquidate part of their interests and scale down their individual investments. In these situations, the firm may sell an interest in the current partnership. On the other hand, if additional capital is needed, adding a partner who will contribute assets may be a proper solution.

For the benefit of the existing partners, the net assets of the current partnership should reflect their current fair values when a new partner is admitted. This may require a revaluation of certain assets. The resultant gain or loss would be apportioned to the current partners in their profit and loss sharing ratio. If the net assets do not reflect their fair values, the new partner may share in gains and losses that developed before admission to the firm. In the following examples of new partner admissions, we assume that the recorded book values of the current partnership's assets do not require restatement.

PURCHASE OF AN INTEREST

Suppose that Ames and Baker have capital balances of $30,000 and $10,000, respectively, and that Ames sells one-half of his interest to Kelsey Carter for $21,000. For Carter to become a partner, both Ames and Baker must consent to the sale. The entry to record Carter's admission would be

E. Ames, Capital	15,000	
K. Carter, Capital		15,000
To record admission of Carter.		

The actual cash amount paid to Ames ($21,000) is entirely a personal matter between the two individuals and is not relevant in recording Carter's admission. Whether an interest is purchased from one partner or several, a transfer of capital is made only for the amounts of the interests purchased without regard to the actual payment made. Suppose that Carter purchased a one-fourth interest in the firm by obtaining one-fourth of each partner's current share. One-fourth interest would amount to $10,000 (one-fourth of $40,000 total capital). The entry for Carter's admission would be

E. Ames, Capital	7,500	
J. Baker, Capital	2,500	
K. Carter, Capital		10,000
To record admission of Carter.		

ADMISSION BY INVESTMENT

When an incoming partner contributes assets to the firm, total capital of the partnership increases. If the current partners' capital balances are realistically stated, the new partner simply contributes assets equal to the desired proportionate interest in the total capital of the new firm. In our example, total capital is $40,000 ($30,000 for Ames and $10,000 for Baker). Carter wants to contribute enough cash to obtain one-third interest in the new firm. The current partners' capital of $40,000 represents two-thirds of the new firm's capital; therefore, Carter should contribute $20,000. The entry for admission would be

Cash	20,000	
K. Carter, Capital		20,000
To record admission of Carter.		

BONUS TO CURRENT PARTNERS

If a partnership interest is especially attractive because of a superior earnings record or the promise of exceptional future earnings, the current partners may require the new partner to pay an additional amount as a **bonus** for admission. Suppose that Ames and Baker required a $35,000 payment for a one-third interest in the new firm. The total capital of the new firm would then be $75,000, of which a one-third interest would be $25,000, as follows:

E. Ames, capital	$30,000
J. Baker, capital	10,000
Present capital	$40,000
Contribution of Carter	35,000
Capital of new firm	$75,000
One-third interest	$25,000

The $10,000 difference between Carter's payment of $35,000 and her interest of $25,000 is a bonus to the current partners, to be divided according to their profit and loss sharing ratio. If the agreement provides for equal sharing, the entry to admit Carter is

Cash	35,000	
E. Ames, Capital		5,000
J. Baker, Capital		5,000
K. Carter, Capital		25,000
To record admission of Carter.		

BONUS TO NEW PARTNER

A firm eager to add a partner who has ready cash, unique skills, management potential, or other desirable characteristics may award the new partner a larger interest than would be warranted by his or her contribution. Because the capital of the new partner will be greater than his or her asset contribution, the current partners must make up the difference (bonus to new partner) by reducing their capital balances. Assume that Carter receives a one-third interest by contributing only $14,000 to the new firm. The capital of the new firm increases to $54,000 ($40,000 + $14,000), of which a one-third interest is $18,000, as shown below:

E. Ames, capital	$30,000
J. Baker, capital	10,000
Present capital	$40,000
Contribution of Carter	14,000
Capital of new firm	$54,000
One-third interest	$18,000

The $4,000 difference between Carter's $14,000 contribution and her $18,000 interest is a bonus to her. Ames and Baker reduce their capital balances accordingly, with amounts based on the profit and loss sharing ratio. With equal sharing, the entry to admit Carter as a partner in the firm is

Cash	14,000	
E. Ames, Capital	2,000	
J. Baker, Capital	2,000	
K. Carter, Capital		18,000
To record admission of Carter.		

RETIREMENT OF A PARTNER

A retiring partner may sell his or her interest to an outsider, sell that interest to one or more of the remaining partners, or receive payment for the interest from partnership funds.

SALE OF PARTNERSHIP INTEREST

OBJECTIVE 6

DESCRIBE the alternatives when a partner retires.

The procedure for recording the sale of a retiring partner's interest to an outsider is similar to that illustrated earlier for the purchase of an interest. Suppose that retiring partner Baker, with the firm's approval, sells his $10,000 interest to Stan Dodge. Regardless of the amount of Dodge's actual payment to Baker, the entry to record Dodge's admission and Baker's departure is

J. Baker, Capital	10,000	
S. Dodge, Capital		10,000
To record Dodge's purchase of Baker's interest.		

If Baker sells his interest to remaining partners Ames and Carter, Baker's interest is transferred to their capital accounts, regardless of the actual amount of the payments. If Baker sells equal portions of his interest to the remaining partners, the entry is

J. Baker, Capital	10,000	
E. Ames, Capital		5,000
K. Carter, Capital		5,000
To record sale of Baker's interest to Ames and Carter.		

PAYMENT FROM PARTNERSHIP FUNDS: SETTLEMENT EXCEEDS CAPITAL BALANCE

A partner's retirement may be an occasion for reviewing partners' capital balances. Because of such factors as appreciation of assets or an exceptional partnership performance record, the capital balances may not provide a realistic basis for determining the value of partnership interests. In such situations, the partners may recognize any amount by which the current fair value of the retiring partner's partnership interest exceeds his or her capital balance by paying a bonus to the retiring partner.

If the retiring partner receives funds from the partnership for his or her interest, any difference between the amount of this interest and the sum paid affects the capital balances of the remaining partners. For example, assume that the capital balances of Ames, Baker, and Carter are $35,000, $15,000, and $25,000, respectively, when Baker retires and that the firm pays $20,000 for Baker's interest. Baker's $5,000 bonus is divided by the other partners according to their profit and loss sharing ratio (assumed here to be equal). The entry would be

E. Ames, Capital	2,500	
K. Carter, Capital	2,500	
J. Baker, Capital	15,000	
Cash		20,000

To record Baker's withdrawal from the partnership.

When the fair value of a retiring partner's interest exceeds his or her related capital balance, the remaining partners might revalue total partnership assets upward proportionately, distribute the increase to all partners in their profit and loss sharing ratio, and then pay the retiring partner an amount equal to his or her new capital balance. Such an approach, however, departs from the principle of historical cost. Although the increased value of the partnership interest is properly considered in settling with the retiring partner, revaluing total partnership assets above their historical cost is not acceptable.

PAYMENT FROM PARTNERSHIP FUNDS: CAPITAL BALANCE EXCEEDS SETTLEMENT

In certain circumstances, a retiring partner may accept a settlement less than his or her capital balance. Examples include a history of poor partnership earnings or recognition of operating disadvantages resulting from the partner's retirement. In such cases, the excess of the retiring partner's capital balance over the settlement constitutes a bonus to the remaining partners. Assume that Baker, who has a capital balance of $15,000, accepts $11,000 rather than $20,000 for his interest. The $4,000 bonus is allocated to the remaining partners in their profit and loss sharing ratio (assumed here to be equal). The entry to record Baker's withdrawal in this case is

J. Baker, Capital	15,000	
E. Ames, Capital		2,000
K. Carter, Capital		2,000
Cash		11,000

To record Baker's withdrawal from the partnership.

POINT OF INTEREST

HOW TO ACHIEVE A PRODUCTIVE PARTNERSHIP

Deborah Heller and Linda Cunningham of Heller, Hunt, and Cunningham of Brookline, Massachusetts, have studied partnerships and have concluded that there are three key dimensions to successful partnerships: (1) the professional competence of all partners, (2) the respect for personality differences among the partners, and (3) a clear, written agreement about the business relationship. This agreement should address (1) each partner's degree of operating autonomy, (2) the business goals of the partnership, (3) the method for determining partner compensation, (4) how different types of managerial decisions will be made and how the firm will be managed, (5) the method for allocating overhead expenses to the individual partners, (6) procedures for entrance and exit of partners, and (7) the methods to be used if the partnership is dissolved.

SOURCE: *Journal of Accountancy,* May 1992, pp. 113–118.

LIQUIDATION OF A PARTNERSHIP

Partners may decide to terminate a partnership for a variety of reasons. For example, the business objectives of the partnership may have been achieved, or competition may have forced the partners to close the business, or the partners may no longer be compatible. When

OBJECTIVE 7

EXPLAIN how partnerships are liquidated.

a partnership is discontinued, the assets are sold, the liabilities are paid, and the remaining cash is distributed to the partners. The conversion of the partnership assets into cash (by selling the assets) generates gains and losses. These gains and losses are carried to the partners' capital accounts (in the established profit and loss sharing ratio), and each partner eventually receives the balance remaining in his or her capital account.

Suppose that Ames, Baker, and Carter share profits and losses in the ratio of 40%, 40%, and 20%, respectively, and that before liquidation the partnership's balance sheet can be summarized as follows (assume that for the final operating period, the partnership books have been adjusted and closed and the profit or loss allocated to each partner):

Cash	$ 15,000	Liabilities	$ 40,000
Other Assets (net)	100,000	E. Ames, Capital	35,000
		J. Baker, Capital	15,000
		K. Carter, Capital	25,000
	$115,000		$115,000

CAPITAL BALANCES EXCEED LOSSES

If Other Assets in the balance sheet in our example are sold for $80,000, the firm sustains a $20,000 loss. Because the partners share the loss, their capital balances are ultimately reduced by the following amounts: Ames, $8,000; Baker, $8,000; and Carter, $4,000. The appropriate entries follow:

Cash	80,000	
Loss on Sale of Assets	20,000	
Other Assets (net)		100,000
To record loss on sale of other assets.		
E. Ames, Capital	8,000	
J. Baker, Capital	8,000	
K. Carter, Capital	4,000	
Loss on Sale of Assets		20,000
To distribute loss on sale of other assets.		

After these entries have been recorded, the firm's balance sheet accounts would be as follows:

Cash	$95,000	Liabilities	$40,000
		E. Ames, Capital	27,000
		J. Baker, Capital	7,000
		K. Carter, Capital	21,000
	$95,000		$95,000

Finally, the entries to pay the liabilities and distribute the remaining cash to the partners are

Liabilities	40,000	
Cash		40,000
To record payment of liabilities.		
E. Ames, Capital	27,000	
J. Baker, Capital	7,000	
K. Carter, Capital	21,000	
Cash		55,000
To record cash distribution to partners.		

Observe that during liquidation, *only gains and losses* are shared in the profit and loss sharing ratio—not the residual cash. Residual cash is distributed to partners *in the amounts of their capital balances* after all gains and losses have been shared.

LOSSES EXCEED PARTNER'S CAPITAL

When liquidation losses occur, a partner's share of losses may exceed his or her capital balance. That partner will be expected to contribute cash to the partnership to offset the capital account debit balance. For example, suppose that in our illustration, the $100,000 of Other Assets is sold for only $60,000. The resulting $40,000 loss on the sale of assets is recorded and then distributed in the 40%:40%:20% sharing ratio, reducing partners' capital accounts as follows: Ames, $16,000; Baker, $16,000; and Carter, $8,000. Entries to record and distribute the loss and to pay the liabilities follow:

Cash	60,000	
Loss on Sale of Assets	40,000	
Other Assets (net)		100,000
To record loss on sale of other assets.		
E. Ames, Capital	16,000	
J. Baker, Capital	16,000	
K. Carter, Capital	8,000	
Loss on Sale of Assets		40,000
To distribute loss on sale of other assets.		
Liabilities	40,000	
Cash		40,000
To record payment of liabilities.		

After recording and distributing the loss on the sale of other assets *and* payment of the liabilities, the following account balances remain:

Cash	$35,000	E. Ames, Capital	$19,000
		J. Baker, Capital	(1,000)
		(debit)	
		K. Carter, Capital	17,000
	$35,000		$35,000

Note that Baker's $16,000 share of the loss on the sale of the other assets absorbs his $15,000 capital balance and leaves a $1,000 capital deficit (debit balance) in his capital account.

    If Baker pays the firm $1,000 to make up his deficit, the resulting $36,000 cash balance is the amount distributed to Ames ($19,000) and Carter ($17,000). If Baker cannot make the contribution, the $1,000 is treated as a loss distributed to Ames and Carter in their profit and loss sharing ratio. Because the ratio of their respective shares is 40:20, Ames sustains 40/60, or two-thirds, of the $1,000 loss and Carter, 20/60, or one-third. Assuming that Baker cannot make the contribution, the entry to redistribute Baker's debit balance is

E. Ames, Capital	667	
K. Carter, Capital	333	
J. Baker, Capital		1,000
To record distribution of Baker's capital deficit to Ames and Carter.		

The $35,000 cash is then paid to Ames and Carter in the amounts of their final capital balances.

E. Ames, Capital	18,333	
K. Carter, Capital	16,667	
Cash		35,000
To record cash distribution to partners.		

STATEMENT OF PARTNERSHIP LIQUIDATION

Liquidation of a partnership can continue over an extended period. To provide interested parties with a comprehensive report of the initial assets and liabilities, the sale of non-cash assets, the payment of liabilities, and the final distribution of cash to the partners, the partnership may prepare a **statement of partnership liquidation.** Using data from our illustration, Exhibit 11-2 presents a statement of partnership liquidation for the Ames, Baker, and Carter partnership. We assume that other assets are sold for $60,000 and that Baker does not make the contribution to cover his $1,000 capital deficit.

EXHIBIT 11–2   Statement of Partnership Liquidation

AMES, BAKER, AND CARTER
STATEMENT OF PARTNERSHIP LIQUIDATION
FROM JANUARY 1 TO MARCH 31, 1996

	Cash	Other Assets	Liabilities	E. Ames, Capital (40%)	J. Baker, Capital (40%)	K. Carter, Capital (20%)	Gain (Loss)
Beginning Balances	$15,000	$100,000	$40,000	$35,000	$15,000	$25,000	
Sale of Other Assets	60,000	(100,000)					($40,000)
	$75,000	$ –0–	$40,000	$35,000	$15,000	$25,000	($40,000)
Allocation of Loss to Partners				(16,000)	(16,000)	(8,000)	40,000
	$75,000		$40,000	$19,000	$(1,000)	$17,000	$ –0–
Payment of Liabilities	(40,000)		(40,000)				
	$35,000		$ –0–	$19,000	$(1,000)	$17,000	
Allocation of Baker's Capital Deficit				(667)	1,000	(333)	
	$35,000			$18,333	$ –0–	$16,667	
Final Distribution of Cash	(35,000)			(18,333)		(16,667)	
	$ –0–			$ –0–		$ –0–	

Observe the following about the statement of partnership liquidation:

1. The statement is dated to reflect the period during which the liquidation took place.

2. The initial numbers on the statement reflect the partnership balance sheet at the beginning of the liquidation.

3. Each line that reflects a step in the liquidation (sale of other assets, allocation of loss to partners, payment of liabilities, allocation of partner's capital deficit, and final distribution of cash) matches related journal entries in the illustration.

4. The statement shows how each step affects the liquidation and is therefore an excellent vehicle for analysis.

FINANCIAL ANALYSIS   DEBT-TO-EQUITY RATIO

OBJECTIVE 8
DEFINE debt-to-equity ratio and **EXPLAIN** its use.

The relationship between a firm's liabilities and its owners' equity is one important indicator of the firm's financial strength. The debt-to-equity ratio measures this relationship. In practice, there are several variations in the computation of this ratio. In its most fundamental form, the **debt-to-equity ratio** is computed as follows:

$$\text{Debt-to-Equity Ratio} = \frac{\text{Total Liabilities}}{\text{Total Owners' Equity}}$$

The debt-to-equity ratio is useful in evaluating all types of entities: sole proprietorships, general partnerships, limited partnerships, limited liability partnerships, limited liability companies, and corporations. A debt-to-equity ratio of 1.0 means a firm has equal amounts of liabilities and owners' equity. A ratio below 1.0 indicates that liabilities are less than owners' equity, and a ratio greater than 1.0 means that liabilities exceed owners' equity.

The debt-to-equity ratio gives potential creditors an indication of the margin of protection available to them (creditors' claims to assets have priority over owners' claims). The lower the ratio, the better a creditor would feel about extending additional credit. As the ratio increases, creditors may charge higher interest rates to compensate for the decreased margin of protection. At some point, the ratio may become so large that it signals creditors that extending additional credit may be unwise.

The interpretation of a firm's debt-to-equity ratio is aided by looking at its trend in recent years (whether it is going up or down) and by comparing it to industry averages. Certain stable industries, such as utilities, tend to have higher debt-to-equity ratios than other industries whose operating results are more volatile. Following are examples of debt-to-equity ratios at a similar point in time for several companies in different industries.

Johnson & Johnson	1.20
Alliance Capital Management L.P.	1.62
Du Pont	2.28
General Mills	3.41
Chrysler Corporation	5.41

KEY POINTS FOR CHAPTER LEARNING OBJECTIVES

1 **DEFINE** the different types of partnerships, **LIST** the characteristics of a partnership, and **DEFINE** a limited liability company (pp. 380–382).
- The three primary types of partnerships are general partnership (all partners have unlimited liability), limited partnership (the general partners have unlimited liability and the limited partners have limited liability), and limited liability partnership (all partners have limited liability).
- All partnerships have a limited life, assets are co-owned by the partners, and the partnership is a nontaxable entity.
- A limited liability company is a hybrid form of organization. It is a nontaxable entity like a partnership, and its owners have limited liability like stockholders in a corporation.

2 **DESCRIBE** the advantages and disadvantages of a partnership and **INTRODUCE** accounting for a partnership (p. 382).
- A partnership is easy and inexpensive to form, partners have fewer constraints on their actions than corporate managers, and a partnership is a nontaxable entity.
- A partnership involves mutual agency, unlimited liability for general partners, and limited life.
- Each partner has a capital account and a drawing account. These accounts are used the same way they are used with a sole proprietorship. Loans to and from partners are placed in separate receivable and payable accounts, separate from receivables from and payables to outsiders.

3 **PRESENT** an overview of the formation of a partnership (pp. 382–383).
- A partnership's books are opened with an entry to record the net contribution of each partner.
- Assets invested in the partnership should be recorded at their current fair value.

4 **ILLUSTRATE** various methods for dividing profits and losses among partners (pp. 383–386).
- Partnership profits and losses are divided among partners according to their sharing agreement. If no sharing agreement exists, profits and losses are divided equally.
- Besides using ratios and percentages in allocating profits and losses, agreements may include salary allowances and interest allowances on capital investments. In certain cases, some partners may receive an increase in capital and others may suffer a decrease when profits and losses are allocated.

5 **PRESENT** the methods for admitting a new partner (pp. 386–388).
- When all or part of a partner's interest is purchased by another party, there is merely a transfer of capital from the selling partner to the other party. Total capital remains unchanged.
- When an incoming partner contributes assets to the firm, he or she is credited with the amount of the investment if there is no bonus arrangement. If the incoming partner is credited with less than the investment, the bonus is credited to current partners in their profit and loss sharing ratio. If the incoming partner is credited with more than the investment, current partners absorb the bonus in their profit and loss sharing ratio.

6 **DESCRIBE** the alternatives when a partner retires (pp. 388–389).
- When a retiring partner sells his or her interest to a new partner or current partners, there is merely a transfer of recorded capital, regardless of the amount paid.

- When payment is made from partnership funds, however, a bonus may be involved. If the settlement exceeds the retiring partner's capital balance, the bonus is absorbed by the remaining partners in their profit and loss sharing ratio. If the capital balance exceeds the settlement, the bonus is credited to the remaining partners in their profit and loss sharing ratio.

7 **EXPLAIN** how partnerships are liquidated (pp. 390–392).

- The following steps are followed in a typical partnership liquidation: (1) noncash assets are sold and any gain or loss on sale is distributed to the partners' capital accounts, (2) liabilities are paid, and (3) partners are paid the amounts in their capital accounts.
- If step 1 results in a deficit for any partner(s) who is unable to make up the deficit, such deficit should be distributed to partners having credit balances in their capital accounts according to their profit and loss sharing ratio before any cash distributions are made to partners.

8 **Financial Analysis**   **DEFINE** *debt-to-equity ratio* and **EXPLAIN** its use (pp. 392–393).

- The debt-to-equity ratio is computed as Total Liabilities / Total Owners' Equity. It indicates the extent that a firm is using debt for financing purposes.

SELF-TEST QUESTIONS FOR REVIEW

(Answers follow the Solution to Demonstration Problem.)

1. Partners A and B have beginning capital balances of $40,000 and $60,000, respectively. Profit and loss sharing is as follows: interest at 20% on beginning capital balances, salaries to A and B of $10,000 and $5,000, respectively, and the remainder shared in the ratio 2:3. How much of $30,000 net income would be distributed to A?
   a. $18,000   **b.** $16,000   **c.** $15,500   **d.** $14,000

2. Partners Hill and Draper have capital balances of $50,000 and $30,000, respectively, and share profits and losses equally. Brown purchases one-half of Hill's interest for $28,000. What entry should be made to record Brown's admission?

a.	Hill, Capital	28,000	
	Brown, Capital		28,000
b.	Cash	28,000	
	Brown, Capital		28,000
c.	Hill, Capital	25,000	
	Brown, Capital		25,000
d.	Hill, Capital	26,500	
	Draper, Capital	1,500	
	Brown, Capital		28,000

3. Bauer and Carr have capital balances of $80,000 and $70,000, respectively, and share profits and losses equally. Drumm invests an amount to give him exactly a one-third interest in the firm. No bonuses are to be awarded to any partners. How much should Drumm invest and how much should be credited to Drumm's capital account?
   a. Drumm should invest $75,000 and be credited with $75,000.
   b. Drumm should invest $50,000 and be credited with $50,000.
   c. Drumm should invest $50,000 and be credited with $75,000.
   d. Drumm should invest $75,000 and be credited with $50,000.

4. Partners Doyle, Katz, and Gibbs have capital balances of $50,000, $60,000, and $70,000, respectively, and share profits and losses in the ratio 3:2:1. Doyle retires and is paid $56,000 with partnership funds. The entry to record Doyle's retirement will include a
   a. Debit to Doyle, Capital for $56,000.
   b. Debit to Katz, Capital for $3,000.
   c. Credit to Katz, Capital for $4,000.
   d. Debit to Gibbs, Capital for $2,000.

5. Partners Hughes, Judd, and Sanchez share profits and losses in the ratio 3:5:2. Just before liquidation, the partnership has the following balance sheet:

Cash	$ 20,000	Hughes, Capital	$ 60,000
Other Assets	140,000	Judd, Capital	20,000
		Sanchez, Capital	80,000
	$160,000		$160,000

   Other Assets are sold for $80,000. Assuming that none of the partners can make up any resulting capital deficit, the final cash distribution to partner Sanchez is
   a. $68,000.   **b.** $64,000.   **c.** $20,000.   **d.** $72,000.

DEMONSTRATION PROBLEM FOR REVIEW

J. Porter and M. Kantor have been partners for several years, operating Fast Moves, a moving business. The business has had its ups and downs but overall has been quite successful. In recognition of Porter's administrative responsibilities, the profit and loss sharing agreement allows her a salary of $5,000, with the remainder shared equally.

On January 1, 1996, Porter and Kantor had capital balances of $14,000 and $9,000, respectively. During 1996, Porter withdrew $4,000 cash from the partnership, and 1996 net income was $11,000. On December 31, 1996, the partnership had the following assets and liabilities: Cash, $4,000; Other Assets, $29,000; and Accounts Payable, $3,000.

Porter and Kantor liquidate the partnership on January 1, 1997. On that date, other assets are sold for $35,000, creditors are paid, and the partners receive the remaining cash.

REQUIRED

a. Prepare a schedule showing how the $11,000 net income for 1996 should be divided between Porter and Kantor.

b. Prepare a statement of partners' capital for 1996.

c. Prepare a balance sheet at December 31, 1996.

d. Prepare the January 1, 1997, journal entries to record the sale of other assets and recognition of any related gain or loss, the distribution of any gain or loss to partners' capital accounts, the payment of liabilities, and the distribution of cash to the partners.

SOLUTION TO DEMONSTRATION PROBLEM

a.

	Porter	Kantor	Total
Earnings to be divided			$11,000
Salary allowance	$5,000		5,000
Remainder			$ 6,000
Remainder divided equally	3,000	$3,000	
Partners' shares	$8,000	$3,000	

b.

FAST MOVES
STATEMENT OF PARTNERS' CAPITAL
FOR THE YEAR 1996

	Porter	Kantor	Total
Capital Balances, January 1, 1996	$14,000	$9,000	$23,000
Add: Net Income for 1996	8,000	3,000	11,000
Totals	$22,000	$12,000	$34,000
Less: Withdrawals	4,000		4,000
Capital Balances, December 31, 1996	$18,000	$12,000	$30,000

c.

FAST MOVES
BALANCE SHEET
DECEMBER 31, 1996

Assets		Liabilities	
Cash	$ 4,000	Accounts Payable	$ 3,000
Other Assets	29,000		
		Owners' Equity	
		J. Porter, Capital $18,000	
		M. Kantor, Capital 12,000	30,000
		Total Liabilities and	
Total Assets	$33,000	Owners' Equity	$33,000

d. **1997**

Jan. 1	Cash	35,000	
	Other Assets		29,000
	Gain on Sale of Assets		6,000
	To record sale of other assets.		

Jan. 1	Gain on Sale of Assets	6,000	
	J. Porter, Capital		3,000
	M. Kantor, Capital		3,000
	To distribute gain on sale of other assets.		
1	Accounts Payable	3,000	
	Cash		3,000
	To record payment of liabilities.		
1	J. Porter, Capital	21,000	
	M. Kantor, Capital	15,000	
	Cash		36,000
	To record cash distribution to partners.		

ANSWERS TO SELF-TEST QUESTIONS

1. b, pp. 384–386   **2.** c, p. 387   **3.** a, p. 387   **4.** d, pp. 388–389   **5.** b, pp. 390–391

GLOSSARY OF KEY TERMS USED IN THIS CHAPTER

articles of copartnership   The formal written agreement among partners setting forth important aspects of the partnership, such as name, nature, duration, and location of the business, capital contributions, duties, and profit and loss ratios (p. 380).

bonus   In the context of partnership admissions, a bonus is the difference between the amount invested by a new partner and the amount credited to the new partner's capital account (p. 387).

debt-to-equity ratio   A ratio that measures the relationship between a firm's liabilities and its owners' equity; the ratio is computed by dividing total liabilities by total owners' equity (p. 392).

general partner   Any partner in a general partnership; also any partner in a limited partnership who has unlimited liability (p. 381).

general partnership   A partnership in which each partner is individually liable for the firm's obligations regardless of the amount of personal investment (p. 380).

interest allowance   A provision in a partnership profit and loss sharing agreement that allows credit for the relative investments of partners (p. 384).

limited liability company   A relatively new form of entity in which each owner's liability for debts of the firm is limited to that owner's investment in the firm; a nontaxable entity like a partnership and accounted for like a partnership (p. 381).

limited liability partnership   A relatively new type of partnership that has no general partners, only limited partners (p. 381).

limited partner   A partner whose liability for debts of the partnership is limited to the amount of his or her investment in the partnership (p. 381).

limited partnership   A partnership in which one class of partner limits its liability for losses to the amount of the limited partners' investment; there must be at least one general partner in a limited partnership (p.381).

partnership   A voluntary association of two or more persons for the purpose of conducting a business for profit (p. 380).

salary allowance   A provision in a partnership profit and loss sharing agreement that allows credit for the partners' personal services to the partnership (p. 384).

statement of partnership liquidation   A comprehensive report on the liquidation of a partnership that includes the initial assets and liabilities, the sale of noncash assets, the payment of liabilities, and the final distribution of cash to the partners (p. 391).

unlimited liability   The characteristic of a partnership in which each partner is individually liable for all of the partnership's debt, regardless of the amount of the partner's investment in the partnership (p. 380).

QUESTIONS

11-1 What is meant by *mutual agency*? By *unlimited liability*?

11-2 A corporation is said to have continuity of existence, whereas a partnership is characterized by a limited life. What are several events that may cause the dissolution of a partnership?

11-3 Porter understands that a partnership is a nontaxable entity and believes that if she does not withdraw any assets from the firm this year, she will not have any taxable income from her partnership activities. Is she correct? Why or why not?

11-4 Carlin invests in his partnership a machine that originally cost him $25,000. At the time of the investment, his personal records carry it at a book value of $13,000. Its current market value is $19,000. At what amount should the partnership record the machine? Why?

11-5 What factors should persons going into partnership consider in deciding how to share profits and losses?

11-6 If a partnership agreement is silent on the sharing of profits and losses, how will they be divided? What if the agreement indicates the method of sharing profits but states nothing about the sharing of losses?

11-7 What are salary allowances? What is the difference between a salary allowance and a salary expense?

11-8 In what ways do the financial statements of a partnership differ from those of a sole proprietorship? What is the purpose of a statement of partners' capital?

11-9 How is the admission of a partner by the purchase of an interest different from an investment in the firm?

11-10 What circumstances might cause (a) current partners to receive a bonus when admitting a new partner and (b) an incoming partner to receive a bonus?

11-11 Boyd and Houk, who share profits and losses equally, admit Lowe as a new partner. Lowe contributes $100,000 for a one-fourth interest in the new firm. The entry to admit Lowe shows a $20,000 bonus each to Boyd and Houk. What is the apparent total capital of the new partnership?

11-12 When a partner retires, are the assets and capital of the partnership reduced? Explain.

11-13 When a partnership liquidates, how do accountants handle the gains and losses generated by selling the assets?

11-14 In a partnership liquidation, the residual cash is distributed to partners in the amounts of their capital balances just prior to the distribution. Why is this the proper distribution procedure?

11-15 Assume that during liquidation, a debit balance arises in a partner's capital account but the partner is unable to contribute any more assets to the partnership. How does the partnership dispose of the debit balance in the capital account?

11-16 How is the *debt-to-equity ratio* calculated? Explain how it is used.

PRINCIPLES DISCUSSION QUESTION

11-17 The operations of the Boston Celtics professional basketball team are organized as a limited partnership. The notes to the financial statements of a recent annual report of the Boston Celtics Limited Partnership contain the following statements regarding revenue and expense recognition:

> Ticket sales and television and radio broadcasting fees generally are recorded as revenues at the time the game to which such proceeds relate is played. Team expenses, principally player and coaches' salaries, related fringe benefits and insurance, and game and playoff expenses, principally National Basketball Association attendance assessments, arena rentals and travel, are recorded as expense on the same basis. Accordingly, advance ticket sales and advance payments on television and radio broadcasting contracts and payments for team and game expenses not earned or incurred are recorded as deferred game revenues and deferred game expenses, respectively, and amortized ratably as regular season games are played.

What are the basic principles of accounting that guide the Boston Celtics Limited Partnership in the handling of its revenue and expense recognition? Briefly explain how these principles impact the Celtics' accounting practices.

EXERCISES

PARTNERSHIP FORMATION
— OBJ. 3 —

11-18 R. Diaz and S. Kaman form a partnership on May 1, 1996. Diaz contributes $120,000 cash, and Kaman contributes the following items from a separate business:

Marketable securities—cost of $14,000, current fair value of $21,000

Equipment—cost of $60,000, accumulated depreciation of $24,000, current fair value of $32,000

Land—cost of $45,000, current fair value of $80,000

Note payable (secured by equipment)—$15,000 assumed by partnership

Prepare the opening general journal entries of the partnership to record the investments of Diaz and Kaman.

PROFIT AND LOSS SHARING
— OBJ. 4 —

11-19 T. Roberts and J. Witmer are partners whose profit and loss sharing agreement gives salary allowances of $50,000 to Roberts and $30,000 to Witmer, with the remainder divided equally.
  a. Net income for 1996 is $116,000. Prepare the general journal entry to distribute the income to Roberts and Witmer at December 31, 1996.
  b. Assume a $40,000 net loss for 1996. Prepare the general journal entry to distribute the loss to Roberts and Witmer at December 31, 1996.

STATEMENT OF PARTNERS'
CAPITAL
— OBJ. 5 —

11-20 Use the following data to prepare a 1996 statement of partners' capital for W. Stevens and S. Jessen, who share profits and losses in the ratio of 60% to Stevens and 40% to Jessen.

W. Stevens, Capital, January 1, 1996	$94,000
S. Jessen, Capital, January 1, 1996	50,000
W. Stevens, Drawing	20,000
S. Jessen, Drawing	26,000
Additional investments by Stevens	7,000
Net income for 1996	50,000

ADMISSION OF A PARTNER
— OBJ. 5 —

11-21 C. Peters and M. Schmidt are partners with capital balances of $180,000 and $120,000, respectively. They share profits and losses in the ratio of 60% to Peters and 40% to Schmidt. J. Walsh receives a one-fourth interest in the firm by investing $140,000 cash on May 4, 1996.
  a. Prepare the general journal entry to record Walsh's admission, assuming that a bonus is allowed Peters and Schmidt.
  b. Briefly explain circumstances that might cause existing partners to receive a bonus when admitting a new partner.

RETIREMENT OF A PARTNER
— OBJ. 6 —

11-22 D. Charles, R. Gibson, and M. Kramer are partners sharing profits and losses in the ratio 5:3:2, respectively. Their capital balances are Charles, $80,000; Gibson, $125,000; and Kramer, $125,000. Charles retires from the firm on June 30, 1996, and is paid $100,000 from partnership funds.
  a. Prepare the general journal entry to record Charles' retirement, assuming that Gibson and Kramer absorb the bonus paid Charles.
  b. Briefly explain circumstances that might cause a retiring partner to receive a bonus.

PARTNERSHIP LIQUIDATION
— OBJ. 7 —

11-23 In the liquidation of the ABC Partnership, noncash assets were sold for $200,000, and the related gain or loss on the sale resulted in debits to the capital accounts of partners A, B, and C for $32,000, $24,000, and $24,000, respectively.
  a. Were the noncash assets sold at a gain or a loss? How do you know? How much was the gain or the loss?
  b. What is the partners' apparent profit and loss sharing ratio?
  c. What was the apparent book value of the noncash assets sold?

PARTNERSHIP LIQUIDATION
— OBJ. 7 —

11-24 Just before liquidation, the balance sheet of the partnership of A. Rosen and W. Travis, who share profits and losses equally, appeared as follows:

Cash	$ 72,000	Liabilities	$ 20,000
Other Assets	128,000	A. Rosen, Capital	120,000
		W. Travis, Capital	60,000
	$200,000		$200,000

  a. If other assets are sold for $120,000, what amounts will Rosen and Travis receive as the final cash distribution?
  b. If other assets are sold for $140,000, what amounts will Rosen and Travis receive as the final cash distribution?
  c. If Rosen receives $102,000 and Travis receives $42,000 as the final (and only) cash distribution, what amount was received from the sale of the other assets?

PROBLEMS

PROFIT AND LOSS SHARING
— OBJ. 4 —

11-25 H. Gordon and L. Madden form a partnership on January 1, 1996, and invest $140,000 and $100,000, respectively. During 1996, the partnership earned a $60,000 net income.
  REQUIRED
  a. Prepare the general journal entry to close the Income Summary account and distribute the $60,000 net income under each of the following independent assumptions:
    1. The partnership agreement is silent on the sharing of profits and losses.
    2. Profits and losses are shared in the ratio of beginning capital balances.

3. Profits and losses are shared by allowing 10% interest on beginning capital balances, with the remainder divided equally.

b. Assume that the partnership had a $36,000 loss during 1996. Prepare the entry to close the Income Summary account and distribute the $36,000 loss under each of the three assumptions in part a.

**PROFIT AND LOSS SHARING
— OBJ. 4 —**

11-26 The capital accounts and the Income Summary account as of December 31, 1996, of the Dole, Fine, and Thomas partnership follow. None of the partners withdrew capital during 1996.

G. DOLE, CAPITAL				J. FINE, CAPITAL		
	1996				1996	
	Jan. 1	48,000			Jan. 1	64,000
	July 1	64,000			Oct. 1	64,000

M. THOMAS, CAPITAL				INCOME SUMMARY		
	1996				1996	
	Jan. 1	160,000			Dec. 31	180,000

REQUIRED

a. Prepare the entry to distribute the $180,000 net income if Dole, Fine, and Thomas share profits and losses:

1. Equally.

2. In the ratio 5:3:2, respectively.

3. In the ratio of *average* capital balances for the year.

4. Under an agreement allowing $40,000 salary to Thomas, 10% interest on *beginning* capital balances, with the remainder shared equally.

b. Assume that net income was $48,000 rather than $180,000. Prepare the entry to distribute the $48,000 earnings if the agreement allows $40,000 salary to Thomas, 10% interest on beginning capital balances, with the remainder shared equally.

**ADMISSION OF A PARTNER
— OBJ. 5 —**

11-27 J. Brady and T. Dalton are partners with capital balances of $160,000 and $128,000, respectively. Profits and losses are shared equally.

REQUIRED

Prepare the entries to record the admission of a new partner, S. Felton, under each of the following separate circumstances:

a. Felton purchases one-half of Dalton's interest, paying Dalton $72,000 personally.

b. Felton invests sufficient funds to receive exactly one-fourth interest in the new partnership. (No bonuses are recorded.)

c. Felton invests $92,000 for a one-fifth interest, with any bonus distributed to the capital accounts of Brady and Dalton.

d. Felton invests $64,000 for a one-fourth interest, with any bonus credited to Felton's capital account.

e. In requirements (c) and (d), what do the terms of admission imply regarding the relative negotiating positions of the new partner and the old partners?

**RETIREMENT OF A PARTNER
— OBJ. 6 —**

11-28 C. Bower, F. Green, and N. Klein are partners with capital balances of $70,000, $40,000, and $50,000, respectively. Profits and losses are shared equally. Klein retires from the firm.

REQUIRED

Record the entries for Klein's retirement in each of the following separate circumstances:

a. Klein's interest is sold to R. Winston, a new partner, for $58,000.

b. Bower and Green each acquire one-half of Klein's interest for $28,000 apiece.

c. Klein receives $58,000 of partnership funds for his interest. The remaining partners absorb the bonus paid Klein.

d. The partners agree that Klein's abrupt retirement presents operating disadvantages and therefore Klein should receive only $46,000 for his interest. Payment is from partnership funds, with any bonuses going to Bower and Green.

**SHARING OF LOSS, ADMISSION
AND WITHDRAWAL OF PARTNERS
— OBJ. 4, 5, 6 —**

11-29 W. Fletcher and S. Marshall formed a partnership on January 1, 1994, with capital investments of $62,000 and $126,000, respectively. The profit and loss sharing agreement allowed Fletcher a salary of $16,000, with the remainder divided equally. During the year, Marshall made withdrawals of $12,000; no other investments or withdrawals were made in 1994. The partnership incurred a net loss of $20,000 in 1994.

On January 1, 1995, J. Kiley was admitted to the partnership. Kiley purchased one-third of Marshall's interest, paying $28,000 directly to Marshall. Fletcher, Marshall, and Kiley agreed to share profits and losses in the ratio 3:5:2, respectively. No provision was made for salaries. The partnership earned a net income of $120,000 in 1995.

On January 1, 1996, Marshall withdrew from the partnership. Marshall received $135,000 of partnership funds for her interest. Fletcher and Kiley absorbed the bonus paid Marshall.

REQUIRED

a. Prepare the December 31, 1994, entry to close the Income Summary account and distribute the $20,000 loss for 1994.

b. Compute the capital balances of Fletcher and Marshall at December 31, 1994.

c. Prepare the entry to record the admission of Kiley on January 1, 1995.

d. Prepare the December 31, 1995, entry to close the Income Summary account and distribute the $120,000 income for 1995.

e. Compute the December 31, 1995, capital balances of Fletcher, Marshall, and Kiley.

f. Prepare the January 1, 1996, entry to record Marshall's withdrawal.

STATEMENT OF PARTNERS' CAPITAL
— OBJ. 4 —

11-30 Litton and Meyer formed a partnership in 1994, agreeing to share profits and losses equally. On December 31, 1994, their capital balances were Litton, $160,000; Meyer, $96,000.

On January 1, 1995, Nelson was admitted to a one-fourth interest in the firm by investing $96,000 cash. Nelson's admission was recorded by according bonuses to Litton and Meyer. The profit and loss sharing agreement of the new partnership allowed salaries of $36,000 to Litton and $44,000 to Nelson, with the remainder divided in the ratio of 3:3:2 among Litton, Meyer, and Nelson, respectively.

Net income for 1995 was $168,000. Litton and Meyer withdrew cash during the year equal to their salary allowances. Immediately after the net income had been closed to the partners' capital accounts, Nelson retired from the firm. Nelson received $130,000 of partnership funds for his interest, and the remaining partners absorbed the bonus paid to him.

REQUIRED

Prepare a statement of partners' capital for 1995.

PARTNERSHIP LIQUIDATION
— OBJ. 7 —

11-31 R. Frain, S. Hawk, and T. Lund are partners who share profits and losses in the ratio of 5:3:2, respectively. Just before the partnership's liquidation, its balance sheet accounts appear as follows:

Cash	$100,000	Accounts Payable	$120,000
Other Assets	300,000	R. Frain, Capital	60,000
		S. Hawk, Capital	120,000
		T. Lund, Capital	100,000
	$400,000		$400,000

REQUIRED

a. Assuming that other assets are sold for $250,000, prepare the entries to record the sale of the other assets and distribute the related loss, pay liabilities, and distribute the remaining cash to the partners on February 15, 1996.

b. Assuming that other assets are sold for $160,000, prepare the entries to record the sale of the other assets and distribute the related loss, pay liabilities, apportion any partner's deficit among the other partners (assuming any such deficit is not made up by the partner involved), and distribute the remaining cash to the appropriate partners on February 15, 1996.

c. Assuming that liquidation procedures occurred between January 1 and February 15, 1996, prepare a statement of partnership liquidation using the data in requirement (b).

SHARING OF LOSS AND PARTNERSHIP LIQUIDATION
— OBJ. 4, 7 —

11-32 G. Abner, H. Boyd, J. Case, and K. Dunn are partners whose profit and loss sharing agreement provides for annual interest at 20% on partners' beginning capital balances, annual salaries of $14,000 and $18,000 to Abner and Case, respectively, with the remainder divided in the ratio of 4:3:2:1, respectively.

Due to a history of modest earnings, they liquidate their partnership at December 31, 1995. Just prior to completing the closing of the partnership books for 1995, the trial balance is summarized as follows:

Debits		**Credits**	
Cash	$148,000	Liabilities	$120,000
Other Assets (net)	220,000	G. Abner, Capital	60,000
G. Abner, Drawing	14,000	H. Boyd, Capital	140,000
J. Case, Drawing	18,000	J. Case, Capital	40,000
Income Summary (loss)	60,000	K. Dunn, Capital	100,000
	$460,000		$460,000

REQUIRED

a. Assuming that none of the partners made any capital contributions during the year, prepare journal entries to complete the closing of the books at December 31, 1995. Then calculate the balances of the capital accounts as of December 31, 1995.

b. Starting with the partnership post-closing trial balance at December 31, 1995, prepare a statement of partnership liquidation, assuming that

1. Other assets were sold for $140,000 cash.
2. All liabilities were paid in cash.
3. Any partner experiencing a capital deficit would be unable to make up the deficit to the partnership.
4. The final distribution of cash to partners was made on February 20, 1996.

ALTERNATE EXERCISES

PARTNERSHIP FORMATION
— OBJ. 3 —

11-18A J. Lopez and W. Garcia form a partnership on July 1, 1996. Lopez contributes $80,000 cash and Garcia contributes the following items from a separate business:

Marketable securities—cost of $15,000, current fair value of $12,000

Equipment—cost of $50,000, accumulated depreciation of $20,000, current fair value of $25,000

Land—cost of $50,000, current fair value of $60,000

Note payable (secured by equipment)—$11,000 assumed by partnership

Prepare the opening general journal entries of the partnership to record the investments of Lopez and Garcia.

PROFIT AND LOSS SHARING
— OBJ. 4 —

11-19A T. Ecker and M. Ward are partners whose profit and loss sharing agreement gives salary allowances of $60,000 to Ecker and $36,000 to Ward, with the remainder divided equally.

a. Net income for 1996 is $144,000. Prepare the general journal entry to distribute the income to Ecker and Ward on December 31, 1996.

b. Assume a $24,000 net loss for 1996. Prepare the general journal entry to distribute the loss to Ecker and Ward on December 31, 1996.

STATEMENT OF PARTNERS'
CAPITAL
— OBJ. 5 —

11-20A Use the following data to prepare a 1996 statement of partners' capital for H. Gomez and C. Bard, who share profits and losses in the ratio of 60% to Gomez and 40% to Bard.

H. Gomez, Capital, January 1, 1996	$90,000
C. Bard, Capital, January 1, 1996	56,000
H. Gomez, Drawing	21,000
C. Bard, Drawing	18,000
Additional investments by Gomez	10,000
Net income for 1996	40,000

ADMISSION OF A PARTNER
— OBJ. 5 —

11-21A B. Falk and T. Hardy are partners with capital balances of $100,000 and $70,000, respectively. They share profits and losses in the ratio of 60% to Falk and 40% to Hardy. J. Jerold receives a one-fourth interest in the firm by investing $90,000 cash on June 15, 1996.

a. Prepare the general journal entry to record Jerold's admission, assuming that a bonus is allowed Falk and Hardy.

b. Briefly explain circumstances that might cause existing partners to receive a bonus when admitting a new partner.

RETIREMENT OF A PARTNER
— OBJ. 6 —

11-22A F. Lane, D. Potter, and L. Neuman are partners sharing profits and losses in the ratio 5:3:2, respectively. Their capital balances are Lane, $120,000; Potter, $180,000; and Neuman, $180,000. Lane retires from the firm on June 30, 1996, and is paid $150,000 from partnership funds.

a. Prepare the general journal entry to record Lane's retirement, assuming that Potter and Neuman absorb the bonus paid Lane.

b. Briefly explain circumstances that might cause a retiring partner to receive a bonus.

PARTNERSHIP LIQUIDATION
— OBJ. 7 —

11-23A In the liquidation of the HJK Partnership, noncash assets were sold for $110,000, and the related gain or loss on the sale resulted in credits to the capital accounts of partners H, J, and K for $15,000, $9,000, and $6,000, respectively.

a. Were the noncash assets sold at a gain or a loss? How do you know? How much was the gain or the loss?

b. What is the partners' apparent profit and loss sharing ratio?

c. What was the apparent book value of the noncash assets sold?

PARTNERSHIP LIQUIDATION
— OBJ. 7 —

11-24A Just before liquidation, the balance sheet of the partnership of T. Harris and C. Moyer, who share profits and losses equally, appeared as follows:

Cash	$ 50,000		Liabilities	$ 11,000
Other Assets	96,000		T. Harris, Capital	90,000
			C. Moyer, Capital	45,000
	$146,000			$146,000

  a. If other assets are sold for $90,000, what amounts will Harris and Moyer receive as the final cash distribution?
  b. If other assets are sold for $105,000, what amounts will Harris and Moyer receive as the final cash distribution?
  c. If Harris receives $76,500 and Moyer receives $31,500 as the final (and only) cash distribution, what amount was received from the sale of the other assets?

ALTERNATE PROBLEMS

PROFIT AND LOSS SHARING
— OBJ. 4 —

11-25A S. Ritter and N. Varney form a partnership on February 1, 1996, and invest $120,000 and $60,000, respectively. During 1996, the partnership earned $48,000 net income.
REQUIRED
  a. Prepare the entry to close the Income Summary account and distribute the $48,000 net income under each of the following independent assumptions:
  1. The partnership agreement is silent on the sharing of profits and losses.
  2. Profits and losses are shared in the ratio of beginning capital balances.
  3. Profits and losses are shared by allowing 10% interest on beginning capital balances with the remainder divided equally.
  b. Assume the partnership had a $24,000 loss in 1996. Prepare the entry to close the Income Summary account and distribute the $24,000 loss under each of the three assumptions in part a.

PROFIT AND LOSS SHARING
— OBJ. 4 —

11-26A The capital accounts and the Income Summary account as of December 31, 1996, of the Baker, Kane, and Quinn partnership follow. None of the partners withdrew capital during 1996.

R. BAKER, CAPITAL			**B. KANE, CAPITAL**	
	1996			1996
	Jan. 1 120,000			Jan. 1 60,000
	Sept. 1 120,000			July 1 40,000

J. QUINN, CAPITAL			**INCOME SUMMARY**	
	1996			1996
	Jan. 1 48,000			Dec. 31 108,000

REQUIRED
  a. Prepare the entry to distribute the $108,000 net income if Baker, Kane, and Quinn share profits and losses:
  1. Equally.
  2. In the ratio 3:2:1, respectively.
  3. In the ratio of *average* capital balances for the year.
  4. Under an agreement allowing $36,000 salary to Baker, 10% interest on *beginning* capital balances, with the remainder shared equally.
  b. Assume that net income was $48,000 rather than $108,000. Prepare the entry to distribute the $48,000 earnings if the agreement allows $36,000 salary to Baker, 10% interest on beginning capital balances, with the remainder shared equally.

ADMISSION OF A PARTNER
— OBJ. 5 —

11-27A A. Curtis and P. James are partners with capital balances of $120,000 and $72,000, respectively. Profits and losses are shared equally.
REQUIRED
Prepare the entries to record the admission of a new partner, D. Pierce, under each of the following separate circumstances:
  a. Pierce purchases one-half of James' interest, paying James $42,000 personally.
  b. Pierce invests sufficient funds to receive exactly one-fourth interest in the new partnership. (No bonuses are recorded.)
  c. Pierce invests $68,000 for a one-fifth interest, with any bonus distributed to the capital accounts of Curtis and James.

d. Pierce invests $56,000 for a one-fourth interest, with any bonus credited to Pierce's capital account.

e. In requirements (c) and (d), what do the terms of admission imply regarding the relative negotiating positions of the new partner and the old partners?

RETIREMENT OF A PARTNER
— OBJ. 6 —

11-28A G. Anderson, K. Carroll, and Q. Warren are partners with capital balances of $120,000, $100,000, and $80,000, respectively. Profits and losses are shared equally. Warren retires from the firm.

REQUIRED

Record the entries for Warren's retirement in each of the following separate circumstances:

a. Warren's interest is sold to V. Hines, a new partner, for $92,000.

b. One-half of Warren's interest is sold to each of the remaining partners for $45,000 apiece.

c. Warren receives $90,000 of partnership funds for her interest. The remaining partners absorb the bonus paid to Warren.

d. The partners agree that Warren's abrupt retirement presents operating disadvantages and therefore Warren should receive only $78,000 for her interest. Payment is from partnership funds.

SHARING OF LOSS, ADMISSION
AND WITHDRAWAL OF PARTNERS
— OBJ. 4, 5, 6 —

11-29A H. Allen and R. Kohl formed a partnership on January 1, 1994, with capital investments of $78,000 and $130,000, respectively. The profit and loss sharing agreement allowed Allen a salary of $24,000 with the remainder divided equally. During the year, Kohl made withdrawals of $18,000; no other investments or withdrawals were made in 1994. The partnership incurred a net loss of $20,000 in 1994.

On January 1, 1995, M. Richards was admitted to the partnership. Richards purchased one-third of Kohl's interest, paying $36,000 directly to Kohl. Allen, Kohl, and Richards agreed to share profits and losses in the ratio 5:3:2, respectively. No provision was made for salaries. The partnership earned a net income of $100,000 in 1995.

On January 1, 1996, Kohl withdrew from the partnership. Kohl received $104,000 of partnership funds for his interest. Allen and Richards absorbed the bonus paid Kohl.

REQUIRED

a. Prepare the December 31, 1994, entry to close the Income Summary account and distribute the $20,000 loss for 1994.

b. Compute the capital balances of Allen and Kohl at December 31, 1994.

c. Prepare the entry to record the admission of Richards on January 1, 1995.

d. Prepare the December 31, 1995, entry to close the Income Summary account and distribute the $100,000 income for 1995.

e. Compute the December 31, 1995, capital balances of Allen, Kohl, and Richards.

f. Prepare the January 1, 1996, entry to record Kohl's withdrawal.

STATEMENT OF PARTNERS'
CAPITAL
— OBJ. 4 —

11-30A Arnold and Brown formed a partnership in 1994, agreeing to share profits and losses equally. On December 31, 1994, their capital balances were Arnold, $140,000; Brown, $108,000.

On January 1, 1995, Carter was admitted to a one-fourth interest in the firm by investing $112,000 cash. Carter's admission was recorded by according bonuses to Arnold and Brown. The profit and loss sharing agreement of the new partnership allowed salaries of $30,000 to Arnold and $36,000 to Carter, with the remainder divided in the ratio 4:3:3 among Arnold, Brown, and Carter, respectively.

Net income for 1995 was $144,000. Arnold and Carter withdrew cash during the year equal to their salary allowances. Immediately after net income had been closed to the partners' capital accounts, Carter retired from the firm. Carter received $118,300 for her interest, and the remaining partners absorbed the bonus paid Carter.

REQUIRED

Prepare a statement of partners' capital for 1995.

PARTNERSHIP LIQUIDATION
— OBJ. 7 —

11-31A H. Cody, T. Lyon, and J. Parker are partners who share profits and losses in the ratio of 5:3:2, respectively. Just before the partnership's liquidation, its balance sheet appears as follows:

Cash	$ 60,000	Accounts Payable	$ 40,000
Other Assets (net)	160,000	H. Cody, Capital	32,000
		T. Lyon, Capital	60,000
		J. Parker, Capital	88,000
	$220,000		$220,000

REQUIRED

a. Assuming that other assets are sold for $140,000, prepare the entries to record the sale of the other assets and distribute the related loss, pay liabilities, and distribute the remaining cash to the partners on February 8, 1996.

b. Assuming that other assets are sold for $88,000, prepare the entries to record the sale of the other assets and distribute the related loss, pay liabilities, apportion any partner's deficit among the other partners (assuming any such deficit is not made up by the partner involved), and distribute the remaining cash to the appropriate partners on February 8, 1996.

c. Assuming that liquidation procedures occurred between January 1 and February 8, 1996, prepare a statement of partnership liquidation using the data in requirement (b).

SHARING OF LOSS AND PARTNERSHIP LIQUIDATION —OBJ. 4, 7 —

11-32A C. Beard, F. Dale, K. Gregg, and N. Ritt are partners whose profit and loss sharing agreement provides for annual interest at 20% on partners' beginning capital balances, annual salaries of $20,000 and $40,000 to Beard and Dale, respectively, with the remainder divided in the ratio of 5:3:1:1, respectively.

Due to a history of modest earnings, they liquidate their partnership on December 31, 1995. Just prior to completing the closing of the partnership books for 1995, the trial balance is summarized as follows:

Cash	$108,000	Liabilities	$ 68,000
Other Assets (net)	320,000	C. Beard, Capital	100,000
Beard, Drawing	40,000	F. Dale, Capital	80,000
Dale, Drawing	60,000	K. Gregg, Capital	200,000
Income Summary (loss)	40,000	N. Ritt, Capital	120,000
	$568,000		$568,000

REQUIRED

a. Assuming that none of the partners made any capital contributions during the year, prepare journal entries to complete the closing of the books at December 31, 1995. Then calculate the balances of the capital accounts at December 31, 1995.

b. Starting with the partnership post-closing trial balance at December 31, 1995, prepare a statement of partnership liquidation, assuming that
1. Other assets were sold for $240,000 cash.
2. All liabilities were paid in cash.
3. Any partner experiencing a capital deficit would be unable to make up the deficit to the partnership.
4. The final distribution of cash to partners was made on January 31, 1996.

CASES

BUSINESS DECISION CASE

Kevin Wong and Jason Marshall were in business for several years, sharing profits and losses equally. Because of Marshall's poor health, they liquidated the partnership. Wong managed the liquidation because Marshall was in the hospital. Just before liquidation, the partnership balance sheet contained the following information:

Cash	$ 80,000	Liabilities	$ 50,000
Other Assets	220,000	Wong, Capital	100,000
		Marshall, Capital	150,000
	$300,000		$300,000

Wong (1) sold the other assets at the best prices obtainable, (2) paid off all the creditors, and (3) divided the remaining cash between Marshall and himself equally, according to their profit and loss sharing ratio.

Marshall received a note from Wong that read "Good news—sold other assets for $250,000. Have $140,000 check waiting for you. Get well soon." Because he will not be released from the hospital for several days, Marshall asks you to review Wong's liquidation and cash distribution procedures.

REQUIRED

Do you approve of Wong's liquidation and cash distribution procedures? Explain. If you believe that Wong made a mistake, what amount of final cash settlement should Marshall receive?

FINANCIAL ANALYSIS CASE

Johnson Controls is an international market leader in automotive seating, control systems, plastic packaging, and automotive batteries. The firm's assets, liabilities, and stockholders' equity (in millions of dollars) for three recent years follow (Year 3 is the most recent year).

	Year 3	Year 2	Year 1
Assets	$3,806.9	$3,230.8	$3,179.5
Liabilities	2,604.1	2,151.8	1,985.3
Stockholders' equity	1,202.8	1,079.0	1,194.2

REQUIRED

a. Compute the debt-to-equity ratio for each of the three years.

b. Assume you are a potential creditor of Johnson Controls. Does the information revealed by the debt-to-equity ratio over the three years influence your credit decision positively or negatively? Comment.

ETHICS CASE   Gary Cunningham and Dennis Stanton are partners in Good Times Recording Studios. Gary manages the New York City office; Dennis manages the Los Angeles office.

Gary borrows $60,000 from a bank in the partnership name, using partnership assets as collateral without discussing it with Dennis. Although Gary is going to use the money for personal reasons, he intends to pay it back promptly and instructs Helen Terry, the accountant, not to bother telling Dennis about the loan.

REQUIRED

What ethical considerations does Helen face? What are her alternatives?

GENERAL MILLS ANNUAL REPORT CASE   Refer to the annual report of General Mills, Inc., presented in Appendix K.

REQUIRED

a. What type of entity is General Mills?

b. Refer to Note 4 of the annual report. Is General Mills involved in any partnerships or joint ventures with other companies? If so, briefly describe them.

c. Refer to Note 10 of the annual report and the May 29, 1994, balance sheet.

1. Describe what is represented by the $122 million classified in the May 29, 1994, balance sheet as Common Stock Subject to Put Options.

2. Note that the Common Stock Subject to Put Options is not classified as part of either total liabilities or total stockholders' equity. Compute the impact on General Mills' debt-to-equity ratio at May 29, 1994, depending on whether the item is classified as a liability or as part of stockholders' equity for purposes of computing the ratio.

12

Corporations: Organization and Capital Stock

CHAPTER LEARNING OBJECTIVES

1 **DEFINE** and **DISCUSS** the corporate form of organization (pp. 407–410).

2 **EXPLAIN** the difference between par and no-par value stock (pp. 410–411).

3 **IDENTIFY** and **DISCUSS** the types of stock and their basic rights (pp. 411–414).

4 **DESCRIBE** the accounting for issuances of stock for cash, for noncash assets, and by bond conversion (pp. 414–416).

5 **DEFINE** and **DISCUSS** stock splits (pp. 416–417).

6 **EXPLAIN** the accounting for treasury stock and donated capital (pp. 417–419).

7 **DEFINE** and **DISCUSS** the terms book value, market value, and liquidation value per share of stock (pp. 420–421).

8 **Financial Analysis** **DEFINE** *return on common stockholders' equity* and **EXPLAIN** its use (p. 421).

CHAPTER FOCUS

Without a doubt, the modern corporation dominates the national and international economic landscape. In the United States, corporations generate well over three-fourths of the combined business receipts of corporations, partnerships, and proprietorships, even though fewer than one of every five businesses is organized as a corporation. The corporate form of organization is used for a variety of business efforts—from the large, multinational corporation with more than a million owners operating in countries all over the world to the small, family-owned business in a single community. In this chapter, we emphasize the organization of the corporation and the accounting procedures for its capital stock transactions.

NATURE AND FORMATION OF A CORPORATION

OBJECTIVE *1*
DEFINE and **DISCUSS** the corporate form of organization.

A **corporation** is a legal entity—an artificial legal "person"—created on the approval of the appropriate governmental authority. The right to conduct business as a corporation is a privilege granted by the state in which the corporation is formed. All states have laws specifying the requirements for creating a corporation. In some instances, such as the formation of a national bank, the federal government must approve the creation of a corporation.

To form a corporation, the incorporators (often at least three are required) must apply for a charter. The incorporators prepare and file the **articles of incorporation,** which delineate the basic structure of the corporation, including the purposes for which it is formed, the amount of capital stock to be authorized, and the number of shares into which the stock is to be divided. If the incorporators meet the requirements of the law, the government issues a charter or certificate of incorporation. After the charter has been granted, the incorporators (or, in some states, the subscribers to the corporation's capital stock) hold an organizational meeting to elect the first board of directors and adopt the corporation's bylaws.

Because assets are essential to corporate operations, the corporation issues *certificates of capital stock* to obtain the necessary funds. As owners of the corporation, *stockholders,* or *shareholders,* are entitled to a voice in the control and management of the company. Stockholders with voting stock may vote on specific issues at the annual meeting and participate in the election of the board of directors. The board of directors establishes the overall policies of the corporation and declares dividends. Normally, the board selects such corporate officers as a president, one or more vice-presidents, a controller, a treasurer, and a secretary. The officers implement the policies of the board of directors and actively manage the day-to-day affairs of the corporation. The other employees of the corporation execute the operating plans and policies developed by management. Exhibit 12-1 depicts the responsibilities of these stakeholders in a corporation.

ADVANTAGES OF THE CORPORATE FORM

A corporation has several organizational advantages compared with a sole proprietorship or partnership. These advantages are discussed in the following sections.

SEPARATE LEGAL ENTITY

A business with a corporate charter is empowered to conduct business affairs apart from its owners. The corporation, as a legal entity, may acquire assets, incur debt, enter into contracts, sue, and be sued—all in its own name. The owners, or stockholders, of the corporation receive stock certificates as evidence of their ownership interests; the stockholders, however, are separate and distinct from the corporation. This characteristic contrasts with proprietorships and partnerships, which are accounting entities but not legal entities apart from their owners.

LIMITED LIABILITY

The liability of shareholders with respect to company affairs is usually limited to their investment in the corporation. In contrast, owners of proprietorships and partnerships can be

407

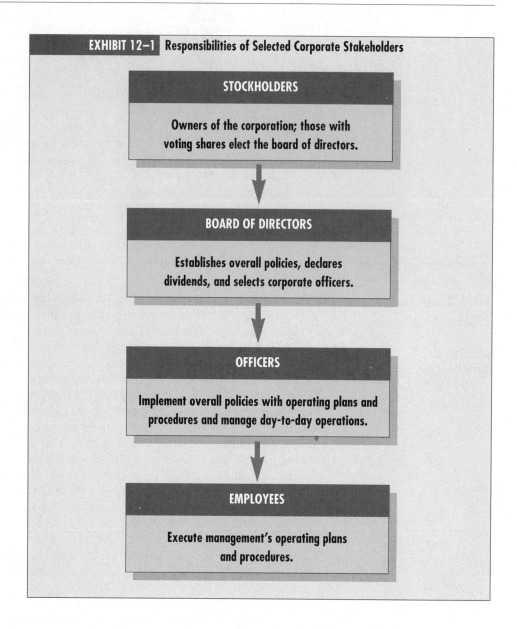

EXHIBIT 12–1 Responsibilities of Selected Corporate Stakeholders

STOCKHOLDERS

Owners of the corporation; those with
voting shares elect the board of directors.

BOARD OF DIRECTORS

Establishes overall policies, declares
dividends, and selects corporate officers.

OFFICERS

Implement overall policies with operating plans and
procedures and manage day-to-day operations.

EMPLOYEES

Execute management's operating plans
and procedures.

held responsible separately and collectively for unsatisfied obligations of the business. Because of the limited liability of corporate shareholders, state laws restrict distributions to shareholders. Most of these laws have fairly elaborate provisions that define the various forms of owners' equity and describe distribution conditions. To protect creditors, state laws limit the distribution of contributed capital. Distributions of retained earnings (undistributed profits) are not legal unless the board of directors formally declares a dividend. Because of the legal delineation of owner capital available for distribution, corporations must maintain careful distinctions in the accounts to identify the different elements of stockholders' equity.

TRANSFERABILITY OF OWNERSHIP

Shares in a corporation may be routinely transferred without affecting the company's operations. The corporation merely notes such transfers of ownership in the stockholder records (ledger). Although a corporation must have stockholder records to notify shareholders of meetings and to pay dividends, the price at which shares transfer between owners is not recognized in the corporation's accounts.

CONTINUITY OF EXISTENCE

Because routine transfers of ownership do not affect a corporation's affairs, the corporation is said to have continuity of existence. In this respect, a corporation is completely different

PRINCIPLE ALERT

ACCOUNTING ENTITY CONCEPT AND GOING CONCERN CONCEPT

Two characteristics of the corporation mesh quite well with the basic principles of accounting. The separate legal status conferred upon the corporation conforms nicely with the *accounting entity concept.* When the corporation is the unit of focus for accounting, the accounting entity concept requires that the economic activity of the corporation be kept separate from the activities of its owners. Legally, the corporate entity is also distinct from its owners. The corporation's continuity of existence aligns well with the *going concern concept,* which assumes that the accounting entity will continue indefinitely into the future. This assumption is strengthened in the corporate setting because legally, the corporation continues as an entity even though its ownership changes.

from a partnership. In a partnership, any change in ownership technically results in discontinuance of the old partnership and formation of a new one. (Many large professional service partnerships, however, follow procedures that provide for continuity with changes in ownership.)

ABSENCE OF MUTUAL AGENCY   The absence of mutual agency for a corporation means that a stockholder, acting as an owner, cannot enter into a contract for the corporation and bind the corporation to the contract. Mutual agency is present in a partnership, however, meaning that every partner is an agent for the firm with the authority to bind the partnership to contracts.

CAPITAL-RAISING CAPABILITY   The limited liability of stockholders and the ease with which shares of stock may be transferred from one investor to another are attractive features to potential stockholders. These characteristics enhance the ability of the corporation to raise large amounts of capital by issuing shares of stock. Because both large and small investors may acquire ownership interests in a corporation, a wide spectrum of potential investors exists. Corporations with thousands of stockholders are not uncommon. The ability to accumulate and use tremendous amounts of capital makes the corporation the dominant form of business organization in the U.S. economy.

DISADVANTAGES OF THE CORPORATE FORM

There are disadvantages to organizing as a corporation rather than as a proprietorship or partnership. We identify three disadvantages here.

ORGANIZATION COSTS   Creating a corporation is more costly than organizing a proprietorship or partnership. The expenditures incurred to organize a corporation are charged to Organization Costs, an intangible asset account. These costs include attorney's fees, fees paid to the state, and costs of promoting the enterprise. Organization costs typically are amortized over a period of 5 to 10 years.

TAXATION   As legal entities, corporations are subject to federal income taxes on their earnings, whether distributed or not. In addition, shareholders must pay income taxes on earnings received as dividends. In many small corporations in which the shareholders themselves manage the business affairs, large salaries may reduce earnings to a point where the double taxation feature is not onerous. However, the firm may have to justify the reasonableness of such salaries to the Internal Revenue Service. Under certain circumstances, a corporation with 35 or fewer shareholders may elect partnership treatment for tax purposes. Although partnerships must submit "information" tax returns, an income tax is not imposed on their earnings. Instead, the partners report their respective shares of partnership earnings on their individual income tax returns.

Usually, corporations are subject to state income taxes in the states in which they are incorporated or are doing business. They may also be subject to real estate, personal property, and franchise taxes.

REGULATION AND SUPERVISION

Corporations are subject to greater degrees of regulation and supervision than are proprietorships and partnerships. Each state has the right to regulate the corporations it charters. State laws limit the powers a corporation may exercise, identify reports that must be filed, and define the rights and liabilities of stockholders. If stock is issued to the public, the corporation must comply with the laws governing the sale of corporate securities. Furthermore, corporations whose stock is listed and traded on organized security exchanges—such as the New York Stock Exchange—are subject to the various reporting and disclosure requirements of these exchanges.

OWNERS' EQUITY AND ORGANIZATIONAL FORMS

Differences arise between the accounting for the owners' equity of a corporation and for that of a sole proprietorship or partnership. In a sole proprietorship, only a single owner's capital account is needed to reflect increases from capital contributions and net earnings as well as decreases from withdrawals and net losses. In practice, many sole proprietors keep a separate drawing account to record withdrawals of cash and other business assets. This separate record is kept only for convenience, however; no subdivision of the owner's capital account is required either by law or by accounting principles.

A similar situation exists in most partnerships, which customarily maintain capital and drawing accounts for each partner. A partnership is simply an association of two or more persons who agree to become joint owners of a business. Because more than one individual is involved in the business, a written agreement should govern the financial participation and business responsibilities of the partners. However, no legal or accounting requirement demands that a distinction be maintained between contributed capital and undistributed earnings.

A corporation, on the other hand, is subject to certain legal restrictions imposed by the government approving its creation. These restrictions focus on the distinction between contributed capital and retained earnings and make accounting for the owners' equity somewhat more complex for corporations than for other types of business organizations. Note that much of the accounting for corporate owners' equity is actually a polyglot of legal prescription and accounting convention. The detailed reporting of stockholders' equity transactions, however, provides analytical information that is often useful and, in many instances, required by law.

In a proprietorship or partnership, the individual owners' capital accounts indicate their relative interests in the business. The stockholders' equity section of a corporate balance sheet does not present individual stockholder accounts. A shareholder, however, can easily compute his or her interest in the corporation by calculating the proportion of the total shares outstanding that his or her shares represent. For example, if only one class of stock is outstanding and it totals 1,000 shares, an individual owning 200 shares has a 20% interest in the corporation's total stockholders' equity, which includes all contributed capital and retained earnings. The dollar amount of this interest, however, is a book amount, rarely coinciding with the market value. A stockholder who liquidates his or her investment would sell it at a price negotiated with a buyer or, if the stock is traded on a stock exchange, at the exchange's quoted market price.

PAR AND NO-PAR VALUE STOCK

OBJECTIVE *2*

EXPLAIN the difference between par and no-par value stock.

The corporate charter may specify a face value, or **par value,** for each share of a stock of any class. In the early days of corporate stock issuances, par value represented the market value of the stock when it was issued. In this century, however, par values have typically been set at amounts well below the stock's market value at date of issue. Par value today, therefore, has no economic significance.

Par value may have legal implications.[1] In some states, par value may represent the minimum amount that must be paid in per share of stock. If stock is issued at a *discount* (that is, at less than par value), the stockholder may have a liability for the discount should creditor claims remain unsatisfied after the company's liquidation. Issuing stock at a discount has been a rare event in this century, though, because boards of directors have generally established par values below market values at time of issue. Following are some examples of corporations whose most basic class of stock (common stock) has a par value below $1.

Corporation	Common Stock Par Value per Share
The Charles Schwab Corporation	$0.01
Lands' End, Inc.	0.01
PepsiCo., Inc.	$0.01\frac{2}{3}$
Pfizer Inc	0.10
The Stride Rite Corporation	0.50
Georgia-Pacific Corporation	0.80

Par value may also be used in some states to define a corporation's legal capital. *Legal capital* is the minimum amount of contributed capital that must remain in the corporation as a margin of protection for creditors. A distribution of assets to stockholders would not be allowed if it reduced stockholders' equity below the amount of legal capital. Given the role that par value may play in defining legal capital, accountants carefully segregate and record the par value of stock transactions in an appropriate capital stock account.

Most states permit the issuance of stock without a par value—that is, **no-par stock.** The company's board of directors usually sets a **stated value** for the no-par stock. In such cases, the stated value will determine the corporation's legal capital. Again, the stated value figure is usually set well below market value at time of issue, but in contrast to par value, the stated value is not printed on the stock certificate. For accounting purposes, stated value amounts are treated in a manner similar to par value amounts. In the absence of a stated value, the entire proceeds from the issuance of no-par stock will likely establish the corporation's legal capital.

TYPES OF STOCK

OBJECTIVE 3

IDENTIFY and **DISCUSS** the types of stock and their basic rights.

The amounts and kinds of stock that a corporation may issue are enumerated in the company's charter. Providing for several classes of stock permits the company to raise capital from different types of investors. The charter also specifies the corporation's **authorized stock**—the maximum number of shares of each class of stock that may be issued. A corporation that wishes to issue more shares than its authorized number must first amend its charter. Shares that have been sold and issued to stockholders constitute the **issued stock** of the corporation. Some of this stock may be repurchased by the corporation. Shares actually held by stockholders are called **outstanding stock,** whereas those reacquired by the corporation (and not retired) are *treasury stock.* We discuss treasury stock later in the chapter.

COMMON STOCK

When only one class of stock is issued, it is called **common stock.** Common shareholders compose the basic ownership class. They have rights to vote, to share in earnings, to participate in additional issues of stock, and—in the case of liquidation—to share in assets after prior claims on the corporation have been settled. We now consider each of these rights.

As the owners of a corporation, the common shareholders elect the board of directors and vote on other matters requiring the approval of owners. Common shareholders are entitled to one vote for each share of stock they own. Owners who do not attend the annual

[1]For a more complete discussion of the legal implications of par value stock, see Philip McGough, "The Legal Significance of the Par Value of Common Stock: What Accounting Educators Should Know," *Issues in Accounting Education,* Fall 1988, pp. 330–350.

stockholders' meetings may vote by proxy (this may be the case for most stockholders in large corporations).

A common stockholder has the right to a proportionate share of the corporation's earnings that are distributed as dividends. All earnings belong to the corporation, however, until the board of directors formally declares a dividend.

Each shareholder of a corporation has a **preemptive right** to maintain his or her proportionate interest in the corporation. If the company issues additional shares of stock, current owners of that type of stock receive the first opportunity to acquire, on a pro rata basis, the new shares. In certain situations, management may request shareholders to waive their preemptive rights. For example, the corporation may wish to issue additional stock to acquire another company. In addition, stockholders of firms incorporated in some states do not receive preemptive rights.

POINT OF INTEREST

PREEMPTIVE RIGHT PREVENTS WEALTH TRANSFER

A major reason for the preemptive right is to protect stockholders against a transfer of wealth to new stockholders. For example, assume that a firm has 10,000 shares of common stock outstanding with a per-share market price of $20. Thus, the firm's total market value is $200,000. If the firm sells another 10,000 common shares at $10 per share (a price below market value), the additional $100,000 cash it received would raise the firm's total market value to $300,000. With a new per-share market value of $15 ($300,000/20,000 shares), the stock issuance causes old stockholders to lose $5 per share and new stockholders to gain $5 per share. The preemptive right prevents the act of selling stock at a price below market value from creating a wealth transfer to new stockholders.

A liquidating corporation converts its assets to a form suitable for distribution, usually cash, which it then distributes to parties having claims on the corporate assets. Any assets remaining after all claims have been satisfied belong to the residual ownership interest in the corporation—the common stockholders. These owners are entitled to the final distribution of the balance of the assets.

A company may occasionally use *classified* common stock; that is, it may issue more than one class of common stock. Two classes of common stock issued are identified as Class A and Class B. The two classes usually differ in either their respective dividend rights or their respective voting powers. Usually, classified common stock is issued when the organizers of the corporation wish to acquire funds from the public while retaining voting control. To illustrate, let us assume that 10,000 shares of Class A stock are issued to the public at $40 per share, and 20,000 shares of Class B stock are issued to the organizers at $5 per share. If each shareholder receives one vote per share of stock, the Class B stockholders have twice as many votes as the Class A stockholders. Yet the total investment of Class B stockholders is significantly less than that of the Class A stockholders. To offset the difference in the voting power per dollar of investment, the Class A stockholders may have better dividend rights, such as being entitled to dividends in early years, whereas the Class B stockholders may not receive dividends until a certain level of earning power is reached.

PREFERRED STOCK

Preferred stock is a class of stock with various characteristics that distinguish it from common stock. Preferred stock has one or more preferences over common stock, usually with reference to (1) dividends and (2) assets when the corporation liquidates. To determine the features of a particular issue, we must examine the stock contract. The majority of preferred issues, however, have certain typical features, which we discuss below.

DIVIDEND PREFERENCE

When the board of directors declares a distribution of earnings, preferred stockholders are entitled to a certain annual amount of dividends before common stockholders receive any distribution. The amount is usually specified in the preferred stock contract as a percentage of the par value of the stock or in dollars per share if the stock does not have a par value. Thus, if the preferred stock has a $100 par value and a 6% dividend rate, the preferred shareholders receive $6 per share in dividends. However, the amount is owed to the stockholders only if declared.

Preferred dividends are usually **cumulative**—that is, regular dividends to preferred stockholders omitted in past years must be paid in addition to the current year's dividend before any distribution is made to common shareholders. If a preferred stock is noncumulative, omitted dividends do not carry forward. Because investors normally consider the noncumulative feature unattractive, noncumulative preferred stock is rarely issued.

To illustrate the difference between cumulative and noncumulative preferred stock, assume that a company ending its second year of operations has outstanding 1,000 shares of $100 par value, 6% preferred stock and 10,000 shares of $20 par value common stock. The company declared no dividends last year. This year a total dividend of $27,000 is declared. The distribution of the $27,000 to the two stockholder classes depends on whether the preferred stock is cumulative or noncumulative. If it is cumulative, preferred shareholders receive $12 per share before common shareholders receive anything.

	Preferred	**Common**	**Total**
Outstanding stock (total par value)	$100,000	$200,000	$300,000
Preferred stock is cumulative			
Preferred dividends in arrears (6%)	$ 6,000		$ 6,000
Regular preferred dividend (6%)	6,000		6,000
Remainder to common		$15,000	15,000
Total distribution	$12,000	$15,000	$27,000
Preferred stock is noncumulative			
Regular preferred dividend (6%)	6,000		6,000
Remainder to common		$21,000	21,000
Total distribution	$6,000	$21,000	$27,000

Dividends in arrears (that is, omitted in past years) on cumulative preferred stock are not an accounting liability and do not appear in the liability section of the balance sheet. They do not become an obligation of the corporation until the board of directors formally declares such dividends. Any arrearages should be disclosed to investors in a footnote to the balance sheet.

Asset Distribution Preference

Preferred stockholders normally have a preference over common stockholders as to the receipt of assets when a corporation liquidates. As the corporation goes out of business, the claims of creditors are settled first. Then preferred stockholders have the right to receive assets equal to the par value of their stock or a larger stated liquidation value per share before any assets are distributed to common stockholders. The preferred stockholders' preference to assets in liquidation also includes any dividends in arrears.

Other Features

Although preferred shareholders do not ordinarily have the right to vote in the election of directors, this right can be accorded by contract. Some state laws require that all stock issued by a corporation be given voting rights. Sometimes, a preferred stock contract confers full or partial voting rights under certain conditions—for example, when dividends have not been paid for a specified period.

Preferred stock contracts may contain features that cause the stock to resemble the common stock equity at one end of a spectrum or a debt obligation at the other end. The stock may, for example, be *convertible* into common stock at some specified rate. With this feature, the market price of the preferred often moves with that of the common. When the price of the common stock rises, the value of the conversion feature is enhanced. Preferred stock may also be convertible into long-term debt securities (bonds).

VOTING RIGHTS AT PORSCHE AG

Actions in 1994 by Porsche AG, the German sports car maker, drew attention to a rule in German corporate law dealing with preferred stock voting rights. In 1994, Porsche announced that it would not pay any dividends on its preferred stock for the second consecutive year (the firm had experienced net losses for three consecutive years). German corporate law grants automatic voting rights to nonvoting preferred stockholders whenever preferred dividends are not paid for two consecutive years. When Porsche resumes its preferred stock dividend payments, the preferred stockholders will lose the voting rights acquired as the result of the company's nonpayment of dividends.

Preferred stock may be *participating*. A participating preferred stock shares dividend distributions with common stock beyond the regular preferred dividend rate. After being allowed its regular dividend preference, the preferred stock does not participate until the common stock is allowed a dividend amount corresponding to the regular preferred dividend rate. At this point, the two classes of stock begin to share the dividend allocation at the same rate. The preferred stock participation feature may be partial (which limits the participation to a certain rate) or full (which places no limit on the rate of participation).

Preferred stock may be *callable,* which means the corporation can redeem the stock after a length of time and at a price specified in the contract. The call feature makes the stock similar to a bond, which frequently is callable or has a limited life. Most preferred stocks are callable, with the call or redemption price set slightly above the original issuance price.

To be successful in selling its preferred stock, a corporation often must cater to current market vogues. Features are added or omitted, depending on market conditions and the desires of the investor group the corporation wishes to attract. Management must balance market requirements with its own goals. Sometimes management must compromise and issue securities that it hopes to change over time, perhaps through conversion or refinancing, to arrive at the desired financial plan.

Preferred stocks appeal to investors who want a steady rate of return that is normally somewhat higher than that on bonds. These investors often believe that preferred stock entails less risk than common stock, although the common will pay off more if the company does well.

From both the legal and the accounting standpoint, preferred stock is part of stockholders' equity. Dividends are distributions of earnings and, unlike interest on bonds, are not shown as expenses on the income statement. Also, because of the legal classification of preferred stock as stockholders' equity, the company cannot deduct dividends as expenses for income tax purposes, whereas interest on debt can be deducted as an expense.

STOCK ISSUANCES FOR CASH

OBJECTIVE 4

DESCRIBE the accounting for issuances of stock for cash, for noncash assets, and by bond conversion.

In issuing its stock, a corporation may use the services of an investment banker, a specialist in marketing securities to investors. The investment banker may *underwrite* a stock issue; that is, the banker buys the stock from the corporation and resells it to investors. The corporation does not risk being unable to sell its stock. The underwriter bears this risk in return for the profits generated by selling the stock to investors at a price higher than that paid the corporation. An investment banker who is unwilling to underwrite a stock issue may handle it on a *best efforts* basis. In this case, the investment banker agrees to sell as many shares as possible at a set price, but the corporation bears the risk of unsold stock.

When capital stock is issued, the appropriate capital stock account is always credited with the par value of the shares, or if the stock is no-par, with its stated value, if any. The asset received for the stock (usually cash) is debited, and any difference is placed in an appropriately named account.

To illustrate the journal entries to record various stock issuances for cash, let us assume that in its first year of operations, a corporation issued two different types of stock, as follows:

1. Issued 1,000 shares of $100 par value, 9% preferred stock at $107 cash per share.

Cash	107,000	
9% Preferred Stock		100,000
Paid-in Capital in Excess of Par Value		7,000

In this transaction, the preferred stock is issued at a premium (that is, at more than par value). The par value of the preferred stock issued is credited to the 9% Preferred Stock account and the $7,000 premium is credited to Paid-in Capital in Excess of Par Value. If there is more than one class of par value stock, the account title may indicate the class of stock to which the premium relates, in this case Paid-in Capital in Excess of Par Value—9% Preferred Stock. An alternative account title for the $7,000 premium is Premium on Preferred Stock. The account title used in the journal entry, however, is more typical.

Should par value stock be issued at less than par, the stock is issued at a discount. The amount of the discount would be debited to an account called Excess of Par Value over Amount Paid In. As noted earlier, issuances of stock for less than par value seldom occur.

2. Issued 30,000 shares of no-par common stock, stated value $5, at $8 cash per share.

Cash	240,000	
Common Stock		150,000
Paid-in Capital in Excess of Stated Value		90,000

When no-par stock has a stated value, as in entry 2, the stated value of the total shares issued is credited to the proper capital stock account, and any additional amount received is credited to an account called Paid-in Capital in Excess of Stated Value. If no stated value for no-par stock exists, the entire proceeds should be credited to the appropriate capital stock account. In entry 2, if the common stock had no stated value, the entire $240,000 amount would have been credited to the Common Stock account.

These two stock issuances are reflected in Exhibit 12-2, which presents the stockholders' equity section in the company's year-end balance sheet. (Retained earnings are assumed to be $25,000.) The stockholders' equity section is divided into two major categories: **1** paid-in capital and **2** retained earnings. **Paid-in capital** is the amount of capital contributed to the corporation by various transactions, such as by issuance of preferred stock and common stock. The capital contributed by owners through the issuance of stock

---

EXHIBIT 12–2 **Stockholders' Equity Section: Various Stock Issuances**

Paid-in Capital			
9% Preferred Stock, $100 Par Value, 1,000 shares authorized, issued, and outstanding		$100,000	
No-Par Common Stock, Stated Value, $5, 40,000 shares authorized; 30,000 shares issued and outstanding		150,000	$250,000
Additional Paid-in Capital			
In Excess of Par Value—Preferred Stock		$ 7,000	
In Excess of Stated Value—Common Stock		90,000	97,000
Total Paid-in Capital			$347,000
2 Retained Earnings			25,000
Total Stockholders' Equity			$372,000

is divided between the legal capital (par or stated value of the stock) and amounts received in excess of the legal capital (or, in rare instances, the discount below legal capital). Later in this chapter we discuss other events (treasury stock transactions and donations) that may increase a corporation's paid-in capital. *Retained earnings* represent the cumulative net earnings and losses of the company that have not been distributed to owners as dividends.

STOCK ISSUANCES FOR ASSETS OTHER THAN CASH

When stock is issued for property other than cash or for services, the accountant must carefully determine the amount recorded. We should not assume that the par or stated value of the shares issued automatically sets a value for the property or services received. In the early years of U.S. corporations, such an assumption frequently resulted in the recording and reporting of excessive asset valuations.

Property or services acquired should be recorded at their current fair value or at the fair value of the stock issued, whichever is more clearly determinable. If the stock is actively traded on a securities exchange, the market price of the stock issued may indicate an appropriate value. For example, if the current market price is $14 per share and 5,000 shares are issued for a parcel of land, this land may be valued, in the absence of other price indicators, at $70,000. An effort should be made, however, to determine a fair value for the property. Certainly, all aspects of the transaction should be carefully scrutinized to ascertain that the number of shares issued was objectively determined. If no market value for the stock is available, we would seek an independently determined value for the property or services received.

Let us suppose the stock issued for the land is $10 par value common stock and its market value is the best indicator of the property's fair value. The entry to record the transaction would be the following:

Land	70,000	
Common Stock		50,000
Paid-in Capital in Excess of Par Value		20,000
To record issuance of 5,000 shares of common stock for land valued at $70,000.		

STOCK ISSUANCES BY BOND CONVERSION

When a corporation issues convertible bonds, it expects to convert them into common stock in the future. Convertible bonds usually include a call provision. When the market value of the stock to be received on conversion is significantly higher than the call price on the bond, a company may force conversion by calling in the bonds. One of the risks of issuing convertible bonds is that the market price of the stock may not increase in the future. Bondholders may then decide it is not to their advantage to convert the bonds, and the company cannot force conversion by exercising the call provision.

The entry to record a bond conversion transfers the book value of the bonds to the common stock accounts. For example, assume that bonds with a face value of $100,000 and a book value of $96,473 are converted into 4,000 shares of $20 par value common stock. The following entry records the conversion:

Bonds Payable	100,000	
Discount on Bonds Payable		3,527
Common Stock		80,000
Paid-in Capital in Excess of Par Value		16,473
To record conversion of bonds into 4,000 shares of $20 par value common stock.		

STOCK SPLITS

OBJECTIVE 5

DEFINE and **DISCUSS** stock splits.

Occasionally, a corporation reduces the par or stated value of its common stock and issues additional shares to its stockholders. This type of transaction, called a **stock split,** does not change the balances of the stockholders' equity accounts—only a memorandum entry is made in the records to show the altered par or stated value of the stock. For example, if a company that has outstanding 10,000 shares of $10 par value common stock announced a 2-for-1 stock split, it would simply reduce the par value of its stock to $5 per share. After the stock split, each shareholder would have twice the number of shares held before the split.

The major reason for a stock split is to reduce the market price of the stock. Some companies like their stock to sell within a certain price range. They may believe that higher prices narrow the breadth of their market, because investors often prefer to buy 100-share lots (purchases of fewer shares are odd-lot purchases and may be subject to higher brokers' fees). Many small investors cannot afford to purchase high-priced stocks in 100-share lots.

When shares are selling below the desired price, a *reverse split* can be accomplished by increasing the par value of the shares and reducing the number outstanding. Such transactions are encountered less frequently than stock splits.

POINT OF INTEREST

"AND HOW WILL YOU BE PAYING FOR YOUR 100 SHARES?"

One company that apparently is not concerned with keeping its market price within an accessible price range is Berkshire Hathaway. A holding company run by well-known investor Warren Buffet, Berkshire Hathaway disdains such maneuvers as stock splits. At the time of this writing, Berkshire Hathaway's per-share market price is $23,000!

TREASURY STOCK

OBJECTIVE 6

EXPLAIN the accounting for treasury stock and donated capital.

When a corporation acquires its own outstanding shares for a purpose other than retiring them, the acquired shares are called **treasury stock.** Treasury stock may be purchased for a variety of reasons, which include reissuing them to officers and employees in profit-sharing schemes or stock-option plans. Whatever the purpose, the corporation is reducing owner capital for a period of time. Consequently, treasury stock is not regarded as an asset. The shares do not carry voting privileges or preemptive rights, are not paid dividends, and do not receive assets on the corporation's liquidation.

POINT OF INTEREST

GREENMAIL

Corporations usually purchase their own stock by buying it through a broker on the open market or by making a tender offer to stockholders. Under a tender offer, the company offers to buy back, within a certain time period and up to a stated limit, shares of its stock at a specified price per share. A third way to acquire treasury stock is to negotiate a purchase from a single large stockholder. In some cases, this latter technique may involve greenmail. *Greenmail* is a ploy in which an investor purchases a sizable number of shares, threatens to try to take control of the company, and then sells the stock back to the company at a premium price. Management pays the premium to entice the investor to "be quiet and go away." For example, to buy off investors on one occasion, Walt Disney Productions paid $325 million—$12 per share above the market price. Payment of an unjustified premium will likely upset other stockholders and may lead to legal action against management.

PURCHASE OF TREASURY STOCK

Accountants commonly record treasury stock at cost, debiting the Treasury Stock account. The account is a contra stockholders' equity account; its balance is deducted when deriving total stockholders' equity in the balance sheet. Suppose a corporation had outstanding 20,000 shares of $10 par value common stock and then purchased 1,000 shares at $12 per share. The entry for the purchase is as follows:

Treasury Stock—Common	12,000	
Cash		12,000
To record purchase of 1,000 shares of treasury stock at $12 per share.		

If a balance sheet is prepared after this transaction, the stockholders' equity section appears as follows (amounts for paid-in capital in excess of par value and retained earnings are assumed):

Stockholders' Equity

Paid-in Capital	
Common Stock, $10 Par Value, authorized and issued 20,000 shares; 1,000 shares in treasury, 19,000 shares outstanding	$200,000
Paid-in Capital in Excess of Par Value	20,000
Total Paid-in Capital	$220,000
Retained Earnings	40,000
	$260,000
Less: Treasury Stock (1,000 shares) at Cost	12,000
Total Stockholders' Equity	$248,000

Note that the $200,000 par value of all *issued* stock is shown, although 1,000 shares are no longer outstanding. The total cost of the 1,000 shares, however, is later deducted as the last component in the presentation of total stockholders' equity.

In this owners' equity situation, the corporation apparently has $40,000 retained earnings unfettered by any legal restrictions; the entire amount might be distributed as dividends if the corporation's cash position permits. In many states, however, the corporation must restrict (reduce) the retained earnings available for declaration of dividends by the cost of any treasury stock held. Then, in our illustration, only $28,000 in retained earnings would be available for dividends. The statutory restriction exists because a corporation that reduces its paid-in capital by purchasing its own shares must protect creditors by "buffering" the reduced capital with its retained earnings in an amount equal to the resources expended.

SALE OF TREASURY STOCK FOR MORE THAN COST

The corporation may accept any price for the sale of treasury stock. Treasury stock transactions are not part of a firm's normal operating activities, and any additional capital obtained from issuing such shares at more than cost is not regarded as earnings and is not added to retained earnings. The corporation should regard any additional amounts paid by subsequent purchasers as paid-in capital. Therefore, increases in capital from the sale of purchased treasury shares are credited to a paid-in capital account such as Paid-in Capital from Treasury Stock.

Let us assume that 500 shares of the treasury stock are sold by the corporation at $13 per share. The entry to record the sale is as follows:

Cash	6,500	
Treasury Stock—Common		6,000
Paid-in Capital from Treasury Stock		500
To record sale of 500 shares of treasury stock at $13 per share.		

Observe that Treasury Stock—Common is credited at the cost price of $12 per share, a basis consistent with the original debit to the account. The excess over cost is credited to Paid-in Capital from Treasury Stock.

SALE OF TREASURY STOCK FOR LESS THAN COST

When treasury stock is sold for an amount less than the treasury stock's cost, the difference first reduces any previously recorded paid-in capital from treasury stock for that class of stock. If there is not enough paid-in capital from treasury stock, the remaining amount is debited to Retained Earnings. To illustrate, assume that the remaining 500 treasury shares from our previous example are sold for $9 per share. The journal entry is as follows:

Cash	4,500	
Paid-in Capital from Treasury Stock	500	
Retained Earnings	1,000	
Treasury Stock—Common		6,000
To record sale of 500 shares of treasury stock at $9 per share.		

DONATED CAPITAL

A corporation may receive an asset as a gift from a governmental unit. A city, for example, may offer a company a land site or a building as an incentive to attract the business to the community. When a donated asset is received from a governmental unit, the corporation records the asset at its fair value and increases **donated capital,** a form of paid-in capital.[2]

PRINCIPLE ALERT

COST PRINCIPLE

A donated asset has no cost to the recipient company. Recording the donated asset at its fair value, then, appears to be a violation of the *cost principle.* Actually, the accounting is a logical extension of the cost principle. In general, assets are to be recorded at their fair value when acquired. Assets are usually acquired in an exchange transaction where cost represents the fair value of the asset as agreed to by both the buyer and seller. In an exchange transaction, then, cost and fair value are equal when the asset is acquired. For a donated asset, cost does not represent the fair value of the asset when it is acquired. In this situation, some measure other than cost is used to determine the asset's fair value at date of acquisition.

Assume that a city donates a plant site to a corporation. An independent appraiser values the land at $26,000, which is accepted by the board of directors as an appropriate valuation. The entry to record the donation is as follows:

Land	26,000	
Donated Capital		26,000
To record receipt of donated land valued at $26,000.		

Exhibit 12-3 illustrates the presentation of donated capital in stockholders' equity, along with examples of other paid-in capital items that we have discussed in this chapter.

EXHIBIT 12-3 Stockholders' Equity Section: Various Paid-in Capital Items		
Paid-in Capital		
6% Preferred Stock, $100 Par Value, 2,000 shares		
authorized, issued, and outstanding	$200,000	
Common Stock, $1 Par Value, 250,000 shares		
authorized; 150,000 shares issued; and 3,000		
shares in the treasury	150,000	$350,000
Additional Paid-in Capital		
In Excess of Par Value—Preferred Stock	$ 30,000	
In Excess of Par Value—Common Stock	455,000	
From Treasury Stock	4,000	
Donated Capital	26,000	515,000
Total Paid-in Capital		$865,000
Retained Earnings		115,000
		$980,000
Less: Treasury Stock (3,000 common shares) at Cost		15,000
Total Stockholders' Equity		$965,000

---

[2]When donated assets are received from a source other than governmental units, the credit must go to a revenue account. *Statement of Financial Accounting Standards No. 116,* "Accounting for Contributions Made and Contributions Received," (Norwalk, CT: Financial Accounting Standards Board, 1993). This standard does not apply to transfers of assets from governmental units to business enterprises.

BOOK VALUE PER SHARE

OBJECTIVE *7*

DEFINE and **DISCUSS** the terms book value, market value, and liquidation value per share of stock.

Book value per share is often calculated for a class of stock, particularly common stock. **Book value per share,** which is the dollar amount of net assets represented by one share of stock, is computed by dividing the amount of stockholders' equity associated with a class of stock by the number of outstanding shares in that class. The computation uses stockholders' equity, because a corporation's net assets (assets – liabilities) equals its stockholders' equity. The measure is based on amounts recorded in the books and presented in the balance sheet—hence, the term *book* value per share.

For example, assume the following stockholders' equity section of a balance sheet:

Stockholders' Equity

Paid-in Capital	
Common Stock, $50 Par Value, 5,000 shares authorized, issued, and outstanding	$250,000
Paid-in Capital in Excess of Par Value	100,000
Total Paid-in Capital	$350,000
Retained Earnings	80,000
Total Stockholders' Equity	$430,000

Because this corporation has only one class of stock, the book value per share is the total stockholders' equity divided by the shares outstanding; that is, $430,000 / 5,000 = $86. Note that the divisor is shares outstanding; it does not include shares of unissued common stock or treasury stock.

To compute book values per share when more than one class of stock is outstanding, we must determine the portion of stockholders' equity attributable to each class of stock. Preferred stocks are assigned the amounts their owners would receive if the corporation liquidated—that is, the liquidation preference of preferred stock plus any dividend arrearages on cumulative stock. The common shares receive the remainder of the stockholders' equity. For example, assume the following stockholders' equity section:

Stockholders' Equity

Paid-in Capital	
9% Preferred Stock, $100 Par Value, 1,000 shares authorized, issued, and outstanding	$100,000
No-par Common Stock, Stated Value $40, 3,000 shares authorized, issued, and outstanding	120,000
Additional Paid-in Capital	
In Excess of Par Value—Preferred Stock	5,000
In Excess of Stated Value—Common Stock	6,000
Total Paid-in Capital	$231,000
Retained Earnings	73,000
Total Stockholders' Equity	$304,000

Assume that the stated liquidation preference is $103 per share for the preferred stock, with no dividends in arrears. The book value per share for the preferred stock, therefore, is also $103. The computation for the book value per share of common stock follows:

Total stockholders' equity	$304,000
Less: Equity applicable to preferred stock (1,000 × $103)	103,000
Equity allocated to common stock	$201,000
Shares of common stock outstanding	3,000
Book value per share of common stock ($201,000/3,000)	$67

The book value per share of common stock may be used in many ways. Management may include the book value per share—and any changes in it for the year—in the annual report to stockholders. Two corporations negotiating a merger through an exchange of stock may find their respective book values per share to be one of several factors influencing the final exchange ratio. Or an individual may acquire an option to buy stock in the future, with the purchase price related to the future book value of the stock. Also, book values are used by many investors in selecting stocks to buy. Such investors concentrate on buying stocks that are selling below or close to their book value because they believe this is the best way to identify undervalued stocks.

MARKET VALUE AND LIQUIDATION VALUE

The book value of common stock is different from its market value and its liquidation value. The **market value per share** is the current price at which the stock may be bought or sold. This price reflects such things as the earnings potential of the company, dividends, book values, capital structure, and general economic conditions. Because book value is only one of several variables influencing market price (and usually not the most significant one at that), market values and book values rarely coincide.

The **liquidation value per share** of common stock is the amount that would be received if the corporation liquidated. The amounts recorded in the books do not portray liquidation proceeds, so no correlation exists between liquidation values and book values of common stocks. Liquidation values may not be easy to determine, but corporate managements must be alert to the relationship between the market value and the approximate liquidation value of their common stock. A corporation whose liquidation value exceeds its market value may be the object of a "raid." A raider acquires control of a corporation (by buying stock at market values) and then liquidates the business (at liquidation values), keeping the difference as a gain.

FINANCIAL ANALYSIS

RETURN ON COMMON STOCKHOLDERS' EQUITY

OBJECTIVE 8

DEFINE return on common stockholders' equity and **EXPLAIN** its use.

A financial ratio of particular interest to common stockholders is the return on common stockholders' equity. This ratio measures the profitability of the common stockholders' equity in the corporation. The **return on common stockholders' equity** is computed as follows:

$$\text{Return on Common Stockholders' Equity} = \frac{\text{Net Income} - \text{Preferred Dividends}}{\text{Average Common Stockholders' Equity}}$$

By subtracting the preferred dividend requirements from net income, the numerator represents the net income available to the common stockholders. The denominator averages the common stockholders' equity for the year (sum the beginning and ending common stockholders' equity and divide the sum by 2). If a corporation has preferred stock outstanding, the common stockholders' equity is computed by subtracting the preferred stockholders' equity (the same equity as is used to compute the preferred stock's book value per share) from total stockholders' equity.

To illustrate the computation of return on common stockholders' equity, we use financial data from a recent annual report of Johnson Controls, Inc., headquartered in Milwaukee, Wisconsin. Johnson Controls manufactures automotive seating systems, environmental control systems, automotive batteries, and plastic packaging. The financial data are as follows (in millions of dollars):

Net income	$ 165.2
Preferred dividends	9.3
Preferred stockholders' equity, beginning of year	168.1
Preferred stockholders' equity, end of year	164.1
Common stockholders' equity, beginning of year	910.9
Common stockholders' equity, end of year	1,038.7

Johnson Controls' return on common stockholders' equity for the year is 16.0%, computed as follows: ($165.2 − $9.3) / [($910.9 + $1,038.7)/2]. This return continues an upward trend for Johnson Controls; two years earlier its return on common stockholders' equity was 12.0% and one year earlier the return was 13.3%.

KEY POINTS FOR CHAPTER LEARNING OBJECTIVES

1 **DEFINE** and **DISCUSS** the corporate form of organization (pp. 407–410).
- A corporation is a separate legal entity chartered by the state in which it is formed or, in some cases, by the federal government.
- The liability of corporate shareholders is usually limited to their ownership investment, whereas claims against partners and sole proprietors may extend to their personal resources.
- Unlike proprietorships and partnerships, corporations must report paid-in capital separately from the accumulated balance of retained earnings. Distributions to shareholders are limited by the amount of retained earnings and other capital as specified by state law.

2 **EXPLAIN** the difference between par and no-par value stock (pp. 410–411).
- Par value is the face value printed on a stock certificate. It has no economic significance but may have legal significance.
- No-par stock has no face value printed on the stock certificate, although generally the board of directors sets a stated value for the stock.

3 **IDENTIFY** and **DISCUSS** the types of stock and their basic rights (pp. 411–414).
- Common stock represents a corporation's basic ownership class of stock.
- Preferred stocks may differ from common stock in any of several characteristics. Typically, preferred stocks have some type of dividend preference and a prior claim to assets in liquidation.

4 **DESCRIBE** the accounting for issuances of stock for cash, for noncash assets, and by bond conversion (pp. 414–416).
- When capital stock is issued in exchange for assets, the appropriate capital stock account is credited with the par or stated value of the shares issued; the asset received for the stock is debited for its fair value; and any difference is placed in an appropriately named account.
- The entry for bond conversion into common stock removes both the appropriate portion of the bonds payable and any related bond premium or bond discount from the accounts at the date of conversion. The par value of common stock issued is recorded, together with the appropriate amount of paid-in capital in excess of par value.

5 **DEFINE** and **DISCUSS** stock splits (pp. 416–417).
- Stock splits change the par or stated value of stock and affect the number of shares outstanding. Only a memorandum notation records stock splits.

6 **EXPLAIN** the accounting for treasury stock and donated capital (pp. 417–419).
- Treasury stock represents reacquired shares of the firm's own stock. It is commonly recorded at cost and deducted in deriving total stockholders' equity in the balance sheet.
- Donated capital results from gifts to the corporation from governmental units that should be recorded at fair value.

7 **DEFINE** and **DISCUSS** the terms book value, market value, and liquidation value per share of stock (pp. 420–421).
- The book value per share of common stock indicates the net assets, based on recorded amounts, associated with a share of common stock. Common stock book values are different from market values or liquidation values.

8 **Financial Analysis** **DEFINE** *return on common stockholders' equity* and **EXPLAIN** its use (p. 421).
- Return on common stockholders' equity is computed as (Net Income – Preferred Dividends)/ Average Common Stockholders' Equity. It indicates the profitability of the common stockholders' equity.

SELF-TEST QUESTIONS FOR REVIEW

(Answers follow the Solution to Demonstration Problem.)

1. What is the usual liability of stockholders for corporation actions?
   a. Unlimited
   b. Limited to the par or stated value of the stock they hold
   c. Limited to the amount of their investment in the corporation
   d. Limited to the amount of the corporation's retained earnings

2. Which type of stock may have dividends in arrears?
   a. Cumulative preferred stock
   b. Common stock
   c. Noncumulative preferred stock
   d. Treasury stock

3. Wyler Company issued 20,000 shares of $10 par value common stock in exchange for a building with a current fair value of $1,000,000. In recording this transaction, what amount should be credited to Paid-in Capital in Excess of Par Value?
   a. $1,000,000
   b. $200,000
   c. $800,000
   d. $980,000

4. Which of the following accounts has a normal debit balance?
   a. Common Stock
   b. Paid-in Capital in Excess of Stated Value
   c. Donated Capital
   d. Treasury Stock

5. Caffey Corporation has a total stockholders' equity of $1,860,000. Caffey has 20,000 shares of $25 par value, 6% preferred stock issued and outstanding, and 60,000 shares of $10 par value common stock issued and outstanding. The preferred stock has a liquidation preference of $27 per share and no dividends in arrears. What is the book value per share of common stock?
   a. $31.00
   b. $22.00
   c. $22.67
   d. $10.00

DEMONSTRATION PROBLEM FOR REVIEW

Following is the stockholders' equity section of Baysite Corporation's December 31, 1996, balance sheet.

Paid-in Capital		
7% Preferred Stock, $50 Par Value, 5,000 shares authorized, issued, and outstanding	$ 250,000	
Common Stock, $6 Par Value, 700,000 shares authorized; 200,000 issued, of which 10,000 shares are in the treasury	1,200,000	$1,450,000
Additional Paid-in Capital		
In Excess of Par Value—Preferred Stock	$ 80,000	
In Excess of Par Value—Common Stock	1,000,000	
From Treasury Stock	22,000	
Donated Capital	75,000	1,177,000
Total Paid-in Capital		$2,627,000
Retained Earnings		2,223,000
		$4,850,000
Less: Treasury Stock (10,000 common shares) at Cost		140,000
Total Stockholders' Equity		$4,710,000

REQUIRED

a. What is Bayside's legal capital at December 31, 1996?
b. What is the number of common shares outstanding at December 31, 1996?
c. What is the average amount per share received from the original issuance of common stock?
d. Assuming that the preferred stock is cumulative with no arrearages, what total dollar amount of preferred dividends needs to be declared at December 31, 1996, before the common stockholders may receive a dividend for 1996?
e. Bayside received a gift of land from a city government in 1995 (the only gift the corporation has ever received). What was the fair value of the land when it was received in 1995?
f. Has Bayside ever sold treasury stock for more than the treasury stock cost when it was acquired? Briefly explain.
g. Assume that Bayside splits its common stock three for one on January 1, 1997. What is the total amount of paid-in capital immediately after the split?

SOLUTION TO DEMONSTRATION PROBLEM

a. $1,450,000 (the par value of the issued preferred stock and common stock).
b. 190,000 shares (200,000 issued common shares less 10,000 shares in the treasury).
c. $11 [($1,200,000 par value of issued shares + $1,000,000 paid-in capital in excess of par value)/ 200,000 issued shares].
d. $17,500 (7% × $250,000).
e. $75,000 (the balance in the Donated Capital account).
f. Yes, the stockholders' equity section shows additional paid-in capital of $22,000 from treasury stock. This type of paid-in capital represents the excess of proceeds from the sale of treasury stock over that treasury stock's cost.
g. $2,627,000 (splitting the common stock does not change any of the account balances composing paid-in capital; the common stock's par value will decrease to $2 per share, and the common shares issued will increase to 600,000).

GLOSSARY OF KEY TERMS USED IN THIS CHAPTER

articles of incorporation A document prepared by persons organizing a corporation in the United States that sets forth the structure and purpose of the corporation and specifics regarding the stock to be issued (p. 407).

authorized stock The maximum number of shares in a class of stock that a corporation may issue (p. 411).

book value per share The dollar amount of net assets represented by one share of stock; computed by dividing the amount of stockholders' equity associated with a class of stock by the outstanding shares of that class of stock (p. 420).

common stock The basic ownership class of corporate capital stock, carrying the rights to vote, share in earnings, participate in future stock issues, and share in any liquidation proceeds after prior claims have been settled (p. 411).

corporation A legal entity created by the granting of a charter from an appropriate governmental authority and owned by stockholders who have limited liability for corporate debt (p. 407).

cumulative (preferred stock) A feature associated with preferred stock whereby any dividends in arrears must be paid before dividends may be paid on common stock (p. 413).

donated capital The amount received by a corporation from the donation of assets by a governmental unit (p. 419).

issued stock Shares of stock that have been sold and issued to stockholders; issued stock may be either outstanding or in the treasury (p. 411).

liquidation value per share The amount that would be received by a holder of a share of stock if the corporation liquidated (p. 421).

market value per share The current price at which shares of stock may be bought or sold (p. 421).

no-par stock Stock that does not have a par value (p. 411).

outstanding stock Shares of stock that are currently owned by stockholders (p. 411).

paid-in capital The amount of capital contributed to a corporation by various transactions; the primary source of paid-in capital is from the issuance of shares of stock (p. 415).

par value (stock) An amount specified in the corporate charter for each share of stock and imprinted on the face of each stock certificate, often determines the legal capital of the corporation (p. 410).

preemptive right The right of a stockholder to maintain his or her proportionate interest in a corporation by having the right to purchase an appropriate share of any new stock issue (p. 412).

preferred stock A class of corportae capital stock typically receiving priority over common stock in dividend payments and distribution of assets should the corporation be liquidated (p. 412).

return on common stockholders' equity A financial ratio computed as (net income – preferred dividends) divided by average common stockholders' equity (p. 421).

stated value A nominal amount that may be assigned to each share of no-par stock and accounted for much as if it were a par value (p. 411).

stock split Additional shares of its own stock issued by a corporation to its current stockholders in proportion to their current ownership interests without changing the balances in the related stockholders' equity accounts. A formal stock split increases the number of shares outstanding and reduces proportionately the stock's per-share par value (p. 416).

treasury stock Shares of outstanding stock that have been acquired by the issuing corporation for purposes other than retiring the stock. Treasury stock is recorded at cost and deducted from stockholders' equity in the balance sheet (p. 417).

QUESTIONS

12-1 What is the meaning of each of the following terms and, when appropriate, how do they interrelate: *corporation, articles of incorporation, corporate charter, board of directors, corporate officers,* and *organization costs*?

12-2 What is meant by the limited liability of a shareholder? Does this characteristic enhance or reduce a corporation's ability to raise capital?

12-3 Contrast the federal income taxation of corporations with that of sole proprietorships and partnerships. Which of the three types of organizations must file a federal income tax return?

12-4 Define *par value stock.* What is the significance of a stock's par value?

12-5 What is the preemptive right of a shareholder?

12-6 What are the basic differences between preferred stock and common stock? What are the typical features of preferred stock?

12-7 What features make preferred stock similar to debt? Similar to common stock?

12-8 What is meant by dividend arrearage on preferred stock? If dividends are two years in arrears on $500,000 of 6% preferred stock and dividends are declared this year, what amount of total dividends must preferred shareholders receive before any distributions can be made to common shareholders?

12-9 Distinguish between authorized stock and issued stock. Why might the number of shares issued be more than the number of shares outstanding?

12-10 What are three different sources of paid-in capital?

12-11 A company acquired machines with a fair value of $90,000 in exchange for 15,000 shares of $5 par value common stock. How should this transaction be recorded in the accounts?

12-12 Define *stock split*. What is the major reason for a stock split?

12-13 Define *treasury stock*. Why might a corporation acquire treasury stock? How is treasury stock shown in the balance sheet?

12-14 If a corporation purchases 600 shares of its own common stock at $10 per share and resells it at $14 per share, where would the $2,400 increase in capital appear in the financial statements? Why is no gain reported?

12-15 A corporation has total stockholders' equity of $4,628,000 and one class of $2 par value common stock. The corporation has 500,000 shares authorized; 300,000 shares issued; 260,000 shares outstanding; and 40,000 shares as treasury stock. What is the book value per share?

12-16 What do the terms *book value, market value,* and *liquidation value per share* of common stock mean?

12-17 Assume that a corporation has preferred stock outstanding. How is the return on common stockholders' equity computed?

PRINCIPLES DISCUSSION QUESTION

12-18 The Financial Accounting Standards Board decided that purchasing treasury stock at a price well above its current market price is evidence the price includes payment for something in addition to the stock acquired (see Point of Interest: Greenmail on page 417). Having the selling shareholder agree to abandon certain acquisition plans or to agree not to purchase additional shares for a stated time period are examples. The FASB concluded that the analysis of this type of treasury stock purchase should result in the treasury stock account being debited for the fair value of the treasury stock purchased. The excess amount paid to elicit certain actions from the selling stockholder must be charged to the current period as an expense. How does this analysis incorporate both the cost principle and the matching concept?

EXERCISES

DIVIDEND DISTRIBUTION
— OBJ. 3 —

12-19 Lakeside Company has outstanding 20,000 shares of $50 par value, 6% cumulative preferred stock and 80,000 shares of $10 par value common stock. The company declared cash dividends amounting to $160,000.
  a. If no arrearage on the preferred stock exists, how much in total dividends, and in dividends per share, is paid to each class of stock?
  b. If one year's dividend arrearage on the preferred stock exists, how much in total dividends, and in dividends per share, is paid to each class of stock?

STOCK ISSUANCES FOR CASH
— OBJ. 4 —

12-20 On June 1, 1996, Finlay, Inc., issued 8,000 shares of $50 par value preferred stock at $68 per share and 12,000 shares of no-par common stock at $10 per share. The common stock has no stated value. All issuances were for cash.
  a. Prepare the general journal entries to record the stock issuances.
  b. Prepare the entry for the issuance of the common stock, assuming that it had a stated value of $5 per share.
  c. Prepare the entry for the issuance of the common stock, assuming that it had a par value of $1 per share.

STOCK SPLIT
— OBJ. 5 —

12-21 On March 1 of the current year, Sentry Corporation has 400,000 shares of $20 par value common stock that are issued and outstanding. The general ledger shows the following account balances relating to the common stock:

Common Stock	$8,000,000
Paid-in Capital in Excess of Par Value	3,400,000

On March 2, Sentry Corporation splits its stock 2 for 1 and reduces the par value to $10 per share.

a. How many shares of common stock are issued and outstanding immediately after the stock split?
b. What is the balance in the Common Stock account immediately after the stock split?
c. What is the balance in the Paid-in Capital in Excess of Par Value account immediately after the stock split?
d. Is a general journal entry required to record the stock split? If yes, prepare the entry.

TREASURY STOCK
— OBJ. 6 —

12-22 Coastal Corporation issued 25,000 shares of $5 par value common stock at $17 per share and 6,000 shares of $50 par value, 8% preferred stock at $78 per share. Later, the company purchased 3,000 shares of its own common stock at $20 per share.

a. Prepare the general journal entries to record the stock issuances and the purchase of the common shares.
b. Assume that Coastal sold 2,000 shares of the treasury stock at $26 per share. Prepare the general journal entry to record the sale of this treasury stock.
c. Assume that Coastal sold the remaining 1,000 shares of treasury stock at $19 per share. Prepare the general journal entry to record the sale of this treasury stock.

DONATED CAPITAL
— OBJ. 6 —

12-23 Prepare the general journal entries (if required) to record the following 1996 transaction relating to Dexter, Inc.

Aug. 12　The government of the community in which Dexter, Inc., is building a new plant donated the land site to the company. The appraised value of the land is $93,000.

Oct.　7　The state completed, at no cost to Dexter, a $600,000 highway exit that makes Dexter's new plant more accessible to customers and suppliers. Although not on Dexter's property, the new exit was an incentive offered by the state to attract Dexter's new plant to the area.

BOOK VALUE PER SHARE
— OBJ. 7 —

12-24 The stockholders' equity section of Caravan Company's balance sheet appears as follows:

Paid-in Capital		
7% Cumulative Preferred Stock, $75 Par Value,		
6,000 shares authorized, issued, and outstanding	$450,000	
No-par Common Stock, $5 Stated Value, 120,000		
shares authorized, issued, and outstanding	600,000	$1,050,000
Additional Paid-in Capital		
In Excess of Par Value—Preferred Stock	$ 90,000	
In Excess of Par Value—Common Stock	750,000	
From Treasury Stock	40,000	880,000
Total Paid-in Capital		$1,930,000
Retained Earnings		2,114,000
Total Stockholders' Equity		$4,044,000

The preferred stock has a liquidation preference of $77 per share, and no dividends are in arrears. Compute the book value per share of the common stock.

PROBLEMS

DIVIDEND DISTRIBUTION
— OBJ. 3 —

12-25 Rydon Corporation began business on March 1, 1995. At that time, it issued 20,000 shares of $60 par value, 7% cumulative preferred stock and 100,000 shares of $5 par value common stock. Through the end of 1997, there has been no change in the number of preferred and common shares outstanding.

REQUIRED

a. Assume that Rydon declared dividends of $0 in 1995, $183,000 in 1996, and $200,000 in 1997. Calculate the total dividends and the dividends per share paid to each class of stock in 1995, 1996, and 1997.
b. Assume that Rydon declared dividends of $0 in 1995, $84,000 in 1996, and $150,000 in 1997. Calculate the total dividends and the dividends per share paid to each class of stock in 1995, 1996, and 1997.

STOCKHOLDERS' EQUITY:
TRANSACTIONS AND BALANCE
SHEET PRESENTATION
— OBJ. 4, 6 —

12-26 Tunic Corporation was organized on April 1, 1996, with an authorization of 25,000 shares of 6%, $50 par value preferred stock and 200,000 shares of $5 par value common stock. During April, the following transactions affecting stockholders' equity occurred:

Apr.　1　Issued 80,000 shares of common stock at $15 cash per share.
　　　3　Issued 2,000 shares of common stock to attorneys and promoters in exchange for their services in organizing the corporation. The services were valued at $31,000.

Apr. 8   Issued 3,000 shares of common stock in exchange for equipment with a fair market value of $48,000.

17   Received land valued at $75,000 as a donation from the city to attract Tunic to its present location. The land will allow Tunic to have adequate parking for its operations.

20   Issued 6,000 shares of preferred stock for cash at $55 per share.

30   Closed the $49,000 net income for April from the Income Summary account to Retained Earnings.

REQUIRED

a. Prepare general journal entries to record the foregoing transactions.
b. Prepare the stockholders' equity section of the balance sheet at April 30, 1996.

STOCKHOLDERS' EQUITY: TRANSACTIONS, BALANCE SHEET PRESENTATION, AND BOOK VALUE PER SHARE — OBJ. 4, 6, 7 —

12-27   The stockholders' equity accounts of Windham Corporation at January 1, 1996, appear below:

8% Preferred Stock, $25 Par Value, 50,000 shares authorized; 6,800 shares issued and outstanding	$170,000
Common Stock, $10 Par Value, 200,000 shares authorized; 50,000 shares issued and outstanding	500,000
Paid-in Capital in Excess of Par Value—Preferred Stock	68,000
Paid-in Capital in Excess of Par Value—Common Stock	200,000
Retained Earnings	270,000

During 1996, the following transactions occurred:

Jan. 10   Issued 28,000 shares of common stock for $17 cash per share.

23   Purchased 8,000 shares of common stock for the treasury at $19 per share.

Mar. 14   Sold one-half of the treasury shares acquired January 23 for $21 per share.

July 15   Issued 3,200 shares of preferred stock to acquire special equipment with a fair market value of $128,000.

Oct. 15   Received a parcel of land valued at $120,000 as a gift from the state.

Nov. 15   Sold 1,000 of the treasury shares acquired January 23 for $24 per share.

Dec. 31   Closed the net income of $59,000 from the Income Summary account to Retained Earnings.

REQUIRED

a. Set up T accounts for the stockholders' equity accounts at the beginning of the year and enter January 1 balances.
b. Prepare general journal entries to record the foregoing transactions and post to T accounts (set up any additional T accounts needed). Determine the ending balances for the stockholders' equity accounts.
c. Prepare the December 31, 1996, stockholders' equity section of the balance sheet.
d. Assume the preferred stock has a liquidation preference of $27 per share. No dividends are in arrears. Compute the book value per share of common stock at December 31, 1996.

STOCKHOLDERS' EQUITY: TRANSACTIONS AND BALANCE SHEET PRESENTATION — OBJ. 4, 5, 6 —

12-28   The stockholders' equity of Summit Corporation at January 1, 1996, follows:

7% Preferred Stock, $100 Par Value, 20,000 shares authorized; 5,000 shares issued and outstanding	$ 500,000
Common Stock, $15 Par Value, 100,000 shares authorized; 40,000 shares issued and outstanding	600,000
Paid-in Capital in Excess of Par Value—Preferred Stock	24,000
Paid-in Capital in Excess of Par Value—Common Stock	360,000
Retained Earnings	325,000
Total Stockholders' Equity	$1,809,000

The following transactions, among others, occurred during the year:

Jan. 12   Announced a 3-for-1 common stock split, reducing the par value of the common stock to $5 per share. The authorization was increased to 300,000 shares.

Mar. 31   Converted $40,000 face value of convertible bonds payable (book value = $43,000) to common stock. Each $1,000 bond converted to 125 shares of common stock.

Apr. 14   Received a plant site valued at $210,000 as a gift from the city.

June 1   Acquired equipment with a fair market value of $60,000 in exchange for 500 shares of preferred stock.

Sept. 1 Acquired 10,000 shares of common stock for cash at $10 per share.
Oct. 12 Sold 1,500 treasury shares at $12 per share.
Nov. 21 Issued 5,000 shares of common stock at $11 cash per share.
Dec. 28 Sold 1,200 treasury shares at $9 per share.
    31 Closed the Income Summary account, with net earnings of $83,000, to Retained Earnings.

REQUIRED

a. Set up T accounts for the stockholders' equity accounts at the beginning of the year and enter January 1 balances.
b. Prepare general journal entries for the given transactions and post them to the T accounts (set up any additional T accounts needed). Determine the ending balances for the stockholders' equity accounts.
c. Prepare the stockholders' equity section of the balance sheet at December 31, 1996.

STOCKHOLDERS' EQUITY: INFORMATION AND ENTRIES FROM COMPARATIVE DATA — OBJ. 4, 6 —

12-29 Comparative stockholders' equity sections from two successive years' balance sheets of Smiley, Inc., are as follows:

	Dec. 31, 1997	Dec. 31, 1996
Paid-in Capital		
8% Preferred Stock, $50 Par Value, authorized 20,000 shares; issued and outstanding, 1996: 8,000 shares; 1997: 12,000 shares	$ 600,000	$ 400,000
Common Stock, No-Par Value, $20 Stated Value, authorized 80,000 shares; issued, 1996: 32,000 shares; 1997: 40,000 shares	800,000	640,000
Additional Paid-in Capital		
In Excess of Par Value—Preferred Stock	224,000	144,000
In Excess of Stated Value—Common Stock	232,000	160,000
From Treasury Stock	21,000	
Donated Capital	80,000	
Retained Earnings	300,000	229,000
		$1,573,000
Less: Treasury Stock (7,000 shares common) at Cost		196,000
Total Stockholders' Equity	$2,257,000	$1,377,000

No dividends were declared or paid during 1997. The company received a donated parcel of land from the city in 1997.

REQUIRED

Prepare the general journal entries for the transactions affecting stockholders' equity that evidently occurred during 1997. Assume that cash was received for stock transactions involving the receipt of an asset.

BOOK VALUE PER SHARE — OBJ. 7 —

12-30 Sanders Corporation has the following stockholders' equity section in its balance sheet:

Paid-in Capital		
7% Preferred Stock, $100 Par Value, 6,000 shares authorized, issued, and outstanding	$600,000	
Common Stock, $5 Par Value, 200,000 shares authorized; 120,000 shares issued and outstanding	600,000	
Additional Paid-in Capital		
In Excess of Par Value—Preferred Stock	30,000	
In Excess of Par Value—Common Stock	840,000	
From Treasury Stock	25,000	$2,095,000
Retained Earnings		767,000
Total Stockholders' Equity		$2,862,000

REQUIRED

For each of the following independent cases, compute the book value per share for the preferred stock and the common stock.

a. The preferred stock is noncumulative and has a liquidation preference of $101 per share.

b. The preferred stock is cumulative and has a liquidation preference per share equal to par value plus dividends in arrears. No dividends are in arrears.

c. The preferred stock is cumulative and has a liquidation preference of $102 per share plus dividends in arrears. Dividends are three years in arrears.

ALTERNATE EXERCISES

DIVIDEND DISTRIBUTION
— OBJ. 3 —

12-19A Bower Corporation has outstanding 15,000 shares of $50 par value, 8% preferred stock and 50,000 shares of $5 par value common stock. During its first three years in business, the firm declared no dividends in the first year, $280,000 of dividends in the second year, and $60,000 of dividends in the third year.

a. If the preferred stock is cumulative, determine the total amount of dividends paid to each class of stock in each of the three years.

b. If the preferred stock is noncumulative, determine the total amount of dividends paid to each class of stock in each of the three years.

CASH AND NONCASH STOCK
ISSUANCES
— OBJ. 4 —

12-20A Chavoy Corporation was organized in 1996. The company's charter authorizes 100,000 shares of $10 par value common stock. On August 1, 1996, the attorney who helped organize the corporation accepted 800 shares of Chavoy common stock as settlement for the services provided (the services were valued at $9,600). On August 15, 1996, Chavoy issued 5,000 common shares for $75,000 cash. On October 15, 1996, Chavoy issued 3,000 common shares to acquire a vacant land site appraised at $48,000. Prepare the general journal entries to record the stock issuances on August 1, August 15, and October 15.

STOCK SPLIT
— OBJ. 5 —

12-21A On September 1, 1996, Oxford Company has 250,000 shares of $15 par value common stock that are issued and outstanding. The general ledger shows the following account balances relating to the common stock:

Common Stock	$3,750,000
Paid-in Capital in Excess of Par Value	$2,250,000

On September 2, Oxford splits its stock 3 for 2 and reduces the par value to $10 per share.

a. How many shares of common stock are issued and outstanding immediately after the stock split?

b. What is the balance in the Common Stock account immediately after the stock split?

c. What is the likely reason that Oxford Company split its stock?

STOCK ISSUANCE AND TREASURY
STOCK
— OBJ. 4, 6 —

12-22A Diva, Inc., recorded certain capital stock transactions shown in the following respective journal entries: (1) issued common stock for $19 cash per share, (2) purchased some treasury shares at $22 per share, and (3) sold some of the treasury shares.

1. Cash	437,000	
Common Stock		46,000
Paid-in Capital in Excess of Par Value		391,000

2. Treasury Stock	77,000	
Cash		77,000

3. Cash	62,400	
Treasury Stock		52,800
Paid-in Capital from Treasury Stock		9,600

a. How many shares were originally issued?

b. What was the par value of the shares issued?

c. How many shares of treasury stock were acquired?

d. How many shares of treasury stock were sold?

e. At what price per share was the treasury stock sold?

DONATED CAPITAL
— OBJ. 6 —

12-23A Prepare the general journal entries (if required) to record the following 1996 transactions related to Flavin Company.

Aug. 10   The company received a parcel of land valued at $125,000 from the city. This gift is an incentive for Flavin to build a new plant in the city.

Aug. 12   The city confirmed that, as an additional incentive for Flavin, it will not levy any real estate taxes on the donated land for the next five years. Flavin estimates it will save $30,000 in real estate taxes over the five-year period.

Book Value per Share
— Obj. 7 —

12-24A The stockholders' equity section of Avalon Corporation's balance sheet appears as follows:

Paid-in Capital	
Common Stock, $1 Par Value, 600,000 shares	
authorized; 400,000 shares issued;	
20,000 shares in the treasury	$ 400,000
Additional Paid-in Capital	
In Excess of Par Value—Common Stock	3,200,000
From Treasury Stock	75,000
Donated Capital	220,000
Total Paid-in Capital	$3,895,000
Retained Earnings	623,800
	$4,518,800
Less: Treasury Stock (20,000 shares) at Cost	240,000
Total Stockholders' Equity	$4,278,800

Compute the book value per share of the common stock.

Alternate Problems

Dividend Distribution
— Obj. 3 —

12-25A Gardner Corporation began business on June 30, 1995. At that time, it issued 18,000 shares of $50 par value, 6%, cumulative preferred stock and 90,000 shares of $10 par value common stock. Through the end of 1997, there has been no change in the number of preferred and common shares outstanding.

Required

a. Assume that Gardner declared dividends of $63,000 in 1995, $0 in 1996, and $378,000 in 1997. Calculate the total dividends and the dividends per share paid to each class of stock in 1995, 1996, and 1997.

b. Assume that Gardner declared dividends of $0 in 1995, $108,000 in 1996, and $189,000 in 1997. Calculate the total dividends and the dividends per share paid to each class of stock in 1995, 1996, and 1997.

Stockholders' Equity: Transactions and Balance Sheet Presentation
— Obj. 4, 6 —

12-26A Beaker Corporation was organized on July 1, 1996, with an authorization of 50,000 shares of $4 no-par value preferred stock ($4 is the annual dividend) and 100,000 shares of $10 par value common stock. During July, the following transactions affecting stockholders' equity occurred:

July 1   Issued 31,000 shares of common stock at $17 cash per share.

     5   The local municipality donated a vacant building to the corporation as an inducement to operate the business in the community. The fair market value of the building was $500,000.

    12   Issued 3,500 shares of common stock in exchange for equipment with a fair market value of $63,000.

    15   Issued 5,000 shares of preferred stock for cash at $44 per share.

    31   Closed the $38,000 net income for July from the Income Summary account to Retained Earnings.

Required

a. Prepare general journal entries to record the foregoing transactions.

b. Prepare the stockholders' equity section of the balance sheet at July 31, 1996.

Stockholders' Equity: Transactions, Balance Sheet Presentation, and Book Value per Share
— Obj. 4, 6, 7 —

12-27A The stockholders' equity accounts of Scott Corporation at January 1, 1996, follow:

Common Stock, $5 Par Value, 350,000 shares authorized;	
150,000 shares issued and outstanding	$750,000
Paid-in Capital in Excess of Par Value	600,000
Retained Earnings	346,000

During 1996, the following transactions occurred:

Jan. 5   Issued 10,000 shares of common stock for $12 cash per share.

    18   Purchased 4,000 shares of common stock for the treasury at $14 cash per share.

Mar. 12   Sold one-fourth of the treasury shares acquired January 18 for $17 per share.

July 17   Sold 500 shares of the remaining treasury stock for $13 per share.

Oct.   1   Issued 5,000 shares of 8%, $25 par value preferred stock for $35 cash per share. These are the first preferred shares issued out of 50,000 authorized shares.

Oct. 20   Received building with an appraised value of $275,000 as a gift from the local government.

Dec. 31   Closed the net income of $72,500 from the Income Summary account to Retained Earnings.

REQUIRED

a. Set up T accounts for the stockholders' equity accounts at the beginning of the year and enter January 1 balances.

b. Prepare general journal entries to record the foregoing transactions and post to T accounts (set up any additional T accounts needed). Determine the ending balances for the stockholders' equity accounts.

c. Prepare the December 31, 1996, stockholders' equity section of the balance sheet.

d. Compute the book value per share of common stock at December 31, 1996. The liquidation preference of the preferred stock is $26 per share. No dividends were declared in 1996. The arrearage on the preferred stock is $2,500 at December 31, 1996.

STOCKHOLDERS' EQUITY: TRANSACTIONS AND BALANCE SHEET PRESENTATION — OBJ. 4, 5, 6 —

12-28A   The following is the stockholders' equity of Clipper Corporation at January 1, 1996:

8% Preferred Stock, $50 Par Value, 10,000 shares authorized; 7,000 shares issued and outstanding	$ 350,000
Common Stock, $20 Par Value, 50,000 shares authorized; 25,000 shares issued and outstanding	500,000
Paid-in Capital in Excess of Par Value—Preferred Stock	70,000
Paid-in Capital in Excess of Par Value—Common Stock	385,000
Retained Earnings	238,000
Total Stockholders' Equity	$1,543,000

The following transactions, among others, occurred during the year:

Jan. 15   Issued 1,000 shares of preferred stock for $62 cash per share.

      20   Issued 4,000 shares of common stock at $36 cash per share.

      31   Converted $20,000 face value of convertible bonds payable (book value = $18,500) to common stock. Each $1,000 bond converted to 25 shares of common stock.

Mar. 10   Received a vacant school building valued at $850,000 as a gift from the city. The company plans to remodel the building for additional office space.

May 18   Announced a 2-for-1 common stock split, reducing the par value of the common stock to $10 per share. The authorization was increased to 100,000 shares.

June 1   Acquired equipment with a fair market value of $40,000 in exchange for 2,000 shares of common stock.

Sept. 1   Purchased 2,500 shares of common stock for the treasury at $18 cash per share.

Oct. 12   Sold 900 treasury shares at $21 per share.

Dec. 22   Issued 500 shares of preferred stock for $59 cash per share.

      28   Sold 1,100 of the remaining treasury shares at $15 per share.

      31   Closed the Income Summary account, with net earnings of $85,000, to Retained Earnings.

REQUIRED

a. Set up T accounts for the stockholders' equity accounts at the beginning of the year and enter January 1 balances.

b. Prepare general journal entries for the given transactions and post them to the T accounts (set up any additional T accounts needed). Determine the ending balances for the stockholders' equity accounts.

c. Prepare the stockholders' equity section of the balance sheet at December 31, 1996.

STOCKHOLDERS' EQUITY: TRANSACTION DESCRIPTIONS FROM ACCOUNT DATA — OBJ. 4, 6 —

12-29A   The following T accounts contain keyed entries representing six transactions involving the stockholders' equity of Riverview, Inc.

CASH			
(1)	80,600	(4)	12,800
(2)	35,000		
(6)	6,080		

LAND			
(3)	93,000		
(5)	88,000		

PREFERRED STOCK, $50 PAR			
		(1)	65,000

PAID-IN CAPITAL IN EXCESS OF PAR VALUE—PREFERRED STOCK			
		(1)	15,600

COMMON STOCK, $10 PAR			
		(2)	35,000
		(3)	60,000

PAID-IN CAPITAL IN EXCESS OF PAR VALUE—COMMON STOCK			
		(3)	33,000

PAID-IN CAPITAL FROM TREASURY STOCK			
		(6)	960

DONATED CAPITAL			
		(5)	88,000

TREASURY STOCK			
(4)	(800 shares of common) 12,800	(6)	5,120

REQUIRED

Using this information, give detailed descriptions, including number of shares and price per share when applicable, for each of the six transactions.

BOOK VALUE PER SHARE
— OBJ. 7 —

12-30A Yambert, Inc., has the following stockholders' equity section in its balance sheet:

Paid-in Capital		
8% Preferred Stock, $50 Par Value, 15,000 shares authorized, issued, and outstanding	$750,000	
Common Stock, $1 Par Value, 800,000 shares authorized; 300,000 shares issued and outstanding	300,000	
Additional Paid-in Capital		
In Excess of Par Value—Preferred Stock	84,000	
In Excess of Par Value—Common Stock	720,000	
Donated Capital	56,000	$1,910,000
Retained Earnings		430,000
Total Stockholders' Equity		$2,340,000

REQUIRED

For each of the following independent cases, compute the book value per share for the preferred stock and the common stock.

a. The preferred stock is noncumulative and has a liquidation preference of $52 per share.
b. The preferred stock is cumulative and has a liquidation preference per share equal to par value plus dividends in arrears. No dividends are in arrears.
c. The preferred stock is cumulative and has a liquidation preference of $51 per share plus dividends in arrears. Dividends are two years in arrears.

CASES

BUSINESS
DECISION CASE

Brett Barr has operated Barr's Hardware very successfully as a sole proprietorship. He believes that the continued growth and success of his business depends on increasing its scale of operations, which requires additional working capital. He also wishes to relocate his store from its rented quarters to a new retail shopping area. After exploring several opportunities that would result in large personal debts, Barr incorporates his business, taking in as stockholders Dr. Alec Frost, who invests cash, and Elise Moore, a real estate developer who owns land and a suitable vacant building in the desired shopping area.

As an initial step, Barr and his attorney secure a corporate charter for Hardware City, Inc., authorizing it to issue 60,000 shares of $10 par value common stock. On June 1, 1996, the date of incorporation, the post-closing trial balance of Barr's Hardware is as follows:

	Debit	Credit
Cash	$ 2,500	
Accounts Receivable	12,200	
Allowance for Uncollectible Accounts		$ 100
Merchandise Inventory	195,000	
Store Equipment	70,000	
Accumulated Depreciation—Store Equipment		34,000
Accounts Payable		8,600
Note Payable (due two years hence)		30,000
B. Barr, Capital		207,000
	$279,700	$279,700

Other details of the agreement follow:

1. After a detailed review of the accounts of Barr's Hardware, the new stockholders agree that
   a. The allowance for uncollectible accounts should increase by $200.
   b. Because of damaged and obsolete goods, the merchandise inventory should be written down by $25,000.
   c. The store equipment will be recorded in the corporate accounts at its fair market value of $40,000 with no accumulated depreciation.
   d. The new corporation assumes at face value the recorded liabilities of the proprietorship.
2. Barr has agreed to accept shares in the new corporation at par value in exchange for his adjusted equity in the assets of the proprietorship. He will purchase for cash at par value any additional shares necessary to bring his total holdings to the next even 100 shares.
3. The total value of Moore's building and land is agreed to be $216,000, of which $30,000 is associated with the land. Moore has agreed to accept stock at $12 per share for her land and building.
4. In an effort to stimulate local business, the Business Development Commission of the local city government has deeded to the corporation, for a token fee of $100, a small strip of land that will provide better delivery access to the rear of Moore's building. The fair value of the parcel is $4,000.
5. Frost has agreed to purchase for cash 7,000 shares at $12 per share.
6. Legal and accounting costs of $7,500 associated with acquiring the corporate charter and issuing the stock are paid from corporate funds. (Treat these as the asset, Organization Costs.)

REQUIRED

a. As Barr's accountant, you must prepare a balance sheet for the new corporation reflecting the shares issued, the parcel of land received from the city, and payment of legal and accounting costs. *Hint:* You may wish to prepare a worksheet with the following headings:

	Barr's Hardware Trial Balance		Adjustments and Organizational Transactions		Hardware City, Inc. Trial Balance	
Accounts	**Dr.**	**Cr.**	**Dr.**	**Cr.**	**Dr.**	**Cr.**

Properly combining and extending the amounts in the first two pairs of columns provide amounts for the trial balance of Hardware City, Inc. When recording Barr's Hardware trial balance, leave extra lines for the several transactions that will affect the Cash and B. Barr, Capital accounts. Also leave extra lines when entering the Common Stock and Paid-in Capital in Excess of Par Value accounts on the worksheet. For purposes of review, you may wish to key your adjustments and transactions to the letters and numbers used in the problem data.

b. In contrast to what they contributed to the corporation, what specifically do Barr and Moore "own" after the incorporation?

c. From Barr's viewpoint, what are the advantages and disadvantages of incorporating the hardware store?

FINANCIAL ANALYSIS CASE Gillette Company, The Procter & Gamble Company, and Colgate-Palmolive Company are three firms in the personal care consumer products industry. During a recent year, the average return on common stockholders' equity for the personal care consumer products industry was 28.1%. In the same year, the relevant financial data for Gillette, Procter & Gamble, and Colgate-Palmolive were as follows (in millions):

	Gillette	Procter & Gamble	Colgate-Palmolive
Preferred stockholders' equity, beginning	$ 99.2	$1,969.0	$ 418.3
Preferred stockholders' equity, ending	99.0	1,942.0	414.3
Preferred dividends	4.7	102.0	21.6
Common stockholders' equity, beginning	1,397.2	5,472.0	2,201.5
Common stockholders' equity, ending	1,380.0	6,890.0	1,460.7
Net income	426.9	2,211.0	548.1

REQUIRED

a. Compute Gillette Company's return on common stockholders' equity.
b. Evaluate Gillette Company's return on common stockholders' equity by comparing it with the following:
1. The average for the personal care consumer products industry.
2. The return earned by The Procter & Gamble Company.
3. The return earned by Colgate-Palmolive Company.
4. The return earned by Gillette Company in the previous year (in the previous year, Gillette's net income was $513.4 million, preferred dividend requirements were $4.8 million, and average common stockholders' equity was $1,227.3 million).

ETHICS CASE

Colin Agee, chairperson of the board of directors and chief executive officer of Image, Inc., is pondering a recommendation to make to the firm's board of directors in response to actions taken by Sam Mecon. Mecon recently informed Agee and other board members that he (Mecon) had purchased 15% of the voting stock of Image at $12 per share and is considering an attempt to take control of the company. His effort to take control would include offering $16 per share to stockholders to induce them to sell shares to him. Mecon also indicated that he would abandon his takeover plans if the company would buy back his stock at a price 50% over its current market price of $13 per share.

Agee views the proposed takeover by Mecon as a hostile maneuver. Mecon has a reputation of identifying companies that are undervalued (that is, their underlying net assets are worth more than the price of the outstanding stock), buying enough stock to take control of such a company, replacing top management, and, on occasion, breaking up the company (that is, selling off the various divisions to the highest bidder). The process has proven profitable to Mecon and his financial backers. Stockholders of the companies taken over also benefited because Mecon paid them attractive prices to buy their stock.

Agee recognizes that Image is currently undervalued by the stock market but believes that eventually the company will significantly improve its financial performance to the long-run benefit of its stockholders.

REQUIRED

What are the ethical issues that Agee should consider in arriving at a recommendation to make to the board of directors regarding Mecon's offer to be "bought out" of his takeover plans?

GENERAL MILLS ANNUAL REPORT CASE

Refer to the annual report of General Mills, Inc., presented in Appendix K. Refer to the consolidated balance sheets, the consolidated statements of earnings, and Note 10.

REQUIRED

a. How many shares of common stock is General Mills authorized to issue? How many common shares are issued at May 29, 1994?
b. What is the par value of General Mills' common stock?
c. How many shares of preferred stock is General Mills authorized to issue? How many preferred shares are issued at May 29, 1994? Is the preferred stock cumulative or noncumulative?
d. How many treasury shares did General Mills purchase on the open market in the 1994 fiscal year? What did General Mills pay to purchase these shares? How many common shares are in the treasury at May 29, 1994?
e. What is General Mills' return on common stockholders' equity for the 1994 fiscal year?

Corporations: Dividends, Retained Earnings, and Earnings Disclosure

CHAPTER LEARNING OBJECTIVES

1 **IDENTIFY** and **DISTINGUISH** between cash dividends and stock dividends (pp. 436–439).

2 **ILLUSTRATE** a retained earnings statement and a statement of stockholders' equity (pp. 439–440).

3 **DISCUSS** the accounting for prior period adjustments, changes in accounting estimates, and the process of restricting retained earnings (pp. 440–442).

4 **IDENTIFY** and **DISCUSS** the content and format of the income statement (pp. 442–448).

5 **IDENTIFY** and **ILLUSTRATE** the computation and disclosure of earnings per share (pp. 448–451).

6 Financial Analysis **DEFINE** *dividend yield* and *dividend payout ratio* and **EXPLAIN** their use (pp. 451–452).

CHAPTER FOCUS

A few years ago, General Motors Corporation reported a net loss of $23.5 billion. A major factor in this loss was a $20.9 billion charge resulting from a change in the accounting principle dealing with postretirement benefits other than pensions. This loss created a debit balance in the corporation's Retained Earnings account; a debit balance in a Retained Earnings account is called a **deficit**. Despite this, General Motors continued to pay over $1 billion of cash dividends to its stockholders.

The preceding events all relate to a corporation's retained earnings. **Retained earnings** represents the stockholders' equity arising from a corporation's retention of assets generated from profit-directed activities. Net income increases retained earnings; net loss and dividends decrease retained earnings. Because net income (or profit) plays a significant role in the functioning of economic activity in the United States, data reported in the income statement are usually considered the most important financial information presented by corporations. Because of the importance of income data, accountants have developed several guidelines for their disclosure. In this chapter, we discuss the accounting guidelines for retained earnings, dividends, and the reporting of information (including changes in accounting principles) in the income statement.

DIVIDENDS

OBJECTIVE *1*
IDENTIFY and **DISTINGUISH** between cash dividends and stock dividends.

Dividends are distributions of assets or stock from a corporation to its stockholders. A corporation can distribute dividends to shareholders only after its board of directors has formally declared a distribution. Dividends are usually paid in cash but may also be property or additional shares of stock in the firm. Legally, declared dividends are an obligation of the firm, and an entry to record the dividend obligation is made on the *declaration date*. Cash and property dividends payable are carried as liabilities, and stock dividends to be issued are shown in the stockholders' equity section of the balance sheet. At the declaration, a *record date* and *payment date* are established. For example, on April 25 (declaration date), the board of directors might declare a dividend payable June 1 (payment date) to those who own stock on May 15 (record date). Stockholders owning stock on the record date receive the dividend even if they dispose of their shares before the payment date. Therefore, shares sold between the record date and payment date are sold *ex-dividend* (without right to the dividend).

Most dividend declarations reduce retained earnings; under certain conditions, however, state laws may permit distributions from paid-in capital. Shareholders should be informed of the source of such dividends, because, in a sense, they are a return of capital rather than a distribution of earnings.

CASH DIVIDENDS

The majority of dividends distributed by corporations are paid in cash. Although companies may pay such dividends annually, many large firms pay quarterly dividends. The Quaker Oats Company and PepsiCo, Inc., for example, usually pay quarterly dividends. Some companies occasionally pay an extra dividend at year-end. Usually this is done when the company wishes to increase the total annual distribution without departing from a standard quarterly amount that was established by custom or announced in advance.

In declaring cash dividends, a company must have both an appropriate amount of retained earnings and the necessary amount of cash. Uninformed investors often believe that a large Retained Earnings balance automatically permits generous dividend distributions. A company, however, may successfully accumulate earnings and at the same time not be sufficiently liquid to pay large dividends. Many companies, especially new firms in growth industries, finance their expansion from assets generated through earnings and pay out small cash dividends or none at all.

Cash dividends are based on the number of shares of stock outstanding. When a company's directors declare a cash dividend, an entry is made debiting Cash Dividends and crediting Dividends Payable. Assume, for example, that a company has outstanding 1,000 shares of $100 par value, 6% preferred stock and 6,000 shares of $10 par value common stock. If the company declares the regular $6 dividend on the preferred stock and a $2 dividend on the common stock, the dividend payment totals $18,000. The following entry is made at the declaration date:

Cash Dividends	18,000	
Dividends Payable—Preferred Stock		6,000
Dividends Payable—Common Stock		12,000
To record declaration of $6 dividend on preferred stock and $2 dividend on common stock.		

The Cash Dividends account is a temporary account that is closed to Retained Earnings at year-end.[1] Dividends Payable—Preferred Stock and Dividends Payable—Common Stock are reported as current liabilities on the balance sheet. On the dividend payment date, the following entry is made:

Dividends Payable—Preferred Stock	6,000	
Dividends Payable—Common Stock	12,000	
Cash		18,000
To record payment of dividends on preferred and common stocks.		

POINT OF INTEREST

DIVIDEND REINVESTMENT PLANS

Most large corporations have dividend reinvestment plans that permit shareholders to use their cash dividends to purchase additional shares of stock directly from the company. These plans are attractive to shareholders because the companies charge little or no commission and may offer a small discount off the stock's current market price. Corporations obtain the stock for participants either by issuing new shares of stock or by buying outstanding stock on the open market. If new shares of stock are issued, the dividend reinvestment plan serves as a low-cost way for the corporation to raise equity capital. If shares are purchased on the open market, the corporation benefits because the frequent reinvestment plan purchases provide market support for the stock's price.

STOCK DIVIDENDS

Companies frequently distribute shares of their own stock as dividends to shareholders in lieu of, or in addition to, cash dividends. A company may issue **stock dividends** when it does not wish to deplete its working capital by paying a cash dividend. Young and growing companies often issue stock dividends, because cash is usually needed to acquire new facilities and to expand. The use of stock dividends is by no means confined to such companies, however.

The accounting for a stock dividend results in a transfer of a portion of retained earnings to the paid-in capital accounts. Thus, distribution of a stock dividend signals management's desire to "plow back" earnings into the company. Although stock dividends may take a number of forms, usually common shares are distributed to common shareholders. We limit our discussion to this type of distribution.

SMALL STOCK DIVIDENDS

Small stock dividends are dividends in which the additional shares issued are fewer than 20–25% of the number previously outstanding. These stock dividends are *recorded at the market value* of the shares involved, causing retained earnings to decrease and paid-in capital to increase by this amount. In some respects, the issuance of new shares in the form of

---

[1]Some companies, especially those paying dividends annually, debit Retained Earnings directly on the dividend declaration date.

a dividend can be viewed as a transaction that avoids the test of the marketplace. If the shareholders receive cash and immediately purchase additional shares of the firm's stock, the purchases are made at market value. Thus, the number of shares issued in exchange for a given amount of retained earnings should be related to the market value of the shares.

To illustrate the entries reflecting a declaration of a small stock dividend, we assume that the stockholders' equity of a company is as follows before declaration of a 10% stock dividend:

Common Stock, $5 Par Value, 20,000 shares issued and outstanding	$100,000
Paid-in Capital in Excess of Par Value	20,000
Total Paid-in Capital	$120,000
Retained Earnings	65,000
Total Stockholders' Equity	$185,000

With 20,000 shares outstanding, declaration of a 10% stock dividend requires the issuance of an additional 2,000 shares. Let us assume that the market price per share is $11. The total market value of the shares to be distributed is $22,000, resulting in the following entry:

Stock Dividends	22,000	
Stock Dividend Distributable		10,000
Paid-in Capital in Excess of Par Value		12,000
To record declaration of 10% stock dividend on common shares.		

The amount of the credit to Stock Dividend Distributable is the par value of the shares to be distributed. If a balance sheet is prepared between the declaration date and the distribution date of a stock dividend, the Stock Dividend Distributable account is shown in stockholders' equity immediately after the Common Stock account. When the stock is distributed, the following entry is made:

Stock Dividend Distributable	10,000	
Common Stock		10,000
To record issuance of stock dividend on common shares.		

The Stock Dividends account is a temporary account that is closed to Retained Earnings at year-end, as shown by the following entry:

Retained Earnings	22,000	
Stock Dividends		22,000
To close the Stock Dividends account.		

After the stock is distributed and the Stock Dividends account is closed, a comparison of the stockholders' equity and outstanding shares before and after the stock dividend appears below. Note that retained earnings decreased $22,000 and paid-in capital increased $22,000, but total stockholders' equity did not change.

	Before Stock Dividend	After Stock Dividend
Common Stock, $5 Par Value	$100,000	$110,000
Paid-in Capital in Excess of Par Value	20,000	32,000
Total Paid-in Capital	$120,000	$142,000
Retained Earnings	65,000	43,000
Total Stockholders' Equity	$185,000	$185,000
Common shares issued and outstanding	20,000	22,000

The relative position of a common shareholder is not altered by the receipt of a common stock dividend. If a 10% stock dividend is distributed, all shareholders increase their proportionate holdings by 10%, and the total stock outstanding is increased in the same proportion. No income is realized by the shareholders. If the stock dividend distributed is not large in relation to the outstanding shares, little or no change may occur in the market value of the stock. If the market value does not decrease and the company continues the same cash dividends per share, shareholders have benefited by the distribution.

LARGE STOCK DIVIDENDS

When the number of shares issued as a stock dividend is large enough to reduce materially the per-share market value, the shareholders may not perceive the same benefits as they do for small stock dividends. Accordingly, the accounting analysis is different for large stock dividends (those over 20–25%). The journal entry to record the declaration of a large stock dividend debits Stock Dividends and credits Stock Dividend Distributable for the *minimum increase in paid-in capital required by law for the issuance of new shares.* Usually this amount is the par or stated value of the stock. Once the stock is issued, the increase in paid-in capital is reflected in the Common Stock account.[2]

RETAINED EARNINGS STATEMENT

OBJECTIVE *2*

ILLUSTRATE a retained earnings statement and a statement of stockholders' equity.

A **retained earnings statement** presents an analysis of the Retained Earnings account for the accounting period. An example of a retained earnings statement is shown in Exhibit 13-1. The statement begins with the retained earnings balance at the beginning of the period **1**, then shows the items that caused retained earnings to change during the period **2**, and ends with the period-end retained earnings balance **3**.

EXHIBIT 13–1	Retained Earnings Statement

GEYSER CORPORATION
RETAINED EARNINGS STATEMENT
FOR THE YEAR ENDED DECEMBER 31, 1996

1 Retained Earnings, January 1, 1996		$48,000
2 Add: Net Income		32,000
		$80,000
Less: Cash Dividends Declared		19,000
3 Retained Earnings, December 31, 1996		$61,000

STATEMENT OF STOCKHOLDERS' EQUITY

Rather than reporting a retained earnings statement, corporations often integrate information about retained earnings into a more comprehensive statement called a **statement of stockholders' equity.** This statement shows an analysis of all components of stockholders' equity for the accounting period. Exhibit 13-2 presents an example of a statement of stockholders' equity. The statement begins with the beginning balances of the various stockholders' equity components **1**, reports the items causing changes in these components **2**, and ends with the period-end balances **3**.

---

[2]A large stock dividend is similar in many respects to a stock split (discussed in the preceding chapter). A stock's par or stated value per share is not changed by a stock dividend; however, a stock split reduces the par or stated value in proportion to the increase in shares of stock. This difference leads to a difference in analysis—only a memorandum entry is made for a stock split, whereas a large stock dividend requires a journal entry to transfer the legal capital of shares to be issued from retained earnings to paid-in capital.

EXHIBIT 13–2   Statement of Stockholders' Equity

GEYSER CORPORATION
STATEMENT OF STOCKHOLDERS' EQUITY
FOR THE YEAR ENDED DECEMBER 31, 1996

	Common Stock	Paid-in Capital in Excess of Par Value	Paid-in Capital from Treasury Stock	Retained Earnings	Treasury Stock	Total
1 Balance, January 1, 1996	$200,000	$120,000	$18,000	$48,000	($14,000)	$372,000
6,000 Common Shares Issued	30,000	24,000				54,000
500 Treasury Shares Issued			2,000		3,500	5,500
2 Net Income				32,000		32,000
Cash Dividends Declared				(19,000)		(19,000)
200 Treasury Shares Acquired					(2,000)	(2,000)
3 Balance, December 31, 1996	$230,000	$144,000	$20,000	$61,000	($12,500)	$442,500

The statement of stockholders' equity in Exhibit 13-2 reveals all of the events affecting the corporation's stockholders' equity during 1996. These events are the issuance of common stock, the issuance of treasury stock, the earning of net income, the declaration of cash dividends, and the acquisition of treasury stock. Note that the information in the Retained Earnings column contains the same information as a retained earnings statement.

PRIOR PERIOD ADJUSTMENTS

OBJECTIVE 3

DISCUSS the accounting for prior period adjustments, changes in accounting estimates, and the process of restricting retained earnings.

Essentially, **prior period adjustments** correct errors made in financial statements of prior periods. Errors may result from mathematical mistakes, oversights, incorrect applications of accounting principles, or improper analyses of existing facts when the financial statements are prepared.

Prior period adjustments are not included in the current year's income statement. Instead, corrections of material errors of past periods are taken directly to Retained Earnings and are reported as adjustments to the beginning balance of Retained Earnings in the current year's retained earnings statement or statement of stockholders' equity. The prior period adjustment should be shown net of any related income tax effects.

For example, assume that Geyser Corporation discovered in 1997 that it charged $10,000 of equipment installation costs on December 31, 1996, to Repairs Expense rather than capitalizing it to the Equipment account. Assuming a 40% income tax rate, 1996 net income was understated by $6,000 (Repairs Expense was overstated $10,000 and Income Tax Expense was understated $4,000.) Because of this error, the company owes another $4,000 of income taxes for 1996. The journal entry in 1997 to correct for the 1996 error is as follows:

Equipment	10,000	
Retained Earnings		6,000
Income Tax Payable		4,000

To correct for error in recording 1996 equipment installation costs.

The company reports the $6,000 prior period adjustment in the 1997 retained earnings statement, as follows:

Retained Earnings, January 1, 1997	$61,000
Add: Correction of Prior Period Equipment Error (net of $4,000 income taxes)	6,000
Adjusted Balance, January 1, 1997	$67,000

ACCOUNTING PERIOD CONCEPT

The treatment of prior period adjustments illustrates the application of the *accounting period concept*. This basic principle of accounting notes that it is possible to segment the continuous economic life of an entity into arbitrary time periods for reporting purposes. Under such a concept, the current period income statement should not contain the effects of an error correction that relates to a prior period income statement. The prior period income statement impact is taken to Retained Earnings because the temporary account balances for all prior periods have been closed to Retained Earnings. Should the prior period income statement be reissued, the specific mistakes it originally contained are corrected.

CHANGES IN ACCOUNTING ESTIMATES

Estimates play an integral part in accounting. In preparing periodic financial statements, we estimate the effects of transactions continuing in the future. For example, we must estimate uncollectible accounts, useful lives of plant and intangible assets, salvage values of plant assets, and product warranty costs. As a normal consequence of such estimates, new information, changed conditions, or more experience may require the revision of previous estimates.

It is important to distinguish a change in accounting estimate from a prior period adjustment because the accounting treatment differs between the two items. The effect of a **change in accounting estimate** should be reflected in the income statements of *current and future periods* to the extent appropriate in each case. The estimated amounts reported in prior period financial statements are not changed. Presumably, the previous estimates were the best possible, given the information then available.

The total impact of some changes in estimates is included in the current year income statement. A revision of an estimated liability recorded in prior periods is one example. Assume that unanticipated cost increases have caused a company to underestimate its liability for product warranty carried into the current year by $900. The estimated liability is revised as follows:

Product Warranty Expense	900	
Estimated Liability for Product Warranty		900
To record change in estimated warranty liability.		

An estimate revision may affect both the period of change and future periods. If so, the effect of the revision should be accounted for over the current and future periods. The revision of depreciation discussed earlier, in the chapter on depreciation methods, illustrates this type of change.

RESTRICTIONS ON RETAINED EARNINGS

Portions of retained earnings are often *restricted* (or *appropriated*), so that these amounts are not available for the declaration of dividends. To the extent that dividends are not declared and paid, assets are kept within the corporation. **Retained earnings restrictions** are usually disclosed in a note to the financial statements and may be voluntary, contractual, or statutory.

Voluntary restrictions are restrictions placed on retained earnings by the board of directors for particular corporate objectives. The board of directors may want to have corporate funds available, for example, to enlarge a plant or to settle a pending lawsuit. By restricting retained earnings, assets needed for these purposes will not be distributed as dividends.

Note, however, that restricting retained earnings for a particular objective restricts only dividend amounts. The restriction does not ensure that specific funds will be available for the stated objective. A company may have a large retained earnings balance without having an ample amount of liquid assets. It is management's responsibility to see that the right kind of assets are available when needed.

Contractual restrictions result from certain types of contracts entered into by a corporation. When a company issues long-term debt, for example, the debt agreement may limit the amount of dividends the company may pay until the debt is settled. This restriction helps protect the availability of the company's working capital for debt payment purposes.

Statutory restrictions are retained earnings restrictions imposed by law. In the previous chapter, we mentioned a statutory restriction in connection with treasury stock purchases: many states require that retained earnings be restricted in an amount equal to the cost of treasury stock purchased by the corporation. This restriction prevents a corporation from distributing assets to stockholders through a combination of dividends and treasury stock purchases that exceeds the retained earnings balance. This restriction, therefore, protects creditors by limiting the assets that may be distributed to owners.

POINT OF INTEREST

EXAMPLE OF RETAINED EARNINGS RESTRICTION

The following financial statement note from an annual report of Donnelly Corporation illustrates the disclosure of a contractual restriction on retained earnings. Donnelly Corporation manufactures automotive mirrors, automotive window systems, and solid-glass coatings for electronics products.

> The various borrowings subject the Company to certain restrictions relating to, among other things, minimum net worth, payment of dividends and maintenance of certain financial ratios. Retained earnings available for dividends at July 2, 1994, are $17.4 million.

Donnelly Corporation's total retained earnings at July 2, 1994, was $49.4 million. Thus, $32 million of retained earnings were not available for dividends.

CONTENT AND FORMAT OF THE INCOME STATEMENT

OBJECTIVE 4
IDENTIFY and **DISCUSS** the content and format of the income statement.

Accountants believe that the income statement is more useful when certain types of transactions and events are reported in separate sections. For this reason, information about extraordinary items, discontinued operations, and effects of changes in accounting principles are disclosed separately in an income statement. Segregating these categories of information from the results of ordinary, continuing operations should make it easier for financial statement users to estimate the future earnings performance of the company.

The creation of several sections in the income statement, however, complicates the reporting of income tax expense. Items affecting the overall amount of income tax expense may appear in more than one section. If this is the case, accountants allocate the income tax expense among those sections of the statement in which the items affecting the tax expense appear.

The income statement's usefulness is also enhanced if it contains information on earnings per share. Accordingly, earnings per share is reported in the income statement immediately after the net income amount.

We now examine these areas in more detail.

TAX ALLOCATION WITHIN A PERIOD

The process of allocating a period's total income tax expense to different sections of an income statement is known as **tax allocation within a period.** This process is necessary when items affecting the income tax amount appear in different income statement sections.

To illustrate, assume that a company will be preparing an income statement with two sections, one section reporting income from ordinary, continuing operations ($100,000 before income taxes) and a second section reporting an extraordinary gain of $20,000 (extraordinary items will be discussed presently). Using a 40% income tax rate, the total income tax expense for the period is $48,000 (40% × $120,000). The $48,000 will be allocated to the two sections of the income statement as shown in the following schedule.

Income Statement Section	Taxable Amount in Section	Income Tax Allocated to Section
Ordinary, continuing operations	$100,000	$40,000
Extraordinary items	20,000	8,000

Now assume that the company had a $30,000 extraordinary loss rather than a $20,000 extraordinary gain. Combining the $30,000 loss with the $100,000 income before income taxes from ordinary, continuing operations gives a total of $70,000 subject to income tax. With a 40% income tax rate, total income tax expense for the period is $28,000 (40% × $70,000). Because the $30,000 extraordinary loss caused a reduction in income taxes, the total tax expense of $28,000 allocated to the two income statement sections consists of a tax expense of $40,000 and a tax reduction of $12,000, as shown in the following schedule.

Income Statement Section	Taxable Amount or (Loss) in Section	Income Tax or (Tax Reduction) Allocated to Section
Ordinary, continuing operations	$100,000	$40,000
Extraordinary items	(30,000)	(12,000)

When tax allocation within a period is used, the income tax amount reported in an income statement section relates only to the revenues, expenses, gains, or losses included in that section. Thus, the income statement section presents a normal relationship between income taxes and the items in that section affecting the tax calculation. Later chapter exhibits will illustrate the income statement presentation of tax allocation within a period.

SECTIONS OF THE INCOME STATEMENT

ORDINARY, CONTINUING OPERATIONS

The first section (and many times the only section) of an income statement presents information on the period's *ordinary, continuing operations*. Either one of two basic formats may be used to report this information: a multiple-step format and a single-step format. Both the multiple-step and single-step formats are acceptable.

MULTIPLE-STEP FORMAT

A **multiple-step income statement** derives one or more intermediate amounts before the final amount for ordinary, continuing income is reported. Examples of intermediate amounts that may be derived are Gross Profit on Sales and Income before Taxes. The following is a brief illustration of a multiple-step income statement:

Sales		$260,000
Cost of Goods Sold		150,000
Gross Profit on Sales		$110,000
Selling Expenses	$32,000	
Administrative Expenses	43,000	75,000
Income before Taxes		$ 35,000
Income Tax Expense		14,000
Net Income		$ 21,000

SINGLE-STEP FORMAT

A **single-step income statement** derives the ordinary, continuing income of the business in one step—by subtracting total expenses from total revenues. A brief single-step income statement follows:

Sales		$260,000
Expenses		
Cost of Goods Sold	$150,000	
Selling Expenses	32,000	
Administrative Expenses	43,000	
Income Tax Expense	14,000	
Total Expenses		239,000
Net Income		$ 21,000

DISCONTINUED OPERATIONS

When a company sells, abandons, or otherwise disposes of a segment of its operations, a **discontinued operations** section of the income statement reports information about the discontinued segment. The discontinued operations section presents two categories of information:

1. The income or loss from the segment's operations for the portion of the year before its discontinuance.
2. The gain or loss from the disposal of the segment.

The section is placed immediately after information about ordinary, continuing operations.

A *segment* of a business is a unit—such as a department or a division—whose activities constitute a separate major line of business or serve a particular class of customer. The assets and operating results of the segment must be clearly distinguishable from the rest of the company. For example, a furniture manufacturing division of a diversified manufacturing company is a segment of the business.

To illustrate the reporting of discontinued operations, we assume that on July 1, 1996, Pacific Corporation sold its Division Y. Exhibit 13-3 illustrates the income statement for Pacific Corporation, including the information about Division Y in the discontinued operations section. From January 1 through June 30, Division Y had operated at a loss, net of taxes, of $24,000 ($40,000 operating loss less a $16,000 reduction in income taxes caused by the operating loss) **1**. The loss, net of taxes, from the sale of the division was $60,000 ($100,000 loss on the sale less a $40,000 reduction in income taxes caused by the loss) **2**. Note that when there is a discontinued operations section, the difference between the ordinary revenues and expenses is labeled Income from Continuing Operations.

EXTRAORDINARY ITEMS

Extraordinary items are transactions and events that are both *unusual in nature* and *occur infrequently.*[3] An item that is unusual in nature is highly abnormal and significantly different from the firm's ordinary and typical activities. To determine a firm's ordinary and typical activities, we must consider such things as the types of operations, lines of business, operating policies, and the environment in which the firm operates. The operating environment includes the characteristics of the industry, the geographic location of the firm's facilities, and the type of government regulations imposed. A transaction or event is considered to occur infrequently if the firm does not expect it to recur in the foreseeable future.

---

[3]*Opinions of the Accounting Principles Board, No. 30,* "Reporting the Results of Operations—Reporting the Effects of Disposal of a Segment of a Business, and Extraordinary, Unusual and Infrequently Occurring Events and Transactions" (New York: American Institute of Certified Public Accountants, 1973).

| EXHIBIT 13–3 | Income Statement Showing Discontinued Operations |

PACIFIC CORPORATION
INCOME STATEMENT
FOR THE YEAR ENDED DECEMBER 31, 1996

Sales		$700,000
Cost of Goods Sold		360,000
Gross Profit on Sales		$340,000
Selling Expenses	$75,000	
Administrative Expenses	45,000	120,000
Income from Continuing Operations before Taxes		$220,000
Income Tax Expense		88,000
Income from Continuing Operations		$132,000
Discontinued Operations		
1 Loss from Operations of Discontinued Division Y (net of $16,000 reduction of income taxes)	$24,000	
2 Loss on Disposal of Division Y (net of $40,000 reduction of income taxes)	60,000	84,000
Net Income		$ 48,000
Earnings per Common Share		
Income from Continuing Operations		$3.30
Discontinued Operations		(2.10)
Net Income		$1.20

The fact that the two criteria—unusual nature and infrequent occurrence—must *both* be present considerably restricts the events and transactions that qualify as extraordinary items. For example, suppose a tobacco grower suffers crop loss from a flood, which normally happens every few years in this area. The history of floods creates a reasonable expectation that another flood will occur in the foreseeable future. The loss, therefore, does not meet the criteria for an extraordinary item. Now consider a different tobacco grower who suffers flood damage to his crop for the first time from a broken dam. The dam is repaired and is not expected to fail in the foreseeable future. The flood loss in this circumstance is an extraordinary item.

Other events that may generate extraordinary losses are earthquakes (but see the next Point of Interest), expropriations of property, and prohibitions under newly enacted laws (such as a government ban on a product currently marketed). An extraordinary gain may result from a nonrecurring sale of an asset never used in operations. Assume that a manufacturing company acquired land several years ago for future use but then changed its plans and held the land for appreciation. If this is the only undeveloped land the company owns and it will not speculate in land in the foreseeable future, any gain from the sale of the land is considered extraordinary.

One exception to the criteria defining extraordinary items relates to gains and losses incurred when a company extinguishes its own debt. These gains and losses are aggregated and, if material, are classified as extraordinary items.[4] An example of a debt extinguishment loss was presented in the chapter on long-term liabilities.

Extraordinary gains and losses are reported in a separate income statement section following the sections on ordinary, continuing operations and discontinued operations (if

---

[4]*Statement of Financial Accounting Standards No. 4,* "Reporting Gains and Losses from Extinguishment of Debt" (Norwalk, CT: Financial Accounting Standards Board, 1975).

present). Exhibit 13-4 is an income statement for a corporation with an extraordinary item. During 1996, Atlantic Corporation, a manufacturing concern, sold a block of common stock of Z Company, a publicly traded company, at a gain of $80,000. The shares of stock were the only security investment the company had ever owned, and it does not plan to acquire other stocks in the foreseeable future. For Atlantic Corporation, this gain is unusual, infrequent, and properly considered an extraordinary item. The gain is reported net of $32,000 of income taxes on the gain, as shown in Exhibit 13-4 **1**.

EXHIBIT 13–4	Income Statement Showing Extraordinary Item, Unusual or Nonrecurring Item, and Change in Accounting Principle

ATLANTIC CORPORATION
INCOME STATEMENT
FOR THE YEAR ENDED DECEMBER 31, 1996

Sales		$1,900,000
Expenses		
Cost of Goods Sold	$1,100,000	
Selling Expenses	195,000	
Administrative Expenses	160,000	
2 Loss from Plant Strike	45,000	
Income Tax Expense	160,000	
Total Expenses		1,660,000
Income before Extraordinary Item and Cumulative Effect of a Change in Accounting Principle		$ 240,000
1 Extraordinary Item		
Gain from Sale of Z Company Stock (net of $32,000 income taxes)		48,000
3 Cumulative Effect on Prior Years of Changing to a Different Depreciation Method (net of $8,000 income taxes)		12,000
Net Income		$ 300,000
Earnings per Common Share		
Income before Extraordinary Item and Cumulative Effect of a Change in Accounting Principle		$2.00
Extraordinary Gain		.40
Cumulative Effect on Prior Years of Changing to a Different Depreciation Method		.10
Net Income		$2.50

UNUSUAL OR NONRECURRING ITEMS

Events and transactions that are unusual *or* nonrecurring, but not both, are not extraordinary items. Accounting guidelines note several examples of gains and losses that are not extraordinary either because they are typical or because they may recur as a result of continuing business activities.[5] Examples of such items are gains and losses from (1) the writedown or write-off of receivables, inventories, and intangible assets; (2) the exchange or translation of foreign currencies; (3) the sale or abandonment of property, plant, or equipment used in the business; (4) the effects of a strike; and (5) the adjustments of long-term

---

[5]*Opinions of the Accounting Principles Board, No. 30.*

contract accruals. An unusual or infrequently occurring item of a material amount should be reported as a separate component of income from ordinary, continuing operations.

Assume that during 1996, Atlantic Corporation incurred a $45,000 loss because of a labor strike at one of its plants. The strike was not part of the company's ordinary activities, but Atlantic Corporation has a history of labor difficulties. Therefore, even though the strike loss was unusual, it was not infrequent because it will likely happen again in the foreseeable future. Because it did not qualify as an extraordinary item, the before-tax amount of the strike loss was reported as a separate item among the ordinary expenses, as shown in Exhibit 13-4 **2**.

POINT OF INTEREST

EARTHQUAKE LOSS FOR DAYTON HUDSON

Dayton Hudson Corporation is a large general merchandise retailer with several chains of department and discount stores. In January 1994, the firm suffered earthquake damage at 11 Target stores and 13 Mervyn's stores in the Los Angeles area. The uninsured earthquake loss totaled $22 million. Dayton Hudson reported the loss as an unusual item in its financial statements. Given the frequency of earthquakes in the Los Angeles area, the earthquake loss did not qualify for classification as an extraordinary item.

CHANGES IN ACCOUNTING PRINCIPLES

Occasionally a company may implement a **change in accounting principle**—that is, switch from one generally accepted method to another.[6] Examples include a change in inventory pricing method—such as from FIFO to weighted average—or a change in depreciation method—such as from double declining balance to straight line.

A fundamental issue in accounting for changes in accounting principles is whether financial statements of prior years (issued in comparative form with the current year statements) should be restated using the new principle. Basically, the answer to this question is no. Concern over the possible dilution of public confidence in financial statements if previously reported statements are changed every time there is change in accounting principle led to this conclusion.

Instead of restating prior year statements, almost all changes in accounting principles introduce a new item into the income statement—the **cumulative effect of a change in principle.** This item represents the total difference in the cumulative income for all prior years had the new principle been used in those years. It is equal to the difference between (1) the retained earnings at the beginning of the year and (2) the retained earnings amount at the beginning of the year had the new principle been used in all years in which the previous principle was followed for the items in question. The cumulative effect is disclosed immediately before the net income figure.

To illustrate the reporting of the cumulative effect of a change in principle, we assume that Atlantic Corporation in Exhibit 13-4 changed its method of depreciating plant equipment in 1996, switching from an accelerated method to the straight-line method. Cumulative income before income taxes for years prior to 1996 would have been $20,000 higher if the straight-line method had been used to depreciate the plant equipment in those years. If we assume an income tax rate of 40%, the $12,000 after-tax amount of the effect of the change in principle would be reported on Atlantic Corporation's income statement as shown in Exhibit 13-4 **3**.

In addition to reporting the cumulative effect, the company should, in a note to the financial statements, justify the change and disclose the effect of the change on the current year income exclusive of the cumulative adjustment. The effect of the change on earnings per share should also be reported.

---

[6]The phrase *generally accepted accounting principles* covers a wide spectrum of accounting guidelines, ranging from basic standards to specific methods. In accounting principle changes, the focus is on changes in specific methods.

Annual financial reports often include financial statements for prior periods for comparative purposes. As noted, these prior period statements are not revised to reflect the new principle adopted this period. For each period reported, however, the net income and the related earnings per share are recomputed as if the new principle had been in effect in that period. Each period's income statement will disclose these recomputed amounts.[7]

CONSISTENCY PRINCIPLE

The *consistency principle* states that, unless otherwise disclosed, financial statements use the same accounting methods from one period to the next. Consistent use of accounting methods enhances the comparability of financial data through time. This basic principle of consistency impacts the accounting for changes in accounting principles in several ways. First, to change an accounting principle, a company must be able to justify that the results under the new principle are preferable. Second, a company must disclose the financial impact and justification for a principle change. Third, even though prior years financial statements are not restated using the new principle, selected financial information (net income and earnings per share) is reported on a consistent basis.

EARNINGS PER SHARE

OBJECTIVE 5

IDENTIFY and **ILLUSTRATE** the computation and disclosure of earnings per share.

A financial statistic of great interest to corporation shareholders and potential investors is the **earnings per share (EPS)** of common stock. Consequently, earnings per share data are widely disseminated, reaching interested persons through such channels as annual stockholder reports, financial newspapers, and financial statistical services. Because this financial information is so important, accounting guidelines require the disclosure of earnings per share data on the income statement.

Earnings per share is computed by dividing the earnings available to common stockholders by the weighted average number of common shares outstanding during the year. The earnings available to common stockholders is the net income less any preferred stock dividend. Thus, the earnings per share computation is as follows:

$$\text{Earnings per Share} = \frac{\text{Net Income} - \text{Preferred Dividends}}{\text{Weighted Average Common Shares Outstanding}}$$

SIMPLE CAPITAL STRUCTURE

In determining the presentation of earnings per share data, accountants distinguish between corporations with simple capital structures and those with complex capital structures. An entity with a **simple capital structure** has no securities outstanding (or agreements to issue securities) that have the potential to dilute (reduce) earnings per share. For example, corporations whose capital structures consist only of common stock or common stock and preferred stock that cannot be converted into common stock have simple capital structures.

A corporation with a simple capital structure computes and presents one earnings per share number. The computation utilizes actual data only (as we shall see shortly, complex capital structure computations incorporate assumed data). To illustrate the calculation for a firm with a simple capital structure, suppose that Owens Corporation had a 1996 net income of $39,000. On January 1, 1996, 10,000 shares of common stock were outstanding. An additional 6,000 common shares were issued on July 1, 1996. The company has no preferred stock.

Because Owens Corporation has no preferred stock, the numerator for the earnings per share calculation will be the $39,000 net income. The computation of average shares out-

---

[7]If the change in accounting principle is mandated by the Financial Accounting Standards Board, this disclosure may not be required (and may even be prohibited).

standing weights the common shares by the length of time they were outstanding. The 1996 weighted average common shares outstanding for Owens Corporation is 13,000, computed as follows:

Shares		Months Outstanding		Share Months
10,000	×	6	=	60,000
16,000	×	6	=	96,000
		12		156,000

$$\text{Weighted Average Common Shares Outstanding} = \frac{156{,}000}{12} = 13{,}000$$

Owens Corporation's 1996 earnings per share, then, is computed as follows:

$$\text{Earnings per Share} = \frac{\$39{,}000 - \$0}{13{,}000} = \$3.00$$

COMPLEX CAPITAL STRUCTURE

An entity with a **complex capital structure** contains one or more securities that have the potential to dilute earnings per share. For example, preferred stock convertible into common stock (convertible preferred stock) or debt convertible into common stock (convertible debt) is a potentially dilutive security because, if converted, each security causes common shares outstanding to increase without providing the corporation with any additional assets to use to generate additional earnings.

A corporation with a complex capital structure presents two earnings per share amounts—a primary earnings per share and a fully diluted earnings per share. The computation of **primary earnings per share** is similar to the earnings per share computation for firms with simple capital structures. The calculation of **fully diluted earnings per share** is based on the assumption that all dilutive securities are converted into common stock (whether or not such conversion is likely). The difference between the two per-share amounts shows the maximum possible dilution in earnings per share from any outstanding dilutive securities.

PRINCIPLE ALERT

FULL DISCLOSURE PRINCIPLE

The *full disclosure principle* lies behind the requirement that corporations with complex capital structures present two earnings per share amounts. The full disclosure principle dictates that all information necessary for the users' understanding of financial statements must be disclosed. Earnings per share is a very important financial statistic for investors. Without the dual presentation of earnings per share, accountants believe that investors may not understand the impact that potentially dilutive securities could have on a firm's earnings per share. The difference between primary and fully diluted earnings per share allows investors to see a worst-case scenario: the maximum potential reduction in earnings per share given the potentially dilutive securities present in a firm's capital structure.

To illustrate the computation of primary and fully diluted earnings per share, let us suppose that Bodeen Company had a net income of $90,000 for 1996. All year the company had 40,000 shares of common stock and 5,000 shares of convertible preferred stock outstanding. The annual dividend on the convertible preferred stock is 80 cents per share, and each share is convertible into two shares of common stock. The convertible preferred stock is a potentially dilutive security.

Bodeen Company's calculation of primary earnings per share is the same as if it had a simple capital structure. Bodeen's preferred stock dividend is $4,000 (5,000 × $0.80) and its weighted average number of actual common shares outstanding is 40,000 (40,000 shares outstanding all year). Thus, primary earnings per share is computed as follows:

$$\text{Primary Earnings per Share} = \frac{\$90,000 - \$4,000}{40,000} = \$2.15$$

The calculation of Bodeen's fully diluted earnings per share incorporates the *assumption* that the preferred stock is converted into common stock at the beginning of 1996. Under this assumption, there would be no 1996 preferred stock dividend. Also under this assumption, the weighted average common shares outstanding would be 50,000 (40,000 actual common shares outstanding all year + 10,000 assumed common shares outstanding all year from the conversion of 5,000 shares of preferred stock). Thus, fully diluted earnings per share is computed as follows:

$$\text{Fully Diluted Earnings per Share} = \frac{\$90,000 - \$0}{50,000} = \$1.80$$

The variety of potentially dilutive securities and of events that affect outstanding common stock can make the computations of earnings per share quite complex. The analysis required for such computations is covered in advanced courses.

ADDITIONAL PER-SHARE DISCLOSURES

The form in which earnings per share are disclosed should correspond to the income statement content. Thus, if a firm reports discontinued operations, earnings per share should be disclosed for income from continuing operations as well as for net income. Companies may also disclose the per-share effect of discontinued operations, although this disclosure is optional. Exhibit 13-3 illustrates an earnings per share presentation with discontinued operations.

Similarly, if a firm reports extraordinary gains or losses, earnings per share should be reported for income before extraordinary items. At the company's option, the per-share effect of each extraordinary item may also be shown. If a firm reports the cumulative effect of a change in an accounting principle, accounting standards require the disclosure of the per-share amount of the cumulative effect. Exhibit 13-4 illustrates the earnings per share presentation for an income statement that contains both an extraordinary item and a change in an accounting principle.

SUMMARY OF THE INCOME STATEMENT

Reporting the income of a corporation with the variety of items discussed in this chapter can be complex. Exhibit 13-5 summarizes these items and indicates their placement on the income statement, the order in which they are normally reported, and whether each is reported before or net of its income tax effect. Each of these items on the statement is keyed with the number of its related explanation.

Note that changes in accounting estimates and unusual *or* nonrecurring items are reported without any related income tax amounts because they are included in the computation of income from continuing operations. Income tax expense in this section relates to all preceding items of revenue and expense. All items below income from continuing operations are reported at amounts net of their income tax effects. The income statement in Exhibit 13-5 is a single-step income statement. Income from continuing operations is computed in one step, subtracting total expenses from sales. A single-step statement may include sections other than income from continuing operations.

Note also that when the income statement contains special sections, the number of per-share disclosures increases. In Exhibit 13-5, the required earnings per share disclosures are per-share amounts for income from continuing operations, income before extraordinary items and cumulative effect of a change in accounting principle, cumulative effect of change in accounting principle, and net income.

EXHIBIT 13–5 Summary of Income Statement Format

EXPLANATIONS

1 Changes in Accounting Estimates

Before-tax amounts are reported as part of related ordinary expenses.

2 Unusual or Nonrecurring Items

Separate before-tax amounts are listed among the ordinary expenses.

3 Income Tax Expense

The initial allocation of income taxes applies to the net of all preceding revenue and expense items. All items below income from continuing operations are reported net of income taxes.

4 Discontinued Operations

Reported separately for the discontinued segment
(a) Gain or loss from operations net of income taxes.
(b) Gain or loss on disposal net of income taxes.

5 Extraordinary Items

Reported net of income taxes.

6 Cumulative Effect of Change in Accounting Principle

Reported net of income taxes as the last item before net income.

7 Earnings per Share

Items in bold type are required disclosures; others are optional. Complex capital structures require reporting of primary and fully diluted earnings per share amounts.

ABC CORPORATION
INCOME STATEMENT
FOR THE YEAR ENDED DECEMBER 31, 1996

Sales		$XXX
Expenses		
1 Ordinary Expenses (including effects of changes in accounting estimates)	$XX	
2 Unusual or Nonrecurring Items	XX	
3 Income Tax Expense	XX	
Total Expenses		XXX
Income from Continuing Operations		$XXX
4 Discontinued Operations		
Gain or Loss from Operations (net of income taxes)	$XX	
Gain or Loss on Disposal (net of income taxes)	XX	XX
Income before Extraordinary Items and Cumulative Effect of a Change in Accounting Principle		$XXX
5 Extraordinary Items (net of income taxes)		XX
6 Cumulative Effect on Prior Years of Change in Accounting Principle (net of income taxes)		XX
Net Income		$XXX
7 Earnings per Common Share		
Income from Continuing Operations		**$X**
Discontinued Operations		X
Income before Extraordinary Items and Cumulative Effect of a Change in Accounting Principle		**$X**
Extraordinary Item		X
Cumulative Effect of Change in Accounting Principle		**X**
Net Income		**$X**

FINANCIAL ANALYSIS

DIVIDEND YIELD AND DIVIDEND PAYOUT RATIO

OBJECTIVE 6
DEFINE dividend yield and dividend payout ratio and **EXPLAIN** their use.

Stock investors differ in their expectations regarding their investments: some investors are primarily interested in appreciation in the market price of the stock, and other investors focus on receiving current income in the form of dividends. Dividend yield and dividend payout ratio are ratios that are helpful to the latter group of investors.

DIVIDEND YIELD **Dividend yield** measures the current rate of return in dividends from an investment in the stock. It is computed by dividing the latest annual dividends per share by the current market price of the stock. Therefore,

$$\text{Dividend Yield} = \frac{\text{Annual Dividends per Share}}{\text{Market Price per Share}}$$

For example, during the fiscal year ending May 31, 1994, Worthington Industries, a manufacturer of steel and plastic products headquartered in Columbus, Ohio, declared cash dividends per common share of $0.367. At May 31, 1994, Worthington's common stock had a per-share market price of $19.75. At May 31, 1994, then, Worthington's dividend yield was $0.367/$19.75 = 1.9%.

Dividend yields are included in the stock tables published in *The Wall Street Journal* and *Barrons,* so it is easy for investors to compare current dividend yields from investments in different stocks. The following are dividend yields for several common stocks from mid-1995.

The Coca-Cola Company	1.5%
GTE	5.7%
IBM Corporation	1.1%
J.C. Penney Company	4.0%
Texaco, Inc.	4.7%
Wal-Mart Stores, Inc.	0.8%

DIVIDEND PAYOUT RATIO

The **dividend payout ratio** is the percentage of earnings available to common stockholders that is paid out as dividends. The ratio is computed as follows:

$$\text{Dividend Payout Ratio} = \frac{\text{Annual Dividends per Share}}{\text{Earnings per Share}}$$

Dividend payout ratios vary considerably among corporations. Companies that are considered "growth" companies often have low payout ratios because they use the assets generated by earnings to help finance their expansion. In contrast, utilities often distribute a high percentage of their earnings as dividends. Utilities generally do much of their financing with long-term debt and, thus, have less need to utilize assets generated by earnings to finance their activities.

Some corporations try to maintain a reasonably constant dividend payout ratio, so their payout ratios do not vary much from one year to the next. Other corporations try to keep the per-share dividend amount either constant or increasing each year at a constant rate. If net income fluctuates quite a bit from year to year, these latter corporations will show dividend payout ratios that are quite variable through time.

Following are the dividend payout ratios of several corporations for a recent year:

Gannett Co., Inc. (newspaper publishing)	41.5%
Intel Corporation (microcomputer products)	3.8%
Interstate Bakeries Corporation (bakery products)	63.5%
Mead Corporation (paper products)	48.1%
The Quaker Oats Company (consumer food products)	82.1%

KEY POINTS FOR CHAPTER LEARNING OBJECTIVES

1 **IDENTIFY** and **DISTINGUISH** between cash dividends and stock dividends (pp. 436–439).
- Cash dividends reduce retained earnings and are a current liability when declared.
- Stock dividends are accounted for by a transfer of retained earnings to the appropriate stock and paid-in capital accounts at the market value of the shares for small stock dividends and at the legal minimum for large stock dividends.

2 **ILLUSTRATE** a retained earnings statement and a statement of stockholders' equity (pp. 439–440).
- A retained earnings statement presents the events causing retained earnings to change during an accounting period.
- A statement of stockholders' equity presents the events causing each component of stockholders' equity (including retained earnings) to change during an accounting period.

3 **DISCUSS** the accounting for prior period adjustments, changes in accounting estimates, and the process of restricting retained earnings (pp. 440–442).
- Prior period adjustments are corrections of material errors made in previous periods. They are taken directly to Retained Earnings.
- The effects of changes in accounting estimates are spread over the appropriate current and future periods.

■ Restrictions placed on retained earnings reduce the amount of retained earnings available for dividends.

4 **IDENTIFY** and **DISCUSS** the content and format of the income statement (pp. 442–448).

■ Tax allocation within a period improves the reporting of income taxes by disclosing both the tax effect and the item causing that effect in the same location in the income statement.

■ The ordinary, continuing income may be reported in a single-step format or in a multiple-step format.

■ Gains and losses from discontinued operations are reported in a special income statement section immediately following income from continuing operations.

■ Extraordinary items are both unusual *and* nonrecurring; they are reported in a separate section of the income statement. Unusual *or* nonrecurring items are not reported in a separate section, but they may be separately identified in the first section of the income statement reporting data on ordinary and continuing operations.

■ The cumulative effects of most changes in accounting principles are disclosed in the income statement in a special section immediately preceding net income.

5 **IDENTIFY** and **ILLUSTRATE** the computation and disclosure of earnings per share (pp. 448–451).

■ Corporations with complex capital structures present data on both primary and fully diluted earnings per share. A single presentation of earnings per share is appropriate for a corporation with a simple capital structure.

■ Per-share amounts in addition to net income per share are reported when there are special sections in the income statement.

6 **Financial Analysis**   **DEFINE** *dividend yield* and *dividend payout ratio* and **EXPLAIN** their use (pp. 451–452).

■ Dividend yield is computed by dividing a stock's annual dividends per share by its current market price. For investors, the ratio identifies the annual rate of return in dividends from an investment in the stock.

■ The dividend payout ratio is computed by dividing the annual dividends per share by the earnings per share.

SELF-TEST QUESTIONS FOR REVIEW

(Answers follow the Solution to Demonstration Problem.)

1. Which of the following events decreases a corporation's stockholders' equity?
   a. A payment of a previously declared cash dividend
   b. A declaration of a 6% stock dividend
   c. A $100,000 retained earnings restriction
   d. A declaration of a $1 cash dividend per share of preferred stock

2. In 1996, Corliss, Inc., discovered that an arithmetic error had been made in 1995, causing 1995's depreciation expense to be overstated. Corliss corrected the error in 1996 with a journal entry that included a credit to Retained Earnings. Which of the following does this situation illustrate?
   a. Prior period adjustment
   b. Change in an accounting estimate
   c. Change in an accounting principle
   d. Restriction on retained earnings

3. Assume that an income statement contains each of the four sections listed below. Which will be the last section in the income statement?
   a. Extraordinary item
   b. Cumulative effect of a change in accounting principle
   c. Income from continuing operations
   d. Discontinued operations

4. Which of the following items will appear in either a single-step or a multiple-step income statement for a merchandising firm?
   a. Restriction of retained earnings
   b. Gross profit on sales
   c. Income before extraordinary item
   d. Prior period adjustment

5. In which of the following situations will a corporation make a dual presentation of earnings per share (primary and fully diluted earnings per share)?
   a. It has two classes of stock outstanding (preferred and common stock).
   b. It uses a multiple-step income statement format.

c. It has a capital structure that contains at least one potentially dilutive security (a complex capital structure).

d. It has restrictions on the amount of earnings that may be paid out as dividends.

DEMONSTRATION PROBLEM FOR REVIEW

Information related to the income and retained earnings of Alpha, Inc., for 1996 is listed below. For simplicity, amounts are limited to three digits. Using these data, prepare a single-step income statement and a retained earnings statement for Alpha, Inc., for 1996. Assume that all changes in income are subject to a 40% income tax rate. Disregard earnings per share disclosures.

Additional uncollectible accounts expense due to revised estimate of percentage of anticipated uncollectible accounts (considered a selling expense)	$ 20	Increase in prior years reported income before income taxes due to change in depreciation method	$ 20
Cost of goods sold	420	Loss from labor strike (considered unusual but recurring)	40
Cash dividends declared	70	Loss from operations of discontinued Beta Division	50
Overstatement of 1995 ending inventory (caused by error)	10	Other operating expenses	230
Gain on condemnation of property (considered unusual and infrequent)	40	Retained earnings balance at end of 1995	454
		Sales	980
Gain on disposal of discontinued Beta Division	80	Selling and administrative expenses (before revised estimate of uncollectible accounts)	170

SOLUTION TO DEMONSTRATION PROBLEM

(Selected computations appear as notes to the financial statements.)

ALPHA, INC.
INCOME STATEMENT
FOR THE YEAR ENDED DECEMBER 31, 1996

Sales		$980
Expenses		
Cost of Goods Sold	$420	
Other Operating Expenses	230	
Selling and Administrative Expenses (Note A)	190	
Loss from Labor Strike	40	
Income Tax Expense (Note B)	40	
Total Expenses		920
Income from Continuing Operations		$ 60
Discontinued Operations		
Loss from Operations of Discontinued Beta Division (net of $20 reduction of income taxes) (Note C)	($ 30)	
Gain on Disposal of Discontinued Beta Division (net of $32 income taxes) (Note D)	48	18
Income before Extraordinary Item and Cumulative Effect of a Change in Accounting Principle		$ 78
Extraordinary Item		
Gain on Condemnation of Property (net of $16 income taxes) (Note E)		24
Cumulative Effect on Prior Years of Changing to a Different Depreciation Method (net of $8 income taxes) (Note F)		12
Net Income		$114

ALPHA, INC.
RETAINED EARNINGS STATEMENT
FOR THE YEAR ENDED DECEMBER 31, 1996

Retained Earnings, January 1, 1996	$454
Less: Correction of Prior Period Inventory Error (net of $4 reduction of income taxes) (Note G)	6
Adjusted Balance, January 1, 1996	$448
Add: Net Income	114
	$562
Less: Cash Dividends Declared	70
Retained Earnings, December 31, 1996	$492

Notes to financial statements

(A) $\$170 + \$20 = \$190$

(B) $40\% [\$980 - (\$420 + \$230 + \$190 + \$40)] = \$40$

(C) $\$50 - [0.4(\$50)] = \$30$

(D) $\$80 - [0.4(\$80)] = \$48$

(E) $\$40 - [0.4(\$40)] = \$24$

(F) $\$20 - [0.4(\$20)] = \$12$

(G) $\$10 - [0.4(\$10)] = \$6$

ANSWERS TO SELF-TEST QUESTIONS

1. d, p. 437   **2.** a, p. 444   **3.** b, p. 447   **4.** c, p. 443   **5.** c, p. 449

GLOSSARY OF KEY TERMS USED IN THIS CHAPTER

change in accounting estimate   A revision of an estimate used in an accounting analysis, such as the revision of the useful life of a plant asset (p. 441).

change in accounting principle   A switch from one generally accepted accounting method to another generally accepted method, such as changing depreciation methods (p. 447).

complex capital structure   A corporate capital structure containing one or more potentially dilutive securities. Complex capital structures normally require a dual presentation of earnings per share (p. 449).

cumulative effect of a change in principle   An item appearing in a separate section of the income statement resulting from a change in accounting principle. It represents the total difference in the cumulative net income for all prior years affected by the change, assuming that the new principle had been used in those years (p. 447).

deficit   A negative (debit) balance in a corporation's Retained Earnings account (p. 436).

discontinued operations   Operating segments of a company that have been sold, abandoned, or disposed of during the accounting period. Related operating income (or loss) and related gains and losses on disposal are reported separately on the income statement (p. 444).

dividend payout ratio   A financial ratio showing the percentage of earnings available to common stockholders that is paid out as dividends; computed as annual dividends per share divided by earnings per share (p. 452).

dividend yield   Annual dividends per share divided by the market price per share (p. 451).

dividends   Distributions of assets (usually cash) or stock from a corporation to its stockholders (p. 436).

earnings per share   A financial ratio computed as net income less preferred stock dividends divided by the weighted average number of common shares outstanding for the period (p. 448).

extraordinary items   Transactions and events that are unusual in nature and occur infrequently. Gains and losses on such items are shown separately, net of tax effects, on the income statement (p. 444).

fully diluted earnings per share   An earnings per share presentation for corporations with complex capital structures that assumes all dilutive securities are converted into common stock (p. 449).

multiple-step income statement   An income statement in which one or more intermediate amounts, such as gross profit on sales, are derived before the ordinary, continuing income is reported (p. 443).

primary earnings per share   One of two earnings per share presentations for corporations with complex capital structures; similar to the single earnings per share that is reported for corporations with simple capital structures (p. 449).

prior period adjustment   The correction of an error made in the financial statements of a prior accounting period (p. 440).

retained earnings   The amount of stockholders' equity resulting from a corporation's retention of assets generated from operating activities (p. 436).

retained earnings restrictions   Voluntary, contractual, or statutory restrictions placed on the availability of retained earnings for dividend declarations (p. 441).

retained earnings statement   A financial statement showing the changes that occurred in retained earnings during the accounting period (p. 439).

simple capital structure   A corporate capital structure that does not contain any securities with the potential to dilute earnings per share (p. 448).

single-step income statement   An income statement in which the ordinary, continuing income is derived in one step by subtracting total expenses from total revenues (p. 444).

statement of stockholders' equity   A financial statement that presents the changes that occurred in all components of stockholders' equity during the accounting period (p. 439).

stock dividends   Additional shares of its own stock issued by a corporation to its current stockholders in proportion to their ownership interests (p. 437).

tax allocation within a period   The apportionment of total income tax expense among the various sections of an income statement (p. 442).

QUESTIONS

13-1 What is a stock dividend? How does a common stock dividend paid to common shareholders affect their respective ownership interests?

13-2 What is the difference between the accounting for a small stock dividend and the accounting for a large stock dividend?

13-3 What information is presented in a retained earnings statement? a statement of stockholders' equity?

13-4 Niro Company discovered this year that a significant portion of its inventory was overlooked during its inventory count at the end of last year. How should the correction of this error be disclosed in the financial statements?

13-5 Distinguish between an error and a change in accounting estimate. How is reporting corrections of errors different from reporting changes in accounting estimates?

13-6 What is a restriction of retained earnings? Why and by whom are such restrictions made?

13-7 Where do the following accounts (and their balances) appear in the balance sheet?
  a. Dividends Payable—Common Stock
  b. Stock Dividend Distributable

13-8 What is meant by *tax allocation within a period*? What is the purpose of this type of tax allocation?

13-9 What is the difference between a single-step income statement and a multiple-step income statement?

13-10 Which one of the following amounts would appear only in a multiple-step income statement?

  Income from continuing operations.
  Income before extraordinary item.
  Gross profit on sales.
  Net income.

13-11 What is a business *segment*? Why are gains and losses from a discontinued segment reported in a separate section of the income statement?

13-12 Define *extraordinary items.* How are extraordinary items shown in the income statement?

13-13 A manufacturing plant of Park Corporation was destroyed by an earthquake, which is rare in the region where the plant was located. Where should this loss be classified in the income statement?

13-14 A Florida citrus grower incurs substantial frost damage to crops. Frost damage typically is experienced every few years. How should the loss on the crops be shown in the income statement?

13-15 This year, Bradley Company switched from the FIFO method of inventory pricing to the weighted average method. Cumulative income before income taxes for previous years would have been $90,000 lower if the weighted average method had been used.

  a. Assuming a 40% income tax rate, how should the effect of this inventory pricing change be shown in the income statement?

  b. If a comparative income statement is presented in the annual report, should Bradley revise last year's income statement using the weighted average method?

13-16 Distinguish between corporations with simple capital structures and those with complex capital structures. What does the type of capital structure imply regarding the presentation of earnings per share data?

13-17 What assumption underlies the computation of fully diluted earnings per share? What does the difference between the amounts of primary earnings per share and fully diluted earnings per share reveal?

13-18 How is a corporation's dividend yield computed?

13-19 Bleaker Company declares and pays its annual dividend near the end of its fiscal year. For the current year, Bleaker's dividend payout ratio was 40%, its earnings per common share was $5.80, and it had 50,000 shares of common stock outstanding all year. What total amount of dividends did Bleaker declare and pay in the current year?

PRINCIPLES DISCUSSION QUESTION

13-20 Werner Enterprises is a common and contract carrier providing truckload transportation services throughout the contiguous 48 states and the southern provinces of Canada. In an annual report to stockholders, Werner discussed the following change in accounting principle:

> In accordance with industry practice, the Company historically recognized operating revenues and related direct costs when freight was picked up for shipment. In January 1992, the Financial Accounting Standards Board Emerging Issues Task Force (EITF) reached a consensus on revenue and expense recognition for freight services in process.
>
> Based on the EITF consensus, the company began recognizing both revenues and direct costs when the shipment is delivered in the year ended February 1992. The cumulative effect of this accounting change on fiscal years prior to the year ended February 1992, was $(1,054,000), net of income taxes of $688,000 or $(.05) per share.

Direct costs are costs that can be readily identified and associated with specific transportation services. Two basic principles of accounting that apply to this change in accounting principle are the revenue recognition principle and the matching concept. Briefly explain how these principles relate to the change described by Werner Enterprises. Where in its financial statements would Werner Enterprises have reported the $(1,054,000) cumulative effect of the change in accounting principle? Briefly describe what this dollar amount represents.

EXERCISES

CASH DIVIDENDS
— OBJ. 1 —

13-21 Sanders Corporation has outstanding 6,000 shares of $50 par value, 6% preferred stock, and 40,000 shares of $1 par value common stock. The company has $328,000 of retained earnings. At year-end, the company declares the regular $3 per share cash dividend on the preferred stock and a $2.20 per share cash dividend on the common stock. Three weeks later, the company pays the dividends.
a. Prepare the journal entry for the declaration of the cash dividends.
b. Prepare the journal entry for the payment of the cash dividends.

STOCK DIVIDENDS
— OBJ. 1 —

13-22 Witt Corporation has outstanding 70,000 shares of $5 par value common stock. At year-end, the company declares a 4% stock dividend. The market price of the stock on the declaration date is $21 per share. Four weeks later, the company issues the shares of stock to shareholders.
a. Prepare the journal entry for the declaration of the stock dividend.
b. Prepare the journal entry for the issuance of the stock dividend.
c. Assume that the company declared a 40% stock dividend rather than a 4% stock dividend. Prepare the journal entries for (1) the declaration of the stock dividend and (2) the issuance of the stock dividend.

RETAINED EARNINGS
STATEMENT
— OBJ. 2 —

13-23 Use the following data to prepare a retained earnings statement for Shepler Corporation for 1996. Assume a 40% income tax rate.

Total retained earnings originally reported at December 31, 1995	$324,000
Cash dividends declared in 1996	75,000
Understatement of 1995 ending inventory discovered late in 1996 (caused by arithmetic errors)	26,000
Net income for 1996	193,000
Stock dividends declared in 1996	30,000

PRIOR PERIOD ADJUSTMENT
— OBJ. 3 —

13-24 Late in 1997, Lowe Corporation receives a notice from the Internal Revenue Service that Lowe had made an arithmetic error on its 1996 income tax return (the multiplication of the income tax rate times taxable income was wrong). As a result, Lowe owes another $8,500 of income taxes for 1996.

a. Prepare the 1997 journal entry to record the additional income taxes owed for 1996.

b. Where will Lowe Corporation report this event in its 1997 financial statements?

INCOME STATEMENT SECTIONS
— OBJ. 4 —

13-25 During the current year, Dale Corporation incurred an extraordinary tornado loss of $300,000 and sold a segment of its business at a gain of $196,000. Until it was sold, the segment had a current period operating loss of $75,000. Also, the company discovered that an error caused last year's ending inventory to be understated by $31,000 (a material amount). The company had $800,000 income from continuing operations for the current year. Prepare the lower part of the income statement, beginning with the $800,000 income from continuing operations. Follow tax allocation procedures, assuming that all changes in income are subject to a 40% income tax rate. Disregard earnings per share disclosures.

ACCOUNTING CHANGES AND
PRIOR PERIOD ADJUSTMENT
— OBJ. 3, 4 —

13-26 For each of the following current year events for Prince, Inc., (1) identify the type of accounting change or other category of event involved, (2) indicate where each would be reported on the current year income or retained earnings statement, and (3) illustrate how each would be disclosed including the relevant dollar amounts. Assume that the income tax rate for all years is 40%.

a. The company changed from the sum-of-the-years'-digits to the straight-line method of depreciating its equipment. Cumulative income before income taxes for prior years would have been $90,000 higher under the straight-line method.

b. The company discovered that, because of a new employee's oversight, depreciation of $30,000 on an addition to the plant had been omitted last year. The amount is material.

c. A patent acquired at a cost of $270,000 five years ago (including the current year) has been amortized under the straight-line method using an estimated useful life of 15 years. In reviewing accounts for the year-end adjustments, the company revised its estimate of the total useful life to 9 years.

EARNINGS PER SHARE
— OBJ. 5 —

13-27 Lucky Corporation began the year with a simple capital structure consisting of 200,000 shares of common stock outstanding. On April 1, 10,000 additional shares were issued, and another 30,000 shares were issued on August 1. The company had a net income for the year of $572,000.

a. Compute the earnings per share of common stock.

b. Assume that the company also had 11,000 shares of 8%, $50 par value cumulative preferred stock outstanding throughout the year. Compute the earnings per share of common stock.

EARNINGS PER SHARE
— OBJ. 5 —

13-28 During 1996, Dogwood Corporation had 125,000 shares of $5 par value common stock and 15,000 shares of 5%, $100 par value convertible preferred stock outstanding. Each share of preferred stock may be converted into two shares of common stock. Dogwood Corporation's 1996 net income was $775,000.

a. Compute the primary earnings per share for 1996.

b. Compute the fully diluted earnings per share for 1996.

PROBLEMS

RETAINED EARNINGS:
TRANSACTIONS AND STATEMENT
— OBJ. 1, 2 —

13-29 The stockholders' equity of Rayburn Corporation at January 1, 1996, appears below.

Common Stock, $5 Par Value, 400,000 shares authorized;	
160,000 shares issued and outstanding	$800,000
Paid-in Capital in Excess of Par Value	920,000
Retained Earnings	513,000

During 1996, the following transactions occurred:

June 7   Declared a 10% stock dividend; market value of the common stock was $11 per share.

      28   Issued the stock dividend declared on June 7.

Dec. 5   Declared a cash dividend of $1.25 per share.

      26   Paid the cash dividend declared on December 5.

      31   Closed the net income of $412,000 from the Income Summary account to Retained Earnings.

      31   Closed the dividend accounts to Retained Earnings.

REQUIRED

a. Prepare general journal entries to record the foregoing transactions.

b. Prepare a retained earnings statement for 1996.

RETAINED EARNINGS:
TRANSACTIONS AND STATEMENT
— OBJ. 1, 2, 3 —

13-30 The stockholders' equity of Cyclone Corporation at January 1, 1996, follows.

6% Preferred Stock, $25 Par Value, 40,000 shares authorized; 20,000 shares issued and outstanding	$ 500,000
Common Stock, $5 Par Value, 300,000 shares authorized; 80,000 shares issued and outstanding	400,000
Paid-in Capital in Excess of Par Value—Common Stock	560,000
Retained Earnings	830,000
Total Stockholders' Equity	$2,290,000

The following transactions, among others, occurred during 1996:

Feb. 10 Discovered that the accountant failed to accrue a $16,000 pollution fine on December 31, 1995. The fine relates to pollution that occurred during 1995, although the fine is not due and payable until June 1996. Pollution fines are not deductible for tax purposes, so this error has no income tax effect.

June 18 Declared a 50% stock dividend on all outstanding shares of common stock. The market value of the stock was $14 per share.

July 1 Issued the stock dividend declared on June 18.

Dec. 20 Declared the annual cash dividend on the preferred stock and a cash dividend of $1.30 per share of common stock, payable on January 20 to stockholders of record on December 28.

   31 Closed the Income Summary account, with net earnings of $379,000, to Retained Earnings.

   31 Closed the dividend accounts to Retained Earnings.

REQUIRED

a. Prepare journal entries to record the foregoing transactions.

b. Prepare a retained earnings statement for 1996.

STOCKHOLDERS' EQUITY:
TRANSACTIONS AND STATEMENT
— OBJ. 1, 2 —

13-31 The stockholders' equity section of Day Corporation's balance sheet at December 31, 1995, follows:

Common Stock, $10 Par Value, 200,000 shares authorized, 35,000 shares issued, 4,000 shares are in the treasury		$350,000
Additional Paid-in Capital		
In Excess of Par Value	$315,000	
From Treasury Stock	18,000	333,000
Retained Earnings (see Note)		298,000
		$981,000
Less: Treasury Stock (4,000 shares) at Cost		84,000
Total Stockholders' Equity		$897,000

Note: The availability of retained earnings for cash dividends is restricted by $84,000 due to the purchase of treasury stock.

The following transactions affecting stockholders' equity occurred during 1996:

Jan. 8 Issued 10,000 shares of previously unissued common stock for $23 cash per share.

Mar. 12 Sold all of the treasury shares for $26 cash per share.

June 30 Declared a 6% stock dividend on all outstanding shares of common stock. The market value of the stock was $30 per share.

July 10 Issued the stock dividend declared on June 30.

Oct. 7 Acquired 1,500 shares of common stock for the treasury at $27 cash per share.

Dec. 18 Declared a cash dividend of 90 cents per outstanding common share, payable on January 9 to stockholders of record on December 31.

   31 Closed the Income Summary account, with net income of $186,000, to Retained Earnings.

   31 Closed the dividend accounts to Retained Earnings.

REQUIRED

a. Prepare journal entries to record the foregoing transactions.

b. Prepare a statement of stockholders' equity for 1996.

INCOME STATEMENT FORMAT
— OBJ. 4 —

13-32 The following information from Belvidere Company's 1996 operations is available:

Administrative expenses	$ 69,000
Cost of goods sold	464,000
Sales	772,000
Flood loss (considered unusual and infrequent)	25,000
Selling expenses	87,000
Interest expense	7,000
Loss from operations of discontinued segment	60,000
Gain on disposal of discontinued segment	40,000
Income taxes	
Amount applicable to ordinary operations	58,000
Reduction applicable to flood loss	10,000
Reduction applicable to loss from operations	
of discontinued segment	24,000
Amount applicable to gain on disposal of	
discontinued segment	16,000

REQUIRED

a. Prepare a multiple-step income statement for 1996. (Disregard earnings per share amounts.)

b. Prepare a single-step income statement for 1996. (Disregard earnings per share amounts.)

EARNINGS PER SHARE
— OBJ. 5 —

13-33 Leland Corporation began 1996 with 120,000 shares of common stock and 16,000 shares of convertible preferred stock outstanding. On March 1 an additional 10,000 shares of common stock were issued. On August 1, another 16,000 shares of common stock were issued. On November 1, 6,000 shares of common stock were acquired for the treasury. The preferred stock has a $2 per-share dividend rate, and each share may be converted into one share of common stock. Leland Corporation's 1996 net income is $501,000.

REQUIRED

a. Compute primary earnings per share for 1996.

b. Compute fully diluted earnings per share for 1996.

c. If the preferred stock were not convertible, Leland Corporation would have a simple capital structure. How would this change Leland's earnings per share presentation?

EARNINGS PER SHARE AND
MULTIPLE-STEP INCOME
STATEMENT
— OBJ. 4, 5 —

13-34 Bowden Corporation discloses earnings per share amounts for extraordinary items. The following summarized data relate to the company's 1996 operations:

Sales	$745,000
Cost of goods sold	450,000
Selling expenses	58,000
Administrative expenses	72,000
Loss from earthquake damages	
(considered unusual and infrequent)	40,000
Loss on sale of equipment	5,000
Income tax expense (not allocated)	48,000
Shares of common stock	
Outstanding at January 1, 1996	15,000 shares
Additional issued at May 1, 1996	7,000 shares
Additional issued at November 1, 1996	2,000 shares

REQUIRED

Prepare a multiple-step income statement for Bowden Corporation for 1996. Assume a 40% income tax rate. Allocate income tax expense within the income statement. Include earnings per share disclosures for 1996 at the bottom of the income statement. Bowden Corporation has no preferred stock.

ALTERNATE EXERCISES

CASH AND STOCK DIVIDENDS
— OBJ. 1 —

13-21A Mandrich Corporation has outstanding 25,000 shares of $10 par value common stock. The company has $405,000 of retained earnings. At year-end, the company declares a cash dividend of $1.90 per share and a 4% stock dividend. The market price of the stock at the declaration date is $35 per share. Four weeks later, the company pays the dividends.
  a. Prepare the journal entry for the declaration of the cash dividend.
  b. Prepare the journal entry for the declaration of the stock dividend.
  c. Prepare the journal entry for the payment of the cash dividend.
  d. Prepare the journal entry for the payment of the stock dividend.

LARGE STOCK DIVIDEND AND
STOCK SPLIT
— OBJ. 1 —

13-22A Key Corporation has 40,000 shares of $10 par value common stock outstanding and retained earnings of $820,000. The company declares a 100% stock dividend. The market price at the declaration date is $17 per share.
  a. Prepare the general journal entries for (1) the declaration of the dividend and (2) the issuance of the dividend.
  b. Assume that the company splits its stock two shares for one share and reduces the par value from $10 to $5 rather than declaring a 100% stock dividend. How does the accounting for the stock split differ from the accounting for the 100% stock dividend?

RETAINED EARNINGS
STATEMENT
— OBJ. 2 —

13-23A Use the following data to prepare a retained earnings statement for Schauer Corporation for 1996. Assume a 40% income tax rate.

Total retained earnings originally reported at December 31, 1995	$347,000
Stock dividends declared in 1996	28,000
Cash dividends declared in 1996	35,000
Understatement of 1995 depreciation expense discovered late in 1996 (caused by arithmetic errors)	8,000
Net income for 1996	94,000

PRIOR PERIOD ADJUSTMENT
— OBJ. 3 —

13-24A Early in 1997, Wall Corporation discovered that its accountant had made an error in determining the firm's interest income for 1996. Due to an arithmetic error, the adjusting entry at the end of 1996 to record interest earned on investments in municipal obligations was understated by $22,000. The interest will be received in December 1997. The interest is exempt from income taxes, so there is no income tax effect.
  a. Prepare the 1997 journal entry to correct the 1996 mistake in recording interest income.
  b. Assume that Wall reported an ending retained earnings balance of $273,000 in its 1996 retained earnings statement. Prepare the first part of the 1997 retained earnings statement to show the correction of the 1997 beginning retained earnings balance.

INCOME STATEMENT SECTIONS
— OBJ. 4 —

13-25A During the current year, Newtech Corporation sold a segment of its business at a loss of $230,000. Until it was sold, the segment had a current period operating loss of $200,000. Also, the company had an extraordinary gain of $90,000 during the year as the result of an expropriation settlement received from a foreign government. The company also changed depreciation methods during the year. Depreciation expense in prior years would have been smaller by $75,000 had the new principle been used in those years. The company has $800,000 income from continuing operations for the current year. Prepare the lower part of the income statement, beginning with the $800,000 income from continuing operations. Follow tax allocation procedures, assuming that all changes in income are subject to a 40% income tax rate. Disregard earnings per share disclosures.

ACCOUNTING CHANGES AND
PRIOR PERIOD ADJUSTMENT
— OBJ. 3, 4 —

13-26A For each of the following current year events for Lordkin, Inc., (1) identify the type of accounting change or other category of event involved, (2) indicate where each would be reported on the current year income or retained earnings statement, and (3) illustrate how each would be disclosed including the relevant dollar amounts. Assume that the income tax rate for all years is 40%.
  a. The company changed from FIFO to the weighted average method of inventory pricing. Cumulative income before income taxes for prior years would have been $80,000 lower under the weighted average method.
  b. The company discovered that depreciation on certain assets had been recorded twice last year. The amount of excess depreciation recorded because of the mistake was $50,000.
  c. The company recorded $450,000 of goodwill 11 years ago (including the current year) and has been amortizing it using the straight-line method over a 20-year period. Upon review, the company now believes the maximum amortization period of 40 years should be used.

EARNINGS PER SHARE
— OBJ. 5 —

13-27A Ewing Corporation began the year with a simple capital structure consisting of 38,000 shares of common stock outstanding. On May 1, 10,000 additional shares were issued, and another 1,000 shares were issued on September 1. The company had a net income for the year of $234,000.

a. Compute the earnings per share of common stock.

b. Assume that the company also had 6,000 shares of 6%, $50 par value cumulative preferred stock outstanding throughout the year. Compute the earnings per share of common stock.

EARNINGS PER SHARE
— OBJ. 5 —

13-28A During 1996, Boxer Corporation had 50,000 shares of $10 par value common stock and 10,000 shares of 8%, $50 par value convertible preferred stock outstanding. Each share of preferred stock may be converted into three shares of common stock. Boxer Corporation's 1996 net income was $440,000.

a. Compute the primary earnings per share for 1996.

b. Compute the fully diluted earnings per share for 1996.

ALTERNATE PROBLEMS

RETAINED EARNINGS:
TRANSACTIONS AND STATEMENT
— OBJ. 1, 2 —

13-29A The stockholders' equity of Striker Corporation at January 1, 1996, appears below.

Common Stock, $10 Par Value, 200,000 shares authorized; 80,000 shares issued and outstanding	$800,000
Paid-in Capital in Excess of Par Value	480,000
Retained Earnings	305,000

During 1996, the following transactions occurred:

May 12   Declared a 7% stock dividend; market value of the common stock was $18 per share.

June 6   Issued the stock dividend declared on May 12.

Dec. 5   Declared a cash dividend of 75 cents per share.

30   Paid the cash dividend declared on December 5.

31   Closed the net income of $283,000 from the Income Summary account to Retained Earnings.

31   Closed the dividend accounts to Retained Earnings.

REQUIRED

a. Prepare general journal entries to record the foregoing transactions.

b. Prepare a retained earnings statement for 1996.

RETAINED EARNINGS:
TRANSACTIONS AND STATEMENT
— OBJ. 1, 2, 3 —

13-30A The stockholders' equity of Elson Corporation at January 1, 1996, is shown below.

5% Preferred Stock, $100 Par Value, 10,000 shares authorized; 4,000 shares issued and outstanding	$ 400,000
Common Stock, $5 Par Value, 200,000 shares authorized; 50,000 shares issued and outstanding	250,000
Paid-in Capital in Excess of Par Value—Preferred Stock	40,000
Paid-in Capital in Excess of Par Value—Common Stock	300,000
Retained Earnings	656,000
Total Stockholders' Equity	$1,646,000

The following transactions, among others, occurred during 1996:

Feb. 12   Elson Corporation carries life insurance on its key officers (with the corporation as beneficiary), and in 1995 it paid insurance premiums of $18,600 covering the three-year period 1995-1997. Today the company discovered that none of the $18,600 had been charged to Insurance Expense in 1995 (it all remained in Prepaid Insurance). These premiums are not deductible for tax purposes, so this error has no tax effect.

Apr. 1   Declared a 100% stock dividend on all outstanding shares of common stock. The market value of the stock was $11 per share.

15   Issued the stock dividend declared on April 1.

Dec. 7   Declared a 3% stock dividend on all outstanding shares of common stock. The market value of the stock was $14 per share.

Dec. 17   Issued the stock dividend declared on December 7.

20   Declared the annual cash dividend on the preferred stock and a cash dividend of 80 cents per common share, payable on January 15 to stockholders of record on December 31.

31   Closed the Income Summary account, with net earnings of $253,000, to Retained Earnings.

31   Closed the dividend accounts to Retained Earnings.

REQUIRED

a. Prepare journal entries to record the foregoing transactions.
b. Prepare a retained earnings statement for 1996.

INCOME STATEMENT AND DIVIDEND RELATIONSHIPS — OBJ. 4, 5 —

13-31A Tricon Company presented the following earnings per share data:

Earnings per Share of Common Stock	
Income before Extraordinary Item	$3.65
Extraordinary Gain (net of tax)	1.10
Net Income	$4.75

The company, which has a simple capital structure, began the year with 56,000 shares of $10 par value common stock and 7,500 shares of 6%, $40 par value preferred stock outstanding. On September 1, an additional 12,000 shares of common stock were issued. Cash dividends were distributed to both preferred and common stockholders.

REQUIRED

a. What is the annual preferred stock dividend requirement?
b. What was the net income for the current year for Tricon Company?
c. What was the amount of the extraordinary gain, net of the tax effect? What was the amount of the gain before the tax effect, assuming a 40% tax rate on the gain?
d. If the tax rate on ordinary income is 40%, what amount of income tax expense was reported in the income before extraordinary item section of the income statement?

SINGLE-STEP INCOME STATEMENT AND RETAINED EARNINGS STATEMENT — OBJ. 2, 4 —

13-32A The information listed below is related to Saglin Corporation's 1996 income and retained earnings.

Administrative expenses	$ 50,000
Stock dividends declared	33,000
Cash dividends declared	18,000
Cost of goods sold	382,000
Understatement of 1995 depreciation expense (caused by an error)	10,000
Increase in prior years income before income taxes due to change in inventory pricing method (from weighted average to FIFO)	55,000
Loss from uninsured portion of brushfire damages (considered unusual but recurring)	19,000
Loss from expropriation of property by foreign government (considered unusual and infrequent)	80,000
Retained earnings (balance at December 31, 1995)	270,000
Sales	636,000
Selling expenses	35,000
Income taxes	
Amount applicable to ordinary operations	60,000
Reduction applicable to loss from expropriation of property	32,000
Amount applicable to increase in prior years income before income taxes due to change in inventory pricing method	22,000
Reduction applicable to 1995 depreciation expense error	4,000

REQUIRED

a. Prepare a single-step income statement for Saglin Corporation for 1996. (Disregard earnings per share amounts.)
b. Prepare a retained earnings statement for Saglin Corporation for 1996.

EARNINGS PER SHARE — OBJ. 5 —

13-33A Island Corporation began the year 1996 with 25,000 shares of common stock and 5,000 shares of convertible preferred stock outstanding. On May 1, an additional 9,000 shares of common stock were issued. On July 1, 6,000 shares of common stock were acquired for the treasury. On September 1, the 6,000 treasury shares of common stock were reissued. The preferred stock has a $4 per-share dividend rate, and each share may be converted into two shares of common stock. Island Corporation's 1996 net income is $230,000.

REQUIRED

a. Compute primary earnings per share for 1996.

b. Compute fully diluted earnings per share for 1996.

c. If the preferred stock were not convertible, Island Corporation would have a simple capital structure. How would this change Island's earnings per share presentation?

EARNINGS PER SHARE AND MULTIPLE-STEP INCOME STATEMENT — OBJ. 4, 5 —

13-34A Garner Corporation discloses earnings per share amounts for extraordinary items. The following summarized data are related to the company's 1996 operations:

Sales	$2,220,000
Cost of goods sold	1,290,000
Selling expenses	180,000
Administrative expenses	143,000
Gain from expropriation of property by foreign government (negotiated settlement; considered unusual and infrequent)	190,000
Loss from plant strike	97,000
Shares of common stock	
Outstanding at January 1, 1996	61,000 shares
Additional issued at April 1, 1996	17,000 shares
Additional issued at August 1, 1996	3,000 shares

REQUIRED

Prepare a multiple-step income statement for Garner Corporation for 1996. Assume a 40% income tax rate. Include earnings per share disclosures for 1996 at the bottom of the income statement. Garner Corporation has no preferred stock.

CASES

BUSINESS DECISION CASE

The stockholders' equity section of Pillar Corporation's comparative balance sheet at the end of 1996 and 1997 is presented below. It is part of the financial data just reviewed at a stockholders' meeting.

	December 31, 1997	December 31, 1996
Common Stock, $10 Par Value, 600,000 shares authorized; issued at December 31, 1997, 275,000 shares; 1996, 250,000 shares	$ 2,750,000	$2,500,000
Paid-in Capital in Excess of Par Value	4,575,000	4,125,000
Retained Earnings (see Note)	2,960,000	2,825,000
Total Stockholders' Equity	$10,285,000	$9,450,000

Note: The availability of retained earnings for cash dividends is restricted by $2,000,000 due to a planned plant expansion.

The following items were also disclosed at the stockholders' meeting: net income for 1997 was $1,220,000; a 10% stock dividend was issued December 14, 1997; when the stock dividend was declared, the market value was $28 per share; the market value per share at December 31, 1997, was $26; management plans to borrow $500,000 to help finance a new plant addition, which is expected to cost a total of $2,300,000; and the customary $1.54 per share cash dividend had been revised to $1.40 when declared and issued the last week of December 1997.

As part of its investor relations program, during the stockholders' meeting management asked stockholders to write any questions they might have concerning the firm's operations or finances. As assistant controller, you are given the stockholders' questions.

REQUIRED

Prepare brief but reasonably complete answers to the following questions:

a. What did Pillar do with the cash proceeds from the stock dividend issued in December?

b. What was my book value per share at the end of 1996 and 1997?

c. I owned 7,500 shares of Pillar in 1996 and have not sold any shares. How much more or less of the corporation do I own at December 31, 1997, and what happened to the market value of my interest in the company?

d. I heard someone say that stock dividends don't give me anything I didn't already have. Why did you issue one? Are you trying to fool us?

e. Instead of a stock dividend, why didn't you declare a cash dividend and let us buy the new shares that were issued?

f. Why are you cutting back on the dividends I receive?

g. If you have $2,000,000 put aside in retained earnings for the new plant addition, which will cost $2,300,000, why are you borrowing $500,000 instead of just the $300,000 needed?

FINANCIAL ANALYSIS CASE I

Following is a listing of the 1994 annual dividends per share of common stock for several major corporations:

Transamerica Corporation (financial services)	$2.00
Southwestern Bell Corporation (communications)	1.65
Honeywell, Inc. (environmental controls)	1.00
Georgia-Pacific Corporation (pulp, paper, and building products)	1.60
Ball Corporation (packaging products)	0.60

At December 31, 1994, the market price per share of common stock for these corporations was as follows:

Transamerica Corporation	$49.75
Southwestern Bell Corporation	43.38
Honeywell, Inc.	38.00
Georgia-Pacific Corporation	79.25
Ball Corporation	36.38

REQUIRED

a. Compute the dividend yield at December 31, 1994, for each of the corporations listed above.

b. At the end of 1994, which corporation had the most attractive dividend yield? the least attractive dividend yield?

c. If dividend income is the investment objective, which variable is more important to an investment decision—dividend yield or dividends per share?

FINANCIAL ANALYSIS CASE II

Listed below are selected financial data for four corporations: Honeywell, Inc. (environmental controls), The Dow Chemical Company (chemicals and plastic products), Osmonics, Inc. (filtration products), and Abbott Laboratories (health care products). These data cover five years (Year 5 is the most recent year; net income in thousands).

	Year 5	Year 4	Year 3	Year 2	Year 1
Honeywell, Inc.					
Net income	$278,900	$322,200	$246,800	$331,100	$381,900
Earnings per common share	$2.15	$2.40	$1.78	$2.35	$2.52
Dividend per common share	$1.00	$0.91	$0.84	$0.77	$0.70
The Dow Chemical Company					
Net income	$938,000	$644,000	$276,000	$942,000	$1,384,000
Earnings per common share	$3.88	$2.33	$0.99	$3.46	$5.10
Dividend per common share	$2.60	$2.60	$2.60	$2.60	$2.60
Osmonics, Inc.					
Net income	$7,895	$1,449	$3,699	$5,879	$5,173
Earnings per common share	$0.63	$0.12	$0.30	$0.47	$0.36
Dividend per common share	$–0–	$–0–	$–0–	$–0–	$–0–
Abbott Laboratories					
Net income*	$1,399,100	$1,239,100	$1,088,700	$965,800	$859,800
Earnings per common share*	$1.69	$1.47	$1.27	$1.11	$0.96
Dividend per common share	$0.68	$0.60	$0.50	$0.42	$0.35

*Before extraordinary gain and accounting change

REQUIRED

a. Compute the dividend payout ratio for each company for each of the five years.

b. Companies may differ in their dividend policy; that is, they may differ in whether they emphasize a constant dividend amount per share, a steady growth in dividend amount per share, a target or constant dividend payout ratio, or some other criterion. Based on the data available, identify what appears to be each of the above firm's dividend policy over the five-year period.

ETHICS CASE

Melanie Samson, vice president and general counsel, chairs the Executive Compensation Committee for Sunlight Corporation. Four and one-half years ago, the compensation committee designed a performance bonus plan for top management that was approved by the board of directors. The plan provides an attractive bonus for top management if the firm's earnings per share grows each year over a five-year period. The plan is now in its fifth year; for the past four years, earnings per share has grown each year. Last year, earnings per share was $1.95 (net income was $7,800,000 and the weighted average common shares outstanding was 4,000,000). Sunlight Corporation has no preferred stock and has had 4,000,000 common shares outstanding for several years. Samson has recently seen an estimate that Sunlight's net income this year will decrease about 5% from last year because of a slight recession in the economy.

Samson is disturbed by an item on the agenda for the board of directors meeting on June 20 and an accompanying note from John Kirk. Kirk is vice president and chief financial officer for Sunlight. Kirk is proposing to the board that Sunlight buy back 600,000 shares of its own common stock on July 1. Kirk's explanation is that the firm's stock is undervalued now and that Sunlight has excess cash on hand. When the stock subsequently recovers in value, Kirk notes, Sunlight will reissue the shares and generate a nice increase in contributed capital.

Kirk's note to Samson merely states, "Look forward to your support of my proposal at the board meeting."

REQUIRED

Why is Samson disturbed by Kirk's proposal and note? What possible ethical problem does Samson face when Kirk's proposal is up for a vote at the board meeting?

GENERAL MILLS ANNUAL REPORT CASE

Refer to the annual report of General Mills, Inc., presented in Appendix K. Refer to the consolidated statement of earnings and Notes 2, 10, 13, 15, and 17.

REQUIRED

a. What is the per-share cash dividend declared by General Mills in fiscal year 1992? 1993? 1994?
b. What is General Mills' earnings per share in fiscal year 1992? 1993? 1994?
c. What is General Mills' dividend payout ratio for fiscal year 1992? 1993? 1994?
d. What is the nature of the $10 million discontinued operations charge in the fiscal year 1992 income statement?
e. Briefly describe the unusual items discussed by General Mills for the 1992–1994 period.
f. General Mills changed two accounting principles in fiscal year 1994: its accounting for postemployment benefits and its accounting for income taxes. What was the cumulative effect on prior years incomes from each of these changes?

Investments and Consolidated Financial Statements

CHAPTER LEARNING OBJECTIVES

1 **IDENTIFY** and **DEFINE** the investment categories for debt and equity securities (pp. 468–470).

2 **DESCRIBE** the accounting for various kinds of debt security investments (pp. 470–474).

3 **DESCRIBE** the accounting for various kinds of equity security investments (pp. 475–479).

4 **DEFINE** parent-subsidiary relationships and **ILLUSTRATE** how their balance sheet data are consolidated (pp. 479–484).

5 **DISCUSS** the treatment of acquisitions when cost exceeds the book value acquired in a subsidiary (pp. 484–485).

6 **EXPLAIN** and **ILLUSTRATE** the consolidation of parent and subsidiary income statements (pp. 485–487).

7 **PROVIDE** an overview of accounting for acquisitions under the pooling of interests method (pp. 487–488).

8 **Financial Analysis** **DEFINE** *price-earnings ratio* and **EXPLAIN** its use (pp. 488–489).

CHAPTER FOCUS

An individual who purchases a government bond or shares of stock is engaging in a transaction that many business entities enter into in significant volume: investments in various securities. In contrast to the individual, though, the business entity must account for investments according to generally accepted accounting principles. The first part of this chapter explains these accounting guidelines for investments.

Among the stock investments held by many corporations are shares that represent a 100% (or a majority) ownership of another company. The financial data for all such investee companies are consolidated with the owner company's financial data when the owner company prepares financial statements. The consolidated financial statements of Union Pacific Corporation, for example, include financial data from such separate companies as a railroad company (Union Pacific Railroad), a natural resources company (Union Pacific Resources), a trucking company (Overnite Transportation), a waste management company (USPCI), a logistics and transportation support company (Skyway Freight Systems), and a computer software company (Union Pacific Technologies). The latter part of this chapter focuses on the nature of and the accounting for consolidated financial statements.

INVESTMENTS

DEBT AND EQUITY SECURITIES

OBJECTIVE *1*
IDENTIFY and **DEFINE** the investment categories for debt and equity instruments.

The resources of a business entity may include investments in one or more types of debt or equity securities. For some industries, such as the insurance industry, investments in debt and equity securities constitute a major portion of total assets. Investments in various debt and equity securities, for example, represent more than 50% of the assets of Transamerica Corporation, one of the world's largest insurance and financial services companies.

A **debt security** refers to a security that creates, for the holder, a creditor relationship with an entity. Examples include U.S. treasury bills, notes, and bonds; U.S. government agency bonds (such as Ginnie Mae bonds); state and local government bonds; corporate bonds; and commercial paper. *Bonds* are long-term debt securities; some bonds, for example, may not mature for 30 to 40 years. *Commercial paper* refers to short-term, unsecured promissory notes (written promises to pay) issued by large corporations.

An **equity security** is a security that represents an ownership interest in an entity. Shares of stock represent ownership interests in a corporation. Investors holding a corporation's *common stock* have the most basic ownership rights; holders of *preferred stock* have some rights that take preference over the common stockholders (such as the right to receive dividends).

Debt and equity securities might be acquired by an investor in the original market; that is, directly from the entity that issues the securities to raise money. When corporations or government agencies need to borrow cash, they offer their debt securities to the general public. This process is called *floating an issue*. When a corporation first issues stock to the general public to raise money, the process is called an *initial public offering* (IPO).

More frequently, though, investors acquire debt and equity securities in the secondary market. The secondary market consists of trades between investors; one investor purchases securities from another investor who wants to sell. Many debt and equity securities are bought and sold on organized exchanges. Stocks and bonds, for example, may trade on a national exchange such as the New York Stock Exchange or the American Stock Exchange (despite their names, both exchanges list a large number of bonds). Stocks and bonds may also trade in a less formal market known as the *over-the-counter* market. Both the buyer and seller of a security normally use the services of a broker to acquire or dispose of their investments.

INVESTMENT CATEGORIES

For accounting purposes, each investment in debt or equity securities is placed in one of five categories: **trading securities, available-for-sale securities, held-to-maturity securities, influential securities,** and **controlling securities.** Of these categories, three are available for debt securities and four are available for equity securities. Exhibit 14-1 shows these investment categories.

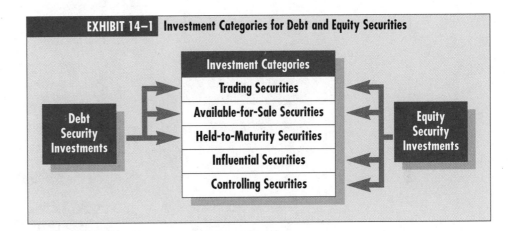

EXHIBIT 14–1 Investment Categories for Debt and Equity Securities

The placement of an investment in the proper category depends on (1) management's intent with respect to selling the investment and (2) the ability to influence or control another entity's activities as a result of an equity investment. Typical evidence of the latter factor is the ownership percentage represented by the equity investment. Exhibit 14-2 defines the five investment categories.

Notice in Exhibit 14-2 that trading securities and available-for-sale securities may include noninfluential equity securities. Noninfluential equity securities refer to stock investments that do not permit the investor to exert any significant influence over the policies of the investee company (the company whose stock is acquired). Accountants consider stock investments noninfluential if the stock purchased is preferred stock (which is nonvoting stock) or less than 20% of a firm's common stock (which is voting stock).

An entity that owns 20% or more of a corporation's voting stock may exert a significant influence on the operating or financial decisions of that company. However, if 50% or less of the total voting stock is owned, the investment does not represent a controlling interest. Voting stock investments in the 20–50% ownership range, therefore, compose the influential securities.

When more than 50% of a corporation's voting stock is owned, the investor is a majority owner and is in a position to control the operating and financial policies of the investee company. These majority-ownership stock investments are classified as controlling securities.[1]

---

[1]The ownership percentages are guidelines only and may be overcome by other factors. In some cases, a company may own more than 20% of another company and still not be able to significantly influence its operating and financial activities. Or effective control of another entity may exist with less than 50% ownership of its stock. For example, ownership of a large minority interest (such as 45%) with other owners widely dispersed and unorganized may provide effective control. The key to proper accounting classification is the presence of significant influence on, or effective control over, another entity.

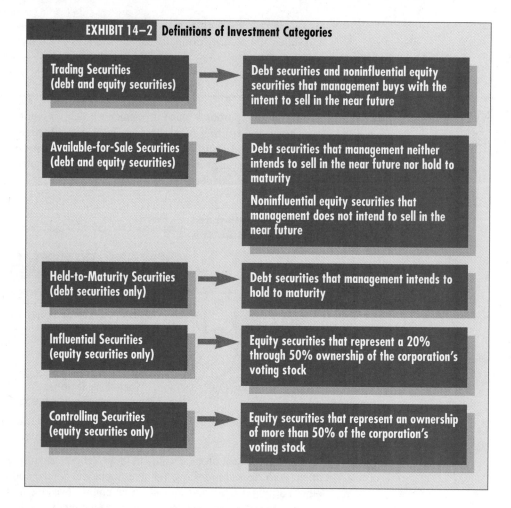

EXHIBIT 14–2 Definitions of Investment Categories

Trading Securities (debt and equity securities)	Debt securities and noninfluential equity securities that management buys with the intent to sell in the near future
Available-for-Sale Securities (debt and equity securities)	Debt securities that management neither intends to sell in the near future nor hold to maturity Noninfluential equity securities that management does not intend to sell in the near future
Held-to-Maturity Securities (debt securities only)	Debt securities that management intends to hold to maturity
Influential Securities (equity securities only)	Equity securities that represent a 20% through 50% ownership of the corporation's voting stock
Controlling Securities (equity securities only)	Equity securities that represent an ownership of more than 50% of the corporation's voting stock

Debt and equity investments are placed in five different categories because accounting guidelines differ among the categories.[2] We will now review these accounting guidelines, looking at debt securities first and then examining equity securities.

INVESTMENTS IN DEBT SECURITIES

OBJECTIVE 2

DESCRIBE the accounting for various kinds of debt security investments.

Investments in debt securities are placed in one of three categories: trading securities, available-for-sale securities, or held-to-maturity securities. The major accounting events related to investments in debt securities are their purchase, the recognition of interest income, their balance sheet valuation, and their sale or their redemption at maturity. Exhibit 14-3 summarizes the accounting guidelines for these events. We will illustrate these guidelines with examples.

PURCHASE Assume that Warner Company purchases $300,000 face value of Natco Company 8% bonds at 98 on July 1, 1997. The bonds pay interest on December 31 and June 30 and mature in 10 years. The brokerage commission is $600. Warner's management considers the bond investment to be divided equally between trading securities, available-for-sale securities, and held-to-maturity securities. Exhibit 14-4 shows the entry to record this purchase. Note that the accounting for the purchase event is the same, regardless of the classification for a bond investment.

---

[2]*Statement of Financial Accounting Standards No. 115,* "Accounting for Certain Investments in Debt and Equity Securities" (Norwalk, CT: Financial Accounting Standards Board, 1993) and *Opinions of the Accounting Principles Board No. 18,* "The Equity Method of Accounting for Investments in Common Stock" (New York: American Institute of CPAs, 1971).

EXHIBIT 14–3 Accounting Guidelines for Investments in Debt Securities

Event/ Accounting Guideline	Trading Securities	Available-for- Sale Securities	Held-to-Maturity Securities
1. Purchase Record at cost, which includes any broker's fees.	X	X	X
2. Recognition of Interest Income Interest accrues daily and is usually recorded when payment is received. Premium or discount on purchase price is not amortized.	X		
Interest accrues daily and is usually recorded when payment is received. Premium or discount on purchase price is amortized as an adjustment of interest income.		X	X
3. Balance Sheet Valuation Measure securities at fair value at balance sheet date. No valuation account to the asset account is used. Changes in fair value are reported in the income statement.	X		
Measure securities at fair value at balance sheet date. Use a valuation account to the asset account. Changes in fair value are reported in stockholders' equity.		X	
Measure securities at amortized cost at balance sheet date.			X
4. (a) Sale Sale proceeds less investment's book value is a realized gain or loss.	X		
Sale proceeds less investment's amortized cost is a realized gain or loss.		X	
(b) Redemption at Maturity At maturity, the investment's book value will equal the redemption proceeds.			X

Natco Company bonds are purchased the first day after an interest payment date, so there is no unpaid interest related to the bonds. If any more time had passed, though, the bond price would include an accrued interest amount. This occurs because the bond seller is entitled to receive the interest earned up to the date of sale. As a result, the purchase price of a bond that is sold between interest payment dates includes not only the current market

EXHIBIT 14–4 Purchase of Debt Securities

1997		
July 1	Bond Investment—Trading (Natco)	98,200
	Bond Investment—Available for Sale (Natco)	98,200
	Bond Investment—Held to Maturity (Natco)	98,200
	Cash	294,600

To record purchase of $300,000 of Natco Company bonds at 98 plus $600 commission [($300,000 × 0.98) + $600 = $294,600].

price but also any interest accrued since the last interest payment date. The bond buyer pays the accrued interest amount to the bond seller, debits the amount to the Bond Interest Receivable account, and then collects it as part of the next interest payment received from the bond issuer. Because the accrued interest purchased by the bond buyer is collected with the next interest payment, the accrued interest is not treated as part of the initial cost of the investment.

RECOGNITION OF INTEREST INCOME

Each $100,000 of Natco Company bonds acquired on July 1, 1997, was purchased at an $1,800 discount ($100,000 – $98,200). This means that the rate of interest in the market on July 1, 1997, was higher than the 8% coupon rate offered on the bonds. For trading securities, any bond discount (or premium) is ignored in accounting for the periodic interest income because management plans to sell the securities in the near future. As such, the effect on net income from ignoring the bond discount (or premium) is immaterial.

For available-for-sale securities and held-to-maturity securities, any bond discount (or premium) is amortized to interest income. This is done to make periodic interest income more accurately reflect the economic reality of the bond investment. The amortization of bond discount causes the periodic interest income to be higher than the semiannual cash receipt of interest. Had bonds been purchased at a premium (more than face value), the premium amortization would cause periodic interest income to be less than the semiannual cash receipt of interest.

Two amortization methods are available for use: the straight-line method and the effective interest method. We shall use the straight-line method here. The *straight-line method* of amortization writes off an equal amount of discount or premium each interest period. Natco Company bonds, when purchased, had 10 years to maturity; interest is paid semiannually, so there are 20 interest periods. Each interest period, $90 ($1,800/20) of discount will be amortized for the available-for-sale securities and the held-to-maturity securities. Each $100,000 (face value) of Natco bonds pays $4,000 interest semiannually (8% × $100,000 × $\frac{1}{2}$). The entries to record interest income at December 31, 1997, are shown in Exhibit 14-5.

EXHIBIT 14–5 | **Recognition of Interest Income on Debt Securities**

1997

Trading Debt Securities

Dec. 31	Cash	4,000	
	Bond Interest Income		4,000
	To record receipt of semiannual interest on $100,000 of trading bonds.		

Available-for-Sale Debt Securities

Dec. 31	Cash	4,000	
	Bond Investment—Available for Sale (Natco)	90	
	Bond Interest Income		4,090
	To record receipt of semiannual interest and discount amortization on $100,000 of available-for-sale bonds.		

Held-to-Maturity Debt Securities

Dec. 31	Cash	4,000	
	Bond Investment—Held to Maturity (Natco)	90	
	Bond Interest Income		4,090
	To record receipt of semiannual interest and discount amortization on $100,000 of held-to-maturity bonds.		

BALANCE SHEET VALUATION

Debt securities are interest rate sensitive: as market interest rates change, the market values of debt securities change. Debt securities that management intends to sell (trading securities) or may sell (available-for-sale securities) are reported in the balance sheet at their

MATERIALITY CONCEPT

Note the role played by the *materiality concept* in determining interest income on trading securities. Because of the short time period that trading securities are held, accountants do not bother to start the amortization of any discount or premium on the debt securities purchased. This simplifies the accounting for these debt securities, yet it causes no significant distortion in the periodic reporting of interest income.

current fair values. If available, quoted market prices provide the best evidence of fair value. Year-end adjusting entries are made to record these current fair values. Current fair value is not a relevant measure for debt securities that management intends to hold to maturity. Thus, no adjustment to fair value is made for held-to-maturity securities.

Assume that a general decline in interest rates cause Natco Company bonds to trade at 99.5 at December 31, 1997. Exhibit 14-6 shows the adjusting entries made on this date to record the relevant fair values.

EXHIBIT 14–6	Balance Sheet Valuation for Debt Securities		
1997			
	Trading Debt Securities		
Dec. 31	Bond Investment—Trading (Natco)	1,300	
	Unrealized Gain on Investments (Income)		1,300
	To adjust trading debt securities to year-end fair value ($99,500 – $98,200 = $1,300 gain).		
	Available-for-Sale Debt Securities		
Dec. 31	Fair Value Adjustment to Bond Investment	1,210	
	Unrealized Gain/Loss on Investments (Equity)		1,210
	To adjust available-for-sale debt securities to year-end fair value ($99,500 – $98,290 = $1,210 gain).		

Fair value changes in securities that are still owned are called *unrealized holding gains and losses*. Unrealized holding gains and losses that relate to trading securities are reported in the income statement. Thus, the $1,300 unrealized gain shown in Exhibit 14-6 is included in Warner's 1997 income statement.

Unrealized holding gains and losses that relate to available-for-sale securities are excluded from the income statement. Instead, their net amount is reported as a separate component of stockholders' equity titled Unrealized Gain/Loss on Investments (Equity). Because these unrealized gains and losses are not included in earnings, the investment's cost must be maintained in the accounts so that a total realized gain or loss can be determined when the investment is sold. Using the valuation account Fair Value Adjustment to Bond Investment permits the maintenance of the investment's cost in the Bond Investment—Available for Sale account.[3] After the adjustments shown in Exhibit 14-6, the December 31, 1997, balance sheet reports the bond investments as follows:

Bond Investment—Trading (Fair value)		$99,500
Bond Investment—Available for Sale (Cost)	$98,290	
Add: Fair Value Adjustment to Bond Investment	1,210	99,500
Bond Investment—Held to Maturity (Cost)		98,290

[3]The cost of trading securities must be maintained for income tax purposes. A fair value valuation account, therefore, may be used in keeping the tax records of trading securities.

CLASSIFICATION OF UNREALIZED GAINS AND LOSSES

Financial institutions manage their interest rate risk by coordinating their holdings of financial assets (loans and investments) and financial liabilities (various borrowings and customer deposits), a practice referred to as *asset/liability management*. This practice caused many accountants to believe that related liabilities should be measured at fair value if available-for-sale investments in debt securities were measured at fair value. Volatility in reported earnings would then be minimized because gains and losses on the liabilities would tend to offset the losses and gains on the debt security investments. The Financial Accounting Standards Board was unable to develop a workable approach for measuring liabilities at fair value. To compensate, the FASB decided to keep the unrealized gains and losses on available-for-sale investments out of the income statement.

SALE OR REDEMPTION AT MATURITY

To complete our illustration, assume that the trading and available-for-sale bond investments are both sold on July 1, 1998, for $99,800 each (after recognizing interest income on June 30, 1998). The remaining bond investment is held to maturity (June 30, 2007), at which time the bonds are redeemed by the issuer for $100,000. Exhibit 14-7 shows the appropriate journal entries related to these events.

EXHIBIT 14–7	Sale or Redemption at Maturity of Debt Securities		
1998			
	Trading Debt Securities		
July 1	Cash	99,800	
	Bond Investment—Trading (Natco)		99,500
	Gain on Sale of Investments		300
	To record sale of trading debt securities for $99,800 ($99,800 – $99,500 = $300 realized gain).		
	Available-for-Sale Debt Securities		
July 1	Cash	99,800	
	Bond Investment—Available for Sale (Natco)		98,380
	Gain on Sale of Investments		1,420
	To record sale of available-for-sale debt securities for $99,800 ($99,800 – $98,380 = $1,420 gain).		
Dec. 31	Unrealized Gain/Loss on Investments (Equity)	1,210	
	Fair Value Adjustment to Bond Investment		1,210
	To adjust these account balances to zero.		
2007			
	Held-to-Maturity Debt Securities		
June 30	Cash	100,000	
	Bond Investment—Held to Maturity (Natco)		100,000
	To record redemption of bonds at maturity.		

In Exhibit 14-7, the $300 gain on the sale of the trading securities is the difference between the $99,800 sales proceeds and the last recorded fair value of $99,500. By July 1, 1998, another $90 of discount amortization would have been recorded on the available-for-sale securities, increasing their amortized cost to $98,380 ($98,290 + $90). The $1,420 gain that is recorded on their sale is the difference between the $99,800 sales proceeds and the amortized cost of $98,380. Because all available-for-sale bonds were sold, the related valuation account and unrealized gain/loss account are adjusted to zero balances at the next adjustment date (December 31, 1998). The completion of the discount amortization on the held-to-maturity bonds brings their amortized cost to $100,000 on June 30, 2007. Thus, there is no gain nor loss from the redemption at maturity of these bonds.

INVESTMENTS IN EQUITY SECURITIES

OBJECTIVE 3

DESCRIBE the accounting for various kinds of equity security investments.

Equity security investments fit into one of four categories: trading securities, available-for-sale securities, influential securities, and controlling securities. The major accounting events related to investments in equity securities are their purchase, the recognition of investment income, their balance sheet valuation, and their sale. Exhibit 14-8 summarizes the accounting guidelines for these events. We will illustrate these guidelines with examples.

EXHIBIT 14–8	Accounting Guidelines for Investments in Equity Securities			
Event/ Accounting Guideline	**Trading Securities**	**Available-for-Sale Securities**	**Influential Securities**	**Controlling Securities**
1. Purchase Record at cost, which includes any broker's fees.	X	X	X	X
2. Recognition of Investment Income Record dividend income when dividends are received.	X	X		
Record equity in investee company's net income as investment income. Decrease investment account for dividends received.			X	X
3. Balance Sheet Valuation Measure securities at fair value at balance sheet date. No valuation account to the investment account is used. Changes in fair value are reported in the income statement.	X			
Measure securities at fair value at balance sheet date. Use a valuation account to the investment account. Changes in fair value are reported in stockholders' equity.		X		
Report securities at book value (cost plus share of investee net income less dividends).			X	
Eliminate investment account as part of consolidation procedures.				X
4. Sale Sale proceeds less investment's book value is a realized gain or loss.	X		X	X
Sale proceeds less investment's cost is a realized gain or loss.		X		

PURCHASE   Assume that Warner Company purchases 1,500 shares of common stock in each of four different companies—Ark, Inc.; Bain, Inc.; Carr, Inc.; and Dot, Inc.—on January 1, 1997. Each investment costs $15,000, including broker's fees. The shares acquired represent 10% of Ark's voting stock, 10% of Bain's voting stock, 25% of Carr's voting stock, and 60% of Dot's voting stock.[4] Only the Ark investment is considered by management to be

---

[4]We assume that the cost of the investments in Carr and Dot are equal to the book value of the underlying net assets of the investee company. This assumption permits us to simplify the illustration of the subsequent accounting for these two investments.

trading securities. Thus, each of these stock investments is placed in a different category. Exhibit 14-9 shows the entry to record these investments. Note that each stock investment is recorded at its cost.

EXHIBIT 14–9	Purchase of Equity Securities		
1997			
Jan. 1	Stock Investment—Trading (Ark)	15,000	
	Stock Investment—Available for Sale (Bain)	15,000	
	Stock Investment—Influential (Carr)	15,000	
	Stock Investment—Controlling (Dot)	15,000	
	Cash		60,000
	To record purchase of 1,500 shares each of Ark, Inc.; Bain, Inc.; Carr, Inc.; and Dot, Inc. common stock for $60,000 ($15,000 for each investment), including broker's fees.		

RECOGNITION OF INVESTMENT INCOME

Each of the four companies earns a 1997 net income of $10,000. Each company also declares a cash dividend of $0.50 per share, which is received by Warner on December 31, 1997. Exhibit 14-10 shows the entries to record this information.

As shown in Exhibit 14-10, the dividends of $750 received on both the Ark and Bain investments are reported as Dividend Income. This is the proper treatment for cash dividends received on trading securities (Ark) and available-for-sale securities (Bain).

When the percentage ownership of voting stock reaches 20% or more, the **equity method** of accounting for the stock investment is used. Under the equity method, the investor company records as income or loss its proportionate share of the net income or net

EXHIBIT 14–10	Recognition of Investment Income on Equity Securities		
1997			
	Trading Equity Securities		
Dec. 31	Cash	750	
	Dividend Income		750
	To record receipt of cash dividend from Ark, Inc.		
	Available-for-Sale Equity Securities		
Dec. 31	Cash	750	
	Dividend Income		750
	To record receipt of cash dividend from Bain, Inc.		
	Influential Equity Securities		
Dec. 31	Stock Investment—Influential (Carr)	2,500	
	Income from Stock Investments		2,500
	To record as income 25% of Carr's 1997 net income of $10,000 (investment balance = $17,500).		
Dec. 31	Cash	750	
	Stock Investment—Influential (Carr)		750
	To record receipt of cash dividend from Carr, Inc. (investment balance = $16,750).		
	Controlling Equity Securities		
Dec. 31	Stock Investment—Controlling (Dot)	6,000	
	Income from Stock Investments		6,000
	To record as income 60% of Dot's 1997 net income of $10,000 (investment balance = $21,000).		
Dec. 31	Cash	750	
	Stock Investment—Controlling (Dot)		750
	To record receipt of cash dividend from Dot, Inc. (investment balance = $20,250).		

loss reported for that period by the company whose stock is held, with the offsetting debit or credit going to the stock investment account. The receipt of cash dividends reduces the stock investment account. *The equity method prevents an investor company from manipulating its own income by the influence it can exercise on the dividend policies of the investee company.*

In Exhibit 14-10, the equity method is used for the Carr stock investment (25% ownership) and Dot stock investment (60% ownership). At December 31, 1997, investment income and the Carr stock investment account are increased by 25% of Carr's 1997 net income (25% × $10,000 = $2,500). The receipt of the $750 cash dividend from Carr reduces the Carr stock investment account. Similarly, the equity method causes a $6,000 increase (60% × $10,000 net income) in both investment income and Dot's stock investment account at December 31, 1997. The $750 cash dividend received from Dot decreases the Dot stock investment account.

BALANCE SHEET VALUATION

The balance sheet valuations for equity trading securities and equity available-for-sale securities are handled in the same manner as the corresponding debt securities. Year-end adjusting entries are made to record these equity securities at current fair values (with quoted market prices being the best evidence of current fair values).

PRINCIPLE ALERT

OBJECTIVITY PRINCIPLE

The standard to measure equity trading securities and equity available-for-sale securities at current fair values applies only to equity securities that have readily determinable fair values. It does not apply to equity investments that would create significant valuation problems, such as equity investments in closely held companies. This represents an application of the *objectivity principle,* which states that accounting entries should be based on objectively determined evidence.

Assume that at December 31, 1997, the fair values of 1,500 shares of Ark common stock and Bain common stock are each $23,000. Exhibit 14-11 shows the adjusting entries made on this date to record the relevant fair values.

EXHIBIT 14–11	Balance Sheet Valuation for Equity Securities		
1997	**Trading Equity Securities**		
Dec. 31	Stock Investment—Trading (Ark)	8,000	
	Unrealized Gain on Investments (Income)		8,000
	To adjust trading stock securities to year-end fair value of $23,000 ($23,000 – $15,000 = $8,000 gain).		
	Available-for-Sale Equity Securities		
Dec. 31	Fair Value Adjustment to Stock Investment	8,000	
	Unrealized Gain/Loss on Investments (Equity)		8,000
	To adjust available-for-sale equity securities (Bain) to year-end fair value of $23,000 ($23,000 – $15,000 = $8,000 gain).		

As is true with debt securities, the $8,000 unrealized holding gain shown in Exhibit 14-11 on the equity trading securities (Ark) is reported in Warner's 1997 income statement. The $8,000 unrealized holding gain on the equity available-for-sale securities (Bain) is reported in the stockholders' equity section of the balance sheet. The valuation account for the Bain stock investment plays the same role as discussed earlier in accounting for debt securities; it permits cost to be maintained in the Stock Investment—Available for Sale account for the available-for-sale securities.

Stock investments accounted for by the equity method are not measured at year-end fair values. Their year-end account balances remain as computed by the equity method ($16,750 for the Carr investment and $20,250 for the Dot investment). For controlling investments, the financial statements of the investee company are usually consolidated with the statements of the investor company. The investment account does not appear in the consolidated statements.

SALE   To complete our illustration, assume that all four stock investments are sold on July 1, 1998. Each of the stock investments is sold for $22,000. Exhibit 14-12 shows the appropriate journal entries related to these events. As shown in Exhibit 14-12, each sale generates a different gain or loss. Even though the basic events relating to each of the stock investments were the same, the accounting guidelines result in quite different analyses.

EXHIBIT 14–12   **Sale of Equity Securities**

1998

Trading Equity Securities

July 1	Cash	22,000	
	Loss on Sale of Investments	1,000	
	Stock Investment—Trading (Ark)		23,000

To record sale of trading equity securities for $22,000 ($22,000 – $23,000 = $1,000 loss).

Available-for-Sale Equity Securities

July 1	Cash	22,000	
	Stock Investment—Available for Sale (Bain)		15,000
	Gain on Sale of Investments		7,000

To record sale of available-for-sale equity securities for $22,000 ($22,000 – $15,000 = $7,000 gain).

Dec. 31	Unrealized Gain/Loss on Investments (Equity)	8,000	
	Fair Value Adjustment to Stock Investment		8,000

To adjust these account balances to zero.

Influential Equity Securities

July 1	Cash	22,000	
	Stock Investment—Influential (Carr)		16,750
	Gain on Sale of Investments		5,250

To record sale of influential equity securities for $22,000 ($22,000 – $16,750 = $5,250 gain).

Controlling Equity Securities

July 1	Cash	22,000	
	Stock Investment—Controlling (Dot)		20,250
	Gain on Sale of Investments		1,750

To record sale of controlling equity securities for $22,000 ($22,000 – $20,250 = $1,750 gain).

Because all available-for-sale stock was sold, the second entry in Exhibit 14-12 for the Bain stock investment eliminates the balances in the related valuation account and unrealized gain/loss account at the next adjustment date (December 31, 1998).

CURRENT AND NONCURRENT CLASSIFICATIONS

Each investment in debt and equity securities must still be classified as either a current asset or a noncurrent asset in the balance sheet. Trading securities are always classified as *current assets*. Held-to-maturity securities are classified as *noncurrent assets* until the last year before maturity. Available-for-sale securities may be classified as either *current* or *noncurrent assets,* depending on management's intentions regarding their sale. Influential invest-

GAINS TRADING

The treatment of unrealized gains and losses on available-for-sale investments permits management to engage in a practice known as "gains trading." Management may select for sale those available-for-sale securities that have unrealized gains, thus converting these gains into gains that appear in the income statement. Available-for-sale investments having unrealized losses are not sold, thus keeping the losses out of the income statement. Gains trading is a management behavior fostered by accounting principles. Many observers believe that it is a practice that gives management too much control over income statement results.

ments are usually classified as *noncurrent assets,* but a current classification is proper if management intends to sell the investments within the next year or operating cycle, whichever is longer. As mentioned earlier, controlling investments do not appear in consolidated financial statements.

DISCLOSURE OF FAIR VALUE

Firms must disclose the fair value of most financial instruments in their financial statements, either in the body of the balance sheet or in the notes to the financial statements.[5] Thus, the fair values of investments in debt and equity securities—other than those accounted for by the equity method—must be disclosed in the financial statements. For trading securities and available-for-sale securities, the carrying value in the balance sheet already shows the fair value. Because held-to-maturity securities are shown in the balance sheet at amortized cost, management must also estimate and disclose their fair value. Quoted market prices, when available, are usually good evidence of fair value.

CONSOLIDATED FINANCIAL STATEMENTS

PARENT-SUBSIDIARY RELATIONSHIP

OBJECTIVE 4
DEFINE parent-subsidiary relationships and **ILLUSTRATE** how their balance sheet data are consolidated.

A corporation that controls other corporations through ownership of the latters' stock is known as a **holding company.** Control over another corporation is ensured through ownership of all or a majority of its voting stock. Another name for a holding company is **parent company,** and the wholly owned or majority-held companies are called **subsidiaries** or **affiliates.** The parent company and each subsidiary company are separate legal entities.

An organizational structure consisting of a parent company and subsidiaries has some advantages over a structure that consists of a single company with separate operating divisions. Two advantages are (1) risk containment and (2) regulatory isolation.

Risk containment: Because it is a separate corporate entity, any obligations of a subsidiary company are legally separated from other business entities. Thus, any sizable claims on the assets of a particular subsidiary (due to a catastrophic loss, for example) cannot be transferred as claims to the assets of other companies. For example, United Asset Management Corporation provides investment management services to institutional clients; the total funds that it manages exceed $105 billion. United Asset Management Corporation is a

---

[5]*Statement of Financial Accounting Standards No. 107,* "Disclosures about Fair Value of Financial Instruments" (Norwalk, CT: Financial Accounting Standards Board, 1991).

holding company operating through 39 separate subsidiaries. Thus, the investment actions of a particular subsidiary do not put at risk the assets that are managed by the other 38 companies.

Regulatory isolation: Certain firms, such as financial institutions, insurance companies, and utilities, operate in industries that are subject to regulatory control by federal or state (or both) agencies. The regulatory agency, for example, may limit the business activities a company can engage in, or it may establish certain financial ratios that the company must maintain. To keep these restrictions or requirements from applying to unrelated operations, the regulated activities are established as a separate subsidiary. For example, Transamerica Corporation (a holding company) conducts its life insurance business through separate life insurance subsidiaries; Citicorp (a holding company) engages in banking through Citibank of New York (a subsidiary); and Southwestern Bell Corporation (a holding company) provides telecommunications through its largest subsidiary, Southwestern Bell Telephone Company.

THE CONSOLIDATED ENTITY

As separate legal entities, a parent company and its subsidiaries maintain their own accounting records and prepare separate financial statements primarily for internal purposes. In the parent company's *separate* financial statements, the ownership of a subsidiary's stock is reported as a stock investment accounted for by the equity method. When the parent company prepares financial statements for shareholders and creditors, however, the financial statements of the parent company and its subsidiaries are combined and reported as a single set of **consolidated financial statements.** When the financial data of these legal entities are consolidated, the resulting statements represent the group as an *economic entity,* as shown in Exhibit 14-13.

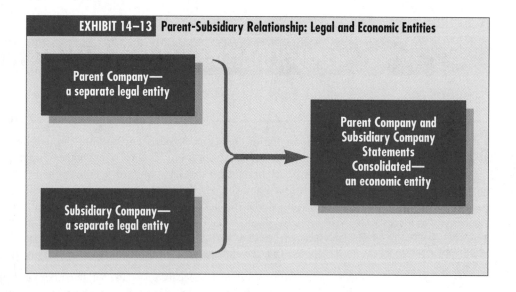

EXHIBIT 14–13 **Parent-Subsidiary Relationship: Legal and Economic Entities**

Consolidated financial statements present both the total resources controlled by a parent company and the aggregate results of the group's operations and cash flows. These amounts are difficult to perceive when viewing only the separate reports of the individual companies. Consolidated statements are particularly valuable to the managers and stockholders of the parent company. In addition, creditors, government agencies, and the general public are informed of the magnitude and scope of an economic enterprise through consolidated statements.

ACCOUNTING ENTITY CONCEPT

The preparation of consolidated financial statements represents an application of the *accounting entity concept.* By viewing the parent company and its subsidiaries as a single economic entity, accountants ignore the legal boundaries of the separate companies. For consolidated financial statements, then, the overall economic entity is the accounting entity. As we shall see shortly, one implication of this perspective is that intercompany financial relationships must be eliminated when consolidated financial statements are prepared.

ACQUISITION OF SUBSIDIARIES

A corporation may obtain a subsidiary either by establishing a new firm and holding more than 50% of its voting stock or by acquiring more than 50% of the voting stock of an existing firm. Both methods have been extensively used. When an existing firm is acquired, however, the method of acquisition may play an important role in the manner of accounting for the subsidiary.

One common method of acquiring an existing firm is to give up cash, other assets, notes, or debt securities. Generally, this is a *purchase* of a subsidiary, and the **purchase method** of reporting is used in consolidated financial statements. We discuss this method of acquisition first. Another method, called *pooling of interests,* involves exchanging stock of the acquiring company for substantially all of the shares of another firm. We discuss the accounting and reporting for pooling of interests later in the chapter.

WHOLLY OWNED SUBSIDIARIES: CONSOLIDATION AT ACQUISITION DATE

The general concept of consolidating affiliated companies is always the same, whether a subsidiary is created or an existing firm is acquired. Intercompany items are eliminated so that the consolidated statements show only the interests of outsiders.

Suppose that P Company purchases 100% of the common stock of an existing firm, Z Company, on January 1, 1996, for $100,000. Z Company's total stockholders' equity of $100,000 is composed of $80,000 of common stock and $20,000 of retained earnings. The entry on P Company's books to record the acquisition debits Stock Investment—Controlling (Z) for $100,000 and credits Cash for $100,000. Z Company makes no entry because payment is made directly to the shareholders of Z Company.

Also assume that on January 1, 1996, P Company loaned Z Company $25,000 cash in exchange for a six-month promissory note. P Company's entry debits Notes Receivable for $25,000 and credits Cash for $25,000; Z Company debits Cash for $25,000 and credits Notes Payable for $25,000.

The balance sheets of the two companies *immediately after the acquisition and loan* are shown in Exhibit 14-14. There are two examples of *reciprocal* items in these balance sheets: (1) the intercompany $25,000 of Notes Receivable for P Company and Notes Payable for Z Company and (2) the $100,000 Stock Investment—Controlling (Z) on P Company's balance sheet and the Common Stock and Retained Earnings ($80,000 + $20,000) on Z Company's balance sheet.

When consolidating the accounts of the two firms, both of the reciprocal situations must be eliminated. Exhibit 14-15 shows the worksheet used to prepare the consolidated balance sheet as of January 1, 1996. A consolidated balance sheet should show receivables and payables only with *outsiders;* otherwise, both total receivables and payables of the consolidated entity are overstated. Therefore, the reciprocal receivable and payable of $25,000 must be eliminated in preparing the consolidated balance sheet. To accomplish this, elimination entry (1) on the worksheet in Exhibit 14-15 debits Notes Payable for $25,000 and credits Notes Receivable for $25,000.

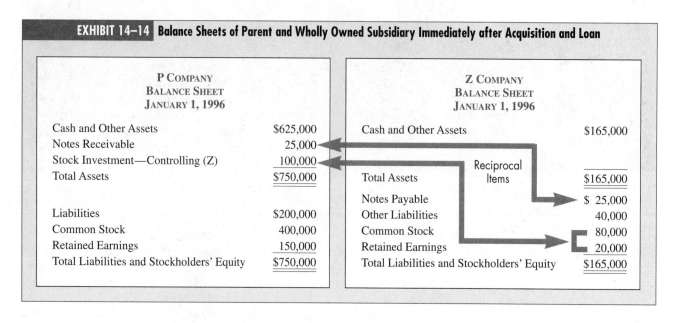

EXHIBIT 14–14 Balance Sheets of Parent and Wholly Owned Subsidiary Immediately after Acquisition and Loan

To avoid double counting assets and stockholders' equity, we must eliminate the reciprocal investment and stockholders' equity accounts. Elimination entry (2) on the worksheet in Exhibit 14-15 does this by debiting Common Stock (Z Company) for $80,000, debiting Retained Earnings (Z Company) for $20,000, and crediting Stock Investment—Controlling (Z) for $100,000. Observe that the stockholders' equity on the consolidated balance sheet is the equity of P Company's stockholders; that is, the *outside* shareholders. The stockholders' equity represented by P Company's ownership of Z Company stock is eliminated. *The intercompany equity existing on the balance sheets is always eliminated.*

EXHIBIT 14–15 Consolidated Balance Sheet Worksheet for Parent and Wholly Owned Subsidiary: Consolidation at Acquisition Date

P AND Z COMPANIES
CONSOLIDATED BALANCE SHEET WORKSHEET
JANUARY 1, 1996

	P Company	Z Company	Eliminations Debit	Eliminations Credit	Consolidated Balance Sheet
Cash and Other Assets	625,000	165,000			790,000
Notes Receivable	25,000	—		(1) 25,000	—
Stock Investment—Controlling (Z)	100,000	—		(2) 100,000	—
	750,000	165,000			790,000
Notes Payable	—	25,000	(1) 25,000		—
Liabilities	200,000	40,000			240,000
Common Stock					
P Company	400,000				400,000
Z Company		80,000	(2) 80,000		—
Retained Earnings					
P Company	150,000				150,000
Z Company		20,000	(2) 20,000		—
	750,000	165,000	125,000	125,000	790,000

MAJORITY-HELD SUBSIDIARIES: CONSOLIDATION AT ACQUISITION DATE

When a firm owns more than a 50% but less than a 100% interest in another firm, the parent company's interest is a *majority interest.* The interest of the other (outside) stockholders of the subsidiary company is called the **minority interest.** In preparing a consolidated balance sheet for a parent company and a majority-held subsidiary, the assets and liabilities of the affiliated companies are combined in the usual way to show their total resources and liabilities. The parent company's equity in the subsidiary at the date of the consolidated statements is eliminated as before, but in this case, the equity represents less than 100% of the subsidiary's common stock and retained earnings. The amount of the subsidiary's common stock and retained earnings not eliminated, which represents the minority interest in the subsidiary, appears on the consolidated balance sheet.

For example, assume that P Company purchased 80% of Q Company's voting stock on January 1, 1996, for $160,000. After the acquisition, the separate balance sheets of the two firms appear as shown in Exhibit 14-16.

EXHIBIT 14–16 **Balance Sheets of Parent and Majority-Held Subsidiary Immediately after Acquisition**

P AND Q COMPANIES
BALANCE SHEETS
JANUARY 1, 1996

	P Company	Q Company
Cash and Other Assets	$590,000	$220,000
Stock Investment—Controlling (Q)	160,000	—
Total Assets	$750,000	$220,000
Liabilities	$200,000	$ 20,000
Common Stock	400,000	150,000
Retained Earnings	150,000	50,000
Total Liabilities and Stockholders' Equity	$750,000	$220,000

Note that Q Company's stockholders' equity is $200,000 ($150,000 Common Stock and $50,000 Retained Earnings). The equity acquired by P Company is therefore $160,000 (80% of $200,000), which is the amount P Company paid for its interest. This intercompany equity at the date of the consolidated statements is eliminated. The remaining 20% minority interest, however, must be shown in the consolidated balance sheet. In other words, the minority, or outside, shareholders have a $40,000 interest in the stockholders' equity of Q Company (20% of $200,000). The worksheet entry to eliminate the intercompany equity and to reflect the minority interest debits Common Stock (Q Company) for $150,000, debits Retained Earnings (Q Company) for $50,000, credits Stock Investment—Controlling (Q) for $160,000, and credits Minority Interest for $40,000. The worksheet from which to prepare the consolidated balance sheet is given in Exhibit 14-17.

A formal consolidated balance sheet for the two companies, prepared from the right-hand column of the worksheet, is given in Exhibit 14-18. Note that the total consolidated stockholders' equity of $590,000 consists of the parent company's common stock and retained earnings (totaling $550,000) and the $40,000 minority interest. Thus, the interests of outside shareholders (the parent firm's shareholders and the subsidiary's minority shareholders) are portrayed in the consolidated balance sheet. Sometimes, in formal consolidated balance sheets, the minority interest amount is shown between the liabilities and the stockholders' equity. Most financial analysts, however, consider the minority interest part of stockholders' equity, and it is probably a better practice to classify it with the stockholders' equity.

EXHIBIT 14–17 Consolidated Balance Sheet Worksheet for Parent and Majority-Held Subsidiary: Consolidation at Acquisition Date

P AND Q COMPANIES
CONSOLIDATED BALANCE SHEET WORKSHEET
JANUARY 1, 1996

	P Company	Q Company	Eliminations Debit	Eliminations Credit	Consolidated Balance Sheet
Cash and Other Assets	590,000	220,000			810,000
Stock Investment—Controlling (Q)	160,000	—		160,000	—
	750,000	220,000			810,000
Liabilities	200,000	20,000			220,000
Minority Interest				40,000	40,000
Common Stock					
P Company	400,000				400,000
Q Company		150,000	150,000		—
Retained Earnings					
P Company	150,000				150,000
Q Company		50,000	50,000		—
	750,000	220,000	200,000	200,000	810,000

EXHIBIT 14–18 Consolidated Balance Sheet of Parent and Majority-Held Subsidiary at Acquisition Date

P AND Q COMPANIES
CONSOLIDATED BALANCE SHEET
JANUARY 1, 1996

Cash and Other Assets	$810,000	Liabilities		$220,000
		Stockholders' Equity		
		Minority Interest	$ 40,000	
		Common Stock	400,000	
		Retained Earnings	150,000	590,000
		Total Liabilities and		
Total Assets	$810,000	Stockholders' Equity		$810,000

DIFFERENCES BETWEEN ACQUISITION COST AND BOOK VALUE

OBJECTIVE 5

DISCUSS the treatment of acquisitions when cost exceeds the book value acquired in a subsidiary.

So far in our examples, we have assumed that the amount paid by the parent company to acquire a particular interest in a subsidiary exactly equals the book value of the interest acquired. In the real world, this rarely happens. In fact, the parent firm almost always pays more for its interest than the book values shown on the subsidiary's balance sheet. This occurs for one of two reasons, or a combination of them. First, the recorded values of the subsidiary's assets are often understated in terms of current fair market values, a common situation given the impact of inflation. Second, the parent firm may be willing to pay an additional amount for an unrecorded asset of the subsidiary—**goodwill**—if the subsidiary's earning power or its potential earning power is higher than normal for similar firms.

Suppose that P Company acquires a 100% interest in Y Company's voting stock for $125,000 when Y Company has the balance sheet shown in Exhibit 14-19. Note that P Company is paying $125,000 for a 100% interest in a firm with a net book value of $100,000. Negotiations for the purchase, however, reveal that Y Company's plant and equipment are undervalued by $15,000 and that its potential for future superior earnings is valued at an additional $10,000.

EXHIBIT 14-19	Balance Sheets of Parent and Wholly Owned Subsidiary at Acquisition Date: Acquisition Cost Exceeds Subsidiary's Book Value

P COMPANY BALANCE SHEET JANUARY 1, 1996		Y COMPANY BALANCE SHEET JANUARY 1, 1996	
Cash and Other Assets	$XXX,XXX	Current Assets	$ 40,000
Stock Investment—Controlling (Y)	125,000	Plant and Equipment	60,000
Total Assets	$XXX,XXX	Total Assets	$100,000
Liabilities	$XXX,XXX	Liabilities	$ —
Common Stock	XXX,XXX	Common Stock	80,000
Retained Earnings	XXX,XXX	Retained Earnings	20,000
Total Liabilities and Stockholders' Equity	$XXX,XXX	Total Liabilities and Stockholders' Equity	$100,000

In preparing a consolidated balance sheet, we make a worksheet entry that eliminates the intercompany equity and reflects the additional asset values established by the acquisition. The entry includes the following debits: Common Stock (Y Company), $80,000; Retained Earnings (Y Company), $20,000; Plant and Equipment, $15,000; and Goodwill from Consolidation, $10,000. A credit of $125,000 is made to Stock Investment—Controlling (Y). Thus, the intercompany equity in the recorded book values of the subsidiary is eliminated, and an additional amount of assets, $25,000, is reflected in the consolidated balance sheet. The goodwill from consolidation[6] appears as an intangible asset on the consolidated balance sheet. In the consolidated statements of subsequent years, the amount paid in excess of the equity acquired in the subsidiary is amortized over the life of the assets to which the amount has been assigned. In the case of goodwill, the period cannot exceed 40 years.

The Demonstration Problem at the end of this chapter illustrates a consolidation that has both a minority interest and goodwill from consolidation.

On occasion, we encounter a situation in which the parent company pays less than the equity acquired for a particular interest in a subsidiary company. If this situation occurs, accounting guidelines attribute the difference to an overvaluation of the subsidiary's noncurrent assets (other than long-term investments in marketable securities). The eliminating entry on the worksheet credits such assets.

CONSOLIDATED INCOME STATEMENT

So far we have dealt only with consolidated balance sheets. Now we look at the problem of consolidating the income statements of affiliated firms. If we wish to show the scope of operations of affiliated companies as an entity, combining the revenues, cost of goods sold,

---

[6]Often this is called *Excess of Cost over Book Value of Investment in Subsidiary.* Many accountants and financial analysts, however, prefer to call it *Goodwill from Consolidation.* Note that the separate balance sheets of P Company and Y Company show no goodwill.

OBJECTIVE 6

EXPLAIN and **ILLUSTRATE** the consolidation of parent and subsidiary income statements.

and expenses of the several companies is logical. In preparing a consolidated income statement, however, we present only the results of transactions with firms and individuals *outside* the entity. Any intercompany transactions—such as intercompany sales and purchases—are eliminated. Likewise, revenue and expense amounts representing services rendered by one firm to an affiliated firm are eliminated.

To illustrate the procedures for preparing a consolidated income statement, we use Exhibit 14-20, the separate income statements of P Company and its 75%-held subsidiary, S Company. For simplicity, we assume that P Company has not yet reflected its 75% share of S Company's net income in its own income statement.[7]

EXHIBIT 14–20 | **Income Statements of Parent and Majority-Held Subsidiary Prior to Consolidation**

P COMPANY INCOME STATEMENT FOR THE YEAR ENDED DECEMBER 31, 1996			S COMPANY INCOME STATEMENT FOR THE YEAR ENDED DECEMBER 31, 1996	
Sales		$500,000	Sales (including $30,000 sold to P Company)	$200,000
Cost of Goods Sold (including $30,000 of purchases from S Company)		300,000	Cost of Goods Sold	140,000
Gross Profit		$200,000	Gross Profit	$ 60,000
Operating Expenses (including income taxes)		160,000	Operating Expenses (including income taxes)	40,000
Net Income		$ 40,000	Net Income	$ 20,000

We have indicated in the income statements that $30,000 of S Company's sales were to P Company. Assume that P Company, in turn, sold all of this merchandise to outsiders. In preparing a consolidated income statement, we must eliminate $30,000 from the sales reported by S Company and from the cost of goods sold reported by P Company. The worksheet from which to prepare a consolidated income statement for the two firms is given in Exhibit 14-21.

In Exhibit 14-20, the $30,000 in S Company's sales and the reciprocal amount in P Company's cost of goods sold have been eliminated so that only sales to outsiders are reflected in the consolidated income statement. Notice that this elimination does not affect consolidated net income, because the same amount is excluded from both sales and cost of goods sold. It does, however, avoid distorting the sales volume and costs of the group. Of the $60,000 aggregate net income of the two firms, the $5,000 minority interest (25% of S Company's net income) is deducted, so the consolidated net income of the affiliated firms is $55,000. Thus, the $55,000 consolidated net income consists of $40,000 (the parent's net income from its own operations) plus $15,000 (the parent's 75% interest in the $20,000 subsidiary net income).

OTHER CONSOLIDATED STATEMENTS

In addition to a consolidated balance sheet and income statement, other consolidated financial statements include a consolidated statement of cash flows, a consolidated statement of retained earnings, and a consolidated statement of stockholders' equity. The preparation of these consolidated statements is beyond the scope of our introductory discussion.

---

[7]If P Company had already included its share of S Company's earnings in its own income statement, this amount would have to be eliminated to avoid double counting when the revenues and expenses of the two firms are consolidated.

| EXHIBIT 14–21 | Consolidated Income Statement Worksheet for Parent and Majority-Held Subsidiary |

P AND S COMPANIES
CONSOLIDATED INCOME STATEMENT WORKSHEET
FOR THE YEAR ENDED DECEMBER 31, 1996

| | | | Eliminations | | Consolidated |
	P Company	S Company	Debit	Credit	Income Statement
Sales	500,000	200,000	30,000		670,000
Cost of Goods Sold	300,000	140,000		30,000	410,000
Gross Profit	200,000	60,000			260,000
Expenses (including income taxes)	160,000	40,000			200,000
Net Income	40,000	20,000			60,000
Minority Interest in Net Income of S Company (25% of $20,000)					(5,000)
Consolidated Net Income					55,000

CONSOLIDATED STATEMENTS: POOLING OF INTERESTS METHOD

OBJECTIVE 7

PROVIDE an overview of accounting for acquisitions under the pooling of interests method.

In all of the foregoing examples, we assumed that an acquiring company *purchased* a controlling interest in the shares of another firm by issuing cash, other assets, or debt. Thus, a purchase and sale transaction occurred, and we used the *purchase method* to prepare consolidated statements.

On the other hand, if the acquiring company obtains substantially all (90% or more) of a subsidiary company's shares by *issuing its own shares* (and by meeting certain other criteria),[8] a **pooling of interests** has occurred. In a pooling of interests, stockholders of the subsidiary company become stockholders of the parent company. Basically, two sets of interests "unite" rather than have a purchase and sale transaction take place.

If a combination is a pooling of interests, the consolidated financial statements are prepared according to the **pooling of interests method.** In a consolidated balance sheet prepared under this method, the *book values* of the affiliated companies are combined. Of course, the market values of each firm's stock play an important part in determining the number of shares exchanged for the subsidiary's shares. However, once the negotiations are completed, the market values of the shares play no role in recording the parent's investment or in preparing consolidated financial statements.

Because the consolidated statements under the pooling of interests method reflect the book values of the subsidiary's assets, we do not revalue these assets, nor does any goodwill (excess of cost over equity acquired) emerge from the consolidation. On the other hand, under the purchase method, the subsidiary's assets are often revalued (almost invariably upward during periods of rising prices), and goodwill often appears in the consolidated balance sheet. Also, the increase in tangible assets and any goodwill are amortized over future periods. Consequently, future yearly consolidated earnings are lower under the purchase method than under the pooling of interests method.

Another facet of the pooling of interests method is that the subsidiary's and the parent's net incomes for the entire period of the acquisition year can be combined regardless of the date of acquisition. For example, suppose that a parent company earned $500,000 net

---

[8]The criteria for determining whether a pooling has occurred are set forth in *Opinions of the Accounting Principles Board, No. 16,* "Business Combinations" (New York: American Institute of Certified Public Accountants, 1970), p. 297.

income in the year that it used a pooling of interests to acquire a 100% interest in a subsidiary that earned $400,000. The acquisition occurred October 1, and the subsidiary's earnings for the last quarter were $100,000. The pooling of interests method combines the subsidiary's entire $400,000 with the parent's earnings, for a total consolidated net income of $900,000. With the purchase method, only the last quarter's earnings of the subsidiary ($100,000) are combined with the parent's $500,000 earnings, for a net income of $600,000.

We summarize the pooling of interests method as follows:

1. With the pooling of interests method, the subsidiary's assets are consolidated at their book value amounts. In contrast with the purchase method, no asset revaluations or goodwill appear in the consolidated balance sheet.

2. Without amortization of revaluation increases or goodwill, the pooling of interests method results in higher future earnings than the purchase method.

3. When the pooling of interests method is used, parent company and subsidiary earnings for the entire year are combined in the year of acquisition. With the purchase method, only the subsidiary's earnings after the acquisition date are included with parent company earnings.

LIMITATIONS OF CONSOLIDATED STATEMENTS

Consolidated statements have certain limitations. The status or performance of weak constituents in a group can be "masked" through consolidation with successful units. Rates of return, other ratios, and trend percentages calculated from consolidated statements may sometimes prove deceptive because they are really composite calculations. Shareholders and creditors of controlled companies who are interested in their legal rights and prerogatives should examine the separate financial statements of the relevant constituent companies.

Supplemental disclosures do improve the quality of consolidated statements, particularly those of *conglomerates,* entities with diversified lines of business. The Financial Accounting Standards Board stipulates that firms disclose information regarding revenues, income from operations, and identifiable assets for significant business segments.

FINANCIAL ANALYSIS

PRICE-EARNINGS RATIO

OBJECTIVE 8
DEFINE price-earnings ratio and **EXPLAIN** its use.

The stock listings in *The Wall Street Journal* contain a column with the heading PE. This column reports a firm's price-earnings ratio, a ratio of particular interest to investors. The **price-earnings ratio** shows the value of common stock in terms of a firm's earnings and is computed as follows:

$$\text{Price-Earnings Ratio} = \frac{\text{Market Price per Common Share}}{\text{Earnings per Share}}$$

The current market price of the firm's common stock and the earnings per share for the most recent four quarters of operations are typically used to calculate this ratio. For firms with complex capital structures, primary earnings per share is used. Also, if a firm's income statement includes data from discontinued operations or extraordinary items, the per-share amount before these items is generally used as the denominator in the ratio.

To illustrate, Lands' End, Inc., reported earnings per share of $1.85 for a recent year. With a market price per share of $30.25 at that time, Lands' End's price-earnings ratio was $30.25/$1.85 = 16. A firm with this ratio is characterized as selling at "16 times earnings" or as having an "earnings multiple" of 16.

After analyzing a firm, an investor may have determined what he or she believes is an appropriate earnings multiple for the firm. The investor then compares it with the actual price-earnings ratio to evaluate whether the firm's stock is overpriced or underpriced.

A high price-earnings ratio for a firm usually indicates that investors expect higher than average earnings growth for the company. Firms in high growth industries, therefore, generally have higher price-earnings ratios than do firms in stable, mature industries. The ratio also varies within an industry, thus indicating the relative attractiveness of firms to investors. For example, in mid-1995, three firms in the computer hardware industry had the following price-earnings ratios: American Power Conversion, 28; IBM, 15; and Apple Computer, 11. The average price-earnings ratio in mid-1995 for the stocks composing Standard & Poor's 500-stock index was 16.7.

KEY POINTS FOR CHAPTER LEARNING OBJECTIVES

1 **IDENTIFY** and **DEFINE** the investment categories for debt and equity securities (pp. 468–470).
■ Debt and equity security investments are placed in one of five categories:
  a. *Trading security,* a debt or equity security that management buys with the intent to sell in the near future.
  b. *Held-to-maturity security,* a debt security that management intends to hold to maturity.
  c. *Available-for-sale security,* a debt security that management neither intends to sell in the near future nor hold to maturity or a noninfluential equity security that management does not intend to sell in the near future.
  d. *Influential security,* an equity security investment that represents a 20% through 50% ownership of a company's voting stock.
  e. *Controlling security,* an equity security investment that represents an ownership of more than 50% of a company's voting stock.

2 **DESCRIBE** the accounting for various kinds of debt security investments (pp. 470–474).
■ Debt trading securities are initially recorded at cost, and interest income is recorded when received. The securities are reported at current fair value in the balance sheet with fair value changes reported in the income statement. When sold, the difference between the sales proceeds and the investment's book value is a realized gain or loss.
■ Debt available-for-sale securities are initially recorded at cost. Interest income is recorded when received, with any premium or discount amortized as an adjustment of interest income. The securities are reported at current fair value in the balance sheet with fair value changes reported in stockholders' equity. When sold, the difference between the sales proceeds and the investment's amortized cost is a realized gain or loss.
■ Debt held-to-maturity securities are initially recorded at cost. Interest income is recorded when received, with any premium or discount amortized as an adjustment of interest income. At maturity, the investment's book value equals the redemption proceeds.

3 **DESCRIBE** the accounting for various kinds of equity security investments (pp. 475–479).
■ Equity trading securities are initially recorded at cost, and dividend income is recorded when received. The securities are reported at current fair value in the balance sheet with fair value changes reported in the income statement. When sold, the difference between the sales proceeds and the investment's book value is a realized gain or loss.
■ Equity available-for-sale securities are initially recorded at cost. Dividend income is recorded when received. The securities are reported at current fair value in the balance sheet with fair value changes reported in stockholders' equity. When sold, the difference between the sales proceeds and the investment's cost is a realized gain or loss.
■ Equity influential securities are initially recorded at cost. Subsequent accounting uses the equity method: the investment account is increased by a proportionate share of the investee company's net income and decreased by the amount of dividends received. When sold, the difference between the sales proceeds and the investment's book value is a realized gain or loss.
■ Equity controlling securities are initially recorded at cost. Subsequent accounting uses the equity method: the investment account is increased by a proportionate share of the investee company's net income and decreased by the amount of dividends received. When consolidated financial statements are prepared, the investment account is eliminated. When sold, the difference between the sales proceeds and the investment's book value is a realized gain or loss.

4 **DEFINE** parent-subsidiary relationships and **ILLUSTRATE** how their balance sheet data are consolidated (pp. 479–484).
■ Two advantages of an organizational structure consisting of a parent company and subsidiaries are risk containment and regulatory isolation.
■ When a consolidated balance sheet is prepared, the intercompany equity on the balance sheets of the parent company and the subsidiary company is eliminated.

- If a subsidiary is majority held, the portion of the subsidiary's stockholders' equity not eliminated is presented in the balance sheet as a minority interest.
- Any amounts owing between the parent and subsidiaries are eliminated in preparing a consolidated balance sheet.

5 **DISCUSS** the treatment of acquisitions when cost exceeds the book value acquired in a subsidiary (pp. 484–485).

- In a purchase combination, the acquiring company initially records its investment at cost. In preparing consolidated statements, any amount in excess of the book value acquired in the subsidiary is allocated among specific assets when possible. Any unallocated amount is goodwill, which must be amortized over a period of years.

6 **EXPLAIN** and **ILLUSTRATE** the consolidation of parent and subsidiary income statements (pp. 485–487).

- A consolidated income statement presents only the results of transactions with firms and individuals outside the entity. Any intercompany transactions, such as intercompany sales and purchases, are eliminated from sales and cost of goods sold.
- After revenues, cost of goods sold, and expenses are combined and a combined net income is determined, any minority interest in the subsidiary's earnings is deducted to determine consolidated net income.

7 **PROVIDE** an overview of accounting for acquisitions under the pooling of interests method (pp. 487–488).

- When an acquiring firm obtains 90% or more of another firm's shares by issuing its own shares, the transaction may be treated as a pooling of interests.
- In a pooling combination, the parent firm records its investment in accordance with the book value of the acquired firm's net assets. Cost (as measured by the market value of shares exchanged) is ignored. The acquired firm's retained earnings at acquisition date are added to those of the acquiring firm in preparing consolidated statements. Earnings of both firms are likewise combined for the period when the acquisition occurred.

8 **Financial Analysis**   **DEFINE** *price-earnings ratio* and **EXPLAIN** its use (pp. 488–489).

- The price-earnings ratio is computed by dividing the current market price per share of common stock by the earnings per share.

SELF-TEST QUESTIONS FOR REVIEW

(Answers follow the Solution to Demonstration Problem.)

1. Snyder, Inc., purchased $100,000 of Dane Company's 8% bonds for $96,400 on January 1, 1996, 15 years before maturity. Snyder plans to hold the bonds to maturity. Snyder records interest and straight-line amortization on interest dates (June 30 and December 31). At December 31, 1996, the bonds have a market value of $97,200. Snyder's balance sheet at December 31, 1996, should report the bonds at
   a. $96,400.   **b.** $96,640.   **c.** $97,200.   **d.** $96,160.

2. A firm purchased noninfluential and noncontrolling stock investments for $65,000. The firm does not intend to sell the investments in the near future. During the year, the firm received dividends totaling $4,000 from these stock investments. At year-end, the stock portfolio had a quoted market value of $68,000. The increase in net income for the year (ignore income taxes) from these stock investments is
   a. $1,000.   **b.** $3,000.   **c.** $4,000.   **d.** $7,000.

3. Artway Company purchased 30% of the voting stock of Barton Company for $60,000 on January 1 of the current year. During the year, Barton Company earned $50,000 net income and paid $15,000 in dividends. At the end of the year, Artway Company's account, Stock Investment—Influential (Barton) should have a balance of
   a. $110,000.   **b.** $70,500.   **c.** $95,000.   **d.** $60,000.

4. X Company purchased an 80% interest in Y Company for $225,000 at the beginning of the current year. At that time, X Company had $500,000 common stock and $150,000 retained earnings, and Y Company had $200,000 common stock and $60,000 retained earnings. On the consolidated balance sheet prepared at the time of the acquisition, consolidated retained earnings should be
   a. $150,000.   **b.** $210,000.   **c.** $198,000.   **d.** $48,000.

5. Brown Company, which owns 70% of Greene Company's voting stock, sold merchandise during the year to Greene Company for $60,000. The merchandise had cost Brown Company $40,000. Greene Company sold all of the merchandise to outsiders during the year. In preparing a consolidated income statement for the year, Brown's sales amount and Greene's cost of goods sold amount should each be reduced by
   a. $60,000.   **b.** $40,000.   **c.** $20,000.   **d.** $28,000.

DEMONSTRATION PROBLEM FOR REVIEW

On January 1, 1997, Montana Company purchased 75% of the common stock of Utah Company for $200,000, after which the separate balance sheets of the two firms were as follows:

MONTANA AND UTAH COMPANIES
BALANCE SHEETS
JANUARY 1, 1997

Assets	Montana	Utah
Accounts Receivable	$ 30,000	$ 25,000
Stock Investment—Controlling (Utah)	200,000	—
Other Assets	270,000	275,000
Total Assets	$500,000	$300,000
Liabilities and Stockholders' Equity		
Accounts Payable	$ 50,000	$ 60,000
Common Stock	350,000	200,000
Retained Earnings	100,000	40,000
Total Liabilities and Stockholders' Equity	$500,000	$300,000

On January 1, 1997, Utah Company owed $7,000 to Montana Company on account for purchases made during 1996. The amount paid by Montana in excess of the equity acquired in Utah is attributable to goodwill.

REQUIRED

Prepare a consolidated balance sheet worksheet at January 1, 1997.

SOLUTION TO DEMONSTRATION PROBLEM

MONTANA AND UTAH COMPANIES
CONSOLIDATED BALANCE SHEET WORKSHEET
JANUARY 1, 1997

	Montana	Utah	Eliminations Debit	Eliminations Credit	Consolidated Balance Sheet
Accounts Receivable	30,000	25,000		(1) 7,000	48,000
Stock Investment—Controlling (Utah)	200,000	—		(2) 200,000	—
Other Assets	270,000	275,000			545,000
Goodwill from Consolidation			(2) 20,000		20,000
	500,000	300,000			613,000
Accounts Payable	50,000	60,000	(1) 7,000		103,000
Minority Interest				(2) 60,000	60,000
Common Stock					
Montana Company	350,000				350,000
Utah Company		200,000	(2) 200,000		—
Retained Earnings					
Montana Company	100,000				100,000
Utah Company		40,000	(2) 40,000		—
	500,000	300,000	267,000	267,000	613,000

Montana Company's January 1, 1997, acquisition of 75% of Utah Company's common stock resulted in goodwill of $20,000 ($200,000 acquisition price – 75% of $240,000 stockholders' equity acquired). At January 1, 1997, the minority interest is $60,000—25% of the $240,000 total stockholders' equity of Utah Company. Elimination entry (1) eliminates the intercompany receivable and payable. Elimination entry (2) eliminates the intercompany equity and establishes the goodwill from consolidation and minority interest.

ANSWERS TO SELF-TEST QUESTIONS

1. b, p. 471   **2.** c, p. 475   **3.** b, p. 476   **4.** a, p. 483   **5.** a, p. 486

Conversion of Foreign Currency Financial Statements

As world trade has grown, so have the number and size of multinational corporations. A **multinational corporation** conducts operations in more than one country by locating branches, divisions, or subsidiaries outside its home country. Exxon Corporation, for example, has divisions and affiliated companies operating in the United States and more than 80 other countries. Exhibit H-1 lists the 10 largest U.S. multinational corporations in 1994.

EXHIBIT H-1	Ten Largest U.S. Multinationals in 1994		
Rank	Company	Foreign Revenue (millions)	Foreign Assets (millions)
1	Exxon	$77,125	$ 50,869
2	General Motors	44,041	50,777
3	Mobil	40,318	24,428
4	IBM	39,934	46,218
5	Ford Motor	38,075	60,610
6	Texaco	24,760	12,910
7	Citicorp	19,703	142,000
8	Chevron	16,533	15,711
9	Philip Morris	16,329	18,025
10	Procter & Gamble	15,650	10,688

Adapted from "The 100 Largest U.S. Multinationals," *Forbes*, July 17, 1995, p. 274. Reprinted by permission.

U.S. multinational corporations frequently use foreign subsidiary companies to conduct their foreign activities. If the foreign subsidiary is more than 50% owned, its financial statements are usually consolidated with the U.S. parent's statements. When the subsidiary's accounting records are kept in the foreign currency, its financial statements must be converted to U.S. dollars before consolidation can occur.

CONVERSION PROCEDURES

Two different procedures may be used to convert foreign financial statements to U.S. dollars:

1. *Translation* procedures.

2. *Remeasurement* procedures.

The **functional currency** of a foreign subsidiary determines which of these two procedures is used. It is defined by the Financial Accounting Standards Board:

An entity's functional currency is the currency of the primary economic environment in which the entity operates; normally, that is the currency of the environment in which an entity primarily generates and expends cash.[1]

Depending on the circumstances, the functional currency may be either the foreign currency or the U.S. dollar. For example, a German subsidiary manufactures and sells its own products. Its expenses, as well as cash generated by its operations, are primarily in German marks and have little impact on its parent's cash flows. This subsidiary's operations are well integrated with the German economy. Thus, its functional currency is the foreign currency (mark). In contrast, consider a German subsidiary that is a sales outlet for its U.S. parent's goods. The subsidiary takes orders, bills and collects the invoice price, warehouses the goods to facilitate delivery, and remits its net cash flows primarily to the parent. This subsidiary is essentially an agent for the parent company. Its functional currency is the U.S. dollar.

The functional currency is also the U.S. dollar for foreign subsidiaries that operate in highly inflationary economies (economies whose cumulative inflation over a three-year period is approximately 100% or more). The U.S. dollar is deemed the functional currency, because it is the more stable currency; the foreign currency is too unstable. Argentina and Brazil are recent examples of countries whose three-year cumulative inflation exceeds 100%.

Once the functional currency is determined, the specific conversion procedures are selected as follows:

1. *Foreign currency is functional currency:* Use translation procedures.

2. *U.S. dollar is functional currency:* Use remeasurement procedures.

To illustrate these two procedures for converting foreign financial statements to U.S. dollars, we assume that Wyso Company was organized in Germany on January 1, 1996, as a wholly owned subsidiary of Minor Corporation, a U.S. company. Wyso's opening balance sheet, in German marks (M), consisted of the following assets and stockholders' equity:

Assets		**Stockholders' Equity**	
Cash	M 40,000	Common Stock	M800,000
Inventory	160,000		
Plant Assets	600,000		
		Total Liabilities and	
Total Assets	M800,000	Stockholders' Equity	M800,000

After one year of operation, Wyso's 1996 income statement and December 31, 1996, balance sheet, in marks, are as follows:

WYSO COMPANY
INCOME STATEMENT
FOR THE YEAR ENDED DECEMBER 31, 1996

Sales		M750,000
Cost of Goods Sold	M500,000	
Depreciation Expense	30,000	
Other Expenses	70,000	
Total Expenses		600,000
Net Income		M150,000

---

[1]*Statement of Financial Accounting Standards No. 52,* "Foreign Currency Translation" (Stamford, CT: Financial Accounting Standards Board, 1981), p. 3.

WYSO COMPANY
BALANCE SHEET
DECEMBER 31, 1996

Assets		Liabilities		
Cash	M 60,000	Accounts Payable		M 30,000
Accounts Receivable (net)	140,000	**Stockholders' Equity**		
Inventory	210,000	Common Stock	M800,000	
Plant Assets (net)	570,000	Retained Earnings	150,000	950,000
		Total Liabilities and		
Total Assets	M980,000	Stockholders' Equity		M980,000

Assume that exchange rates for the mark are as follows:

January 1, 1996	$0.64
Average for 1996	0.60
December 31, 1996	0.56

TRANSLATION PROCEDURES

Assume that Wyso Company's operations are fully integrated with Germany's economy. Thus, its functional currency is the mark and translation procedures are used. **Translation procedures** convert foreign financial statements to U.S. dollars as follows:

1. All asset and liability accounts are converted using the exchange rate at the balance sheet date (current rate).

2. Capital stock accounts are converted using the exchange rate on the date the stock was issued (historical rate).

3. All revenue and expense accounts are converted using the exchange rate at the date these items were recognized. If revenues and expenses are generated in a relatively uniform pattern during the year, an average exchange rate for the year may be used (average rate).

The purpose of these translation procedures is to retain, in the converted data, the financial results and relationships among assets and liabilities that were created by the subsidiary's operation in its foreign environment.

Exhibit H-2 shows these translation procedures applied to Wyso Company's financial statements. Note the $70,000 **translation adjustment** in the exhibit, shown as a reduction of stockholders' equity in U.S. dollars. Translation procedures create a translation adjustment. The translation adjustment balances the balance sheet and occurs because the same exchange rate is not used to convert all accounts. The $70,000 may be calculated as follows:

Common Stock × (Historical Rate – Current Rate)	
M800,000 × ($0.64 – $0.56) =	$64,000
Net Income × (Average Rate – Current Rate)	
M150,000 × ($0.60 – $0.56) =	6,000
Translation adjustment	$70,000

The translation adjustment is reported as a separate component of stockholders' equity. Depending on the direction of exchange rate changes, it may reduce (as in our illustration) or increase stockholders' equity.

REMEASUREMENT PROCEDURES

Now assume that Wyso Company's operations are essentially a direct extension of Minor Corporation's (the parent) activities. In this circumstance, Wyso's functional currency is the U.S. dollar and remeasurement procedures are used. **Remeasurement procedures** convert foreign financial statements to U.S. dollars as follows:

1. Monetary asset and liability accounts (basically all cash, receivables, and payables) are converted using the exchange rate at the balance sheet date (current rate).

2. All other balance sheet accounts are converted using the exchange rate in effect when the item was initially recorded on the books (historical rate).

EXHIBIT H–2	Translation of Wyso Company Financial Statements, December 31, 1996 German Mark = Functional Currency		

	German Marks	Exchange Rate	U.S. Dollars
Balance Sheet			
Cash	M 60,000	$0.56	$ 33,600
Accounts Receivable (net)	140,000	0.56	78,400
Inventory	210,000	0.56	117,600
Plant Assets (net)	570,000	0.56	319,200
Total	M980,000		$548,800
Accounts Payable	M 30,000	0.56	$ 16,800
Common Stock	800,000	0.64	512,000
Retained Earnings	150,000	See Net Income	90,000
Translation Adjustment			(70,000)
Total	M980,000		$548,800
Income Statement			
Sales	M750,000	0.60	$450,000
Cost of Goods Sold	M500,000	0.60	$300,000
Depreciation Expense	30,000	0.60	18,000
Other Expenses	70,000	0.60	42,000
Total Expenses	M600,000		$360,000
Net Income	M150,000		$ 90,000

3. Revenue and expense accounts are converted using the exchange rate related to the transaction. Generally, the average exchange rate for the period is used. However, expenses that relate to assets converted at historical rates are converted at the appropriate historical rate. Depreciation expense and cost of goods sold are in this latter category.

The objective of these remeasurement procedures is to produce the same U.S. dollar financial statements as if the foreign entity's accounting records had been initially maintained in the U.S. dollar.

Exhibit H-3 shows these remeasurement procedures applied to Wyso Company's financial statements. An exchange rate of $0.58 applies to the ending inventory (the average exchange rate during the latter part of the year when the ending inventory was acquired). Under the perpetual FIFO method used by Wyso, the average exchange rate that relates to the 1996 cost of goods sold is $0.61. Also, note the $14,000 foreign exchange loss among the income statement expenses in U.S. dollars.[2] Remeasurement procedures produce foreign gains or losses: the effects on assets and liabilities of exchange rate changes. These foreign exchange gains and losses are included in net income.

GENERALLY ACCEPTED ACCOUNTING PRINCIPLES

At present, there are no international accounting principles that are broadly accepted and enforced. Accounting principles vary among countries because legal, economic, and regulatory systems differ, just as social values and traditions do. Foreign company financial statements, therefore, may vary in some respects from U.S. generally accepted accounting principles. If they do, the statements must be changed to conform to U.S. generally accepted accounting principles *before* the conversion to U.S. dollars may occur.

---

[2]The $14,000 foreign exchange loss is the amount needed to obtain a $69,800 net income. When transferred to retained earnings, the $69,800 balances the balance sheet.

EXHIBIT H–3	Remeasurement of Wyso Company Financial Statements, December 31, 1996
	U.S. Dollar = Functional Currency

Balance Sheet	German Marks	Exchange Rate	U.S. Dollars
Cash	M 60,000	$0.56	$ 33,600
Accounts Receivable (net)	140,000	0.56	78,400
Inventory	210,000	0.58	121,800
Plant Assets (net)	570,000	0.64	364,800
Total	M980,000		$598,600
Accounts Payable	M 30,000	0.56	$ 16,800
Common Stock	800,000	0.64	512,000
Retained Earnings	150,000	See Net Income	69,800
Total	M980,000		$598,600
Income Statement			
Sales	M750,000	0.60	$450,000
Cost of Goods Sold	M500,000	0.61	$305,000
Depreciation Expense	30,000	0.64	19,200
Other Expenses	70,000	0.60	42,000
Foreign Exchange Loss			14,000
Total Expenses	M600,000		$380,200
Net Income	M150,000		$ 69,800

GLOSSARY OF KEY TERMS USED IN THIS CHAPTER AND APPENDIX

affiliates   Corporations that have at least a majority of their voting stock owned by another company; also called *subsidiaries* (p. 479).

available-for-sale securities   Debt securities and noninfluential equity securities that management does not intend to sell in the near future nor hold to maturity (p. 469).

consolidated financial statements   Financial statements prepared with intercompany (reciprocal) accounts eliminated to portray the financial position, results of operations, and cash flows of two or more affiliated companies as a single economic entity (p. 480).

controlling securities   Equity securities that represent an ownership of more than 50% of a corporation's voting stock (p. 469).

debt security   A security that creates, for the holder, a creditor relationship with an entity (p. 468).

equity method   A method of accounting by a parent company for investments in subsidiary companies by which the parent's share of subsidiary income or loss is periodically recorded in the parent company investment account (p. 476).

equity security   A security that represents an ownership interest in an entity (p. 468).

functional currency   The currency of the primary economic environment in which a foreign entity operates (p. 492).

goodwill   The value that derives from a firm's ability to earn more than a normal rate of return on the fair market value of its specific, identifiable net assets. Goodwill is recognized only when it is acquired through the purchase of another entity (p. 484).

held-to-maturity securities   Debt securities that management intends to hold to maturity (p. 469).

holding company   A corporation that controls other corporations through ownership of the latters' stock (p. 479).

influential securities   Equity securities that represent a 20% through 50% ownership of a corporation's voting stock (p. 469).

minority interest   The portion of capital stock in a subsidiary corporation that is not owned by the controlling (parent) company (p. 483).

multinational corporation   A corporation that conducts operations in more than one country by locating branches, divisions, or subsidiaries outside its home country (p. 492).

parent company   A company holding all or a majority of the voting stock of another company, which is called an *affiliate* or a *subsidiary* (p. 479).

pooling of interests   Uniting the ownership interests of two or more companies through the exchange of 90% or more of the firms' voting stock (p. 487).

pooling of interests method The method used to prepare consolidated financial statements for a business combination treated as a pooling of interests. Under this method, the book values of the affiliated companies are combined in the consolidated balance sheet and annual earnings are combined in the income statement in the year of acquisition (p. 487).

price-earnings ratio A financial ratio computed as the current market price per common share divided by the earnings per share (p. 488).

purchase method The method used to prepare consolidated financial statements for a business combination treated as a purchase transaction. Under this method, the net assets of the acquired company appear at fair market value in the consolidated balance sheet and goodwill from consolidation appears if the purchase price exceeds the fair market value of the specific net assets acquired (p. 481).

remeasurement procedures A process of converting foreign currency financial statements to U.S. dollars that essentially produces the same U.S. dollar financial statements as if the foreign entity's records had been initially maintained in U.S. dollars (p. 494).

subsidiaries Corporations that have at least a majority of their voting stock owned by another company; also called *affiliates* (p. 479).

trading securities Debt securities and noninfluential equity securities that management buys with the intent to sell in the near future (p. 469).

translation adjustment A component of stockholders' equity (either an increase or a decrease) resulting from the use of translation procedures to convert foreign currency financial statements. The adjustment arises because the same exchange rate is not used to convert all accounts (p. 494).

translation procedures A process of converting foreign currency financial statements to U.S. dollars that retains, in the converted data, the financial results and relationships among assets and liabilities that were created by the entity's operations in its foreign environment (p. 494).

QUESTIONS

14-1 Debt security investments are placed in one of three investment categories. What are these three categories?

14-2 Equity security investments are placed in one of four investment categories. What are these four categories?

14-3 Caldwell Company invests in bonds at a premium. Caldwell does not intend to sell the bonds in the near future, nor does it intend to hold the bonds to maturity. Should the bond premium be amortized? What measure should be used to report these bonds in the year-end balance sheet?

14-4 What measure should be used to report trading securities in the balance sheet? Available-for-sale securities? Held-to-maturity securities?

14-5 What is an unrealized holding gain? Unrealized holding loss?

14-6 Where are unrealized holding gains and losses related to trading securities reported in the financial statements? Where are unrealized holding gains and losses related to available-for-sale securities reported in the financial statements?

14-7 What is an influential stock investment? Describe the accounting procedures used for such investments.

14-8 On January 1 of the current year, Mower Company purchased 40% of the common stock of Starr Company for $250,000. During the year, Starr had $80,000 of net income and paid $60,000 in cash dividends. At year-end, what amount should appear in Mower's balance sheet for its investment in Starr?

14-9 What accounting procedures are used when a stock investment represents more than 50% of the investee company's voting stock?

14-10 What is the purpose of consolidated financial statements?

14-11 What are two advantages to organizing as a parent company with subsidiaries rather than organizing as a single company with divisions? Briefly explain the advantages.

14-12 In a recent annual report, the consolidated financial statements of Overseas Shipholding Group, Inc., show an asset Investment in Celebrity Cruise Lines, Inc. This investment represents a 50% ownership interest in Celebrity Cruise Lines. Explain why the accounts of Celebrity Cruise Lines are not consolidated with the accounts of Overseas Shipholding Group and its other subsidiaries. On what accounting basis is the investment in Celebrity Cruise Lines carried?

14-13 What is the difference between a purchase acquisition and a pooling of interests?

14-14 P Company purchases all of the common stock of S Company for $750,000 when S Company has $300,000 of common stock and $450,000 of retained earnings. If a consolidated balance sheet is prepared immediately after the acquisition, what amounts are eliminated in preparing it?

14-15 Baxter, Inc., owns 100% of Technocel Company. At year-end, Technocel owes Baxter $75,000, terms n/60. If a consolidated balance sheet is prepared at year-end, how is the $75,000 handled? Why?

14-16 P Company purchases 80% of S Company's common stock for $600,000 when S Company has $300,000 of common stock and $450,000 of retained earnings. If a consolidated balance sheet is prepared immediately after the acquisition, what amounts are eliminated in preparing this statement? What amount of minority interest appears in the consolidated balance sheet?

14-17 Madd Company purchased an interest in West Company for $650,000 when West Company had $400,000 of common stock and $220,000 of retained earnings.
   a. If Madd Company had acquired a 100% interest in West Company, what amount of Goodwill from Consolidation would appear on the consolidated balance sheet? (Assume that West's assets are fairly valued.)
   b. If Madd had acquired only a 75% interest in West Company, what amount of Goodwill from Consolidation would appear?

14-18 Nelson Company purchased a 90% interest in Wells Company on January 1 of the current year. Nelson Company had $600,000 net income for the current year before reflecting its share of Wells Company's net income. If Wells Company had net income of $150,000 for the year, what is the consolidated net income for the year?

14-19 Kern Company, which owns 75% of Snell Company, sold merchandise during the year to Snell Company for $100,000. The merchandise cost Kern Company $70,000. If Snell Company in turn sold all of the merchandise to outsiders for $125,000, what eliminating entry related to these transactions does Kern make in preparing a consolidated income statement for the year?

14-20 P Company acquired 100% of S Company on September 1 of the current year. Why might the consolidated earnings of the two firms for the current year be higher if the transaction is treated as a pooling of interests rather than as a purchase?

14-21 What are the inherent limitations of consolidated financial statements?

14-22 How is a corporation's *price-earnings ratio* computed?

PRINCIPLES DISCUSSION QUESTION

14-23 Peugeot S.A. is incorporated in France and manufactures the Peugeot and Citroen automobiles. Peugeot S.A. prepares its financial statements in conformity with accounting principles in France and the United States. In accordance with French accounting principles, Peugeot S.A. does not consolidate its majority-owned banking and finance subsidiaries. To conform to U.S. accounting principles, it presents financial statements in a note that do consolidate the banking and finance subsidiaries. What is the rationale for not consolidating the banking and finance subsidiaries? Peugeot's consolidated net income is the same whether or not the banking and finance subsidiaries are consolidated. Why?

EXERCISES

DEBT SECURITY—TRADING — OBJ. 2 —

14-24 Gressens Company had the following transactions and adjustments related to a bond investment:

1996

Oct. 1   Purchased $500,000 face value of Skyline, Inc.'s 7% bonds at 97 plus a brokerage commission of $1,000. The bonds pay interest on September 30 and March 31 and mature in 20 years. Gressens Company expects to sell the bonds in the near future.

Dec. 31   Made the adjusting entry to record interest earned on investment in the Skyline bonds. (Gressens does not make reversing entries.)

     31   Made the adjusting entry to record the current fair value of the Skyline bonds. At December 31, 1996, the market value of the Skyline bonds was $490,000.

1997

Mar. 31   Received the semiannual interest payment on investment in the Skyline bonds.

Apr. 1   Sold the Skyline bond investment for $492,300 cash.

Record, in general journal form, these transactions and adjustments of Gressens Company.

DEBT SECURITY—AVAILABLE FOR SALE — OBJ. 2 —

14-25 Hilyn Company had the following transactions and adjustments related to a bond investment:

1996

Jan. 1   Purchased $800,000 face value of Cynad, Inc.'s 9% bonds at 99 plus a brokerage commission of $1,400. The bonds pay interest on June 30 and December 31 and mature in 15 years. Hilyn does not expect to sell the bonds in the near future, nor does it intend to hold the bonds to maturity.

June 30 Received the semiannual interest payment on the Cynad bonds and amortized the bond discount for six months. Hilyn uses the straight-line method to amortize bond discounts and premiums.

Dec. 31 Received the semiannual interest payment on the Cynad bonds and amortized the bond discount for six months.

31 Made the adjusting entry to record the current fair value of the Cynad bonds. At December 31, 1996, the market value of the Cynad bonds was $790,000.

1997

June 30 Received the semiannual interest payment on the Cynad bonds and amortized the bond discount for six months.

July 1 Sold the Cynad bond investment for $792,500 cash.

Dec. 31 Made the adjusting entry to eliminate balances from Fair Value Adjustment to Bond Investment account and Unrealized Gain/Loss on Investments (Equity) account.

Record, in general journal form, these transactions and adjustments of Hilyn Company.

DEBT SECURITY—HELD TO MATURITY
— OBJ. 2 —

14-26 Kurl Company had the following transactions and adjustments related to a bond investment:

1996

Jan. 1 Purchased $600,000 face value of Sphere, Inc.'s 9% bonds at 102 plus a brokerage commission of $900. The bonds pay interest on June 30 and December 31 and mature in 10 years. Kurl expects to hold the bonds to maturity.

June 30 Received the semiannual interest payment on the Sphere bonds and amortized the bond premium for six months. Kurl uses the straight-line method to amortize bond discounts and premiums.

2005

Dec. 31 Received the semiannual interest payment on the Sphere bonds and amortized the bond premium for six months.

31 Received the principal amount in cash on maturity date of the Sphere bonds.

Record, in general journal form, these transactions and adjustments of Kurl Company.

EQUITY SECURITY—TRADING
— OBJ. 3 —

14-27 Glass Company had the following transactions and adjustment related to a stock investment:

1996

Nov. 15 Purchased 6,000 shares of Erie, Inc.'s common stock at $12 per share plus a brokerage commission of $750. Glass expects to sell the stock in the near future.

Dec. 22 Received a cash dividend of $1.10 per share of common stock from Erie.

31 Made the adjusting entry to reflect year-end fair value of the stock investment in Erie. The year-end market price of the Erie common stock is $11.25 per share.

1997

Jan. 20 Sold all 6,000 shares of the Erie common stock for $66,900.

Record, in general journal form, these transactions and adjustment of Glass Company.

EQUITY SECURITY—AVAILABLE FOR SALE
— OBJ. 3 —

14-28 Refer to the data for Glass Company in Exercise 14-27. Assume that when the shares were purchased, management did not intend to sell the stock in the near future. Record the transactions and adjustment for Glass Company under this assumption. In addition, prepare any adjusting entry needed at December 31, 1997.

EQUITY SECURITY— INFLUENTIAL
— OBJ. 3 —

14-29 Dunn Company had the following transactions and adjustment related to a stock investment:

1996

Jan. 15 Purchased 12,000 shares of Van, Inc.'s common stock at $9 per share plus a brokerage commission of $900. These shares represent a 30% ownership of Van's common stock.

Dec. 31 Received a cash dividend of $1.25 per share of common stock from Van.

31 Made the adjusting entry to reflect income from the Van stock investment. Van's 1996 net income is $80,000.

1997

Jan. 20 Sold all 12,000 shares of the Van common stock for $120,500.

Record, in general journal form, these transactions and adjustment of Dunn Company.

ELIMINATING ENTRY AND STOCKHOLDERS' EQUITY IN CONSOLIDATION
— OBJ. 4 —

14-30 On January 1 of the current year, Halen Company purchased all of the common shares of Jolson Company for $575,000 cash. On this date, the stockholders' equity of Halen Company consisted of $600,000 in common stock and $310,000 in retained earnings. Jolson Company had $350,000 in common stock and $225,000 in retained earnings.

a. Give the worksheet eliminating entry to prepare a consolidated balance sheet on the acquisition date.
b. What amount of total stockholders' equity appears on the consolidated balance sheet?

STOCKHOLDERS' EQUITY IN CONSOLIDATED BALANCE SHEET — OBJ. 4 —

14-31 Baylor Company purchased 75% of the common stock of Reed Company for $600,000 in cash when the stockholders' equity of Reed Company consisted of $500,000 in common stock and $300,000 in retained earnings. On the acquisition date, the stockholders' equity of Baylor Company consisted of $900,000 in common stock and $440,000 in retained earnings. Prepare the stockholders' equity section in the consolidated balance sheet as of the acquisition date.

ELIMINATING ENTRY INCLUDING ASSET REVALUATION AND GOODWILL — OBJ. 5 —

14-32 On January 1 of the current year, Pyramid Company purchased all of the common shares of Pound Company for $500,000 cash and notes. Balance sheets of the two firms immediately after the acquisition were as follows:

	Pyramid	Pound
Current Assets	$1,700,000	$120,000
Stock Investment—Controlling (Pound)	500,000	—
Plant and Equipment (net)	3,000,000	410,000
Total Assets	$5,200,000	$530,000
Liabilities	$ 700,000	$ 90,000
Common Stock	3,500,000	400,000
Retained Earnings	1,000,000	40,000
Total Liabilities and Stockholders' Equity	$5,200,000	$530,000

During the negotiations for the purchase, Pound's plant and equipment were appraised at $425,000. Furthermore, Pyramid concluded that an additional $45,000 demanded by Pound's shareholders was warranted because Pound's earning power was somewhat better than the industry average. Prepare the worksheet eliminating entry needed to prepare a consolidated balance sheet on the acquisition date.

ELIMINATING ENTRY FOR INTERCOMPANY SALES — OBJ. 6 —

14-33 Pate Company has an 80% interest in Benson Company. During the current year, Benson Company sold merchandise costing $44,000 to Pate Company for $80,000. Assuming that Pate Company sold all of the merchandise to outsiders for $116,000, what worksheet eliminating entry should be made in preparing a consolidated income statement for the period?

TRANSLATION PROCEDURES — APPENDIX H —

14-34 Assume that translation procedures are being used to convert the financial statements of a foreign subsidiary to U.S. dollars. Indicate which exchange rate—current, historical, or average for the year—should be used to convert each of the following categories of accounts:
a. Assets.
b. Liabilities.
c. Capital stock.
d. Revenues generated uniformly throughout the year.
e. Expenses incurred uniformly throughout the year.

PROBLEMS

ANALYSIS OF BOND INVESTMENTS — OBJ. 2 —

14-35 Columbia Company began operations in 1996 and by year-end (December 31) had made six bond investments. Year-end information on these bond investments follows.

Company	Face Value	Cost or Amortized Cost	Year-End Market Value	Classification
Ling, Inc.	$100,000	$102,400	$105,300	Trading
Wren, Inc.	$250,000	$262,500	$270,000	Trading
Olanamic, Inc.	$200,000	$197,000	$199,000	Available for sale
Fossil, Inc.	$150,000	$154,000	$160,000	Available for sale
Meander, Inc.	$100,000	$101,200	$102,400	Held to maturity
Resin, Inc.	$140,000	$136,000	$137,000	Held to maturity

REQUIRED

a. At what total amount will the trading bond investments be reported in the December 31, 1996, balance sheet?

b. At what total amount will the available-for-sale bond investments be reported in the December 31, 1996, balance sheet?

c. At what total amount will the held-to-maturity bond investments be reported in the December 31, 1996, balance sheet?

d. What total amount of unrealized holding gains or unrealized holding losses related to bond investments will appear in the 1996 income statement?

e. What total amount of unrealized holding gains or unrealized holding losses related to bond investments will appear in the stockholders' equity section of the December 31, 1996, balance sheet?

f. What total amount of fair value adjustment to bond investments will appear in the December 31, 1996, balance sheet? Which category of bond investments does the fair value adjustment relate to? Does the fair value adjustment increase or decrease the financial statement presentation of these bond investments?

BOND INVESTMENT ENTRIES
— OBJ. 2 —

14-36 The following transactions and adjustments relate to bond investments acquired by Bloom Corporation.

1996

June 30   Purchased $200,000 face value of Dynamo, Inc.'s 20-year, 9% bonds dated June 30, 1996, for $215,200 cash. Interest is paid December 31 and June 30. Investment is classified in the available-for-sale category.

Dec. 31   Received the semiannual interest payment from Dynamo and amortized the bond premium (straight-line method).

    31   Purchased $300,000 face value of Link, Inc.'s 10-year, 7% bonds dated December 31, 1996, for $297,000 cash. Interest is paid June 30 and December 31. Investment is classified in the held-to-maturity category.

    31   Made the adjusting entry to record the current fair value of the Dynamo bonds. At December 31, 1996, their market value was $216,000.

1997

June 30   Received the semiannual interest payment from Dynamo and amortized the bond premium.

    30   Received the semiannual interest payment from Link and amortized the bond discount (straight-line method).

July 1   Sold the Dynamo bonds for $216,500.

Oct. 31   Purchased $60,000 face value of Taxco, Inc.'s 5-year, 8% bonds dated October 31, 1997, for $60,500. Interest is paid April 30 and October 31. Investment is classified in the trading category.

Dec. 31   Received the semiannual interest payment from Link and amortized the bond discount.

    31   Made the adjusting entry to record interest earned on investment in the Taxco bonds.

    31   Made the adjusting entry to record the current fair value of the Taxco bonds. At December 31, 1997, the market value of these bonds was $59,200.

    31   Made the adjusting entry to eliminate balances in Fair Value Adjustment to Bond Investment account and Unrealized Gain/Loss on Investments (Equity) account.

REQUIRED

Prepare the journal entries to record these transactions and adjustments.

STOCK INVESTMENT ENTRIES
— OBJ. 3 —

14-37 The following transactions and adjustments relate to stock investments made by Steen Corporation.

1996

July 1   Purchased, as a stock investment, 1,000 shares of Polk, Inc.'s common stock for $66,200 cash. The investment, which is noninfluential and noncontrolling, is classified in the trading category.

Oct. 1   Purchased, as stock investments, 3,000 shares of Wynn, Inc.'s common stock for $78,000 cash and 2,000 shares of Maple, Inc.'s common stock for $64,000 cash. These investments, which are noninfluential and noncontrolling, are classified in the available-for-sale category. (Note: Use two investment accounts.)

Nov. 9   Received a cash dividend of 90 cents per share on the Wynn stock.

Dec. 31   Made the adjusting entry to record the current fair value of the Polk stock. At December 31, 1996, the stock has a market value of $63.00 per share.

31   Made adjusting entry to record the current fair values of Wynn and Maple stocks. At December 31, 1996, the Wynn stock has a market value of $27.50 per share and the Maple stock has a market value of $31.00 per share. (*Note:* Make one adjusting entry for the portfolio of available-for-sale stocks.)

1997

Feb. 1   Sold the Polk stock for $62 per share.

Dec. 31   Made adjusting entry to record the current fair values of the Wynn and Maple stocks. At December 31, 1997, the per-share market values are Wynn, $30.00 and Maple, $33.00. (*Note:* Be sure to allow for the adjustment made at December 31, 1996.)

REQUIRED

Prepare the journal entries to record these transactions and adjustments.

CONTRASTING ENTRIES FOR STOCK INVESTMENTS: TRADING AND EQUITY METHODS — OBJ. 3 —

14-38 On January 2, 1996, Trubek Corporation purchased, as a stock investment, 10,000 shares of Forge Company common stock for $15 per share, including commissions and taxes. On December 31, 1996, Forge announced a net income of $80,000 for the year and a dividend of $1.10 per share, payable January 20, 1997, to stockholders of record on January 10, 1997. At December 31, 1996, the market value of Forge's stock was $19 per share. Trubek received its dividend on January 23, 1997.

REQUIRED

a. Assume that the stock acquired by Trubek represents 15% of Forge's voting stock and is classified in the trading category. Prepare all journal entries appropriate for this investment, beginning with the purchase on January 2, 1996, and ending with the receipt of the dividend on January 23, 1997. (Trubek recognizes dividend income when received.)

b. Assume that the stock acquired by Trubek represents 25% of Forge's voting stock. Prepare all journal entries appropriate for this investment, beginning with the purchase on January 2, 1996, and ending with the receipt of the dividend on January 23, 1997.

DETERMINING ELIMINATIONS AND CONSOLIDATED DATA ON DATE OF ACQUISITION (WHOLLY OWNED SUBSIDIARY) — OBJ. 4, 5 —

14-39 Elder Company purchased all of Hart Company's common stock for cash on January 1, 1997, after which the separate balance sheets of the two corporations appeared as follows:

ELDER AND HART COMPANIES
BALANCE SHEETS
JANUARY 1, 1997

	Elder	Hart
Stock Investment—Controlling (Hart)	$ 600,000	—
Other Assets	2,300,000	$700,000
Total Assets	$2,900,000	$700,000
Liabilities	$ 900,000	$160,000
Common Stock	1,400,000	300,000
Retained Earnings	600,000	240,000
Total Liabilities and Stockholders' Equity	$2,900,000	$700,000

During the negotiations for the purchase, Elder determined that the appraised value of Hart's Other Assets amounted to $720,000.

REQUIRED

a. Prepare the worksheet entry to eliminate the intercompany equity and to reflect the appraised value of Hart's assets.

b. What amount of total assets should appear on a January 1 consolidated balance sheet?

c. What amount of total stockholders' equity should appear on a January 1 consolidated balance sheet?

PREPARING CONSOLIDATED BALANCE SHEET WORKSHEET ON ACQUISITION DATE (MINORITY INTEREST) — OBJ. 4, 5 —

14-40 On January 1, 1997, Katt Company purchased 85% of the common stock of Harbor Company for $580,000 cash, after which the separate balance sheets of the two firms were as follows:

KATT AND HARBOR COMPANIES
BALANCE SHEETS
JANUARY 1, 1997

	Katt	Harbor
Stock Investment—Controlling (Harbor)	$ 580,000	—
Other Assets	1,220,000	$800,000
Total Assets	$1,800,000	$800,000
Liabilities	$ 410,000	$200,000
Common Stock	1,000,000	380,000
Retained Earnings	390,000	220,000
Total Liabilities and Stockholders' Equity	$1,800,000	$800,000

REQUIRED

Prepare a consolidated balance sheet worksheet at January 1, 1997. Assume that any amount paid by Katt in excess of the equity acquired in Harbor's net assets is attributable to goodwill.

PREPARING CONSOLIDATED INCOME STATEMENT WORKSHEET
— OBJ. 6 —

14-41 Oxford Company owns 75% of the common stock of Cherokee Company. The income statements of the two companies for 1997 follow. In its income statement, Oxford has not recorded its share of Cherokee's net income.

OXFORD AND CHEROKEE COMPANIES
INCOME STATEMENTS
FOR THE YEAR ENDED DECEMBER 31, 1997

	Oxford	Cherokee
Sales	$630,000	$280,000
Cost of Goods Sold	420,000	160,000
Gross Profit	$210,000	$120,000
Expenses (including income taxes)	100,000	72,000
Net Income	$110,000	$ 48,000

During the year, Oxford sold merchandise to Cherokee for $70,000, which had cost Oxford $44,000. Cherokee sold all of this merchandise to outsiders for $110,000.

REQUIRED

Prepare a consolidated income statement worksheet for 1997.

PURCHASE VERSUS POOLING OF INTERESTS
— OBJ. 7 —

14-42 On December 31, 1996, Ross Company issued shares of its common stock to acquire all of the outstanding common stock of Lance Company. Selected accounts at December 31, 1996, for Ross, Lance, and from the consolidated balance sheet follow.

	Ross	Lance	Consolidated
Cash	$ 50,000	$20,000	$ 70,000
Accounts Receivable	75,000	30,000	90,000
Accounts Payable	33,000	20,000	38,000
Retained Earnings	120,000	80,000	200,000

REQUIRED

a. Is the acquisition of Lance by Ross a purchase or a pooling of interests? Explain.
b. What are the amounts of intercompany receivables and payables at December 31?
c. Net incomes for 1996 are Ross, $124,000 and Lance, $55,000. What is the 1996 consolidated net income? Explain.

CONVERSION OF FOREIGN CURRENCY FINANCIAL STATEMENTS: TRANSLATION PROCEDURES
— APPENDIX H —

14-43 Zurich Company was organized in Switzerland on January 1, 1997, as a wholly owned subsidiary of Starr, Inc., a U.S. company. Zurich's opening balance sheet, in Swiss francs (SF), consisted of the following assets and stockholders' equity:

Assets		Stockholders' Equity	
Cash	SF 30,000	Common Stock	SF700,000
Inventory	120,000		
Plant Assets	550,000		
		Total Liabilities and	
Total Assets	SF700,000	Stockholders' Equity	SF700,000

Zurich's 1997 income statement and December 31, 1997, balance sheet, in Swiss francs, follow:

ZURICH COMPANY
INCOME STATEMENT
FOR THE YEAR ENDED DECEMBER 31, 1997

Sales		SF850,000
Cost of Goods Sold	SF600,000	
Depreciation Expense	50,000	
Other Expenses	40,000	
Total Expenses		690,000
Net Income		SF160,000

ZURICH COMPANY
BALANCE SHEET
DECEMBER 31, 1997

Assets		**Liabilities**		
Cash	SF 60,000	Accounts Payable		SF 30,000
Accounts Receivable (net)	150,000	**Stockholders' Equity**		
Inventory	180,000	Common Stock	SF700,000	
Plant Assets (net)	500,000	Retained Earnings	160,000	860,000
		Total Liabilities and		
Total Assets	SF890,000	Stockholders' Equity		SF890,000

Assume the following exchange rates for the Swiss franc:

January 1, 1997	$0.78
Average for 1997	0.75
December 31, 1997	0.72

REQUIRED

Assume that the functional currency for Zurich is the Swiss franc. Use translation procedures to convert Zurich's 1997 income statement and December 31, 1997, balance sheet to U.S. dollars. Follow the format of Exhibit H-2.

ALTERNATE EXERCISES

DEBT SECURITY—TRADING
— OBJ. 2 —

14-24A Sanders, Inc., had the following transactions and adjustments related to a bond investment:

1996

Nov. 1 Purchased $300,000 face value of Batem, Inc.'s 9% bonds at 102 plus a brokerage commission of $900. The bonds pay interest on October 31 and April 30 and mature in 15 years. Sanders expects to sell the bonds in the near future.

Dec. 31 Made the adjusting entry to record interest earned on investment in the Batem bonds. (Sanders does not make reversing entries.)

    31 Made the adjusting entry to record the current fair value of the Batem bonds. At December 31, 1996, the market value of the Batem bonds was $301,500.

1997

Apr. 30 Received the semiannual interest payment on investment in the Batem bonds.

May 1 Sold the Batem bond investment for $300,900 cash.

Record, in general journal form, these transactions and adjustments of Sanders Company.

DEBT SECURITY—AVAILABLE
FOR SALE
— OBJ. 2 —

14-25A Witt Company had the following transactions and adjustments related to a bond investment:

1996

Jan. 1 Purchased $600,000 face value of Chevy, Inc.'s 8% bonds at 101 plus a brokerage commission of $1,400. The bonds pay interest on June 30 and December 31 and mature in 10 years. Witt does not expect to sell the bonds in the near future, nor does it intend to hold the bonds to maturity.

June 30 Received the semiannual interest payment on the Chevy bonds and amortized the bond premium for six months. Witt uses the straight-line method to amortize bond discounts and premiums.

Dec. 31 Received the semiannual interest payment on the Chevy bonds and amortized the bond premium for six months.

31 Made the adjusting entry to record the current fair value of the Chevy bonds. At December 31, 1996, the market value of the Chevy bonds was $609,000.

1997

June 30 Received the semiannual interest payment on the Chevy bonds and amortized the bond premium for six months.

July 1 Sold the Chevy bond investment for $608,500 cash.

Dec. 31 Made the adjusting entry to eliminate balances from Fair Value Adjustment to Bond Investment account and Unrealized Gain/Loss on Investments (Equity) account.

Record, in general journal form, these transactions and adjustments of Witt Company.

DEBT SECURITY—HELD TO MATURITY
— OBJ. 2 —

14-26A Shepler Company had the following transactions and adjustments related to a bond investment:

1996

Jan. 1 Purchased $250,000 face value of Lowe, Inc.'s 6% bonds at 98 plus a brokerage commission of $500. The bonds pay interest on June 30 and December 31 and mature in 15 years. Shepler expects to hold the bonds to maturity.

June 30 Received the semiannual interest payment on the Lowe bonds and amortized the bond discount for six months. Shepler uses the straight-line method to amortize bond discounts and premiums.

2010

Dec. 31 Received the semiannual interest payment on the Lowe bonds and amortized the bond discount for six months.

31 Received the principal amount in cash on maturity date of the Lowe bonds.

Record, in general journal form, these transactions and adjustments of Shepler Company.

EQUITY SECURITY—TRADING
— OBJ. 3 —

14-27A Dale Company had the following transactions and adjustment related to a stock investment:

1996

Nov. 15 Purchased 5,000 shares of Lake, Inc.'s common stock at $16 per share plus a brokerage commission of $900. Dale Company expects to sell the stock in the near future.

Dec. 22 Received a cash dividend of $1.25 per share of common stock from Lake.

31 Made the adjusting entry to reflect year-end fair value of the stock investment in Lake. The year-end market price of the Lake common stock is $17.50 per share.

1997

Jan. 20 Sold all 5,000 shares of the Lake common stock for $86,400.

Record, in general journal form, these transactions and adjustment of Dale Company.

EQUITY SECURITY—AVAILABLE FOR SALE
— OBJ. 3 —

14-28A Refer to the data for Dale Company in Exercise 14-27A. Assume that when the shares were purchased, management did not intend to sell the stock in the near future. Record the transactions and adjustment for Dale Company under this assumption. In addition, prepare any adjusting entry needed at December 31, 1997.

EQUITY SECURITY— INFLUENTIAL
— OBJ. 3 —

14-29A Prince Company had the following transactions and adjustment related to a stock investment:

1996

Jan. 15 Purchased 15,000 shares of Park, Inc.'s common stock at $8 per share plus a brokerage commission of $1,000. These shares represent a 25% ownership of the Park common stock.

Dec. 31 Received a cash dividend of $0.80 per share of common stock from Park.

31 Made the adjusting entry to reflect income from the Park stock investment. Park's 1996 net income is $120,000.

1997

Jan. 20 Sold all 15,000 shares of the Park common stock for $132,000.

Record, in general journal form, the above transactions and adjustment of Prince Company.

ELIMINATING ENTRIES FOR CONSOLIDATED BALANCE SHEET — OBJ. 4 —

14-30A On January 1, 1997, Pratt Corporation purchased all of the common stock of Steere Company for $550,000. On this same date, Steere Company borrowed $45,000 from Pratt Corporation and signed a promissory note agreeing to repay the money plus interest in six months. Steere Company's stockholders' equity on January 1, 1997, consisted of $250,000 of common stock and $300,000 of retained earnings. Prepare the worksheet eliminating entries needed to prepare a consolidated balance sheet on January 1, 1997.

ELIMINATING ENTRIES FOR CONSOLIDATED BALANCE SHEET — OBJ. 4 —

14-31A On July 1, 1997, Travis Company purchased 80% of the common stock of Kiley Company for $480,000 cash when the stockholders' equity of Kiley consisted of $275,000 in common stock and $325,000 in retained earnings. Also on July 1, 1997, Travis purchased $65,000 of supplies on account from Kiley ($65,000 was also Kiley's cost). Prepare the worksheet eliminating entries needed to prepare a consolidated balance sheet on July 1, 1997.

ELIMINATING ENTRY INCLUDING ASSET REVALUATION AND GOODWILL — OBJ. 5 —

14-32A On January 1, 1997, Gem Company purchased for $450,000 cash a 70% stock interest in Alpine, Inc., which then had common stock of $420,000 and retained earnings of $140,000. Balance sheets of the two companies immediately after the acquisition were as follows:

	Gem	Alpine
Current Assets	$200,000	$160,000
Stock Investment—Controlling (Alpine)	450,000	—
Plant and Equipment (net)	265,000	460,000
Total Assets	$915,000	$620,000
Liabilities	$ 50,000	$ 60,000
Common Stock	700,000	420,000
Retained Earnings	165,000	140,000
Total Liabilities and Stockholders' Equity	$915,000	$620,000

Sixty percent of the amount paid by Gem in excess of the equity acquired is attributed to undervalued plant and equipment; the other 40% is based on Alpine's potential for future superior earning power. Prepare the worksheet eliminating entry needed to prepare a consolidated balance sheet on the acquisition date.

ELIMINATING ENTRY FOR INTERCOMPANY SALES — OBJ. 6 —

14-33A Skinner Company has a 90% interest in Flint Company. During the current year, Skinner sold merchandise costing $90,000 to Flint for $150,000. Assuming that Flint sold all of the merchandise to outsiders for $190,000, what worksheet eliminating entry should be made in preparing a consolidated income statement for the period?

REMEASUREMENT PROCEDURES — APPENDIX H —

14-34A Assume that remeasurement procedures are being used to convert the financial statements of a foreign subsidiary to U.S. dollars. Indicate which exchange rate—current, historical, or average for the year—should be used to convert each of the following categories of accounts.
a. Monetary assets and liabilities.
b. Assets and liabilities that are not monetary.
c. Capital stock.
d. Revenues generated uniformly throughout the year.
e. Expenses incurred uniformly throughout the year (other than depreciation expense and cost of goods sold).
f. Depreciation expense and cost of goods sold.

ALTERNATE PROBLEMS

14-35A Discovery Company began operations in 1996 and, by year-end (December 31), had made six stock investments. Year-end information on these stock investments follows.

ANALYSIS OF STOCK INVESTMENTS — OBJ. 3 —

Company	Cost or Equity (as appropriate)	Year-End Market Value	Classification
Lisle, Inc.	$ 68,000	$ 65,300	Trading
Owl, Inc.	$162,500	$160,000	Trading
Bionamic, Inc.	$197,000	$192,000	Available for sale
Foote, Inc.	$157,000	$154,700	Available for sale
Buckley, Inc.	$100,000	$102,400	Influential
Riccer, Inc.	$136,000	$133,200	Influential

REQUIRED

a. At what total amount will the trading stock investments be reported in the December 31, 1996, balance sheet?

b. At what total amount will the available-for-sale stock investments be reported in the December 31, 1996, balance sheet?

c. At what total amount will the influential stock investments be reported in the December 31, 1996, balance sheet?

d. What total amount of unrealized holding gains or unrealized holding losses related to stock investments will appear in the 1996 income statement?

e. What total amount of unrealized holding gains or unrealized holding losses related to stock investments will appear in the stockholders' equity section of the December 31, 1996, balance sheet?

f. What total amount of fair value adjustment to stock investments will appear in the December 31, 1996, balance sheet? Which category of stock investments does the fair value adjustment relate to? Does the fair value adjustment increase or decrease the financial statement presentation of these stock investments?

BOND INVESTMENT ENTRIES — OBJ. 2 —

14-36A The following transactions and adjustments relate to bond investments acquired by Jackson Corporation.

1996

June 30   Purchased $100,000 face value of Alamo, Inc.'s 20-year, 7% bonds dated June 30, 1996, for $97,200 cash. Interest is paid December 31 and June 30. Investment is classified in the available-for-sale category.

Dec. 31   Received the semiannual interest payment from Alamo and amortized the bond discount (straight-line method).

      31   Purchased $300,000 face value of Lyme, Inc.'s 10-year, 8% bonds dated December 31, 1996, for $304,000 cash. Interest is paid June 30 and December 31. Investment is classified in the held-to-maturity category.

      31   Made the adjusting entry to record the current fair value of the Alamo bonds. At December 31, 1996, their market value was $96,400.

1997

June 30   Received the semiannual interest payment from Alamo and amortized the bond discount.

      30   Received the semiannual interest payment from Lyme and amortized the bond premium (straight-line method).

July   1   Sold Alamo bonds for $96,500.

Oct. 31   Purchased $80,000 face value of Weir, Inc.'s 5-year, 7.5% bonds dated October 31, 1997, for $79,000. Interest is paid April 30 and October 31. Investment is classified in the trading category.

Dec. 31   Received the semiannual interest payment from Lyme and amortized the bond premium.

      31   Made the adjusting entry to record interest earned on investment in the Weir bonds.

      31   Made the adjusting entry to record the current fair value of Weir bonds. At December 31, 1997, the market value of these bonds was $79,900.

      31   Made the adjusting entry to eliminate balances in Fair Value Adjustment to Bond Investment account and Unrealized Gain/Loss on Investments (Equity) account.

REQUIRED

Prepare the journal entries to record these transactions and adjustments.

STOCK INVESTMENT ENTRIES — OBJ. 3 —

14-37A The following transactions and adjustments relate to stock investments made by Kramer Corporation.

1996

July   1   Purchased, as a stock investment, 2,000 shares of Cook, Inc.'s common stock for $96,200 cash. The investment, which is noninfluential and noncontrolling, is classified in the trading category.

Oct.   1   Purchased, as stock investments, 1,000 shares of Fox, Inc.'s common stock for $28,000 cash and 5,000 shares of Dent, Inc.'s common stock for $75,000 cash. These investments, which are noninfluential and noncontrolling, are classified in the available-for-sale category. (Note: Use two investment accounts.)

Nov.   9   Received a cash dividend of 70 cents per share on the Dent stock.

Dec. 31 Made the adjusting entry to record the current fair value of the Cook stock. At December 31, 1996, the stock has a market value of $50.50 per share.

31 Made the adjusting entry to record the current fair values of the Fox and Dent stocks. At December 31, 1996, the Fox stock has a market value of $26.25 per share and the Dent stock has a market value of $14.00 per share. (*Note:* Make one adjusting entry for the portfolio of available-for-sale stocks.)

1997

Feb. 1 Sold the Cook stock for $52 per share.

Dec. 31 Made adjusting entry to record the current fair values of Fox and Dent stocks. At December 31, 1997, the per-share market values are Fox, $25.00 and Dent, $12.00. (*Note:* Be sure to allow for the adjustment made at December 31, 1996.)

REQUIRED

Prepare the journal entries to record these transactions and adjustments.

CONTRASTING ENTRIES FOR STOCK INVESTMENTS: TRADING AND EQUITY METHODS — OBJ. 3 —

14-38A On January 2, 1996, Clemens, Inc., purchased, as a stock investment, 20,000 shares of Baer, Inc.'s common stock for $21 per share, including commissions and taxes. On December 31, 1996, Baer announced a net income of $280,000 for the year and a dividend of 80 cents per share, payable January 15, 1997, to stockholders of record on January 5, 1997. At December 31, 1996, the market value of Baer's stock was $18 per share. Clemens received its dividend on January 18, 1997.

REQUIRED

a. Assume that the stock acquired by Clemens represents 10% of Baer's voting stock and is classified in the trading category. Prepare all journal entries appropriate for this investment, beginning with the purchase on January 2, 1996, and ending with the receipt of the dividend on January 18, 1997. (Clemens recognizes dividend income when received.)

b. Assume that the stock acquired by Clemens represents 40% of Baer's voting stock. Prepare all journal entries appropriate for this investment, beginning with the purchase on January 2, 1996, and ending with the receipt of the dividend on January 18, 1997.

DETERMINING ELIMINATIONS AND CONSOLIDATED DATA ON DATE OF ACQUISITION (MAJORITY-HELD SUBSIDIARY) — OBJ. 4, 5 —

14-39A Skokie Company purchased 70% of Lavin Company's voting stock on January 1, 1997, after which the separate balance sheets of the two companies appeared as follows:

SKOKIE AND LAVIN COMPANIES
BALANCE SHEETS
JANUARY 1, 1997

	Skokie	Lavin
Stock Investment—Controlling (Lavin)	$ 800,000	—
Other Assets	2,200,000	$920,000
Total Assets	$3,000,000	$920,000
Liabilities	$ 500,000	$100,000
Common Stock	700,000	450,000
Retained Earnings	1,800,000	370,000
Total Liabilities and Stockholders' Equity	$3,000,000	$920,000

In purchasing Lavin's shares, Skokie attributed the excess of the amount paid over the equity acquired in Lavin entirely to that company's superior earning potential.

REQUIRED

a. Prepare the worksheet entry to eliminate the intercompany equity and to reflect the goodwill.

b. What amount of total assets should appear on a January 1 consolidated balance sheet?

c. What amount of total stockholders' equity should appear on a January 1 consolidated balance sheet?

PREPARING CONSOLIDATED BALANCE SHEET WORKSHEET ON DATE OF ACQUISITION (MINORITY INTEREST) — OBJ. 4, 5 —

14-40A On January 1, 1997, Weaver, Inc., purchased 75% of the voting stock of Ogden, Inc., for $530,000, after which the separate balance sheets of the two companies were as follows:

WEAVER, INC., AND OGDEN, INC.
BALANCE SHEETS
JANUARY 1, 1997

	Weaver	Ogden
Accounts Receivable	$ 90,000	$ 50,000
Stock Investment—Controlling (Ogden)	630,000	—
Other Assets	995,000	850,000
Total Assets	$1,715,000	$900,000
Accounts Payable	$ 200,000	$140,000
Common Stock	900,000	600,000
Retained Earnings	615,000	160,000
Total Liabilities and Stockholders' Equity	$1,715,000	$900,000

At January 1, 1997, Ogden owed $15,000 to Weaver on account for purchases made during 1996.

REQUIRED

Prepare a consolidated balance sheet worksheet at January 1, 1997. Assume that any amount paid by Weaver in excess of the equity acquired in Ogden is attributable to a $25,000 undervaluation of Ogden's other assets and the existence of goodwill (for the remainder).

PREPARING CONSOLIDATED INCOME STATEMENT WORKSHEET — OBJ. 6 —

14-41A Kline Company purchased a 60% interest in Voight Company on January 1, 1996. The income statements for the two companies for 1996 follow. Kline has not recorded its share of Voight's net income.

KLINE AND VOIGHT COMPANIES
INCOME STATEMENTS
FOR THE YEAR ENDED DECEMBER 31, 1996

	Kline	Voight
Sales	$980,000	$540,000
Cost of Goods Sold	620,000	320,000
Gross Profit	$360,000	$220,000
Operating Expenses (including income taxes)	270,000	160,000
Net Income	$ 90,000	$ 60,000

Voight did not pay any dividends in 1996. During the year, Kline sold merchandise costing $58,000 to Voight for $94,000, all of which Voight sold to outsiders for $130,000.

REQUIRED

Prepare a consolidated income statement worksheet for 1996.

PURCHASE VERSUS POOLING OF INTERESTS — OBJ. 7 —

14-42A On December 31, 1996, Ryan Company purchased, for cash, all of the outstanding common stock of Lemke Company. Selected accounts at December 31, 1996, for Ryan, Lemke, and from the consolidated balance sheet follow.

	Ryan	Lemke	Consolidated
Cash	$ 65,000	$ 15,000	$ 80,000
Notes Receivable	110,000	30,000	40,000
Notes Payable	25,000	150,000	75,000
Retained Earnings	120,000	80,000	120,000

REQUIRED

a. Is the acquisition of Lemke by Ryan a purchase or a pooling of interests? Explain.

b. What are the amounts of intercompany receivables and payables at December 31?

c. Net incomes for 1996 are Ryan, $144,000 and Lemke, $66,000. What is the 1996 consolidated net income? Explain.

CONVERSION OF FOREIGN CURRENCY FINANCIAL STATEMENTS: REMEASUREMENT PROCEDURES — APPENDIX H —

14-43A Refer to the data given for Zurich Company in Problem 14-43. In addition, the historical exchange rate applicable to the ending inventory is $0.73, and the historical exchange rate applicable to the cost of goods sold is $0.76.

REQUIRED

Assume that the functional currency for Zurich is the U.S. dollar. Use remeasurement procedures to convert Zurich's 1997 income statement and December 31, 1997, balance sheet to U.S. dollars. There is a 1997 foreign exchange loss of $7,500 from the remeasurement procedures. Follow the format of Exhibit H-3.

CASES

BUSINESS DECISION CASE

Redding, Inc., manufactures heating and cooling systems. It has a 75% interest in Guardian Company, which manufactures thermostats, switches, and other controls for heating and cooling products. It also has a 100% interest in Redding Finance Company, created by the parent company to finance sales of its products to contractors and other consumers. The parent company's only other investment is a 25% interest in the common stock of Dawson, Inc., which produces certain circuits used by Redding, Inc. A condensed consolidated balance sheet of the entity for the current year follows:

REDDING, INC., AND SUBSIDIARIES
CONSOLIDATED BALANCE SHEET
DECEMBER 31, 1996

Assets

Current Assets	$19,300,000
Stock Investment—Influential (Dawson)	2,600,000
Other Assets	71,400,000
Excess of Cost over Equity Acquired in Net Assets of Guardian Company	1,700,000
Total Assets	$95,000,000

Liabilities and Stockholders' Equity

Current Liabilities		$10,300,000
Long-Term Liabilities		14,200,000
Stockholders' Equity		
Minority Interest	$ 3,800,000	
Common Stock	50,000,000	
Retained Earnings	16,700,000	70,500,000
Total Liabilities and Stockholders' Equity		$95,000,000

This balance sheet, along with other financial statements, was furnished to shareholders before their annual meeting, and all shareholders were invited to submit questions to be answered at the meeting. As chief financial officer of Redding, you have been appointed to respond to the questions at the meeting.

REQUIRED

Answer the following stockholder questions.
a. What is meant by *consolidated* financial statements?
b. Why is the investment in Dawson shown on the consolidated balance sheet, but the investments in Guardian and Redding Finance are omitted?
c. Explain the meaning of the asset Excess of Cost over Equity Acquired in Net Assets of Guardian Company.
d. What is meant by *minority interest* and to what company is this account related?

FINANCIAL ANALYSIS CASE

The Home Depot, Inc., and Tiffany & Co. are both specialty retailers. The Home Depot, headquartered in Atlanta, sells home improvement materials and supplies; Tiffany, headquartered in New York City, specializes in fine jewelry, china, crystal, and silver. As is typical of retailers, each company ends its fiscal year a few weeks after the December holiday season. The Home Depot's fiscal year ends on the Sunday nearest January 31 and Tiffany's fiscal year ends on January 31. Neither company has any outstanding preferred stock. For a recent period of four consecutive quarters, the two companies reported the following quarterly primary earnings per share (most recent quarter shown first):

	Home Depot	Tiffany
Quarterly primary earnings per share for quarter ending in		
July	$0.39	$0.22
April	0.31	0.12
January	0.25	1.14
October	0.24	0.21

A few weeks after the July quarterly earnings per share data were released, the common stocks of the two companies were trading at the following per share prices: The Home Depot, $44.13; Tiffany & Co., $37.38.

REQUIRED

a. Using the preceding data, compute the price-earnings ratio for The Home Depot.

b. Using the preceding data, compute the price-earnings ratio for Tiffany.

c. At the time of the above price-earnings ratios, which of the two companies was apparently favored more by investors?

ETHICS CASE   Shawn Webster, controller of Nexgen, Inc., has asked his assistant, Dawn Cryor, for suggestions as to how the company can improve its financial performance for the year. The company is in the last quarter of the year and projections to the end of the year show the company will have a net loss of about $400,000.

"My suggestion," said Cryor, "is that we sell 1,000 of the 200,000 common shares of Blaney Company that we own. The 200,000 shares gives us a 20% ownership of Blaney, and we have been using the equity method to account for this investment. We have owned this stock a long time and the current market value of the 200,000 shares is about $750,000 above our book value for the stock."

"That sale will only generate a gain of about $3,750," replied Webster.

"The rest of the story," continued Cryor, "is that once we sell the 1,000 shares, we will own less than 20% of Blaney. We can then reclassify the remaining 199,000 shares from the influential category to the trading category. Once in the trading category, we value the stocks at their current fair value, include the rest of the $750,000 gain in this year's income statement, and finish the year with a healthy net income."

"But," responded Webster, "we aren't going to sell all the Blaney stock; 1,000 shares maybe, but certainly not any more. We own that stock because they are a long-term supplier of ours. Indeed, we even have representation on their board of directors. The 199,000 shares do not belong in the trading category."

Cryor rolled her eyes and continued, "The classification of an investment as trading or not depends on management's intent. This year-end we claim it was our intent to sell the stock. Next year we change our minds and take the stock out of the trading category. Generally accepted accounting principles can't legislate management intent, nor can our outside auditors read our minds. Besides, why shouldn't we take advantage of the flexibility in GAAP to avoid reporting a net loss for this year?"

REQUIRED

a. Should generally accepted accounting principles permit management's intent to influence accounting classifications and measurements?

b. Is it ethical for Shawn Webster to implement the recommendation of Dawn Cryor?

GENERAL MILLS ANNUAL REPORT CASE   Refer to the annual report of General Mills, Inc., presented in Appendix K.

REQUIRED

a. Refer to Note 1 to the financial statements. What principles of consolidation were followed by General Mills? Does General Mills have any goodwill from consolidation in its balance sheet? Over what time period does General Mills amortize goodwill?

b. General Mills owns 50% of Cereal Partners Worldwide (a joint venture with Nestlé, S.A.) and 40.5% of Snack Ventures Europe (a joint venture with PepsiCo Foods International). Neither of these affiliates is consolidated into General Mills' consolidated financial statements. Why? Would PepsiCo, Inc. (100% owner of PepsiCo Foods International), consolidate the financial data of Snack Ventures Europe into PepsiCo, Inc.'s consolidated financial statements? Why?

c. Refer to Note 6. What dollar amount is reported for investments in and advances to affiliates as of May 29, 1994? Are these investments reported at their fair value? What method is used to account for the investments in these joint ventures?

d. General Mills owns The Olive Garden and Red Lobster restaurant chains at May 29, 1994. The balance sheet does not show any investment in these two entities, nor are they discussed in Note 6 dealing with investments in affiliates. Why?

e. Refer to Note 6. What dollar amount of marketable investments does General Mills report as of May 29, 1994? Are these investments reported at their fair value?

f. Refer to the statement of cash flows. For the year ended May 29, 1994, did General Mills have a cash inflow or cash outflow related to its transactions in marketable investments? How much?

Statement of Cash Flows

CHAPTER LEARNING OBJECTIVES

1 **PROVIDE** a basis for understanding a statement of cash flows (pp. 514–519).

2 **DISCUSS** the preparation of a statement of cash flows using the indirect method (pp. 519–526).

3 **DISCUSS** the preparation of a statement of cash flows using the direct method (pp. 526–532).

4 **Financial Analysis** **DEFINE** *operating cash flow to current liabilities ratio* and *operating cash flow to capital expenditures ratio* and **EXPLAIN** their use (pp. 532–533).

CHAPTER FOCUS

Do you maintain a checkbook in which you record the checks you write and the bank deposits you make? If so, you are keeping a record of your cash flows—the checks you write are cash outflows and your bank deposits are cash inflows. Business entities also experience cash inflows and cash outflows. They do more than just record their cash flows, however, because accounting standards require that a related financial statement be prepared. The **statement of cash flows** is a basic financial statement that summarizes information about the flow of cash into and out of a company. In this chapter, we discuss the interpretation and preparation of the statement of cash flows.

The statement of cash flows complements the balance sheet and the income statement. The balance sheet reports the company's financial position at a point in time (the end of each period) whereas the statement of cash flows explains the change in one component of financial position—cash—from one balance sheet date to the next. The income statement reveals the results of the company's operating activities for the period, and these operating activities are a major contributor to the change in cash reported in the statement of cash flows.

CASH AND CASH EQUIVALENTS

OBJECTIVE *1*

PROVIDE a basis for understanding a statement of cash flows.

Financial managers manage cash and marketable securities together. They hold marketable securities either (1) as a substitute for cash or (2) as a short-term investment. The substitute cash holdings are liquidated whenever the firm needs cash for its regular operating activities. The short-term investments exist to provide funds for a known future cash need (such as a quarterly income tax payment) or to earn a return on excess funds available for short periods in seasonal or cyclical businesses.

Accountants recognize that many firms may hold securities that are viewed as the equivalent of cash. Accordingly, the statement of cash flows is to explain the change in a firm's cash *and* cash equivalents. **Cash equivalents** are short-term, highly liquid investments that are (1) easily convertible into a known cash amount and (2) close enough to maturity so that their market value is not sensitive to interest rate changes (generally, investments with initial maturities of three months or less).[1]

Treasury bills, commercial paper (short-term notes issued by corporations) and money market funds are typical examples of cash equivalents. Yet firms may differ as to which investments they consider to be the equivalent of cash. Thus, the Financial Accounting Standards Board requires each firm to disclose its policy for deciding which investments are treated as cash equivalents. Further, the period-end cash and cash equivalents reported in a statement of cash flows must agree with the amount of cash and cash equivalents reported in the firm's balance sheet.

When preparing a statement of cash flows, the cash and cash equivalents are added together and treated as a single sum. This is done because the purchase and sale of investments in cash equivalents are considered to be part of a firm's overall management of cash rather than a source or use of cash. As statement users evaluate and project cash flows, for example, it should not matter whether the cash is on hand, deposited in a bank account, or invested in cash equivalents. Transfers back and forth between a firm's Cash account and its investments in cash equivalents, therefore, are not treated as cash inflows and cash outflows in its statement of cash flows.

When discussing the statement of cash flows, accountants generally use the word *cash* rather than the term *cash and cash equivalents*. We will follow the same practice in this chapter.

---

[1]*Statement of Financial Accounting Standards No. 95,* "Statement of Cash Flows" (Stamford, CT: Financial Accounting Standards Board, 1987), par. 8.

CASH EQUIVALENT DEFINITIONS

PepsiCo, Inc., the beverage and restaurant company, states in the notes to its financial statements: "Cash equivalents represent funds temporarily invested (with original maturities not exceeding three months) as part of PepsiCo's management of day-to-day operating cash receipts and disbursements. All other investment portfolios, primarily held outside the U.S., are classified as short-term investments."

International Game Technology manufactures gaming machines and proprietory gaming software systems. In some gaming jurisdictions, the company operates its proprietory software. In its financial statement notes, the company observes that its cash and cash equivalents include "cash required for funding current systems jackpot payments as well as purchasing investments to meet obligations for making payments to jackpot winners. Cash in excess of daily requirements is generally invested in various marketable securities. If these securities have original maturities of three months or less, they are considered cash equivalents."

CLASSIFICATIONS IN THE STATEMENT OF CASH FLOWS

A statement of cash flows classifies cash receipts and payments into three major categories: operating activities, investing activities, and financing activities. Grouping cash flows into these categories identifies the effects on cash of each of the major activities of a firm. The combined effects on cash of all three categories explain the net change in cash for the period. The period's net change in cash is then reconciled with the beginning and ending amounts of cash. Exhibit 15-1 illustrates the basic format for a statement of cash flows.

EXHIBIT 15–1	Format for the Statement of Cash Flows

SAMPLE COMPANY
STATEMENT OF CASH FLOWS
FOR THE YEAR ENDED DECEMBER 31, 1997

Cash Flows from Operating Activities		
(DETAILS OF NET CASH FLOW FROM OPERATING ACTIVITIES)	$XXX	
Net Cash Provided (Used) by Operating Activities		$XXX
Cash Flows from Investing Activities		
(DETAILS OF INDIVIDUAL INVESTING CASH INFLOWS AND OUTFLOWS)	$XXX	
Net Cash Provided (Used) by Investing Activities		XXX
Cash Flows from Financing Activities		
(DETAILS OF INDIVIDUAL FINANCING CASH INFLOWS AND OUTFLOWS)	$XXX	
Net Cash Provided (Used) by Financing Activities		XXX
Net Increase (Decrease) in Cash		$XXX
Cash at Beginning of Year		XXX
Cash at End of Year		$XXX

OPERATING ACTIVITIES

A company's income statement reflects the transactions and events that constitute its operating activities. Generally, the cash effects of these transactions and events determine the net cash flow from operating activities. The usual focus of a firm's operating activities is on selling goods or rendering services. Cash flows from **operating activities** are defined broadly enough, however, to include any cash receipts or payments that are not classified as investing or financing activities. For example, cash received as lawsuit settlements and cash payments to charity are treated as cash flows from operating activities. The following are examples of cash inflows and outflows relating to operating activities.

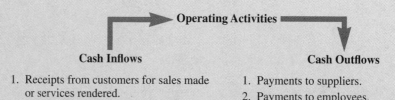

INVESTING ACTIVITIES   A firm's transactions involving (1) the acquisition and disposal of plant assets and intangible assets, (2) the purchase and sale of stocks, bonds, and other securities (that are not cash equivalents), and (3) the lending and subsequent collection of money constitute the basic components of its **investing activities.**[2] The related cash receipts and payments appear in the investing activities section of the statement of cash flows. Examples of these cash flows follow.

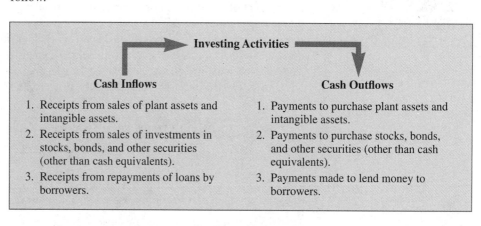

FINANCING ACTIVITIES   A firm engages in **financing activities** when it obtains resources from owners, returns resources to owners, borrows resources from creditors, and repays amounts borrowed. Cash flows related to these events are reported in the financing activities section of the statement of cash flows. Examples of these cash flows are listed below.

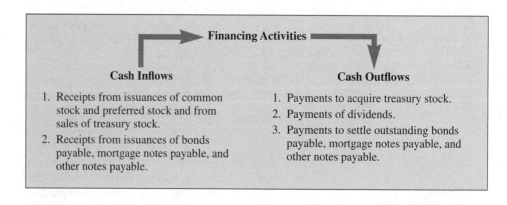

---

[2]There are exceptions to the classification of these events as investing activities. For example, the purchase and sale of mortgage loans by a mortgage banker and the purchase and sale of securities in the trading account of a broker and dealer in securities represent operating activities for these businesses.

Observe that paying cash to settle such obligations as accounts payable, wages payable, interest payable, and income tax payable are operating activities, not financing activities. Also observe that cash received as interest and dividends and cash paid as interest are classified as cash flows from operating activities.

ILLUSTRATION OF CLASSIFICATION USEFULNESS

The classification of cash flows into three categories of activities helps financial statement users interpret cash flow data. To illustrate, assume that companies D, E, and F are similar companies operating in the same industry. Each company showed a $100,000 cash increase during the current year. Information from their current year statements of cash flows is summarized below.

	Company		
	D	**E**	**F**
Net Cash Provided by Operating Activities	$100,000	$ –0–	$ –0–
Cash Flows from Investing Activities			
Sale of Plant Assets	–0–	100,000	–0–
Cash Flows from Financing Activities			
Issuance of Notes Payable	–0–	–0–	100,000
Net Increase in Cash	$100,000	$100,000	$100,000

Although each company's cash increase was the same, the source of the increase varied by company. This variation affects the analysis of the cash flow data, particularly for potential short-term creditors who must evaluate the likelihood of obtaining repayment in the future for any funds loaned to the company. Based only on these cash flow data, a potential creditor would feel more comfortable lending money to D than to either E or F. D's cash increase came from its operating activities, whereas both E and F could only break even on their cash flows from operations. E's cash increase came from the sale of plant assets, a source that is not likely to recur regularly. F's cash increase came entirely from borrowed funds. F faces additional cash burdens in the future when the interest and principal payments on the note payable become due.

NONCASH INVESTING AND FINANCING ACTIVITIES

A secondary objective of cash flow reporting is to present summary information about a firm's investing and financing activities. Of course, many of these activities affect cash and are therefore already included in the investing and financing sections of the statement of cash flows. Some significant investing and financing events, however, do not affect current cash flows. Examples of **noncash investing and financing activities** are the issuance of stocks or bonds in exchange for plant assets or intangible assets, the exchange of long-term assets for other long-term assets, and the conversion of long-term debt into common stock. Information about these events must be reported as a supplement to the statement of cash flows.

Noncash investing and financing transactions generally do affect future cash flows, however. Issuing bonds payable to acquire equipment, for example, requires future cash payments for interest and principal on the bonds. On the other hand, converting bonds payable into common stock eliminates future cash payments related to the bonds. Knowledge of these types of events, therefore, should be helpful to users of cash flow data who wish to assess a firm's future cash flows.

The information on noncash investing and financing transactions is disclosed in a schedule that is separate from the statement of cash flows. The separate schedule may be placed immediately below the statement of cash flows, or it may be placed among the notes to the financial statements.

OBJECTIVITY PRINCIPLE

As noted by the *objectivity principle,* the usefulness of financial statements is enhanced when the underlying data are objective and verifiable. Measuring cash and the changes in cash are among the most objective measurements that accountants make. The statement of cash flows, therefore, is the most objective financial statement required by generally accepted accounting principles. This characteristic of the statement of cash flows is welcomed by those investors and creditors interested in evaluating the quality of a firm's income.

USEFULNESS OF THE STATEMENT OF CASH FLOWS

The Financial Accounting Standards Board believes that one objective of financial reporting is to help external users assess the amount, timing, and uncertainty of future cash flows to the enterprise.[3] These assessments, in turn, help users evaluate their own prospective cash receipts from their investments in, or loans to, the firm. Although statements of cash flows report past cash flows, these statements should be useful for assessing the future cash flows of firms.

A statement of cash flows shows the periodic cash effects of a firm's operating, investing, and financing activities. Distinguishing among these different categories of cash flows helps users compare, evaluate, and predict cash flows. With cash flow information, creditors and investors are better able to assess a firm's ability to settle its liabilities and pay its dividends. A firm's need for outside financing may also be better evaluated. Over time, the statement of cash flows permits users to observe and analyze management's investing and financing policies.

A statement of cash flows also provides information useful in evaluating a firm's financial flexibility. *Financial flexibility* is a firm's ability to generate sufficient amounts of cash to respond to unanticipated needs and opportunities. Information about past cash flows, particularly cash flows from operations, helps in assessing financial flexibility. An evaluation of a firm's ability to survive an unexpected drop in demand, for example, may include a review of its past cash flows from operations. The larger these cash flows, the greater will be the firm's ability to withstand adverse changes in economic conditions. Other financial statements, particularly the balance sheet and its notes, also contain information useful for judging financial flexibility.

Some investors and creditors find the statement of cash flows useful in evaluating the "quality" of a firm's income. As we know, determining income under accrual accounting procedures requires many accruals, deferrals, allocations, and valuations. These adjustment and measurement procedures introduce more subjectivity into income determination than some financial statement users prefer. These users relate a more objective performance measure—cash flow from operations—to net income. To these users, the higher this ratio is, the higher is the quality of the income.

NET CASH FLOW FROM OPERATING ACTIVITIES

The first section of a statement of cash flows presents a firm's net cash flow from operating activities. *Two alternative formats are used to report the net cash flow from operating activities: the indirect method and the direct method. Both methods report the same amount of net cash flow from operating activities.*

---

[3]*Statement of Financial Accounting Concepts No. 1,* "Objectives of Financial Reporting by Business Enterprises" (Stamford, CT: Financial Accounting Standards Board, 1978), p. 18. The FASB also believes that information should be reported about earnings. It notes that earnings measured by accrual accounting are a better indicator of periodic financial performance than information about current cash receipts and payments.

The *indirect method* (or *reconciliation method*) starts with net income and applies a series of adjustments to net income to convert it to a cash-basis income number, which is the net cash flow from operating activities. The adjustments to net income do not represent specific cash flows, however, so the indirect method does not report any detail concerning individual operating cash inflows and outflows.

In contrast, the *direct method* shows individual amounts of cash inflows and cash outflows for the major operating activities. The net difference between these inflows and outflows is the net cash flow from operating activities.

The Financial Accounting Standards Board encourages companies to use the direct method but permits the use of the indirect method. Despite the FASB's preference for the direct method, accountants estimate that *more than 95% of companies preparing the statement of cash flows use the indirect method.* The indirect method is popular because (1) it is easier and less expensive to prepare than the direct method and (2) the direct method requires a supplemental disclosure showing the indirect method.

The remainder of this chapter discusses the preparation of the statement of cash flows. *The indirect method is discussed first, followed by the direct method. These discussions are independent of each other; either one provides complete coverage of the preparation of the statement of cash flows.*

POINT OF INTEREST

COMPARISON OF ACCRUAL AND CASH-BASIS AMOUNTS

Accountants compute net income, shown on the income statement, using accrual accounting procedures. The net cash flow from operating activities, presented on the cash flow statement, represents a cash-basis amount. There is no necessary relationship between the two numbers. Compared with net income, the net cash flow from operating activities may be larger, smaller, or about the same amount. Financial data from recent annual reports of three companies bear this out.

	Net Income or (Loss)	Net Cash Provided (Used) by Operating Activities
Boise Cascade Corporation	($ 77,140,000)	$131,221,000
Cisco Systems, Inc.	$171,955,000	$176,010,000
Best Buy Co., Inc.	$ 19,855,000	($ 31,049,000)

PREPARING THE STATEMENT OF CASH FLOWS UNDER THE INDIRECT METHOD

OBJECTIVE 2

DISCUSS the preparation of a statement of cash flows using the indirect method.

To prepare a statement of cash flows, we need a firm's income statement, comparative balance sheets, and some additional data taken from the accounting records. Exhibit 15-2 presents this information for Bennett Company. We use these data to prepare Bennett's 1997 statement of cash flows using the indirect method.

Bennett's statement of cash flows explains the $25,000 increase in cash that occurred during 1997 (from $10,000 to $35,000) by classifying the firm's cash flows into operating, investing, and financing categories. To get the information to construct the statement, therefore, we do the following:

1. *Use the indirect method to determine the net cash flow from operating activities.* In doing this, we apply a series of adjustments to the firm's net income. The adjustments include changes in various current asset and current liability accounts.

2. *Determine cash flows from investing activities.* We do this by analyzing changes in the noncash asset accounts not used in the indirect method.

3. *Determine cash flows from financing activities.* We do this by analyzing changes in the liability and stockholders' equity accounts not used in the indirect method.

EXHIBIT 15–2 Financial Data of Bennett Company

BENNETT COMPANY
INCOME STATEMENT
FOR THE YEAR ENDED DECEMBER 31, 1997

Sales		$250,000
Cost of Goods Sold	$148,000	
Wages Expense	52,000	
Insurance Expense	5,000	
Depreciation Expense	10,000	
Income Tax Expense	11,000	
Gain on Sale of Land	(8,000)	218,000
Net Income		$ 32,000

Additional Data for 1997

1. At year-end, purchased long-term stock investments for cash.
2. Sold land costing $20,000 for $28,000 cash.
3. At year-end, acquired $60,000 patent by issuing common stock at par.
4. All accounts payable relate to merchandise purchases.
5. Issued common stock at par for $10,000 cash.
6. Declared and paid cash dividends of $13,000.

BENNETT COMPANY
BALANCE SHEETS

	Dec. 31, 1997	Dec. 31, 1996
Assets		
Cash	$ 35,000	$ 10,000
Accounts Receivable	39,000	34,000
Inventory	54,000	60,000
Prepaid Insurance	17,000	4,000
Long-Term Investments	15,000	—
Plant Assets	180,000	200,000
Accumulated Depreciation	(50,000)	(40,000)
Patent	60,000	—
Total Assets	$350,000	$268,000
Liabilities and Stockholders' Equity		
Accounts Payable	$ 10,000	$ 19,000
Income Tax Payable	5,000	3,000
Common Stock	260,000	190,000
Retained Earnings	75,000	56,000
Total Liabilities and Stockholders' Equity	$350,000	$268,000

NET CASH FLOW FROM OPERATING ACTIVITIES UNDER THE INDIRECT METHOD

The **indirect method** presents the net cash flow from operating activities by applying a series of adjustments to net income to convert it to a cash-basis amount. The adjustment amounts represent differences between revenues, expenses, gains, and losses recorded under accrual accounting and the related operating cash inflows and outflows. The adjustments are added to or subtracted from net income, depending on whether the related cash flow is more or less than the accrual amount. Exhibit 15-3 portrays this process.

EXHIBIT 15–3 The Indirect Method

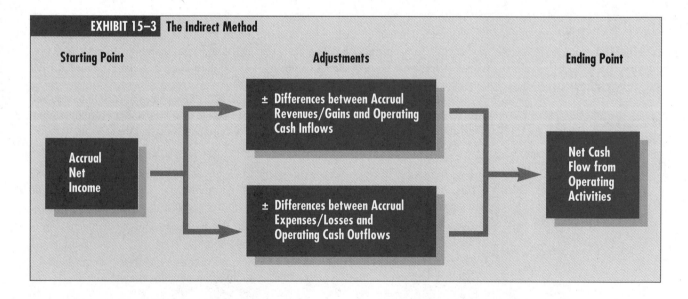

CONVERT NET INCOME TO NET CASH FLOW FROM OPERATING ACTIVITIES

Exhibit 15-4 summarizes the specific adjustments to convert net income to a corresponding net cash flow from operating activities. The first several adjustments cover depreciation expense, amortization expense, depletion expense, and gains and losses from investing and financing activities. The remaining adjustments relate to various current assets and current liabilities. Note that all current asset changes are handled the same way (add decreases and subtract increases) and all current liability changes are handled the same way (add increases and subtract decreases).

EXHIBIT 15–4	Indirect Method Conversion Schedule: Adjustments to Convert Net Income to Net Cash Flow from Operating Activities

Add to Net Income	Deduct from Net Income
Depreciation Expense	
Amortization Expense	
Depletion Expense	
Losses (investing/financing)	Gains (investing/financing)
Decrease in Accounts Receivable	Increase in Accounts Receivable
Decrease in Inventory	Increase in Inventory
Decrease in Prepaid Expenses	Increase in Prepaid Expenses
Increase in Accounts Payable	Decrease in Accounts Payable
Increase in Accrued Liabilities	Decrease in Accrued Liabilities

If there is a net loss for the period, the indirect method begins with the net loss. It is possible for the net amount of add-backs to exceed the loss so that there is a positive net cash flow from operating activities even when there is an accrual net loss.

BENNETT COMPANY EXAMPLE

We will now explain these adjustments and illustrate them with Bennett Company's data from Exhibit 15-2.

DEPRECIATION, AMORTIZATION, AND DEPLETION EXPENSES   Depreciation, amortization, and depletion expenses represent write-offs of previously recorded assets; they are totally noncash expenses. These expenses, therefore, represent an excess of accrual expenses over related cash outflows. Because depreciation, amortization, and depletion expenses are subtracted in computing net income, we add these expenses to net income as we convert it to a related net operating cash flow. Adding these expenses to net income cancels out their effect on net income, which means they have no effect on the amount of net cash flow from operating activities.

Bennett Company had $10,000 of 1997 depreciation expense, so this amount is added to Bennett's net income of $32,000.

Net Income	$32,000
Add: Depreciation	10,000

GAINS AND LOSSES RELATED TO INVESTING OR FINANCING ACTIVITIES   The income statement may contain gains and losses that relate to investing or financing activities. Gains and losses from the sale of investments, plant assets, or intangible assets illustrate gains and losses from investing activities. A gain or loss from the retirement of bonds payable is an example of a financing gain or loss. The full cash flow from these types of events is reported in the investing or financing sections of the statement of cash flows. Therefore, the effect of the related gains or losses on net income must be eliminated as we convert net income to a net cash flow from operating activities. To eliminate their impact on net income, gains are subtracted and losses are added to net income.

Bennett Company had an $8,000 gain from the sale of land in 1997. This gain relates to an investing activity, so it is subtracted from Bennett's net income.

Net Income	**$32,000**
Add: Depreciation	**10,000**
Deduct: Gain on Sale of Land	**(8,000)**

ACCOUNTS RECEIVABLE CHANGE   Sales on account increase accounts receivable; cash collections on account decrease accounts receivable. If, overall, accounts receivable decrease during a year, then cash collections from customers must exceed sales revenue by the amount of the decrease. Because sales are added in computing net income, the period's decrease in accounts receivable is added to net income. In essence, this adjustment replaces the sales amount with the larger amount of cash collections from customers.

If accounts receivable increase during a year, then sales revenue must exceed the cash collections from customers by the amount of the increase. Because sales are added in computing net income, the period's increase in accounts receivable is subtracted from net income as we convert it to a net cash flow from operating activities. In essence, this adjustment replaces the sales amount with the smaller amount of cash collections from customers.

Bennett's accounts receivable increased $5,000 during 1997, so this increase is subtracted from net income under the indirect method.

Net Income	**$32,000**
Add: Depreciation	**10,000**
Deduct: Gain on Sale of Land	**(8,000)**
Deduct: Accounts Receivable Increase	**(5,000)**

INVENTORY CHANGE   The adjustment for an inventory change is one of two adjustments to net income that together cause the cost of goods sold expense to be replaced by an amount representing the cash paid during the period for merchandise purchased. The second adjustment, which we shall examine shortly, is for the change in accounts payable. The effect of the inventory adjustment alone is to adjust net income for the difference between the cost of goods sold and the cost of merchandise purchased during the period.

The cost of merchandise purchased increases inventory; the cost of goods sold decreases inventory. An overall decrease in inventory during a period must mean, therefore, that the cost of merchandise purchased was less than the cost of goods sold by the amount of the decrease. Because cost of goods sold was subtracted in computing net income, the inventory decrease is added to net income. After this adjustment, the effect of the cost of goods sold on net income has been replaced by the smaller cost of merchandise purchased.

Similarly, if inventory increased during a period, the cost of merchandise purchased must be larger than the cost of goods sold by the amount of the increase. To replace the cost of goods sold with the cost of merchandise purchased, the inventory increase is subtracted from net income.

Bennett's inventory decreased $6,000 during 1997, so this decrease is added to net income.

Net Income	$32,000
Add: Depreciation	10,000
Deduct: Gain on Sale of Land	(8,000)
Deduct: Accounts Receivable Increase	(5,000)
Add: Inventory Decrease	6,000

PREPAID EXPENSES CHANGE   Cash prepayments of various expenses increase a firm's prepaid expenses. When the related expenses for the period are subsequently recorded, the prepaid expenses decrease. An overall decrease in prepaid expenses for a period means that the cash prepayments were less than the related expenses. Because the expenses were subtracted in determining net income, the indirect method adds the decrease in prepaid expenses to net income as it is converted to a cash flow amount. The effect of the addition is to replace the expense amount with the smaller cash payment amount.

Similarly, an increase in prepaid expenses is subtracted from net income because an increase means that the cash prepayments during the year were more than the related expenses. Bennett's prepaid insurance increased $13,000 during 1997, so this increase is deducted from net income.

Net Income	$32,000
Add: Depreciation	10,000
Deduct: Gain on Sale of Land	(8,000)
Deduct: Accounts Receivable Increase	(5,000)
Add: Inventory Decrease	6,000
Deduct: Prepaid Insurance Increase	(13,000)

ACCOUNTS PAYABLE CHANGE   When merchandise is purchased on account, accounts payable increase by the amount of the goods' cost. Accounts payable decrease when cash payments are made to settle the accounts. An overall decrease in accounts payable during a year means that cash payments for purchases were more than the cost of the purchases. An accounts payable decrease, therefore, is subtracted from net income under the indirect method. The deduction, in effect, replaces the cost of merchandise purchased with the larger cash payments for merchandise purchased. (Recall that the earlier inventory adjustment replaced the cost of goods sold with the cost of merchandise purchased.)

In contrast, an increase in accounts payable means that cash payments for purchases were less than the cost of purchases during the period. Thus, an accounts payable increase is added to net income as it is converted to a net cash flow from operating activities.

Bennett Company shows a $9,000 decrease in accounts payable during 1997. This decrease is subtracted from net income.

Net Income	$32,000
Add: Depreciation	10,000
Deduct: Gain on Sale of Land	(8,000)
Deduct: Accounts Receivable Increase	(5,000)
Add: Inventory Decrease	6,000
Deduct: Prepaid Insurance Increase	(13,000)
Deduct: Accounts Payable Decrease	(9,000)

ACCRUED LIABILITIES CHANGE   Changes in accrued liabilities are interpreted the same way as changes in accounts payable. A decrease means that cash payments exceeded the related expense amounts; an increase means that cash payments were less than the related expenses. Decreases are subtracted from net income; increases are added to net income.

Bennett has one accrued liability, Income Tax Payable, and it increased by $2,000 during 1997. The $2,000 increase is added to net income.

Net Income	**$32,000**
Add: Depreciation	**10,000**
Deduct: Gain on Sale of Land	**(8,000)**
Deduct: Accounts Receivable Increase	**(5,000)**
Add: Inventory Decrease	**6,000**
Deduct: Prepaid Insurance Increase	**(13,000)**
Deduct: Accounts Payable Decrease	**(9,000)**
Add: Income Tax Payable Increase	**2,000**

We have now identified the proper adjustments to convert Bennett's net income to its net cash flow from operating activities. The operating activities section of the statement of cash flows appears as follows under the indirect method:

Net Income	$32,000
Add (Deduct) Items to Convert Net Income to Cash Basis	
Depreciation	10,000
Gain on Sale of Land	(8,000)
Accounts Receivable Increase	(5,000)
Inventory Decrease	6,000
Prepaid Insurance Increase	(13,000)
Accounts Payable Decrease	(9,000)
Income Tax Payable Increase	2,000
Net Cash Provided by Operating Activities	$15,000

CASH FLOWS FROM INVESTING ACTIVITIES

ANALYZE CHANGES IN REMAINING NONCASH ASSET ACCOUNTS

Investing activities cause changes in asset accounts. Usually the accounts affected other than cash are noncurrent asset accounts such as plant assets and long-term investments, although short-term investment accounts may also be affected. To determine the cash flows from investing activities, *we analyze the changes in all noncash asset accounts not used in computing the net cash flow from operating activities*. Our objective is to identify any investing cash flows related to these changes. Related contra asset accounts should also be analyzed.

BENNETT COMPANY EXAMPLE

ANALYZE CHANGE IN LONG-TERM INVESTMENTS   Bennett's comparative balance sheets show that long-term investments increased $15,000 during 1997. The increase means that investments must have been purchased, and the additional data indicates that cash was spent to purchase long-term stock investments. Purchasing stock is an investing activity. Thus, a $15,000 purchase of stock investments will be shown as a cash outflow from investing activities in the statement of cash flows.

ANALYZE CHANGE IN PLANT ASSETS   Bennett's plant assets decreased $20,000 during 1997. Plant assets decrease as the result of disposals, and the additional data for Bennett Company indicate that land was sold for cash in 1997. Selling land is an investing activity. Thus, the sale of land for $28,000 will be shown as a cash inflow from investing activities in the statement of cash flows.

ANALYZE CHANGE IN ACCUMULATED DEPRECIATION   Bennett's accumulated depreciation increased $10,000 during 1997. Accumulated depreciation increases when depreciation expense is recorded. Bennett's 1997 depreciation expense was $10,000, so the total change in accumulated depreciation is the result of the recording of depreciation expense. As previously discussed, there is no cash flow related to the recording of depreciation expense.

ANALYZE CHANGE IN PATENT   We see from the comparative balance sheets that Bennett had an increase of $60,000 in the patent category. The increase means that a patent was acquired, and the additional data indicate that common stock was issued to obtain a patent. This event is a noncash investing (acquiring a patent) and financing (issuing common stock) transaction that must be disclosed as supplementary information to the statement of cash flows.

CASH FLOWS FROM FINANCING ACTIVITIES

ANALYZE CHANGES IN REMAINING LIABILITY AND STOCKHOLDERS' EQUITY ACCOUNTS

Financing activities cause changes in liability and stockholders' equity accounts. Usually the accounts affected are noncurrent accounts such as bonds payable and common stock, although a current liability such as short-term notes payable may also be affected. To determine the cash flows from financing activities, *we analyze the changes in all liability and stockholders' equity accounts that were not used in computing the net cash flow from operating activities.* Our objective is to identify any financing cash flows related to these changes.

BENNETT COMPANY EXAMPLE

ANALYZE CHANGE IN COMMON STOCK   Bennett's common stock increased $70,000 during 1997. Common stock increases when shares of stock are issued. As noted in discussing the patent increase, common stock with a $60,000 par value was issued in exchange for a patent. This event is disclosed as a noncash investing and financing transaction. The other $10,000 increase in common stock, as noted in the additional data, resulted from an issuance of stock for cash. Issuing common stock is a financing activity, so a $10,000 cash inflow from a stock issuance appears as a financing activity in the statement of cash flows.

ANALYZE CHANGE IN RETAINED EARNINGS   Retained earnings grew from $56,000 to $75,000 during 1997—a $19,000 increase. This increase is the net result of Bennett's $32,000 of net income (which increased retained earnings) and a $13,000 cash dividend (which decreased retained earnings). Because every item in Bennett's income statement was considered in computing the net cash provided by operating activities, only the cash dividend remains to be considered at this point. Paying a cash dividend is a financing activity. Thus, a $13,000 cash dividend appears as a cash outflow from financing activities in the statement of cash flows.

We have now completed the analysis of all of Bennett's noncash balance sheet accounts and can prepare the 1997 statement of cash flows. Exhibit 15-5 shows this statement.

If there are cash inflows and outflows from similar types of investing and financing activities, the inflows and outflows are reported separately (rather than reporting only the net difference). For example, proceeds from the sale of plant assets are reported separately from outlays made to acquire plant assets. Similarly, funds borrowed are reported separately from debt repayments, and proceeds from issuing stock are reported separately from outlays to acquire treasury stock.

SEPARATE DISCLOSURES UNDER THE INDIRECT METHOD

When the indirect method is used in the statement of cash flows, three separate disclosures are required: (1) two specific operating cash outflows—cash paid for interest and cash paid for income taxes, (2) a schedule or description of all noncash investing and financing transactions, and (3) the firm's policy for determining which highly liquid, short-term investments are treated as cash equivalents.

The firm's policy regarding cash equivalents is placed in the financial statement notes. The other two separate disclosures may be placed in the notes, or they may be shown at the bottom of the statement of cash flows.

BENNETT COMPANY EXAMPLE

Bennett Company incurred no interest cost during 1997. It did pay income taxes, however. Our discussion of the $2,000 change in Income Tax Payable during 1997 revealed that the

EXHIBIT 15–5	Statement of Cash Flows under the Indirect Method with Supplemental Disclosures

BENNETT COMPANY
STATEMENT OF CASH FLOWS
FOR THE YEAR ENDED DECEMBER 31, 1997

Net Cash Flow from Operating Activities

Net Income	$32,000	
Add (Deduct) Items to Convert Net Income to Cash Basis		
Depreciation	10,000	
Gain on Sale of Land	(8,000)	
Accounts Receivable Increase	(5,000)	
Inventory Decrease	6,000	
Prepaid Insurance Increase	(13,000)	
Accounts Payable Decrease	(9,000)	
Income Tax Payable Increase	2,000	
Net Cash Provided by Operating Activities		$15,000
Cash Flows from Investing Activities		
Purchase of Stock Investments	($15,000)	
Sale of Land	28,000	
Net Cash Provided by Investing Activities		13,000
Cash Flows from Financing Activities		
Issuance of Common Stock	$10,000	
Payment of Dividends	(13,000)	
Net Cash Used by Financing Activities		(3,000)
Net Increase in Cash		$25,000
Cash at Beginning of Year		10,000
Cash at End of Year		$35,000

Supplemental Information

Supplemental Cash Flow Disclosure

Cash Paid for Income Taxes	$ 9,000

Schedule of Noncash Investing and Financing Activities

Issuance of Common Stock to Acquire Patent	$60,000

increase meant that cash tax payments were less than income tax expense by the amount of the increase. Income tax expense was $11,000, so the cash paid for income taxes was $2,000 less than $11,000, or $9,000.

Bennett Company did have one noncash investing and financing event during 1997: the issuance of common stock to acquire a patent. This event, as well as the cash paid for income taxes, is disclosed as supplemental information to the statement of cash flows in Exhibit 15-5.

PREPARING THE STATEMENT OF CASH FLOWS UNDER THE DIRECT METHOD

OBJECTIVE 3

DISCUSS the preparation of a statement of cash flows using the direct method.

To prepare a statement of cash flows, we need a firm's income statement, comparative balance sheets, and some additional data taken from the accounting records. Exhibit 15-6 presents this information for Bennett Company. We use these data to prepare Bennett's 1997 statement of cash flows using the direct method.

Bennett's statement of cash flows will explain the $25,000 increase in cash that occurred during 1997 (from $10,000 to $35,000) by classifying the firm's cash flows into operating, investing, and financing categories. To get the information to construct the statement, therefore, we do the following:

| EXHIBIT 15–6 | Financial Data of Bennett Company |

BENNETT COMPANY
INCOME STATEMENT
FOR THE YEAR ENDED DECEMBER 31, 1997

Sales		$250,000
Cost of Goods Sold	$148,000	
Wages Expense	52,000	
Insurance Expense	5,000	
Depreciation Expense	10,000	
Income Tax Expense	11,000	
Gain on Sale of Land	(8,000)	218,000
Net Income		$ 32,000

Additional Data for 1997

1. At year end, purchased long-term stock investments for cash.
2. Sold land costing $20,000 for $28,000 cash.
3. At year-end, acquired $60,000 patent by issuing common stock at par.
4. All accounts payable relate to merchandise purchases.
5. Issued common stock at par for $10,000 cash.
6. Declared and paid cash dividends of $13,000.

BENNETT COMPANY
BALANCE SHEETS

	Dec. 31, 1997	Dec. 31, 1996
Assets		
Cash	$ 35,000	$ 10,000
Accounts Receivable	39,000	34,000
Inventory	54,000	60,000
Prepaid Insurance	17,000	4,000
Long-Term Investments	15,000	—
Plant Assets	180,000	200,000
Accumulated Depreciation	(50,000)	(40,000)
Patent	60,000	—
Total Assets	$350,000	$268,000
Liabilities and Stockholders' Equity		
Accounts Payable	$10,000	$19,000
Income Tax Payable	5,000	3,000
Common Stock	260,000	190,000
Retained Earnings	75,000	56,000
Total Liabilities and Stockholders' Equity	$350,000	$268,000

1. *Use the direct method to determine the individual cash flows from operating activities.* In doing this, we use changes that occurred during 1997 in various current asset and current liability accounts.

2. *Determine cash flows from investing activities.* We do this by analyzing changes in the noncash asset accounts not used in the direct method.

3. *Determine cash flows from financing activities.* We do this by analyzing changes in the liability and stockholders' equity accounts not used in the direct method.

NET CASH FLOW FROM OPERATING ACTIVITIES UNDER THE DIRECT METHOD

The **direct method** presents the net cash flow from operating activities by showing the major categories of operating cash receipts and payments. The operating cash receipts and payments are usually determined by converting the accrual revenues and expenses to corresponding cash amounts. It is efficient to do it this way, because the accrual revenues and expenses are readily available in the income statement.

CONVERT REVENUES AND EXPENSES TO CASH FLOWS

Exhibit 15-7 summarizes the procedures for converting individual income statement items to corresponding cash flows from operating activities.

BENNETT COMPANY EXAMPLE

We now explain and illustrate the process of converting Bennett Company's 1997 revenues and expenses to corresponding cash flows from operating activities.

CONVERT SALES TO CASH RECEIVED FROM CUSTOMERS   During 1997, accounts receivable increased $5,000. This increase means that during 1997, cash collections on account (which

EXHIBIT 15–7	Direct Method Conversion Schedule: Adjustments to Convert Income Statement Items to Operating Activity Cash Flows

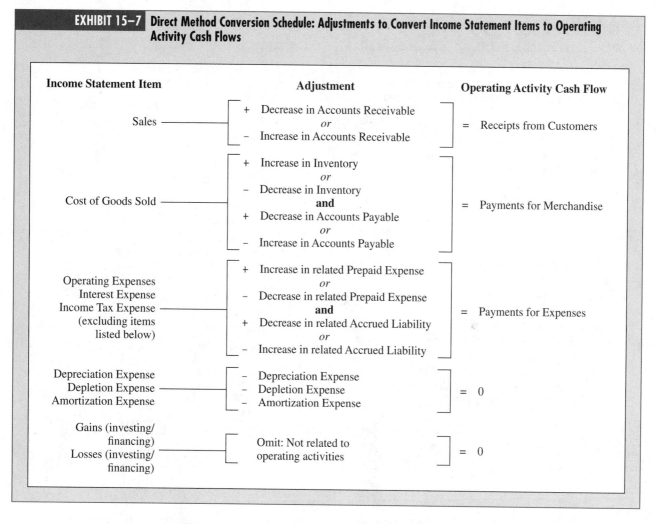

decrease accounts receivable) were less than credit sales (which increase accounts receivable). We compute cash received from customers, then, as follows:[4]

Sales	$250,000
− Increase in accounts receivable	(5,000)
= Cash received from customers	$245,000

CONVERT COST OF GOODS SOLD TO CASH PAID FOR MERCHANDISE PURCHASED   The conversion of cost of goods sold to cash paid for merchandise purchased is a two-step process. First, cost of goods sold is adjusted for the change in inventory to determine the amount of purchases during the year. Then the purchases amount is adjusted for the change in accounts payable to derive the cash paid for merchandise purchased.

Inventory decreased from $60,000 to $54,000 during 1997. This $6,000 decrease indicates that the cost of goods sold exceeded the cost of goods purchased during the year. The year's purchases amount is computed as follows:

Cost of goods sold	$148,000
− Decrease in inventory	(6,000)
= Purchases	$142,000

During 1997, accounts payable decreased $9,000. This decrease reflects the fact that cash payments for merchandise purchased on account (which decrease accounts payable)

---

[4]This computation assumes that no accounts were written off as uncollectible during the period. The impact on the computation of an allowance account and uncollectible accounts expense is beyond the scope of this discussion.

exceeded purchases on account (which increase accounts payable). The cash paid for merchandise purchased, therefore, is computed as follows:

Purchases	$142,000
+ Decrease in accounts payable	9,000
= Cash paid for merchandise purchased	$151,000

CONVERT WAGES EXPENSE TO CASH PAID TO EMPLOYEES   No adjustment to wages expense is needed. The absence of any beginning or ending accrued liability for wages payable means that wages expense and cash paid to employees as wages are the same amount: $52,000.

CONVERT INSURANCE EXPENSE TO CASH PAID FOR INSURANCE   Prepaid insurance increased $13,000 during 1997. The $13,000 increase reflects the excess of cash paid for insurance during 1997 (which increases prepaid insurance) over the year's insurance expense (which decreases prepaid insurance). Starting with insurance expense, then, the cash paid for insurance is computed as follows:

Insurance expense	$ 5,000
+ Increase in prepaid insurance	13,000
= Cash paid for insurance	$18,000

ELIMINATE DEPRECIATION EXPENSE AND OTHER NONCASH OPERATING EXPENSES   Depreciation expense is a noncash expense. Because it does not represent a cash payment, depreciation expense is completely eliminated as we convert accrual expense amounts to the corresponding amounts of cash payments. If Bennett Company had any amortization expense or depletion expense, it also would be eliminated for the same reason. The amortization of an intangible asset and the depletion of a natural resource are entirely noncash expenses.

CONVERT INCOME TAX EXPENSE TO CASH PAID FOR INCOME TAXES   The increase in income tax payable from $3,000 at December 31, 1996, to $5,000 at December 31, 1997, means that 1997's income tax expense (which increases income tax payable) was $2,000 more than 1997's tax payments (which decrease income tax payable). If we start with income tax expense, then we calculate cash paid for income taxes in the following manner:

Income tax expense	$11,000
− Increase in income tax payable	(2,000)
= Cash paid for income taxes	$ 9,000

OMIT GAINS AND LOSSES RELATED TO INVESTING AND FINANCING ACTIVITIES   The income statement may contain gains and losses related to investing or financing activities. Examples include gains and losses from the sale of plant assets and gains and losses from the retirement of bonds payable. Because these gains and losses are not related to operating activities, we ignore them as we convert income statement items to various cash flows from operating activities. The cash flows relating to these gains and losses are reported in the investing activities or financing activities sections of the statement of cash flows.

Bennett Company had an $8,000 gain from the sale of land in 1997. This gain resulted from an investing activity; no related cash flow appears within the operating activities category.

We have now applied the proper adjustments to convert each accrual revenue and expense to the corresponding operating cash flow. We use these individual cash flows to prepare the operating activities section of the statement of cash flows. This section appears as follows:

Cash Received from Customers		$245,000
Cash Paid for Merchandise Purchased	$151,000	
Cash Paid to Employees	52,000	
Cash Paid for Insurance	18,000	
Cash Paid for Income Taxes	9,000	230,000
Net Cash Provided by Operating Activities		$ 15,000

POINT OF INTEREST

DIRECT METHOD USERS

A small proportion of companies use the direct method in their reporting of net cash flows from operating activities. Among the companies that use the direct method are

Compaq Computer Corporation

Cray Research, Inc.

Office Depot, Inc.

Wausau Paper Mills Company

CASH FLOWS FROM INVESTING ACTIVITIES

ANALYZE CHANGES IN REMAINING NONCASH ASSET ACCOUNTS

Investing activities cause changes in asset accounts. Usually the accounts affected other than cash are noncurrent asset accounts such as plant assets and long-term investments, although short-term investment accounts may also be affected. To determine the cash flows from investing activities, *we analyze the changes in all noncash asset accounts not used in computing the net cash flow from operating activities.* Our objective is to identify any investing cash flows related to these changes. Related contra asset accounts should also be analyzed.

BENNETT COMPANY EXAMPLE

ANALYZE CHANGE IN LONG-TERM INVESTMENTS Bennett's comparative balance sheets show that long-term investments increased $15,000 during 1997. The increase means that investments must have been purchased, and the additional data indicate that cash was spent to purchase long-term stock investments. Purchasing stock is an investing activity. Thus, a $15,000 purchase of stock investments is shown as a cash outflow from investing activities in the statement of cash flows.

ANALYZE CHANGE IN PLANT ASSETS Bennett's plant assets decreased $20,000 during 1997. Plant assets decrease as the result of disposals, and the additional data for Bennett Company indicate that land was sold for cash in 1997. Selling land is an investing activity. Thus, the sale of land for $28,000 is shown as a cash inflow from investing activities in the statement of cash flows.

ANALYZE CHANGE IN ACCUMULATED DEPRECIATION Bennett's accumulated depreciation increased $10,000 during 1997. Accumulated depreciation increases when depreciation expense is recorded. Bennett's 1997 depreciation expense was $10,000, so the total change in accumulated depreciation is the result of the recording of depreciation expense. As previously discussed, there is no cash flow related to the recording of depreciation expense.

ANALYZE CHANGE IN PATENT We see from the comparative balance sheets that Bennett had an increase of $60,000 in the patent category. The increase means that a patent was acquired, and the additional data indicate that common stock was issued to obtain a patent. This event is a noncash investing (acquiring a patent) and financing (issuing common stock) transaction that must be disclosed as supplementary information to the statement of cash flows.

CASH FLOWS FROM FINANCING ACTIVITIES

ANALYZE CHANGES IN REMAINING LIABILITY AND STOCKHOLDERS' EQUITY ACCOUNTS

Financing activities cause changes in liability and stockholders' equity accounts. Usually the accounts affected are noncurrent accounts such as bonds payable and common stock, although a current liability such as short-term notes payable may also be affected. To determine the cash flows from financing activities, *we analyze the changes in all liability and stockholders' equity accounts that were not used in computing the net cash flow from operating activities.* Our objective is to identify any financing cash flows related to these changes.

BENNETT COMPANY EXAMPLE

ANALYZE CHANGE IN COMMON STOCK   Bennett's common stock increased $70,000 during 1997. Common stock increases when shares of stock are issued. As noted in discussing the patent increase, common stock with a $60,000 par value was issued in exchange for a patent. This event is disclosed as a noncash investing and financing transaction. The other $10,000 increase in common stock, as noted in the additional data, resulted from an issuance of stock for cash. Issuing common stock is a financing activity, so a $10,000 cash inflow from a stock issuance appears as a financing activity in the statement of cash flows.

ANALYZE CHANGE IN RETAINED EARNINGS   Retained earnings grew from $56,000 to $75,000 during 1997—a $19,000 increase. This increase is the net result of Bennett's $32,000 of net income (which increased retained earnings) and a $13,000 cash dividend (which decreased retained earnings). Because every item in Bennett's income statement was considered in computing the net cash provided by operating activities, only the cash dividend remains to be considered at this point. Paying a cash dividend is a financing activity. Thus, a $13,000 cash dividend appears as a cash outflow from financing activities in the statement of cash flows.

We have now completed the analysis of all of Bennett's noncash balance sheet accounts and can prepare the 1997 statement of cash flows. Exhibit 15-8 shows this statement.

EXHIBIT 15–8	Statement of Cash Flows under the Direct Method with Supplemental Disclosure

BENNETT COMPANY
STATEMENT OF CASH FLOWS
FOR THE YEAR ENDED DECEMBER 31, 1997

Cash Flows from Operating Activities		
Cash Received from Customers		$245,000
Cash Paid for Merchandise Purchased	$151,000	
Cash Paid to Employees	52,000	
Cash Paid for Insurance	18,000	
Cash Paid for Income Taxes	9,000	230,000
Net Cash Provided by Operating Activities		$ 15,000
Cash Flows from Investing Activities		
Purchase of Stock Investments	($ 15,000)	
Sale of Land	28,000	
Net Cash Provided by Investing Activities		13,000
Cash Flows from Financing Activities		
Issuance of Common Stock	$ 10,000	
Payment of Dividends	(13,000)	
Net Cash Used by Financing Activities		(3,000)
Net Increase in Cash		$ 25,000
Cash at Beginning of Year		10,000
Cash at End of Year		$ 35,000

Supplemental Information

Schedule of Noncash Investing and Financing Activities

Issuance of Common Stock to Acquire Patent	$ 60,000

If there are cash inflows and outflows from similar types of investing and financing activities, the inflows and outflows are reported separately (rather than reporting only the net difference). For example, proceeds from the sale of plant assets are reported separately from outlays made to acquire plant assets. Similarly, funds borrowed are reported separately from debt repayments, and proceeds from issuing stock are reported separately from outlays to acquire treasury stock.

SEPARATE DISCLOSURES UNDER THE DIRECT METHOD

When the direct method is used in the statement of cash flows, three separate disclosures are required: (1) a reconciliation of net income to the net cash flow from operating activities, (2) a schedule or description of all noncash investing and financing transactions, and (3) the firm's policy for determining which highly liquid, short-term investments are treated as cash equivalents.

The firm's policy regarding cash equivalents is placed in the financial statement notes. The other two separate disclosures may be placed in the notes, or they may be shown at the bottom of the statement of cash flows.

The required reconciliation is the indirect method of computing the cash flow from operating activities. *Thus, when the direct method is used in the statement of cash flows, the indirect method is a required separate disclosure.* We discuss the indirect method earlier in this chapter. We do not illustrate the disclosure here; an example appears on page 524.

BENNETT COMPANY EXAMPLE

Bennett Company did have one noncash investing and financing event during 1997: the issuance of common stock to acquire a patent. This event is disclosed as supplemental information to the statement of cash flows in Exhibit 15-8.

FINANCIAL ANALYSIS

OPERATING CASH FLOW TO CURRENT LIABILITIES RATIO AND OPERATING CASH FLOW TO CAPITAL EXPENDITURES RATIO

OBJECTIVE 4

DEFINE the operating cash flow to current liabilities ratio and the operating cash flow to capital expenditures ratio and **EXPLAIN** their use.

Data from the statement of cash flows enter into various financial ratios. Two such ratios are the operating cash flow to current liabilities ratio and the operating cash flow to capital expenditures ratio.

OPERATING CASH FLOW TO CURRENT LIABILITIES RATIO

Two measures previously introduced—the current ratio and the quick ratio—emphasize the relationship of current assets to current liabilities in an attempt to measure the ability of the firm to liquidate current liabilities when they become due. The **operating cash flow to current liabilities ratio** is another measure of ability to liquidate current liabilities. The ratio is calculated as follows:

$$\begin{array}{c} \text{Operating Cash Flow} \\ \text{to Current Liabilities} \\ \text{Ratio} \end{array} = \frac{\text{Net Cash Flow from Operating Activities}}{\text{Average Current Liabilities}}$$

Net cash flow from operating activities is obtained from the statement of cash flows. The net cash flow from operating activities represents the excess amount of cash derived from operations during the year after deducting working capital needs and payments required on current liabilities. The denominator is the average of the beginning and ending current liabilities for the year.

The following amounts (in thousands of dollars) were taken from recent financial statements for Gannett Co., Inc., a diversified news and information company that publishes *USA Today:*

Net cash flow from operating activities	$714,297
Current liabilities at beginning of the year	455,139
Current liabilities at end of the year	527,054

The operating cash flow to current liabilities ratio would be calculated as follows:

$$\$714,297/[(\$455,139 + \$527,054)/2] = 1.45$$

Gannett's operating cash flow to current liabilities ratio for the preceding year was 1.51. The higher this ratio, the stronger is a firm's ability to settle current liabilities as they become due. The decline in Gannett's ratio from 1.51 to 1.45, however, is not necessarily a sign of financial weakness. A ratio of 0.5 is considered a strong ratio so Gannett's ratio of 1.45 would be interpreted as very strong.

OPERATING CASH FLOW TO CAPITAL EXPENDITURES RATIO

To remain competitive, an entity must be able to replace, and expand when appropriate, its property, plant, and equipment. A ratio that helps assess a firm's ability to do this is the **operating cash flow to capital expenditures ratio,** which is computed as follows:

$$\text{Operating Cash Flow to Capital Expenditures Ratio} = \frac{\text{Net Cash Flow from Operating Activities}}{\text{Annual Capital Expenditures}}$$

The numerator in this ratio comes from the first section of the statement of cash flows—the section reporting the net cash flow from operating activities. Information for the denominator may be found in one or more places in the financial statements and related disclosures. Data on capital expenditures are part of the required industry segment disclosures in the notes to the financial statements.[5] Capital expenditures may also be shown in the investing activities section of the statement of cash flows. Also, capital expenditures often appear in the comparative selected financial data presented as supplementary information to the financial statements. Finally, management's discussion and analysis of the statements may identify the annual capital expenditures.

A ratio in excess of 1.0 means that the firm's current operating activities are providing cash in excess of the amount needed to provide the desired level of plant capacity and would normally be considered a sign of financial strength. This ratio may also be viewed as an indicator of long-term solvency—a ratio exceeding 1.0 means that there is an operating cash flow in excess of capital needs that may be used to repay outstanding long-term debt.

The interpretation of this ratio for a firm is influenced by its trend in recent years, the ratio size being achieved by other firms in the same industry, and the stage of the firm's life cycle. A firm in the early stages of its life cycle—when periods of rapid expansion may occur—may be expected to experience a lower ratio than a firm in the mature stage of its life cycle—when maintenance of plant capacity may be more likely than expansion of capacity.

To illustrate the ratio's computation, Abbott Laboratories (a manufacturer of pharmaceutical and other health care products) reported capital expenditures in a recent year of $952,732,000. In the same year, Abbott's net cash flow from operating activities was $1,846,909,000. Abbott's operating cash flow to capital expenditures ratio for that year was $1,846,909,000/$952,732,000 = 1.94. Following are recent operating cash flow to capital expenditures ratios for several companies:

The Quaker Oats Company (consumer grocery products)	3.24
Lockheed Corporation (aerospace)	2.48
Norfolk Southern Corporation (freight transportation services)	1.31
Federal Mogul Corporation (precision parts)	0.50
Ben & Jerry's Homemade, Inc. (ice cream products)	0.41

KEY POINTS FOR CHAPTER LEARNING OBJECTIVES

1 **PROVIDE** a basis for understanding a statement of cash flows (pp. 514–519).
- A statement of cash flows explains the net increase or decrease in cash and cash equivalents during the period.
- A statement of cash flows separates cash flows into operating, investing, and financing categories.

[5]Segment disclosures are discussed in Appendix J.

- A secondary objective of cash flow reporting is to provide information about a firm's investing and financing activities. A required supplemental disclosure reports noncash investing and financing activities.
- A statement of cash flows should help users compare, evaluate, and predict a firm's cash flows and also help evaluate its financial flexibility.

2 **DISCUSS** the preparation of a statement of cash flows using the indirect method (pp. 519–526).
- The indirect method reconciles net income to net cash flow from operating activities.
- A firm using the indirect method must separately disclose the cash paid for interest and the cash paid for income taxes.

3 **DISCUSS** the preparation of a statement of cash flows using the direct method (pp. 526–532).
- The direct method shows the major categories of operating cash receipts and payments.
- The FASB encourages use of the direct method but permits use of either the direct or the indirect method.
- A firm using the direct method must separately disclose the reconciliation of net income to net cash flow from operating activities.

4 **Financial Analysis**   **DEFINE** the *operating cash flow to current liabilities ratio* and *the operating cash flow to capital expenditures ratio* and **EXPLAIN** their use (pp. 532–533).
- The operating cash flow to current liabilities ratio is calculated by dividing net cash flow from operating activities by the average current liabilities for the year.
- The operating cash flow to current liabilities ratio is a measure of a firm's ability to liquidate its current liabilities.
- The operating cash flow to capital expenditures ratio is computed by dividing a firm's net cash flow from operating activities by its annual capital expenditures.
- The operating cash flow to capital expenditures ratio helps assess a firm's (1) ability to maintain its plant capacity and (2) long-run solvency.

SELF-TEST QUESTIONS FOR REVIEW

(Answers follow Solution to Demonstration Problem 2.)

1. Which of the following is not disclosed in a statement of cash flows?
   a. A transfer of cash to a cash equivalent investment
   b. The amount of cash on hand at year-end
   c. Cash outflows from investing activities during the period
   d. Cash inflows from financing activities during the period

2. Which of the following events will appear in the cash flows from investing activities section of the statement of cash flows?
   a. Cash received as interest
   b. Cash received from issuance of common stock
   c. Cash purchase of truck
   d. Cash payment of dividends

3. Which of the following events will appear in the cash flows from financing activities section of the statement of cash flows?
   a. Cash purchase of equipment
   b. Cash purchase of bonds issued by another company
   c. Cash received as repayment for funds loaned
   d. Cash purchase of treasury stock

4. Tyler Company has a net income of $49,000 and the following related items:

Depreciation expense	$ 5,000
Accounts receivable increase	2,000
Inventory decrease	10,000
Accounts payable decrease	4,000

   Using the indirect method, what is Tyler's net cash flow from operations?
   a. $42,000   **b.** $46,000   **c.** $58,000   **d.** $38,000

5. Which of the following methods will disclose the cash received from customers in the statement of cash flows?
   a. Indirect method
   b. Reconciliation method
   c. Direct method
   d. Both direct and indirect methods

DEMONSTRATION PROBLEM 1 FOR REVIEW: THE INDIRECT METHOD

Terry Company's 1997 income statement and comparative balance sheets at December 31, 1997 and 1996, are as follows:

TERRY COMPANY
INCOME STATEMENT
FOR THE YEAR ENDED DECEMBER 31, 1997

Sales		$385,000
Dividend Income		5,000
		$390,000
Cost of Goods Sold	$233,000	
Wages Expense	82,000	
Advertising Expense	10,000	
Depreciation Expense	11,000	
Income Tax Expense	17,000	
Loss on Sale of Investments	2,000	355,000
Net Income		$ 35,000

TERRY COMPANY
BALANCE SHEETS

Assets	Dec. 31, 1997	Dec. 31, 1996
Cash	$ 8,000	$ 12,000
Accounts Receivable	22,000	28,000
Inventory	94,000	66,000
Prepaid Advertising	12,000	9,000
Long-Term Investments—Available for Sale	30,000	41,000
Fair Value Adjustment to Investments	—	(1,000)
Plant Assets	178,000	130,000
Accumulated Depreciation	(72,000)	(61,000)
Total Assets	$272,000	$224,000

Liabilities and Stockholders' Equity		
Accounts Payable	$ 27,000	$ 14,000
Wages Payable	6,000	2,500
Income Tax Payable	3,000	4,500
Common Stock	139,000	125,000
Retained Earnings	97,000	79,000
Unrealized Loss on Investments	—	(1,000)
Total Liabilities and Stockholders' Equity	$272,000	$224,000

Cash dividends of $17,000 were declared and paid during 1997. Plant assets were purchased for cash, and, later in the year, additional common stock was issued for cash. Investments costing $11,000 were sold for cash at a $2,000 loss; an unrealized loss of $1,000 on these investments had been recorded in 1996 (at December 31, 1997, the cost and fair value of unsold investments are equal).

REQUIRED

a. Compute the change in cash that occurred during 1997.
b. Prepare a 1997 statement of cash flows using the indirect method.

SOLUTION TO DEMONSTRATION PROBLEM 1

a. $8,000 ending balance – $12,000 beginning balance = $4,000 decrease in cash
b. 1. Use the indirect method to determine the net cash flow from operating activities.
- The adjustments to convert Terry Company's net income of $35,000 to a net cash provided by operating activities of $38,000 are shown in the following statement of cash flows.

2. Analyze changes in remaining noncash asset (and contra asset) accounts to determine cash flows from investing activities.
- Long-Term Investments: $11,000 decrease resulted from sale of investments for cash at a $2,000 loss. Cash received from sale of investments = $9,000 ($11,000 cost – $2,000 loss).

- Fair Value Adjustment to Investments: $1,000 decrease resulted from the elimination of this account balance (and the Unrealized Loss on Investments) at the end of 1997. No cash flow effect.
- Plant Assets: $48,000 increase resulted from purchase of plant assets for cash. Cash paid to purchase plant assets = $48,000.
- Accumulated Depreciation: $11,000 increase resulted from the recording of 1997 depreciation. No cash flow effect.

3. Analyze changes in remaining liability and stockholders' equity accounts to determine cash flows from financing activities.

- Common Stock: $14,000 increase resulted from the issuance of stock for cash. Cash received from issuance of common stock = $14,000.
- Retained Earnings: $18,000 increase resulted from net income of $35,000 and dividend declaration of $17,000. Cash paid as dividends = $17,000.
- Unrealized Loss on Investments: $1,000 decrease resulted from the elimination of this account balance (and the Fair Value Adjustment to Investments) at the end of 1997. No cash flow effect.

The statement of cash flows is as follows:

TERRY COMPANY
STATEMENT OF CASH FLOWS
FOR THE YEAR ENDED DECEMBER 31, 1997

Net Cash Flow from Operating Activities

Net Income	$35,000	
Add (Deduct) Items to Convert Net Income to Cash Basis		
Depreciation	11,000	
Loss on Sale of Investments	2,000	
Accounts Receivable Decrease	6,000	
Inventory Increase	(28,000)	
Prepaid Advertising Increase	(3,000)	
Accounts Payable Increase	13,000	
Wages Payable Increase	3,500	
Income Tax Payable Decrease	(1,500)	
Net Cash Provided by Operating Activities		$38,000
Cash Flows from Investing Activities		
Sale of Investments	$ 9,000	
Purchase of Plant Assets	(48,000)	
Net Cash Used by Investing Activities		(39,000)
Cash Flows from Financing Activities		
Issuance of Common Stock	$14,000	
Payment of Dividends	(17,000)	
Net Cash Used by Financing Activities		(3,000)
Net Decrease in Cash		($ 4,000)
Cash at Beginning of Year		12,000
Cash at End of Year		$ 8,000

DEMONSTRATION PROBLEM 2 FOR REVIEW: THE DIRECT METHOD

Refer to the data for Terry Company presented in Demonstration Problem 1.

REQUIRED

a. Compute the change in cash that occurred during 1997.
b. Prepare a 1997 statement of cash flows using the direct method.

SOLUTION TO DEMONSTRATION PROBLEM 2

a. $8,000 ending balance – $12,000 beginning balance = $4,000 decrease in cash
b. 1. Use the direct method to determine the individual cash flows from operating activities.
   - $385,000 Sales + $6,000 Accounts Receivable decrease = $391,000 Cash Received from Customers
   - $5,000 Dividend Income = $5,000 Cash Received as Dividends
   - $233,000 Cost of Goods Sold + $28,000 Inventory increase – $13,000 Accounts Payable increase = $248,000 Cash Paid for Merchandise Purchased
   - $82,000 Wages Expense – $3,500 Wages Payable increase = $78,500 Cash Paid to Employees

- $10,000 Advertising Expense + $3,000 Prepaid Advertising increase = $13,000 Cash Paid for Advertising
- $17,000 Income Tax Expense + $1,500 Income Tax Payable decrease = $18,500 Cash Paid for Income Taxes

2. Analyze changes in remaining noncash asset (and contra asset) accounts to determine cash flows from investing activities.
   - Long-Term Investments: $11,000 decrease resulted from sale of investments for cash at a $2,000 loss. Cash received from sale of investments = $9,000 ($11,000 cost – $2,000 loss).
   - Fair Value Adjustment to Investments: $1,000 decrease resulted from the elimination of this account balance (and the Unrealized Loss on Investments) at the end of 1997. No cash flow effect.
   - Plant Assets: $48,000 increase resulted from purchase of plant assets for cash. Cash paid to purchase plant assets = $48,000.
   - Accumulated Depreciation: $11,000 increase resulted from the recording of 1997 depreciation. No cash flow effect.

3. Analyze changes in remaining liability and stockholders' equity accounts to determine cash flows from financing activities.
   - Common Stock: $14,000 increase resulted from the issuance of stock for cash. Cash received from issuance of common stock = $14,000.
   - Retained Earnings: $18,000 increase resulted from net income of $35,000 and dividend declaration of $17,000. Cash paid as dividends = $17,000.
   - Unrealized Loss on Investments: $1,000 decrease resulted from the elimination of this account balance (and the Fair Value Adjustment to Investments) at the end of 1997. No cash flow effect.

The statement of cash flows is as follows:

TERRY COMPANY
STATEMENT OF CASH FLOWS
FOR THE YEAR ENDED DECEMBER 31, 1997

Cash Flows from Operating Activities

Cash Received from Customers	$391,000	
Cash Received as Dividends	5,000	$396,000
Cash Paid for Merchandise Purchased	$248,000	
Cash Paid to Employees	78,500	
Cash Paid for Advertising	13,000	
Cash Paid for Income Taxes	18,500	358,000
Net Cash Provided by Operating Activities		$ 38,000

Cash Flows from Investing Activities

Sale of Investments	$ 9,000	
Purchase of Plant Assets	(48,000)	
Net Cash Used by Investing Activities		(39,000)

Cash Flows from Financing Activities

Issuance of Common Stock	$ 14,000	
Payment of Dividends	(17,000)	
Net Cash Used by Financing Activities		(3,000)
Net Decrease in Cash		($ 4,000)
Cash at Beginning of Year		12,000
Cash at End of Year		$ 8,000

ANSWERS TO SELF-TEST QUESTIONS   **1.** a, p. 514   **2.** c, p. 516   **3.** d, p. 516   **4.** c, p. 521   **5.** c, p. 528

I

T-Account Approach to Preparing the Statement of Cash Flows under the Indirect Method

Some accountants prefer to use a T-account approach to accumulate the information needed for a statement of cash flows. In this appendix, we explain the T-account approach for a statement of cash flows prepared using the indirect method.

FIVE STEPS IN THE T-ACCOUNT APPROACH UNDER THE INDIRECT METHOD

Preparing a statement of cash flows under the indirect method and the related separate disclosures using a T-account approach involves five steps:

1. Set up a large T account for Cash showing the net change in cash that occurred during the year.
2. Set up T accounts for all other balance sheet accounts showing the net change in each account that occurred during the year.
3. Record entries in the T accounts to account for and explain the net change that occurred in each account.
4. Prepare the statement of cash flows using information from the Cash T account.
5. Determine the information for the required separate disclosures.

ILLUSTRATION OF T-ACCOUNT APPROACH

We illustrate the T-account approach for the indirect method using the data for Superior Corporation presented in Exhibit I-1.

STEP 1

Set up a large T account labeled Cash and enter the period's net change in cash in the account—a cash increase is entered on the debit side and a cash decrease is entered on the credit side. Superior Corporation's cash increased $12,000 during 1997, so $12,000 is entered on the debit side and identified as "Net Change." Place a single rule beneath this entry to separate it from the analyzing entries that will be reflected in the account.

Divide the T account into the following six categories, leaving space for entries in each category:

Debit Side	Credit Side
Operating Activities—Increases	Operating Activities—Decreases
Investing Activities—Increases	Investing Activities—Decreases
Financing Activities—Increases	Financing Activities—Decreases

STEP 2

Set up T accounts for each remaining balance sheet account and enter the period's net change on the appropriate side of each account. During 1997, Superior Corporation's ac-

EXHIBIT I–1 Financial Data of Superior Corporation

SUPERIOR CORPORATION
INCOME STATEMENT
FOR THE YEAR ENDED DECEMBER 31, 1997

Sales		$360,000
Cost of Goods Sold	$200,000	
Wages and Other Operating Expenses	78,000	
Depreciation Expense	13,000	
Interest Expense	10,000	
Income Tax Expense	12,000	
Gain on Sale of Equipment	(16,000)	
Loss on Bond Retirement*	9,000	306,000
Net Income		$ 54,000

SUPERIOR CORPORATION
BALANCE SHEET

Assets	Dec. 31, 1997	Dec. 31, 1996	Increase (Decrease)
Current Assets			
Cash	$ 25,000	$ 13,000	$ 12,000
Accounts Receivable (net)	55,000	60,000	(5,000)
Inventory	94,000	80,000	14,000
Prepaid Expenses	13,000	10,000	3,000
Total Current Assets	$187,000	$163,000	$ 24,000
Plant Assets			
Building and Equipment	$418,000	$333,000	$ 85,000
Accumulated Depreciation	(75,000)	(68,000)	7,000
Total Plant Assets	$343,000	$265,000	$ 78,000
Total Assets	$530,000	$428,000	$102,000
Liabilities and Stockholders' Equity			
Current Liabilities			
Accounts Payable	$ 32,000	$ 42,000	($ 10,000)
Interest Payable	1,000	3,000	(2,000)
Income Tax Payable	2,000	1,000	1,000
Total Current Liabilities	$ 35,000	$ 46,000	($ 11,000)
Long-Term Debt			
Bonds Payable	$ 40,000	$120,000	($ 80,000)
Stockholders' Equity			
Common Stock ($10 par value)	$350,000	$200,000	$150,000
Retained Earnings	105,000	62,000	43,000
Total Stockholders' Equity	$455,000	$262,000	$193,000
Total Liabilities and Stockholders' Equity	$530,000	$428,000	$102,000

Additional Data for 1997

1. Sold equipment having a book value of $4,000 ($10,000 cost – $6,000 accumulated depreciation) for $20,000 cash.
2. Purchased new equipment for $65,000 cash.
3. Retired $80,000 of bonds payable for $89,000 cash.
4. Acquired equipment worth $30,000 by issuing 3,000 shares of common stock.
5. Issued additional common stock at par for $120,000 cash.
6. Declared and paid cash dividends of $11,000.

*If material, this loss is extraordinary. Separate disclosure of cash flows relating to extraordinary items is not required. For simplicity, a separate extraordinary section is not used here.

counts receivable decreased $5,000, so $5,000 is entered on the credit side of the Accounts Receivable T account; inventory increased $14,000, so $14,000 is entered on the debit side of the Inventory T account, and so on. Place a single rule beneath the net change entered in each account.

Exhibit I-2 shows the T accounts for Superior Corporation after all the net changes have been entered and ruled. The net change for each account is the *target number* for that account. Our objective is to analyze all changes in the noncash balance sheet accounts to determine the events affecting cash flows. Entries recorded in each account will eventually equal that account's target number. Our analysis is complete when the target numbers in all T accounts equal the net balances of the entries in the T accounts.

STEP 3

Record entries in the T accounts to account for and explain the net changes in the accounts. These entries are placed directly into the T accounts; for ease of study, we also present them in a general journal format. Entries to the Cash T account need a descriptive label because this account provides the data for the statement of cash flows.

EXHIBIT 1–2   Cash Flows T Accounts after Entry of Net Changes for Superior Corporation

CASH

Net Change	12,000	

Operating Activities—Increases	Operating Activities—Decreases

Investing Activities—Increases	Investing Activities—Decreases

Financing Activities—Increases	Financing Activities—Decreases

ACCOUNTS RECEIVABLE

	Net Change	5,000

INVENTORY

Net Change	14,000	

PREPAID EXPENSES

Net Change	3,000	

BUILDING AND EQUIPMENT

Net Change	85,000	

ACCUMULATED DEPRECIATION

	Net Change	7,000

ACCOUNTS PAYABLE

	Net Change	10,000

INTEREST PAYABLE

Net Change	2,000	

INCOME TAX PAYABLE

	Net Change	1,000

BONDS PAYABLE

Net Change	80,000	

COMMON STOCK

	Net Change	150,000

RETAINED EARNINGS

	Net Change	43,000

The T-account entries are divided into two sets. The *first set* of entries determines the net cash flow from operating activities using the indirect method. The indirect method begins with net income (or net loss) and applies a series of adjustments to convert the net income (or net loss) to a cash amount. (These adjustments are summarized in Exhibit 15-4 on page 521.) When these adjustments deal with gains and losses related to investing and financing activities, the T-account entry presents the entire transaction. The *second set* of entries explains the remaining changes in the T accounts.

Entries 1–10 compose the first set of entries and determine the net cash flow from operating activities for Superior Corporation. (You should trace each entry into the completed T-account analysis shown in Exhibit I-3 on page 543.)

T-Account Entries Only

1. Cash—Operating Activities (Net Income)   54,000
     Retained Earnings   54,000

This entry establishes net income as the starting point for computing the net cash flow from operating activities and shows the increase in retained earnings caused by the period's net income.

2. Cash—Operating Activities (Depreciation)   13,000
     Accumulated Depreciation   13,000

The period's depreciation expense is added to net income in computing the net cash flow from operating activities. Depreciation expense also increased accumulated depreciation.

3. Cash—Investing Activities (Sale of Equipment)   20,000
     Accumulated Depreciation   6,000
        Building and Equipment   10,000
        Cash—Operating Activities (Gain on Sale of Equipment)   16,000

This entry reflects the sale of equipment and its impact on cash flows. The sale provided cash from investing activities of $20,000. The $16,000 gain on sale of equipment is deducted from net income in determining the net cash flow from operating activities.

4. Bonds Payable   80,000
     Cash—Operating Activities (Loss on Bond Retirement)   9,000
        Cash—Financing Activities (Retirement of Bonds Payable)   89,000

The retirement of bonds payable is a financing activity that used $89,000 of cash. The $9,000 loss on bond retirement is added to net income in computing the net cash flow from operating activities.

5. Cash—Operating Activities (Accounts Receivable Decrease)   5,000
     Accounts Receivable   5,000

A decrease in accounts receivable is added to net income in computing the net cash flow from operating activities.

6. Inventory   14,000
     Cash—Operating Activities (Inventory Increase)   14,000

An increase in inventory is deducted from net income in computing the net cash flow from operating activities.

7. Prepaid Expenses   3,000
     Cash—Operating Activities (Prepaid Expenses Increase)   3,000

An increase in prepaid expenses is deducted from net income in computing the net cash flow from operating activities.

8. Accounts Payable   10,000
    Cash—Operating Activities (Accounts Payable Decrease)   10,000

A decrease in accounts payable is deducted from net income in computing the net cash flow from operating activities.

9. Interest Payable   2,000
    Cash—Operating Activities (Interest Payable Decrease)   2,000

A decrease in interest payable is deducted from net income in computing the net cash flow from operating activities.

10. Cash—Operating Activities (Income Tax Payable Increase)   1,000
    Income Tax Payable   1,000

An increase in income tax payable is added to net income in computing the net cash flow from operating activities.

At this point, all of the T-account entries affecting the net cash flow from operating activities have been recorded. Any noncash T account whose target amount does not equal the entries to date is identified. For Superior Corporation, these accounts are Building and Equipment, Common Stock, and Retained Earnings. The transactions affecting these accounts are reviewed and T-account entries are then prepared to explain these remaining changes. Entries 11–14 are the second set of T-account entries for Superior Corporation; they explain the remaining changes in the T accounts.

11. Building and Equipment   65,000
    Cash—Investing Activities (Purchase of Equipment)   65,000

The purchase of equipment for $65,000 increased the Building and Equipment account and used cash for an investing activity.

12. Building and Equipment   30,000
    Common Stock   30,000

This entry reconstructs the entry for the acquisition of equipment in exchange for common stock. This event is a noncash investing and financing transaction that must be disclosed in a supplemental schedule. We highlight the T-account entry with an asterisk (*) to identify it as an event requiring special disclosure treatment.

13. Cash—Financing Activities (Issuance of Common Stock)   120,000
    Common Stock   120,000

The issuance of common stock was a financing activity that provided $120,000 of cash.

14. Retained Earnings   11,000
    Cash—Financing Activities (Payment of Dividends)   11,000

The $11,000 dividend declared and paid in 1997 reduced retained earnings and used cash for a financing activity.

After these 14 entries, the T-account entries equal the target amounts for all of the noncash balance sheet accounts. The entries in the Cash T account should also equal the target amount; we total the debit entries and credit entries to confirm this. The totals show the following:

Cash debit entries	$222,000
Cash credit entries	210,000
Cash target amount—debit	$ 12,000

Exhibit I-3 shows the T accounts with all of the entries recorded in the accounts. We are now ready to prepare the statement of cash flows.

EXHIBIT I–3	Completed Cash Flows T-Account Analysis for Superior Corporation

CASH

Net Change	12,000		

Operating Activities—Increases		Operating Activities—Decreases	
(1) Net Income	54,000	(3) Gain on Sale of Equipment	16,000
(2) Depreciation	13,000	(6) Inventory Increase	14,000
(4) Loss on Bond Retirement	9,000	(7) Prepaid Expenses Increase	3,000
(5) Accounts Receivable Decrease	5,000	(8) Accounts Payable Decrease	10,000
(10) Income Tax Payable Increase	1,000	(9) Interest Payable Decrease	2,000
Investing Activities—Increases		Investing Activities—Decreases	
(3) Sale of Equipment	20,000	(11) Purchase of Equipment	65,000
Financing Activities—Increases		Financing Activities—Decreases	
(13) Issuance of Common Stock	120,000	(4) Retirement of Bonds Payable	89,000
	222,000	(14) Payment of Dividends	11,000
			210,000

ACCOUNTS RECEIVABLE

		Net Change	5,000
		(5)	5,000

INVENTORY

Net Change	14,000		
(6)	14,000		

PREPAID EXPENSES

Net Change	3,000		
(7)	3,000		

BUILDING AND EQUIPMENT

Net Change	85,000		
(11)	65,000	(3)	10,000
(12)*	30,000		

ACCUMULATED DEPRECIATION

		Net Change	7,000
(3)	6,000	(2)	13,000

ACCOUNTS PAYABLE

Net Change	10,000		
(8)	10,000		

INTEREST PAYABLE

Net Change	2,000		
(9)	2,000		

INCOME TAX PAYABLE

		Net Change	1,000
		(10)	1,000

BONDS PAYABLE

Net Change	80,000		
(4)	80,000		

COMMON STOCK

		Net Change	150,000
		(12)*	30,000
		(13)	120,000

RETAINED EARNINGS

		Net Change	43,000
(14)	11,000	(1)	54,000

STEP 4

Prepare the statement of cash flows from the information in the Cash T account. This T account provides the adjustments necessary to reconcile net income to the net cash flow from operating activities. It also provides the various cash inflows and outflows from the investing activities and the financing activities. The sum of the operating, investing, and financing cash flows will equal the period's change in cash. In the statement of cash flows, the change in cash is reconciled with the beginning and ending cash balances. The statement of cash flows for Superior Corporation, using the indirect method, is shown in Exhibit I-4.

EXHIBIT I–4   **Statement of Cash Flows under the Indirect Method with Supplemental Disclosures**

SUPERIOR CORPORATION
STATEMENT OF CASH FLOWS
FOR THE YEAR ENDED DECEMBER 31, 1997

Net Cash Flow from Operating Activities

Net Income	$ 54,000	
Add (Deduct) Items to Convert Net Income to Cash Basis		
Depreciation	13,000	
Gain on Sale of Equipment	(16,000)	
Loss on Bond Retirement	9,000	
Accounts Receivable Decrease	5,000	
Inventory Increase	(14,000)	
Prepaid Expenses Increase	(3,000)	
Accounts Payable Decrease	(10,000)	
Interest Payable Decrease	(2,000)	
Income Tax Payable Increase	1,000	
Net Cash Provided by Operating Activities		$37,000
Cash Flows from Investing Activities		
Sale of Equipment	$ 20,000	
Purchase of Equipment	(65,000)	
Net Cash Used by Investing Activities		(45,000)
Cash Flows from Financing Activities		
Issuance of Common Stock	$120,000	
Retirement of Bonds Payable	(89,000)	
Payment of Dividends	(11,000)	
Net Cash Provided by Financing Activities		20,000
Net Increase in Cash		$12,000
Cash at Beginning of Year		13,000
Cash at End of Year		$25,000

Supplemental Information

Supplemental Cash Flow Disclosures

Cash Paid for Interest	$12,000
Cash Paid for Income Taxes	11,000

Schedule of Noncash Investing and Financing Activities

Issuance of Common Stock to Acquire Equipment	$30,000

STEP 5

Determine the information for the required separate disclosures. Cash paid for interest is computed by adjusting interest expense for the change during the year in interest payable.

Superior Corporation's 1997 cash paid for interest is $12,000 ($10,000 + $2,000). Cash paid for income taxes is computed by adjusting income tax expense for the change during the year in income tax payable. Superior Corporation's 1997 cash paid for income taxes is $11,000 ($12,000 – $1,000). Exhibit I-4 shows these amounts as supplemental disclosures to the statement of cash flows.

The noncash investing and financing transactions are identified in the T accounts (the entries containing an asterisk identify these events). Exhibit I-4 shows the supplemental disclosure of Superior Corporation's one noncash investing and financing transaction: the $30,000 issuance of common stock to acquire equipment.

Superior Corporation has no short-term investments, so a separate disclosure to indicate which highly liquid, short-term investments are treated as cash equivalents is not needed.

GLOSSARY OF KEY TERMS USED IN THIS CHAPTER AND APPENDIX

cash equivalents   Short-term, highly liquid investments that firms acquire with temporarily idle cash to earn interest on these excess funds. To qualify as a cash equivalent, an investment must be easily convertible into a known amount of cash and be close enough to maturity so that its market value is not sensitive to interest rate changes (p. 524).

direct method   A presentation of net cash flow from operating activities in a statement of cash flows that shows the major categories of operating cash receipts and payments (p. 527).

financing activities   A section in the statement of cash flows that reports cash flows associated with obtaining resources from owners and creditors, returning resources to owners, and repaying amounts borrowed (p. 516).

indirect method   A presentation of net cash flow from operating activities in a statement of cash flows that begins with net income and applies a series of adjustments to convert the net income to a cash basis amount. Also known as the *reconciliation method* (p. 520).

investing activities   A section in the statement of cash flows that reports cash flows involving (1) the purchase and sale of plant and intangible assets, (2) the purchase and sale of stocks, bonds, and other securities, and (3) the lending and subsequent collection of money (p. 516).

noncash investing and financing activities   Investing activities and financing activities that do not affect current cash flows; information about these events must be reported as a supplement to the statement of cash flows (p. 517).

operating activities   A section in the statement of cash flows that reports cash flows from all activities that are not classified as investing or financing activities. Generally, the activities reported in the income statement constitute a company's operating activities (p. 515).

operating cash flow to capital expenditures ratio   A financial ratio calculated by dividing a firm's net cash flow from operating activities by its annual capital expenditures (p. 533).

operating cash flow to current liabilities ratio   A financial ratio calculated by dividing net cash flow from operating activities by the average current liabilities for the year (p. 532).

statement of cash flows   A financial statement showing a firm's cash inflows and cash outflows for a specific period, classified into operating, investing, and financing categories (p. 514).

QUESTIONS

15-1 What is the definition of *cash equivalents?* Give three examples of cash equivalents.

15-2 Why are cash equivalents included with cash in a statement of cash flows?

15-3 What are the three major types of activities classified on a statement of cash flows? Give an example of a cash inflow and a cash outflow in each classification.

15-4 In which of the three activity categories of a statement of cash flows would each of the following items appear? Indicate for each item whether it represents a cash inflow or a cash outflow:
a. Cash purchase of equipment.
b. Cash collection on loans.
c. Cash dividends paid.
d. Cash dividends received.
e. Cash proceeds from issuing stock.
f. Cash receipts from customers.
g. Cash interest paid.
h. Cash interest received.

15-5 Traverse Company acquired a $3,000,000 building by issuing $3,000,000 worth of bonds payable. In terms of cash flow reporting, what type of transaction is this? What special disclosure requirements apply to a transaction of this type?

15-6 Why are noncash investing and financing transactions disclosed as supplemental information to a statement of cash flows?

15-7 Why is a statement of cash flows a useful financial statement?

15-8 What is the difference between the direct method and the indirect method of presenting net cash flow from operating activities?

15-9 In determining net cash flow from operating activities using the indirect method, why must we add depreciation back to net income? Give an example of another item that is added back to net income under the indirect method.

15-10 Vista Company sold for $98,000 cash land originally costing $70,000. The company recorded a gain on the sale of $28,000. How is this event reported in a statement of cash flows using the indirect method?

15-11 A firm uses the indirect method. Using the following information, what is its net cash flow from operating activities?

Net income	$88,000
Accounts receivable decrease	13,000
Inventory increase	9,000
Accounts payable decrease	3,500
Income tax payable increase	1,500
Depreciation expense	6,000

15-12 What separate disclosures are required for a company that reports a statement of cash flows using the indirect method?

15-13 If a business had a net loss for the year, under what circumstances would the statement of cash flows show a positive net cash flow from operating activities?

15-14 A firm is converting its accrual revenues to corresponding cash amounts using the direct method. Sales on the income statement are $925,000. Beginning and ending accounts receivable on the balance sheet are $58,000 and $44,000, respectively. What is the amount of cash received from customers?

15-15 A firm reports $86,000 wages expense in its income statement. If beginning and ending wages payable are $3,900 and $2,800, respectively, what is the amount of cash paid to employees?

15-16 A firm reports $43,000 advertising expense in its income statement. If beginning and ending prepaid advertising are $6,000 and $7,600, respectively, what is the amount of cash paid for advertising?

15-17 Rusk Company sold equipment for $5,100 cash that had cost $35,000 and had $29,000 of accumulated depreciation. How is this event reported in a statement of cash flows using the direct method?

15-18 What separate disclosures are required for a company that reports a statement of cash flows using the direct method?

15-19 How is the *operating cash flow to current liabilities ratio* calculated? Explain its use.

15-20 How is the *operating cash flow to capital expenditures ratio* calculated? Explain its use.

PRINCIPLES DISCUSSION QUESTION

15-21 The statement of cash flows provides information that may be useful in predicting future cash flows, evaluating financial flexibility, assessing liquidity, and identifying financing needs. It is not, however, the best financial statement for learning about a firm's financial performance during a period; information about periodic financial performance is provided by the income statement. Two basic principles—the revenue recognition principle and the matching concept—work to distinguish the income statement from the statement of cash flows. (a) Define the revenue recognition principle and the matching concept. (b) Briefly explain how these two principles work to make the income statement a better report on periodic financial performance than the statement of cash flows.

EXERCISES

CLASSIFICATION OF CASH FLOWS
— OBJ. 1 —

15-22 For each of the items below, indicate whether the cash flow relates to an operating activity, an investing activity, or a financing activity.
  a. Cash receipts from customers for services rendered.
  b. Sale of long-term investments for cash.
  c. Acquisition of plant assets for cash.
  d. Payment of income taxes.
  e. Bonds payable issued for cash.
  f. Payment of cash dividends declared in previous year.
  g. Purchase of short-term investments (not cash equivalents) for cash.

CLASSIFICATION OF CASH FLOWS
— OBJ. 1 —

15-23 For each of the items below, indicate whether it is (1) a cash flow from an operating activity, (2) a cash flow from an investing activity, (3) a cash flow from a financing activity, (4) a noncash investing and financing activity, or (5) none of the above.
  a. Paid cash to retire bonds payable at a loss.
  b. Received cash as settlement of a lawsuit.
  c. Acquired a patent in exchange for common stock.
  d. Received advance payments from customers on orders for custom-made goods.
  e. Gave large cash contribution to local university.
  f. Invested cash in 60-day commercial paper (a cash equivalent).

NET CASH FLOW FROM OPERATING ACTIVITIES (INDIRECT METHOD)
— OBJ. 2 —

15-24 Lincoln Company, a sole proprietorship that owns no plant assets, had the following income statement for the current year:

Sales		$750,000
Cost of Goods Sold	$470,000	
Wages Expense	110,000	
Rent Expense	42,000	
Insurance Expense	15,000	637,000
Net Income		$113,000

Additional information about the company follows:

	End of Year	Beginning of Year
Accounts Receivable	$54,000	$49,000
Inventory	60,000	66,000
Prepaid Insurance	8,000	7,000
Accounts Payable	22,000	18,000
Wages Payable	9,000	11,000

Use the preceding information to calculate the net cash flow from operating activities using the indirect method.

STATEMENT OF CASH FLOWS (INDIRECT METHOD)
— OBJ. 2 —

15-25 Use the following information about Lund Corporation for 1997 to prepare a statement of cash flows using the indirect method.

Accounts payable increase	$ 9,000
Accounts receivable increase	4,000
Accrued liabilities decrease	3,000
Amortization expense	6,000
Cash balance, beginning of 1997	22,000
Cash balance, end of 1997	15,000
Cash paid as dividends	29,000
Cash paid to purchase land	90,000
Cash paid to retire bonds payable at par	60,000
Cash received from issuance of common stock	35,000
Cash received from sale of equipment	17,000

Depreciation expense	$29,000
Gain on sale of equipment	4,000
Inventory decrease	13,000
Net income	76,000
Prepaid expenses increase	2,000

OPERATING CASH FLOWS (DIRECT METHOD) — OBJ. 3 —

15-26 Calculate the cash flow asked for in each of the following cases.

a. Cash paid for advertising:

Advertising expense	$62,000
Prepaid advertising, January 1	11,000
Prepaid advertising, December 31	15,000

b. Cash paid for income taxes:

Income tax expense	$29,000
Income tax payable, January 1	7,100
Income tax payable, December 31	4,900

c. Cash paid for merchandise purchased:

Cost of goods sold	$180,000
Inventory, January 1	30,000
Inventory, December 31	25,000
Accounts payable, January 1	10,000
Accounts payable, December 31	12,000

STATEMENT OF CASH FLOWS (DIRECT METHOD) — OBJ. 3 —

15-27 Use the following information about the 1997 cash flows of Mason Corporation to prepare a statement of cash flows using the direct method.

Cash balance, end of 1997	$ 12,000
Cash paid to employees and suppliers	148,000
Cash received from sale of land	40,000
Cash paid to acquire treasury stock	10,000
Cash balance, beginning of 1997	16,000
Cash received as interest	6,000
Cash paid as income taxes	11,000
Cash paid to purchase equipment	89,000
Cash received from customers	194,000
Cash received from issuing bonds payable	30,000
Cash paid as dividends	16,000

OPERATING CASH FLOWS (DIRECT METHOD) — OBJ. 3 —

15-28 Refer to the information in Exercise 15-24. Calculate the net cash flow from operating activities using the direct method. Show a related cash flow for each revenue and expense.

INVESTING AND FINANCING CASH FLOWS — OBJ. 2, 3 —

15-29 During 1997, Paxon Corporation's Long-Term Investments account (at cost) increased $15,000, the net result of purchasing stocks costing $80,000 and selling stocks costing $65,000 at a $6,000 loss. Also, the Bonds Payable account decreased $40,000, the net result of issuing $100,000 of bonds at 103 and retiring bonds with a face value (and book value) of $140,000 at a $9,000 gain. What items and amounts will appear in the (a) cash flows from investing activities and the (b) cash flows from financing activities sections of a 1997 statement of cash flows?

PROBLEMS

STATEMENT OF CASH FLOWS
(INDIRECT METHOD)
— OBJ. 2 —

15-30 Wolff Company's 1997 income statement and comparative balance sheets at December 31 of 1997 and 1996 are shown below.

WOLFF COMPANY
INCOME STATEMENT
FOR THE YEAR ENDED DECEMBER 31, 1997

Sales		$635,000
Cost of Goods Sold	$430,000	
Wages Expense	86,000	
Insurance Expense	8,000	
Depreciation Expense	17,000	
Interest Expense	9,000	
Income Tax Expense	29,000	579,000
Net Income		$ 56,000

WOLFF COMPANY
BALANCE SHEETS

Assets	Dec. 31, 1997	Dec. 31, 1996
Cash	$ 11,000	$ 5,000
Accounts Receivable	41,000	32,000
Inventory	90,000	60,000
Prepaid Insurance	5,000	7,000
Plant Assets	250,000	195,000
Accumulated Depreciation	(68,000)	(51,000)
Total Assets	$329,000	$248,000

Liabilities and Stockholders' Equity		
Accounts Payable	$ 7,000	$ 10,000
Wages Payable	9,000	6,000
Income Tax Payable	7,000	8,000
Bonds Payable	130,000	75,000
Common Stock	90,000	90,000
Retained Earnings	86,000	59,000
Total Liabilities and Stockholders' Equity	$329,000	$248,000

Cash dividends of $29,000 were declared and paid during 1997. Plant assets were purchased for cash and bonds payable were issued for cash. Bond interest is paid semi-annually on June 30 and December 31. Accounts payable relate to merchandise purchases.

REQUIRED

a. Compute the change in cash that occurred during 1997.

b. Prepare a 1997 statement of cash flows using the indirect method.

STATEMENT OF CASH FLOWS
(INDIRECT METHOD)
— OBJ. 2 —

15-31 Arctic Company's 1997 income statement and comparative balance sheets at December 31 of 1997 and 1996 follow.

ARCTIC COMPANY
INCOME STATEMENT
FOR THE YEAR ENDED DECEMBER 31, 1997

Sales		$728,000
Cost of Goods Sold	$534,000	
Wages Expense	190,000	
Advertising Expense	31,000	
Depreciation Expense	22,000	
Interest Expense	18,000	
Gain on Sale of Land	(25,000)	770,000
Net Loss		($ 42,000)

ARCTIC COMPANY
BALANCE SHEETS

Assets	Dec. 31, 1997	Dec. 31, 1996
Cash	$ 49,000	$ 28,000
Accounts Receivable	42,000	50,000
Inventory	107,000	113,000
Prepaid Advertising	10,000	13,000
Plant Assets	360,000	222,000
Accumulated Depreciation	(78,000)	(56,000)
Total Assets	$490,000	$370,000

Liabilities and Stockholders' Equity

	Dec. 31, 1997	Dec. 31, 1996
Accounts Payable	$ 17,000	$ 31,000
Interest Payable	6,000	—
Bonds Payable	200,000	—
Common Stock	245,000	245,000
Retained Earnings	52,000	94,000
Treasury Stock	(30,000)	—
Total Liabilities and Stockholders' Equity	$490,000	$370,000

During 1997, Arctic sold land for $70,000 cash that had originally cost $45,000. Arctic also purchased equipment for cash, acquired treasury stock for cash, and issued bonds payable for cash. Accounts payable relate to merchandise purchases.

REQUIRED

a. Compute the change in cash that occurred during 1997.

b. Prepare a 1997 statement of cash flows using the indirect method.

STATEMENT OF CASH FLOWS (INDIRECT METHOD)
— OBJ. 2 —

15-32 Dairy Company's 1997 income statement and comparative balance sheets at December 31 of 1997 and 1996 follow.

DAIRY COMPANY
INCOME STATEMENT
FOR THE YEAR ENDED DECEMBER 31, 1997

Sales		$700,000
Cost of Goods Sold	$440,000	
Wages and Other Operating Expenses	95,000	
Depreciation Expense	22,000	
Goodwill Amortization Expense	7,000	
Interest Expense	10,000	
Income Tax Expense	36,000	
Loss on Bond Retirement	5,000	615,000
Net Income		$ 85,000

DAIRY COMPANY
BALANCE SHEETS

Assets	Dec. 31, 1997	Dec. 31, 1996
Cash	$ 27,000	$ 18,000
Accounts Receivable	53,000	48,000
Inventory	103,000	109,000
Prepaid Expenses	12,000	10,000
Plant Assets	360,000	336,000
Accumulated Depreciation	(87,000)	(84,000)
Goodwill	43,000	50,000
Total Assets	$511,000	$487,000

Liabilities and Stockholders' Equity

Accounts Payable	$ 32,000	$ 26,000
Interest Payable	4,000	7,000
Income Tax Payable	6,000	8,000
Bonds Payable	60,000	120,000
Common Stock	252,000	228,000
Retained Earnings	157,000	98,000
Total Liabilities and Stockholders' Equity	$511,000	$487,000

During the year, the company sold for $17,000 cash old equipment that had cost $36,000 and had $19,000 accumulated depreciation. New equipment worth $60,000 was acquired in exchange for $60,000 of bonds payable. Bonds payable of $120,000 were retired for cash at a loss. A $26,000 cash dividend was declared and paid in 1997. All stock issuances were for cash.

REQUIRED

a. Compute the change in cash that occurred in 1997.
b. Prepare a 1997 statement of cash flows using the indirect method.
c. Prepare separate schedules showing (1) cash paid for interest and for income taxes and (2) noncash investing and financing transactions.

STATEMENT OF CASH FLOWS
(INDIRECT METHOD)
— OBJ. 2 —

15-33 Rainbow Company's income statement for 1997 and comparative balance sheets at December 31 of 1997 and 1996 follow.

RAINBOW COMPANY
INCOME STATEMENT
FOR THE YEAR ENDED DECEMBER 31, 1997

Sales		$750,000
Dividend Income		15,000
		$765,000
Cost of Goods Sold	$440,000	
Wages and Other Operating Expenses	130,000	
Depreciation Expense	39,000	
Patent Amortization Expense	7,000	
Interest Expense	13,000	
Income Tax Expense	44,000	
Loss on Sale of Equipment	5,000	
Gain on Sale of Investments	(10,000)	668,000
Net Income		$ 97,000

RAINBOW COMPANY
BALANCE SHEETS

Assets	Dec. 31, 1997	Dec. 31, 1996
Cash and Cash Equivalents	$ 19,000	$ 25,000
Accounts Receivable	40,000	30,000
Inventory	103,000	77,000
Prepaid Expenses	10,000	6,000
Long-Term Investments—Available for Sale	—	50,000
Fair Value Adjustment to Investments	—	7,000
Land	190,000	100,000
Buildings	445,000	350,000
Accumulated Depreciation—Buildings	(91,000)	(75,000)
Equipment	179,000	225,000
Accumulated Depreciation—Equipment	(42,000)	(46,000)
Patents	50,000	32,000
Total Assets	$903,000	$781,000

Liabilities and Stockholders' Equity

Accounts Payable	$ 20,000	$ 16,000
Interest Payable	6,000	5,000
Income Tax Payable	8,000	10,000
Bonds Payable	155,000	125,000
Preferred Stock ($100 par value)	100,000	75,000
Common Stock ($5 par value)	379,000	364,000
Paid-in Capital in Excess of Par Value—Common	133,000	124,000
Retained Earnings	102,000	55,000
Unrealized Gain on Investments	—	7,000
Total Liabilities and Stockholders' Equity	$903,000	$781,000

During the year, the following transactions occurred:

1. Sold long-term investments costing $50,000 for $60,000 cash. Unrealized gains totaling $7,000 related to these investments had been recorded in earlier years. At year-end, the fair value adjustment and unrealized gain account balances were eliminated.
2. Purchased land for cash.
3. Capitalized an expenditure made to improve the building.
4. Sold equipment for $14,000 cash that originally cost $46,000 and had $27,000 accumulated depreciation.
5. Issued bonds payable at face value for cash.
6. Acquired a patent with a fair value of $25,000 by issuing 250 shares of preferred stock at par value.
7. Declared and paid a $50,000 cash dividend.
8. Issued 3,000 shares of common stock for cash at $8 per share.
9. Recorded depreciation of $16,000 on buildings and $23,000 on equipment.

REQUIRED

a. Compute the change in cash and cash equivalents that occurred during 1997.
b. Prepare a 1997 statement of cash flows using the indirect method.
c. Prepare separate schedules showing (1) cash paid for interest and for income taxes and (2) noncash investing and financing transactions.

STATEMENT OF CASH FLOWS
(DIRECT METHOD)
— OBJ. 3 —

15-34 Refer to the data given for Wolff Company in Problem 15-30.
REQUIRED
a. Compute the change in cash that occurred during 1997.
b. Prepare a 1997 statement of cash flows using the direct method.

STATEMENT OF CASH FLOWS
(DIRECT METHOD)
— OBJ. 3 —

15-35 Refer to the data given for Arctic Company in Problem 15-31.
REQUIRED
a. Compute the change in cash that occurred during 1997.
b. Prepare a 1997 statement of cash flows using the direct method.

STATEMENT OF CASH FLOWS
(DIRECT METHOD)
— OBJ. 3 —

15-36 Refer to the data given for Dairy Company in Problem 15-32.
REQUIRED
a. Compute the change in cash that occurred in 1997.
b. Prepare a 1997 statement of cash flows using the direct method. Use one cash outflow for "cash paid for wages and other operating expenses." Accounts payable relate to inventory purchases only.
c. Prepare separate schedules showing (1) a reconciliation of net income to net cash flow from operating activities (see Exhibit 15-4, page 521) and (2) noncash investing and financing transactions.

STATEMENT OF CASH FLOWS
(DIRECT METHOD)
— OBJ. 3 —

15-37 Refer to the data given for Rainbow Company in Problem 15-33.
REQUIRED
a. Compute the change in cash that occurred in 1997.
b. Prepare a 1997 statement of cash flows using the direct method. Use one cash outflow for "cash paid for wages and other operating expenses." Accounts payable relate to inventory purchases only.
c. Prepare separate schedules showing (1) a reconciliation of net income to net cash flow from operating activities (see Exhibit 15-4, page 521) and (2) noncash investing and financing transactions.

**STATEMENT OF CASH FLOWS
(INDIRECT METHOD) USING
T-ACCOUNT APPROACH
— APPENDIX I —**

15-38 Refer to the data given for Wolff Company in Problem 15-30.
REQUIRED
a. Use the T-account approach to compile data for a statement of cash flows using the indirect method.
b. Prepare a 1997 statement of cash flows using the indirect method.

**STATEMENT OF CASH FLOWS
(INDIRECT METHOD) USING
T-ACCOUNT APPROACH
— APPENDIX I —**

15-39 Refer to the data given for Arctic Company in Problem 15-31.
REQUIRED
a. Use the T-account approach to compile data for a statement of cash flows using the indirect method.
b. Prepare a 1997 statement of cash flows using the indirect method.

**STATEMENT OF CASH FLOWS
(INDIRECT METHOD) USING
T-ACCOUNT APPROACH
— APPENDIX I —**

15-40 Refer to the data given for Dairy Company in Problem 15-32.
REQUIRED
a. Use the T-account approach to compile data for a statement of cash flows using the indirect method.
b. Prepare a 1997 statement of cash flows using the indirect method.
c. Prepare separate schedules showing (1) cash paid for interest and for income taxes and (2) noncash investing and financing transactions.

**STATEMENT OF CASH FLOWS
(INDIRECT METHOD) USING
T-ACCOUNT APPROACH
— APPENDIX I —**

15-41 Refer to the data given for Rainbow Company in Problem 15-33.
REQUIRED
a. Use the T-account approach to compile data for a statement of cash flows using the indirect method.
b. Prepare a 1997 statement of cash flows using the indirect method.
c. Prepare separate schedules showing (1) cash paid for interest and for income taxes and (2) noncash investing and financing transactions.

ALTERNATE EXERCISES

**CLASSIFICATION OF CASH
FLOWS
— OBJ. 1 —**

15-22A For each of the items below, indicate whether the cash flow relates to an operating activity, an investing activity, or a financing activity.
a. Cash loaned to borrowers.
b. Cash paid as interest on bonds payable.
c. Cash received from issuance of preferred stock.
d. Cash paid as state income taxes.
e. Cash received as dividends on stock investments.
f. Cash paid to acquire treasury stock.
g. Cash paid to acquire franchise to distribute a product line.

**CLASSIFICATION OF CASH
FLOWS
— OBJ. 1 —**

15-23A For each of the items below, indicate whether it is (1) a cash flow from an operating activity, (2) a cash flow from an investing activity, (3) a cash flow from a financing activity, (4) a noncash investing and financing activity, or (5) none of the above.
a. Received cash as interest earned on bond investment.
b. Received cash as refund from supplier.
c. Borrowed cash from bank on six-month note payable.
d. Exchanged, at a gain, stock held as an investment for a parcel of land.
e. Invested cash in a money market fund (cash may be easily withdrawn from the fund).
f. Loaned cash to help finance the start of a new biotechnology firm.

**NET CASH FLOW FROM
OPERATING ACTIVITIES
(INDIRECT METHOD)
— OBJ. 2 —**

15-24A The following information was obtained from Galena Company's comparative balance sheets.

	Dec. 31, 1997	Dec. 31, 1996
Cash	$ 19,000	$ 9,000
Accounts Receivable	44,000	35,000
Inventory	55,000	49,000
Prepaid Rent	6,000	8,000
Long-Term Investments	21,000	34,000
Plant Assets	150,000	106,000
Accumulated Depreciation	(40,000)	(32,000)
Accounts Payable	24,000	20,000

	Dec. 31, 1997	Dec. 31, 1996
Income Tax Payable	$ 4,000	$ 6,000
Common Stock	121,000	92,000
Retained Earnings	106,000	91,000

Assume that Galena Company's 1997 income statement showed depreciation expense of $8,000, a gain on sale of investments of $9,000, and a net income of $45,000. Calculate the net cash flow from operating activities using the indirect method.

NET CASH FLOW FROM OPERATING ACTIVITIES (INDIRECT METHOD) — OBJ. 2 —

15-25A Cairo Company had a $21,000 net loss from operations for 1997. Depreciation expense for 1997 was $8,600 and a 1997 dividend of $6,000 was declared and paid. Balances of the current asset and current liability accounts at the beginning and end of 1997 are as follows:

	End	Beginning
Cash	$ 3,500	$ 7,000
Accounts Receivable	16,000	25,000
Inventory	50,000	53,000
Prepaid Expenses	6,000	9,000
Accounts Payable	12,000	8,000
Accrued Liabilities	5,000	7,600

Did Cairo Company's 1997 operating activities provide or use cash? Use the indirect method to determine your answer.

OPERATING CASH FLOWS (DIRECT METHOD) — OBJ. 3 —

15-26A Calculate the cash flow asked for in each of the following cases.
a. Cash paid for rent:

Rent expense	$60,000
Prepaid rent, January 1	10,000
Prepaid rent, December 31	8,000

b. Cash received as interest:

Interest income	$16,000
Interest receivable, January 1	3,000
Interest receivable, December 31	3,700

c. Cash paid for merchandise purchased:

Cost of goods sold	$98,000
Inventory, January 1	19,000
Inventory, December 31	22,000
Accounts payable, January 1	11,000
Accounts payable, December 31	7,000

OPERATING CASH FLOWS (DIRECT METHOD) — OBJ. 3 —

15-27A Howell Company's current year income statement contains the following data:

Sales	$825,000
Cost of Goods Sold	550,000
Gross Profit	$275,000

Howell's comparative balance sheets show the following data (accounts payable relate to merchandise purchases):

	End of Year	Beginning of Year
Accounts Receivable	$ 71,000	$60,000
Inventory	109,000	96,000
Prepaid Expenses	3,000	8,000
Accounts Payable	31,000	37,000

Compute Howell's current-year cash received from customers and cash paid for merchandise purchased.

**STATEMENT OF CASH FLOWS
(DIRECT METHOD)
— OBJ. 3 —**

15-28A Use the following information about the 1997 cash flows of Gilbert Corporation to prepare a statement of cash flows using the direct method.

Cash balance, end of 1997	$ 30,000
Cash paid to employees and suppliers	151,000
Cash received from sale of equipment	98,000
Cash paid to retire bonds payable	70,000
Cash balance, beginning of 1997	20,000
Cash paid as interest	7,000
Cash paid as income taxes	24,000
Cash paid to purchase patent	66,000
Cash received from customers	216,000
Cash received from issuing common stock	35,000
Cash paid as dividends	21,000

**INVESTING AND FINANCING
CASH FLOWS
— OBJ. 2, 3 —**

15-29A Refer to the information in Exercise 15-24A. During 1997, Galena Company purchased plant assets for cash, sold investments for cash (the entire $9,000 gain developed during 1997), and issued common stock for cash. The firm also declared and paid cash dividends in 1997. What items and amounts will appear in (a) the cash flows from investing activities and (b) the cash flows from financing activities sections of a 1997 statement of cash flows?

ALTERNATE PROBLEMS

**STATEMENT OF CASH FLOWS
(INDIRECT METHOD)
— OBJ. 2 —**

15-30A Rural Company's 1997 income statement and comparative balance sheets at December 31 of 1997 and 1996 are shown below.

**RURAL COMPANY
INCOME STATEMENT
FOR THE YEAR ENDED DECEMBER 31, 1997**

Sales		$630,000
Cost of Goods Sold	$376,000	
Wages Expense	107,000	
Depreciation Expense	20,000	
Rent Expense	28,000	
Income Tax Expense	31,000	562,000
Net Income		$ 68,000

**RURAL COMPANY
BALANCE SHEETS**

Assets	Dec. 31, 1997	Dec. 31, 1996
Cash	$ 20,000	$ 37,000
Accounts Receivable	52,000	60,000
Inventory	137,000	110,000
Prepaid Rent	14,000	12,000
Plant Assets	420,000	300,000
Accumulated Depreciation	(125,000)	(105,000)
Total Assets	$518,000	$414,000

Liabilities and Stockholders' Equity		
Accounts Payable	$ 29,000	$ 17,000
Wages Payable	12,000	7,000
Income Tax Payable	5,000	8,000
Common Stock	294,000	252,000
Paid-in Capital in Excess of Par Value	72,000	58,000
Retained Earnings	106,000	72,000
Total Liabilities and Stockholders' Equity	$518,000	$414,000

Cash dividends of $34,000 were declared and paid during 1997. Plant assets were purchased for cash and additional common stock was issued for cash. Accounts payable relate to merchandise purchases.

REQUIRED

a. Compute the change in cash that occurred during 1997.

b. Prepare a 1997 statement of cash flows using the indirect method.

STATEMENT OF CASH FLOWS
(INDIRECT METHOD)
— OBJ. 2 —

15-31A Sweet Company's 1997 income statement and comparative balance sheets at December 31 of 1997 and 1996 are presented below.

SWEET COMPANY
INCOME STATEMENT
FOR THE YEAR ENDED DECEMBER 31, 1997

Sales		$946,000
Cost of Goods Sold	$507,000	
Wages Expense	203,000	
Depreciation Expense	60,000	
Insurance Expense	13,000	
Interest Expense	12,000	
Income Tax Expense	57,000	
Gain on Sale of Equipment	(16,000)	836,000
Net Income		$110,000

SWEET COMPANY
BALANCE SHEETS

Assets	Dec. 31, 1997	Dec. 31, 1996
Cash	$ 23,000	$ 31,000
Accounts Receivable	68,000	43,000
Inventory	177,000	126,000
Prepaid Insurance	9,000	11,000
Plant Assets	887,000	770,000
Accumulated Depreciation	(189,000)	(175,000)
Total Assets	$975,000	$806,000

Liabilities and Stockholders' Equity		
Accounts Payable	$ 37,000	$ 27,000
Interest Payable	5,000	—
Income Tax Payable	12,000	16,000
Bonds Payable	135,000	80,000
Common Stock	660,000	585,000
Retained Earnings	178,000	98,000
Treasury Stock	(52,000)	—
Total Liabilities and Stockholders' Equity	$975,000	$806,000

During the year, Sweet Company sold equipment for $27,000 cash that originally cost $57,000 and had $46,000 accumulated depreciation. New equipment was purchased for cash. Bonds payable and common stock were issued for cash. Cash dividends of $30,000 were declared and paid. At the end of the year, shares of treasury stock were purchased for cash. Accounts payable relate to merchandise purchases.

REQUIRED

a. Compute the change in cash that occurred during 1997.

b. Prepare a 1997 statement of cash flows using the indirect method.

STATEMENT OF CASH FLOWS
(INDIRECT METHOD)
— OBJ. 2 —

15-32A Huber Company's 1997 income statement and comparative balance sheets at December 31 of 1997 and 1996 follow.

HUBER COMPANY
INCOME STATEMENT
FOR THE YEAR ENDED DECEMBER 31, 1997

Sales		$800,000
Cost of Goods Sold	$530,000	
Wages and Other Operating Expenses	172,000	
Depreciation Expense	27,000	
Patent Amortization Expense	6,000	
Interest Expense	18,000	
Income Tax Expense	25,000	
Gain on Exchange of Land for Patent	(36,000)	742,000
Net Income		$ 58,000

HUBER COMPANY
BALANCE SHEETS

Assets	Dec. 31, 1997	Dec. 31, 1996
Cash	$ 34,000	$ 16,000
Accounts Receivable	64,000	49,000
Inventory	85,000	64,000
Land	117,000	160,000
Building and Equipment	441,000	361,000
Accumulated Depreciation	(120,000)	(100,000)
Patent	73,000	—
Total Assets	$694,000	$550,000

Liabilities and Stockholders' Equity		
Accounts Payable	$ 36,000	$ 26,000
Interest Payable	13,000	5,000
Income Tax Payable	7,000	12,000
Bonds Payable	175,000	75,000
Common Stock	350,000	350,000
Retained Earnings	113,000	82,000
Total Liabilities and Stockholders' Equity	$694,000	$550,000

During 1997, $27,000 of cash dividends were declared and paid. A patent valued at $79,000 was obtained in exchange for land. Equipment that originally cost $20,000 and had $7,000 accumulated depreciation was sold for $13,000 cash. Bonds payable were sold for cash and cash was used to pay for structural improvements to the building.

REQUIRED

a. Compute the change in cash that occurred during 1997.
b. Prepare a 1997 statement of cash flows using the indirect method.
c. Prepare separate schedules showing (1) cash paid for interest and for income taxes and (2) noncash investing and financing transactions.

STATEMENT OF CASH FLOWS
(INDIRECT METHOD)
— OBJ. 2 —

15-33A Towne Company's income statement for 1997 and comparative balance sheets at December 31 of 1997 and 1996 follow.

TOWNE COMPANY
INCOME STATEMENT
FOR THE YEAR ENDED DECEMBER 31, 1997

Service Fees Earned		$317,000
Dividend and Interest Income		14,000
		$331,000
Wages and Other Operating Expenses	$285,000	
Depreciation Expense	52,000	
Franchise Amortization Expense	10,000	
Loss on Sale of Equipment	7,000	
Gain on Sale of Investments	(17,000)	337,000
Net Loss		($ 6,000)

TOWNE COMPANY
BALANCE SHEETS

Assets	Dec. 31, 1997	Dec. 31, 1996
Cash	$ 43,000	$ 36,000
Accounts Receivable	13,000	18,000
Interest Receivable	—	4,000
Prepaid Expenses	16,000	8,000
Long-Term Investments—Available for Sale	—	70,000
Fair Value Adjustment to Investments	—	10,000
Plant Assets	696,000	655,000
Accumulated Depreciation	(234,000)	(185,000)
Franchise	91,000	29,000
Total Assets	$625,000	$645,000

Liabilities and Stockholders' Equity		
Accrued Liabilities	$ 12,000	$ 14,000
Notes Payable	—	27,000
Common Stock ($10 par value)	595,000	535,000
Retained Earnings	38,000	59,000
Unrealized Gain on Investments	—	10,000
Treasury Stock	(20,000)	—
Total Liabilities and Stockholders' Equity	$625,000	$645,000

During the year, the following transactions occurred:
1. Sold equipment for $9,000 cash that originally cost $19,000 and had $3,000 accumulated depreciation.
2. Sold long-term investments that had cost $70,000 for $87,000 cash. Unrealized gains totaling $10,000 related to these investments had been recorded in earlier years. At year-end, the fair value adjustment and unrealized gain account balances were eliminated.
3. Paid cash to extend the company's exclusive franchise for another three years.
4. Paid off a note payable at the bank on January 1.
5. Declared and paid a $15,000 dividend.
6. Purchased treasury stock for cash.
7. Acquired land valued at $60,000 by issuing 6,000 shares of common stock.

REQUIRED
a. Compute the change in cash that occurred in 1997.
b. Prepare a 1997 statement of cash flows using the indirect method.
c. Prepare a supplemental disclosure showing noncash investing and financing transactions.

STATEMENT OF CASH FLOWS
(DIRECT METHOD)
— OBJ. 3 —

15-34A Refer to the data given for Rural Company in Problem 15-30A.
REQUIRED
a. Compute the change in cash that occurred during 1997.
b. Prepare a 1997 statement of cash flows using the direct method.

STATEMENT OF CASH FLOWS (**DIRECT METHOD**) — **OBJ. 3** —	**15-35A** Refer to the data given for Sweet Company in Problem 15-31A. **REQUIRED** **a.** Compute the change in cash that occurred during 1997. **b.** Prepare a 1997 statement of cash flows using the direct method.
STATEMENT OF CASH FLOWS (**DIRECT METHOD**) — **OBJ. 3** —	**15-36A** Refer to the data given for Huber Company in Problem 15-32A. **REQUIRED** **a.** Compute the change in cash that occurred during 1997. **b.** Prepare a 1997 statement of cash flows using the direct method. Use one cash outflow for "cash paid for wages and other operating expenses." Accounts payable relate to inventory purchases only. **c.** Prepare separate schedules showing (1) a reconciliation of net income to net cash flow from operating activities (see Exhibit 15-4, page 521) and (2) noncash investing and financing transactions.
STATEMENT OF CASH FLOWS (**DIRECT METHOD**) — **OBJ. 3** —	**15-37A** Refer to the data given for Towne Company in Problem 15-33A. **REQUIRED** **a.** Compute the change in cash that occurred during 1997. **b.** Prepare a 1997 statement of cash flows using the direct method. Use one cash outflow for "cash paid for wages and other operating expenses." **c.** Prepare separate schedules showing (1) a reconciliation of net loss to net cash flow from operating activities (see Exhibit 15-4, page 521) and (2) noncash investing and financing transactions.
STATEMENT OF CASH FLOWS (**INDIRECT METHOD**) **USING** **T-ACCOUNT APPROACH** — **APPENDIX I** —	**15-38A** Refer to the data given for Rural Company in Problem 15-30A. **REQUIRED** **a.** Use the T-account approach to compile data for a statement of cash flows using the indirect method. **b.** Prepare a 1997 statement of cash flows using the indirect method.
STATEMENT OF CASH FLOWS (**INDIRECT METHOD**) **USING** **T-ACCOUNT APPROACH** — **APPENDIX I** —	**15-39A** Refer to the data given for Sweet Company in Problem 15-31A. **REQUIRED** **a.** Use the T-account approach to compile data for a statement of cash flows using the indirect method. **b.** Prepare a 1997 statement of cash flows using the indirect method.
STATEMENT OF CASH FLOWS (**INDIRECT METHOD**) **USING** **T-ACCOUNT APPROACH** — **APPENDIX I** —	**15-40A** Refer to the data given for Huber Company in Problem 15-32A. **REQUIRED** **a.** Use the T-account approach to compile data for a statement of cash flows using the indirect method. **b.** Prepare a 1997 statement of cash flows using the indirect method. **c.** Prepare separate schedules showing (1) cash paid for interest and for income taxes and (2) noncash investing and financing transactions.
STATEMENT OF CASH FLOWS (**INDIRECT METHOD**) **USING** **T-ACCOUNT APPROACH** — **APPENDIX I** —	**15-41A** Refer to the data given for Towne Company in Problem 15-33A. **REQUIRED** **a.** Use the T-account approach to compile data for a statement of cash flows using the indirect method. **b.** Prepare a 1997 statement of cash flows using the indirect method. **c.** Prepare a supplemental disclosure showing noncash investing and financing transactions.

CASES

BUSINESS DECISION CASE

Recently hired as assistant controller for Finite, Inc., you are sitting next to the controller as she responds to questions at the annual stockholders' meeting. The firm's financial statements contain a statement of cash flows prepared using the indirect method. A stockholder raises his hand.

Stockholder: "I notice depreciation expense is shown as an addition in the calculation of the net cash flow from operating activities."

Controller: "That's correct."

Stockholder: "What depreciation method do you use?"

Controller: "We use the straight-line method for all plant assets."

Stockholder: "Well, why don't you switch to an accelerated depreciation method, such as double declining balance, increase the annual depreciation amount, and thus increase the net cash flow from operating activities?"

The controller pauses, turns to you, and replies, "My assistant will answer your question."

REQUIRED

Prepare an answer to the stockholder's question.

FINANCIAL ANALYSIS CASE

Parker Hannifin Corporation, headquartered in Cleveland, Ohio, manufactures motion control and fluid system components for a variety of industrial users. The firm's financial statements for three recent years contain the following data (Year 3 is the most recent year; dollar amounts in thousands):

	Year 3	Year 2	Year 1
Current assets at year-end	$1,018,354	$1,056,443	$1,055,776
Current liabilities at year-end	504,444	468,254	358,729
Current liabilities at beginning of year	468,254	358,729	345,594
Cash provided by operating activities	259,204	229,382	235,186
Capital expenditures	99,914	91,484	84,955

a. Compute Parker Hannifin's current ratio (current assets/current liabilities) for Years 1, 2, and 3.
b. Compute Parker Hannifin's operating cash flow to current liabilities ratio for Years 1, 2, and 3.
c. Comment on the three-year trend in Parker Hannifin's current ratio and operating cash flow to current liabilities ratio. Do the trends in these two ratios reinforce each other or contradict each other as indicators of Parker Hannifin's ability to pay its current liabilities?
d. Compute Parker Hannifin's operating cash flow to capital expenditures ratio for Years 1, 2, and 3. Comment on the strength of this ratio over the three-year period.

ETHICS CASE

Due to an economic recession, Anton Corporation faces severe cash flow problems. Management forecasts that payments to some suppliers will have to be delayed for several months. Jay Newton, controller, has asked his staff for suggestions on selecting the suppliers for which payments will be delayed.

"That's a fairly easy decision," observes Tim Haslem. "Some suppliers charge interest if our payment is late, but others do not. We should pay those suppliers that charge interest and delay payments to the ones that do not charge interest. If we do this, the savings in interest charges will be quite substantial."

"I disagree," states Tara Wirth. "That position is too 'bottom line' oriented. It's not fair to delay payments only to suppliers who don't charge interest for late payments. Most suppliers in that category are ones we have dealt with for years; selecting these suppliers would be taking advantage of the excellent relationships we have developed over the years. The fair thing to do is to make pro rata payments to each supplier."

"Well, making pro rata payments to each supplier means that *all* our suppliers will be upset because no one receives full payment," comments Sue Myling. "I believe it is most important to maintain good relations with our long-term suppliers; we should pay them currently and delay payments to our newer suppliers. The interest costs we end up paying these newer suppliers is the price we must pay to keep our long-term relationships solid."

REQUIRED

Which suppliers should Jay Newton select for delayed payments? Discuss.

GENERAL MILLS ANNUAL REPORT CASE

Refer to the annual report of General Mills, Inc., presented in Appendix K.

REQUIRED

a. Refer to Note 1. How does General Mills define its cash equivalents?
b. What method does General Mills use to report its net cash provided by operating activities?
c. What is the change in cash and cash equivalents experienced by General Mills during fiscal 1994? What is the amount of cash and cash equivalents at May 29, 1994?
d. Refer to Note 11. How much cash did General Mills pay for interest (net of amount capitalized) in 1994? What was the 1994 interest expense (net of amount capitalized)?
e. Refer to Note 15. How much cash did General Mills pay for income taxes in 1994? What was the 1994 income tax expense?
f. Refer to the Eleven Year Summary. How many times in the period 1984–1994 was General Mills' ratio of operating cash flow to capital expenditures less than 1.0? Identify the years where the ratio is less than 1.0.
g. Compute General Mills' 1994 operating cash flow to current liabilities ratio.

Analysis and Interpretation of Financial Statements

CHAPTER LEARNING OBJECTIVES

1 IDENTIFY sources of financial information for analysts and DESCRIBE horizontal analysis of financial statements (pp. 562–567).

2 DESCRIBE vertical analysis of financial statements (pp. 567–569).

3 DEFINE and DISCUSS financial ratios for analyzing profitability (pp. 569–572).

4 DEFINE and DISCUSS financial ratios for analyzing short-term liquidity (pp. 572–575).

5 DEFINE and DISCUSS financial ratios for analyzing long-term solvency (pp. 575–577).

6 DEFINE and DISCUSS financial ratios for analysis by common stock investors (pp. 577–579).

7 DISCUSS the limitations of financial analysis (p. 579).

CHAPTER FOCUS

Many individuals and groups, including managers, owners, prospective investors, creditors, labor unions, governmental agencies, and the public, are interested in the data appearing in a firm's financial statements. These parties are usually interested in the profitability and financial strength of the firm in question, although such factors as size, growth, and the firm's efforts to meet its social responsibilities may also be of interest. Managers, owners, and prospective investors may ask the following questions: How do profits this year compare with those of previous years? How do profits compare with those of other firms in the same industry? Creditors may ask: Will our debt be repaid on time? Will the interest payments be met? Unions may ask: How can we show that the firm can support a particular wage increase? Regulatory agencies may ask: What rate of return is the firm earning? These kinds of questions can be answered by interpreting the data in financial reports.

Various techniques are used to analyze and interpret financial statement data. In the following pages, we concentrate on some widely used methods of evaluation. In many cases, management may profitably use these techniques to plan and control its own operations, but in this discussion, our viewpoint is primarily that of an outsider.

SOURCES OF INFORMATION

OBJECTIVE *1*

IDENTIFY sources of financial information for analysts and **DESCRIBE** horizontal analysis of financial statements.

Except for closely held companies, business firms publish financial statements at least annually. Most large companies also issue them quarterly. Normally, annual statements are attested to by certified public accountants, and the careful analyst reads the accountants' opinion to determine the reliability of the given data. Companies listed on stock exchanges submit annual statements to the Securities and Exchange Commission (SEC). These statements, which are available to any interested party, are generally more useful than annual reports because they furnish a greater amount of detail. Even more detail can be found in *prospectuses* submitted to the SEC by certain companies issuing large amounts of new securities.

For data not provided by the financial statements, a trained analyst has a number of sources: personal interviews with company management, contacts with research organizations, trade association data, computer databases, and subscriptions to financial services that periodically publish analytical data for many firms. The analyst also can obtain useful information from financial newspapers, such as *The Wall Street Journal* and *Barron's,* and from magazines devoted to financial and economic reporting, such as *Business Week* and *Forbes.* The analyst may want to compare the performance of a particular firm with that of the industry. Data on industry norms, median ratios by industry, and other relationships are available from such agencies as Dun & Bradstreet and Robert Morris Associates. In addition, some brokerage firms compile various industry norms and average ratios from their own computer databases.

POINT OF INTEREST

DISCLOSURE SEC DATABASE

An example of a computer database is the Disclosure SEC Database maintained by Disclosure Incorporated of Bethesda, Maryland. Compiled primarily from documents filed with the Securities and Exchange Commission, the database contains 250 fields of information about virtually all public companies in the United States. The information, available online and via CD-ROM, is divided into three main categories: corporate resume, textual, and financial. The corporate resume section presents such data as address, ticker symbol, business description, and auditor. Textual information includes data on officers, directors, and subsidiaries as well as the complete financial statements and related footnotes. Financial information includes data on financial statement components, ratios, stock prices, dividends, and earnings.

ANALYTICAL TECHNIQUES

Absolute dollar amounts of profits, sales, assets, and other key data are not meaningful when studied individually. For example, knowing that a company's annual earnings are $1 million is of little value unless these earnings can be related to other data. A $1 million profit might represent excellent performance for a company with less than $10 million in invested capital. On the other hand, such earnings would be meager for a firm that has several hundred million dollars in invested capital. Thus, the most significant information derived in analysis concerns the relationships between two or more variables, such as earnings to assets, earnings to sales, and earnings to stockholders' investment. To describe these relationships clearly and to make comparisons easy, the analyst states these relationships in terms of ratios and percentages.

For example, we might express the relationship of $15,000 in earnings to $150,000 in sales as a 10% ($15,000/$150,000) rate of earnings on sales. To describe the relationship between sales of $150,000 and inventory of $20,000, we might use a ratio or a percentage; ($150,000/$20,000) may be expressed as 7.5, 7.5:1, or 750%.

Changes in selected items compared in successive financial statements are often expressed as percentages. For example, if a firm's earnings increased from $40,000 last year to $48,000 this year, the $8,000 increase related to last year (the base year) is expressed as a 20% increase ($8,000/$40,000). To express a dollar increase or decrease as a percentage, however, the analyst must make the base-year amount a positive figure. If, for example, a firm had a net loss of $4,000 in one year and earnings of $20,000 in the next, the $24,000 increase cannot be expressed as a percentage. Similarly, if a firm showed no marketable securities in last year's balance sheet but showed $15,000 of such securities in this year's statement, the $15,000 increase cannot be expressed as a percentage.

When evaluating a firm's financial statements for two or more years, analysts often use **horizontal analysis.** This type of analysis is useful in detecting improvement or deterioration in a firm's performance and in spotting trends. The term **vertical analysis** describes the study of a single year's financial statements.

HORIZONTAL ANALYSIS

COMPARATIVE FINANCIAL STATEMENTS

The form of horizontal analysis encountered most often is **comparative financial statements** for two or more years, showing dollar and/or percentage changes for important items and classification totals. Dollar increases and decreases are divided by the earliest year's data to obtain percentage changes. The 1995 and 1996 financial statements of Alliance Company, an electronic components and accessories manufacturer, are shown in Exhibits 16-1, 16-2, and 16-3. We use the data in these statements throughout this chapter to illustrate various analytical techniques.

When examining financial statements, the analyst focuses immediate attention on significant items only. Although percentage changes are helpful in identifying items to focus on, sometimes they may be misleading. An unusually large percentage change may occur primarily because the dollar amount of the base year is small. This is illustrated by the percentage increase exceeding 1,787% for net cash provided by financing activities (Exhibit 16-3). Large percentage changes also frequently occur in items whose dollar amounts may not be significant compared with other items on the statements. For example, although a large percentage change in Alliance Company's balance sheet occurred in Prepaid Expenses (Exhibit 16-1), the analyst would scarcely notice this item in an initial examination of changes. Instead, attention would be directed first to changes in totals: current assets, total assets, current liabilities, and so on. Next, changes in significant individual items, such as receivables and inventory, would be examined. These changes may be related to certain changes in income statement items or cash flows to determine whether they are favorable.

For example, Alliance Company's total assets increased 17.4% (Exhibit 16-1), and net sales increased 29.7% (Exhibit 16-2). A fairly large percentage increase in sales was supported by a much smaller rate of increase in assets. Furthermore, the 19.0% increase in inventory was also considerably less than the increase in sales. These results reflect favorably on the firm's performance. In addition, the 29.7% increase in sales was accompanied

EXHIBIT 16–1 Example of Comparative Balance Sheets Showing Dollar and Percentage Changes

ALLIANCE COMPANY
COMPARATIVE BALANCE SHEETS
(THOUSANDS OF DOLLARS)

	Dec. 31, 1996	Dec. 31, 1995	Increase (Decrease)	Percent Change
Assets				
Current Assets				
Cash and Cash Equivalents	$ 5,500	$ 4,200	$ 1,300	31.0%
Investments—Trading (at market)	2,500	—	2,500	—
Accounts Receivable (net)	59,600	52,000	7,600	14.6
Inventory [lower of cost (first-in, first-out) or market]	75,000	63,000	12,000	19.0
Prepaid Expenses	900	600	300	50.0
Total Current Assets	$143,500	$119,800	$23,700	19.8
Long-Term Investments (at market)	800	—	800	—
Property, Plant, and Equipment (net of accumulated depreciation)	48,000	44,000	4,000	9.1
Total Assets	$192,300	$163,800	$28,500	17.4
Liabilities				
Current Liabilities				
Notes Payable	$ 3,500	$ 3,000	$ 500	16.7
Accounts Payable	25,100	24,100	1,000	4.1
Accrued Liabilities	30,000	27,300	2,700	9.9
Total Current Liabilities	$ 58,600	$ 54,400	$ 4,200	7.7
Long-Term Liabilities				
12% Debenture Bonds Payable	25,000	20,000	5,000	25.0
Total Liabilities	$ 83,600	$ 74,400	$ 9,200	12.4
Stockholders' Equity				
10% Preferred Stock, $100 Par Value	$ 8,000	$ 8,000	$ —	—
Common Stock, $5 Par Value	20,000	14,000	6,000	42.9
Additional Paid-in Capital	6,600	5,500	1,100	36.4
Retained Earnings	74,100	61,900	12,200	19.7
Total Stockholders' Equity	$108,700	$ 89,400	$19,300	21.6
Total Liabilities and Stockholders' Equity	$192,300	$163,800	$28,500	17.4

by an increase in accounts receivable of only 14.6%; on the surface, the company's sales growth was not associated with a relaxation in credit policy.

We see on the income statement that the 38.9% gross profit increase outstripped the rate of increase in sales, indicating a higher mark-up rate in 1996. Net income, however, increased only 21.8%; therefore, expenses must have grown disproportionately. Indeed, selling and administrative expenses increased 44.7% and 52.3%, respectively. Further, the net cash provided by operating activities decreased 28.5% (Exhibit 16-3). This is not a favor-

EXHIBIT 16–2 Examples of Comparative Income and Retained Earnings Statements Showing Dollar and Percentage Changes

ALLIANCE COMPANY
COMPARATIVE INCOME STATEMENTS
(THOUSANDS OF DOLLARS)

	Year Ended Dec. 31, 1996	Year Ended Dec. 31, 1995	Increase (Decrease)	Percent Change
Net Sales	$415,000	$320,000	$95,000	29.7%
Cost of Goods Sold	290,000	230,000	60,000	26.1
Gross Profit on Sales	$125,000	$ 90,000	$35,000	38.9
Operating Expenses				
Selling Expenses	$ 39,500	$ 27,300	$12,200	44.7
Administrative Expenses	49,640	32,600	17,040	52.3
Total Operating Expenses	$ 89,140	$ 59,900	$29,240	48.8
Income before Interest Expense and Income Taxes	$ 35,860	$ 30,100	$ 5,760	19.1
Interest Expense	3,000	2,400	600	25.0
Income before Income Taxes	$ 32,860	$ 27,700	$ 5,160	18.6
Income Tax Expense	14,100	12,300	1,800	14.6
Net Income	$ 18,760	$ 15,400	$ 3,360	21.8
Earnings per Share	$5.28	$5.21		
Dividends per Share	1.44	0.85		

ALLIANCE COMPANY
COMPARATIVE RETAINED EARNINGS STATEMENTS
(THOUSANDS OF DOLLARS)

	Year Ended Dec. 31, 1996	Year Ended Dec. 31, 1995	Increase (Decrease)	Percent Change
Retained Earnings, January 1	$61,900	$49,680	$12,220	24.6%
Add: Net Income	18,760	15,400	3,360	21.8
Total	$80,660	$65,080	$15,580	23.9
Less: Dividends				
On Preferred Stock	$ 800	$ 800	$ —	—
On Common Stock	5,760	2,380	3,380	142.0
Total	$ 6,560	$ 3,180	$ 3,380	106.3
Retained Earnings, December 31	$74,100	$61,900	$12,200	19.7

able sign; combined with the 7.7% increase in current liabilities, it may signal a problem developing in the firm's ability to pay off its current obligations as they become due.

From this limited analysis of comparative financial statements, an analyst may conclude that operating performance for 1996 was generally favorable when compared with that for 1995. Further analysis using some of the techniques summarized later in the chapter, however, may cause the analyst to modify that opinion. The foregoing analysis has revealed two reservations: selling and administrative expenses increased at a fairly high rate and net cash provided by operating activities decreased even though net income increased.

TREND ANALYSIS   To observe percentage changes over time in selected data, analysts compute **trend percentages.** Most companies provide summaries of data for the past 5 or 10 years in their annual reports. With such information, the analyst may examine changes over a period longer

EXHIBIT 16–3 Example of Comparative Statements of Cash Flows Showing Dollar and Percentage Changes

ALLIANCE COMPANY
COMPARATIVE STATEMENTS OF CASH FLOWS
(THOUSANDS OF DOLLARS)

	Year Ended Dec. 31, 1996	Year Ended Dec. 31, 1995	Increase (Decrease)	Percent Change
Net Cash Flow from Operating Activities				
Net Income	$ 18,760	$ 15,400		
Add (Deduct) Items to Convert Net Income to Cash Basis				
Depreciation	3,000	2,800		
Accounts Receivable Increase	(7,600)	(4,000)		
Inventory Increase	(12,000)	(8,400)		
Prepaid Expenses Increase	(300)	—		
Accounts Payable Increase	1,000	200		
Accrued Liabilities Increase	2,700	1,780		
Net Cash Provided by Operating Activities	$ 5,560	$ 7,780	($2,220)	(28.5)%
Cash Flows from Investing Activities				
Purchase of Trading Investments	($ 2,500)	$ —	2,500	—
Purchase of Long-Term Investments	(800)	—	800	—
Purchase of Property, Plant, and Equipment	(7,000)	(7,700)	(700)	(9.1)
Net Cash Used by Investing Activities	($10,300)	($ 7,700)	2,600	33.8
Cash Flows from Financing Activities				
Borrowing on Notes Payable	$ 500	$ 500	—	—
Issuance of Bonds Payable	5,000	3,000	2,000	66.7
Issuance of Common Stock	7,100	—	7,100	—
Payment of Dividends	(6,560)	(3,180)	3,380	106.3
Net Cash Provided by Financing Activities	$ 6,040	$ 320	5,720	1,787.5
Net Increase in Cash and Cash Equivalents	$ 1,300	$ 400		
Cash and Cash Equivalents at Beginning of Year	4,200	3,800		
Cash and Cash Equivalents at End of Year	$ 5,500	$ 4,200		

than two years. For example, suppose you were interested in sales and earnings trends for Alliance Company for the past five years. The following are the dollar data for the years 1992–1996):

ALLIANCE COMPANY
ANNUAL PERFORMANCE (MILLIONS OF DOLLARS)

	1992	1993	1994	1995	1996
Sales	$202.0	$215.0	$243.0	$320.0	$415.0
Net income	10.9	11.7	13.5	15.4	18.8

These data suggest a fairly healthy growth pattern for this company, but we can determine the pattern of change from year to year more precisely by calculating trend percentages. To do this, we select a *base year* and then divide the data for each of the other years by the base-year data. The resultant figures are actually indexes of the changes occurring throughout the period. If we choose 1992 as the base year, all data for 1993 through 1996 will be related to 1992, which is represented as 100%.

To create the following table, we divided each year's sales—from 1993 through 1996—by $202, the 1992 sales in millions of dollars. Similarly, the net incomes for 1993 through 1996 were divided by $10.9, the 1992 net income in millions of dollars.

CONSISTENCY PRINCIPLE

Horizontal analysis interprets a firm's financial data through two or more years by looking at dollar changes, percentage changes, and/or trend percentages. The usefulness of horizontal analysis relies on the *consistency principle*. This basic accounting principle requires the use of the same accounting methods from one period to the next or, if a firm finds it necessary to change a method, the disclosure of the financial effects of a change. The consistency principle assures analysts that, unless otherwise disclosed, financial changes through time represent underlying economic changes.

ALLIANCE COMPANY
ANNUAL PERFORMANCE (PERCENTAGE OF BASE YEAR)

	1992	1993	1994	1995	1996
Sales	100	106	120	158	205
Net income	100	107	124	141	172

The trend percentages reveal that the growth in earnings outstripped the growth in sales for 1993 and 1994 and then fell below the sales growth in the last two years. We saw in our analysis of comparative statements that a disproportionate increase in selling and administrative expenses emerged in 1996. We might therefore analyze the 1995 data to determine whether net income was affected for the same reason or whether the reduced growth was caused by other factors.

We must exercise care in interpreting trend percentages. Remember that all index percentages are related to the *base year*. Therefore, the change between the 1993 sales index (106%) and the 1994 sales index (120%) represents a 14% increase in terms of *base year* dollars. To express the increase as a percentage of 1993 dollars, we divide the 14% increase by the 106% 1993 sales index to obtain an increase of 13%. We must also be careful to select a *representative* base year. For example, consider the following sales and earnings data during the identical period for a competing company, Century Company.

CENTURY COMPANY
ANNUAL PERFORMANCE

	1992	1993	1994	1995	1996
Sales (millions of dollars)	$192.3	$204.4	$225.0	$299.0	$414.6
Percentage of base year	100	106	117	155	216
Net income (millions of dollars)	$ 1.9	$ 3.0	$ 4.0	$ 6.5	$ 10.0
Percentage of base year	100	158	210	342	526

Note that Century's sales growth pattern is similar to Alliance's. When judged from trend percentages, however, Century's net income growth is more than three times that of Alliance. Using an unrepresentative base year for Century—when earnings were depressed—makes the earnings trend misleading. In 1992, Century earned less than 1% of sales ($1.9/$192.3). But in the later years of the period, a more normal relationship between earnings and sales prevailed, and earnings were roughly 2–$2\frac{1}{2}$% of sales. The earnings/sales relationship for Alliance was relatively normal in 1992.

Other data that the analyst may relate to sales and earnings over a period of years include total assets, plant investment, and expenditures for research and development.

VERTICAL ANALYSIS

OBJECTIVE 2

DESCRIBE vertical analysis of financial statements.

The relative importance of various items in financial statements for a single year can be highlighted by showing them as percentages of a key figure. A financial statement that presents the various items as percentages of a key figure is called a **common-size financial statement.** Net sales (or net revenues) is the key figure used in a common-size income statement; total assets is the typical key figure used in a common-size balance sheet.

A financial statement may present both the dollar amounts and common-size percentages. For example, Exhibit 16-4 presents Alliance Company's 1996 income statement in dollars and common-size percentages. The common-size percentages show each item in the income statement as a percentage of net sales.

EXHIBIT 16–4 **Example of Income Statement with Common-Size Percentages**

ALLIANCE COMPANY
INCOME STATEMENT WITH COMMON-SIZE PERCENTAGES
FOR THE YEAR ENDED DECEMBER 31, 1996
(THOUSANDS OF DOLLARS)

Net Sales	$415,000	100.0%
Cost of Goods Sold	290,000	69.9
Gross Profit on Sales	$125,000	30.1%
Operating Expenses		
Selling Expenses	$ 39,500	9.5%
Administrative Expenses	49,640	12.0
Total Operating Expenses	$ 89,140	21.5%
Income before Interest and Taxes	$ 35,860	8.6%
Interest Expense	3,000	0.7
Income before Income Taxes	$ 32,860	7.9%
Income Tax Expense	14,100	3.4
Net Income	$ 18,760	4.5%

Alliance's common-size income statements for 1995 and 1996 are compared with those for Century in Exhibit 16-5. We see in Exhibit 16-5 that Century has a smaller gross profit percentage than does Alliance. The disparity might be due either to lower sales prices or higher production costs for Century. Selling and administrative expenses as a percentage of

---

EXHIBIT 16–5 **Examples of Common-Size Comparative Income Statements**

ALLIANCE AND CENTURY COMPANIES
COMMON-SIZE COMPARATIVE INCOME STATEMENTS
(PERCENTAGE OF NET SALES)

	Alliance Company		Century Company	
	Year Ended Dec. 31, 1996	Year Ended Dec. 31, 1995	Year Ended Dec. 31, 1996	Year Ended Dec. 31, 1995
Net Sales	100.0%	100.0%	100.0%	100.0%
Cost of Goods Sold	69.9	71.9	73.8	74.9
Gross Profit on Sales	30.1%	28.1%	26.2%	25.1%
Operating Expenses				
Selling Expenses	9.5%	8.5%	8.6%	8.2%
Administrative Expenses	12.0	10.2	12.3	11.4
Total Operating Expenses	21.5%	18.7%	20.9%	19.6%
Income before Interest and Taxes	8.6%	9.4%	5.3%	5.5%
Interest Expense	0.7	0.8	1.0	0.8
Income before Income Taxes	7.9%	8.6%	4.3%	4.7%
Income Tax Expense	3.4	3.8	2.1	2.3
Net Income	4.5%	4.8%	2.2%	2.4%

sales are fairly comparable, except that, combined, they are a higher percentage of the sales dollar for Alliance than for Century in 1996. Interest expense as a percentage of sales in 1996 is somewhat higher for Century than for Alliance. If we consider Century's low rate of net income to net sales (2.2% in 1996), the interest percentage is significant. Yet Alliance Company's higher rate of net income to net sales (about double that of Century Company) is due mainly to its better gross profit margin.

We may also use common-size percentages to analyze balance sheet data, although less successfully than with income statement data. For example, if for a period of several years we state current assets and long-term assets as a percentage of total assets, we can determine whether a company is becoming more or less liquid. The best use of common-size percentages with balance sheet data is probably with the sources of capital (equities). The proportions of the total capital supplied by short-term creditors, long-term creditors, preferred stockholders, and common stockholders of Alliance Company are shown below for 1996:

	Amount (Millions of Dollars)	Common-Size Percentage
Current debt	$ 58.6	30.5%
Long-term debt	25.0	13.0
Preferred stock equity	8.0	4.1
Common stock equity	100.7	52.4
	$192.3	100.0%

POINT OF INTEREST

ANNUAL REPORTS AS COLLECTIBLES

Annual reports to stockholders are generally most useful and valuable to readers because of the financial information they contain. On occasion, though, an annual report has intrinsic value as a collectible item. For example, the early comic-book style annual reports of Marvel Entertainment Group, parent company to such comic book heroes as Spider-Man and the X-Men, are valued in the $200–$300 range. A 1960s Rolls-Royce Ltd. annual report, in good condition, commands more than $100 in the collectibles market.

Source: "Annual Reports With Value," *Kiplinger's Personal Finance Magazine,* March 1995, p. 84.

ANALYSIS OF PROFITABILITY

OBJECTIVE 3

DEFINE and **DISCUSS** financial ratios for analyzing profitability.

We have introduced a number of financial ratios in the preceding chapters. At this point, we will classify the ratios by their overall objective and review their computations by calculating them for a single company. Alliance Company's financial statements provide the data for the calculations (all dollar amounts are in thousands). Also, representative industry averages will be presented when available.[1]

Several ratios assist in evaluating how efficiently and effectively a firm operates in its quest for profits; in other words, these ratios analyze various aspects of a firm's profitability. These ratios are (1) gross profit percentage, (2) return on sales, (3) asset turnover, (4) return on assets, and (5) return on common stockholders' equity.

GROSS PROFIT PERCENTAGE

The **gross profit percentage** is a closely watched ratio for retailers and manufacturers. The ratio is computed as follows:

$$\text{Gross Profit Percentage} = \frac{\text{Gross Profit on Sales}}{\text{Net Sales}}$$

This ratio reflects the net impact on profitability of changes in a firm's pricing structure, sales mix, and merchandise costs. Both managers and analysts monitor movements in the gross profit percentage.

---

[1]Although assumed, the industry averages are derived from data for manufacturers of electronic components and accessories compiled by Robert Morris Associates, Dun & Bradstreet, and Standard & Poor's Compustat Services.

Alliance's common-size income statements (Exhibit 16-5) reveal that its gross profit percentage improved from 28.1% in 1995 to 30.1% in 1996. These percentages are derived using the following amounts:

	1996	1995
Gross profit	$125,000	$ 90,000
Net sales	415,000	320,000
Gross profit percentage	30.1%	28.1%
Industry average	33.1%	

Although Alliance's ratio improved, the 1996 ratio falls below the industry average.

RETURN ON SALES

Another important measure of operating performance is **return on sales.** An overall test of operating efficiency, this ratio reveals the percentage of each dollar of net sales that remains as profit. Return on sales is computed as follows:

$$\text{Return on Sales} = \frac{\text{Net Income}}{\text{Net Sales}}$$

When common-size income statements are available, return on sales equals the net income percentage. Alliance's common-size income statements (Exhibit 16-5) reveal that its return on sales decreased from 4.8% in 1995 to 4.5% in 1996. These percentages are computed using the following amounts:

	1996	1995
Net income	$ 18,760	$ 15,400
Net sales	415,000	320,000
Return on sales	4.5%	4.8%
Industry average	3.9%	

The decline in return on sales is unfavorable, particularly in light of the gross profit percentage increase from 1995 to 1996. This is further evidence that Alliance's selling and administrative expenses increased at a relatively high rate during 1996. Even at that, however, Alliance's 1996 return on sales exceeds the industry average.

Return on sales and gross profit percentages should be used only when analyzing similar companies in the same industry or when comparing different periods for the same company (as above). These ratios vary widely by industry. Retail jewelers, for example, have much larger gross profit percentages (industry average around 44%) and returns on sales (industry average around 5%) than retail grocers (industry averages are about 20% for gross profit percentage and about 2% for return on sales). Averages for these industries would also be expected to vary significantly in the next ratio we consider, asset turnover.

ASSET TURNOVER

Asset turnover measures how efficiently a firm uses its assets to generate sales revenue. The ratio is computed as follows:

$$\text{Asset Turnover} = \frac{\text{Net Sales}}{\text{Average Total Assets}}$$

The following calculations are for Alliance Company (total assets were $146,100 at the end of 1994):

		1996	1995
Net sales		$415,000	$320,000
Total assets:			
Beginning of year	(a)	163,800	146,100
End of year	(b)	192,300	163,800
Average [(a + b)/2]		178,050	154,950
Asset turnover		2.33	2.07
Industry average		2.0	

Alliance's asset turnover increased from 1995 to 1996, indicating that assets were used more efficiently in 1996 to generate sales revenue. The 1996 ratio also exceeds the industry average.

Some industries that are characterized by low gross profit percentages and returns on sales manage relatively high asset turnovers. Retail grocers, for example, typically turn over assets five to six times per year. In contrast, retail jewelers average one to two asset turnovers per year.

RETURN ON ASSETS The rate of return on total assets, generally called **return on assets,** is an overall measure of a firm's profitability and efficiency. It shows the rate of profit earned per dollar of assets under a firm's control. Return on assets is calculated as follows:[2]

$$\text{Return on Assets} = \frac{\text{Net Income}}{\text{Average Total Assets}}$$

Alliance's return on assets is calculated as follows:

	1996	1995
Net income	$ 18,760	$ 15,400
Average total assets *(see asset turnover calculation)*	178,050	154,950
Return on assets	10.5%	9.9%
Industry average	8.1%	

Alliance Company improved its return on assets to 10.5% in 1996, a return that is nicely above the industry average.

The return on assets summarizes, in one ratio, the impact of two component ratios: return on sales and asset turnover. Return on assets is the product of these latter ratios, as follows:

Ratio title:	Return on Sales ×	Asset Turnover	=	Return on Assets
Ratio computation:	$\dfrac{\text{Net Income}}{\text{Net Sales}} \times$	$\dfrac{\text{Net Sales}}{\text{Average Total Assets}}$	=	$\dfrac{\text{Net Income}}{\text{Average Total Assets}}$
Alliance Company:	4.5% ×	2.33	=	10.5%

RETURN ON COMMON STOCKHOLDERS' EQUITY The **return on common stockholders' equity** measures the ultimate profitability of the ownership interest held by common stockholders. The ratio shows the percentage of profit earned on each dollar of common stockholders' equity. The return is earned on the stockholders' equity invested throughout the year, so the ratio uses the average common stockholders' equity, as follows:

$$\frac{\text{Return on Common}}{\text{Stockholder's Equity}} = \frac{\text{Net Income} - \text{Preferred Dividends}}{\text{Average Common Stockholders' Equity}}$$

The return on common stockholders' equity for Alliance Company is calculated below (common stockholders' equity was $69,180 at the end of 1994):

		1996	1995
Net income		$ 18,760	$15,400
Less: Preferred dividends		800	800
Common stock earnings		$ 17,960	$14,600
Common stockholders' equity			
Beginning of year	(a)	$ 81,400	$69,180
End of year	(b)	100,700	81,400
Average [(a + b)/2]		91,050	75,290
Return on common stockholders' equity		19.7%	19.4%
Industry average		16.0%	

---

[2]An alternative computation adds interest expense to net income in the ratio's numerator. This variation keeps the method of financing the assets from influencing the ratio.

Alliance's return on common stockholders' equity improved slightly from 1995 to 1996; it also exceeds the industry average for 1996.

ANALYSIS OF SHORT-TERM LIQUIDITY

OBJECTIVE *4*

DEFINE and **DISCUSS** financial ratios for analyzing short-term liquidity.

A firm's *working capital* is the difference between its current assets and current liabilities. Adequate working capital enables a firm to meet its current obligations on time and take advantage of available discounts. Shortages of working capital can sometimes force a company into disadvantageous borrowing at inopportune times and unfavorable interest rates. Many long-term debt contracts contain provisions that require the borrowing firm to maintain an adequate working capital position.

The adequacy of a firm's working capital is best judged by examining various financial relationships in addition to calculating the working capital amount. For example, compare the following working capital positions of Alliance Company and Dover Company:

	(Thousands of Dollars)	
	Alliance	**Dover**
Current assets	$143,500	$988,700
Current liabilities	58,600	903,800
Working capital	$ 84,900	$ 84,900

Both firms have the same amount of working capital, yet their working capital positions are not equal. Alliance's working capital exceeds its current liabilities whereas Dover's working capital is less than 10% of its current liabilities.

Analysis of a firm's short-term liquidity utilizes several financial ratios that relate to various aspects of working capital. These ratios are (1) current ratio, (2) quick ratio, (3) operating cash flow to current liabilities ratio, (4) accounts receivable turnover and average collection period, and (5) inventory turnover and days' sales in inventory.

CURRENT RATIO

The **current ratio** is simply the current assets divided by the current liabilities.

$$\text{Current Ratio} = \frac{\text{Current Assets}}{\text{Current Liabilities}}$$

This ratio is a widely used measure of a firm's ability to meet its current obligations on time and to have funds readily available for current operations. The following calculations show that Alliance Company improved its current ratio to 2.45 (or 2.45:1) in 1996.

	1996	**1995**
Current assets	$143,500	$119,800
Current liabilities	58,600	54,400
Current ratio	2.45	2.20
Industry average	2.1	

Evaluating the adequacy of a firm's current ratio may involve comparing it with the recent past (Alliance's current ratio went up in 1996) or with an industry average (Alliance's ratio exceeds the industry average). What is considered an appropriate current ratio varies by industry. A service firm with little inventory, such as a car wash service, is expected to have a smaller current ratio than does a firm carrying a large inventory, such as a hardware retailer. At the end of a recent year, for example, the median current ratio for the car wash industry was 0.9; the median current ratio for the retail hardware industry was 2.4. The composition of current assets, therefore, influences the evaluation of short-term liquidity. The quick ratio, which we discuss next, considers the composition of current assets.

QUICK RATIO

The **quick ratio** (or *acid-test ratio*) shows the relationship between a firm's liquid, or *quick,* assets and its current liabilities. Quick assets are cash and cash equivalents, short-term investments, and current receivables. Compared with the current ratio, the main item omitted is inventory. Prepaid items are also omitted, but they are usually not large relative to inventory. The quick ratio may give a better picture than the current ratio of a company's ability to meet current debts and to take advantage of discounts offered by creditors. The quick ratio and the current ratio together indicate the influence of the inventory figure in the company's working capital position. For example, a company might have an acceptable current ratio, but if its quick ratio falls much below 1.0, the analyst might be uneasy about the size of the inventory and analyze the inventory position more carefully. The 1.0 rule of thumb for the quick ratio is an arbitrary standard used only to alert the analyst to the need for further scrutiny.

The quick ratio is computed as follows:

$$\text{Quick Ratio} = \frac{\text{Cash and Cash Equivalents} + \text{Short-Term Investments} + \text{Current Receivables}}{\text{Current Liabilities}}$$

We calculate the quick ratio for Alliance Company as follows:

	1996	1995
Cash and cash equivalents, trading investments, and accounts receivable	$67,600	$56,200
Current liabilities	58,600	54,400
Quick ratio	1.15	1.03
Industry average	1.2	

Alliance's quick ratio improved from 1995 to 1996, and its 1996 quick ratio of 1.15 is consistent with the industry average of 1.2.

OPERATING CASH FLOW TO CURRENT LIABILITIES RATIO

Ultimately, cash is needed to settle current liabilities. Another ratio dealing with the ability to pay current liabilities as they become due focuses on the firm's cash flow from operations. The **operating cash flow to current liabilities ratio** is calculated as follows:

$$\frac{\text{Operating Cash Flow to}}{\text{Current Liabilities Ratio}} = \frac{\text{Net Cash Flow from Operating Activities}}{\text{Average Current Liabilities}}$$

Working capital components are constantly changing as a firm engages in its operating activities—inventory is bought and sold, services are rendered, receivables are collected, employees work, suppliers provide various goods and services, and payments are made to employees and suppliers. This ratio relates the net cash available as a result of these activities for a year to the average current liabilities outstanding during the period. The higher the ratio, the stronger the firm's ability to settle current liabilities as they become due.

Alliance's operating cash flow to current liabilities ratio is computed as follows (current liabilities at the end of 1994 were $51,920; no industry average is available):

		1996	1995
Net cash flow from operating activities		$ 5,560	$ 7,780
Current liabilities			
Beginning of year	(a)	54,400	51,920
End of year	(b)	58,600	54,400
Average [(a + b)/2]		56,500	53,160
Operating cash flow to current liabilities ratio		0.10	0.15

Alliance's ratio worsened from 1995 to 1996, a result of both a decline in cash provided by operating activities and an increase in average current liabilities.

ACCOUNTS RECEIVABLE TURNOVER

The speed with which accounts receivable are collected is of interest in evaluating short-term liquidity. **Accounts receivable turnover** indicates how many times a year a firm collects its average receivables and, thus, measures how fast a firm converts its accounts receivable into cash. Accounts receivable turnover is computed as follows:

$$\text{Accounts Receivable Turnover} = \frac{\text{Net Sales}}{\text{Average Accounts Receivable}}$$

The accounts receivable turnover for Alliance Company is computed below (accounts receivable at the end of 1994 were $48,000):

		1996	1995
Net sales		$415,000	$320,000
Average accounts receivable (net)			
Beginning of year	(a)	52,000	48,000
End of year	(b)	59,600	52,000
Average [(a + b)/2]		55,800	50,000
Accounts receivable turnover		7.44	6.40
Industry average		7.0	

The higher the accounts receivable turnover is, the faster accounts receivable are being converted into cash. Alliance's turnover increased from 6.40 in 1995 to 7.44 in 1996, which is an improvement in the ratio. Alliance's 1996 accounts receivable turnover is also above the industry average of 7.0 for the year.

AVERAGE COLLECTION PERIOD

A variation (or extension) of accounts receivable turnover is the **average collection period.** The average collection period, sometimes called *days' sales outstanding,* shows how many days it takes on average to collect an account receivable. It is computed as follows:

$$\text{Average Collection Period} = \frac{365}{\text{Accounts Receivable Turnover}}$$

Alliance Company's average collection period is calculated as follows:

	1996	1995
Average collection period		
1996: 365/7.44; 1995: 365/6.40	49.1 days	57.0 days
Industry average	52.1 days	

Alliance reduced its average collection period by almost eight days during 1996, so that it is three days less than the industry average. This may have resulted from such actions as a tightening of credit standards or a shortening of the credit period. Or it may reflect that customers have improved their cash flows and are thus able to pay more promptly. Knowledge of Alliance's credit terms would permit us to evaluate its average collection period further. If, for example, Alliance's credit terms are net 30 days, then an average collection period of 49.1 days indicates that it has a problem with slow-paying customers. On the other hand, if the terms are that payment is due within 45 days, then the 1996 average collection period shows no particular problem with the speed of collection.

INVENTORY TURNOVER

An analyst concerned about a company's inventory position may compute the company's **inventory turnover.** This figure indicates whether the inventory amount is disproportionate to the amount of sales. Excessive inventories not only tie up company funds and increase storage costs but may also lead to subsequent losses if the goods become outdated or unsalable. The computation of inventory turnover is as follows:

$$\text{Inventory Turnover} = \frac{\text{Cost of Goods Sold}}{\text{Average Inventory}}$$

Using this measure for Alliance Company gives the following results (inventory at the end of 1994 was $54,600):

		1996	1995
Cost of goods sold		$290,000	$230,000
Inventory			
Beginning of year	(a)	63,000	54,600
End of year	(b)	75,000	63,000
Average [(a + b)/2]		69,000	58,800
Inventory turnover		4.20	3.91
Industry average		4.6	

Alliance improved its inventory turnover from 1995 to 1996. Its 1996 inventory turnover of 4.20, however, is below the industry average of 4.6.

We use cost of goods sold in the calculation because the inventory measure in the denominator is a *cost* figure; we should therefore use a cost figure in the numerator. However, some financial information services use net sales instead of cost of goods sold to calculate inventory turnover. Analysts who compare a firm's inventory turnover with industry averages should be alert to how the industry average for inventory turnover is computed.

Usually, the average inventory is obtained by adding the year's beginning and ending inventories and dividing by 2. Because inventories taken at the beginning and end of the year are likely to be lower than the typical inventory, an unrealistically high turnover ratio may result. We should use a 12-month average if monthly inventory figures are available. Furthermore, we should be careful in calculating inventory turnover ratios for companies that use last-in, first-out inventory measurement methods, because the inventory amounts may deviate substantially from current costs.

A low inventory turnover can result from an overextended inventory position or from inadequate sales volume. For this reason, appraisal of inventory turnover should be accompanied by scrutiny of the quick ratio and analysis of trends in both inventory and sales.

DAYS' SALES IN INVENTORY

Days' sales in inventory is derived from a firm's inventory turnover. It shows how many days it takes a firm to sell its average inventory and is computed as follows:

$$\text{Days' Sales in Inventory} = \frac{365}{\text{Inventory Turnover}}$$

Days' sales in inventory for Alliance Company is calculated below:

	1996	**1995**
Days' sales in inventory		
1996: 365/4.20; 1995: 365/3.91	86.9 days	93.4 days
Industry average	79.3 days	

Alliance decreased the time it takes to sell its average inventory from 93.4 days in 1995 to 86.9 days in 1996. Even with this improvement, however, Alliance's length of time exceeds the industry average by more than seven days.

By combining days' sales in inventory with the average collection period, we can estimate the average time period running from the acquisition of inventory to the eventual collection of cash. In 1996, for example, it took Alliance 136.0 days (86.9 days' sales in inventory + 49.1 days for the average collection period) to sell its average inventory and collect the related cash from its customers. Although this time period exceeds the industry average of 131.4 days by more than four days, it is more than two weeks shorter than Alliance's 1995 time period of 150.4 days (93.4 days + 57.0 days). Alliance has improved its performance in this area, but there apparently is still room for more improvement.

ANALYSIS OF LONG-TERM SOLVENCY

The preceding set of ratios examined a firm's short-term liquidity. Another set of ratios analyzes long-term solvency. Ratios in the latter group are the (1) debt-to-equity ratio, (2) times interest earned ratio, and (3) operating cash flow to capital expenditures ratio.

DEBT-TO-EQUITY RATIO

OBJECTIVE 5
DEFINE and **DISCUSS** financial ratios for analyzing long-term solvency.

The **debt-to-equity ratio** looks at the financial structure of a firm by relating total liabilities to total owners' equity, as follows:

$$\text{Debt-to-Equity Ratio} = \frac{\text{Total Liabilities}}{\text{Total Owners' Equity}}$$

We use year-end balances for the elements in this ratio rather than averages because we are interested in the capital structure at a particular point in time. The total owners' equity for a corporation is its total stockholders' equity.

The debt-to-equity ratio gives potential creditors an indication of the margin of protection available to them (creditors' claims to assets have priority over owners' claims). The lower the ratio, the better the protection being provided to creditors. A firm with a low ratio usually has more flexibility in seeking borrowed funds than does a firm with a high ratio.

Alliance Company's debt-to-equity ratio is computed as follows:

	1996	1995
Total liabilities (year-end)	$ 83,600	$74,400
Total stockholders' equity (year-end)	108,700	89,400
Debt-to-equity ratio	0.77	0.83
Industry average	0.98	

Alliance's debt-to-equity ratio dropped from 0.83 in 1995 to 0.77 in 1996; the 1996 ratio is also below the industry average. Both the trend in the ratio and its relationship to the industry average would be interpreted as positive aspects of the firm's long-term financial strength.

POINT OF INTEREST

MICROSOFT'S DEBT/EQUITY STATUS

Some corporations enjoy the luxury of having no long-term debt in their financial structure. In its fiscal 1994 balance sheet, for example, Microsoft Corporation reported no long-term liabilities. A computer software company, Microsoft had total assets of $5,363,000,000, current liabilities of $913,000,000 and stockholders' equity of $4,450,000,000 at fiscal 1994 year-end. Microsoft's debt-to-equity ratio at that point was $913,000,000/$4,450,000,000 = 0.21. In addition to this very strong debt-to-equity ratio, Microsoft's cash and short-term investments at the same point in time were 67% of its total assets!

TIMES INTEREST EARNED RATIO

To evaluate further the size of a company's debt, an analyst may observe the relationship of interest charges to earnings. For example, an extremely high debt-to-equity ratio for a company may indicate heavy borrowing. However, if its earnings are sufficient, even in poor years, to meet the interest charges on the debt several times over, the analyst may regard the situation quite favorably.

Analysts, particularly long-term creditors, almost always calculate the **times interest earned ratio.** This ratio is determined by dividing the income before interest expense and income taxes by the annual interest expense:

$$\text{Times Interest Earned Ratio} = \frac{\text{Income before Interest Expense and Income Taxes}}{\text{Interest Expense}}$$

The computations for Alliance Company are as follows:

	1996	1995
Income before interest expense and income taxes	$35,860	$30,100
Interest expense	3,000	2,400
Times interest earned ratio	11.95	12.54
Industry average	3.2	

Alliance's income available to meet interest charges each year was approximately 12 times the amount of its interest expense. The 1996 ratio is well above the industry average. Alliance has an exceptionally good margin of safety. Generally speaking, a company that earns its interest several times before taxes in its poor years is regarded as a satisfactory risk by long-term creditors.

OPERATING CASH FLOW TO CAPITAL EXPENDITURES RATIO

The ability of a firm's operations to provide sufficient cash to replace, and expand when appropriate, its property, plant, and equipment is shown by the **operating cash flow to capital expenditures ratio.** To the extent that acquisitions of plant assets can be financed out of cash provided by operating activities, a firm does not have to use other financing sources, such as long-term debt. The ratio is calculated as follows:

$$\text{Operating Cash Flow to Capital Expenditures Ratio} = \frac{\text{Net Cash Flow from Operating Activities}}{\text{Annual Capital Expenditures}}$$

A ratio of 1.0 means that the firm's current operating activities are providing sufficient cash to provide the desired level of plant capacity. A ratio in excess of 1.0 means that there is net cash available from operations in excess of plant asset needs that may be used for other purposes, such as retiring long-term debt.

The operating cash flow to capital expenditures ratio for Alliance Company is computed below (no industry average is available):

	1996	1995
Net cash flow from operating activities	$5,560	$7,780
Annual capital expenditures (see Exhibit 16-3)	7,000	7,700
Operating cash flow to capital expenditures ratio	0.79	1.01

Alliance's ratio decreased from 1.01 in 1995 to 0.79 in 1996. Although annual capital expenditures decreased from 1995 to 1996, the net cash flow from operating activities decreased even more.

ANALYSIS FOR COMMON STOCK INVESTORS

Present and potential common stockholders share an interest with other parties in analyzing the profitability, short-term liquidity, and long-term solvency of a corporation. There are other financial ratios, however, that are primarily of interest to common stockholders. These ratios are (1) earnings per share, (2) price-earnings ratio, (3) dividend yield, and (4) dividend payout ratio.

EARNINGS PER SHARE

OBJECTIVE 6
DEFINE and **DISCUSS** financial ratios for analysis by common stock investors.

Because stock market prices are quoted on a per-share basis, the reporting of **earnings per share** of common stock is useful to investors. Our discussion of earnings per share in an earlier chapter noted that the computation for corporations with simple capital structures is as follows:

$$\text{Earnings per Share} = \frac{\text{Net Income} - \text{Preferred Dividends}}{\text{Weighted Average Common Shares Outstanding}}$$

Earnings per share must be reported on the income statement, so the analyst does not have to compute this ratio. Alliance Company's income statements show the following earnings per share (Exhibit 16-2; no industry average is available):

	1996	1995
Earnings per share	$5.28	$5.21

Even though Alliance's net income increased almost 22% in 1996, earnings per share increased only slightly because a large number of additional common shares were issued during the year.

PRICE-EARNINGS RATIO

The **price-earnings ratio** is the result of dividing the market price of a share of common stock by the earnings per share.

$$\text{Price-Earnings Ratio} = \frac{\text{Market Price per Share}}{\text{Earnings per Share}}$$

For many analysts and investors, this ratio is an important tool in assessing stock values. For example, after evaluating the strong and weak points of several companies in an industry, the analyst may compare price-earnings ratios to determine the "best buy."

When determining the price-earnings ratio, we customarily use the latest market price and the earnings per share for the last four quarters of a company's operations. Alliance's price-earnings ratios at the end of 1995 and 1996 are computed as follows (year-end market prices follow):

	1996	1995
Market price per share (at year-end)	$55.50	$53.75
Earnings per share	5.28	5.21
Price-earnings ratio	10.5	10.3
Industry average	12	

The market price of a share of Alliance's common stock was slightly more than 10 times the amount that share earned in both 1995 and 1996. Alliance's price-earnings ratio at the end of 1996 is a little below the industry average.

DIVIDEND YIELD

Investors' expectations vary a great deal with personal economic circumstances and with the overall economic outlook. Some investors are more interested in the price appreciation of a stock investment than in present income in the form of dividends. When shares are disposed of in the future, the capital gains provision of the income tax laws may tax any gains at a rate that is lower than the rate applied to other income. Other investors are more concerned with dividends than with price appreciation. Such investors desire a high **dividend yield** on their investments. Dividend yield is calculated by dividing the current annual dividends per share by the current price of the stock:

$$\text{Dividend Yield} = \frac{\text{Annual Dividends per Share}}{\text{Market Price per Share}}$$

Alliance's dividend yields per common share are computed as follows (dividends per share are disclosed in Exhibit 16-2; no industry average is available):

	1996	1995
Annual dividends per share	$ 1.44	$ 0.85
Market price per share (at year-end)	55.50	53.75
Dividend yield	2.6%	1.6%

Even though Alliance's dividend yield was higher at the end of 1996 than it was at the end of 1995, the dividend yields for both years are considered low.

DIVIDEND PAYOUT RATIO

Investors who emphasize the yield on their investments may also be interested in a firm's **dividend payout ratio,** which is the percentage of the common stock earnings paid out in dividends. The payout ratio indicates whether a firm has a conservative or a liberal dividend policy and may also indicate whether the firm is conserving funds for internal financing of growth. We calculate the dividend payout ratio as follows:

$$\text{Dividend Payout Ratio} = \frac{\text{Annual Dividends per Share}}{\text{Earnings per Share}}$$

Alliance Company's dividend payout ratios are calculated as follows (no industry average is available):

	1996	1995
Annual dividends per share	$1.44	$0.85
Earnings per share	5.28	5.21
Dividend payout ratio	27.3%	16.3%

Alliance increased its dividend payout ratio in 1996 compared with 1995. The payout ratios in both years, however, would be considered relatively low.

Payout ratios for typical, seasoned industrial corporations vary between 40% and 60%. Many corporations, however, need funds for internal financing of growth and pay out little or nothing in dividends. At the other extreme, some companies—principally utility companies—may pay out as much as 70% or 80% of their earnings. Utilities have less need to retain funds for growth because the bulk of their financing is through long-term debt.

POINT OF INTEREST

INTERPRETING A LOW AVERAGE DIVIDEND YIELD

Over the past few decades, the dividend yield of the stocks composing the Dow Jones Industrial Average has averaged around 4.4%. With this knowledge, many financial analysts consider a low average dividend yield for the stock market (below 3%) to be a sign that stocks are priced too high. Yields, they believe, will eventually rise to the long-term average, either through falling stock prices or increasing dividends. Other analysts believe the significant stock buyback programs of many companies, which began about 15 years ago, reduce the negative implications of low average dividend yields. In addition to providing another way (besides dividends) for corporations to transfer assets to stockholders, many stock buyback programs have helped buoy their company's stock price.

Source: Anita Raghavan, "Industrials' Low Dividend Yield Sparks Worries over Valuation," *The Wall Street Journal,* January 17, 1994; and Anita Raghavan, "As Companies Turn to Stock Buybacks, Some Market Bulls Spot 'Hidden Yield,' " *The Wall Street Journal,* May 2, 1994.

LIMITATIONS OF FINANCIAL ANALYSIS

OBJECTIVE 7
DISCUSS the limitations of financial analysis.

The ratios, percentages, and other relationships we have described in this chapter are merely the result of analytical techniques. They may only isolate areas requiring further investigation. Moreover, we must interpret them with due consideration to general economic conditions, conditions of the industry in which the companies operate, and the positions of individual companies within the industry.

We should also be aware of the inherent limitations of financial statement data. Problems of comparability are frequently encountered. Companies otherwise similar may use different accounting methods, which can cause problems in comparing certain key relationships. For instance, inventory turnover is different for a company using LIFO inventory costing than for one using FIFO. Inflation may distort certain computations, especially those resulting from horizontal analysis. For example, trend percentages calculated from data unadjusted for inflation may be deceptive.

We must be careful even when comparing companies in a particular industry. Such factors as size, diversity of product, and mode of operations can make the firms completely dissimilar. Some firms, particularly conglomerates, are difficult to classify by industry. If segment information—particularly product-line data—is available, the analyst may compare the statistics for several industries. Often, trade associations prepare industry statistics that are stratified by size of firm or type of product, making analysis easier.

KEY POINTS FOR CHAPTER LEARNING OBJECTIVES

1 **IDENTIFY** sources of financial information for analysts and **DESCRIBE** horizontal analysis of financial statements (pp. 562–567).
  ■ Data sources include published financial statements, filings with the SEC, and statistics available from financial services.
  ■ A common form of horizontal analysis is inspecting dollar and percentage changes in comparative financial statements for two or more years.
  ■ Analyzing trend percentages of key figures, such as net sales, net income, and total assets for a number of years, related to a base year, is often useful.

2 **Describe** vertical analysis of financial statements (pp. 567–569).
- Vertical analysis deals with the relationships of financial statement data for a single year.
- Common-size statements express items on a financial statement as a percentage of a key item, such as expressing income statement items as a percentage of net sales.

3 **Define** and **Discuss** financial ratios for analyzing profitability (pp. 569–572).
- Ratios for analyzing profitability are gross profit percentage, return on sales, asset turnover, return on assets, and return on common stockholders' equity.

4 **Define** and **Discuss** financial ratios for analyzing short-term liquidity (pp. 572–575).
- Ratios for analyzing short-term liquidity are current ratio, quick ratio, operating cash flow to current liabilities ratio, accounts receivable turnover, average collection period, inventory turnover, and days' sales in inventory.

5 **Define** and **Discuss** financial ratios for analyzing long-term solvency (pp. 575–577).
- Ratios for analyzing long-term solvency are debt-to-equity ratio, times interest earned ratio, and operating cash flow to capital expenditures ratio.

6 **Define** and **Discuss** financial ratios for analysis by common stock investors (pp. 577–579).
- Ratios of particular interest to common stock investors are earnings per share, price-earnings ratio, dividend yield, and dividend payout ratio.

7 **Discuss** the limitations of financial analysis (p. 579).
- When analyzing statements, one must be aware of the firm's accounting methods, the effects of inflation, and the difficulty of identifying a firm's industry classification.

Summary of Financial Statement Ratios

Analysis of Profitability

$$\text{Gross Profit Percentage} = \frac{\text{Gross Profit on Sales}}{\text{Net Sales}}$$

$$\text{Return on Sales} = \frac{\text{Net Income}}{\text{Net Sales}}$$

$$\text{Asset Turnover} = \frac{\text{Net Sales}}{\text{Average Total Assets}}$$

$$\text{Return on Assets} = \frac{\text{Net Income}}{\text{Average Total Assets}}$$

$$\text{Return on Common Stockholders' Equity} = \frac{\text{Net Income} - \text{Preferred Dividends}}{\text{Average Common Stockholders' Equity}}$$

Analysis of Short-Term Liquidity

$$\text{Current Ratio} = \frac{\text{Current Assets}}{\text{Current Liabilities}}$$

$$\text{Quick Ratio} = \frac{\text{Cash and Cash Equivalents} + \text{Short-Term Investments} + \text{Current Receivables}}{\text{Current Liabilities}}$$

$$\frac{\text{Operating Cash Flow to}}{\text{Current Liabilities Ratio}} = \frac{\text{Net Cash Flow from Operating Activities}}{\text{Average Current Liabilities}}$$

$$\text{Accounts Receivable Turnover} = \frac{\text{Net Sales}}{\text{Average Accounts Receivable}}$$

$$\text{Average Collection Period} = \frac{365}{\text{Accounts Receivable Turnover}}$$

$$\text{Inventory Turnover} = \frac{\text{Cost of Goods Sold}}{\text{Average Inventory}}$$

$$\text{Days' Sales in Inventory} = \frac{365}{\text{Inventory Turnover}}$$

ANALYSIS OF LONG-TERM SOLVENCY

$$\text{Debt-to-Equity Ratio} = \frac{\text{Total Liabilities}}{\text{Total Owners' Equity}}$$

$$\text{Times Interest Earned Ratio} = \frac{\text{Income before Interest Expense and Income Taxes}}{\text{Interest Expense}}$$

$$\begin{array}{c}\text{Operating Cash Flow to}\\\text{Capital Expenditures Ratio}\end{array} = \frac{\text{Net Cash Flow from Operating Activities}}{\text{Annual Capital Expenditures}}$$

ANALYSIS FOR COMMON STOCK INVESTORS

$$\text{Earnings per Share} = \frac{\text{Net Income} - \text{Preferred Dividends}}{\text{Weighted Average Common Shares Outstanding}}$$

$$\text{Price-Earnings Ratio} = \frac{\text{Market Price per Share}}{\text{Earnings per Share}}$$

$$\text{Dividend Yield} = \frac{\text{Annual Dividends per Share}}{\text{Market Price per Share}}$$

$$\text{Dividend Payout Ratio} = \frac{\text{Annual Dividends per Share}}{\text{Earnings per Share}}$$

SELF-TEST QUESTIONS FOR REVIEW

(Answers follow the Solution to Demonstration Problem.)

All of the self-test questions are based on the following data:

THERMO COMPANY
BALANCE SHEET
DECEMBER 31, 1996

Cash	$ 40,000	Current Liabilities	$ 80,000
Accounts Receivable (net)	80,000	10% Bonds Payable	120,000
Inventory	130,000	Common Stock	200,000
Plant and Equipment (net)	250,000	Retained Earnings	100,000
		Total Liabilities and	
Total Assets	$500,000	Stockholders' Equity	$500,000

Net sales for 1996 were $800,000, gross profit was $320,000, and net income was $36,000. The income tax rate was 40%. A year ago accounts receivable (net) were $76,000, inventory was $110,000, and common stockholders' equity was $260,000. The bonds payable were outstanding all year and 1996 interest expense was $12,000.

1. The current ratio of Thermo Company at 12/31/96, calculated from these data, was 3.13, and the working capital was $170,000. Which of the following would happen if the firm paid $20,000 of its current liabilities on January 1, 1997?
   a. Both the current ratio and the working capital would decrease.
   b. Both the current ratio and the working capital would increase.
   c. The current ratio would increase, but the working capital would remain the same.
   d. The current ratio would increase, but the working capital would decrease.
2. What was the firm's inventory turnover for 1996?
   a. 6.67   b. 4   c. 6   d. 3.69
3. What was the firm's return on common stockholders' equity for 1996?
   a. 25.7%   b. 12.9%   c. 17.1%   d. 21.4%
4. What was the firm's average collection period for receivables for 1996?
   a. 36.5 days   b. 37.4 days   c. 35.6 days   d. 18.3 days
5. What was the firm's times interest earned ratio for 1996?
   a. 4   b. 3   c. 5   d. 6

DEMONSTRATION PROBLEM FOR REVIEW

Knox Instruments, Inc., is a manufacturer of various medical and dental instruments. Financial statement data for the firm follow.

1996	(Thousands of Dollars, except per-share amount)
Net Sales	$200,000
Cost of Goods Sold	98,000
Net Income	10,750
Dividends	4,200
Net Cash Provided by Operating Activities	7,800
Earnings per Share	3.07

KNOX INSTRUMENTS, INC.
BALANCE SHEETS
(THOUSANDS OF DOLLARS)

Assets	Dec. 31, 1996	Dec. 31, 1995
Cash	$ 3,000	$ 2,900
Accounts Receivable (net)	28,000	28,800
Inventory	64,000	44,000
Total Current Assets	$ 95,000	$ 75,700
Plant Assets (net)	76,000	67,300
Total Assets	$171,000	$143,000

Liabilities and Stockholders' Equity		
Current Liabilities	$ 45,200	$ 39,750
10% Bonds Payable	20,000	14,000
Total Liabilities	$ 65,200	$ 53,750
Common Stock, $10 Par Value	$ 40,000	$ 30,000
Retained Earnings	65,800	59,250
Total Stockholders' Equity	$105,800	$ 89,250
Total Liabilities and Stockholders' Equity	$171,000	$143,000

REQUIRED

a. Using the given data, calculate items 1 through 9 for 1996. Compare the performance of Knox Instruments, Inc., with the following industry averages and comment on its operations.

	Median Ratios for the Industry
1. Current ratio	2.7
2. Quick ratio	1.6
3. Average collection period	73 days
4. Inventory turnover	2.3
5. Operating cash flow to current liabilities ratio	NA
6. Debt-to-equity ratio	0.50
7. Return on assets	4.9%
8. Return on common stockholders' equity	10.2%
9. Return on sales	4.1%

b. Calculate the dividends paid per share of common stock. (Use average number of shares outstanding during the year.) What was the dividend payout ratio?

c. If the 1996 year-end price per share of common stock is $25, what is (1) the price-earnings ratio? (2) the dividend yield?

SOLUTION TO DEMONSTRATION PROBLEM

a. 1. Current Ratio $= \dfrac{\$95,000}{\$45,200} = 2.10$

2. Quick Ratio $= \dfrac{\$31,000}{\$45,200} = 0.69$

3. Average Collection Period:

$$\text{Accounts Receivable Turnover} = \frac{\$200,000}{(\$28,800 + \$28,000)/2} = 7.04$$

$$\text{Average Collection Period} = \frac{365}{7.04} = 51.8 \text{ days}$$

4. Inventory Turnover $= \dfrac{\$98,000}{(\$44,000 + \$64,000)/2} = 1.81$

5. Operating Cash Flow to Current Liabilities Ratio $= \dfrac{\$7,800}{(\$39,750 + \$45,200)/2} = 0.18$

6. Debt-to-Equity Ratio $= \dfrac{\$65,200}{\$105,800} = 0.62$

7. Return on Assets $= \dfrac{\$10,750}{(\$143,000 + \$171,000)/2} = 6.8\%$

8. Return on Common Stockholders' Equity $= \dfrac{\$10,750}{(\$89,250 + \$105,800)/2} = 11.0\%$

9. Return on Sales $= \dfrac{\$10,750}{\$200,000} = 5.4\%$

Although the firm's current ratio, 2.10, is below the industry median, it is still acceptable. However, the quick ratio, 0.69, is far below the industry median. This indicates that the inventory (which is omitted from this calculation) is excessive; this is borne out by the firm's inventory turnover of 1.81 times, which compares with the industry median of 2.3 times. The firm's average collection period of 51.8 days is significantly better than the industry median of 73 days. No industry median is available for the operating cash flow to current liabilities ratio. The debt-to-equity ratio of 0.62 indicates that the firm has proportionately more debt in its capital structure than the median industry firm, which has a debt-to-equity ratio of 0.50. The firm's operations appear efficient, because its return on assets, return on common stockholders' equity, and return on sales all exceed the industry medians.

b. Average number of shares outstanding = (4,000,000 + 3,000,000)/2 = 3,500,000 shares.
$4,200,000 dividends/3,500,000 shares = $1.20 dividends per share.
Dividend payout ratio = $1.20/$3.07 = 39.1%.

c. Price-earnings ratio = $25/$3.07 = 8.1.
Dividend yield = $1.20/$25 = 4.8%.

ANSWERS TO SELF-TEST QUESTIONS

1. c, p. 572   **2.** b, p. 574   **3.** b, p. 571   **4.** c, p. 574   **5.** d, p. 576

Financial Statement Disclosures

Disclosures related to financial statements fall into one of three categories: (1) parenthetical disclosures on the face of the financial statements, (2) notes to the financial statements, and (3) supplementary information. Most disclosures amplify or explain information contained in the financial statements. Some disclosures, however, add new kinds of information.

PARENTHETICAL DISCLOSURES

Parenthetical disclosures are placed next to an account title or other descriptive label in the financial statements. Their purpose is to provide succinctly some additional detail about the item. The information disclosed parenthetically could instead be disclosed by a note to the statements. The selection of the particular disclosure technique is at the discretion of individual companies. Because they are presented on the face of the financial statements, parenthetical disclosures probably stand a better chance of being noticed by statement readers than do disclosures in the notes.

Several types of parenthetical disclosures follow, illustrated with examples that relate to topics we have discussed in earlier chapters.

1. A parenthetical disclosure may report *contra asset amounts,* such as the allowance for uncollectible accounts or accumulated depreciation.

	1996	1995
Accounts Receivable, less allowances for uncollectible accounts (1996—$30,000; 1995—$26,500)	$215,000	$174,000
Plant and Equipment, less accumulated depreciation (1996—$530,000; 1995—$450,000)	997,000	892,000

2. The *measurement technique* used may be revealed by a parenthetical disclosure.

	1996	1995
Inventories (at last-in, first-out cost)	$620,000	$710,000
Intangibles (cost less amortization to date)	75,000	80,000

3. An *alternate financial measure* for the item reported may be disclosed parenthetically.

	1996	1995
Short-Term Stock Investments, at market (cost, $250,000 at December 31, 1996, and $600,000 at December 31, 1995)	$270,000	$625,000
Inventories (at last-in, first-out cost; cost using first-in, first-out would have been: 1996—$1,200,000, 1995—$1,000,000)	950,000	800,000

4. A parenthetical disclosure may report an *amount that is not otherwise separately reported,* such as the amount of interest capitalized during the year.

	1996	1995
Interest Expense (net of capitalized amounts of $29,000 and $11,000, respectively)	$187,000	$162,000

5. Accounts that have been combined and reported as *a single figure in the financial statements may be broken down* in a parenthetical disclosure.

	1996	1995
Cash and Cash Equivalents (including short-term investments of $300,000 and $270,000 at December 31, 1996 and 1995, respectively)	$540,000	$420,000

NOTES TO FINANCIAL STATEMENTS

Although much information is gathered, summarized, and reported in financial statements, the statements alone are limited in their ability to convey a complete picture of a firm's financial status. *Notes* are added to financial statements to help fill in the gaps. In fact, accountants have given so much attention to financial statement notes in recent years that today it is not unusual for the notes to take up more space than the statements themselves. Notes may cover a wide variety of topics. Typically, they deal with significant accounting policies, explanations of complex or special transactions, details of reported amounts, commitments, contingencies, segments, quarterly data, and subsequent events.

SIGNIFICANT ACCOUNTING POLICIES

Accounting principles contain several instances for which alternative procedures are acceptable. For example, there are several acceptable depreciation and inventory pricing methods, and there are different ways to convert financial data of foreign subsidiaries to U.S. dollars. The particular procedures selected obviously affect the financial data presented. Further, unique or complex events may require innovative applications of accounting principles. Knowledge of a firm's specific accounting principles and methods of applying these principles helps users understand the financial statements. Accordingly, these principles and methods are disclosed in a **summary of significant accounting policies.** The summary is either the initial note to the financial statements or immediately precedes the notes. The number of policies listed, of course, varies from firm to firm, but the policies relating to inventory pricing methods, depreciation methods, and consolidation practices are invariably included.

For example, a recent annual report of Honeywell, Inc., contains the following description of its depreciation and amortization policies (Honeywell manufactures control components and systems for residential and commercial applications):

> Property is carried at cost and depreciated primarily using the straight-line method over estimated useful lives of 10 to 40 years for buildings and improvements, and three to 15 years for machinery and equipment.
> Intangibles are carried at cost and amortized over their estimated useful lives of not more than 40 years for goodwill, three to 17 years for patents, licenses and trademarks, and six to 24 years for software and other intangibles.

EXPLANATIONS OF COMPLEX OR SPECIAL TRANSACTIONS

The complexity of certain transactions means that not all important aspects are likely to be reflected in the accounts. Financial statement notes, therefore, report the additional relevant details about such transactions. Typical examples include notes discussing financial aspects of pension plans, profit-sharing plans, acquisitions of other companies, borrowing agreements, stock option and other incentive plans, and income taxes.

Transactions with related parties are special transactions requiring disclosure in the financial statement notes.[1] *Related-party transactions* include transactions between a firm and its (1) principal owners, (2) members of management, (3) subsidiaries, or (4) affiliates. The transactions may be sales or purchases of property, leases, borrowings or lendings, and the like. These transactions are not arm's length transactions; that is, they are not between

---

[1] *Statement of Financial Accounting Standards No. 57,* "Related Party Disclosures" (Stamford, CT: Financial Accounting Standards Board, 1982).

independent parties each acting in its own best interests (as is true in most transactions). Because of the relationships between the parties, one party may exert significant influence over the other party and the results may differ from what would occur in an arm's length transaction (for example, the interest rate for funds borrowed may be below the current market rate). A user trying to compare a firm's financial data with that of prior periods or other similar companies will find related-party information useful. It may help identify and explain differences in the data.

To illustrate, a recent annual report of Best Buy Co., Inc., contains the following description of a related-party transaction (Best Buy sells consumer electronics, major appliances, home office products, entertainment software, and related accessories):

> Five stores are leased from the Company's CEO and principal stockholder, his spouse, or partnerships in which he is a partner. Rent expense under these leases during the last three fiscal years was as follows (in thousands):

	1994	1993	1992
Minimum rentals	$1,049	$1,051	$1,049
Percentage rentals	423	405	388
	$1,472	$1,456	$1,437

DETAILS OF REPORTED AMOUNTS

Financial statements often summarize several groups of accounts into a single dollar amount. For example, a balance sheet may show as one asset an amount labeled *Property, Plant, and Equipment,* or it may list *Long-Term Debt* as a single amount among the liabilities. These aggregated amounts may be sufficient for some financial statement users, but others want more detail about these items. Notes will report this detail, presenting schedules that list the types and amounts of property, plant, and equipment and long-term debt. Other items that may be summarized in the financial statements and detailed in the notes include inventories, other current assets, notes payable, accrued liabilities, owners' equity, and income tax expense.

The notes to General Mills' annual report (see Appendix K) contain several examples of financial statement items that are detailed, including inventories (note 5), land, buildings and equipment (note 6), notes payable (note 7), long-term debt (note 8), and income taxes (note 15).

COMMITMENTS

A firm may have contractual arrangements existing at a balance sheet date in which both parties to the contract still have acts to perform. If performance under these **commitments** will have a significant financial impact on the firm, the existence and nature of the commitments should be disclosed in the financial statement notes. Examples of commitments reported in notes are commitments under operating leases, contracts to purchase materials or equipment, contracts to construct facilities, salary commitments to executives, commitments to retire or redeem stock, and commitments to deliver goods.

A recent annual report of Kimberly-Clark Corporation—a producer of tissue products (such as Kleenex), newsprint, and papers—includes the following example of significant purchase commitments:

> The Corporation has entered into long-term contracts for the purchase of certain raw materials. Minimum purchase commitments, at current prices, are approximately $230 million in 1994 and $190 million in each of the years 1995 and 1996. In no year are these purchase commitments expected to exceed usage requirements.

CONTINGENCIES

We discussed contingent liabilities in an earlier chapter. As noted there, if the future event that would turn a contingency into an obligation is not likely to occur, or if the liability amount cannot be reasonably estimated, the **contingency** is disclosed parenthetically or in a note to the financial statements. Typical contingencies disclosed in notes are lawsuits, environmental cleanup, possible income tax assessments, credit guarantees, and discounted notes receivable.

Union Pacific Corporation, a firm engaged in rail transportation, trucking, and natural resources, reported the following contingencies in a recent annual report:

> There are various lawsuits pending against the Corporation and certain of its subsidiaries. The Corporation is also subject to Federal, state and local environmental laws and regulations, and is currently participating in the investigation and remediation of numerous sites. Where the remediation costs can be reasonably determined, and where such remediation is probable, the Corporation has recorded a liability. At December 31, 1993, the Corporation has accrued $181 million for estimated future environmental costs and believes it is reasonably possible that actual environmental costs could be lower than the recorded cost or as much as 50% higher. The Corporation has also entered into commitments and provided guarantees for specific financial and contractual obligations of its subsidiaries and affiliates. The Corporation does not expect that the lawsuits, environmental costs, commitments or guarantees will have a material adverse effect on its consolidated financial position or its results of operations.

SEGMENTS

Many firms diversify their activities and operate in several different industries. The firms' financial statements combine information from all operations into aggregate amounts. This complicates the users' ability to analyze the statements because the interpretation of financial data is influenced by the industry in which a firm operates. Different industries face different types of risk and have different rates of profitability. In making investment and lending decisions, users evaluate risk and required rates of return. Having financial data available by industry segments is helpful to such evaluations.

The FASB recognizes the usefulness of industry data to investors and lenders. Public companies with significant operations in more than one industry must report certain information by industry **segments.** Typically, these disclosures are in the financial statement notes. The major disclosures by industry segment are revenue, operating profit or loss, identifiable assets (the assets used by the segment), capital expenditures, and depreciation.

Other types of segment data may also be disclosed. Business operations in different parts of the world are subject to different risks and opportunities for growth. Thus, public firms with significant operations in foreign countries must report selected financial data by foreign geographic area. The data disclosed are revenue, operating profit or loss (or other profitability measure), and identifiable assets. Also, if a firm has export sales or sales to a single customer that are 10% or more of total revenue, the amount of such sales must be separately disclosed.

An example of the latter type of segment disclosure is Ben & Jerry's Homemade, Inc., which reported the following segment information in a recent annual report (Ben & Jerry's makes and sells premium ice cream):

> The Company's most significant customer, Dreyer's Ice Cream, Inc., accounted for 54% or $76.4 million of net sales in 1993, 49% or $65.0 million in 1992 and 44% or $42.3 million in 1991.

Note 18 to General Mills' financial statements in its 1994 annual report (see Appendix K) illustrates segment disclosures by industry and foreign versus domestic.

QUARTERLY DATA

Interim financial reports cover periods shorter than one year. Companies that issue interim reports to investors and others generally do so quarterly. These reports provide users with timely information on a firm's progress and are most useful in predicting what the annual financial results will be. The SEC requires certain companies to disclose selected quarterly financial data in their annual reports to stockholders. Included among the notes, the data reported for each quarter include sales, gross profit, net income, and earnings per share. **Quarterly data** permit users to analyze such things as the seasonal nature of operations, the impact of diversification on quarterly activity, and whether the firm's activities lead or lag general economic trends.

Note 19 to General Mills' financial statements (see Appendix K) illustrates a disclosure of quarterly data for a two-year period.

SUBSEQUENT EVENTS

If a company issues a large amount of securities or suffers a casualty loss after the balance sheet date, this information should be reported in a note to the readers, even though the situation arose subsequent to the balance sheet date. Firms are responsible for disclosing any significant events that occur between the balance sheet date and the date the financial statements are issued. This guideline recognizes that it takes several weeks for financial statements to be prepared and audited before they are issued. Events occurring during this period that may have a material effect on the firm's operations are certainly of interest to readers and should be disclosed. Other examples of **subsequent events** requiring disclosure are sales of assets, significant changes in long-term debt, and acquisitions of other companies.

For example, Eastman Kodak Company, whose main products include photographic films and cameras, reported the following subsequent event in its 1993 annual report:

> The Company announced on March 2, 1994 that it has elected to redeem the zero coupon convertible subordinated debentures due 2011 on April 1, 1994. The redemption price is $312.14 per debenture. Each debenture may be converted into the Company's common stock at a conversion rate of 6.944 shares per debenture at any time before the close of business on April 1, 1994.

SUPPLEMENTARY INFORMATION

Supplementing the financial statements are several additional disclosures—management's financial discussion and analysis of the statements, selected financial data covering a 5- to 10-year period, and perhaps information on the impact of inflation. These *supplementary* disclosures are either required of certain companies by the SEC or recommended (but not required) by the FASB.

MANAGEMENT'S DISCUSSION AND ANALYSIS

Management may increase the usefulness of financial statements by sharing some of their knowledge about the company's financial condition and operations. This is the purpose of the disclosure devoted to management's discussion and analysis. In this supplement to the financial statements, management identifies and comments on events and trends influencing the firm's liquidity, operating results, and financial resources. Management's closeness to the company not only gives it insights unavailable to outsiders but also may introduce certain biases into the analysis. Nonetheless, management's comments, interpretations, and explanations should contribute to a better understanding of the financial statements.

COMPARATIVE SELECTED FINANCIAL DATA

The analysis of financial performance is enhanced if a firm's financial data for several years are available. By analyzing trends over time, the analyst learns much more about a company than is possible from only a single year's data. Year-to-year changes may give clues as to future growth or may highlight areas for concern. Corporate annual reports to stockholders present complete financial statements in comparative form, showing the current year and one or two preceding years. Beyond this, however, the financial statements are supplemented by a summary of selected key financial statistics for a 5- or 10-year period. The financial data presented in this historical summary usually include sales, net income, dividends, earnings per share, working capital, and total assets.

INFLATION ACCOUNTING

Inflation has an impact on virtually every aspect of economic affairs, including investment decisions, pricing policies, marketing strategies, and salary and wage negotiations. Persons making economic decisions utilize financial data prepared by accountants. Conventional financial statements, however, contain no explicit adjustments for the impact of inflation on the financial data. In response to this, the FASB encourages companies to disclose supplementary information about the effects of changing prices on the firm's financial data.[2]

The U.S. rate of inflation in the 1990s has been low, so financial statement users are not demanding information on the impact of changing prices. Because there is a cost to compiling this type of information, few companies are voluntarily making the supplementary disclosures recommended by the FASB. Should the rate of inflation increase to the point where disclosures are required, the current recommended disclosures will be the likely starting point for the development of the required disclosures.

The preceding catalogue of parenthetical disclosures, notes, and supplementary information demonstrates the breadth and detail of data that accompany a set of financial statements. To some, the vast and increasing array of financial statement disclosures threatens to turn a wealth of information into an information "overload." Whether there is too much information, of course, depends on the needs and financial sophistication of users. Nonetheless, it should be clear that much may be learned by reading these disclosures.

GLOSSARY OF KEY TERMS USED IN THIS CHAPTER AND APPENDIX

accounts receivable turnover Annual net sales divided by average accounts receivable (net) (p. 573).

asset turnover Net income divided by average total assets (p. 570).

average collection period 365 days divided by accounts receivable turnover (p. 574).

commitments A contractual arrangement by which both parties to the contract still have acts to perform (p. 586).

common-size financial statement A financial statement in which each item is presented as a percentage of a key figure (p. 567).

comparative financial statements A form of horizontal analysis involving comparison of two or more periods' financial statements showing dollar and/or percentage changes (p. 563).

contingency A possible future event; significant contingent liabilities must be disclosed in the notes to the financial statements (p. 586).

current ratio A firm's current assets divided by its current liabilities (p. 572).

days' sales in inventory 365 days divided by inventory turnover (p. 575).

debt-to-equity ratio A firm's total liabilities divided by its total owners' equity (p. 575).

dividend payout ratio Annual dividends per share divided by the earnings per share (p. 578).

dividend yield Annual dividends per share divided by the market price per share (p. 578).

earnings per share Net income less preferred stock dividends divided by the weighted average common shares outstanding for the period (p. 577).

gross profit percentage Gross profit on sales divided by net sales (p. 569).

horizontal analysis Analysis of a firm's financial statements that covers two or more years (p. 563).

inventory turnover Cost of goods sold divided by average inventory (p. 574).

operating cash flow to capital expenditures ratio A firm's net cash flow from operating activities divided by its annual capital expenditures (p. 577).

operating cash flow to current liabilities ratio A firm's net cash flow from operating activities divided by its average current liabilities (p. 573).

price-earnings ratio Current market price per common share divided by earnings per share (p. 577).

quarterly data Selected quarterly financial information that is reported in annual reports to stockholders (p. 587).

quick ratio Quick assets (that is, cash and cash equivalents, short-term investments, and current receivables) divided by current liabilities (p. 572).

return on assets Net income divided by average total assets (p. 571).

return on common stockholders' equity Net income less preferred stock dividends divided by average common stockholders' equity (p. 571).

return on sales Net income divided by net sales (p. 570).

segments Subdivisions of a firm for which supplemental financial information is disclosed (p. 587).

subsequent events Events occurring shortly after a fiscal year-end that will be reported as supplemental information to the financial statements of the year just ended (p. 588).

---

[2]*Statement of Financial Accounting Standards No. 89,* "Financial Reporting and Changing Prices" (Stamford, CT: Financial Accounting Standards Board, 1986).

summary of significant accounting policies A financial statement disclosure, usually the initial note to the statements, that identifies the major accounting policies and procedures used by the firm (p. 585).

times interest earned ratio Income before interest expense and income taxes divided by interest expense (p. 576).

trend percentages A comparison of the same financial item over two or more years stated as a percentage of a base-year amount (p. 565).

vertical analysis Analysis of a firm's financial statements that focuses on the statements of a single year (p. 563).

QUESTIONS

16-1 How do horizontal analysis and vertical analysis of financial statements differ?

16-2 "Analysts should focus attention on each item showing a large percentage change from one year to the next." Is this statement correct? Comment.

16-3 What are trend percentages and how are they calculated? What pitfalls must an analyst avoid when preparing trend percentages?

16-4 What are common-size financial statements and how are they used?

16-5 What item is the key figure (that is, 100%) in a common-size income statement? a common-size balance sheet?

16-6 During the past year, Lite Company had net income of $5 million, and Scanlon Company had net income of $8 million. Both companies manufacture electrical components for the building trade. What additional information would you need to compare the profitability of the two companies? Discuss your answer.

16-7 Under what circumstances can return on sales be used to appraise the profitability of a company? Can this ratio be used to compare the profitability of companies from different industries? Explain.

16-8 What is the relationship between asset turnover, return on assets, and return on sales?

16-9 For 1997, Blare Company had a return on sales of 6.5% and an asset turnover of 2.40. What is Blare's 1997 return on assets?

16-10 What does the return on common stockholders' equity measure?

16-11 How does the quick ratio differ from the current ratio?

16-12 For each of the following ratios, is a high ratio or low ratio considered, in general, a positive sign?
   a. Current ratio.
   b. Quick ratio.
   c. Operating cash flow to current liabilities ratio.
   d. Accounts receivable turnover.
   e. Average collection period.
   f. Inventory turnover.
   g. Days' sales in inventory.

16-13 What is the significance of the debt-to-equity ratio and how is it computed?

16-14 Why do we determine the times interest earned ratio and how is it calculated?

16-15 What does the operating cash flow to capital expenditures ratio measure?

16-16 Clair, Inc., earned $4.50 per share of common stock in the current year and paid dividends of $2.34 per share. The most recent market price of the common stock is $46.80 per share. What are its (a) price-earnings ratio, (b) dividend yield, and (c) dividend payout ratio?

16-17 What are two inherent limitations of financial statement data?

PRINCIPLES DISCUSSION QUESTION

16-18 The notes to the financial statements in the 1994 annual report of The Coca-Cola Company state the following:

> Certain amounts in the prior years' financial statements have been reclassified to conform to the current year presentation.

What basic accounting principle is responsible for the reclassification of prior years' data by Coca-Cola? How does this action by Coca-Cola improve the usefulness of its financial data?

EXERCISES

**COMPARATIVE INCOME
STATEMENTS
— OBJ. 1 —**

16-19 Consider the following income statement data from Ross Company for 1996 and 1997.

	1997	1996
Sales	$525,000	$450,000
Cost of Goods Sold	336,000	279,000
Selling Expenses	105,000	99,000
Administrative Expenses	60,000	54,000
Income Tax Expense	7,800	5,400

a. Prepare a comparative income statement, showing increases and decreases in dollars and in percentages.
b. Comment briefly on the changes between the two years.

**COMMON-SIZE INCOME
STATEMENTS
— OBJ. 2 —**

16-20 Refer to the income statement data given in Exercise 16-19.
a. Prepare common-size income statements for each year.
b. Compare the common-size income statements and comment briefly.

**RATIOS ANALYZING
PROFITABILITY
— OBJ. 3 —**

16-21 The following information is available for Buhler Company:

Annual Data	1997	1996
Net sales	$8,600,000	$8,000,000
Gross profit on sales	3,053,000	2,736,000
Net income	567,600	488,000

Year-End Data	**Dec. 31, 1997**	**Dec. 31, 1996**
Total assets	$6,500,000	$6,100,000
Common stockholders' equity	3,800,000	3,200,000

Calculate the following ratios for 1997:
a. Gross profit percentage.
b. Return on sales.
c. Asset turnover.
d. Return on assets.
e. Return on common stockholders' equity (Buhler Company has no preferred stock outstanding).

**WORKING CAPITAL AND
SHORT-TERM LIQUIDITY
RATIOS
— OBJ. 4 —**

16-22 Bell Company has a current ratio of 2.85 (2.85:1) on December 31, 1997. On that date its current assets are as follows:

Cash	$ 26,400
Short-term investments	49,000
Accounts receivable (net)	169,000
Inventory	200,000
Prepaid expenses	11,600
	$456,000

Bell Company's current liabilities at December 31, 1996, were $135,000 and during 1997 its operating activities provided a net cash flow of $50,000.
a. What are the firm's current liabilities on December 31, 1997?
b. What is the firm's working capital on December 31, 1997?
c. What is the quick ratio on December 31, 1997?
d. What is the 1997 operating cash flow to current liabilities ratio?

**RECEIVABLE AND
INVENTORY RATIOS
— OBJ. 4 —**

16-23 Bell Company, whose current assets at December 31, 1997, are shown in Exercise 16-22, had 1997 net sales of $950,000 and cost of goods sold of $552,900. At January 1, 1997, accounts receivable (net) were $155,000 and inventory was $194,000.
a. What is the 1997 accounts receivable turnover?
b. What is the 1997 average collection period?
c. What is the 1997 inventory turnover?
d. What is the 1997 days' sales in inventory?

**RATIOS ANALYZING
LONG-TERM SOLVENCY
— OBJ. 5 —**

16-24 The following information is available for Antler Company:

Annual Data	1996	1995
Interest expense	$ 88,000	$ 82,000
Income tax expense	203,500	185,000
Net income	496,500	395,000
Capital expenditures	320,000	400,000
Net cash provided by operating activities	425,000	390,000

Year-End Data	Dec. 31, 1996	Dec. 31, 1995
Total liabilities	$2,200,000	$1,900,000
Total owners' equity	4,000,000	3,600,000

Calculate the following:
a. 1996 year-end debt-to-equity ratio.
b. 1996 times interest earned ratio.
c. 1996 operating cash flow to capital expenditures ratio.

**RATIOS FOR COMMON STOCK
INVESTORS
— OBJ. 6 —**

16-25 Kluster Corporation has only common stock issued and outstanding. The firm reported earnings per share of $5.10 for 1997. During 1997, Kluster paid dividends of $2.04 per share. On December 31, 1997, the current market price of the stock was $63 per share. Calculate the following:
a. 1997 year-end price-earnings ratio.
b. 1997 dividend yield.
c. 1997 dividend payout ratio.

**FINANCIAL STATEMENT NOTES
— APPENDIX J —**

16-26 Notes to financial statements present information on significant accounting policies, complex or special transactions, details of reported amounts, commitments, contingencies, segments, quarterly data, and subsequent events. Indicate which type of note disclosure is illustrated by each of the following notes.
a. The company has agreed to purchase seven EMB-120 aircraft and related spare parts. The aggregate cost of these aircraft is approximately $35,500,000, subject to a cost escalation provision. The aircraft are scheduled to be delivered over the next two fiscal years.
b. The company has deferred certain costs related to major accounting and information systems enhancements that are anticipated to benefit future years. Upon completion, the related cost is amortized over a period not exceeding five years.
c. The company has guaranteed loans and leases of independent distributors approximating $26,800,000 as of December 31 of the current year.
d. An officer of the company is also a director of a major raw material supplier of the company. The amount of raw material purchases from this supplier approximated $365,000 in the current year.

PROBLEMS

16-27 Net sales, net income, and total asset figures for Vibrant Controls, Inc., for five consecutive years are given below (Vibrant manufactures pollution controls):

**TREND PERCENTAGES
— OBJ. 1 —**

Annual Amounts (Thousands of Dollars)

	1993	1994	1995	1996	1997
Net sales	$71,500	$79,800	$84,250	$88,400	$94,700
Net income	3,200	3,650	3,900	4,160	4,790
Total assets	42,500	45,400	48,700	51,000	54,900

REQUIRED
a. Calculate trend percentages, using 1993 as the base year.
b. Calculate the return on sales for each year. (Rates above 2.8% are considered good for manufacturers of pollution controls; rates above 6.4% are considered very good.)
c. Comment on the results of your analysis.

**CHANGES IN VARIOUS RATIOS
— OBJ. 1, 3, 4, 5 —**

16-28 Selected information follows for Brimmer Company, taken from the 1996 and 1997 financial statements:

	1997	1996
Net sales	$910,000	$840,000
Cost of goods sold	575,000	542,000
Interest expense	20,000	20,000
Income tax expense	27,000	24,000
Net income	61,000	52,000
Net cash flow from operating activities	65,000	55,000
Capital expenditures	42,000	45,000
Accounts receivable (net), December 31	126,000	120,000
Inventory, December 31	196,000	160,000
Common stockholders' equity, December 31	450,000	400,000
Total assets, December 31	730,000	660,000

REQUIRED

a. Calculate the following ratios for 1997. The 1996 results are given for comparative purposes.

	1996
1. Gross profit percentage	35.5%
2. Return on assets	8.3%
3. Return on sales	6.2%
4. Return on common stockholders' equity (no preferred stock was outstanding)	13.9%
5. Accounts receivable turnover	8.00
6. Average collection period	45.6 days
7. Inventory turnover	3.61
8. Times interest earned ratio	4.80
9. Operating cash flow to capital expenditures ratio	1.22

b. Comment on the changes between the two years.

RATIOS FROM COMPARATIVE AND COMMON-SIZE DATA — OBJ. 1, 2, 3, 4, 5 —

16-29 Consider the following financial statements for Waverly Company for 1996 and 1997.

During 1997, management obtained additional bond financing to enlarge its production facilities. The company faced higher production costs during the year for such things as fuel, materials, and freight. Because of temporary government price controls, a planned price increase on products was delayed several months.

As a holder of both common and preferred stock, you analyze the financial statements for 1996 and 1997.

WAVERLY COMPANY
BALANCE SHEETS
(THOUSANDS OF DOLLARS)

Assets	Dec. 31, 1997	Dec. 31, 1996
Cash and Cash Equivalents	$ 18,000	$ 12,000
Accounts Receivable (net)	55,000	43,000
Inventory	120,000	105,000
Prepaid Expenses	20,000	14,000
Plant and Other Assets (net)	471,000	411,000
Total Assets	$684,000	$585,000

Liabilities and Stockholders' Equity	Dec. 31, 1997	Dec. 31, 1996
Current Liabilities	$ 90,000	$ 82,000
10% Bonds Payable	225,000	160,000
9% Preferred Stock, $50 Par Value	75,000	75,000
Common Stock, $10 Par Value	200,000	200,000
Retained Earnings	94,000	68,000
Total Liabilities and Stockholders' Equity	$684,000	$585,000

WAVERLY COMPANY
INCOME STATEMENTS
(THOUSANDS OF DOLLARS)

	1997	1996
Sales	$820,000	$678,000
Cost of Goods Sold	541,200	433,920
Gross Profit on Sales	$278,800	$244,080
Selling and Administrative Expenses	171,400	149,200
Income before Interest Expense and		
Income Taxes	$107,400	$ 94,880
Interest Expense	22,500	16,000
Income before Income Taxes	$ 84,900	$ 78,880
Income Tax Expense	22,900	21,300
Net Income	$ 62,000	$ 57,580
Other Financial Data (thousands of dollars)		
Net Cash Provided by Operating Activities	$ 65,200	$ 60,500
Preferred Dividends	6,750	6,750

REQUIRED

a. Calculate the following for each year: current ratio, quick ratio, operating cash flow to current liabilities ratio (current liabilities were $78,000,000 at December 31, 1995), inventory turnover (inventory was $87,000,000 at December 31, 1995), debt-to-equity ratio, times interest earned ratio, return on assets (total assets were $493,000,000 at December 31, 1995), and return on common stockholders' equity (common stockholders' equity was $236,000,000 at December 31, 1995).

b. Calculate common-size percentages for each year's income statement.

c. Comment on the results of your analysis.

CONSTRUCTING STATEMENTS
FROM RATIO DATA
— OBJ. 3, 4 —

16-30 The following are the 1996 financial statements for Omicron Company, with almost all dollar amounts missing.

OMICRON COMPANY
BALANCE SHEET
DECEMBER 31, 1996

Cash	$?	Current Liabilities	$?
Accounts Receivable (net)	?	8% Bonds Payable	?
Inventory	?	Common Stock	?
Equipment (net)	?	Retained Earnings	900,000
		Total Liabilities and	
Total Assets	$5,900,000	Stockholders' Equity	$5,900,000

OMICRON COMPANY
INCOME STATEMENT
FOR THE YEAR ENDED DECEMBER 31, 1996

Net Sales	$?
Cost of Goods Sold	?
Gross Profit	?
Selling and Administrative Expenses	?
Income before Interest Expense and Income Taxes	?
Interest Expense	80,000
Income before Income Taxes	?
Income Tax Expense (30%)	?
Net Income	$560,000

The following information is available about Omicron Company's 1996 financial statements:

1. Quick ratio, 0.90.

2. Inventory turnover (inventory at January 1, 1996, was $924,000), 5 times.

3. Return on sales, 8.0%.

4. Accounts receivable turnover [accounts receivable (net) at January 1, 1996, were $860,000], 8 times.
5. Gross profit percentage, 32%.
6. Return on common stockholders' equity (common stockholders' equity at January 1, 1996, was $3,300,000), 16%.
7. The interest expense relates to the bonds payable that were outstanding all year.

REQUIRED

Compute the missing amounts, and complete the financial statements of Omicron Company. *Hint:* Complete the income statement first.

RATIOS COMPARED WITH INDUSTRY AVERAGES
— OBJ. 3, 4, 5 —

16-31 Because you own common stock of Phantom Corporation, a paper manufacturer, you are analyzing the firm's performance for the most recent year. The following data are taken from the firm's latest annual report.

	Dec. 31, This Year	Dec. 31, Last Year
Quick Assets	$ 600,000	$ 552,000
Inventory and Prepaid Expenses	372,000	312,000
Other Assets	4,788,000	4,176,000
Total Assets	$5,760,000	$5,040,000
Current Liabilities	$ 624,000	$ 540,000
10% Bonds Payable	1,440,000	1,440,000
8% Preferred Stock, $100 Par Value	480,000	480,000
Common Stock, $10 Par Value	2,700,000	2,160,000
Retained Earnings	516,000	420,000
Total Liabilities and Stockholders' Equity	$5,760,000	$5,040,000

For this year, net sales amount to $11,280,000, net income is $573,600, and preferred dividends declared and paid are $38,400.

REQUIRED

a. Calculate the following for this year:
   1. Return on sales.
   2. Return on assets.
   3. Return on common stockholders' equity.
   4. Quick ratio.
   5. Current ratio.
   6. Debt-to-equity ratio.
b. Trade association statistics and information provided by credit agencies reveal the following data on industry norms:

	Median	Upper Quartile
Return on sales	4.9%	8.6%
Return on assets	6.5%	11.2%
Return on common stockholders' equity	10.6%	17.3%
Quick ratio	1.0	1.8
Current ratio	1.8	3.0
Debt-to-equity ratio	1.08	0.66

Compare Phantom Corporation's performance with industry performance.

RATIOS COMPARED WITH INDUSTRY AVERAGES
— OBJ. 3, 4, 5, 6 —

16-32 Packard Plastics, Inc., manufactures various plastic and synthetic products. Financial statement data for the firm are as follows:

	1997 (Thousands of Dollars, except Earnings per Share)
Net Sales	$815,000
Cost of Goods Sold	540,000
Net Income	50,500
Dividends	14,000
Earnings per Share	4.04

PACKARD PLASTICS, INC.
BALANCE SHEETS
(THOUSANDS OF DOLLARS)

	Dec. 31, 1997	Dec. 31, 1996
Assets		
Cash	$ 4,100	$ 2,700
Accounts Receivable (net)	66,900	60,900
Inventory	148,000	140,000
Total Current Assets	$219,000	$203,600
Plant Assets (net)	215,000	194,000
Other Assets	5,300	3,900
Total Assets	$439,300	$401,500
Liabilities and Stockholders' Equity		
Notes Payable—Banks	$ 31,000	$ 25,000
Accounts Payable	27,600	23,000
Accrued Liabilities	25,100	24,800
Total Current Liabilities	$ 83,700	$ 72,800
10% Bonds Payable	150,000	150,000
Total Liabilities	$233,700	$222,800
Common Stock, $10 Par Value (12,500,000 shares)	$125,000	$125,000
Retained Earnings	80,600	53,700
Total Stockholders' Equity	$205,600	$178,700
Total Liabilities and Stockholders' Equity	$439,300	$401,500

REQUIRED

a. Using the given data, calculate items 1 through 8 below for 1997. Compare the performance of Packard Plastics, Inc., with the following industry averages and comment on its operations.

	Median Ratios for Manufacturers of Plastic and Synthetic Products
1. Quick ratio	1.2
2. Current ratio	1.9
3. Accounts receivable turnover	7.9
4. Inventory turnover	7.8
5. Debt-to-equity ratio	0.95
6. Gross profit percentage	32.7%
7. Return on sales	3.5%
8. Return on assets	6.3%

b. Calculate the dividends paid per share of common stock. What was the dividend payout ratio?

c. If the most recent price per share of common stock is $47.75, what is the price-earnings ratio? The dividend yield?

FINANCIAL STATEMENT NOTES:
QUARTERLY DATA
— APPENDIX J —

16-33 Actual recent quarterly data are presented below for Company A and Company B. One of these companies is Gibson Greetings, Inc., which manufactures and sells greeting cards. The other company is Hon Industries, Inc., which manufactures and sells office furniture. Both companies are on a calendar-year basis.

	(Amounts in Thousands)				
	First Quarter	Second Quarter	Third Quarter	Fourth Quarter	Year
Company A					
Net Sales	$186,111	$177,537	$203,070	$213,608	$780,326
Gross profit	55,457	53,643	64,024	69,374	242,498

Company B

Net sales	$ 84,896	$ 83,796	$142,137	$235,336	$546,165
Gross profit	53,900	52,983	66,018	104,961	277,862

REQUIRED

a. Compute the percent of annual net sales generated each quarter by Company A. Round to the nearest percent.
b. Compute the percent of annual net sales generated each quarter by Company B. Round to the nearest percent.
c. Which company has the most seasonal business? Briefly explain.
d. Which company is Gibson Greetings, Inc.? Hon Industries, Inc.? Briefly explain.
e. Which company's interim quarterly data are probably most useful for predicting annual results? Briefly explain.

ALTERNATE EXERCISES

COMPARATIVE BALANCE SHEET — OBJ. 1 —

16-19A Consider the following balance sheet data for Best Buy Co., Inc., an electronics and major appliance retailer, at February 26, 1994, and February 27, 1993 (amounts in thousands):

	Feb. 26, 1994	Feb. 27, 1993
Cash and Cash Equivalents	$ 59,872	$ 7,138
Receivables	52,944	37,968
Merchandise Inventories	637,950	249,991
Other Current Assets	13,844	9,829
Current Assets	$764,610	$304,926
Property and Equipment (net)	172,724	126,442
Other Assets	15,160	7,774
Total Assets	$952,494	$439,142
Current Liabilities	$402,028	$186,005
Long-Term Liabilities	239,022	70,854
Total Liabilities	$641,050	$256,859
Common Stock	$ 2,087	$ 1,149
Additional Paid-in Capital	224,089	137,151
Retained Earnings	85,268	43,983
Total Stockholders' Equity	$311,444	$182,283
Total Liabilities and Stockholders' Equity	$952,494	$439,142

a. Prepare a comparative balance sheet, showing increases in dollars and percentages.
b. Comment briefly on the changes between the two years.

COMMON-SIZE BALANCE SHEETS — OBJ. 2 —

16-20A Refer to the balance sheet data given in Exercise 16-19A.
a. Prepare common-size balance sheets for each year (use total assets as the base amount for computing percentages).
b. Compare the common-size balance sheets and comment briefly.

RATIOS ANALYZING PROFITABILITY — OBJ. 3 —

16-21A The following information is available for Crest Company:

Annual Data	1997	1996
Net sales	$6,400,000	$6,000,000
Cost of goods sold	4,006,400	3,720,000
Net income	307,200	264,000

Year-End Data	Dec. 31, 1997	Dec. 31, 1996
Total assets	$2,850,000	$2,360,000
Common stockholders' equity	1,900,000	1,800,000

Calculate the following ratios for 1997:
a. Gross profit percentage.
b. Return on sales.

     c. Asset turnover.

     d. Return on assets.

     e. Return on common stockholders' equity (Crest Company declared and paid preferred dividends of $25,000 in 1997).

WORKING CAPITAL AND SHORT-TERM LIQUIDITY RATIOS
— OBJ. 4 —

16-22A Favor Company has a current ratio of 2.08 (2.08:1) on December 31, 1996. On that date its current assets are as follows:

Cash and cash equivalents	$ 28,000
Short-term investments	87,000
Accounts receivable (net)	125,000
Inventory	178,500
Prepaid expenses	9,980
	$428,480

Favor Company's current liabilities at December 31, 1995, were $192,000 and during 1996 its operating activities provided a net cash flow of $33,830.

a. What are the firm's current liabilities on December 31, 1996?

b. What is the firm's working capital on December 31, 1996?

c. What is the quick ratio on December 31, 1996?

d. What is the 1996 operating cash flow to current liabilities ratio?

RECEIVABLE AND INVENTORY RATIOS
— OBJ. 4 —

16-23A Favor Company, whose current assets at December 31, 1996, are shown in Exercise 16-22A, had 1996 net sales of $522,750 and cost of goods sold of $345,900. At January 1, 1996, accounts receivable (net) were $121,000 and inventory was $165,700.

a. What is the 1996 accounts receivable turnover?

b. What is the 1996 average collection period?

c. What is the 1996 inventory turnover?

d. What is the 1996 days' sales in inventory?

RATIOS ANALYZING LONG-TERM SOLVENCY
— OBJ. 5 —

16-24A The following information is available for Percy Company:

Annual Data	1996	1995
Interest expense	$ 175,000	$ 166,000
Income tax expense	126,000	117,000
Net income	294,000	273,000
Capital expenditures	440,000	350,000
Net cash provided by operating activities	247,000	223,000

Year-End Data	Dec. 31, 1996	Dec. 31, 1995
Total liabilities	$3,300,000	$2,900,000
Total owners' equity	2,200,000	1,900,000

Calculate the following:

a. 1996 year-end debt-to-equity ratio.

b. 1996 times interest earned ratio.

c. 1996 operating cash flow to capital expenditures ratio.

RATIOS FOR COMMON STOCK INVESTORS
— OBJ. 6 —

16-25A Henshue Corporation has only common stock issued and outstanding. The firm reported earnings per share of $1.80 for 1997. During 1997, Henshue paid dividends of $0.81 per share. On December 31, 1997, the current market price of the stock was $35.15 per share. Calculate the following:

a. 1997 year-end price-earnings ratio.

b. 1997 dividend yield.

c. 1997 dividend payout ratio.

FINANCIAL STATEMENT NOTES
— APPENDIX J —

16-26A Notes to financial statements present information on significant accounting policies, complex or special transactions, details of reported amounts, commitments, contingencies, segments, quarterly data, and subsequent events. Indicate which type of note disclosure is illustrated by each of the following notes.

a. Sales by the Farm and Equipment segment to independent dealers are recorded at the time of shipment to those dealers. Sales through company-owned retail stores are recorded at the time of sale to retail customers.

b. Members of the board of directors, the advisory board, and employees are not charged the vendor's commission on property sold at auction for their benefit. (From the notes of an auctioneer company.)

c. Sales to an airline company accounted for approximately 43% of the company's net sales in the current year.

d. The company's product liability insurance coverage with respect to insured events occurring after January 1 of the current year is substantially less than the amount of that insurance available in the recent past. The company is now predominantly self-insured in this area. The reduction in insurance coverage reflects trends in the liability insurance field generally and is not unique to the company.

ALTERNATE PROBLEMS

**TREND PERCENTAGES
— OBJ. 1 —**

16-27A Sales of automotive products for Ford Motor Company and General Motors Corporation for the five years 1989–1993 follow:

	Sales of Automotive Products (Millions of Dollars)				
	1989	**1990**	**1991**	**1992**	**1993**
Ford Motor Company	$82,879	$81,844	$72,051	$ 84,407	$ 91,568
General Motors Corporation	99,106	97,312	94,828	103,005	108,027

Net sales for Pfizer Inc and Abbott Laboratories for the five years 1989–1993 follow:

	Net Sales (Millions of Dollars)				
	1989	**1990**	**1991**	**1992**	**1993**
Pfizer Inc	$5,672	$6,406	$6,950	$7,230	$7,478
Abbott Laboratories	5,380	6,159	6,877	7,852	8,408

REQUIRED

a. Calculate trend percentages for all four companies, using 1989 as the base year.
b. Comment on the trend percentages of Ford Motor Company and General Motors Corporation.
c. Comment on the trend percentages of Pfizer Inc and Abbot Laboratories.

**CHANGES IN VARIOUS RATIOS
— OBJ. 1, 3, 4, 5 —**

16-28A Selected information follows for Cycle Company, taken from the 1996 and 1997 financial statements:

	1997	1996
Net sales	$675,000	$520,000
Cost of goods sold	407,700	310,000
Interest expense	18,000	14,000
Income tax expense	6,200	5,100
Net income	24,600	20,300
Net cash flow from operating activities	29,500	26,500
Capital expenditures	40,000	25,000
Accounts receivable (net), December 31	182,000	128,000
Inventory, December 31	225,000	180,000
Common stockholders' equity, December 31	205,000	165,000
Total assets, December 31	460,000	350,000

REQUIRED

a. Calculate the following ratios for 1997. The 1996 results are given for comparative purposes.

	1996
1. Gross profit percentage	40.4%
2. Return on assets	6.3%
3. Return on sales	3.9%
4. Return on common stockholders' equity (no preferred stock was outstanding)	14.0%
5. Accounts receivable turnover	4.77
6. Average collection period	76.5 days
7. Inventory turnover	2.07
8. Times interest earned ratio	2.81
9. Operating cash flow to capital expenditures ratio	1.06

b. Comment on the changes between the two years.

RATIOS FROM COMPARATIVE AND COMMON-SIZE DATA — OBJ. 1, 2, 3, 4, 5 —

16-29A Consider the following financial statements for Vega Company for 1996 and 1997.

During 1997, management obtained additional bond financing to enlarge its production facilities. The plant addition produced a new high-margin product, which is supposed to improve the average rate of gross profit and return on sales.

As a potential investor, you analyze the financial statements for 1996 and 1997.

VEGA COMPANY
BALANCE SHEETS
(THOUSANDS OF DOLLARS)

Assets	Dec. 31, 1997	Dec. 31, 1996
Cash	$ 21,000	$ 16,100
Accounts Receivable (net)	39,000	21,400
Inventory	105,000	72,000
Prepaid Expenses	1,500	3,000
Plant and Other Assets (net)	463,500	427,500
Total Assets	$630,000	$540,000

Liabilities and Stockholders' Equity		
Current Liabilities	$ 76,000	$ 45,000
9% Bonds Payable	187,500	150,000
8% Preferred Stock, $50 Par Value	60,000	60,000
Common Stock, $10 Par Value	225,000	225,000
Retained Earnings	81,500	60,000
Total Liabilities and Stockholders' Equity	$630,000	$540,000

VEGA COMPANY
INCOME STATEMENTS
(THOUSANDS OF DOLLARS)

	1997	1996
Sales	$840,000	$697,500
Cost of Goods Sold	552,000	474,000
Gross Profit on Sales	$288,000	$223,500
Selling and Administrative Expenses	231,000	174,000
Income before Interest Expense and Income Taxes	$ 57,000	$ 49,500
Interest Expense	16,800	13,500
Income before Income Taxes	$ 40,200	$ 36,000
Income Tax Expense	14,100	12,600
Net Income	$ 26,100	$ 23,400
Other Financial Data (thousands of dollars)		
Net Cash Provided by Operating Activities	$ 30,000	$ 25,000
Preferred Dividends	4,800	4,800

REQUIRED

a. Calculate the following for each year: current ratio, quick ratio, operating cash flow to current liabilities ratio (current liabilities were $42 million at December 31, 1995), inventory turnover (inventory was $68 million at December 31, 1995), debt-to-equity ratio, times interest earned ratio, return on assets (total assets were $472 million at December 31, 1995), and return on common stockholders' equity (common stockholders' equity was $266 million at December 31, 1995).

b. Calculate common-size percentages for each year's income statement.

c. Comment on the results of your analysis.

CONSTRUCTING STATEMENTS FROM RATIO DATA — OBJ. 3, 4 —

16-30A The following are the 1996 financial statements for Timber Company, with almost all dollar amounts missing.

TIMBER COMPANY
BALANCE SHEET
DECEMBER 31, 1996

Cash	$?	Current Liabilities	$?
Accounts Receivable (net)	?	10% Bonds Payable	144,000
Inventory	?	Common Stock	?
Equipment (net)	?	Retained Earnings	48,000
		Total Liabilities and	
Total Assets	$576,000	Stockholders' Equity	$576,000

TIMBER COMPANY
INCOME STATEMENT
FOR THE YEAR ENDED DECEMBER 31, 1996

Net Sales	$?
Cost of Goods Sold	?
Gross Profit on Sales	?
Selling and Administrative Expenses	?
Income before Interest Expense and Income Taxes	?
Interest Expense	?
Income before Income Taxes	?
Income Tax Expense (35%)	?
Net Income	$ 70,200

The following information is available about Timber Company's 1996 financial statements:
1. Quick ratio, 1.65.
2. Current ratio, 3.15.
3. Return on sales, 7.5%.
4. Return on common stockholders' equity (common stockholders' equity at January 1, 1996, was $342,000), 20%.
5. Gross profit percentage, 30%.
6. Accounts receivable turnover [accounts receivable (net) at January 1, 1996, were $97,200], 10 times.
7. The interest expense relates to the bonds payable that were outstanding all year.

REQUIRED
Compute the missing amounts, and complete the financial statements of Timber Company.

**RATIOS COMPARED WITH
INDUSTRY AVERAGES
— OBJ. 3, 4, 5 —**

16-31A You are analyzing the performance of Lumite Corporation, a manufacturer of personal care products, for the most recent year. The following data are taken from the firm's latest annual report.

	Dec. 31, This Year	Dec. 31, Last Year
Quick Assets	$ 290,000	$ 250,000
Inventory and Prepaid Expenses	945,000	820,000
Other Assets	4,165,000	3,700,000
Total Assets	$5,400,000	$4,770,000
Current Liabilities	$ 500,000	$ 400,000
10% Bonds Payable	1,300,000	1,300,000
7% Preferred Stock	900,000	900,000
Common Stock, $5 Par Value	1,900,000	1,800,000
Retained Earnings	800,000	370,000
Total Liabilities and Stockholders' Equity	$5,400,000	$4,770,000

For this year, net sales amount to $8,600,000, net income is $675,000, and preferred dividends declared and paid are $63,000.

REQUIRED
a. Calculate the following for this year:
   1. Return on sales.
   2. Return on assets.

3. Return on common stockholders' equity.
4. Quick ratio.
5. Current ratio.
6. Debt-to-equity ratio.

b. Trade association statistics and information provided by credit agencies reveal the following data on industry norms:

	Median	Upper Quartile
Return on sales	3.7%	10.6%
Return on assets	5.8%	14.2%
Return on common stockholders' equity	18.5%	34.2%
Quick ratio	1.0	1.8
Current ratio	2.2	3.7
Debt-to-equity ratio	1.07	0.37

Compare Lumite Corporation's performance with industry performance.

RATIOS COMPARED WITH INDUSTRY AVERAGES — OBJ. 3, 4, 5, 6 —

16-32A Avery Instruments, Inc., is a manufacturer of various measuring and controlling instruments. Financial statement data for the firm are as follows:

	1997 (Thousands of Dollars, except Earnings per Share)
Net Sales	$210,000
Cost of Goods Sold	125,000
Net Income	8,300
Dividends	2,600
Earnings per Share	4.15

AVERY INSTRUMENTS, INC.
BALANCE SHEETS
(THOUSANDS OF DOLLARS)

Assets	Dec. 31, 1997	Dec. 31, 1996
Cash	$ 18,300	$ 18,000
Accounts Receivable (net)	46,000	41,000
Inventory	39,500	43,700
Total Current Assets	$103,800	$102,700
Plant Assets (net)	52,600	50,500
Other Assets	15,600	13,800
Total Assets	$172,000	$167,000

Liabilities and Stockholders' Equity		
Notes Payable—Banks	$ 6,000	$ 6,000
Accounts Payable	22,500	18,700
Accrued Liabilities	16,500	21,000
Total Current Liabilities	$ 45,000	$ 45,700
9% Bonds Payable	40,000	40,000
Total Liabilities	$ 85,000	$ 85,700
Common Stock, $25 Par Value (2,000,000 shares)	$ 50,000	$ 50,000
Retained Earnings	37,000	31,300
Total Stockholders' Equity	$ 87,000	$ 81,300
Total Liabilities and Stockholders' Equity	$172,000	$167,000

REQUIRED

a. Using the given data, calculate items 1 through 8 on the next page for 1997. Compare the performance of Avery Instruments, Inc., with the following industry averages and comment on its operations.

	Median Ratios for Manufacturers of Measuring and Controlling Instruments
1. Quick ratio	1.3
2. Current ratio	2.4
3. Accounts receivable turnover	5.9 times
4. Inventory turnover	3.5 times
5. Debt-to-equity ratio	0.73
6. Gross profit percentage	42.8%
7. Return on sales	4.5%
8. Return on assets	7.6%

b. Calculate the dividends paid per share of common stock. What was the dividend payout ratio?

c. If the most recent price per share of common stock is $62.25, what is the price-earnings ratio? The dividend yield?

FINANCIAL STATEMENT NOTES: QUARTERLY DATA — APPENDIX J —

16-33A Actual recent quarterly data are presented below for Company C and Company D. One of these companies is Toys "R" Us, a children's specialty retail chain. The company's fiscal year ends on the Saturday nearest to January 31. The other company is The Gillette Company. Gillette manufactures and sells blades, razors, and toiletries. Gillette is on a calendar-year basis.

	(Amounts in Millions)				
	First Quarter	Second Quarter	Third Quarter	Fourth Quarter	Year
Company C					
Net sales	$1,216.6	$1,237.3	$1,339.7	$1,617.2	$5,410.8
Gross profit	753.1	773.6	839.0	1,000.8	3,366.5
Company D					
Net sales	$1,172.5	$1,249.1	$1,345.8	$3,401.8	$7,169.2
Gross profit	362.5	384.6	423.2	1,030.3	2,200.6

REQUIRED

a. Compute the percentage of annual net sales generated each quarter by Company C. Round to the nearest percent.

b. Compute the percentage of annual net sales generated each quarter by Company D. Round to the nearest percent.

c. Which company has the most seasonal business? Briefly explain.

d. Which company is Toys "R" Us? The Gillette Company? Briefly explain.

CASES

BUSINESS DECISION CASE

Crescent Paints, Inc., a paint manufacturer, has been in business five years. The company has had modest profits and has experienced few operating difficulties until this year (1997), when president Alice Becknell discusses her company's working capital problems with you, a loan officer at Granite Bank. Becknell explains that expanding her firm has created difficulties in meeting obligations when they come due and in taking advantage of cash discounts offered by manufacturers for timely payment. She would like to borrow $50,000 from Granite Bank. At your request, Becknell submits the following financial data for the past two years:

	1996	1995
Net sales	$2,000,000	$1,750,000
Cost of goods sold	1,320,000	1,170,000
Net income	42,000	33,600
Dividends	22,000	18,000
December 31, 1994, data		
Total assets		$1,100,000
Accounts receivable (net)		205,000
Inventory		350,000

CRESCENT PAINTS, INC.
BALANCE SHEETS

	Dec. 31, 1996	Dec. 31, 1995
Assets		
Cash	$ 31,000	$ 50,000
Accounts Receivable (net)	345,000	250,000
Inventory	525,000	425,000
Prepaid Expenses	11,000	6,000
Total Current Assets	$ 912,000	$ 731,000
Plant Assets (net)	483,000	444,000
Total Assets	$1,395,000	$1,175,000
Liabilities and Stockholders' Equity		
Notes Payable—Banks	$ 100,000	$ 35,000
Accounts Payable	244,000	190,000
Accrued Liabilities	96,000	85,000
Total Current Liabilities	$ 440,000	$ 310,000
10% Mortgage Payable	190,000	250,000
Total Liabilities	$ 630,000	$ 560,000
Common Stock	$ 665,000	$ 535,000
Retained Earnings	100,000	80,000
Total Stockholders' Equity	$ 765,000	$ 615,000
Total Liabilities and Stockholders' Equity	$1,395,000	$1,175,000

You calculate the following items for both years from the given data and compare them with the median ratios for paint manufacturers provided by a commercial credit firm:

	Median Ratios for Paint Manufacturers
1. Current ratio	2.5
2. Quick ratio	1.3
3. Accounts receivable turnover	8.1
4. Average collection period	44.9 days
5. Inventory turnover	4.9
6. Debt-to-equity ratio	0.78
7. Return on assets	4.8%
8. Return on sales	2.4%

REQUIRED

Based on your analysis, decide whether and under what circumstances you would grant Becknell's request for a loan. Explain the reasons for your decision.

ETHICS CASE   Chris Nelson, new assistant controller for Grand Company, is preparing for the firm's year-end closing procedures. On December 30, 1996, a memorandum from the controller directed Nelson to make a journal entry debiting Cash and crediting Long-Term Advances to Officers for $1,000,000. Not finding the $1,000,000 in the cash deposit prepared for the bank that day, Nelson went to the controller for a further explanation. In response, the controller took from her desk drawer a check for $1,000,000 payable to Grand Company from Jason Grand, chief executive officer of the firm. Attached to the check was a note from Jason Grand saying that if this check were not needed to return it to him next week.

"This check is paying off a $1,000,000 advance the firm made to Jason Grand six years ago," stated the controller. "Mr. Grand has done this every year since the advance; each time we have returned the check to him in January of the following year. We plan to do so again this time. In fact, when Mr. Grand retires in four years, I expect the board of directors will forgive this advance. However, if the firm really needed the cash, we would deposit the check."

"Then why go through this charade each year?" inquired Nelson.

"It dresses up our year-end balance sheet," replied the controller. "Certain financial statement ratios are improved significantly. Further, the notes to the financial statements don't have to reveal a related-party loan. Lots of firms engage in year-end transactions designed to dress up their financial statements."

REQUIRED

a. What financial statement ratios are improved by making the journal entry contained in the controller's memorandum?

b. Is the year-end handling of Jason Grand's advance an ethical practice? Discuss.

GENERAL MILLS ANNUAL REPORT CASE

Refer to the actual financial statements of General Mills, Inc., for fiscal years 1993 and 1994 presented in Appendix K at the end of the textbook. General Mills is headquartered in Minneapolis, Minnesota. About 65% of its 1993 and 1994 sales were in consumer foods, with the remaining sales in restaurant operations. The firm has about 27% of the U.S. cereal market. Some of its major brands are Cheerios, Wheaties, Yoplait, Betty Crocker, and Gold Medal. Restaurants operated include The Olive Garden and Red Lobster chains.

REQUIRED

a. For both fiscal years (1993 and 1994), compute (or identify) the following financial ratios:

1. Gross profit percentage.
2. Return on sales.
3. Asset turnover.
4. Return on assets.
5. Return on common stockholders' equity.
6. Current ratio.
7. Quick ratio.
8. Operating cash flow to current liabilities ratio (May 31, 1992, current liabilities = $1,371.7 million).
9. Accounts receivable turnover (May 31, 1992, accounts receivable = $291.9 million).
10. Average collection period.
11. Inventory turnover (May 31, 1992, inventory = $487.2 million).
12. Days' sales in inventory.
13. Debt-to-equity ratio (include Common Stock Subject to Put Options in total liabilities).
14. Times interest earned ratio.
15. Operating cash flow to capital expenditures ratio.
16. Earnings per share.
17. Price-earnings ratio. (Use the high stock price in the fourth quarter each year.)
18. Dividend yield.
19. Dividend payout ratio.

b. Comment briefly on the changes from fiscal 1993 to fiscal 1994 in the ratios computed above.

K

Financial Statements and Related Disclosures from the 1994 Annual Report of General Mills, Inc.

The financial statements and related disclosures from the 1994 annual report of General Mills, Inc. are presented in this appendix. General Mills is headquartered in Minneapolis, Minnesota. During 1993 and 1994, General Mills' primary lines of business were consumer foods and restaurants; about 65% of its sales were in consumer foods with the remaining 35% coming from its restaurants. Some of its major consumer food brands during this period were Cheerios, Wheaties, Yoplait, Betty Crocker, and Gold Medal. Its major restaurant chains were The Olive Garden and Red Lobster.

The information presented consists of management's discussion of results of operations and financial condition, the report of management responsibilities, the report of the audit committee, the independent auditor's report, the consolidated financial statements, the notes to the consolidated financial statements, and selected financial data and other statistics for an eleven-year period.

MANAGEMENT DISCUSSION OF RESULTS OF OPERATIONS AND FINANCIAL CONDITION

General Mills' financial goal is to achieve performance that places us in the top 10 percent of major American companies, ranked by the combination of growth in earnings per share and return on capital. Over the past five years, our earnings per share have grown at a 13 percent compound rate and our after-tax return on capital has averaged 21 percent, both before unusual items. Meeting our financial objectives is the key to providing superior returns to shareholders.

Results of Operations

In 1994, sales rose 5 percent to $8.52 billion. Earnings per share from continuing operations were $2.95 compared to $3.10 in 1993. After-tax earnings were $469.7 million compared to $506.1 million a year ago. Results for 1994 include an unusual after-tax charge of $87.1 million, or 55 cents per share, to cover estimated costs associated with the actions of an independent licensed contractor who made an improper pesticide substitution in treating some of our oat supplies. See note two to the consolidated financial statements for further discussion. We voluntarily suspended production and shipments of oat-containing products for a period of time during the first quarter of 1995 while resolving this issue; therefore, there will be a negative impact on 1995 first-quarter volume and earnings. There was an unusual net after-tax charge in 1993 of $57.3 million, or 35 cents per share, primarily for restructuring actions at consumer foods manufacturing facilities as well as selected restaurant unit closings.

Segment operating results are summarized in note eighteen to the consolidated financial statements on page 32.

Consumer Foods' sales grew 3 percent in 1994 to $5.55 billion with domestic packaged foods unit volume increasing 3 percent. Operating profits decreased 1 percent excluding unusual items from both years. In 1994, there was an unusual charge of $146.9 million related to the improper pesticide application as noted above. Included in operating profits for 1993 were unusual items totaling $33.4 million for increasing manufacturing productivity, and our share of streamlining and tax-reorganization costs associated with the formation of Snack Ventures Europe (SVE), our joint venture with PepsiCo Foods International. Including the unusual items, operating profits for 1994 decreased to $653.1 million.

Big G's 1994 operating profit decline reflected the year-long cereal market promotional escalation and the fourth-quarter impact of our pricing and promotional actions. In a departure from recent cereal industry practices, the Company announced actions in April 1994 to reduce spending on inefficient cereal couponing and price promotion, and to reduce prices on our largest cereal brands by an average of 11 percent. These actions were designed to deliver consumer value more directly and efficiently, and are anticipated to have positive profit impact in 1995, but are expected to be volume and market share neutral.

Yoplait yogurt, Betty Crocker Products, Gorton's seafood and Canada Foods posted double-digit operating profit gains for the year. SVE showed an excellent increase in operating profits and volume, and expanded beyond its original six European markets to Italy.

CPW, our cereal joint venture with Nestlé, continued to demonstrate progress in existing markets and expanded operations to Belgium, Switzerland, Austria, Greece and Chile during the year. Consumer Foods' operating profits include a loss of $30.3 million in 1994 and $30.6 million in 1993 for General Mills' share of CPW's losses. The developmental spending burden for CPW is expected to moderate as initial operations in European markets approach profitability in 1995.

In 1993, Consumer Foods' sales and operating profits grew 3 percent and 11 percent (excluding unusual items), respectively, led by Betty Crocker Products, Big G cereals, Yoplait yogurt, Foodservice, Gorton's seafood and Canada Foods.

Restaurants' sales grew 8 percent in 1994 to $2.96 billion. An operating profit gain of 3 percent before unusual items in the prior year was achieved despite disappointing results at The Olive Garden and the effects of unprecedented harsh winter weather. A net total of 115 new restaurants were opened in North America. Red Lobster's profits increased strongly as new menu items, improved service and a new decor package favorably influenced results. The Olive Garden's profits were lower, due to a decline in average unit sales that resulted primarily from not updating the successful concept soon enough to meet changing consumer expectations. China Coast commenced broader market expansion in 1994. Twenty new units were opened during the year with plans calling for faster expansion during 1995. Including the unusual items for last year, operating profits increased 21 percent.

In 1993, Restaurants' sales and operating profits before unusual items increased 8 percent and 11 percent, respectively. Results reflected good gains by The Olive Garden and good overall performance by Red Lobster. Together, The Olive Garden and Red Lobster added 112 new units in North America. Results for Canadian restaurants improved versus the prior year, but still trailed expectations. A charge of $30.6 million was recorded in 1993 for closing 31 Red Lobster and The Olive Garden units in the United States and Canada. Including the charge, operating profits decreased 5 percent.

Interest expense in 1994 was $115.6 million, an increase of $27.3 million from the prior year due to borrowing to fund purchases of common shares for treasury. The 1993 interest expense of $88.3 million was $12.4 million greater than 1992 primarily due to funding purchases of common shares for treasury. Interest income of $14.7 million in 1993 was $3.0 million less than the prior year reflecting lower rates.

The effective tax rates in 1994 and 1993 were 37.6 percent and 40.0 percent, respectively. Excluding the unusual items in both years, the rates were 38.1 percent and 38.2 percent in 1994 and 1993, respectively. The federal tax law changes in 1993 did not have a significant impact on 1994, but are expected to have a slight negative impact in the future.

It is management's view that changes in the rate of inflation have not had a significant effect on profitability from continuing operations over the three most recent years. Management attempts to minimize the effects of inflation through appropriate planning and operating practices.

The Financial Accounting Standards Board issued Statement of Financial Accounting Standards No. 115, "Accounting for Certain Investments in Debt and Equity Securities," in May 1993. The American Institute of Certified Public Accountants issued Statement of Position 93-7, "Reporting on Advertising Costs," in December 1993. Neither of these statements will have a significant impact on the Company when adopted.

Financial Condition

The Company intends to manage its businesses and financial ratios so as to maintain a strong "A" bond rating, which allows access to financing at reasonable costs. Currently, General Mills' publicly issued long-term debt carries "A1" (Moody's Investors Services, Inc.) and "A+" (Standard & Poor's Corporation) ratings. Our commercial paper has ratings of "P-1" (Moody's) and "A-1" (Standard & Poor's) in the United States and "R-1 (middle)" in Canada from Dominion Bond Rating Service.

General Mills' financial condition remains strong. As important measures of financial strength, the Company focuses on the cash flow to debt and fixed charge coverage ratios, which were 46 percent and 6.2 times, respectively, in 1994. The purchase of 2.4 million shares of common stock for our treasury increased debt and reduced equity by $145.7 million, contributing to a debt to capital ratio of 65 percent.

The composition of the Company's capital structure is shown in the accompanying table.

Capital Structure

In Millions	May 29, 1994	May 30, 1993
Notes payable	$ 433.3	$ 339.6
Current portion of long-term debt	115.2	64.3
Long-term debt	1,417.2	1,268.3
Deferred income taxes - tax leases	189.8	195.6
Total debt	2,155.5	1,867.8
Debt adjustments:		
Leases - debt equivalent	434.4	428.8
Domestic cash equivalents	-	(109.4)
Marketable investments	(196.1)	(137.0)
Adjusted debt	2,393.8	2,050.2
Common stock subject to put options	122.0	-
Stockholders' equity	1,151.2	1,218.5
Total capital	$3,667.0	$3,268.7

We selectively use derivatives to hedge financial risks, primarily interest rate volatility and foreign currency fluctuations. The derivatives are generally treated as hedges for accounting purposes. We manage our debt structure through both issuance of fixed and floating-rate debt as well as the use of derivatives. The debt equivalent of our leases and deferred income taxes related to tax leases are both fixed-rate obligations. The table below, when reviewed in conjunction with the capital structure table, shows the composition of our debt structure including the impact of derivatives.

Debt Structure

In Millions	May 29, 1994		May 30, 1993	
Floating-rate debt	$ 733.4	31%	$ 534.9	26%
Fixed-rate debt	1,036.2	43	890.9	43
Leases - debt equivalent	434.4	18	428.8	21
Deferred income taxes - tax leases	189.8	8	195.6	10
Total debt	$2,393.8	100%	$2,050.2	100%

Commercial paper has historically been our primary source of short-term financing. Bank credit lines are maintained to ensure availability of short-term funds on an as-needed basis. In June 1994, our fee-paid credit lines were increased from $500.0 million to $650.0 million.

Our shelf registration statement permits issuance of up to $222.1 million net proceeds in unsecured debt securities. The shelf registration authorizes a medium-term note program that provides additional flexibility in accessing the debt markets.

Sources and uses of cash in the past three years are shown in the accompanying table. Operations generated $29.2 million less cash in 1994 than in the previous year primarily due to an increase in inventory levels. We purchased various marketable investments to take advantage of interest rate spreads.

Capital expenditures in 1995 are estimated to be approximately $525 million; an additional $50 million capital investment is anticipated for our joint ventures, principally CPW. In July 1994, the Company purchased 976,000 shares of common stock for $56.4 million as privately placed put options were exercised. The unusual item recorded in 1994 will be substantially included in 1995 as cash outflow. As a result, the Company is anticipating a net cash outflow in 1995 and will borrow either short- or long-term, depending on market conditions.

Cash Sources (Uses)

In Millions	1994	1993	1992
From operations	$ 830.7	$ 859.9	$ 771.6
Fixed assets and other investments-net	(732.1)	(714.4)	(725.7)
From dispositions of businesses	-	-	77.7
Change in marketable investments	(50.1)	(69.7)	-
Increase in outstanding debt-net	287.7	585.7	91.0
Common stock issued	13.3	32.3	39.3
Treasury stock purchases	(145.7)	(420.2)	(40.1)
Dividends paid	(299.4)	(274.8)	(245.2)
Other	(4.2)	(7.4)	(7.9)
Decrease in cash and cash equivalents	$ (99.8)	$ (8.6)	$ (39.3)

REPORT OF MANAGEMENT RESPONSIBILITIES

The management of General Mills, Inc. is responsible for the fairness and accuracy of the consolidated financial statements. The consolidated financial statements have been prepared in accordance with generally accepted accounting principles, using management's best estimates and judgments where appropriate. The financial information throughout this report is consistent with our consolidated financial statements.

Management has established a system of internal controls that provides reasonable assurance that assets are adequately safeguarded, and transactions are recorded accurately, in all material respects, in accordance with management's authorization. We maintain a strong audit program that independently evaluates the adequacy and effectiveness of internal controls. Our internal controls provide for appropriate separation of duties and responsibilities, and there are documented policies regarding utilization of Company assets and proper financial reporting. These formally stated and regularly communicated policies demand high ethical conduct from all employees.

The Audit Committee of the Board of Directors meets regularly to determine that management, internal auditors and independent auditors are properly discharging their duties regarding internal control and financial reporting. The independent auditors, internal auditors and employees have full and free access to the Audit Committee at any time.

KPMG Peat Marwick, independent certified public accountants, are retained to audit the consolidated financial statements. Their report follows.

H. B. Atwater, Jr.
Chairman of the Board and Chief Executive Officer

S. W. Sanger
President

M. H. Willes
Vice Chairman

REPORT OF THE AUDIT COMMITTEE

The Audit Committee of the Board of Directors is composed of six outside directors. Its primary function is to oversee the Company's system of internal controls, financial reporting practices and audits to ensure their quality, integrity and objectivity are sufficient to protect stockholder assets.

The Audit Committee met twice during 1994 to review the overall audit scope, plans and results of the internal auditor and independent auditor, the Company's internal controls, emerging accounting issues, officer and director expenses, audit fees, goodwill and other intangible values, and the audits of the pension plans. The Committee also met separately without management present and with the independent auditors to discuss the audit. Acting with the other Board members, the Committee reviewed the Company's annual financial state-ments and approved them before issuance. Audit Committee meeting results were reported to the full Board of Directors. The Audit Committee recommended to the Board that KPMG Peat Marwick be reappointed for 1995, subject to the approval of stockholders at the annual meeting.

The Audit Committee is satisfied that the internal control system is adequate and that the stockholders of General Mills are protected by appropriate accounting and auditing procedures.

M. D. Rose
Chairman, Audit Committee

INDEPENDENT AUDITORS' REPORT

The Stockholders and the Board of Directors
of General Mills, Inc.:

We have audited the accompanying consolidated balance sheets of General Mills, Inc. and subsidiaries as of May 29, 1994 and May 30, 1993, and the related consolidated statements of earnings and cash flows for each of the fiscal years in the three-year period ended May 29, 1994. These consolidated financial statements are the responsibility of the Company's management. Our responsibility is to express an opinion on these consolidated financial statements based on our audits.

We conducted our audits in accordance with generally accepted auditing standards. Those standards require that we plan and perform the audit to obtain reasonable assurance about whether the financial statements are free of material misstatement. An audit includes examining, on a test basis, evidence supporting the amounts and disclosures in the financial statements. An audit also includes assessing the accounting principles used and significant estimates made by management, as well as evaluating the overall financial statement presentation. We believe that our audits provide a reasonable basis for our opinion.

In our opinion, the consolidated financial statements referred to above present fairly, in all material respects, the financial position of General Mills, Inc. and subsidiaries as of May 29, 1994 and May 30, 1993, and the results of their operations and their cash flows for each of the fiscal years in the three-year period ended May 29, 1994 in conformity with generally accepted accounting principles.

As discussed in notes thirteen and fifteen to the consolidated financial statements, the Company adopted the provisions of the Financial Accounting Standards Board's Statements of Financial Accounting Standards No. 112, Employers' Accounting for Postemployment Benefits, and No. 109, Accounting for Income Taxes, in fiscal 1994.

KPMG Peat Marwick

Minneapolis, Minnesota
July 29, 1994

CONSOLIDATED STATEMENTS OF EARNINGS

	Fiscal Year Ended		
In Millions, Except per Share Data	May 29, 1994	May 30, 1993	May 31, 1992
Continuing Operations:			
Sales	$8,516.9	$8,134.6	$7,777.8
Costs and Expenses:			
Cost of sales	4,458.2	4,297.6	4,123.2
Selling, general and administrative	2,755.5	2,578.2	2,516.3
Depreciation and amortization	303.8	274.2	247.4
Interest, net	99.2	73.6	58.2
Unusual expenses (income)	146.9	67.0	(11.8)
Total Costs and Expenses	7,763.6	7,290.6	6,933.3
Earnings from Continuing Operations before Taxes	753.3	844.0	844.5
Income Taxes	283.6	337.9	338.9
Earnings from Continuing Operations	469.7	506.1	505.6
Discontinued Operations after Taxes	-	-	(10.0)
Cumulative Effect to May 31, 1993 of Accounting Changes	.2	-	-
Net Earnings	$ 469.9	$ 506.1	$ 495.6
Earnings per Share:			
Continuing operations	$ 2.95	$ 3.10	$ 3.05
Discontinued operations	-	-	(.06)
Cumulative effect of accounting changes	-	-	-
Net Earnings per Share	$ 2.95	$ 3.10	$ 2.99
Average Number of Common Shares	159.1	163.1	165.7

See accompanying notes to consolidated financial statements.

CONSOLIDATED BALANCE SHEETS

In Millions	May 29, 1994	May 30, 1993
Assets		
Current Assets:		
Cash and cash equivalents	$ .2	$ 100.0
Receivables, less allowance for doubtful accounts of $4.4 in 1994 and $4.3 in 1993	309.7	287.4
Inventories	488.3	439.0
Prepaid expenses and other current assets	110.6	108.2
Deferred income taxes	220.4	142.3
Total Current Assets	1,129.2	1,076.9
Land, Buildings and Equipment, at cost	3,092.6	2,859.6
Other Assets	976.5	714.3
Total Assets	$5,198.3	$4,650.8
Liabilities and Equity		
Current Liabilities:		
Accounts payable	$ 650.4	$ 617.0
Current portion of long-term debt	115.2	64.3
Notes payable	433.3	339.6
Accrued taxes	178.3	139.7
Accrued payroll	165.6	158.8
Other current liabilities	289.3	239.4
Total Current Liabilities	1,832.1	1,558.8
Long-term Debt	1,417.2	1,268.3
Deferred Income Taxes	297.4	262.0
Deferred Income Taxes–Tax Leases	189.8	195.6
Other Liabilities	188.6	147.6
Total Liabilities	3,925.1	3,432.3
Common Stock Subject to Put Options	122.0	-
Stockholders' Equity:		
Cumulative preference stock, none issued	-	-
Common stock, 204.2 shares issued	251.0	358.7
Retained earnings	2,457.9	2,284.5
Less common stock in treasury, at cost, shares of 45.7 in 1994 and 43.7 in 1993	(1,334.4)	(1,196.4)
Unearned compensation and other	(160.2)	(167.5)
Cumulative foreign currency adjustment	(63.1)	(60.8)
Total Stockholders' Equity	1,151.2	1,218.5
Total Liabilities and Equity	$5,198.3	$4,650.8

See accompanying notes to consolidated financial statements.

CONSOLIDATED STATEMENTS OF CASH FLOWS

	Fiscal Year Ended		
In Millions	May 29, 1994	May 30, 1993	May 31, 1992
Cash Flows - Operating Activities:			
Earnings from continuing operations	$469.9	$506.1	$505.6
Adjustments to reconcile earnings to cash flow:			
Depreciation and amortization	303.8	274.2	247.4
Deferred income taxes	(27.8)	40.8	13.5
Change in current assets and liabilities,			
net of effects from business acquired	(72.0)	2.5	20.0
Unusual expenses	146.9	57.3	-
Other, net	15.2	(15.0)	3.9
Cash provided by continuing operations	836.0	865.9	790.4
Cash used by discontinued operations	(5.3)	(6.0)	(18.8)
Net Cash Provided by Operating Activities	830.7	859.9	771.6
Cash Flows - Investment Activities:			
Purchases of land, buildings and equipment	(559.5)	(623.8)	(695.3)
Investments in businesses, intangibles and affiliates, net of dividends	(140.8)	(55.8)	(30.6)
Purchases of marketable investments	(83.8)	(82.8)	(6.9)
Proceeds from sale of marketable investments	33.7	13.1	6.9
Proceeds from disposal of land, buildings and equipment	7.2	5.2	8.1
Proceeds from dispositions	-	-	77.7
Other, net	(39.0)	(40.0)	(7.9)
Net Cash Used by Investment Activities	(782.2)	(784.1)	(648.0)
Cash Flows - Financing Activities:			
Increase in notes payable	93.2	207.6	150.3
Issuance of long-term debt	273.6	422.6	188.7
Payment of long-term debt	(79.1)	(44.5)	(248.0)
Common stock issued	13.3	32.3	39.3
Purchases of common stock for treasury	(145.7)	(420.2)	(40.1)
Dividends paid	(299.4)	(274.8)	(245.2)
Other, net	(4.2)	(7.4)	(7.9)
Net Cash Used by Financing Activities	(148.3)	(84.4)	(162.9)
Decrease in Cash and Cash Equivalents	(99.8)	(8.6)	(39.3)
Cash and Cash Equivalents - Beginning of Year	100.0	.5	39.8
Reclassification of Marketable Investment	-	108.1	-
Cash and Cash Equivalents - End of Year	$ .2	$100.0	$ .5
Cash Flow from Changes in Current Assets and Liabilities:			
Receivables	$ (17.3)	$ (44.7)	$ 2.1
Inventories	(111.0)	28.7	.6
Prepaid expenses and other current assets	(5.1)	4.6	(8.9)
Accounts payable	33.2	9.0	54.5
Other current liabilities	28.2	4.9	(28.3)
Change in Current Assets and Liabilities	$ (72.0)	$ 2.5	$ 20.0

See accompanying notes to consolidated financial statements.

NOTES TO CONSOLIDATED FINANCIAL STATEMENTS

[1] Summary of Significant Accounting Policies

A. Principles of Consolidation. The consolidated financial statements include the following domestic and foreign operations: parent company and 100% owned subsidiaries, and General Mills' investment in and share of net earnings or losses of 20-50% owned companies.

Our fiscal year ends on the last Sunday in May. Years 1994 and 1993 each consisted of 52 weeks and 1992 consisted of 53 weeks.

B. Land, Buildings, Equipment and Depreciation. Buildings and equipment are depreciated over estimated useful lives ranging from three to 50 years, primarily using the straight-line method. Accelerated depreciation methods are generally used for income tax purposes.

When an item is sold or retired, the accounts are relieved of its cost and related accumulated depreciation; the resulting gains and losses, if any, are recognized.

C. Inventories. Inventories are valued at the lower of cost or market. Certain domestic inventories are valued using the LIFO method, while other inventories are generally valued using the FIFO method.

D. Intangible Assets. Goodwill represents the difference between purchase prices of acquired companies and the related fair values of net assets acquired and accounted for by the purchase method of accounting. Goodwill acquired after October 1970 is amortized on a straight-line basis over 40 years or less.

Intangible assets include an amount that offsets a minimum liability recorded for a pension plan with assets less than accumulated benefits as required by Financial Accounting Standard No. 87.

The costs of patents, copyrights and other intangible assets are amortized evenly over their estimated useful lives.

The Audit Committee of the Board of Directors annually reviews goodwill and other intangibles. At its meeting on April 25, 1994, the Board of Directors affirmed that the remaining amounts of these assets have continuing value.

E. Research and Development. All expenditures for research and development are charged against earnings in the year incurred. The charges for 1994, 1993 and 1992 were $63.6 million, $60.1 million and $62.1 million, respectively.

F. Earnings per Share. Earnings per share has been determined by dividing the appropriate earnings by the weighted average number of common shares outstanding during the year. Common share equivalents were not material.

G. Foreign Currency Translation. For most foreign operations, local currencies are considered the functional currency. Assets and liabilities are translated using the exchange rates in effect at the balance sheet date. Results of operations are translated using the average exchange rates prevailing throughout the period. Translation effects are accumulated in the foreign currency adjustment in stockholders' equity.

Gains and losses from foreign currency transactions are generally included in net earnings for the period.

H. Interest Rate Swap Agreements. Any interest rate differential on an interest rate swap is recognized as an adjustment of interest expense or income over the term of the agreement. We enter into these agreements with a diversified group of highly-rated financial institutions. We are exposed to credit loss in the event of nonperformance by the other parties to these agreements. However, we do not anticipate any losses.

The fair value of interest rate swaps is the estimated amount we would receive or pay to replace the swap agreements, taking into consideration current interest rates. This estimated amount was immaterial at May 29, 1994.

I. Statements of Cash Flows. For purposes of the statement of cash flows, we consider all investments purchased with a maturity of three months or less to be cash equivalents.

[2] Unusual Items

In 1994, we recorded an after-tax charge of $87.1 million ($.55 per share) to cover estimated costs associated with the actions of an independent licensed contractor who made an improper substitution of a pesticide in treating some of our oat supplies, a portion of which were used in production. While the substitution presented no consumer health or safety issues, the pesticide had not been registered for use on oats and thus its application represented a FDA regulatory violation. Due to a lengthy government approval process for registration, the affected finished oat-products inventory would be past the Company's freshness standard dates. Therefore, the charge includes costs associated with disposition of the finished oat products and oats inventory as well as other related expenses. Several consumer class action lawsuits have been filed in connection with this matter. The Company believes these lawsuits are without merit and will not have any material impact on the financial condition of the Company.

We recorded restructuring charges in 1993 related primarily to restaurant closings in the U.S. and Canada, costs for increasing Consumer Foods manufacturing productivity and efficiency, and our share of streamlining and tax reorganization costs associated with the formation of Snack Ventures Europe.

These charges resulted in a reduction in net earnings of $57.3 million ($.35 per share). These actions were substantially completed in 1994.

In 1992, we recognized a gain on the sale of the stock of our Spanish frozen food subsidiary, Preparados y Congelados Alimenticios, S.A. (PYCASA) and also recorded charges primarily related to restructuring of Betty Crocker packaged mixes production, European food operations, and Consumer Foods national sales organization, and the call of our 9 3/8% sinking fund debentures. These transactions resulted in no net effect on earnings.

[3] Foreign Exchange

We selectively hedge the potential effect of foreign currency fluctuations related to operating activities and net investments in foreign operations by entering into foreign exchange contracts with major financial institutions. Realized and unrealized gains and losses on contracts that hedge operating activities are recognized currently in net earnings. Realized and unrealized gains and losses on contracts that hedge net investments are recognized in the foreign currency adjustment in stockholders' equity.

The components of our net foreign investment exposure by geographic region are as follows:

In Millions	May 29, 1994	May 30, 1993
Europe	$118.3	$103.9
North/South America	43.3	41.7
Asia	12.1	13.0
Total exposure	173.7	158.6
After-tax hedges	(30.2)	(134.1)
Net exposure	$143.5	$ 24.5

At May 29, 1994, we had forward contracts maturing in 1995 to sell $59.5 million and purchase $7.5 million of foreign currencies. We also had foreign currency put options expiring in 1995 of $26.8 million. The fair value of these contracts is based on third-party quotes and is immaterial at May 29, 1994.

[4] Acquisition and Investments

We purchased the Colombo yogurt business for approximately $75.0 million from a U.S. subsidiary of Bongrain S.A. effective December 1993. Colombo has a refrigerated yogurt business in the Northeast and is a leading producer of soft frozen yogurt, as well as premium hard pack frozen yogurt. The transaction did not have any material effect on our 1994 earnings.

During 1994 and 1993, we made capital contributions and advances of $48.3 million and $66.1 million, respectively, to Cereal Partners Worldwide (CPW), our joint venture with Nestlé, S.A.

In 1993, we entered into a joint venture, Snack Ventures Europe (SVE), with PepsiCo Foods International to merge six existing Continental European snack operations (three from each company) into one company to develop, manufacture and market snack foods. We own 40.5 percent of SVE. The merger was effective July 1992. We reclassified the net individual assets and liabilities of our operations to investment in affiliates and excluded the noncash transaction from our statement of cash flows.

[5] Inventories

The components of inventories are as follows:

In Millions	May 29, 1994	May 30, 1993
Raw materials, work in process and supplies	$245.0	$206.2
Finished goods	249.3	252.6
Grain	47.0	40.5
Reserve for LIFO valuation method	(53.0)	(60.3)
Total inventories	$488.3	$439.0

At May 29, 1994 and May 30, 1993, respectively, inventories of $245.1 million and $244.5 million were valued at LIFO.

[6] Balance Sheet Information

The components of certain balance sheet items are as follows:

In Millions	May 29, 1994	May 30, 1993
Land, Buildings and Equipment:		
Land	$ 360.9	$ 302.3
Buildings	1,655.6	1,452.6
Equipment	2,373.8	2,048.1
Construction in progress	299.5	436.5
Total land, buildings and equipment	4,689.8	4,239.5
Less accumulated depreciation	(1,597.2)	(1,379.9)
Net land, buildings and equipment	$3,092.6	$2,859.6
Other Assets:		
Prepaid pension	$ 288.0	$ 257.4
Marketable investments, at cost	196.1	137.0
Investments in and advances to affiliates	188.3	163.9
Intangible assets	157.3	70.6
Miscellaneous	146.8	85.4
Total other assets	$ 976.5	$ 714.3

Based on quoted market prices, the fair value of the marketable investments was $231.4 million at May 29, 1994 and $186.9 million at May 30, 1993.

We have interest rate and currency swap agreements related to marketable investments that convert fixed interest rates to variable interest rates and foreign currencies to U.S. dollars on a notional amount of $81.9 million. These agreements mature from December 1994 to January 2001.

[7] Notes Payable

The components of notes payable are as follows:

In Millions	May 29, 1994	May 30, 1993
U.S. commercial paper	$339.2	$255.5
Canadian commercial paper	83.3	75.9
Financial institutions	260.8	208.2
Amount reclassified to long-term debt	(250.0)	(200.0)
Total notes payable	$433.3	$339.6

To ensure availability of funds, we maintain bank credit lines sufficient to cover our outstanding commercial paper. As of May 29, 1994, we had $500.0 million fee-paid lines and $179.4 million uncommitted, no-fee lines available in the U.S. and Canada. In addition, other foreign subsidiaries had unused credit lines of $37.1 million.

We have a revolving credit agreement expiring in 1999 that provides for the fee-paid credit lines. This agreement provides us with the ability to refinance short-term borrowings on a long-term basis, and therefore we have reclassified a portion of our notes payable to long-term debt.

We occasionally enter into swap agreements to lock in interest rates on notes payable that may result in fixed rates higher than short-term rates. At May 29, 1994 we had interest rate swap agreements on a notional amount of $145.0 million that convert an average interest rate of 2.8% to an average interest rate of 5.7%. These agreements mature from June 1994 to August 1994. At May 30, 1993 we had interest rate swap agreements on a notional amount of $169.0 million that converted an average interest rate of 3.3% to an average interest rate of 7.9%.

We purchased and sold interest rate cap agreements, expiring in May 1995, on a notional amount of $200.0 million with strike rates of 5.0% and 6.5%, respectively. These agreements limit our exposure to an increase in short-term interest rates. If rates are between 5.0-6.5%, our rate is limited to 5.0%; if rates are greater than 6.5%, our rate will be 150 basis points less than market rates until the agreements expire.

[8] Long-term Debt

In Millions	May 29, 1994	May 30, 1993
4.3% to 9.1% medium-term notes, due 1994 to 2033	$1,080.3	$ 918.3
Zero coupon notes, yield 11.1%, $327.0 due August 15, 2013	41.4	47.1
ESOP loan guaranty, variable rate (3.7% at May 29, 1994), due December 31, 2007	50.0	50.0
8.3% ESOP loan guaranty, due through June 30, 2007	78.3	82.0
Zero coupon notes yield 11.7%, $64.4 due August 15, 2004	20.2	18.0
Notes payable, reclassified	250.0	200.0
Other	12.2	17.2
	1,532.4	1,332.6
Less amounts due within one year	(115.2)	(64.3)
Total long-term debt	$1,417.2	$1,268.3

Our shelf registration statement permits the issuance of up to $222.1 million net proceeds in unsecured debt securities to reduce short-term debt and for other general corporate purposes. This registration includes a medium-term note program that allows us to issue debt quickly for various amounts and at various rates and maturities.

In 1994, we issued $217.9 million of debt under our medium-term note program with maturities from one to 40 years and interest rates from 4.3% to 7.3%. In 1993, $366.7 million of debt was issued under this program with maturities from one to 30 years and interest rates from 3.5% to 8.6%.

We had interest rate swap agreements that convert an average interest rate of 5.5% to an average interest rate of 3.2% on $162.9 million notional amount of medium-term notes. These agreements mature from October 1994 to January 1999. In 1994, we sold a swap option that gives the holder the right, if exercised, to receive a fixed payment of 6.8% and pay a floating rate based on commercial paper on a notional amount of $21.3 million from February 1995 until February 1997. At May 30, 1993 we had interest rate swap agreements that converted an average interest rate of 5.4% to an average interest rate of 2.9% on $120.0 million notional amount of medium-term notes.

In 1992, we called our 9 3/8% sinking fund debentures due March 1, 2009 (see note two). This transaction resulted in a decrease in net earnings of $3.5 million ($.02 per share).

The Company has guaranteed the debt of the Employee Stock Ownership Plans; therefore, the loans are reflected on our consolidated balance sheets as long-term debt with a related offset in stockholders' equity, "Unearned compensation and other."

Based on borrowing rates currently available for debt with similar terms and average maturities, the fair value of our long-term debt, excluding current portion, was $1,476.4 million at May 29, 1994 and $1,413.4 million at May 30, 1993.

The sinking fund and principal payments due on long-term debt are (in millions) $115.2, $72.0, $94.2, $101.0 and $99.7 in years ending 1995, 1996, 1997, 1998 and 1999, respectively. The notes payable that are reclassified under our revolving credit agreement are not included in these principal payments.

Our marketable investments include zero coupon U.S. Treasury securities. These investments are intended to provide the funds for the payment of principal and interest for the zero coupon notes due August 15, 2013 and 2004.

[9] Stock Options

The following table contains information on stock options:

	Shares	Average Option Price per Share
Granted		
1994	4,868,098	$63.22
1993	3,384,144	66.64
1992	2,574,008	58.29
Exercised		
1994	562,714	$31.08
1993	1,962,063	22.90
1992	1,026,760	19.64
Expired		
1994	459,800	$62.56
1993	288,907	61.63
1992	175,804	39.12
Outstanding at year end		
1994	18,009,478	$49.52
1993	14,163,894	44.50
1992	13,030,720	35.88
Exercisable at year end		
1994	10,278,466	$38.73
1993	9,488,948	36.23
1992	8,938,384	28.71

A total of 10,622,403 shares (including 2,535,750 shares for salary replacement options and 321,164 shares for restricted stock) are available for grants of options or restricted stock to employees under our 1990 and 1993 stock plans through October 1, 1998. An additional 3,083,400 shares are available for grants on a one-for-one basis as common stock shares are repurchased by the Company. The options may be granted at a price not less than 100% of fair market value on the date the option is granted. Options now outstanding include some granted under the 1980, 1984 and 1988 option plans, under which no further options or other rights may be granted. All options expire within 10 years plus one month after the date of grant. The plans provide for full vesting of the option in the event there is a change of control.

The 1993 plan permits awards of restricted stock to key employees subject to a restricted period and a purchase price, if any, to be paid by the employee as determined by the Compensation Committee of the Board of Directors. Most of the restricted stock awards require the employee to deposit personally owned shares (on a one-for-one basis) with the Company during the restricted period. In 1994, grants of 95,685 shares of restricted stock were made and on May 29, 1994, there were 188,822 of such shares outstanding.

The 1988 plan also permitted the granting of performance units corresponding to stock options granted. The value of performance units will be determined by return on equity and growth in earnings per share measured against preset goals over three-year performance periods. For seven years after a performance period, holders may elect to receive the value of performance units (with interest) as an alternative to exercising corresponding stock options. On May 29, 1994, there were 2,894,984 outstanding options with corresponding performance units or performance unit accounts.

A total of 52,300 shares are available for grants of options and restricted stock to non-employee directors until September 30, 1995 under a separate 1990 stock plan. Each newly elected non-employee director is granted an option to purchase 2,500 shares at fair market value on the date of grant. Options expire 10 years after the date of grant. Each year 400 shares of restricted stock will be awarded to each non-employee director, restricted until the later of the expiration of one year or completion of service on the Board of Directors.

[10] Stockholders' Equity and Put Options

In Millions, Except per Share Data

	$.10 Par Value Common Stock (One Billion Shares Authorized)				Retained Earnings	Unearned Compensation and Other	Cumulative Foreign Currency Adjustment	Total
	Issued		Treasury					
	Shares	Amount	Shares	Amount				
Balance at May 26, 1991	204.2	$320.2	(39.1)	$ (777.4)	$1,795.5	$(177.6)	$(47.2)	$1,113.5
Net earnings					495.6			495.6
Cash dividends declared ($1.48 per share), net of income taxes of $3.1					(242.1)			(242.1)
Stock option, profit sharing and ESOP plans		23.4	1.1	21.5				44.9
Shares purchased on open market			(.7)	(47.0)				(47.0)
Unearned compensation related to restricted stock awards						(4.3)		(4.3)
Earned compensation						9.6		9.6
Translation adjustments, net of income taxes of $.7							(6.7)	(6.7)
Amount charged to gain on sale of foreign operation							7.4	7.4
Balance at May 31, 1992	204.2	343.6	(38.7)	(802.9)	2,049.0	(172.3)	(46.5)	1,370.9
Net earnings					506.1			506.1
Cash dividends declared ($1.68 per share), net of income taxes of $4.2					(270.6)			(270.6)
Stock option, profit sharing and ESOP plans		15.1	1.3	19.7				34.8
Shares purchased on open market			(6.3)	(413.2)				(413.2)
Unearned compensation related to restricted stock awards						(3.2)		(3.2)
Earned compensation						9.6		9.6
Minimum pension liability adjustment						(1.6)		(1.6)
Translation adjustments, net of income tax benefit of $2.0							(14.3)	(14.3)
Balance at May 30, 1993	204.2	358.7	(43.7)	(1,196.4)	2,284.5	(167.5)	(60.8)	1,218.5
Net earnings					469.9			469.9
Cash dividends declared ($1.88 per share), net of income taxes of $2.9					(296.5)			(296.5)
Stock option, profit sharing and ESOP plans		8.0	.4	7.5				15.5
Shares purchased on open market			(2.4)	(145.7)				(145.7)
Put option premium		6.3		.2				6.5
Transfer of put options		(122.0)						(122.0)
Unearned compensation related to restricted stock awards						(3.9)		(3.9)
Earned compensation						9.6		9.6
Minimum pension liability adjustment						1.6		1.6
Translation adjustments, net of income taxes of $4.2							(2.3)	(2.3)
Balance at May 29, 1994	204.2	$251.0	(45.7)	$(1,334.4)	$2,457.9	$(160.2)	$(63.1)	$1,151.2

Cumulative preference stock of 5.0 million shares, without par value, is authorized but unissued.

We have a shareholder rights plan that entitles each outstanding share of common stock to one-fourth of a right. Each right entitles the holder to purchase one one-hundredth of a share of cumulative preference stock (or, in certain circumstances, common stock or other securities), exercisable upon the occurrence of certain events. The rights are not transferable apart from the common stock until a person or group has acquired 20% or more, or makes a tender offer for 20% or more, of the common stock. If the Company is then acquired in a merger or other business combination transaction, each right will entitle the holder (other than the acquiring company) to receive, upon exercise, common stock of either the Company or the acquiring company having a value equal to two times the exercise price of the right. The rights are redeemable by the Board in certain circumstances and expire on March 7, 1996. At May 29, 1994, there were 39.6 million rights issued and outstanding.

The Board of Directors has authorized the repurchase, from time to time, of common stock for our treasury, provided that the number of shares held in treasury shall not exceed 60.0 million.

Through private placements, we issued put options that entitle the holder to sell shares of our common stock to us, at a specified price, if the holder exercises the option. In 1994, we issued put options for 2.6 million shares for $6.5 million in premiums. As of May 29, 1994, put options for 2.2 million shares remain outstanding at strike prices ranging from $50.00

to $59.99 per share with exercise dates from July 1994 to March 1995. The amount related to our potential obligation has been transferred from stockholders' equity to "Common Stock Subject to Put Options."

[11] Interest Expense

The components of net interest expense are as follows:

	Fiscal Year		
In Millions	1994	1993	1992
Interest expense	$121.7	$99.8	$89.5
Capitalized interest	(6.1)	(11.5)	(13.6)
Interest income	(16.4)	(14.7)	(17.7)
Interest expense, net	$ 99.2	$73.6	$58.2

During 1994, 1993 and 1992, we paid interest (net of amount capitalized) of $99.0 million, $77.0 million and $70.7 million, respectively.

[12] Retirement Plans

We have defined benefit plans covering most employees. Benefits for salaried employees are based on length of service and final average compensation. The hourly plans include various monthly amounts for each year of credited service. Our funding policy is consistent with the funding requirements of federal law and regulations. Our principal plan covering salaried employees has a provision that any excess pension assets would be vested in plan participants if the plan is terminated within five years of a change in control. Plan assets consist principally of listed equity securities and corporate obligations, and U.S. government securities.

Components of net pension income are as follows:

	Fiscal Year		
Expense (Income) in Millions	1994	1993	1992
Service cost–benefits earned	$ 19.1	$ 14.7	$ 14.2
Interest cost on projected benefit obligation	57.8	52.6	51.2
Actual return on plan assets	(50.5)	(136.6)	(75.0)
Net amortization and deferral	(47.0)	38.3	(26.1)
Net pension expense (income)	$(20.6)	$(31.0)	$(35.7)

The weighted-average discount rate and rate of increase in future compensation levels used in determining the actuarial present value of the benefit obligations were 8.8% and 4.6% in 1994, and 8.5% and 5.1% in 1993, respectively. The expected long-term rate of return on assets was 10.4%.

The funded status of the plans and the amount recognized on the consolidated balance sheets (as determined as of May 31, 1994 and 1993) are as follows:

In Millions	May 29, 1994		May 30, 1993	
	Assets Exceed Accumulated Benefits	Accumulated Benefits Exceed Assets	Assets Exceed Accumulated Benefits	Accumulated Benefits Exceed Assets
Actuarial present value of benefit obligations:				
Vested benefits	$572.7	$24.1	$545.5	$ 12.1
Nonvested benefits	55.9	3.3	55.0	2.3
Accumulated benefit obligations	628.6	27.4	600.5	14.4
Projected benefit obligation	688.4	30.3	680.9	18.8
Plan assets at fair value	920.8	10.7	921.6	-
Plan assets in excess of (less than) the projected benefit obligation	232.4	(19.6)	240.7	(18.8)
Unrecognized prior service cost	31.4	2.9	40.1	.3
Unrecognized net loss	148.1	10.7	125.3	6.0
Recognition of minimum liability	-	(10.1)	-	(10.7)
Unrecognized transition (asset) liability	(130.6)	6.2	(148.7)	8.8
Prepaid (accrued) pension cost	$281.3	$ (9.9)	$257.4	$(14.4)

We have defined contribution plans covering salaried and non-union employees. Contributions are determined by matching a percentage of employee contributions. Such plans had net assets of $665.3 million at May 31, 1994. Expense recognized in 1994, 1993 and 1992 was $6.7 million, $9.6 million and $12.7 million, respectively.

Within our defined contribution plans we have Employee Stock Ownership Plans (ESOPs). These ESOPs borrowed funds guaranteed by the Company with terms described in the long-term debt footnote, as well as originally borrowed $35.0 million from the Company at a variable interest rate. At May 29, 1994, the interest rate was 4.6% with outstanding amounts of $21.0 million due December 2014 and $7.2 million with sinking fund payments to June 2015. Compensation expense is recognized as contributions are accrued. Our contributions to the plans, plus the dividends accumulated on the common stock held by the ESOPs, are used to pay principal, interest and expenses of the plans. As loan payments are made, common stock is allocated to ESOP participants. In 1994, 1993 and 1992, the ESOPs incurred interest expense of $9.0 million, $9.6 million and $11.3 million, respectively, and used dividends received of $8.9 million, $8.2 million and $7.8 million and contributions received from the Company of $7.4 million, $7.4 million and $7.1 million, respectively, to pay principal and interest on their debt.

[13] Other Postretirement and Postemployment Benefits

We sponsor several plans that provide health care benefits to the majority of our retirees. The salaried plan is contributory with retiree contributions based on years of service.

We fund plans for certain employees and retirees on an annual basis. In 1994, 1993 and 1992 we contributed $38.3 million, $30.6 million and $4.2 million, respectively. Plan assets consist principally of listed equity securities and U.S. government securities.

Components of the postretirement health care expense are as follows:

	Fiscal Year		
Expense (Income) in Millions	1994	1993	1992
Service cost—benefits earned	$ 5.6	$ 3.6	$3.5
Interest cost on accumulated benefit obligation	14.0	11.0	9.7
Actual return on plan assets	(1.5)	(3.9)	(3.0)
Net amortization and deferral	(4.5)	(1.0)	(1.2)
Net postretirement expense	$13.6	$ 9.7	$9.0

The funded status of the plans and the amount recognized on our consolidated balance sheets are as follows:

In Millions	May 29, 1994		May 30, 1993
	Assets Exceed Accumulated Benefits	Accumulated Benefits Exceed Assets	Accumulated Benefits Exceed Assets
Accumulated benefit obligations:			
Retirees	$ 36.3	$ 48.7	$ 80.0
Fully eligible active employees	12.7	8.0	19.3
Other active employees	27.0	48.5	70.4
Accumulated benefit obligations	76.0	105.2	169.7
Plan assets at fair value	89.3	7.4	60.8
Accumulated benefit obligations in excess of (less than) plan assets	(13.3)	97.8	108.9
Unrecognized prior service cost	.1	12.2	14.3
Unrecognized net loss	(28.1)	(27.7)	(51.1)
Accrued (prepaid) postretirement benefits	$(41.3)	$ 82.3	$ 72.1

The discount rates used in determining the actuarial present value of the benefit obligations were 8.8% and 8.5% in 1994 and 1993, respectively. The expected long-term rate of return on assets was 10%.

The health care cost trend rate increase in the per capita charges for benefits ranged from 6.2% to 9.8% for 1995 depending on the medical service category. The rates gradually decrease to 4.4% to 5.7% for 2007 and remain at that level thereafter. If the health care cost trend rate increased by one percentage point in each future year, the aggregate of the service and interest cost components of postretirement expense would increase for 1994 by $3.1 million and the accumulated benefit obligation as of May 29, 1994 would increase by $24.6 million.

In 1994, we adopted Statement of Financial Accounting Standards (SFAS) No. 112, "Employers' Accounting for Postemployment Benefits." The cumulative effect as of May 31, 1993 of changing to the accrual basis for severance and disability costs was a decrease in net earnings of $17.3 million ($.11 per share).

[14] Profit-sharing Plans

We have profit-sharing plans to provide incentives to key individuals who have the greatest potential to contribute to current earnings and successful future operations. These plans were approved by the Board of Directors upon recommendation of the Compensation Committee. The awards under these plans depend on profit performance in relation to pre-established goals. The plans are administered by the Compensation Committee, which consists solely of outside directors. Profit-sharing expense, including performance unit accruals, was $1.7 million, $7.3 million and $8.8 million in 1994, 1993 and 1992, respectively.

[15] Income Taxes

We adopted SFAS No. 109, "Accounting for Income Taxes" as of May 31, 1993. The adoption of SFAS 109 changed our method of accounting for income taxes from the deferred method to the asset and liability method. Deferred income taxes reflect the differences between assets and liabilities recognized for financial reporting purposes and amounts recognized for tax purposes measured using the current enacted tax rates. The cumulative effect of adoption was an increase in net earnings of $17.5 million ($.11 per share).

The components of earnings before income taxes and the income taxes thereon are as follows:

	Fiscal Year		
In Millions	1994	1993	1992
Earnings (loss) before income taxes:			
U.S.	$746.4	$887.2	$818.3
Foreign	6.9	(43.2)	26.2
Total earnings before income taxes	$753.3	$844.0	$844.5
Income taxes:			
Current:			
Federal	$246.5	$243.1	$254.0
State and local	60.9	60.2	55.1
Foreign	4.0	(6.2)	16.3
Total current	311.4	297.1	325.4
Deferred (principally U.S.)	(27.8)	40.8	13.5
Total income taxes	$283.6	$337.9	$338.9

During 1994, income tax benefits of $3.5 million were allocated to stockholders' equity. These benefits were attributable to the exercise of employee stock options, dividends paid on unallocated ESOP shares and translation adjustments.

During 1994, 1993 and 1992, we paid income taxes of $273.8 million, $268.3 million and $326.4 million, respectively.

In prior years we purchased certain income tax items from other companies through tax lease transactions. Total current income taxes charged to earnings reflect the amounts attributable to operations and have not been materially affected by these tax leases. Actual current taxes payable on 1994, 1993 and 1992 operations were increased by approximately $10 million, $10 million and $8 million, respectively, due to the effect of tax leases. These tax payments do not affect taxes for statement of earnings purposes since they repay tax benefits realized in prior years. The repayment liability is classified as "Deferred Income Taxes–Tax Leases."

The following table reconciles the U.S. statutory income tax rate with the effective income tax rate:

In Millions	Fiscal Year		
	1994	1993	1992
U.S. statutory rate	35.0%	34.0%	34.0%
State and local income taxes, net of federal tax benefits	5.0	5.2	4.9
Other, net	(2.4)	.8	1.2
Effective income tax rate	37.6%	40.0%	40.1%

The tax effects of temporary differences that give rise to deferred tax assets and liabilities at May 29, 1994 are as follows:

In Millions	
Accrued liabilities	$129.1
Unusual charge for oats	59.8
Compensation and employee benefits	59.6
Disposition liabilities	37.5
Foreign tax loss carryforward	16.2
Other	13.6
Gross deferred tax assets	315.8
Depreciation	219.5
Prepaid pension asset	112.0
Intangible assets	12.7
Other	37.5
Gross deferred tax liabilities	381.7
Valuation allowance	11.1
Net deferred tax liability	$ 77.0

As of May 29, 1994, we have foreign operating loss carryovers for tax purposes of $40.9 million, which will expire as follows if not offset against future taxable income: $11.0 million in 1998, $9.3 million in 1999, $10.9 million in 2000 and $9.7 million in 2001.

We have not recognized a deferred tax liability for unremitted earnings of $60.1 million for our foreign operations because we do not expect those earnings to become taxable to us in the foreseeable future. A determination of the potential liability is not practicable. If a portion were to be remitted, we believe income tax credits would substantially offset any resulting tax liability.

[16] Leases and Other Commitments

An analysis of rent expense by property leased follows:

In Millions	Fiscal Year		
	1994	1993	1992
Restaurant space	$41.2	$39.5	$33.9
Warehouse space	13.8	13.0	12.6
Equipment	10.6	10.6	8.3
Other	3.9	5.5	5.4
Total rent expense	$69.5	$68.6	$60.2

Some leases require payment of property taxes, insurance and maintenance costs in addition to the rent payments. Contingent and escalation rent in excess of minimum rent payments and sublease income netted in rent expense were insignificant.

Noncancelable future lease commitments are (in millions) $60.6 in 1995, $56.2 in 1996, $52.0 in 1997, $46.9 in 1998, $43.6 in 1999 and $236.5 after 1999, with a cumulative total of $495.8.

We are contingently liable under guarantees and comfort letters for $88.5 million. The guarantees and comfort letters are issued to support borrowing arrangements, primarily for our joint ventures.

[17] Discontinued Operations

We recorded a net after-tax charge related to previously discontinued operations of $10.0 million ($.06 per share) in 1992. This charge primarily related to a lease adjustment with the R. H. Macy Company, which is operating under bankruptcy law protection.

[18] Segment Information

In Millions

	Consumer Foods	Restaurants	Unallocated Corporate Items (a)	Consolidated Total
Sales				
1994	$5,553.9	$2,963.0		$8,516.9
1993	5,397.2	2,737.4		8,134.6
1992	5,233.8	2,544.0		7,777.8
Operating Profits				
1994	653.1(b)	219.4	$(119.2)	753.3
1993	772.6(c)	181.4(c)	(110.0)	844.0
1992	744.3(d)	190.8	(90.6)	844.5
Identifiable Assets				
1994	2,820.8	1,834.9	542.6	5,198.3
1993	2,576.4	1,605.0	469.4	4,650.8
1992	2,481.2	1,419.3	404.5	4,305.0
Capital Expenditures				
1994	207.7	343.3	8.5	559.5
1993	321.6	301.2	1.0	623.8
1992	397.1	297.0	1.2	695.3
Depreciation and Amortization				
1994	176.6	125.4	1.8	303.8
1993	155.8	116.8	1.6	274.2
1992	142.2	101.0	4.2	247.4

	U.S.A.	Foreign	Unallocated Corporate Items (a)	Consolidated Total
Sales				
1994	$8,172.1	$344.8		$8,516.9
1993	7,719.4	415.2		8,134.6
1992	7,039.6	738.2		7,777.8
Operating Profits				
1994	875.6(b)	(3.1)	$(119.2)	753.3
1993	997.1(c)	(43.1)(c)	(110.0)	844.0
1992	896.3(d)	38.8 (d)	(90.6)	844.5
Identifiable Assets				
1994	4,297.6	358.1	542.6	5,198.3
1993	3,828.3	353.1	469.4	4,650.8
1992	3,452.2	448.3	404.5	4,305.0

(a) Corporate expenses reported here include net interest expense and general corporate expenses.
(b) Consumer Foods operating profits include a charge of $146.9 million for unusual items described in note two.
(c) Consumer Foods and Restaurants operating profits include a charge of $33.4 million and $30.6 million, respectively, (U.S.A. $35.5 million; Foreign $28.5 million) for unusual items.
(d) Consumer Foods operating profits include a net gain of $17.5 million (U.S.A. $20.5 million loss; Foreign $38.0 million gain) for unusual items.

[19] Quarterly Data (unaudited)

Summarized quarterly data for 1994 and 1993 follows:

In Millions, Except per Share and Market Price Amounts	First Quarter 1994	First Quarter 1993	Second Quarter 1994	Second Quarter 1993	Third Quarter 1994	Third Quarter 1993	Fourth Quarter 1994	Fourth Quarter 1993	Total Year 1994	Total Year 1993
Sales	$2,089.8	$2,019.6	$2,182.2	$2,096.9	$2,101.4	$2,010.7	$2,143.5	$2,007.4	$8,516.9	$8,134.6
Gross profit (a)	1,011.7	977.3	1,055.1	1,016.6	994.6	941.4	997.3	901.7	4,058.7	3,837.0
Earnings from operations	165.6	159.6	140.7	138.1	145.0	140.9(b)	18.4(c)	67.5(d)	469.7	506.1
Earnings per share from operations	1.04	.97	.88	.85	.91	.86	.12	.42	2.95	3.10
Cumulative effect of accounting changes	.2	-	-	-	-	-	-	-	.2	-
Net earnings	165.8	159.6	140.7	138.1	145.0	140.9	18.4	67.5	469.9	506.1
Net earnings per share	1.04	.97	.88	.85	.91	.86	.12	.42	2.95	3.10
Dividends per share	.47	.42	.47	.42	.47	.42	.47	.42	1.88	1.68
Market price of common stock:										
High	68 3/4	71 1/8	67 3/4	73 7/8	63	72 1/2	57	74 1/8	68 3/4	74 1/8
Low	56 7/8	62	59 5/8	64 1/2	55 1/2	65	49 7/8	64 1/8	49 7/8	62

(a) Before charges for depreciation.
(b) Includes an after-tax loss of $8.7 million ($.05 per share) for a restructuring charge for SVE.
(c) Includes an after-tax loss of $87.1 million ($.55 per share) related to the improper treatment of oat supplies.
(d) Includes an after-tax loss of $47.0 million ($.29 per share) for restructuring charges related to restaurant closings and Consumer Foods manufacturing costs.

ELEVEN YEAR FINANCIAL SUMMARY AS REPORTED

In Millions, Except per Share Data	May 29, 1994	May 30, 1993	May 31, 1992	May 26, 1991	May 27, 1990	May 28, 1989	May 29, 1988	May 31, 1987	May 25, 1986	May 26, 1985	May 27, 1984
Financial Results											
Earnings (loss) per share (a)	$ 2.95	$ 3.10	$ 2.99	$ 2.87	$ 2.32	$ 2.53	$ 1.63	$ 1.25	$ 1.03	$ (.41)	$ 1.24
Return on average equity	37.7%	39.1%	39.9%	49.2%	49.5%	60.0%	41.1%	31.4%	21.5%	(6.5)%	19.0%
Dividends per share (a)	1.88	1.68	1.48	1.28	1.10	.94	.80	.625	.565	.56	.51
Sales (b)	8,516.9	8,134.6	7,777.8	7,153.2	6,448.3	5,620.6	5,178.8	5,189.3	4,586.6	4,285.2	5,600.8
Costs and expenses:											
Cost of sales (b)	4,458.2	4,297.6	4,123.2	3,722.1	3,485.1	3,114.8	2,847.8	2,834.0	2,563.9	2,474.8	3,165.9
Selling, general and administrative (b)	2,902.4	2,645.2	2,504.5	2,386.0	2,138.0	1,808.5	1,710.5	1,757.5	1,547.2	1,443.9	1,841.7
Depreciation and amortization (b)	303.8	274.2	247.4	218.4	180.1	152.3	140.0	131.7	113.1	110.4	133.1
Interest (b)(c)	99.2	73.6	58.2	61.1	32.4	27.5	37.7	32.9	38.8	60.2	61.4
Earnings before income taxes (b)	753.3(e)	844.0(f)	844.5	765.6	612.7	517.5	442.8	433.2	323.6	195.9(h)	398.7
Net earnings (loss)	469.9	506.1	495.6	472.7	381.4	414.3(g)	283.1	222.0	183.5	(72.9)(i)	233.4
Net earnings (loss) as a percent of sales	5.5%	6.2%	6.4%	6.6%	5.9%	7.4%	5.5%	4.3%	4.0%	(1.7)%	4.2%
Weighted average number of common shares (a)	159.1	163.1	165.7	164.5	164.4	163.9	174.0	177.5	178.5	179.0	187.5
Taxes (income, payroll, property, etc.) per share (a)(b)	2.98	3.14	3.09	2.77	2.29	1.98	1.66	1.80	1.33	1.00	1.56
Financial Position											
Total assets	5,198.3	4,650.8	4,305.0	3,901.8	3,289.5	2,888.1	2,671.9	2,280.4	2,086.2	2,662.6	2,858.1
Land, buildings and equipment, net	3,092.6	2,859.6	2,648.6	2,241.3	1,934.5	1,588.1	1,376.4	1,249.5	1,084.9	956.0	1,229.4
Working capital at year end	(702.9)	(481.9)	(337.1)	(190.1)	(263.1)	(197.1)	(205.5)	(57.1)	41.6	229.4	244.5
Long-term debt, excluding current portion	1,417.2	1,268.3	920.5	879.0	688.5	536.3	361.5	285.5	458.3	449.5	362.6
Stockholders' equity	1,151.2	1,218.5	1,370.9	1,113.5	809.7	731.9	648.5	730.4	682.5	1,023.3	1,224.6
Stockholders' equity per share (a)	7.26	7.59	8.28	6.74	4.96	4.54	3.88	4.14	3.81	5.76	6.76
Other Statistics											
Cash provided by operations (b)	836.0	865.9	790.4	548.6	657.1	527.3	329.9	442.9	466.5	150.4	236.1
Total dividends	299.4	274.8	245.2	210.6	180.8	154.4	139.3	110.8	100.9	100.4	96.0
Gross capital expenditures (d)	559.5	623.8	695.3	554.6	540.0	442.4	410.7	329.1	244.9	209.7	282.4
Research and development (b)	63.6	60.1	62.1	57.0	48.2	41.2	40.7	38.3	41.7	38.7	63.5
Advertising media expenditures (b)	409.5	395.4	426.8	419.6	394.9	336.5	345.9	330.0	317.0	274.3	349.6
Wages, salaries and employee benefits (b)	1,490.0	1,433.2	1,398.5	1,331.6	1,171.5	987.1	911.3	958.6	895.8	860.2	1,121.6
Number of employees (b)	125,670	121,290	111,501	108,077	97,238	83,837	74,453	65,619	62,056	63,162	80,297
Accumulated LIFO reserve	53.0	60.3	67.0	75.9	71.4	65.5	53.0	51.5	45.8	47.5	79.7
Common stock price range (a)	68 3/4	74 1/8	75 7/8	60 7/8	39 5/8	33 7/8	31	28	20	15 1/8	14 1/4
	49 7/8	62	54 1/4	37 7/8	31 3/8	22 3/8	20 3/8	18 1/2	13	11 7/8	10 3/8

(a) Years prior to 1991 have been adjusted for the two-for-one stock splits in November 1990 and 1986.
(b) Includes continuing operations only; years prior to 1989 include the discontinued cafeteria-style restaurant and frozen novelties operations, years prior to 1988 include the discontinued specialty retailing apparel operations, years prior to 1987 include the discontinued furniture operations, and years prior to 1985 include the discontinued toy, fashion and specialty retailing non-apparel operations.
(c) Interest expense is net of interest income; years prior to 1986 are interest expense only with interest income included in selling, general and administrative.
(d) Includes capital expenditures of continuing operations and discontinued operations through the date disposition was authorized.
(e) Includes pretax unusual expense of $146.9 million.
(f) Includes pretax restructuring charge of $67.0 million.
(g) Includes after-tax discontinued operations income of $169.0 million and cumulative effect of accounting change charge of $70.0 million.
(h) Includes pretax restructuring charge of $75.8 million.
(i) Includes after-tax discontinued operations charge of $188.3 million.

FINANCIAL DATA FOR CONTINUING OPERATIONS

In Millions, Except per Share Data	Fiscal Year Ended				
	May 29, 1994	May 30, 1993	May 31, 1992	May 26, 1991	May 27, 1990
Sales	$8,516.9	$8,134.6	$7,777.8	$7,153.2	$6,448.3
Earnings after taxes	469.7	506.1	505.6	464.2	373.7
Earnings per share	2.95	3.10	3.05	2.82	2.27